I0130742

SHARP FAMILY

PATRICK COUNTY, VIRGINIA TO LAUDERDALE COUNTY, ALABAMA AND BEYOND

REMEMBERING THOSE WHO HAVE GONE BEFORE US

BY DAVID GUY SHARP

© Copyright 2009
Bluewater Publications
Protected

All rights reserved. No part of this publication may be reproduced or
transmitted in any form or by any means, electronic or mechanical,
including photocopying, recording, or by any information storage and
retrieval system, without prior written permission from the Publisher.

Published by:
Bluewater Publications
1812 CR 111
Killen, Alabama 35645
www.BluewaterPublications.com

David Guy Sharp and his beloved wife, Audrey Cordelia Montgomery Sharp

Introduction

David Guy Sharp was born 2 June 1927 in Lauderdale County, Alabama. He is the son of Guy Thomas Sharp and Vivian May and grew up in the Petersville and Underwood communities of Lauderdale County.

After his school days, David served in the U. S. Navy at two different times. The first time was 1945 – 46. Then he was married to Audrey Cordelia Montgomery on 3 February 1950. After his marriage he then re-entered the navy.

David worked for the Tennessee Valley Association, after his service in the navy. His last employment was with the U. S. Post Office. While working at the post office, Mary Threet Sharp brought him some family information. That was when he became interested in genealogy.

In 1974 David started searching for information on his ancestors. That search has lasted approximately twenty-five years. Many hours have been spent in libraries, court houses and graveyards. There were numerous phone calls to make and families to visit. David found many relatives that he did not know he had.

There are two items that are in David's possession that he cherishes very much. He has a muzzle loader rifle that belonged to his great granddaddy, Charles W. Sharp, Jr., or his great-great granddaddy, Charles W. Sharp, Sr. The other item is Charles W. Sharp, Jr.'s Bible, with all the family information filled in.

Anyone related to the Sharp family will benefit greatly from all of David's years of hard work. His love for family history will be appreciated by many people in the future.

Acknowledgements

Many thanks go to all those people, who graciously contributed information, pictures and their time to the printing of this book. Special thanks go to Dan Wood, Sharon Wood, Doris McMillan, Rufus South, Bill Weaver, William Lindsey McDonald, Mildred Gean Mason, and Larry Sharp. Without your valuable assistance to David, this book of genealogy could not have been completed.

Disclaimer

The contributors to this book have been many. Some have been family, who knew the information first hand. Some were friends and neighbors. However, much of the information has come from research done in libraries, court house records, microfilm and the internet.

Numerous hours have been spent trying to publish the book as accurately as possible. There are probably many misspelled names, incorrect dates, or other information that was incorrectly given to the compilers of the book. We apologize for any such errors, and have done our best to avoid them. The typist may have misread some of the information and we apologize for that, also.

Table of Contents

Note: A plus sign (+) by a name indicates the person is married and there is more information on that person's family.

Sharp Family
England to Virginia

**William Sharp was born about 1580 in England.

General Notes: Arrived on HMS Starr - May 1620...taken from papers of Steve Sharp, Germantown, TN.

William married **Elizabeth Parker**. Elizabeth was born about 1595 in England.

General Notes: Arrived on HMS Bonaventure...1620...Steve Sharp, Germantown, TN.

M i. **Issac Sharp** was born about 1618 in England.

Issac Sharp (*William*[1]) was born about 1618 in England.

Issac married **Ann Turner**.
M i. **Robert Sharp Sr.** was born about 1645 in Henrico County, VA.

Robert Sharp Sr. (*Issac*[2], *William*[1]) was born about 1645 in Henrico County, VA.

Robert married someone.
M i. **Robert Sharp Jr.** was born about 1686 in Henrico County, VA.

Robert Sharp Jr. (*Robert Sr.*[3], *Issac*[2], *William*[1]) was born about 1686 in Henrico County, VA.

Robert married **Sarah Woodson**.
M i. **William Sharp** was born between 1700 and 1728 in Henrico County, VA.

William Sharp (*Robert Jr.*[4], *Robert Sr.*[3], *Issac*[2], *William*[1]) was born between 1700 and 1728 in Henrico County, VA.

William married **Elizabeth *Unk**.
M i. **Richard Sharp** was born in 1730 and died in 1823.

Richard Sharp (*William*[5], *Robert Jr.*[4], *Robert Sr.*[3], *Issac*[2], *William*[1]) was born in 1730 and died in 1823.

Richard married **Agnes *Unk**.
M i. **John Sharp Sr.** was born in 1755 in Chesterfield County, VA and died 29 May 1834 in Abingdon, Patrick County, VA.

John Sharp Sr. (*Richard*[6], *William*[5], *Robert Jr.*[4], *Robert Sr.*[3], *Issac*[2], *William*[1]) was born in 1755 in Chesterfield County, VA and died 29 May 1834 in Abingdon, Patrick County, VA.

General Notes: John Sharp moved from Chesterfield County, Virginia to Buckingham County, Virginia where he married. He was living in Bedford County, Virginia when he joined the war effort on April 03, 1781. John fought at Yorktown and Guilford County Courthouse during the revolutionary war. He applied for pension November 13, 1832 in Patrick County, Virginia. John died in 1834.

John married **Frances Walthall** 1 Jan 1766 in Buckingham County, VA. Frances was born in 1749.
M i. **Thomas Sharp**.
   Thomas married **Lucina Reynolds** 12 Jan 1809 in Abingdon, Patrick County, VA.
F ii. **Ruth Sharp**.
   Ruth married **William Crum** 13 Aug 1813 in Abingdon, Patrick County, VA.
F iii. **Lucy Sharp**.
   Lucy married **George Lackey** 7 Oct 1795 in Abingdon, Patrick County, VA.

M	iv.	**Joseph Sharp**.

Joseph married **Sally Shelton** 29 Jul 1813 in Abingdon, Patrick County, VA.

M	v.	**Leonard Sharp**.
F	vi.	**Viny Sharp**.
M	vii.	**John Sharp Jr.** was born in Abingdon, Patrick County, VA.

John married **Susanna Medley** 7 Dec 1796 in Abingdon, Patrick County, VA.

M	viii.	**Robert Sharp** was born about 1770 and died 28 Oct 1814 in Norfolk, VA.

Robert married **Phillioena Peney Shelton** 17 Aug 1796 in Abingdon, Patrick County, VA. Phillioena was born in 1775 in Abingdon, Patrick County, VA and died 1 Feb 1856 in Abingdon, Patrick County, VA.

M	ix.	**Charles W. Sharp Sr.** was born 25 Dec 1777 in Abingdon, Patrick County, VA, died in 1867, and was buried in the Arbor between Murphy's Chapel and the Charlie Whitten Place.

** The above generations are being included for research purposes.
They have not been researched or proven by David Sharp or the compilers of this book.
It is thought that Charles Sharp, Sr. is the 9th son of John and Frances Walthall Sharp, Sr.

Descendants of Charles W. & Matilda Anglin Sharp, Sr.

First Generation

10. Charles W. Sharp Sr. (*John Sr.* [1]) was born 25 Dec 1777 in Abingdon, Patrick County, VA, died in 1867, and was buried in the Arbor between Murphy's Chapel and the Charlie Whitten Place.

General Notes: Charles Sharp, Sr. was born in Virginia December 25, 1777 and Matilda Anglin who was the daughter of Adron and Elizabeth Anglin was born May 7, 1788 in Virginia.
The Alabama territory was created by an act of Congress on March 3, 1817. William Wyatt Bibb of Georgia was appointed territorial Governor by President James Monroe. Lauderdale County was created January 19, 1818.
Charles Sharp, Sr. it was thought came from Petersburg, Virginia in 1818. The Sharp's Mill was named for his son David Allen Sharp. Descended from the Sharp's of Horton in Yorkshire, England, aka 'Sharpe' left England and went to Ireland to escape religious persecution.
This information from: "A History of Florence, Alabama" By: Jill K, Garrett printed 1968

The following taken from papers that Bert Wood gave me... Sharon Wood
Adron had a nickname as Ade. Robert's nickname was Bob. A man killed Uncle Robert on a Sunday morning over an argument about a mule that had strayed to his house and the man claimed the mule. His wife was named Betsy and they did not have any children. After his death she later married a man by the name of Jones. Uncle Granville had one son who married and had one little boy.
Aunt Mary married a man by the name of Jonathan Young. She died rather young leaving two children.
Charles and Matilda Anglin Sharp came to Alabama from Richmond and Petersburg, Va.

Great-Grandma Matilda Anglin Sharp was living with her youngest daughter, Eliza Jane White (Ella White's mother) when she died. She lived to be 110 years of age, still had her teeth and didn't have to use glasses.
Charles and Matilda Sharp are buried at the Arbor between Murphy's Chapel and the Charlie Whitten place. Charles Sharp mentioned as a son of Charles and Matilda married Mary Angeline Dowdy and they are buried in the private cemetery in the yard of Miss Johnnie Dowdy.
Some of the Sharps are buried on Brush Creek. According to one person I contacted there are some graves supposed to be those of Joseph Sharp buried on a hill above the cemetery. It was during a rainy season and the cemetery was full of water and they buried these others on top of the hill. The grandparents of Beulah Sharp and the great grandparents of Orville O. Sharp are supposed to be buried in this Sharp cemetery. There are no tombstones in this cemetery but a Mr. Wheeler Jones knows a lot about who is buried there.

Co. D 9th Alabama Infantry, under Captain J. Butler Hooston

Pictured in both pictures below on left is William Lindsey McDonald, great-great-grandson of Charles and Matilda Sharp. On the right is William Claude "Billy" Wood, Jr., great-great-great-grandson of Charles and Matilda. They are shown at the erecting of tombs for Charles and Matilda, which were purchased by several descendants of their grandparents. The graves are located in an arbor close to Murphy's Chapel Church on County Road 8, in Lauderdale County, Alabama. Some have called the site the Cody Cemetery, as there are grave markers with the Cody name on them there. The picture to the left is of Charles W. Sharp, Senior's tomb and the one to the right is the tomb of Matilda Anglin Sharp.

Charles married **Matilda Anglin**, daughter of **Adron Anglin Jr.** and **Elizabeth W. Harbour**, 20 Aug 1807 in Abingdon, Patrick County, VA. Matilda was born 7 May 1788 in Richmond, VA, died in 1898, and was buried in the Arbor between Murphy's Chapel and the Charlie Whitten Place.

General Notes: She was living with her youngest daughter, Eliza Jane White when she died. She lived to be a 110 years old, had her teeth and didn't wear glasses.

+   20 F   i.   **Frances (Frankie) Sharp** was born 28 Oct 1808 in Abingdon, Patrick County, VA, died about 1879, and was buried in Wright Cemetery, Wright, Lauderdale County, AL.

+   21 M   ii. **Adron (Edwin/Ade) Sharp Sr.** was born 21 Aug 1810 in Abingdon, Patrick County, VA, died 4 Dec 1882, and was buried in Oak Hill Cemetery, Booneville, Logan County, AR.

+   22 M   iii. **John Sharp Sr.** was born 5 Sep 1814 in Petersburg, VA and died about 23 Nov 1867 in Lauderdale County, AL.

+   23 M   iv. **Robert (Bob) T. Sharp** was born 7 May 1809 in Virginia, died 12 May 1867, and was buried in Austin Cemetery, Lauderdale County, AL.

+   24 F   v.   **Mary E. Sharp** was born 27 Mar 1819 in Lauderdale County, AL, died between 1847 and 1850, and was buried in Alabama.

+   25 M   vi. **Joseph (Joe) Sharp** was born 14 May 1821 in Lauderdale County, AL, died 2 Sep 1874, and was buried in Wheeler Jones Place, Lauderdale County, AL.

    26 M   vii. **Greenville Penn Sharp** was born 24 Jan 1829 in Lauderdale County, AL.

General Notes: "Whereabouts unknown. Do not have any info on Greenville Penn Sharp. He may have been named after a Greenville Penn that had signed a legal paper in VA for Charles Sharp. Names: Charles Sharp, Henry Fulcher, to Hezekiah Mankin, dated Oct 15, 1807, Patrick County, VA. Deed book, 1807-1817, pg 74-75.
Samuel Staples, Robert Sharp, John Turner Greenville Penn..." David Sharp

+	27	M	viii.	**Charles W. Sharp II** was born 12 Feb 1830 in Lauderdale County, AL, died 23 Jul 1889, and was buried in Dowdy Cemetery, Lauderdale County, AL.
+	28	F	ix.	**Matilda Sharp** was born 30 Sep 1832 in Lauderdale County, AL and died in Apr 1857.
+	29	F	x.	**Eliza Jane Sharp** was born 12 Sep 1835 in Lauderdale County, AL, died 21 Mar 1909, and was buried in Lauderdale County, AL.
+	30	M	xi.	**David Allen Sharp** was born 27 Feb 1841 in Lauderdale County, AL, died 3 Jun 1906, and was buried in Florence City Cemetery, Florence, Lauderdale County, AL.

Second Generation

12. Frances Sharp (*Robert^2, John Sr.^{1}*).

Frances married **Armstead W. Newman** 10 Jan 1837 in Abingdon, Patrick County, VA.

	31	F	i.	**Lavenia Newman** was born in 1840.
	32	F	ii.	**Parthenia Newman** was born in 1842.
	33	F	iii.	**Nancy Newman** was born in 1845.
	34	M	iv.	**Samuel Newman** was born in 1849.

13. Jane Sharp (*Robert^2, John Sr.^{1}*).

Jane married **Frederick Gilbert**.

14. Nancy Sharp (*Robert^2, John Sr.^{1}*).

Nancy married **William Sandefur** 29 Sep 1827 in Abingdon, Patrick County, VA.

15. Hannah Sharp (*Robert^2, John Sr.^{1}*) was born in 1795.

Hannah married **William Walker Tuggle Sr.**. William was born in 1777.

| + | 35 | F | i. | **Mary Ann Tuggle**. |
| + | 36 | M | ii. | **William Walker Tuggle Jr.** |

16. Lucy Sharp (*Robert^2, John Sr.^{1}*) was born in 1798 in Virginia.

Lucy married **Samuel Gilbert** 6 Mar 1823 in Abingdon, Patrick County, VA. Samuel was born in 1795 in Virginia.

+	37	M	i.	**Robert Gilbert** was born in 1820 in Virginia.
	38	M	ii.	**George Gilbert** was born in 1830.
	39	F	iii.	**Minerva Gilbert** was born in 1833.
+	40	M	iv.	**Samuel L. Gilbert** was born in 1836 in Virginia.
	41	F	v.	**Emily F. Gilbert** was born in 1839.
	42	F	vi.	**Lovenia Gilbert** was born in 1846.

17. Sally Sharp (*Robert^2, John Sr.^{1}*) was born 12 Mar 1801 in Abingdon, Patrick County, VA and died in Jul 1891 in Abingdon, Patrick County, VA.

Sally married **Harbert Shelton** 6 Jan 1825 in Abingdon, Patrick County, VA. Harbert was born in 1801 in Abingdon, Patrick County, VA.

	43	M	i.	**Samuel Shelton** was born in 1833.
	44	F	ii.	**Penah Shelton** was born in 1835.
	45	M	iii.	**Bass Shelton** was born in 1837.
	46	F	iv.	**Octavia Shelton** was born in 1842.

18. Samuel Sharp (*Robert^2, John Sr.^{1}*) was born between 1804 and 1806 in Abingdon, Patrick County, VA and died in Feb 1849 in Van Buren County, MO.

Samuel married **Frances Thurmon Lyon** 19 Mar 1828 in Abingdon, Patrick County, VA. Frances was born in Sep 1809 in Abingdon, Patrick County, VA.

47	F	i.	**Jane Sharp** was born in 1829.
48	F	ii.	**Mary Ellen Sharp** was born in 1832.

19. Louvenia Sharp (*Robert*[2], *John Sr.*[1]) was born in 1814 in Abingdon, Patrick County, VA.

Louvenia married **Mark Plaster** 13 Sep 1836 in Abingdon, Patrick County, VA. Mark was born in 1814 in Abingdon, Patrick County, VA.

49	M	i.	**Mark Plaster Jr.** was born in 1833.
50	F	ii.	**Ruhaney Plaster** was born in 1838.
51	F	iii.	**Eliza Plaster** was born in 1840.
52	M	iv.	**Robert Plaster** was born in 1843.
53	M	v.	**Samuel Plaster** was born in 1844.
54	F	vi.	**Lucy Plaster** was born in 1847.

20. Frances (Frankie) Sharp (*Charles W. Sr.*[2], *John Sr.*[1]) was born 28 Oct 1808 in Abingdon, Patrick County, VA, died about 1879, and was buried in Wright Cemetery, Wright, Lauderdale County, AL.

General Notes: "According to records, she was 13 yrs, 7 mos old when married..." Sharon Wood

Frances married **Phillip Lindsey**, son of **John L. Lindsey** and **Rebecca Anderson**, 22 May 1822 in Lauderdale County, AL. Phillip was born in 1804 in Newberry County, VA, died about 1891, and was buried in Wright Cemetery, Wright, Lauderdale County, AL.

General Notes: During the Yankee Occupation of 1864, the soldiers had very little food.
The following story appeared in the East Lauderdale News on October 27, 1988:
On the first day of General Hatch's arrival at Waterloo in early January, some 200 of his men under the command of a Lieutenant camped at the home of Phillip Lindsey. Lindsey's 120 acre farm was four miles from Waterloo, and 3 miles from Hatch's headquarters. The Lieut. slept in the house that night with the family. The next morning as they were leaving they took about everything in the way of food that they could find. Phillip Lindsey filed a claim against the Federal Government in 1876 listing the following items and their value:

5100# of salted pork from the smokehouse	$667.00
50 Bu of corn from the crib at the house	$50.00
500 Bundles of fodder from the barn	$15.00
3 stands of beehives	$50.00
100# of honey	$20.00
40 gals of molasses taken away in utensils	$40.00
50# of potatoes dug from garden by soldiers	$25.00
1,000# of cotton in seed (burned at site)	$300.00
1,000 newly cut fence rails (burned at site)	$30.00

Slaughtered a milk cow and 2 heifers
Slaughtered all the hogs on the place
Later that same day other soldiers overtook Lindsey's son, John, on his way to the mill at Brush Creek and confiscated a clay bank mare worth $200.00

Lindsey was refused time and again because he had 3 sons in the Confederate Army and owned slaves. He never gave up. However, each time the courts turned him down he would file again, and as late as 1891 he was resubmitting his claim.
The Baptist churches at Gravelly Springs and Waterloo were torn down and the lumber used in the construction of barracks and stables. In fact, hardly a barn or outbuilding was left standing for miles around.

Files on record in Washington reveal that a large number of families at the Waterloo and Gravelly Springs area filed claims after the war. Some of these were: Ann Carr, James Johnson, John Higgins, Calvin Higgins, James Bevis, and John Perryman. A hundred years later these files were restricted and almost inaccessible to the general public. Very few claims of this nature were honored.

In 1912 the United States made some settlements of claims dating from the Civil War. Two claims from Lauderdale County were among those settled in January 1912. Gravelly Springs Baptist Church received $725.00 and the Waterloo Missionary Baptist Church $615.56.

In the 1866 tax census Phillip had 200 acres in Waterloo district. The Phillip Lindsey farm was located at the spring where Barton Branch begins, just over the hill from where Adron Sharp and sons had property.

"Phillip Lindsey was my great - great grandfather. He was a teenager when he came with his parents as early immigrants to Middle Tennessee. My grandfather remembered his grandfather telling how the young people and the men walked most of the way, riding in wagons only when the weather was bad.

To begin this narrative, let me say that Phillip was called "Drummer". My grandfather thought that his nickname came about because Phillip would 'sell' the corn meal produced at his grist mill. Another relative, Miss Johnnie Dowdy, had this same theory. Incidentally, I have an iron fireplace shovel made by Phillip in his combined blacksmith shop and grist mill. It was carefully handed down in our family through his granddaughter, Aunt Fannie Holt.

Philip Lindsey had a reputation of being strong -willed and quite independent. Official records of the U.S. Government bear this out. It took a good many years to get a copy of his Civil War Claim because of restrictions about the release of such documents. However, I do have the complete file in my archives; it takes up an entire section of one of my library shelves. Phillip made a claim for the amount of $1.327.00 in damages inflicted against him by the U.S. Army during the Civil War. This case came before the Court of Claims on June 3, 1886. It was denied because he was a slave holder and he had sons who fought in the Confederate Army. Phillip appealed his decision. In fact, over a period of five years every time his claim was turned down he would file an appeal. Because of his persistent efforts, though, he finally was awarded partial reimbursement for the damages. This announcement is found in the Saturday, March 21, 1891, edition of the Florence Times; "under the "Bowman Act" of Congress, Mr. Phillips Lindsey of Lauderdale has been allowed by the court of claims $331, for supplies taken during the war". Sadly our Phillip did not live to receive his money. Perhaps there was a long delay in processing the payment following action by the court. This could account for a record I discovered at the courthouse whereby two of Phillip's sons, Adron and Caleb, filed a complaint against their father's attorney, Culter Smith for embossing these funds. What a sad commentary. Culter Smith was considered one of Florence's better attorneys as well as a member in good standing at the First United Methodist Church.

William Lindsey McDonald and William Claude "Billy" Wood, Jr. shown erecting tombs for Frances "Frankie" Sharp Lindsey and Phillip Lindsey, in the Wright Cemetery

Great -great grandpa Lindsey's claim was based upon the following event during the Civil War. In January, 1865, U.S. General James H. Wilson brought his Calvary corps to Gravelly Springs for training prior to his raid into South Alabama and Georgia. on the first day of their arrival, the commander of Wilson's Fifth Division, Brigadier General Edward Hatch, sent out raiding parties to confiscate food and other valuables. The following is Phillip's written statement as to what Calvary at his farm located near the Wright community.

"I lived in Lauderdale County, Alabama, during the war and owned 120 acres of land and lived on my own place. I rented land in the bottom for raising corn; it was situated four miles east of Waterloo, Alabama. I farmed all during the war and was present and saw all the property taken by General Hatch's command camped about three miles from me, they passed my house; all that was taken the first and second days after the command came; took all the pork I salted for my own use; I had weighted and salted up to 100 pounds...they took my corn I had raised, 500 bushels; about 250 bushels had been cribbed at the house...I had counted 500 bundles of fodder into the stable loft....my creatures were all running in the field. The General gave me a safe guard to hall 250 bushels of corn to the house that had been cribbed in the bottom field...they killed my milch cow and....three heifers which would have averaged 300 pounds each, they took one barrel of molasses; took it away in buckets, pans and canteens; the first day they took one clay bank three year old mare; I had been offered $200 fifty times for her; my son was riding her to mill when the army took her; my wife was sick and I had no chance to go and try to get the mare back. I have forgotten how many hogs they killed; had a great many. I had spayed sows, barrows and 16 shoats that would have weighted 50 - 60 pounds each. I guessed at the honey; there were 14 gums; they got it all; they were rich looking gums, as rich as ever I saw in my life. I have put down 50 bushels of potatoes....from a patch from which I generally got more than 100 bushels. The soldiers burned 1,000 rails; I know there were 1,000 because I cut and split 1,000 to make the fence. I think there were 200 men present; I only saw a Lieutenant in command. He stayed at my house. They came to my house that night. He said he belonged to Hatch's command. I never knew his name. I have never taken the benefit of the bankrupt law; never got receipts of this property."

Phillip Lindsey was married to Frankie Sharp on May 22, 1822. She was the oldest child of Charles and Matilda Anglin Sharp, who had settled in Lauderdale County about 1820, from Patrick County, Virginia. The original Sharp home was on the Natchez trace where Charles operated a farm and grist mill on Cypress Creek not far from the Lindsey place at Cypress Inn. Charles and Matilda Sharp were my great-great-great grandparents. They both were descended from Revolutionary War soldiers. Charles was a son of John Sharp who was born about 1755 in Chesterfield County, Virginia; John served in the Revolutionary War. (John Sharp's wife was named Frances. His granddaughter, who was my Great-great Grandmother, Frances Sharp Lindsey, was a daughter of Adron Angling of Patrick County, Virginia, also a veteran of the Revolution. Adron Anglin, was born in 1761 and died August 31, 1849 was a son of Phillip Anglin. Our Phillip and Frances Lindsey named their son Adron Lindsey (my great- grandfather) for her father Adron Anglin.

Phillip and Frances Lindsey made their home in Wayne County, Tennessee, a few miles west of Cypress Inn from 1822 until 1855. This was located in a green valley surrounded by rolling hills. Phillip's grist mill and blacksmith shop were alongside Lindsey Creek that flowed through their farm. I located this place during the 1950's by following Miss Johnnie Dowdy's directions. "Turn north off of the road that connects Threet's Crossroads and Murphy's Chapel. The old Phillip Lindsey place is located at the bottom of the hill not far from the Pine Hill Church of Christ". Miss Johnnie was related through the Sharps. Part of the old log house, she said, was underneath a dwelling; the log portion had been added to and covered over. However, this place has disappeared in more recent years. It is hard to tell where the Tennessee- Alabama line is in relation to this homestead. However, Phillip Lindsey was shown in 1830 and 1940 census records for Wayne County,

Now, I'm getting ahead of my story, but let me say that our Sharp ancestors sold their farm and grist mill on the Natchez Trace in January 1836, to William Waldripe (for $201.50). Earlier, they had sold part of their farm to a man named Young. They moved that same year (1836) to Brush Creek, a few miles to north of Wright Community on County Road 8.

The above information about the Sharp family has a direct bearing on our Lindsey's as well. Frances and Phillip Lindsey apparently liked this area north of the Wright Community where her parents had relocated. So, in 1855, they pulled up stakes and moved to a farm just south of the Sharp place. Phillip acquired two tracts through the Homestead Act that year and added to it four years later for a total of 160 acres. This is where they were when the Yankees came. Martin and Dawn Hardy now own the old Phillip Lindsey place. It is located near County Road 8 and Brush

Creek a few miles north of Wright. A number of old ruins, including the root cellar, can be observed near where the house once stood. I do not know the year Great-great grandmother Frances Lindsay died; she was 60 years of age at the time of the 1870 census. Great-great grandfather Phillip Lindsey died about 1891 or 1892. They are buried somewhere in the area of Wright, perhaps in the small Sharp Cemetery, a few miles northeast of their home..." see 'The Legacy of Our Lindsey's' by William Lindsey McDonald.

"It was later learned that Phillip and Frankie Lindsey were buried at Wright Cemetery, Lauderdale County, Alabama and tombstones have been erected there..." Millie Mason

+   55   M   i.   **Caleb (Calip) Lindsey** was born 2 May 1827 in Cypress Inn, Wayne County, TN, died 25 Jun 1904, and was buried in Florence City Cemetery, Florence, Lauderdale County, AL.
+   56   M   ii.   **Andrew Jackson Lindsey** was born in 1829 in Cypress Inn, Wayne County, TN, died 17 Jul 1863, and was buried in National Cemetery, Finns Point, NJ.
+   57   M   iii.   **Sylvester (Sill) B. Lindsey** was born 14 Jul 1830 in Cypress Inn, Wayne County, TN, died 14 Jan 1892, and was buried in Wright Cemetery, Wright, Lauderdale County, AL.
+   58   M   iv.   **Adron Leonard Lindsey Sr.** was born in 1835 in Cypress Inn, Wayne County, TN, died 16 Jan 1924, and was buried in Florence City Cemetery, Florence, Lauderdale County, AL.
+   59   M   v.   **Robert Lindsey** was born in 1839 in Cypress Inn, Wayne County, TN, died in 1924, and was buried in Florence City Cemetery, Florence, Lauderdale County, AL.
     60   F   vi.   **Mary Polly Lindsey** was born in 1842 in Lauderdale County, AL and died in 1842 in Lauderdale County, AL.

General Notes: "Mary died in infancy. The next child was named in her memory"...William McDonald

+   61   F   vii.   **Mary M. (Polly II) Lindsey** was born about 1844 in Waterloo, Lauderdale County, AL, died 5 Jan 1920, and was buried in Murphy's Chapel Cemetery, Lauderdale County, AL.
     62   M   viii. **Thomas Lindsey** was born in 1844 in Cypress Inn, Wayne County, TN.
+   63   M   ix.   **John S. Lindsey** was born in 1845 in Lauderdale County, AL.

Adron Edwin "Ade" Sharp, born 21 Aug. 1810, in Abingdon, Patrick County, VA

21. Adron (Edwin/Ade) Sharp Sr. (*Charles W. Sr.* [2], *John Sr.* [1]) was born 21 Aug 1810 in Abingdon, Patrick County, VA, died 4 Dec 1882, and was buried in Oak Hill Cemetery, Booneville, Logan County, AR.

General Notes: Adron came to Lauderdale County, Alabama in 1820 with his parents Charles and Matilda Anglin Sharp from Petersburg, Virginia who were married August 20, 1807 in Patrick County, Virginia. Adron was born in Patrick Co. on August 21, 1810 and was the second oldest of eleven children born to Charles and Matilda Sharp.

Adron Sharp came to Alabama from Virginia about 1818 - 1820 with his parents. Probably came for the offer of free or very cheap land in the area ready for statehood. He was married in 1828 to Martha Lamb. He apparently was a man of means; he had what some called a plantation on Brush Creek about three miles north of the Tennessee River. The old home has been moved and restored and is located on Alabama State road #20 about 4 miles west of Florence. Adron had a mill on the creek, I am not sure of all the workings of the mill. But it definitely was a grist mill. This mill was burned by the Yankee occupation forces, probably in late 1864. They took him and his horse. The officer told the soldiers if they even heard gunfire to kill old man Sharp. I heard recently the grinding wheel is still in the area of the mill.

See more under son Charles' wife Matilda Boles notes.
*According to "History of Florence, Alabama"
By: Jill K. Garrett

LAST WILL AND TESTAY£NT OF ADRON SHARP
Source: Probate Box No. Logan County Courthouse, Paris, Arkansas
KNOW all men by these presents, that I, ADRON SHARP of Booneville in the County of Logan and State of Arkansas, being of sound and disposing mind and memory, do make and publish this my last will and testament hereby revoking all former wills by me at any time heretofore made.
1. I hereby constitute and appoint my wife ZELINE M. SHARP to be the sole executor of my last will, directing my said executrix to pay all my just debts and funeral expenses, out of my Estate.
2. After the payment of my said debts and funeral expenses, I give to my said wife ZELINE M. SHARP all the livestock that I may own at the time of my decease to use or dispose of as she may please for her sole use and benefit, also all the household and kitchen furniture and wearing apparel together with all the tools implements or personal property to me belonging at the time of my decease, also all the crop or produce growing or otherwise at said time.
3. I devise to my said wife all my real estate, to wit; beginning at the southeast corner of Section (31) Township (6) North, Range (27) West, thence North (92) ninety two rods to a rock in the South (79½) west (160) one hundred and sixty rods to a stake in said road, thence South (66) sixty six rods to a stake on the south boundary of said Section, thence East (160) one hundred and sixty rods to the place of beginning, containing (78) seventy -eight acres, all in southeast ¼ of said section, also all that portion of the southeast of the southwest quarter of Section thirty -one (31), Township (6) six North of Range Twenty-seven (27) West, that lies East of the middle channel of the Booneville Creek and south of the main road that runs East and West through said land containing five acres, more or less to have and to hold for her sole use and benefit during her natural life... At her decease said real estate to my children and respectively to share and share alike.
In testimony whereof, hereby set my hand and publish and declare this to be my last
Will and Testament in the presence of the witnesses named below this 6 day of
February 1882.
Signed ADRON SHARP
Signed published and declared by the said ADRON SHARP as and for his last will and testament in presence of us, who in his and in the presence of each other, and at his request have I our names as witnesses hereto.
John Rhyne
Saml. P. Florence
G.W. Evans

Probate records book "D", page 517, Paris, Logan County, Arkansas.
Will: probate box 139, Paris Courthouse, Arkansas Feb 1882.

The Sharp House
It is believed that Adron Sharp lived in this house, as well as other Sharp family members.

Adron married **Martha Ann Lamb**, daughter of **James Lamb** and **Margaret (Peggy) Wood**, 25 Jan 1828 in Lauderdale County, AL. Martha was born in 1810 in Williamson County, TN, died in 1870, and was buried in Gravely Springs Cemetery, Lauderdale County, AL.

General Notes: "My dad, Jesse Bert Wood, was told by Mr. Wheeler Jones that Martha Lamb Sharp and her mother (Margaret) are buried just east of Wright Cemetery on the bank of Brush Creek. He said the graves were approximately 250 feet north of Waterloo Road and west of the creek bank on a level spot not far from the creek.

I believe Martha was raised around Wright; there are many Lamb names in the 1850 Lauderdale County Census. The area where Adron Sharp and other Sharps had property on Brush Creek also had a number of Lambs living there. The church was called Lambs Chapel. Mr. Jones also said Adron Sharp was very good to his slaves. He had a portion of all food set aside for them but Martha would sell it without his knowledge and threaten the Negroes if they told Adron about it...." Dan Wood

This picture is believed to have been taken around 1907 in Booneville (Mixon Valley) Arkansas. This is Adron and Matilda Sharp's house.

The women on the left side of the porch is unknow. The young girl holding a doll on the right side of the porch is Florence Sharp. The man on the left side is Mundrow Sharp. Next to him is Virge Sharp. The little boy with the two dogs is Kelly C. Sharp which is my Great Grandfather. In the wagon is Claude Sharp. He is the older boy. And next to him is Aide Sharp. Behind the wagon by the fence are the parents, Matilda is on the left and Adron is on the right.

+ 64 M i. **James (Jim) Charles Sharp Sr.** was born in 1829 in Gravely Springs, Lauderdale County, AL, died 7 May 1894, and was buried in Lauderdale County, AL.

+ 65 M ii. **Charles (Charlie) A. Sharp** was born 12 Feb 1830 in Wright, Lauderdale County, AL, died 23 Nov 1882, and was buried in Oak Hill Cemetery, Booneville, Logan County, AR.

+ 66 F iii. **Elizabeth Mae (Lizzie) Sharp** was born in 1833 in Wright, Lauderdale County, AL and died before 1888 in Lee County, AR.

67 F iv. **Margaret Sharp** was born in 1837 in Wright, Lauderdale County, AL.

+ 68 F v. **Rutha (Ruthey) Barton Sharp** was born in May 1841 in Waterloo, Lauderdale County, AL, died in Nov 1903, and was buried in Wright Cemetery, Wright, Lauderdale County, AL.

+ 69 F vi. **Matilda Sharp** was born in Mar 1843 in Wright, Lauderdale County, AL.

70 M vii. **Adron Edwin (Eddie) Sharp Jr.** was born in 1845 in Waterloo, Lauderdale County, AL, died in 1882, and was buried in Oak Hill Cemetery, Booneville, Logan County, AR.

Adron next married **Zeline M. Potts** 3 Sep 1873 in Lauderdale County, AL. Zeline was born in 1833, died 28 Nov 1882, and was buried in Webb City, AR.

22. John Sharp Sr. (*Charles W. Sr.* [2], *John Sr.* [1]) was born 5 Sep 1814 in Petersburg, VA and died about 23 Nov 1867 in Lauderdale County, AL.

John married **Nancy Balentine** 26 Jan 1836. Nancy was born in 1819 in South Carolina and died in Lauderdale County, AL.

+	71	F	i.	**Mary Eliza Sharp** was born in Lauderdale County, AL, died 2 Jul 1908, and was buried in Murphy's Chapel Cemetery, Lauderdale County, AL.
+	72	F	ii.	**Sarah (Sallie) Sharp** was born about 1838 in Lauderdale County, AL.
+	73	F	iii.	**Elizabeth (Lizzie) May Sharp** was born 18 Sep 1840 in Lauderdale County, AL, died 20 Jan 1915, and was buried in Wright Cemetery, Wright, Lauderdale County, AL.
+	74	M	iv.	**Carroll Ira (Buck) Sharp** was born 11 Jan 1842 in Alabama, died 1 Aug 1896, and was buried in Wright Cemetery, Wright, Lauderdale County, AL.
+	75	F	v.	**Martha J. Sharp** was born in 1845 in Alabama.
+	76	F	vi.	**Eliza Sharp** was born in 1846 in Lauderdale County, AL and died about 1862 in Lauderdale County, AL.
+	77	M	vii.	**David (Dave) Owen Sharp** was born in 1852 in Lauderdale County, AL.
+	78	M	viii.	**John Sharp Jr.** was born in Mar 1854 in Lauderdale County, AL.
+	79	M	ix.	**William (Candy) Erwin Sharp** was born 7 Jun 1857 in Lauderdale County, AL, died 17 Nov 1938, and was buried in Florence City Cemetery, Florence, Lauderdale County, AL.
+	80	M	x.	**Richard Gaines Sharp** was born between Jan 1858 and 1859 in Lauderdale County, AL.

23. Robert (Bob) T. Sharp (*Charles W. Sr.* [2], *John Sr.* [1]) was born 7 May 1809 in Virginia, died 12 May 1867, and was buried in Austin Cemetery, Lauderdale County, AL.

General Notes: "Robert's nickname was Bob. A man killed Uncle Robert on Sunday morning over an argument about a mule which had strayed to his house and the man claimed the mule. His wife's name was Betsy and they did not have any children. After his death she later married a man by the name of Jones...." Bert Wood

Robert married **Elizabeth (Betsy) *Unk** before 1850. Elizabeth was born in 1824 in Alabama.

24. Mary E. Sharp (*Charles W. Sr.* [2], *John Sr.* [1]) was born 27 Mar 1819 in Lauderdale County, AL, died between 1847 and 1850, and was buried in Alabama.

Mary married **Jonathan Butler Young** 27 Sep 1835 in Lauderdale County, AL. Jonathan was born in 1818 in Tennessee.

	81	F	i.	**Matilda Young** was born in 1838.
	82	M	ii.	**Charles Young** was born in 1840.
	83	M	iii.	**James Young** was born in 1842.
+	84	F	iv.	**Julia Ann Young** was born about 1845 in Alabama, died 28 Oct 1907, and was buried in Murphy's Chapel Cemetery, Lauderdale County, AL.
	85	F	v.	**Mary Ann Young** was born in 1847.

25. Joseph (Joe) Sharp (*Charles W. Sr.* [2], *John Sr.* [1]) was born 14 May 1821 in Lauderdale County, AL, died 2 Sep 1874, and was buried in Wheeler Jones Place, Lauderdale County, AL.

Charles W. Sharp, Jr. and Mary Angeline Dowdy Sharp

General Notes: "David states that he is buried in a cemetery on Brush Creek behind the Wheeler Jones Farm House. Joe owned this place before Wheeler and has some children buried there also. No markers. Think that this is possibly located on County Road 8 and is being currently worked on. There are several stones here and a sign that reads Sharp..." Sharon Wood

Joseph married **Emily S. Hutton** between 1842 and 1843. Emily was born in 1825 in Tennessee and was buried in Wheeler Jones Place, Lauderdale County, AL.

    86 M i. **Charles Sharp** was born about 1844 in Tennessee.

    87 M ii. **Namon Sharp** was born about 1848 in Lauderdale County, AL.

    88 F iii. **Alcy Sharp** was born about 1850 in Alabama.

+   89 F iv. **Harriett Matilda Sharp** was born in 1853 in Lauderdale County, AL.

+   90 M v. **Berry Nolan Sharp** was born 15 Dec 1859 in Lauderdale County, AL, died 21 Sep 1945, and was buried in Stoney Point Cemetery, Lauderdale County, AL.

+   91 M vi. **Benjamin Franklin Sharp** was born 5 Feb 1865 in Lauderdale County, AL, died 19 Apr 1914, and was buried in Wesley Chapel Cemetery, Lauderdale County, AL.

27. Charles W. Sharp II (*Charles W. Sr.*[2], *John Sr.*[1]) was born 12 Feb 1830 in Lauderdale County, AL, died 23 Jul 1889, and was buried in Dowdy Cemetery, Lauderdale County, AL.

    General Notes: CSA, 9th Tennessee Calvary, Company B

Charles married **Julia Sharp**. Julia was born in 1832 in Alabama.
    92 M i. **Reuben Sharp** was born in 1849 in Alabama.

Charles next married **Mary Angeline Dowdy**, daughter of **Thomas Dowdy** and **Margaret Brown**, 20 Jan 1851 in Lauderdale County, AL. Mary was born in 1834 in Lauderdale County, AL, died 18 Dec 1888, and was buried in Dowdy Cemetery, Lauderdale County, AL.

+   93 M i. **John Levi Sharp** was born 20 May 1852 in Lauderdale County, AL and died 22 Aug 1920 in McQueen, AR.

+   94 F ii. **Amanda Jane Sharp** was born 29 Oct 1855 in Lauderdale County, AL and was buried in Wesley Chapel Cemetery, Lauderdale County, AL.

+   95 F iii. **Mary Elizabeth (Molly) Sharp** was born 14 Aug 1865 in Lauderdale County, AL, died 26 Jul 1961, and was buried in Graham Cemetery, Hardin County, TN.

+   96 M iv. **Charles Franklin Sharp** was born 3 Nov 1866 in Lauderdale County, AL, died 29 Apr 1932, and was buried in Fairmont Cemetery, San Angelo, TX.

+   97 F v. **Rachel Ann (Babe) Sharp** was born 17 May 1868 in Lauderdale County, AL, died 24 Jun 1957, and was buried in Dowdy Cemetery, Lauderdale County, AL.

| + | 98 | M | vi. | **Thomas (Tom) Erwin Sharp** was born 3 Oct 1869 in Lauderdale County, AL, died 13 Jun 1940, and was buried in Murphy's Chapel Cemetery, Lauderdale County, AL. |
| | | | | |

Charles and Mary Angeline Dowdy Sharp home

+	99	M	vii.	**Richard (Dick) Allen Sharp** was born 7 Oct 1872 in Lauderdale County, AL and was buried in Nashville, Davidson County, TN.
+	100	F	viii.	**Alice J. Sharp** was born 7 Apr 1873 in Lauderdale County, AL and was buried in Lake Charles, LA.
	101	F	ix.	**Lydia Sharp** was born 3 Mar 1875.
	102	F	x.	**Bossie Sharp** was born 24 Jun 1876.

28. Matilda Sharp (*Charles W. Sr. [2], John Sr. [1]*) was born 30 Sep 1832 in Lauderdale County, AL and died in Apr 1857.

Matilda married **Thomas Jefferson Dowdy**, son of **Thomas Dowdy** and **Margaret Brown**, 21 Sep 1852 in Lauderdale County, AL. Thomas was born in 1831 in Lauderdale County, AL.

+	103	F	i.	**Laura Belle Dowdy** was born about 1853 in Lauderdale County, AL and died 7 Feb 1937 in Booneville, MS.
	104	M	ii.	**Franklin Dowdy** was born in 1854 in Alabama and died 10 Oct 1915.
	105	F	iii.	**Mary Dowdy** was born in 1857 in Alabama.

29. Eliza Jane Sharp (*Charles W. Sr. [2], John Sr. [1]*) was born 12 Sep 1835 in Lauderdale County, AL, died 21 Mar 1909, and was buried in Lauderdale County, AL.

Eliza married **William White** 21 Mar 1856 in Lauderdale County, AL. William was born about 1835 in Tennessee, died in 1880, and was buried in Alabama.

	106	F	i.	**Mary Ann White** was born in 1856 in Lauderdale County, AL.
+	107	F	ii.	**Matilda Ann White** was born 2 Oct 1858 in Lauderdale County, AL, died 24 Oct 1937, and was buried in Murphy's Chapel Cemetery, Lauderdale County, AL.
	108	M	iii.	**John B. White** was born in 1861 in Lauderdale County, AL, died in 1924, and was buried in Lauderdale County, AL.
	109	M	iv.	**Robert F. White** was born in 1867 in Lauderdale County, AL.
+	110	F	v.	**Martha Jane White** was born 19 Jan 1869 in Lauderdale County, AL, died 7 Nov 1952, and was buried in Montgomery, AL.
+	111	F	vi.	**Ella Prooterwill White** was born 9 Sep 1871 in Lauderdale County, AL, died 14 Mar 1965, and was buried in Murphy's Chapel Cemetery, Lauderdale County, AL.
	112	M	vii.	**Edmon R. White** was born in 1876 in Lauderdale County, AL.

30. David Allen Sharp (*Charles W. Sr. [2], John Sr. [1]*) was born 27 Feb 1841 in Lauderdale County, AL, died 3 Jun 1906, and was buried in Florence City Cemetery, Florence, Lauderdale County, AL.

General Notes: Served in CSA, 9th Tennessee Calvary, Company B

"David Allen Sharp was in the Civil War, his son Andrew Jefferson Sharp, Sr. was in the Spanish-American War. They are buried side by side in the Florence Cemetery..." David Sharp

David married **Susan Tabatha Geans**, daughter of **Jesse P. Geans** and **Unknown**, in Selmer, McNairy County, TN. Susan was born 15 Dec 1838 in Tennessee, died 4 Jun 1917, and was buried in Florence City Cemetery, Florence, Lauderdale County, AL.

	113	M	i.	**Robert O. Sharp** was born 7 Apr 1865 in Lauderdale County, AL, died 31 Jan 1888, and was buried in Florence City Cemetery, Florence, Lauderdale County, AL.
+	114	M	ii.	**William (Bill) Edgar Sharp** was born 3 Sep 1866 in Lauderdale County, AL, died 2 Sep 1937, and was buried in Florence City Cemetery, Florence, Lauderdale County, AL.
+	115	M	iii.	**James (Jim) Hulet Sharp** was born in Jul 1870 in Lauderdale County, AL and was buried in Stoney Point Cemetery, Lauderdale County, AL.
+	116	M	iv.	**Joseph (Joe) Powers Sharp Sr.** was born 1 Jul 1873 in Lauderdale County, AL, died 23 Nov 1959, and was buried in Stoney Point Cemetery, Lauderdale County, AL.
+	117	M	v.	**Andrew Jefferson Sharp Sr.** was born 4 Feb 1877 in Lauderdale County, AL, died 29 Oct 1931, and was buried in Florence City Cemetery, Florence, Lauderdale County, AL.
	118	M	vi.	**Timothy Sharp** was born 23 Apr 1881 in Lauderdale County, AL, died in Dec 1881, and was buried in Macedonia Cemetery, Lauderdale County, AL.

Third Generation

35. Mary Ann Tuggle (*Hannah Sharp³, Robert², John Sr.¹*).

Mary married **Jefferson Davis Holyfield**.

36. William Walker Tuggle Jr. (*Hannah Sharp³, Robert², John Sr.¹*).

William married someone.
| | 119 | F | i. | **Harriet Tuggle** was born in 1852. |

37. Robert Gilbert (*Lucy Sharp³, Robert², John Sr.¹*) was born in 1820 in Virginia.

Robert married **Jane *Unk**. Jane was born in 1829 in Virginia.
| | 120 | M | i. | **John F. Gilbert** was born in 1848. |
| | 121 | F | ii. | **Ann Gilbert** was born in 1851. |

40. Samuel L. Gilbert (*Lucy Sharp³, Robert², John Sr.¹*) was born in 1836 in Virginia.

Samuel married **Martha J. *Unk**. Martha was born in 1825.
| | 122 | M | i. | **William P. Gilbert** was born in 1847. |
| | 123 | M | ii. | **John A. Gilbert** was born in 1852. |

55. Caleb (Calip) Lindsey (*Frances (Frankie) Sharp³, Charles W. Sr.², John Sr.¹*) was born 2 May 1827 in Cypress Inn, Wayne County, TN, died 25 Jun 1904, and was buried in Florence City Cemetery, Florence, Lauderdale County, AL.

General Notes: Co. J 76th Regiment, Missouri Militia, U.S. Calvary then Co E, 6th Regiment, Missouri Militia Calvary...notes of David Sharp.

"Caleb was in the Union Army, Company E, 6th Missouri Militia Calvary in the Civil War.
Caleb was the oldest child of Phillip and Frankie Lindsey. Born in 1827 near Cypress Inn, he died in 1904 and was buried on the East side of the Florence City Cemetery. The carver did such a terrible job that one has to decipher what is on the stone. It should be replaced by a Civil War marker that the government will furnish free of charge.
In his younger days, Caleb migrated to the Osage River in Missouri and at one time or another lived near Warsaw and Sedalia. His first marriage was to Frances Bush. They had four children, all born in Missouri. Following her death, he was soon married again, this time to Nancy Jane Gregg. She was born May 2, 1848, in Greene County, Missouri. She died October 27, 1898 and is buried beside Caleb. There were 10 children by this second marriage. I knew a number of Caleb's children. Two of his sons were married to my Father's aunts, making us double kin. One son, David, often told exciting stories about growing up in Missouri

where they were neighbors to Jesse James' mother. One of his favorite tales was about Jesse James "bumping" him on his knees when he was a child, pretending that he was riding a horse. (This was before Jesse and Frank James became infamous outlaws)

Caleb enrolled in Company J, 76th Regiment, Missouri Militia, U.S. Calvary, on Dec 5, 1862. He later served in Company E, 6th Regiment, Missouri Militia Calvary. This caused a problem in our family in that his Alabama brothers were in the Confederate Army. My Grandfather Lindsey told a story about his Uncle Caleb's Yankee unit was in the local area at one occasion, allowing him to visit his mother and father on Brush Creek. By chance, his brother, Adron came home on furlough at the same time. As Adron approached the house, Caleb fled out the back door and into the woods, leaving his hat behind. The Yankee hat was the first thing Adron spotted when he entered the room. When I was a little fellow, I wondered what my Great- Grandfather Adron would have done had he met his brother that day rather than finding his hat.

After the war, Caleb and Nancy Jane left their farm in Missouri. His family said they 'just moved away without selling the farm'. They traveled in covered wagons to Tennessee where Caleb bought another farm. This place was called Missionary Springs near Cypress Inn, not far from where he was born. In 1890, he acquired 159.05 acres under the Homestead Act; this farm (S.E. 1/4 Section 11, Township 1, South, Range 13 West) near Savannah Highway in Lauderdale County about twelve or thirteen miles from Florence. He sold this farm around 1897 and bought a place on Sweetwater avenue in Florence where he died in 1904. When my Grandfather Leonard Lindsey moved to Florence from Waterloo in 1899 to work at the Florence Wagon Works he lived with his Uncle Caleb at this place. This was when he met my Grandmother Lucy Lavinia Johnson..." see 'The Legacy of Our Lindsey's' by William Lindsey McDonald.

Caleb married **Frances (Lucy Ann) Bush** about 1845 in Alabama. Frances was born in 1818 in Tennessee, died 27 Oct 1898, and was buried in Wright Cemetery, Wright, Lauderdale County, AL. Another name for Frances was Francis (Lucy Ann) Bush.

+ 124 F i. **Nancy (Fannie) Paralee Lindsey** was born 22 Apr 1847 in Tennessee and died 5 Mar 1923.
+ 125 M ii. **John Phillip Lindsey II** was born 14 Nov 1848 in Lauderdale County, AL, died 16 Feb 1917, and was buried in Florence City Cemetery, Florence, Lauderdale County, AL.
+ 126 M iii. **Joseph A. Lindsey** was born in May 1850 in Missouri.
+ 127 M iv. **David A. Lindsey** was born in Dec 1861 in Warsaw, MO, died 25 May 1934, and was buried in Florence City Cemetery, Florence, Lauderdale County, AL.

Caleb next married **Nancy Jane Gregg** about 1862 in Lauderdale County, AL. Nancy was born 2 May 1848 in Green County, MO, died 27 Oct 1898, and was buried in Florence City Cemetery, Florence, Lauderdale County, AL.

+ 128 M i. **John L. Lindsey** died 7 Jun 1937 and was buried in Dalton, GA.
  129 M ii. **Charles Lindsey** was born in 1867 and died in 1871.

> General Notes: "The story of "Little Charlie" is sad. On a cold winter day he strayed from home and became lost in the deep Missouri woods. Search parties - soldiers from a nearby camp - eventually found him, but Little Charlie developed pneumonia from the exposure and died a few days before his fourth birthday..." William McDonald

  130 F iii. **Janie Margaret Lindsey** was born 1 Feb 1869 in Sedalia, MO, died in 1941, and was buried in Florence City Cemetery, Florence, Lauderdale County, AL.

> General Notes: "Janie was never married and lived with her sister, Tellie Myrick..." William McDonald

+ 131 F iv. **Mollie Elizabeth Lindsey** was born 11 Mar 1871, died 30 Aug 1907, and was buried in Florence City Cemetery, Florence, Lauderdale County, AL.
+ 132 F v. **America Lindsey** was born in 1873 in Lauderdale County, AL and died in 1925.
+ 133 F vi. **Lula Mae Lindsey** was born 21 Feb 1876 and died 12 Jan 1948.
+ 134 F vii. **Tellie Dora Lindsey** was born 8 Jan 1879 in Lauderdale County, AL, died 24 Aug 1949, and was buried in Florence City Cemetery, Florence, Lauderdale County, AL.
+ 135 M viii. **Robert Andrew Lindsey** was born 27 Jan 1880 in Lauderdale County, AL, died 27 Jan 1932, and was buried in Florence City Cemetery, Florence, Lauderdale County, AL.
+ 136 M ix. **Alonzo Brown Lindsey** was born 16 Nov 1887 in Lauderdale County, AL, died 30 Aug 1954, and was buried in Greenview Memorial Park, Florence, Lauderdale County, AL.
+ 137 M x. **Edgar Floyd Lindsey Sr.** was born 11 Mar 1893 in Lauderdale County, AL, died 8 Jan 1951, and was buried in New Orleans, LA.

56. Andrew Jackson Lindsey (*Frances (Frankie) Sharp* [3], *Charles W. Sr.* [2], *John Sr.* [1]) was born in 1829 in Cypress Inn, Wayne County, TN, died 17 Jul 1863, and was buried in National Cemetery, Finns Point, NJ.

General Notes: "Andrew was in the Confederate Army, Company G, 27th Alabama Infantry Regiment. He was captured at Raymond, Mississippi, on May 17, 1863 and sent to Ft Delaware, Delaware, where he died July 17, 1863. I have corresponded with Fort Delaware and they sent me photos of a monument which has Uncle Jack's name inscribed among the other prisoners who died there during the war. There is little question as to how he came by his name in that he was born about the year 1829 while Andrew Jackson was in the White House. On September 28, 1853, he was married to Nancy Jane Murphy who was of the family that gave its name to Murphy's Cross Roads and Murphy's Chapel Free Will Baptist Church. I know very little about Uncle Jack other than my Grandfather said that he had fought for the Confederacy. When Milton Burks was pastor at Liberty Baptist Church in the 1960's he permitted me to look at the early church records. There were two incidents involving a gentleman named Jackson Lindley who may or may not have been our Andrew Jackson Lindsey (It was not unusual for our Lindsey name to be misspelled in early records). The first was his trial in November 1852: "We took up the report on Jackson Lindley for drinking too much liquor, and laid it over until the next meeting" at the next session Jackson Lindley was "excluded for disorderly conduct". This church was organized, May 22, 1852, about twenty miles from Florence - seventeen miles out the Savannah Highway and three miles north on the old Natchez Trace. In 1868, it was moved to Threet's Crossroads (formerly called Russell's Crossroads). Jackson and Nancy Jane Lindsey had at least two children, Caleb and Merry Dee. I wish I knew more about Uncle Jack and his family. They must surely have moved to another state...." William McDonald

Thursday, August 13, 1998 ------------ Florence, Alabama Times Daily by Bill McDonald

Jack Lindsey Mystery Has Been Solved
"This story is about Jack Lindsey, who went to war and was never seen or heard from again. Now, more than 130 years later, the mystery of what happened to him has been resolved.
Born as Andrew Jackson Lindsey in 1829 at Cypress Inn, Tennessee, Jack's parents were Phillips and Frankie Sharp Lindsey. His family later settled on the Barton Branch in the Wright Community near Waterloo.
In 1853, Jack and Nancy Jane Murphy of the Murphy's Chapel Community exchanged their wedding vows. Soon afterwards they were residing on a small farm near the Russell Crossroads Northwest of Florence. This is where Jack, Nancy Jane and their two small children were living when the war erupted, an event that changed their lives forever.
It was on Christmas Eve 1861 when Jack and his brother, Adron, made their way to Florence to be sworn in as members of the newly organized 27th Alabama Infantry Regiment by the local recruiting officer, Alabama Militia Gen. Samuel Weakley.
They were assigned to Company C. This was Captain E.B. Thompsons's outfit. He lived near the Oakland Community.
Both brothers were armed with a hunting knife and Higgins long rifle .These had been made during their boyhood years by old Alexander Higgins in Waterloo. Adron recalled he also brought along a bullet mold, shot pouch and powder flask. Two days after their enlistment they along with others were placed aboard boats at the Florence Port and sent to Fort Helman, Kentucky.
After most of the 27th Regiment had been captured at the fall of Fort Donelson in February 1862, Adron was detached as a wagoner and pioneer, with duties that involved building bridges and pontoons. It was more than a year later when his brother Jack disappeared.
Facts surrounding the mystery of what happened to Jack Lindsey began unfolding recently when the Florence-Lauderdale Public Library acquired the Confederate Microfilms from the National Archives. Military records revealed that he had been captured near Raymond, Mississippi on May 17, 1863 and sent to Fort Delaware, Del.
Two months later he died and was buried in the nearby National Cemetery at Finn's Point, New Jersey.
Following this discovery, an inquiry was made to the Fort Delaware Society. This organization was founded in 1950 with the Mission of preserving the Old Fort as well as the memories of those who were part of this history.
They quickly responded with information about Private Lindsey and the 12,500 Confederate prisoners who were imprisoned there in the summer of 1863. Lindsey had been among the 2,700 soldiers who died at Fort Delaware during the Civil War. Accompanying photographs from the Fort Delaware Society shows that the Confederate dead are beautifully memorialized by the name of each soldier inscribed on a large marble monument. This is enclosed inside a white, Romanesque rotunda inside the National Cemetery. Among those listed is the name of Private A. J. Lindsey. This ends the story of what happened to Jack Lindsey.

Although written in tragedy, its sadness has been somewhat softened over many years by the love and care of strangers who knew only his name and his identification as a confederate soldier...." William McDonald

Andrew married **Nancy Jane Murphy**, daughter of **John Murphy** and **Alley (Ailey) Welch**, 30 Sep 1853 in Lauderdale County, AL. Nancy was born in Aug 1837 in Alabama and died in 1910 in Alabama.

| | 138 | M | i. | **Caleb Lindsey** was born between 1854 and 1855 in Lauderdale County, AL. |
| + | 139 | M | ii. | **Maraday (Merry Dee) Lindsey** was born in May 1854 in Lauderdale County, AL and died in Mississippi. |

57. Sylvester (Sill) B. Lindsey (*Frances (Frankie) Sharp* [3], *Charles W. Sr.* [2], *John Sr.* [1]) was born 14 Jul 1830 in Cypress Inn, Wayne County, TN, died 14 Jan 1892, and was buried in Wright Cemetery, Wright, Lauderdale County, AL.

General Notes: "In 1850 Census Sylvester Lindsey was listed living in a house listed as a Private Entertainment House. He was listed as a cooper (barrel maker). Sylvester was a mail carrier. He went to Florence one day and picked up the mail and returned the next. He also took passengers. A newspaper advertisement read: "Attention Travelers! During low water in the river, I will leave Waterloo with my nice spring wagon every Monday, Wednesday and Friday at 9:00 A.M. through to Florence by 5:00 P.M. Returning I will leave Florence on Tuesday, Thursday and Saturday at 9:00 A.M. and get to Waterloo at 5:00 P.M. Charge for passenger and 50 pounds baggage $2.00 each way... Sill B. Lindsey

He served in the Fourth Alabama Calvary. He often told of fighting in the battles of Little Bear Creek and Town Creek. He boasted of being at Shiloh under Fighting Joe Wheeler and of riding with Forrest in the capture of Colonel Abel Streight in his famous raid across Sand Mountain. He was married to Hannah Less, a distant cousin of General Robert E. Lee.

Sylvester B. Lindsey, II was a veteran of the Confederate Army. A member of the 4th Alabama Calvary, he was under Brigadier General Philip Dale Roddey of Moulton, Alabama. Roddey was known as the "Defender of North Alabama". Uncle Sill told of fighting in the Battles of Little Bear Creek and Town Creek. He was at Shiloh and with General Joe Wheeler in the famous raid into Tennessee. In April, 1863, he rode with Forest in the capture of Colonel Streight in his raid across Sand Mountain. He and his brother, Adron, my great- grandfather, were in the Battle of Franklin, Tennessee but in different commands. Sylvester's widow, Hannah, filed for a Confederate pension following his death; he died January 24, 1890..." David Sharp

Sylvester married **Hannah Neamah Lee**, daughter of **John (Jackie) David Lee** and **Amy Ray**, 7 Jan 1853 in Lauderdale County, AL. Hannah was born in 1832 in Lauderdale County, AL, died after 24 Jan 1890, and was buried in Wright Cemetery, Wright, Lauderdale County, AL.

General Notes: "The legacy of Hannah Lee is most interesting in that she was related to the Byrds of Virginia and a distant cousin of General Robert E. Lee. Her father, John Lee, of Brush Creek in West Lauderdale County, was a son of Michael Byrd Lee who was descended from William Lee I (born 1597 and died 1653). This William was a brother to Richard Lee I (born in 1602 and died in 1664). Richard Lee I was a direct ancestor of the famous Lees of Virginia. The name "Green Berry" in our Lindsey's began with this generation and can be traced back through a number of generations among the Lees who named their sons both Green and Berry"...William McDonald

+	140	M	i.	**Greenberry Lee Lindsey Sr.** was born 14 Nov 1854 in Lauderdale County, AL, died 12 Nov 1930, and was buried in Wright Cemetery, Wright, Lauderdale County, AL.
	141	F	ii.	**Mary (Polly) Lindsey** was born in 1856 in Lauderdale County, AL.
	142	F	iii.	**Martha (Bettie) Lindsey** was born in 1859 in Lauderdale County, AL.
+	143	F	iv.	**Julie (Julia) Lindsey** was born in Jun 1860 in Lauderdale County, AL and died 3 Mar 1937.
+	144	M	v.	**Adron (Little Ade) Lindsey** was born in Oct 1863 in Lauderdale County, AL, died in 1945, and was buried in John Lay Cemetery, Etheridge, TN.
+	145	M	vi.	**John H. Lindsey** was born in 1866 in Lauderdale County, AL.
+	146	F	vii.	**Matilda Lindsey** was born in 1868 in Lauderdale County, AL.

58. Adron Leonard Lindsey Sr. (*Frances (Frankie) Sharp* [3], *Charles W. Sr.* [2], *John Sr.* [1]) was born in 1835 in Cypress Inn, Wayne County, TN, died 16 Jan 1924, and was buried in Florence City Cemetery, Florence, Lauderdale County, AL.

General Notes: From biographical sketches of Lauderdale County Civil War Soldiers:
Adron L. Lindsey of Bluff Creek area, near Wright, served in Co. C, 27th Alabama Infantry.
"While he was in service, records show that his wife and three children, ages, 7, 6 and 2 had been harassed so frequently by the numerous raids, the county made purchases of $158.50 worth of supplies for the family. Materials thus purchased included 800 pounds of pork, 35 bushels of meal, 200 pounds of flour, salt, cotton and shoes. Similar entries were recorded for 751 families.

'The Confederate Soldier'
   My Great-grandfather Adron Leonard Lindsey, Sr. was born at Cypress Inn, Tennessee, in February, 1835. His parents were Phillip Lindsey and Frankie Sharp Lindsey. His name Adron was often spelled "Adrian", in fact, he used this spelling as well as his nickname "Aid" in the later years of his life. His mother named him in honor of her brother, Adron Sharp, and her grandfather Adron Anglin. The name Adron has been carried through many generations in our family....
   ...As a young boy Adron went to work for Josiah Higgins who operated a large farm north of Waterloo on Second Creek. Josiah became his father-in-law on April 8. 1861. War clouds were gathering. Adron was 23 years of age, and his bride, Martha Jane Higgins, was one year younger. I have published the story of our Higgins Family, in which I related the story about Martha Jane being a half -blood Chickasaw Indian. (Her mother, Chealty Higgins, was a full- blooded Chickasaw born on Koger Island in 1811 or 1813.) Family tradition has it that Chealty and her daughters, who fortunately inherited her features, were unusually graceful and beautiful. This characteristic agrees with what Albert James Pickett observed in his early history of Alabama. He described the Chickasaw female as "cleanly, industrious and generally good-looking".

"Great -Grandpa's War Experiences"
   "Adron Lindsey lived to be 89 years of age and was living with my Grandparents when he died. In his last days he was quite feeble and would sit for hours in a rocking chair in the front parlor. His young grandchildren would sometimes run through the house which would disturb the old fellow. These abrupt noises seemed to bring back memories from his war years. at such events he would bang the floor with his walking cane and yell, "The Yankees are coming! The Yankees are coming!" My dear Mother said that when a little girl she was afraid of her grandfather Lindsey.
   Adron and Martha had been married a little over eight months when he went to war. He was sworn in on Christmas Eve, 1861, by General Samuel Weakley of Florence. Adron L. Lindsey was assigned to the 27th Alabama Infantry Regiment. One of the privileges at that time was that volunteers could select their company; Adron picked Company C, commanded by Captain Thompson who operated a large plantation near Oakland.
   Adron furnished his own weapons which included a long hunting knife and a Kentucky rifle, both made by Alexander Higgins at the blacksmith shop on Josiah Higgins' farm. Old Alexander Higgins was Martha Jane Lindsey's Grandfather. Adron also brought along his own bullet mold, shot pouch and powder flask.
   The 27th Regiment assembled at Florence on the day after Christmas at which time they were placed aboard boats and sent to Fort Heiman, Kentucky. Great-grandfather was captured, along with most all of his regiment, following the fall of Fort Donelson. They were sent to Camp Douglas, Illinois, where they remained until exchanged the following September.
   After the 27th was re- organized, Adron was assigned as wagoner and from time to time was detailed to other commands as a Pioneer, which in our modern army relates to military engineering - building bridges, pontoons, camp sites, etc.
   Great -grandpa Lindsey was in ten major battles and many skirmishes. One historian estimated that the 27th Infantry marched more than 5,000 miles from the time it left home until its surrender. The major battles great -grandpa fought in were: Baker's Creek, Baton Rouge, Jackson, Resaca, New Hope Church, Peace Tree Creek, Ezra Church, Franklin and Nashville. Adron was wounded at Baton Rouge in June, 1863; a wagon ran over him, breaking an arm at the elbow and a leg at his ankle. He sometimes talked about being on the line of battle for four weeks without let -up around Atlanta in July 1864. All but three members of his company were killed in the Battle of Franklin. Great -grandpa remained with his unit until almost the very end - serving for more than three years. He was captured near Demopolis in April, 1865. He often told of how he had been without food or sleep for three days and three nights prior to his capture. The Yankees gave him a choice as to whether to eat or sleep first, he said as hungry as he was, he chose first to sleep under a tree where he remained almost all day before he lined up for chow late in the afternoon. Adron walked home to Waterloo from Demopolis. He said that he had no shoes and was barefoot. He hitched a ride near Montgomery on a wagon and rode some two or three miles. All the rest of the trip was on foot.

Martha Jane remained on her father's farm while her husband was away at war. A daughter, Lucretia, whom we knew as "Aunt Lula" was born during this time. Martha Jane's father, Josiah Higgins, was captured at Waterloo in August, 1862, for firing on a Yankee boat. He was sent to a prison in Alton, Illinois. Josiah was transferred in October of that year to St Louis, Missouri and from there released and allowed to return home to Waterloo.

Adron and Martha Jane lived at a number of places following the war years. When my Grandfather - their youngest child - was born, they were living in the Wright Community. I have visited this old place a number of times. It was a log structure with a large open hall between the rooms, called a "dog trot". This house is now gone but it stood almost across the highway from the Wright Cemetery near the junction of County Road 8. When Pickwick Lake was formed about 1937, it created a small peninsula where the lake came almost up to the house.

They later moved to Manbone Creek where they were living in 1888 when Martha Jane died. My Grandfather was only nine years old at the time. Great-grandmother Martha Jane was buried on top of a high and steep hill overlooking her father's farm at Second Creek. Here she rests in the Simpson/Whitten Cemetery beside her father and mother and her sister, Ellender Elizabeth Tune. In 1990, my brothers, John and Tom and I placed markers on Martha Jane's grave along with markers for her parents, Josiah and Chealty Higgins.

Adron was soon married to a widow, Isabel Culver, who was called "Belle". She was born in August 1844 or 1845 and listed her age as 45 years in the 1900 census. Belle had a number of children by a previous marriage. One son was Washington Culver, the father of Ezra L. Culver, an outstanding business leader at Florence.

Old Palestine Methodist Church in those days was near Manbone Cave not far from the Lindsey home. Great-grandpa joined this church in his old days. He enjoyed talking about the minister and repeating the text used that day. I have forgotten the name of the minister, but the text he used was from Joshua 24:15 "...choose you this day whom you will serve..."

Adron applied for and was granted a Confederate pension (Application Number 9201) in 1899. He listed his illness as "rheumatism" and gave "Waterloo" as his post office address. He was 64 years of age at the time and listed his assets as: 1 mule $30; 1 cow and calf $20; 5 hogs $5; 1 clock $1; household and kitchen furniture $50; 1 farm wagon $15 and tools $4. I have a copy of a letter dated October 14, 1900, written on the stationary of "W.T. McCorkle Drugs and Stationary, Waterloo, Alabama". It was signed by "A. L. Lindsey, Sr." and addressed to "Judge John J. Mitchell" at Florence. This letter was a request as follows, "You will please send me the amount due me from the state by Mr. Phillips'. Mr. Phillips was the mail carrier between Florence and Waterloo.

Late in life, Adron and Belle moved to Florence. The old veteran, Adron "Adrian" L. Lindsey, died January 16, 1924 and was buried in Soldier's Rest, a Confederate Cemetery near the back of the Florence Cemetery. A beautiful marble stone marks his final resting place. We have a large painting of Great-grandfather Lindsey hanging in our stairwell. The photograph from which this painting was created was made about 1920 when he was 85 years old. In the painting he is dressed in his ceremonial Confederate Uniform worn in those days to conventions and gatherings of old soldiers. The Confederate Battle Flag forms the background for this portrait...." see 'The Legacy of Our Lindsey's' by William Lindsey McDonald.

Adron married **Martha Jane Higgins**, daughter of **Josiah Higgins** and **Charlotte Smith (Chealty) Chickasaw**, 7 Apr 1861 in Lauderdale County, AL. Martha was born about 1837 in Lauderdale County, AL, died in 1888, and was buried in Whitten Cemetery, Lauderdale County, AL.

+ 147 F i. **Lucretia (Lula) Lindsey** was born 3 Apr 1863 in Lauderdale County, AL and died 15 Apr 1940 in Savannah, Hardin County, TN.

+ 148 M ii. **Calvin Lindsey** was born about 1868 in Lauderdale County, AL, died in 1894, and was buried in Tyronza Cemetery, Tyronza, Poinsett County, AR.

+ 149 F iii. **Mary (Polly) Lindsey** was born in 1870 in Lauderdale County, AL.

+ 150 M iv. **Hunter Lindsey** was born in 1876 in Wright, Lauderdale County, AL, died in 1900, and was buried in Wright Cemetery, Wright, Lauderdale County, AL.

+ 151 M v. **Adron Leonard (Green) Lindsey Jr.** was born 21 Jan 1878 in Wright, Lauderdale County, AL, died 30 May 1960, and was buried in Florence City Cemetery, Florence, Lauderdale County, AL.

Adron next married **Isabell (Belle) Culver**. Isabell was born in Aug 1844 in Alabama.

59. Robert Lindsey (*Frances (Frankie) Sharp [3], Charles W. Sr. [2], John Sr. [1]*) was born in 1839 in Cypress Inn, Wayne County, TN, died in 1924, and was buried in Florence City Cemetery, Florence, Lauderdale County, AL.

General Notes: "Robert Lindsey, born about 1832 or 1833, was the fourth son of Phillip and Frankie Sharp Lindsey. My Grandfather mentioned once that his Uncle Robert was a soldier in the Civil War. However, I have no information as to when or what unit. Robert was married twice. His first wife died in childbirth. He was married the second time on December 21, 1855, to Sarah Freeman. Sarah was born in 1837. Robert listed his occupation as farmer in both the 1860 and 1870 census records.." William McDonald

Robert married ***Unk**.

General Notes: This first wife died in childbirth. Name is unknown. Mary was her child.

    152   F   i.   **Mary Lindsey** was born in 1852.

Robert next married **Sarah Freeman** 21 Dec 1855 in Lauderdale County, AL. Sarah was born about 1837 in Alabama.

+   153 F   i.   **Nancy Lindsey** was born about 1856 in Alabama.
     154 M ii.   **William Lindsey** was born about 1857 in Alabama.
+   155 M iii. **Johnathan Lindsey Jr.** was born about 1860 in Alabama.
+   156 M iv. **Calvin Lindsey** was born about 1862 in Alabama.
     157 F   v.   **Leanna Lindsey** was born about 1868 in Alabama.

61. Mary M. (Polly II) Lindsey (*Frances (Frankie) Sharp*[3], *Charles W. Sr.*[2], *John Sr.*[1]) was born about 1844 in Waterloo, Lauderdale County, AL, died 5 Jan 1920, and was buried in Murphy's Chapel Cemetery, Lauderdale County, AL.

Front: William "Billy" M. Young, Mary "Polly" Lindsey Young, Elizabeth "Lizzie" Young (Bill's Sister)
Back standing: Hubert Young, Lee Young and Nan Young Bevis

General Notes: "Mary Lindsey, II, born in 1844, was named in honor of her sister Mary who died in infancy two years before the second Mary's birth. Both Mary's were called 'Polly". This Polly was married to William Young at the end of the Civil War. William was a farmer and they made their home at Gravelly Springs..." William McDonald

Mary married **William (Billy) M. Young**, son of **Elijah Young** and **Mary Jane Lamb**, 24 Dec 1865 in Lauderdale County, AL. William was born 10 Jun 1836 in Lauderdale County, AL, died 30 Dec 1904, and was buried in Murphy's Chapel Cemetery, Lauderdale County, AL.

General Notes: "William served in the Civil War. Info as follows: Pvt. Co. C.27th Alabama Infantry, C.S.A. A memorial tomb has been placed at his grave in the Murphy's Chapel Cemetery. At a re-enactment of a Civil War Battle, a flag was presented to Ronnie Brown, William's great-great-grandson..." William McDonald

     158 U   i.   **Infant Young**.
     159 U   ii.   **Infant Young**.
     160 U iii. **Infant Young**.
+   161 F   iv. **Eddie Young** was born 5 Aug 1866 in Gravely Springs, Lauderdale County, AL, died 5 Oct 1933, and was buried in Murphy's Chapel Cemetery, Lauderdale County, AL.
+   162 F   v.   **Mary Francis (Molly) Young** was born 9 Nov 1867 in Lauderdale County, AL, died 14 Apr 1900, and was buried in Murphy's Chapel Cemetery, Lauderdale County, AL.
+   163 F   vi. **Roxie Leona Young** was born

19 Oct 1868 in Gravely Springs, Lauderdale County, AL, died 19 Jan 1951, and was buried in Murphy's Chapel Cemetery, Lauderdale County, AL.

+ 164 F vii. **Delia (Dee) Young** was born 19 Oct 1869 in Gravely Springs, Lauderdale County, AL, died in 1897, and was buried in Murphy's Chapel Cemetery, Lauderdale County, AL.

+ 165 F viii. **Lou Young** was born 11 Jul 1870 in Lauderdale County, AL, died 31 Dec 1952, and was buried in Murphy's Chapel Cemetery, Lauderdale County, AL.

+ 166 M ix. **William (Bill) Young** was born 15 Mar 1873 in Lauderdale County, AL, died 14 Nov 1941, and was buried in Pleasant Hill Cemetery, Lauderdale County, AL.

+ 167 F x. **Nancy (Nan) Young** was born 15 Mar 1874 in Lauderdale County, AL, died 17 Feb 1914, and was buried in Murphy's Chapel Cemetery, Lauderdale County, AL.

+ 168 F xi. **Dora Lee Young** was born 13 Jun 1876 in Lauderdale County, AL, died 21 May 1922, and was buried in Mt. Olive Cemetery, Lauderdale County, AL.

169 M xii. **Hurbert Franklin Young** was born 30 Apr 1881 in Lauderdale County, AL, died 27 Nov 1927, and was buried in Murphy's Chapel Cemetery, Lauderdale County, AL.

+ 170 M xiii. **Lee Jackson Young** was born in 1883 in Lauderdale County, AL, died 4 Oct 1962, and was buried in St. Joseph Valley Cemetery, Mishawaka, IN.

63. John S. Lindsey (*Frances (Frankie) Sharp[3], Charles W. Sr.[2], John Sr.[1]*) was born in 1845 in Lauderdale County, AL.

General Notes: "John, the youngest child of Phillip and Frankie, was not old enough to fight in the Civil War. He helped his father on the farm all during the war years. On November 19, 1886, he gave a deposition about his experiences in the winter of 1865 when federal soldiers raided his father's farm (this document is filed with Phillip Lindsey's Claim in Washington).

J. A. Lindsey testifies: Age 33; farmer; residence, Waterloo, Alabama; interested and related to the claimant as a son; I lived in Waterloo, Alabama, during the war with my father; do not know how much property father had at the outbreak of the war; I know of property being taken from home by the Union Army during the war; of my own personal knowledge there was taken from him one milch cow, 2 heifers, 50 bushels of corn, 1200 lbs pork, about 500 bundles fodder, one mare of the value of $200, 40 gallons molasses, 100 lbs honey, 50 bushels potatoes, 1000 rails and some cotton in the seed, about 800 lbs or more. The mare was on Brush Creek when she was taken; I was riding her at the time; I know they took 1,000 rails because I helped make one thousand to replace the amount taken; two heifers were worth $30; the milk cow that was taken was worth $20, the 50 bushels corn $25, the 1200 lbs fodder $96, the 500 bundles fodder $5; 40 gallons molasses 75 cents gallon, $30; the 100 lbs honey, 10 cents per pound, $10; the 50 bushels potatoes at 50 cents, $25; 1,000 rails at 75 cents per hundred, $7.50; the 800 lbs seed cotton at $6 pound, $68.

Cross examination: Soldiers that took the cotton burned about three -fourths of it; I cannot tell what they did with the honey and molasses. I was 12 or 13 years old at the beginning of the war; I was 33 years old at my last birthday; do not know of anything further in relation to this case.

This statement was of it to the one he had made at an earlier date when the claim was originally filed. However, here are more interesting excerpts.

"There was a good pile of it (salted pork)...I saw it taken from the smokehouse; it was carried away on horses; Lieutenant was with the command; had camped at father's house; meat was taken away with them in the morning...."

"I was on the mare when she was taken; the command met me and made me get down; they took the mare, saddle, bridle and blanket; clay bank mare three years old..." William McDonald

John married **Martha C. Gooch**, daughter of **Johnson Gooch** and **Dicy *Unk**, 19 May 1867 in Lauderdale County, AL. Martha was born in 1847 in Alabama.

+ 171 F i. **Harriet Lutisha Lindsey** was born in 1867 in Alabama.

172 M ii. **William Lindsey** was born in 1868 in Lauderdale County, AL.

173 M iii. **John Lindsey** was born in 1869 in Alabama.

174 M iv. **Henry Lindsey** was born in 1870 in Lauderdale County, AL.

+ 175 F v. **Louisa F. Lindsey** was born 9 May 1872 in Lauderdale County, AL, died 13 Jan 1931, and was buried in Snyder, Scurry County, TX.

+ 176 F vi. **Ellie Lindsey** was buried in Forrest City, St. Francis County, AR.

+ 177 F vii. **Sarah Lindsey**.

178 F viii. **Dee Lindsey**.

179 F ix. **Dicey Lindsey**.

180 F x. **Leora Lindsey**.

+	181	F	xi.	**Lara Lindsey.**
	182	F	xii.	**Leatha Lindsey.**
	183	M	xiii.	**Albert Lindsey.**

64. James (Jim) Charles Sharp Sr. (*Adron (Edwin/Ade) Sr.[3], Charles W. Sr.[2], John Sr.[1]*) was born in 1829 in Gravely Springs, Lauderdale County, AL, died 7 May 1894, and was buried in Lauderdale County, AL.

James married **Melissa Ann Wood**, daughter of **Bennett A. Wood** and **Margaret Ford**, 10 Apr 1852 in Lauderdale County, AL. Melissa was born 10 Apr 1852 in Wright, Lauderdale County, AL and died in 1872.

+	184	M	i.	**Robert Patton Sharp** was born 12 Feb 1854 in Wright, Lauderdale County, AL, died 6 Dec 1912, and was buried in Savannah, Hardin County, TN.
+	185	M	ii.	**John Thomas (Tom) Sharp** was born 6 Sep 1855 in Wright, Lauderdale County, AL, died 22 Jul 1895, and was buried in Wright Cemetery, Wright, Lauderdale County, AL.
+	186	F	iii.	**Matilda Ann Sharp** was born in Jan 1858 in Wright, Lauderdale County, AL, died in 1927, and was buried in Gravely Springs Cemetery, Lauderdale County, AL.
+	187	M	iv.	**Owen Bennett (Doc) Sharp** was born 23 Dec 1860 in Wright, Lauderdale County, AL, died 21 Apr 1923, and was buried in Wright Cemetery, Wright, Lauderdale County, AL.
+	188	M	v.	**James Charles Sharp Jr.** was born 8 Apr 1861 in Wright, Lauderdale County, AL, died in 1939, and was buried in Wesley Chapel Cemetery, Lauderdale County, AL.
+	189	F	vi.	**Margaret E. Sharp** was born about 1866 in Wright, Lauderdale County, AL and died in Texas.
	190	M	vii.	**Eddie Sharp** was born about 1868 in Wright, Lauderdale County, AL.

General Notes: "Eddie and James C. lived at Gravelly Springs. He sent James to get some fresh water from the spring a couple of hundred yards away. James came back and found him by a rail fence with his throat cut. It is said that he killed himself..." Doris McMillan

James next married **Maryjane America Smith**, daughter of **John Smith** and **Katherine (Katty) Swinford**, 21 Mar 1878 in Lauderdale County, AL. Maryjane was born 19 Apr 1860 in Lauderdale County, AL, died 2 Feb 1944, and was buried in Oak Grove Cemetery, Lauderdale County, AL.

+	191	M	i.	**Charles W. Sharp** was born 25 May 1879 in Lauderdale County, AL, died 16 Feb 1924, and was buried in Oak Grove Cemetery, Lauderdale County, AL.
+	192	M	ii.	**Joseph (Joe) Sidney Sharp** was born 28 Sep 1880 in Lauderdale County, AL, died 17 Dec 1966, and was buried in Milledgeville Cemetery, Hardin County, TN.
+	193	F	iii.	**Elizabeth (Roxie) Belle Sharp** was born 15 Jun 1882 in Lauderdale County, AL, died 25 Jan 1957, and was buried in Oak Grove Cemetery, Lauderdale County, AL.
	194	F	iv.	**Minnie Jane Sharp** was born 15 Apr 1884 in Lauderdale County, AL, died 22 Oct 1948, and was buried in Oak Grove Cemetery, Lauderdale County, AL.
+	195	M	v.	**Louis (Bud) Wheeler Sharp** was born 19 May 1887 in Lauderdale County, AL, died 17 Feb 1943, and was buried in Oak Grove Cemetery, Lauderdale County, AL.
+	196	F	vi.	**Etta C. Sharp** was born in Nov 1888 in Lauderdale County, AL and died 18 May 1920.
+	197	F	vii.	**Mary Elizabeth Sharp** was born in Feb 1891 in Lauderdale County, AL.
+	198	F	viii.	**Margie (Lady) J. Sharp** was born in Aug 1892 in Lauderdale County, AL, died 11 Apr 1936, and was buried in Oak Grove Cemetery, Lauderdale County, AL.

James Charles Sharp, Sr. and his second wife, Maryjane America Smith Sharp

65. Charles (Charlie) A. Sharp (*Adron (Edwin/Ade) Sr.*³*, Charles W. Sr.*²*, John Sr.*¹) was born 12 Feb 1830 in Wright, Lauderdale County, AL, died 23 Nov 1882, and was buried in Oak Hill Cemetery, Booneville, Logan County, AR.

Charles married **Julia *Unk** about 1848. Julia was born about 1837 and died about 1855.
   199 F   i.   **Robin Sharp** was born in 1849 in Lauderdale County, AL and was buried in Booneville, Logan County, AR.

Charles next married **Matilda Boles**, daughter of **Gustavous Adolphus Boles** and **Charlotte *Unk**, about 1861 in Booneville, Logan County, AR. Matilda was born 5 Apr 1837 in South Carolina, died 22 Feb 1916, and was buried in Oak Hill Cemetery, Booneville, Logan County, AR.

> General Notes: Matilda Boles Sharp came to Greene County, Arkansas in the early 1860's with her husband Charles Sharp.
> He enlisted into Company "D" 5th Arkansas Infantry at Little Rock on March 15, 1863 to serve a period of one year or more.
> Matilda, being left alone with an infant daughter, Mary Ann, walked all the way back to Lauderdale County, Alabama to be with her family, Mr. and Mrs. Gustavus Adolphus Boles (approximately 200 miles).
> The year of 1882 was a very difficult period for the Sharp's. Charles Sharp's father, Adron had come to Logan County, Arkansas to be near his son. Adron had married Zelene M. Potts after the death of his first wife Martha Lamb.
> The fall and winter of 1882 brought a flu (or grippe as it was sometimes called) epidemic. Charles died first on November 23, 1882 then on November 28, 1882 Zelene died, Adron completed a terrible 11 day period when he died on December 4, 1882.

+ 200 F   i.   **Mary Ann Sharp** was born 27 Aug 1862 in Lauderdale County, AL and died 30 Jan 1936 in Booneville, Logan County, AR.
+ 201 F   ii.   **Clarissa Sharp** was born 20 Aug 1865 in Logan County, AR.
+ 202 M   iii.   **Lil Adron Sharp** was born 1 Feb 1867 in Booneville, Logan County, AR.
+ 203 M   iv.   **Pugh Cannon Sharp** was born 31 Dec 1868 in Logan County, AR.
+ 204 F   v.   **Martha (Mattie) Sharp** was born 19 Jan 1871 in Logan County, AR.

+ 205 F vi. **Ellar Louise Sharp** was born 8 Apr 1872 in Logan County, AR.
+ 206 M vii. **William L. Sharp** was born 13 Apr 1875 in Logan County, AR.
+ 207 M viii. **Carol (Fuzzy) Louis Sharp** was born 7 Apr 1879 in Booneville, Logan County, AR and died 1 Aug 1952 in Woodlake, Tulare County, CA.

66. Elizabeth Mae (Lizzie) Sharp (*Adron (Edwin/Ade) Sr.*[3]*, Charles W. Sr.*[2]*, John Sr.*[1]) was born in 1833 in Wright, Lauderdale County, AL and died before 1888 in Lee County, AR.

   Elizabeth married **William (Bill) Jefferson Hill** about 1853 in Lee County, AR. William was born in Mar 1830 in Lauderdale County, AL and died in 1911 in Lee County, AR.
   208 F i. **Martha Hill** was born in 1854 in Lauderdale County, AL.
   209 F ii. **Francis Ruth Hill** was born in 1856 in Lauderdale County, AL.
   210 F iii. **Matilda Hill** was born in 1859 in Lauderdale County, AL.
+ 211 F iv. **Leanna Hill** was born 8 Apr 1861 in Lauderdale County, AL and died 6 Dec 1925 in Forrest City, St. Francis County, AR.
+ 212 F v. **Polly Hill** was born in 1864 in Lauderdale County, AL.
   213 F vi. **Laura Hill** was born in 1868 in Lauderdale County, AL.
   214 F vii. **Ida E. Hill** was born in 1871 in Lauderdale County, AL.

Bennett Hampton "Hamp" Wood and Rutha Barton Sharp Wood

68. Rutha (Ruthey) Barton Sharp (*Adron (Edwin/Ade) Sr.*[3]*, Charles W. Sr.*[2]*, John Sr.*[1]) was born in May 1841 in Waterloo, Lauderdale County, AL, died in Nov 1903, and was buried in Wright Cemetery, Wright, Lauderdale County, AL.

Rutha married **Bennett Hampton (Hamp) Wood**, son of **Bennett A. Wood** and **Margaret Ford**, 24 Apr 1856 in Lauderdale County, AL. Bennett was born 24 Mar 1838 in Alabama, died 15 Apr 1907, and was buried in Oak Grove Cemetery, Lauderdale County, AL.

General Notes: For further information on this branch of the family tree please see 'In the Beginning …1798 to 1998' by Sharon Wood and Doris McMillan.

69. Matilda Sharp (*Adron (Edwin/Ade) Sr.*[3]*, Charles W. Sr.*[2]*, John Sr.*[1]) was born in Mar 1843 in Wright, Lauderdale County, AL.

   Matilda married **Jefferson Thomas Reaves** 4 Mar 1857 in Lauderdale County, AL. Jefferson was born about 1838 in Alabama.
   215 M i. **Adron Reaves** was born about 1858 in Gravely Springs, Lauderdale County, AL.
   216 F ii. **Martha Reaves** was born about 1860 in Gravely Springs, Lauderdale County, AL.

71. Mary Eliza Sharp (*John Sr.*[3]*, Charles W. Sr.*[2]*, John Sr.*[1]) was born in Lauderdale County, AL, died 2 Jul 1908, and was buried in Murphy's Chapel Cemetery, Lauderdale County, AL.

   Mary married **James Robert Murphy Sr.**, son of **John Murphy** and **Alley (Ailey) Welch**, 17 Jun 1855 in Lauderdale County, AL. James was born 4 Sep 1831 in Lauderdale County, AL, died 11 Feb 1911, and was buried in Murphy's Chapel Cemetery, Lauderdale County, AL.
+ 217 F i. **Amanda Louisa Murphy** was born in 1857 in Lauderdale County, AL.
+ 218 M ii. **John Carroll Murphy** was born in 1859 in Lauderdale County, AL.
   219 M iii. **Marion E. Murphy** was born in 1860 in Lauderdale County, AL.

| | 220 | F | iv. | **Laura E. Murphy** was born 4 Oct 1862 in Lauderdale County, AL, died 25 Sep 1896, and was buried in Murphy's Chapel Cemetery, Lauderdale County, AL. |

+ 220 F iv. **Laura E. Murphy** was born 4 Oct 1862 in Lauderdale County, AL, died 25 Sep 1896, and was buried in Murphy's Chapel Cemetery, Lauderdale County, AL.

+ 221 F v. **Dorothy (Dolly) Elizabeth Murphy** was born 29 Jul 1864 in Lauderdale County, AL, died 18 Dec 1942, and was buried in Stoney Point Cemetery, Lauderdale County, AL.

+ 222 F vi. **Alice Murphy** was born in 1867 in Lauderdale County, AL.

+ 223 M vii. **David Murphy** was born in 1869 in Lauderdale County, AL.

+ 224 F viii. **Ida Murphy** was born in 1872 in Lauderdale County, AL.

225 M ix. **James R. Murphy Jr.** was born in 1878 in Lauderdale County, AL.

72. Sarah (Sallie) Sharp (*John Sr.³, Charles W. Sr.², John Sr.¹*) was born about 1838 in Lauderdale County, AL.

Sarah married **George J. Minton**, son of **John Minton** and **Sina *Unk**, 24 Oct 1853 in Lauderdale County, AL. George was born about 1828 in South Carolina.

226 F i. **Rosilee Minton** was born in 1857 in Alabama.

227 F ii. **Harriet Minton** was born about 1858 in Alabama.

228 F iii. **Cynthia Minton** was born about 1860 in Alabama.

229 F iv. **Julia Minton** was born about 1862 in Alabama.

230 F v. **Laura Minton** was born about 1865 in Alabama.

73. Elizabeth (Lizzie) May Sharp (*John Sr.³, Charles W. Sr.², John Sr.¹*) was born 18 Sep 1840 in Lauderdale County, AL, died 20 Jan 1915, and was buried in Wright Cemetery, Wright, Lauderdale County, AL.

Elizabeth married **Richard Washington Wright**, son of **Moses Wright** and **Sarah Anna Wilson**, 22 Dec 1868 in Lauderdale County, AL. Richard was born 7 Sep 1836 in Nashville, Davidson County, TN, died 25 Jun 1918, and was buried in Wright Cemetery, Wright, Lauderdale County, AL.

General Notes: PVT Co I 35th Alabama Infantry CSA

231 F i. **Nancy Minnie Irvin Wright** was born 15 Nov 1869 in Lauderdale County, AL, died 2 Aug 1877, and was buried in Wright, Lauderdale County, AL.

232 F ii. **Ida Mae Wright** was born 25 Mar 1873 in Lauderdale County, AL, died 6 Sep 1925, and was buried in Wright Cemetery, Wright, Lauderdale County, AL.

233 F iii. **Carrie Emma Wright** was born 25 May 1874 in Lauderdale County, AL, died 26 Jul 1877, and was buried in Lauderdale County, AL.

+ 234 M iv. **George Moses (Mode) Wright** was born 27 Aug 1877 in Wright, Lauderdale County, AL, died 2 Feb 1955, and was buried in Wright Cemetery, Wright, Lauderdale County, AL.

+ 235 M v. **James Phillip Wright** was born 12 Mar 1879 in Lauderdale County, AL, died in 1958, and was buried in Florence, Lauderdale County, AL.

+ 236 F vi. **Martha (Mattie) Jane Wright** was born 29 Jan 1882 in Lauderdale County, AL, died 21 Apr 1911, and was buried in Wright Cemetery, Wright, Lauderdale County, AL.

74. Carroll Ira (Buck) Sharp (*John Sr.³, Charles W. Sr.², John Sr.¹*) was born 11 Jan 1842 in Alabama, died 1 Aug 1896, and was buried in Wright Cemetery, Wright, Lauderdale County, AL.

Carroll married **Ann Caroline (Callie) Howell**, daughter of **William Phillip Howell** and **Mary Wesson**, 15 Aug 1865 in Lauderdale County, AL. Ann was born in 1846 in Alabama, died in 1934, and was buried in Wright Cemetery, Wright, Lauderdale County, AL.

237 M i. **William (Willie) Carrol Sharp** was born in 1866 in Lauderdale County, AL and died 4 May 1898 in Lauderdale County, AL.

+ 238 M ii. **Lee Sharp** was born in 1868 in Alabama.

+ 239 M iii. **John (Buck) Phillip Sharp** was born 9 Jan 1870 in Lauderdale County, AL, died 2 Mar 1949, and was buried in Wright Cemetery, Wright, Lauderdale County, AL.

+ 240 F iv. **Lilly B. Sharp** was born in 1873 in Alabama.

75. Martha J. Sharp (*John Sr.³, Charles W. Sr.², John Sr.¹*) was born in 1845 in Alabama.

Martha married **William Whitten** 17 Apr 1863 in Lauderdale County, AL.

76. Eliza Sharp (*John Sr.³, Charles W. Sr.², John Sr.¹*) was born in 1846 in Lauderdale County, AL and died about 1862 in Lauderdale County, AL.

Eliza married **Edmond Ruthin Till**. Edmond was born 14 Sep 1836 in Waterloo, Lauderdale County, AL, died 20 Sep 1910, and was buried in Canaan Cemetery, Lauderdale County, AL.

    241 M   i.   **Cart Till**.
    242 M   ii.   **Gaines Till**.
    243 M   iii.   **Charner Till** was born about 1862.

77. David (Dave) Owen Sharp (*John Sr.*[3], *Charles W. Sr.*[2], *John Sr.*[1]) was born in 1852 in Lauderdale County, AL.

David married **Martha (Mattie) Jane Carr**, daughter of **Joseph Price Carr Sr.** and **Julia Ann Lee**, 30 Nov 1874 in Lauderdale County, AL. Martha was born 18 Sep 1854 in Lauderdale County, AL.

+ 244 M   i.   **John (Johnny) L. Sharp** was born in 1877 in Lauderdale County, AL.
    245 F   ii.   **Nancy (Nannie) A. Sharp** was born in Sep 1878 in Lauderdale County, AL.
    246 M   iii.   **Butler P. Sharp** was born in Sep 1881 in Lauderdale County, AL.
+ 247 M   iv.   **Arnold B. Sharp** was born in Sep 1884 in Lauderdale County, AL.
+ 248 M   v.   **Turner Morris Sharp** was born in Feb 1887 in Lauderdale County, AL and died 3 Feb 1930.
+ 249 M   vi.   **Homer D. Sharp** was born in Aug 1888 in Lauderdale County, AL.
+ 250 M   vii. **Clyde Sharp** was born in Jun 1894 in Lauderdale County, AL.

78. John Sharp Jr. (*John Sr.*[3], *Charles W. Sr.*[2], *John Sr.*[1]) was born in Mar 1854 in Lauderdale County, AL.

John married **Josephine (Josie) Anderson** 23 Sep 1875 in Lauderdale County, AL. Josephine was born in Apr 1856 in Tennessee.

+ 251 F   i.   **Bertie Sharp** was born in Aug 1876 in Lauderdale County, AL.
    252 F   ii.   **Miner Sharp** was born in 1878 in Lauderdale County, AL.
    253 M   iii.   **Walker Sharp** was born in Oct 1882 in Lauderdale County, AL.
+ 254 F   iv.   **Lizzie Sharp** was born in Mar 1885 in Lauderdale County, AL.
    255 M   v.   **Turner Sharp** was born in Sep 1888 in Lauderdale County, AL.
    256 F   vi.   **Pearl Sharp** was born in Jan 1894 in Lauderdale County, AL.
    257 F   vii. **Ruby Sharp** was born in Apr 1896 in Lauderdale County, AL.

79. William (Candy) Erwin Sharp (*John Sr.*[3], *Charles W. Sr.*[2], *John Sr.*[1]) was born 7 Jun 1857 in Lauderdale County, AL, died 17 Nov 1938, and was buried in Florence City Cemetery, Florence, Lauderdale County, AL.

William married **Tennapee (Tennie) Candace Anderson**, daughter of **Charlie Anderson** and ***Unk**, 7 Sep 1876 in Lauderdale County, AL. Tennapee was born 19 Apr 1860 in Lauderdale County, AL, died 16 May 1946, and was buried in Florence City Cemetery, Florence, Lauderdale County, AL.

+ 258 M   i.   **Charlie William Sharp** was born 4 Jul 1877 in Lauderdale County, AL, died 26 Feb 1910, and was buried in Pettus Cemetery, Lexington, AL.
+ 259 F   ii.   **Dollie E. Sharp** was born 23 Apr 1880 in Lauderdale County, AL, died 5 Jul 1956, and was buried in Florence City Cemetery, Florence, Lauderdale County, AL.
+ 260 M   iii.   **Richard Owen Sharp** was born 15 Apr 1882 in Wright, Lauderdale County, AL, died 25 Jan 1950, and was buried in Rosewood Cemetery, Waco, TX.
+ 261 F   iv.   **Beulah L. Sharp** was born 1 Mar 1884 in Lauderdale County, AL, died 21 Dec 1972, and was buried in Walston Cemetery, Oakland, Lauderdale County, AL.
+ 262 M   v.   **Charner Leander Sharp Sr.** was born 22 Jun 1886 in Lauderdale County, AL, died 14 Oct 1951, and was buried in Florence City Cemetery, Florence, Lauderdale County, AL.
+ 263 M   vi.   **Clarence Morris Sharp** was born 22 May 1889 in Lauderdale County, AL, died 9 Feb 1929, and was buried in Florence City Cemetery, Florence, Lauderdale County, AL.
+ 264 M   vii. **Robert Irwin Sharp** was born 22 Sep 1893 in Lauderdale County, AL and died 17 Sep 1975 in Waco, McLennan County, TX.
+ 265 M   viii. **Burt Hilliard Sharp Sr.** was born 10 Sep 1894 in Lauderdale County, AL and died 25 Apr 1966 in Weirton, WV.
+ 266 F   ix.   **Myrtle Mabel (Mae) Sharp** was born 14 Jul 1896 in Lauderdale County, AL and died 15 Nov 1944 in Waco, McLennan County, TX.
+ 267 F   x.   **Virginia (Emma) Sharp** was born 7 Jun 1900 in Lauderdale County, AL, died 8 Jan 1975, and was buried in Holy Cross Cemetery, Cleveland, OH.

268 M xi. **Dalton Sharp** was born 10 Aug 1902 in Lauderdale County, AL, died 7 Oct 1904, and was buried in Florence City Cemetery, Florence, Lauderdale County, AL.

80. Richard Gaines Sharp (*John Sr.*[3], *Charles W. Sr.*[2], *John Sr.*[1]) was born between Jan 1858 and 1859 in Lauderdale County, AL.

Richard married **Amanda Lee Young** 25 Dec 1895 in Lauderdale County, AL.

84. Julia Ann Young (*Mary E. Sharp*[3], *Charles W. Sr.*[2], *John Sr.*[1]) was born about 1845 in Alabama, died 28 Oct 1907, and was buried in Murphy's Chapel Cemetery, Lauderdale County, AL.

Julia married **Owen Bartley Young Sr.**, son of **Elijah Young** and **Mary Jane Lamb**, 11 Sep 1876 in Lauderdale County, AL. Owen was born about 1852 in Lauderdale County, AL, died 25 Mar 1939, and was buried in Murphy's Chapel Cemetery, Lauderdale County, AL.

+ 269 M i. **James Wylie (Jim) Young** was born 20 Mar 1878 in Lauderdale County, AL, died 11 Jul 1959, and was buried in Murphy's Chapel Cemetery, Lauderdale County, AL.
+ 270 M ii. **Hulet Edward Young** was born 18 May 1882 in Lauderdale County, AL, died 27 Jan 1956, and was buried in Cloverdale COC Cemetery, Lauderdale County, AL.
+ 271 M iii. **Turner Andrew Young** was born about 1888 in Lauderdale County, AL, died in May 1968, and was buried in Greenview Memorial Park, Florence, Lauderdale County, AL.
   272 F iv. **Nora Young** was born 28 Aug 1888 in Lauderdale County, AL, died 26 Nov 1915, and was buried in Murphy's Chapel Cemetery, Lauderdale County, AL.
+ 273 M v. **Cleave Homer Young** was born 3 Sep 1892 in Lauderdale County, AL, died 20 Mar 1960 in Lauderdale County, AL, and was buried in Indiana.
+ 274 M vi. **Wheeler Young** was born 3 May 1896 in Lauderdale County, AL, died 6 Apr 1975, and was buried in Seattle, WA.
+ 275 F vii. **Ada V. Young** was born 28 Jan 1900 in Lauderdale County, AL and died in Dec 1974 in Lauderdale County, AL.
   276 M viii. **Robert (Bob) E. Young** was born 29 Apr 1900 in Lauderdale County, AL and died 13 May 1962 in South Bend, IN.

89. Harriett Matilda Sharp (*Joseph (Joe)*[3], *Charles W. Sr.*[2], *John Sr.*[1]) was born in 1853 in Lauderdale County, AL.

Harriett married **Robert F. Palmer** 13 Feb 1872 in Lauderdale County, AL.

90. Berry Nolan Sharp (*Joseph (Joe)*[3], *Charles W. Sr.*[2], *John Sr.*[1]) was born 15 Dec 1859 in Lauderdale County, AL, died 21 Sep 1945, and was buried in Stoney Point Cemetery, Lauderdale County, AL.

Berry married **Dorothy (Dolly) Elizabeth Murphy**, daughter of **James Robert Murphy Sr.** and **Mary Eliza Sharp**, 13 Dec 1879 in Lauderdale County, AL. Dorothy was born 29 Jul 1864 in Lauderdale County, AL, died 18 Dec 1942, and was buried in Stoney Point Cemetery, Lauderdale County, AL.

+ 277 F i. **Mollie Jo Sharp** was born 15 Mar 1883 in Lauderdale County, AL, died 1 Mar 1961, and was buried in Stoney Point Cemetery, Lauderdale County, AL.
+ 278 M ii. **James David Sharp** was born 1 Apr 1885 in Lauderdale County, AL, died 14 Jun 1945, and was buried in Stoney Point Cemetery, Lauderdale County, AL.
+ 279 F iii. **Eula Elizabeth Sharp** was born 6 Mar 1887 in Lauderdale County, AL, died 13 Jul 1977, and was buried in Stoney Point Cemetery, Lauderdale County, AL.
   280 F iv. **Nancy Hattie Sharp** was born 16 Feb 1889, died 3 Feb 1916, and was buried in Stoney Point Cemetery, Lauderdale County, AL.
   281 F v. **Roxie Ida Sharp** was born 1 Feb 1891, died 16 Mar 1916, and was buried in Stoney Point Cemetery, Lauderdale County, AL.
+ 282 M vi. **Charles Robert Sharp** was born 25 Jan 1893 in Lauderdale County, AL, died 7 Aug 1983, and was buried in Stoney Point Cemetery, Lauderdale County, AL.
+ 283 F vii. **Lovie Francis Sharp** was born 27 Aug 1895 in Lauderdale County, AL, died 14 Aug 1979, and was buried in Stoney Point Cemetery, Lauderdale County, AL.
   284 M viii. **Carroll L. Sharp** was born 31 Oct 1897, died 2 Dec 1968, and was buried in Stoney Point Cemetery, Lauderdale County, AL.
+ 285 F ix. **Muncie Venetta Sharp** was born 3 Feb 1901 in Lauderdale County, AL, died 20 Jun 1987, and was buried in Stoney Point Cemetery, Lauderdale County, AL.

286 M x. **William Benton Sharp** was born 23 Oct 1903, died 6 Mar 1916, and was buried in Stoney Point Cemetery, Lauderdale County, AL.

91. Benjamin Franklin Sharp (*Joseph (Joe)* [3]*, Charles W. Sr.* [2]*, John Sr.* [1]) was born 5 Feb 1865 in Lauderdale County, AL, died 19 Apr 1914, and was buried in Wesley Chapel Cemetery, Lauderdale County, AL.

Benjamin married **Ida Malissie Eveline Clanton**, daughter of **James R. Clanton** and **Manerva E. Gray**, 29 Mar 1883 in Lauderdale County, AL. Ida was born 1 Jan 1865 in Alabama, died 2 Aug 1939, and was buried in Wesley Chapel Cemetery, Lauderdale County, AL.

General Notes: "Ida Clanton was supposed to be part Cherokee Indian"…David Sharp

	287	F	i.	**Lillie F. Sharp** was born in Jan 1884 in Alabama.
+	288	M	ii.	**James Leander Sharp** was born 28 Aug 1885 in Lauderdale County, AL, died 16 Aug 1918, and was buried in Wesley Chapel Cemetery, Lauderdale County, AL.
+	289	M	iii.	**Joseph Homer Sharp** was born in Aug 1890 in Lauderdale County, AL, died in 1968, and was buried in Wesley Chapel Cemetery, Lauderdale County, AL.
+	290	F	iv.	**Nora E. Sharp** was born 21 Mar 1892 in Lauderdale County, AL, died 4 Apr 1983, and was buried in Florence City Cemetery, Florence, Lauderdale County, AL.
+	291	M	v.	**Berry Robert Sharp** was born in Mar 1894 in Lauderdale County, AL, died in 1963, and was buried in Wesley Chapel Cemetery, Lauderdale County, AL.
+	292	F	vi.	**Ethel Belle Sharp** was born 26 Nov 1896 in Lauderdale County, AL, died 4 Jul 1982, and was buried in Wesley Chapel Cemetery, Lauderdale County, AL.
+	293	M	vii.	**Marvin Frank Sharp Sr.** was born 28 Feb 1900 in Lauderdale County, AL, died in 1950, and was buried in Wesley Chapel Cemetery, Lauderdale County, AL.
+	294	F	viii.	**Maggie Leona Sharp** was born in 1903 in Lauderdale County, AL, died in 1985, and was buried in Wesley Chapel Cemetery, Lauderdale County, AL.

93. John Levi Sharp (*Charles W. II* [3]*, Charles W. Sr.* [2]*, John Sr.* [1]) was born 20 May 1852 in Lauderdale County, AL and died 22 Aug 1920 in McQueen, AR.

General Notes: "After his son, Charles, was killed in a knife fight over a cigar by Dean. It was reported that John Levi said that if he stayed here he would kill Dean. He sold his farm in Colbert County and left Alabama. The farm is now part of Reynolds Plant...." David Sharp

John married **Mary Alice Dowdy** 13 Feb 1876 in Wayne County, TN. Mary was born about 1856 in Lauderdale County, AL.

295 M i. **Jack Sharp** was born in 1879 in Lauderdale County, AL.

General Notes: "At Pearl Harbor (ship attack). He was a POW in another battle after WW II. He has not been heard from again..." David Sharp

+	296	M	ii.	**William F. Sharp** was born in Apr 1880 in Lauderdale County, AL and died in Waco, McLennan County, TX.
+	297	F	iii.	**Donna L. Sharp** was born in Dec 1882 in Lauderdale County, AL and was buried in Coos Bay Cemetery, Coos, OR.
+	298	M	iv.	**Charles Edward (Eddie) Sharp** was born in Nov 1884 in Lauderdale County, AL, died 25 Dec 1905, and was buried in Wright Cemetery, Wright, Lauderdale County, AL.

John next married **Mary Jane (Mollie) Chaney** 24 Oct 1886 in Lauderdale County, AL. Mary was born in 1856 in Alabama and died after 1887.

299 F i. **Daughter Sharp** was born about 1887.

John next married **Bessie Marie Holloway**, daughter of **John Holloway** and **Unknown**, 27 Jan 1903 in Lauderdale County, AL. Bessie was born 19 Oct 1882 in Hardin County, TN, died 28 Jan 1961, and was buried in Los Angeles, CA.

	300	M	i.	**Jack Sharp**.
+	301	F	ii.	**Mary Lee Sharp** was born 8 Jun 1905 in Sheffield, Colbert County, AL and died 15 May 1967 in Los Angeles, CA.
+	302	M	iii.	**Jason Levi Sharp** was born 23 Dec 1906 in Sheffield, Colbert County, AL.

+ 303 F iv. **Alice Maxwell Sharp** was born 22 Mar 1911 in Sheffield, Colbert County, AL, died 11 Oct 1985, and was buried in Visalia, Tulare, CA.

304 M v. **Vernon Sharp** was born about 1913 in Alabama and was buried in DeQueen, AR.

94. Amanda Jane Sharp (*Charles W. II³, Charles W. Sr.², John Sr.¹*) was born 29 Oct 1855 in Lauderdale County, AL and was buried in Wesley Chapel Cemetery, Lauderdale County, AL.

Amanda married **John Craven Box**, son of **George Daily Box** and **Elizabeth T. Graven**, 2 Jan 1880 in Lauderdale County, AL. John was born 27 Feb 1857 in Pontotoc County, MS, died 8 Dec 1918, and was buried in Pleasant Hill Cemetery, Lauderdale County, AL.

+ 305 M i. **James (Jim) W. Box** was born 24 Sep 1880 in Lake Charles, LA, died 26 Nov 1925, and was buried in Pleasant Hill Cemetery, Lauderdale County, AL.

306 F ii. **Baby Box**.

95. Mary Elizabeth (Molly) Sharp (*Charles W. II³, Charles W. Sr.², John Sr.¹*) was born 14 Aug 1865 in Lauderdale County, AL, died 26 Jul 1961, and was buried in Graham Cemetery, Hardin County, TN.

Mary married **John Henry Anderson**, son of **John Joseph Anderson** and **Sarah Adelene Gresham**, 5 Feb 1885 in Lauderdale County, AL. John was born 6 Sep 1855 in Palestine, TX, died 23 May 1923, and was buried in Gresham Cemetery, Lauderdale County, AL.

+ 307 M i. **Charles David Anderson Sr.** was born 2 Dec 1885 in Lauderdale County, AL, died 30 Aug 1974, and was buried in Greenview Memorial Park, Florence, Lauderdale County, AL.

+ 308 M ii. **Robert (Bud) Henry Anderson** was born 17 Mar 1887 in Lauderdale County, AL, died 23 Dec 1957, and was buried in Greenview Memorial Park, Florence, Lauderdale County, AL.

309 M iii. **Perry Price Anderson** was born 17 Jul 1889 in Lauderdale County, AL, died 12 Feb 1914, and was buried in Gresham Cemetery, Lauderdale County, AL.

310 F iv. **Ester Pearl Anderson** was born 8 May 1891 in Lauderdale County, AL, died 12 Jul 1908, and was buried in Gresham Cemetery, Lauderdale County, AL.

+ 311 F v. **Mary Adeline (Addie) Anderson** was born 6 May 1892 in Lauderdale County, AL, died 20 Mar 1936, and was buried in Gresham Cemetery, Lauderdale County, AL.

312 M vi. **Earl B. Anderson** was born 12 Jan 1895 in Lauderdale County, AL, died 17 Sep 1904, and was buried in Gresham Cemetery, Lauderdale County, AL.

+ 313 M vii. **Emmett Anderson** was born 20 Jul 1897 in Lauderdale County, AL, died 4 Aug 1983, and was buried in Greenview Memorial Park, Florence, Lauderdale County, AL.

+ 314 M viii. **Marvin Robert Anderson** was born 31 Jul 1902 in Lauderdale County, AL and was buried in Olney, IL.

+ 315 F ix. **Moodie Bell Anderson** was born 18 May 1905, died 8 Nov 1995, and was buried in Gresham Cemetery, Lauderdale County, AL.

96. Charles Franklin Sharp (*Charles W. II³, Charles W. Sr.², John Sr.¹*) was born 3 Nov 1866 in Lauderdale County, AL, died 29 Apr 1932, and was buried in Fairmont Cemetery, San Angelo, TX.

Charles married **Nancy Elizabeth (Lizzie) McPeters**, daughter of **William A. McPeters** and **Serena Ann Phillips**, 22 Dec 1887 in Lauderdale County, AL. Nancy was born 23 Aug 1866 in Lauderdale County, AL and died 15 Jul 1899.

+ 316 M i. **William Lee Sharp** was born 2 Aug 1890 in Lauderdale County, AL, died 12 May 1931, and was buried in El Bethel Cemetery, Lamar County, Paris, TX.

+ 317 F ii. **Alma Derry Sharp** was born 30 Sep 1894 in Lauderdale County, AL.

97. Rachel Ann (Babe) Sharp (*Charles W. II³, Charles W. Sr.², John Sr.¹*) was born 17 May 1868 in Lauderdale County, AL, died 24 Jun 1957, and was buried in Dowdy Cemetery, Lauderdale County, AL.

Rachel married **William Alexander Dowdy**, son of **John Thomas Dowdy** and **Sarah J. Threet**, 24 Dec 1893 in Paris, Lamar County, TX. William was born 24 Feb 1858 in Lauderdale County, AL, died 1 May 1932, and was buried in Dowdy Cemetery, Lauderdale County, AL.

318 M i. **William Floyd Dowdy** was born 21 Mar 1894 in Lauderdale County, AL, died 19 Jan 1911, and was buried in Dowdy Cemetery, Lauderdale County, AL.

+ 319 M ii. **Hosea (Hozie) Durille Dowdy** was born 1 Feb 1896 in Lauderdale County, AL, died 1 Feb 1973, and was buried in Pine Hill Cemetery, Lauderdale County, AL.

320 M iii. **Charlie Avery D. Dowdy** was born 7 Apr 1900 in Lauderdale County, AL.

321	F	iv.	**Infant Daughter Dowdy** was born 18 Mar 1903 in Lauderdale County, AL, died 17 Jul 1903, and was buried in Dowdy Cemetery, Lauderdale County, AL.
322	M	v.	**Infant Son Dowdy** was born 30 Apr 1905 in Lauderdale County, AL, died 1 May 1905, and was buried in Dowdy Cemetery, Lauderdale County, AL.
+ 323	F	vi.	**Johnnie Charles Dowdy** was born 17 Dec 1908 in Lauderdale County, AL, died 22 Dec 1989, and was buried in Tri-Cities Memorial Gardens, Florence, Lauderdale County, AL.

98. Thomas (Tom) Erwin Sharp (*Charles W. II^3, Charles W. Sr.^{2}, John Sr.^{1}*) was born 3 Oct 1869 in Lauderdale County, AL, died 13 Jun 1940, and was buried in Murphy's Chapel Cemetery, Lauderdale County, AL.

Thomas married **Sarah Lavinia (Vina) Carr**, daughter of **Joseph Price Carr Sr.** and **Julia Ann Lee**, 6 Feb 1892 in Lauderdale County, AL. Sarah was born 9 Jul 1872 in Lauderdale County, AL, died 21 Sep 1949, and was buried in Murphy's Chapel Cemetery, Lauderdale County, AL.

+ 324	F	i.	**Pearl Etoile Sharp** was born 24 Nov 1892 in Lauderdale County, AL, died 11 Feb 1975, and was buried in Florence City Cemetery, Florence, Lauderdale County, AL.
325	F	ii.	**A. Maud Sharp** was born 24 Feb 1895 in Lauderdale County, AL, died 4 Oct 1896, and was buried in Murphy's Chapel Cemetery, Lauderdale County, AL.
+ 326	F	iii.	**Linnie Mae Sharp** was born 19 Apr 1897 in Lauderdale County, AL, died 16 Oct 1974, and was buried in Murphy's Chapel Cemetery, Lauderdale County, AL.
+ 327	M	iv.	**Guy Thomas Sharp** was born 23 Aug 1899 in Lauderdale County, AL, died 20 Apr 1960, and was buried in Greenview Memorial Park, Florence, Lauderdale County, AL.
328	F	v.	**Theresa A. Sharp** was born 30 Nov 1901 in Lauderdale County, AL, died 14 Jan 1906, and was buried in Murphy's Chapel Cemetery, Lauderdale County, AL.
329	M	vi.	**Vernon R. Sharp** was born 8 Sep 1903 in Lauderdale County, AL, died 27 Nov 1903, and was buried in Murphy's Chapel Cemetery, Lauderdale County, AL.
+ 330	F	vii.	**Wylodean Marie Sharp** was born 3 Aug 1912 in Lauderdale County, AL, died 14 Sep 1974, and was buried in Greenview Memorial Park, Florence, Lauderdale County, AL.
+ 331	M	viii.	**Ellis Eugene Sharp** was born 3 Jun 1915 in Lauderdale County, AL, died 31 Jan 1968, and was buried in Greenview Memorial Park, Florence, Lauderdale County, AL.

99. Richard (Dick) Allen Sharp (*Charles W. II^3, Charles W. Sr.^{2}, John Sr.^{1}*) was born 7 Oct 1872 in Lauderdale County, AL and was buried in Nashville, Davidson County, TN.

Richard married **Amanda Lee Young** 25 Dec 1895 in Lauderdale County, AL. Amanda was born in Oct 1878 in Tennessee and was buried in Murphy's Chapel Cemetery, Lauderdale County, AL.

| 332 | F | i. | **Nellie L. Sharp** was born in Nov 1897 in Lauderdale County, AL. |
| + 333 | M | ii. | **Dalton Sharp** was born in May 1899 in Lauderdale County, AL. |

Richard next married **Rachel A. Young** 5 Jan 1903 in Lauderdale County, AL. Rachel was born in 1875 in Lauderdale County, AL, died in 1914, and was buried in Wesley Chapel Cemetery, Lauderdale County, AL.

| 334 | F | i. | **Elizabeth Sharp** was buried in Wesley Chapel Cemetery, Lauderdale County, AL. |
| 335 | F | ii. | **Clora Sharp** was born in 1909. |

Richard next married **Dorothy Hyde**, daughter of **William Hyde** and **Martha A. *Unk**, 15 Jul 1914 in Lauderdale County, AL. Dorothy was born 11 Nov 1893 in Lauderdale County, AL, died 15 Jun 1970, and was buried in Lindsey Chapel Cemetery, Lauderdale County, AL.

100. Alice J. Sharp (*Charles W. II^3, Charles W. Sr.^{2}, John Sr.^{1}*) was born 7 Apr 1873 in Lauderdale County, AL and was buried in Lake Charles, LA.

Alice married **Joe Hopper** 11 Feb 1887 in Lauderdale County, AL.

Alice next married **James Andrew Oneal** 7 Nov 1888 in Wayne County, TN. James was born about 1870 and died before 1910.

| 336 | M | i. | **Boy Oneal**. |

Alice next married **J. W. Dehart** after 1891.

103. Laura Belle Dowdy (*Matilda Sharp^3, Charles W. Sr.^{2}, John Sr.^{1}*) was born about 1853 in Lauderdale County, AL and died 7 Feb 1937 in Booneville, MS.

General Notes: "Laura Belle Dowdy's mother came from a very outstanding southern family. The Adron Sharps owned a big southern plantation near Gravelly Springs, Alabama near Florence. Her mother was truly a southern belle. Laura's mother ran away from home at a very young age and married Mr. Dowdy, a poor man whom she loved dearly but could not accept his way of life as she had been reared in a home of wealth, culture and refinement. She died at a young age. Laura was her oldest daughter. Laura often visited at the Sharp plantation as a child; they had many slaves but were good to them.

During the Civil War, Laura remembered trembling with fear when they would hear the rumble and beat of the soldier's horses coming. They would hide their food and valuables. One dark night three Yankee prisoners were brought to her grandfather's house. The grownups got up so the prisoners could lie down and rest as they were very tired. A short time afterwards a man who lived near was captured by the Yankees, he told the officer if they would release him, he would tell him something. He told the officer that Adron Sharp had carried three Yankee soldiers up the hollow and killed them, instantly the man was released. The Yankees rode straight to the Sharp plantation and made Adron Sharp a prisoner, setting fire to his grist mill and feed barns. They went into the house and carried the piano out on the lawn and splintered it with rocks. They set fire in the house. They rode away with Adron Sharp leaving his wife and Mammy Cella pleading and crying. The slaves soon diminished the fire in the house but the mill and barn had already burned down.

Months passed without a word from Adron Sharp. Late one evening he came limping into the house. Albert a young Negro slave saw him coming, he raised his arms and shouted, 'Mars Adrons' comin, I'm telling ya'. Great rejoicing was underway that night as they thought he was dead. He sat in his favorite chair and told how the three prisoners he was accused of killing escaped returned to the camp where he was held prisoner. Of course, there was some explaining to do. The three solders told how they were entertained in the Sharp home, the best food set before them, etc. Upon hearing this the officer told Adron to go home and kill his betrayer the minute he arrived, which he had no thought of doing. He was happy to be getting home as he was an old man and feeble. Laura made her home with a granddaughter, Mrs. Norwood McCarly. She is buried in Booneville Cemetery, Booneville, Mississippi, She died on Feb 7, 1937, at age 89..." David Sharp

Laura married **Franklin B. Kilpatrick**, son of **John Kilpatrick** and **Nacny Selph**. Franklin was buried in Colbert County, AL.

    337 F   i.   **Daughter Kilpatrick**.

107. Matilda Ann White (*Eliza Jane Sharp^3, Charles W. Sr.^{2}, John Sr.^{1}*) was born 2 Oct 1858 in Lauderdale County, AL, died 24 Oct 1937, and was buried in Murphy's Chapel Cemetery, Lauderdale County, AL.

Matilda married **John Nicholas Young** in Jan 1877 in Lauderdale County, AL. John was born 11 Apr 1858 in Lauderdale County, AL, died 25 Aug 1928, and was buried in Murphy's Chapel Cemetery, Lauderdale County, AL.

	338	U	i.	**Infant Young** was buried in Murphy's Chapel Cemetery, Lauderdale County, AL.
	339	U	ii.	**Infant Young** was buried in Murphy's Chapel Cemetery, Lauderdale County, AL.
+	340	M	iii.	**William C. Young** was born about 1879 in Lauderdale County, AL, died 14 Jan 1934, and was buried in St. Joseph County, IN.
+	341	F	iv.	**Cora Young** was born 7 Jan 1883 in Lauderdale County, AL, died 17 Sep 1943, and was buried in Wright Cemetery, Wright, Lauderdale County, AL.
+	342	M	v.	**John Robert Young** was born 8 Apr 1884 in Lauderdale County, AL, died 12 Feb 1950, and was buried in Wright Cemetery, Wright, Lauderdale County, AL.
	343	F	vi.	**Eula Young** was born 7 Apr 1887, died 12 Oct 1890, and was buried in Murphy's Chapel Cemetery, Lauderdale County, AL.
+	344	F	vii.	**Florence Beulah Young** was born 16 Aug 1887 in Lauderdale County, AL, died 12 Oct 1969, and was buried in Murphy's Chapel Cemetery, Lauderdale County, AL.
+	345	F	viii.	**Lillian Ella Young** was born 27 Jul 1891 in Lauderdale County, AL, died 20 Jan 1954, and was buried in Cloverdale COC Cemetery, Lauderdale County, AL.
+	346	M	ix.	**Andrew Cleveland Young** was born 20 Aug 1894 in Lauderdale County, AL, died 16 Jun 1968, and was buried in Greenview Memorial Park, Florence, Lauderdale County, AL.
+	347	M	x.	**Clarence W. Young** was born 26 Sep 1897 in Lauderdale County, AL, died 2 Mar 1985, and was buried in Williams Chapel Cemetery, Lauderdale County, AL.
+	348	F	xi.	**Edna G. (Birdie) Young** was born 3 Sep 1900 in Alabama, died in 1986, and was buried in Indiana.

110. Martha Jane White (*Eliza Jane Sharp³, Charles W. Sr.², John Sr.¹*) was born 19 Jan 1869 in Lauderdale County, AL, died 7 Nov 1952, and was buried in Montgomery, AL.

Martha married **Lawson Benjamin Hinton** 23 Feb 1886 in Lauderdale County, AL. Lawson was born in Jul 1869 in Tennessee, died 2 Feb 1902, and was buried in Waterloo, Lauderdale County, AL.

+	349	F	i.	**Rosa Hinton** was born 28 Mar 1890 in Lauderdale County, AL, died 8 Mar 1987, and was buried in Lauderdale County, AL.
+	350	M	ii.	**Jones Henry Hinton** was born 3 Aug 1891 in Lauderdale County, AL, died in 1985, and was buried in Lauderdale County, AL.
	351	F	iii.	**Pallie Hinton** was born in Oct 1893 in Lauderdale County, AL.
	352	F	iv.	**Pearl Hinton** was born in Nov 1894 in Lauderdale County, AL.
	353	M	v.	**Barnie Hinton** was born in Apr 1895 in Lauderdale County, AL.
+	354	F	vi.	**Bonnie Ethel Hinton** was born 6 Apr 1896 in Hardin County, TN, died 1 Nov 1980, and was buried in Birmingham, Jefferson County, AL.
+	355	F	vii.	**Vernon L. B. Hinton** was born 19 Jul 1902 in Lauderdale County, AL, died 22 Feb 1987, and was buried in Montgomery, AL.

111. Ella Prooterwill White (*Eliza Jane Sharp³, Charles W. Sr.², John Sr.¹*) was born 9 Sep 1871 in Lauderdale County, AL, died 14 Mar 1965, and was buried in Murphy's Chapel Cemetery, Lauderdale County, AL.

Ella married **John Butler Young**, son of **Joseph Young** and **Mary L. Whitten**, 7 Feb 1894 in Lauderdale County, AL. John was born 17 Aug 1870 in Lauderdale County, AL, died 2 Feb 1935, and was buried in Murphy's Chapel Cemetery, Lauderdale County, AL.

| + | 356 | M | i. | **Charles Westbrook Young Sr.** was born 25 Sep 1895 in Lauderdale County, AL, died 7 Aug 1983, and was buried in Lauderdale County, AL. |
| + | 357 | F | ii. | **Gladys Myrtle Young** was born 16 Jul 1897 in Lauderdale County, AL, died 22 Sep 1993 in Lauderdale County, AL, and was buried in Murphy's Chapel Cemetery, Lauderdale County, AL. |

114. William (Bill) Edgar Sharp (*David Allen³, Charles W. Sr.², John Sr.¹*) was born 3 Sep 1866 in Lauderdale County, AL, died 2 Sep 1937, and was buried in Florence City Cemetery, Florence, Lauderdale County, AL.

William married **Cynthia Emanola Morrison**, daughter of **Zebulon Pike Morrison** and ***Unk**, 11 Mar 1892 in Lauderdale County, AL. Cynthia was born 8 Jan 1872 in Lauderdale County, AL, died 24 Jan 1929, and was buried in Florence City Cemetery, Florence, Lauderdale County, AL.

+	358	F	i.	**Virginia (Virgie) A. Sharp** was born in Feb 1892 in Lauderdale County, AL.
+	359	F	ii.	**Mary M. Sharp** was born in Dec 1895 in Lauderdale County, AL.
+	360	M	iii.	**Edgar Chisholm Sharp Sr.** was born in Oct 1898 in Lauderdale County, AL, died 14 Nov 1981, and was buried in Houston, TX.
+	361	F	iv.	**Minnie Louise Sharp** was born 1 Jun 1905 in Lauderdale County, AL, died 8 Aug 1968, and was buried in Roselawn Cemetery, Athens, AL.
	362	F	v.	**Blanche Anderson Sharp** was born 7 Sep 1907 in Lauderdale County, AL and died 6 Oct 1914.

115. James (Jim) Hulet Sharp (*David Allen³, Charles W. Sr.², John Sr.¹*) was born in Jul 1870 in Lauderdale County, AL and was buried in Stoney Point Cemetery, Lauderdale County, AL.

James married **Ida Lula Blanton**, daughter of **R. Ben Blanton** and **Nancy G. Young**, 16 Feb 1898 in Lauderdale County, AL. Ida was born in Jan 1875 in Lauderdale County, AL, died 4 Jan 1950, and was buried in Stoney Point Cemetery, Lauderdale County, AL.

	363	F	i.	**Vera L. Sharp** was born 19 Apr 1899 in Lauderdale County, AL and died 22 Jun 1902.
+	364	M	ii.	**James Buford Sharp Sr.** was born 11 Jan 1904 in Lauderdale County, AL.
	365	M	iii.	**Oscar Sharp** was born in Apr and died 29 Dec 1901.

116. Joseph (Joe) Powers Sharp Sr. (*David Allen³, Charles W. Sr.², John Sr.¹*) was born 1 Jul 1873 in Lauderdale County, AL, died 23 Nov 1959, and was buried in Stoney Point Cemetery, Lauderdale County, AL.

Joseph married **Sarah M. Denson** 9 Dec 1890 in Lauderdale County, AL. Sarah was born 21 Aug 1874 in Lauderdale County, AL, died 4 Oct 1903, and was buried in Stoney Point Cemetery, Lauderdale County, AL.

366	M	i.	**David E. Sharp** was born 1 May 1894 in Lauderdale County, AL, died 4 Oct 1898, and was buried in Stoney Point Cemetery, Lauderdale County, AL.
367	M	ii.	**Thomas D. Sharp** was born 1 May 1894 in Lauderdale County, AL, died 6 Oct 1896, and was buried in Stoney Point Cemetery, Lauderdale County, AL.
+ 368	M	iii.	**Robert Owen Sharp** was born 21 Aug 1895 in Lauderdale County, AL, died 8 Jun 1981, and was buried in Stoney Point Cemetery, Lauderdale County, AL.
+ 369	M	iv.	**Eugene (Dock) Neal Sharp** was born 19 Jun 1898 in Lauderdale County, AL, died 7 Nov 1987, and was buried in Stoney Point Cemetery, Lauderdale County, AL.
+ 370	F	v.	**Cynthia Emmanola Sharp** was born 11 Aug 1899 in Lauderdale County, AL, died 9 Dec 1984, and was buried in Stoney Point Cemetery, Lauderdale County, AL.

Joseph next married **Amanda (Mandie) Westmoreland**. Amanda was born 17 Mar 1868, died 1 Sep 1913, and was buried in New Pisgah AME Church Cemetery, Lauderdale County, AL.

General Notes: "She was a black deaf mute, also a cook and housekeeper for Joseph Sharp..." David Sharp

| + 371 | M | i. | **Frank Littleton Sharp** was born in 1905 in Lauderdale County, AL and died in 1968. |

Joseph next married **Nancy (Mattie) George Holland**, daughter of **John Holland** and **Mollie Sample**, 5 May 1905 in Lauderdale County, AL. Nancy was born 14 Mar 1883 in Lauderdale County, AL, died 10 Jun 1963, and was buried in Stoney Point Cemetery, Lauderdale County, AL.

+ 372	F	i.	**Mayro Sharp** was born 30 Jul 1906 in Lauderdale County, AL, died 18 Nov 2002, and was buried in Stoney Point Cemetery, Lauderdale County, AL.
+ 373	M	ii.	**Joseph Powers (J. P.) Sharp Jr.** was born 31 May 1909 in Lauderdale County, AL, died 29 Apr 1977, and was buried in Stoney Point Cemetery, Lauderdale County, AL.
+ 374	M	iii.	**David (Big David) Roderick Sharp** was born 30 May 1912 in Lauderdale County, AL, died 2 Dec 2002, and was buried in Stoney Point Cemetery, Lauderdale County, AL.

117. Andrew Jefferson Sharp Sr. (*David Allen*[3], *Charles W. Sr.*[2], *John Sr.*[1]) was born 4 Feb 1877 in Lauderdale County, AL, died 29 Oct 1931, and was buried in Florence City Cemetery, Florence, Lauderdale County, AL.

Andrew married **Margaret (Maggie) Virginia Underwood**, daughter of **James F. Underwood** and **Rachel Catherine Sharpston**, 17 Jun 1903 in Lauderdale County, AL. Margaret was born 6 Oct 1885 in Lauderdale County, AL, died 9 Jun 1954, and was buried in Greenview Memorial Park, Florence, Lauderdale County, AL.

+ 375	F	i.	**Lyda Mae Sharp** was born 7 Jul 1904 in Lauderdale County, AL and died 14 Sep 1963 in Natchez, MS.
+ 376	F	ii.	**Kathleen Lamar Sharp** was born 29 Sep 1906 in Lauderdale County, AL and died in Jan 1987 in Alexandria, LA.
+ 377	F	iii.	**Dorothy Elizabeth Sharp** was born 25 Oct 1908 in Lauderdale County, AL, died 27 Nov 1994, and was buried in Alexandria, LA.
+ 378	F	iv.	**Virginia Rebecca Sharp** was born 25 Jun 1910 in Lauderdale County, AL and died about 1988 in Mobile, AL.
+ 379	F	v.	**Evelyn Marie (Verna) Sharp** was born 30 Apr 1912 in Lauderdale County, AL and died 1 Jan 1990 in Houston, TX.
380	F	vi.	**Fay Jefferson Sharp** was born about 1914 in Lauderdale County, AL and died about 1915 in Lauderdale County, AL.
+ 381	M	vii.	**Andrew Jefferson Sharp Jr.** was born 20 Apr 1916 in Lauderdale County, AL, died 25 Sep 1974, and was buried in Oakwood Cemetery, Sheffield, Colbert County, AL.
+ 382	F	viii.	**Helen Margaret Sharp** was born 2 Sep 1921 in Lauderdale County, AL.

Fourth Generation

124. Nancy (Fannie) Paralee Lindsey (*Caleb (Calip) Lindsey*[4], *Frances (Frankie) Sharp*[3], *Charles W. Sr.*[2], *John Sr.*[1]) was born 22 Apr 1847 in Tennessee and died 5 Mar 1923. Another name for Nancy was Nancy Paralee (Fannie) Lindsey.

General Notes: "Nancy was married to Aaron B. Brown Holt, veteran of Company H, 2nd U.S. Tennessee Mounted Infantry. There were no children although he has a daughter, Ellen (born 1869 and died 1930) by a previous marriage. My heirloom iron fireplace shovel, made by my Great -Great grandfather Phillip Lindsey came to me by way of Nancy Fannie Holt. She had given it to her nephew, Ed Lindsey, following Ed's death, his wife, Annie presented it to me. Brown and Fannie Holt lived in a large two story house near what is now the Florence Boulevard overpass at Royal Avenue. Following Brown's death, Fannie's young brother, David and his wife, Melissa, took care of Fannie who was an invalid. Fannie willed her farm to David and Melissa...." William McDonald

Nancy married **Aaron Von Brown Holt** 4 Sep 1865. Aaron was born 23 Mar 1846 in Wayne County, TN.

General Notes: "Co. H, 2nd U.S. Tennessee Mounted Infantry..." David Sharp

125. John Phillip Lindsey II (*Caleb (Calip) Lindsey*[4], *Frances (Frankie) Sharp*[3], *Charles W. Sr.*[2], *John Sr.*[1]) was born 14 Nov 1848 in Lauderdale County, AL, died 16 Feb 1917, and was buried in Florence City Cemetery, Florence, Lauderdale County, AL. Another name for John was John Philip Lindsey II.

John married **Ella C. Diakus**, daughter of ***Unk Diakus** and **Unknown**, 15 Sep 1897 in Lauderdale County, AL. Ella was born 9 Feb 1857 in Missouri, died 3 Jan 1942, and was buried in Florence City Cemetery, Florence, Lauderdale County, AL.

- + 383 M i. **George W. Lindsey** was born in Feb 1873 in Missouri.
- + 384 F ii. **Lucelle (Lucy) Lindsey** was born in Aug 1875 in Lauderdale County, AL, died in 1954, and was buried in Florence City Cemetery, Florence, Lauderdale County, AL.
- + 385 M iii. **Willie C. (Will) Lindsey** was born in Feb 1879 in Lauderdale County, AL.
- + 386 F iv. **Lizzie O. Lindsey** was born in Sep 1883 in Lauderdale County, AL.
- + 387 M v. **Ernest Lindsey** was born in Apr 1886 in Lauderdale County, AL.
-   388 F vi. **Mary (Mittie) Lindsey** was born in Nov 1887 in Alabama and was buried in Florence City Cemetery, Florence, Lauderdale County, AL.
-   389 F vii. **Ola Lindsey**.
-   390 F viii. **Ellie Lindsey**.

126. Joseph A. Lindsey (*Caleb (Calip) Lindsey*[4], *Frances (Frankie) Sharp*[3], *Charles W. Sr.*[2], *John Sr.*[1]) was born in May 1850 in Missouri.

Joseph married **Fannie Bauchman** 30 Oct 1876 in Lauderdale County, AL. Fannie was born in 1855.

- + 391 M i. **David (Dave) Lindsey** was born in Aug 1876 in Lauderdale County, AL, died 26 Aug 1947, and was buried in Florence City Cemetery, Florence, Lauderdale County, AL.
- + 392 F ii. **Lillie Mae Lindsey** was born in 1880.
-   393 M iii. **Wheeler Lindsey** was born in Jan 1884.
- + 394 M iv. **J. Lewis Lindsey** was born in 1885.
- + 395 F v. **Emma Lindsey** was born in Feb 1887.
- + 396 F vi. **Ada Bell Lindsey** was born in Mar 1888 in Lauderdale County, AL, died in 1958, and was buried in Florence City Cemetery, Florence, Lauderdale County, AL.
- + 397 M vii. **Lee Willie Lindsey** was born in Feb 1892, died in 1965, and was buried in Burnt Church Cemetery, Russellville, AL.

127. David A. Lindsey (*Caleb (Calip) Lindsey*[4], *Frances (Frankie) Sharp*[3], *Charles W. Sr.*[2], *John Sr.*[1]) was born in Dec 1861 in Warsaw, MO, died 25 May 1934, and was buried in Florence City Cemetery, Florence, Lauderdale County, AL.

General Notes: "David and Melissa assisted other members of the Redding family in caring for my father whose mother died when he was five years of age. As I have already recounted, David's sister, Nancy Fannie Holt, willed her home and farm to him and his wife. The land that David farmed was part of what was known as the old Simpson Plantation. It was located west of the Sweetwater Plantation. I remember picking cotton on his field where the modern Darby Drive now joins Florence Boulevard.

Melissa died January 26, 1933, and David died May 25, 1934; they are buried in the Florence Cemetery. Their funerals were at their home. David's casket was on the front lawn and the preacher spoke from the porch. I shall not forget the drama that came into being when he ended his message. Cousin Dewey came out of the house and placed an old quilt inside the casket before it was finally closed. This family heirloom had been quilted by David's Grandmother (who was my great-great-grandmother Frankie Sharp Lindsey). It seems there was contention among the heirs as to which daughter-in-law would inherit grandmother's quilt; so the matter was resolved by burying it with David. A number of years following this event, David's home burned, consuming other valuable heirlooms that had once belonged to Phillip and Frankie Lindsey..." William McDonald

David married **Melissa Redding**, daughter of **Duncan Redding** and **Tabitha Ann Adair**, 26 Sep 1877 in Lauderdale County, AL. Melissa was born in 1860, died 26 Jan 1933, and was buried in Florence City Cemetery, Florence, Lauderdale County, AL.

+ 398 M i. **Albert Curtis Lindsey** was born in 1880 in Lauderdale County, AL, died 16 Aug 1952, and was buried in Florence City Cemetery, Florence, Lauderdale County, AL.
+ 399 M ii. **Edward (Ed) Price Lindsey** was born in 1899 in Lauderdale County, AL, died 5 May 1976, and was buried in Tri-Cities Memorial Gardens, Florence, Lauderdale County, AL.

128. John L. Lindsey (*Caleb (Calip) Lindsey*[4], *Frances (Frankie) Sharp*[3], *Charles W. Sr.*[2], *John Sr.*[1]) died 7 Jun 1937 and was buried in Dalton, GA.

John married **Mary Beckman** 5 Jun 1904 in Lauderdale County, AL.
400 M i. **Earl Lindsey.**
401 M ii. **Hubert Lindsey.**
402 F iii. **Louise Lindsey.**
403 F iv. **Alma Lindsey.**
404 M v. **Elvin Lindsey.**
405 M vi. **William A. Lindsey.**
406 F vii. **Sara Francis Lindsey.**

131. Mollie Elizabeth Lindsey (*Caleb (Calip) Lindsey*[4], *Frances (Frankie) Sharp*[3], *Charles W. Sr.*[2], *John Sr.*[1]) was born 11 Mar 1871, died 30 Aug 1907, and was buried in Florence City Cemetery, Florence, Lauderdale County, AL.

Mollie married **William W. Bennett** 18 Dec 1890 in Lauderdale County, AL.
+ 407 F i. **Mary Mable Bennett.**
+ 408 M ii. **Roy Bennett.**
+ 409 M iii. **Oscar Lee Bennett Sr.** was born in 1892 and died in 1957.

132. America Lindsey (*Caleb (Calip) Lindsey*[4], *Frances (Frankie) Sharp*[3], *Charles W. Sr.*[2], *John Sr.*[1]) was born in 1873 in Lauderdale County, AL and died in 1925.

America married **Tom Mitchum** 29 Jan 1898 in Lauderdale County, AL. Tom was born in 1867 and died in 1939.
+ 410 M i. **Floyd Mitchum.**
+ 411 F ii. **Tellie Ruth Mitchum.**
+ 412 F iii. **Nellie Mitchum** was born 11 Apr 1894 and died 26 Mar 1983.
+ 413 M iv. **Bufford Lee Mitchum** was born 2 Nov 1903 in Lauderdale County, AL, died 20 Dec 1964, and was buried in Tri-Cities Memorial Gardens, Florence, Lauderdale County, AL.

133. Lula Mae Lindsey (*Caleb (Calip) Lindsey*[4], *Frances (Frankie) Sharp*[3], *Charles W. Sr.*[2], *John Sr.*[1]) was born 21 Feb 1876 and died 12 Jan 1948.

General Notes: "Lula was Caleb's fourth child by his second marriage. She was born February 21, 18876, and died January 12, 1948. Cousin Lula was married to William Henry Holt. His elder brother, Brown Holt, was married to Lula's half -sister, Fannie. Following William's death, Cousin Lula and her son, Cecil, operated a grocery store on Sweetwater Avenue across from the Cherry Cotton Mill. They built a home near the store according to plans William had made prior to his death. Their second home on the old Jackson Highway was also constructed from William's drawings..." William McDonald

Lula married **William Henry Holt** 29 Jan 1898 in Lauderdale County, AL. William was born 28 Dec 1872 and died 19 Jan 1926.
+ 414 F i. **Grace E. Holt** was born in 1892 and died 6 May 1942.
+ 415 M ii. **William Cecil Holt.**

134. Tellie Dora Lindsey (*Caleb (Calip) Lindsey[4], Frances (Frankie) Sharp[3], Charles W. Sr.[2], John Sr.[1]*) was born 8 Jan 1879 in Lauderdale County, AL, died 24 Aug 1949, and was buried in Florence City Cemetery, Florence, Lauderdale County, AL.

Tellie married **John Steven Myrick** 22 Aug 1911 in Lauderdale County, AL. John was born 10 Nov 1886 in Franklin County, AL, died 27 Feb 1968, and was buried in Florence City Cemetery, Florence, Lauderdale County, AL.

> General Notes: "John was ticket agent for the L & N Railroad in East Florence for almost half a century. They had a daughter, Reba Ruth, who died June 25, 1914, at the age of almost ten months. Cousin Rivers Lindsey, Sr., remembered that his Cousin Tellie Lindsey taught at the old log school that was given to the Oakland community by his family. In their early years, Tellie and John made their home in one of the houses built by her father on Sweetwater Avenue..." William McDonald

    416 F   i.   **Reba Ruth Myrick** was born 19 Aug 1913 in Lauderdale County, AL and died 25 Jun 1914.

135. Robert Andrew Lindsey (*Caleb (Calip) Lindsey[4], Frances (Frankie) Sharp[3], Charles W. Sr.[2], John Sr.[1]*) was born 27 Jan 1880 in Lauderdale County, AL, died 27 Jan 1932, and was buried in Florence City Cemetery, Florence, Lauderdale County, AL.

> General Notes: "Robert and his brother, David, were married to sisters, and both families helped rear my father. Dad's first cousins were almost as my uncles and aunts. During the hard years of the Depression my family moved to that part of Robert's place known as the "wood lot". Uncle Robert farmed Patton Island and drove a large wagon pulled by two mules, Sam and Ada. Late in the day as Uncle Rob passed our home, he would sing out "Little Willie Wooden Leg!" This was my invitation to climb up on the wagon and ride beside him to the barn. I cherish those wonderful memories. One time a flash flood almost isolated Uncle Rob on the island. Sam and Ada managed to swim the channel at the last minute before the entire island was inundated. Uncle Rob said that Ada almost gave up the struggle, but was urged on by Sam. Uncle Rob and Aunt Lottie had four children...." William McDonald

Robert married **Charlotte Redding** 29 Sep 1907 in Lauderdale County, AL. Charlotte was born 23 Mar 1885, died 23 Jan 1938, and was buried in Florence City Cemetery, Florence, Lauderdale County, AL.

      417 M   i.   **Andrew Charles Lindsey** was born 25 Sep 1908 in Lauderdale County, AL, died 19 Aug 1925, and was buried in Florence City Cemetery, Florence, Lauderdale County, AL.

+ 418 F   ii.   **Mazie Aileen Lindsey** was born 11 Nov 1909 in Lauderdale County, AL, died 13 Sep 1970, and was buried in Florence City Cemetery, Florence, Lauderdale County, AL.

+ 419 M   iii.   **Dewey Caleb Lindsey** was born 30 Jan 1911 in Lauderdale County, AL, died 13 Dec 1970, and was buried in Florence City Cemetery, Florence, Lauderdale County, AL.

+ 420 M   iv.   **Donald Edward Lindsey Sr.** was born 15 Dec 1912 in Lauderdale County, AL, died 21 Jul 1964, and was buried in Greenview Memorial Park, Florence, Lauderdale County, AL.

136. Alonzo Brown Lindsey (*Caleb (Calip) Lindsey[4], Frances (Frankie) Sharp[3], Charles W. Sr.[2], John Sr.[1]*) was born 16 Nov 1887 in Lauderdale County, AL, died 30 Aug 1954, and was buried in Greenview Memorial Park, Florence, Lauderdale County, AL.

Alonzo married **Laura May Gist** 6 Apr 1907 in Lauderdale County, AL. Laura was born 2 May 1888, died 21 Jun 1958, and was buried in Greenview Memorial Park, Florence, Lauderdale County, AL.

+ 421 M   i.   **Chester B. Lindsey** was born 24 Nov 1907 in Lauderdale County, AL, died 22 Nov 1979, and was buried in Arlington Cemetery, Mt. Pleasant, TN.

+ 422 F   ii.   **Nellie Mauvaline Lindsey** was born 24 Sep 1909 in Lauderdale County, AL, died 2 May 1954, and was buried in Greenview Memorial Park, Florence, Lauderdale County, AL.

      423 F   iii.   **Annie Lorene Lindsey** was born 9 Oct 1911 in Lauderdale County, AL, died 22 Apr 1915, and was buried in Florence City Cemetery, Florence, Lauderdale County, AL.

+ 424 F   iv.   **Elsie Lindsey** was born 8 Nov 1913 in Lauderdale County, AL.

+ 425 F   v.   **Lula Mae Lindsey** was born 19 Feb 1916 in Lauderdale County, AL and died 12 Jun 1969.

+ 426 F   vi.   **Doris Lindsey** was born 25 May 1919 in Lauderdale County, AL, died 20 Feb 1998, and was buried in Greenview Memorial Park, Florence, Lauderdale County, AL.

+ 427 M vii.   **Thomas Arnett Lindsey** was born 5 May 1921 in Lauderdale County, AL.

137. Edgar Floyd Lindsey Sr. (*Caleb (Calip) Lindsey [4], Frances (Frankie) Sharp [3], Charles W. Sr. [2], John Sr. [1]*) was born 11 Mar 1893 in Lauderdale County, AL, died 8 Jan 1951, and was buried in New Orleans, LA.

Edgar married **Lilly Goins** 24 Jan 1912 in Lauderdale County, AL.

Edgar next married **Rena Thomason**. Rena was born 10 Apr 1900 in Colbert County, AL, died 29 Oct 1966, and was buried in New Orleans, LA.

| | 428 | M | i. | **Edgar Floyd (E. F.) Lindsey Jr.** was born 3 Mar 1924 in Lauderdale County, AL. |
| + | 429 | F | ii. | **Evie Jane Lindsey** was born 27 Jul 1926 in Birmingham, Jefferson County, AL. |

139. Maraday (Merry Dee) Lindsey (*Andrew Jackson Lindsey [4], Frances (Frankie) Sharp [3], Charles W. Sr. [2], John Sr. [1]*) was born in May 1854 in Lauderdale County, AL and died in Mississippi.

Maraday married **Bettie Thompson** 3 Feb 1878 in Hardin County, TN. Bettie was born in Feb 1862 in Hardin County, TN.

+	430	M	i.	**Millard Lindsey** was born in Feb 1883 in Alabama, died 1 Oct 1945, and was buried in Crittenden Memorial Park, Marion, AR.
+	431	M	ii.	**Thomas G. Lindsey** was born in Jun 1885 in Mississippi.
+	432	F	iii.	**Effie C. M. Lindsey** was born in Aug 1887 in Alabama.
+	433	M	iv.	**Hector J. Lindsey** was born in Jan 1890 in Alabama.
	434	F	v.	**Willie May Lindsey** was born in Jan 1892 in Alabama.
	435	F	vi.	**Ollie Lou Lindsey** was born in Feb 1895 in Alabama.

> General Notes: "Mom thinks she married a Sam Oliver. Kids Jessie Belle, Mary, Alice, a couple of boys..." Debbie Wasserburger

	436	F	vii.	**Joyce Lindsey** was born in Oct 1898 in Alabama and died in 1910 in Alabama.
	437	F	viii.	**Beulah Lindsey** was born in 1900 in Alabama.
	438	M	ix.	**Dudley Lindsey** was born in 1903 in Alabama.

140. Greenberry Lee Lindsey Sr. (*Sylvester (Sill) B. Lindsey [4], Frances (Frankie) Sharp [3], Charles W. Sr. [2], John Sr. [1]*) was born 14 Nov 1854 in Lauderdale County, AL, died 12 Nov 1930, and was buried in Wright Cemetery, Wright, Lauderdale County, AL.

> General Notes: "Greenberry Lindsey, Sr., lived north of Waterloo near the junction of Manbone and Second Creeks, where the old well and foundation of the chimney can be seen today. Greenberry and my great-grandfather Lindsey were close ..." William McDonald
>
> "Greenberry, Sr. and Nancy Bruce marriage records in Blue Book in Vault, p 131. Copy of book that was burned...." David Sharp

Greenberry married **Nancy Bruce**, daughter of **Baylis Bruce Sr.** and **Elizabeth *Unk**, 25 Dec 1878 in Lauderdale County, AL. Nancy was born in 1854 in Lauderdale County, AL, died in 1900, and was buried in Wright Cemetery, Wright, Lauderdale County, AL.

+	439	M	i.	**Kerom William Lindsey** was born 17 Jan 1880 in Lauderdale County, AL, died 25 Oct 1957, and was buried in Wright Cemetery, Wright, Lauderdale County, AL.
+	440	M	ii.	**Samuel S. Lindsey** was born 16 Oct 1882 in Lauderdale County, AL, died 20 Jan 1917, and was buried in Wright Cemetery, Wright, Lauderdale County, AL.
+	441	M	iii.	**John David Lindsey** was born in Jan 1885 in Tyronza, Poinsett County, AR, died 28 Jan 1947, and was buried in Tyronza Cemetery, Tyronza, Poinsett County, AR.
+	442	M	iv.	**Greenberry Lee Lindsey Jr.** was born 19 Nov 1886 in Lauderdale County, AL, died 15 Nov 1974, and was buried in Wright Cemetery, Wright, Lauderdale County, AL.
+	443	F	v.	**Elizabeth (Lizzie) Lindsey** was born in Apr 1889 in Alabama.
+	444	F	vi.	**Hannah Margaret Lindsey** was born in Jul 1894 in Lauderdale County, AL.
+	445	M	vii.	**Bruce Lindsey** was born in Aug 1896 in Lauderdale County, AL.

Greenberry next married **Emma White** 12 Nov 1930 in Lauderdale County, AL. Emma was born in 1881 in Tennessee, died 1 Jun 1942, and was buried in Decatur, Morgan County, AL.

| | 446 | F | i. | **Nancy Elizabeth Lindsey**. |
| + | 447 | F | ii. | **Etta Lindsey** was born about 1914 in Alabama. |

143. Julie (Julia) Lindsey (*Sylvester (Sill) B. Lindsey ^{4}, Frances (Frankie) Sharp ^{3}, Charles W. Sr. ^{2}, John Sr. ^{1}*) was born in Jun 1860 in Lauderdale County, AL and died 3 Mar 1937.

Julie married **George W. Milford**, son of **Anaziah Douglas (A. D.) Milford** and **Minerva Caroline Aikens**, 30 Aug 1883 in Lauderdale County, AL. George was born 12 Mar 1862 in Florence, Lauderdale County, AL, died in May 1930, and was buried in Gravely Springs Cemetery, Lauderdale County, AL.

+   448   F   i.   **Mollie L. Milford** was born 23 Jan 1885 in Lauderdale County, AL and died before 1 Apr 1969.

   449   F   ii.   **George Eddie Milford** was born 11 Apr 1886 in Lauderdale County, AL and died 20 Jan 1887 in Lauderdale County, AL.

   450   F   iii.   **Allie Lee Milford** was born 28 Jun 1888 in Lauderdale County, AL and died 18 Jul 1890 in Lauderdale County, AL.

+   451   F   iv.   **Ruby P. Milford** was born 8 Apr 1893 in Lauderdale County, AL.

+   452   F   v.   **Pearlie Ann Milford** was born 20 Sep 1895 in Lauderdale County, AL, died 31 Mar 1969, and was buried in Wright Cemetery, Wright, Lauderdale County, AL.

   453   F   vi.   **Olivia Pinkney Milford** was born 3 Apr 1898 in Lauderdale County, AL and died 16 Dec 1900 in Lauderdale County, AL.

144. Adron (Little Ade) Lindsey (*Sylvester (Sill) B. Lindsey ^{4}, Frances (Frankie) Sharp ^{3}, Charles W. Sr. ^{2}, John Sr. ^{1}*) was born in Oct 1863 in Lauderdale County, AL, died in 1945, and was buried in John Lay Cemetery, Etheridge, TN.

General Notes: "... Adron was known as "Little Aid" and was named for my Great- grandfather Adron Lindsey (who was Little Aid's uncle). Little Aid was living at Waterloo at the time of the 1900 census. He soon afterwards moved to Florence and was employed at the Florence Wagon Works. He convinced my Grandfather Lindsey to come to Florence and assisted in finding work for him at the wagon factory. I remember seeing Little Aid when I was a child. My impression of him will always be 'a man with a beard driving a small wagon pulled by a mule and heading toward East Hill'...." William McDonald

Adron married **Ida V. Crittenden**, daughter of **John Wesley Crittenden** and **Hester Ann Sharp**, 30 Dec 1885 in Lauderdale County, AL. Ida was born in Sep 1869 in Alabama, died 9 May 1939, and was buried in John Lay Cemetery, Etheridge, TN.

+   454   F   i.   **Margie L. Lindsey** was born in Oct 1888 in Alabama.

+   455   F   ii.   **Carrie M. Lindsey** was born in Oct 1890 in Alabama.

+   456   F   iii.   **Amy Gertrude Lindsey** was born in Dec 1892 and was buried in Harvey Cemetery, Whitehead, Rogersville, AL.

+   457   M   iv.   **Turner Lindsey** was born in Nov 1894 in Lauderdale County, AL.

+   458   F   v.   **Viola Lindsey** was born in Jan 1896 in Lauderdale County, AL.

+   459   F   vi.   **Zula Mason Lindsey** was born in Apr 1899.

+   460   F   vii.   **Estelle Lindsey** was born in 1902 and died in 1983 in Lawrenceburg, Lawrence County, TN.

+   461   F   viii.   **Mary Odelle Lindsey** was born in 1905.

+   462   F   ix.   **Almeda Lindsey** was born in 1910.

+   463   M   x.   **Jesse Mack Lindsey** was born in 1912, died 23 Sep 1992, and was buried in John Lay Cemetery, Etheridge, TN.

   464   M   xi.   **Bayles R. Lindsey** was born in 1914.

Adron next married **Isabelle Hopson** 20 Sep 1888 in Lauderdale County, AL.

145. John H. Lindsey (*Sylvester (Sill) B. Lindsey ^{4}, Frances (Frankie) Sharp ^{3}, Charles W. Sr. ^{2}, John Sr. ^{1}*) was born in 1866 in Lauderdale County, AL.

General Notes: "1910 census showed John Lindsey born around 1862 and Martha born around 1882, with children: Verta M. 6 years old, b 1904, James P. 4 years old, b 1906, Johnnie B 11/12 years old, about 1909. (David Sharp thinks this may be the children of this John and Martha, John, son of Sylvester Lindsey..." William McDonald

John married **Ellen D. Ady** 9 May 1888 in Lauderdale County, AL.

John next married **Martha C. Johnson** 5 Sep 1900 in Lauderdale County, AL.

146. Matilda Lindsey (*Sylvester (Sill) B. Lindsey [4], Frances (Frankie) Sharp [3], Charles W. Sr. [2], John Sr. [1]*) was born in 1868 in Lauderdale County, AL.

Matilda married **W. S. Whitsett** 1 Apr 1897 in Lauderdale County, AL.

147. Lucretia (Lula) Lindsey (*Adron Leonard Lindsey Sr. [4], Frances (Frankie) Sharp [3], Charles W. Sr. [2], John Sr. [1]*) was born 3 Apr 1863 in Lauderdale County, AL and died 15 Apr 1940 in Savannah, Hardin County, TN.

General Notes:

"Lucretia, whom I knew as "Aunt Lula" was born in April, 1862. She was one -fourth blood Chickasaw and looked very much the part. As a boy I was spellbound when we visited her because of her striking features. She was of dark complexion and had high cheek bones as did her Native -American ancestors. Her hair was long and straight and hung over her shoulders and although she was quite elderly when I knew her, there was not on gray hair to be seen. I recall her hair being so unusually black that it glistened in the sunlight. On March 30, 1881, she married Christopher C. Haynes of Waterloo. Criss, as he was called, was a widower some twelve years her senior.

Lula reared a total of twelve children, including the three who were her first husband's previous marriage. Six were by her first husband and the last three were by her second marriage.

I do not remember when Aunt Lula died, it must have been during the early years of WWII when gas was rationed and it was difficult to travel. I'm not sure now but I think she was living in Tyronza, Arkansas at the time of her death. We have lost contact with most all of Aunt Lula's family. However there are two descendants who live in Florence. Jack Haynes, son of

L-R Josie Etta Haynes Kirkland, Leonard A. Haynes and Lou Tishie Haynes Tacker

either Elbert or Dick Haynes, is a great -grandson of Criss and Lula. Jack and his wife, Jill, own the Haynes Specialty Shop on North Court Street. This business was established by Jack's mother, Ruth, who is now deceased. Another great -grandson is Edward Haynes who lives on Dixie Avenue.

Lula and Criss lived at various times in Waterloo and on a farm near Waterloo. When I was a boy, Great -aunt Lula was a widow and lived, as I remember, on a farm.

Criss died sometime between 1890 and 1896. Afterwards, Lula married her former brother-in-law, Edward B. Taylor, on November 18, 1896. Ed Taylor's first wife was Lula's younger sister, Mary. Ed Taylor was also a cousin to Criss Haynes.

I have already mentioned Criss's children by his first marriage; William, Ida and Wiley Elbert. I do not know what happened to Willie and Ida, however, Wiley was living with Lula and Edward at the time of the 1900 census, (this was of course after his father's death)..." William McDonald

Lucretia married **Christopher (Criss) Columbus Haynes**, son of **Henry Harvey Haynes** and **Nancy Turpin**, 30 Mar 1881 in Lauderdale County, AL. Christopher was born in 1850 in Alabama and died between 1890 and 1896.

+	465	F	i.	**Josie Etta Haynes** was born 6 Mar 1883 in Lauderdale County, AL, died 13 Aug 1964, and was buried in Mt. Zion Cemetery, Hardin County, TN.

+ 465 F i. **Josie Etta Haynes** was born 6 Mar 1883 in Lauderdale County, AL, died 13 Aug 1964, and was buried in Mt. Zion Cemetery, Hardin County, TN.

+ 466 M ii. **Clarence Haynes** was born 3 Jan 1882 in Waterloo, Lauderdale County, AL, died 10 Jul 1960, and was buried in Tyronza Cemetery, Tyronza, Poinsett County, AR.

+ 467 F iii. **Lou Tishie Haynes** was born 18 May 1885, died 9 Sep 1974, and was buried in Mt. Zion Cemetery, Hardin County, TN.

+ 468 F iv. **Roxie W. Haynes** was born in Feb 1886 and was buried in Tyronza Cemetery, Tyronza, Poinsett County, AR.

469 M v. **Columbus C. Haynes** was born in Jun 1888 and was buried in Arkansas.

+ 470 M vi. **Leonard A. Haynes** was born in Aug 1890 and was buried in Memphis, Shelby County, TN.

Lucretia next married **Edward (Edwin/Ed) Taylor** 16 Nov 1896 in Lauderdale County, AL. Edward was born in 1873 in Wayne County, TN.

+ 471 F i. **Elza Raider Taylor** was born in 1898 in Alabama.

+ 472 F ii. **Martha (Mattie) Inez Taylor** was born 29 Mar 1900 in Lauderdale County, AL, died 6 Nov 1993, and was buried in Oak Grove Cemetery, Lauderdale County, AL.

+ 473 M iii. **George Willis Taylor** was born 28 Feb 1931 in Tennessee, died 5 Apr 1995, and was buried in Rhodesville Cemetery, Lauderdale County, AL.

148. Calvin Lindsey (*Adron Leonard Lindsey Sr.*^{4}, *Frances (Frankie) Sharp*^{3}, *Charles W. Sr.*^{2}, *John Sr.*^{1}) was born about 1868 in Lauderdale County, AL, died in 1894, and was buried in Tyronza Cemetery, Tyronza, Poinsett County, AR.

Calvin married **Dora Hooden**.

149. Mary (Polly) Lindsey (*Adron Leonard Lindsey Sr.*^{4}, *Frances (Frankie) Sharp*^{3}, *Charles W. Sr.*^{2}, *John Sr.*^{1}) was born in 1870 in Lauderdale County, AL.

General Notes: "It was said in the family that she was 'the fairest of all'. She had the prominent features of the Chickasaws inherited from her grandmother. According to one story, little Mary and her grandmother, Chealty, had a very close relationship and for some reason, perhaps when her mother was ill, she lived with her grandmother for a time. Mary was married to Edward Taylor and died during childbirth; as far as I know she left no surviving children. A number of years after Mary's death, her husband married her older sister, Lucretia (Lula)...." William McDonald

Mary married **Edward (Edwin/Ed) Taylor** 14 Mar 1894 in Lauderdale County, AL. Edward was born in 1873 in Wayne County, TN.

150. Hunter Lindsey (*Adron Leonard Lindsey Sr.*^{4}, *Frances (Frankie) Sharp*^{3}, *Charles W. Sr.*^{2}, *John Sr.*^{1}) was born in 1876 in Wright, Lauderdale County, AL, died in 1900, and was buried in Wright Cemetery, Wright, Lauderdale County, AL.

General Notes: "On January 9, 1898, Great Uncle Hunter was married to Laura Saddler in the home of her father, John Saddler, of the Wright community. Dr. Ben Lee, a local physician and Presbyterian minister, read the vows. Hunter died soon afterwards and is buried alongside the Saddler family in the Wright Cemetery. Hunter's untimely death occurred while my grandfather Lindsey was away in Texas. Consequently, he did not know where his brother was buried until about 1958 when Cousin Kern Lindsey pointed out the grave to us when we were visiting there. Papa and I placed a marker on Hunter's grave, but I cannot now locate it...." William McDonald

Hunter married **Laura Ethel Saddler**, daughter of **John Wesley Saddler Sr.** and **Melissa Evelyn (Aunt Eb) Wood**, 8 Jan 1898 in Lauderdale County, AL. Laura was born 6 Apr 1882 in Wright, Lauderdale County, AL, died 24 Mar 1947, and was buried in Wright Cemetery, Wright, Lauderdale County, AL.

+ 474 F i. **Winnie E. Lindsey** was born in Apr 1899 in Lauderdale County, AL, died in 1928, and was buried in Wright Cemetery, Wright, Lauderdale County, AL.

151. Adron Leonard (Green) Lindsey Jr. (*Adron Leonard Lindsey Sr.*[4]*, Frances (Frankie) Sharp*[3]*, Charles W. Sr.*[2]*, John Sr.*[1]) was born 21 Jan 1878 in Wright, Lauderdale County, AL, died 30 May 1960, and was buried in Florence City Cemetery, Florence, Lauderdale County, AL.

> General Notes:
> "My Grandfather Lindsey was known as Leonard; he never used his full name - Adron Leonard Lindsey, Jr. His grocery store had large letters across the front that read; "L. Lindsey Grocery". The folks he grew up with at Waterloo called him "Len". His children knew him as Papa and those of us who were his grandchildren always called him "Papa Lindsey".
> Leonard Lindsey was born in a two room log house at the Wright Community near Waterloo, Alabama on January 21, 1878. This house was located alongside Lauderdale County Road 14 almost at the junction of Roads 14 and 8 and almost directly across from the Wright Cemetery. One might say, too, that this house with a 'dog trot' between the two large rooms overlooked the mouth of Brush Creek. When TVA completed its Pickwick Dam about 1937, the backwater that created Pickwick Lake formed a small peninsula that almost isolated the house by waters on three sides.
> Leonard grew to manhood at his father's farm on Manbone Creek north of Waterloo. He labored on the farm for the family. He also cut cross ties that sold for 25 cents each. There was a buyer in those days at Waterloo who shipped the ties down the river by boat.
> Papa said that things were so hard during Reconstruction that it was necessary to ration the wearing of clothes. While plowing in isolated fields and cutting cross ties in the deep woods, he would hang his trousers on a tree limb and work in his shirt tail. He only had one pair of shoes. On Sundays he would walk barefoot until almost within sight of the church at which time he would stop and put on his shoes.
> Papa's school sessions were held in the Palestine Methodist Church near the junction of Manbone and Second Creeks. His favorite teacher was Miss Mary Houston. She was of the family of Alabama Governor George Smith Houston who grew up at his father's Wildwood Plantation at Gravelly Springs.
> Papa and I visited Miss Mary and her sister, Martha, when they were quite elderly. They were living then under extremely poor and in very primitive circumstances on a high hill near Wright. Papa would take them food and other necessities; I well remember how he would leave money in their room after we had our prayer and were getting ready to leave.
> Leonard's mother, Martha Jane, died when he was nine years old. My Grandpa's only clear memory of his mother was at the times he helped to wash clothes in the spring branch. Papa showed me the rock where his mother had to 'beat' her clothes before scrubbing them in the water.
> Dr. Sullivan, a local physician at Waterloo, tried to adopt Papa but his father would not agree. Papa often spoke of this and would say '....if this happened I could have gone to college to become a Methodist preacher'.
> Papa's father, Adron L. Lindsey, Sr., was soon remarried - to a widow with children of her own. She mistreated Papa and seldom permitted him to eat with the family. As he and I stood at the old home one day, he told this story: "I remember plowing all day, from sun -up until sun -set. My stepmother would not fix lunch for me to carry to the field. When I came in late in the day, tired and hungry, my supper would be waiting on a rafter in the barn. It usually consisted of cold peas in a fruit jar with a small piece of corn bread. I would wait until the last minute to look up at the rafter, in hopes that she would call me to eat a warm meal with the others...." William McDonald

Adron married **Lucy Lavinia Johnson**, daughter of **Franklin Pierce Johnson** and **Mary Ellender McCuan**, 9 Nov 1902 in Lauderdale County, AL. Lucy was born 23 Apr 1885 in Lauderdale County, AL, died 30 Oct 1951, and was buried in Florence City Cemetery, Florence, Lauderdale County, AL.

+ 475 F i. **Carmel Lindsey** was born 11 Dec 1903 in Lauderdale County, AL, died 8 Jan 1968, and was buried in Greenview Memorial Park, Florence, Lauderdale County, AL.

+ 476 M ii. **Carlos (Bill) Lindsey** was born 17 Feb 1907 in Lauderdale County, AL, died 19 Jul 1974, and was buried in Pleasant Hill Cemetery, Lauderdale County, AL.

+ 477 F iii. **Pauline Myran Lindsey** was born 15 Mar 1910 in Lauderdale County, AL, died 6 Mar 1964, and was buried in Pleasant Hill Cemetery, Lauderdale County, AL.

+ 478 F iv. **Laura Lindsey** was born 12 Aug 1912 in Lauderdale County, AL, died 10 Oct 1991, and was buried in Greenview Memorial Park, Florence, Lauderdale County, AL.

+ 479 M v. **Nelson McCaun Lindsey** was born 26 Mar 1915 in Lauderdale County, AL, died 30 Dec 1978, and was buried in Oakwood Cemetery, Sheffield, Colbert County, AL.
+ 480 M vi. **Howard Shannon Lindsey** was born 11 Apr 1917 in Lauderdale County, AL.
+ 481 M vii. **Marvin Glenn Lindsey** was born 4 Nov 1919 in Lauderdale County, AL.
+ 482 M viii. **Claude Raymond Lindsey Sr.** was born 24 Apr 1922 in Lauderdale County, AL.
  483 F ix. **Mary Ellender Lindsey** was born 12 Jun 1928 in Lauderdale County, AL and died 10 Oct 1995.

153. Nancy Lindsey (*Robert Lindsey*[4]*, Frances (Frankie) Sharp*[3]*, Charles W. Sr.*[2]*, John Sr.*[1]) was born about 1856 in Alabama.

Nancy married **Francis M. Young** 25 Sep 1873 in Lauderdale County, AL.

155. Johnathan Lindsey Jr (*Robert Lindsey*[4]*, Frances (Frankie) Sharp*[3]*, Charles W. Sr.*[2]*, John Sr.*[1]) was born about 1860 in Alabama.

Johnathan married **Mary Parker** 16 Dec 1880 in Lauderdale County, AL.

156. Calvin Lindsey (*Robert Lindsey*[4]*, Frances (Frankie) Sharp*[3]*, Charles W. Sr.*[2]*, John Sr.*[1]) was born about 1862 in Alabama.

Calvin married **C. M. Horton** 20 Jan 1889 in Lauderdale County, AL.

161. Eddie Young (*Mary M. (Polly II) Lindsey*[4]*, Frances (Frankie) Sharp*[3]*, Charles W. Sr.*[2]*, John Sr.*[1]) was born 5 Aug 1866 in Gravely Springs, Lauderdale County, AL, died 5 Oct 1933, and was buried in Murphy's Chapel Cemetery, Lauderdale County, AL.

Eddie married **Mack Edward Young**, son of **Devenport (Deb) Young** and **Catherine Richardson**, 15 Nov 1881 in Lauderdale County, AL. Mack was born 14 Jan 1868 in Lauderdale County, AL, died 6 Dec 1944, and was buried in Murphy's Chapel Cemetery, Lauderdale County, AL.
+ 484 M i. **Grover Cleveland Young** was born 9 Nov 1892 in Lauderdale County, AL, died 3 Feb 1936, and was buried in Pensacola, Escambia County, FL.
+ 485 M ii. **William (Bill) Mack Young** was born 17 May 1894 in Lauderdale County, AL, died 8 Dec 1971, and was buried in Tri-Cities Memorial Gardens, Florence, Lauderdale County, AL.
+ 486 F iii. **Nellie Bell Young** was born 3 Sep 1895 in Lauderdale County, AL, died 22 Aug 1945, and was buried in Mishawaka, St Joseph County, IN.
+ 487 M iv. **Earnest Edward Young** was born 3 May 1900 in Lauderdale County, AL, died 6 Aug 1971, and was buried in Murphy's Chapel Cemetery, Lauderdale County, AL.
+ 488 F v. **Willie Leona Young** was born 28 Sep 1907 in Lauderdale County, AL, died 5 Jan 2001, and was buried in Murphy's Chapel Cemetery, Lauderdale County, AL.
+ 489 M vi. **Odus Clarence Young Sr.** was born 7 Mar 1909 in Lauderdale County, AL, died 1 Jun 1968, and was buried in Murphy's Chapel Cemetery, Lauderdale County, AL.

Mack Edward Young and Eddie Young Family
Front: Mack holding Willie Young Witt, Ernest Young, Eddie (Young) Young
Back Row: Nellie Young Biggs, Cleveland Young, William Young. Odus not born yet.

162. Mary Francis (Molly) Young (*Mary M. (Polly II) Lindsey* [4], *Frances (Frankie) Sharp* [3], *Charles W. Sr.* [2], *John Sr.* [1]) was born 9 Nov 1867 in Lauderdale County, AL, died 14 Apr 1900, and was buried in Murphy's Chapel Cemetery, Lauderdale County, AL. Another name for Mary was Mary Frances (Mollie) Young.

Mary married **John Lindley Dearen**, son of **Hopkins Lee Dearen** and **Nancy Caroline White**, 18 Jan 1891 in Lauderdale County, AL. John was born 14 Apr 1861 in Hardin County, TN, died 15 Nov 1953, and was buried in Murphy's Chapel Cemetery, Lauderdale County, AL.

+	490	F	i.

+ 490 F i.   **Jessie Bell Dearen** was born 2 Nov 1891 in Waterloo, Lauderdale County, AL, died 5 Feb 1955, and was buried in Florence City Cemetery, Florence, Lauderdale County, AL.

+ 491 M ii.   **William Lee Dearen** was born 8 Jun 1893 in Lauderdale County, AL and died in Oct 1981 in Waco, McLennan County, TX.

+ 492 F iii.   **Minnie Pearl Dearen** was born 18 Dec 1894 in Lauderdale County, AL, died 5 May 1983, and was buried in Williams Chapel Cemetery, Lauderdale County, AL.

+ 493 M iv.   **James Edgar Dearen** was born 15 Apr 1897 in Lauderdale County, AL, died 5 Dec 1964 in Marlin, TX, and was buried in Hamilton Cemetery, Corsicana, TX.

+ 494 F v.   **Clara Edna Dearen** was born 21 Nov 1898 in Lauderdale County, AL, died 19 Jul 1978, and was buried in Murphy's Chapel Cemetery, Lauderdale County, AL.

John Lindley Dearen, son of **Hopkins Lee Dearen** and **Nancy Caroline White**, next married **Ollie B. Young.** Ollie was born 10 Sep 1881 in Waterloo, Lauderdale County, AL, died 1 Jan 1947, and was buried
in Tyronza Cemetery, Tyronza, Poinsett County, AR.

- **Margie Etta Dearen** was born 8 Sep 1902.
  Margie married **Sam Jones Morgan** 7 Aug 1930 in Tyronza, Poinsett County,   AR.

- **John Garland Dearen** was born 28 Feb 1905 in Wright, Lauderdale County, AL and died in Mar 1978.

    John married **Lenora Manley**.
    John next married **Lillian *Unk**.

- **Roy Edwin Dearen** was born 21 Apr 1907 in Waterloo, Lauderdale County, AL, died 2 May 1988, and was buried in Tyronza Cemetery, Tyronza, Poinsett County, AR.
  > Roy married **Toy Katherine Rook** 3 Mar 1929 in Tyronza, Poinsett County, AR.

- **Mary Gladis Dearen** was born 4 Apr 1909 in Waterloo, Lauderdale County, AL and died 19 Jan 1999 in Ft Oglethorpe, GA.
  > Mary married **Pat Ellis**.
- **Addie Louise Dearen** was born 31 Jul 1911 in Waterloo, Lauderdale County, AL.
  > Addie married **Isaac Benton Young**.

- **Bobby Glenn Young Sr.** was born 7 Jan 1937 in Manila, Mississippi County, AR

- **James Lindley (Jay) Dearen** was born 11 Jul 1913.
  > James married **Lucille Rook**.

- **Era Marie Dearen** was born 19 May 1915.
  > Era married **Carlos Posey**.

- **Nancy Leverne Dearen** was born 10 Aug 1918 in Waterloo, Lauderdale County, AL and died 24 Apr 2001 in West Memphis, Crittenden County, AR.
  > Nancy married **William Mullins Crockett** 27 Sep 1929 in Hernando, MS.
  > William was born 2 Nov 1908 in Dallas, MS and died in Dec 1965 in West Memphis, Crittenden County, AR.

- **Robert Clearmont Dearen** was born 19 Oct 1922 in Waterloo, Lauderdale County, AL and died 12 Apr 2000 in Memphis, Shelby County, TN.
  > Robert married **Louis Evelyn Young** 16 Dec 1949. Louis was born 22 Jul 1928 and died 15 Jan 1996.

Delia "Dee" Young and Mary Frances "Molly" Young Dearen

John Lindley Dearen's 14 children shown by his casket. L-R Jessie Murphy, Garland, Lee, Ed, Minnie Sego, Clearmont, Jim, Jay, Clara South, Era Posey, Margie Morgan, Gladys Patton, Laverne Crockett and Addie Young. John had five children by Molly. After Mollie died he married her cousin, Ollie Young and they had nine children. This was the only time that all 14 children had ever been together at the same time.

163. Roxie Leona Young (*Mary M. (Polly II) Lindsey[4], Frances (Frankie) Sharp[3], Charles W. Sr.[2], John Sr.[1]*) was born 19 Oct 1868 in Gravely Springs, Lauderdale County, AL, died 19 Jan 1951, and was buried in Murphy's Chapel Cemetery, Lauderdale County, AL.

Roxie married **John Allen Ticer**, son of **Robert Clark Ticer I** and **Sarah A. Foust**, 27 Dec 1888 in Lauderdale County, AL. John was born 22 Dec 1863 in Hardin County, TN, died 1 Apr 1931, and was buried in Murphy's Chapel Cemetery, Lauderdale County, AL.

+ 495 F i. **Florence L. Ticer** was born 25 Oct 1889 in Lauderdale County, AL, died 23 May 1955, and was buried in Williams Chapel Cemetery, Lauderdale County, AL.

+ 496 M ii. **Robert Clark Ticer II** was born 12 Feb 1892 in Lauderdale County, AL, died 26 Jan 1966, and was buried in Williams Chapel

John Allen Ticer, Roxie Leona Young Ticer and family

45

Cemetery, Lauderdale County, AL.

| | 497 | M | iii. | **J. Turner Ticer** was born 18 Feb 1894 in Lauderdale County, AL, died 15 Feb 1902, and was buried in Murphy's Chapel Cemetery, Lauderdale County, AL. |

+ 497 M iii. **J. Turner Ticer** was born 18 Feb 1894 in Lauderdale County, AL, died 15 Feb 1902, and was buried in Murphy's Chapel Cemetery, Lauderdale County, AL.

+ 498 F iv. **Mary Ann Ticer** was born 23 Mar 1896 in Lauderdale County, AL, died 7 Apr 1951, and was buried in Richardson Cemetery, Lauderdale County, AL.

499 F v. **Mamie Ticer** was born 19 Apr 1898 in Lauderdale County, AL, died 30 Oct 1945 in Lauderdale County, AL, and was buried in Williams Chapel Cemetery, Lauderdale County, AL.

+ 500 F vi. **Ada Bell Ticer** was born 28 Jan 1900 in Lauderdale County, AL, died 31 Dec 1974, and was buried in Williams Chapel Cemetery, Lauderdale County, AL.

+ 501 M vii. **David (Dave) Washington Ticer** was born 10 Mar 1902 in Lauderdale County, AL, died 3 Mar 1960, and was buried in Williams Chapel Cemetery, Lauderdale County, AL.

+ 502 F viii. **Myrtle S. Ticer** was born 3 Mar 1904 in Lauderdale County, AL, died 5 Jan 1931, and was buried in Williams Chapel Cemetery, Lauderdale County, AL.

+ 503 F ix. **Lillian T. Ticer** was born 27 Apr 1906 in Lauderdale County, AL, died 1 May 1984, and was buried in Wright Cemetery, Wright, Lauderdale County, AL.

+ 504 F x. **Lois V. Ticer** was born in 1909 in Lauderdale County, AL and died 18 Dec 1984.

+ 505 F xi. **Pearl Etta Ticer** was born 24 Aug 1911 in Lauderdale County, AL, died 28 Nov 1992, and was buried in Murphy's Chapel Cemetery, Lauderdale County, AL.

164. Delia (Dee) Young (*Mary M. (Polly II) Lindsey[4], Frances (Frankie) Sharp[3], Charles W. Sr.[2], John Sr.[1]*) was born 19 Oct 1869 in Gravely Springs, Lauderdale County, AL, died in 1897, and was buried in Murphy's Chapel Cemetery, Lauderdale County, AL.

Delia married **Samuel Douglas Milford**, son of **Anaziah Douglas (A. D.) Milford** and **Minerva Caroline Aikens**, 16 May 1888 in Lauderdale County, AL. Samuel was born 20 Jan 1864 in Lauderdale County, AL, died 14 Sep 1947, and was buried in Forrest Hill Cemetery, Jonesboro, AR.

+ 506 F i. **Hettie Milford** was born 28 Jun 1889 in Gravely Springs, Lauderdale County, AL, died 1 Oct 1985, and was buried in Forrest Hill Mid Town Cemetery, Memphis, TN.

+ 507 F ii. **Etta Lee Milford** was born 12 Jul 1890 in Rhodesville, Lauderdale County, AL, died 21 Feb 1985, and was buried in Chapel Hill Memorial Garden, Osceola, IN.

165. Lou Young (*Mary M. (Polly II) Lindsey[4], Frances (Frankie) Sharp[3], Charles W. Sr.[2], John Sr.[1]*) was born 11 Jul 1870 in Lauderdale County, AL, died 31 Dec 1952, and was buried in Murphy's Chapel Cemetery, Lauderdale County, AL.

Lou married **James (Jim) Calvin Young Jr.**, son of **James Calvin Young Sr.** and **Mary Ann Jones**, 25 Dec 1890 in Lauderdale County, AL. James was born 11 Mar 1865 in Pulaski, TN, died 26 Jan 1925, and was buried in Murphy's Chapel Cemetery, Lauderdale County, AL.

+ 508 F i. **Ada Young** was born 28 Mar 1892 in Lauderdale County, AL, died 1 Apr 1975, and was buried in Greenview Memorial Park, Florence, Lauderdale County, AL.

+ 509 M ii. **Dave D. Young** was born 22 Feb 1896 in Lauderdale County, AL, died 9 Feb 1956, and was buried in Greenview Memorial Park, Florence, Lauderdale County, AL.

510 M iii. **Dewey Young** was born 10 Dec 1899 in Lauderdale County, AL, died 24 May 1904, and was buried in Murphy's Chapel Cemetery, Lauderdale County, AL.

+ 511 F iv. **Verna Virella Young** was born 25 Oct 1902 in Lauderdale County, AL, died 9 Sep 1975, and was buried in Mt. Zion Cemetery, Lauderdale County, AL.

+ 512 F v. **Mary Etta Young** was born 28 Nov 1908 in Lauderdale County, AL, died 24 Oct 1990, and was buried in Greenview Memorial Park, Florence, Lauderdale County, AL.

+ 513 F vi. **Della Young** was born 30 Dec 1912 in Lauderdale County, AL, died 12 May 2003, and was buried in Greenview Memorial Park, Florence, Lauderdale County, AL.

166. William (Bill) Young (*Mary M. (Polly II) Lindsey[4], Frances (Frankie) Sharp[3], Charles W. Sr.[2], John Sr.[1]*) was born 15 Mar 1873 in Lauderdale County, AL, died 14 Nov 1941, and was buried in Pleasant Hill Cemetery, Lauderdale County, AL.

William married **Pamphelia Graves** 23 Aug 1900 in Lauderdale County, AL. Pamphelia was born 13 Jul 1868 in Lauderdale County, AL, died 21 Jan 1924, and was buried in Pleasant Hill Cemetery, Lauderdale County, AL.

514 M i. **Marvin Young** was born in Lauderdale County, AL.

515 M ii. **Condy Young**.

+ 516 F iii. **Lavenia Young**.
+ 517 F iv. **Reba Young**.
  518 M v. **Garland Young** was born in 1907.
+ 519 F vi. **Vivian Young** was born 27 Mar 1910, died 22 May 1953, and was buried in Pleasant Hill Cemetery, Lauderdale County, AL.

167. Nancy (Nan) Young (*Mary M. (Polly II) Lindsey*[4]*, Frances (Frankie) Sharp*[3]*, Charles W. Sr.*[2]*, John Sr.*[1]) was born 15 Mar 1874 in Lauderdale County, AL, died 17 Feb 1914, and was buried in Murphy's Chapel Cemetery, Lauderdale County, AL.

    Nancy married **James Celia Bevis**, son of **James Bevis** and **Martha *Unk**, 4 Oct 1900 in Lauderdale County, AL. James was born 16 May 1859 in Lauderdale County, AL, died 8 Jun 1945, and was buried in Macedonia Cemetery, Lauderdale County, AL. Another name for James was *Unk Bevis.
+ 520 M i. **Arbie Bevis** was born 22 Jan 1910 in Lauderdale County, AL, died 11 Jun 1965, and was buried in Pine Hill Cemetery, Lauderdale County, AL.

168. Dora Lee Young (*Mary M. (Polly II) Lindsey*[4]*, Frances (Frankie) Sharp*[3]*, Charles W. Sr.*[2]*, John Sr.*[1]) was born 13 Jun 1876 in Lauderdale County, AL, died 21 May 1922, and was buried in Mt. Olive Cemetery, Lauderdale County, AL.

    Dora married **Edward Rufus Parnell** 3 Feb 1897 in Lauderdale County, AL. Edward was born 10 Jan 1873 in Lauderdale County, AL, died 19 Sep 1945, and was buried in Pine Log Cemetery, Brookland, AR.
  521 F i. **Ethel Parnell**.
+ 522 M ii. **Alonzo Parnell** was born 27 Jul 1899.
+ 523 M iii. **Elbert Parnell** was born 24 Sep 1901.
+ 524 M iv. **Lee Parnell** was born 19 Oct 1903.
  525 M v. **Turner W. Parnell** was born 22 Jun 1905, died in Dec 1906, and was buried in Mt. Olive Cemetery, Lauderdale County, AL.
+ 526 F vi. **Vertia Thora Parnell** was born 28 Nov 1911 in Lauderdale County, AL.
+ 527 F vii. **Aladee Parnell** was born 8 Apr 1914, died in 1936, and was buried in Pine Hill Cemetery, Lauderdale County, AL.
  528 F viii. **Oma Mae Parnell** was born 24 May 1918 in Lauderdale County, AL, died 8 Feb 1919, and was buried in Mt. Olive Cemetery, Lauderdale County, AL.

Lee Jackson and Ethel Rogers Young family. Back: L-R Monser, Lee, Ethel, and Hosea Young
Front: Tove McFall, and Pearl Sharp

170. Lee Jackson Young (*Mary M. (Polly II) Lindsey [4], Frances (Frankie) Sharp [3], Charles W. Sr. [2], John Sr. [1]*) was born in 1883 in Lauderdale County, AL, died 4 Oct 1962, and was buried in St. Joseph Valley Cemetery, Mishawaka, IN.

    Lee married **Ethel Rogers**, daughter of **Robert Chris (Bob) Rogers** and **Abigail (Abbie) Randolph**, 26 Apr 1907 in Lutts, Wayne County, TN. Ethel was born 25 Feb 1892 in Lauderdale County, AL, died 6 Sep 1976, and was buried in St. Joseph Valley Cemetery, Mishawaka, IN.

+	529	F	i.	**Toye R. Young** was born about 1908 in Lauderdale County, AL, died 1 Nov 1998, and was buried in John Lay Cemetery, Etheridge, TN.
+	530	F	ii.	**Pearl V. Young** was born 25 Dec 1910 in Lauderdale County, AL, died 11 Feb 1992, and was buried in Lawrenceburg, Lawrence County, TN.
+	531	M	iii.	**Hosea Leba Young** was born 27 May 1913 in Lauderdale County, AL, died 4 Mar 1990, and was buried in Fairview Cemetery, Mishawaka, IN.
+	532	M	iv.	**Monser Lee Young** was born 19 Jun 1915 in Lauderdale County, AL, died 12 Oct 2000, and was buried in Fairview Cemetery, Mishawaka, IN.

171. Harriet Lutisha Lindsey (*John S. Lindsey [4], Frances (Frankie) Sharp [3], Charles W. Sr. [2], John Sr. [1]*) was born in 1867 in Alabama.

    Harriet married **William Joseph Jasper Long** 23 Dec 1885 in Lauderdale County, AL. William was born in 1865.

175. Louisa F. Lindsey (*John S. Lindsey [4], Frances (Frankie) Sharp [3], Charles W. Sr. [2], John Sr. [1]*) was born 9 May 1872 in Lauderdale County, AL, died 13 Jan 1931, and was buried in Snyder, Scurry County, TX.

    Louisa married **William R. Wood** 9 May 1890 in Marian, Lee County, AR. William was born 22 Feb 1868 in Lauderdale County, AL, died 17 Apr 1954 in Oklahoma City, Oklahoma County, OK, and was buried in Snyder, Scurry County, TX.

+	533	M	i.	**John Hampton (Charlie) Wood** was born 16 Mar 1892 in Florence, Lauderdale County, AL, died 4 Feb 1979, and was buried in Snyder, Scurry County, TX.
+	534	M	ii.	**William Hunter Wood** was born 20 Dec 1894 in Forrest City, St. Francis County, AR, died 3 Mar 1962, and was buried in Oklahoma City, Oklahoma County, OK.
+	535	F	iii.	**Bertha Mae Wood** was born 25 Feb 1896 in Lauderdale County, AL and died 1 Dec 1921 in Plainview, Lea County, NM.
	536	F	iv.	**Mittie Ethel Wood** was born 13 Oct 1899 and died 25 Aug 1918 in White County, AR.
+	537	F	v.	**Ada Evelyn Wood** was born 24 Oct 1902 in Florence, Lauderdale County, AL, died 6 May 1941, and was buried in Snyder, Scurry County, TX.
+	538	M	vi.	**Otha Oneal Wood** was born 20 Nov 1904 in Arkansas, died 25 Feb 1990, and was buried in North Kearn Cemetery, Delano, Kearn County, CA.
+	539	M	vii.	**Elmer Cecil Wood** was born 8 Feb 1907, died 15 Jul 1980 in McCloud, OK, and was buried in Snyder, Scurry County, TX.
+	540	M	viii.	**Lemuel Carl Wood** was born 24 Nov 1910 in Griffithville, White County, AR, died 7 Feb 1989, and was buried in Snyder, Scurry County, TX.

176. Ellie Lindsey (*John S. Lindsey [4], Frances (Frankie) Sharp [3], Charles W. Sr. [2], John Sr. [1]*) was buried in Forrest City, St. Francis County, AR.

    Ellie married ***Unk Waterman**.

177. Sarah Lindsey (*John S. Lindsey [4], Frances (Frankie) Sharp [3], Charles W. Sr. [2], John Sr. [1]*).

    Sarah married ***Unk Moore**.

181. Lara Lindsey (*John S. Lindsey [4], Frances (Frankie) Sharp [3], Charles W. Sr. [2], John Sr. [1]*).

    Lara married ***Unk Compton**.

184. Robert Patton Sharp (*James (Jim) Charles Sr.*[4]*, Adron (Edwin/Ade) Sr.*[3]*, Charles W. Sr.*[2]*, John Sr.*[1]) was born 12 Feb 1854 in Wright, Lauderdale County, AL, died 6 Dec 1912, and was buried in Savannah, Hardin County, TN.

> General Notes: "When Robert Patton Sharp was born, a politician named "Patton" was campaigning and asked James and Melissa Sharp if they would name him "Patton" that when he became governor of Alabama he would educate him. He was elected Governor and kept his word.
> Robert Patton sharp was educated at State Normal College at Florence, Alabama. (Now known as The University of North Alabama) Robert Patton served as Governor of Alabama starting in 1865...." Dan Wood

> Robert married **Mary (Mollie) Elizabeth Carr**, daughter of **Joseph Price Carr Sr.** and **Julia Ann Lee**, 9 Feb 1879 in Lauderdale County, AL. Mary was born 21 Sep 1863 in Gravely Springs, Lauderdale County, AL, died 26 May 1932, and was buried in Savannah, Hardin County, TN.

+	541 F	i.	**Viney Viola Sharp** was born 26 Nov 1879 in Lauderdale County, AL, died 18 Jul 1902, and was buried in Gravely Springs Cemetery, Lauderdale County, AL.
	542 M	ii.	**Kirk Jackson Sharp** was born 22 Oct 1881 in Lauderdale County, AL and died 9 Jan 1883.
+	543 F	iii.	**Carrie Eudora Sharp** was born 12 Oct 1883 in Lauderdale County, AL, died 3 Jun 1964, and was buried in Florence City Cemetery, Florence, Lauderdale County, AL.
+	544 M	iv.	**Oscar Eldred Sharp** was born 10 May 1886 in Lauderdale County, AL and died 7 Jul 1943 in Memphis, Shelby County, TN.
+	545 M	v.	**Robert Marvin Sharp Sr.** was born 21 Mar 1888 in Lauderdale County, AL and died 18 Nov 1957 in Hardin County, TN.
+	546 F	vi.	**Virgie Lenora Sharp** was born 24 Aug 1890 in Lauderdale County, AL and died 13 Sep 1938.
	547 F	vii.	**Stella Irine Sharp** was born 10 Jan 1893 in Lauderdale County, AL and died 9 Oct 1893.
	548 F	viii.	**Bertha Blanche Sharp** was born 24 Jul 1894 in Lauderdale County, AL and died 16 Jun 1896.
+	549 F	ix.	**Ella Myrtle Sharp** was born 17 Jan 1897 in Lauderdale County, AL and died 28 Mar 1984 in Memphis, Shelby County, TN.
+	550 F	x.	**Lizzie Oneita Sharp** was born 7 Oct 1899 in Lauderdale County, AL and died 29 Aug 1960.
+	551 F	xi.	**Annie Inez Sharp** was born 16 Jun 1902 in Lauderdale County, AL, died 26 Jun 1979, and was buried in Memorial Park, Memphis, TN.
+	552 F	xii.	**Ida Lois Sharp** was born 12 Dec 1905 in Savannah, Hardin County, TN, died 28 Aug 1993, and was buried in Greenview Memorial Park, Florence, Lauderdale County, AL.

185. John Thomas (Tom) Sharp (*James (Jim) Charles Sr.*[4]*, Adron (Edwin/Ade) Sr.*[3]*, Charles W. Sr.*[2]*, John Sr.*[1]) was born 6 Sep 1855 in Wright, Lauderdale County, AL, died 22 Jul 1895, and was buried in Wright Cemetery, Wright, Lauderdale County, AL.

> General Notes: His children Bertha, Thomas, Mina, Bailey, Daisy & Maggie allegedly lost their minds.
> Obit for Edgar list Jim as only brother alive. Sisters: Mrs. Ernest Warhurst, Mrs. G. B. Lindsey and Mrs. Nina

John Thomas Sharp and Susan Elizabeth "Betty" Johnson Sharp

Hairell...

John married **Susan Elizabeth (Betty) Johnson** 31 Dec 1872 in Lauderdale County, AL. Susan was born 23 Aug 1858 in Arkansas, died 19 Feb 1940, and was buried in Wright Cemetery, Wright, Lauderdale County, AL.

+ 553 F i. **Lillian Anna (Lillie) Sharp** was born 10 Aug 1875 in Lauderdale County, AL, died 19 Jun 1944, and was buried in Milledgeville Cemetery, Hardin County, TN.

Betty Johnson Sharp and Family

+ 554 F ii. **Maggie Sharp** was born in Jun 1877 in Alabama, died in 1913, and was buried in Wright Cemetery, Wright, Lauderdale County, AL.

+ 555 M iii. **Hallie (Hal) B. Sharp** was born 28 Jul 1880 in Lauderdale County, AL, died 30 Nov 1951, and was buried in Florence City Cemetery, Florence, Lauderdale County, AL.

+ 556 F iv. **Daisy L. Sharp** was born in May 1882 in Lauderdale County, AL, died 24 Feb 1933, and was buried in Tuscaloosa Brice Hospital Cemetery.

+ 557 F v. **Mattie A. Sharp** was born in Jun 1885 in Gravely Springs, Lauderdale County, AL, died 23 Feb 1965, and was buried in Oak Grove Cemetery, Lauderdale County, AL.

+ 558 M vi. **James (Swagger) Sharp** was born 24 May 1886 in Lauderdale County, AL, died 31 Mar 1973, and was buried in Wright Cemetery, Wright, Lauderdale County, AL.

+ 559 M vii. **Thomas Leslie (Peck) Sharp** was born 17 Dec 1887 in Lauderdale County, AL, died 1 Jan 1963, and was buried in Wright Cemetery, Wright, Lauderdale County, AL.

+ 560 F viii. **Bertha Sharp** was born in May 1890 in Alabama.

+ 561 M ix. **Edgar Lee Sharp** was born 28 Jan 1891 in Lauderdale County, AL, died 15 Jan 1965, and was buried in Wright Cemetery, Wright, Lauderdale County, AL.

+ 562 F x. **Quinnie Vester Sharp** was born 20 Sep 1892 in Lauderdale County, AL, died 7 May 1980, and was buried in Wright Cemetery, Wright, Lauderdale County, AL.

+ 563 F xi. **Minor (Mina) Houston Sharp** was born 18 Feb 1894 in Lauderdale County, AL, died 1 Mar 1978, and was buried in Wright Cemetery, Wright, Lauderdale County, AL.

564 M xii. **Bailey (Ballie) Sharp** was born 15 Sep 1895 in Waterloo, Lauderdale County, AL, died 25 Feb 1916, and was buried in Wright Cemetery, Wright, Lauderdale County, AL.

General Notes: "Mr. Wheeler Jones told Jesse Bert Wood, "That Bailey was in church and just went crazy, and he died on the way to the insane asylum..." Dan Wood

186. Matilda Ann Sharp (*James (Jim) Charles Sr.* [4], *Adron (Edwin/Ade) Sr.* [3], *Charles W. Sr.* [2], *John Sr.* [1]) was born in Jan 1858 in Wright, Lauderdale County, AL, died in 1927, and was buried in Gravely Springs Cemetery, Lauderdale County, AL.

Matilda married **George Robert (Dan) Bruce**, son of **Pinkton (Pinkerton) Bruce** and **Nancy Rhodes**, 27 Dec 1879 in Lauderdale County, AL. George was born in Oct 1858 in Lauderdale County, AL, died in 1931, and was buried in Gravely Springs Cemetery, Lauderdale County, AL.

+ 565 M i. **James Pinkney Bruce Sr.** was born 3 May 1881 in Lauderdale County, AL, died in 1958, and was buried in Wesley Chapel Cemetery, Lauderdale County, AL.

+ 566 M ii. **Robert William Bruce** was born 14 Apr 1883 in Lauderdale County, AL, died 9 Dec 1962, and was buried in Murphy's Chapel Cemetery, Lauderdale County, AL.

+ 567 F iii. **Lilly Eddie Levie Bruce** was born 22 Apr 1886 in Lauderdale County, AL and died 9 Jan 1959 in Memphis, Shelby County, TN.

+ 568 M iv. **George Owen Bruce** was born 27 Aug 1890 in Lauderdale County, AL, died in 1931, and was buried in Gravely Springs Cemetery, Lauderdale County, AL.

+ 569 F v. **Margie Ann (Marjorie) Bruce** was born 9 Aug 1893 in Gravely Springs, Lauderdale County, AL, died 26 Mar 1940, and was buried in Oak Grove Cemetery, Lauderdale County, AL.

Back L-R: Dee Long, Lilly Bruce Long, Billy, George and Margie Bruce.
Seated: George "Dan" Robert Bruce, Ann Sharp Bruce, James and Dora Smith Bruce
Children: Turner Long, Pearl Bruce, and Willie Bruce. About 1910

187. Owen Bennett (Doc) Sharp (*James (Jim) Charles Sr. [4], Adron (Edwin/Ade) Sr. [3], Charles W. Sr. [2], John Sr. [1]*) was born 23 Dec 1860 in Wright, Lauderdale County, AL, died 21 Apr 1923, and was buried in Wright Cemetery, Wright, Lauderdale County, AL.

General Notes: Information from his grandson: Owen Sharp was known by most people around Wright, Alabama as "Doc". He was crippled and walked on the side of his feet. He went insane and attempted to cut his throat. He passed away in an insane asylum located in Tuscaloosa, Alabama in 1923.

Owen married **Mary Frances (Fannie) Wiley**, daughter of **Wm Jasper Newton Wiley** and **Carolyn Courtney Fulmer**, 15 Jan 1883 in Lauderdale County, AL. Mary was born 8 Feb 1861 in Lauderdale County, AL, died 18 Dec 1943, and was buried in Wright Cemetery, Wright, Lauderdale County, AL.

+ 570 F i. **Virgie Lenoria (Nora) Sharp** was born 25 Apr 1884 in Wright, Lauderdale County, AL, died 25 Dec 1963, and was buried in Wright Cemetery, Wright, Lauderdale County, AL.

+ 571 M ii. **Lee Hal Sharp** was born 15 Feb 1886 in Lauderdale County, AL, died 16 Mar 1951, and was buried in Wright Cemetery, Wright, Lauderdale County, AL.

+ 572 F iii. **May N. (Nettie) Sharp** was born 8 Jul 1888 in Alabama, died 18 Nov 1950, and was buried in Wright Cemetery, Wright, Lauderdale County, AL.

+ 573 F iv. **Ada Irene Sharp** was born 3 Apr 1890 in Lauderdale County, AL, died 6 Apr 1979, and was buried in Greenview Memorial Park, Florence, Lauderdale County, AL.

+ 574 M v. **Harrell Emmett Sharp** was born 2 May 1892 in Lauderdale County, AL, died 3 Feb 1946, and was buried in Wright Cemetery, Wright, Lauderdale County, AL.

+ 575 F vi. **Mildred Sharp** was born 15 Feb 1894 in Lauderdale County, AL, died 26 Nov 1964, and was buried in Oak Grove Cemetery, Lauderdale County, AL.

+ 576 F vii. **Mason Sharp** was born 15 Feb 1894 in Lauderdale County, AL.

188. James Charles Sharp Jr. (*James (Jim) Charles Sr.*[4]*, Adron (Edwin/Ade) Sr.*[3]*, Charles W. Sr.*[2]*, John Sr.*[1]) was born 8 Apr 1861 in Wright, Lauderdale County, AL, died in 1939, and was buried in Wesley Chapel Cemetery, Lauderdale County, AL.

James married **Lizzie (Pearl) R. Palmer**, daughter of **Henry W. Palmer** and **Mary E. Young**, 16 Nov 1900 in Lauderdale County, AL. Lizzie was born 10 Aug 1877 in Lauderdale County, AL, died 20 Mar 1947, and was buried in Wesley Chapel Cemetery, Lauderdale County, AL.

James Charles Sharp and Lizzie R. Palmer Sharp

+ 577 F i. **Lillie May Sharp** was born 15 May 1902 in Lauderdale County, AL, died 21 Mar 1982, and was buried in New Hope Cemetery, Lauderdale County, AL.

+ 578 M ii. **Turner Lee Sharp** was born 25 Jun 1906 in Wright, Lauderdale County, AL, died 9 Aug 1990, and was buried in Macedonia Cemetery, Lauderdale County, AL.

+ 579 M iii. **James (Little James) Robert Sharp** was born 20 Jul 1908 in Wright, Lauderdale County, AL, died 6 Jan 1982, and was buried in Macedonia Cemetery, Lauderdale County, AL.

+ 580 F iv. **Minor Lucille Sharp** was born 1 Dec 1911 in Wright, Lauderdale County, AL, died 30 Jul 1987, and was buried in Tri-Cities Memorial Gardens, Florence, Lauderdale County, AL.

+ 581 F v. **Maggie Lorene Sharp** was born 15 Nov 1917 in Wright, Lauderdale County, AL, died 9 Apr 1963, and was buried in Macedonia Cemetery, Lauderdale County, AL.

189. Margaret E. Sharp (*James (Jim) Charles Sr.*[4]*, Adron (Edwin/Ade) Sr.*[3]*, Charles W. Sr.*[2]*, John Sr.*[1]) was born about 1866 in Wright, Lauderdale County, AL and died in Texas.

Margaret married **Lee Young**, son of **James Wiley Young** and **Sarah Elizabeth Bowles**, 3 Mar 1887 in Lauderdale County, AL.

191. Charles W. Sharp (*James (Jim) Charles Sr.*[4]*, Adron (Edwin/Ade) Sr.*[3]*, Charles W. Sr.*[2]*, John Sr.*[1]) was born 25 May 1879 in Lauderdale County, AL, died 16 Feb 1924, and was buried in Oak Grove Cemetery, Lauderdale County, AL.

Charles married **Alice A. Smith**, daughter of **Henry Littleton Smith** and **Louisa Dock (Loudocky) Burns**, 9 Apr 1899 in Wayne County, TN. Alice was born 12 Aug 1877 in Lauderdale County, AL, died 10 May 1935, and was buried in Oak Grove Cemetery, Lauderdale County, AL.

+ 582 M i. **Elmer Sharp** was born 29 Aug 1900 in Lauderdale County, AL, died 30 Jul 1962 in South Bend, St Joseph County, IN, and was buried in Oak Grove Cemetery, Lauderdale County, AL.

+ 583 M ii. **Brother Sharp** was born 12 Feb 1903 in Wright, Lauderdale County, AL, died in Mar 1976, and was buried in Oak Grove Cemetery, Lauderdale County, AL.

+ 584 M iii. **William Hubert Sharp** was born 5 Sep 1905 in Lauderdale County, AL, died 12 Jun 1989, and was buried in Oak Grove Cemetery, Lauderdale County, AL.

+ 585 F iv. **Aurelia Sharp** was born 13 Jul 1908 in Lauderdale County, AL, died 10 Mar 1990, and was buried in Oak Grove Cemetery, Lauderdale County, AL.

+ 586 F v. **Audry Sharp** was born 26 Nov 1912 in Waterloo, Lauderdale County, AL, died 16 Sep 1998, and was buried in Young Cemetery, Waterloo, Lauderdale County, AL.

587 F vi. **Dorothy Sharp** was born 21 Jun 1914 in Lauderdale County, AL, died 10 Jul 1937, and was buried in Oak Grove Cemetery, Lauderdale County, AL.

+ 588 F vii. **Eura (Eurie) Sharp** was born 29 Aug 1919 in Lauderdale County, AL, died 4 Aug 1998, and was buried in Murphy's Chapel Cemetery, Lauderdale County, AL.

192. Joseph (Joe) Sidney Sharp (*James (Jim) Charles Sr.*[4], *Adron (Edwin/Ade) Sr.*[3], *Charles W. Sr.*[2], *John Sr.*[1]) was born 28 Sep 1880 in Lauderdale County, AL, died 17 Dec 1966, and was buried in Milledgeville Cemetery, Hardin County, TN.

Joseph married **Julia (Junnie) C. Rogers**, daughter of **Albert Beverly Thomas Rogers** and **Elizabeth Ann Moore**, 16 Mar 1901 in Lauderdale County, AL. Julia was born in Jun 1880 in Lauderdale County, AL, died 17 Mar 1928, and was buried in Milledgeville Cemetery, Hardin County, TN.

+ 589 F i. **Annie Maudie Rogers Sharp** was born in Jun 1898 in Lauderdale County, AL.

+ 590 M ii. **Lawrence P. Sharp** was born about 1902 in Lauderdale County, AL and died in 1974 in McNairy County, TN.

+ 591 M iii. **Roosevelt (Vel) Sharp** was born about 1905 in Lauderdale County, AL.

+ 592 M iv. **Joseph (Jodie) Floyd Sharp** was born 17 Nov 1908 in McNairy County, TN and died in May 1984 in Colbert County, AL.

593 M v. **Jesse James O. Sharp** was born about 1911 in McNairy County, TN.

594 F vi. **Gladys E. Sharp** was born about 1913 in McNairy County, TN.

595 F vii. **Earline (Effie) L. Sharp** was born about 1915 in McNairy County, TN.

+ 596 M viii. **Russell Larry Sharp Sr.** was born 17 Feb 1917 in McNairy County, TN and died 30 Mar 1944 in McNairy County, TN.

597 F ix. **Hycanth Sharp** was born about 1920 in McNairy County, TN.

598 F x. **Loree Sharp** was born about 1922 in McNairy County, TN.

599 M xi. **Infant Sharp** was born 1 May 1924 in McNairy County, TN and died 13 May 1928 in McNairy County, TN.

600 M xii. **Infant Sharp** was born 5 Mar 1926 in McNairy County, TN and died in McNairy County, TN.

601 M xiii. **Infant Sharp** was born about 1928 in McNairy County, TN and died about 1928 in McNairy County, TN.

193. Elizabeth (Roxie) Belle Sharp (*James (Jim) Charles Sr.*[4], *Adron (Edwin/Ade) Sr.*[3], *Charles W. Sr.*[2], *John Sr.*[1]) was born 15 Jun 1882 in Lauderdale County, AL, died 25 Jan 1957, and was buried in Oak Grove Cemetery, Lauderdale County, AL.

Elizabeth married **William Jefferson (Jeff) Crider**, son of **George Washington Crider** and **Mary K. (Polly) Holt**, 18 Jan 1901 in Lauderdale County, AL. William was born 5 Mar 1880 in Lauderdale County, AL, died 3 Dec 1963, and was buried in Oak Grove Cemetery, Lauderdale County, AL.

+ 602 M i. **Marvin Turner Crider** was born 24 Jun 1902 in Lauderdale County, AL, died 6 Oct 1982, and was buried in Old Pleasant Hill Cemetery, Iuka, MS.

+ 603 F ii. **Fannie Elizabeth (Sister) Crider** was born 5 Jul 1903 in Lauderdale County, AL, died 17 Nov 1993, and was buried in Oak Grove Cemetery, Lauderdale County, AL.

+ 604 M iii. **John Richard Crider** was born 12 Jan 1905 in Gravely Springs, Lauderdale County, AL, died 2 Jan 1995, and was buried in Oak Grove Cemetery, Lauderdale County, AL.

+ 605 F iv. **Mary Etta (Virgie) Crider** was born 6 Oct 1906 in Lauderdale County, AL, died 24 Oct 1966, and was buried in Oak Grove Cemetery, Lauderdale County, AL.

+ 606 F v. **Bertha Mae Crider** was born 10 Oct 1909 in Gravely Springs, Lauderdale County, AL and died 19 Jan 1977.

+ 607 M vi. **Edgar Louis (Ed) Crider** was born 28 Mar 1911 in Lauderdale County, AL, died 6 Apr 1978, and was buried in Oak Grove Cemetery, Lauderdale County, AL.

+ 608 F vii. **Annie Viola Crider** was born 7 Jul 1915 in Lauderdale County, AL, died 12 Mar 1972, and was buried in Oak Grove Cemetery, Lauderdale County, AL.

+ 609 M viii. **James Albert Crider** was born in 1919 in Gravely Springs, Lauderdale County, AL.

+ 610 F ix. **Edith Louise Crider** was born 15 Aug 1921 in Gravely Springs, Lauderdale County, AL, died 30 Mar 1998, and was buried in Harmony Hill Cemetery, Burnsville, Tishomingo County, MS.

195. Louis (Bud) Wheeler Sharp (*James (Jim) Charles Sr.⁴, Adron (Edwin/Ade) Sr.³, Charles W. Sr.², John Sr.¹*) was born 19 May 1887 in Lauderdale County, AL, died 17 Feb 1943, and was buried in Oak Grove Cemetery, Lauderdale County, AL.

    Louis married **Ada (Adar) Elizabeth Hill**, daughter of **William (Bill) Hill** and **Caroline Young**, 18 Oct 1906 in Lauderdale County, AL. Ada was born 9 Jun 1895 in Lauderdale County, AL, died 13 Jan 1960, and was buried in Oak Grove Cemetery, Lauderdale County, AL.

    611 F i. **Lilly Sharp** was born in Lauderdale County, AL and died at 6 months.

    612 M ii. **Infant Son Sharp** was born in Lauderdale County, AL.

+ 613 M iii. **William Herbert (Hubbard) Sharp** was born 12 Oct 1909 in Florence, Lauderdale County, AL, died 16 Jul 2004, and was buried in Oak Grove Cemetery, Lauderdale County, AL.

    614 M iv. **Earl Sharp** was born about 1913 in Lauderdale County, AL.

+ 615 F v. **Pearlie Elizabeth Sharp** was born 27 Jun 1914 in Lauderdale County, AL, died 22 Jun 1988, and was buried in Wright Cemetery, Wright, Lauderdale County, AL.

+ 616 M vi. **Loye Arvel Sharp** was born 1 Mar 1916 in Gravely Springs, Lauderdale County, AL, died 29 Oct 2004, and was buried in Oak Grove Cemetery, Lauderdale County, AL.

+ 617 M vii. **Lawrence (Toby) Eldred Sharp** was born 22 May 1919 in Lauderdale County, AL, died 14 May 1994, and was buried in Oak Grove Cemetery, Lauderdale County, AL.

196. Etta C. Sharp (*James (Jim) Charles Sr.⁴, Adron (Edwin/Ade) Sr.³, Charles W. Sr.², John Sr.¹*) was born in Nov 1888 in Lauderdale County, AL and died 18 May 1920.

    Etta married **James Foust** 1 Sep 1905 in Lauderdale County, AL.

    618 F i. **Etta Foust**.

197. Mary Elizabeth Sharp (*James (Jim) Charles Sr.⁴, Adron (Edwin/Ade) Sr.³, Charles W. Sr.², John Sr.¹*) was born in Feb 1891 in Lauderdale County, AL.

    Mary married **Carl Lutts**.

+ 619 F i. **Myrtle Lutts** was born 13 Mar 1912 in Lauderdale County, AL, died 29 Jan 1940, and was buried in Oak Grove Cemetery, Lauderdale County, AL.

198. Margie (Lady) J. Sharp (*James (Jim) Charles Sr.⁴, Adron (Edwin/Ade) Sr.³, Charles W. Sr.², John Sr.¹*) was born in Aug 1892 in Lauderdale County, AL, died 11 Apr 1936, and was buried in Oak Grove Cemetery, Lauderdale County, AL.

    Margie married **Presley (Press) Harrison Allison**, son of **P. R. Allison** and **Mable *Unk**, 30 Aug. Presley was born 27 Feb 1888 in Savannah, TN, died 20 Apr 1936, and was buried in Oak Grove Cemetery, Lauderdale County, AL.

+ 620 M i. **Raymond Andrew Allison** was born 25 May 1911 in Tennessee, died 3 Mar 1977, and was buried in Oak Grove Cemetery, Lauderdale County, AL.

+ 621 F ii. **Carrie Etta Allison** was born 22 Jan 1913 in Hardin County, TN, died 31 Jan 1960, and was buried in Macedonia Cemetery, Lauderdale County, AL.

    622 M iii. **Lewis Allison** was born 22 Jul 1915, died 6 Sep 1916, and was buried in Oak Grove Cemetery, Lauderdale County, AL.

+ 623 F iv. **Lady Jewel Allison** was born 15 Jul 1917 in Waterloo, Lauderdale County, AL, died 21 Aug 1979, and was buried in Tyronza Cemetery, Tyronza, Poinsett County, AR.

    624 M v. **Press C. Allison** was born about 1918 in Alabama.

+ 625 M vi. **Andy J. Allison** was born 9 Mar 1919 in Lauderdale County, AL, died 10 Apr 1974, and was buried in Tyronza Cemetery, Tyronza, Poinsett County, AR.

+ 626 M vii. **William Turner Allison** was born 3 Jul 1921 in Gravely Springs, Lauderdale County, AL, died 11 Feb 1999, and was buried in Oak Grove Cemetery, Lauderdale County, AL.

+	627	F	viii.	**Vertie Mae Allison** was born 22 Feb 1922 in Lauderdale County, AL, died 7 Jul 2002, and was buried in Oak Grove Cemetery, Lauderdale County, AL.
+	628	F	ix.	**Elizabeth Earline Allison** was born 7 Feb 1923 in Lauderdale County, AL, died 13 Apr 1999, and was buried in Oak Grove Cemetery, Lauderdale County, AL.
+	629	F	x.	**Clara Estelle Allison** was born 9 Jul 1924 in Lauderdale County, AL.
+	630	M	xi.	**Velty Hoover Allison** was born 4 Aug 1929 in Lauderdale County, AL, died 18 Nov 2002, and was buried in Oak Grove Cemetery, Lauderdale County, AL.
+	631	M	xii.	**Earl Alvin Allison** was born 4 May 1932 in Lauderdale County, AL.
	632	M	xiii.	**Melvin Allison** was born 29 Jun 1935 in Lauderdale County, AL, died 15 Mar 1938, and was buried in Oak Grove Cemetery, Lauderdale County, AL.

200. Mary Ann Sharp (*Charles (Charlie) A.*[4]*, Adron (Edwin/Ade) Sr.*[3]*, Charles W. Sr.*[2]*, John Sr.*[1]) was born 27 Aug 1862 in Lauderdale County, AL and died 30 Jan 1936 in Booneville, Logan County, AR.

Mary married **James Miller McConnell**, son of **Miller (Mid) C. McConnell** and **Lavis Elizabeth Davis**, 21 Feb 1878 in Mixon, Logan County, AR. James was born 1 Feb 1855 in Mt. Ida, Montgomery County, AR and died 18 Apr 1930 in Fort Smith, AR.

	633	F	i.	**Matilda Elizabeth McConnell** was born 23 Apr 1879 in Booneville, Logan County, AR and died 4 Jul 1891.
+	634	M	ii.	**Charlie McConnell** was born 16 Jul 1881 in Booneville, Logan County, AR and died 14 Feb 1923.
	635	M	iii.	**Adron McConnell**.
	636	F	iv.	**Ester McConnell**.
	637	M	v.	**Ezra McConnell**.
+	638	M	vi.	**Jesse Robert McConnell** was born 8 Mar 1887 in Booneville, Logan County, AR, died 28 Aug 1959, and was buried in Fort Smith, AR.
	639	F	vii.	**Mattie McConnell**.

201. Clarissa Sharp (*Charles (Charlie) A.*[4]*, Adron (Edwin/Ade) Sr.*[3]*, Charles W. Sr.*[2]*, John Sr.*[1]) was born 20 Aug 1865 in Logan County, AR.

Clarissa married **J. Matt House** 23 Oct 1884 in Booneville, Logan County, AR.

202. Lil Adron Sharp (*Charles (Charlie) A.*[4]*, Adron (Edwin/Ade) Sr.*[3]*, Charles W. Sr.*[2]*, John Sr.*[1]) was born 1 Feb 1867 in Booneville, Logan County, AR.

Lil married **Elizabeth Matilda Voyles**, daughter of **Jacob Voyles** and **Elizabeth Trout**, 30 Nov 1888 in Booneville, Logan County, AR. Elizabeth was born 25 Sep 1869 in Booneville, Logan County, AR and died 1 Jun 1935 in Booneville, Logan County, AR.

+	640	M	i.	**Mundrow Sharp**.
+	641	M	ii.	**Virgil Sharp** was born in Feb 1892.
+	642	M	iii.	**Claude V. Sharp** was born in Jul 1894.
+	643	F	iv.	**Florence Sharp** was born in May 1897.
+	644	M	v.	**Kelly C. Sharp** was born in Arkansas and was buried in Arkansas.
+	645	M	vi.	**Ade Leonard Sharp** was born in Sep 1889.
+	646	M	vii.	**Biven Sharp** was born in 1906.

203. Pugh Cannon Sharp (*Charles (Charlie) A.*[4]*, Adron (Edwin/Ade) Sr.*[3]*, Charles W. Sr.*[2]*, John Sr.*[1]) was born 31 Dec 1868 in Logan County, AR.

General Notes: "Pugh Cannon Sharp was named after James Pugh Cannon, who was in the Confederate Army with Adrian L. Lindsey. This name also appears on several legal documents..." David Sharp

Pugh married **Ivy Jarvis** 31 Jul 1901 in Greenwood, AR.

204. Martha (Mattie) Sharp (*Charles (Charlie) A.*[4]*, Adron (Edwin/Ade) Sr.*[3]*, Charles W. Sr.*[2]*, John Sr.*[1]) was born 19 Jan 1871 in Logan County, AR.

General Notes: Moved to Oklahoma Territory...David Sharp

Martha married **Spencer (Charles) Weedle** 14 Jun 1888 in Logan County, AR.

205. Ellar Louise Sharp (*Charles (Charlie) A.*[4], *Adron (Edwin/Ade) Sr.*[3], *Charles W. Sr.*[2], *John Sr.*[1]) was born 8 Apr 1872 in Logan County, AR.

Ellar married **William (Bill) Ward** 7 Sep 1890 in Booneville, Logan County, AR.

206. William L. Sharp (*Charles (Charlie) A.*[4], *Adron (Edwin/Ade) Sr.*[3], *Charles W. Sr.*[2], *John Sr.*[1]) was born 13 Apr 1875 in Logan County, AR.

General Notes: "Moved to Poteau, Oklahoma..." David Sharp

William married **Node Pool** in Booneville, Logan County, AR.

207. Carol (Fuzzy) Louis Sharp (*Charles (Charlie) A.*[4], *Adron (Edwin/Ade) Sr.*[3], *Charles W. Sr.*[2], *John Sr.*[1]) was born 7 Apr 1879 in Booneville, Logan County, AR and died 1 Aug 1952 in Woodlake, Tulare County, CA.

Carol married **Mary Lee Verna (Vernie) Poole**, daughter of **Moses Greenworth Poole** and **Missouri Elvina Eddy**, 9 Mar 1899 in Booneville, Logan County, AR. Mary was born in 1878 in Booneville, Logan County, AR and died in Woodlake, Tulare County, CA.

+ 647 M i. **Verbie Anter Sharp** was born 16 Mar 1901 in Kula Chaha, La Flore County, Indian Territory, died 3 Feb 1974 in Carney, Lincoln County, OK, and was buried in Carney Cemetery, Lincoln County, OK.

648 M ii. **Vasser Newt Sharp** was born 8 Oct 1903 and died in 1977 in Visalia, Tulare, CA.

649 F iii. **Velmar Mirl Sharp** was born 5 Aug 1907 and died in 1974 in Woodlake, Tulare County, CA.

650 M iv. **Oscar Vansler Sharp** was born 29 Nov 1911 and died in 1969 in Atascadero, CA (cremated).

651 F v. **Eva Agnes Sharp** was born 25 Jan 1920 and was buried in Comanche, OK.

211. Leanna Hill (*Elizabeth Mae (Lizzie) Sharp*[4], *Adron (Edwin/Ade) Sr.*[3], *Charles W. Sr.*[2], *John Sr.*[1]) was born 8 Apr 1861 in Lauderdale County, AL and died 6 Dec 1925 in Forrest City, St. Francis County, AR.

Leanna married **William Edward Dover** 3 May 1882 in Lee County, AR. William was born 28 Jan 1862 in Phillips County, AR and died 28 Jul 1919 in Forrest City, St. Francis County, AR.

+ 652 M i. **Adron Pension Dover** was born 19 Sep 1884 in Phillips County, AR, died 9 Apr 1928, and was buried in St. Frances County, AR.

+ 653 F ii. **Josephine Dover** was born 12 Aug 1888 in Phillips, St Frances County, AR and died 11 Dec 1967 in St. Frances County, AR.

+ 654 F iii. **Gertrude Dover** was born 27 Mar 1890 in Palestine, St Francis County, AR and died 28 Jul 1916 in St. Frances County, AR.

655 M iv. **Eurwin Dover** was born 12 Jan 1893 in Palestine, St Francis County, AR and died in 1893 in Palestine, St Francis County, AR.

+ 656 F v. **Jenetta Dover** was born 6 Mar 1895 in Palestine, St Francis County, AR and died 31 Mar 1974 in Palestine, St Francis County, AR.

+ 657 F vi. **Hattie Dover** was born 12 Oct 1898 in Palestine, St Francis County, AR and died 11 Apr 1968 in St. Frances County, AR.

658 F vii. **Blanche Dover** was born 25 Jul 1900 in Palestine, St Francis County, AR and died 2 Jul 1987 in Mission Hills, Santa Barbara, CA.

659 F viii. **Estell Dover** was born 12 Aug 1902 in Palestine, St Francis County, AR and died in 1902 in St. Frances County, AR.

+ 660 F ix. **Florence Dover** was born 19 Jul 1904 in Palestine, St Francis County, AR and died 20 Mar 1976 in St. Frances County, AR.

661 M x. **Gaylord Dover** was born 12 Oct 1908.

212. Polly Hill (*Elizabeth Mae (Lizzie) Sharp*[4], *Adron (Edwin/Ade) Sr.*[3], *Charles W. Sr.*[2], *John Sr.*[1]) was born in 1864 in Lauderdale County, AL.

Polly married **Marin Blount** 3 Nov 1882 in Lee County, AR.

217. Amanda Louisa Murphy (*Mary Eliza Sharp*[4]*, John Sr.*[3]*, Charles W. Sr.*[2]*, John Sr.*[1]) was born in 1857 in Lauderdale County, AL.

Amanda married **Marion Young**.

218. John Carroll Murphy (*Mary Eliza Sharp*[4]*, John Sr.*[3]*, Charles W. Sr.*[2]*, John Sr.*[1]) was born in 1859 in Lauderdale County, AL.

John married **Callie *Unk**.

220. Laura E. Murphy (*Mary Eliza Sharp*[4]*, John Sr.*[3]*, Charles W. Sr.*[2]*, John Sr.*[1]) was born 4 Oct 1862 in Lauderdale County, AL, died 25 Sep 1896, and was buried in Murphy's Chapel Cemetery, Lauderdale County, AL.

Laura married **William Turner Carr**, son of **Joseph Price Carr Sr.** and **Julia Ann Lee**, 2 Jan 1881 in Lauderdale County, AL. William was born 1 Jun 1858 in Lauderdale County, AL, died 11 May 1940, and was buried in Murphy's Chapel Cemetery, Lauderdale County, AL.

+	662	M	i.	**Griffith Putman Carr** was born 13 Jan 1882 in Lauderdale County, AL and died 1 Aug 1951.
+	663	M	ii.	**Andrew J. Carr** was born in 1884 in Lauderdale County, AL and died 27 Aug 1962 in Savannah, TN.
+	664	M	iii.	**Noah Edgar Carr** was born in 1886 in Lauderdale County, AL.
+	665	M	iv.	**Lee Shelton Carr** was born in 1887 in Lauderdale County, AL.
+	666	F	v.	**Mamie Etta Carr** was born 4 Sep 1888 in Lauderdale County, AL.
+	667	F	vi.	**Minnie Ada Carr** was born 1 Aug 1890 in Lauderdale County, AL.
	668	F	vii.	**Ruby Whiton Carr** was born 10 Aug 1893 in Lauderdale County, AL, died 14 Jan 1914, and was buried in Murphy's Chapel Cemetery, Lauderdale County, AL.

221. Dorothy (Dolly) Elizabeth Murphy (*Mary Eliza Sharp*[4]*, John Sr.*[3]*, Charles W. Sr.*[2]*, John Sr.*[1]) was born 29 Jul 1864 in Lauderdale County, AL, died 18 Dec 1942, and was buried in Stoney Point Cemetery, Lauderdale County, AL.

Dorothy married **Berry Nolan Sharp**, son of **Joseph (Joe) Sharp** and **Emily S. Hutton**, 13 Dec 1879 in Lauderdale County, AL. Berry was born 15 Dec 1859 in Lauderdale County, AL, died 21 Sep 1945, and was buried in Stoney Point Cemetery, Lauderdale County, AL.
(Duplicate Line. See Person 90)

222. Alice Murphy (*Mary Eliza Sharp*[4]*, John Sr.*[3]*, Charles W. Sr.*[2]*, John Sr.*[1]) was born in 1867 in Lauderdale County, AL.

Alice married **Lee Dowdy**.

223. David Murphy (*Mary Eliza Sharp*[4]*, John Sr.*[3]*, Charles W. Sr.*[2]*, John Sr.*[1]) was born in 1869 in Lauderdale County, AL.

David married **Dora South**.

224. Ida Murphy (*Mary Eliza Sharp*[4]*, John Sr.*[3]*, Charles W. Sr.*[2]*, John Sr.*[1]) was born in 1872 in Lauderdale County, AL.

Ida married ***Unk White**.

234. George Moses (Mode) Wright (*Elizabeth (Lizzie) May Sharp*[4]*, John Sr.*[3]*, Charles W. Sr.*[2]*, John Sr.*[1]) was born 27 Aug 1877 in Wright, Lauderdale County, AL, died 2 Feb 1955, and was buried in Wright Cemetery, Wright, Lauderdale County, AL.

George married **Virgie Lenoria (Nora) Sharp**, daughter of **Owen Bennett (Doc) Sharp** and **Mary Frances (Fannie) Wiley**, 30 Dec 1911 in Lauderdale County, AL. Virgie was born 25 Apr 1884 in Wright, Lauderdale County, AL, died 25 Dec 1963, and was buried in Wright Cemetery, Wright, Lauderdale County, AL.

669	M	i.	**Paul Winford Wright** was born 15 Jun 1913 in Lauderdale County, AL, died 2 Mar 1988, and was buried in Greenview Memorial Park, Florence, Lauderdale County, AL.
670	M	ii.	**Louis Almon Wright** was born 14 Dec 1914 in Lauderdale County, AL, died 3 Feb 1992, and was buried in Greenview Memorial Park, Florence, Lauderdale County, AL.
671	F	iii.	**Elizabeth (Lizzie) Frances Wright** was born 16 Dec 1915 in Lauderdale County, AL, died 1 Oct 2004, and was buried in Greenview Memorial Park, Florence, Lauderdale County, AL.
+ 672	F	iv.	**Mason Louise Wright** was born 13 Jan 1918 in Wright, Lauderdale County, AL, died 25 Feb 1999 in Lauderdale County, AL, and was buried in Greenview Memorial Park, Florence, Lauderdale County, AL.
+ 673	F	v.	**Etta Buna Wright** was born 9 May 1919 in Waterloo, Lauderdale County, AL, died 10 Jun 1979, and was buried in Tri-Cities Memorial Gardens, Florence, Lauderdale County, AL.
+ 674	F	vi.	**Mattie May Wright** was born 15 Dec 1922 in Waterloo, Lauderdale County, AL and died 24 Feb 1999.

235. James Phillip Wright (*Elizabeth (Lizzie) May Sharp^4, John Sr.^{3}, Charles W. Sr.^{2}, John Sr.^{1}*) was born 12 Mar 1879 in Lauderdale County, AL, died in 1958, and was buried in Florence, Lauderdale County, AL.

James married **Annie Myrtle Pace**, daughter of **James Asgood Andrew Pace** and **Mary Josephine Quillen**, 22 May 1908. Annie was born 5 Nov 1888 in Franklin County, AL and was buried in Florence, Lauderdale County, AL.

+ 675	F	i.	**Edith Louise Wright** was born 17 Jan 1911 in Lauderdale County, AL.

236. Martha (Mattie) Jane Wright (*Elizabeth (Lizzie) May Sharp^4, John Sr.^{3}, Charles W. Sr.^{2}, John Sr.^{1}*) was born 29 Jan 1882 in Lauderdale County, AL, died 21 Apr 1911, and was buried in Wright Cemetery, Wright, Lauderdale County, AL.

Martha married **Henry Wade Wesson**, son of **Nathaniel Joseph Wesson** and **Emma Potts**, 16 Sep 1900 in Lauderdale County, AL. Henry was born 14 May 1876 in Wright, Lauderdale County, AL, died 8 Sep 1947, and was buried in Wright Cemetery, Wright, Lauderdale County, AL.

+ 676	F	i.	**Elizabeth (Lizzie) Inez Wesson** was born 29 May 1902 in Lauderdale County, AL.
+ 677	F	ii.	**Hazel Wright Wesson** was born 25 Nov 1903 in Lauderdale County, AL and died in Aug 1997.
+ 678	M	iii.	**Rawley (Roy) Archibald Wesson** was born 24 Nov 1905 in Lauderdale County, AL and died 31 Jul 1992.
+ 679	M	iv.	**Joseph Phillip Wesson** was born 18 Mar 1908 in Lauderdale County, AL and died in 1983.
680	M	v.	**Benjamin (Bennie) Russell Wesson** was born 28 Feb 1911 in Lauderdale County, AL, died 14 Jul 1911, and was buried in Wright Cemetery, Wright, Lauderdale County, AL.

238. Lee Sharp (*Carroll Ira (Buck)^4, John Sr.^{3}, Charles W. Sr.^{2}, John Sr.^{1}*) was born in 1868 in Alabama.

Lee married **Minnie *Unk**.

239. John (Buck) Phillip Sharp (*Carroll Ira (Buck)^4, John Sr.^{3}, Charles W. Sr.^{2}, John Sr.^{1}*) was born 9 Jan 1870 in Lauderdale County, AL, died 2 Mar 1949, and was buried in Wright Cemetery, Wright, Lauderdale County, AL.

John married **Laura Moody Faires** 25 Dec 1896 in Lauderdale County, AL. Laura was born 19 May 1874 in Tennessee, died 26 Feb 1966, and was buried in Wright Cemetery, Wright, Lauderdale County, AL.

+ 681	F	i.	**Callie Louise Sharp** was born in 1900 in Alabama.
+ 682	M	ii.	**Ben Faires Sharp** was born in 1902 in Lauderdale County, AL, died 8 Oct 1949, and was buried in John Lay Cemetery, Etheridge, TN.
+ 683	M	iii.	**Lee Howell (Hal) Sharp** was born in 1904 in Lauderdale County, AL.
+ 684	F	iv.	**Gladys Lillian Sharp** was born in 1912 in Lauderdale County, AL.
685	F	v.	**Mary Sharp** was born in 1918.

240. Lilly B. Sharp (*Carroll Ira (Buck)^4, John Sr.^{3}, Charles W. Sr.^{2}, John Sr.^{1}*) was born in 1873 in Alabama.

Lilly married ***Unk Meadows**.

+ 686	F	i.	**Ida Lee Meadows**.

244. John (Johnny) L. Sharp (*David (Dave) Owen⁴, John Sr.³, Charles W. Sr.², John Sr.¹*) was born in 1877 in Lauderdale County, AL.

    John married **Jennie *Unk** in 1900. Jennie was born in 1887 in Texas.
687	M	i.	**George Sharp** was born about 1904 in Texas.
688	F	ii.	**Lillian Sharp** was born about 1905 in Texas.
689	F	iii.	**Clara Mae Sharp** was born about 1908 in Texas.
690	M	iv.	**Bob Henry Sharp** was born about 1910 in Texas.
691	F	v.	**Louise Sharp** was born about 1917 in Texas.
692	M	vi.	**Clyde Sharp** was born about 1918 in Texas.

247. Arnold B. Sharp (*David (Dave) Owen⁴, John Sr.³, Charles W. Sr.², John Sr.¹*) was born in Sep 1884 in Lauderdale County, AL.

    Arnold married **Lena *Unk** in 1906. Lena was born about 1888 in Kentucky.
693	M	i.	**Arthur Sharp** was born about 1907 in Texas.
694	F	ii.	**Iva Sharp** was born about 1908 in Texas.

248. Turner Morris Sharp (*David (Dave) Owen⁴, John Sr.³, Charles W. Sr.², John Sr.¹*) was born in Feb 1887 in Lauderdale County, AL and died 3 Feb 1930.

    Turner married **Maud *Unk** in 1905. Maud was born in 1890 in Tennessee.
695	F	i.	**Eva Sharp** was born about 1911 in Texas.
696	F	ii.	**Lizzie Sharp** was born about 1913 in Texas.

249. Homer D. Sharp (*David (Dave) Owen⁴, John Sr.³, Charles W. Sr.², John Sr.¹*) was born in Aug 1888 in Lauderdale County, AL.

    Homer married **Ella *Unk**. Ella was born in 1889 in Alabama.
697	M	i.	**E. C. Sharp**.

250. Clyde Sharp (*David (Dave) Owen⁴, John Sr.³, Charles W. Sr.², John Sr.¹*) was born in Jun 1894 in Lauderdale County, AL.

    Clyde married **Jessie *Unk**.

251. Bertie Sharp (*John Jr.⁴, John Sr.³, Charles W. Sr.², John Sr.¹*) was born in Aug 1876 in Lauderdale County, AL.

    Bertie married **W. L. Callahan** 11 Jun 1901 in Lauderdale County, AL.

254. Lizzie Sharp (*John Jr.⁴, John Sr.³, Charles W. Sr.², John Sr.¹*) was born in Mar 1885 in Lauderdale County, AL.

    Lizzie married **Samuel L. Poole** 26 May 1904 in Lauderdale County, AL.

258. Charlie William Sharp (*William (Candy) Erwin⁴, John Sr.³, Charles W. Sr.², John Sr.¹*) was born 4 Jul 1877 in Lauderdale County, AL, died 26 Feb 1910, and was buried in Pettus Cemetery, Lexington, AL.

    Charlie married **Mary Jane Vanpelt**, daughter of **David Vanpelt** and **Eliza Jane Gray**, 1 Oct 1902 in Lauderdale County, AL. Mary was born between Feb 1880 and 1885 in Lauderdale County, AL and was buried in Center Hill Cemetery, Lauderdale County, AL.
+	698	F	i.	**Minnie Jane Sharp** was born 3 Sep 1903 in Lauderdale County, AL, died 1 Oct 1972, and was buried in Tri-Cities Memorial Gardens, Florence, Lauderdale County, AL.
+	699	M	ii.	**Owen Lee Sharp** was born 30 Jun 1905 in Lauderdale County, AL, died 21 May 1976, and was buried in Center Hill Cemetery, Lauderdale County, AL.
+	700	M	iii.	**Donald Edward Sharp** was born 21 May 1907 in Lauderdale County, AL, died 12 Sep 1994, and was buried in Center Hill Cemetery, Lauderdale County, AL.

+ 701 M iv. **Charles Price Sharp** was born about 1909 in Lauderdale County, AL, died 19 Aug 1991, and was buried in Pettus Cemetery, Lexington, AL.

259. Dollie E. Sharp (*William (Candy) Erwin⁴, John Sr.³, Charles W. Sr.², John Sr.¹*) was born 23 Apr 1880 in Lauderdale County, AL, died 5 Jul 1956, and was buried in Florence City Cemetery, Florence, Lauderdale County, AL.

Dollie married **William T. Bounds**, son of **John Bounds** and **Lina C. Eaves**, 31 Oct 1905 in Lauderdale County, AL. William was born 2 Jan 1875 in Lauderdale County, AL, died 23 Dec 1915, and was buried in Florence City Cemetery, Florence, Lauderdale County, AL.
    702 M i. **Thomas Evertt Bounds** was born 1 Jun 1907 in Lauderdale County, AL, died 11 Apr 1909, and was buried in Florence City Cemetery, Florence, Lauderdale County, AL.
+ 703 F ii. **Emily Louise Bounds** was born 16 Aug 1910 in Lauderdale County, AL.

260. Richard Owen Sharp (*William (Candy) Erwin⁴, John Sr.³, Charles W. Sr.², John Sr.¹*) was born 15 Apr 1882 in Wright, Lauderdale County, AL, died 25 Jan 1950, and was buried in Rosewood Cemetery, Waco, TX.

Richard married **Izora Isabelle Bounds**, daughter of **John Bounds** and **Lina C. Eaves**, 7 Jan 1904 in Lauderdale County, AL. Izora was born 4 Jun 1883 in Lauderdale County, AL, died 23 Jul 1905, and was buried in Florence City Cemetery, Florence, Lauderdale County, AL.
+ 704 M i. **Orville Owen Sharp** was born 28 Jan 1905 in Lauderdale County, AL, died 11 Jun 1957, and was buried in Florence City Cemetery, Florence, Lauderdale County, AL.

Richard next married **Ada Blanton**, daughter of **R. Ben Blanton** and **Nancy G. Young**, 1 Oct 1907 in Lauderdale County, AL. Ada was born 6 Aug 1876 in Lauderdale County, AL, died 16 May 1946, and was buried in Rosewood Cemetery, Waco, TX.
+ 705 M i. **Richard Orlando Sharp** was born 18 Dec 1907 in Colbert County, AL and died 25 Jan 1950.
+ 706 M ii. **Franklin Earl Sharp** was born 1 Feb 1910 in Lorene, TX.
+ 707 F iii. **Alma Bertha Sharp** was born 6 Jan 1913 in Robinson, TX.
+ 708 F iv. **Edith Elaine Sharp** was born 10 Jun 1915 in Gholson, TX.

261. Beulah L. Sharp (*William (Candy) Erwin⁴, John Sr.³, Charles W. Sr.², John Sr.¹*) was born 1 Mar 1884 in Lauderdale County, AL, died 21 Dec 1972, and was buried in Walston Cemetery, Oakland, Lauderdale County, AL.

Beulah married **Solomon L. Call**, son of **Robert T. Call** and **Julia Garner**, 14 Jul 1906 in Lauderdale County, AL. Solomon was born 3 Jun 1884 in Lauderdale County, AL, died 7 Dec 1958, and was buried in Walston Cemetery, Oakland, Lauderdale County, AL.
+ 709 F i. **Bessie Virgil Call** was born 14 Apr 1904 in Lauderdale County, AL.
+ 710 M ii. **Robert Turner Call** was born 24 Apr 1907 in Lauderdale County, AL and was buried in Cleveland, OH.
+ 711 F iii. **Ida Mae Call** was born 28 Jul 1908 in Lauderdale County, AL.
+ 712 M iv. **Floyd William Call** was born 29 Aug 1910 in Lauderdale County, AL, died in 1956, and was buried in Walston Cemetery, Oakland, Lauderdale County, AL.
+ 713 F v. **Dorothy Louise Call** was born 24 Oct 1912 in Lauderdale County, AL.
+ 714 F vi. **Daisy Ruth Call** was born 20 Jun 1916 in Lauderdale County, AL.
+ 715 M vii. **Roy Lee Call** was born 26 Apr 1920 in Lauderdale County, AL, died 14 Apr 1977, and was buried in Tri-Cities Memorial Gardens, Florence, Lauderdale County, AL.
+ 716 M viii. **Ervin Howard Call** was born 7 Jan 1922 in Lauderdale County, AL.
    717 F ix. **Clara Dean Call** was born 3 Feb 1926, died in 1928, and was buried in Walston Cemetery, Oakland, Lauderdale County, AL.

262. Charner Leander Sharp Sr. (*William (Candy) Erwin⁴, John Sr.³, Charles W. Sr.², John Sr.¹*) was born 22 Jun 1886 in Lauderdale County, AL, died 14 Oct 1951, and was buried in Florence City Cemetery, Florence, Lauderdale County, AL.

Charner married **Mattie Mae Elmore**.
+ 718 M i. **Dalton Sharp** was born 12 Sep 1908 and died in Aug 1962.

Charner next married **Blanche Lorene Dowdy**, daughter of **Jesse A. Dowdy** and **Myra Till**, 3 Aug 1935 in Colbert County, AL. Blanche was born 3 Sep 1898 in Lauderdale County, AL, died 23 Jul 1992, and was buried in Florence City Cemetery, Florence, Lauderdale County, AL.

+ 719 F i. **Verna Lorena Sharp** was born 30 Jul 1936 in Cleveland, OH.
+ 720 F ii. **Virginia Mae Sharp** was born 21 Nov 1938 in Cleveland, OH.
+ 721 M iii. **Charner Leander Sharp Jr.** was born 21 Jan 1939 in Cleveland, OH.

263. Clarence Morris Sharp (*William (Candy) Erwin [4], John Sr. [3], Charles W. Sr. [2], John Sr. [1]*) was born 22 May 1889 in Lauderdale County, AL, died 9 Feb 1929, and was buried in Florence City Cemetery, Florence, Lauderdale County, AL.

Clarence married **Martha *Unk**.

264. Robert Irwin Sharp (*William (Candy) Erwin [4], John Sr. [3], Charles W. Sr. [2], John Sr. [1]*) was born 22 Sep 1893 in Lauderdale County, AL and died 17 Sep 1975 in Waco, McLennan County, TX.

Robert married **Myrtle Guderian**. Myrtle died 23 May 1969 in Waco, McLennan County, TX.

265. Burt Hilliard Sharp Sr. (*William (Candy) Erwin [4], John Sr. [3], Charles W. Sr. [2], John Sr. [1]*) was born 10 Sep 1894 in Lauderdale County, AL and died 25 Apr 1966 in Weirton, WV.

Burt married **Katherine (Katie) Evelyn Garrett** in Waco, McLennan County, TX. Katherine was born in 1896 in Carters Creek, TN and died 15 Oct 1961 in Weirton, WV.

722 M i. **Burt H. Sharp Jr.** was born 15 Sep.
+ 723 M ii. **William (Billy) Brevard Sharp** was born 17 Nov 1920 in Cleveland, OH and died 23 Nov 1993 in Weirton, WV (cremated).
+ 724 M iii. **Thomas Milton Sharp** was born 11 Mar 1927 in Cleveland, OH.
+ 725 F iv. **Pauline (Polly) Elaine Sharp** was born 23 Jul 1931 in Cleveland, OH.

266. Myrtle Mabel (Mae) Sharp (*William (Candy) Erwin [4], John Sr. [3], Charles W. Sr. [2], John Sr. [1]*) was born 14 Jul 1896 in Lauderdale County, AL and died 15 Nov 1944 in Waco, McLennan County, TX.

Myrtle married **Charlie Glatz**. Charlie was buried in Waco, McLennan County, TX.

267. Virginia (Emma) Sharp (*William (Candy) Erwin [4], John Sr. [3], Charles W. Sr. [2], John Sr. [1]*) was born 7 Jun 1900 in Lauderdale County, AL, died 8 Jan 1975, and was buried in Holy Cross Cemetery, Cleveland, OH.

Virginia married **Anthony W. Stepwith**. Anthony died 18 Apr 1964 and was buried in Cleveland, OH.

726 M i. **Sonny Stepwith** died 6 Mar 1964 and was buried in Cleveland, OH.
+ 727 F ii. **Eleanor Stepwith**.

269. James Wylie (Jim) Young (*Julia Ann Young [4], Mary E. Sharp [3], Charles W. Sr. [2], John Sr. [1]*) was born 20 Mar 1878 in Lauderdale County, AL, died 11 Jul 1959, and was buried in Murphy's Chapel Cemetery, Lauderdale County, AL.

James married **Florence Beulah Young**, daughter of **John Nicholas Young** and **Matilda Ann White**, 2 Apr 1904 in Lauderdale County, AL. Florence was born 16 Aug 1887 in Lauderdale County, AL, died 12 Oct 1969, and was buried in Murphy's Chapel Cemetery, Lauderdale County, AL.

728 F i. **Infant Daughter Young**.
729 M ii. **Bert Edward Young** was born 29 Sep 1905 in Lauderdale County, AL, died 2 Mar 1970, and was buried in Murphy's Chapel Cemetery, Lauderdale County, AL.
+ 730 F iii. **Mae Belle Young** was born 4 Jan 1907 in Lauderdale County, AL, died 11 Jun 1985, and was buried in Murphy's Chapel Cemetery, Lauderdale County, AL.
+ 731 F iv. **Nomer Marie Young** was born 21 Feb 1909 in Lauderdale County, AL, died 25 Dec 1997, and was buried in Murphy's Chapel Cemetery, Lauderdale County, AL.
+ 732 F v. **Mozella Young** was born 18 Dec 1911 in Lauderdale County, AL, died 1 Oct 2001, and was buried in Murphy's Chapel Cemetery, Lauderdale County, AL.
+ 733 M vi. **James Nicklaus Young** was born 30 Jan 1912 in Lauderdale County, AL, died 8 Nov 1997, and was buried in Murphy's Chapel Cemetery, Lauderdale County, AL.

+ 734 M vii. **Ellie Bert Young** was born 23 Oct 1913 in Lauderdale County, AL, died 25 Aug 1993, and was buried in Murphy's Chapel Cemetery, Lauderdale County, AL.

+ 735 M viii. **Paul Mansel Young** was born 26 May 1917 in Lauderdale County, AL, died 5 Aug 1975, and was buried in Murphy's Chapel Cemetery, Lauderdale County, AL.

+ 736 F ix. **Hazel Inez Young** was born 26 May 1919 in Lauderdale County, AL.

737 M x. **Elvin Bay Young** was born 1 Jan 1921 in Lauderdale County, AL, died 13 Jan 1922 in Lauderdale County, AL, and was buried in Murphy's Chapel Cemetery, Lauderdale County, AL.

+ 738 M xi. **Lawrence Arnold Young** was born about 1924 in Lauderdale County, AL, died 12 Nov 2000, and was buried in Mt. Pleasant Cemetery, Lauderdale County, AL.

+ 739 F xii. **Irene Beulah Young** was born 5 Dec 1926 in Florence, Lauderdale County, AL.

270. Hulet Edward Young (*Julia Ann Young*[4], *Mary E. Sharp*[3], *Charles W. Sr.*[2], *John Sr.*[1]) was born 18 May 1882 in Lauderdale County, AL, died 27 Jan 1956, and was buried in Cloverdale COC Cemetery, Lauderdale County, AL.

Hulet married **Lillian Ella Young**, daughter of **John Nicholas Young** and **Matilda Ann White**, 22 Jan 1907 in Lauderdale County, AL. Lillian was born 27 Jul 1891 in Lauderdale County, AL, died 20 Jan 1954, and was buried in Cloverdale COC Cemetery, Lauderdale County, AL.

+ 740 F i. **Eula Beatrice Young** was born 16 Nov 1907 in Lauderdale County, AL, died 2 Jan 2000, and was buried in Murphy's Chapel Cemetery, Lauderdale County, AL.

+ 741 F ii. **Carrie Ann Young** was born 21 May 1909 in Lauderdale County, AL, died 25 May 1984, and was buried in Cloverdale COC Cemetery, Lauderdale County, AL.

+ 742 F iii. **Myrtle Lena Young** was born 8 Mar 1911 in Lauderdale County, AL, died 6 Jan 2004, and was buried in Greenview Memorial Park, Florence, Lauderdale County, AL.

+ 743 M iv. **Arnold Edward (Ed) Young** was born 15 Jun 1912 in Lauderdale County, AL, died 20 Aug 1976, and was buried in Cloverdale COC Cemetery, Lauderdale County, AL.

+ 744 F v. **Bertha Young** was born 23 Jan 1914 in Lauderdale County, AL, died 2 Apr 1981, and was buried in Murphy's Chapel Cemetery, Lauderdale County, AL.

+ 745 M vi. **Boss C. Young** was born 13 Apr 1916 in Lauderdale County, AL, died 19 Apr 1944, and was buried in Murphy's Chapel Cemetery, Lauderdale County, AL.

+ 746 F vii. **Vertie Mae Young** was born 20 May 1918 in Lauderdale County, AL, died 13 Feb 1998, and was buried in Tri-Cities Memorial Gardens, Florence, Lauderdale County, AL.

747 U viii. **Infant Young** was born 24 Jun 1920, died 24 Jun 1920, and was buried in Murphy's Chapel Cemetery, Lauderdale County, AL.

+ 748 F ix. **Rachel Nell Young** was born 30 May 1922 in Lauderdale County, AL, died 16 Apr 2000, and was buried in Greenview Memorial Park, Florence, Lauderdale County, AL.

+ 749 M x. **Joe L. Young** was born 9 Feb 1925 in Lauderdale County, AL, died 9 Dec 1976, and was buried in Greenview Memorial Park, Florence, Lauderdale County, AL.

+ 750 M xi. **Grady L. Young** was born 12 Oct 1931 in Lauderdale County, AL, died 24 Jan 1972, and was buried in Cloverdale COC Cemetery, Lauderdale County, AL.

271. Turner Andrew Young (*Julia Ann Young*[4], *Mary E. Sharp*[3], *Charles W. Sr.*[2], *John Sr.*[1]) was born about 1888 in Lauderdale County, AL, died in May 1968, and was buried in Greenview Memorial Park, Florence, Lauderdale County, AL.

Turner married **Bessie Etta Mary Ann Rogers**, daughter of **Robert Chris (Bob) Rogers** and **Abigail (Abbie) Randolph**, 21 Dec 1909 in Lauderdale County, AL. Bessie was born 20 Jun 1894 in Alabama, died 3 Jul 1982, and was buried in Greenview Memorial Park, Florence, Lauderdale County, AL.

+ 751 M i. **Bobby Turner Young** was born in Lauderdale County, AL.

+ 752 F ii. **Virgie Ione Young** was born 22 Oct 1911 in Lauderdale County, AL.

+ 753 M iii. **Marvin Andrew (Tuck) Young** was born 16 Jul 1914 in Lauderdale County, AL and died in Feb 1972 in Lauderdale County, AL.

+ 754 F iv. **Myrtle Mae Young** was born about 1916 in Lauderdale County, AL, died 10 Nov 2000, and was buried in Greenview Memorial Park, Florence, Lauderdale County, AL.

755 F v. **Clara D. Young** was born about 1918 in Alabama.

+ 756 F vi. **Gladys Lee Young** was born 16 May 1919 in Lauderdale County, AL.

+ 757 M vii. **Noah Sewell Young** was born about 1921, died 10 Mar 2008 in Lauderdale County, AL, and was buried in Greenview Memorial Park, Florence, Lauderdale County, AL.

+ 758 M viii. **Cecil Arthur Young** was born 2 Jul 1925 in Mishawaka, St Joseph County, IN.

273. Cleave Homer Young (*Julia Ann Young*[4], *Mary E. Sharp*[3], *Charles W. Sr.*[2], *John Sr.*[1]) was born 3 Sep 1892 in Lauderdale County, AL, died 20 Mar 1960 in Lauderdale County, AL, and was buried in Indiana.

Cleave married **Cornelia B. Rogers**, daughter of **Robert Chris (Bob) Rogers** and **Abigail (Abbie) Randolph**, 20 Feb 1916 in Lauderdale County, AL. Cornelia was born 17 Apr 1899 in Lauderdale County, AL, died 15 Feb 1918, and was buried in Murphy's Chapel Cemetery, Lauderdale County, AL.

+ 759 F i. **Clara Belle Young** was born 25 Jul 1917 in Lauderdale County, AL.

Cleave next married **Edna G. (Birdie) Young**, daughter of **John Nicholas Young** and **Matilda Ann White**, 20 Jan 1920 in Lauderdale County, AL. Edna was born 3 Sep 1900 in Alabama, died in 1986, and was buried in Indiana.

+ 760 F i. **Christine Young** was born about 1920.
+ 761 F ii. **Virginia Young** was born about 1922.
  762 M iii. **John Ray Young** was born about 1923.
  763 M iv. **Ralph Earl Young** was born 26 Dec 1925.
+ 764 M v. **Douglas C. Young Sr.**
  765 M vi. **Fred Young**.
+ 766 M vii. **Larry Joe Young** was born 7 Mar 1943 in St. Joseph County, IN and died 28 Sep 2004 in Niles, MI.

Cleave next married **Lillian Mitchell** after 1920.

274. Wheeler Young (*Julia Ann Young*[4], *Mary E. Sharp*[3], *Charles W. Sr.*[2], *John Sr.*[1]) was born 3 May 1896 in Lauderdale County, AL, died 6 Apr 1975, and was buried in Seattle, WA.

Wheeler married **Mamie Young**, daughter of **William C. Young** and **Ella Elizabeth Saddler**, 8 Jan 1918 in Lauderdale County, AL. Mamie was born 30 Jun 1903 in Florence, Lauderdale County, AL, died 29 Jun 1942, and was buried in Fairview Cemetery, Mishawaka, IN.

+ 767 M i. **Kerry W. Young** was born 27 Nov 1918 in Lauderdale County, AL, died 15 Apr 1983, and was buried in Fairview Cemetery, Mishawaka, IN.
+ 768 F ii. **Ruth Young** was born 8 Oct 1920 in Lauderdale County, AL, died 7 Jul 1979, and was buried in Kirkland Cemetery, Kirkland, WA.
+ 769 F iii. **Dorothy Young** was born 7 Apr 1923 in Lauderdale County, AL, died 28 Mar 1975, and was buried in Kirkland Cemetery, Kirkland, WA.
+ 770 F iv. **Catherine (Katie) Young** was born in Feb 1927 in St. Joseph County, IN.

275. Ada V. Young (*Julia Ann Young*[4], *Mary E. Sharp*[3], *Charles W. Sr.*[2], *John Sr.*[1]) was born 28 Jan 1900 in Lauderdale County, AL and died in Dec 1974 in Lauderdale County, AL.

Ada married ***Unk**.
  771 F i. **Edith Mae Young** was born in 1923.
  772 F ii. **T. Elnora Young** was born in Jan 1927.

277. Mollie Jo Sharp (*Berry Nolan*[4], *Joseph (Joe)*[3], *Charles W. Sr.*[2], *John Sr.*[1]) was born 15 Mar 1883 in Lauderdale County, AL, died 1 Mar 1961, and was buried in Stoney Point Cemetery, Lauderdale County, AL.

Mollie married **William (Will) Jacob Stutts**, son of **John Stutts** and **Elizabeth *Unk**, 8 May 1905 in Colbert County, AL. William was born 27 Oct 1876 in Wayne County, TN, died 11 Sep 1963, and was buried in Stoney Point Cemetery, Lauderdale County, AL.

+ 773 M i. **Daniel Oneal Stutts Sr.** was born 25 Jan 1914 in Birmingham, Jefferson County, AL.

278. James David Sharp (*Berry Nolan*[4], *Joseph (Joe)*[3], *Charles W. Sr.*[2], *John Sr.*[1]) was born 1 Apr 1885 in Lauderdale County, AL, died 14 Jun 1945, and was buried in Stoney Point Cemetery, Lauderdale County, AL.

James married **Fannie Ethel Stutts**, daughter of **William Joel Stutts** and **Dorinda Elizabeth Brumley**, 1 Dec 1909 in Lauderdale County, AL. Fannie was born 13 Sep 1888 in Wayne County, TN, died 28 Feb 1967, and was buried in Stoney Point Cemetery, Lauderdale County, AL.

  774 M i. **Howard Ernest Sharp** was born 26 Mar 1911 in Lauderdale County, AL, died 31 Mar 1982, and was buried in Stoney Point Cemetery, Lauderdale County, AL.

| + | 775 | M | ii. | **James Wesley Sharp** was born 20 Nov 1912 in Lauderdale County, AL, died 20 Feb 1998, and was buried in Stoney Point Cemetery, Lauderdale County, AL. |

  776 M iii. **William Berry Sharp** was born 15 Mar 1915 in Wayne County, TN, died in Mar 1916, and was buried in Stoney Point Cemetery, Lauderdale County, AL.

+ 777 M iv. **Clyde Joel (Link) Sharp** was born 23 Feb 1917 in Iron City, Wayne County, TN, died 23 Oct 2000, and was buried in Green Acres Mortuary.

+ 778 F v. **Velma Nadine Sharp** was born 13 Dec 1919 in Lauderdale County, AL, died 26 Dec 1972, and was buried in Stoney Point Cemetery, Lauderdale County, AL.

+ 779 M vi. **Ray Thomas Sharp** was born 24 Mar 1922 in Lauderdale County, AL, died 15 Sep 2004, and was buried in Mishawaka Cemetery, Mishawaka, IN.

+ 780 M vii. **Paul Edward Sharp Sr.** was born 25 Sep 1925 in Lauderdale County, AL, died 10 Nov 1989, and was buried in Greenview Memorial Park, Florence, Lauderdale County, AL.

+ 781 M viii. **Vernon Stults Sharp Sr.** was born 5 May 1927 in Lauderdale County, AL, died 1 Jul 2003, and was buried in St. Joseph Valley Cemetery, Mishawaka, IN.

+ 782 F ix. **Kathryn Etoil Sharp** was born 1 Jan 1931 in Lauderdale County, AL.

279. Eula Elizabeth Sharp (*Berry Nolan [4], Joseph (Joe) [3], Charles W. Sr. [2], John Sr. [1]*) was born 6 Mar 1887 in Lauderdale County, AL, died 13 Jul 1977, and was buried in Stoney Point Cemetery, Lauderdale County, AL.

Eula married **Levi (Lee) Grant Wilkes I**, son of **John Francis M. Wilkes** and **Mary E. Farmer**, 25 May 1907 in Lauderdale County, AL. Levi was born 12 Dec 1872 in Lauderdale County, AL, died 2 Nov 1937, and was buried in Stoney Point Cemetery, Lauderdale County, AL.

+ 783 M i. **James Chambers Wilkes** was born 30 Dec 1908 in Lauderdale County, AL, died 20 Jul 1998, and was buried in Colbert Memorial Gardens, Colbert County, AL.

+ 784 M ii. **Elting Wilkes** was born 24 May 1910 in Lauderdale County, AL, died 9 Jan 2003, and was buried in Savannah Memorial Gardens, Hardin County, TN.

+ 785 M iii. **Levi (Lee) Grant Wilkes II** was born 9 Feb 1912 in Lauderdale County, AL, died 18 May 1991, and was buried in Stoney Point Cemetery, Lauderdale County, AL.

+ 786 F iv. **Ruby Crystine Wilkes** was born 27 Dec 1914 in Lauderdale County, AL and died 17 Jan 2003 in Memphis, Shelby County, TN.

+ 787 F v. **Lovie Lucille Wilkes** was born 28 Jun 1917 in Lauderdale County, AL, died 10 Feb 2002, and was buried in Stoney Point Cemetery, Lauderdale County, AL.

+ 788 M vi. **Earl Berry Wilkes** was born 17 Aug 1919 in Lauderdale County, AL.

+ 789 M vii. **Rufus Jackson Wilkes** was born 5 Mar 1924 in Lauderdale County, AL, died 27 Jan 2003, and was buried in Greenview Memorial Park, Florence, Lauderdale County, AL.

282. Charles Robert Sharp (*Berry Nolan [4], Joseph (Joe) [3], Charles W. Sr. [2], John Sr. [1]*) was born 25 Jan 1893 in Lauderdale County, AL, died 7 Aug 1983, and was buried in Stoney Point Cemetery, Lauderdale County, AL.

Charles married **Betsie Ettie Townsley**, daughter of **James Fernnado Buckingham Townsley** and **Elizabeth Lizzie Pruitt**, 12 Jun 1915 in Lauderdale County, AL. Betsie was born 7 Mar 1892 in Lauderdale County, AL, died 18 May 1920, and was buried in Stoney Point Cemetery, Lauderdale County, AL.

+ 790 M i. **Charles Roy Sharp** was born 25 Aug 1916 in Lauderdale County, AL, died 27 Jul 1986, and was buried in Stoney Point Cemetery, Lauderdale County, AL.

Charles next married **Sarah Pearl Balentine**, daughter of **Sidney Houston Balentine** and **Mollie Melinda McCorkle**, 4 May 1921 in Lauderdale County, AL. Sarah was born 5 Apr 1904 in Lauderdale County, AL, died 15 Nov 1982, and was buried in Stoney Point Cemetery, Lauderdale County, AL.

+ 791 F i. **Elizabeth Sharp** was born 26 Feb 1920 in Lauderdale County, AL.

+ 792 M ii. **Berry Robert Sharp** was born 28 Dec 1924 in Colbert County, AL, died 18 Jun 1985, and was buried in Stoney Point Cemetery, Lauderdale County, AL.

+ 793 F iii. **Deedie P. Sharp** was born 20 Sep 1928 in Lauderdale County, AL.

+ 794 M iv. **Billy Eugene Sharp** was born 27 Feb 1932 in Lauderdale County, AL.

283. Lovie Francis Sharp (*Berry Nolan [4], Joseph (Joe) [3], Charles W. Sr. [2], John Sr. [1]*) was born 27 Aug 1895 in Lauderdale County, AL, died 14 Aug 1979, and was buried in Stoney Point Cemetery, Lauderdale County, AL.

Lovie married **Ollie Mitchell Statom I**, son of **James A. Statom** and **Lucy McCuan**, 14 Jun 1919 in Lauderdale County, AL. Ollie was born 28 Oct 1889 in Lauderdale County, AL, died 5 Feb 1964, and was buried in Stoney Point Cemetery, Lauderdale County, AL.

+ 795 M i. **Ollie Mitchell Statom II** was born 28 Aug 1926 in Lauderdale County, AL, died 8 Jul 2000, and was buried in Stoney Point Cemetery, Lauderdale County, AL.

285. Muncie Venetta Sharp (*Berry Nolan*[4], *Joseph (Joe)*[3], *Charles W. Sr.*[2], *John Sr.*[1]) was born 3 Feb 1901 in Lauderdale County, AL, died 20 Jun 1987, and was buried in Stoney Point Cemetery, Lauderdale County, AL.

Muncie married **John Price Statom Sr.**, son of **James A. Statom** and **Lucy McCuan**, 2 Sep 1918 in Lauderdale County, AL. John was born 4 Apr 1899 in Lauderdale County, AL, died 26 Jul 1973, and was buried in Stoney Point Cemetery, Lauderdale County, AL.

+ 796 M i. **Nolan Sharp Statom** was born 11 Sep 1919 in Lauderdale County, AL, died 9 May 2002, and was buried in Greenview Memorial Park, Florence, Lauderdale County, AL.
+ 797 F ii. **Lois Katherine Statom** was born 15 Sep 1921 in Lauderdale County, AL, died 2 Apr 1970, and was buried in Stoney Point Cemetery, Lauderdale County, AL.
+ 798 F iii. **Hilda Mae Statom** was born 14 Apr 1923 in Black Oak, AR.
+ 799 F iv. **Dolly Francis Statom** was born 28 Jan 1925 in Lauderdale County, AL.
+ 800 M v. **John Price Statom Jr.** was born 5 Apr 1927 in Lauderdale County, AL.
+ 801 F vi. **Mattie Jo Statom** was born 10 Jul 1930 in Lauderdale County, AL.
+ 802 F vii. **Betty Ruth Statom** was born 19 Mar 1932 in Lauderdale County, AL.

288. James Leander Sharp (*Benjamin Franklin*[4], *Joseph (Joe)*[3], *Charles W. Sr.*[2], *John Sr.*[1]) was born 28 Aug 1885 in Lauderdale County, AL, died 16 Aug 1918, and was buried in Wesley Chapel Cemetery, Lauderdale County, AL.

James married **Lousindy (Lula) Cathrine Keeton**, daughter of **John (Jack) N. Keeton** and **Emma Nard**, 28 Nov 1909 in Lauderdale County, AL. Lousindy was born 15 Aug 1894 in Lauderdale County, AL and was buried in Flatwoods Cemetery, Lawrenceburg, TN.

+ 803 M i. **James Dalton Sharp** was born 18 Oct 1910 in Lauderdale County, AL, died 24 Jan 1987, and was buried in Wesley Chapel Cemetery, Lauderdale County, AL.
+ 804 F ii. **Thelma Mae Sharp** was born 24 Dec 1912 in Lauderdale County, AL, died 7 Apr 1999, and was buried in Rail Road Church Cemetery, Wayne County, TN.
+ 805 F iii. **Pauline Sharp** was born 18 Apr 1914 in Lauderdale County, AL and died in 1986.
+ 806 F iv. **Vella Ruth Sharp** was born 2 Sep 1917 in Lauderdale County, AL.

289. Joseph Homer Sharp (*Benjamin Franklin*[4], *Joseph (Joe)*[3], *Charles W. Sr.*[2], *John Sr.*[1]) was born in Aug 1890 in Lauderdale County, AL, died in 1968, and was buried in Wesley Chapel Cemetery, Lauderdale County, AL.

Joseph married **Ella F. Willis**, daughter of **Wesley Willis** and **Mary *Unk**, 27 Dec 1911 in Lauderdale County, AL. Ella was born in 1889 in Alabama, died 12 Jan 1978, and was buried in Wesley Chapel Cemetery, Lauderdale County, AL.

290. Nora E. Sharp (*Benjamin Franklin*[4], *Joseph (Joe)*[3], *Charles W. Sr.*[2], *John Sr.*[1]) was born 21 Mar 1892 in Lauderdale County, AL, died 4 Apr 1983, and was buried in Florence City Cemetery, Florence, Lauderdale County, AL.

Nora married **Samuel Pugh Thrasher**, son of **W. T. (Billy) Thrasher** and **M. Fanny Anderson**, 29 Aug 1917 in Lauderdale County, AL. Samuel was born 19 Aug 1894 in Lauderdale County, AL, died 7 May 1981, and was buried in Florence City Cemetery, Florence, Lauderdale County, AL.

+ 807 F i. **Mary Katherine Thrasher** was born 17 Jul 1918 in Lauderdale County, AL.

291. Berry Robert Sharp (*Benjamin Franklin*[4], *Joseph (Joe)*[3], *Charles W. Sr.*[2], *John Sr.*[1]) was born in Mar 1894 in Lauderdale County, AL, died in 1963, and was buried in Wesley Chapel Cemetery, Lauderdale County, AL.

Berry married **Etoile May**, daughter of **Emmit May** and **Annie Belle Willis**, 19 Mar 1914 in Lauderdale County, AL. Etoile was born in May 1893 in Lauderdale County, AL, died in 1926, and was buried in Wesley Chapel Cemetery, Lauderdale County, AL.

+ 808 M i. **Edwin Robert Sharp** was born 15 Feb 1917 in Lauderdale County, AL, died 1 Oct 1998, and was buried in Wesley Chapel Cemetery, Lauderdale County, AL.
+ 809 M ii. **William Frank Sharp** was born 25 Oct 1921 in Cloverdale, Lauderdale County, AL, died 17 Jun 1996, and was buried in Greenview Memorial Park, Florence, Lauderdale County, AL.

Berry next married **Inez Paulk**, daughter of **Guy J. Paulk** and **Mattie Koonce**, 3 Jun 1927 in Lauderdale County, AL. Inez was born 6 Oct 1904 in Lauderdale County, AL, died 17 Nov 1991, and was buried in Wesley Chapel Cemetery, Lauderdale County, AL.

+   810   M   i.   **Noel Sharp**.
+   811   M   ii.   **Guy Owen Sharp** was born 25 Jan 1933 in Oklahoma City, Oklahoma County, OK.

292. Ethel Belle Sharp (*Benjamin Franklin*[4], *Joseph (Joe)*[3], *Charles W. Sr.*[2], *John Sr.*[1]) was born 26 Nov 1896 in Lauderdale County, AL, died 4 Jul 1982, and was buried in Wesley Chapel Cemetery, Lauderdale County, AL.

Ethel married **William Edward Cagle Sr.**, son of ***Unk Cagle** and **Clara E. O'Kelley**, 8 Dec 1917 in Lauderdale County, AL. William was born 17 Aug 1893 in Lauderdale County, AL, died 23 Feb 1972, and was buried in Wesley Chapel Cemetery, Lauderdale County, AL.

+   812   F   i.   **Beatrice E. Cagle** was born 17 Dec 1918 in Lauderdale County, AL, died 2 Dec 2007, and was buried in Mt. Tabor Cemetery, Lauderdale County, AL.
+   813   M   ii.   **Lloyd Brooke Cagle** was born 15 Jul 1921 in Lauderdale County, AL, died 31 Jul 1991, and was buried in Greenview Memorial Park, Florence, Lauderdale County, AL.
+   814   F   iii.   **Evelyn Clara Cagle** was born 24 Jun 1924 in Lauderdale County, AL, died 11 Aug 2000, and was buried in Johnsons Crossroads Cemetery, Lauderdale County, AL.
+   815   F   iv.   **Francis Jeanette Cagle** was born 25 Jul 1926 in Lauderdale County, AL, died 25 Jul 1994, and was buried in Johnsons Crossroads Cemetery, Lauderdale County, AL.
+   816   M   v.   **William Edward Cagle Jr.** was born 22 Apr 1929 in Lauderdale County, AL.
+   817   F   vi.   **Fayna (Faye) Cagle** was born 14 Feb 1936 in Lauderdale County, AL.

293. Marvin Frank Sharp Sr. (*Benjamin Franklin*[4], *Joseph (Joe)*[3], *Charles W. Sr.*[2], *John Sr.*[1]) was born 28 Feb 1900 in Lauderdale County, AL, died in 1950, and was buried in Wesley Chapel Cemetery, Lauderdale County, AL.

Marvin married **Mary Ellen Holliman**, daughter of **Curry Holliman** and **Martha Gray**, 10 Sep 1921 in Lauderdale County, AL. Mary was born 3 Nov 1894 in Lauderdale County, AL, died 18 Jan 1989, and was buried in Wesley Chapel Cemetery, Lauderdale County, AL.

+   818   F   i.   **Celia Frances Sharp** was born 8 May 1921 in Lauderdale County, AL, died 31 Jul 1988, and was buried in Greenview Memorial Park, Florence, Lauderdale County, AL.
+   819   M   ii.   **Marvin (Billy) Frank Sharp Jr.** was born 5 Jul 1926 in Lauderdale County, AL, died 17 May 1999, and was buried in Colbert Memorial Gardens, Colbert County, AL.

294. Maggie Leona Sharp (*Benjamin Franklin*[4], *Joseph (Joe)*[3], *Charles W. Sr.*[2], *John Sr.*[1]) was born in 1903 in Lauderdale County, AL, died in 1985, and was buried in Wesley Chapel Cemetery, Lauderdale County, AL.

Maggie married **Vernel Andrew Hill**, son of **Jolly Hill** and **Sabrina Tant**, 22 Jul 1920 in Lauderdale County, AL. Vernel died 3 Mar 1948 and was buried in Oak Grove Cemetery, Lauderdale County, AL.

+   820   M   i.   **Donald J. Hill** was born 28 Jul 1921 in Lauderdale County, AL, died 1 Jan 1975, and was buried in Florence City Cemetery, Florence, Lauderdale County, AL.
+   821   F   ii.   **Mary Opel Hill** was born 7 Feb 1923 in Lauderdale County, AL.
+   822   M   iii.   **Raymond A. Hill** was born 28 Oct 1923 in Lauderdale County, AL, died 3 Jun 1993, and was buried in Greenview Memorial Park, Florence, Lauderdale County, AL.

Maggie next married **Blant Burgess** 21 Apr 1934 in Lauderdale County, AL. Blant was born 9 Mar 1899, died 13 Mar 1952, and was buried in Wesley Chapel Cemetery, Lauderdale County, AL.

296. William F. Sharp (*John Levi*[4], *Charles W. II*[3], *Charles W. Sr.*[2], *John Sr.*[1]) was born in Apr 1880 in Lauderdale County, AL and died in Waco, McLennan County, TX.

William married **Madgie D. Milton** 31 Mar 1901 in Lauderdale County, AL. Madgie was born about 1885 in Lauderdale County, AL and died in Texas.

   823   M   i.   **Roy Sharp**.

297. Donna L. Sharp (*John Levi*[4], *Charles W. II*[3], *Charles W. Sr.*[2], *John Sr.*[1]) was born in Dec 1882 in Lauderdale County, AL and was buried in Coos Bay Cemetery, Coos, OR.

     General Notes: "David Sharp has note: Dona was a school teacher, went to Texas with Willie and his wife, then she went to Coos Bay, Oregon. Married a man by the name of Wyatt, divorced him. She died and was buried at Coos Bay Cemetery. 1911 will of Dowdy & Sharp had Dona listed as Dona Handley, working in a logging camp as a cook...." Sharon Wood

Donna married ***Unk Wyatt**.

298. Charles Edward (Eddie) Sharp (*John Levi*[4], *Charles W. II*[3], *Charles W. Sr.*[2], *John Sr.*[1]) was born in Nov 1884 in Lauderdale County, AL, died 25 Dec 1905, and was buried in Wright Cemetery, Wright, Lauderdale County, AL.

Charles married **Mattie J. Jones**, daughter of **Will Jones** and **Unknown**, 4 May 1902 in Lauderdale County, AL.
+ 824 M i. **Turner L. Sharp Sr.** was born 11 Apr 1903 in Lauderdale County, AL, died 23 Aug 1934, and was buried in Centenary Cemetery, Lutts, Wayne County, TN.
+ 825 M ii. **Dalton R. Sharp** was born 27 Apr 1905 in Lauderdale County, AL, died 31 Jan 1942 in Mishawaka, St Joseph County, IN, and was buried in Lauderdale County, AL.

301. Mary Lee Sharp (*John Levi*[4], *Charles W. II*[3], *Charles W. Sr.*[2], *John Sr.*[1]) was born 8 Jun 1905 in Sheffield, Colbert County, AL and died 15 May 1967 in Los Angeles, CA.

Mary married **William Massey** before 1941.

Mary next married **J. C. Howell** 3 Mar 1941 in Oklahoma City, Oklahoma County, OK. J. was born 7 Jun 1898 and was buried in Los Angeles, CA.

302. Jason Levi Sharp (*John Levi*[4], *Charles W. II*[3], *Charles W. Sr.*[2], *John Sr.*[1]) was born 23 Dec 1906 in Sheffield, Colbert County, AL.

Jason married **Gladys *Unk**.
826 F i. **Linda Sharp** was born 12 Sep 1976 in Los Angeles, CA and was buried in Riverside, CA.

303. Alice Maxwell Sharp (*John Levi*[4], *Charles W. II*[3], *Charles W. Sr.*[2], *John Sr.*[1]) was born 22 Mar 1911 in Sheffield, Colbert County, AL, died 11 Oct 1985, and was buried in Visalia, Tulare, CA.

Alice married **William Henry Hill** 23 Apr 1929 in Oklahoma City, Oklahoma County, OK. William was born 8 Dec 1903 in Plainview, Yell, AR, died 8 Oct 1985, and was buried in Lancaster, Los Angeles, CA.
+ 827 M i. **Charles Henry Hill Sr.** was born 10 Nov 1930 in Wichita, Sedgwick, KS.
+ 828 F ii. **Rita Faye Hill** was born 27 Mar 1934 in Oklahoma City, Oklahoma County, OK.
+ 829 F iii. **Elsie Marie Hill** was born 31 Aug 1937 in Los Angeles, CA.

305. James (Jim) W. Box (*Amanda Jane Sharp*[4], *Charles W. II*[3], *Charles W. Sr.*[2], *John Sr.*[1]) was born 24 Sep 1880 in Lake Charles, LA, died 26 Nov 1925, and was buried in Pleasant Hill Cemetery, Lauderdale County, AL.

James married **Moody Carroll** 4 Aug 1904 in Lauderdale County, AL. Moody was born 12 Feb 1879 in Lauderdale County, AL, died 28 Nov 1943, and was buried in Pleasant Hill Cemetery, Lauderdale County, AL.
+ 830 F i. **Willie Carmen Box** was born 28 Dec 1906 in Lauderdale County, AL, died 13 Jan 1944, and was buried in New Hope Cemetery, Lauderdale County, AL.
+ 831 F ii. **Gladys Box** was born in 1910 in Alabama.
+ 832 M iii. **John Carroll (J. C.) Box Sr.** was born 15 Sep 1910 in Lauderdale County, AL, died 16 Mar 1965, and was buried in Pleasant Hill Cemetery, Lauderdale County, AL.
+ 833 F iv. **Stella Mae Box** was born in Jun 1916 in Lauderdale County, AL.
834 F v. **Mutell Sue Box** was born in 1919 in Alabama.

307. Charles David Anderson Sr. (*Mary Elizabeth (Molly) Sharp*[4], *Charles W. II*[3], *Charles W. Sr.*[2], *John Sr.*[1]) was born 2 Dec 1885 in Lauderdale County, AL, died 30 Aug 1974, and was buried in Greenview Memorial Park, Florence, Lauderdale County, AL.

Charles married **Ora Lee Matheny**, daughter of **William Harrison Matheny** and **Ann Purser**, 26 Dec 1907 in Lauderdale County, AL. Ora was born 26 Feb 1888 in Lauderdale County, AL, died 6 Mar 1970, and was buried in Greenview Memorial Park, Florence, Lauderdale County, AL.

+	835	M	i.	**Herschel D. Anderson** was born 8 Feb 1909 in Lauderdale County, AL, died 20 Oct 1931, and was buried in Gresham Cemetery, Lauderdale County, AL.
	836	F	ii.	**Bessie Anderson** was born 10 Jun 1910 in Lauderdale County, AL, died 10 Jul 1911, and was buried in Gresham Cemetery, Lauderdale County, AL.
+	837	M	iii.	**Robert Perry Anderson** was born 16 Sep 1912 in Lauderdale County, AL, died 20 Jan 1936, and was buried in Gresham Cemetery, Lauderdale County, AL.
+	838	F	iv.	**Vera Anderson** was born 8 Sep 1913 in Lauderdale County, AL.
+	839	F	v.	**Ester Marie Anderson** was born 17 Apr 1914 in Lauderdale County, AL.
+	840	M	vi.	**John William Anderson** was born 12 Mar 1916 in Lauderdale County, AL.
+	841	F	vii.	**Lillian Anderson** was born 14 May 1920 in Lauderdale County, AL.
+	842	F	viii.	**Christine Anderson** was born 26 Dec 1921 in Lauderdale County, AL.
+	843	F	ix.	**Geneva Anderson** was born 23 Aug 1924 in Lauderdale County, AL.
+	844	F	x.	**Ruby Anderson** was born 23 Sep 1926 in Lauderdale County, AL.
	845	F	xi.	**Lila Ruth Anderson** was born 13 Feb 1928 in Lauderdale County, AL.
+	846	F	xii.	**Lucille Anderson** was born 4 Sep 1929 in Lauderdale County, AL.
+	847	M	xiii.	**Charles David Anderson Jr.** was born 30 Aug 1931 in Lauderdale County, AL.

308. Robert (Bud) Henry Anderson (*Mary Elizabeth (Molly) Sharp*[4]*, Charles W. II*[3]*, Charles W. Sr.*[2]*, John Sr.*[1]) was born 17 Mar 1887 in Lauderdale County, AL, died 23 Dec 1957, and was buried in Greenview Memorial Park, Florence, Lauderdale County, AL.

Robert married **Essie Amanda Fulmer**, daughter of **George Washington Fulmer** and **Mary Alice Bevis**, 28 Sep 1913 in Lauderdale County, AL. Essie was born 4 Mar 1886 in Lauderdale County, AL, died 12 Jun 1951, and was buried in Greenview Memorial Park, Florence, Lauderdale County, AL.

+	848	F	i.	**Maxine Anderson** was born 7 Jul 1915 in Lauderdale County, AL.
+	849	F	ii.	**Mary Alice Anderson** was born 26 Dec 1916 in Lauderdale County, AL, died 24 Apr 1994, and was buried in Greenview Memorial Park, Florence, Lauderdale County, AL.
+	850	F	iii.	**Francis Geraldine Anderson** was born 27 Mar 1920 in Lauderdale County, AL, died 26 Jan 1981, and was buried in Greenview Memorial Park, Florence, Lauderdale County, AL.
+	851	M	iv.	**Robert (Bob) Fulmer Anderson** was born 4 Jan 1922 in Lauderdale County, AL, died 26 Nov 1993, and was buried in Greenview Memorial Park, Florence, Lauderdale County, AL.
+	852	F	v.	**Helen Elizabeth Anderson** was born 21 Apr 1926 in Lauderdale County, AL.
+	853	M	vi.	**Gene Tunney Anderson Sr.** was born 25 Sep 1929 in Lauderdale County, AL, died 31 Jul 1999, and was buried in Greenview Memorial Park, Florence, Lauderdale County, AL.

311. Mary Adeline (Addie) Anderson (*Mary Elizabeth (Molly) Sharp*[4]*, Charles W. II*[3]*, Charles W. Sr.*[2]*, John Sr.*[1]) was born 6 May 1892 in Lauderdale County, AL, died 20 Mar 1936, and was buried in Gresham Cemetery, Lauderdale County, AL.

Mary married **Jesse T. Saxton** 18 Mar 1907 in Lauderdale County, AL. Jesse was born 28 Sep 1887 in Detroit, Wayne County, MI, died 21 Apr 1939, and was buried in Gresham Cemetery, Lauderdale County, AL.

	854	M	i.	**Floyd Saxton.**
	855	F	ii.	**Thelma Saxton.**
+	856	M	iii.	**Earl B. Saxton** was born 26 Dec 1911 in Lauderdale County, AL and died 23 Aug 1969 in Detroit, Wayne County, MI.
+	857	M	iv.	**Jess Lloyd Saxton Sr.** was born 25 Apr 1913 in Nashville, Davidson County, TN.

313. Emmett Anderson (*Mary Elizabeth (Molly) Sharp*[4]*, Charles W. II*[3]*, Charles W. Sr.*[2]*, John Sr.*[1]) was born 20 Jul 1897 in Lauderdale County, AL, died 4 Aug 1983, and was buried in Greenview Memorial Park, Florence, Lauderdale County, AL.

Emmett married **Gladys Beavers** 13 Oct 1921 in Lauderdale County, AL. Gladys was born 6 Mar 1898 and died 25 Nov 1933.

Emmett next married **Cornelius Carroll** after 1926. Cornelius was born 21 Dec 1910.

314. Marvin Robert Anderson (*Mary Elizabeth (Molly) Sharp*[4]*, Charles W. II*[3]*, Charles W. Sr.*[2]*, John Sr.*[1]) was born 31 Jul 1902 in Lauderdale County, AL and was buried in Olney, IL.

Marvin married **Lillie Mae Riley** 9 Jul 1925. Lillie was born 13 Jan 1908 in Lauderdale County, AL, died 27 Sep 1949, and was buried in Gresham Cemetery, Lauderdale County, AL.

+ 858 M i. **John Edward Anderson** was born 16 Jul 1926 in Lauderdale County, AL.
+ 859 F ii. **Marion Ruth Anderson** was born 8 Feb 1930 in Detroit, Wayne County, MI.
+ 860 F iii. **Marvelen Anderson** was born 31 Aug 1936 in Lauderdale County, AL.
+ 861 F iv. **Jeanett Anderson** was born 4 Aug 1942 in Lauderdale County, AL.

Marvin next married **Ruby Jones** after 1925.

Marvin next married **Virginia Offield** after 1925.

315. Moodie Bell Anderson (*Mary Elizabeth (Molly) Sharp*[4], *Charles W. II*[3], *Charles W. Sr.*[2], *John Sr.*[1]) was born 18 May 1905, died 8 Nov 1995, and was buried in Gresham Cemetery, Lauderdale County, AL.

Moodie married **Joe E. Woolwright** 9 Jul 1927.

316. William Lee Sharp (*Charles Franklin*[4], *Charles W. II*[3], *Charles W. Sr.*[2], *John Sr.*[1]) was born 2 Aug 1890 in Lauderdale County, AL, died 12 May 1931, and was buried in El Bethel Cemetery, Lamar County, Paris, TX.

William married **Lillian Cleo Martin**, daughter of **Charles Martin** and **Mary Jane Troup**, 30 Jul 1916 in Paris, Lamar County, TX. Lillian was born 8 Jun 1897 in McMinville, Warren County, TN, died 23 Sep 1980, and was buried in Memorial Park Cemetery, Paris, TX.

+ 862 M i. **Charles William Sharp** was born 28 Apr 1919 in Paris, Lamar County, TX, died 27 Sep 1989, and was buried in Paris, Lamar County, TX.
+ 863 F ii. **Mary Elizabeth Sharp** was born 4 Apr 1926 in Paris, Lamar County, TX, died in 1945, and was buried in Evergreen Cemetery, Paris, TX.
+ 864 F iii. **Virginia Lee Sharp** was born 15 May 1927 in Paris, Lamar County, TX.

317. Alma Derry Sharp (*Charles Franklin*[4], *Charles W. II*[3], *Charles W. Sr.*[2], *John Sr.*[1]) was born 30 Sep 1894 in Lauderdale County, AL.

Alma married **James Matthew White** 4 Jun 1911 in Paris, Lamar County, TX.

319. Hosea (Hozie) Durille Dowdy (*Rachel Ann (Babe) Sharp*[4], *Charles W. II*[3], *Charles W. Sr.*[2], *John Sr.*[1]) was born 1 Feb 1896 in Lauderdale County, AL, died 1 Feb 1973, and was buried in Pine Hill Cemetery, Lauderdale County, AL.

Hosea married **Virginia (Virgie) Balentine**, daughter of **John Rich Balentine** and **Nancy Jane Henson**, 15 Dec 1918 in Wayne County, TN. Virginia was born in 1903 in Lauderdale County, AL, died 8 Jan, and was buried in Pine Hill Cemetery, Lauderdale County, AL.

+ 865 F i. **Clora Ovrille Dowdy** was born 27 May 1919 in Lauderdale County, AL, died 14 Mar 1973, and was buried in Macedonia Cemetery, Lauderdale County, AL.
+ 866 M ii. **James Floyd Dowdy Sr.** was born 8 Jan 1921 in Lauderdale County, AL and died 30 Mar 1987 in Huntsville, Madison County, AL.
+ 867 F iii. **Juanita Ventelle Dowdy** was born 3 Apr 1923 in Lauderdale County, AL.
  868 M iv. **Horace Loyd Dowdy** was born 3 Apr 1925 in Lauderdale County, AL, died 22 Dec 1946, and was buried in Murphy's Chapel Cemetery, Lauderdale County, AL.
+ 869 F v. **Addye Faye Dowdy** was born 4 Nov 1934 in Lauderdale County, AL.

323. Johnnie Charles Dowdy (*Rachel Ann (Babe) Sharp*[4], *Charles W. II*[3], *Charles W. Sr.*[2], *John Sr.*[1]) was born 17 Dec 1908 in Lauderdale County, AL, died 22 Dec 1989, and was buried in Tri-Cities Memorial Gardens, Florence, Lauderdale County, AL.

Johnnie married **James C. Morris Sr.**.

324. Pearl Etoile Sharp (*Thomas (Tom) Erwin*[4], *Charles W. II*[3], *Charles W. Sr.*[2], *John Sr.*[1]) was born 24 Nov 1892 in Lauderdale County, AL, died 11 Feb 1975, and was buried in Florence City Cemetery, Florence, Lauderdale County, AL.

Pearl married **Ellis Franklin Hill**, son of **Walter Hill** and **Ella Love Webb**, 24 Dec 1927 in Russellville, Franklin County, AL. Ellis was born 18 Jul 1897 in Clark City, AL, died 27 Nov 1953, and was buried in Florence City Cemetery, Florence, Lauderdale County, AL.

326. Linnie Mae Sharp (*Thomas (Tom) Erwin*[4]*, Charles W. II*[3]*, Charles W. Sr.*[2]*, John Sr.*[1]) was born 19 Apr 1897 in Lauderdale County, AL, died 16 Oct 1974, and was buried in Murphy's Chapel Cemetery, Lauderdale County, AL.

Linnie married **Carter Blessin Stults**, son of **Joel Thomas Stults** and **Orenda Orlando Bromley**, 22 Nov 1914 in Lauderdale County, AL. Carter was born 6 Oct 1893 in Wayne County, TN, died 21 May 1958, and was buried in Greenview Memorial Park, Florence, Lauderdale County, AL.

+ 870 F i. **Mary Louise Stults** was born 6 Oct 1916 in Lauderdale County, AL, died 31 Oct 2004, and was buried in Greenview Memorial Park, Florence, Lauderdale County, AL.
+ 871 M ii. **Thomas Joel Stults** was born 1 Sep 1922 in Lauderdale County, AL, died 21 Feb 1989, and was buried in Mt. Zion Cemetery, Wayne County, TN.
+ 872 F iii. **Julia Christine Stults** was born 16 Jul 1924 in Lauderdale County, AL, died 19 Sep 1981, and was buried in Greenview Memorial Park, Florence, Lauderdale County, AL.
+ 873 M iv. **John Bobby Stults** was born 19 Apr 1932 in Lauderdale County, AL, died 19 Dec 1990, and was buried in Greenview Memorial Park, Florence, Lauderdale County, AL.

Linnie next married ***Unk Ward**.

327. Guy Thomas Sharp (*Thomas (Tom) Erwin*[4]*, Charles W. II*[3]*, Charles W. Sr.*[2]*, John Sr.*[1]) was born 23 Aug 1899 in Lauderdale County, AL, died 20 Apr 1960, and was buried in Greenview Memorial Park, Florence, Lauderdale County, AL.

Guy married **Vivian May**, daughter of **David Monroe May** and **Violet Catherine Broadfoot**, 13 Dec 1925 in Iuka, Tishomingo County, MS. Vivian was born 25 Aug 1906 in Lauderdale County, AL, died 7 Nov 1991, and was buried in Wesley Chapel Cemetery, Lauderdale County, AL.

+ 874 M i. **David Guy Sharp** was born 2 Jun 1927 in Lauderdale County, AL.
+ 875 M ii. **Tommy Gerald Sharp** was born 15 Sep 1933 in Russellville, Franklin County, AL, died 19 Aug 2008, and was buried in Eastern Gate Memorial Gardens, Pensacola, FL.
+ 876 F iii. **Nancy Kay Sharp** was born 21 Jul 1944 in Lauderdale County, AL.

330. Wylodean Marie Sharp (*Thomas (Tom) Erwin*[4]*, Charles W. II*[3]*, Charles W. Sr.*[2]*, John Sr.*[1]) was born 3 Aug 1912 in Lauderdale County, AL, died 14 Sep 1974, and was buried in Greenview Memorial Park, Florence, Lauderdale County, AL.

Wylodean married **Hershel Price Davis**, son of **John Henry Davis** and **Sara Chappel May**, 19 Dec 1931 in Lauderdale County, AL. Hershel was born 25 Sep 1910 in Lauderdale County, AL, died 26 Feb 1981, and was buried in Greenview Memorial Park, Florence, Lauderdale County, AL.

331. Ellis Eugene Sharp (*Thomas (Tom) Erwin*[4]*, Charles W. II*[3]*, Charles W. Sr.*[2]*, John Sr.*[1]) was born 3 Jun 1915 in Lauderdale County, AL, died 31 Jan 1968, and was buried in Greenview Memorial Park, Florence, Lauderdale County, AL.

Ellis married **Maxine Flora Collie**, daughter of **Walter J. Collie** and **Donna H. Harrison**, 19 Mar 1936 in Lauderdale County, AL. Maxine was born 8 Nov 1918 in Clifton, TN, died 20 Apr 2005, and was buried in Greenview Memorial Park, Florence, Lauderdale County, AL.

+ 877 M i. **Walter Eugene Sharp** was born 13 Jun 1938 in Lauderdale County, AL.
+ 878 F ii. **Donna Joyce Sharp** was born 14 Sep 1940 in Springfield, OH.

333. Dalton Sharp (*Richard (Dick) Allen*[4]*, Charles W. II*[3]*, Charles W. Sr.*[2]*, John Sr.*[1]) was born in May 1899 in Lauderdale County, AL.

General Notes: "see notes on Dad..." Sharon Wood

Dalton married **Lottie Coleman** about 1925 in Alabama. Lottie was born about 1905 in Alabama.

879 F i. **Elizabeth Sharp**.

340. William C. Young (*Matilda Ann White* [4], *Eliza Jane Sharp* [3], *Charles W. Sr.* [2], *John Sr.* [1]) was born about 1879 in Lauderdale County, AL, died 14 Jan 1934, and was buried in St. Joseph County, IN.

William married **Ella Elizabeth Saddler**, daughter of **John Wesley Saddler Sr.** and **Melissa Evelyn (Aunt Eb) Wood**, 21 Sep 1896 in Lauderdale County, AL. Ella was born 15 Apr 1879 in Wright, Lauderdale County, AL, died 9 Jun 1944, and was buried in St. Joseph County, IN.

John Wesley Saddler, Jr. and Melissa Evelyn Wood

+	880	M	i.	**J. Patton (Pat) Young** was born in 1900 in Lauderdale County, AL and died in 1986 in Mishawaka, St Joseph County, IN.
+	881	F	ii.	**Mamie Young** was born 30 Jun 1903 in Florence, Lauderdale County, AL, died 29 Jun 1942, and was buried in Fairview Cemetery, Mishawaka, IN.
+	882	M	iii.	**William Dalton Young** was born in 1906 in Lauderdale County, AL, died 10 May 1967, and was buried in Mishawaka, St Joseph County, IN.
	883	F	iv.	**Mary Etta Young** was born in 1911 in Lauderdale County, AL. .
+	884	F	v.	**Ella Mae Young** was born 15 May 1913 in Lauderdale County, AL, died 8 Nov 1989, and was buried in Mishawaka, St Joseph County, IN.

341. Cora Young (*Matilda Ann White* [4], *Eliza Jane Sharp* [3], *Charles W. Sr.* [2], *John Sr.* [1]) was born 7 Jan 1883 in Lauderdale County, AL, died 17 Sep 1943, and was buried in Wright Cemetery, Wright, Lauderdale County, AL.

Cora married **John Wesley Saddler Jr.**, son of **John Wesley Saddler Sr.** and **Melissa Evelyn (Aunt Eb) Wood**, 19 Mar 1900 in Lauderdale County, AL. John was born 8 Jul 1880 in Wright, Lauderdale County, AL, died 22 Jan 1949, and was buried in Wright Cemetery, Wright, Lauderdale County, AL.

	885	M	i.	**Infant Son Saddler** was born 20 Aug 1901, died 20 Aug 1901, and was buried in Wright Cemetery, Wright, Lauderdale County, AL.
	886	M	ii.	**Donald Saddler** was born 8 Oct 1901, died 8 Jul 1906, and was buried in Wright Cemetery, Wright, Lauderdale County, AL.
+	887	F	iii.	**Lady Goldie Saddler** was born 6 Feb 1903 in Lauderdale County, AL, died 7 Jan 1967, and was buried in Richardson Cemetery, Lauderdale County, AL.
+	888	F	iv.	**Vera Alean Saddler** was born in 1910 in Lauderdale County, AL and was buried in Mishawaka, St Joseph County, IN.
+	889	M	v.	**James Louie Saddler** was born 6 Aug 1912 in Lauderdale County, AL, died 25 Feb 1936, and was buried in Wright Cemetery, Wright, Lauderdale County, AL.

342. John Robert Young (*Matilda Ann White[4], Eliza Jane Sharp[3], Charles W. Sr.[2], John Sr.[1]*) was born 8 Apr 1884 in Lauderdale County, AL, died 12 Feb 1950, and was buried in Wright Cemetery, Wright, Lauderdale County, AL.

> John married **Della Parrish** in 1905 in Lauderdale County, AL. Della was born 2 Dec 1886 in Lauderdale County, AL, died 9 Jul 1911, and was buried in Wright Cemetery, Wright, Lauderdale County, AL.

> John next married **Callie Fielder**, daughter of **James Boyd Fielder** and **Harriet Estelle McCorkle**, 29 Dec 1919 in Lauderdale County, AL. Callie was born 2 May 1889 in Lauderdale County, AL, died 23 Jul 1981, and was buried in Williams Chapel Cemetery, Lauderdale County, AL.

	890	M	i.	**Fay Young**.
	891	M	ii.	**John Young**.
	892	M	iii.	**Marvin Young** was born about 1907 in Alabama.
+	893	M	iv.	**Doyle Lee Young** was born 18 Jul 1913 in Lauderdale County, AL, died 30 Jan 1991, and was buried in Wright Cemetery, Wright, Lauderdale County, AL.
	894	F	v.	**Etoile Young** was born about 1916 in Alabama.
+	895	F	vi.	**Jewel Estelle Young** was born 28 Sep 1920 in Lauderdale County, AL, died 4 Dec 2004, and was buried in Greenview Memorial Park, Florence, Lauderdale County, AL.
+	896	M	vii.	**Robert Vernon Young** was born 4 Apr 1923 in Waterloo, Lauderdale County, AL, died 9 Jul 2000, and was buried in Williams Chapel Cemetery, Lauderdale County, AL.

344. Florence Beulah Young (*Matilda Ann White[4], Eliza Jane Sharp[3], Charles W. Sr.[2], John Sr.[1]*) was born 16 Aug 1887 in Lauderdale County, AL, died 12 Oct 1969, and was buried in Murphy's Chapel Cemetery, Lauderdale County, AL.

> Florence married **James Wylie (Jim) Young**, son of **Owen Bartley Young Sr.** and **Julia Ann Young**, 2 Apr 1904 in Lauderdale County, AL. James was born 20 Mar 1878 in Lauderdale County, AL, died 11 Jul 1959, and was buried in Murphy's Chapel Cemetery, Lauderdale County, AL.
> **(Duplicate Line. See Person 269)**

345. Lillian Ella Young (*Matilda Ann White[4], Eliza Jane Sharp[3], Charles W. Sr.[2], John Sr.[1]*) was born 27 Jul 1891 in Lauderdale County, AL, died 20 Jan 1954, and was buried in Cloverdale COC Cemetery, Lauderdale County, AL.

> Lillian married **Hulet Edward Young**, son of **Owen Bartley Young Sr.** and **Julia Ann Young**, 22 Jan 1907 in Lauderdale County, AL. Hulet was born 18 May 1882 in Lauderdale County, AL, died 27 Jan 1956, and was buried in Cloverdale COC Cemetery, Lauderdale County, AL.
> **(Duplicate Line. See Person 270)**

346. Andrew Cleveland Young (*Matilda Ann White[4], Eliza Jane Sharp[3], Charles W. Sr.[2], John Sr.[1]*) was born 20 Aug 1894 in Lauderdale County, AL, died 16 Jun 1968, and was buried in Greenview Memorial Park, Florence, Lauderdale County, AL.

> Andrew married **Alice Leona Fielder**, daughter of **James Boyd Fielder** and **Harriet Estelle McCorkle**, 12 Jan 1916 in Lauderdale County, AL. Alice was born 31 Oct 1891 in Alabama, died in Nov 1969, and was buried in Greenview Memorial Park, Florence, Lauderdale County, AL.

+	897	M	i.	**Arnold Andrew Young** was born 13 Nov 1918 in Waterloo, Lauderdale County, AL, died 7 Apr 2001, and was buried in Greenview Memorial Park, Florence, Lauderdale County, AL.

347. Clarence W. Young (*Matilda Ann White[4], Eliza Jane Sharp[3], Charles W. Sr.[2], John Sr.[1]*) was born 26 Sep 1897 in Lauderdale County, AL, died 2 Mar 1985, and was buried in Williams Chapel Cemetery, Lauderdale County, AL.

> Clarence married **Ada Bell Ticer**, daughter of **John Allen Ticer** and **Roxie Leona Young**, 14 Nov 1915 in Lauderdale County, AL. Ada was born 28 Jan 1900 in Lauderdale County, AL, died 31 Dec 1974, and was buried in Williams Chapel Cemetery, Lauderdale County, AL.

+	898	F	i.	**Annie Mae Young** was born in Waterloo, Lauderdale County, AL.
+	899	M	ii.	**Hubert F. Young**.
+	900	M	iii.	**William (Bill) Young** was born 20 Oct 1916 in Lauderdale County, AL, died 24 Jun 1985, and was buried in Mishawaka, St Joseph County, IN.

| | 901 | M | iv. | **Clarence Roy Young** was born 25 May 1918 in Lauderdale County, AL, died 16 Nov 1985, and was buried in Greenview Memorial Park, Florence, Lauderdale County, AL. |

+ 901 M iv. **Clarence Roy Young** was born 25 May 1918 in Lauderdale County, AL, died 16 Nov 1985, and was buried in Greenview Memorial Park, Florence, Lauderdale County, AL.

902 M v. **Melvin Young** was born in 1922 in Lauderdale County, AL, died in 1924, and was buried in Williams Chapel Cemetery, Lauderdale County, AL.

+ 903 M vi. **John David Young** was born 30 Apr 1924 in Lauderdale County, AL.

+ 904 F vii. **Doris (Susie) Opel Young** was born in 1926 in Lauderdale County, AL, died 28 Jun 1999, and was buried in Williams Chapel Cemetery, Lauderdale County, AL.

905 M viii. **Lamar Young** was born in 1929 in Lauderdale County, AL, died in 1930, and was buried in Williams Chapel Cemetery, Lauderdale County, AL.

348. Edna G. (Birdie) Young (*Matilda Ann White⁴, Eliza Jane Sharp³, Charles W. Sr.², John Sr.¹*) was born 3 Sep 1900 in Alabama, died in 1986, and was buried in Indiana.

Edna married ***Unk**.

+ 906 F i. **Marie Mae Young** was born 2 Jan 1916 in Waterloo, Lauderdale County, AL and died 25 Nov 2000 in South Bend, IN.

Edna next married **Cleave Homer Young**, son of **Owen Bartley Young Sr.** and **Julia Ann Young**, 20 Jan 1920 in Lauderdale County, AL. Cleave was born 3 Sep 1892 in Lauderdale County, AL, died 20 Mar 1960 in Lauderdale County, AL, and was buried in Indiana.
(Duplicate Line. See Person 273)

349. Rosa Hinton (*Martha Jane White⁴, Eliza Jane Sharp³, Charles W. Sr.², John Sr.¹*) was born 28 Mar 1890 in Lauderdale County, AL, died 8 Mar 1987, and was buried in Lauderdale County, AL.

Rosa married **John Golden** about 1915. John was born in 1885 in Alabama.

+ 907 F i. **Florence Golden** was born in 1917 and died in 1989.

+ 908 M ii. **John Golden**.

909 M iii. **Willis Golden**.

350. Jones Henry Hinton (*Martha Jane White⁴, Eliza Jane Sharp³, Charles W. Sr.², John Sr.¹*) was born 3 Aug 1891 in Lauderdale County, AL, died in 1985, and was buried in Lauderdale County, AL.

Jones married **Annie Mae Byard** about 1915.

+ 910 M i. **Jones Carlton Hinton** was born in 1919.

+ 911 M ii. **Curtis Melvin Hinton Sr.** was born in 1921.

+ 912 F iii. **Vernon Juanita Hinton** was born in 1923.

+ 913 F iv. **Gloria Mae Hinton** was born in 1925.

+ 914 M v. **Lloyd Thurston Hinton Sr.** was born in 1927.

+ 915 F vi. **Ola Roselyn Hinton** was born in 1929.

916 M vii. **Gene Arnold Hinton** was born in 1931 and died in 1933.

+ 917 F viii. **Martha Ann Hinton** was born in 1934.

354. Bonnie Ethel Hinton (*Martha Jane White⁴, Eliza Jane Sharp³, Charles W. Sr.², John Sr.¹*) was born 6 Apr 1896 in Hardin County, TN, died 1 Nov 1980, and was buried in Birmingham, Jefferson County, AL.

Bonnie married **Reginal Ballard** in 1917.

355. Vernon L. B. Hinton (*Martha Jane White⁴, Eliza Jane Sharp³, Charles W. Sr.², John Sr.¹*) was born 19 Jul 1902 in Lauderdale County, AL, died 22 Feb 1987, and was buried in Montgomery, AL.

Vernon married **Charles M. Wilkerson**.

+ 918 M i. **Fred Lewis Wilkerson** was born in 1917 and died in 1993.

+ 919 M ii. **Charles B. Wilkerson** was born in 1919.

+ 920 M iii. **Johnnie B. Wilkerson** was born in 1922 and died in 1990.

+ 921 M iv. **Reginal Lawson Wilkerson** was born in 1926 and died in 1978.

922 M v. **Lloyd J. Wilkerson** was born in 1928 and died in 1935.

+ 923 M vi. **William J. Wilkerson** was born in 1930 and died in 1970.

356. Charles Westbrook Young Sr. (*Ella Prooterwill White^4, Eliza Jane Sharp^3, Charles W. Sr.^{2}, John Sr.^{1}*) was born 25 Sep 1895 in Lauderdale County, AL, died 7 Aug 1983, and was buried in Lauderdale County, AL.

Charles married **Minnie Mae Stevenson** 20 Dec 1919 in Lauderdale County, AL. Minnie was born 25 Apr 1902 in Lauderdale County, AL, died 10 Sep 1977, and was buried in Murphy's Chapel Cemetery, Lauderdale County, AL.

	924	M	i.	**Richard Earl Young** was born in 1921 in Lauderdale County, AL and died in 1988.
+	925	F	ii.	**Mary Addalian Young** was born in 1923 in Lauderdale County, AL.
+	926	M	iii.	**Charles Westbrook Young Jr.** was born in 1927 in Lauderdale County, AL.
+	927	M	iv.	**Paul Ray Young I** was born in 1929 in Lauderdale County, AL.
+	928	F	v.	**Opal Christine Young** was born in 1931 in Lauderdale County, AL.
+	929	M	vi.	**Joseph Inloe Young I** was born in 1936.

357. Gladys Myrtle Young (*Ella Prooterwill White^4, Eliza Jane Sharp^3, Charles W. Sr.^{2}, John Sr.^{1}*) was born 16 Jul 1897 in Lauderdale County, AL, died 22 Sep 1993 in Lauderdale County, AL, and was buried in Murphy's Chapel Cemetery, Lauderdale County, AL.

Gladys married **Roy Lincoln Ellison**, son of **Walter James Ellison** and **Abigail Fulton**, 25 Oct 1955 in Lauderdale County, AL. Roy was born 26 Nov 1901 in Hebron, NE.

358. Virginia (Virgie) A. Sharp (*William (Bill) Edgar^4, David Allen^3, Charles W. Sr.^{2}, John Sr.^{1}*) was born in Feb 1892 in Lauderdale County, AL.

Virginia married **William Donley Irby** 29 Sep 1919 in Lauderdale County, AL. William was born in Tennessee.

| + | 930 | F | i. | **Francis Adele Irby** was born in Memphis, Shelby County, TN and died in 1989. |

359. Mary M. Sharp (*William (Bill) Edgar^4, David Allen^3, Charles W. Sr.^{2}, John Sr.^{1}*) was born in Dec 1895 in Lauderdale County, AL.

Mary married **Sam Clifford Hunt Sr.** 8 Jan 1925 in Lauderdale County, AL. Sam was buried in Florida.

| + | 931 | M | i. | **Sam Clifford Hunt Jr.** |

360. Edgar Chisholm Sharp Sr. (*William (Bill) Edgar^4, David Allen^3, Charles W. Sr.^{2}, John Sr.^{1}*) was born in Oct 1898 in Lauderdale County, AL, died 14 Nov 1981, and was buried in Houston, TX.

Edgar married **Emma Lile Drisdale**, daughter of **William E. Drisdale** and **Emma Allison**, 25 Apr 1922 in Lauderdale County, AL. Emma was born 29 Mar 1900 in Colbert County, AL.

| + | 932 | M | i. | **Edgar Chisholm Sharp Jr.** was born 10 Feb 1926 in Lauderdale County, AL. |

361. Minnie Louise Sharp (*William (Bill) Edgar^4, David Allen^3, Charles W. Sr.^{2}, John Sr.^{1}*) was born 1 Jun 1905 in Lauderdale County, AL, died 8 Aug 1968, and was buried in Roselawn Cemetery, Athens, AL.

Minnie married **Milton Stribling (Strip) Killen Sr.**, son of **James Sharp Killen** and **Jennie Peden**, 16 Mar 1926 in Lauderdale County, AL. Milton was born 5 Jul 1903 in Lauderdale County, AL, died 5 Nov 1963, and was buried in Roselawn Cemetery, Athens, AL.

+	933	M	i.	**Milton Stribling Killen Jr.** was born 1 Jul 1927 in Lauderdale County, AL.
+	934	M	ii.	**William (Billy) Sharp Killen** was born 9 Apr 1929 in Lauderdale County, AL.
+	935	M	iii.	**Jimmy Eugene Killen** was born 2 Mar 1931 in Lauderdale County, AL.
+	936	M	iv.	**Don Sherron Killen** was born 28 Nov 1934 in Lauderdale County, AL.

364. James Buford Sharp Sr. (*James (Jim) Hulet^4, David Allen^3, Charles W. Sr.^{2}, John Sr.^{1}*) was born 11 Jan 1904 in Lauderdale County, AL.

James married **Nettie Grace Dickson**, daughter of **Lemuel Forrest Dickson** and **Emma Virginia Brown**, 26 Dec 1927. Nettie was born 8 Aug 1903 in Colbert County, AL and was buried in Oakwood Cemetery, Sheffield, Colbert County, AL.

| + | 937 | M | i. | **James Buford Sharp Jr.** was born 30 Oct 1928 in Colbert County, AL, died 17 Aug 2003, and was buried in Tri-Cities Memorial Gardens, Florence, Lauderdale County, AL. |

+ 938 M ii. **Joseph (Joe) Dickson Sharp** was born 27 Mar 1931 in Lauderdale County, AL, died 24 Nov 1997, and was buried in Florence City Cemetery, Florence, Lauderdale County, AL.

+ 939 M iii. **John Alvin Sharp Sr.** was born 18 Sep 1935 in Colbert County, AL.

368. Robert Owen Sharp (*Joseph (Joe) Powers Sr.*[4], *David Allen*[3], *Charles W. Sr.*[2], *John Sr.*[1]) was born 21 Aug 1895 in Lauderdale County, AL, died 8 Jun 1981, and was buried in Stoney Point Cemetery, Lauderdale County, AL.

Robert married **Helen Elizabeth Scott** 2 Dec 1925 in Lauderdale County, AL. Helen was born 7 May 1898 in Illinois, died 8 Jun 1981, and was buried in Stoney Point Cemetery, Lauderdale County, AL.

369. Eugene (Dock) Neal Sharp (*Joseph (Joe) Powers Sr.*[4], *David Allen*[3], *Charles W. Sr.*[2], *John Sr.*[1]) was born 19 Jun 1898 in Lauderdale County, AL, died 7 Nov 1987, and was buried in Stoney Point Cemetery, Lauderdale County, AL.

Eugene married **Mary Elizabeth Martin**, daughter of **F. T. Martin** and **Margaret Aldridge**, 23 Nov 1941 in Lauderdale County, AL. Mary was born 6 Sep 1907 in Colbert County, AL, died 15 May 1987, and was buried in Stoney Point Cemetery, Lauderdale County, AL.

370. Cynthia Emmanola Sharp (*Joseph (Joe) Powers Sr.*[4], *David Allen*[3], *Charles W. Sr.*[2], *John Sr.*[1]) was born 11 Aug 1899 in Lauderdale County, AL, died 9 Dec 1984, and was buried in Stoney Point Cemetery, Lauderdale County, AL.

Cynthia married **Charles Gomer Stewart** 26 Nov 1924 in Lauderdale County, AL. Charles was born in Lauderdale County, AL and was buried in Stoney Point Cemetery, Lauderdale County, AL.

+ 940 F i. **Mallie Denson Stewart** was born 30 Apr 1933 in Lauderdale County, AL.

371. Frank Littleton Sharp (*Joseph (Joe) Powers Sr.*[4], *David Allen*[3], *Charles W. Sr.*[2], *John Sr.*[1]) was born in 1905 in Lauderdale County, AL and died in 1968.

Frank married **Bessie Shoemaker** 3 Nov 1931 in Lauderdale County, AL.

Frank next married **Sarah Ingram**.

Frank next married **Julie Shoemaker** 26 May 1934 in Lauderdale County, AL.

372. Mayro Sharp (*Joseph (Joe) Powers Sr.*[4], *David Allen*[3], *Charles W. Sr.*[2], *John Sr.*[1]) was born 30 Jul 1906 in Lauderdale County, AL, died 18 Nov 2002, and was buried in Stoney Point Cemetery, Lauderdale County, AL.

Mayro married **Walter W. Hale Jr.**, son of **Walter William Hale Sr.** and **Lola Elizabeth Cox**, 4 May 1928 in Colbert County, AL. Walter was born 3 Aug 1904 in Lauderdale County, AL, died 26 Jun 1999, and was buried in Stoney Point Cemetery, Lauderdale County, AL.

+ 941 M i. **William Holland Hale** was born 29 Jun 1929 in Lauderdale County, AL, died 3 Mar 1997, and was buried in Greenview Memorial Park, Florence, Lauderdale County, AL.

373. Joseph Powers (J. P.) Sharp Jr. (*Joseph (Joe) Powers Sr.*[4], *David Allen*[3], *Charles W. Sr.*[2], *John Sr.*[1]) was born 31 May 1909 in Lauderdale County, AL, died 29 Apr 1977, and was buried in Stoney Point Cemetery, Lauderdale County, AL.

Joseph married **Carrie Morrow**, daughter of **James Madison Morrow** and **Rosie Beckman**, 28 Feb 1931 in Lauderdale County, AL. Carrie was born 24 Dec 1909 in Lauderdale County, AL, died 13 Jul 1992, and was buried in Stoney Point Cemetery, Lauderdale County, AL.

+ 942 M i. **Ralph Morrow Sharp** was born 19 Nov 1932 in Lauderdale County, AL.

+ 943 M ii. **Billy Joe Sharp** was born 10 Sep 1935 in Lauderdale County, AL, died 22 Dec 2000, and was buried in Tri-Cities Memorial Gardens, Florence, Lauderdale County, AL.

+ 944 M iii. **Daniel C. Sharp** was born 26 May 1936 in Lauderdale County, AL.

374. David (Big David) Roderick Sharp (*Joseph (Joe) Powers Sr.* [4]*, David Allen* [3]*, Charles W. Sr.* [2]*, John Sr.* [1]) was born 30 May 1912 in Lauderdale County, AL, died 2 Dec 2002, and was buried in Stoney Point Cemetery, Lauderdale County, AL.

David married **Virginia White Thrasher**, daughter of **Samuel David Thrasher** and **Leola Emma White**, 9 Jul 1939 in Lauderdale County, AL. Virginia was born 5 Apr 1917 in Lauderdale County, AL.
+ 945 M i. **Ronald Gene Sharp** was born 13 Mar 1941 in Lauderdale County, AL.
+ 946 F ii. **Angelia Gail Sharp** was born 12 Dec 1948 in Lauderdale County, AL.

375. Lyda Mae Sharp (*Andrew Jefferson Sr.* [4]*, David Allen* [3]*, Charles W. Sr.* [2]*, John Sr.* [1]) was born 7 Jul 1904 in Lauderdale County, AL and died 14 Sep 1963 in Natchez, MS.

Lyda married **Lanie G. Sharp**, son of **D. H. Sharp** and **Z. E. *Unk**, 10 Dec 1924 in Colbert County, AL. Lanie was born about 1900 in Guys, TN and died about 1994 in Savannah, TN.
+ 947 F i. **Betty Jane Sharp** was born 11 May 1927.
+ 948 M ii. **John David Sharp** was born 10 Apr 1931 in Monroe, LA.

376. Kathleen Lamar Sharp (*Andrew Jefferson Sr.* [4]*, David Allen* [3]*, Charles W. Sr.* [2]*, John Sr.* [1]) was born 29 Sep 1906 in Lauderdale County, AL and died in Jan 1987 in Alexandria, LA.

Kathleen married **Milton Carter** 8 May 1930 in Colbert County, AL. Milton died about 1985 in Alexandria, LA.

Kathleen next married **Cary C. Fuller** about 1960. Cary died about 1984 in Alexandria, LA.

377. Dorothy Elizabeth Sharp (*Andrew Jefferson Sr.* [4]*, David Allen* [3]*, Charles W. Sr.* [2]*, John Sr.* [1]) was born 25 Oct 1908 in Lauderdale County, AL, died 27 Nov 1994, and was buried in Alexandria, LA.

Dorothy married **Harold V. Anderson** about 1930. Harold was born in Colorado.

378. Virginia Rebecca Sharp (*Andrew Jefferson Sr.* [4]*, David Allen* [3]*, Charles W. Sr.* [2]*, John Sr.* [1]) was born 25 Jun 1910 in Lauderdale County, AL and died about 1988 in Mobile, AL.

Virginia married **Ralph Williams**.

Virginia next married **Paul Nichols Sr.** 24 Oct 1928.
+ 949 M i. **Paul Nichols Jr.**

379. Evelyn Marie (Verna) Sharp (*Andrew Jefferson Sr.* [4]*, David Allen* [3]*, Charles W. Sr.* [2]*, John Sr.* [1]) was born 30 Apr 1912 in Lauderdale County, AL and died 1 Jan 1990 in Houston, TX.

Evelyn married **Clarence Blake Watson** about 1935. Clarence was buried in Houston, TX.
+ 950 F i. **Kathleen Margaret Watson**.

381. Andrew Jefferson Sharp Jr. (*Andrew Jefferson Sr.* [4]*, David Allen* [3]*, Charles W. Sr.* [2]*, John Sr.* [1]) was born 20 Apr 1916 in Lauderdale County, AL, died 25 Sep 1974, and was buried in Oakwood Cemetery, Sheffield, Colbert County, AL.

Andrew married **Edna Pearl Smith**, daughter of **Calvin Horton Smith** and **Annie Mae Allen**, 18 Aug 1944 in Colbert County, AL. Edna was born 2 Feb 1917 in Belen, NM, died 17 Feb 2004, and was buried in Oak Grove Cemetery, Lauderdale County, AL.
+ 951 M i. **Andrew Jefferson Sharp III** was born 5 Mar 1949 in Alabama.
  952 F ii. **Margaret Anne Sharp**.

Andrew next married **Frances Christinson Hillis** about 1973.

382. Helen Margaret Sharp (*Andrew Jefferson Sr.* [4]*, David Allen* [3]*, Charles W. Sr.* [2]*, John Sr.* [1]) was born 2 Sep 1921 in Lauderdale County, AL.

Helen married **John Stuart Paton Sr.** in Jul 1943 in New Orleans, LA.

Helen next married **Bennett Otho White** in Jun 1948 in Houston, TX.

Helen next married **William Fleetwood Simmons** 22 Nov 1952 in Baton Rouge, LA. William was born 16 Jul 1911 in Boyce, LA, died 3 Aug 1987, and was buried in Alexandria, LA.

+ 953 M i. **John William Paton Simmons** was born 10 Aug 1944 in New Orleans, LA.
+ 954 F ii. **Rebecca Gail White Simmons** was born 16 Mar 1949 in Houston, TX.

Fifth Generation

383. George W. Lindsey (*John Phillip Lindsey II*[5], *Caleb (Calip) Lindsey*[4], *Frances (Frankie) Sharp*[3], *Charles W. Sr.*[2], *John Sr.*[1]) was born in Feb 1873 in Missouri.

George married **Mary (Becky) Williams** 15 Sep 1897 in Lauderdale County, AL. Mary was born in 1876 in Alabama.

+ 955 M i. **Marvin Elmer Lindsey** was born 8 Apr 1905 in Lauderdale County, AL, died 1 Nov 1983, and was buried in Wesley Chapel Cemetery, Lauderdale County, AL.
+ 956 F ii. **Carrie M. Lindsey** was born in 1908 in Lauderdale County, AL.
+ 957 M iii. **Aubra Lee Lindsey** was born in 1910 in Lauderdale County, AL.
  958 M iv. **Clifford Lindsey** was born in 1911 in Lauderdale County, AL.
+ 959 F v. **Mamie G. Lindsey** was born in 1913 in Lauderdale County, AL.

384. Lucelle (Lucy) Lindsey (*John Phillip Lindsey II*[5], *Caleb (Calip) Lindsey*[4], *Frances (Frankie) Sharp*[3], *Charles W. Sr.*[2], *John Sr.*[1]) was born in Aug 1875 in Lauderdale County, AL, died in 1954, and was buried in Florence City Cemetery, Florence, Lauderdale County, AL.

Lucelle married **Leonard Riley** 2 Nov 1899 in Lawrence County, TN. Leonard was born in May 1876 in Lawrence County, TN, died in 1952, and was buried in Florence City Cemetery, Florence, Lauderdale County, AL.

+ 960 F i. **Mittie Rebecca Riley**.
+ 961 F ii. **Ora Gladys Riley** was born 18 May 1903 in Franklin County, AL and died in Dec 1985.
+ 962 F iii. **Nellie Catherine Riley** was born 17 Feb 1905 in Franklin County, AL and died 26 Feb 1984.
+ 963 F iv. **Beulah Riley** was born 13 Dec 1907 in Franklin County, AL and died 10 Jul 1984.
  964 F v. **Lillie Riley** was born in 1910 in Franklin County, AL and died before 1984.
  965 F vi. **Velmer Riley** was born in 1911 in Franklin County, AL and died before 1984.
+ 966 M vii. **Claude Edward Riley** was born 9 Feb 1913 in Franklin County, AL and died before 1984.
  967 M viii. **William Floyd Riley** was born in 1916.

385. Willie C. (Will) Lindsey (*John Phillip Lindsey II*[5], *Caleb (Calip) Lindsey*[4], *Frances (Frankie) Sharp*[3], *Charles W. Sr.*[2], *John Sr.*[1]) was born in Feb 1879 in Lauderdale County, AL.

Willie married **Ankie Williams** 4 Apr 1905 in Lauderdale County, AL.

386. Lizzie O. Lindsey (*John Phillip Lindsey II*[5], *Caleb (Calip) Lindsey*[4], *Frances (Frankie) Sharp*[3], *Charles W. Sr.*[2], *John Sr.*[1]) was born in Sep 1883 in Lauderdale County, AL.

Lizzie married **Millard O. Nelson** 6 Apr 1912 in Lauderdale County, AL.

387. Ernest Lindsey (*John Phillip Lindsey II*[5], *Caleb (Calip) Lindsey*[4], *Frances (Frankie) Sharp*[3], *Charles W. Sr.*[2], *John Sr.*[1]) was born in Apr 1886 in Lauderdale County, AL.

Ernest married **Delphia Scott** 18 Sep 1906 in Lauderdale County, AL.

391. David (Dave) Lindsey (*Joseph A. Lindsey*[5], *Caleb (Calip) Lindsey*[4], *Frances (Frankie) Sharp*[3], *Charles W. Sr.*[2], *John Sr.*[1]) was born in Aug 1876 in Lauderdale County, AL, died 26 Aug 1947, and was buried in Florence City Cemetery, Florence, Lauderdale County, AL.

General Notes: "David Lindsey was a minister of the Freewill Baptist Church. Information for David taken off tomb in Florence Cemetery. East side on hillside of the road..." David Sharp

David married **Mattie Diakus**, daughter of ***Unk Diakus** and **Unknown**.

968 M i. **Luther Lindsey**.

> General Notes: "Luther retired from the U. S. Army, was a Sgt. Lived in Washington, D. C. ..." Millie Mason

969 M ii. **Clarence Lindsey**.

> General Notes: "Lived in Baltimore, Maryland..." Millie Mason

970 M iii. **Henry Lindsey**.

> General Notes: Henry lives in California. Notes from David Sharp. "I found a Henry Lindsey that married an Elizabeth Burns on Feb 26, 1927 in Lauderdale County, Alabama, book 32, pg 298.

+ 971 F iv. **Nora Louise Lindsey**.
+ 972 F v. **Loraine Lindsey**.

392. Lillie Mae Lindsey (*Joseph A. Lindsey[5], Caleb (Calip) Lindsey[4], Frances (Frankie) Sharp[3], Charles W. Sr.[2], John Sr.[1]*) was born in 1880.

Lillie married **John H. Goodman** 2 Apr 1925 in Lauderdale County, AL.

394. J. Lewis Lindsey (*Joseph A. Lindsey[5], Caleb (Calip) Lindsey[4], Frances (Frankie) Sharp[3], Charles W. Sr.[2], John Sr.[1]*) was born in 1885.

J. married **Kate Robinett** 20 Jul 1907.
+ 973 M i. **Katen Lewis Lindsey** was born 12 Apr 1908 in Wayne County, TN, died 2 May 1998, and was buried in Collinwood Cemetery, Collinwood, TN.

395. Emma Lindsey (*Joseph A. Lindsey[5], Caleb (Calip) Lindsey[4], Frances (Frankie) Sharp[3], Charles W. Sr.[2], John Sr.[1]*) was born in Feb 1887.

Emma married **Thomas E. Arnett** 28 Sep 1902 in Lauderdale County, AL. Thomas was born in Mississippi.

396. Ada Bell Lindsey (*Joseph A. Lindsey[5], Caleb (Calip) Lindsey[4], Frances (Frankie) Sharp[3], Charles W. Sr.[2], John Sr.[1]*) was born in Mar 1888 in Lauderdale County, AL, died in 1958, and was buried in Florence City Cemetery, Florence, Lauderdale County, AL.

Ada married **Houston Alfred Hall** 28 Sep 1902 in Lauderdale County, AL. Houston was born in 1883, died in 1929, and was buried in Florence City Cemetery, Florence, Lauderdale County, AL.
+ 974 M i. **Lester Lawrence Hall Sr.** was born 11 Apr 1917 in Lauderdale County, AL, died 9 Jan 1990, and was buried in Pleasant Hill Freewill Baptist Cemetery, Cherokee, Colbert County, AL.
+ 975 M ii. **Floyd Edward Hall Sr.** was born 15 Sep 1919 in Lauderdale County, AL, died 15 Jun 1994, and was buried in Florence City Cemetery, Florence, Lauderdale County, AL.
+ 976 M iii. **Hubert F. Hall** was born 11 Dec 1920 in Lauderdale County, AL, died 25 May 1957, and was buried in Tri-Cities Memorial Gardens, Florence, Lauderdale County, AL.

397. Lee Willie Lindsey (*Joseph A. Lindsey[5], Caleb (Calip) Lindsey[4], Frances (Frankie) Sharp[3], Charles W. Sr.[2], John Sr.[1]*) was born in Feb 1892, died in 1965, and was buried in Burnt Church Cemetery, Russellville, AL.

Lee married **Rosa Shook** 19 Nov 1910 in Lauderdale County, AL.
+ 977 F i. **Reba Lindsey**.
+ 978 F ii. **Pearl Lindsey**.

| 979 | F | iii. | **Louise Lindsey.** |

General Notes: "Residence: Russellville, Alabama..." Millie Mason

| 980 | M | iv. | **Floyd Lindsey.** |

General Notes: "Residence: Chicago, Illinois..." Millie Mason

+	981	M	v.	**Herschel Lee Lindsey** was born 25 Oct 1926 in Lauderdale County, AL, died 22 May 1988, and was buried in K. P. Cemetery, Killen, AL.
	982	M	vi.	**Paul J. Lindsey.**
	983	M	vii.	**Emmit Lindsey.**

General Notes: "Residence: Anniston, Alabama..." Millie Mason

| 984 | M | viii. | **Emory Lindsey.** |

General Notes: "Residence: Russellville, Alabama..." Millie Mason

398. Albert Curtis Lindsey (*David A. Lindsey[5], Caleb (Calip) Lindsey[4], Frances (Frankie) Sharp[3], Charles W. Sr.[2], John Sr.[1]*) was born in 1880 in Lauderdale County, AL, died 16 Aug 1952, and was buried in Florence City Cemetery, Florence, Lauderdale County, AL.

Albert married **Lucille Morrison** 6 Apr 1909 in Lauderdale County, AL. Lucille was born in Lauderdale County, AL, died 16 Jan 1987, and was buried in Lindsey Chapel Cemetery, Lauderdale County, AL.

+	985	F	i.	**Ethel M. Lindsey** was born 3 Dec 1897 in Lauderdale County, AL, died 16 Jan 1987, and was buried in Lindsey Chapel Cemetery, Lauderdale County, AL.
+	986	M	ii.	**Charles Edward Lindsey** was born 7 Nov 1904, died 20 Mar 1942, and was buried in Florence City Cemetery, Florence, Lauderdale County, AL.
+	987	M	iii.	**Dalton Allen Lindsey** was born 10 Nov 1910, died 6 Nov 1976, and was buried in Tri-Cities Memorial Gardens, Florence, Lauderdale County, AL.

399. Edward (Ed) Price Lindsey (*David A. Lindsey[5], Caleb (Calip) Lindsey[4], Frances (Frankie) Sharp[3], Charles W. Sr.[2], John Sr.[1]*) was born in 1899 in Lauderdale County, AL, died 5 May 1976, and was buried in Tri-Cities Memorial Gardens, Florence, Lauderdale County, AL.

General Notes: "Funeral service was preached by Wm Lindsey McDonald..." Millie Mason

Edward married **Annie Laura Butler**, daughter of **Bob Butler** and **Mary Nipper**, 20 Jul 1925 in Lauderdale County, AL. Annie was born 2 Sep 1905 in Lauderdale County, AL, died 27 Feb 1991, and was buried in Tri-Cities Memorial Gardens, Florence, Lauderdale County, AL.

General Notes: "Annie was descended from Gabriel Butler who was one of the earliest settlers of Lauderdale County. Funeral service was preached by Wm Lindsey McDonald..." Millie Mason

| | 988 | F | i. | **Mildred Etoyl Lindsey** was born in 1927 in Lauderdale County, AL. |
| + | 989 | M | ii. | **Clifton D. Lindsey** was born 23 Mar 1930 in Lauderdale County, AL. |

407. Mary Mable Bennett (*Mollie Elizabeth Lindsey[5], Caleb (Calip) Lindsey[4], Frances (Frankie) Sharp[3], Charles W. Sr.[2], John Sr.[1]*).

Mary married **Don Eagle** 11 Jan 1920 in Lauderdale County, AL.

| + | 990 | F | i. | **Miriam Ann Eagle.** |
| + | 991 | F | ii. | **Carolyn Virginia Eagle** died 1 Mar 2000 and was buried in Tri-Cities Memorial Gardens, Florence, Lauderdale County, AL. |

408. Roy Bennett (*Mollie Elizabeth Lindsey[5], Caleb (Calip) Lindsey[4], Frances (Frankie) Sharp[3], Charles W. Sr.[2], John Sr.[1]*).

Roy married ***Unk.**
   992 F   i.   **Allison Bennett.**
   993 F   ii.   **Jean Marie Bennett.**
   994 F   iii.   **Barbara Sue Bennett.**

409. Oscar Lee Bennett Sr. (*Mollie Elizabeth Lindsey*[5], *Caleb (Calip) Lindsey*[4], *Frances (Frankie) Sharp*[3], *Charles W. Sr.*[2], *John Sr.*[1]) was born in 1892 and died in 1957.

Oscar married ***Unk.**
   995 F   i.   **Mary Bennett.**
   996 M   ii.   **Martin Bennett.**
   997 M   iii.   **Oscar Lee Bennett Jr.**

410. Floyd Mitchum (*America Lindsey*[5], *Caleb (Calip) Lindsey*[4], *Frances (Frankie) Sharp*[3], *Charles W. Sr.*[2], *John Sr.*[1]).

Floyd married **Gertrude Trammel.**
   998 F   i.   **Marguerite Mitchum.**

Floyd next married **Grace Hensley.**
   999   M   i.   **Bobby Mitchum.**
  1000 F   ii.   **Glenda Mitchum.**
  1001 M   iii.   **Tommy Mitchum.**

411. Tellie Ruth Mitchum (*America Lindsey*[5], *Caleb (Calip) Lindsey*[4], *Frances (Frankie) Sharp*[3], *Charles W. Sr.*[2], *John Sr.*[1]).

Tellie married **Robert L. Puteet** 15 Apr 1824 in Lauderdale County, AL.
  1002 F   i.   **Sarah Francis Puteet.**
  1003 M   ii.   **Robert (Bobby) Lain Puteet.**

412. Nellie Mitchum (*America Lindsey*[5], *Caleb (Calip) Lindsey*[4], *Frances (Frankie) Sharp*[3], *Charles W. Sr.*[2], *John Sr.*[1]) was born 11 Apr 1894 and died 26 Mar 1983.

Nellie married **Oatly Franklin Romine**, son of **Peter Francis Romine** and **Louisa Francis Overby**, 21 Aug 1911 in Lauderdale County, AL. Oatly was born 28 Feb 1888 in Lauderdale County, AL and died 14 Jun 1961.
+ 1004 M   i.   **Howard James Romine** was born 30 Jun 1915 in Lauderdale County, AL, died 8 Feb 1996, and was buried in Richardson Cemetery, Lauderdale County, AL.
+ 1005 M   ii.   **Richard Leland Romine** was born 25 Mar 1925 in Lauderdale County, AL, died 17 Nov 1982, and was buried in Tri-Cities Memorial Gardens, Florence, Lauderdale County, AL.

413. Bufford Lee Mitchum (*America Lindsey*[5], *Caleb (Calip) Lindsey*[4], *Frances (Frankie) Sharp*[3], *Charles W. Sr.*[2], *John Sr.*[1]) was born 2 Nov 1903 in Lauderdale County, AL, died 20 Dec 1964, and was buried in Tri-Cities Memorial Gardens, Florence, Lauderdale County, AL.

Bufford married **Montez Bruce**, daughter of **Unknown** and **Willie Mae Cottle**, 17 Nov 1929 in Tallahassee, AL. Montez was born 17 Nov 1908 in Tallahassee, AL, died 6 Apr 2000, and was buried in Tri-Cities Memorial Gardens, Florence, Lauderdale County, AL.
+ 1006 F   i.   **Barbara B. Mitchum** was born 9 Apr 1937 in Madison County, AL.

Bufford next married **Etheline *Unk.**

414. Grace E. Holt (*Lula Mae Lindsey*[5], *Caleb (Calip) Lindsey*[4], *Frances (Frankie) Sharp*[3], *Charles W. Sr.*[2], *John Sr.*[1]) was born in 1892 and died 6 May 1942.

Grace married **Charles E. Howell** 12 Jul 1914 in Lauderdale County, AL. Charles was born in 1892 and died 6 May 1942.
  1007 F   i.   **Winifred Louise Howell.**

General Notes: "Winifred was a TVA employee for many years..." Millie Mason

    1008 M   ii.   **Charles Edward Howell.**

415. William Cecil Holt (*Lula Mae Lindsey*[5], *Caleb (Calip) Lindsey*[4], *Frances (Frankie) Sharp*[3], *Charles W. Sr.*[2], *John Sr.*[1]).

William married **Elizabeth Cromwell** 23 Dec 1920 in Lauderdale County, AL.
+ 1009 M   i.   **William Charles Holt.**
    1010 F   ii.   **Cecilia Ann Holt.**

William next married **Vivian Beatrice Holtsford**, daughter of **B. M. Holtsford** and **Velma Williams**, 25 Dec 1941. Vivian was born 9 Mar 1907 in St. Joseph, TN.

418. Mazie Aileen Lindsey (*Robert Andrew Lindsey*[5], *Caleb (Calip) Lindsey*[4], *Frances (Frankie) Sharp*[3], *Charles W. Sr.*[2], *John Sr.*[1]) was born 11 Nov 1909 in Lauderdale County, AL, died 13 Sep 1970, and was buried in Florence City Cemetery, Florence, Lauderdale County, AL.

Mazie married **Virgil Ellis Carter**, son of **Robert Franklin Carter** and **Martha Evelyn Williams**, 10 May 1935 in Lauderdale County, AL. Virgil was born 14 Nov 1909 in Lauderdale County, AL, died 16 Jun 1988, and was buried in Florence City Cemetery, Florence, Lauderdale County, AL.
    1011 M   i.   **Stephen (Chipper) L. Carter** was born 11 Aug 1949 in Lauderdale County, AL, died 27 Mar 1997, and was buried in Florence City Cemetery, Florence, Lauderdale County, AL.

419. Dewey Caleb Lindsey (*Robert Andrew Lindsey*[5], *Caleb (Calip) Lindsey*[4], *Frances (Frankie) Sharp*[3], *Charles W. Sr.*[2], *John Sr.*[1]) was born 30 Jan 1911 in Lauderdale County, AL, died 13 Dec 1970, and was buried in Florence City Cemetery, Florence, Lauderdale County, AL.

General Notes: "In the last years of Dewey's life we would gather at my Daddy's shop on Saturday mornings, which became almost a family ritual. The last time I saw Cousin Dewey was at the nursing home a few weeks before his death. As I was preparing to leave his bedside, I asked if I could do anything. He replied, "I would like a good cup of coffee". I'm glad I was able to fulfill that last wish..." William McDonald

Dewey married **Thelma Katherine Bloss**, daughter of **J. B. Bloss** and **Lydia Pearl Pilkington**, 20 Feb 1954. Thelma was born 26 Sep 1913 in Columbia, TN, died 4 Sep 2000, and was buried in Florence City Cemetery, Florence, Lauderdale County, AL.

420. Donald Edward Lindsey Sr. (*Robert Andrew Lindsey*[5], *Caleb (Calip) Lindsey*[4], *Frances (Frankie) Sharp*[3], *Charles W. Sr.*[2], *John Sr.*[1]) was born 15 Dec 1912 in Lauderdale County, AL, died 21 Jul 1964, and was buried in Greenview Memorial Park, Florence, Lauderdale County, AL.

Donald married **Elizabeth Horton**, daughter of **George Horton** and **Maudie Sherrill**, 13 Apr 1935. Elizabeth was born 13 Apr 1919 in Wayne County, TN.
+ 1012 M   i.   **Donald Edward Lindsey Jr.** was born 15 Oct 1935 in Lauderdale County, AL, died 8 Oct 2008 in Lauderdale County, AL, and was buried in Greenview Memorial Park, Florence, Lauderdale County, AL.
+ 1013 F   ii.   **Rebecca Ann Lindsey** was born 16 Sep 1942 in Lauderdale County, AL.

421. Chester B. Lindsey (*Alonzo Brown Lindsey*[5], *Caleb (Calip) Lindsey*[4], *Frances (Frankie) Sharp*[3], *Charles W. Sr.*[2], *John Sr.*[1]) was born 24 Nov 1907 in Lauderdale County, AL, died 22 Nov 1979, and was buried in Arlington Cemetery, Mt. Pleasant, TN.

Chester married **Fronia C. Hudson**, daughter of **Samuel Hudson** and **Fronia Perryman**, 4 Sep 1934 in Lauderdale County, AL. Fronia was born 7 Mar 1911 in Killen, AL, died 10 Jan 1999, and was buried in Arlington Cemetery, Mt. Pleasant, TN.
+ 1014 F   i.   **Carolyn Lindsey** was born 14 Aug 1936 in Lauderdale County, AL.

422. Nellie Mauvaline Lindsey (*Alonzo Brown Lindsey[5], Caleb (Calip) Lindsey[4], Frances (Frankie) Sharp[3], Charles W. Sr.[2], John Sr.[1]*) was born 24 Sep 1909 in Lauderdale County, AL, died 2 May 1954, and was buried in Greenview Memorial Park, Florence, Lauderdale County, AL.

Nellie married **John Earl Prater** 30 Mar 1929 in Las Vegas, NV. John was buried in Jasper, TX.
+ 1015 F   i.   **Bettye Jean Prater** was born 25 Jul 1931 in Lauderdale County, AL.

424. Elsie Lindsey (*Alonzo Brown Lindsey[5], Caleb (Calip) Lindsey[4], Frances (Frankie) Sharp[3], Charles W. Sr.[2], John Sr.[1]*) was born 8 Nov 1913 in Lauderdale County, AL.

Elsie married **Alva A. Bradfield** 4 Apr 1940. Alva was born 27 Mar 1903 and died 4 Sep 1983.

425. Lula Mae Lindsey (*Alonzo Brown Lindsey[5], Caleb (Calip) Lindsey[4], Frances (Frankie) Sharp[3], Charles W. Sr.[2], John Sr.[1]*) was born 19 Feb 1916 in Lauderdale County, AL and died 12 Jun 1969.

Lula married **Lester Hawkins Thomason**, son of **Robert Lee Thomason** and **Evie Duncan**, 23 Dec in Lauderdale County, AL. Lester was born 25 Nov 1901 in Colbert County, AL and died 8 Jan 1967.

426. Doris Lindsey (*Alonzo Brown Lindsey[5], Caleb (Calip) Lindsey[4], Frances (Frankie) Sharp[3], Charles W. Sr.[2], John Sr.[1]*) was born 25 May 1919 in Lauderdale County, AL, died 20 Feb 1998, and was buried in Greenview Memorial Park, Florence, Lauderdale County, AL.

Doris married **Andrew (Andy) Anderer**.
+ 1016 F   i.   **Laura Francis Anderer** was born 11 Oct.

427. Thomas Arnett Lindsey (*Alonzo Brown Lindsey[5], Caleb (Calip) Lindsey[4], Frances (Frankie) Sharp[3], Charles W. Sr.[2], John Sr.[1]*) was born 5 May 1921 in Lauderdale County, AL.

General Notes: "Thomas was a star football player at Coffee High School before WWII. He is a retired law enforcement officer in Macon, Georgia..." William McDonald

Thomas married **Hattie M. Pace**. Hattie was born 4 Oct 1917 in Gray, GA.
+ 1017 M   i.   **Thomas Alonzo Lindsey** was born 9 Feb 1945 in Macon, GA.
+ 1018 M   ii.   **Ronald Gregg Lindsey** was born 1 Feb 1948 in Macon, GA.
+ 1019 M   iii.   **Donald Pace Lindsey** was born 1 Feb 1948 in Macon, GA.
+ 1020 F   iv.   **Angelia Dee Lindsey** was born 20 Mar 1953 in Macon, GA.

429. Evie Jane Lindsey (*Edgar Floyd Lindsey Sr.[5], Caleb (Calip) Lindsey[4], Frances (Frankie) Sharp[3], Charles W. Sr.[2], John Sr.[1]*) was born 27 Jul 1926 in Birmingham, Jefferson County, AL.

Evie married **William Marsh Torbett**, son of **Unknown** and **Unknown**. William was born 6 May 1925 in Rogers, AR.
+ 1021 M   i.   **Harry Lindsey Torbett** was born 28 Jun 1954 in Alexandria, LA.
+ 1022 M   ii.   **John William Torbett** was born 9 Aug 1962 in Alexandria, LA.

430. Millard Lindsey (*Maraday (Merry Dee) Lindsey[5], Andrew Jackson Lindsey[4], Frances (Frankie) Sharp[3], Charles W. Sr.[2], John Sr.[1]*) was born in Feb 1883 in Alabama, died 1 Oct 1945, and was buried in Crittenden Memorial Park, Marion, AR.

Millard married **Sarah Minnie Lee Weathers** 4 Jul 1906 in Cherokee, Colbert County, AL. Sarah was born 11 Aug 1887 in Lincoln County, TN, died 7 Nov 1967, and was buried in Crittenden Memorial Park, Marion, AR.
+ 1023 F   i.   **Lilly Mae Lindsey** was born 6 Jul 1907 in Colbert County, AL, died 4 Feb 1961, and was buried in Barton Cemetery, Colbert County, AL.
+ 1024 F   ii.   **Viola Beatrice Lindsey** was born 20 Dec 1910 in Cherokee, Colbert County, AL, died 18 Mar 1990, and was buried in Barton Cemetery, Colbert County, AL.
+ 1025 F   iii. **Ola Mae Lindsey** was born 5 Apr 1915 in Colbert County, AL.
+ 1026 F   iv.   **Bessie Lee Lindsey** was born 14 Jul 1917 in Colbert County, AL, died 1 Jul 1993, and was buried in Crittenden Memorial Park, Marion, AR.

+ 1027 F   v.   **Dixie Lindsey** was born 31 Jan 1918, died 18 Aug 1997, and was buried in Crittenden Memorial Park, Marion, AR.
+ 1028 F   vi.   **Lucille Lindsey** was born 20 Mar 1920 in Colbert County, AL.
+ 1029 F   vii. **Dorothy Lindsey** was born 10 Nov 1922, died 5 Mar 1988, and was buried in Crittenden Memorial Park, Marion, AR.
+ 1030 M   viii. **Pete (J. R.) Lindsey** was born in 1924 and died in 1979.

431. Thomas G. Lindsey (*Maraday (Merry Dee) Lindsey[5], Andrew Jackson Lindsey[4], Frances (Frankie) Sharp[3], Charles W. Sr.[2], John Sr.[1]*) was born in Jun 1885 in Mississippi.

Thomas married **Ada (Adder) *Unk** in 1918. Ada was born about 1900 in Alabama.

1031 F   i.   **Nora Lindsey** was born in 1909 in Alabama.
1032 M   ii.   **Curtis Lindsey** was born in 1916 in Alabama.
1033 M   iii. **Ellis Lindsey** was born in 1917 in Alabama.
1034 F   iv.   **Pearlie Lindsey** was born in 1919 in Alabama.
1035 F   v.   **Velma Lindsey** was born in 1921.
1036 M   vi.   **Thomas Lindsey** was born in 1923.
1037 M   vii. **Buford Lindsey** was born in 1925.
1038 M   viii. **Arnold Lindsey** was born in 1929.

432. Effie C. M. Lindsey (*Maraday (Merry Dee) Lindsey[5], Andrew Jackson Lindsey[4], Frances (Frankie) Sharp[3], Charles W. Sr.[2], John Sr.[1]*) was born in Aug 1887 in Alabama.

Effie married **Frank Roberts** in 1903. Frank was born in 1887 in Alabama.

433. Hector J. Lindsey (*Maraday (Merry Dee) Lindsey[5], Andrew Jackson Lindsey[4], Frances (Frankie) Sharp[3], Charles W. Sr.[2], John Sr.[1]*) was born in Jan 1890 in Alabama.

Hector married **Vernice Murphy** 30 Mar 1912 in Colbert County, AL.
1039 M   i.   **Robert Lindsey** was born in 1913 in Alabama.
1040 F   ii.   **Lorane Lindsey** was born in 1917 in Alabama.

439. Kerom William Lindsey (*Greenberry Lee Lindsey Sr.[5], Sylvester (Sill) B. Lindsey[4], Frances (Frankie) Sharp[3], Charles W. Sr.[2], John Sr.[1]*) was born 17 Jan 1880 in Lauderdale County, AL, died 25 Oct 1957, and was buried in Wright Cemetery, Wright, Lauderdale County, AL.

General Notes: "Kern Lindsey, born about 1880, was the oldest child. He was married to his cousin Nettie Sharp. (She was first cousin-once-removed to his brother, Sam's wife, Mattie and also to Quinnie, wife of Kern's brother, Greenberry). Kern and Nettie lived at Wright when I knew them. Cousin Kern was a big help to me in the location of a number of old graves in our family cemeteries. Kern and Nettie had one son, Coleman Lindsey, whom I knew at the Tennessee Valley Authority..." William McDonald.

Kerom married **May N. (Nettie) Sharp**, daughter of **Owen Bennett (Doc) Sharp** and **Mary Frances (Fannie) Wiley**, 2 Aug 1907 in Lauderdale County, AL. May was born 8 Jul 1888 in Alabama, died 18 Nov 1950, and was buried in Wright Cemetery, Wright, Lauderdale County, AL.
+ 1041 M   i.   **Coleman Edison Lindsey** was born 4 Jul 1909 in Wright, Lauderdale County, AL, died 15 Feb 1981, and was buried in Wright Cemetery, Wright, Lauderdale County, AL.

440. Samuel S. Lindsey (*Greenberry Lee Lindsey Sr.[5], Sylvester (Sill) B. Lindsey[4], Frances (Frankie) Sharp[3], Charles W. Sr.[2], John Sr.[1]*) was born 16 Oct 1882 in Lauderdale County, AL, died 20 Jan 1917, and was buried in Wright Cemetery, Wright, Lauderdale County, AL.

Samuel married **Mattie A. Sharp**, daughter of **John Thomas (Tom) Sharp** and **Susan Elizabeth (Betty) Johnson**, 19 Mar 1901 in Lauderdale County, AL. Mattie was born in Jun 1885 in Gravely Springs, Lauderdale County, AL, died 23 Feb 1965, and was buried in Oak Grove Cemetery, Lauderdale County, AL.
+ 1042 M   i.   **Clyde Roosevelt Lindsey** was born 17 Oct 1901 in Waterloo, Lauderdale County, AL, died 28 Sep 1979, and was buried in Wright Cemetery, Wright, Lauderdale County, AL.
1043 F   ii.   **Linnie I. Lindsey** was born in 1904 in Waterloo, Lauderdale County, AL.
+ 1044 F   iii. **Mattie Sue (Susie) Lindsey** was born 9 Jul 1906 in Waterloo, Lauderdale County, AL.

1045 M iv. **Howard Lindsey** was born in 1908.
1046 M v. **Homer Lindsey**.

441. John David Lindsey (*Greenberry Lee Lindsey Sr.* [5], *Sylvester (Sill) B. Lindsey* [4], *Frances (Frankie) Sharp* [3], *Charles W. Sr.* [2], *John Sr.* [1]) was born in Jan 1885 in Tyronza, Poinsett County, AR, died 28 Jan 1947, and was buried in Tyronza Cemetery, Tyronza, Poinsett County, AR.

"He was married to Lannie Joiner whom our folks said 'came from the bend of the river area' in West Lauderdale. John and Lannie moved to Arkansas where they are buried..." William McDonald

John married **Lannie L. Milford**, daughter of **James William Milford** and **Martha Jane Clanton**, 26 Dec 1905 in Lauderdale County, AL. Lannie was born 29 Jul 1886 in Lauderdale County, AL, died 19 Mar 1957, and was buried in Tyronza Cemetery, Tyronza, Poinsett County, AR.

+ 1047 F i. **Georgia Mae Lindsey** was born 6 May 1907 and died 18 Apr 1979 in Michigan City, IN.
+ 1048 M ii. **James Alex Lindsey** was born about 1909 in Arkansas and died in Holland, MI.
+ 1049 M iii. **Edgar Bruce Lindsey** was born 23 Apr 1913 in Deckerville, AR, died 5 Apr 1990, and was buried in Corinth, Alcorn County, MS.
   1050 M iv. **Alvin Lindsey** was born in Tyronza, Poinsett County, AR and died in Elm Loum County, IL.
+ 1051 M v. **Donald Lindsey** was buried in Illinois.
+ 1052 M vi. **John Henry Lindsey** was born 8 Feb in Arkansas.
+ 1053 F vii. **Bessie Lindsey** was born 24 Nov in Alabama.
+ 1054 F viii. **Mary Lindsey** was born 7 Apr 1920.
+ 1055 F ix. **Bonnie Lindsey** was born 28 Aug 1922 in Arkansas.

442. Greenberry Lee Lindsey Jr. (*Greenberry Lee Lindsey Sr.* [5], *Sylvester (Sill) B. Lindsey* [4], *Frances (Frankie) Sharp* [3], *Charles W. Sr.* [2], *John Sr.* [1]) was born 19 Nov 1886 in Lauderdale County, AL, died 15 Nov 1974, and was buried in Wright Cemetery, Wright, Lauderdale County, AL.

General Notes: "I remember Greenberry as the barber in Waterloo, Alabama..." Dan Wood

"He was born in December 1887 (his tomb stone says Nov 19, 1886). Cousin Greenberry served as the barber for Waterloo for over 50 years and was known as the sage of the community. I can remember when he rode a bicycle from Wright to Waterloo every day. In his older years, he walked that long trip regardless of the weather. He lived more than 90 years and was a kind, wise, friendly and delightful man. Greenberry was married to his cousin Quinnie Vester Sharp, who was a sister to Sam Lindsey's wife, Mattie.
Someone told me years ago that Greenberry knew more about the Lindseys and Sharps than any living soul. I wish he had written a book, but as far as I know he carried all this valuable knowledge in his head. I'm indebted to him for many of the things I'm now able to write about our Lindseys and Sharps.
Cousins Greenberry and Quinnie lived on one of the most picturesque places in this part of the country. On one of our visits our daughter Nancy went wading in the creek with Cousin Greenberry, while her mother and I watched from the kitchen above. You can well imagine how terrified we were when we spotted a large cotton mouth moccasin only a couple of feet from where they were wading. My Granddaddy Lindsey - cousin to both Greenberry and Quinnie - was often invited in the summers for supper at their home. Their kind invitations included me. On one visit we learned that cousin Quinnie had been fasting for three days in preparation for a revival at the Methodist Church. I've often thought about that gracious soul and how hungry she must have been as she prepared such sumptuous meals for Papa and me. ..." William McDonald

Greenberry married **Quinnie Vester Sharp**, daughter of **John Thomas (Tom) Sharp** and **Susan Elizabeth (Betty) Johnson**, 26 May 1913 in Lauderdale County, AL. Quinnie was born 20 Sep 1892 in Lauderdale County, AL, died 7 May 1980, and was buried in Wright Cemetery, Wright, Lauderdale County, AL.

+ 1056 M i. **Ralph Nolan Lindsey** was born 15 Jun 1915 in Lauderdale County, AL.
+ 1057 F ii. **Mary Bernease Lindsey** was born 19 Feb 1922 in Lauderdale County, AL, died 8 Jul 2002, and was buried in Greenview Memorial Park, Florence, Lauderdale County, AL.

443. Elizabeth (Lizzie) Lindsey (*Greenberry Lee Lindsey Sr.* [5], *Sylvester (Sill) B. Lindsey* [4], *Frances (Frankie) Sharp* [3], *Charles W. Sr.* [2], *John Sr.* [1]) was born in Apr 1889 in Alabama.

Elizabeth married ***Unk Wood**.

444. Hannah Margaret Lindsey (*Greenberry Lee Lindsey Sr.[5], Sylvester (Sill) B. Lindsey[4], Frances (Frankie) Sharp[3], Charles W. Sr.[2], John Sr.[1]*) was born in Jul 1894 in Lauderdale County, AL.

General Notes: "Lived in Birmingham, Alabama..." Millie Mason

Hannah married ***Unk Atkinson**.
+ 1058 F i. **Alberta Atkinson**.
+ 1059 M ii. **Fred Atkinson**.

Hannah next married ***Unk Godfrey**.

445. Bruce Lindsey (*Greenberry Lee Lindsey Sr.[5], Sylvester (Sill) B. Lindsey[4], Frances (Frankie) Sharp[3], Charles W. Sr.[2], John Sr.[1]*) was born in Aug 1896 in Lauderdale County, AL.

Bruce married ***Unk**.
1060 M i. **Robert Lindsey**.

General Notes: "Robert, while temporarily taking care if a friend's grocery store in Birmingham, was robbed and murdered..." William McDonald

447. Etta Lindsey (*Greenberry Lee Lindsey Sr.[5], Sylvester (Sill) B. Lindsey[4], Frances (Frankie) Sharp[3], Charles W. Sr.[2], John Sr.[1]*) was born about 1914 in Alabama.

Etta married ***Unk Joiner**.

448. Mollie L. Milford (*Julie (Julia) Lindsey[5], Sylvester (Sill) B. Lindsey[4], Frances (Frankie) Sharp[3], Charles W. Sr.[2], John Sr.[1]*) was born 23 Jan 1885 in Lauderdale County, AL and died before 1 Apr 1969.

Mollie married **John Huskie**.
1061 F i. **Alberta Milford**.

Mollie next married ***Unk Scott**.

Mollie next married ***Unk**.

451. Ruby P. Milford (*Julie (Julia) Lindsey[5], Sylvester (Sill) B. Lindsey[4], Frances (Frankie) Sharp[3], Charles W. Sr.[2], John Sr.[1]*) was born 8 Apr 1893 in Lauderdale County, AL.

Ruby married **Walter Smith**.

452. Pearlie Ann Milford (*Julie (Julia) Lindsey[5], Sylvester (Sill) B. Lindsey[4], Frances (Frankie) Sharp[3], Charles W. Sr.[2], John Sr.[1]*) was born 20 Sep 1895 in Lauderdale County, AL, died 31 Mar 1969, and was buried in Wright Cemetery, Wright, Lauderdale County, AL.

Pearlie married **Jack Johnson**. Jack was born in 1884, died in 1954, and was buried in Wright Cemetery, Wright, Lauderdale County, AL.
1062 M i. **Joe Johnson**.
1063 M ii. **Virgil Johnson**.
+ 1064 F iii. **Nell Johnson**.
+ 1065 F iv. **Estell Johnson** was born 10 Apr 1919 in Lauderdale County, AL.
+ 1066 M v. **James Edward Johnson** was born 10 Sep 1924 in Lauderdale County, AL, died 13 May 1978, and was buried in Murphy's Chapel Cemetery, Lauderdale County, AL.

454. Margie L. Lindsey (*Adron (Little Ade) Lindsey[5], Sylvester (Sill) B. Lindsey[4], Frances (Frankie) Sharp[3], Charles W. Sr.[2], John Sr.[1]*) was born in Oct 1888 in Alabama.

Margie married **William C. Isbell** 9 Jun 1905 in Lauderdale County, AL.
1067 M i. **Earl Isbell**.

Margie next married **Joseph Callahan**.

455. Carrie M. Lindsey (*Adron (Little Ade) Lindsey*[5], *Sylvester (Sill) B. Lindsey*[4], *Frances (Frankie) Sharp*[3], *Charles W. Sr.*[2], *John Sr.*[1]) was born in Oct 1890 in Alabama.

Carrie married **James Bradley** 1 Jan 1904 in Lauderdale County, AL.

456. Amy Gertrude Lindsey (*Adron (Little Ade) Lindsey*[5], *Sylvester (Sill) B. Lindsey*[4], *Frances (Frankie) Sharp*[3], *Charles W. Sr.*[2], *John Sr.*[1]) was born in Dec 1892 and was buried in Harvey Cemetery, Whitehead, Rogersville, AL.

Amy married **Simpson Tate**. Simpson was buried in Harvey Cemetery, Whitehead, Rogersville, AL.
+ 1068 F i. **Edna Mae Tate**.
+ 1069 F ii. **Cornelia Tate**.

Amy next married **Edgar Ross Pierce**.
+ 1070 M i. **Ray Pierce** was born 17 Oct 1921 in Lawrence County, TN.
+ 1071 F ii. **Susie Belle Pierce** was born 22 Apr 1923 in Lauderdale County, AL.
+ 1072 F iii. **Mildred Lucille Pierce** was born 10 Jun 1922 in Lauderdale County, AL and was buried in Greenview Memorial Park, Florence, Lauderdale County, AL.
+ 1073 F iv. **Julie Blance Pierce** was born 2 Mar 1926 in Lauderdale County, AL.
+ 1074 M v. **Raymond Ross Pierce** was born 20 Mar 1927 in Lawrence County, TN.
+ 1075 F vi. **Jessie Imogene Pierce** was born 3 Nov 1928 in Lawrence County, TN.
+ 1076 F vii. **Bobbie Lee Pierce** was born 2 Sep 1930 in Lawrence County, TN, died 17 May 2000, and was buried in Kidd Cemetery, Lawrence County, TN.
+ 1077 M viii. **Jesse Sewell Pierce** was born 20 Jan 1933 in Lawrence County, TN.

457. Turner Lindsey (*Adron (Little Ade) Lindsey*[5], *Sylvester (Sill) B. Lindsey*[4], *Frances (Frankie) Sharp*[3], *Charles W. Sr.*[2], *John Sr.*[1]) was born in Nov 1894 in Lauderdale County, AL.

General Notes: "Turner was Little Aid's fourth child. He was married to Minnie Weathers who was descended from an early Rogersville family....The road between Rogersville and the Toonersville Community - Turner Lindsey Road - was named for him. Turner and Minnie had a daughter, Robbie Nell, who lived in Florida. Turner, as I recall, died while visiting Robbie Nell a number of years ago..." William McDonald

Turner married **Minnie Lee Weathers**, daughter of **Bayless Edward Weathers** and **Mary E. Springer**, 22 Aug 1914 in Lauderdale County, AL. Minnie was born 19 Apr 1896 in Rogersville, Lauderdale County, AL, died 18 Jul 1975, and was buried in McCartney Cemetery.
1078 F i. **Robbi Nell Lindsey** was born in Aug 1926.

458. Viola Lindsey (*Adron (Little Ade) Lindsey*[5], *Sylvester (Sill) B. Lindsey*[4], *Frances (Frankie) Sharp*[3], *Charles W. Sr.*[2], *John Sr.*[1]) was born in Jan 1896 in Lauderdale County, AL.

Viola married **Ollie E. Bills** 11 Aug 1918 in Lauderdale County, AL. Ollie was born in Laurel, MS.
1079 M i. **Marlon Bills**.
1080 F ii. **Virginia Bills**.
+ 1081 F iii. **Evelyn Bills**.
1082 F iv. **Fleeda Bills**.
1083 F v. **Elizabeth Bills**.

459. Zula Mason Lindsey (*Adron (Little Ade) Lindsey*[5], *Sylvester (Sill) B. Lindsey*[4], *Frances (Frankie) Sharp*[3], *Charles W. Sr.*[2], *John Sr.*[1]) was born in Apr 1899.

Zula married **Amon Pierce**.

460. Estelle Lindsey (*Adron (Little Ade) Lindsey*[5], *Sylvester (Sill) B. Lindsey*[4], *Frances (Frankie) Sharp*[3], *Charles W. Sr.*[2], *John Sr.*[1]) was born in 1902 and died in 1983 in Lawrenceburg, Lawrence County, TN.

Estelle married **Herbert Wilborn**.

461. Mary Odelle Lindsey (*Adron (Little Ade) Lindsey*[5], *Sylvester (Sill) B. Lindsey*[4], *Frances (Frankie) Sharp*[3], *Charles W. Sr.*[2], *John Sr.*[1]) was born in 1905.

Mary married **Will Locke**.
+ 1084 F i. **Ann Locke**.

462. Almeda Lindsey (*Adron (Little Ade) Lindsey*[5], *Sylvester (Sill) B. Lindsey*[4], *Frances (Frankie) Sharp*[3], *Charles W. Sr.*[2], *John Sr.*[1]) was born in 1910.

Almeda married **Scott Harrison**.

463. Jesse Mack Lindsey (*Adron (Little Ade) Lindsey*[5], *Sylvester (Sill) B. Lindsey*[4], *Frances (Frankie) Sharp*[3], *Charles W. Sr.*[2], *John Sr.*[1]) was born in 1912, died 23 Sep 1992, and was buried in John Lay Cemetery, Etheridge, TN.

Jesse married **Nellie McMullens** in 1960 in Yorktown, IN. Nellie was born in Indiana, died 5 Feb 1998, and was buried in Garden & Memorial Cemetery, Muncie, IN.

465. Josie Etta Haynes (*Lucretia (Lula) Lindsey*[5], *Adron Leonard Lindsey Sr.*[4], *Frances (Frankie) Sharp*[3], *Charles W. Sr.*[2], *John Sr.*[1]) was born 6 Mar 1883 in Lauderdale County, AL, died 13 Aug 1964, and was buried in Mt. Zion Cemetery, Hardin County, TN.

> General Notes: "When I was a boy we visited Cousin Josie when she lived in the old Major Witherspoon house, one of the earliest homes built in Waterloo. It was a two- story log house with a two- story front porch. I was fascinated with this old place. My Grandfather Lindsey and I often went to see Josie. Following Pap's death, I visited with her a number of times. Cousin Josie died in 1962 and was buried in the Mt Zion Church of Christ Cemetery. She was survived by three daughters, two sons, twelve grandchildren, and sixteen great -grandchildren...." William McDonald

Josie married **Iric Kirkland** 25 Jan 1901. Iric was buried in Mt. Zion Cemetery, Hardin County, TN.
1085 M i. **Leonard Kirkland**.
1086 F ii. **Lillian Kirkland**.
1087 M iii. **Lee Kirkland**.
1088 F iv. **Edna Kirkland**.
1089 F v. **Stella Kirkland**.

Josie next married **Henry Barrier**. Henry was born 15 Apr 1872 and died in Sep 1947.
+ 1090 F i. ***Unk Barrier**.
+ 1091 F ii. **Bernice Barrier**.
+ 1092 F iii. ***Unk Barrier**.
+ 1093 M iv. **Henry Olen Barrier** was born in 1920 and died in Apr 1980.

466. Clarence Haynes (*Lucretia (Lula) Lindsey*[5], *Adron Leonard Lindsey Sr.*[4], *Frances (Frankie) Sharp*[3], *Charles W. Sr.*[2], *John Sr.*[1]) was born 3 Jan 1882 in Waterloo, Lauderdale County, AL, died 10 Jul 1960, and was buried in Tyronza Cemetery, Tyronza, Poinsett County, AR.

Clarence married **Edna Pearl Perkins**, daughter of **James Wesley Perkins** and **Rebecca P. Gray**, 28 Feb 1909. Edna was born 11 Nov 1893 in Waterloo, Lauderdale County, AL, died 29 Mar 1976, and was buried in Tyronza Cemetery, Tyronza, Poinsett County, AR.
+ 1094 F i. **Carmel Inez Haynes** was born 5 Dec 1909 in Lauderdale County, AL and died 8 Jan 1968.
+ 1095 M ii. **Edwin Lenard Haynes** was born 20 Feb 1911 in Waterloo, Lauderdale County, AL, died 12 Jul 1979, and was buried in Tyronza Cemetery, Tyronza, Poinsett County, AR.
+ 1096 M iii. **Doyle Odell Haynes** was born 30 May 1913 in Waterloo, Lauderdale County, AL.
+ 1097 M iv. **Weldon Lewis Haynes** was born 16 Aug 1919 in Tyronza, Poinsett County, AR, died 11 Mar 1988, and was buried in Luxoro Cemetery, Luxora, AR.

+ 1098 M v.   **James Purnell Haynes** was born 14 Nov 1930 in Tyronza, Poinsett County, AR, died 5 Nov 1986, and was buried in Ripley Memorial Cemetery, Ripley, TN.

467. Lou Tishie Haynes (*Lucretia (Lula) Lindsey*[5], *Adron Leonard Lindsey Sr.*[4], *Frances (Frankie) Sharp*[3], *Charles W. Sr.*[2], *John Sr.*[1]) was born 18 May 1885, died 9 Sep 1974, and was buried in Mt. Zion Cemetery, Hardin County, TN.

Lou married **Donald Tacker**. Donald was born in 1883, died in 1939, and was buried in Mt. Zion Cemetery, Hardin County, TN.

     1099 F   i.   **Lillie Tacker**.
+ 1100 F   ii.   **Dora Inez Tacker** was born 11 Aug 1906 and died 26 Nov.
+ 1101 F   iii. **Tennie Louise Tacker** was born 24 Sep 1909 and died 28 May 2000.
+ 1102 F   iv.   **Virgie Hazel Tacker** was born 22 Jul 1914 and died 6 Mar 1990.
+ 1103 F   v.   **Mary Bastine Tacker** was born 28 Nov 1916 and died 17 Dec 1996.
+ 1104 M   vi.   **Harold D. Tacker** was born in 1921 and died in 1975.

468. Roxie W. Haynes (*Lucretia (Lula) Lindsey*[5], *Adron Leonard Lindsey Sr.*[4], *Frances (Frankie) Sharp*[3], *Charles W. Sr.*[2], *John Sr.*[1]) was born in Feb 1886 and was buried in Tyronza Cemetery, Tyronza, Poinsett County, AR.

Roxie married **Luther Gammel**. Luther was buried in Tyronza Cemetery, Tyronza, Poinsett County, AR.

470. Leonard A. Haynes (*Lucretia (Lula) Lindsey*[5], *Adron Leonard Lindsey Sr.*[4], *Frances (Frankie) Sharp*[3], *Charles W. Sr.*[2], *John Sr.*[1]) was born in Aug 1890 and was buried in Memphis, Shelby County, TN.

Leonard married **Thelma *Unk**.

471. Elza Raider Taylor (*Lucretia (Lula) Lindsey*[5], *Adron Leonard Lindsey Sr.*[4], *Frances (Frankie) Sharp*[3], *Charles W. Sr.*[2], *John Sr.*[1]) was born in 1898 in Alabama.

Elza married **Frank Wood**.

     1105 M   i.   **Ralph Wood**.
     1106 M   ii.   **Carlos Wood**.
     1107 M   iii. **Roy Lynn Wood**.

472. Martha (Mattie) Inez Taylor (*Lucretia (Lula) Lindsey*[5], *Adron Leonard Lindsey Sr.*[4], *Frances (Frankie) Sharp*[3], *Charles W. Sr.*[2], *John Sr.*[1]) was born 29 Mar 1900 in Lauderdale County, AL, died 6 Nov 1993, and was buried in Oak Grove Cemetery, Lauderdale County, AL.

Martha married **Floyde Leonard Wood**, son of **James Hampton (Jim) Wood Sr.** and **Mary (Mollie) Taylor**, about 1918. Floyde was born 1 Mar 1897 in Wright, Lauderdale County, AL, died 27 Jan 1971, and was buried in Oak Grove Cemetery, Lauderdale County, AL.

     1108 F   i.   **Mary Lou Wood** was born 27 Mar 1920 in Lauderdale County, AL, died 27 Jun 1920, and was buried in Lauderdale County, AL.
+ 1109 M   ii.   **Fred Amos Wood** was born 26 Jan 1921 in Wright, Lauderdale County, AL, died 29 Aug 1976, and was buried in Oak Grove Cemetery, Lauderdale County, AL.
+ 1110 F   iii. **Ruby Mae Wood** was born 19 Mar 1923 in Lauderdale County, AL, died 20 Dec 1996, and was buried in Wesley Chapel Cemetery, Lauderdale County, AL.
+ 1111 M   iv.   **Floyde Virgil Wood** was born 15 Jun 1925 in Lauderdale County, AL, died 9 May 1984, and was buried in Oak Grove Cemetery, Lauderdale County, AL.
+ 1112 F   v.   **Annie Ruth Wood** was born 13 Aug 1927 in Lauderdale County, AL, died 18 Aug 2006, and was buried in Murphy's Chapel Cemetery, Lauderdale County, AL.
+ 1113 M   vi.   **Glen Wood** was born 6 May 1929 in Lauderdale County, AL, died 7 May 2002, and was buried in Stoney Point Cemetery, Lauderdale County, AL.
+ 1114 F   vii. **Elza Darlene Wood** was born 29 Mar 1931 in Lauderdale County, AL, died 4 Apr 2009, and was buried in Pine Hill Cemetery, Lauderdale County, AL.
     1115 M   viii. **Grady Wood** was born 2 Mar 1933, died 15 Jul 1933, and was buried in Lauderdale County, AL.
+ 1116 F   ix.   **Josephine Wood** was born 28 Jun 1934 in Lauderdale County, AL.

1117	F	x.	**Barbara Wood** was born 26 Feb 1936 in Lauderdale County, AL, died 2 May 1936, and was buried in Lauderdale County, AL.
+ 1118	M	xi.	**James Edward Wood** was born 22 May 1937 in Lauderdale County, AL, died 11 Sep 1990, and was buried in Oak Grove Cemetery, Lauderdale County, AL.
+ 1119	M	xii.	**Harold Taylor Wood** was born 8 Oct 1939 in Lauderdale County, AL, died 27 Mar 2004, and was buried in Oak Grove Cemetery, Lauderdale County, AL.

473. George Willis Taylor (*Lucretia (Lula) Lindsey*[5]*, Adron Leonard Lindsey Sr.*[4]*, Frances (Frankie) Sharp*[3]*, Charles W. Sr.*[2]*, John Sr.*[1]) was born 28 Feb 1931 in Tennessee, died 5 Apr 1995, and was buried in Rhodesville Cemetery, Lauderdale County, AL.

George married **Maude Elizabeth (Libby) Fowler**, daughter of ***Unk Fowler** and ***Unk**, 13 Mar 1954. Maude was born 17 Sep 1937, died 2 Nov 2001, and was buried in Rhodesville Cemetery, Lauderdale County, AL.

General Notes: Obituary, Times Daily, Florence, Lauderdale County, Alabama

"Elizabeth "Libby" Taylor, 64, Florence, died Saturday, Nov. 3, 2001, after an extended illness. Visitation was Sunday at the residence. The funeral will be at 2 p.m. today at Souls Harbor Apostolic Church, with burial in Rhodesville United Methodist Church Cemetery. The body will be at the church one hour before the service. Officiating at the funeral will be Brother Bobby Crosswhite and Tim Hollis.

Mrs. Taylor is survived by her sons, Steve Taylor, Florence, Andy Taylor, Florence; daughters, Cathy Lambert, Waterloo, Lisa Wallace, Rogersville, and Amanda Hill, Florence; foster sons, William Richards, Dale Richards and Carl Richards, Tuscumbia; sister, Mamie Turner, Texas, stepsister, Patricia King, Lawrenceburg, Tenn; brothers, Russell Fowler, Indiana, Raymond Fowler, Ohio; 13 grandchildren; seven great -grandchildren.

Mrs. Taylor was preceded in death by her husband, George W. Taylor, and a grandchild, Steven.

Pallbearers will include Donny Taylor, Mike Taylor, Lonnie Taylor, Curtis Hill, Craig Taylor, Mike Lard, Billy Taylor, Justin Hill. Honorary pallbearers will include Bradley Lard, Ramon Lambert, Will Vickers.

Mrs. Taylor was retired as a bus driver for the Lauderdale County Board of Education and drove a bus to Central High School. She was a member of the Souls Harbor Apostolic Church. Greenview Funeral Home of Florence is directing."

+ 1120	F	i.	**Amanda Taylor**.
+ 1121	F	ii.	**Lisa Taylor**.
1122	M	iii.	**Andy Taylor**.
1123	M	iv.	**Steve Taylor**.
+ 1124	F	v.	**Cathy Taylor**.

474. Winnie E. Lindsey (*Hunter Lindsey*[5]*, Adron Leonard Lindsey Sr.*[4]*, Frances (Frankie) Sharp*[3]*, Charles W. Sr.*[2]*, John Sr.*[1]) was born in Apr 1899 in Lauderdale County, AL, died in 1928, and was buried in Wright Cemetery, Wright, Lauderdale County, AL.

Winnie married **Marvin Smith**, son of **Harvey Hamilton Smith** and **Sarah E. Davis**, 16 May 1918 in Lauderdale County, AL. Marvin was born 8 Jan 1898 in Waterloo, Lauderdale County, AL, died 14 Mar 1963, and was buried in Tyronza Cemetery, Tyronza, Poinsett County, AR.

+ 1125	F	i.	**Christine Smith** was born 5 Jan 1922 in Waterloo, Lauderdale County, AL.

475. Carmel Lindsey (*Adron Leonard (Green) Lindsey Jr.*[5]*, Adron Leonard Lindsey Sr.*[4]*, Frances (Frankie) Sharp*[3]*, Charles W. Sr.*[2]*, John Sr.*[1]) was born 11 Dec 1903 in Lauderdale County, AL, died 8 Jan 1968, and was buried in Greenview Memorial Park, Florence, Lauderdale County, AL.

Carmel married **Hardie Raymond Springer**, son of **Bedford Forrest Springer** and **Amanda Killen**. Hardie was born 18 Mar 1902 in Lauderdale County, AL, died 8 Mar 1985, and was buried in Greenview Memorial Park, Florence, Lauderdale County, AL.

General Notes: "Hardie owned and operated Florence's first, and for many years, the town's only Gulf Service Station for more than half a century. Springer's Gulf was originally where the

Lauderdale County Courthouse is now located. It later was at the present site of the Florence-Lauderdale Public Library..." William McDonald

+ 1126 M i. **Raymond Glenn Springer** was born 18 Dec 1927 in Lauderdale County, AL.

476. Carlos (Bill) Lindsey (*Adron Leonard (Green) Lindsey Jr.*[5], *Adron Leonard Lindsey Sr.*[4], *Frances (Frankie) Sharp*[3], *Charles W. Sr.*[2], *John Sr.*[1]) was born 17 Feb 1907 in Lauderdale County, AL, died 19 Jul 1974, and was buried in Pleasant Hill Cemetery, Lauderdale County, AL.

General Notes: "Carlos was with General Patton's Third army when they linked with the Russians during WWII. He was highly decorated for heroism while his company was holding a bridge for the army to cross the Rhine..." William McDonald

Carlos married **Fannie Katherine Boyd**, daughter of **Charles Boyd** and **May Overton**, about 1926. Fannie was born 10 Jul 1910 in Wayne County, TN, died 2 Jun 1976, and was buried in K. P. Cemetery, Killen, AL.

+ 1127 F i. **Dolly Katherine Lindsey** was born 13 Sep 1927 in Lauderdale County, AL, died 8 Dec 2000, and was buried in Tri-Cities Memorial Gardens, Florence, Lauderdale County, AL.
+ 1128 M ii. **Jack Clayton Lindsey** was born 1 Jan 1935 in Lauderdale County, AL.

477. Pauline Myran Lindsey (*Adron Leonard (Green) Lindsey Jr.*[5], *Adron Leonard Lindsey Sr.*[4], *Frances (Frankie) Sharp*[3], *Charles W. Sr.*[2], *John Sr.*[1]) was born 15 Mar 1910 in Lauderdale County, AL, died 6 Mar 1964, and was buried in Pleasant Hill Cemetery, Lauderdale County, AL.

Pauline married **William Ervin McDonald**, son of **Jessie McDonald** and **Lillie Redding**, 19 Nov 1926 in Lauderdale County, AL. William was born 10 Nov 1903 in Lauderdale County, AL, died 11 Nov 1990, and was buried in Pleasant Hill Cemetery, Lauderdale County, AL.

General Notes: "In early days William was employed in the construction of Wilson Dam and at the Riverton, Alabama, lock. He served also on the lock at Cape Cod in Massachusetts. He was one of TVA's first employees at the Chemical Plant in 1933. Following retirement from TVA, William Ervin McDonald was a merchant at Central Heights near Florence..." William McDonald

+ 1129 M i. **William Lindsey McDonald** was born 7 Jun 1927 in Florence, Lauderdale County, AL.
+ 1130 M ii. **Jimmy Joe McDonald** was born 24 Jul 1929 in Lauderdale County, AL.
+ 1131 M iii. **Marvin McDaniel McDonald** was born 25 Mar 1931 in Lauderdale County, AL, died 17 Apr 1994, and was buried in Pleasant Hill Cemetery, Lauderdale County, AL.
+ 1132 M iv. **Bobby Jeffrey McDonald** was born 19 May 1935 in Lauderdale County, AL.
+ 1133 F v. **Virginia Lee McDonald** was born 18 Sep 1938 in Lauderdale County, AL.
+ 1134 M vi. **John Nelson McDonald Sr.** was born 9 Jul 1943 in Lauderdale County, AL.
+ 1135 M vii. **Thomas Glenn McDonald** was born 22 Oct 1945 in Lauderdale County, AL.

478. Laura Lindsey (*Adron Leonard (Green) Lindsey Jr.*[5], *Adron Leonard Lindsey Sr.*[4], *Frances (Frankie) Sharp*[3], *Charles W. Sr.*[2], *John Sr.*[1]) was born 12 Aug 1912 in Lauderdale County, AL, died 10 Oct 1991, and was buried in Greenview Memorial Park, Florence, Lauderdale County, AL.

Laura married **James Franklin Hall Sr.**, son of **Will Hall** and **Nannie Mae Freeman**, 28 Feb 1929 in Lauderdale County, AL. James was born 3 Nov 1910 in Lauderdale County, AL, died 16 Feb 1986, and was buried in Greenview Memorial Park, Florence, Lauderdale County, AL.

+ 1136 M i. **Ray Arlen Hall** was born 24 Sep 1930 in Lauderdale County, AL.
+ 1137 M ii. **James Franklin Hall Jr.** was born 4 Apr 1934 in Lauderdale County, AL.
+ 1138 M iii. **Howard Thomas Hall** was born 24 Aug 1936 in Lauderdale County, AL.

479. Nelson McCaun Lindsey (*Adron Leonard (Green) Lindsey Jr.*[5], *Adron Leonard Lindsey Sr.*[4], *Frances (Frankie) Sharp*[3], *Charles W. Sr.*[2], *John Sr.*[1]) was born 26 Mar 1915 in Lauderdale County, AL, died 30 Dec 1978, and was buried in Oakwood Cemetery, Sheffield, Colbert County, AL.

Nelson married **Mary Virginia Mason**, daughter of **Walter Frederick Mason** and **Annie Mae Holt**, 21 Dec 1939 in Colbert County, AL. Mary was born 8 Aug 1918 in Lauderdale County, AL.

+ 1139 F i. **Mary Nell Lindsey** was born 10 Aug 1941 in Colbert County, AL.

+ 1140 F ii. **Mae Virginia Lindsey** was born 25 Feb 1946 in Colbert County, AL.
+ 1141 F iii. **Linda Sue Lindsey** was born 22 Mar 1954 in Colbert County, AL.

480. Howard Shannon Lindsey (*Adron Leonard (Green) Lindsey Jr.*[5], *Adron Leonard Lindsey Sr.*[4], *Frances (Frankie) Sharp*[3], *Charles W. Sr.*[2], *John Sr.*[1]) was born 11 Apr 1917 in Lauderdale County, AL.

General Notes: "Howard and Lorine were career employees with the National Space Program in Florida. Howard is also a retired Chief Warrant Officer who served with the U. S. Army Signal Corps for more than twenty years and is a veteran of WWII and the Korean War...." William McDonald

Howard married **Bertha Lorine Sutton** 15 Jun 1940. Bertha was born 13 Jun 1920, died 7 Dec 1991, and was buried in Melbourne, FL.
+ 1142 M i. **Howard Carlos Lindsey** was born 24 Apr 1941 in Columbus, GA.
+ 1143 F ii. **Iris Gail Lindsey** was born 30 Nov 1942 in Columbus, GA.
  1144 M iii. **James Leonard Lindsey** was born 31 May 1949 in Trieste, Italy, died 30 Sep 1963, and was buried in Melbourne, FL.

481. Marvin Glenn Lindsey (*Adron Leonard (Green) Lindsey Jr.*[5], *Adron Leonard Lindsey Sr.*[4], *Frances (Frankie) Sharp*[3], *Charles W. Sr.*[2], *John Sr.*[1]) was born 4 Nov 1919 in Lauderdale County, AL.

Marvin married **Betty Jean Gullett** 18 Aug 1946. Betty was born 22 Feb 1927 in Camden, TN.
+ 1145 M i. **Richard G. Lindsey** was born 26 Jan 1947, died 6 Oct 1992, and was buried in Valhalla Memorial Gardens, Huntsville, AL.
+ 1146 F ii. **Andrea Ophelia Ellender Lindsey** was born 16 Aug 1948.
+ 1147 F iii. **Brenda Jean Lindsey** was born 16 Apr 1951.

482. Claude Raymond Lindsey Sr. (*Adron Leonard (Green) Lindsey Jr.*[5], *Adron Leonard Lindsey Sr.*[4], *Frances (Frankie) Sharp*[3], *Charles W. Sr.*[2], *John Sr.*[1]) was born 24 Apr 1922 in Lauderdale County, AL.

Claude married **Mary Lois Williams**, daughter of **W. T. Williams** and *Unk, 26 Jun 1939 in Lafayette, GA. Mary was born 11 Feb 1923 in Lauderdale County, AL.
+ 1148 M i. **William Richard Lindsey** was born 31 Aug 1939 in Lauderdale County, AL.

Claude next married **Eloise Keech Brown**. Eloise was born 18 Feb 1928 in Montgomery, AL.
+ 1149 F i. **Patricia Elois Lindsey** was born 5 Sep 1947.
+ 1150 F ii. **Lucy Claudette Lindsey** was born 3 Jan 1950.
+ 1151 M iii. **Claude Raymond Lindsey Jr.** was born 10 Mar 1953 in Montgomery, AL.
+ 1152 F iv. **Judith (Judy) Lynn Lindsey** was born 27 May 1955 in Montgomery, AL.
  1153 F v. **Julia Suzanne Lindsey** was born 24 Jun 1960 in San Antonio, TX, died 16 Dec 1991, and was buried in Union Grove United Methodist Cemetery, Eclectic, AL.

General Notes: "Julia was a full- time Alabama National Guard Sergeant. She met a tragic death at Montgomery, Alabama, on the night of December 16, 1991. While on her way to a friend's house, she was killed as the result of a random shooting by three black men who drove up beside her as she was waiting for a traffic light. Julia is buried in the Union Grove United Methodist Church cemetery at Eclectic, a few miles from Wetumpka, Alabama..." William McDonald

  1154 M vi. **Mark Howard Lindsey** was born 11 Mar 1964 in Tinker AFB, Oklahoma City, OK and died 10 Oct 1995.

484. Grover Cleveland Young (*Eddie Young*[5], *Mary M. (Polly II) Lindsey*[4], *Frances (Frankie) Sharp*[3], *Charles W. Sr.*[2], *John Sr.*[1]) was born 9 Nov 1892 in Lauderdale County, AL, died 3 Feb 1936, and was buried in Pensacola, Escambia County, FL.

Grover married **Lullie Garner**. Lullie was born in Lauderdale County, AL.

485. William (Bill) Mack Young (*Eddie Young*[5], *Mary M. (Polly II) Lindsey*[4], *Frances (Frankie) Sharp*[3], *Charles W. Sr.*[2], *John Sr.*[1]) was born 17 May 1894 in Lauderdale County, AL, died 8 Dec 1971, and was buried in Tri-Cities Memorial Gardens, Florence, Lauderdale County, AL.

William married **Clura Mae Moore**, daughter of **George Will Moore** and **Emma White**, 26 Jul 1919 in Lauderdale County, AL. Clura was born 30 May 1902 in Lauderdale County, AL, died 11 Aug 1992, and was buried in Tri-Cities Memorial Gardens, Florence, Lauderdale County, AL.

+ 1155 F i. **Jewel Dean Young** was born 2 Dec 1919 in Lauderdale County, AL, died 2 Jun 2000, and was buried in Tri-Cities Memorial Gardens, Florence, Lauderdale County, AL.

+ 1156 M ii. **Melvin Eugene Young** was born 15 Mar 1926 in Lauderdale County, AL and was buried in Stutts Road Cemetery, Greenhill, Lauderdale County, AL.

+ 1157 F iii. **Ruby Dale Young** was born 11 Nov 1931 in Lauderdale County, AL and was buried in Lauderdale County, AL.

+ 1158 M iv. **James Robert Young** was born 15 Aug 1935 in Lauderdale County, AL.

+ 1159 F v. **Shirley Ann Young** was born 11 Feb 1939 in Lauderdale County, AL.

486. Nellie Bell Young (*Eddie Young⁵, Mary M. (Polly II) Lindsey⁴, Frances (Frankie) Sharp³, Charles W. Sr.², John Sr.¹*) was born 3 Sep 1895 in Lauderdale County, AL, died 22 Aug 1945, and was buried in Mishawaka, St Joseph County, IN.

Nellie married **Royal N. R. Biggs** 20 Feb 1919 in Lauderdale County, AL. Royal was buried in Mishawaka, St Joseph County, IN.

+ 1160 F i. **Clara Kay Biggs**.
1161 M ii. **Edward (Eddie) Biggs**.
1162 M iii. **William Biggs**.
1163 F iv. **Ruby Biggs**.

487. Earnest Edward Young (*Eddie Young⁵, Mary M. (Polly II) Lindsey⁴, Frances (Frankie) Sharp³, Charles W. Sr.², John Sr.¹*) was born 3 May 1900 in Lauderdale County, AL, died 6 Aug 1971, and was buried in Murphy's Chapel Cemetery, Lauderdale County, AL.

Earnest married **Maudie Alice Bevis**, daughter of **Matthew M. Bevis** and **Dora K. Young**, 29 Oct 1921 in Lauderdale County, AL. Maudie was born 16 Jun 1903 in Lauderdale County, AL, died 8 Sep 1957, and was buried in Murphy's Chapel Cemetery, Lauderdale County, AL.

1164 M i. **Douglas E. Young** was born in Lauderdale County, AL and was buried in Murphy's Chapel Cemetery, Lauderdale County, AL.

+ 1165 M ii. **Cecil Lloyd Young** was born 22 Dec 1926 in Lauderdale County, AL, died 7 Mar 2002, and was buried in Greenview Memorial Park, Florence, Lauderdale County, AL.

+ 1166 M iii. **Jay Fred Young** was born 28 May 1929 in Lauderdale County, AL.

+ 1167 M iv. **Doyal Lee Young Sr.** was born 28 Aug 1937 in Lauderdale County, AL, died 10 Jan 1994, and was buried in Murphy's Chapel Cemetery, Lauderdale County, AL.

+ 1168 M v. **Harold Moore Young** was born 27 Oct 1942 in Lauderdale County, AL.

+ 1169 F vi. **Hazel Joyce Young** was born 16 Oct 1944 in Lauderdale County, AL.

488. Willie Leona Young (*Eddie Young⁵, Mary M. (Polly II) Lindsey⁴, Frances (Frankie) Sharp³, Charles W. Sr.², John Sr.¹*) was born 28 Sep 1907 in Lauderdale County, AL, died 5 Jan 2001, and was buried in Murphy's Chapel Cemetery, Lauderdale County, AL.

Willie married **Dewey Marlin Witt**, son of **Johnny R. Witt** and **Susie Ann Balentine**, 23 Dec 1934 in Lauderdale County, AL. Dewey was born 3 May 1909 in Lauderdale County, AL, died 30 May 1989, and was buried in Murphy's Chapel Cemetery, Lauderdale County, AL.

+ 1170 F i. **Elsie Irene Witt** was born 1 Feb 1936 in Lauderdale County, AL.
1171 M ii. **Charles D. Witt** was born 6 Dec 1946 in Lauderdale County, AL, died 23 May 2002, and was buried in Murphy's Chapel Cemetery, Lauderdale County, AL.

489. Odus Clarence Young Sr. (*Eddie Young⁵, Mary M. (Polly II) Lindsey⁴, Frances (Frankie) Sharp³, Charles W. Sr.², John Sr.¹*) was born 7 Mar 1909 in Lauderdale County, AL, died 1 Jun 1968, and was buried in Murphy's Chapel Cemetery, Lauderdale County, AL.

Odus married **Nettie Bethel Bruce**, daughter of **Robert William Bruce** and **Mamie Rogers**, 30 Oct 1927 in Waynesboro, TN. Nettie was born 26 Jul 1911 in Lauderdale County, AL, died 9 Jan 1998, and was buried in Murphy's Chapel Cemetery, Lauderdale County, AL.

+ 1172 F i. **Macil Bethrine Young** was born 25 Mar 1928 in Lauderdale County, AL, died 21 Jan 1995, and was buried in Canaan Cemetery, Lauderdale County, AL.

+ 1173 F ii. **Carlene Vernial Young** was born 31 Mar 1933 in Lauderdale County, AL.

+ 1174 M iii. **Clarence William (C. W.) Young** was born 14 Apr 1937 in Lauderdale County, AL and died 15 Jun 1998 in Lauderdale County, AL.

+ 1175 M iv. **Melvin Lee Young** was born 16 Oct 1939 in Lauderdale County, AL, died 4 Aug 1993, and was buried in McKinney Cemetery, Rogersville, TN.

   1176 M v. **Odus Clarence Young Jr.** was born in 1940 in Lauderdale County, AL, died 15 Jun 1998, and was buried in Lauderdale County, AL.

490. Jessie Bell Dearen (*Mary Francis (Molly) Young ^{5}, Mary M. (Polly II) Lindsey ^{4}, Frances (Frankie) Sharp ^{3}, Charles W. Sr. ^{2}, John Sr. ^{1}*) was born 2 Nov 1891 in Waterloo, Lauderdale County, AL, died 5 Feb 1955, and was buried in Florence City Cemetery, Florence, Lauderdale County, AL.

Jessie married **Jones Elbert Murphy**, son of **Carroll Murphy** and **Sara McKelvey**, 9 Aug 1908 in Lauderdale County, AL. Jones was born 14 May 1889 in Lauderdale County, AL, died 16 May 1959, and was buried in Florence City Cemetery, Florence, Lauderdale County, AL.

+ 1177 M i. **Robert Arnold Murphy** was born 25 Jul 1909 in Lauderdale County, AL, died 13 Aug 1990, and was buried in Greenview Memorial Park, Florence, Lauderdale County, AL.

   1178 F ii. **Mary Etta Murphy** was born 12 Nov 1910 in Lauderdale County, AL, died 26 Nov 2000, and was buried in Florence City Cemetery, Florence, Lauderdale County, AL.

+ 1179 M iii. **Doyal Lee Murphy** was born 24 Sep 1913 in Lauderdale County, AL, died 27 Mar 1948, and was buried in Florence City Cemetery, Florence, Lauderdale County, AL.

+ 1180 F iv. **Jenny Ione Murphy** was born 22 Feb 1916 in Waco, McLennan County, TX, died 15 Apr 2001, and was buried in Mt. Zion Cemetery, Lauderdale County, AL.

+ 1181 M v. **Karl Jones Murphy** was born 23 Oct 1917 in Lorena, TX, died 13 Nov 1992, and was buried in Tri-Cities Memorial Gardens, Florence, Lauderdale County, AL.

+ 1182 F vi. **Ora Kyleene Murphy** was born 27 May 1920 in Lauderdale County, AL.

491. William Lee Dearen (*Mary Francis (Molly) Young ^{5}, Mary M. (Polly II) Lindsey ^{4}, Frances (Frankie) Sharp ^{3}, Charles W. Sr. ^{2}, John Sr. ^{1}*) was born 8 Jun 1893 in Lauderdale County, AL and died in Oct 1981 in Waco, McLennan County, TX.

William married **Lena Pack**, daughter of **J. L. Pack** and **Mae Harris**. Lena was born in 1898 in Waco, McLennan County, TX and died in Apr 1972 in Waco, McLennan County, TX.

+ 1183 F i. **Hazel Inez Dearen** was born 14 Aug 1917 in Waco, McLennan County, TX.

+ 1184 F ii. **Mildred Pauline Dearen** was born 29 Sep 1919 in Waco, McLennan County, TX.

+ 1185 F iii. **Vera Mae Dearen** was born 29 Sep 1922 in Waco, McLennan County, TX.

492. Minnie Pearl Dearen (*Mary Francis (Molly) Young ^{5}, Mary M. (Polly II) Lindsey ^{4}, Frances (Frankie) Sharp ^{3}, Charles W. Sr. ^{2}, John Sr. ^{1}*) was born 18 Dec 1894 in Lauderdale County, AL, died 5 May 1983, and was buried in Williams Chapel Cemetery, Lauderdale County, AL.

Minnie married **Tommie Boise Sego**, son of **George Washington Sego** and **Virginia Alice Jackson**, 1 May 1910 in Lauderdale County, AL. Tommie was born 24 May 1890 in Lauderdale County, AL, died 1 Apr 1983, and was buried in Williams Chapel Cemetery, Lauderdale County, AL.

+ 1186 F i. **Della V. Abilene Sego** was born 14 Mar 1911 in Lauderdale County, AL, died 23 Feb 1997, and was buried in Murphy's Chapel Cemetery, Lauderdale County, AL.

+ 1187 F ii. **Mary Alice Sego** was born 19 Jun 1913 in Lauderdale County, AL, died 28 Nov 1994, and was buried in Chapel Hills Memorial Gardens, Mishawaka, IN.

+ 1188 F iii. **Frances Boyce Sego** was born 1 Mar 1915 in Waterloo, Lauderdale County, AL.

   1189 M iv. **Johnnie W. Sego** was born 4 Nov 1918 in Lauderdale County, AL, died 29 Jun 1920, and was buried in Williams Chapel Cemetery, Lauderdale County, AL.

+ 1190 M v. **Willie Doyal Sego** was born 25 Mar 1924 in Lauderdale County, AL, died 15 Nov 2002, and was buried in Crestwood Cemetery, Gadsden, AL.

+ 1191 F vi. **Clara Bell Sego** was born 18 May 1928 in Waterloo, Lauderdale County, AL.

493. James Edgar Dearen (*Mary Francis (Molly) Young* [5]*, Mary M. (Polly II) Lindsey* [4]*, Frances (Frankie) Sharp* [3]*, Charles W. Sr.* [2]*, John Sr.* [1]) was born 15 Apr 1897 in Lauderdale County, AL, died 5 Dec 1964 in Marlin, TX, and was buried in Hamilton Cemetery, Corsicana, TX.

James married **Margie White**.
1192 M i. **William Merle Dearen** was born 14 Mar 1922 in Waco, McLennan County, TX.

James next married **Jimmie Lee Perkins**, daughter of **James Perkins** and **Sarah Gray**, 4 Nov 1933 in Corsicana, Navarro County, TX.
+ 1193 M i. **John Lemuel Dearen** was born 25 Jul 1934 in Waco, McLennan County, TX.
+ 1194 M ii. **Edgar Lee Dearen** was born 15 Oct 1936 in Corsicana, Navarro County, TX.
+ 1195 F iii. **Nancy Ray Dearen** was born 15 Sep 1938 in Corsicana, Navarro County, TX.
+ 1196 F iv. **Martha Dearen** was born 31 Dec 1939 in Corsicana, Navarro County, TX and died 22 Oct 1997 in Corsicana, Navarro County, TX.

494. Clara Edna Dearen (*Mary Francis (Molly) Young* [5]*, Mary M. (Polly II) Lindsey* [4]*, Frances (Frankie) Sharp* [3]*, Charles W. Sr.* [2]*, John Sr.* [1]) was born 21 Nov 1898 in Lauderdale County, AL, died 19 Jul 1978, and was buried in Murphy's Chapel Cemetery, Lauderdale County, AL.

General Notes: "Clara was about 1 1/2 years old when her mother died. A niece of John Dearen, Carrie and husband Charles Murphy took her in and raised her...info from Elijah Young book..." Sharon Wood

Clara married **James Claude South**, son of **John T. South** and **Hattie Dowdy**, 8 Jan 1918 in Lauderdale County, AL. James was born 30 Nov 1892 in Lauderdale County, AL, died 15 Sep 1971, and was buried in Murphy's Chapel Cemetery, Lauderdale County, AL.
1197 M i. **James South** was born 10 Oct 1918 in Lauderdale County, AL, died 14 Oct 1923, and was buried in Murphy's Chapel Cemetery, Lauderdale County, AL.
1198 M ii. **Infant South** was born 27 Aug 1931 in Lauderdale County, AL, died 27 Aug 1931, and was buried in Murphy's Chapel Cemetery, Lauderdale County, AL.
+ 1199 M iii. **Rufus Allen South** was born 20 Dec 1933 in Lauderdale County, AL.
+ 1200 F iv. **Eva Leigh South** was born 2 Feb 1939 in Lauderdale County, AL, died 5 Jul 1972, and was buried in Murphy's Chapel Cemetery, Lauderdale County, AL.

495. Florence L. Ticer (*Roxie Leona Young* [5]*, Mary M. (Polly II) Lindsey* [4]*, Frances (Frankie) Sharp* [3]*, Charles W. Sr.* [2]*, John Sr.* [1]) was born 25 Oct 1889 in Lauderdale County, AL, died 23 May 1955, and was buried in Williams Chapel Cemetery, Lauderdale County, AL.

Florence married **A. J. (Will) Dailey Sr.** 20 Nov 1909 in Lauderdale County, AL. A. was buried in White's Creek Cemetery, Hardin County, TN.
+ 1201 M i. **William (Doc) Turner Dailey Sr.** was born 6 Dec 1911 in Lauderdale County, AL, died 7 Sep 1974, and was buried in Cloverdale COC Cemetery, Lauderdale County, AL.

Florence next married **Andrew Jackson Dennis**, son of **John Dennis** and **Suzann Tidwell**, 7 Mar 1915 in Tennessee. Andrew was born 4 Mar 1883 in Alabama, died 11 Aug 1971, and was buried in Piney Grove Cemetery, Lauderdale County, AL.
+ 1202 M i. **Clarence L. V. Dennis** was born 20 Sep 1915 in Lauderdale County, AL, died 6 Apr 1990 in Lauderdale County, AL, and was buried in Greenview Memorial Park, Florence, Lauderdale County, AL.
+ 1203 M ii. **John Albert Dennis** was born in 1917 in Lauderdale County, AL, died 3 Apr 1983, and was buried in Tri-Cities Memorial Gardens, Florence, Lauderdale County, AL.
+ 1204 M iii. **Dalton L. Dennis** was born 25 Jun 1919 in Lauderdale County, AL.
+ 1205 F iv. **Christine Dennis** was born 16 Jun 1921 in Hardin County, TN.
+ 1206 M v. **Troy Burlon Dennis** was born 18 Jul 1923 in Hardin County, TN, died 5 Jul 1992, and was buried in Tri-Cities Memorial Gardens, Florence, Lauderdale County, AL.
+ 1207 M vi. **Curtis Dennis** was born 20 Oct 1925 in Waterloo, Lauderdale County, AL.
+ 1208 F vii. **Dorothy W. Dennis** was born 7 Jul 1933 in Hardin County, TN.

496. Robert Clark Ticer II (*Roxie Leona Young[5], Mary M. (Polly II) Lindsey[4], Frances (Frankie) Sharp[3], Charles W. Sr.[2], John Sr.[1]*) was born 12 Feb 1892 in Lauderdale County, AL, died 26 Jan 1966, and was buried in Williams Chapel Cemetery, Lauderdale County, AL.

Robert married **Virgie E. May**, daughter of **Taylor May** and **Ida *Unk**, 19 May 1918 in Lauderdale County, AL. Virgie was born 22 Nov 1899 in Lauderdale County, AL, died 8 Mar 1966, and was buried in Williams Chapel Cemetery, Lauderdale County, AL.

+ 1209 F i. **Elsie Irene Ticer** was born in Apr 1920 in Waterloo, Lauderdale County, AL, died in Apr 1989, and was buried in Osceola, Elkhart County, IN.
+ 1210 M ii. **Raymond Cecil Ticer Sr.** was born 10 May 1922 in Lauderdale County, AL, died 21 Feb 1989, and was buried in Shady Grove Cemetery, Colbert County, AL.
+ 1211 M iii. **James Allen Ticer** was born 4 Jul 1924 in Waterloo, Lauderdale County, AL, died 20 Oct 1998, and was buried in Williams Chapel Cemetery, Lauderdale County, AL.
+ 1212 F iv. **Joy M. Ticer** was born 27 Oct 1926 in Waterloo, Lauderdale County, AL.
+ 1213 F v. **Velva Ticer** was born 6 Jan 1928 in Waterloo, Lauderdale County, AL.
+ 1214 M vi. **Arnold Lee Ticer** was born 5 May 1931 in Waterloo, Lauderdale County, AL.
+ 1215 F vii. **Doris (Elwee) Ticer** was born 19 Oct 1933 in Waterloo, Lauderdale County, AL.
+ 1216 M viii. **Robert Ernest Ticer** was born 3 Feb 1937 in Waterloo, Lauderdale County, AL and was buried in Eudora, AR.

498. Mary Ann Ticer (*Roxie Leona Young[5], Mary M. (Polly II) Lindsey[4], Frances (Frankie) Sharp[3], Charles W. Sr.[2], John Sr.[1]*) was born 23 Mar 1896 in Lauderdale County, AL, died 7 Apr 1951, and was buried in Richardson Cemetery, Lauderdale County, AL.

Mary married **Jasper Clarence Weaver**, son of **John Sidney Weaver** and **Nellie R. White**, 13 Aug 1916 in Lauderdale County, AL. Jasper was born 30 May 1896 in Hardin County, TN, died 18 Apr 1968, and was buried in Richardson Cemetery, Lauderdale County, AL.

+ 1217 F i. **Virtie Viola Weaver** was born 5 Jul 1918 in Lauderdale County, AL.
+ 1218 F ii. **Roxie Lucille Weaver** was born 22 Jun 1921 in Lauderdale County, AL, died 2 Apr 1993, and was buried in Chapel Hills Memorial Gardens, Mishawaka, IN.
+ 1219 F iii. **Clara Oneita Weaver** was born 17 Aug 1925 in Lauderdale County, AL.
+ 1220 M iv. **James Paul Weaver** was born 8 Nov 1927 in Lauderdale County, AL.
+ 1221 M v. **William Clarence Weaver** was born 15 Oct 1931 in Lauderdale County, AL.
+ 1222 F vi. **Mary June Weaver** was born 30 Mar 1934 in Lauderdale County, AL, died 28 Apr 2004, and was buried in Chapel Hills Memorial Gardens, Mishawaka, IN.

500. Ada Bell Ticer (*Roxie Leona Young[5], Mary M. (Polly II) Lindsey[4], Frances (Frankie) Sharp[3], Charles W. Sr.[2], John Sr.[1]*) was born 28 Jan 1900 in Lauderdale County, AL, died 31 Dec 1974, and was buried in Williams Chapel Cemetery, Lauderdale County, AL.

Ada married **Clarence W. Young**, son of **John Nicholas Young** and **Matilda Ann White**, 14 Nov 1915 in Lauderdale County, AL. Clarence was born 26 Sep 1897 in Lauderdale County, AL, died 2 Mar 1985, and was buried in Williams Chapel Cemetery, Lauderdale County, AL.
(Duplicate Line. See Person 347)

501. David (Dave) Washington Ticer (*Roxie Leona Young[5], Mary M. (Polly II) Lindsey[4], Frances (Frankie) Sharp[3], Charles W. Sr.[2], John Sr.[1]*) was born 10 Mar 1902 in Lauderdale County, AL, died 3 Mar 1960, and was buried in Williams Chapel Cemetery, Lauderdale County, AL.

David married **Erma Lillian Smith**, daughter of **Joseph Spencer Smith** and **Alice Elizabeth Norad**, 23 Jan 1933 in Lauderdale County, AL. Erma was born 24 Jun 1906 in Russ Chapel, TN, died 22 Jul 1998, and was buried in Richardson Cemetery, Lauderdale County, AL.

+ 1223 M i. **Bobby Joe Ticer** was born 26 Oct 1933 in Saltillo, TN, died 16 Apr 1997, and was buried in Richardson Cemetery, Lauderdale County, AL.
+ 1224 M ii. **Montie Wayne Ticer** was born 19 Apr 1936 in Lauderdale County, AL, died 16 Nov 1985, and was buried in Richardson Cemetery, Lauderdale County, AL.
+ 1225 F iii. **Peggy Ann Ticer** was born 7 Dec 1938 in Lauderdale County, AL.

502. Myrtle S. Ticer (*Roxie Leona Young[5], Mary M. (Polly II) Lindsey[4], Frances (Frankie) Sharp[3], Charles W. Sr.[2], John Sr.[1]*) was born 3 Mar 1904 in Lauderdale County, AL, died 5 Jan 1931, and was buried in Williams Chapel Cemetery, Lauderdale County, AL.

Myrtle married **William Claude Goodman Sr.** 25 Feb 1920 in Lauderdale County, AL. William was born 7 Dec 1902 in Lauderdale County, AL, died 29 Nov 1952, and was buried in Williams Chapel Cemetery, Lauderdale County, AL.

+ 1226 F   i.   **Deaner Beatrice Goodman** was born 15 Feb 1915.
  1227 M   ii. **Clifford Lee Goodman** was born 21 Jan 1921 in Lauderdale County, AL, died 19 Dec 1991, and was buried in Williams Chapel Cemetery, Lauderdale County, AL.
  1228 M   iii. **William Claude Goodman Jr.** was born 8 Jan 1927 in Lauderdale County, AL, died 4 Nov 1989, and was buried in Williams Chapel Cemetery, Lauderdale County, AL.
  1229 M   iv. **Rayborn Eugene Goodman** was born 27 May 1929 in Lauderdale County, AL, died 3 Oct 1987, and was buried in Williams Chapel Cemetery, Lauderdale County, AL.
+ 1230 F   v.   **Earline Inese Goodman** was born in Lauderdale County, AL, died in Oct 1951, and was buried in Stoney Point Cemetery, Lauderdale County, AL.

503. Lillian T. Ticer (*Roxie Leona Young[5], Mary M. (Polly II) Lindsey[4], Frances (Frankie) Sharp[3], Charles W. Sr.[2], John Sr.[1]*) was born 27 Apr 1906 in Lauderdale County, AL, died 1 May 1984, and was buried in Wright Cemetery, Wright, Lauderdale County, AL.

Lillian married **Homer Lee Jones**, son of **Johnny Weakley Jones I** and **Dora E. Reeder**, 24 May 1924 in Lauderdale County, AL. Homer was born 26 Nov 1896 in Lauderdale County, AL, died 1 Dec 1969, and was buried in Wright Cemetery, Wright, Lauderdale County, AL.

  1231 M   i.   **Dalton Earl Jones** was born 19 Mar 1925 in Lauderdale County, AL, died 20 Feb 1939, and was buried in Wright Cemetery, Wright, Lauderdale County, AL.
+ 1232 F   ii.   **Gladys Marie Jones** was born 26 Feb 1927 in Lauderdale County, AL.
  1233 M   iii. **Vernon Lee Jones** was born 9 Apr 1929 in Lauderdale County, AL.
+ 1234 M   iv.   **James Ellis Jones** was born 30 May 1931 in Lauderdale County, AL, died 2 Jan 1985, and was buried in Wright Cemetery, Wright, Lauderdale County, AL.
+ 1235 M   v.   **Charles Edward Jones** was born 16 Sep 1935 in Lauderdale County, AL.
+ 1236 F   vi.   **Nina Faye Jones** was born 6 Oct 1937 in Lauderdale County, AL.
+ 1237 M   vii. **Roy Lynn Jones** was born 20 Jan 1940 in Lauderdale County, AL.
+ 1238 M   viii. **Kenneth Ray Jones** was born 2 Oct 1942 in Lauderdale County, AL, died 7 Mar 1970, and was buried in Wright Cemetery, Wright, Lauderdale County, AL.

504. Lois V. Ticer (*Roxie Leona Young[5], Mary M. (Polly II) Lindsey[4], Frances (Frankie) Sharp[3], Charles W. Sr.[2], John Sr.[1]*) was born in 1909 in Lauderdale County, AL and died 18 Dec 1984.

Lois married **Arthur H. Peters**. Arthur was born in 1909 and died in 1958.

505. Pearl Etta Ticer (*Roxie Leona Young[5], Mary M. (Polly II) Lindsey[4], Frances (Frankie) Sharp[3], Charles W. Sr.[2], John Sr.[1]*) was born 24 Aug 1911 in Lauderdale County, AL, died 28 Nov 1992, and was buried in Murphy's Chapel Cemetery, Lauderdale County, AL.

Pearl married **Benjamin Franklin Brown Sr.**, son of **Marvin Francis Brown** and **Clara South**, 23 Aug 1930 in Lauderdale County, AL. Benjamin was born 26 Sep 1911 in Lauderdale County, AL, died 5 Feb 1988 in Birmingham, Jefferson County, AL, and was buried in Murphy's Chapel Cemetery, Lauderdale County, AL.

+ 1239 F   i.   **Jimmie Nell Brown** was born 15 Dec 1936 in Lauderdale County, AL.
+ 1240 M   ii.   **Benjamin Franklin Brown Jr.** was born 21 May 1939 in Lauderdale County, AL.
+ 1241 M   iii. **Ronnie Lowell Brown** was born 7 Jun 1941 in Lauderdale County, AL.
+ 1242 F   iv.   **Dorothy (Dottie) Norene Brown** was born 24 Nov 1943 in Lauderdale County, AL.

506. Hettie Milford (*Delia (Dee) Young[5], Mary M. (Polly II) Lindsey[4], Frances (Frankie) Sharp[3], Charles W. Sr.[2], John Sr.[1]*) was born 28 Jun 1889 in Gravely Springs, Lauderdale County, AL, died 1 Oct 1985, and was buried in Forrest Hill Mid Town Cemetery, Memphis, TN.

Hettie married **Burton Elias Chambers**. Burton was born 28 Jan 1880 in Fayette County, TN.

  1243 F   i.   **Mary Chambers** was born 12 Aug 1908.

1244	M	ii.	**Samuel Elias Chambers**.
+ 1245	F	iii.	**Princess Inez Chambers**.
1246	M	iv.	**Burton Chambers**.
+ 1247	M	v.	**Milford Faxon Chambers**.
1248	M	vi.	**Hubert Chambers**.
+ 1249	M	vii.	**Woodrow Chambers** was born in 1917 in Memphis, Shelby County, TN, died 14 Jan 1998, and was buried in Ashland Cemetery, Ashland, MS.

Hettie next married **Ewing Lamar Maupin Sr.** 18 Aug 1925 in Marion, Crittenden County, AR. Ewing was born in 1879 in Richmond , KY.

1250	M	i.	**Ewing Lamar Maupin Jr.**
+ 1251	F	ii.	**Elizabeth Virgina Maupin** was born 27 Jun 1929 in Memphis, Shelby County, TN.
+ 1252	F	iii.	**Jo Anna Maupin** was born 20 Oct 1934 in Memphis, Shelby County, TN.

507. Etta Lee Milford (*Delia (Dee) Young⁵, Mary M. (Polly II) Lindsey⁴, Frances (Frankie) Sharp³, Charles W. Sr.², John Sr.¹*) was born 12 Jul 1890 in Rhodesville, Lauderdale County, AL, died 21 Feb 1985, and was buried in Chapel Hill Memorial Garden, Osceola, IN.

Etta married **James Frederick (Fred) Perkins** 20 Feb 1908 in Tyronza, Poinsett County, AR. James was born 31 Jul 1881 in Tyronza, Poinsett County, AR, died 7 Jun 1932 in Trumann, AR, and was buried in Arkansas.

+ 1253	F	i.	**Elsie Perkins** was born 28 Apr 1909 in Tyronza, Poinsett County, AR.
+ 1254	F	ii.	**Nancy Delia (Dee) Perkins** was born 3 Dec 1910 in Magazine, AR.
+ 1255	M	iii.	**James Douglas Perkins** was born 23 Sep 1912 in Magazine, AR and died 23 Nov 1978 in St. Joseph County, IN.
+ 1256	M	iv.	**Woodrow Wilson Perkins** was born 12 Oct 1914 in Vineyard, Phillips, AR and died in Jul 1975 in Jonesboro, Craighead County, AR.
+ 1257	F	v.	**Freddie Perkins** was born 25 Dec 1917 in Arkansas.
+ 1258	M	vi.	**Samuel Burton Perkins** was born 23 Aug 1919 in Weona, Poinsett County, AR and died 18 Sep 1981 in Indiana.
+ 1259	F	vii.	**Annie Lue Perkins** was born 28 Aug 1923 in Weona, Poinsett County, AR, died 22 Dec 2004, and was buried in Chapel Hill Memorial Garden, Osceola, IN.
1260	M	viii.	**Joseph Lee Perkins** was born 25 Sep 1925 in Weona, Poinsett County, AR and died 7 Mar 1926 in Weona, Poinsett County, AR.

Etta next married **Charlie F. Glass** in Feb 1943 in Trumann, AR. Charlie died in 1958.

508. Ada Young (*Lou Young⁵, Mary M. (Polly II) Lindsey⁴, Frances (Frankie) Sharp³, Charles W. Sr.², John Sr.¹*) was born 28 Mar 1892 in Lauderdale County, AL, died 1 Apr 1975, and was buried in Greenview Memorial Park, Florence, Lauderdale County, AL.

Ada married **Johnny Weakley Jones II**, son of **Johnny Weakley Jones I** and **Dora E. Reeder**, 9 Jan 1914 in Lauderdale County, AL. Johnny was born 10 Apr 1887 in Lauderdale County, AL, died 9 Jan 1968, and was buried in Greenview Memorial Park, Florence, Lauderdale County, AL.

1261	F	i.	**Infant Jones** was born 5 Dec 1914 in Lauderdale County, AL, died 27 Dec 1914, and was buried in Murphy's Chapel Cemetery, Lauderdale County, AL.
+ 1262	M	ii.	**Robert Dalton Jones** was born 20 Jun 1916 in Lauderdale County, AL.
+ 1263	F	iii.	**Mary Louise Jones** was born 11 Jul 1918 in Lauderdale County, AL, died 7 Dec 2001, and was buried in Greenview Memorial Park, Florence, Lauderdale County, AL.

509. Dave D. Young (*Lou Young⁵, Mary M. (Polly II) Lindsey⁴, Frances (Frankie) Sharp³, Charles W. Sr.², John Sr.¹*) was born 22 Feb 1896 in Lauderdale County, AL, died 9 Feb 1956, and was buried in Greenview Memorial Park, Florence, Lauderdale County, AL.

Dave married **Ester Whitten**, daughter of **William T. Whitten** and **Mary B. Lovelace**, 7 Oct 1923 in Lauderdale County, AL. Ester was born 4 Jan 1903 in Lauderdale County, AL, died 23 Oct 1993, and was buried in Greenview Memorial Park, Florence, Lauderdale County, AL.

511. Verna Virella Young (*Lou Young[5], Mary M. (Polly II) Lindsey[4], Frances (Frankie) Sharp[3], Charles W. Sr.[2], John Sr.[1]*) was born 25 Oct 1902 in Lauderdale County, AL, died 9 Sep 1975, and was buried in Mt. Zion Cemetery, Lauderdale County, AL.

Verna married **McArthur Andrew Billingsley** 23 Feb 1923 in Lauderdale County, AL. McArthur was born 7 Jan 1888 in Lauderdale County, AL, died 7 Aug 1968, and was buried in Mt. Zion Cemetery, Lauderdale County, AL.

+ 1264 M i. **Millard Horace Billingsley** was born 7 Feb 1924 in Lauderdale County, AL.
+ 1265 M ii. **James (Pete) Marshall Billingsley** was born 22 Jan 1926 in Lauderdale County, AL, died 22 Aug 1980, and was buried in Mt. Zion Cemetery, Lauderdale County, AL.
+ 1266 M iii. **William Eugene Billingsley** was born 1 Apr 1930 in Lauderdale County, AL.
+ 1267 M iv. **Grady Earl Billingsley** was born 10 Dec 1931 in Lauderdale County, AL.
+ 1268 M v. **Thomas Moore Billingsley** was born 18 Mar 1933 in Lauderdale County, AL.

512. Mary Etta Young (*Lou Young[5], Mary M. (Polly II) Lindsey[4], Frances (Frankie) Sharp[3], Charles W. Sr.[2], John Sr.[1]*) was born 28 Nov 1908 in Lauderdale County, AL, died 24 Oct 1990, and was buried in Greenview Memorial Park, Florence, Lauderdale County, AL.

Mary married **Thomas Clyde (T. C.) Witt Sr.**, son of **Johnny R. Witt** and **Susie Ann Balentine**, 9 Aug 1925 in Lauderdale County, AL. Thomas was born 11 Aug 1905 in Lauderdale County, AL, died 15 Feb 1989, and was buried in Greenview Memorial Park, Florence, Lauderdale County, AL.

+ 1269 F i. **Ruth Vernet Witt** was born 11 Jun 1927 in Lauderdale County, AL.
+ 1270 M ii. **James Arnold Witt** was born 21 Feb 1929 in Lauderdale County, AL.
+ 1271 M iii. **Virgil David Witt** was born 12 Feb 1931 in Lauderdale County, AL, died 14 Jan 1963, and was buried in Greenview Memorial Park, Florence, Lauderdale County, AL.
+ 1272 F iv. **Ila Jean Witt** was born 3 Mar 1933 in Lauderdale County, AL.
+ 1273 F v. **Betty Lou Witt** was born 2 Feb 1935 in Lauderdale County, AL.
+ 1274 F vi. **Carolyn Sue Witt** was born 22 Aug 1937 in Lauderdale County, AL.
+ 1275 F vii. **Dorothy Jo Witt** was born 12 Nov 1939 in Lauderdale County, AL.
+ 1276 M viii. **Thomas Clyde (T. C.) Witt Jr.** was born 12 Feb 1942 in Lauderdale County, AL.
+ 1277 F ix. **Mary Etta Witt** was born 27 Feb 1944 in Lauderdale County, AL.
+ 1278 F x. **Virginia Francine Witt** was born 12 Feb 1947 in Lauderdale County, AL and was buried in Greenview Memorial Park, Florence, Lauderdale County, AL.
+ 1279 M xi. **Danny Price Witt** was born 7 Sep 1950 in Lauderdale County, AL.
+ 1280 F xii. **Shirley Diane Witt** was born 22 Aug 1952 in Lauderdale County, AL.

513. Della Young (*Lou Young[5], Mary M. (Polly II) Lindsey[4], Frances (Frankie) Sharp[3], Charles W. Sr.[2], John Sr.[1]*) was born 30 Dec 1912 in Lauderdale County, AL, died 12 May 2003, and was buried in Greenview Memorial Park, Florence, Lauderdale County, AL.

Della married **Marvin Virgil Lovelace**, son of **Bennett Pope Lovelace** and **Linnie Ann Hayes**, 1 Mar 1931. Marvin was born 24 Feb 1911 in Lauderdale County, AL, died 6 Jul 1969, and was buried in Greenview Memorial Park, Florence, Lauderdale County, AL.

+ 1281 F i. **Billie Faye Lovelace** was born 19 Feb 1938 in Lauderdale County, AL.
+ 1282 F ii. **Barbara Jean Lovelace** was born 24 Nov 1939 in Lauderdale County, AL.

516. Lavenia Young (*William (Bill) Young[5], Mary M. (Polly II) Lindsey[4], Frances (Frankie) Sharp[3], Charles W. Sr.[2], John Sr.[1]*).

Lavenia married **William Lewis Watkins** 29 Jun 1929 in Lauderdale County, AL.

517. Reba Young (*William (Bill) Young[5], Mary M. (Polly II) Lindsey[4], Frances (Frankie) Sharp[3], Charles W. Sr.[2], John Sr.[1]*).

Reba married **W. N. Bysom**.

519. Vivian Young (*William (Bill) Young[5], Mary M. (Polly II) Lindsey[4], Frances (Frankie) Sharp[3], Charles W. Sr.[2], John Sr.[1]*) was born 27 Mar 1910, died 22 May 1953, and was buried in Pleasant Hill Cemetery, Lauderdale County, AL.

Vivian married **W. L. Dunmire**.

520. Arbie Bevis (*Nancy (Nan) Young[5], Mary M. (Polly II) Lindsey[4], Frances (Frankie) Sharp[3], Charles W. Sr.[2], John Sr.[1]*) was born 22 Jan 1910 in Lauderdale County, AL, died 11 Jun 1965, and was buried in Pine Hill Cemetery, Lauderdale County, AL.

Arbie married **Sarah Ellon *Unk**. Sarah was born 22 Sep 1911, died 26 Jul 1941, and was buried in Pine Hill Cemetery, Lauderdale County, AL.

522. Alonzo Parnell (*Dora Lee Young[5], Mary M. (Polly II) Lindsey[4], Frances (Frankie) Sharp[3], Charles W. Sr.[2], John Sr.[1]*) was born 27 Jul 1899.

Alonzo married **Retha Hairrell** 26 Dec 1920.
1283	M	i.	**Jack Parnell.**
+ 1284	M	ii.	**Doyle Parnell.**
1285	M	iii.	**Howard Parnell.**
1286	M	iv.	**Lenny Parnell.**
1287	F	v.	**Christeen Parnell.**
1288	M	vi.	**J. C. Parnell.**

523. Elbert Parnell (*Dora Lee Young[5], Mary M. (Polly II) Lindsey[4], Frances (Frankie) Sharp[3], Charles W. Sr.[2], John Sr.[1]*) was born 24 Sep 1901.

General Notes: "Elbert & wife had eight children..." Millie Mason

Elbert married **Birdia Hairell** 31 Oct 1920.

524. Lee Parnell (*Dora Lee Young[5], Mary M. (Polly II) Lindsey[4], Frances (Frankie) Sharp[3], Charles W. Sr.[2], John Sr.[1]*) was born 19 Oct 1903.

General Notes: "Lee & wife had 13 children...." Millie Mason

Lee married **Cora Mae Randolph** 12 Sep 1925.

526. Vertia Thora Parnell (*Dora Lee Young[5], Mary M. (Polly II) Lindsey[4], Frances (Frankie) Sharp[3], Charles W. Sr.[2], John Sr.[1]*) was born 28 Nov 1911 in Lauderdale County, AL.

Vertia married **Charles Gordon Bracken** 21 Aug 1930.
1289	M	i.	**Gordon Bracken.**
1290	M	ii.	**James Edward Bracken.**
1291	F	iii.	**Joanne Bracken.**
+ 1292	F	iv.	**Sharon Sue Bracken.**

527. Aladee Parnell (*Dora Lee Young[5], Mary M. (Polly II) Lindsey[4], Frances (Frankie) Sharp[3], Charles W. Sr.[2], John Sr.[1]*) was born 8 Apr 1914, died in 1936, and was buried in Pine Hill Cemetery, Lauderdale County, AL.

Aladee married **William Webster** 6 Apr 1930.

529. Toye R. Young (*Lee Jackson Young[5], Mary M. (Polly II) Lindsey[4], Frances (Frankie) Sharp[3], Charles W. Sr.[2], John Sr.[1]*) was born about 1908 in Lauderdale County, AL, died 1 Nov 1998, and was buried in John Lay Cemetery, Etheridge, TN.

Toye married **Aaron Burr McFall**, son of **Unknown** and **Unknown**. Aaron was born about 1884 in Lawrenceburg, Lawrence County, TN, died in 1963, and was buried in John Lay Cemetery, Etheridge, TN.

+ 1293 F   i.   **Katherine McFall** was born in Waterloo, Lauderdale County, AL.

+ 1294 M   ii.   **Hershel Eugene McFall**.

Toye next married **C. A. Crowell**.

530. Pearl V. Young (*Lee Jackson Young⁵, Mary M. (Polly II) Lindsey⁴, Frances (Frankie) Sharp³, Charles W. Sr.², John Sr.¹*) was born 25 Dec 1910 in Lauderdale County, AL, died 11 Feb 1992, and was buried in Lawrenceburg, Lawrence County, TN.

Pearl married **Dalton R. Sharp**, son of **Charles Edward (Eddie) Sharp** and **Mattie J. Jones**, 31 Jul 1927 in St. Joseph County, IN. Dalton was born 27 Apr 1905 in Lauderdale County, AL, died 31 Jan 1942 in Mishawaka, St Joseph County, IN, and was buried in Lauderdale County, AL.

+ 1295 M   i.   **Virgil Lee Sharp** was born 20 Jun 1928 in Mishawaka, St Joseph County, IN.

Pearl next married **Crosby Mattox** after 1942 in Tennessee.

531. Hosea Leba Young (*Lee Jackson Young⁵, Mary M. (Polly II) Lindsey⁴, Frances (Frankie) Sharp³, Charles W. Sr.², John Sr.¹*) was born 27 May 1913 in Lauderdale County, AL, died 4 Mar 1990, and was buried in Fairview Cemetery, Mishawaka, IN.

Hosea married **Vera May Holcombe** 13 Oct 1933 in Lauderdale County, AL. Vera was born 5 Jun 1914 in Lauderdale County, AL, died 12 Jan 1972, and was buried in Southlawn Cemetery, South Bend, St Joseph County, IN.

+ 1296 M   i.   **Ronnie Lowell Young** was born 16 Sep 1934 in Mishawaka, St Joseph County, IN, died 20 Sep 2000, and was buried in Williams Chapel Cemetery, Lauderdale County, AL.

+ 1297 M   ii.   **James Lee Young** was born 28 Nov 1941 in Mishawaka, St Joseph County, IN.

+ 1298 M   iii.   **Donnie D. Young** was born 10 Mar 1944 in Mishawaka, St Joseph County, IN.

+ 1299 M   iv.   **Larry T. Young** was born 14 May 1947 in Mishawaka, St Joseph County, IN.

Hosea next married **Verda M. Snow**, daughter of **William Snow** and **Mary B. Wakelandis**, 13 Oct 1973 in St. Joseph County, IN. Verda was born 4 Jan 1912 in Linton, IN, died 14 Jul 1994, and was buried in Fairview Cemetery, Mishawaka, IN.

+ 1300 F   i.   **Shirley Young** was born 4 Nov.

532. Monser Lee Young (*Lee Jackson Young⁵, Mary M. (Polly II) Lindsey⁴, Frances (Frankie) Sharp³, Charles W. Sr.², John Sr.¹*) was born 19 Jun 1915 in Lauderdale County, AL, died 12 Oct 2000, and was buried in Fairview Cemetery, Mishawaka, IN.

Monser married **Juanita Faye Geist** 30 Aug 1941 in St. Joseph County, IN. Juanita was born 7 May 1917 in Mongo, IN, died 1 Dec 1994, and was buried in Fairview Cemetery, Mishawaka, IN.

   1301 M   i.   **Lee C. Young** was born 7 Mar 1956 in St. Joseph County, IN.

533. John Hampton (Charlie) Wood (*Louisa F. Lindsey⁵, John S. Lindsey⁴, Frances (Frankie) Sharp³, Charles W. Sr.², John Sr.¹*) was born 16 Mar 1892 in Florence, Lauderdale County, AL, died 4 Feb 1979, and was buried in Snyder, Scurry County, TX.

John married **Lola Smith**, daughter of **Dill Smith** and **Martha Eveline Sands**, 28 Feb 1914 in Searcy, White County, AR. Lola was born 28 Feb and died 3 Mar 1962.

+ 1302 F   i.   **Opal Wood** was born 24 Oct 1917.

+ 1303 M   ii.   **John Franklin Wood** was born 27 Nov 1928.

534. William Hunter Wood (*Louisa F. Lindsey⁵, John S. Lindsey⁴, Frances (Frankie) Sharp³, Charles W. Sr.², John Sr.¹*) was born 20 Dec 1894 in Forrest City, St. Francis County, AR, died 3 Mar 1962, and was buried in Oklahoma City, Oklahoma County, OK.

William married **Bertha *Unk**.

535. Bertha Mae Wood (*Louisa F. Lindsey [5], John S. Lindsey [4], Frances (Frankie) Sharp [3], Charles W. Sr. [2], John Sr. [1]*) was born 25 Feb 1896 in Lauderdale County, AL and died 1 Dec 1921 in Plainview, Lea County, NM.

Bertha married **Clyde Clanton**, son of **Eli Clanton** and **Mary Jones**, 17 May 1914 in Judsonia, White County, AR. Clyde was born 27 Oct 1894 in Walter, White County, AR and died 25 Dec 1989.
+ 1304 F   i.   **Delora May Clanton** was born 27 May 1915 in Griffithville, White County, AR.
+ 1305 M   ii.   **William Carl Clanton** was born 8 Feb 1917 in Kent County, TX.
+ 1306 M   iii.   **Murrell Wilson Clanton** was born 10 Mar 1919.

537. Ada Evelyn Wood (*Louisa F. Lindsey [5], John S. Lindsey [4], Frances (Frankie) Sharp [3], Charles W. Sr. [2], John Sr. [1]*) was born 24 Oct 1902 in Florence, Lauderdale County, AL, died 6 May 1941, and was buried in Snyder, Scurry County, TX.

Ada married **Earl Edward Rinehart**, son of **Ocie Columbus Rinehart** and **Cora May Johnson**, 31 Aug 1931 in Snyder, Scurry County, TX. Earl was born 11 Apr 1908 in Gustine, Comanche County, TX, died 23 Apr 1963 in Hermleigh, TX, and was buried in Snyder, Scurry County, TX.
   1307 F   i.   **Infant Daughter Rinehart** was born 3 Aug 1932 and died 3 Aug 1932 in Snyder, Scurry County, TX.
+ 1308 M   ii.   **Wallace Harold Rinehart** was born 28 Nov 1934 in Snyder, Scurry County, TX.
+ 1309 M   iii.   **William Porter Rinehart** was born 9 Apr 1941 in Snyder, Scurry County, TX.

538. Otha Oneal Wood (*Louisa F. Lindsey [5], John S. Lindsey [4], Frances (Frankie) Sharp [3], Charles W. Sr. [2], John Sr. [1]*) was born 20 Nov 1904 in Arkansas, died 25 Feb 1990, and was buried in North Kearn Cemetery, Delano, Kearn County, CA.

Otha married **Anna *Unk**.

539. Elmer Cecil Wood (*Louisa F. Lindsey [5], John S. Lindsey [4], Frances (Frankie) Sharp [3], Charles W. Sr. [2], John Sr. [1]*) was born 8 Feb 1907, died 15 Jul 1980 in McCloud, OK, and was buried in Snyder, Scurry County, TX.

Elmer married **Wilma Martin**.
   1310 M   i.   **Bobby Wood**.

540. Lemuel Carl Wood (*Louisa F. Lindsey [5], John S. Lindsey [4], Frances (Frankie) Sharp [3], Charles W. Sr. [2], John Sr. [1]*) was born 24 Nov 1910 in Griffithville, White County, AR, died 7 Feb 1989, and was buried in Snyder, Scurry County, TX.

Lemuel married **Essie Belle Rinehart**, daughter of **Ocie Columbus Rinehart** and **Cora May Johnson**, 9 Mar 1929 in Snyder, Scurry County, TX. Essie was born 16 Mar 1915 in Sidney, Comanche County, TX.
+ 1311 F   i.   **Evelyn May Wood** was born 4 Mar 1930 in Snyder, Scurry County, TX, died 9 Aug 1987, and was buried in Lubbock, Lubbock County, TX.
+ 1312 M   ii.   **Daryl Elmer Wood** was born 28 Jun 1932 in Snyder, Scurry County, TX.

541. Viney Viola Sharp (*Robert Patton [5], James (Jim) Charles Sr. [4], Adron (Edwin/Ade) Sr. [3], Charles W. Sr. [2], John Sr. [1]*) was born 26 Nov 1879 in Lauderdale County, AL, died 18 Jul 1902, and was buried in Gravely Springs Cemetery, Lauderdale County, AL.

Viney married **Samuel Lewis Bruce**, son of **Kern Bruce** and **Mary Scott**. Samuel was born 25 Mar 1877 in Lauderdale County, AL, died 20 Dec 1954, and was buried in Greenview Memorial Park, Florence, Lauderdale County, AL.
+ 1313 F   i.   **Laverne Bruce** was born 4 Nov 1896 in Lauderdale County, AL, died 20 Nov 1975, and was buried in Elmwood Cemetery, Birmingham, AL.
+ 1314 F   ii.   **Patricia Bruce** was born 26 Nov 1897 in Lauderdale County, AL, died 24 Mar 1979, and was buried in Birmingham, Jefferson County, AL.
+ 1315 M   iii.   **Lewis Bruce** was born 24 Oct 1901 in Lauderdale County, AL, died 23 May 1974, and was buried in Gravely Springs Cemetery, Lauderdale County, AL.

543. Carrie Eudora Sharp (*Robert Patton* [5], *James (Jim) Charles Sr.* [4], *Adron (Edwin/Ade) Sr.* [3], *Charles W. Sr.* [2], *John Sr.* [1]) was born 12 Oct 1883 in Lauderdale County, AL, died 3 Jun 1964, and was buried in Florence City Cemetery, Florence, Lauderdale County, AL.

  Carrie married **George Edgar Pickens**, son of **William David Benton Pickens** and **Amanda Joe Faires**, 28 Dec 1898 in Lauderdale County, AL. George was born 12 Dec 1877 in Lauderdale County, AL, died 20 Nov 1949, and was buried in Florence City Cemetery, Florence, Lauderdale County, AL.

  + 1316 F   i.   **Nellie Mae Pickens** was born 22 Sep 1900 in Lauderdale County, AL.
  + 1317 F   ii.   **Stella Iown Pickens** was born 16 Jul 1902 in Lauderdale County, AL, died 6 Apr 1975, and was buried in Florence, Lauderdale County, AL.
  + 1318 F   iii. **Era Viola Pickens** was born 31 Oct 1905 in Lauderdale County, AL and died 24 May 1988.
  + 1319 M   iv.   **Casey Watson Pickens** was born 1 Jan 1908 in Savannah, Hardin County, TN and died 21 Jan 1991.
  + 1320 M   v.   **Cecil Edgar Pickens** was born 12 Mar 1910 in Lauderdale County, AL and died 17 Nov 1973.
  + 1321 M   vi.   **Joe Wilson Pickens** was born 11 Nov 1912 in Lauderdale County, AL.

544. Oscar Eldred Sharp (*Robert Patton* [5], *James (Jim) Charles Sr.* [4], *Adron (Edwin/Ade) Sr.* [3], *Charles W. Sr.* [2], *John Sr.* [1]) was born 10 May 1886 in Lauderdale County, AL and died 7 Jul 1943 in Memphis, Shelby County, TN.

  Oscar married **Madge Counts**.
  1322 F   i.   **Mary Elizabeth Sharp** died at 4 weeks.
  + 1323 M   ii.   **Glen Wilson Sharp** was born 17 Jul 1918 in Ft Smith, AR and died in 2000.

  Oscar next married **Bessie Counts**.

  Oscar next married **Roxie Mae Shore** 17 Jul 1926 in Marian, Lee County, AR. Roxie died 30 Jun 1975 in Marian, Lee County, AR.
  + 1324 M   i.   **Leon Wallace Sharp** was born 5 Sep 1926 in Marian, Lee County, AR and died 1 Apr 1983.
  + 1325 M   ii.   **Joseph Patton Sharp** was born 26 Aug 1929 in Marian, Lee County, AR, died in 2000, and was buried in Marian, Lee County, AR.

545. Robert Marvin Sharp Sr. (*Robert Patton* [5], *James (Jim) Charles Sr.* [4], *Adron (Edwin/Ade) Sr.* [3], *Charles W. Sr.* [2], *John Sr.* [1]) was born 21 Mar 1888 in Lauderdale County, AL and died 18 Nov 1957 in Hardin County, TN.

  Robert married **Edna Kirby** 29 Mar 1912 in Hardin County, TN. Edna was born 21 Oct 1894 in Savannah, Hardin County, TN and died 17 Dec 1961 in Loudon, TN.
  1326 F   i.   **Bernice Estelle Sharp** was born 31 Mar 1913 in Savannah, Hardin County, TN and died 18 Feb 1921.
  + 1327 F   ii.   **Thelma Cornelia Sharp** was born 24 Oct 1914 in Savannah, Hardin County, TN.
  + 1328 M   iii. **Robert Marvin Sharp Jr.** was born 30 Apr 1916 in Savannah, Hardin County, TN.
  + 1329 F   iv.   **Freda Rae Sharp** was born 30 May 1921 in Tyronza, Poinsett County, AR.
  + 1330 M   v.   **James Patton Sharp** was born 18 Apr 1925 in Etowah, AR and died 3 Mar 1982.
  + 1331 M   vi.   **Thomas Earle (Tommy) Sharp** was born 10 Nov 1927.
  + 1332 F   vii. **Melverda Sharp** was born 18 Sep 1932.

546. Virgie Lenora Sharp (*Robert Patton* [5], *James (Jim) Charles Sr.* [4], *Adron (Edwin/Ade) Sr.* [3], *Charles W. Sr.* [2], *John Sr.* [1]) was born 24 Aug 1890 in Lauderdale County, AL and died 13 Sep 1938.

  Virgie married **Marion Andrew Handley** 24 May 1905. Marion was born 1 Aug 1878 and died 29 May 1952.
  + 1333 F   i.   **Irene Handley** was born 17 May 1906.
  1334 F   ii.   **Pauline Handley**.
  + 1335 F   iii. **Trula Handley**.

549. Ella Myrtle Sharp (*Robert Patton* [5], *James (Jim) Charles Sr.* [4], *Adron (Edwin/Ade) Sr.* [3], *Charles W. Sr.* [2], *John Sr.* [1]) was born 17 Jan 1897 in Lauderdale County, AL and died 28 Mar 1984 in Memphis, Shelby County, TN.

  Ella married **William Robert Ashburn** 12 Nov 1916 in Lauderdale County, AL. William was born 5 Mar 1894 in Frenchmans Bayou, AR and died 6 Jun 1981 in Memphis, Shelby County, TN.

+ 1336 M i. **Fay Ashburn.**
+ 1337 F ii. **Virginia Ashburn.**

550. Lizzie Oneita Sharp (*Robert Patton[5], James (Jim) Charles Sr.[4], Adron (Edwin/Ade) Sr.[3], Charles W. Sr.[2], John Sr.[1]*) was born 7 Oct 1899 in Lauderdale County, AL and died 29 Aug 1960.

Lizzie married **Carl C. Gammill** 7 Mar 1915. Carl was born 11 Sep 1883 and died 27 May 1974.
+ 1338 M i. **Robert Arthur Gammill** was born 18 Aug 1918.
+ 1339 M ii. **Bernis Carl Gammill** was born 5 Apr 1921 and died 18 Jan 1965.
+ 1340 F iii. **Ora Elizabeth Gammill** was born 13 Feb 1925.

551. Annie Inez Sharp (*Robert Patton[5], James (Jim) Charles Sr.[4], Adron (Edwin/Ade) Sr.[3], Charles W. Sr.[2], John Sr.[1]*) was born 16 Jun 1902 in Lauderdale County, AL, died 26 Jun 1979, and was buried in Memorial Park, Memphis, TN.

Annie married **Arch Falls.**

Annie next married **Frank Cameron Waggener.** Frank was born 27 May 1898, died 8 Feb 1967, and was buried in Elmwood Cemetery, Memphis, TN.
+ 1341 M i. **Frank Wilson Waggener Sr.** was born 23 May 1924 in Memphis, Shelby County, TN.
+ 1342 F ii. **Gwendolyn Waggener** was born 18 Aug 1926.

Annie next married **Louis Jasper Rochelle**, son of **Thomas Edward Rochelle** and **Rosa Ebray**, 15 May 1936 in Marion, Crittenden County, AR. Louis was born 23 Jul 1894 in Nunnaly, TN.
+ 1343 F i. **Barbara Ann Rochelle** was born 12 Dec 1939 in Memphis, Shelby County, TN.

552. Ida Lois Sharp (*Robert Patton[5], James (Jim) Charles Sr.[4], Adron (Edwin/Ade) Sr.[3], Charles W. Sr.[2], John Sr.[1]*) was born 12 Dec 1905 in Savannah, Hardin County, TN, died 28 Aug 1993, and was buried in Greenview Memorial Park, Florence, Lauderdale County, AL.

Ida married **Orlan Wesley Givens**, son of **Franklin Givens** and **Lucy Phillips**, 5 Jun 1923 in Lauderdale County, AL. Orlan was born 21 Sep 1904 in Lauderdale County, AL, died 23 Mar 1981, and was buried in Greenview Memorial Park, Florence, Lauderdale County, AL.
+ 1344 F i. **Mary Virginia Givens** was born 15 Mar 1924 in Florence, Lauderdale County, AL.
+ 1345 M ii. **Robert Orlan Givens Sr.** was born 5 Sep 1925 in Florence, Lauderdale County, AL, died 18 Dec 1991, and was buried in New Hollywood Cemetery, Elizabeth City, NC.
+ 1346 M iii. **Thomas Edsel Givens** was born 14 Nov 1927 in Florence, Lauderdale County, AL.
+ 1347 F iv. **Francis Ann Givens** was born 21 Nov 1930 in Memphis, Shelby County, TN.
+ 1348 M v. **Billy Fred Givens** was born 22 Dec 1932 in Memphis, Shelby County, TN.

553. Lillian Anna (Lillie) Sharp (*John Thomas (Tom)[5], James (Jim) Charles Sr.[4], Adron (Edwin/Ade) Sr.[3], Charles W. Sr.[2], John Sr.[1]*) was born 10 Aug 1875 in Lauderdale County, AL, died 19 Jun 1944, and was buried in Milledgeville Cemetery, Hardin County, TN.

Lillian married **Benjamin Franklin Rogers**, son of **Albert Beverly Thomas Rogers** and **Elizabeth Ann Moore**, 22 Sep 1900 in Lauderdale County, AL. Benjamin was born 27 Mar 1872 in Lauderdale County, AL, died 17 Sep 1959, and was buried in Milledgeville Cemetery, Hardin County, TN.
+ 1349 F i. **Velma Rogers.**

Back: Junie Rogers Sharp, Ben Franklin Rogers and wife Lillie Ann Sharp Rogers
Front: Albert, Annie Maude Rogers, daughter of Junie, Eliza Ann Moore Rogers
On Ben and Lillie's wedding day.

+ 1350 M ii. **Emmet P. Rogers** was born 26 Jun 1902 in Lauderdale County, AL and died 23 Jun 1962 in McNairy County, TN.

1351 M iii. **William Robert (Bob) Rogers** was born in 1904 in McNairy County, TN and died 12 Oct 1991 in Tennessee.

+ 1352 M iv. **Edmon (Eddie) Falmer Rogers** was born 26 Sep 1905 in Tennessee and died 8 Oct 1980 in McNairy County, TN.

+ 1353 M v. **Claudie Thomas Rogers** was born in 1907 in McNairy County, TN and died in 1987 in Hardin County, TN.

+ 1354 M vi. **Clydie B. Rogers** was born in 1909 in McNairy County, TN and died 4 Sep 1999 in Adamsville, McNairy County, TN.

+ 1355 M vii. **Robert W. Rogers** was born in Hardin County, TN and died 12 Oct 1991 in Hardin County, TN.

1356 M viii. **Woodson Chris Rogers** was born 10 Nov 1910 in McNairy County, TN, died 7 May 1939, and was buried in Milledgeville Cemetery, Hardin County, TN.

554. Maggie Sharp (*John Thomas (Tom)* [5], *James (Jim) Charles Sr.* [4], *Adron (Edwin/Ade) Sr.* [3], *Charles W. Sr.* [2], *John Sr.* [1]) was born in Jun 1877 in Alabama, died in 1905, and was buried in Wright Cemetery, Wright, Lauderdale County, AL.

Maggie married **Milton Sarah Holcombe** 5 Jan 1898 in Lauderdale County, AL. Milton was born in 1874 in Florence, Lauderdale County, AL, died in 1911, and was buried in Wright Cemetery, Wright, Lauderdale County, AL.

+ 1357 M i. **Ernest Powers Holcombe** was born 9 Oct 1898 in Florence, Lauderdale County, AL, died 5 Jan 1978, and was buried in Williams Chapel Cemetery, Lauderdale County, AL.

+ 1358 M ii. **Elmer Patford Holcombe** was born 1 Feb 1903 in Florence, Lauderdale County, AL, died 17 Oct 1980, and was buried in Walston Cemetery, Oakland, Lauderdale County, AL.

+ 1359 M iii. **Hubert Lee Holcombe** was born 21 Aug 1904 in Florence, Lauderdale County, AL, died 30 Jun 1955, and was buried in Williams Chapel Cemetery, Lauderdale County, AL.

Milton Sarah Holcombe next married **Owen Carson** 14 May 1909 in Lauderdale County, AL.

1360 F i. **Atheleen Carson.**

555. Hallie (Hal) B. Sharp (*John Thomas (Tom)* [5], *James (Jim) Charles Sr.* [4], *Adron (Edwin/Ade) Sr.* [3], *Charles W. Sr.* [2], *John Sr.* [1]) was born 28 Jul 1880 in Lauderdale County, AL, died 30 Nov 1951, and was buried in Florence City Cemetery, Florence, Lauderdale County, AL.

Hallie married **Lula Lucretia Pickens**, daughter of **William David Benton Pickens** and **Amanda Joe Faires**, 17 Jan 1898 in Lauderdale County, AL. Lula was born 28 Dec 1881 in Lauderdale County, AL, died 6 Jan 1978, and was buried in Florence City Cemetery, Florence, Lauderdale County, AL.

1361 F i. **Viola Waymon Sharp** was born 25 Apr 1899 in Lauderdale County, AL, died 9 Jul 1900, and was buried in Wright Cemetery, Wright, Lauderdale County, AL.

+ 1362 M ii. **Jesse Thomas Sharp Sr.** was born 10 Feb 1901 in Lauderdale County, AL, died 19 Sep 1990, and was buried in Rogersville Civitan Cemetery, Lauderdale County, AL.

+ 1363 M iii. **Vessey David Sharp** was born 4 Dec 1902 in Waterloo, Lauderdale County, AL, died 28 Aug 1953, and was buried in Rogersville Civitan Cemetery, Lauderdale County, AL.

+ 1364 F iv. **Letha Birdie Sharp** was born 28 Jul 1904 in Lauderdale County, AL, died 17 Apr 2003, and was buried in Florence City Cemetery, Florence, Lauderdale County, AL.

+ 1365 F v. **Mary Zethayr Sharp** was born 29 Jun 1906 in Waterloo, Lauderdale County, AL, died 5 Apr 1997, and was buried in Rogersville Civitan Cemetery, Lauderdale County, AL.

+ 1366 M vi. **Fred Noel Sharp Sr.** was born 7 Jun 1909 in Waterloo, Lauderdale County, AL, died 23 May 1973, and was buried in Florence City Cemetery, Florence, Lauderdale County, AL.

+ 1367 F vii. **Thursa Lou Sharp** was born 5 Jun 1911 in Lauderdale County, AL, died in 1997, and was buried in Rogersville Civitan Cemetery, Lauderdale County, AL.

+ 1368 F viii. **Leona May Sharp** was born 27 Jul 1915 in Lauderdale County, AL, died 23 Sep 2003, and was buried in Florence City Cemetery, Florence, Lauderdale County, AL.

556. Daisy L. Sharp (*John Thomas (Tom)*^{5}, *James (Jim) Charles Sr.*^{4}, *Adron (Edwin/Ade) Sr.*^{3}, *Charles W. Sr.*^{2}, *John Sr.*^{1}) was born in May 1882 in Lauderdale County, AL, died 24 Feb 1933, and was buried in Tuscaloosa Brice Hospital Cemetery.

Daisy married **Felix M. Gean**, son of **Wylie Henderson Gean** and **Nancy Whitaker**, 20 Jan 1900 in Lauderdale County, AL. Felix was born 25 Oct 1879 in Lutts, Wayne County, TN, died 27 Nov 1936, and was buried in Mt. Hope Cemetery, Anson County, TX.

1369 M i. **Curtis Gean** was born in 1905 in Oklahoma.

557. Mattie A. Sharp (*John Thomas (Tom)*^{5}, *James (Jim) Charles Sr.*^{4}, *Adron (Edwin/Ade) Sr.*^{3}, *Charles W. Sr.*^{2}, *John Sr.*^{1}) was born in Jun 1885 in Gravely Springs, Lauderdale County, AL, died 23 Feb 1965, and was buried in Oak Grove Cemetery, Lauderdale County, AL.

Mattie married **Samuel S. Lindsey**, son of **Greenberry Lee Lindsey Sr.** and **Nancy Bruce**, 19 Mar 1901 in Lauderdale County, AL. Samuel was born 16 Oct 1882 in Lauderdale County, AL, died 20 Jan 1917, and was buried in Wright Cemetery, Wright, Lauderdale County, AL. **(Duplicate Line. See Person 440)**

558. James (Swagger) Sharp (*John Thomas (Tom)*^{5}, *James (Jim) Charles Sr.*^{4}, *Adron (Edwin/Ade) Sr.*^{3}, *Charles W. Sr.*^{2}, *John Sr.*^{1}) was born 24 May 1886 in Lauderdale County, AL, died 31 Mar 1973, and was buried in Wright Cemetery, Wright, Lauderdale County, AL.

Felix and Daisy L. Sharp Gean

James married **Lillie Evelyn Saddler**, daughter of **John Wesley Saddler Sr.** and **Melissa Evelyn (Aunt Eb) Wood**, 24 Feb 1909 in Lauderdale County, AL. Lillie was born 13 Jun 1889 in Wright, Lauderdale County, AL, died 23 Feb 1974, and was buried in Wright Cemetery, Wright, Lauderdale County, AL.

+ 1370 M i. **John Edward Sharp** was born 9 Jan 1910 in Lauderdale County, AL, died 17 Mar 1993, and was buried in St. Joseph Valley Cemetery, Mishawaka, IN.

+ 1371 M ii. **Homer Carroll Sharp** was born 18 Jul 1913 in Lauderdale County, AL, died 30 Oct 1992, and was buried in Rose Lawn Cemetery, Decatur, AL.

+ 1372 F iii. **Bessie Etoil Sharp** was born 9 Sep 1914 in Lauderdale County, AL, died 8 Mar 2002, and was buried in Oak Grove Cemetery, Lauderdale County, AL.

+ 1373 F iv. **Annie May Sharp** was born 13 Jan 1917 in Alabama.

+ 1374 F v. **Mollie Nell Sharp** was born 19 Jun 1920 in Lauderdale County, AL.

+ 1375 F vi. **Rachel Violet Sharp** was born 18 Feb 1923 in Lauderdale County, AL.

+ 1376 M vii. **James Loyal Sharp** was born 12 Jun 1927 in Lauderdale County, AL.

+ 1377 F viii. **Aileen Beulah Sharp** was born 24 Feb 1927 in Waterloo, Lauderdale County, AL.

559. Thomas Leslie (Peck) Sharp (*John Thomas (Tom)* [5], *James (Jim) Charles Sr.* [4], *Adron (Edwin/Ade) Sr.* [3], *Charles W. Sr.* [2], *John Sr.* [1]) was born 17 Dec 1887 in Lauderdale County, AL, died 1 Jan 1963, and was buried in Wright Cemetery, Wright, Lauderdale County, AL.

Thomas married **Mollie F. Handback**, daughter of **Samuel E. Handback** and **Elizabeth *Unk**, 23 Dec 1908 in Lauderdale County, AL. Mollie was born 25 Sep 1891 in Lauderdale County, AL, died 21 Feb 1913, and was buried in Wright Cemetery, Wright, Lauderdale County, AL.

+ 1378 M i. **Ellie Berry Sharp Sr.** was born 11 Jul 1910 in Lauderdale County, AL, died 26 Feb 1975, and was buried in Wright Cemetery, Wright, Lauderdale County, AL.

+ 1379 M ii. **Earl Leslie Sharp** was born 15 Sep 1912 in Wright, Lauderdale County, AL, died 20 Jan 1999, and was buried in Wright Cemetery, Wright, Lauderdale County, AL.

Thomas next married **Lida Mae Gammill**. Lida was born 24 Feb 1913 in Lauderdale County, AL and died 16 Oct 1974 in Lauderdale County, AL.

1380 M i. **Vernon Sharp** was born 11 Mar 1917 in Lauderdale County, AL, died 15 Jun 1918, and was buried in Wright Cemetery, Wright, Lauderdale County, AL.

+ 1381 M ii. **Virgil Sharp** was born 12 Feb 1918 in Lauderdale County, AL and died in 1969.

+ 1382 F iii. **Wilma Lutell Sharp** was born 2 Dec 1920 in Savannah, TN.

+ 1383 M iv. **Selbert Sharp** was born 28 Apr 1921 in Savannah, TN.

+ 1384 M v. **Ray Sharp** was born 22 Mar 1924 in Savannah, TN.

+ 1385 M vi. **Robert (Bob) Sharp** was born 9 Sep 1926 in Savannah, TN and died in 1999 in Memphis, Shelby County, TN.

+ 1386 M vii. **Murray Sharp** was born 18 Jun 1928 in Savannah, TN.

+ 1387 M viii. **Broadus Sharp** was born 1 Apr 1930 in Lauderdale County, AL.

1388 M ix. **Lawrence Sharp** was born in 1933 in Lauderdale County, AL, died in 1935, and was buried in Wright Cemetery, Wright, Lauderdale County, AL.

1389 F x. **Eloise Sharp** was born in 1934 in Lauderdale County, AL, died in 1935, and was buried in Wright Cemetery, Wright, Lauderdale County, AL.

Thomas next married **Clara Herston**, daughter of **R. P. Herston** and **Sara *Unk**, 20 May 1940 in Colbert County, AL. Clara was born 7 Apr 1900 and was buried in Center Star Cemetery, Lauderdale County, AL.

+ 1390 F i. **Brenda Joyce Sharp** was born 16 Aug 1941 in Colbert County, AL.

+ 1391 F ii. **Judy Amisonia Sharp** was born 26 Mar 1943 in Colbert County, AL.

560. Bertha Sharp (*John Thomas (Tom)* [5], *James (Jim) Charles Sr.* [4], *Adron (Edwin/Ade) Sr.* [3], *Charles W. Sr.* [2], *John Sr.* [1]) was born in May 1890 in Alabama.

Bertha married **Linus Ticer** 22 Dec 1906 in Lauderdale County, AL.

Bertha next married **Robert E. Woodward** 7 Dec 1921 in Lauderdale County, AL.

561. Edgar Lee Sharp (*John Thomas (Tom)* [5], *James (Jim) Charles Sr.* [4], *Adron (Edwin/Ade) Sr.* [3], *Charles W. Sr.* [2], *John Sr.* [1]) was born 28 Jan 1891 in Lauderdale County, AL, died 15 Jan 1965, and was buried in Wright Cemetery, Wright, Lauderdale County, AL.

Edgar married **Lonie Alberta Glasscock**, daughter of **John Elijah Glasscock** and **Mollie Lugenia Morse**, 31 Mar 1914 in Lauderdale County, AL. Lonie was born 23 Jan 1892 in Blount County, AL, died 19 Mar 1981, and was buried in Wright Cemetery, Wright, Lauderdale County, AL.

| 1392 | F | i. | **Lillian Veatrice Sharp** was born 4 May 1914 in Lauderdale County, AL and died 4 May 1914 in Lauderdale County, AL. |

+ 1393 M ii. **Terry Lee Sharp** was born 13 Sep 1915 in Lauderdale County, AL, died 14 Jan 1994, and was buried in Greenview Memorial Park, Florence, Lauderdale County, AL.

+ 1394 M iii. **Doyle Woodrow Sharp** was born 22 Feb 1917 in Lauderdale County, AL, died 15 Nov 1987 in Lauderdale County, AL, and was buried in Greenview Memorial Park, Florence, Lauderdale County, AL.

+ 1395 F iv. **Mary Elizabeth Sharp** was born 16 Nov 1918 in Lauderdale County, AL, died 10 Oct 1976, and was buried in Greenview Memorial Park, Florence, Lauderdale County, AL.

+ 1396 F v. **Annie Bell Sharp** was born 11 Jun 1920 in Lauderdale County, AL, died 8 Mar 2009, and was buried in Greenview Memorial Park, Florence, Lauderdale County, AL.

+ 1397 F vi. **Edna Idelle Sharp** was born 23 Jun 1922 in Lauderdale County, AL, died 18 Jul 1997, and was buried in Rhodesville Cemetery, Lauderdale County, AL.

+ 1398 F vii. **Julia Edneta Sharp** was born 23 Dec 1924 in Lauderdale County, AL and was buried in Wright Cemetery, Wright, Lauderdale County, AL.

+ 1399 M viii. **John Thomas Sharp** was born 26 Oct 1927 in Lauderdale County, AL, died 7 Mar 2001, and was buried in Greenview Memorial Park, Florence, Lauderdale County, AL.

+ 1400 F ix. **Ellen Emogene Sharp** was born 12 Apr 1932 in Lauderdale County, AL.

Back: Doyal, Dell, Annabelle, Julia, Mary Elizabeth, Lillian and Terry Sharp
Front: John Thomas, Edgar, Lonnie Glasscock and Emogene Sharp

562. Quinnie Vester Sharp (*John Thomas (Tom)^5, James (Jim) Charles Sr.^{4}, Adron (Edwin/Ade) Sr.^{3}, Charles W. Sr.^{2}, John Sr.^{1}*) was born 20 Sep 1892 in Lauderdale County, AL, died 7 May 1980, and was buried in Wright Cemetery, Wright, Lauderdale County, AL.

Quinnie married **Greenberry Lee Lindsey Jr.**, son of **Greenberry Lee Lindsey Sr.** and **Nancy Bruce**, 26 May 1913 in Lauderdale County, AL. Greenberry was born 19 Nov 1886 in Lauderdale County, AL, died 15 Nov 1974, and was buried in Wright Cemetery, Wright, Lauderdale County, AL.
(Duplicate Line. See Person 442)

563. Minor (Mina) Houston Sharp (*John Thomas (Tom)^5, James (Jim) Charles Sr.^{4}, Adron (Edwin/Ade) Sr.^{3}, Charles W. Sr.^{2}, John Sr.^{1}*) was born 18 Feb 1894 in Lauderdale County, AL, died 1 Mar 1978, and was buried in Wright Cemetery, Wright, Lauderdale County, AL.

Minor married **Emmett Comer Hairell**, son of **William (Billy) Hairell** and **Cynthia Hairell**, 9 Oct 1916 in Lauderdale County, AL. Emmett was born 21 Nov 1893, died 23 Oct 1939, and was buried in Mt. Olive Cemetery, Lauderdale County, AL.

+ 1401 F i. **Dorothy Maurita Hairell** was born 17 Sep 1918 in Waterloo, Lauderdale County, AL.
+ 1402 F ii. **Idna Cynthia Hairell** was born 20 Feb 1922 in Lauderdale County, AL.

565. James Pinkney Bruce Sr. (*Matilda Ann Sharp*[5], *James (Jim) Charles Sr.*[4], *Adron (Edwin/Ade) Sr.*[3], *Charles W. Sr.*[2], *John Sr.*[1]) was born 3 May 1881 in Lauderdale County, AL, died in 1958, and was buried in Wesley Chapel Cemetery, Lauderdale County, AL.

James married **Dora Chlora Lee Smith**, daughter of **Henry Littleton Smith** and **Louisa Dock (Loudocky) Burns**, 29 Mar 1899 in Lauderdale County, AL. Dora was born in Mar 1881 in Lauderdale County, AL, died in 1964, and was buried in Wesley Chapel Cemetery, Lauderdale County, AL.

+ 1403 M i. **Willie Clyde Bruce** was born about 1901 in Alabama.
+ 1404 F ii. **Pearl I. Bruce** was born about 1904 in Alabama.
+ 1405 F iii. **Jewell Bruce** was born about 1906 in Alabama.
+ 1406 M iv. **James Pinkney Bruce Jr.** was born 20 Jun 1909 in Lauderdale County, AL.
+ 1407 M v. **Riggle Bruce** was born 13 Feb 1913 in Lauderdale County, AL and died 14 Aug 1993.
+ 1408 M vi. **John Gilbert Bruce Sr.** was born 25 Apr 1915 in Lauderdale County, AL, died 2 Feb 1986, and was buried in Williams Chapel Cemetery, Lauderdale County, AL.
+ 1409 F vii. **Cleona Bruce** was born in 1918 in Lauderdale County, AL, died in 1997, and was buried in Tri-Cities Memorial Gardens, Florence, Lauderdale County, AL.
+ 1410 F viii. **Mary Leona Bruce** was born about 1919 in Alabama.
  1411 F ix. **Margaret L. Bruce** was born about 1919 in Alabama.
  1412 M x. **Edsel Glenn Bruce** was born 1 Jan 1925, died 26 Dec 1949, and was buried in Wesley Chapel Cemetery, Lauderdale County, AL.

566. Robert William Bruce (*Matilda Ann Sharp*[5], *James (Jim) Charles Sr.*[4], *Adron (Edwin/Ade) Sr.*[3], *Charles W. Sr.*[2], *John Sr.*[1]) was born 14 Apr 1883 in Lauderdale County, AL, died 9 Dec 1962, and was buried in Murphy's Chapel Cemetery, Lauderdale County, AL.

Robert married **Mamie Rogers**, daughter of **John T. Rogers** and **Tabitha Jane Randolph**, 22 Apr 1910 in Lauderdale County, AL. Mamie was born 25 Sep 1889 in Lauderdale County, AL, died 29 Jun 1968, and was buried in Murphy's Chapel Cemetery, Lauderdale County, AL.

+ 1413 F i. **Nettie Bethel Bruce** was born 26 Jul 1911 in Lauderdale County, AL, died 9 Jan 1998, and was buried in Murphy's Chapel Cemetery, Lauderdale County, AL.
+ 1414 M ii. **Amos Jerry Bruce Sr.** was born 17 Dec 1913 in Lauderdale County, AL.
+ 1415 F iii. **Naomi Deborah Bruce** was born 7 Jan 1915 in Lauderdale County, AL.
+ 1416 M iv. **Paul Byrum Bruce** was born 24 Nov 1916 in Lauderdale County, AL, died 9 Aug 1980, and was buried in Murphy's Chapel Cemetery, Lauderdale County, AL.
+ 1417 M v. **Reeder Warner Bruce** was born 9 Sep 1918 in Lauderdale County, AL, died 11 Jan 2008, and was buried in Greenview Memorial Park, Florence, Lauderdale County, AL.
+ 1418 M vi. **Robert Cyrus Bruce** was born 22 Sep 1919 in Lauderdale County, AL, died 5 Aug 1971 in Oak Ridge, TN, and was buried in Solway Church Cemetery, Oak Ridge, TN.
+ 1419 M vii. **Harding Abel Bruce** was born 24 Oct 1922 in Lauderdale County, AL, died 10 May 1997, and was buried in Murphy's Chapel Cemetery, Lauderdale County, AL.
+ 1420 F viii. **Viola T. Bruce** was born 8 Dec 1924 in Lauderdale County, AL, died 13 Oct 1995, and was buried in Murphy's Chapel Cemetery, Lauderdale County, AL.
  1421 M ix. **Durwood Wiliiam Bruce** was born 24 Oct 1927 in Lauderdale County, AL, died 31 Mar 1997, and was buried in Murphy's Chapel Cemetery, Lauderdale County, AL.
+ 1422 M x. **John C. Bruce** was born 10 Jul 1932 in Lauderdale County, AL, died 24 Nov 2008, and was buried in Chapel Hill Memorial Garden, Osceola, IN.

Robert William Bruce and Mamie Rogers Bruce Family

Back: Nettie Young, Amos, Naomi Mason, Byrum, and Cyrus Bruce
Front: Reeder, Abel, Viola Melton, Durwood and John Bruce

567. Lilly Eddie Levie Bruce (*Matilda Ann Sharp*[5]*, James (Jim) Charles Sr.*[4]*, Adron (Edwin/Ade) Sr.*[3]*, Charles W. Sr.*[2]*, John Sr.*[1]) was born 22 Apr 1886 in Lauderdale County, AL and died 9 Jan 1959 in Memphis, Shelby County, TN.

Lilly married **William Dee Long** in 1902 in Tishomingo, MS. William was born in 1880 in Alabama.

+ 1423 M i. **Turner Cuelell Long** was born 2 Aug 1903 in Lauderdale County, AL and died 4 Apr 1984 in Sugar Tree, TN.
+ 1424 F ii. **Magie Estelle Long** was born 27 Apr 1905 in Gill, AR and died 20 Mar 1955 in Memphis, Shelby County, TN.
+ 1425 F iii. **Abbie Leona Long** was born 7 Jul 1907 in Cross County, AR and died about 1995 in Batesville, MS.
+ 1426 F iv. **Carrie D. Long** was born about 1909 in Cross County, AR.
+ 1427 F v. **Lillian Long** was born 25 Dec 1912 in Cross County, AR and died in California.
+ 1428 F vi. **Virginia Long** was born 14 Dec 1914 in Cross County, AR.
+ 1429 M vii. **John Long** was born 18 Nov 1916 in Cross County, AR and died about 1990 in Memphis, Shelby County, TN.
+ 1430 M viii. **James Ireis Long** was born 25 Jan 1919 in Cross County, AR.
+ 1431 M ix. **Ernest Steven Long Sr.** was born about 1920 in Memphis, Shelby County, TN.
+ 1432 F x. **Margie Grace Long** was born 4 May 1923 in Memphis, Shelby County, TN.

Lilly next married **David John Boldger** after 1951 in Memphis, Shelby County, TN.

568. George Owen Bruce (*Matilda Ann Sharp*[5]*, James (Jim) Charles Sr.*[4]*, Adron (Edwin/Ade) Sr.*[3]*, Charles W. Sr.*[2]*, John Sr.*[1]) was born 27 Aug 1890 in Lauderdale County, AL, died in 1931, and was buried in Gravely Springs Cemetery, Lauderdale County, AL.

George married **Lula Pearl Crider**, daughter of **George Washington Crider** and **Mary K. (Polly) Holt**, 24 May 1916 in Lauderdale County, AL. Lula was born in 1893 in Lauderdale County, AL, died in 1924, and was buried in Gravely Springs Cemetery, Lauderdale County, AL.

+ 1433 F i. **Leacia Mae Bruce** was born 25 May 1922 in Lauderdale County, AL.
+ 1434 M ii. **Jessie D. Bruce** was born 28 Feb 1928 in Lauderdale County, AL.

569. Margie Ann (Marjorie) Bruce (*Matilda Ann Sharp*[5], *James (Jim) Charles Sr.*[4], *Adron (Edwin/Ade) Sr.*[3], *Charles W. Sr.*[2], *John Sr.*[1]) was born 9 Aug 1893 in Gravely Springs, Lauderdale County, AL, died 26 Mar 1940, and was buried in Oak Grove Cemetery, Lauderdale County, AL.

Margie married **Finis Leonard (Phiney/Slim) Wood**, son of **John Pugh Wood** and **Sarah (Sallie) Frances Elizabeth Milford**, 24 Sep 1912 in Lauderdale County, AL. Finis was born 13 Nov 1891 in Gravely Springs, Lauderdale County, AL, died 4 Sep 1962, and was buried in Barton Cemetery, Colbert County, AL.

+ 1435	F	i.	**Lady Carrie Wood** was born 4 Aug 1913 in Gravely Springs, Lauderdale County, AL, died 22 Sep 1996, and was buried in Oak Grove Cemetery, Lauderdale County, AL.
+ 1436	F	ii.	**Pearlie Mae Wood** was born 1 May 1915 in Gravely Springs, Lauderdale County, AL, died 26 Feb 2003, and was buried in Oak Grove Cemetery, Lauderdale County, AL.
+ 1437	M	iii.	**Claude Ellis Wood Sr.** was born 26 Apr 1917 in Gravely Springs, Lauderdale County, AL, died 30 Jan 2006, and was buried in Oak Grove Cemetery, Lauderdale County, AL.
+ 1438	M	iv.	**Leonard Earl Wood** was born 4 Jun 1919 in Gravely Springs, Lauderdale County, AL, died 30 Oct 2001, and was buried in Oak Grove Cemetery, Lauderdale County, AL.
+ 1439	F	v.	**Pauline Inez Wood** was born 1 May 1921 in Gravely Springs, Lauderdale County, AL, died 17 Feb 2007, and was buried in Oak Grove Cemetery, Lauderdale County, AL.
+ 1440	F	vi.	**Onita Katherine (Neat) Wood** was born 7 Jul 1924 in Gravely Springs, Lauderdale County, AL.
+ 1441	M	vii.	**Wallace Ray Wood** was born 10 May 1929 in Gravely Springs, Lauderdale County, AL, died 1 Mar 1980, and was buried in Oak Grove Cemetery, Lauderdale County, AL.

570. Virgie Lenoria (Nora) Sharp (*Owen Bennett (Doc)*[5], *James (Jim) Charles Sr.*[4], *Adron (Edwin/Ade) Sr.*[3], *Charles W. Sr.*[2], *John Sr.*[1]) was born 25 Apr 1884 in Wright, Lauderdale County, AL, died 25 Dec 1963, and was buried in Wright Cemetery, Wright, Lauderdale County, AL.

Virgie married **George Moses (Mode) Wright**, son of **Richard Washington Wright** and **Elizabeth (Lizzie) May Sharp**, 30 Dec 1911 in Lauderdale County, AL. George was born 27 Aug 1877 in Wright, Lauderdale County, AL, died 2 Feb 1955, and was buried in Wright Cemetery, Wright, Lauderdale County, AL. **(Duplicate Line. See Person 234)**

571. Lee Hal Sharp (*Owen Bennett (Doc)*[5], *James (Jim) Charles Sr.*[4], *Adron (Edwin/Ade) Sr.*[3], *Charles W. Sr.*[2], *John Sr.*[1]) was born 15 Feb 1886 in Lauderdale County, AL, died 16 Mar 1951, and was buried in Wright Cemetery, Wright, Lauderdale County, AL.

Lee married **Lillie Smith**, daughter of **William (Bill) Smith** and **Fannie Parrish**, 2 Aug 1907 in Lauderdale County, AL. Lillie was born 18 May 1888 in Lauderdale County, AL, died 20 Jun 1988, and was buried in Greenview Memorial Park, Florence, Lauderdale County, AL.

1442	F	i.	**Girtie (Eirtie) M. Sharp** was born 19 Oct 1909 in Lauderdale County, AL, died 10 May 1990, and was buried in Greenview Memorial Park, Florence, Lauderdale County, AL.
+ 1443	F	ii.	**Fannie Birdie Sharp** was born 15 Apr 1910 in Lauderdale County, AL.
+ 1444	M	iii.	**Reeder Earl Sharp** was born 1 Jul 1913 in Lauderdale County, AL, died 4 Dec 1938, and was buried in Wright Cemetery, Wright, Lauderdale County, AL.
+ 1445	F	iv.	**Grace Leona Sharp** was born 8 Jun 1918 in Waterloo, Lauderdale County, AL.

572. May N. (Nettie) Sharp (*Owen Bennett (Doc)*[5], *James (Jim) Charles Sr.*[4], *Adron (Edwin/Ade) Sr.*[3], *Charles W. Sr.*[2], *John Sr.*[1]) was born 8 Jul 1888 in Alabama, died 18 Nov 1950, and was buried in Wright Cemetery, Wright, Lauderdale County, AL.

May married **Kerom William Lindsey**, son of **Greenberry Lee Lindsey Sr.** and **Nancy Bruce**, 2 Aug 1907 in Lauderdale County, AL. Kerom was born 17 Jan 1880 in Lauderdale County, AL, died 25 Oct 1957, and was buried in Wright Cemetery, Wright, Lauderdale County, AL. **(Duplicate Line. See Person 439)**

573. Ada Irene Sharp (*Owen Bennett (Doc)*[5], *James (Jim) Charles Sr.*[4], *Adron (Edwin/Ade) Sr.*[3], *Charles W. Sr.*[2], *John Sr.*[1]) was born 3 Apr 1890 in Lauderdale County, AL, died 6 Apr 1979, and was buried in Greenview Memorial Park, Florence, Lauderdale County, AL.

Ada married **James Fletcher Glasscock**, son of **John Elijah Glasscock** and **Mollie Lugenia Morse**, 7 Sep 1909 in Lauderdale County, AL. James was born 23 Mar 1888 in Lauderdale County, AL, died 9 Oct 1971, and was buried in Greenview Memorial Park, Florence, Lauderdale County, AL.

+ 1446 F   i.   **Ethel Lucille Glasscock** was born 18 Sep 1910 in Lauderdale County, AL, died 8 Jun 1987, and was buried in Greenview Memorial Park, Florence, Lauderdale County, AL.

+ 1447 F   ii.   **Vivian Veatrice Glasscock** was born 16 May 1913 in Lauderdale County, AL, died 28 Mar 1998 in Lauderdale County, AL, and was buried in Greenview Memorial Park, Florence, Lauderdale County, AL.

+ 1448 F   iii. **Irene Glasscock** was born 21 May 1916 in Lauderdale County, AL, died 23 Dec 1952, and was buried in Greenview Memorial Park, Florence, Lauderdale County, AL.

  1449 F   iv.   **Irella Glasscock** was born 21 May 1916, died 29 Mar 2004, and was buried in Greenview Memorial Park, Florence, Lauderdale County, AL.

+ 1450 M   v.   **Fred Glasscock Sr.** was born 11 May 1919 in Lauderdale County, AL, died 9 Jun 1995, and was buried in Greenview Memorial Park, Florence, Lauderdale County, AL.

+ 1451 M   vi.   **James Arnold Glasscock** was born 31 Oct 1921 in Lauderdale County, AL, died 8 Dec 1992, and was buried in Greenview Memorial Park, Florence, Lauderdale County, AL.

+ 1452 M   vii. **Harold Owen Glasscock** was born 27 Jul 1924 in Lauderdale County, AL, died 10 Feb 1999, and was buried in Greenview Memorial Park, Florence, Lauderdale County, AL.

+ 1453 M   viii. **William Boyce Glasscock** was born 14 Feb 1927 in Lauderdale County, AL, died 13 Sep 1991, and was buried in Greenview Memorial Park, Florence, Lauderdale County, AL.

574. Harrell Emmett Sharp (*Owen Bennett (Doc)^5, James (Jim) Charles Sr.^{4}, Adron (Edwin/Ade) Sr.^{3}, Charles W. Sr.^{2}, John Sr.^{1}*) was born 2 May 1892 in Lauderdale County, AL, died 3 Feb 1946, and was buried in Wright Cemetery, Wright, Lauderdale County, AL.

Harrell married **Lula Ann Wood**, daughter of **James Hampton (Jim) Wood Sr.** and **Mary (Mollie) Taylor**, 11 Oct 1915 in Lauderdale County, AL. Lula was born 6 Feb 1887 in Wright, Lauderdale County, AL, died 22 Feb 1941, and was buried in Wright Cemetery, Wright, Lauderdale County, AL.

+ 1454 F   i.   **Lois Etoile Sharp** was born 19 Dec 1916 in Lauderdale County, AL, died 28 Jul 1990, and was buried in Macedonia Cemetery, Lauderdale County, AL.

+ 1455 F   ii.   **Mary Helen Sharp** was born 7 Sep 1919 in Waterloo, Lauderdale County, AL, died 26 Aug 2003, and was buried in Greenview Memorial Park, Florence, Lauderdale County, AL.

  1456 F   iii. **Oneal Wood Sharp** was born 20 Jul 1921 in Lauderdale County, AL, died 20 Jul 1921, and was buried in Wright Cemetery, Wright, Lauderdale County, AL.

  1457 F   iv.   **Elrea Wood Sharp** was born 3 May 1923 in Lauderdale County, AL, died 3 May 1923, and was buried in Wright Cemetery, Wright, Lauderdale County, AL.

575. Mildred Sharp (*Owen Bennett (Doc)^5, James (Jim) Charles Sr.^{4}, Adron (Edwin/Ade) Sr.^{3}, Charles W. Sr.^{2}, John Sr.^{1}*) was born 15 Feb 1894 in Lauderdale County, AL, died 26 Nov 1964, and was buried in Oak Grove Cemetery, Lauderdale County, AL.

Mildred married **James Hampton (Jim) Wood Jr.**, son of **James Hampton (Jim) Wood Sr.** and **Mary (Mollie) Taylor**, 19 Oct 1912 in Lauderdale County, AL. James was born 3 Mar 1890 in Wright, Lauderdale County, AL, died 30 Mar 1971, and was buried in Oak Grove Cemetery, Lauderdale County, AL.

  1458 M   i.   **Garlin Wood** was born 24 Jan 1914 in Lauderdale County, AL, died 12 Mar 1931, and was buried in Oak Grove Cemetery, Lauderdale County, AL.

  1459 M   ii.   **Infant Son Wood** was born in 1915 in Lauderdale County, AL, died in 1915, and was buried in Oak Grove Cemetery, Lauderdale County, AL.

+ 1460 M   iii. **Curtis (Slick) Wood** was born 30 Jun 1917 in Lauderdale County, AL, died 17 Feb 2000, and was buried in Oak Grove Cemetery, Lauderdale County, AL.

+ 1461 F   iv.   **Mary Edith (Tootsie) Wood** was born 31 Jan 1921 in Lauderdale County, AL and died 2 Feb 2007.

+ 1462 M   v.   **Ray Wood** was born 9 Feb 1921 in Lauderdale County, AL, died 31 Oct 1991, and was buried in Greenview Memorial Park, Florence, Lauderdale County, AL.

+ 1463 M   vi.   **Joseph Wood** was born 13 Mar 1928 in Lauderdale County, AL and died 25 Jan 1993 in Lauderdale County, AL (cremated).

+ 1464 F   vii. **Erlene Wood** was born 24 Oct 1934 in Lauderdale County, AL.

+ 1465 M   viii. **Rassie Wood** was born 23 Apr 1937 in Lauderdale County, AL, died 7 Jan 1987, and was buried in Oak Grove Cemetery, Lauderdale County, AL.

576. Mason Sharp (*Owen Bennett (Doc)*[5], *James (Jim) Charles Sr.*[4], *Adron (Edwin/Ade) Sr.*[3], *Charles W. Sr.*[2], *John Sr.*[1]) was born 15 Feb 1894 in Lauderdale County, AL.

Mason married **William (Will) Isley** 18 Oct 1919 in Lauderdale County, AL. William was born in 1890.

577. Lillie May Sharp (*James Charles Jr.*[5], *James (Jim) Charles Sr.*[4], *Adron (Edwin/Ade) Sr.*[3], *Charles W. Sr.*[2], *John Sr.*[1]) was born 15 May 1902 in Lauderdale County, AL, died 21 Mar 1982, and was buried in New Hope Cemetery, Lauderdale County, AL.

Lillie married **Elmer J. Cummings**, son of **David Cummings** and **Mary Ann Qualls**, 8 Dec 1919 in Lauderdale County, AL. Elmer was born 8 Apr 1895 in Lauderdale County, AL, died 15 May 1960, and was buried in Hollands Creek Cemetery, Hardin County, TN.

+ 1466   F   i.   **Mary Frances Cummings** was born 9 Jul 1919 in Lauderdale County, AL.
+ 1467   M   ii.   **Lucian Jones (Jay) Cummings I** was born 8 Jul 1927 in Lauderdale County, AL, died 24 Oct 1990, and was buried in New Hope Cemetery, Lauderdale County, AL.
+ 1468   M   iii.   **Paul Lee Cummings** was born 25 Aug 1929 in Lauderdale County, AL.

578. Turner Lee Sharp (*James Charles Jr.*[5], *James (Jim) Charles Sr.*[4], *Adron (Edwin/Ade) Sr.*[3], *Charles W. Sr.*[2], *John Sr.*[1]) was born 25 Jun 1906 in Wright, Lauderdale County, AL, died 9 Aug 1990, and was buried in Macedonia Cemetery, Lauderdale County, AL.

General Notes: Obituary - Times Daily, Florence, Lauderdale County, Alabama

"Killen - The graveside service for Turner Lee Sharp, 85, Lauderdale Christian Nursing Home, will be at 3 p.m. today at Macedonia Cemetery with Fred Dillon officiating, Spry Funeral Home, Sheffield, will direct. He died Thursday, Aug. 9, 1990, at his residence.
He was a native of Lauderdale County and a member of Macedonia Church of Christ. He was the son of the late "Big" Jim and Lizzie Sharp and was a former employee of the Alabama Highway Department.
Survivors include his wife, Pearl Daniels Sharp, Florence; sons, Marvin Lee Sharp, Douglas Sharp, both of Florence, James Earl Sharp, Nashville, Tenn., Elvin Sharp, Decatur, Frederick Sharp, Waynesboro, Tenn.; daughters, Jean Sharp Salter, Lois Flippoe Parrish, Barbara Sharp, all of Florence; 15 grandchildren; two great -grandchildren; nieces and nephews.
Bearers will be Robert Sharp, Loyd Sharp, Cecil Sharp, Clyde Sharp, Jeff Sharp, Frankie Willard, Skipper Thomas and Jack May.

Turner married **Minnie Pearl Daniels**, daughter of **John Daniel** and **Lizzie Hipps**, 4 Dec 1937 in Lauderdale County, AL. Minnie was born 29 Jul 1919 in Lauderdale County, AL, died 28 Aug 2003, and was buried in Macedonia Cemetery, Lauderdale County, AL.

+ 1469   F   i.   **Lillie Earline (Jean) Sharp** was born 21 Sep 1938 in Lauderdale County, AL.
+ 1470   M   ii.   **Marvin Lee Sharp** was born 13 Jan 1940 in Lauderdale County, AL.
+ 1471   M   iii.   **James Earl Sharp** was born 27 Jun 1941 in Lauderdale County, AL.
  1472   M   iv.   **Elvin Eugene Sharp** was born 24 Nov 1944 in Lauderdale County, AL.
+ 1473   M   v.   **Ernest Frederick Sharp** was born 21 Jul 1945 in Lauderdale County, AL.
+ 1474   M   vi.   **Harold Douglas Sharp** was born 21 Jan 1946 in Lauderdale County, AL, died 24 Dec 2005, and was buried in Macedonia Cemetery, Lauderdale County, AL.
  1475   F   vii.   **Barbara Gail Sharp** was born 19 May 1949 in Lauderdale County, AL.
+ 1476   F   viii.   **Lois Darnell Sharp** was born 16 Apr 1953 in Lauderdale County, AL.

579. James (Little James) Robert Sharp (*James Charles Jr.*[5], *James (Jim) Charles Sr.*[4], *Adron (Edwin/Ade) Sr.*[3], *Charles W. Sr.*[2], *John Sr.*[1]) was born 20 Jul 1908 in Wright, Lauderdale County, AL, died 6 Jan 1982, and was buried in Macedonia Cemetery, Lauderdale County, AL.

James married **Carrie Lee Brown**, daughter of **Lewis Brown** and **Mary Frances Young**, 9 Nov 1928 in Lauderdale County, AL. Carrie was born 12 Apr 1911 in Lauderdale County, AL, died 14 Apr 1990, and was buried in Macedonia Cemetery, Lauderdale County, AL.

+ 1477   M   i.   **Clarence Earl Sharp** was born 11 Jun 1929 in Lauderdale County, AL, died 24 Feb 1998, and was buried in Greenview Memorial Park, Florence, Lauderdale County, AL.

+ 1478 M ii. **James Loyd Sharp** was born 28 Nov 1930 in Lauderdale County, AL, died 5 Aug 2001, and was buried in Woodlawn Cemetery, Woodlawn, TN.

+ 1479 M iii. **Robert Lee Sharp** was born 21 Oct 1932 in Lauderdale County, AL.

+ 1480 M iv. **Clyde Ray Sharp** was born 11 Apr 1936 in Lauderdale County, AL, died 3 Oct 1998, and was buried in Macedonia Cemetery, Lauderdale County, AL.

+ 1481 F v. **Pearl Rebecca Sharp** was born 18 Feb 1937 in Lauderdale County, AL.

+ 1482 M vi. **Cecil Moore Sharp** was born 11 Jan 1943 in Lauderdale County, AL.

580. Minor Lucille Sharp (*James Charles Jr.*[5], *James (Jim) Charles Sr.*[4], *Adron (Edwin/Ade) Sr.*[3], *Charles W. Sr.*[2], *John Sr.*[1]) was born 1 Dec 1911 in Wright, Lauderdale County, AL, died 30 Jul 1987, and was buried in Tri-Cities Memorial Gardens, Florence, Lauderdale County, AL.

Minor married **George Elmer Cobb**, son of **Richard S. Cobb** and **Mary Rebecca *Unk**, 14 Dec 1929 in Wayne County, TN. George was born 27 May 1889 in Lauderdale County, AL, died 7 Nov 1971, and was buried in Tri-Cities Memorial Gardens, Florence, Lauderdale County, AL.

+ 1483 F i. **Emmy Luetellace (Lou) Cobb** was born 30 Nov 1930.

+ 1484 F ii. **Villace Lorene Cobb** was born 21 Mar 1932.

+ 1485 F iii. **Julia Loretta Cobb** was born 4 Dec 1933 in Lauderdale County, AL, died 16 Feb 1993, and was buried in Wesley Chapel Cemetery, Lauderdale County, AL.

581. Maggie Lorene Sharp (*James Charles Jr.*[5], *James (Jim) Charles Sr.*[4], *Adron (Edwin/Ade) Sr.*[3], *Charles W. Sr.*[2], *John Sr.*[1]) was born 15 Nov 1917 in Wright, Lauderdale County, AL, died 9 Apr 1963, and was buried in Macedonia Cemetery, Lauderdale County, AL.

Maggie married **James Willis Keel** 21 May 1937 in Lauderdale County, AL. James was born 8 Mar 1898 in Gillis Mills, TN, died 22 Sep 1979, and was buried in Macedonia Cemetery, Lauderdale County, AL.

+ 1486 F i. **Helen Marie Keel** was born 14 Nov 1938 in Lauderdale County, AL.

+ 1487 M ii. **James Walbert Keel** was born 19 May 1940 in Lauderdale County, AL.

1488 M iii. **Gerold B. Keel** was born 1 Jun 1944 in Lauderdale County, AL, died 28 Sep 1944, and was buried in Macedonia Cemetery, Lauderdale County, AL.

1489 M iv. **Jerry C. Keel** was born 1 Jun 1944 in Lauderdale County, AL, died 15 Jun 1944, and was buried in Macedonia Cemetery, Lauderdale County, AL.

+ 1490 F v. **Joyce Lorene Keel** was born 5 Jun 1946 in Lauderdale County, AL.

+ 1491 F vi. **Lois Laverne Keel** was born 20 Oct 1947 in Lauderdale County, AL.

1492 M vii. **Ottis Willis Keel** was born 2 Dec 1948 in Lauderdale County, AL.

+ 1493 F viii. **Linda Kay Keel** was born 7 Jul 1950 in Lauderdale County, AL.

582. Elmer Sharp (*Charles W.*[5], *James (Jim) Charles Sr.*[4], *Adron (Edwin/Ade) Sr.*[3], *Charles W. Sr.*[2], *John Sr.*[1]) was born 29 Aug 1900 in Lauderdale County, AL, died 30 Jul 1962 in South Bend, St Joseph County, IN, and was buried in Oak Grove Cemetery, Lauderdale County, AL.

Elmer married **Mamie Lee Milford**, daughter of **Thomas Douglas Milford** and **Laura Ann Minton**, 16 Aug 1919 in Lauderdale County, AL. Mamie was born 24 May 1897 in Gravely Springs, Lauderdale County, AL, died 11 Apr 1959 in South Bend, St Joseph County, IN, and was buried in Oak Grove Cemetery, Lauderdale County, AL.

+ 1494 F i. **Ruby Pauline Sharp** was born 28 Jan 1922 in Lauderdale County, AL, died 24 Mar 2003, and was buried in Greenview Memorial Park, Florence, Lauderdale County, AL.

+ 1495 F ii. **Mary Madgalene Sharp** was born 29 Jul 1926 in Lauderdale County, AL.

+ 1496 M iii. **William (Bill) Harvel Sharp** was born 11 Mar 1927 in Lauderdale County, AL.

+ 1497 M iv. **Curtis Corbin Sharp** was born 15 Nov 1928 in Lauderdale County, AL.

+ 1498 F v. **Agnes Geneva Sharp** was born 3 May 1931 in Lauderdale County, AL.

+ 1499 M vi. **James Earl Sharp** was born in Aug 1933 in Lauderdale County, AL.

1500 F vii. **Infant Daughter Sharp** was born 24 Jan 1936 in Lauderdale County, AL, died 27 Jan 1936, and was buried in Oak Grove Cemetery, Lauderdale County, AL.

+ 1501 F viii. **Vivian Katherine Sharp** was born 30 Jun 1937 in Lauderdale County, AL.

+ 1502 F ix. **Rachel Ruth Sharp** was born 19 Feb 1942 in Lauderdale County, AL.

Elmer next married **Emma Vandusan**.

583. Brother Sharp (*Charles W.[5], James (Jim) Charles Sr.[4], Adron (Edwin/Ade) Sr.[3], Charles W. Sr.[2], John Sr.[1]*) was born 12 Feb 1903 in Wright, Lauderdale County, AL, died in Mar 1976, and was buried in Oak Grove Cemetery, Lauderdale County, AL.

Brother married **Mary Opal Saddler**, daughter of **Charles Pugh Saddler** and **Mary Etta Wesson**, 2 Oct 1937 in Lauderdale County, AL. Mary was born 4 Feb 1919 in Lauderdale County, AL.

Brother next married **Viola White**, daughter of **Alvie White** and **Katie Jones**, in Lauderdale County, AL. Viola was born in 1913, died in Mar 1976, and was buried in Oak Grove Cemetery, Lauderdale County, AL.

584. William Hubert Sharp (*Charles W.[5], James (Jim) Charles Sr.[4], Adron (Edwin/Ade) Sr.[3], Charles W. Sr.[2], John Sr.[1]*) was born 5 Sep 1905 in Lauderdale County, AL, died 12 Jun 1989, and was buried in Oak Grove Cemetery, Lauderdale County, AL.

William married **Beadie May (Beckie) Wood**, daughter of **Albert Weaver Wood** and **Nancy Elizabeth Bruce**, 27 Oct 1927 in Lauderdale County, AL. Beadie was born 12 May 1910 in Gravely Springs, Lauderdale County, AL, died 21 Jan 1997, and was buried in Oak Grove Cemetery, Lauderdale County, AL.

- + 1503 M   i.   **W. C. Sharp** was born 9 Sep 1927 in Lauderdale County, AL.
- + 1504 F   ii. **Dorothy Virginia Sharp** was born 17 Aug 1930 in Lauderdale County, AL, died 8 Nov 2007, and was buried in Cloverdale COC Cemetery, Lauderdale County, AL.
- + 1505 F   iii. **Gladys Corrine Sharp** was born 24 Dec 1934 in Gravely Springs, Lauderdale County, AL, died 8 Mar 1966, and was buried in Murphy's Chapel Cemetery, Lauderdale County, AL.
- + 1506 F   iv. **Sarah Ruth Sharp** was born 29 Mar 1935 in Lauderdale County, AL.
- + 1507 F   v.   **Betty May Sharp** was born 5 Sep 1937 in Lauderdale County, AL.
- + 1508 M   vi. **Jack Jonah Sharp** was born 15 Sep 1938 in Lauderdale County, AL.
- + 1509 M   vii. **Billy Joe Sharp** was born 9 Dec 1943 in Lauderdale County, AL.
- + 1510 M   viii. **William Edward (Tiny) Sharp** was born 26 Jun 1946 in Lauderdale County, AL.

585. Aurelia Sharp (*Charles W.[5], James (Jim) Charles Sr.[4], Adron (Edwin/Ade) Sr.[3], Charles W. Sr.[2], John Sr.[1]*) was born 13 Jul 1908 in Lauderdale County, AL, died 10 Mar 1990, and was buried in Oak Grove Cemetery, Lauderdale County, AL.

Aurelia married **Owen Bartley Young Jr.**, son of **Owen Bartley Young Sr.** and **Rosie E. Mann**, 16 Oct 1938 in Lauderdale County, AL. Owen was born 2 May 1918 in Lauderdale County, AL. Another name for Owen is Owen B. Young Jr.

- 1511 F   i.   **Infant Daughter Young** was born about 1939, died about 1939, and was buried in Oak Grove Cemetery, Lauderdale County, AL.
- + 1512 M   ii. **Fred Demphis Young** was born 8 Feb 1940 in Lauderdale County, AL.
- + 1513 F   iii. **Mary Rachel Young** was born 24 Oct 1943 in Lauderdale County, AL.
- + 1514 F   iv. **Robbie Lou Young** was born 2 Sep 1946.

586. Audry Sharp (*Charles W.[5], James (Jim) Charles Sr.[4], Adron (Edwin/Ade) Sr.[3], Charles W. Sr.[2], John Sr.[1]*) was born 26 Nov 1912 in Waterloo, Lauderdale County, AL, died 16 Sep 1998, and was buried in Young Cemetery, Waterloo, Lauderdale County, AL.

Audry married **William (Bill) Young**, son of **Owen Bartley Young Sr.** and **Rosie E. Mann**, 7 Nov 1931 in Lauderdale County, AL. William was born 14 Nov 1914 in Waterloo, Lauderdale County, AL, died 14 Feb 2007, and was buried in Young Cemetery, Waterloo, Lauderdale County, AL.

- + 1515 M   i.   **William Roland Young** was born 19 Nov 1935 in Lauderdale County, AL.
- + 1516 M   ii. **Cletus Dempsey (Skeet) Young** was born 3 Nov 1937 in Lauderdale County, AL.
- + 1517 F   iii. **Bonnie Mae Young** was born 4 Aug 1941 in Lauderdale County, AL.
- 1518 F   iv. **Shirley Ann Young** was born 3 Oct 1943 in Lauderdale County, AL.
- + 1519 F   v.   **Jewel Dean Young** was born 8 Oct 1944 in Lauderdale County, AL, died 2 Jun 2000, and was buried in Tri-Cities Memorial Gardens, Florence, Lauderdale County, AL.
- + 1520 F   vi. **Barbara Sue Young** was born 12 Jun 1947 in Lauderdale County, AL.

588. Eura (Eurie) Sharp (*Charles W.[5], James (Jim) Charles Sr.[4], Adron (Edwin/Ade) Sr.[3], Charles W. Sr.[2], John Sr.[1]*) was born 29 Aug 1919 in Lauderdale County, AL, died 4 Aug 1998, and was buried in Murphy's Chapel Cemetery, Lauderdale County, AL.

Eura married **Ellie Bert Young**, son of **James Wylie (Jim) Young** and **Florence Beulah Young**, 25 Jul 1938 in Lauderdale County, AL. Ellie was born 23 Oct 1913 in Lauderdale County, AL, died 25 Aug 1993, and was buried in Murphy's Chapel Cemetery, Lauderdale County, AL.

+ 1521 M   i.   **James Charles (J. C.) Young** was born 26 Oct 1940 in Florence, Lauderdale County, AL.
+ 1522 F   ii.   **Alice Beulah Young** was born 5 Aug 1942 in Lauderdale County, AL.
+ 1523 F   iii.   **Agnes Gwindolin Young** was born 9 Apr 1945 in Lauderdale County, AL.
+ 1524 M   iv.   **Donald Kenneth Young** was born 9 Jan 1948 in Lauderdale County, AL.
+ 1525 F   v.   **Dorothy Mae Young** was born 26 May 1949 in Lauderdale County, AL.
+ 1526 F   vi.   **Deborah Sue Young** was born 9 May 1955 in Lauderdale County, AL.
+ 1527 M   vii. **Johnny Lynn Young** was born 29 Jul 1957 in Lauderdale County, AL, died 15 Mar 1994, and was buried in Murphy's Chapel Cemetery, Lauderdale County, AL.

589. Annie Maudie Rogers Sharp (*Joseph (Joe) Sidney^5, James (Jim) Charles Sr.^{4}, Adron (Edwin/Ade) Sr.^{3}, Charles W. Sr.^{2}, John Sr.^{1}*) was born in Jun 1898 in Lauderdale County, AL.

Annie married ***Unk Frazier** about 1920 in Tennessee.

590. Lawrence P. Sharp (*Joseph (Joe) Sidney^5, James (Jim) Charles Sr.^{4}, Adron (Edwin/Ade) Sr.^{3}, Charles W. Sr.^{2}, John Sr.^{1}*) was born about 1902 in Lauderdale County, AL and died in 1974 in McNairy County, TN.

Lawrence married **Martha Hollin** about 1922 in Tennessee. Martha was born 13 Mar 1890 in Tennessee and died 7 Nov 1976 in Tennessee.

591. Roosevelt (Vel) Sharp (*Joseph (Joe) Sidney^5, James (Jim) Charles Sr.^{4}, Adron (Edwin/Ade) Sr.^{3}, Charles W. Sr.^{2}, John Sr.^{1}*) was born about 1905 in Lauderdale County, AL.

Roosevelt married **Marye *Unk** about 1930 in Tennessee. Marye was born 25 Jul 1905 and died 29 Sep 1936 in McNairy County, TN.

  1528 M   i.   **Infant Sharp** was born in 1936 in Tennessee, died in 1936, and was buried in Milledgeville Cemetery, Hardin County, TN.

592. Joseph (Jodie) Floyd Sharp (*Joseph (Joe) Sidney^5, James (Jim) Charles Sr.^{4}, Adron (Edwin/Ade) Sr.^{3}, Charles W. Sr.^{2}, John Sr.^{1}*) was born 17 Nov 1908 in McNairy County, TN and died in May 1984 in Colbert County, AL.

Joseph married **Celia Ilene Doss**, daughter of **Johnny Buford Doss** and **Della Reid**, 3 Mar 1984 in Colbert County, AL. Celia was born 19 Nov 1913 in McNairy County, TN.

596. Russell Larry Sharp Sr. (*Joseph (Joe) Sidney^5, James (Jim) Charles Sr.^{4}, Adron (Edwin/Ade) Sr.^{3}, Charles W. Sr.^{2}, John Sr.^{1}*) was born 17 Feb 1917 in McNairy County, TN and died 30 Mar 1944 in McNairy County, TN.

Russell married **Wilma *Unk** about 1942.

  1529 M   i.   **Russell Larry Sharp Jr.** was born 24 Oct 1943 in McNairy County, TN, died 30 Mar 1944, and was buried in Milledgeville Cemetery, Hardin County, TN.

602. Marvin Turner Crider (*Elizabeth (Roxie) Belle Sharp^5, James (Jim) Charles Sr.^{4}, Adron (Edwin/Ade) Sr.^{3}, Charles W. Sr.^{2}, John Sr.^{1}*) was born 24 Jun 1902 in Lauderdale County, AL, died 6 Oct 1982, and was buried in Old Pleasant Hill Cemetery, Iuka, MS.

Marvin married **Mason Addie Milford**, daughter of **Thomas Douglas Milford** and **Laura Ann Minton**, 30 Aug 1919 in Lauderdale County, AL. Mason was born 6 Aug 1899 in Gravely Springs, Lauderdale County, AL, died 11 Apr 1984, and was buried in Old Pleasant Hill Cemetery, Iuka, MS.

+ 1530 F   i.   **Etta Mae Crider** was born 14 Jul 1920 in Lauderdale County, AL.
+ 1531 F   ii.   **Catherine Lorene Crider** was born 31 Jul 1925 in Lauderdale County, AL.
+ 1532 F   iii.   **Ruth C. Crider** was born 25 Sep 1929 in Lauderdale County, AL.
+ 1533 M   iv.   **Paul Evertt Crider** was born 31 Jul 1935 in Lauderdale County, AL.
+ 1534 F   v.   **Ima Jean Crider** was born 9 Apr 1940 in Tishomingo, MS.

603. Fannie Elizabeth (Sister) Crider (*Elizabeth (Roxie) Belle Sharp⁵, James (Jim) Charles Sr.⁴, Adron (Edwin/Ade) Sr.³, Charles W. Sr.², John Sr.¹*) was born 5 Jul 1903 in Lauderdale County, AL, died 17 Nov 1993, and was buried in Oak Grove Cemetery, Lauderdale County, AL.

Fannie married **Benjamin McKinley Wood**, son of **John Pugh Wood** and **Sarah (Sallie) Frances Elizabeth Milford**, 16 Dec 1925 in Lauderdale County, AL. Benjamin was born 26 Dec 1898 in Lauderdale County, AL, died 20 Aug 1981, and was buried in Milford Cemetery, Lauderdale County, AL.

+ 1535 M i. **Paul Douglas Wood Sr.** was born 24 Feb 1930 in Lauderdale County, AL, died 2 Oct 1960, and was buried in Oak Grove Cemetery, Lauderdale County, AL.
+ 1536 M ii. **Rufus Ezra Wood** was born 19 Sep 1931 in Lauderdale County, AL, died 19 Dec 2005, and was buried in Milford Cemetery, Lauderdale County, AL.
+ 1537 M iii. **Eldred McKinley Wood** was born 25 Aug 1934 in Lauderdale County, AL.

604. John Richard Crider (*Elizabeth (Roxie) Belle Sharp⁵, James (Jim) Charles Sr.⁴, Adron (Edwin/Ade) Sr.³, Charles W. Sr.², John Sr.¹*) was born 12 Jan 1905 in Gravely Springs, Lauderdale County, AL, died 2 Jan 1995, and was buried in Oak Grove Cemetery, Lauderdale County, AL.

John married **Helen Alean Woodfin**, daughter of **Zebbie D. Woodfin** and **Thula Mae Smith**, 31 Dec 1955. Helen was born 27 Dec 1918 in Limestone County, AL, died 16 Mar 1996, and was buried in Macedonia Cemetery, Lauderdale County, AL.

+ 1538 F i. **Betty Ann Crider** was born 10 Jul 1956 in Lauderdale County, AL.

605. Mary Etta (Virgie) Crider (*Elizabeth (Roxie) Belle Sharp⁵, James (Jim) Charles Sr.⁴, Adron (Edwin/Ade) Sr.³, Charles W. Sr.², John Sr.¹*) was born 6 Oct 1906 in Lauderdale County, AL, died 24 Oct 1966, and was buried in Oak Grove Cemetery, Lauderdale County, AL.

Mary married **Charlie Hampton Wood**, son of **Charles Wayne Wood** and **Mary Elizabeth (Lizzie) Herron**, 26 Jul 1924 in Lauderdale County, AL. Charlie was born 10 Sep 1903 in Wright, Lauderdale County, AL, died 12 Jan 1969, and was buried in Oak Grove Cemetery, Lauderdale County, AL. Another name for Charlie was Charles Hampton (Charlie) Wood.

+ 1539 F i. **Hazel Irene Wood** was born 29 Oct 1925 in Lauderdale County, AL, died 13 Apr 1994, and was buried in Oak Grove Cemetery, Lauderdale County, AL.
+ 1540 M ii. **Charles William Wood** was born 5 Apr 1927 in Lauderdale County, AL, died 21 Nov 1993, and was buried in Oak Grove Cemetery, Lauderdale County, AL.
+ 1541 F iii. **Edith Inez Wood** was born 19 Jan 1929 in Lauderdale County, AL.
+ 1542 M iv. **Carl Thomas Wood** was born 8 Oct 1930 in Wright, Lauderdale County, AL.
+ 1543 M v. **Louis Cola Wood** was born 10 Jun 1935 in Wright, Lauderdale County, AL.
+ 1544 F vi. **Betty Sue Wood** was born 21 May 1939 in Wright, Lauderdale County, AL.
+ 1545 F vii. **Rachel Anna Wood** was born 12 Oct 1945 in Wright, Lauderdale County, AL.

606. Bertha Mae Crider (*Elizabeth (Roxie) Belle Sharp⁵, James (Jim) Charles Sr.⁴, Adron (Edwin/Ade) Sr.³, Charles W. Sr.², John Sr.¹*) was born 10 Oct 1909 in Gravely Springs, Lauderdale County, AL and died 19 Jan 1977.

Bertha married **Arthur (Arter) Peden** 18 Jul 1930 in Lauderdale County, AL.

1546 M i. **Infant Peden** was born 4 Oct 1930, died in 1930, and was buried in Oak Grove Cemetery, Lauderdale County, AL.

Bertha next married **Clyde Wilhite** 18 Jul 1930 in Lauderdale County, AL.

607. Edgar Louis (Ed) Crider (*Elizabeth (Roxie) Belle Sharp⁵, James (Jim) Charles Sr.⁴, Adron (Edwin/Ade) Sr.³, Charles W. Sr.², John Sr.¹*) was born 28 Mar 1911 in Lauderdale County, AL, died 6 Apr 1978, and was buried in Oak Grove Cemetery, Lauderdale County, AL.

Edgar married **Rejoyce Maree (Joyce) Wood**, daughter of **Hurbert (Herb) Lee Wood** and **Ozella (Ella) Perkins**, 10 Oct 1936 in Lauderdale County, AL. Rejoyce was born 2 Jul 1913 in Lauderdale County, AL, died 29 Jan 1973, and was buried in Oak Grove Cemetery, Lauderdale County, AL.

1547	M	i.	**Infant Son Crider** was born in 1936, died in 1936, and was buried in Oak Grove Cemetery, Lauderdale County, AL.
+ 1548	M	ii.	**Edward Joyce (E. J.) Crider** was born 7 Apr 1941 in Lauderdale County, AL.
+ 1549	M	iii.	**Donald Fay Crider** was born 24 Sep 1943 in Lauderdale County, AL.

608. Annie Viola Crider (*Elizabeth (Roxie) Belle Sharp[5], James (Jim) Charles Sr.[4], Adron (Edwin/Ade) Sr.[3], Charles W. Sr.[2], John Sr.[1]*) was born 7 Jul 1915 in Lauderdale County, AL, died 12 Mar 1972, and was buried in Oak Grove Cemetery, Lauderdale County, AL.

Annie married ***Unk Newcomb**.

Annie next married **Doyle Holliman**, son of **June Holliman** and **Katie Wright**, 4 Aug 1947 in Lauderdale County, AL. Doyle was born 24 Apr 1912 in Lauderdale County, AL, died 11 Mar 1984, and was buried in Canaan Cemetery, Lauderdale County, AL.

609. James Albert Crider (*Elizabeth (Roxie) Belle Sharp[5], James (Jim) Charles Sr.[4], Adron (Edwin/Ade) Sr.[3], Charles W. Sr.[2], John Sr.[1]*) was born in 1919 in Gravely Springs, Lauderdale County, AL.

James married **Ruth Clark**.

+ 1550	F	i.	**Lois Crider** was born in 1939.
1551	F	ii.	**Patricia Crider**.
1552	F	iii.	**Dorothy Crider**.
+ 1553	F	iv.	**Peggy Crider**.
1554	M	v.	**James Owen Crider**.

610. Edith Louise Crider (*Elizabeth (Roxie) Belle Sharp[5], James (Jim) Charles Sr.[4], Adron (Edwin/Ade) Sr.[3], Charles W. Sr.[2], John Sr.[1]*) was born 15 Aug 1921 in Gravely Springs, Lauderdale County, AL, died 30 Mar 1998, and was buried in Harmony Hill Cemetery, Burnsville, Tishomingo County, MS.

Edith married **John Wesley Lambert** 3 Nov 1940 in Iuka, Tishomingo County, MS. John was born 26 Aug 1914, died 30 Oct 1993, and was buried in Harmony Hill Cemetery, Burnsville, Tishomingo County, MS.

+ 1555	F	i.	**Bonnie Sue Lambert**.
+ 1556	F	ii.	**Shirley Olivia Lambert**.
1557	M	iii.	**Charles Wesley Lambert**.
+ 1558	F	iv.	**Debra Ann Lambert**.
+ 1559	M	v.	**William Dan Lambert** was born 21 Jun 1954, died 12 Nov 1986, and was buried in Harmony Hill Cemetery, Burnsville, Tishomingo County, MS.
1560	M	vi.	**Dennis Ray Lambert** was born 27 Jun 1957, died 3 Sep 1984, and was buried in Harmony Hill Cemetery, Burnsville, Tishomingo County, MS.

613. William Herbert (Hubbard) Sharp (*Louis (Bud) Wheeler[5], James (Jim) Charles Sr.[4], Adron (Edwin/Ade) Sr.[3], Charles W. Sr.[2], John Sr.[1]*) was born 12 Oct 1909 in Florence, Lauderdale County, AL, died 16 Jul 2004, and was buried in Oak Grove Cemetery, Lauderdale County, AL.

William married **Flora Wood**, daughter of **Charles Wayne Wood** and **Mary Elizabeth (Lizzie) Herron**, 4 Aug 1928 in Lauderdale County, AL. Flora was born 6 Mar 1910 in Wright, Lauderdale County, AL, died 22 Jan 1988, and was buried in Oak Grove Cemetery, Lauderdale County, AL.

+ 1561	F	i.	**Agnes Lorene Sharp** was born 30 Jul 1930 in Lauderdale County, AL.
+ 1562	M	ii.	**Ofard William Sharp** was born 23 Aug 1931 in Lauderdale County, AL, died 7 May 2005, and was buried in Tyronza Cemetery, Tyronza, Poinsett County, AR.
+ 1563	F	iii.	**Hazel Erline Sharp** was born 4 Jun 1934 in Lauderdale County, AL.
+ 1564	M	iv.	**Franklin (Duce) Sharp** was born 8 Sep 1936 in Lauderdale County, AL, died 1 Oct 1999, and was buried in Oak Grove Cemetery, Lauderdale County, AL.
+ 1565	M	v.	**Charles Hampton Sharp** was born 5 Feb 1939 in Lauderdale County, AL.
1566	M	vi.	**Walter David Sharp** was born 26 Feb 1946 in Lauderdale County, AL, died 10 Jan 1969, and was buried in Oak Grove Cemetery, Lauderdale County, AL.
+ 1567	M	vii.	**Amos Earl Sharp** was born in Lauderdale County, AL.

615. Pearlie Elizabeth Sharp (*Louis (Bud) Wheeler*[5], *James (Jim) Charles Sr.*[4], *Adron (Edwin/Ade) Sr.*[3], *Charles W. Sr.*[2], *John Sr.*[1]) was born 27 Jun 1914 in Lauderdale County, AL, died 22 Jun 1988, and was buried in Wright Cemetery, Wright, Lauderdale County, AL.

Pearlie married **Huell Wood**, son of **Bennett Arvil (Ben) Wood** and **Mittie Lou Wood**, 5 Feb 1936 in Lauderdale County, AL. Huell was born 7 Sep 1916 in Lauderdale County, AL, died 17 May 2000, and was buried in Wright Cemetery, Wright, Lauderdale County, AL.

616. Loye Arvel Sharp (*Louis (Bud) Wheeler*[5], *James (Jim) Charles Sr.*[4], *Adron (Edwin/Ade) Sr.*[3], *Charles W. Sr.*[2], *John Sr.*[1]) was born 1 Mar 1916 in Gravely Springs, Lauderdale County, AL, died 29 Oct 2004, and was buried in Oak Grove Cemetery, Lauderdale County, AL.

Loye married **Pearlie Mae Wood**, daughter of **Finis Leonard (Phiney/Slim) Wood** and **Margie Ann (Marjorie) Bruce**, 18 Oct 1935 in Lauderdale County, AL. Pearlie was born 1 May 1915 in Gravely Springs, Lauderdale County, AL, died 26 Feb 2003, and was buried in Oak Grove Cemetery, Lauderdale County, AL.

+ 1568	M	i.	**Rufus Eldred Sharp** was born 3 Oct 1936 in Gravely Springs, Lauderdale County, AL.
+ 1569	F	ii.	**Lola Mae Sharp** was born 16 Mar 1938 in Gravely Springs, Lauderdale County, AL.
+ 1570	M	iii.	**Millard Woodrow Sharp** was born 21 Feb 1940 in Gravely Springs, Lauderdale County, AL.
+ 1571	M	iv.	**Ralph Arvel Sharp** was born 15 Nov 1942 in Gravely Springs, Lauderdale County, AL.
+ 1572	F	v.	**Carolyn Lois Sharp** was born 24 Nov 1944 in Gravely Springs, Lauderdale County, AL.
+ 1573	F	vi.	**Sally Ann (Mavis) Sharp** was born 27 Oct 1946 in Gravely Springs, Lauderdale County, AL.
+ 1574	M	vii.	**Berlon Ray Sharp** was born 13 Sep 1948 in Gravely Springs, Lauderdale County, AL.

617. Lawrence (Toby) Eldred Sharp (*Louis (Bud) Wheeler*[5], *James (Jim) Charles Sr.*[4], *Adron (Edwin/Ade) Sr.*[3], *Charles W. Sr.*[2], *John Sr.*[1]) was born 22 May 1919 in Lauderdale County, AL, died 14 May 1994, and was buried in Oak Grove Cemetery, Lauderdale County, AL.

Lawrence married **Pauline Inez Wood**, daughter of **Finis Leonard (Phiney/Slim) Wood** and **Margie Ann (Marjorie) Bruce**. Pauline was born 1 May 1921 in Gravely Springs, Lauderdale County, AL, died 17 Feb 2007, and was buried in Oak Grove Cemetery, Lauderdale County, AL.

1575	F	i.	**Infant Daughter Wood** was born 21 Jul 1937 in Lauderdale County, AL, died 21 Jul 1937, and was buried in Oak Grove Cemetery, Lauderdale County, AL.
+ 1576	F	ii.	**Clara Sue (Susie) Wood** was born 12 Feb 1940 in Lauderdale County, AL, died 24 Jan 1994, and was buried in Oak Grove Cemetery, Lauderdale County, AL.
+ 1577	M	iii.	**Stevie Lawrence Wood** was born 13 Jul 1947 in Florence, Lauderdale County, AL.
+ 1578	F	iv.	**Patsy Ann Wood** was born 14 Oct 1949 in Florence, Lauderdale County, AL.

Lawrence next married **Fannie Elizabeth Ezekiel**, daughter of **Jesse James Ezekiel** and **Dewey Leora Wood**, 24 Dec 1940 in Lauderdale County, AL. Fannie was born 13 Jul 1922 in Lauderdale County, AL.

+ 1579	F	i.	**Ruby Nell Sharp** was born 29 Oct 1941 in Lauderdale County, AL, died 23 Feb 1974 in Mishawaka, St Joseph County, IN, and was buried in Oak Grove Cemetery, Lauderdale County, AL.
+ 1580	M	ii.	**Tony Leon Sharp** was born 28 Jun 1944 in Lauderdale County, AL.
+ 1581	F	iii.	**Doris Etoyle Sharp** was born 7 Jul 1946 in Lauderdale County, AL.
+ 1582	M	iv.	**Alfred Donald Sharp** was born 20 Dec 1947 in Lauderdale County, AL, died 28 Aug 1978, and was buried in Oak Grove Cemetery, Lauderdale County, AL.
+ 1583	F	v.	**Cathy Deloris Sharp** was born 22 Feb 1952 in Lauderdale County, AL.
+ 1584	M	vi.	**Juston Leveril Sharp** was born 19 Nov 1953 in Lauderdale County, AL, died 21 May 1999, and was buried in Oak Grove Cemetery, Lauderdale County, AL.
+ 1585	M	vii.	**Danny Wayne Sharp** was born 25 Apr 1956 in Lauderdale County, AL, died 20 Dec 1992, and was buried in Oak Grove Cemetery, Lauderdale County, AL.
+ 1586	F	viii.	**Melba Rose Sharp** was born 13 Mar 1959 in Lauderdale County, AL.
+ 1587	F	ix.	**Tammy Loudean Sharp** was born 16 Apr 1962 in Lauderdale County, AL.

619. Myrtle Lutts (*Mary Elizabeth Sharp*[5], *James (Jim) Charles Sr.*[4], *Adron (Edwin/Ade) Sr.*[3], *Charles W. Sr.*[2], *John Sr.*[1]) was born 13 Mar 1912 in Lauderdale County, AL, died 29 Jan 1940, and was buried in Oak Grove Cemetery, Lauderdale County, AL.

Myrtle married **Doyle Lee Young**, son of **John Robert Young** and **Callie Fielder**, 28 Dec 1935 in Lauderdale County, AL. Doyle was born 18 Jul 1913 in Lauderdale County, AL, died 30 Jan 1991, and was buried in Wright Cemetery, Wright, Lauderdale County, AL.

+ 1588 M i. **Carl Robert Young** was born 26 Nov 1937 in Lauderdale County, AL, died 8 Mar 2008 in Lauderdale County, AL, and was buried in Central Heights Community Cemetery, Lauderdale County, AL.

+ 1589 F ii. **Laura Young**.

+ 1590 F iii. **Rita Mae Young**.

+ 1591 F iv. **June Young**.

620. Raymond Andrew Allison (*Margie (Lady) J. Sharp^5, James (Jim) Charles Sr.^{4}, Adron (Edwin/Ade) Sr.^{3}, Charles W. Sr.^{2}, John Sr.^{1}*) was born 25 May 1911 in Tennessee, died 3 Mar 1977, and was buried in Oak Grove Cemetery, Lauderdale County, AL.

Raymond married **Bama Inez Ingram**, daughter of **Lige Ingram** and **Lue Ella Hale**, 24 Aug 1928 in Lauderdale County, AL. Bama was born 23 Jun 1909 in Lauderdale County, AL, died 24 Dec 1979, and was buried in Oak Grove Cemetery, Lauderdale County, AL.

+ 1592 F i. **Ruby Lucille Allison** was born 26 Jul 1929 in Lauderdale County, AL.

1593 F ii. **Christine Allison** was born 29 Sep 1930 in Lauderdale County, AL, died 28 Oct 1930, and was buried in Oak Grove Cemetery, Lauderdale County, AL.

+ 1594 F iii. **Lois Evelyn Allison** was born 5 Nov 1932 in Lauderdale County, AL.

+ 1595 F iv. **Elsie Gertrude Allison** was born 4 Dec 1934 in Lauderdale County, AL.

+ 1596 M v. **Harve Harrison Allison** was born 2 Feb 1936 in Lauderdale County, AL, died 17 Jun 1991, and was buried in Oak Grove Cemetery, Lauderdale County, AL.

+ 1597 M vi. **Marcus Andrew Allison** was born 7 Sep 1938 in Lauderdale County, AL, died 29 Oct 2005, and was buried in Tri-Cities Memorial Gardens, Florence, Lauderdale County, AL.

+ 1598 M vii. **Connie Eugene Allison** was born 28 Dec 1941 in Lauderdale County, AL.

+ 1599 M viii. **Vernon Lee Allison** was born 2 Jan 1943 in Lauderdale County, AL.

1600 M ix. **Ray Allison** was born 15 Jun 1944, died 15 Jun 1944, and was buried in Oak Grove Cemetery, Lauderdale County, AL.

+ 1601 M x. **Rayburn Leon Allison** was born 13 Jun 1946 in Lauderdale County, AL.

+ 1602 F xi. **Sandra Gail Allison** was born 4 Jan 1951 in Lauderdale County, AL.

621. Carrie Etta Allison (*Margie (Lady) J. Sharp^5, James (Jim) Charles Sr.^{4}, Adron (Edwin/Ade) Sr.^{3}, Charles W. Sr.^{2}, John Sr.^{1}*) was born 22 Jan 1913 in Hardin County, TN, died 31 Jan 1960, and was buried in Macedonia Cemetery, Lauderdale County, AL.

Carrie married **Everett Owen Poole**, son of **James A. Poole** and **Virginia Bevis**, 24 Dec 1941 in Lauderdale County, AL. Everett was born 15 Mar 1889 in Lauderdale County, AL, died 5 May 1982, and was buried in Macedonia Cemetery, Lauderdale County, AL.

+ 1603 F i. **Betty Sue Poole** was born 20 Nov 1942 in Lauderdale County, AL.

+ 1604 M ii. **Jimmy Carl Poole** was born 6 Aug 1949 in Lauderdale County, AL.

623. Lady Jewel Allison (*Margie (Lady) J. Sharp^5, James (Jim) Charles Sr.^{4}, Adron (Edwin/Ade) Sr.^{3}, Charles W. Sr.^{2}, John Sr.^{1}*) was born 15 Jul 1917 in Waterloo, Lauderdale County, AL, died 21 Aug 1979, and was buried in Tyronza Cemetery, Tyronza, Poinsett County, AR.

Lady married **John Robert Wood**, son of **Charles Wayne Wood** and **Mary Elizabeth (Lizzie) Herron**, 25 Nov 1933 in Lauderdale County, AL. John was born 21 Sep 1912 in Wright, Lauderdale County, AL, died 15 Oct 1994, and was buried in Tyronza Cemetery, Tyronza, Poinsett County, AR.

+ 1605 F i. **Virginia Elizabeth Wood** was born 24 Mar 1935 in Waterloo, Lauderdale County, AL.

+ 1606 F ii. **Nettie Louise Wood** was born 1 Jun 1936 in Waterloo, Lauderdale County, AL.

+ 1607 F iii. **Rachel Kathrine Wood** was born 29 Jan 1938 in Waterloo, Lauderdale County, AL.

+ 1608 F iv. **Robbie Etoil Wood** was born 23 May 1940 in Waterloo, Lauderdale County, AL.

+ 1609 F v. **Thelma Jean Wood** was born 4 Apr 1942 in Waterloo, Lauderdale County, AL.

+ 1610 F vi. **Nadine Wood** was born 1 Jul 1943 in Waterloo, Lauderdale County, AL.

+ 1611 F vii. **Clara Nell Wood** was born 17 Dec 1945 in Waterloo, Lauderdale County, AL.

+ 1612 F viii. **Nancy Carolyn Wood** was born 5 Oct 1947 in Waterloo, Lauderdale County, AL.

1613 F ix. **Judy Mae Wood** was born 6 Mar 1949 in Waterloo, Lauderdale County, AL, died 21 Jul 1949, and was buried in Oak Grove Cemetery, Lauderdale County, AL.

1614 M x. **Robert Earl Wood** was born 31 Mar 1952 in Tyronza, Poinsett County, AR, died 31 Mar 1952, and was buried in Tyronza Cemetery, Tyronza, Poinsett County, AR.

+ 1615 M xi. **Robert David Wood** was born 28 Aug 1956 in Memphis, Shelby County, TN.

625. Andy J. Allison (*Margie (Lady) J. Sharp* [5], *James (Jim) Charles Sr.* [4], *Adron (Edwin/Ade) Sr.* [3], *Charles W. Sr.* [2], *John Sr.* [1]) was born 9 Mar 1919 in Lauderdale County, AL, died 10 Apr 1974, and was buried in Tyronza Cemetery, Tyronza, Poinsett County, AR.

Andy married **Della Hubbard**, daughter of **John Washington Hubbard** and **Bertha M. Milford**, 30 Jul 1939 in Lauderdale County, AL. Della was born in 1920.

626. William Turner Allison (*Margie (Lady) J. Sharp* [5], *James (Jim) Charles Sr.* [4], *Adron (Edwin/Ade) Sr.* [3], *Charles W. Sr.* [2], *John Sr.* [1]) was born 3 Jul 1921 in Gravely Springs, Lauderdale County, AL, died 11 Feb 1999, and was buried in Oak Grove Cemetery, Lauderdale County, AL.

William married **Onita Katherine (Neat) Wood**, daughter of **Finis Leonard (Phiney/Slim) Wood** and **Margie Ann (Marjorie) Bruce**, 30 Aug 1943 in Lauderdale County, AL. Onita was born 7 Jul 1924 in Gravely Springs, Lauderdale County, AL.

+ 1616 M i. **Melvin Jack Allison Sr.** was born 9 Jun 1943 in Florence, Lauderdale County, AL.

1617 M ii. **Howard Neal Allison** was born 2 Aug 1944 in Florence, Lauderdale County, AL.

+ 1618 M iii. **Lonnie Edward Allison** was born 20 Aug 1946 in Florence, Lauderdale County, AL.

+ 1619 M iv. **Tony William Allison** was born 2 Aug 1948 in Florence, Lauderdale County, AL.

+ 1620 F v. **Clara Jane Allison** was born 5 Aug 1957 in Florence, Lauderdale County, AL.

627. Vertie Mae Allison (*Margie (Lady) J. Sharp* [5], *James (Jim) Charles Sr.* [4], *Adron (Edwin/Ade) Sr.* [3], *Charles W. Sr.* [2], *John Sr.* [1]) was born 22 Feb 1922 in Lauderdale County, AL, died 7 Jul 2002, and was buried in Oak Grove Cemetery, Lauderdale County, AL.

Vertie married **Arthur Lee (Dick) Smith**, son of **Jimmy Ottis (Ott) Smith** and **Susie Terry**, 27 Nov 1938 in Lauderdale County, AL. Arthur was born 17 Sep 1917 in Lauderdale County, AL.

+ 1621 F i. **Evelyn Irene Smith** was born 31 Dec 1939 in Lauderdale County, AL.

+ 1622 M ii. **Charles Leon Smith** was born 27 Jul 1943 in Lauderdale County, AL.

+ 1623 F iii. **Wanda Sue Smith** was born 17 Feb 1946 in Lauderdale County, AL.

+ 1624 F iv. **Margie Ruth Smith** was born 21 Jul 1948 in Lauderdale County, AL.

+ 1625 M v. **Travis Lynn Smith** was born 23 Aug 1958 in Lauderdale County, AL.

+ 1626 F vi. **Vicki Kay Smith** was born 10 Jul 1961 in Lauderdale County, AL.

+ 1627 M vii. **Ricky Dale Smith** was born 15 Jan 1963 in Lauderdale County, AL.

628. Elizabeth Earline Allison (*Margie (Lady) J. Sharp* [5], *James (Jim) Charles Sr.* [4], *Adron (Edwin/Ade) Sr.* [3], *Charles W. Sr.* [2], *John Sr.* [1]) was born 7 Feb 1923 in Lauderdale County, AL, died 13 Apr 1999, and was buried in Oak Grove Cemetery, Lauderdale County, AL.

Elizabeth married **Fred Amos Wood**, son of **Floyde Leonard Wood** and **Martha (Mattie) Inez Taylor**, 7 Nov 1942 in Lauderdale County, AL. Fred was born 26 Jan 1921 in Wright, Lauderdale County, AL, died 29 Aug 1976, and was buried in Oak Grove Cemetery, Lauderdale County, AL.

+ 1628 M i. **Fred Calvin Wood** was born 16 Jun 1946 in Lauderdale County, AL.

+ 1629 M ii. **Jerry Wayne Wood** was born 15 Jan 1948 in Lauderdale County, AL.

+ 1630 M iii. **Kenneth Carroll Wood** was born 10 Jan 1950 in Lauderdale County, AL.

+ 1631 M iv. **Gerald Glenn Wood** was born 14 Jan 1953 in Lauderdale County, AL.

+ 1632 F v. **Elizabeth Ann Wood** was born 6 Jun 1956 in Lauderdale County, AL.

+ 1633 M vi. **Lowell Dale Wood** was born 1 Nov 1959 in Lauderdale County, AL.

+ 1634 M vii. **Ronnie Earl Wood** was born 27 Aug 1969 in Lauderdale County, AL.

629. Clara Estelle Allison (*Margie (Lady) J. Sharp* [5], *James (Jim) Charles Sr.* [4], *Adron (Edwin/Ade) Sr.* [3], *Charles W. Sr.* [2], *John Sr.* [1]) was born 9 Jul 1924 in Lauderdale County, AL.

Clara married **Ray Wood**, son of **James Hampton (Jim) Wood Jr.** and **Mildred Sharp**, 21 Nov 1942 in Lauderdale County, AL. Ray was born 9 Feb 1921 in Lauderdale County, AL, died 31 Oct 1991, and was buried in Greenview Memorial Park, Florence, Lauderdale County, AL.

+ 1635 F i. **Clara Jean (Jeannie) Wood** was born 14 Feb 1947 in Lauderdale County, AL.
+ 1636 M ii. **Dennis Ray Wood** was born 30 Jan 1948 in Lauderdale County, AL, died 19 Feb 2003, and was buried in Greenview Memorial Park, Florence, Lauderdale County, AL.
+ 1637 F iii. **Shirley Ann Wood** was born 24 Aug 1949 in Lauderdale County, AL.
+ 1638 F iv. **Martha Jane Wood** was born 9 Jul 1952 in Lauderdale County, AL.
+ 1639 M v. **Timothy (Tim) Michael Wood** was born 22 Mar 1956 in Lauderdale County, AL.

630. Velty Hoover Allison (*Margie (Lady) J. Sharp*[5], *James (Jim) Charles Sr.*[4], *Adron (Edwin/Ade) Sr.*[3], *Charles W. Sr.*[2], *John Sr.*[1]) was born 4 Aug 1929 in Lauderdale County, AL, died 18 Nov 2002, and was buried in Oak Grove Cemetery, Lauderdale County, AL.

Velty married **Ethel Imogene Reeves**. Ethel was born 23 Aug 1933 in Lauderdale County, AL, died 27 Apr 1990, and was buried in Oak Grove Cemetery, Lauderdale County, AL.

+ 1640 F i. **Linda Gail Allison** was born 1 Oct 1950 in Lauderdale County, AL.

Velty next married **Mamie Baugus**.

631. Earl Alvin Allison (*Margie (Lady) J. Sharp*[5], *James (Jim) Charles Sr.*[4], *Adron (Edwin/Ade) Sr.*[3], *Charles W. Sr.*[2], *John Sr.*[1]) was born 4 May 1932 in Lauderdale County, AL.

Earl married **Darnell Eunice Burbank**, daughter of **Ethridge John Burbank** and **Erma Jane Davis**, 24 Dec 1949 in Iuka, Tishomingo County, MS. Darnell was born 14 Feb 1932 in Lauderdale County, AL.

+ 1641 M i. **Earl Steven Allison** was born 2 Nov 1950 in South Bend, St Joseph County, IN.
+ 1642 F ii. **Rosa Rita Allison** was born 18 Jan 1952 in Mishawaka, St Joseph County, IN.
  1643 M iii. **Jerry Lynn Allison** was born 21 Mar 1955, died 26 Jun 1969, and was buried in Oak Grove Cemetery, Lauderdale County, AL.

634. Charlie McConnell (*Mary Ann Sharp*[5], *Charles (Charlie) A.*[4], *Adron (Edwin/Ade) Sr.*[3], *Charles W. Sr.*[2], *John Sr.*[1]) was born 16 Jul 1881 in Booneville, Logan County, AR and died 14 Feb 1923.

Charlie married **Lulu Appleton** 22 Dec 1904.

638. Jesse Robert McConnell (*Mary Ann Sharp*[5], *Charles (Charlie) A.*[4], *Adron (Edwin/Ade) Sr.*[3], *Charles W. Sr.*[2], *John Sr.*[1]) was born 8 Mar 1887 in Booneville, Logan County, AR, died 28 Aug 1959, and was buried in Fort Smith, AR.

Jesse married **Nola Eugene Foster**, daughter of **Buck Byrum Foster** and **Luna Eugenia Barlow**, 26 Feb 1911 in Booneville, Logan County, AR. Nola was born 2 Oct 1893 in Booneville, Logan County, AR.

+ 1644 M i. **Foster Woodrow McConnell Sr.** was born 21 Mar 1912 in Booneville, Logan County, AR.

640. Mundrow Sharp (*Lil Adron*[5], *Charles (Charlie) A.*[4], *Adron (Edwin/Ade) Sr.*[3], *Charles W. Sr.*[2], *John Sr.*[1]).

Mundrow married **Bonnie Dorrough**.

Mundrow next married **Martha Bailey**.

641. Virgil Sharp (*Lil Adron*[5], *Charles (Charlie) A.*[4], *Adron (Edwin/Ade) Sr.*[3], *Charles W. Sr.*[2], *John Sr.*[1]) was born in Feb 1892.

Virgil married **Annie K. Kihilling**.

642. Claude V. Sharp (*Lil Adron*[5], *Charles (Charlie) A.*[4], *Adron (Edwin/Ade) Sr.*[3], *Charles W. Sr.*[2], *John Sr.*[1]) was born in Jul 1894.

Claude married **Willie Maxwell**.

643. Florence Sharp (*Lil Adron⁵, Charles (Charlie) A.⁴, Adron (Edwin/Ade) Sr.³, Charles W. Sr.², John Sr.¹*) was born in May 1897.

Florence married **Lester Maxwell**.

644. Kelly C. Sharp (*Lil Adron⁵, Charles (Charlie) A.⁴, Adron (Edwin/Ade) Sr.³, Charles W. Sr.², John Sr.¹*) was born in Arkansas and was buried in Arkansas.

Kelly married **Ruth Maxwell** in Arkansas. Ruth was buried in Arkansas.

1645	M	i.	**John Q. Sharp** was born in Arkansas.
1646	M	ii.	**Dale Sharp** was born in Arkansas and was buried in Arkansas.
1647	F	iii.	**Rebba Sharp** was born in Arkansas.
+ 1648	M	iv.	**Hayden D. T. Sharp** was born in Arkansas and died in 1983 in Arkansas.
1649	F	v.	**Gwen Sharp** was born in Arkansas.
1650	M	vi.	**Billy Wayne Sharp** was born in Arkansas and was buried in Arkansas.

645. Ade Leonard Sharp (*Lil Adron⁵, Charles (Charlie) A.⁴, Adron (Edwin/Ade) Sr.³, Charles W. Sr.², John Sr.¹*) was born in Sep 1889.

Ade married **Archie Lewis**.

646. Biven Sharp (*Lil Adron⁵, Charles (Charlie) A.⁴, Adron (Edwin/Ade) Sr.³, Charles W. Sr.², John Sr.¹*) was born in 1906.

Biven married **Ida L. Bobbett**.

647. Verbie Anter Sharp (*Carol (Fuzzy) Louis⁵, Charles (Charlie) A.⁴, Adron (Edwin/Ade) Sr.³, Charles W. Sr.², John Sr.¹*) was born 16 Mar 1901 in Kula Chaha, La Flore County, Indian Territory, died 3 Feb 1974 in Carney, Lincoln County, OK, and was buried in Carney Cemetery, Lincoln County, OK.

Verbie married **Nancy Taylor**, daughter of **George W. Taylor** and **Unknown**, 17 Sep 1920 in Poteau, Le Flore County, OK. Nancy was born in Cherry Grove, AR.

+ 1651	F	i.	**Genoa V. Sharp** was born 16 Aug 1921.
+ 1652	M	ii.	**OssaLee Sharp** was born 8 Aug 1923 and died 2 Jan 2005 in Visalia, Tulare, CA.
+ 1653	F	iii.	**Mirlacoys Sharp** was born 19 Mar 1926.
+ 1654	M	iv.	**Verbie Anter Sharp Jr.** was born 11 Apr 1929 and died 4 Jun 2008 in Bakersville, CA.
+ 1655	M	v.	**Bobby Ray Sharp** was born 3 Apr 1931 in Hope, Stephens County, OK and died 24 Jan 2002 in Stephens County, OK.

652. Adron Pension Dover (*Leanna Hill⁵, Elizabeth Mae (Lizzie) Sharp⁴, Adron (Edwin/Ade) Sr.³, Charles W. Sr.², John Sr.¹*) was born 19 Sep 1884 in Phillips County, AR, died 9 Apr 1928, and was buried in St. Frances County, AR.

Adron married **Annie French** 5 Mar 1907 in St. Frances County, AR. Annie was born in 1888 in St. Frances County, AR.

653. Josephine Dover (*Leanna Hill⁵, Elizabeth Mae (Lizzie) Sharp⁴, Adron (Edwin/Ade) Sr.³, Charles W. Sr.², John Sr.¹*) was born 12 Aug 1888 in Phillips, St Frances County, AR and died 11 Dec 1967 in St. Frances County, AR.

Josephine married **Marcus Thigpen** 14 Oct 1906 in St. Frances County, AR. Marcus was born in 1884 in Palestine, St Francis County, AR.

654. Gertrude Dover (*Leanna Hill⁵, Elizabeth Mae (Lizzie) Sharp⁴, Adron (Edwin/Ade) Sr.³, Charles W. Sr.², John Sr.¹*) was born 27 Mar 1890 in Palestine, St Francis County, AR and died 28 Jul 1916 in St. Frances County, AR.

Gertrude married **Tom Grimes**. Tom was born in 1886 in Palestine, St Francis County, AR.

656. Jenetta Dover (*Leanna Hill⁵, Elizabeth Mae (Lizzie) Sharp⁴, Adron (Edwin/Ade) Sr.³, Charles W. Sr.², John Sr.¹*) was born 6 Mar 1895 in Palestine, St Francis County, AR and died 31 Mar 1974 in Palestine, St Francis County, AR.

Jenetta married **Samuel Jackson Jones** 22 Nov 1910 in St. Frances County, AR. Samuel was born 10 Jan 1893 in St. Frances County, AR and died 3 Dec 1968 in St. Frances County, AR.

1656	M	i.	**Paul Jones** was born 23 Sep 1912 in Palestine, St Francis County, AR and died 6 Oct 1972 in St. Frances County, AR.
1657	M	ii.	**Stanley Jones** was born 7 Apr 1917 in Palestine, St Francis County, AR and died in Nov 1917 in St. Frances County, AR.
1658	M	iii.	**William Anderson Jones** was born 29 Sep 1919 in Palestine, St Francis County, AR and died 10 Jul 1971 in West Memphis, Crittenden County, AR.
1659	M	iv.	**Douglas Fairbanks Jones** was born 1 Apr 1926 in Palestine, St Francis County, AR and died 4 Aug 1985 in St. Frances County, AR.
1660	F	v.	**Anna Bell Jones** was born 22 Sep 1928 in Palestine, St Francis County, AR.

657. Hattie Dover (*Leanna Hill⁵, Elizabeth Mae (Lizzie) Sharp⁴, Adron (Edwin/Ade) Sr.³, Charles W. Sr.², John Sr.¹*) was born 12 Oct 1898 in Palestine, St Francis County, AR and died 11 Apr 1968 in St. Frances County, AR.

Hattie married **Frank Jones** 3 Oct 1911 in St. Frances County, AR. Frank was born in 1894 in Palestine, St Francis County, AR.

660. Florence Dover (*Leanna Hill⁵, Elizabeth Mae (Lizzie) Sharp⁴, Adron (Edwin/Ade) Sr.³, Charles W. Sr.², John Sr.¹*) was born 19 Jul 1904 in Palestine, St Francis County, AR and died 20 Mar 1976 in St. Frances County, AR.

Florence married **Bob Alsoup**. Bob was born in 1900 in Palestine, St Francis County, AR.

662. Griffith Putman Carr (*Laura E. Murphy⁵, Mary Eliza Sharp⁴, John Sr.³, Charles W. Sr.², John Sr.¹*) was born 13 Jan 1882 in Lauderdale County, AL and died 1 Aug 1951.

Griffith married **LaDonia Pittman** 14 Mar 1907 in Oklahoma.

1661	M	i.	**Glenn Carr**.
1662	F	ii.	**Meryl Carr**.
1663	F	iii.	**Edith Carr**.

663. Andrew J. Carr (*Laura E. Murphy⁵, Mary Eliza Sharp⁴, John Sr.³, Charles W. Sr.², John Sr.¹*) was born in 1884 in Lauderdale County, AL and died 27 Aug 1962 in Savannah, TN.

Andrew married **Bess Morrow** in 1914.

1664	M	i.	**Douglas Carr**.
1665	F	ii.	**Ruby Carr**.

664. Noah Edgar Carr (*Laura E. Murphy⁵, Mary Eliza Sharp⁴, John Sr.³, Charles W. Sr.², John Sr.¹*) was born in 1886 in Lauderdale County, AL.

Noah married **Bess Brewer**.

1666	M	i.	**James Carr**.
1667	M	ii.	**Edward Carr**.
1668	F	iii.	**Hazel Carr**.

665. Lee Shelton Carr (*Laura E. Murphy⁵, Mary Eliza Sharp⁴, John Sr.³, Charles W. Sr.², John Sr.¹*) was born in 1887 in Lauderdale County, AL.

Lee married **Lillian Durham**.

1669	M	i.	**Doyle Carr**.
1670	F	ii.	**Edith Carr**.

```
1671  F    iii.   Odessia Carr.
1672  F    iv.    Zelma Carr.
1673  F    v.     Thelma Carr.
1674  F    vi.    Iva Lee Carr.
1675  M    vii.   Griffin Carr.
```

666. Mamie Etta Carr (*Laura E. Murphy*[5], *Mary Eliza Sharp*[4], *John Sr.*[3], *Charles W. Sr.*[2], *John Sr.*[1]) was born 4 Sep 1888 in Lauderdale County, AL.

Mamie married **Clifford Linam**.
```
1676  M    i.     Earl Linam.
1677  M    ii.    Clarence Linam.
1678  M    iii.   Roy Linam.
1679  F    iv.    Mamie Etta Linam.
```

667. Minnie Ada Carr (*Laura E. Murphy*[5], *Mary Eliza Sharp*[4], *John Sr.*[3], *Charles W. Sr.*[2], *John Sr.*[1]) was born 1 Aug 1890 in Lauderdale County, AL.

Minnie married **Edgar Adkisson**.
```
1680  M    i.     Lewis Adkisson.
1681  M    ii.    Clark Adkisson.
1682  M    iii.   Talmadge Adkisson.
1683  M    iv.    Roy Adkisson.
1684  F    v.     Juanita Adkisson.
1685  F    vi.    Thelma Adkisson.
```

672. Mason Louise Wright (*George Moses (Mode) Wright*[5], *Elizabeth (Lizzie) May Sharp*[4], *John Sr.*[3], *Charles W. Sr.*[2], *John Sr.*[1]) was born 13 Jan 1918 in Wright, Lauderdale County, AL, died 25 Feb 1999 in Lauderdale County, AL, and was buried in Greenview Memorial Park, Florence, Lauderdale County, AL.

General Notes: Obituary - Times Daily, Florence, Lauderdale County, Alabama

"Mrs. Louise White, 81, passed away on Thursday, Feb. 25, 1999, at ECM Hospital after a brief illness. The family will receive friends at Elkins Funeral Home, Florence, Friday evening, Feb. 26, from 6 p.m. until 8 p.m. At Mrs. White's request, there will be only a graveside ceremony at Greenview Memorial Gardens on Saturday, Feb. 27, at 11 a.m. with Bro. Emerald Bailey officiating.
Mrs. White was a lifelong resident of the Wright Community. She was preceded in death by a sister, Etta Hanback, and two brothers, Paul Winford and Louis Almon Wright. Mrs. White also was preceded in death by her son, Jerry Travis White on Feb. 15, 1998. Mrs. White's favorite hobby was reading the Bible and she had read it through numerous times.
She is survived by her husband of 54 years, Jessie L. White of Waterloo; sisters, Elizabeth Wright, Waterloo, and Mattie Mae Elliot, Leighton; granddaughter, Sandi Tubbs; and great -granddaughter, Lauren Nicole Tubbs.
Pallbearers will include Larry Cole, Robert Cole, Tommy Elliot, Glenn Stevenson, Leonard Berryman and Edwin White. Honorary pallbearers include Charles Hanback and David Elliot.
Memorials may be made to The Memorial and Honor Program, St. Jude Children's Research Hospital, 501 St. Jude Place, Memphis, Tenn., 38105-1905."

Mason married **Jesse Lee White**, son of **Jones Oscar White** and **Laura B. Robertson**, 13 Sep 1944 in Lauderdale County, AL. Jesse was born 6 Aug 1918 in Lauderdale County, AL, died 13 Nov 2001 in Lauderdale County, AL, and was buried in Greenview Memorial Park, Florence, Lauderdale County, AL.
```
+ 1686  M   i.    Jerry Travis White was born 14 Aug 1946 in Lauderdale County, AL, died 15 Feb 1998 in
                  Lauderdale County, AL, and was buried in Greenview Memorial Park, Florence, Lauderdale
                  County, AL.
```

673. Etta Buna Wright (*George Moses (Mode) Wright*[5], *Elizabeth (Lizzie) May Sharp*[4], *John Sr.*[3], *Charles W. Sr.*[2], *John Sr.*[1]) was born 9 May 1919 in Waterloo, Lauderdale County, AL, died 10 Jun 1979, and was buried in Tri-Cities Memorial Gardens, Florence, Lauderdale County, AL.

Etta married **Lee Ellis Hanback**, son of **James Stanton Hanback** and **Daisy Elizabeth Sharp**, 3 Sep 1936 in Lauderdale County, AL. Lee was born 25 Jan 1915 in Waterloo, Lauderdale County, AL, died 2 Jan 2005, and was buried in Tri-Cities Memorial Gardens, Florence, Lauderdale County, AL.

+ 1687 M i. **Charles Boyce Hanback** was born 14 Dec 1937 in Lauderdale County, AL.

674. Mattie May Wright (*George Moses (Mode) Wright⁵, Elizabeth (Lizzie) May Sharp⁴, John Sr.³, Charles W. Sr.², John Sr.¹*) was born 15 Dec 1922 in Waterloo, Lauderdale County, AL and died 24 Feb 1999.

Mattie married **Thomas Ralph Elliott Sr.**, son of **Sammie E. Elliott** and **Mary Annie Gibbs**, 2 Mar 1938 in Lauderdale County, AL. Thomas was born 14 Jun 1916 in Cherokee, Colbert County, AL, died 23 Feb 2000, and was buried in Oakwood Cemetery, Sheffield, Colbert County, AL.

 1688 F i. **Wanda Louise Elliott** was born 26 Dec 1940 in Lauderdale County, AL and died 29 Dec 1940 in Lauderdale County, AL.
+ 1689 F ii. **Patsy Ann Elliott** was born 21 Feb 1942 in Colbert County, AL.
+ 1690 F iii. **Linda May Elliott** was born 16 Jan 1948 in Colbert County, AL.
+ 1691 M iv. **David Ralph Elliott** was born 14 Apr 1957 in Colbert County, AL.
+ 1692 M v. **Thomas (Tommy) Douglas Elliott** was born 10 Nov 1960 in Colbert County, AL.

675. Edith Louise Wright (*James Phillip Wright⁵, Elizabeth (Lizzie) May Sharp⁴, John Sr.³, Charles W. Sr.², John Sr.¹*) was born 17 Jan 1911 in Lauderdale County, AL.

Edith married **Joseph (Joe) S. Redd**, son of **Robert Carroll Redd** and **America Pogue**, 23 Dec 1933 in Lauderdale County, AL. Joseph was born 24 Sep 1908 in Nashville, Davidson County, TN, died 14 Aug 1994, and was buried in Florence, Lauderdale County, AL.

+ 1693 M i. **Robert Carroll Redd** was born 24 Sep 1946 in Lauderdale County, AL.

676. Elizabeth (Lizzie) Inez Wesson (*Martha (Mattie) Jane Wright⁵, Elizabeth (Lizzie) May Sharp⁴, John Sr.³, Charles W. Sr.², John Sr.¹*) was born 29 May 1902 in Lauderdale County, AL.

Elizabeth married **Arthur James Williams Sr.** in 1927.
+ 1694 F i. **Jane Anne Williams** was born in 1929 in Lauderdale County, AL.
+ 1695 M ii. **Arthur J. Williams Jr.** was born in 1931 in Lauderdale County, AL.

677. Hazel Wright Wesson (*Martha (Mattie) Jane Wright⁵, Elizabeth (Lizzie) May Sharp⁴, John Sr.³, Charles W. Sr.², John Sr.¹*) was born 25 Nov 1903 in Lauderdale County, AL and died in Aug 1997.

Hazel married **Donald Arthur Boggess Sr.** about 1925. Donald was born in 1900 in Alabama.
+ 1696 M i. **Donald Arthur Boggess Jr.** was born in 1928 and died in 1991.
+ 1697 F ii. **Dorothy Ann Boggess** was born in 1938.

678. Rawley (Roy) Archibald Wesson (*Martha (Mattie) Jane Wright⁵, Elizabeth (Lizzie) May Sharp⁴, John Sr.³, Charles W. Sr.², John Sr.¹*) was born 24 Nov 1905 in Lauderdale County, AL and died 31 Jul 1992.

Rawley married **Tyra Ann Jordan**.
+ 1698 M i. **John Phillip Wesson** was born 5 Oct 1945 in Lauderdale County, AL.
 1699 M ii. **James Wade Wesson** was born 30 Jan 1951 in Lauderdale County, AL.

679. Joseph Phillip Wesson (*Martha (Mattie) Jane Wright⁵, Elizabeth (Lizzie) May Sharp⁴, John Sr.³, Charles W. Sr.², John Sr.¹*) was born 18 Mar 1908 in Lauderdale County, AL and died in 1983.

Joseph married **Margaret Louise Cronk**.
+ 1700 M i. **Walter Wade Wesson** was born in 1934.
+ 1701 F ii. **Phyllis Fay Wesson** was born in 1951.

681. Callie Louise Sharp (*John (Buck) Phillip⁵, Carroll Ira (Buck)⁴, John Sr.³, Charles W. Sr.², John Sr.¹*) was born in 1900 in Alabama.

Callie married **Nathan M. North**, son of **Ira North** and **Betty Gooch**, 17 Mar 1942 in Lauderdale County, AL. Nathan was born 6 Feb 1886 in Lawrence County, TN.

682. Ben Faires Sharp (*John (Buck) Phillip* [5], *Carroll Ira (Buck)* [4], *John Sr.* [3], *Charles W. Sr.* [2], *John Sr.* [1]) was born in 1902 in Lauderdale County, AL, died 8 Oct 1949, and was buried in John Lay Cemetery, Etheridge, TN.

Ben married **Pearl Belle Balentine**, daughter of **John Rich Balentine** and **Nancy Jane Henson**, 24 Dec 1932 in Lauderdale County, AL. Pearl was born 15 Feb 1904 in Lauderdale County, AL, died 22 Dec 1993, and was buried in John Lay Cemetery, Etheridge, TN.

+	1702	F	i.	**Jo Carolyn Sharp** was born 9 Nov 1935 in Lauderdale County, AL.
+	1703	M	ii.	**John Phillip Sharp** was born 30 Apr 1937 in Lauderdale County, AL.
+	1704	M	iii.	**Ben Travis (Benny) Sharp** was born 1 Dec 1940 in Lauderdale County, AL.
	1705	M	iv.	**David Lawrence Sharp** was born 30 May 1944 in Lauderdale County, AL, died 24 May 2002, and was buried in John Lay Cemetery, Etheridge, TN.

683. Lee Howell (Hal) Sharp (*John (Buck) Phillip* [5], *Carroll Ira (Buck)* [4], *John Sr.* [3], *Charles W. Sr.* [2], *John Sr.* [1]) was born in 1904 in Lauderdale County, AL.

Lee married **Mary Frances Carroll**, daughter of **James Thomas Carroll** and **Mary Dixie Rhodes**, 15 Feb 1936 in Colbert County, AL. Mary was born in 1906 in Lauderdale County, AL, died 10 Apr 1991, and was buried in Lawrenceburg Memorial Gardens, Lawrenceburg, TN.

+	1706	F	i.	**Mary Frances Sharp** was born 28 Jun 1939 in Lawrenceburg, Lawrence County, TN.
+	1707	F	ii.	**Nancy Lee Sharp** was born 20 Feb 1942 in Lawrenceburg, Lawrence County, TN.
+	1708	F	iii.	**Susan Sharp** was born 22 Nov 1948 in Lawrenceburg, Lawrence County, TN.

684. Gladys Lillian Sharp (*John (Buck) Phillip* [5], *Carroll Ira (Buck)* [4], *John Sr.* [3], *Charles W. Sr.* [2], *John Sr.* [1]) was born in 1912 in Lauderdale County, AL.

Gladys married **John Lester Price Jr.**, son of **John Lester Price Sr.** and **Unknown**.

+	1709	F	i.	**Marilyn Sharpe Price** was born 25 Mar 1941 in West Palm Beach, FL.

686. Ida Lee Meadows (*Lilly B. Sharp* [5], *Carroll Ira (Buck)* [4], *John Sr.* [3], *Charles W. Sr.* [2], *John Sr.* [1]).

Ida married ***Unk Kinkle**.

698. Minnie Jane Sharp (*Charlie William* [5], *William (Candy) Erwin* [4], *John Sr.* [3], *Charles W. Sr.* [2], *John Sr.* [1]) was born 3 Sep 1903 in Lauderdale County, AL, died 1 Oct 1972, and was buried in Tri-Cities Memorial Gardens, Florence, Lauderdale County, AL.

Minnie married **William (Willie) Lee Killen**, son of **John Henry Killen** and **Sally Mae Jones**, 6 Jul 1918 in Lauderdale County, AL. William died 28 Dec 1974 and was buried in Granny Richardson Cemetery, Killen, AL.

+	1710	F	i.	**Clara May Killen** was born 19 Jul 1918 in Lauderdale County, AL.
+	1711	F	ii.	**Ida Odell Killen** was born 2 May 1921 in Lauderdale County, AL.
+	1712	F	iii.	**Mary Dalphine Killen** was born 7 Aug 1926 in Lauderdale County, AL.
+	1713	F	iv.	**June (Betty) Eleanor Killen** was born 12 Jun 1929 in Lauderdale County, AL.
+	1714	M	v.	**William (Buddy) Doyce Killen** was born 13 Nov 1932 in Lauderdale County, AL.
+	1715	F	vi.	**Juanita Joice Killen** was born 13 Nov 1932 in Lauderdale County, AL.
+	1716	M	vii.	**Harold Burt Killen** was born 27 Sep 1934 in Lauderdale County, AL, died 15 Apr 2003, and was buried in Greenview Memorial Park, Florence, Lauderdale County, AL.
	1717	F	viii.	**Carol Killen** was born 26 Sep 1937 in Lauderdale County, AL and died in 1937 in Lauderdale County, AL.

699. Owen Lee Sharp (*Charlie William* [5], *William (Candy) Erwin* [4], *John Sr.* [3], *Charles W. Sr.* [2], *John Sr.* [1]) was born 30 Jun 1905 in Lauderdale County, AL, died 21 May 1976, and was buried in Center Hill Cemetery, Lauderdale County, AL.

Owen married **Annie Lee Davis** 23 Oct 1925 in Lauderdale County, AL. Annie was born 4 Apr 1906, died 27 Feb 1931, and was buried in Granny Richardson Cemetery, Killen, AL.

Owen next married **Irene Michael**.

+ 1718 M i. **William Delton Sharp** was born 12 Dec 1934 in Lauderdale County, AL and died 24 Mar 2007 in Lauderdale County, AL.
+ 1719 F ii. **Alvie Sharp**.
+ 1720 F iii. **Iatrice Sharp**.

700. Donald Edward Sharp (*Charlie William [5], William (Candy) Erwin [4], John Sr. [3], Charles W. Sr. [2], John Sr. [1]*) was born 21 May 1907 in Lauderdale County, AL, died 12 Sep 1994, and was buried in Center Hill Cemetery, Lauderdale County, AL.

Donald married **Jennie Hester Hill**, daughter of **John Quincey Hill** and **Judith Elizabeth Richardson**, 6 Aug 1927. Jennie was born 15 Oct 1907 in Lauderdale County, AL.

> General Notes: Obituary - Times Daily, Florence, Lauderdale County, Alabama
> November 4, 2008
>
> "Jennie Hester Hill Sharp, age 101, of Greenhill, Ala., passed away Sunday, Nov. 2, 2008, of a brief illness at Lauderdale Christian Nursing Home. She was a native of Lauderdale County, Ala., a housewife and a member of Center Hill Church of Christ.
> Survivors are daughters, Eloise Snoddy, of Florence, Ala., Austelene Johnston, of Killen, Ala.; seven grandchildren; and 13 great -grandchildren.
> She was preceded in death by her husband, Dan Sharp; parents, John Q. Hill and Judith Elizabeth Hill; son, Robert Earl Sharp; a grandson, Christopher Michael Sharp; and one great-grand-child, Kayla Michelle Ensey; seven brothers and four sisters.
> The funeral service will be at 2 p.m. Wednesday, Nov. 5, 2008, at Greenhill Funeral Home Chapel, with Brother Jimmy Wisdom officiating. Burial will follow at Center Hill Cemetery. Visitation will be from noon - 2 p.m. Wednesday, Nov. 5, 2008, at Greenhill Funeral Home.
> Pallbearers are Henry Allen, Oscar LeMay, R.V. Hill, Randall Hill, Eric Snoddy and John Johnston. Honorary pallbearers are Leon LeMay, Travis Hill, Clifford Sharp, Fred Allen, Billy Ray Hill, James Hill, Doyle Hill, Harlon Hill, Coleman Sharp and Kenneth Sharp.
> Special thanks to the staff of Lauderdale Christian Nursing Home for the 17 years of loving care shown to our mother, also for all the many friends who visited her and the phone calls received during her stay at the nursing home. Greenhill Funeral Home is in charge of all arrangements."

+ 1721 M i. **Robert Earl Sharp** was born 12 May 1928 in Lauderdale County, AL, died 24 Dec 1997, and was buried in Center Hill Cemetery, Lauderdale County, AL.
+ 1722 F ii. **Gloria Eloise Sharp** was born 19 Nov 1937 in Lauderdale County, AL.
+ 1723 F iii. **Ethel Austelene Sharp** was born 31 Dec 1941 in Lauderdale County, AL.

701. Charles Price Sharp (*Charlie William [5], William (Candy) Erwin [4], John Sr. [3], Charles W. Sr. [2], John Sr. [1]*) was born about 1909 in Lauderdale County, AL, died 19 Aug 1991, and was buried in Pettus Cemetery, Lexington, AL.

Charles married **Lizzie Gray**, daughter of **Gilbert Gray** and **Ester *Unk**, 25 Nov 1927 in Lauderdale County, AL. Lizzie was born 23 Dec 1907, died 11 Jul 1999, and was buried in Pettus Cemetery, Lexington, AL.

+ 1724 M i. **Kennis Coleman Sharp** was born 4 Jul 1925 in Lexington, Lauderdale County, AL.
+ 1725 M ii. **Charles Clifford Sharp** was born 13 Nov 1932 in Lexington, Lauderdale County, AL.
+ 1726 M iii. **James Kenneth (Moose) Sharp** was born 4 Jun 1944 in Lexington, Lauderdale County, AL.

703. Emily Louise Bounds (*Dollie E. Sharp [5], William (Candy) Erwin [4], John Sr. [3], Charles W. Sr. [2], John Sr. [1]*) was born 16 Aug 1910 in Lauderdale County, AL.

Emily married **Lawson Spence Wilson**, son of **Eliza Henry Wilson** and **Cora Frye**, 21 Jul 1935 in Roswell, GA. Lawson was born 22 Jul 1906 in Tennessee, died 20 Oct 1978, and was buried in Tri-Cities Memorial Gardens, Florence, Lauderdale County, AL.

+ 1727 F i. **Nancy Spence Wilson** was born 4 Aug 1947 in Lauderdale County, AL.
+ 1728 F ii. **Emily Elizabeth Wilson** was born 9 Jul 1949 in Lauderdale County, AL.

704. Orville Owen Sharp (*Richard Owen [5], William (Candy) Erwin [4], John Sr. [3], Charles W. Sr. [2], John Sr. [1]*) was born 28 Jan 1905 in Lauderdale County, AL, died 11 Jun 1957, and was buried in Florence City Cemetery, Florence, Lauderdale County, AL.

Orville married **Mary Ethel Threet**, daughter of **William Johnson Threet** and **Fannie Florence Caperton**, 4 Oct 1930 in Colbert County, AL. Mary was born 6 Sep 1905 in Lauderdale County, AL, died 6 Feb 1989, and was buried in Florence City Cemetery, Florence, Lauderdale County, AL.

705. Richard Orlando Sharp (*Richard Owen⁵, William (Candy) Erwin⁴, John Sr.³, Charles W. Sr.², John Sr.¹*) was born 18 Dec 1907 in Colbert County, AL and died 25 Jan 1950.

Richard married **Rosemary Sunderhaus**, daughter of **Edward Benjamin Sunderhaus** and **Mary Agnes Brown**. Rosemary was born 6 May 1911 in Hamilton, OH.
+ 1729 F   i.   **Patricia Louise Mary Sharp** was born 25 Mar 1937 in Cuyahoga County, OH.
  1730 F   ii.   **Priscilla Agnes Sharp** was born 26 Jan 1943 in Cuyahoga County, OH.

706. Franklin Earl Sharp (*Richard Owen⁵, William (Candy) Erwin⁴, John Sr.³, Charles W. Sr.², John Sr.¹*) was born 1 Feb 1910 in Lorene, TX.

Franklin married **Alma Parker** 20 Dec 1938.

707. Alma Bertha Sharp (*Richard Owen⁵, William (Candy) Erwin⁴, John Sr.³, Charles W. Sr.², John Sr.¹*) was born 6 Jan 1913 in Robinson, TX.

Alma married **Luther H. Hargrove** 8 Feb 1937.

708. Edith Elaine Sharp (*Richard Owen⁵, William (Candy) Erwin⁴, John Sr.³, Charles W. Sr.², John Sr.¹*) was born 10 Jun 1915 in Gholson, TX.

Edith married **William C. Mullins** 25 Dec 1937.

709. Bessie Virgil Call (*Beulah L. Sharp⁵, William (Candy) Erwin⁴, John Sr.³, Charles W. Sr.², John Sr.¹*) was born 14 Apr 1904 in Lauderdale County, AL.

Bessie married **David Lambert**.
+ 1731 F   i.   **Reta Lambert**.

710. Robert Turner Call (*Beulah L. Sharp⁵, William (Candy) Erwin⁴, John Sr.³, Charles W. Sr.², John Sr.¹*) was born 24 Apr 1907 in Lauderdale County, AL and was buried in Cleveland, OH.

Robert married **Myrtle Hunt**.
  1732 M   i.   **Bobby Call**.
  1733 F   ii.   **Doris Ann Call**.

711. Ida Mae Call (*Beulah L. Sharp⁵, William (Candy) Erwin⁴, John Sr.³, Charles W. Sr.², John Sr.¹*) was born 28 Jul 1908 in Lauderdale County, AL.

Ida married **Lee Riley Cox**, son of **Key Cox** and **Mary Stewart**, 28 Feb 1924 in Lauderdale County, AL. Lee was born 30 Nov 1902 in Lauderdale County, AL, died 16 Aug 1938, and was buried in Walston Cemetery, Oakland, Lauderdale County, AL.
+ 1734 M   i.   **Elbert Turner Cox Sr.** was born 13 Oct 1924 in Lauderdale County, AL, died 25 Aug 1994, and was buried in Tri-Cities Memorial Gardens, Florence, Lauderdale County, AL.
+ 1735 M   ii.   **Lee Douglas Cox** was born 16 Dec 1925 in Lauderdale County, AL, died 31 Oct 1985, and was buried in Tri-Cities Memorial Gardens, Florence, Lauderdale County, AL.

Ida next married **Benton Killen**.

712. Floyd William Call (*Beulah L. Sharp⁵, William (Candy) Erwin⁴, John Sr.³, Charles W. Sr.², John Sr.¹*) was born 29 Aug 1910 in Lauderdale County, AL, died in 1956, and was buried in Walston Cemetery, Oakland, Lauderdale County, AL.

Floyd married **Myra Smith** 9 Oct 1930 in Lauderdale County, AL.

1736 M   i.   **George William Call**.

713. Dorothy Louise Call (*Beulah L. Sharp⁵, William (Candy) Erwin⁴, John Sr.³, Charles W. Sr.², John Sr.¹*) was born 24 Oct 1912 in Lauderdale County, AL.

Dorothy married **C. B. Kinsolving**.

714. Daisy Ruth Call (*Beulah L. Sharp⁵, William (Candy) Erwin⁴, John Sr.³, Charles W. Sr.², John Sr.¹*) was born 20 Jun 1916 in Lauderdale County, AL.

Daisy married **William Winston Rice**, son of **John Robert Rice** and **Mary F. Whitten**. William was born in 1910 in Lauderdale County, AL.
+ 1737 M   i.   **Johnny Winston Rice** was born in Lauderdale County, AL.

715. Roy Lee Call (*Beulah L. Sharp⁵, William (Candy) Erwin⁴, John Sr.³, Charles W. Sr.², John Sr.¹*) was born 26 Apr 1920 in Lauderdale County, AL, died 14 Apr 1977, and was buried in Tri-Cities Memorial Gardens, Florence, Lauderdale County, AL.

Roy married **Lois Marie Murphy**, daughter of **Lee Murphy** and **Ada Hayes**, 18 Feb 1941 in Lauderdale County, AL. Lois was born in Aug 1920 in Lauderdale County, AL, died 14 Aug 1980, and was buried in Tri-Cities Memorial Gardens, Florence, Lauderdale County, AL.
+ 1738 M   i.   **David Lee Call** was born 18 Feb 1941 in Lauderdale County, AL.
+ 1739 F   ii.   **Linda Call** was born 4 May 1946 in Lauderdale County, AL.
+ 1740 F   iii.   **Connie Lynn Call** was born 19 Nov 1950 in Lauderdale County, AL.
+ 1741 M   iv.   **Dennis Howard Call** was born 30 Nov 1953 in Lauderdale County, AL.

716. Ervin Howard Call (*Beulah L. Sharp⁵, William (Candy) Erwin⁴, John Sr.³, Charles W. Sr.², John Sr.¹*) was born 7 Jan 1922 in Lauderdale County, AL.

Ervin married **Irene Higgins**.
+ 1742 F   i.   **Greta Call**.

Ervin next married **Francis Crosswhite**.

718. Dalton Sharp (*Charner Leander Sr.⁵, William (Candy) Erwin⁴, John Sr.³, Charles W. Sr.², John Sr.¹*) was born 12 Sep 1908 and died in Aug 1962.

Dalton married **Matilda Powal**, daughter of **Edward Powal** and **Helen Scholtz**. Matilda was born 18 May 1908.
+ 1743 F   i.   **Penelope Anne Sharp** was born 16 Dec 1948.

719. Verna Lorena Sharp (*Charner Leander Sr.⁵, William (Candy) Erwin⁴, John Sr.³, Charles W. Sr.², John Sr.¹*) was born 30 Jul 1936 in Cleveland, OH.

Verna married **James Howard Grigsby Sr.**, son of **Arthur Eugene Grigsby** and **Pearl Gladys Gist**, 29 Oct 1953 in Lauderdale County, AL. James was born 22 Feb 1935 in Lauderdale County, AL.
+ 1744 M   i.   **James Howard Grigsby Jr.** was born 19 Mar 1957 in Tuscan, AZ.
+ 1745 M   ii.   **Michael Owen Grigsby** was born 16 Apr 1958 in Selma, AL.

720. Virginia Mae Sharp (*Charner Leander Sr.⁵, William (Candy) Erwin⁴, John Sr.³, Charles W. Sr.², John Sr.¹*) was born 21 Nov 1938 in Cleveland, OH.

Virginia married **Bobby Sherrill Walker**, son of **Lee Elton Walker** and **Ruth Lucille Nuszbomb**, 25 May 1959 in Lauderdale County, AL. Bobby was born 4 Aug 1937 in Rogersville, Lauderdale County, AL.
+ 1746 F   i.   **Elisa Lynn Walker** was born 8 Dec 1959 in Lauderdale County, AL.

721. Charner Leander Sharp Jr. (*Charner Leander Sr.⁵, William (Candy) Erwin⁴, John Sr.³, Charles W. Sr.², John Sr.¹*) was born 21 Jan 1939 in Cleveland, OH.

Charner married **Yvonne Baich**, daughter of **Dan Baich** and **Unknown**, 7 Jul 1966 in South Bend, IN.

1747 M i. **Daniel Lee Sharp** was born 8 Feb 1968 in South Bend, IN.
+ 1748 F ii. **Susanne Marie Sharp** was born 29 Aug 1971 in Lauderdale County, AL.

Charner next married **Lois Irons** 19 Apr 1994 in Polaski.

723. William (Billy) Brevard Sharp (*Burt Hilliard Sr.*[5], *William (Candy) Erwin*[4], *John Sr.*[3], *Charles W. Sr.*[2], *John Sr.*[1]) was born 17 Nov 1920 in Cleveland, OH and died 23 Nov 1993 in Weirton, WV (cremated).

William married **Frances Hughes**, daughter of **Glenn Hughes** and **Frances *Unk**, 8 Jan 1944 in Elkins, WV. Frances was born 20 Oct 1924 in Waynesboro, PA.
+ 1749 F i. **Kathleen Sharp** was born 29 Jul 1942 in Lackwana, NY.
+ 1750 M ii. **William Daniel Sharp** was born 21 Dec 1947 in Steubenville, Jefferson County, OH.
+ 1751 F iii. **Pamela Sharp** was born 29 Jul 1949 in Steubenville, OH.

724. Thomas Milton Sharp (*Burt Hilliard Sr.*[5], *William (Candy) Erwin*[4], *John Sr.*[3], *Charles W. Sr.*[2], *John Sr.*[1]) was born 11 Mar 1927 in Cleveland, OH.

Thomas married **Elizabeth Mickey**, daughter of **Frank Mickey** and **Lois Collins**, 24 Nov 1956 in Virginia. Elizabeth was born 24 Jul 1932 in Steubenville, OH.
+ 1752 F i. **Shelly Sharp** was born 19 Oct 1957.
+ 1753 F ii. **Kathy Sharp** was born 13 Jan 1962.

725. Pauline (Polly) Elaine Sharp (*Burt Hilliard Sr.*[5], *William (Candy) Erwin*[4], *John Sr.*[3], *Charles W. Sr.*[2], *John Sr.*[1]) was born 23 Jul 1931 in Cleveland, OH.

Pauline married **Joseph Fabian Sr.**, son of **Michael Fabian** and **Katie Fabian**, 18 Nov 1961. Joseph was born 27 Jun 1926 in Calliers, WV.
+ 1754 F i. **Cynthia L. Fabian** was born 11 Jun 1952 in Steubenville, OH.
+ 1755 M ii. **Donald N. Fabian** was born 11 Jun 1953 in Steubenville, OH.
1756 M iii. **Joseph Fabian Jr.** was born 24 Apr 1962 in Steubenville, OH.

727. Eleanor Stepwith (*Virginia (Emma) Sharp*[5], *William (Candy) Erwin*[4], *John Sr.*[3], *Charles W. Sr.*[2], *John Sr.*[1]).

Eleanor married ***Unk Schverman**.
1757 F i. **Mary Ann Schverman**.
1758 M ii. **Paul Schverman**.
1759 M iii. **Danny Schverman**.
1760 F iv. **Laura Schverman**.

730. Mae Belle Young (*James Wylie (Jim) Young*[5], *Julia Ann Young*[4], *Mary E. Sharp*[3], *Charles W. Sr.*[2], *John Sr.*[1]) was born 4 Jan 1907 in Lauderdale County, AL, died 11 Jun 1985, and was buried in Murphy's Chapel Cemetery, Lauderdale County, AL.

Mae married **Homer Lee Witt**, son of **Johnny R. Witt** and **Susie Ann Balentine**, 22 Aug 1927 in Lauderdale County, AL. Homer was born 18 Aug 1899 in Lauderdale County, AL, died 30 Jan 1945, and was buried in Murphy's Chapel Cemetery, Lauderdale County, AL.
+ 1761 M i. **Johnny Ray Witt** was born 8 Jun 1930 in Lauderdale County, AL, died 7 Jan 2005, and was buried in Murphy's Chapel Cemetery, Lauderdale County, AL.
+ 1762 F ii. **Letha Helen Witt** was born 19 Jan 1935 in Lauderdale County, AL, died 9 Oct 2005, and was buried in Murphy's Chapel Cemetery, Lauderdale County, AL.
+ 1763 F iii. **Eva Witt** was born 25 Oct 1937 in Lauderdale County, AL.
+ 1764 F iv. **Rachel Lee Witt** was born 2 Apr 1942 in Lauderdale County, AL, died 3 Nov 2000, and was buried in Murphy's Chapel Cemetery, Lauderdale County, AL.

731. Nomer Marie Young (*James Wylie (Jim) Young*[5], *Julia Ann Young*[4], *Mary E. Sharp*[3], *Charles W. Sr.*[2], *John Sr.*[1]) was born 21 Feb 1909 in Lauderdale County, AL, died 25 Dec 1997, and was buried in Murphy's Chapel Cemetery, Lauderdale County, AL.

Nomer married **Elbert Grady Smith**, son of **Menzo Lester Smith** and **Ida D. Horton**, 1 May 1927 in Lauderdale County, AL. Elbert was born 5 Dec 1907 in McNairy County, TN, died 23 Oct 1980, and was buried in Murphy's Chapel Cemetery, Lauderdale County, AL.

	1765	F	i.	**Beddie May Smith** was born 4 Jul 1928 in Lauderdale County, AL, died 14 Oct 1929, and was buried in Murphy's Chapel Cemetery, Lauderdale County, AL.
+	1766	F	ii.	**Gladys Marie Smith** was born 19 Mar 1930 in Lauderdale County, AL.
+	1767	M	iii.	**Randle Arnold Smith** was born 14 Jun 1932 in Lauderdale County, AL, died 8 Apr 2001, and was buried in Murphy's Chapel Cemetery, Lauderdale County, AL.
+	1768	M	iv.	**Jimmy Lester (JL) Smith** was born 20 Feb 1935 in Lauderdale County, AL, died 10 Feb 2006, and was buried in Murphy's Chapel Cemetery, Lauderdale County, AL.
+	1769	F	v.	**Ruth Lucille Smith** was born 12 Sep 1937 in Lauderdale County, AL, died 24 May 2000, and was buried in Murphy's Chapel Cemetery, Lauderdale County, AL.
+	1770	F	vi.	**Beulah Estelle Smith** was born 21 Mar 1941 in Alabama.
+	1771	M	vii.	**Grady Elbert Smith** was born 4 Jan 1945 in Lauderdale County, AL.

732. Mozella Young (*James Wylie (Jim) Young*^{5}, *Julia Ann Young*^{4}, *Mary E. Sharp*^{3}, *Charles W. Sr.*^{2}, *John Sr.*^{1}) was born 18 Dec 1911 in Lauderdale County, AL, died 1 Oct 2001, and was buried in Murphy's Chapel Cemetery, Lauderdale County, AL.

Mozella married **Marvin John Smith Sr.**, son of **Wheeler Turner Smith** and **Leona J. Murphy**, 30 Nov 1928 in Lauderdale County, AL. Marvin was born 24 Apr 1908 in Lauderdale County, AL, died 2 Sep 1965, and was buried in Murphy's Chapel Cemetery, Lauderdale County, AL.

+	1772	M	i.	**Edwin Smith** was born 31 Oct 1929.
	1773	M	ii.	**Marvin John Smith Jr.** was born 15 Feb 1931 in Lauderdale County, AL, died 17 Feb 1931, and was buried in Murphy's Chapel Cemetery, Lauderdale County, AL.
+	1774	F	iii.	**Lavada (Slick) Smith** was born 22 Jul 1932.
+	1775	F	iv.	**Eulalia (Curly) Smith** was born 22 Jul 1932 in Lauderdale County, AL, died 3 Sep 1995, and was buried in South Bend, St Joseph County, IN.
+	1776	M	v.	**Joseph Wheeler Smith** was born 28 Nov 1937 in Lauderdale County, AL.

733. James Nicklaus Young (*James Wylie (Jim) Young*^{5}, *Julia Ann Young*^{4}, *Mary E. Sharp*^{3}, *Charles W. Sr.*^{2}, *John Sr.*^{1}) was born 30 Jan 1912 in Lauderdale County, AL, died 8 Nov 1997, and was buried in Murphy's Chapel Cemetery, Lauderdale County, AL.

James married **Either Katherine Smith**, daughter of **Menzo Lester Smith** and **Mary M. Rainey**, 9 Oct 1937 in Lauderdale County, AL. Either was born 6 Feb 1921 in Lauderdale County, AL.

734. Ellie Bert Young (*James Wylie (Jim) Young*^{5}, *Julia Ann Young*^{4}, *Mary E. Sharp*^{3}, *Charles W. Sr.*^{2}, *John Sr.*^{1}) was born 23 Oct 1913 in Lauderdale County, AL, died 25 Aug 1993, and was buried in Murphy's Chapel Cemetery, Lauderdale County, AL.

Ellie married **Eura (Eurie) Sharp**, daughter of **Charles W. Sharp** and **Alice A. Smith**, 25 Jul 1938 in Lauderdale County, AL. Eura was born 29 Aug 1919 in Lauderdale County, AL, died 4 Aug 1998, and was buried in Murphy's Chapel Cemetery, Lauderdale County, AL.
(Duplicate Line. See Person 588)

735. Paul Mansel Young (*James Wylie (Jim) Young*^{5}, *Julia Ann Young*^{4}, *Mary E. Sharp*^{3}, *Charles W. Sr.*^{2}, *John Sr.*^{1}) was born 26 May 1917 in Lauderdale County, AL, died 5 Aug 1975, and was buried in Murphy's Chapel Cemetery, Lauderdale County, AL.

Paul married **Lora Ruth Jones**, daughter of **Hurse Jones** and **Mamie Raines**, 24 May 1941 in Lauderdale County, AL. Lora was born 14 Apr 1921 in Lauderdale County, AL, died in Oct, and was buried in Florence City Cemetery, Florence, Lauderdale County, AL.

| + | 1777 | F | i. | **Margaret Young**. |
| + | 1778 | F | ii. | **Christine Young**. |

Paul next married **Alma June Wylie**.

| + | 1779 | F | i. | **Loretta Young** was born 6 Oct 1954 in Lauderdale County, AL. |
| + | 1780 | F | ii. | **Paulette Young** was born 1 Nov 1955 in Lauderdale County, AL. |

+ 1781 F iii. **Barbara Lynn Young** was born 4 Nov 1957 in Lauderdale County, AL.
+ 1782 F iv. **Cathy Young**.
+ 1783 F v. **Elsie Sue Young** was born 23 Apr 1963 in Lauderdale County, AL, died in Apr 2002, and was buried in Florence City Cemetery, Florence, Lauderdale County, AL.
  1784 M vi. **Paul Steven Young**.

736. Hazel Inez Young (*James Wylie (Jim) Young*[5], *Julia Ann Young*[4], *Mary E. Sharp*[3], *Charles W. Sr.*[2], *John Sr.*[1]) was born 26 May 1919 in Lauderdale County, AL.

Hazel married **Robert Houston Jones**, son of **Sam Houston Jones** and **Mammie Whitten**, 27 Nov 1940 in Lauderdale County, AL. Robert was born 12 Oct 1916 in Cloverdale, Lauderdale County, AL, died 26 Jul 2006, and was buried in Bethel Berry Cemetery, Lauderdale County, AL.
  1785 F i. **Bobbie Sue Jones**.
+ 1786 F ii. **Betty Lou Jones**.
+ 1787 M iii. **Jim Robert Jones**.

738. Lawrence Arnold Young (*James Wylie (Jim) Young*[5], *Julia Ann Young*[4], *Mary E. Sharp*[3], *Charles W. Sr.*[2], *John Sr.*[1]) was born about 1924 in Lauderdale County, AL, died 12 Nov 2000, and was buried in Mt. Pleasant Cemetery, Lauderdale County, AL.

Lawrence married **Nancy Vertie McGee**, daughter of **James William McGee** and **Nora Williams**, 5 Feb 1974. Nancy was born 13 Sep 1924 in Lexington, Lauderdale County, AL, died 28 Jun 2000, and was buried in Mt. Pleasant Cemetery, Lauderdale County, AL.

739. Irene Beulah Young (*James Wylie (Jim) Young*[5], *Julia Ann Young*[4], *Mary E. Sharp*[3], *Charles W. Sr.*[2], *John Sr.*[1]) was born 5 Dec 1926 in Florence, Lauderdale County, AL.

Irene married **Dewey Thomas McKelvey**, son of **Johnny F. McKelvey** and **Mollie Lovelace**, 28 Jul 1947 in Lauderdale County, AL. Dewey was born 27 Mar 1923 in Lauderdale County, AL, died 29 Jan 1993, and was buried in Cloverdale COC Cemetery, Lauderdale County, AL.
+ 1788 M i. **Larry Steven McKelvey** was born 4 Jan 1948 in Lauderdale County, AL.
  1789 M ii. **Ricky Dewey McKelvey** was born 29 May 1966 in Lauderdale County, AL.

740. Eula Beatrice Young (*Hulet Edward Young*[5], *Julia Ann Young*[4], *Mary E. Sharp*[3], *Charles W. Sr.*[2], *John Sr.*[1]) was born 16 Nov 1907 in Lauderdale County, AL, died 2 Jan 2000, and was buried in Murphy's Chapel Cemetery, Lauderdale County, AL.

Eula married **Robert Owen Scott** 17 Nov 1930 in Lauderdale County, AL. Robert was born 25 Sep 1909 in Lauderdale County, AL, died 18 Sep 1992, and was buried in Murphy's Chapel Cemetery, Lauderdale County, AL.
+ 1790 M i. **Bobby Moore Scott** was born 16 Jun 1937.
+ 1791 M ii. **Gary Lance Scott** was born 5 Nov 1939.
+ 1792 M iii. **Daniel Scott** was born 6 Jan 1943 in Lauderdale County, AL.
+ 1793 M iv. **David Scott** was born 6 Jan 1943 in Lauderdale County, AL.
+ 1794 F v. **Peggy Jo Scott** was born 19 Nov 1944 in Lauderdale County, AL.
+ 1795 M vi. **James Owen Scott** was born 22 Jul 1946.
+ 1796 F vii. **Julia Earline Scott** was born 20 May 1948 in Lauderdale County, AL.
+ 1797 M viii. **James (Jim) Allen Scott** was born 8 Sep 1949 in Lauderdale County, AL.
  1798 M ix. **Steve Yogi Scott** was born 29 Nov 1954.

741. Carrie Ann Young (*Hulet Edward Young*[5], *Julia Ann Young*[4], *Mary E. Sharp*[3], *Charles W. Sr.*[2], *John Sr.*[1]) was born 21 May 1909 in Lauderdale County, AL, died 25 May 1984, and was buried in Cloverdale COC Cemetery, Lauderdale County, AL.

Carrie married **William (Doc) Turner Dailey Sr.**, son of **A. J. (Will) Dailey Sr.** and **Florence L. Ticer**, 13 May 1928 in Lauderdale County, AL. William was born 6 Dec 1911 in Lauderdale County, AL, died 7 Sep 1974, and was buried in Cloverdale COC Cemetery, Lauderdale County, AL.
+ 1799 F i. **Josephine Oneada Dailey** was born 25 May 1929 in Lauderdale County, AL, died 19 May 2004, and was buried in Cloverdale COC Cemetery, Lauderdale County, AL.

+ 1800 F ii. **Margaret Louise Dailey** was born 10 Dec 1932 in Lauderdale County, AL, died 28 Nov 1995, and was buried in Memorial Cemetery, Savannah, Hardin County, TN.

+ 1801 M iii. **William Turner Dailey Jr.** was born 25 Jan 1939 in Lauderdale County, AL, died 24 Apr 2008, and was buried in Cloverdale COC Cemetery, Lauderdale County, AL.

1802 F iv. **Mary Ann Dailey** was born 31 Dec 1943 in Lauderdale County, AL.

1803 M v. **Jerry Lynn Dailey** was born 8 Feb 1946 in Lauderdale County, AL.

742. Myrtle Lena Young (*Hulet Edward Young*[5], *Julia Ann Young*[4], *Mary E. Sharp*[3], *Charles W. Sr.*[2], *John Sr.*[1]) was born 8 Mar 1911 in Lauderdale County, AL, died 6 Jan 2004, and was buried in Greenview Memorial Park, Florence, Lauderdale County, AL.

Myrtle married **James Douglas Balentine**, son of **Phillip S. Balentine** and **Mary L. Wallace**, 16 Nov 1937 in Lauderdale County, AL. James was born 10 Apr 1914 in Lauderdale County, AL, died 11 Sep 2000, and was buried in Greenview Memorial Park, Florence, Lauderdale County, AL.

+ 1804 M i. **James Leon Balentine** was born 26 Apr 1940 in Lauderdale County, AL, died 31 Aug 2004, and was buried in Greenview Memorial Park, Florence, Lauderdale County, AL.

1805 M ii. **William Kenneth Balentine** was born 4 Aug 1942 in Lauderdale County, AL.

1806 F iii. **Mary Lillian Balentine** was born 25 Jul 1943 in Lauderdale County, AL.

+ 1807 F iv. **Dorothy (Dot) Gloria Balentine** was born 21 Apr 1945 in Lauderdale County, AL.

+ 1808 F v. **Janice June Balentine** was born 17 Jun 1947 in Lauderdale County, AL.

743. Arnold Edward (Ed) Young (*Hulet Edward Young*[5], *Julia Ann Young*[4], *Mary E. Sharp*[3], *Charles W. Sr.*[2], *John Sr.*[1]) was born 15 Jun 1912 in Lauderdale County, AL, died 20 Aug 1976, and was buried in Cloverdale COC Cemetery, Lauderdale County, AL.

Arnold married **Reba Jean Johnson**, daughter of **Dave Andrew Johnson** and **Edna Hill**, 13 Dec 1935 in Lauderdale County, AL. Reba was born 7 Jun 1916 in Lauderdale County, AL, died 28 Aug 1997, and was buried in Cloverdale COC Cemetery, Lauderdale County, AL.

+ 1809 M i. **Boyce Edward Young** was born 21 Oct 1936 in Lauderdale County, AL.

744. Bertha Young (*Hulet Edward Young*[5], *Julia Ann Young*[4], *Mary E. Sharp*[3], *Charles W. Sr.*[2], *John Sr.*[1]) was born 23 Jan 1914 in Lauderdale County, AL, died 2 Apr 1981, and was buried in Murphy's Chapel Cemetery, Lauderdale County, AL.

Bertha married **Olen L. Witt**, son of **Johnny R. Witt** and **Susie Ann Balentine**, 3 Apr 1932 in Lauderdale County, AL. Olen was born 30 Nov 1912 in Lauderdale County, AL, died 19 Jun 1986, and was buried in Murphy's Chapel Cemetery, Lauderdale County, AL.

1810 M i. **Johnny Hulet Witt** was born 4 Jul 1935, died 23 Jun 1963, and was buried in Murphy's Chapel Cemetery, Lauderdale County, AL.

+ 1811 F ii. **Polly Ann Witt** was born 4 Sep 1940 in Lauderdale County, AL, died 13 Aug 1992, and was buried in Murphy's Chapel Cemetery, Lauderdale County, AL.

1812 F iii. **Johnelle Witt**.

745. Boss C. Young (*Hulet Edward Young*[5], *Julia Ann Young*[4], *Mary E. Sharp*[3], *Charles W. Sr.*[2], *John Sr.*[1]) was born 13 Apr 1916 in Lauderdale County, AL, died 19 Apr 1944, and was buried in Murphy's Chapel Cemetery, Lauderdale County, AL.

Boss married **Mattie Sue (Susie) Lindsey**, daughter of **Samuel S. Lindsey** and **Mattie A. Sharp**, 6 Mar 1926 in Lauderdale County, AL. Mattie was born 9 Jul 1906 in Waterloo, Lauderdale County, AL.

746. Vertie Mae Young (*Hulet Edward Young*[5], *Julia Ann Young*[4], *Mary E. Sharp*[3], *Charles W. Sr.*[2], *John Sr.*[1]) was born 20 May 1918 in Lauderdale County, AL, died 13 Feb 1998, and was buried in Tri-Cities Memorial Gardens, Florence, Lauderdale County, AL.

Vertie married **Ernest Balentine**, son of **Robert Balentine** and **Mattie Beavers**, 9 Dec 1937 in Lauderdale County, AL. Ernest was born 22 May 1919 in Lauderdale County, AL, died 28 Nov 1988, and was buried in Tri-Cities Memorial Gardens, Florence, Lauderdale County, AL.

1813 M i. **Thomas Lynn Balentine**.

748. Rachel Nell Young (*Hulet Edward Young^5, Julia Ann Young^4, Mary E. Sharp^3, Charles W. Sr.^{2}, John Sr.^{1}*) was born 30 May 1922 in Lauderdale County, AL, died 16 Apr 2000, and was buried in Greenview Memorial Park, Florence, Lauderdale County, AL.

    Rachel married **Robert Murray White**, son of **Jones Oscar White** and **Laura B. Robertson**, 23 Mar 1946 in Lauderdale County, AL. Robert was born 19 Jun 1921 in Lauderdale County, AL.

+ 1814 M   i.   **Randy Harris White** was born 3 Jul 1953 in Lauderdale County, AL.
+ 1815 F   ii.   **Robbie White**.
+ 1816 F   iii. **Nancy White**.

749. Joe L. Young (*Hulet Edward Young^5, Julia Ann Young^4, Mary E. Sharp^3, Charles W. Sr.^{2}, John Sr.^{1}*) was born 9 Feb 1925 in Lauderdale County, AL, died 9 Dec 1976, and was buried in Greenview Memorial Park, Florence, Lauderdale County, AL.

    Joe married **Rebecca Ann Murphy**, daughter of **Eldridge (Ajax) Murphy** and **Verna Weaver**, 25 Jun 1949 in Iuka, Tishomingo County, MS. Rebecca was born 8 Sep 1933 in Lauderdale County, AL.

+ 1817 M   i.   **Larry Joe Young** was born 26 Jan 1951 in Lauderdale County, AL.
+ 1818 M   ii.   **Ronnie Dale Young** was born 24 May 1953 in Lauderdale County, AL.

750. Grady L. Young (*Hulet Edward Young^5, Julia Ann Young^4, Mary E. Sharp^3, Charles W. Sr.^{2}, John Sr.^{1}*) was born 12 Oct 1931 in Lauderdale County, AL, died 24 Jan 1972, and was buried in Cloverdale COC Cemetery, Lauderdale County, AL.

    Grady married **Martha Ann Blount**.

+ 1819 F   i.   **Deborah Young**.
  1820 M   ii.   **Darrell Lee Young**.

751. Bobby Turner Young (*Turner Andrew Young^5, Julia Ann Young^4, Mary E. Sharp^3, Charles W. Sr.^{2}, John Sr.^{1}*) was born in Lauderdale County, AL.

    Bobby married **Joyce Beasley**.

  1821 F   i.   **Regina Young**.
  1822 M   ii.   **Ricky Young**.
  1823 F   iii. **Sandra Young**.
  1824 M   iv. **Terry Young**.
  1825 F   v.   **Robin Young**.

    Bobby next married **Laura Johnson**.

752. Virgie Ione Young (*Turner Andrew Young^5, Julia Ann Young^4, Mary E. Sharp^3, Charles W. Sr.^{2}, John Sr.^{1}*) was born 22 Oct 1911 in Lauderdale County, AL.

    Virgie married **Robert Perry Anderson**, son of **Charles David Anderson Sr.** and **Ora Lee Matheny**. Robert was born 16 Sep 1912 in Lauderdale County, AL, died 20 Jan 1936, and was buried in Gresham Cemetery, Lauderdale County, AL.

+ 1826 F   i.   **Betsy (Bessie Bob) Anderson** was born 23 Jan 1934.
  1827 M   ii.   **Jimmy Earl Anderson** was born 19 Jun 1936 in Lauderdale County, AL, died 24 Aug 1957, and was buried in Greenview Memorial Park, Florence, Lauderdale County, AL.

    Virgie next married **Joseph Buford Patrick Sr.**.

  1828 M   i.   **Joseph Buford (Jb) Patrick Jr.**
+ 1829 F   ii.   **Patricia Carolyn Patrick** was born 19 Dec 1949 in Lauderdale County, AL.

753. Marvin Andrew (Tuck) Young (*Turner Andrew Young^5, Julia Ann Young^4, Mary E. Sharp^3, Charles W. Sr.^{2}, John Sr.^{1}*) was born 16 Jul 1914 in Lauderdale County, AL and died in Feb 1972 in Lauderdale County, AL.

    Marvin married **Ruth Campbell**.

  1830 M   i.   **Billy Young**.
  1831 M   ii.   **Tommy Young**.

754. Myrtle Mae Young (*Turner Andrew Young[5], Julia Ann Young[4], Mary E. Sharp[3], Charles W. Sr.[2], John Sr.[1]*) was born about 1916 in Lauderdale County, AL, died 10 Nov 2000, and was buried in Greenview Memorial Park, Florence, Lauderdale County, AL.

Myrtle married **Claude Ellis Holt**. Claude was born 28 May 1915 in Lauderdale County, AL, died 30 Oct 1985, and was buried in Greenview Memorial Park, Florence, Lauderdale County, AL.

	1832	F	i.	**Jean Holt.**
+	1833	F	ii.	**Joyce Holt.**
	1834	M	iii.	**John E. Holt.**
+	1835	F	iv.	**Mary Ann Holt.**
+	1836	F	v.	**Nancy Holt.**
+	1837	F	vi.	**Bobbie Holt.**
	1838	F	vii.	**Kathy Holt.**
+	1839	F	viii.	**Penny Holt.**

756. Gladys Lee Young (*Turner Andrew Young[5], Julia Ann Young[4], Mary E. Sharp[3], Charles W. Sr.[2], John Sr.[1]*) was born 16 May 1919 in Lauderdale County, AL.

Gladys married **James Maxwell Cooper**, son of **Joe Cooper** and **Mary Koonce**. James was born 9 Oct 1916 in Lauderdale County, AL and died 7 Sep 1991 in Lauderdale County, AL.

+	1840	M	i.	**Joe Benny Cooper** was born in 1940 in Lauderdale County, AL.
+	1841	M	ii.	**James Steven (Steve) Cooper** was born 4 Jul 1951 in Lauderdale County, AL.

757. Noah Sewell Young (*Turner Andrew Young[5], Julia Ann Young[4], Mary E. Sharp[3], Charles W. Sr.[2], John Sr.[1]*) was born about 1921, died 10 Mar 2008 in Lauderdale County, AL, and was buried in Greenview Memorial Park, Florence, Lauderdale County, AL.

Noah married **Ann Clemmons**, daughter of **Clyde Clemmons** and **Mary Alice Pitman**, in 1945 in Lauderdale County, AL. Ann was born in 1919.

+	1842	M	i.	**Donny Joe Young.**

758. Cecil Arthur Young (*Turner Andrew Young[5], Julia Ann Young[4], Mary E. Sharp[3], Charles W. Sr.[2], John Sr.[1]*) was born 2 Jul 1925 in Mishawaka, St Joseph County, IN.

Cecil married **Helen Boyd**.

1843	M	i.	**Roger Young.**
1844	F	ii.	**Martha Young.**
1845	F	iii.	**Connie Young.**
1846	F	iv.	**Julia Young.**
1847	M	v.	**Phillip Young.**

759. Clara Belle Young (*Cleave Homer Young[5], Julia Ann Young[4], Mary E. Sharp[3], Charles W. Sr.[2], John Sr.[1]*) was born 25 Jul 1917 in Lauderdale County, AL.

Clara married **Charles Dewey Miles**, son of **Charlie Miles** and **Belle Vickery**, 27 Jan 1940 in Lauderdale County, AL. Charles was born 2 May 1916 in Lauderdale County, AL, died in Indiana, and was buried in Muncie, Delaware County, IN.

+	1848	M	i.	**Charles Dennis Miles** was born 10 Apr 1941 in Indiana and died 29 Aug 2005 in Muncie, Delaware County, IN.
+	1849	F	ii.	**Mary Francis Miles** was born 21 Apr 1943 in Indiana.
+	1850	M	iii.	**Billy Ray Miles** was born 12 Feb 1948 in Indiana.
+	1851	F	iv.	**Sandra Kay Miles** was born 22 Oct 1949 in California.
+	1852	F	v.	**Bonnie Fay Miles** was born 19 Dec 1952 in California.

760. Christine Young (*Cleave Homer Young[5], Julia Ann Young[4], Mary E. Sharp[3], Charles W. Sr.[2], John Sr.[1]*) was born about 1920.

Christine married **James Ardis Dowdy**, son of **Willie M. Dowdy** and **Minnie Ida Witt**. James was born 21 Mar 1920 in Lauderdale County, AL, died 9 Jul 1996, and was buried in Fairview Cemetery, Mishawaka, IN. Another name for James was James A. Dowdy.

1853 M i. **James Don Dowdy** was born in 1938 in Alabama.

761. Virginia Young (*Cleave Homer Young*[5], *Julia Ann Young*[4], *Mary E. Sharp*[3], *Charles W. Sr.*[2], *John Sr.*[1]) was born about 1922.

Virginia married **Mack Barkley**.

Virginia next married ***Unk Perkins**.

764. Douglas C. Young Sr. (*Cleave Homer Young*[5], *Julia Ann Young*[4], *Mary E. Sharp*[3], *Charles W. Sr.*[2], *John Sr.*[1]).

Douglas married **Sally Werntz**.
1854 F i. **Douglas C. Young Jr.**

766. Larry Joe Young (*Cleave Homer Young*[5], *Julia Ann Young*[4], *Mary E. Sharp*[3], *Charles W. Sr.*[2], *John Sr.*[1]) was born 7 Mar 1943 in St. Joseph County, IN and died 28 Sep 2004 in Niles, MI.

Larry married **Rose *Unk**.
+ 1855 F i. **Melissa Young**.

767. Kerry W. Young (*Wheeler Young*[5], *Julia Ann Young*[4], *Mary E. Sharp*[3], *Charles W. Sr.*[2], *John Sr.*[1]) was born 27 Nov 1918 in Lauderdale County, AL, died 15 Apr 1983, and was buried in Fairview Cemetery, Mishawaka, IN.

Kerry married **Ann Artusi** 31 Aug 1940 in Mishawaka, St Joseph County, IN.
+ 1856 M i. **Michael Young Sr.**
+ 1857 M ii. **Ronald Young** was born 18 Jul 1946 in Mishawaka, St Joseph County, IN and died 13 May 1992 in Mishawaka, St Joseph County, IN.

768. Ruth Young (*Wheeler Young*[5], *Julia Ann Young*[4], *Mary E. Sharp*[3], *Charles W. Sr.*[2], *John Sr.*[1]) was born 8 Oct 1920 in Lauderdale County, AL, died 7 Jul 1979, and was buried in Kirkland Cemetery, Kirkland, WA.

Ruth married ***Unk Fain**.

769. Dorothy Young (*Wheeler Young*[5], *Julia Ann Young*[4], *Mary E. Sharp*[3], *Charles W. Sr.*[2], *John Sr.*[1]) was born 7 Apr 1923 in Lauderdale County, AL, died 28 Mar 1975, and was buried in Kirkland Cemetery, Kirkland, WA.

Dorothy married ***Unk Cox**.

770. Catherine (Katie) Young (*Wheeler Young*[5], *Julia Ann Young*[4], *Mary E. Sharp*[3], *Charles W. Sr.*[2], *John Sr.*[1]) was born in Feb 1927 in St. Joseph County, IN.

Catherine married ***Unk Wilkins**.

Catherine next married **Larry Dewitt**.
1858 F i. **Vicki Dewitt**.

773. Daniel Oneal Stutts Sr. (*Mollie Jo Sharp*[5], *Berry Nolan*[4], *Joseph (Joe)*[3], *Charles W. Sr.*[2], *John Sr.*[1]) was born 25 Jan 1914 in Birmingham, Jefferson County, AL.

General Notes: This child was adopted by William and Mollie Stutts. His mother was Nancy Hattie (Mollie Jo's sister) His father was a Matheney? They were not married.

Daniel married **Lillian Maye Giles**, daughter of **Leon Dotson Giles** and **Maggie Myrtle Bowles**, 6 May 1933 in Colbert County, AL. Lillian was born 22 Jan 1914 in Colbert County, AL.
+ 1859 M i. **Daniel Oneal Stutts Jr.** was born 17 Jan 1934 in Colbert County, AL.

+ 1860 F ii. **Dolly Jane Stutts** was born 21 Apr 1936 in Colbert County, AL.

775. James Wesley Sharp (*James David*[5], *Berry Nolan*[4], *Joseph (Joe)*[3], *Charles W. Sr.*[2], *John Sr.*[1]) was born 20 Nov 1912 in Lauderdale County, AL, died 20 Feb 1998, and was buried in Stoney Point Cemetery, Lauderdale County, AL.

James married **Ruby Idella Martin**, daughter of **Therman Alvin Martin** and **Beulah Frances Troop**, 16 Jun 1946 in Lauderdale County, AL. Ruby was born 28 Feb 1922 in Lawrence County, TN, died 9 Sep 2004, and was buried in Stoney Point Cemetery, Lauderdale County, AL.

+ 1861 M i. **James Alvin Sharp Sr.** was born 27 Apr 1948 in Lauderdale County, AL.
+ 1862 F ii. **Wanda Marie Sharp** was born 11 Aug 1949 in Lauderdale County, AL.
+ 1863 M iii. **Roger Wayne Sharp** was born 19 Nov 1951 in Lauderdale County, AL.
+ 1864 F iv. **Sandra Louise Sharp** was born 11 Sep 1953 in Lauderdale County, AL.
+ 1865 M v. **Albert Leon Sharp** was born 11 Sep 1955 in Lauderdale County, AL.

777. Clyde Joel (Link) Sharp (*James David*[5], *Berry Nolan*[4], *Joseph (Joe)*[3], *Charles W. Sr.*[2], *John Sr.*[1]) was born 23 Feb 1917 in Iron City, Wayne County, TN, died 23 Oct 2000, and was buried in Green Acres Mortuary.

Clyde married **Audrey Ellen Smith**, daughter of **Marion Luther Smith** and **Ella Sue Danner**, 23 Jul 1940 in Lauderdale County, AL. Audrey was born 17 Jul 1921 in Colbert County, AL.

+ 1866 M i. **David Lynn Sharp** was born 18 Mar 1941 in Lauderdale County, AL.
+ 1867 M ii. **Robert Owen Sharp** was born 14 Feb 1942 in Lauderdale County, AL.
+ 1868 M iii. **James Kenneth Sharp** was born 19 Dec 1944 in Lauderdale County, AL.

Clyde next married **Dorothy Marvell Elliot** 18 Oct 1947 in Tempe, AZ. Dorothy was born 30 Oct 1919 in River Falls, Pierce County, WI.

778. Velma Nadine Sharp (*James David*[5], *Berry Nolan*[4], *Joseph (Joe)*[3], *Charles W. Sr.*[2], *John Sr.*[1]) was born 13 Dec 1919 in Lauderdale County, AL, died 26 Dec 1972, and was buried in Stoney Point Cemetery, Lauderdale County, AL.

Velma married **William Oscar Turbyfill**, son of **Robert Miles Turbyfill** and **Carrie Lavenia Hughes**, 5 Nov 1939 in Lauderdale County, AL. William was born 10 Dec 1916 in Russellville, Franklin County, AL, died 26 Dec 1972, and was buried in Stoney Point Cemetery, Lauderdale County, AL.

+ 1869 F i. **Betty Lou Turbyfill** was born 16 Dec 1941 in Russellville, Franklin County, AL.
+ 1870 M ii. **Donald Eugene Turbyfill** was born 26 Sep 1943 in Lauderdale County, AL.
+ 1871 F iii. **Clara Dean Turbyfill** was born 3 Apr 1944 in Lauderdale County, AL.
+ 1872 M iv. **Thomas (Tommy) Ray Turbyfill** was born 14 Sep 1947 in Lauderdale County, AL.
+ 1873 M v. **Charles Robert Turbyfill** was born 18 Jun 1949 in Lauderdale County, AL, died 25 Oct 2000, and was buried in Stoney Point Cemetery, Lauderdale County, AL.
+ 1874 F vi. **Mary Nell Turbyfill** was born 17 Mar 1951 in Lauderdale County, AL.
+ 1875 M vii. **Jerry Lynn Turbyfill** was born 6 Jan 1953 in Lauderdale County, AL, died 15 Aug 2003 in Shreveport, LA, and was buried in Stoney Point Cemetery, Lauderdale County, AL.
  1876 M viii. **Norris Turbyfill**.

779. Ray Thomas Sharp (*James David*[5], *Berry Nolan*[4], *Joseph (Joe)*[3], *Charles W. Sr.*[2], *John Sr.*[1]) was born 24 Mar 1922 in Lauderdale County, AL, died 15 Sep 2004, and was buried in Mishawaka Cemetery, Mishawaka, IN.

Ray married **Helen Sue Southern**, daughter of **William R. Southern** and **Virgie M. Bevis**. Helen was born 4 Oct 1932 in Wayne County, TN.

  1877 F i. **Debbie Ray Sharp** was born 10 Apr 1953 in Mishawaka, St Joseph County, IN.
  1878 F ii. **Patty Sue Sharp** was born 26 Mar 1955 in Lauderdale County, AL, died in Feb 1988, and was buried in Mishawaka Cemetery, Mishawaka, IN.

780. Paul Edward Sharp Sr. (*James David*[5], *Berry Nolan*[4], *Joseph (Joe)*[3], *Charles W. Sr.*[2], *John Sr.*[1]) was born 25 Sep 1925 in Lauderdale County, AL, died 10 Nov 1989, and was buried in Greenview Memorial Park, Florence, Lauderdale County, AL.

Paul married **Fay Wilcoxson**, daughter of **Jesse D. Wilcoxson** and **Lola Briggs**, 14 Oct 1950 in Lauderdale County, AL. Fay was born 20 Nov 1931 in Lauderdale County, AL, died 22 Sep 2007, and was buried in Greenview Memorial Park, Florence, Lauderdale County, AL.

+ 1879 M i. **Paul Edward Sharp Jr.** was born 10 Sep 1958 in Lauderdale County, AL.
+ 1880 M ii. **James Briggs Sharp** was born 9 Dec 1963 in Lauderdale County, AL.

781. Vernon Stults Sharp Sr. (*James David^5, Berry Nolan^4, Joseph (Joe)^3, Charles W. Sr.^{2}, John Sr.^{1}*) was born 5 May 1927 in Lauderdale County, AL, died 1 Jul 2003, and was buried in St. Joseph Valley Cemetery, Mishawaka, IN.

Vernon married **Sylvia *Unk**. Sylvia was buried in St. Joseph Valley Memorial Park, Mishawaka, IN.

1881 M i. **Brian Sharp**.
1882 M ii. **Vernon Stults Sharp Jr.**
1883 F iii. **Jeanell Sharp**.

782. Kathryn Etoil Sharp (*James David^5, Berry Nolan^4, Joseph (Joe)^3, Charles W. Sr.^{2}, John Sr.^{1}*) was born 1 Jan 1931 in Lauderdale County, AL.

Kathryn married **Marvin Robert Lansdell Jr.**, son of **Marvin Robert Lansdell Sr.** and **Ina Mae Evans**, 30 Dec 1950 in Lauderdale County, AL. Marvin was born 11 Sep 1929 in Town Creek, Lawrence County, AL.

+ 1884 M i. **Robert Steven Lansdell** was born 17 Mar 1953 in Lauderdale County, AL.
+ 1885 M ii. **Michael Lee Lansdell** was born 3 Jul 1956 in Lauderdale County, AL.
+ 1886 F iii. **Kathy Diane Lansdell** was born 15 Dec 1958 in Lauderdale County, AL.

783. James Chambers Wilkes (*Eula Elizabeth Sharp^5, Berry Nolan^4, Joseph (Joe)^3, Charles W. Sr.^{2}, John Sr.^{1}*) was born 30 Dec 1908 in Lauderdale County, AL, died 20 Jul 1998, and was buried in Colbert Memorial Gardens, Colbert County, AL.

James married **Leona Narmore**, daughter of **William (Bill) M. Narmore** and **Annie Ellidge**, 12 Mar 1947 in Lauderdale County, AL. Leona was born 3 Aug 1912 in Colbert County, AL, died 4 Jul 1996, and was buried in Colbert Memorial Gardens, Colbert County, AL.

+ 1887 M i. **James Riley Wilkes** was born 20 Jan 1930 in Colbert County, AL.
+ 1888 F ii. **Shirley Jean Wilkes** was born 1 Sep 1935 in Colbert County, AL.

784. Elting Wilkes (*Eula Elizabeth Sharp^5, Berry Nolan^4, Joseph (Joe)^3, Charles W. Sr.^{2}, John Sr.^{1}*) was born 24 May 1910 in Lauderdale County, AL, died 9 Jan 2003, and was buried in Savannah Memorial Gardens, Hardin County, TN.

Elting married **Agnes Irene Williams**, daughter of **Chloe Wheeler Williams** and **Beulah Mae Shelby**, 10 Dec 1932 in Hardin County, TN. Agnes was born 11 Oct 1913 in Savannah, Hardin County, TN, died 18 Jan 2002, and was buried in Savannah Memorial Gardens, Hardin County, TN.

1889 M i. **Edwin Fay Wilkes** was born 23 Feb 1934 in Lauderdale County, AL and died 4 Jan 1940.
+ 1890 F ii. **Annie Mae Wilkes** was born 23 Feb 1934 in Lauderdale County, AL.
+ 1891 M iii. **Jimmy Carroll Wilkes** was born 25 Oct 1938 in Lauderdale County, AL.
+ 1892 F iv. **Patsy Lee Wilkes** was born 30 Apr 1944 in Lauderdale County, AL.
+ 1893 M v. **Joe Wheeler Wilkes** was born 29 Jan 1949 in Lauderdale County, AL.

785. Levi (Lee) Grant Wilkes II (*Eula Elizabeth Sharp^5, Berry Nolan^4, Joseph (Joe)^3, Charles W. Sr.^{2}, John Sr.^{1}*) was born 9 Feb 1912 in Lauderdale County, AL, died 18 May 1991, and was buried in Stoney Point Cemetery, Lauderdale County, AL.

Levi married **Vernice Louise Black** 11 Jun 1936 in Lauderdale County, AL. Vernice was born 7 Nov 1915 in Lauderdale County, AL, died 19 Jul 1943, and was buried in Stoney Point Cemetery, Lauderdale County, AL.

+ 1894 M i. **Aubrey Neal Wilkes** was born 2 Oct 1938 in Lauderdale County, AL.
+ 1895 F ii. **Mary Lee Wilkes** was born 18 May 1940 in Lauderdale County, AL.
+ 1896 M iii. **Levi Grant Wilkes III** was born 4 Jul 1943 in Lauderdale County, AL.

Levi next married **Edna Pauline Burchell** in Iuka, Tishomingo County, MS. Edna was born 30 Jul 1919 in Grainger County, TN.

786. Ruby Crystine Wilkes (*Eula Elizabeth Sharp*[5], *Berry Nolan*[4], *Joseph (Joe)*[3], *Charles W. Sr.*[2], *John Sr.*[1]) was born 27 Dec 1914 in Lauderdale County, AL and died 17 Jan 2003 in Memphis, Shelby County, TN.

> Ruby married **Rufus H. Whitten** 7 Jul 1931 in Lauderdale County, AL.
> 1897 F   i.   **Nina Ruth Whitten**.

> Ruby next married **Alfred Eugene Costner**. Alfred was born 17 Aug 1917, died 25 May 1957, and was buried in Stoney Point Cemetery, Lauderdale County, AL.

787. Lovie Lucille Wilkes (*Eula Elizabeth Sharp*[5], *Berry Nolan*[4], *Joseph (Joe)*[3], *Charles W. Sr.*[2], *John Sr.*[1]) was born 28 Jun 1917 in Lauderdale County, AL, died 10 Feb 2002, and was buried in Stoney Point Cemetery, Lauderdale County, AL.

> Lovie married **Ernest C. Whitten**, son of **Earley B. Whitten** and **Myrtle B. White**, 29 Apr 1955 in Lauderdale County, AL. Ernest was born 30 Jul 1926 in Lauderdale County, AL.

788. Earl Berry Wilkes (*Eula Elizabeth Sharp*[5], *Berry Nolan*[4], *Joseph (Joe)*[3], *Charles W. Sr.*[2], *John Sr.*[1]) was born 17 Aug 1919 in Lauderdale County, AL.

> Earl married **Vernon Jaynes**, daughter of **Otis Theo Jaynes** and **Cordelia Whittaker**, 15 Jun 1940 in Lauderdale County, AL. Vernon was born 24 Jun 1922 in Lauderdale County, AL, died 24 Dec 2001, and was buried in Stoney Point Cemetery, Lauderdale County, AL.
> + 1898 F   i.   **Bonnie Faye Wilkes** was born 6 Jun 1942 in Lauderdale County, AL.
>   1899 M   ii. **Edward Earl Wilkes** was born 15 Nov 1946 in Lauderdale County, AL, died 17 Nov 1946, and was buried in Stoney Point Cemetery, Lauderdale County, AL.
> + 1900 M   iii. **Charles Ashley Wilkes Sr.** was born 3 Nov 1948 in Lauderdale County, AL.

789. Rufus Jackson Wilkes (*Eula Elizabeth Sharp*[5], *Berry Nolan*[4], *Joseph (Joe)*[3], *Charles W. Sr.*[2], *John Sr.*[1]) was born 5 Mar 1924 in Lauderdale County, AL, died 27 Jan 2003, and was buried in Greenview Memorial Park, Florence, Lauderdale County, AL.

> Rufus married **Julia Christine Stults**, daughter of **Carter Blessin Stults** and **Linnie Mae Sharp**, 8 Nov 1941 in Lauderdale County, AL. Julia was born 16 Jul 1924 in Lauderdale County, AL, died 19 Sep 1981, and was buried in Greenview Memorial Park, Florence, Lauderdale County, AL.
> + 1901 M   i.   **John Jackson Wilkes Sr.** was born 10 Oct 1942 in Lauderdale County, AL.
> + 1902 M   ii. **Rufus Grant Wilkes** was born 8 May 1944 in Lauderdale County, AL.

790. Charles Roy Sharp (*Charles Robert*[5], *Berry Nolan*[4], *Joseph (Joe)*[3], *Charles W. Sr.*[2], *John Sr.*[1]) was born 25 Aug 1916 in Lauderdale County, AL, died 27 Jul 1986, and was buried in Stoney Point Cemetery, Lauderdale County, AL.

> Charles married **Gladys Marie Wallace**, daughter of **James William Wallace** and **Ida Dean Gooch**, 28 Mar 1937 in Lauderdale County, AL. Gladys was born 29 Jun 1918 in Lauderdale County, AL, died 1 Jul 2003, and was buried in Stoney Point Cemetery, Lauderdale County, AL.
> + 1903 M   i.   **Robert Norman Sharp** was born 23 Feb 1940 in Lauderdale County, AL, died 20 Feb 1988, and was buried in Stoney Point Cemetery, Lauderdale County, AL.
> + 1904 M   ii. **Jerry Clayton Sharp** was born 31 Jan 1941 in Lauderdale County, AL.
> + 1905 M   iii. **Charles Timothy Sharp** was born 12 Mar 1941 in Lauderdale County, AL.
> + 1906 F   iv. **Candace Marie Sharp** was born 5 Jan 1958 in Lauderdale County, AL, died 24 Apr 2004, and was buried in Stoney Point Cemetery, Lauderdale County, AL.

791. Elizabeth Sharp (*Charles Robert*[5], *Berry Nolan*[4], *Joseph (Joe)*[3], *Charles W. Sr.*[2], *John Sr.*[1]) was born 26 Feb 1920 in Lauderdale County, AL.

> Elizabeth married **Hershel H. Dodd**, son of **Clifford Dodd** and **Ola Leadford**, 7 Jan 1939 in Lauderdale County, AL. Hershel was born 26 Oct 1919 in Lauderdale County, AL, died 22 Dec 1998, and was buried in Stoney Point Cemetery, Lauderdale County, AL.
> + 1907 M   i.   **Jimmy Howard Dodd** was born 2 Jul 1947 in Lauderdale County, AL.
> + 1908 M   ii. **Danny Rae Dodd** was born 30 Mar 1949 in Lauderdale County, AL.

+ 1909 M iii. **Roger Anthony Dodd** was born 22 Aug 1954 in Lauderdale County, AL.

792. Berry Robert Sharp (*Charles Robert*[5], *Berry Nolan*[4], *Joseph (Joe)*[3], *Charles W. Sr.*[2], *John Sr.*[1]) was born 28 Dec 1924 in Colbert County, AL, died 18 Jun 1985, and was buried in Stoney Point Cemetery, Lauderdale County, AL.

Berry married **Roberta Irons**, daughter of **Robert Lee Irons** and **Cora Belle Fowler**, 16 Oct 1948 in Iuka, Tishomingo County, MS. Roberta was born 11 Jul 1931 in Lauderdale County, AL.
+ 1910 M i. **Robert (Bobby) Michael Sharp** was born 25 Oct 1955 in Lauderdale County, AL.
+ 1911 M ii. **Johnny Phillip Sharp** was born 13 Feb 1959 in Lauderdale County, AL.

793. Deedie P. Sharp (*Charles Robert*[5], *Berry Nolan*[4], *Joseph (Joe)*[3], *Charles W. Sr.*[2], *John Sr.*[1]) was born 20 Sep 1928 in Lauderdale County, AL.

Deedie married **Forrest B. Gibbs**, son of **William Alton Gibbs** and **Margaret Brown**, 13 Mar 1960 in Orlando, FL. Forrest was born in Columbia, TN and died 13 Jul 1977 in Columbia, TN.
+ 1912 F i. **Sandra Dee Gibbs** was born 7 Feb 1961 in Murfreesboro, TN.
+ 1913 M ii. **Jeffrey Brown Gibbs** was born 25 Sep 1964 in Lauderdale County, AL.

Deedie next married **Elton McDaniel**.

794. Billy Eugene Sharp (*Charles Robert*[5], *Berry Nolan*[4], *Joseph (Joe)*[3], *Charles W. Sr.*[2], *John Sr.*[1]) was born 27 Feb 1932 in Lauderdale County, AL.

Billy married **Christa Leona Retherford**, daughter of **Coy B. Retherford** and **Geraldine Scott**, 13 Oct 1956. Christa was born 20 Oct 1935 in Panama City, FL, died 15 Feb 1991, and was buried in Stoney Point Cemetery, Lauderdale County, AL.
+ 1914 M i. **Charles (Chuck) Ray Sharp** was born 5 Sep 1955 in Jefferson County, AL.
  1915 M ii. **Mark Stephen Sharp** was born 3 Jan 1957 in Lauderdale County, AL.

Billy next married **Barbara Jean McClusky** 18 Mar 1992 in Lauderdale County, AL.

795. Ollie Mitchell Statom II (*Lovie Francis Sharp*[5], *Berry Nolan*[4], *Joseph (Joe)*[3], *Charles W. Sr.*[2], *John Sr.*[1]) was born 28 Aug 1926 in Lauderdale County, AL, died 8 Jul 2000, and was buried in Stoney Point Cemetery, Lauderdale County, AL.

Ollie married **Martha Ernestine Roberts**, daughter of **Ernest Ray Roberts** and **Genieve Williams**, 9 Sep 1946 in Iuka, Tishomingo County, MS. Martha was born 5 Jan 1928 in Lauderdale County, AL, died 9 Feb 2000, and was buried in Stoney Point Cemetery, Lauderdale County, AL.
  1916 M i. **Ollie Mitchell Statom III** was born 31 Jul 1947 in Lauderdale County, AL.
+ 1917 M ii. **Robert Michael Statom** was born 31 Dec 1949 in Lauderdale County, AL.

796. Nolan Sharp Statom (*Muncie Venetta Sharp*[5], *Berry Nolan*[4], *Joseph (Joe)*[3], *Charles W. Sr.*[2], *John Sr.*[1]) was born 11 Sep 1919 in Lauderdale County, AL, died 9 May 2002, and was buried in Greenview Memorial Park, Florence, Lauderdale County, AL.

Nolan married **Lois Juanita Moore**, daughter of **Maxie B. Moore** and **Mary Alice Watkin**, 7 Jun 1941 in Lauderdale County, AL. Lois was born 24 Mar 1921 in Lauderdale County, AL.
+ 1918 F i. **Martha Ann Statom** was born 18 Jan 1942 in Lauderdale County, AL.
+ 1919 F ii. **Frances Kay Statom** was born 17 Dec 1943 in Lauderdale County, AL.

797. Lois Katherine Statom (*Muncie Venetta Sharp*[5], *Berry Nolan*[4], *Joseph (Joe)*[3], *Charles W. Sr.*[2], *John Sr.*[1]) was born 15 Sep 1921 in Lauderdale County, AL, died 2 Apr 1970, and was buried in Stoney Point Cemetery, Lauderdale County, AL.

Lois married **Roy Wilson Hodges**, son of **Chester Roy Hodges** and **Stella Nichols**, 21 Oct 1939 in Lauderdale County, AL. Roy was born 2 Jan 1918 in Woodville, AL.
+ 1920 M i. **Roy Wade Hodges** was born 6 Sep 1940 in Lauderdale County, AL.
+ 1921 M ii. **Larry Joe Hodges** was born 30 Jun 1942 in Lauderdale County, AL.

+ 1922 M iii. **Johnny Dale Hodges** was born 22 Aug 1947 in Lauderdale County, AL.

798. Hilda Mae Statom (*Muncie Venetta Sharp*[5]*, Berry Nolan*[4]*, Joseph (Joe)*[3]*, Charles W. Sr.*[2]*, John Sr.*[1]) was born 14 Apr 1923 in Black Oak, AR.

Hilda married **Earl Douglas Zahnd I**, son of **J. A. Zahnd** and **Mattie B. Wallace**, 6 Sep 1941 in Lauderdale County, AL. Earl was born 28 Sep 1922 in Lauderdale County, AL, died 9 Sep 2004, and was buried in Lauderdale County, AL.
+ 1923 M i. **Earl Douglas Zahnd II** was born 26 Jul 1943 in Lauderdale County, AL, died 26 Apr 1999, and was buried in Greenview Memorial Park, Florence, Lauderdale County, AL.
+ 1924 M ii. **Philip Gene Zahnd Sr.** was born 3 Mar 1947 in Lauderdale County, AL.

799. Dolly Francis Statom (*Muncie Venetta Sharp*[5]*, Berry Nolan*[4]*, Joseph (Joe)*[3]*, Charles W. Sr.*[2]*, John Sr.*[1]) was born 28 Jan 1925 in Lauderdale County, AL.

Dolly married **James Ervin Hickman Sr.**, son of **Rufus T. Hickman** and **Nannie Kellun**, 13 Sep 1947 in Lauderdale County, AL. James was born 30 Jan 1916 in Lynnville, TN, died 25 Mar 1999, and was buried in Greenview Memorial Park, Florence, Lauderdale County, AL.
+ 1925 M i. **James Ervin Hickman Jr.** was born 28 Jun 1952 in Lauderdale County, AL.
1926 F ii. **Beverly Jane Hickman** was born 4 Jan 1955 in Bridgeport, AL.
1927 M iii. **Joel Scott Hickman** was born 29 Sep 1960 in Paducah, KY.

800. John Price Statom Jr. (*Muncie Venetta Sharp*[5]*, Berry Nolan*[4]*, Joseph (Joe)*[3]*, Charles W. Sr.*[2]*, John Sr.*[1]) was born 5 Apr 1927 in Lauderdale County, AL.

John married **Alice Elizabeth Simmons**, daughter of **Luther Simmons** and **Minnie Austin**, 1 Jul 1949 in Lauderdale County, AL. Alice was born 13 Feb 1930 in Lauderdale County, AL.
1928 M i. **John Tracey Statom** was born 12 Nov 1960 in Lauderdale County, AL.
+ 1929 M ii. **Sterling Josh Statom** was born 4 Nov 1964 in Lauderdale County, AL.

801. Mattie Jo Statom (*Muncie Venetta Sharp*[5]*, Berry Nolan*[4]*, Joseph (Joe)*[3]*, Charles W. Sr.*[2]*, John Sr.*[1]) was born 10 Jul 1930 in Lauderdale County, AL.

Mattie married **Raymond C. Berkey**, son of **Albert Berkey** and **Arda Mae Miles**, 5 Jun 1948 in Colbert County, AL. Raymond was born 26 Aug 1927 in Lauderdale County, AL.
+ 1930 F i. **Patricia Gail Berkey** was born 24 Mar 1949 in Lauderdale County, AL.
1931 M ii. **Ronald Chas Berkey** was born 5 Nov 1951 in Lauderdale County, AL.
+ 1932 F iii. **Denise Lynne Berkey** was born 24 Aug 1957 in Lauderdale County, AL.

Mattie next married ***Unk Campbell**.

802. Betty Ruth Statom (*Muncie Venetta Sharp*[5]*, Berry Nolan*[4]*, Joseph (Joe)*[3]*, Charles W. Sr.*[2]*, John Sr.*[1]) was born 19 Mar 1932 in Lauderdale County, AL.

Betty married **Harold Lee James**, son of **Robert Enoch James** and **Erma Odel Lancaster**, 16 Jan 1951 in Colbert County, AL. Harold was born 24 Feb 1930 in Red Bay, Franklin County, AL.
+ 1933 F i. **Jennifer Leigh James** was born 20 Jul 1956 in Lauderdale County, AL.
1934 F ii. **Joni Lisa James** was born 19 Sep 1959.
+ 1935 M iii. **Jerry Glynn James** was born 20 Apr 1962 in Lauderdale County, AL.
+ 1936 M iv. **Joey Kynn James** was born 20 Apr 1962 in Lauderdale County, AL.

803. James Dalton Sharp (*James Leander*[5]*, Benjamin Franklin*[4]*, Joseph (Joe)*[3]*, Charles W. Sr.*[2]*, John Sr.*[1]) was born 18 Oct 1910 in Lauderdale County, AL, died 24 Jan 1987, and was buried in Wesley Chapel Cemetery, Lauderdale County, AL.

James married **Lila Virginia Montgomery**, daughter of **Miley Greenberry Montgomery** and **Flora Hall**, 28 Jan 1928 in Lauderdale County, AL. Lila was born 16 Nov 1909 in Lauderdale County, AL, died 2 Mar 2001, and was buried in Wesley Chapel Cemetery, Lauderdale County, AL.

+ 1937 M   i.   **Harry Lee Sharp** was born 6 Mar 1929 in Lauderdale County, AL and died 15 Sep 1988 in South Bend, IN (cremated).

  1938 M   ii.   **James David Sharp** was born 21 Mar 1932 in Lauderdale County, AL, died in May 1932, and was buried in Wesley Chapel Cemetery, Lauderdale County, AL.

+ 1939 F   iii.   **Helen Elizabeth Sharp** was born 22 Jul 1934 in Lauderdale County, AL.

+ 1940 M   iv.   **Bobby Montgomery Sharp** was born 25 Feb 1937 in Lauderdale County, AL.

+ 1941 F   v.   **Martha Wilhelminia Sharp** was born 7 Oct 1939 in Lauderdale County, AL.

+ 1942 M   vi.   **Richard Lynn (Rick) Sharp** was born 25 Jan 1953 in Lauderdale County, AL.

804. Thelma Mae Sharp (*James Leander* [5], *Benjamin Franklin* [4], *Joseph (Joe)* [3], *Charles W. Sr.* [2], *John Sr.* [1]) was born 24 Dec 1912 in Lauderdale County, AL, died 7 Apr 1999, and was buried in Rail Road Church Cemetery, Wayne County, TN.

Thelma married **Clemeth Issac Dixon**, son of **Virgil Commadore Dixon** and **Betty Copeland**, 25 Apr 1925 in Lawrenceburg, Lawrence County, TN. Clemeth was born 9 Aug 1902 in Wayne County, TN, died 13 Nov 1991, and was buried in Rail Road Church Cemetery, Wayne County, TN.

+ 1943 F   i.   **Audrey Ruth Dixon** was born 2 Nov 1938 in Lawrenceburg, Lawrence County, TN.

+ 1944 M   ii.   **Robert Dale Dixon** was born 30 Mar 1947 in Lawrenceburg, Lawrence County, TN.

805. Pauline Sharp (*James Leander* [5], *Benjamin Franklin* [4], *Joseph (Joe)* [3], *Charles W. Sr.* [2], *John Sr.* [1]) was born 18 Apr 1914 in Lauderdale County, AL and died in 1986.

Pauline married **Roy Davis**. Roy was born in Lawrenceburg, Lawrence County, TN.

806. Vella Ruth Sharp (*James Leander* [5], *Benjamin Franklin* [4], *Joseph (Joe)* [3], *Charles W. Sr.* [2], *John Sr.* [1]) was born 2 Sep 1917 in Lauderdale County, AL.

Vella married **Bonnie Gray**.

807. Mary Katherine Thrasher (*Nora E. Sharp* [5], *Benjamin Franklin* [4], *Joseph (Joe)* [3], *Charles W. Sr.* [2], *John Sr.* [1]) was born 17 Jul 1918 in Lauderdale County, AL.

Mary married **Coy E. Smith**, son of **Marion Smith** and **Ollie Cecil**, 29 Apr 1939 in Lauderdale County, AL. Coy was born 31 Jul 1918 in Lauderdale County, AL.

+ 1945 M   i.   **Samuel (Sammie) Coy Smith** was born 10 Apr 1942 in Lauderdale County, AL.

+ 1946 F   ii.   **Debora Louise Smith** was born 1 Oct 1952 in Lauderdale County, AL.

808. Edwin Robert Sharp (*Berry Robert* [5], *Benjamin Franklin* [4], *Joseph (Joe)* [3], *Charles W. Sr.* [2], *John Sr.* [1]) was born 15 Feb 1917 in Lauderdale County, AL, died 1 Oct 1998, and was buried in Wesley Chapel Cemetery, Lauderdale County, AL.

Edwin married **Mary Blanche Campbell**, daughter of **J. Wesley Campbell** and **Ada Oakley**, 18 Dec 1937 in Lauderdale County, AL. Mary was born 14 Oct 1917 in Lauderdale County, AL, died 14 Jun 1950, and was buried in Wesley Chapel Cemetery, Lauderdale County, AL.

+ 1947 F   i.   **Brenda Sharp**.

+ 1948 F   ii.   **Myra Sharp**.

+ 1949 F   iii.   **Wanda Sharp**.

+ 1950 M   iv.   **William David Sharp** was born 28 Jul 1940 in Lauderdale County, AL.

+ 1951 M   v.   **James Robert Sharp Sr.** was born 25 Dec 1944 in Lauderdale County, AL.

809. William Frank Sharp (*Berry Robert* [5], *Benjamin Franklin* [4], *Joseph (Joe)* [3], *Charles W. Sr.* [2], *John Sr.* [1]) was born 25 Oct 1921 in Cloverdale, Lauderdale County, AL, died 17 Jun 1996, and was buried in Greenview Memorial Park, Florence, Lauderdale County, AL.

William married **Jewell Ihone Quillen**, daughter of **Otis L. Quillen** and **Nannie Burns**, 26 Jan 1943 in Lauderdale County, AL. Jewell was born 5 Jan 1923 in Maud, AL.

+ 1952 F   i.   **Linda Ann Sharp** was born 9 Sep 1944 in Lauderdale County, AL.

810. Noel Sharp (*Berry Robert* [5], *Benjamin Franklin* [4], *Joseph (Joe)* [3], *Charles W. Sr.* [2], *John Sr.* [1]).

General Notes: "Lives in Nevada..." David Sharp

Noel married **Anna *Unk**.

811. Guy Owen Sharp (*Berry Robert^5, Benjamin Franklin^4, Joseph (Joe)^3, Charles W. Sr.^{2}, John Sr.^{1}*) was born 25 Jan 1933 in Oklahoma City, Oklahoma County, OK.

General Notes: "Lives in Las Vegas, Nevada..." David Sharp

Guy married **Joy Lee Henderson**, daughter of **William Henderson** and **Unknown**, in 1956 in Reno, NV. Joy was born in Orange County, CA.
1953　M　i.　**Randy Len Sharp** was born 1 Nov 1956 in Reno, NV.

Guy next married **Renee L. Gregoire**, daughter of **Robert Gregoire** and **Gertrude Fulton**, 6 Nov 1976 in Las Vegas, NV. Renee was born 8 Nov 1940 in Trumansburg, NY.

812. Beatrice E. Cagle (*Ethel Belle Sharp^5, Benjamin Franklin^4, Joseph (Joe)^3, Charles W. Sr.^{2}, John Sr.^{1}*) was born 17 Dec 1918 in Lauderdale County, AL, died 2 Dec 2007, and was buried in Mt. Tabor Cemetery, Lauderdale County, AL.

Beatrice married **George Henry Lard**, son of **Garfield Lard** and **Mattie Rhodes**, 8 May 1937 in Lauderdale County, AL. George was born 17 Aug 1914 in Lauderdale County, AL.
+　1954　M　i.　**James Edward Lard** was born 22 Mar 1938 in Lauderdale County, AL, died 14 Jul 1991, and was buried in Mt. Tabor Cemetery, Lauderdale County, AL.
+　1955　F　ii.　**Myra Elyne Lard** was born 28 Sep 1939 in Lauderdale County, AL.
+　1956　M　iii.　**Jackie Leon Lard** was born 15 Feb 1942 in Lauderdale County, AL.
+　1957　F　iv.　**Lynda Gale Lard** was born 13 Nov 1944 in Lauderdale County, AL.
+　1958　F　v.　**Vivi Don Lard** was born 25 Jan 1946 in Lauderdale County, AL.
　　1959　M　vi.　**Dwight David Lard** was born 8 Nov 1947 in Lauderdale County, AL.
+　1960　M　vii.　**Odis (Dale) Lard** was born 11 Sep 1951 in Lauderdale County, AL.

813. Lloyd Brooke Cagle (*Ethel Belle Sharp^5, Benjamin Franklin^4, Joseph (Joe)^3, Charles W. Sr.^{2}, John Sr.^{1}*) was born 15 Jul 1921 in Lauderdale County, AL, died 31 Jul 1991, and was buried in Greenview Memorial Park, Florence, Lauderdale County, AL.

Lloyd married **Ester Marie Daniel**, daughter of **Modie Bentley Daniel** and **Ada Cobb**, 12 Jul 1943 in Lauderdale County, AL. Ester was born 16 Oct 1924 in Lauderdale County, AL.
+　1961　M　i.　**Lindon Loyd Cagle** was born 26 Nov 1944 in Lauderdale County, AL.

Lloyd next married **Alma Evelene Hanback**, daughter of **Jessie L. Hanback** and **Thuney Etta Holt**, 27 Jul 1963 in Lauderdale County, AL.

Lloyd next married **Helen Clemons**, daughter of **James Thomas Clemons** and **Roxie Bell Smith**, 11 Dec 1969 in Lauderdale County, AL. Helen was born 31 Mar 1924 in Waterloo, Lauderdale County, AL.

Lloyd next married **Leona Ruth Robinson**, daughter of **Leroy Robinson** and **Mable Dixon**, 11 Jul 1975 in Lauderdale County, AL.

814. Evelyn Clara Cagle (*Ethel Belle Sharp^5, Benjamin Franklin^4, Joseph (Joe)^3, Charles W. Sr.^{2}, John Sr.^{1}*) was born 24 Jun 1924 in Lauderdale County, AL, died 11 Aug 2000, and was buried in Johnsons Crossroads Cemetery, Lauderdale County, AL.

Evelyn married **Albert Russell**, son of ***Unk Russell** and **Ora Herston**, 30 Aug 1947. Albert was born 19 Jan 1920 in Marked Tree, Poinsett County, AR, died 4 Nov 1995, and was buried in Johnsons Crossroads Cemetery, Lauderdale County, AL.
+　1962　F　i.　**Shirley Ann Russell** was born 25 Oct 1943 in Lauderdale County, AL.
+　1963　F　ii.　**Rebecca Russell** was born in Lauderdale County, AL.
+　1964　F　iii.　**Kathy Russell** was born in Lauderdale County, AL.
　　1965　M　iv.　**Don Russell** was born in Lauderdale County, AL.

+ 1966 M   v.   **James Albert Russell Sr.** was born 14 Oct 1950 in Lauderdale County, AL.

815. Francis Jeanette Cagle (*Ethel Belle Sharp*[5]*, Benjamin Franklin*[4]*, Joseph (Joe)*[3]*, Charles W. Sr.*[2]*, John Sr.*[1]) was born 25 Jul 1926 in Lauderdale County, AL, died 25 Jul 1994, and was buried in Johnsons Crossroads Cemetery, Lauderdale County, AL.

Francis married **Claude O. Lard**, son of **Garfield Lard** and **Mattie Rhodes**, 10 Dec 1942 in Lauderdale County, AL. Claude was born 4 Mar 1921 in Lauderdale County, AL.
+ 1967 F   i.   **Myra Lynn Lard** was born 26 Jun 1957 in Lauderdale County, AL.

Francis next married **Clifford McKelvey**.

Francis next married **Ed Louie Crider** 3 Jul 1973 in Lauderdale County, AL.

816. William Edward Cagle Jr. (*Ethel Belle Sharp*[5]*, Benjamin Franklin*[4]*, Joseph (Joe)*[3]*, Charles W. Sr.*[2]*, John Sr.*[1]) was born 22 Apr 1929 in Lauderdale County, AL.

William married **Nellie Jane Kelley**, daughter of **Wiley Edward Kelley** and **Mary Mymer Goodman**, 19 Aug 1950 in Iuka, Tishomingo County, MS. Nellie was born 22 Nov 1931 in Lauderdale County, AL.
+ 1968 M   i.   **Harold Ray Cagle** was born 28 Jul 1951 in Lauderdale County, AL.
+ 1969 F   ii.   **Mary Diane Cagle** was born 6 Oct 1952 in Lauderdale County, AL.
+ 1970 F   iii. **Teresa Yvonne Cagle** was born 20 Jun 1955 in Peoria, IL.
+ 1971 F   iv.   **Melissa Rene Cagle** was born 22 Aug 1959 in Peoria, IL.
   1972 M   v.   **David Leon Cagle** was born 7 May 1962.
+ 1973 F   vi.   **Delora Jean Cagle** was born 11 Sep 1964 in Peoria, IL.
+ 1974 F   vii. **Denise Lynn Cagle** was born 11 Sep 1964 in Peoria, IL.

817. Fayna (Faye) Cagle (*Ethel Belle Sharp*[5]*, Benjamin Franklin*[4]*, Joseph (Joe)*[3]*, Charles W. Sr.*[2]*, John Sr.*[1]) was born 14 Feb 1936 in Lauderdale County, AL.

Fayna married **Jack Charles Lawson**, son of **Robert William Lawson** and **Clara Jones**, 14 Apr 1950 in Iuka, Tishomingo County, MS. Jack was born 7 Jul 1938 in Lauderdale County, AL.
+ 1975 M   i.   **Charles William Lawson** was born 17 Jan 1952 in Lauderdale County, AL.
+ 1976 F   ii.   **Cathy Sue Lawson** was born 7 May 1954 in Lauderdale County, AL.
+ 1977 M   iii. **Larry Steven Lawson** was born 25 Jul 1959 in Lauderdale County, AL.
   1978 M   iv.   **Michael Shane Lawson** was born 2 Oct 1963 in Lauderdale County, AL.

Fayna next married **Charles Elbert Glover** 15 Aug 1977 in Lauderdale County, AL. Charles was born 1 Feb 1932 in Lauderdale County, AL.

818. Celia Frances Sharp (*Marvin Frank Sr.*[5]*, Benjamin Franklin*[4]*, Joseph (Joe)*[3]*, Charles W. Sr.*[2]*, John Sr.*[1]) was born 8 May 1921 in Lauderdale County, AL, died 31 Jul 1988, and was buried in Greenview Memorial Park, Florence, Lauderdale County, AL.

Celia married ***Unk**.

Celia next married **Al Bergbauger**.

819. Marvin (Billy) Frank Sharp Jr. (*Marvin Frank Sr.*[5]*, Benjamin Franklin*[4]*, Joseph (Joe)*[3]*, Charles W. Sr.*[2]*, John Sr.*[1]) was born 5 Jul 1926 in Lauderdale County, AL, died 17 May 1999, and was buried in Colbert Memorial Gardens, Colbert County, AL.

Marvin married **Mary Elizabeth Peck**, daughter of **Granville Allison Peck** and **Susie Ann Myrick**, 3 Mar 1947 in Lauderdale County, AL. Mary was born 1 Oct 1927 in Lauderdale County, AL.
   1979 M   i.   **Donald (Donnie) Edward Sharp** was born 25 Dec 1947 in Lauderdale County, AL.

Marvin next married **Joan Mills**, daughter of **Joe H. Mills** and **Vester Johnson**, 5 Jan 1954 in Colbert County, AL. Joan was born 6 Nov 1932 in Colbert Memorial Gardens, Colbert County, AL.
   1980 F   i.   **Marva Kim Sharp** was born 9 Feb 1955 in Lauderdale County, AL.

Marvin next married **Genevia *Unk**. Genevia was buried in Colbert Memorial Gardens, Colbert County, AL.

820. Donald J. Hill (*Maggie Leona Sharp^5, Benjamin Franklin^4, Joseph (Joe)^3, Charles W. Sr.^{2}, John Sr.^{1}*) was born 28 Jul 1921 in Lauderdale County, AL, died 1 Jan 1975, and was buried in Florence City Cemetery, Florence, Lauderdale County, AL.

Donald married **Mary Katherine Worsham**, daughter of **V. E. Worsham** and **Lizzie Bell Thomas**, 25 Oct 1947 in Lauderdale County, AL. Mary was born 16 Feb 1926 in Lauderdale County, AL.
+ 1981 M   i.   **Melvin Douglas Hill** was born 17 Nov 1948 in Lauderdale County, AL.

821. Mary Opel Hill (*Maggie Leona Sharp^5, Benjamin Franklin^4, Joseph (Joe)^3, Charles W. Sr.^{2}, John Sr.^{1}*) was born 7 Feb 1923 in Lauderdale County, AL.

Mary married **Aubrey Ray Cobb**, son of **Willis E. Cobb** and **Dollie Riddle**, 19 Oct 1941 in Colbert County, AL. Aubrey was born 27 Dec 1920 in Lauderdale County, AL.
1982 M   i.   **Donnie Ray Cobb**.

Mary next married **Virgil Vinson Kelley**, son of **Sammy T. Kelley** and **Inez Isabell Montgomery**. Virgil was born 26 Mar 1920 in Wayne County, TN.
+ 1983 M   i.   **Paul Eugene Kelley** was born 6 Apr 1949 in Lauderdale County, AL.
+ 1984 F   ii.   **Joyce Lynn Kelley** was born 10 Oct 1954 in Lauderdale County, AL.

822. Raymond A. Hill (*Maggie Leona Sharp^5, Benjamin Franklin^4, Joseph (Joe)^3, Charles W. Sr.^{2}, John Sr.^{1}*) was born 28 Oct 1923 in Lauderdale County, AL, died 3 Jun 1993, and was buried in Greenview Memorial Park, Florence, Lauderdale County, AL.

Raymond married **Francis Mullins**.
1985 M   i.   **John Arthur Hill** was born 7 Nov 1949 in Miami, FL.
1986 F   ii.   **Beverly Diane Hill** was born 2 Oct 1954.

824. Turner L. Sharp Sr. (*Charles Edward (Eddie)^5, John Levi^4, Charles W. II^3, Charles W. Sr.^{2}, John Sr.^{1}*) was born 11 Apr 1903 in Lauderdale County, AL, died 23 Aug 1934, and was buried in Centenary Cemetery, Lutts, Wayne County, TN.

Turner married **Lillie Gean**, daughter of **Henry Gean** and **Sallie Martin**, 20 Sep 1926 in Lauderdale County, AL. Lillie was born 17 Nov 1899 in Alabama, died 7 Jan 1966, and was buried in Graham Cemetery, Hardin County, TN.
+ 1987 M   i.   **Turner L. Sharp Jr.** died about 1995.
+ 1988 M   ii.   **Vernon Howard Sharp** was born 2 Jan 1929 in Mishawaka, St Joseph County, IN, died 15 Jan 1996, and was buried in Memory Gardens, Savannah, Hardin County, TN.

825. Dalton R. Sharp (*Charles Edward (Eddie)^5, John Levi^4, Charles W. II^3, Charles W. Sr.^{2}, John Sr.^{1}*) was born 27 Apr 1905 in Lauderdale County, AL, died 31 Jan 1942 in Mishawaka, St Joseph County, IN, and was buried in Lauderdale County, AL.

Dalton married **Pearl V. Young**, daughter of **Lee Jackson Young** and **Ethel Rogers**, 31 Jul 1927 in St. Joseph County, IN. Pearl was born 25 Dec 1910 in Lauderdale County, AL, died 11 Feb 1992, and was buried in Lawrenceburg, Lawrence County, TN.
(Duplicate Line. See Person 530)

827. Charles Henry Hill Sr. (*Alice Maxwell Sharp^5, John Levi^4, Charles W. II^3, Charles W. Sr.^{2}, John Sr.^{1}*) was born 10 Nov 1930 in Wichita, Sedgwick, KS.

Charles married **Wilhemina Guadalupe Tavarez** 26 Mar 1955 in Los Angeles, CA. Wilhemina was born 16 Sep 1934 in Oakland, Alameda County, CA.
+ 1989 M   i.   **Charles Henry Hill Jr.** was born 26 Nov 1957 in Long Beach, Los Angeles, CA.
+ 1990 F   ii.   **Paula Elaine Hill** was born 10 Aug 1960 in Long Beach, Los Angeles, CA.

828. Rita Faye Hill (*Alice Maxwell Sharp^5, John Levi^4, Charles W. II^3, Charles W. Sr.^{2}, John Sr.^{1}*) was born 27 Mar 1934 in Oklahoma City, Oklahoma County, OK.

Rita married **Clell Marker Greene Sr.** 12 Nov 1952 in Los Angeles, CA. Clell was born 22 May 1934 in Driggs, Teton, ID.

	1991	F	i.	**Adell Marie Greene** was born 2 Sep 1955 in Lynnwood, Los Angeles, CA.
+	1992	M	ii.	**David Craig Greene I** was born 20 Apr 1957 in Los Angeles, CA.
+	1993	M	iii.	**Clell Marker Greene Jr.** was born 26 Apr 1962 in Redondo Beach, Los Angeles, CA.

829. Elsie Marie Hill (*Alice Maxwell Sharp^5, John Levi^4, Charles W. II^3, Charles W. Sr.^{2}, John Sr.^{1}*) was born 31 Aug 1937 in Los Angeles, CA.

Elsie married **Gerald Joseph Twiss** 21 Oct 1961 in Mohave Kern, CA. Gerald was born 18 Mar 1934 in Athol, Spink, SD.

1994 M i. **William Michael Twiss** was born 23 Jun 1962 in Redondo Beach, Los Angeles, CA.
1995 M ii. **Bradley Joseph Twiss** was born 18 Dec 1968 in Redondo Beach, Los Angeles, CA.

830. Willie Carmen Box (*James (Jim) W. Box^5, Amanda Jane Sharp^4, Charles W. II^3, Charles W. Sr.^{2}, John Sr.^{1}*) was born 28 Dec 1906 in Lauderdale County, AL, died 13 Jan 1944, and was buried in New Hope Cemetery, Lauderdale County, AL.

Willie married **Buford Clyde Blackburn**, son of **Sampson Emmitt Blackburn** and **Ella Mae Wesson**, 27 Jul 1929 in Lauderdale County, AL. Buford was born 2 Dec 1908 in Lauderdale County, AL, died 29 Aug 2001, and was buried in New Hope Cemetery, Lauderdale County, AL.

+ 1996 M i. **Charles Everett Blackburn** was born 17 Apr 1942 in Lauderdale County, AL, died 7 Nov 1999, and was buried in New Hope Cemetery, Lauderdale County, AL.

831. Gladys Box (*James (Jim) W. Box^5, Amanda Jane Sharp^4, Charles W. II^3, Charles W. Sr.^{2}, John Sr.^{1}*) was born in 1910 in Alabama.

Gladys married **Andrew Williams** 11 Dec 1928 in Lauderdale County, AL.

832. John Carroll (J. C.) Box Sr. (*James (Jim) W. Box^5, Amanda Jane Sharp^4, Charles W. II^3, Charles W. Sr.^{2}, John Sr.^{1}*) was born 15 Sep 1910 in Lauderdale County, AL, died 16 Mar 1965, and was buried in Pleasant Hill Cemetery, Lauderdale County, AL.

John married **Mary Ethel Williams**, daughter of **Robert Oscar Williams** and **Ida Whitehead**, 26 Jul 1930 in Lauderdale County, AL. Mary was born 10 Jul 1910 in Lauderdale County, AL, died 15 Dec 1991, and was buried in Pleasant Hill Cemetery, Lauderdale County, AL.

+ 1997 F i. **Ruby Louise Box** was born 15 Feb 1933.
+ 1998 M ii. **Thomas Carroll Box** was born 4 Aug 1934 in Lauderdale County, AL.
+ 1999 M iii. **Donald Andrew Box** was born 28 Nov 1935 in Lauderdale County, AL.
+ 2000 F iv. **Rose Mary Box** was born 9 May 1949.

833. Stella Mae Box (*James (Jim) W. Box^5, Amanda Jane Sharp^4, Charles W. II^3, Charles W. Sr.^{2}, John Sr.^{1}*) was born in Jun 1916 in Lauderdale County, AL.

Stella married **Hagan Smith** 22 Feb 1936.

835. Herschel D. Anderson (*Charles David Anderson Sr.^{5}, Mary Elizabeth (Molly) Sharp^4, Charles W. II^3, Charles W. Sr.^{2}, John Sr.^{1}*) was born 8 Feb 1909 in Lauderdale County, AL, died 20 Oct 1931, and was buried in Gresham Cemetery, Lauderdale County, AL.

Herschel married **Ruby Crosswhite** 6 Dec 1929 in Lauderdale County, AL.

+ 2001 F i. **Clara Ruth Anderson**.

837. Robert Perry Anderson (*Charles David Anderson Sr.*^{5}, *Mary Elizabeth (Molly) Sharp*^{4}, *Charles W. II*^{3}, *Charles W. Sr.*^{2}, *John Sr.*^{1}) was born 16 Sep 1912 in Lauderdale County, AL, died 20 Jan 1936, and was buried in Gresham Cemetery, Lauderdale County, AL.

Robert married **Virgie Ione Young**, daughter of **Turner Andrew Young** and **Bessie Etta Mary Ann Rogers**. Virgie was born 22 Oct 1911 in Lauderdale County, AL.
(Duplicate Line. See Person 752)

838. Vera Anderson (*Charles David Anderson Sr.*^{5}, *Mary Elizabeth (Molly) Sharp*^{4}, *Charles W. II*^{3}, *Charles W. Sr.*^{2}, *John Sr.*^{1}) was born 8 Sep 1913 in Lauderdale County, AL.

Vera married **Hines Gray**, son of **Henry Gray** and **Martha Hamm**, 14 Aug 1937 in Colbert County, AL. Hines was born 19 Jan 1892 in Lauderdale County, AL, died 3 Dec 1951, and was buried in Greenview Memorial Park, Florence, Lauderdale County, AL.
+ 2002   M   i.   **John Hines Gray** was born 27 May 1939 in Lauderdale County, AL.
+ 2003   M   ii.   **Charles Leon Gray** was born 2 May 1943 in Lauderdale County, AL.

Vera next married **Dubert Eddy**.

839. Ester Marie Anderson (*Charles David Anderson Sr.*^{5}, *Mary Elizabeth (Molly) Sharp*^{4}, *Charles W. II*^{3}, *Charles W. Sr.*^{2}, *John Sr.*^{1}) was born 17 Apr 1914 in Lauderdale County, AL.

Ester married **Elmer Johnson**, son of **Zeb Johnson** and **Hattie Hinton**, 10 May 1931 in Lauderdale County, AL. Elmer was born 22 Jul 1909 in Lutts, Wayne County, TN.

840. John William Anderson (*Charles David Anderson Sr.*^{5}, *Mary Elizabeth (Molly) Sharp*^{4}, *Charles W. II*^{3}, *Charles W. Sr.*^{2}, *John Sr.*^{1}) was born 12 Mar 1916 in Lauderdale County, AL.

John married **Violet Turpen**, daughter of **William O. Turpen** and **Effie May Freeman**, 10 May 1941 in Lauderdale County, AL. Violet was born 29 Apr 1922 in Lauderdale County, AL.
+ 2004   M   i.   **David Eugene Anderson Sr.** was born 21 Feb 1942 in Nashville, Davidson County, TN.

841. Lillian Anderson (*Charles David Anderson Sr.*^{5}, *Mary Elizabeth (Molly) Sharp*^{4}, *Charles W. II*^{3}, *Charles W. Sr.*^{2}, *John Sr.*^{1}) was born 14 May 1920 in Lauderdale County, AL.

Lillian married **Thomas Alton Coleman** 6 Sep 1938 in Lauderdale County, AL.
2005   F   i.   **Rachel Ann Coleman**.
2006   M   ii.   **Wade Coleman**.
2007   F   iii.   **Betty Coleman**.
2008   M   iv.   **Michael Coleman**.
2009   F   v.   **Gail Coleman**.
2010   M   vi.   **Ricky Coleman**.
2011   M   vii.   **William (Billy) Coleman**.
2012   F   viii.   **Linda Coleman**.

842. Christine Anderson (*Charles David Anderson Sr.*^{5}, *Mary Elizabeth (Molly) Sharp*^{4}, *Charles W. II*^{3}, *Charles W. Sr.*^{2}, *John Sr.*^{1}) was born 26 Dec 1921 in Lauderdale County, AL.

Christine married **John Joyner** in 1936.
+ 2013   F   i.   **Inesse Joyner**.
+ 2014   M   ii.   **Gerald Joyner**.
2015   F   iii.   **Linda Joyner**.
2016   F   iv.   **Sandra Joyner**.

Christine next married **Nolan Rayburn** after 1936.

Christine next married **Elbert Anglin** after 1937.
2017   M   i.   **Lee Anglin**.

Christine next married **Fred *Unk** after 1938.

843. Geneva Anderson (*Charles David Anderson Sr.*[5]*, Mary Elizabeth (Molly) Sharp*[4]*, Charles W. II*[3]*, Charles W. Sr.*[2]*, John Sr.*[1]) was born 23 Aug 1924 in Lauderdale County, AL.

Geneva married **Joe Treviso** 19 Mar 1944.

2018	F	i.	**Joda Treviso.**
+ 2019	F	ii.	**Martha Treviso.**
2020	F	iii.	**Lidia Treviso.**

844. Ruby Anderson (*Charles David Anderson Sr.*[5]*, Mary Elizabeth (Molly) Sharp*[4]*, Charles W. II*[3]*, Charles W. Sr.*[2]*, John Sr.*[1]) was born 23 Sep 1926 in Lauderdale County, AL.

Ruby married **Lurlan Leathard Gean**, son of **Henry Letherd Gean** and **Ida Florence Vinson**, 7 Aug 1945. Lurlan was born 28 Feb 1922.

+ 2021	M	i.	**Larry David Gean** was born 9 Aug 1946 in South Bend, St Joseph County, IN.
+ 2022	F	ii.	**Cheryl Darline Gean** was born 7 Dec 1949 in South Bend, St Joseph County, IN.
+ 2023	M	iii.	**Kenneth Edward Gean** was born 8 Sep 1951 in South Bend, St Joseph County, IN.
+ 2024	F	iv.	**Wanda Gail Gean** was born 8 Nov 1957 in South Bend, St Joseph County, IN.

846. Lucille Anderson (*Charles David Anderson Sr.*[5]*, Mary Elizabeth (Molly) Sharp*[4]*, Charles W. II*[3]*, Charles W. Sr.*[2]*, John Sr.*[1]) was born 4 Sep 1929 in Lauderdale County, AL.

Lucille married **James Cecil Balentine Jr.**, son of **James Cecil Balentine Sr.** and **Pearl Winborn**, 13 Mar 1948. James was born 28 Nov 1926, died 15 Feb 1989, and was buried in Macedonia Cemetery, Lauderdale County, AL.

+ 2025	F	i.	**Katherine Jean Balentine** was born in Feb 1945 in Lauderdale County, AL.
+ 2026	F	ii.	**Carolyn Joan Balentine** was born 2 May 1949 in Lauderdale County, AL.
+ 2027	F	iii.	**Marilyn Jo Balentine** was born 8 Apr 1954 in Lauderdale County, AL.
+ 2028	F	iv.	**Martha Lee Balentine** was born 14 Mar 1956 in Lauderdale County, AL.
2029	F	v.	**Cindy Lou Balentine** was born 11 Mar 1958.
2030	F	vi.	**Debra Annette Balentine** was born in Oct 1962.

847. Charles David Anderson Jr. (*Charles David Anderson Sr.*[5]*, Mary Elizabeth (Molly) Sharp*[4]*, Charles W. II*[3]*, Charles W. Sr.*[2]*, John Sr.*[1]) was born 30 Aug 1931 in Lauderdale County, AL.

Charles married **Virginia Shirley** 2 Oct 1948.

2031	M	i.	**Bradley Anderson** was born in 1969.

Charles next married **Elgenia Darby** after 1948.

Charles next married **Ruth *Unk** after 1948.

848. Maxine Anderson (*Robert (Bud) Henry Anderson*[5]*, Mary Elizabeth (Molly) Sharp*[4]*, Charles W. II*[3]*, Charles W. Sr.*[2]*, John Sr.*[1]) was born 7 Jul 1915 in Lauderdale County, AL.

Maxine married **James Earl Romine**, son of **John Soloman Romine** and **Mable Chester Hale**, 29 Mar 1940 in Lauderdale County, AL. James was born 23 Jul 1914 in Lauderdale County, AL.

+ 2032	F	i.	**Charlotte Earl Romine** was born 7 Jan 1945 in Lauderdale County, AL.
2033	M	ii.	**James Thomas Romine** was born 12 Dec 1948 in Lauderdale County, AL and died 29 Feb 1964.

849. Mary Alice Anderson (*Robert (Bud) Henry Anderson*[5]*, Mary Elizabeth (Molly) Sharp*[4]*, Charles W. II*[3]*, Charles W. Sr.*[2]*, John Sr.*[1]) was born 26 Dec 1916 in Lauderdale County, AL, died 24 Apr 1994, and was buried in Greenview Memorial Park, Florence, Lauderdale County, AL.

Mary married **James William Winter**, son of **James Winter** and **Dolly Olive**, 31 Oct 1937 in Lauderdale County, AL. James was born 29 Jul 1916 in Colbert County, AL.

+ 2034 M i. **James Larry Winter** was born 15 Mar 1943 in Nashville, Davidson County, TN.

850. Francis Geraldine Anderson (*Robert (Bud) Henry Anderson*[5], *Mary Elizabeth (Molly) Sharp*[4], *Charles W. II*[3], *Charles W. Sr.*[2], *John Sr.*[1]) was born 27 Mar 1920 in Lauderdale County, AL, died 26 Jan 1981, and was buried in Greenview Memorial Park, Florence, Lauderdale County, AL.

Francis married **Lester Eugene Womble**, son of **Lester Womble** and ***Unk McKelvey**, in 1939. Lester was born 21 Jan 1915 in Lauderdale County, AL, died 13 Jun 1961, and was buried in Greenview Memorial Park, Florence, Lauderdale County, AL.

+ 2035 M i. **Kenneth Gene Womble** was born 20 May 1940.
2036 M ii. **William Russell Womble** was born 21 Jun 1949.

851. Robert (Bob) Fulmer Anderson (*Robert (Bud) Henry Anderson*[5], *Mary Elizabeth (Molly) Sharp*[4], *Charles W. II*[3], *Charles W. Sr.*[2], *John Sr.*[1]) was born 4 Jan 1922 in Lauderdale County, AL, died 26 Nov 1993, and was buried in Greenview Memorial Park, Florence, Lauderdale County, AL.

Robert married **Dorothy Ann Phelps**, daughter of **Bruce Whiting Phelps** and **Annie Margie Bowes**, 16 Feb 1946 in Lauderdale County, AL. Dorothy was born 12 Nov 1928 in Atlanta, Fulton County, GA, died 24 Jan 2002, and was buried in Greenview Memorial Park, Florence, Lauderdale County, AL.

+ 2037 M i. **James Robert Anderson** was born 5 Jan 1947 in Lauderdale County, AL.
+ 2038 M ii. **Phillip Edward Anderson** was born 15 Oct 1949 in Lauderdale County, AL.
+ 2039 M iii. **Stephen Gary Anderson** was born 27 May 1951 in Lauderdale County, AL.
+ 2040 M iv. **Timothy Milton Anderson** was born 11 Oct 1958 in Lauderdale County, AL.
+ 2041 F v. **Mary Ann Anderson** was born 28 Jan 1960 in Lauderdale County, AL.
+ 2042 M vi. **Mark Van Anderson** was born 28 Jan 1960 in Lauderdale County, AL.
+ 2043 M vii. **David Claude Anderson** was born 5 Sep 1961 in Lauderdale County, AL.

852. Helen Elizabeth Anderson (*Robert (Bud) Henry Anderson*[5], *Mary Elizabeth (Molly) Sharp*[4], *Charles W. II*[3], *Charles W. Sr.*[2], *John Sr.*[1]) was born 21 Apr 1926 in Lauderdale County, AL.

Helen married **Allen Wesson**.

Helen next married **Robert E. Moore**.

Helen next married **Walden McMillan**.

853. Gene Tunney Anderson Sr. (*Robert (Bud) Henry Anderson*[5], *Mary Elizabeth (Molly) Sharp*[4], *Charles W. II*[3], *Charles W. Sr.*[2], *John Sr.*[1]) was born 25 Sep 1929 in Lauderdale County, AL, died 31 Jul 1999, and was buried in Greenview Memorial Park, Florence, Lauderdale County, AL.

Gene married **Betty Lou Simpson**, daughter of **Fred Simpson** and **Lena Henson**, 6 Sep 1952 in Corinth, Alcorn County, MS. Betty was born 25 Sep 1934 in Colbert County, AL.

+ 2044 F i. **Shelia Dianne Anderson** was born 23 Jan 1954 in Lauderdale County, AL.
2045 F ii. **Amanda Kay Anderson** was born 4 Jun 1955 in Lauderdale County, AL.
2046 M iii. **Gene Tunney (Bud) Anderson Jr.** was born 18 Oct 1963 in Lauderdale County, AL.

856. Earl B. Saxton (*Mary Adeline (Addie) Anderson*[5], *Mary Elizabeth (Molly) Sharp*[4], *Charles W. II*[3], *Charles W. Sr.*[2], *John Sr.*[1]) was born 26 Dec 1911 in Lauderdale County, AL and died 23 Aug 1969 in Detroit, Wayne County, MI.

Earl married **Lucille Sims** in 1929.
2047 M i. **Gerald Saxton**.

Earl next married **Helen Austin** in 1932. Helen died 30 Dec 1946.

Earl next married **Mary *Unk** after 1946.

857. Jess Lloyd Saxton Sr. (*Mary Adeline (Addie) Anderson^5, Mary Elizabeth (Molly) Sharp^4, Charles W. II^3, Charles W. Sr.^{2}, John Sr.^{1}*) was born 25 Apr 1913 in Nashville, Davidson County, TN.

Jess married **Helen Naples**, daughter of **Albert Naples** and **Mary Grace Pamella**, 14 Oct 1939 in Bowling Green, KY. Helen was born 2 Aug 1916 in Wheeling, WV.

+ 2048 F i. **Mary Adeline Saxton**.
+ 2049 M ii. **Jess Lloyd Saxton Jr.**
  2050 F iii. **Lois Susan Saxton** was born 14 Oct 1950 in Detroit, Wayne County, MI.

858. John Edward Anderson (*Marvin Robert Anderson^5, Mary Elizabeth (Molly) Sharp^4, Charles W. II^3, Charles W. Sr.^{2}, John Sr.^{1}*) was born 16 Jul 1926 in Lauderdale County, AL.

John married **Dorothy Menges**.

859. Marion Ruth Anderson (*Marvin Robert Anderson^5, Mary Elizabeth (Molly) Sharp^4, Charles W. II^3, Charles W. Sr.^{2}, John Sr.^{1}*) was born 8 Feb 1930 in Detroit, Wayne County, MI.

Marion married **David Hunt**.

860. Marvelen Anderson (*Marvin Robert Anderson^5, Mary Elizabeth (Molly) Sharp^4, Charles W. II^3, Charles W. Sr.^{2}, John Sr.^{1}*) was born 31 Aug 1936 in Lauderdale County, AL.

Marvelen married **Steven Davey**.

861. Jeanett Anderson (*Marvin Robert Anderson^5, Mary Elizabeth (Molly) Sharp^4, Charles W. II^3, Charles W. Sr.^{2}, John Sr.^{1}*) was born 4 Aug 1942 in Lauderdale County, AL.

Jeanett married **Ronald Conway**.

862. Charles William Sharp (*William Lee^5, Charles Franklin^4, Charles W. II^3, Charles W. Sr.^{2}, John Sr.^{1}*) was born 28 Apr 1919 in Paris, Lamar County, TX, died 27 Sep 1989, and was buried in Paris, Lamar County, TX.

Charles married **Dona Jane Crumley** 25 Dec 1940 in Amarillo, TX. Dona was born 6 Jul 1923 in Paris, Lamar County, TX.

+ 2051 M i. **Scott Lee Sharp** was born 13 Aug 1945 in Paris, Lamar County, TX.
+ 2052 F ii. **Susan Sharp** was born 12 Dec 1954 in Paris, Lamar County, TX.

863. Mary Elizabeth Sharp (*William Lee^5, Charles Franklin^4, Charles W. II^3, Charles W. Sr.^{2}, John Sr.^{1}*) was born 4 Apr 1926 in Paris, Lamar County, TX, died in 1945, and was buried in Evergreen Cemetery, Paris, TX.

Mary married **Jack A. Warner** in Oct 1944.

864. Virginia Lee Sharp (*William Lee^5, Charles Franklin^4, Charles W. II^3, Charles W. Sr.^{2}, John Sr.^{1}*) was born 15 May 1927 in Paris, Lamar County, TX.

Virginia married **Buryl O. Hutto** 16 May 1950. Buryl was born 20 Jun 1925 in Rockford, Lamar County, TX.

+ 2053 M i. **Victor Barney Hutto**.
+ 2054 M ii. **Bruce Hutto**.

865. Clora Ovrille Dowdy (*Hosea (Hozie) Durille Dowdy^5, Rachel Ann (Babe) Sharp^4, Charles W. II^3, Charles W. Sr.^{2}, John Sr.^{1}*) was born 27 May 1919 in Lauderdale County, AL, died 14 Mar 1973, and was buried in Macedonia Cemetery, Lauderdale County, AL.

Clora married **Herschel Clyde Wright**, son of **Clyde Wright** and **Camilla Joiner**, 8 Apr 1939 in Lauderdale County, AL. Herschel was born 20 Jan 1918, died 18 Nov 1986, and was buried in Macedonia Cemetery, Lauderdale County, AL.

+ 2055 M i. **Jerry Wade Wright** was born 9 Nov 1940 in Lauderdale County, AL.

+ 2056 M ii. **Timothy Elliot Wright** was born 5 Sep 1943 in Lauderdale County, AL.

+ 2057 M iii. **Horace Lanny Wright** was born 20 Oct 1947 in Lauderdale County, AL.

866. James Floyd Dowdy Sr. (*Hosea (Hozie) Durille Dowdy*[5], *Rachel Ann (Babe) Sharp*[4], *Charles W. II*[3], *Charles W. Sr.*[2], *John Sr.*[1]) was born 8 Jan 1921 in Lauderdale County, AL and died 30 Mar 1987 in Huntsville, Madison County, AL.

James married **Shirley Frances Mason**, daughter of **Earl Mason** and **Dora Stack**, 17 Nov 1943 in Denver, CO. Shirley was born 23 Sep 1925 in Denver, CO.

+ 2058 M i. **James Floyd Dowdy Jr.** was born 9 Aug 1948 in Denver, CO.

+ 2059 F ii. **Dorlea Francis Dowdy** was born 26 Mar 1950 in Denver, CO.

+ 2060 M iii. **Kenneth Herschel Dowdy** was born 8 Dec 1952 in Denver, CO.

867. Juanita Ventelle Dowdy (*Hosea (Hozie) Durille Dowdy*[5], *Rachel Ann (Babe) Sharp*[4], *Charles W. II*[3], *Charles W. Sr.*[2], *John Sr.*[1]) was born 3 Apr 1923 in Lauderdale County, AL.

Juanita married **Edward Walker Slaughter**, son of **Frank Vitalis Slaughter** and **Nellie Mae Morrison**, 12 Sep 1947 in Lauderdale County, AL. Edward was born 29 Jan 1919 in Colbert County, AL.

2061 M i. **James Edward Slaughter** was born 25 Jun 1953 in Lauderdale County, AL.

+ 2062 M ii. **Michael Robin Slaughter** was born 30 Mar 1959 in Lauderdale County, AL.

869. Addye Faye Dowdy (*Hosea (Hozie) Durille Dowdy*[5], *Rachel Ann (Babe) Sharp*[4], *Charles W. II*[3], *Charles W. Sr.*[2], *John Sr.*[1]) was born 4 Nov 1934 in Lauderdale County, AL.

Addye married **Ralph D. Hanback**, son of **Roy Lee Hanback** and **Thelma Marion Stewart**, 24 Nov 1952 in Lauderdale County, AL. Ralph was born 13 Jun 1931 in Lauderdale County, AL.

+ 2063 M i. **John Stewart Hanback** was born 7 Nov 1958 in Huntsville, Madison County, AL.

+ 2064 M ii. **Barry Lee Hanback** was born 22 Sep 1961 in Huntsville, Madison County, AL.

870. Mary Louise Stults (*Linnie Mae Sharp*[5], *Thomas (Tom) Erwin*[4], *Charles W. II*[3], *Charles W. Sr.*[2], *John Sr.*[1]) was born 6 Oct 1916 in Lauderdale County, AL, died 31 Oct 2004, and was buried in Greenview Memorial Park, Florence, Lauderdale County, AL.

Mary married **Archie Hopson Watkins**, son of **Tom Watkins** and **Francis Hill**, 28 Jan 1933 in Lauderdale County, AL. Archie was born 31 Dec 1913 in Lauderdale County, AL, died 20 May 1956, and was buried in Greenview Memorial Park, Florence, Lauderdale County, AL.

+ 2065 F i. **Omi Jean Watkins** was born 16 Nov 1935 in Lauderdale County, AL.

+ 2066 F ii. **Earline Watkins** was born 2 Nov 1938 in Lauderdale County, AL.

+ 2067 F iii. **Bobbie Sue Watkins** was born 5 Jul 1942 in Lauderdale County, AL, died 23 Sep 2000, and was buried in Greenview Memorial Park, Florence, Lauderdale County, AL.

+ 2068 M iv. **Charles Lee Watkins** was born 2 Feb 1948 in Lauderdale County, AL.

871. Thomas Joel Stults (*Linnie Mae Sharp*[5], *Thomas (Tom) Erwin*[4], *Charles W. II*[3], *Charles W. Sr.*[2], *John Sr.*[1]) was born 1 Sep 1922 in Lauderdale County, AL, died 21 Feb 1989, and was buried in Mt. Zion Cemetery, Wayne County, TN.

Thomas married **Laura Annie Medley**, daughter of **Samuel Medley** and **Lucinda Watkins**, 10 May 1941 in Wayne County, TN. Laura was born 5 Jun 1922 in Lauderdale County, AL.

+ 2069 F i. **Tommie Jo Stults** was born 16 Feb 1942 in Lauderdale County, AL, died 16 Feb 1984, and was buried in Mt. Zion Cemetery, Wayne City, TN.

+ 2070 M ii. **Sammy Carter Stults Sr.** was born 20 Jan 1944 in Lauderdale County, AL.

+ 2071 M iii. **Horace Calvin Stults Sr.** was born 5 Jul 1949 in Lauderdale County, AL.

+ 2072 F iv. **Judith Ann (Judy) Stults** was born 1 Sep 1953 in Lauderdale County, AL, died 25 Jan 2003, and was buried in Mt. Zion Cemetery, Wayne City, TN.

872. Julia Christine Stults (*Linnie Mae Sharp*[5], *Thomas (Tom) Erwin*[4], *Charles W. II*[3], *Charles W. Sr.*[2], *John Sr.*[1]) was born 16 Jul 1924 in Lauderdale County, AL, died 19 Sep 1981, and was buried in Greenview Memorial Park, Florence, Lauderdale County, AL.

Julia married **Rufus Jackson Wilkes**, son of **Levi (Lee) Grant Wilkes I** and **Eula Elizabeth Sharp**, 8 Nov 1941 in Lauderdale County, AL. Rufus was born 5 Mar 1924 in Lauderdale County, AL, died 27 Jan 2003, and was buried in Greenview Memorial Park, Florence, Lauderdale County, AL.
(Duplicate Line. See Person 789)

Julia next married **Raymond (Ray) Berry**.

873. John Bobby Stults (*Linnie Mae Sharp* [5], *Thomas (Tom) Erwin* [4], *Charles W. II* [3], *Charles W. Sr.* [2], *John Sr.* [1]) was born 19 Apr 1932 in Lauderdale County, AL, died 19 Dec 1990, and was buried in Greenview Memorial Park, Florence, Lauderdale County, AL.

John married **Betty Jean Wallace**, daughter of **James Thomas Wallace** and **Velma Linville**. Betty was born 5 Apr 1934 in Lauderdale County, AL.
+ 2073 F i. **Teresa Jean Stults** was born 6 Apr 1953 in Lauderdale County, AL.
+ 2074 F ii. **Debra Lynn Stults** was born 12 Apr 1956 in Lauderdale County, AL.
+ 2075 F iii. **Janice Faye Stults** was born 9 Mar 1957 in Lauderdale County, AL.

874. David Guy Sharp (*Guy Thomas* [5], *Thomas (Tom) Erwin* [4], *Charles W. II* [3], *Charles W. Sr.* [2], *John Sr.* [1]) was born 2 Jun 1927 in Lauderdale County, AL.

David married **Audrey Cordelia Montgomery**, daughter of **Henry Harrison Montgomery Sr.** and **Addie Lee Darby**, 3 Feb 1950 in Iuka, Tishomingo County, MS. Audrey was born 18 Mar 1934 in Lauderdale County, AL, died 17 Feb 2009, and was buried in Cherokee Memorial Park, Colbert County, AL.

David Guy Sharp holding a rifle that was handed down to him by his dad, Guy Thomas Sharp. The rifle belonged to Charles Sharp, Sr.

Cordelia Montgomery Sharp, the first motorcycle policewoman in Florence, AL

Ticket to ride

First woman motorcycle officer in Florence looks back on career and her 15 minutes of fame

By Bernie Delinski
STAFF WRITER

FLORENCE

The woman on the 46-year-old black-and-white program carried an air of confidence and grace as she responded to the questions.

The celebrity panel tried to glean information about her profession by asking various questions.

Eventually, the woman smiled and nodded her head as the panel was told they had guessed her profession: a motorcycle police officer for the Florence Police Department.

That confidence and grace haven't left Cordelia Sharp as she recalls that Feb. 14, 1960, nationwide taping of the game show,

"What's My Line?"

"I wasn't nervous, I just went along with the show," Sharp recalls. "I just acted like I knew what I was doing there."

The notion of a woman motorcycle officer was foreign nationwide in 1960, but not in Florence, where four motorcycle officers were women.

In fact, David Sharp says, a woman in their neighborhood told his wife about an opening the department.

The woman and Cordelia Sharp both were hired for the positions.

Still, it was unusual enough to garner the attention of the nationwide game show, which invited her to be a panelist.

Sharp's husband, David Sharp, recently showed Florence police a tape of the show, while gathering clippings and other information for a scrapbook of his wife's police career.

Police Chief Rick Singleton sat in on the viewing. "When I saw it, I thought, 'I just have to let everyone in our department see this,'" Singleton recalls.

That's just what he did Sunday, showing the segment of the show during the department's annual meeting.

POLICE continued on 4

Cordelia Sharp with "What's My Line?" host John Daly during the show's broadcast.

Cordelia Montgomery Sharp on "What's My Line" TV show (*Florence Times Daily*)

General Notes: Obituary - Times Daily, Florence, Lauderdale County, Alabama
2-18-2009
"Cordelia Montgomery Sharp, age 74, of Florence, Ala., passed away Tuesday, Feb. 17, 2009. Her family will receive friends Thursday, Feb. 19, 2009, from 1 - 2 p.m. at Morrison Funeral Home, of Cherokee. Her funeral service will follow in the funeral home chapel, with Dr. Tom Whatley officiating. Burial will be in Cherokee Memorial Park.

She was a native of Lauderdale County and a member of Central Baptist Church. She was preceded in death by her sister, Ethel Gertrude Stowe; brothers, Lee, Henry and Graford Montgomery; granddaughter, Nikky Waldrep; and son-in-law Larry Waldrep.

She is survived by her husband, David Guy Sharp; daughter, Patsy Waldrep; granddaughter, Holly Morrison and husband, Mike; great -grandchildren, Alex, Rhett and Braden Morrison.

Pallbearers are Kenny Stowe, Joe Willis, Tim Wright, Chris May, Clyde Richard, and great - grandsons, Alex, Rhett and Braden.

In lieu of flowers, memorials may be made to St. Jude Children's Research Hospital, Memorial and Honor Program, 501 St. Jude Place, Memphis, TN 38105-1942, or Coalition of Alzheimer and Related Disorders, P.O. Box 1608, Florence, AL 35631.

The family would like to express sincere appreciation to Glenwood Nursing Home for their exceptional care and love given to Mrs. Sharp; also the compassion shown her family, during these past few months. Morrison Funeral Home, of Cherokee, is directing."

+ 2076 F i. **Patsy Marie Sharp** was born 24 Jan 1952 in Lauderdale County, AL.

875. Tommy Gerald Sharp (*Guy Thomas[5], Thomas (Tom) Erwin[4], Charles W. II[3], Charles W. Sr.[2], John Sr.[1]*) was born 15 Sep 1933 in Russellville, Franklin County, AL, died 19 Aug 2008, and was buried in Eastern Gate Memorial Gardens, Pensacola, FL.

General Notes: Obituary - Times Daily, Florence, Lauderdale County, Alabama

"Tommy G. Sharp, 74, of Pace, Fla., formerly of Lauderdale County, passed away Tuesday, Aug. 19, 2008. His funeral service will be Friday, Aug. 22, 2008, at 10 a. m. in the chapel of Eastern Gate Funeral Home, of Pensacola, Fla., with burial in Eastern Gate Memorial Gardens.

He proudly served his country in the U. S. Navy for three years. He was preceded in death by his parents, Guy Sharp and Vivian Patterson, and his grandson, Sean Thomas Cannon.

Survivors include his daughter, Robin Beasley and husband, Jackie, of Pensacola, Fla.; brother, David G. Sharp and wife, Cordelia; and sister, Nancy Reese."

Tommy married **Myra Catherine Carroll**, daughter of **Reeder Edward Carroll** and **Vera Womble**, 3 Sep 1960 in Lauderdale County, AL. Myra was born 3 Apr 1941 in Lauderdale County, AL.
+ 2077 F i. **Robbie Dawn Sharp** was born 15 Sep 1965 in Pensacola, Escambia County, FL.

876. Nancy Kay Sharp (*Guy Thomas[5], Thomas (Tom) Erwin[4], Charles W. II[3], Charles W. Sr.[2], John Sr.[1]*) was born 21 Jul 1944 in Lauderdale County, AL.

Nancy married **Johnny Wayne Murphy**, son of **John Franklin Murphy** and **Sally Myrtle Marler**, 2 Jun 1964 in Lauderdale County, AL. Johnny was born 3 Jul 1942 in Lauderdale County, AL.
+ 2078 F i. **Angelia Leigh Murphy** was born 9 Sep 1965 in Lauderdale County, AL.
  2079 M ii. **Daryl Wayne Murphy** was born 1 Jan 1970 in Nashville, Davidson County, TN, died 29 Nov 1991, and was buried in Summerville Park Memorial Cemetery, SC.
  2080 F iii. **Kristy Lynn Murphy** was born 5 Nov 1973 in Charlotte, NC.

877. Walter Eugene Sharp (*Ellis Eugene[5], Thomas (Tom) Erwin[4], Charles W. II[3], Charles W. Sr.[2], John Sr.[1]*) was born 13 Jun 1938 in Lauderdale County, AL.

Walter married **Jeanetta Irene Parker**, daughter of **Edward B. Parker** and **Nina Travis**, 29 Jun 1957 in Lauderdale County, AL. Jeanetta was born 14 Jan 1939 in Paris, Henry County, TN.
+ 2081 F i. **Cindy Ann Sharp** was born 20 Apr 1958 in Lauderdale County, AL.

878. Donna Joyce Sharp (*Ellis Eugene[5], Thomas (Tom) Erwin[4], Charles W. II[3], Charles W. Sr.[2], John Sr.[1]*) was born 14 Sep 1940 in Springfield, OH.

Donna married **James Lindsey (Bo) Vinson**, son of **Louis Andrew Vinson** and **Dimple Laverne Curtis**, 5 Jan 1959 in Decatur, Morgan County, AL. James was born 11 Apr 1939 in Colbert County, AL.

+ 2082 M   i.   **James Donald (Donnie) Vinson** was born 23 Oct 1959 in Florence, Lauderdale County, AL.
+ 2083 F   ii.   **Andrea Jean Vinson** was born 30 Oct 1961 in Florence, Lauderdale County, AL.
+ 2084 F   iii.   **Melanie Lynne Vinson** was born 5 Feb 1963 in Florence, Lauderdale County, AL.

880. J. Patton (Pat) Young (*William C. Young* [5], *Matilda Ann White* [4], *Eliza Jane Sharp* [3], *Charles W. Sr.* [2], *John Sr.* [1]) was born in 1900 in Lauderdale County, AL and died in 1986 in Mishawaka, St Joseph County, IN.

J. married **Madge Carpenter** 28 Mar 1931. Madge was born in 1911 and died in 1993 in Mishawaka, St Joseph County, IN.

2085 M   i.   ***Unk Young** was born 6 Jan 1931.

J. next married **Elizabeth Weston**.

881. Mamie Young (*William C. Young* [5], *Matilda Ann White* [4], *Eliza Jane Sharp* [3], *Charles W. Sr.* [2], *John Sr.* [1]) was born 30 Jun 1903 in Florence, Lauderdale County, AL, died 29 Jun 1942, and was buried in Fairview Cemetery, Mishawaka, IN.

Mamie married **Wheeler Young**, son of **Owen Bartley Young Sr.** and **Julia Ann Young**, 8 Jan 1918 in Lauderdale County, AL. Wheeler was born 3 May 1896 in Lauderdale County, AL, died 6 Apr 1975, and was buried in Seattle, WA.
(Duplicate Line. See Person 274)

882. William Dalton Young (*William C. Young* [5], *Matilda Ann White* [4], *Eliza Jane Sharp* [3], *Charles W. Sr.* [2], *John Sr.* [1]) was born in 1906 in Lauderdale County, AL, died 10 May 1967, and was buried in Mishawaka, St Joseph County, IN.

William married **Marguerite Smith** 17 Jan 1930 in St. Joseph County, IN.

884. Ella Mae Young (*William C. Young* [5], *Matilda Ann White* [4], *Eliza Jane Sharp* [3], *Charles W. Sr.* [2], *John Sr.* [1]) was born 15 May 1913 in Lauderdale County, AL, died 8 Nov 1989, and was buried in Mishawaka, St Joseph County, IN.

Ella married **Darrell C. Sowders** 21 Mar 1941 in Ohio. Darrell was born 13 Mar 1917, died 21 Sep 1981, and was buried in Mishawaka, St Joseph County, IN.

2086 M   i.   **James Sowders**.
+ 2087 M   ii.   **Charles Sowders**.
2088 M   iii.   **Lamar S. Sowders**.

887. Lady Goldie Saddler (*Cora Young* [5], *Matilda Ann White* [4], *Eliza Jane Sharp* [3], *Charles W. Sr.* [2], *John Sr.* [1]) was born 6 Feb 1903 in Lauderdale County, AL, died 7 Jan 1967, and was buried in Richardson Cemetery, Lauderdale County, AL.

Lady married **James (Jim) W. Boatright**, son of **James Madison Boatright** and **Elizabeth Taylor**, 11 Aug 1919 in Lauderdale County, AL. James was born 15 Sep 1891 in Colbert County, AL, died 23 Oct 1968, and was buried in Richardson Cemetery, Lauderdale County, AL.

+ 2089 M   i.   **James Hoyt Boatright Sr.** was born 26 Jul 1920 in Wright, Lauderdale County, AL.
+ 2090 F   ii.   **Wernita Elizabeth Boatright** was born 3 Nov 1922 in Lauderdale County, AL.
+ 2091 M   iii.   **Donald Douglas Boatright** was born 16 Jan 1930 in Lauderdale County, AL.

888. Vera Alean Saddler (*Cora Young* [5], *Matilda Ann White* [4], *Eliza Jane Sharp* [3], *Charles W. Sr.* [2], *John Sr.* [1]) was born in 1910 in Lauderdale County, AL and was buried in Mishawaka, St Joseph County, IN.

Vera married **Ernest M. Pruitt** 17 Oct 1930 in Lauderdale County, AL.

+ 2092 F   i.   **Wanda Joy Pruitt**.

889. James Louie Saddler (*Cora Young[5], Matilda Ann White[4], Eliza Jane Sharp[3], Charles W. Sr.[2], John Sr.[1]*) was born 6 Aug 1912 in Lauderdale County, AL, died 25 Feb 1936, and was buried in Wright Cemetery, Wright, Lauderdale County, AL.

James married **Louise Fisher**, daughter of **John Anderson Fisher** and **Timpest Beadle**, 13 Nov 1931 in Lauderdale County, AL. Louise was born 17 Nov 1913 in Lawrence County, TN.

+ 2093 M i. **James Lewis Saddler** was born 6 Jul 1932 in Lauderdale County, AL.

893. Doyle Lee Young (*John Robert Young[5], Matilda Ann White[4], Eliza Jane Sharp[3], Charles W. Sr.[2], John Sr.[1]*) was born 18 Jul 1913 in Lauderdale County, AL, died 30 Jan 1991, and was buried in Wright Cemetery, Wright, Lauderdale County, AL.

Doyle married **Myrtle Lutts**, daughter of **Carl Lutts** and **Mary Elizabeth Sharp**, 28 Dec 1935 in Lauderdale County, AL. Myrtle was born 13 Mar 1912 in Lauderdale County, AL, died 29 Jan 1940, and was buried in Oak Grove Cemetery, Lauderdale County, AL.
(Duplicate Line. See Person 619)

Doyle next married **Dorothy Betty White**, daughter of **Dempsey Dave White** and **Lucinda Ida Young**, 4 Jan 1944 in Lauderdale County, AL. Dorothy was born 27 Feb 1916 in Lauderdale County, AL, died 8 Dec 1992, and was buried in Wright Cemetery, Wright, Lauderdale County, AL.

895. Jewel Estelle Young (*John Robert Young[5], Matilda Ann White[4], Eliza Jane Sharp[3], Charles W. Sr.[2], John Sr.[1]*) was born 28 Sep 1920 in Lauderdale County, AL, died 4 Dec 2004, and was buried in Greenview Memorial Park, Florence, Lauderdale County, AL.

Jewel married **Terry Lee Sharp**, son of **Edgar Lee Sharp** and **Lonie Alberta Glasscock**, 23 Dec 1944 in Lauderdale County, AL. Terry was born 13 Sep 1915 in Lauderdale County, AL, died 14 Jan 1994, and was buried in Greenview Memorial Park, Florence, Lauderdale County, AL.

+ 2094 M i. **Larry Dennis Sharp** was born 17 Sep 1945 in Lauderdale County, AL.
+ 2095 F ii. **Roberta Nathalie Sharp** was born 21 Aug 1951 in Lauderdale County, AL.
  2096 F iii. **Roma Jane Sharp** was born 4 May 1954 in Lauderdale County, AL.

896. Robert Vernon Young (*John Robert Young[5], Matilda Ann White[4], Eliza Jane Sharp[3], Charles W. Sr.[2], John Sr.[1]*) was born 4 Apr 1923 in Waterloo, Lauderdale County, AL, died 9 Jul 2000, and was buried in Williams Chapel Cemetery, Lauderdale County, AL.

General Notes: Obituary - Times Daily, Florence, Lauderdale County, Alabama

"Robert Vernon Young, 77, Waterloo, died Saturday, July 9, 2000, after an extended illness. Visitation will be 6 – 9 p.m. today at Greenview Funeral Home. The funeral will be at 10 a.m. Wednesday at the funeral home chapel with burial in Williams Chapel Cemetery. Officiating at the funeral will be Vance Hutton and David Rushlow.
Mr. Young was a native and lifelong resident of the Waterloo community.
He is survived by his wife of 54 years, Sarah F. Strange Young, Waterloo; son, Robert Erskin Hisey, a nephew whom he raised as a son, Waterloo; sister, Jewell Sharp, Florence; brothers, Fay Young, Florence, John Young, Mishawaka, Ind.; grandchildren, Tanya Hisey White, Waterloo, Melissa Grove, Plymouth, Ind., Jamie KayHisey, Florence, Ashley Hisey, Plymouth, Matthew Hisey, Plymouth; nephew, Carl Young, Waterloo; eight great -grandchildren; several nieces and nephews.
Mr. Young was preceded in death by his parents, Robert and Callie Young; brothers, Doyle and Marvin Young; and sister, Etoile Young.
Pallbearers will include Daniel Holcombe, Danny Wade Barrier, Keith Barrier, Mark Barrier, David Hutton, Terry Duboise.
Mr. Young retired from the forestry commission as a forest manager after 25 years. He was a member of the Church of Christ and was a disabled veteran of World War II.
Mr. Young was a beloved husband, father and grandfather. He loved his wife, son and grandchildren. He always gave to others without thoughts of himself. He was unselfish, kind, generous and loving. Robert Vernon Young will always be remembered, always be missed and always be loved.
Greenview Funeral Home of Florence is directing."

Robert married **Sarah Frances Strange** about 1946. Sarah was born 1 Aug 1926.

2097 M   i.   **Robert Erskin Hisey**.

897. Arnold Andrew Young (*Andrew Cleveland Young^5, Matilda Ann White^4, Eliza Jane Sharp^3, Charles W. Sr.^{2}, John Sr.^{1}*) was born 13 Nov 1918 in Waterloo, Lauderdale County, AL, died 7 Apr 2001, and was buried in Greenview Memorial Park, Florence, Lauderdale County, AL.

Arnold married **Clarita May Thompson**, daughter of **James Rodger Thompson** and **Clara Moyers**, 28 Oct 1945 in Athens, Limestone County, AL. Clarita was born 1 May 1918 in Athens, Limestone County, AL, died 16 Nov 2007, and was buried in Greenview Memorial Park, Florence, Lauderdale County, AL.

+ 2098 F   i.   **Linda Arnalla Young** was born 8 Jul 1947 in Athens, Limestone County, AL.

898. Annie Mae Young (*Clarence W. Young^5, Matilda Ann White^4, Eliza Jane Sharp^3, Charles W. Sr.^{2}, John Sr.^{1}*) was born in Waterloo, Lauderdale County, AL.

Annie married **William Roy Parrish** 8 Apr 1936. William was born in 1913.

Annie next married **Arthur Wyman** 11 Jun 1983 in Benton Harbor, MI.

899. Hubert F. Young (*Clarence W. Young^5, Matilda Ann White^4, Eliza Jane Sharp^3, Charles W. Sr.^{2}, John Sr.^{1}*).

Hubert married **June *Unk**.

900. William (Bill) Young (*Clarence W. Young^5, Matilda Ann White^4, Eliza Jane Sharp^3, Charles W. Sr.^{2}, John Sr.^{1}*) was born 20 Oct 1916 in Lauderdale County, AL, died 24 Jun 1985, and was buried in Mishawaka, St Joseph County, IN.

William married **Lucille Hanback**.

2099 F   i.   **Linda R. Young**.
2100 M   ii.   **Paul Young**.
2101 M   iii.   **Danny Young**.
2102 F   iv.   **Marilyn Young**.

William next married **Ann Aldrich** 29 Apr 1961.

901. Clarence Roy Young (*Clarence W. Young^5, Matilda Ann White^4, Eliza Jane Sharp^3, Charles W. Sr.^{2}, John Sr.^{1}*) was born 25 May 1918 in Lauderdale County, AL, died 16 Nov 1985, and was buried in Greenview Memorial Park, Florence, Lauderdale County, AL.

Clarence married **Clara Lorene Seaton**, daughter of **William (Willie) Richard Seaton** and **Carrie Mildred Smith**, 6 Jun 1936 in Lauderdale County, AL. Clara was born 25 May 1920 in Lauderdale County, AL, died 7 Aug 1978, and was buried in Greenview Memorial Park, Florence, Lauderdale County, AL.

+ 2103 F   i.   **Tempie Voliun Young** was born 22 Dec 1937 in Lauderdale County, AL.
+ 2104 M   ii.   **Roy Lewis Young** was born 9 Aug 1943 in Lauderdale County, AL.
+ 2105 M   iii.   **Phillip Dale Young** was born 11 Mar 1950 in Lauderdale County, AL.

Clarence next married **Frankie Keith McClain**, daughter of **Charlie McClain** and **Alta Mae Smith**, 28 Sep 1979 in Lauderdale County, AL. Frankie was born 9 Dec 1933 in Savannah, TN.

903. John David Young (*Clarence W. Young^5, Matilda Ann White^4, Eliza Jane Sharp^3, Charles W. Sr.^{2}, John Sr.^{1}*) was born 30 Apr 1924 in Lauderdale County, AL.

John married **Ruby Elizabeth Sego**, daughter of **Louis Sego** and **Elizabeth Jones**, 28 Aug 1943 in Lauderdale County, AL. Ruby was born 11 Jan 1916 in Lauderdale County, AL.

+ 2106 F   i.   **Judith Ann Young** was born 5 Jan 1947 in Lauderdale County, AL, died 21 Jan 1993, and was buried in Mishawaka, St Joseph County, IN.
+ 2107 F   ii.   **Glenda Sue Young** was born 23 Jul 1949 in Lauderdale County, AL.
+ 2108 F   iii.   **Reba Kay Young** was born 3 Dec 1952 in Mishawaka, St Joseph County, IN.
+ 2109 F   iv.   **Rose Marie Young** was born 11 Aug 1954 in Mishawaka, St Joseph County, IN.

904. Doris (Susie) Opel Young (*Clarence W. Young^5, Matilda Ann White^4, Eliza Jane Sharp^3, Charles W. Sr.^{2}, John Sr.^{1}*) was born in 1926 in Lauderdale County, AL, died 28 Jun 1999, and was buried in Williams Chapel Cemetery, Lauderdale County, AL.

Doris married ***Unk Belew**.

906. Marie Mae Young (*Edna G. (Birdie) Young^5, Matilda Ann White^4, Eliza Jane Sharp^3, Charles W. Sr.^{2}, John Sr.^{1}*) was born 2 Jan 1916 in Waterloo, Lauderdale County, AL and died 25 Nov 2000 in South Bend, IN.

Marie married **Robert (Bob) Ellie Hawkins**, son of **John Hawkins** and **Ada Frances Saddler**, 15 Jul 1937 in Lauderdale County, AL. Robert was born 20 Nov 1909 in Waterloo, Lauderdale County, AL and died 26 Dec 1990 in Florence, Lauderdale County, AL.

+ 2110 F i. **Patsy Hawkins**.
  2111 M ii. **Jack Hawkins**.

907. Florence Golden (*Rosa Hinton^5, Martha Jane White^4, Eliza Jane Sharp^3, Charles W. Sr.^{2}, John Sr.^{1}*) was born in 1917 and died in 1989.

Florence married **Floyd Teer**.
+ 2112 F i. **Bonnie Iness Teer**.
  2113 M ii. **Willis Golden**.
  2114 M iii. **John Golden**.

908. John Golden (*Rosa Hinton^5, Martha Jane White^4, Eliza Jane Sharp^3, Charles W. Sr.^{2}, John Sr.^{1}*).

John married ***Unk**.
+ 2115 F i. **Martha Janice Golden** was born in 1953.
  2116 M ii. **Myron Dennis Golden** was born in 1953 and died in 1976.

910. Jones Carlton Hinton (*Jones Henry Hinton^5, Martha Jane White^4, Eliza Jane Sharp^3, Charles W. Sr.^{2}, John Sr.^{1}*) was born in 1919.

Jones married **Mary Louise Hanks**.
+ 2117 M i. **Larry Carlton Hinton** was born in 1944.
+ 2118 F ii. **Anita Louise Hinton** was born in 1947.
+ 2119 M iii. **James Arnold Hinton** was born in 1948.

911. Curtis Melvin Hinton Sr. (*Jones Henry Hinton^5, Martha Jane White^4, Eliza Jane Sharp^3, Charles W. Sr.^{2}, John Sr.^{1}*) was born in 1921.

Curtis married **Francis Virginia Green**.
+ 2120 M i. **Curtis Melvin Hinton Jr.** was born in 1947.
+ 2121 F ii. **Cynthia Ann Hinton** was born in 1952.
  2122 M iii. **Robert Lewis Hinton** was born in 1955.
+ 2123 F iv. **Candy Jones Hinton** was born in 1958.
+ 2124 F v. **Wendy Estelle Hinton** was born in 1965.

912. Vernon Juanita Hinton (*Jones Henry Hinton^5, Martha Jane White^4, Eliza Jane Sharp^3, Charles W. Sr.^{2}, John Sr.^{1}*) was born in 1923.

Vernon married **Hubert Jeffrey Burson Sr.**.
+ 2125 M i. **Hubert Jeffrey Burson Jr.** was born in 1943.
+ 2126 F ii. **Linda Kay Burson** was born in 1944.
+ 2127 F iii. **Gloria Jean Burson** was born in 1946.
+ 2128 F iv. **Roslyn Darleen Burson** was born in 1947.

913. Gloria Mae Hinton (*Jones Henry Hinton^5, Martha Jane White^4, Eliza Jane Sharp^3, Charles W. Sr.^{2}, John Sr.^{1}*) was born in 1925.

Gloria married **Joseph Norman Hearin II**.
+ 2129 M i. **Joseph Norman Hearin III** was born in 1947.

914. Lloyd Thurston Hinton Sr. (*Jones Henry Hinton^5, Martha Jane White^4, Eliza Jane Sharp^3, Charles W. Sr.^{2}, John Sr.^{1}*) was born in 1927.

Lloyd married **Rachel Ann George**.
+ 2130 F i. **Norma Susan Hinton** was born in 1949.
+ 2131 M ii. **Lloyd Thurston Hinton Jr.** was born in 1951.
+ 2132 M iii. **Richard George Hinton** was born in 1952.
+ 2133 M iv. **Britt Hinton** was born in 1955.

915. Ola Roselyn Hinton (*Jones Henry Hinton^5, Martha Jane White^4, Eliza Jane Sharp^3, Charles W. Sr.^{2}, John Sr.^{1}*) was born in 1929.

Ola married **Herbert Johnson**.
+ 2134 F i. **Rita Charlotte Johnson** was born in 1953.

Ola next married **Charles Frederick Rohde Jr.**.

917. Martha Ann Hinton (*Jones Henry Hinton^5, Martha Jane White^4, Eliza Jane Sharp^3, Charles W. Sr.^{2}, John Sr.^{1}*) was born in 1934.

Martha married **Raymond Lewis Gamell**.

918. Fred Lewis Wilkerson (*Vernon L. B. Hinton^5, Martha Jane White^4, Eliza Jane Sharp^3, Charles W. Sr.^{2}, John Sr.^{1}*) was born in 1917 and died in 1993.

Fred married **Jessie Margaret Foster**.

919. Charles B. Wilkerson (*Vernon L. B. Hinton^5, Martha Jane White^4, Eliza Jane Sharp^3, Charles W. Sr.^{2}, John Sr.^{1}*) was born in 1919.

Charles married **Ellie Juanita Spivey**.
+ 2135 F i. **Vernon Annette Wilkerson** was born in 1940.
2136 M ii. **Charles Richard Wilkerson** was born in 1941.
2137 F iii. **Janice Marie Wilkerson** was born in 1951.

920. Johnnie B. Wilkerson (*Vernon L. B. Hinton^5, Martha Jane White^4, Eliza Jane Sharp^3, Charles W. Sr.^{2}, John Sr.^{1}*) was born in 1922 and died in 1990.

Johnnie married **Dortha Joyce McCarley**.

921. Reginal Lawson Wilkerson (*Vernon L. B. Hinton^5, Martha Jane White^4, Eliza Jane Sharp^3, Charles W. Sr.^{2}, John Sr.^{1}*) was born in 1926 and died in 1978.

Reginal married **Della Vel Smith**.

923. William J. Wilkerson (*Vernon L. B. Hinton^5, Martha Jane White^4, Eliza Jane Sharp^3, Charles W. Sr.^{2}, John Sr.^{1}*) was born in 1930 and died in 1970.

William married **Jeanette Thorton**.
2138 M i. **Michael Dale Wilkerson**.

925. Mary Addalian Young (*Charles Westbrook Young Sr.*[5], *Ella Prooterwill White*[4], *Eliza Jane Sharp*[3], *Charles W. Sr.*[2], *John Sr.*[1]) was born in 1923 in Lauderdale County, AL.

Mary married **Maurice Wellington McLam** in 1951.

926. Charles Westbrook Young Jr. (*Charles Westbrook Young Sr.*[5], *Ella Prooterwill White*[4], *Eliza Jane Sharp*[3], *Charles W. Sr.*[2], *John Sr.*[1]) was born in 1927 in Lauderdale County, AL.

Charles married **Beverly Ann Kyle** 20 Feb 1953 in St. Joseph County, IN.
2139 M   i.   **Douglas Young**.
2140 M   ii.   **Kevin Young**.

927. Paul Ray Young I (*Charles Westbrook Young Sr.*[5], *Ella Prooterwill White*[4], *Eliza Jane Sharp*[3], *Charles W. Sr.*[2], *John Sr.*[1]) was born in 1929 in Lauderdale County, AL.

Paul married **Lila Mae Hodges** in 1951. Lila was born 25 Oct 1936, died 6 Jan 2006, and was buried in Murphy's Chapel Cemetery, Lauderdale County, AL.
+ 2141 M   i.   **Paul Ray Young II** was born 15 Dec 1952 in Lauderdale County, AL and died 15 Dec 2006 in Lauderdale County, AL.
2142 F   ii.   **Alana Young**.
2143 M   iii.   **Jon David Young**.
2144 M   iv.   **Donnie Young**.
2145 F   v.   **Pamela Young**.
2146 F   vi.   **Mary Young**.

928. Opal Christine Young (*Charles Westbrook Young Sr.*[5], *Ella Prooterwill White*[4], *Eliza Jane Sharp*[3], *Charles W. Sr.*[2], *John Sr.*[1]) was born in 1931 in Lauderdale County, AL.

Opal married **Thomas Arthur Cummings**.

929. Joseph Inloe Young I (*Charles Westbrook Young Sr.*[5], *Ella Prooterwill White*[4], *Eliza Jane Sharp*[3], *Charles W. Sr.*[2], *John Sr.*[1]) was born in 1936.

Joseph married **Ruth Ann Carles**.
+ 2147 M   i.   **Jim I. Young Jr.** was born 12 Jul 1956 in Indiana.

Joseph next married **Madeline V. Thomas**.
+ 2148 M   i.   **Joseph (Jody) Inloe Young II** was born 22 Dec 1967 in Lauderdale County, AL.

930. Francis Adele Irby (*Virginia (Virgie) A. Sharp*[5], *William (Bill) Edgar*[4], *David Allen*[3], *Charles W. Sr.*[2], *John Sr.*[1]) was born in Memphis, Shelby County, TN and died in 1989.

Francis married **Edward Chastagner**.

931. Sam Clifford Hunt Jr. (*Mary M. Sharp*[5], *William (Bill) Edgar*[4], *David Allen*[3], *Charles W. Sr.*[2], *John Sr.*[1]).

Sam married **Shirley *Unk**.

932. Edgar Chisholm Sharp Jr. (*Edgar Chisholm Sr.*[5], *William (Bill) Edgar*[4], *David Allen*[3], *Charles W. Sr.*[2], *John Sr.*[1]) was born 10 Feb 1926 in Lauderdale County, AL.

Edgar married **Catherine Duffy Johnson** 1 Dec 1951 in Houston, TX. Catherine was born 29 Sep 1923 in Dallas, TX.
+ 2149 F   i.   **Sarah Duffy Sharp** was born 18 Feb 1957 in Houston, TX.
+ 2150 M   ii.   **Edgar Chisholm Sharp III** was born 7 Jun 1960 in Houston, TX.

933. Milton Stribling Killen Jr. (*Minnie Louise Sharp*[5], *William (Bill) Edgar*[4], *David Allen*[3], *Charles W. Sr.*[2], *John Sr.*[1]) was born 1 Jul 1927 in Lauderdale County, AL.

Milton married **Ann Clementine Reid**, daughter of **Julius C. Reid** and **Eva Dell Carpenter**, 8 Oct 1950 in Lauderdale County, AL. Ann was born 6 Sep 1931 in Vina, AL.

+	2151	F	i.	**Melinda Ann Killen** was born 31 Dec 1953 in Lauderdale County, AL.
+	2152	M	ii.	**Milton Reid Killen** was born 31 Jan 1958 in Toledo, OH.
+	2153	F	iii.	**Elyse Carpenter Killen** was born 3 Oct 1961 in Verdun, France.

934. William (Billy) Sharp Killen (*Minnie Louise Sharp*[5], *William (Bill) Edgar*[4], *David Allen*[3], *Charles W. Sr.*[2], *John Sr.*[1]) was born 9 Apr 1929 in Lauderdale County, AL.

William married **Ann Jeanette Dodd** 9 Apr 1951 in Colorado Springs, CO. Ann was born about 1930 in Columbus, OH.

	2154	M	i.	**William Sharp Killen Jr.**
+	2155	F	ii.	**Laura Kathleen Killen** was born 8 Oct 1953 in Lauderdale County, AL.
	2156	M	iii.	**Steven Blaine Killen** was born in Dec 1954 in Lauderdale County, AL.
+	2157	F	iv.	**Jenny Louise Killen** was born 24 Aug 1958 in Athens, Limestone County, AL.
	2158	M	v.	**James Striblin Killen** was born 16 Oct 1968 in Athens, Limestone County, AL.

William next married **Martha Jane Fulton** 19 Sep 1977 in Cape Girardeau, MO. Martha was born in Cape Girardeau, MO.

	2159	F	i.	**Jennifer Lynn Griffith** was born 9 Feb 1973 in Ft Leonardwood, MO.
	2160	M	ii.	**Jordan Lincoln Killen** was born 8 Feb 1981 in Memphis, Shelby County, TN.

935. Jimmy Eugene Killen (*Minnie Louise Sharp*[5], *William (Bill) Edgar*[4], *David Allen*[3], *Charles W. Sr.*[2], *John Sr.*[1]) was born 2 Mar 1931 in Lauderdale County, AL.

Jimmy married **Lona Boeswetter**, daughter of **Otto Boeswetter** and **Eva Jones**, 22 May 1952 in Lauderdale County, AL. Lona was born 13 Nov 1928 in Athens, Limestone County, AL.

+	2161	M	i.	**Billy Eugene Killen** was born 17 Jan 1953 in Athens, Limestone County, AL.
+	2162	F	ii.	**Brenda Maxine Killen** was born 20 Jun 1954 in Athens, Limestone County, AL.

936. Don Sherron Killen (*Minnie Louise Sharp*[5], *William (Bill) Edgar*[4], *David Allen*[3], *Charles W. Sr.*[2], *John Sr.*[1]) was born 28 Nov 1934 in Lauderdale County, AL.

Don married **Jeanette Franks**.

+	2163	F	i.	**Debra Killen** was born 2 Oct 1952 in Athens, Limestone County, AL.

Don next married **Helen Howard**, daughter of **Thomas Eroy Howard** and **Nell Grubbs**, 10 May 1961 in Athens, Limestone County, AL. Helen was born 28 Jun 1929 in Limestone County, AL.

	2164	F	i.	**Donna S. Killen** was born 8 Jan 1965 in Athens, Limestone County, AL.
	2165	M	ii.	**Thomas B. Killen** was born 23 Jan 1972 in Athens, Limestone County, AL.

937. James Buford Sharp Jr. (*James Buford Sr.*[5], *James (Jim) Hulet*[4], *David Allen*[3], *Charles W. Sr.*[2], *John Sr.*[1]) was born 30 Oct 1928 in Colbert County, AL, died 17 Aug 2003, and was buried in Tri-Cities Memorial Gardens, Florence, Lauderdale County, AL.

James married **Laura Jean Gay**, daughter of **Samuel Albert Gay** and **Norva Williams**, 6 Jan 1951 in Lauderdale County, AL. Laura was born 5 Apr 1930 in Brilliant, AL.

+	2166	M	i.	**William Paul Sharp** was born 11 Nov 1951 in Colbert County, AL.
	2167	F	ii.	**Betty Ann Sharp** was born 16 May 1955 in Colbert County, AL.
+	2168	F	iii.	**Linda Gay Sharp** was born 31 Aug 1956 in Colbert County, AL.
+	2169	F	iv.	**Nancy Lynn Sharp** was born 20 Apr 1961 in Lauderdale County, AL.

938. Joseph (Joe) Dickson Sharp (*James Buford Sr.*[5], *James (Jim) Hulet*[4], *David Allen*[3], *Charles W. Sr.*[2], *John Sr.*[1]) was born 27 Mar 1931 in Lauderdale County, AL, died 24 Nov 1997, and was buried in Florence City Cemetery, Florence, Lauderdale County, AL.

Joseph married **Lidie Jean Staggs**, daughter of **Clifford Dalton Staggs** and **Polly Marinda Gargas**, 3 May 1958 in Lauderdale County, AL. Lidie was born 29 Apr 1937 in Lauderdale County, AL.

+ 2170 F i. **Melanie Jane Sharp** was born 4 Jul 1964 in Lauderdale County, AL.
+ 2171 F ii. **Jo Lynn Sharp** was born 28 Feb 1971 in Lauderdale County, AL.

939. John Alvin Sharp Sr. (*James Buford Sr.*[5], *James (Jim) Hulet*[4], *David Allen*[3], *Charles W. Sr.*[2], *John Sr.*[1]) was born 18 Sep 1935 in Colbert County, AL.

John married **Betty Jane Nichols**, daughter of **Gilbert C. Nichols** and **Edna Baker**, 21 Aug 1959 in Lauderdale County, AL. Betty was born 8 Apr 1934 in Lauderdale County, AL.

+ 2172 F i. **Susanne Sharp** was born 25 Feb 1962 in Lauderdale County, AL.
+ 2173 M ii. **John Alvin Sharp Jr.** was born 26 Jun 1973 in Lauderdale County, AL.

940. Mallie Denson Stewart (*Cynthia Emmanola Sharp*[5], *Joseph (Joe) Powers Sr.*[4], *David Allen*[3], *Charles W. Sr.*[2], *John Sr.*[1]) was born 30 Apr 1933 in Lauderdale County, AL.

Mallie married **Edward Branden Akers**, son of **Noel Akers** and **Louise *Unk**, 28 Jan 1951. Edward was born 15 Sep 1930 in Hohenwald, TN, died 24 Jun 1992, and was buried in Barrancas National Cemetery, Pensacola, FL.

+ 2174 M i. **Robert Denson Akers** was born 22 Aug 1952 in Lauderdale County, AL.
+ 2175 F ii. **Ellen Louise Akers** was born 6 Dec 1954 in Jacksonville, FL.
+ 2176 F iii. **Peggy Leigh Akers** was born 3 May 1956 in San Diego, CA.
+ 2177 F iv. **Theresa Ann Akers** was born 15 Jun 1957 in San Diego, CA.

941. William Holland Hale (*Mayro Sharp*[5], *Joseph (Joe) Powers Sr.*[4], *David Allen*[3], *Charles W. Sr.*[2], *John Sr.*[1]) was born 29 Jun 1929 in Lauderdale County, AL, died 3 Mar 1997, and was buried in Greenview Memorial Park, Florence, Lauderdale County, AL.

William married **Joyce Hayes**, daughter of **Freddie Hayes** and **Pauline Irons**, 18 Feb 1950 in Lauderdale County, AL. Joyce was born 24 Apr 1930 in Lauderdale County, AL.

+ 2178 F i. **Joyelyn Holland Hale** was born 17 Aug 1955 in Lauderdale County, AL.

942. Ralph Morrow Sharp (*Joseph Powers (J. P.) Jr.*[5], *Joseph (Joe) Powers Sr.*[4], *David Allen*[3], *Charles W. Sr.*[2], *John Sr.*[1]) was born 19 Nov 1932 in Lauderdale County, AL.

Ralph married **Mildred Hayes**, daughter of **Jesse Raymond Hayes** and **Linnie Mae Montgomery**.

+ 2179 F i. **Debra Arlene Sharp** was born 17 Sep 1956 in Lauderdale County, AL.
+ 2180 M ii. **Eddie D. Sharp** was born 18 Aug 1957 in Lauderdale County, AL.
  2181 M iii. **Randy Keith Sharp** was born 4 Jul 1959 in Lauderdale County, AL.
+ 2182 M iv. **Ralph David Sharp** was born 26 Aug 1968 in St. Joseph County, IN.

Ralph next married **Brenda Parsons**.

943. Billy Joe Sharp (*Joseph Powers (J. P.) Jr.*[5], *Joseph (Joe) Powers Sr.*[4], *David Allen*[3], *Charles W. Sr.*[2], *John Sr.*[1]) was born 10 Sep 1935 in Lauderdale County, AL, died 22 Dec 2000, and was buried in Tri-Cities Memorial Gardens, Florence, Lauderdale County, AL.

Billy married **Mildred Lorene Givens**, daughter of **James Walter Givens** and **Mary Geneva Chambers**, 14 Apr 1963 in Lauderdale County, AL. Mildred was born 23 Aug 1945 in Lauderdale County, AL.

+ 2183 F i. **Tina Kaye Sharp** was born 30 Jan 1964 in Lauderdale County, AL.
+ 2184 F ii. **Pamela Diane Sharp** was born 4 Oct 1965 in Lauderdale County, AL.
+ 2185 F iii. **Vicky Robin Sharp** was born 11 Jun 1967 in Lauderdale County, AL.
+ 2186 F iv. **Natasha Jo Sharp** was born 21 Aug 1977 in Lauderdale County, AL.

944. Daniel C. Sharp (*Joseph Powers (J. P.) Jr.*[5], *Joseph (Joe) Powers Sr.*[4], *David Allen*[3], *Charles W. Sr.*[2], *John Sr.*[1]) was born 26 May 1936 in Lauderdale County, AL.

Daniel married **Audrey Pauline (Pat) Gilmore**, daughter of **Cordis Dee Gilmore** and **Bessie Florence Heard**, 22 Nov 1956 in Iuka, Tishomingo County, MS. Audrey was born 13 May 1937 in Savannah, TN.

+ 2187 F i. **Cynthia (Cindy) Robyn Sharp** was born 2 May 1961 in Lauderdale County, AL.
+ 2188 F ii. **Kelli Layne Sharp** was born 22 May 1969 in Lauderdale County, AL.

945. Ronald Gene Sharp (*David (Big David) Roderick⁵, Joseph (Joe) Powers Sr.⁴, David Allen³, Charles W. Sr.², John Sr.¹*) was born 13 Mar 1941 in Lauderdale County, AL.

Ronald married **Mary Marie Burns**, daughter of **Cecil C. Burns** and **Ida Simmons**, 24 Dec 1960 in Lauderdale County, AL. Mary was born 29 Jun 1944 in Wayne County, TN.
+ 2189 F i. **Mary Jacqueline (Jackie) Sharp** was born 29 Nov 1964 in Lauderdale County, AL.

Ronald next married **Mary Caroline Roden**, daughter of **Thomas Alvine Roden** and **Olivia Odell Hammond**, 12 Nov 1971 in Lauderdale County, AL. Mary was born 22 Aug 1947 in Lauderdale County, AL.
+ 2190 F i. **Amy Janice Sharp** was born 25 Mar 1977 in Lauderdale County, AL.

946. Angelia Gail Sharp (*David (Big David) Roderick⁵, Joseph (Joe) Powers Sr.⁴, David Allen³, Charles W. Sr.², John Sr.¹*) was born 12 Dec 1948 in Lauderdale County, AL.

Angelia married **John Joe Peters**, son of **Phillip J. Peters** and **Maud Bogus**, 20 Mar 1970 in Lauderdale County, AL. John was born 28 Jun 1944 in Lauderdale County, AL.
2191 M i. **Phillip David Peters** was born 30 Jan 1971 in Lauderdale County, AL.
+ 2192 F ii. **Julie Deann Peters** was born 16 Jul 1974 in Lauderdale County, AL.

947. Betty Jane Sharp (*Lyda Mae Sharp⁵, Andrew Jefferson Sr.⁴, David Allen³, Charles W. Sr.², John Sr.¹*) was born 11 May 1927.

Betty married **William G. Tate** 6 Oct 1956. William was born 6 Jan 1907.
+ 2193 F i. **Lyda Kathleen Tate** was born 5 Dec 1957.
+ 2194 F ii. **Marie Lynn Tate** was born 18 May 1959.
+ 2195 F iii. **Stacy Leigh Tate** was born 24 Feb 1967.

948. John David Sharp (*Lyda Mae Sharp⁵, Andrew Jefferson Sr.⁴, David Allen³, Charles W. Sr.², John Sr.¹*) was born 10 Apr 1931 in Monroe, LA.

John married **Sue *Unk**. Sue was born in Monroe, LA.
+ 2196 F i. **Linda Sharp**.
+ 2197 M ii. **Donald Sharp**.
+ 2198 F iii. **Karen Diana Sharp**.
+ 2199 M iv. **Paul David Sharp**.

949. Paul Nichols Jr. (*Virginia Rebecca Sharp⁵, Andrew Jefferson Sr.⁴, David Allen³, Charles W. Sr.², John Sr.¹*).

Paul married **Mimi *Unk**.
2200 M i. **James (Jimmy) Nichols**.
2201 M ii. **John Nichols**.
2202 F iii. **Mary Virginia Nichols**.
2203 F iv. **Vicki Nichols**.
2204 F v. **Paula Nichols**.

950. Kathleen Margaret Watson (*Evelyn Marie (Verna) Sharp⁵, Andrew Jefferson Sr.⁴, David Allen³, Charles W. Sr.², John Sr.¹*).

Kathleen married **Ron Lauguter**.
+ 2205 F i. **Lisa Lauguter**.
+ 2206 F ii. **Rhonda Lauguter**.

951. Andrew Jefferson Sharp III (*Andrew Jefferson Jr.⁵, Andrew Jefferson Sr.⁴, David Allen³, Charles W. Sr.², John Sr.¹*) was born 5 Mar 1949 in Alabama.

Andrew married **Linda *Unk**.
2207 F i. **Jennifer Eliza Sharp.**
2208 M ii. **Andrew (Andy) Joseph Sharp.**
2209 M iii. **Nathan Allen Sharp.**

953. John William Paton Simmons (*Helen Margaret Sharp* [5], *Andrew Jefferson Sr.* [4], *David Allen* [3], *Charles W. Sr.* [2], *John Sr.* [1]) was born 10 Aug 1944 in New Orleans, LA.

John married **Glenda Carol Van Hoof-White**. Glenda was born 31 Jul 1943.
2210 M i. **Donald Wayne Simmons** was born 8 Mar 1962.
+ 2211 M ii. **Gary Allen Simmons** was born 3 Jun 1964.

954. Rebecca Gail White Simmons (*Helen Margaret Sharp* [5], *Andrew Jefferson Sr.* [4], *David Allen* [3], *Charles W. Sr.* [2], *John Sr.* [1]) was born 16 Mar 1949 in Houston, TX.

Rebecca married **Lloyd Lee Anderson** 12 Sep 1968.
2212 F i. **Laura Kathleen Anderson** was born 28 Jun 1974 in Longview, WA.

Sixth Generation

955. Marvin Elmer Lindsey (*George W. Lindsey* [6], *John Phillip Lindsey II* [5], *Caleb (Calip) Lindsey* [4], *Frances (Frankie) Sharp* [3], *Charles W. Sr.* [2], *John Sr.* [1]) was born 8 Apr 1905 in Lauderdale County, AL, died 1 Nov 1983, and was buried in Wesley Chapel Cemetery, Lauderdale County, AL.

Marvin married **Brella Palmer**, daughter of **William O. Palmer** and **Elizabeth Francis Brewer**, 20 Nov 1932 in Lauderdale County, AL. Brella was born 9 Jul 1908 in Lauderdale County, AL, died 19 Nov 1986, and was buried in Wesley Chapel Cemetery, Lauderdale County, AL.
+ 2213 M i. **George William Lindsey** was born 1 Jul 1935 in Lauderdale County, AL.
+ 2214 F ii. **Mary Elizabeth Lindsey** was born 30 Oct 1940 in Lauderdale County, AL.
+ 2215 F iii. **Robbie Lee Lindsey** was born 19 Oct 1945 in Lauderdale County, AL.

956. Carrie M. Lindsey (*George W. Lindsey* [6], *John Phillip Lindsey II* [5], *Caleb (Calip) Lindsey* [4], *Frances (Frankie) Sharp* [3], *Charles W. Sr.* [2], *John Sr.* [1]) was born in 1908 in Lauderdale County, AL.

Carrie married **James Bradley** 31 Dec 1931 in Lauderdale County, AL.

957. Aubra Lee Lindsey (*George W. Lindsey* [6], *John Phillip Lindsey II* [5], *Caleb (Calip) Lindsey* [4], *Frances (Frankie) Sharp* [3], *Charles W. Sr.* [2], *John Sr.* [1]) was born in 1910 in Lauderdale County, AL.

Aubra married **Mae Hayes** 27 Dec 1925 in Lauderdale County, AL.

Aubra next married **Cordelia Allred**, daughter of **Isaac Newton Allred** and **Lannie Lee Matthews**, 5 Sep 1946 in Lauderdale County, AL. Cordelia was born in Loretto, Lawrence County, TN.

959. Mamie G. Lindsey (*George W. Lindsey* [6], *John Phillip Lindsey II* [5], *Caleb (Calip) Lindsey* [4], *Frances (Frankie) Sharp* [3], *Charles W. Sr.* [2], *John Sr.* [1]) was born in 1913 in Lauderdale County, AL.

Mamie married **Columbus Guyse** 23 Aug 1022 in Lauderdale County, AL.

960. Mittie Rebecca Riley (*Lucelle (Lucy) Lindsey* [6], *John Phillip Lindsey II* [5], *Caleb (Calip) Lindsey* [4], *Frances (Frankie) Sharp* [3], *Charles W. Sr.* [2], *John Sr.* [1]).

Mittie married **William Olive**.

Mittie next married ***Unk Rogers**.

Mittie next married ***Unk Blevins**.

961. Ora Gladys Riley (*Lucelle (Lucy) Lindsey*[6], *John Phillip Lindsey II*[5], *Caleb (Calip) Lindsey*[4], *Frances (Frankie) Sharp*[3], *Charles W. Sr.*[2], *John Sr.*[1]) was born 18 May 1903 in Franklin County, AL and died in Dec 1985.

Ora married **David Blevins**.

962. Nellie Catherine Riley (*Lucelle (Lucy) Lindsey*[6], *John Phillip Lindsey II*[5], *Caleb (Calip) Lindsey*[4], *Frances (Frankie) Sharp*[3], *Charles W. Sr.*[2], *John Sr.*[1]) was born 17 Feb 1905 in Franklin County, AL and died 26 Feb 1984.

Nellie married **Thomas Williams**.

963. Beulah Riley (*Lucelle (Lucy) Lindsey*[6], *John Phillip Lindsey II*[5], *Caleb (Calip) Lindsey*[4], *Frances (Frankie) Sharp*[3], *Charles W. Sr.*[2], *John Sr.*[1]) was born 13 Dec 1907 in Franklin County, AL and died 10 Jul 1984.

Beulah married **Arsen Ault**.

966. Claude Edward Riley (*Lucelle (Lucy) Lindsey*[6], *John Phillip Lindsey II*[5], *Caleb (Calip) Lindsey*[4], *Frances (Frankie) Sharp*[3], *Charles W. Sr.*[2], *John Sr.*[1]) was born 9 Feb 1913 in Franklin County, AL and died before 1984.

Claude married **Lorene Martha Tubbs** 19 Oct 1940.

971. Nora Louise Lindsey (*David (Dave) Lindsey*[6], *Joseph A. Lindsey*[5], *Caleb (Calip) Lindsey*[4], *Frances (Frankie) Sharp*[3], *Charles W. Sr.*[2], *John Sr.*[1]).

Nora married **A. H. Wilson**.

972. Loraine Lindsey (*David (Dave) Lindsey*[6], *Joseph A. Lindsey*[5], *Caleb (Calip) Lindsey*[4], *Frances (Frankie) Sharp*[3], *Charles W. Sr.*[2], *John Sr.*[1]).

Loraine married ***Unk McKelvey**.

973. Katen Lewis Lindsey (*J. Lewis Lindsey*[6], *Joseph A. Lindsey*[5], *Caleb (Calip) Lindsey*[4], *Frances (Frankie) Sharp*[3], *Charles W. Sr.*[2], *John Sr.*[1]) was born 12 Apr 1908 in Wayne County, TN, died 2 May 1998, and was buried in Collinwood Cemetery, Collinwood, TN.

Katen married **Christine *Unk**. Christine died 26 Jan 1999 and was buried in Collinwood Cemetery, Lauderdale County, AL.
+ 2216 F i. **Rachel June Lindsey**.

974. Lester Lawrence Hall Sr. (*Ada Bell Lindsey*[6], *Joseph A. Lindsey*[5], *Caleb (Calip) Lindsey*[4], *Frances (Frankie) Sharp*[3], *Charles W. Sr.*[2], *John Sr.*[1]) was born 11 Apr 1917 in Lauderdale County, AL, died 9 Jan 1990, and was buried in Pleasant Hill Freewill Baptist Cemetery, Cherokee, Colbert County, AL.

Lester married **Annie Mae Lamb**, daughter of **Johnny Franklin Lamb** and **Martha Nora Wallace**. Annie was born 4 Jun 1915 in Colbert County, AL, died 3 Oct 1995, and was buried in Pleasant Hill Freewill Baptist Cemetery, Cherokee, Colbert County, AL.
+ 2217 F i. **Shirley Ann Hall** was born 16 Jun 1944 in Lauderdale County, AL.
  2218 F ii. **Glenda Dale Hall** was born 4 Aug 1946 in Lauderdale County, AL.
+ 2219 M iii. **Lester Lawrence Hall Jr.** was born 5 Jun 1948 in Lauderdale County, AL.
+ 2220 F iv. **Dovie Leigh Hall** was born 13 Aug 1949 in Lauderdale County, AL.
+ 2221 M v. **Johnny Houston Hall** was born 14 Feb 1951 in Lauderdale County, AL.
+ 2222 F vi. **Robin Michele Hall** was born 22 Jan 1953 in Lauderdale County, AL.
+ 2223 F vii. **Carlene Hall** was born 28 Mar 1955 in Ann Harber, MI.
  2224 F viii. **Martha Bell Hall** was born in 1956 and died in 1957.

975. Floyd Edward Hall Sr. (*Ada Bell Lindsey*[6], *Joseph A. Lindsey*[5], *Caleb (Calip) Lindsey*[4], *Frances (Frankie) Sharp*[3], *Charles W. Sr.*[2], *John Sr.*[1]) was born 15 Sep 1919 in Lauderdale County, AL, died 15 Jun 1994, and was buried in Florence City Cemetery, Florence, Lauderdale County, AL.

Floyd married **Susie Jane Melton**, daughter of **John T. Melton** and **Rosie Lee Austin**, 18 Nov 1939 in Lauderdale County, AL. Susie was born 23 Feb 1924 in Hardin County, TN.

+ 2225 M i. **Floyd Edward Hall Jr.** was born 5 Sep 1940 in Lauderdale County, AL.
+ 2226 F ii. **Clara Mae Hall** was born 11 Sep 1942 in Lauderdale County, AL.
+ 2227 F iii. **Sara Jane Hall** was born 24 Aug 1944 in Lauderdale County, AL.

Floyd next married **Olivia Margaret Schaut**, daughter of **Joseph Schaut** and **Unknown**, 20 Jan 1947 in Lauderdale County, AL. Olivia was born 15 Apr 1926 in Lauderdale County, AL, died 10 Jul 1958, and was buried in Tri-Cities Memorial Gardens, Florence, Lauderdale County, AL.

+ 2228 M i. **Wayne Joseph Hall** was born 26 Feb 1949 in Lauderdale County, AL.
+ 2229 F ii. **Barbara Kaye Hall** was born 8 Jul 1952 in Lauderdale County, AL.
+ 2230 M iii. **Jerry Michael Hall** was born 9 Mar 1955 in Lauderdale County, AL.

Floyd next married **Zillah Leland** 8 Apr 1959. Zillah was born 28 Sep 1921 in Lawrence County, TN.

976. Hubert F. Hall (*Ada Bell Lindsey*[6], *Joseph A. Lindsey*[5], *Caleb (Calip) Lindsey*[4], *Frances (Frankie) Sharp*[3], *Charles W. Sr.*[2], *John Sr.*[1]) was born 11 Dec 1920 in Lauderdale County, AL, died 25 May 1957, and was buried in Tri-Cities Memorial Gardens, Florence, Lauderdale County, AL.

General Notes: "Hubert was a fireman. He died in the line of duty..." Millie Mason

Hubert married **Velma Mae McBride**, daughter of **Edward McBride** and **Delphea Goings**, 30 Aug 1941 in Lauderdale County, AL. Velma was born 6 Jun 1922 in Lauderdale County, AL.

Hubert next married **Deloris Regina Schut**, daughter of **Joseph B. Schut** and **Annie Marie Donaver**, 16 Jun 1948 in Iuka, Tishomingo County, MS. Deloris was born 23 Oct 1930 in Lauderdale County, AL.

977. Reba Lindsey (*Lee Willie Lindsey*[6], *Joseph A. Lindsey*[5], *Caleb (Calip) Lindsey*[4], *Frances (Frankie) Sharp*[3], *Charles W. Sr.*[2], *John Sr.*[1]).

General Notes: "Residence: Huntsville, Alabama..." Millie Mason

Reba married **A. M. Kelley**.

978. Pearl Lindsey (*Lee Willie Lindsey*[6], *Joseph A. Lindsey*[5], *Caleb (Calip) Lindsey*[4], *Frances (Frankie) Sharp*[3], *Charles W. Sr.*[2], *John Sr.*[1]).

General Notes: "Residence: Chicago, Illionois..." Millie Mason

Pearl married **Elmer Adamson**.

981. Herschel Lee Lindsey (*Lee Willie Lindsey*[6], *Joseph A. Lindsey*[5], *Caleb (Calip) Lindsey*[4], *Frances (Frankie) Sharp*[3], *Charles W. Sr.*[2], *John Sr.*[1]) was born 25 Oct 1926 in Lauderdale County, AL, died 22 May 1988, and was buried in K. P. Cemetery, Killen, AL.

Herschel married **Ethel Marie Reed**, daughter of **Arther Reed** and **Lady Ruth Jones**. Ethel was born 21 Mar 1933 in Decatur, Morgan County, AL.

  2231 F i. **Janie Marie Lindsey.**
+ 2232 F ii. **Judy Jane Lindsey.**
  2233 F iii. **Wanda Gail Lindsey.**
  2234 F iv. **Jewell Lee Lindsey.**

985. Ethel M. Lindsey (*Albert Curtis Lindsey*^{6}*, David A. Lindsey*^{5}*, Caleb (Calip) Lindsey*^{4}*, Frances (Frankie) Sharp*^{3}*, Charles W. Sr.*^{2}*, John Sr.*^{1}) was born 3 Dec 1897 in Lauderdale County, AL, died 16 Jan 1987, and was buried in Lindsey Chapel Cemetery, Lauderdale County, AL.

    Ethel married **Rufus J. Garrett**, son of **William R. Garrett** and **Lizzie *Unk**, 3 Jul 1919 in Lauderdale County, AL. Rufus was born 23 Feb 1898 in Lauderdale County, AL, died 15 Jun 1975, and was buried in Lindsey Chapel Cemetery, Lauderdale County, AL.

+ 2235   F   i.   **Jewell Virgie Garrett** was born 23 Dec 1922 in Lauderdale County, AL.

986. Charles Edward Lindsey (*Albert Curtis Lindsey*^{6}*, David A. Lindsey*^{5}*, Caleb (Calip) Lindsey*^{4}*, Frances (Frankie) Sharp*^{3}*, Charles W. Sr.*^{2}*, John Sr.*^{1}) was born 7 Nov 1904, died 20 Mar 1942, and was buried in Florence City Cemetery, Florence, Lauderdale County, AL.

    Charles married **Myrtle Lou Ruple**, daughter of **Tom Ruple** and **Ida Stanfield**, 19 Apr 1924 in Lauderdale County, AL. Myrtle was born 28 Jul 1902 in Lauderdale County, AL, died 26 Jul 1969, and was buried in Florence City Cemetery, Florence, Lauderdale County, AL.

+ 2236   F   i.   **Edna Juanita Lindsey** was born 19 Sep 1924 in Lauderdale County, AL.
+ 2237   M   ii.   **Gentry Aaron Lindsey** was born 2 Feb 1927 in Lauderdale County, AL.
+ 2238   F   iii.   **Mable Lindsey** was born 16 Oct 1930 in Lauderdale County, AL.
+ 2239   F   iv.   **Margaret Marie Lindsey** was born 23 Jan 1933 in Lauderdale County, AL.
+ 2240   F   v.   **Sarah Melissa Lindsey** was born in Lauderdale County, AL.
+ 2241   F   vi.   **Charles Roberta Lindsey** was born 19 Jul 1942 in Lauderdale County, AL.

987. Dalton Allen Lindsey (*Albert Curtis Lindsey*^{6}*, David A. Lindsey*^{5}*, Caleb (Calip) Lindsey*^{4}*, Frances (Frankie) Sharp*^{3}*, Charles W. Sr.*^{2}*, John Sr.*^{1}) was born 10 Nov 1910, died 6 Nov 1976, and was buried in Tri-Cities Memorial Gardens, Florence, Lauderdale County, AL.

    Dalton married **Flora Izadora Wright**, daughter of **Jess Wright** and **Kathy Oneal**, 21 Jul 1932. Flora was born 5 Nov 1915, died 5 Nov 1980, and was buried in Tri-Cities Memorial Gardens, Florence, Lauderdale County, AL.

+ 2242   F   i.   **Helen Louise Lindsey** was born 10 Oct 1932 in Lauderdale County, AL.
+ 2243   M   ii.   **Carl Dewey Lindsey** was born 3 Apr 1937 in Lauderdale County, AL.

989. Clifton D. Lindsey (*Edward (Ed) Price Lindsey*^{6}*, David A. Lindsey*^{5}*, Caleb (Calip) Lindsey*^{4}*, Frances (Frankie) Sharp*^{3}*, Charles W. Sr.*^{2}*, John Sr.*^{1}) was born 23 Mar 1930 in Lauderdale County, AL.

    Clifton married **Jenell Spain**, daughter of **Noah Thomas Spain** and **Mary Alice Jackson**, 30 Nov 1956 in Lauderdale County, AL. Jenell was born 17 Sep 1931 in Winston County, AL.

+ 2244   F   i.   **Cheryl Dianne Gables Lindsey** was born 15 Apr 1952 in Jasper, Walker County, AL.
+ 2245   F   ii.   **Debra Kaye Lindsey** was born 2 Aug 1957 in Lauderdale County, AL.
+ 2246   F   iii.   **Susan Renee Lindsey** was born 13 May 1959 in Lauderdale County, AL.

990. Miriam Ann Eagle (*Mary Mable Bennett*^{6}*, Mollie Elizabeth Lindsey*^{5}*, Caleb (Calip) Lindsey*^{4}*, Frances (Frankie) Sharp*^{3}*, Charles W. Sr.*^{2}*, John Sr.*^{1}).

    Miriam married **Thomas Thorne Sr.**.

2247   F   i.   **Janie Alberta Thorne**.
2248   M   ii.   **Thomas Thorne Jr.**

991. Carolyn Virginia Eagle (*Mary Mable Bennett*^{6}*, Mollie Elizabeth Lindsey*^{5}*, Caleb (Calip) Lindsey*^{4}*, Frances (Frankie) Sharp*^{3}*, Charles W. Sr.*^{2}*, John Sr.*^{1}) died 1 Mar 2000 and was buried in Tri-Cities Memorial Gardens, Florence, Lauderdale County, AL.

    Carolyn married **Charles W. Suggs Jr.**.

+ 2249   F   i.   **Kathleen Ann Suggs**.
+ 2250   F   ii.   **Sandra Lee Suggs**.
+ 2251   F   iii.   **Mary Louise Suggs**.
2252   M   iv.   **Michael T. Suggs**.

2253 M v. **Patrick D. Suggs.**

Carolyn next married ***Unk Pepper.**
+ 2254 M i. **Michael T. Pepper.**
+ 2255 M ii. **Patrick D. Pepper.**

1004. Howard James Romine (*Nellie Mitchum* [6], *America Lindsey* [5], *Caleb (Calip) Lindsey* [4], *Frances (Frankie) Sharp* [3], *Charles W. Sr.* [2], *John Sr.* [1]) was born 30 Jun 1915 in Lauderdale County, AL, died 8 Feb 1996, and was buried in Richardson Cemetery, Lauderdale County, AL.

Howard married **Henrietta Kathleen McCorkle**, daughter of **J. H. McCorkle** and **Linnie Belle Bevis**, 9 Jun 1940 in Lauderdale County, AL. Henrietta was born 23 Dec 1918 in Lauderdale County, AL.
   2256 M i. **James Howard Romine** was born 15 Jul 1944 in Portsmouth, VA.
+ 2257 F ii. **Linda Faye Romine** was born 4 Apr 1946 in Lauderdale County, AL.
+ 2258 F iii. **Donna Diane Romine** was born 28 Aug 1947 in Lauderdale County, AL.
   2259 F iv. **Kathy Raynell Romine** was born 28 Feb 1952 in Benton, KY.

1005. Richard Leland Romine (*Nellie Mitchum* [6], *America Lindsey* [5], *Caleb (Calip) Lindsey* [4], *Frances (Frankie) Sharp* [3], *Charles W. Sr.* [2], *John Sr.* [1]) was born 25 Mar 1925 in Lauderdale County, AL, died 17 Nov 1982, and was buried in Tri-Cities Memorial Gardens, Florence, Lauderdale County, AL.

Richard married **Rose Marie Morris**, daughter of **Homer Morris** and **Marie Haverwas**, 29 Feb 1944 in San Diego, CA. Rose was born 4 Feb 1925 in Lauderdale County, AL, died 7 Jun 1989, and was buried in Tri-Cities Memorial Gardens, Florence, Lauderdale County, AL.
+ 2260 F i. **Susan Marie Romine** was born 22 Sep 1945 in Colbert County, AL.
+ 2261 M ii. **Richard Morris Romine** was born 8 Aug 1948 in Lauderdale County, AL.
   2262 M iii. **Paul Franklin Romine** was born 10 Jun 1952 in Lauderdale County, AL.
+ 2263 M iv. **William Dean Romine** was born 6 Sep 1954 in Lauderdale County, AL.

1006. Barbara B. Mitchum (*Bufford Lee Mitchum* [6], *America Lindsey* [5], *Caleb (Calip) Lindsey* [4], *Frances (Frankie) Sharp* [3], *Charles W. Sr.* [2], *John Sr.* [1]) was born 9 Apr 1937 in Madison County, AL.

Barbara married **Jerry Trapp Crowell Sr.**, son of **Edward Crowell** and **Mae James**, 27 Nov 1954 in Lauderdale County, AL. Jerry was born 14 Apr 1935 in Colbert County, AL and died 25 Oct 1982.
+ 2264 M i. **Jerry Trapp Crowell Jr.** was born 23 Dec 1956 in Lauderdale County, AL.
+ 2265 F ii. **Marilyn Leigh Crowell** was born 15 Jul 1960 in Lauderdale County, AL.

1009. William Charles Holt (*William Cecil Holt* [6], *Lula Mae Lindsey* [5], *Caleb (Calip) Lindsey* [4], *Frances (Frankie) Sharp* [3], *Charles W. Sr.* [2], *John Sr.* [1]).

William married **Carolyn *Unk**.

1012. Donald Edward Lindsey Jr. (*Donald Edward Lindsey Sr.* [6], *Robert Andrew Lindsey* [5], *Caleb (Calip) Lindsey* [4], *Frances (Frankie) Sharp* [3], *Charles W. Sr.* [2], *John Sr.* [1]) was born 15 Oct 1935 in Lauderdale County, AL, died 8 Oct 2008 in Lauderdale County, AL, and was buried in Greenview Memorial Park, Florence, Lauderdale County, AL.

Donald married **Opal Asaline Russell**, daughter of **Fred Russell** and **Fannie Belle Haskins**, 24 Jul 1955 in Iuka, Tishomingo County, MS. Opal was born 2 Apr 1933 in Lauderdale County, AL.
+ 2266 M i. **Donald Edward Lindsey III** was born 1 Sep 1956 in Lauderdale County, AL.
+ 2267 M ii. **Robert Russell Lindsey** was born 22 Sep 1958 in Lauderdale County, AL.
+ 2268 F iii. **Laurel Lee Lindsey** was born 1 Jul 1963 in Lauderdale County, AL.

1013. Rebecca Ann Lindsey (*Donald Edward Lindsey Sr.* [6], *Robert Andrew Lindsey* [5], *Caleb (Calip) Lindsey* [4], *Frances (Frankie) Sharp* [3], *Charles W. Sr.* [2], *John Sr.* [1]) was born 16 Sep 1942 in Lauderdale County, AL.

Rebecca married **Billy Clay Cofield** 29 May 1961 in Lauderdale County, AL. Billy was born 23 Mar 1932 in Franklin County, AL.

+ 2269 F   i.   **Beth May Cofield** was born 14 Apr 1962 in Lauderdale County, AL.
+ 2270 F   ii.   **Crystal Alese Cofield** was born 5 Sep 1963 in Lauderdale County, AL.
+ 2271 F   iii. **Lee Ann Cofield** was born 18 Nov 1965 in Lauderdale County, AL.

1014. Carolyn Lindsey (*Chester B. Lindsey^6, Alonzo Brown Lindsey^5, Caleb (Calip) Lindsey^4, Frances (Frankie) Sharp^3, Charles W. Sr.^{2}, John Sr.^{1}*) was born 14 Aug 1936 in Lauderdale County, AL.

Carolyn married **William (Pete) Harvey Wilson**, son of **Cecil Howard Wilson** and **Myrtle Alice Linvile**, 24 Feb 1951 in Iuka, Tishomingo County, MS. William was born 19 Jul 1931 in Lauderdale County, AL, died 10 Jul 1986, and was buried in Florence City Cemetery, Florence, Lauderdale County, AL.
+ 2272 M   i.   **William Ricky (Ric) Wilson** was born 20 Jul 1953 in Lauderdale County, AL.

Carolyn next married **James Martin Roy**, son of **Guy Roy** and **Margaret Green**, 10 May 1972 in Las Vegas, NV. James was born 9 Sep 1926 in Nashville, Davidson County, TN.
2273 M   i.   **James Matthew Roy** was born 27 Sep 1973 in Mt. Pleasant, TN.
2274 M   ii.   **Samuel Martin Roy** was born 17 Feb 1976 in Mt. Pleasant, TN.

1015. Bettye Jean Prater (*Nellie Mauvaline Lindsey^6, Alonzo Brown Lindsey^5, Caleb (Calip) Lindsey^4, Frances (Frankie) Sharp^3, Charles W. Sr.^{2}, John Sr.^{1}*) was born 25 Jul 1931 in Lauderdale County, AL.

Bettye married **Charles Glenn Edwards**. Charles was born 8 Dec 1937 in McKinney, Collin County, TX.
2275 F   i.   **Reate Lynn Edwards** was born 12 Jan 1961 in Weisbaden, Germany.
2276 M   ii.   **David Edwards**.

1016. Laura Francis Anderer (*Doris Lindsey^6, Alonzo Brown Lindsey^5, Caleb (Calip) Lindsey^4, Frances (Frankie) Sharp^3, Charles W. Sr.^{2}, John Sr.^{1}*) was born 11 Oct.

Laura married **Kevin Kilgore**.
2277 M   i.   **Austin Philip Kilgore** was born in Conroe, TX.
2278 F   ii.   **Gillian Cecelia Kilgore** was born in Woodland, TX.

1017. Thomas Alonzo Lindsey (*Thomas Arnett Lindsey^6, Alonzo Brown Lindsey^5, Caleb (Calip) Lindsey^4, Frances (Frankie) Sharp^3, Charles W. Sr.^{2}, John Sr.^{1}*) was born 9 Feb 1945 in Macon, GA.

Thomas married **Sandra McCrane**. Sandra was born 26 Dec 1946 in Ft Gaines, GA.
2279 F   i.   **Christy Robin Lindsey** was born 12 Apr 1974 in Americus, GA.

1018. Ronald Gregg Lindsey (*Thomas Arnett Lindsey^6, Alonzo Brown Lindsey^5, Caleb (Calip) Lindsey^4, Frances (Frankie) Sharp^3, Charles W. Sr.^{2}, John Sr.^{1}*) was born 1 Feb 1948 in Macon, GA.

Ronald married **Karen *Unk**.
2280 F   i.   **Karey Lindsey** was born 3 Oct in Fitsgerald, GA.
+ 2281 M   ii.   **Ronald Joseph Lindsey** was born 29 Aug in Fitsgerald, GA.

1019. Donald Pace Lindsey (*Thomas Arnett Lindsey^6, Alonzo Brown Lindsey^5, Caleb (Calip) Lindsey^4, Frances (Frankie) Sharp^3, Charles W. Sr.^{2}, John Sr.^{1}*) was born 1 Feb 1948 in Macon, GA.

Donald married **Cheryl Toney**. Cheryl was born 6 Dec 1946 in Athens, GA.
2282 F   i.   **Sherrie Denise Lindsey** was born 24 Aug 1970 in Platsburg, NY.
2283 F   ii.   **Amy Nacole Lindsey** was born 23 Mar 1976 in Macon, GA.
2284 F   iii. **Tina Ann Lindsey** was born 14 Jul 1979 in Macon, GA.

1020. Angelia Dee Lindsey (*Thomas Arnett Lindsey^6, Alonzo Brown Lindsey^5, Caleb (Calip) Lindsey^4, Frances (Frankie) Sharp^3, Charles W. Sr.^{2}, John Sr.^{1}*) was born 20 Mar 1953 in Macon, GA.

Angelia married **Anthony Bare**. Anthony was born in Macon, GA.

Angelia next married **Dewey Pope**.

+ 2285 M i. **Anthony Shane Lindsey Pope** was born 25 Apr 1972 in Macon, GA.

2286 F ii. **Mya Lindsey Pope** was born 16 Apr 1992.

1021. Harry Lindsey Torbett (*Evie Jane Lindsey*[6], *Edgar Floyd Lindsey Sr.*[5], *Caleb (Calip) Lindsey*[4], *Frances (Frankie) Sharp*[3], *Charles W. Sr.*[2], *John Sr.*[1]) was born 28 Jun 1954 in Alexandria, LA.

Harry married **Melanie *Unk**. Melanie was born 15 Oct in Winfield, AL.

2287 F i. **Lauren H. Torbett** was born 8 Sep 1982 in Alexandria, LA.

2288 M ii. **William B. Torbett** was born 18 Aug 1987 in Alexandria, LA.

1022. John William Torbett (*Evie Jane Lindsey*[6], *Edgar Floyd Lindsey Sr.*[5], *Caleb (Calip) Lindsey*[4], *Frances (Frankie) Sharp*[3], *Charles W. Sr.*[2], *John Sr.*[1]) was born 9 Aug 1962 in Alexandria, LA.

John married **Candy Champion**. Candy was born 17 Feb 1969 in West Monroe, LA.

1023. Lilly Mae Lindsey (*Millard Lindsey*[6], *Maraday (Merry Dee) Lindsey*[5], *Andrew Jackson Lindsey*[4], *Frances (Frankie) Sharp*[3], *Charles W. Sr.*[2], *John Sr.*[1]) was born 6 Jul 1907 in Colbert County, AL, died 4 Feb 1961, and was buried in Barton Cemetery, Colbert County, AL.

Lilly married **Henry Fletcher May**. Henry was born 17 May 1894, died 31 Jan 1969, and was buried in Union Hill Cemetery, Franklin County, AL.

2289 F i. **Infant Daughter May** was buried in Watson Cemetery, Franklin County, AL.

+ 2290 M ii. **James William May Sr.** was born 5 Oct 1926 in Franklin County, AL, died 25 Nov 1985, and was buried in Union Hill Cemetery, Franklin County, AL.

2291 M iii. **Harold Dean (Bobo) May** was born 16 Jun 1934, died 29 Jul 1978, and was buried in Barton Cemetery, Colbert County, AL.

Lilly next married **John R. (Mac) McCleskey**.

1024. Viola Beatrice Lindsey (*Millard Lindsey*[6], *Maraday (Merry Dee) Lindsey*[5], *Andrew Jackson Lindsey*[4], *Frances (Frankie) Sharp*[3], *Charles W. Sr.*[2], *John Sr.*[1]) was born 20 Dec 1910 in Cherokee, Colbert County, AL, died 18 Mar 1990, and was buried in Barton Cemetery, Colbert County, AL.

Viola married **Finis Leonard (Phiney/Slim) Wood**, son of **John Pugh Wood** and **Sarah (Sallie) Frances Elizabeth Milford**, 13 Dec 1931 in Iuka, Tishomingo County, MS. Finis was born 13 Nov 1891 in Gravely Springs, Lauderdale County, AL, died 4 Sep 1962, and was buried in Barton Cemetery, Colbert County, AL.

+ 2292 F i. **Virginia Nell Wood** was born 22 Mar 1933 in Cherokee, Colbert County, AL, died 29 Mar 1991, and was buried in Barton Cemetery, Colbert County, AL.

+ 2293 F ii. **Sarah Elizabeth (Lib) Wood** was born 8 Sep 1934 in Cherokee, Colbert County, AL, died 6 May 2005, and was buried in Barton Cemetery, Colbert County, AL.

+ 2294 F iii. **Shirley Jean Wood** was born 19 Jul 1936 in Cherokee, Colbert County, AL, died 13 Dec 1998, and was buried in Barton Cemetery, Colbert County, AL.

+ 2295 F iv. **Beatrice Marie Wood** was born 15 Sep 1937 in Cherokee, Colbert County, AL.

+ 2296 M v. **Jack Leon Wood** was born 20 Oct 1939 in Cherokee, Colbert County, AL.

+ 2297 F vi. **Patsy Faye Wood** was born 30 Apr 1941 in Cherokee, Colbert County, AL.

2298 M vii. **Winston Churchill Wood** was born 24 Feb 1944 in Cherokee, Colbert County, AL, died 3 Oct 1946, and was buried in Barton Cemetery, Colbert County, AL.

2299 M viii. **Franklin Delano Wood** was born 24 Feb 1944 in Cherokee, Colbert County, AL, died 27 Jun 1944, and was buried in Barton Cemetery, Colbert County, AL.

+ 2300 F ix. **Barbara Gail (Cookie) Wood** was born 14 Sep 1945 in Cherokee, Colbert County, AL.

2301 F x. **Claudette Wood** was born 28 Apr 1948 in Cherokee, Colbert County, AL, died 28 Apr 1948, and was buried in Barton Cemetery, Colbert County, AL.

2302 F xi. **Paulette Wood** was born 28 Apr 1948 in Cherokee, Colbert County, AL, died 28 Apr 1948, and was buried in Barton Cemetery, Colbert County, AL.

Viola next married **Ervin Ralph (Red) Worsham** about 1966. Ervin was born 12 Jul 1918 in Cherokee, Colbert County, AL, died 18 Mar 1978, and was buried in Barton Cemetery, Colbert County, AL.

+ 2303 M   i.   **David Leon Wood Worsham** was born 11 Aug 1971 in Colbert County, AL, died 6 Feb 1999, and was buried in Barton Cemetery, Colbert County, AL.

1025. Ola Mae Lindsey (*Millard Lindsey^6, Maraday (Merry Dee) Lindsey^5, Andrew Jackson Lindsey^4, Frances (Frankie) Sharp^3, Charles W. Sr.^{2}, John Sr.^{1}*) was born 5 Apr 1915 in Colbert County, AL.

Ola married ***Unk Burns**.
  2304 F   i.   **Helen Burns**.
+ 2305 F   ii. **Geraldine Burns**.
  2306 F   iii. **Mary Burns**.
  2307 M   iv. **Lester Burns**.
  2308 M   v.   **Chester Burns**.
  2309 M   vi. **Vester Burns**.

Ola next married **Leslie Gray**.

1026. Bessie Lee Lindsey (*Millard Lindsey^6, Maraday (Merry Dee) Lindsey^5, Andrew Jackson Lindsey^4, Frances (Frankie) Sharp^3, Charles W. Sr.^{2}, John Sr.^{1}*) was born 14 Jul 1917 in Colbert County, AL, died 1 Jul 1993, and was buried in Crittenden Memorial Park, Marion, AR.

Bessie married **James Aubry Morgan Sr.**. James was born 19 Aug 1917, died 14 Aug 1994, and was buried in Crittenden Memorial Park, Marion, AR.
+ 2310 F   i.   **Evaline Morgan**.
+ 2311 F   ii.   **Dorothy Lorraine Morgan**.
+ 2312 F   iii. **Sue Morgan**.
+ 2313 F   iv.   **Peggy Morgan**.
  2314 M   v.   **James Edward Morgan**.
+ 2315 F   vi.   **Betty Jo Morgan**.
  2316 M   vii. **Jerry Wayne Morgan**.
  2317 M   viii. **James Aubry Morgan Jr.** was born 14 Aug 1942, died 26 Aug 1984, and was buried in Crittenden Memorial Park, Marion, AR.
+ 2318 M   ix.   **Charles Edward Morgan** was born 27 May 1951 in Turrell, Crittenden County, AR.

1027. Dixie Lindsey (*Millard Lindsey^6, Maraday (Merry Dee) Lindsey^5, Andrew Jackson Lindsey^4, Frances (Frankie) Sharp^3, Charles W. Sr.^{2}, John Sr.^{1}*) was born 31 Jan 1918, died 18 Aug 1997, and was buried in Crittenden Memorial Park, Marion, AR.

Dixie married **Tommy Gelitha Burns Sr.**. Tommy was born 3 Oct 1910, died 1 Apr 1987, and was buried in Crittenden Memorial Park, Marion, AR.
  2319 M   i.   **Tommy Gelitha Burns Jr.**
  2320 M   ii.   **James Billy Burns**.
  2321 F   iii. **Joyce Sue Burns**.
  2322 M   iv.   **Allen Wayne Burns**.
  2323 M   v.   **Rodney Perry Burns**.
  2324 F   vi.   **Peggy Lou Burns**.
  2325 F   vii. **Edna Joe Burns**.

1028. Lucille Lindsey (*Millard Lindsey^6, Maraday (Merry Dee) Lindsey^5, Andrew Jackson Lindsey^4, Frances (Frankie) Sharp^3, Charles W. Sr.^{2}, John Sr.^{1}*) was born 20 Mar 1920 in Colbert County, AL.

Lucille married **Bob Salter**.
  2326 F   i.   **Betty Jean Salter**.
  2327 M   ii.   **James Earl Salter**.

1029. Dorothy Lindsey (*Millard Lindsey^6, Maraday (Merry Dee) Lindsey^5, Andrew Jackson Lindsey^4, Frances (Frankie) Sharp^3, Charles W. Sr.^{2}, John Sr.^{1}*) was born 10 Nov 1922, died 5 Mar 1988, and was buried in Crittenden Memorial Park, Marion, AR.

Dorothy married **Bob Nelson**.

2328 M i. **Richard Nelson**.

Dorothy next married ***Unk Proctor**.

Dorothy next married ***Unk Tankersley**.

1030. Pete (J. R.) Lindsey (*Millard Lindsey*[6], *Maraday (Merry Dee) Lindsey*[5], *Andrew Jackson Lindsey*[4], *Frances (Frankie) Sharp*[3], *Charles W. Sr.*[2], *John Sr.*[1]) was born in 1924 and died in 1979.

Pete married **Mamie Jean**. Mamie was born 11 Jul 1928, died 9 May 1952, and was buried in Crittenden Memorial Park, Marion, AR.
2329 F i. **Patsy Lindsey**.
2330 M ii. **Ralph Lindsey**.

Pete next married **Bunnie *Unk**.

1041. Coleman Edison Lindsey (*Kerom William Lindsey*[6], *Greenberry Lee Lindsey Sr.*[5], *Sylvester (Sill) B. Lindsey*[4], *Frances (Frankie) Sharp*[3], *Charles W. Sr.*[2], *John Sr.*[1]) was born 4 Jul 1909 in Wright, Lauderdale County, AL, died 15 Feb 1981, and was buried in Wright Cemetery, Wright, Lauderdale County, AL.

Coleman married **Virgie Elizabeth Clemons**, daughter of **James Thomas Clemons** and **Roxie Bell Smith**, 19 Apr 1936 in Lauderdale County, AL. Virgie was born 9 Nov 1915 in Florence, Lauderdale County, AL, died 22 Apr 2004, and was buried in Wright Cemetery, Wright, Lauderdale County, AL.
+ 2331 F i. **Kathyleen Lindsey** was born 2 Feb 1937 in Lauderdale County, AL.
+ 2332 M ii. **Owen Wayne Lindsey** was born 16 Aug 1941 in Lauderdale County, AL.
  2333 F iii. **Jeanetta Lindsey** was born 9 Jul 1950 in Lauderdale County, AL.

1042. Clyde Roosevelt Lindsey (*Samuel S. Lindsey*[6], *Greenberry Lee Lindsey Sr.*[5], *Sylvester (Sill) B. Lindsey*[4], *Frances (Frankie) Sharp*[3], *Charles W. Sr.*[2], *John Sr.*[1]) was born 17 Oct 1901 in Waterloo, Lauderdale County, AL, died 28 Sep 1979, and was buried in Wright Cemetery, Wright, Lauderdale County, AL. Another name for Clyde was Clyde R. Lindsey.

Clyde married **Jewel G. Ticer**, daughter of **Ottis C. Ticer** and **Verta E. Robertson**, 24 Dec 1924 in Lauderdale County, AL. Jewel was born 16 Nov 1908 in Lauderdale County, AL, died 23 Jan 1998, and was buried in Wright Cemetery, Wright, Lauderdale County, AL.
+ 2334 M i. **Lynwood Clyde Lindsey** was born 5 May 1928 in Lauderdale County, AL, died 19 May 1967, and was buried in Wright Cemetery, Wright, Lauderdale County, AL.

1044. Mattie Sue (Susie) Lindsey (*Samuel S. Lindsey*[6], *Greenberry Lee Lindsey Sr.*[5], *Sylvester (Sill) B. Lindsey*[4], *Frances (Frankie) Sharp*[3], *Charles W. Sr.*[2], *John Sr.*[1]) was born 9 Jul 1906 in Waterloo, Lauderdale County, AL.

Mattie married **Boss C. Young**, son of **Hulet Edward Young** and **Lillian Ella Young**, 6 Mar 1926 in Lauderdale County, AL. Boss was born 13 Apr 1916 in Lauderdale County, AL, died 19 Apr 1944, and was buried in Murphy's Chapel Cemetery, Lauderdale County, AL.
(Duplicate Line. See Person 745)

1047. Georgia Mae Lindsey (*John David Lindsey*[6], *Greenberry Lee Lindsey Sr.*[5], *Sylvester (Sill) B. Lindsey*[4], *Frances (Frankie) Sharp*[3], *Charles W. Sr.*[2], *John Sr.*[1]) was born 6 May 1907 and died 18 Apr 1979 in Michigan City, IN.

Georgia married **Willie Smith Joiner**, son of **James William Joiner** and **Margaret Elizabeth Barker**, 15 Dec 1930 in Tyronza, Poinsett County, AR. Willie was born 2 Dec 1903 in Lauderdale County, AL and died 26 Jan 1976 in Michigan City, IN.
  2335 F i. **Doris Elouise Joiner** was born 13 May 1933 in Tyronza, Poinsett County, AR and died 21 Jun 1933.
+ 2336 M ii. **Wallace Wilbur Joiner** was born 27 Jan 1935.
+ 2337 F iii. **June Jenette Joiner** was born 11 Oct 1937.

1048. James Alex Lindsey (*John David Lindsey*^{6}, *Greenberry Lee Lindsey Sr.*^{5}, *Sylvester (Sill) B. Lindsey*^{4}, *Frances (Frankie) Sharp*^{3}, *Charles W. Sr.*^{2}, *John Sr.*^{1}) was born about 1909 in Arkansas and died in Holland, MI.

James married **Bertha *Unk.**

2338 M i. **Lindsey** was born 5 Mar 1931, died in Sep, and was buried in Tyronza Cemetery, Tyronza, Poinsett County, AR.

1049. Edgar Bruce Lindsey (*John David Lindsey*^{6}, *Greenberry Lee Lindsey Sr.*^{5}, *Sylvester (Sill) B. Lindsey*^{4}, *Frances (Frankie) Sharp*^{3}, *Charles W. Sr.*^{2}, *John Sr.*^{1}) was born 23 Apr 1913 in Deckerville, AR, died 5 Apr 1990, and was buried in Corinth, Alcorn County, MS.

Edgar married **Thurza Dean**, daughter of **Charles Mack Dean** and **Martha Smallwood**, 8 Aug 1931 in Lauderdale County, AL. Thurza was born 27 Oct 1915 in Lauderdale County, AL, died 7 Sep 1962, and was buried in Florence City Cemetery, Florence, Lauderdale County, AL.

+ 2339 M i. **Charles David Lindsey Sr.** was born 25 Apr 1933 in Lauderdale County, AL.
+ 2340 M ii. **Raymond Oneal Lindsey** was born 18 Jul 1936 in Lauderdale County, AL.
+ 2341 F iii. **Patricia Ann Lindsey** was born 20 Apr 1944 in Lauderdale County, AL.

Edgar next married **Mae Richardson**, daughter of **Robert Richardson** and **Millie Landers**, 9 Feb 1940 in Chicago, IL. Mae was born 3 Feb 1921 in Lauderdale County, AL.

+ 2342 M i. **James Bruce Lindsey** was born 11 May 1951 in Chicago, IL.

1051. Donald Lindsey (*John David Lindsey*^{6}, *Greenberry Lee Lindsey Sr.*^{5}, *Sylvester (Sill) B. Lindsey*^{4}, *Frances (Frankie) Sharp*^{3}, *Charles W. Sr.*^{2}, *John Sr.*^{1}) was buried in Illinois.

Donald married **Mable Garrett.**

+ 2343 F i. **Louise Lindsey.**

1052. John Henry Lindsey (*John David Lindsey*^{6}, *Greenberry Lee Lindsey Sr.*^{5}, *Sylvester (Sill) B. Lindsey*^{4}, *Frances (Frankie) Sharp*^{3}, *Charles W. Sr.*^{2}, *John Sr.*^{1}) was born 8 Feb in Arkansas.

General Notes: "Lived in Melrose Park, Illinois..." Millie Mason

John married **Martha Foy** 1 Sep 1951.

1053. Bessie Lindsey (*John David Lindsey*^{6}, *Greenberry Lee Lindsey Sr.*^{5}, *Sylvester (Sill) B. Lindsey*^{4}, *Frances (Frankie) Sharp*^{3}, *Charles W. Sr.*^{2}, *John Sr.*^{1}) was born 24 Nov in Alabama.

General Notes: "Lived in Chicago..." Millie Mason

Bessie married **Johnnie Marmol.**

1054. Mary Lindsey (*John David Lindsey*^{6}, *Greenberry Lee Lindsey Sr.*^{5}, *Sylvester (Sill) B. Lindsey*^{4}, *Frances (Frankie) Sharp*^{3}, *Charles W. Sr.*^{2}, *John Sr.*^{1}) was born 7 Apr 1920.

General Notes: "Lived at Cicero, Illinois..." Millie Mason

Mary married **Leo Smith.**

1055. Bonnie Lindsey (*John David Lindsey*^{6}, *Greenberry Lee Lindsey Sr.*^{5}, *Sylvester (Sill) B. Lindsey*^{4}, *Frances (Frankie) Sharp*^{3}, *Charles W. Sr.*^{2}, *John Sr.*^{1}) was born 28 Aug 1922 in Arkansas.

General Notes: "Lived at Clay City, Kentucky..." Millie Mason

Bonnie married **Kernest Collier.**

1056. Ralph Nolan Lindsey (*Greenberry Lee Lindsey Jr.*[6], *Greenberry Lee Lindsey Sr.*[5], *Sylvester (Sill) B. Lindsey*[4], *Frances (Frankie) Sharp*[3], *Charles W. Sr.*[2], *John Sr.*[1]) was born 15 Jun 1915 in Lauderdale County, AL.

Ralph married **Lucille Futrell**, daughter of **William P. Futrell** and **Lona Smith**, 17 Jun 1946 in Lauderdale County, AL. Lucille was born 22 Jan 1924 in Lauderdale County, AL.

2344　M　i.　**Gregory Darrell Lindsey** was born 14 Dec 1969 in Colbert County, AL.

1057. Mary Bernease Lindsey (*Greenberry Lee Lindsey Jr.*[6], *Greenberry Lee Lindsey Sr.*[5], *Sylvester (Sill) B. Lindsey*[4], *Frances (Frankie) Sharp*[3], *Charles W. Sr.*[2], *John Sr.*[1]) was born 19 Feb 1922 in Lauderdale County, AL, died 8 Jul 2002, and was buried in Greenview Memorial Park, Florence, Lauderdale County, AL.

Mary married **Robert Arnold Austin**, son of **James Robert Austin** and **Minnie Salinia Gooch**, 9 May 1945 in Lauderdale County, AL. Robert was born 1 Apr 1918 in Lauderdale County, AL, died 17 May 2002, and was buried in Greenview Memorial Park, Florence, Lauderdale County, AL.

2345　F　i.　**Linda Gail Austin** was born 2 Nov 1949 in Lauderdale County, AL.
2346　M　ii.　**Robert Kevin Austin** was born 17 Mar 1958 in Lauderdale County, AL.

1058. Alberta Atkinson (*Hannah Margaret Lindsey*[6], *Greenberry Lee Lindsey Sr.*[5], *Sylvester (Sill) B. Lindsey*[4], *Frances (Frankie) Sharp*[3], *Charles W. Sr.*[2], *John Sr.*[1]).

Alberta married **Eustis Blount**.
2347　M　i.　**Ronald Atkinson**.

1059. Fred Atkinson (*Hannah Margaret Lindsey*[6], *Greenberry Lee Lindsey Sr.*[5], *Sylvester (Sill) B. Lindsey*[4], *Frances (Frankie) Sharp*[3], *Charles W. Sr.*[2], *John Sr.*[1]).

Fred married ***Unk**.
2348　M　i.　**Larry Atkinson**.
2349　M　ii.　**Hubert Atkinson**.

1064. Nell Johnson (*Pearlie Ann Milford*[6], *Julie (Julia) Lindsey*[5], *Sylvester (Sill) B. Lindsey*[4], *Frances (Frankie) Sharp*[3], *Charles W. Sr.*[2], *John Sr.*[1]).

Nell married **B. L. Darby**.

1065. Estell Johnson (*Pearlie Ann Milford*[6], *Julie (Julia) Lindsey*[5], *Sylvester (Sill) B. Lindsey*[4], *Frances (Frankie) Sharp*[3], *Charles W. Sr.*[2], *John Sr.*[1]) was born 10 Apr 1919 in Lauderdale County, AL.

Estell married **Mack Carroll** 30 Jun 1944 in Lauderdale County, AL. Mack was born 22 Mar 1894 in Texas.

1066. James Edward Johnson (*Pearlie Ann Milford*[6], *Julie (Julia) Lindsey*[5], *Sylvester (Sill) B. Lindsey*[4], *Frances (Frankie) Sharp*[3], *Charles W. Sr.*[2], *John Sr.*[1]) was born 10 Sep 1924 in Lauderdale County, AL, died 13 May 1978, and was buried in Murphy's Chapel Cemetery, Lauderdale County, AL.

James married **Mable Christine *Unk**. Mable was born 12 May 1926, died 1 Mar 1994, and was buried in Murphy's Chapel Cemetery, Lauderdale County, AL.

+ 2350　F　i.　**Wanda Gail Johnson**.
2351　M　ii.　**John Edward Johnson Jr.**
2352　M　iii.　**Roger Johnson**.
2353　M　iv.　**David Jerome Johnson**.

1068. Edna Mae Tate (*Amy Gertrude Lindsey*[6], *Adron (Little Ade) Lindsey*[5], *Sylvester (Sill) B. Lindsey*[4], *Frances (Frankie) Sharp*[3], *Charles W. Sr.*[2], *John Sr.*[1]).

Edna married **Hopson Price**.

1069. Cornelia Tate (*Amy Gertrude Lindsey*[6], *Adron (Little Ade) Lindsey*[5], *Sylvester (Sill) B. Lindsey*[4], *Frances (Frankie) Sharp*[3], *Charles W. Sr.*[2], *John Sr.*[1]).

Cornelia married ***Unk Pricer**.

1070. Ray Pierce (*Amy Gertrude Lindsey*[6], *Adron (Little Ade) Lindsey*[5], *Sylvester (Sill) B. Lindsey*[4], *Frances (Frankie) Sharp*[3], *Charles W. Sr.*[2], *John Sr.*[1]) was born 17 Oct 1921 in Lawrence County, TN.

Ray married **Valleria Mitchell**.
2354　F　i.　**Bertha Joyce Pierce**.
2355　M　ii.　**Billy Ray Pierce**.

1071. Susie Belle Pierce (*Amy Gertrude Lindsey*[6], *Adron (Little Ade) Lindsey*[5], *Sylvester (Sill) B. Lindsey*[4], *Frances (Frankie) Sharp*[3], *Charles W. Sr.*[2], *John Sr.*[1]) was born 22 Apr 1923 in Lauderdale County, AL.

Susie married **James Henry Carson Johnston**, son of **William T. Johnston** and **Sarah E. Phillips**, 13 Oct 1944 in Lauderdale County, AL. James was born 21 Jul 1915 in Lexington, Lauderdale County, AL.
+ 2356　F　i.　**Rebecca Ann Johnston** was born 13 Oct 1948 in Colbert County, AL.
+ 2357　M　ii.　**William (Bill) Ross Johnston** was born 3 Jan 1952 in Colbert County, AL.
+ 2358　M　iii.　**James Maurice Johnston** was born 3 Mar 1961 in Lauderdale County, AL.

1072. Mildred Lucille Pierce (*Amy Gertrude Lindsey*[6], *Adron (Little Ade) Lindsey*[5], *Sylvester (Sill) B. Lindsey*[4], *Frances (Frankie) Sharp*[3], *Charles W. Sr.*[2], *John Sr.*[1]) was born 10 Jun 1922 in Lauderdale County, AL and was buried in Greenview Memorial Park, Florence, Lauderdale County, AL.

Mildred married **Roy James Pigg**, son of **Jessie James Pigg** and **Mary Elizabeth Putman**, 27 Jul 1940 in Lauderdale County, AL. Roy was born 29 May 1918 in Lauderdale County, AL and was buried in Greenview Memorial Park, Florence, Lauderdale County, AL.
2359　M　i.　**Roy Glenn Pigg**.
2360　F　ii.　**Mary Pigg**.
+ 2361　F　iii.　**Betty Dean Pigg**.

Mildred next married **Virgil Newberry**.

Mildred next married **George Jessie Gentile**, son of **Jesse Gentile** and **Maria Mascia**, 15 Jun 1970 in Lauderdale County, AL. George was born 20 May 1914 in Manhattan, NY.

1073. Julie Blance Pierce (*Amy Gertrude Lindsey*[6], *Adron (Little Ade) Lindsey*[5], *Sylvester (Sill) B. Lindsey*[4], *Frances (Frankie) Sharp*[3], *Charles W. Sr.*[2], *John Sr.*[1]) was born 2 Mar 1926 in Lauderdale County, AL.

Julie married **Alfred White**.

1074. Raymond Ross Pierce (*Amy Gertrude Lindsey*[6], *Adron (Little Ade) Lindsey*[5], *Sylvester (Sill) B. Lindsey*[4], *Frances (Frankie) Sharp*[3], *Charles W. Sr.*[2], *John Sr.*[1]) was born 20 Mar 1927 in Lawrence County, TN.

Raymond married **Nadine Baggett**.
2362　F　i.　**Denise Pierce**.
2363　M　ii.　**Timothy Pierce**.

1075. Jessie Imogene Pierce (*Amy Gertrude Lindsey*[6], *Adron (Little Ade) Lindsey*[5], *Sylvester (Sill) B. Lindsey*[4], *Frances (Frankie) Sharp*[3], *Charles W. Sr.*[2], *John Sr.*[1]) was born 3 Nov 1928 in Lawrence County, TN.

Jessie married **Clayton Sanker**.
2364　M　i.　**Phillip Sanker**.
2365　F　ii.　**Lisa Lynn Sanker**.

1076. Bobbie Lee Pierce (*Amy Gertrude Lindsey*[6], *Adron (Little Ade) Lindsey*[5], *Sylvester (Sill) B. Lindsey*[4], *Frances (Frankie) Sharp*[3], *Charles W. Sr.*[2], *John Sr.*[1]) was born 2 Sep 1930 in Lawrence County, TN, died 17 May 2000, and was buried in Kidd Cemetery, Lawrence County, TN.

Bobbie married **Homer Clyde Perkins Jr.**, son of **Homer Perkins** and **Ada Webb**, 28 Feb 1946 in Lauderdale County, AL. Homer was born 16 Nov 1921 in Waterloo, Lauderdale County, AL, died 15 Nov 1986, and was buried in Kidd Cemetery, Lawrence County, TN.

- \+ 2366 F i. **Karen Anne Perkins** was born 8 Jan 1947 in Lawrence County, TN.
- \+ 2367 F ii. **Connie Lee Perkins** was born 23 Jul 1949 in Lawrence County, TN.
- \+ 2368 F iii. **Dianna Lynn Perkins** was born 10 Apr 1951 in Muncie, Delaware County, IN.
- \+ 2369 M iv. **Homer Clyde Perkins III** was born 27 Oct 1953 in Muncie, Delaware County, IN.
- \+ 2370 F v. **Pamela Sue Perkins** was born 27 Oct 1955 in Muncie, Delaware County, IN.

1077. Jesse Sewell Pierce (*Amy Gertrude Lindsey*[6], *Adron (Little Ade) Lindsey*[5], *Sylvester (Sill) B. Lindsey*[4], *Frances (Frankie) Sharp*[3], *Charles W. Sr.*[2], *John Sr.*[1]) was born 20 Jan 1933 in Lawrence County, TN.

Jesse married **Roberta Tarpley**.

- 2371 F i. **Vickey Pierce**.
- 2372 F ii. **Judy Pierce**.
- 2373 M iii. **Jesse Pierce Jr.**

1081. Evelyn Bills (*Viola Lindsey*[6], *Adron (Little Ade) Lindsey*[5], *Sylvester (Sill) B. Lindsey*[4], *Frances (Frankie) Sharp*[3], *Charles W. Sr.*[2], *John Sr.*[1]).

Evelyn married **Robert Davis**.

Evelyn next married **Wilkes Smith**.

- \+ 2374 F i. **Betty Smith**.
- \+ 2375 F ii. **Dollie Smith**.

1084. Ann Locke (*Mary Odelle Lindsey*[6], *Adron (Little Ade) Lindsey*[5], *Sylvester (Sill) B. Lindsey*[4], *Frances (Frankie) Sharp*[3], *Charles W. Sr.*[2], *John Sr.*[1]).

Ann married **Bill Tidwell**.

General Notes: "Lived in Nashville..." Millie Mason

1090. *Unk Barrier (*Josie Etta Haynes*[6], *Lucretia (Lula) Lindsey*[5], *Adron Leonard Lindsey Sr.*[4], *Frances (Frankie) Sharp*[3], *Charles W. Sr.*[2], *John Sr.*[1]).

*Unk married **Robert E. Bird**.

1091. Bernice Barrier (*Josie Etta Haynes*[6], *Lucretia (Lula) Lindsey*[5], *Adron Leonard Lindsey Sr.*[4], *Frances (Frankie) Sharp*[3], *Charles W. Sr.*[2], *John Sr.*[1]).

Bernice married **Horace Beard**.

- 2376 F i. **Polly Beard**.
- 2377 F ii. **Sharon Beard**.

1092. *Unk Barrier (*Josie Etta Haynes*[6], *Lucretia (Lula) Lindsey*[5], *Adron Leonard Lindsey Sr.*[4], *Frances (Frankie) Sharp*[3], *Charles W. Sr.*[2], *John Sr.*[1]).

*Unk married **Albert Reynolds**.

1093. Henry Olen Barrier (*Josie Etta Haynes*[6], *Lucretia (Lula) Lindsey*[5], *Adron Leonard Lindsey Sr.*[4], *Frances (Frankie) Sharp*[3], *Charles W. Sr.*[2], *John Sr.*[1]) was born in 1920 and died in Apr 1980.

Henry married **Lady Maude Wesson**, daughter of **Unknown** and **Unknown**.

   2378 M   i.   **Charles Barrier.**
   2379 F   ii.   **Jimmie Barrier.**
+ 2380 F   iii.   **Mary Ann Barrier.**
+ 2381 F   iv.   **Donna Sue Barrier** was born 27 Mar 1948 in Lauderdale County, AL.

1094. Carmel Inez Haynes (*Clarence Haynes*[6], *Lucretia (Lula) Lindsey*[5], *Adron Leonard Lindsey Sr.*[4], *Frances (Frankie) Sharp*[3], *Charles W. Sr.*[2], *John Sr.*[1]) was born 5 Dec 1909 in Lauderdale County, AL and died 8 Jan 1968.

> General Notes: "She writes...Edwin, Doyle and I were born in Waterloo. We lived in town in the house with Grandpa and Grandma (Criss & Lula Haynes) and also lived with them at their farm home. She added that her father, Clarence Haynes, moved his family to Nixon, Tennessee...then we moved to Arkansas in October 1916...." William McDonald

Carmel married **Grady Floyd Odum**. Grady was born 15 Mar, died 11 Aug 1973, and was buried in Forest Hills, South Cemetery, Memphis, TN.

+ 2382 M   i.   **Harry Wilbern Odum Sr.** was born 26 Oct 1931 in Tyronza, Poinsett County, AR.

1095. Edwin Lenard Haynes (*Clarence Haynes*[6], *Lucretia (Lula) Lindsey*[5], *Adron Leonard Lindsey Sr.*[4], *Frances (Frankie) Sharp*[3], *Charles W. Sr.*[2], *John Sr.*[1]) was born 20 Feb 1911 in Waterloo, Lauderdale County, AL, died 12 Jul 1979, and was buried in Tyronza Cemetery, Tyronza, Poinsett County, AR.

Edwin married **Lillian Inez Lawson** 10 Dec 1939. Lillian was born 8 Nov in Wayne County, TN, died 25 May 1982, and was buried in Tyronza Cemetery, Tyronza, Poinsett County, AR.

   2383 M   i.   **Bobby Gene Haynes** died 6 Jul 1983 and was buried in Tyronza Cemetery, Tyronza, Poinsett County, AR.
+ 2384 F   ii.   **Joyce Ann Haynes** was born in Tyronza, Poinsett County, AR.

1096. Doyle Odell Haynes (*Clarence Haynes*[6], *Lucretia (Lula) Lindsey*[5], *Adron Leonard Lindsey Sr.*[4], *Frances (Frankie) Sharp*[3], *Charles W. Sr.*[2], *John Sr.*[1]) was born 30 May 1913 in Waterloo, Lauderdale County, AL.

Doyle married **Ruth Virginia Hughes**. Ruth was born 1 Nov 1912 in Mammoth Springs, Fulton County, AR.

   2385 F   i.   **Rebecca Lee Haynes** was born 11 Apr 1948 in Craighead County, AR, died 7 Aug 1948, and was buried in Tyronza Cemetery, Tyronza, Poinsett County, AR.
+ 2386 M   ii.   **Gary Doyle Haynes** was born 12 Dec 1950 in Memphis, Shelby County, TN.

1097. Weldon Lewis Haynes (*Clarence Haynes*[6], *Lucretia (Lula) Lindsey*[5], *Adron Leonard Lindsey Sr.*[4], *Frances (Frankie) Sharp*[3], *Charles W. Sr.*[2], *John Sr.*[1]) was born 16 Aug 1919 in Tyronza, Poinsett County, AR, died 11 Mar 1988, and was buried in Luxoro Cemetery, Luxora, AR.

Weldon married **Helen Gladys Perry** 8 Oct 1943. Helen was born 16 Aug in Louisiana, died 6 Nov 1958, and was buried in Memorial Park, West Memphis, AR.

+ 2387 F   i.   **Linda Sue Haynes** was born 31 Mar 1943 in Craighead County, AR.
+ 2388 F   ii.   **Phyllis Kay Haynes** was born 6 Mar 1946 in California.

1098. James Purnell Haynes (*Clarence Haynes*[6], *Lucretia (Lula) Lindsey*[5], *Adron Leonard Lindsey Sr.*[4], *Frances (Frankie) Sharp*[3], *Charles W. Sr.*[2], *John Sr.*[1]) was born 14 Nov 1930 in Tyronza, Poinsett County, AR, died 5 Nov 1986, and was buried in Ripley Memorial Cemetery, Ripley, TN.

James married **Georgia Weston** in 1949.

   2389 F   i.   **Kathy Jane Haynes** was born 13 Oct 1950 in Tyronza, Poinsett County, AR.
   2390 F   ii.   **Carol Suzanne Haynes** was born 17 Sep 1953 in Tyronza, Poinsett County, AR.

James next married **Jo Anne Barham**.

   2391 F   i.   **Leigh Ann Haynes** was born 18 Oct 1972 in Crittenden County, AR.

1100. Dora Inez Tacker (*Lou Tishie Haynes*[6], *Lucretia (Lula) Lindsey*[5], *Adron Leonard Lindsey Sr.*[4], *Frances (Frankie) Sharp*[3], *Charles W. Sr.*[2], *John Sr.*[1]) was born 11 Aug 1906 and died 26 Nov.

Dora married **Grady Thomas Harmon** 9 Sep 1925. Grady was born 21 Jul 1903 and died 22 Jun 1948.

+ 2392 F i. **Mary Lou Faye Harmon** was born 16 Sep 1926.
+ 2393 F ii. **Gradie Marguerite Harmon** was born 9 Nov 1929.
+ 2394 M iii. **Billy Thomas Harmon Sr.** was born 7 Dec 1933 and died 21 Jun 2001.
  2395 M iv. **Jimmy Donald Harmon** was born 26 Aug 1938 and died 22 Jul 1999.
+ 2396 M v. **Odie Jack Harmon** was born 25 Jul 1941.
+ 2397 M vi. **Harold Mack Harmon** was born 22 Mar 1944.
+ 2398 F vii. **Norma Jean Harmon** was born 5 Jan 1948.

1101. Tennie Louise Tacker (*Lou Tishie Haynes*[6], *Lucretia (Lula) Lindsey*[5], *Adron Leonard Lindsey Sr.*[4], *Frances (Frankie) Sharp*[3], *Charles W. Sr.*[2], *John Sr.*[1]) was born 24 Sep 1909 and died 28 May 2000.

Tennie married **Daniel Lawson Borden** 2 Oct 1927. Daniel was born 14 Feb 1909 and died 11 Nov 1968.

  2399 F i. **Betty Borden.**
  2400 M ii. **Dannie Borden.**

1102. Virgie Hazel Tacker (*Lou Tishie Haynes*[6], *Lucretia (Lula) Lindsey*[5], *Adron Leonard Lindsey Sr.*[4], *Frances (Frankie) Sharp*[3], *Charles W. Sr.*[2], *John Sr.*[1]) was born 22 Jul 1914 and died 6 Mar 1990.

Virgie married **Lameul Wolf** 6 Apr 1935. Lameul was born 6 Sep 1912 and died 4 May 1978.

  2401 F i. **Donnie Lou Wolf.**
  2402 M ii. **Billy Wolf.**
  2403 F iii. **Martha Ann Wolf.**

1103. Mary Bastine Tacker (*Lou Tishie Haynes*[6], *Lucretia (Lula) Lindsey*[5], *Adron Leonard Lindsey Sr.*[4], *Frances (Frankie) Sharp*[3], *Charles W. Sr.*[2], *John Sr.*[1]) was born 28 Nov 1916 and died 17 Dec 1996.

Mary married **Robert Morris.** Robert was born in 1910 and died in 1979.

  2404 M i. **Charles Morris** was born 6 Dec 1944 and died 5 Jun 2004.

1104. Harold D. Tacker (*Lou Tishie Haynes*[6], *Lucretia (Lula) Lindsey*[5], *Adron Leonard Lindsey Sr.*[4], *Frances (Frankie) Sharp*[3], *Charles W. Sr.*[2], *John Sr.*[1]) was born in 1921 and died in 1975.

Harold married **Dorothy Ferrell.**

  2405 M i. **Loyd T. Tacker.**
  2406 F ii. **Rebecca Tacker.**
  2407 M iii. **James Boyd Tacker.**
  2408 F iv. **Retta Sue Tacker.**
  2409 M v. **Harold D. Tacker Jr.**

1109. Fred Amos Wood (*Martha (Mattie) Inez Taylor*[6], *Lucretia (Lula) Lindsey*[5], *Adron Leonard Lindsey Sr.*[4], *Frances (Frankie) Sharp*[3], *Charles W. Sr.*[2], *John Sr.*[1]) was born 26 Jan 1921 in Wright, Lauderdale County, AL, died 29 Aug 1976, and was buried in Oak Grove Cemetery, Lauderdale County, AL.

Fred married **Elizabeth Earline Allison**, daughter of **Presley (Press) Harrison Allison** and **Margie (Lady) J. Sharp**, 7 Nov 1942 in Lauderdale County, AL. Elizabeth was born 7 Feb 1923 in Lauderdale County, AL, died 13 Apr 1999, and was buried in Oak Grove Cemetery, Lauderdale County, AL.
(Duplicate Line. See Person 628)

1110. Ruby Mae Wood (*Martha (Mattie) Inez Taylor*[6], *Lucretia (Lula) Lindsey*[5], *Adron Leonard Lindsey Sr.*[4], *Frances (Frankie) Sharp*[3], *Charles W. Sr.*[2], *John Sr.*[1]) was born 19 Mar 1923 in Lauderdale County, AL, died 20 Dec 1996, and was buried in Wesley Chapel Cemetery, Lauderdale County, AL.

Ruby married **James Leo Winborn**, son of **Edward Homer Winborn** and **Elsie Elizabeth Wood**, 21 Oct 1942 in Lauderdale County, AL. James was born 7 Nov 1923 in Gravely Springs, Lauderdale County, AL, died 19 Dec 1990, and was buried in Wesley Chapel Cemetery, Lauderdale County, AL.

+ 2410 F i. **Glenda Gayle Winborn** was born in Lauderdale County, AL.

| + | 2411 | F | ii. | **Wanda Sue Winborn** was born in Lauderdale County, AL. |

+ 2411 F ii. **Wanda Sue Winborn** was born in Lauderdale County, AL.

2412 M iii. **Wilson Leo Winborn** was born 15 Apr 1945 in Gravely Springs, Lauderdale County, AL, died 2 Jan 1952, and was buried in Wesley Chapel Cemetery, Lauderdale County, AL.

+ 2413 M iv. **Willard Leon (Pete) Winborn** was born 27 Nov 1946 in Lauderdale County, AL.

+ 2414 M v. **Douglas Ray Winborn** was born 16 Jul 1948 in Lauderdale County, AL.

+ 2415 F vi. **Martha Faye Winborn** was born 9 Jun 1953 in Lauderdale County, AL.

2416 M vii. **Jimmy Glenn Winborn** was born 3 May 1956 in Lauderdale County, AL, died 24 Oct 1957, and was buried in Wesley Chapel Cemetery, Lauderdale County, AL.

2417 M viii. **Donnie Joe Winborn** was born 6 May 1968 in Lauderdale County, AL, died 6 Feb 1969, and was buried in Wesley Chapel Cemetery, Lauderdale County, AL.

1111. Floyde Virgil Wood (*Martha (Mattie) Inez Taylor*[6]*, Lucretia (Lula) Lindsey*[5]*, Adron Leonard Lindsey Sr.*[4]*, Frances (Frankie) Sharp*[3]*, Charles W. Sr.*[2]*, John Sr.*[1]) was born 15 Jun 1925 in Lauderdale County, AL, died 9 May 1984, and was buried in Oak Grove Cemetery, Lauderdale County, AL.

Floyde married **Gertrude Carter**, daughter of **Oscar W. Carter** and **Ella Bell Smith**, about 1952. Gertrude was born 7 Sep 1935 in Elkhart, Elkhart County, IN, died 11 Jul 1970, and was buried in Elkhart, Elkhart County, IN.

+ 2418 F i. **Sandra (Sandy) Jean Wood** was born 22 Dec 1954.

+ 2419 F ii. **Patricia (Pat) Wood** was born 21 Mar 1959.

Floyde next married ***Unk**.

Floyde next married **Sandra Kay Upthegrove**, daughter of **Osceola Upthegrove** and **Ella Forst**, 12 May 1975 in Lauderdale County, AL. Sandra was born 25 Oct 1943 in Palm Beach, FL.

1112. Annie Ruth Wood (*Martha (Mattie) Inez Taylor*[6]*, Lucretia (Lula) Lindsey*[5]*, Adron Leonard Lindsey Sr.*[4]*, Frances (Frankie) Sharp*[3]*, Charles W. Sr.*[2]*, John Sr.*[1]) was born 13 Aug 1927 in Lauderdale County, AL, died 18 Aug 2006, and was buried in Murphy's Chapel Cemetery, Lauderdale County, AL.

Annie married **Paul Byrum Bruce**, son of **Robert William Bruce** and **Mamie Rogers**, 30 Oct 1947 in Lauderdale County, AL. Paul was born 24 Nov 1916 in Lauderdale County, AL, died 9 Aug 1980, and was buried in Murphy's Chapel Cemetery, Lauderdale County, AL.

+ 2420 F i. **Brenda Ruth Bruce** was born 19 Nov 1948 in Lauderdale County, AL.

+ 2421 M ii. **Michael Wayne Bruce** was born 30 May 1951 in Lauderdale County, AL.

+ 2422 F iii. **Barbara Sue Bruce** was born 30 Oct 1954 in Lauderdale County, AL.

+ 2423 M iv. **John Daniel Bruce** was born 23 Jun 1958 in Lauderdale County, AL.

+ 2424 M v. **David Paul Bruce** was born 9 Jul 1961 in Lauderdale County, AL.

+ 2425 M vi. **Terry Lynn Bruce** was born 24 Dec 1964 in Lauderdale County, AL.

+ 2426 F vii. **Becky Lou Bruce** was born 11 Dec 1966 in Lauderdale County, AL.

1113. Glen Wood (*Martha (Mattie) Inez Taylor*[6]*, Lucretia (Lula) Lindsey*[5]*, Adron Leonard Lindsey Sr.*[4]*, Frances (Frankie) Sharp*[3]*, Charles W. Sr.*[2]*, John Sr.*[1]) was born 6 May 1929 in Lauderdale County, AL, died 7 May 2002, and was buried in Stoney Point Cemetery, Lauderdale County, AL.

Glen married **Geneva Arelia Underwood**, daughter of **William McKinley Underwood** and **Arelia Jeanetta Jackson**, 11 Jul 1953 in Iuka, Tishomingo County, MS. Geneva was born 29 Dec 1934 in Lauderdale County, AL.

+ 2427 F i. **Karen Denise Wood** was born 24 Sep 1954 in Lauderdale County, AL.

+ 2428 F ii. **Glenna Joy Wood** was born 25 Jan 1956 in Lauderdale County, AL.

+ 2429 M iii. **Kent Maurice Wood** was born 3 Feb 1958 in Lauderdale County, AL.

+ 2430 M iv. **Barry Keith Wood** was born 14 Jan 1960 in Lauderdale County, AL.

+ 2431 F v. **Lisa Rene Wood** was born 21 Mar 1962 in Lauderdale County, AL.

1114. Elza Darlene Wood (*Martha (Mattie) Inez Taylor*[6]*, Lucretia (Lula) Lindsey*[5]*, Adron Leonard Lindsey Sr.*[4]*, Frances (Frankie) Sharp*[3]*, Charles W. Sr.*[2]*, John Sr.*[1]) was born 29 Mar 1931 in Lauderdale County, AL, died 4 Apr 2009, and was buried in Pine Hill Cemetery, Lauderdale County, AL.

Elza married **James David Hipps**, son of **William Reeder Hipps** and **Hattie Bevis**, 18 Aug 1951 in Iuka, Tishomingo County, MS. James was born 14 Feb 1931 in Lauderdale County, AL, died 11 Apr 1994, and was buried in Pine Hill Cemetery, Lauderdale County, AL.

+ 2432 F   i.   **Debra Lynn Hipps** was born 22 May 1952 in Lauderdale County, AL.
+ 2433 F   ii.   **Jackie Diane Hipps** was born 9 Oct 1954 in Lauderdale County, AL.
+ 2434 F   iii. **Nancy Carol Hipps** was born 21 Jan 1961 in Lauderdale County, AL.
+ 2435 M   iv.   **Jesse James (Jamie) Hipps** was born 2 May 1965 in Lauderdale County, AL.

1116. Josephine Wood (*Martha (Mattie) Inez Taylor*^{6}, *Lucretia (Lula) Lindsey*^{5}, *Adron Leonard Lindsey Sr.*^{4}, *Frances (Frankie) Sharp*^{3}, *Charles W. Sr.*^{2}, *John Sr.*^{1}) was born 28 Jun 1934 in Lauderdale County, AL.

Josephine married **Owen Cole** about 1955.

+ 2436 M   i.   **Danny Joe Cole** was born 7 Nov 1955.
  2437 M   ii.   **Billy Ray Cole** was born 3 Dec 1956 in Indiana and died 3 Dec 1956 in Indiana.

Josephine next married **Ralph Glenn Pulley**. Ralph was born 27 May 1942.

1118. James Edward Wood (*Martha (Mattie) Inez Taylor*^{6}, *Lucretia (Lula) Lindsey*^{5}, *Adron Leonard Lindsey Sr.*^{4}, *Frances (Frankie) Sharp*^{3}, *Charles W. Sr.*^{2}, *John Sr.*^{1}) was born 22 May 1937 in Lauderdale County, AL, died 11 Sep 1990, and was buried in Oak Grove Cemetery, Lauderdale County, AL.

James married **Brenda Mae Grimes**, daughter of **Fletcher Grimes** and **Edna Matthews**, 15 Aug 1962 in Lauderdale County, AL. Brenda was born 19 Sep 1943 in Lauderdale County, AL.

+ 2438 M   i.   **James Gregory Wood** was born 6 Mar 1963.
  2439 M   ii.   **Brian Keith Wood** was born 12 Jul 1968.
  2440 M   iii. **Ryan Lee Wood** was born 12 Jul 1968.

1119. Harold Taylor Wood (*Martha (Mattie) Inez Taylor*^{6}, *Lucretia (Lula) Lindsey*^{5}, *Adron Leonard Lindsey Sr.*^{4}, *Frances (Frankie) Sharp*^{3}, *Charles W. Sr.*^{2}, *John Sr.*^{1}) was born 8 Oct 1939 in Lauderdale County, AL, died 27 Mar 2004, and was buried in Oak Grove Cemetery, Lauderdale County, AL.

Harold married **Mary Richardson**.

Harold next married **Sue Anderson**. Sue was born 8 Dec 1946.

+ 2441 M   i.   **Harold Wade Wood** was born 20 Jun 1975.

1120. Amanda Taylor (*George Willis Taylor*^{6}, *Lucretia (Lula) Lindsey*^{5}, *Adron Leonard Lindsey Sr.*^{4}, *Frances (Frankie) Sharp*^{3}, *Charles W. Sr.*^{2}, *John Sr.*^{1}).

Amanda married ***Unk Hill**.

1121. Lisa Taylor (*George Willis Taylor*^{6}, *Lucretia (Lula) Lindsey*^{5}, *Adron Leonard Lindsey Sr.*^{4}, *Frances (Frankie) Sharp*^{3}, *Charles W. Sr.*^{2}, *John Sr.*^{1}).

Lisa married ***Unk Wallace**.

1124. Cathy Taylor (*George Willis Taylor*^{6}, *Lucretia (Lula) Lindsey*^{5}, *Adron Leonard Lindsey Sr.*^{4}, *Frances (Frankie) Sharp*^{3}, *Charles W. Sr.*^{2}, *John Sr.*^{1}).

Cathy married ***Unk Lambert**.

1125. Christine Smith (*Winnie E. Lindsey*^{6}, *Hunter Lindsey*^{5}, *Adron Leonard Lindsey Sr.*^{4}, *Frances (Frankie) Sharp*^{3}, *Charles W. Sr.*^{2}, *John Sr.*^{1}) was born 5 Jan 1922 in Waterloo, Lauderdale County, AL.

Christine married **Jessie Mitchell**, son of **Jim Mitchell** and **Martha Fielder**, 30 Dec 1940 in Lauderdale County, AL. Jessie was born 27 May 1916 in Waterloo, Lauderdale County, AL.

1126. Raymond Glenn Springer (*Carmel Lindsey*[6], *Adron Leonard (Green) Lindsey Jr.*[5], *Adron Leonard Lindsey Sr.*[4], *Frances (Frankie) Sharp*[3], *Charles W. Sr.*[2], *John Sr.*[1]) was born 18 Dec 1927 in Lauderdale County, AL.

Raymond married **Betty Garrison** 3 Jul 1953.
   2442 M   i.   **Raymond Winston Springer** was born 21 May 1955.

1127. Dolly Katherine Lindsey (*Carlos (Bill) Lindsey*[6], *Adron Leonard (Green) Lindsey Jr.*[5], *Adron Leonard Lindsey Sr.*[4], *Frances (Frankie) Sharp*[3], *Charles W. Sr.*[2], *John Sr.*[1]) was born 13 Sep 1927 in Lauderdale County, AL, died 8 Dec 2000, and was buried in Tri-Cities Memorial Gardens, Florence, Lauderdale County, AL.

Dolly married **Paul Jerome Haeger**, son of **Lewis Haeger** and **Mary Copos**, 20 Mar 1958 in Iuka, Tishomingo County, MS. Paul was born 21 Mar 1929 in Lauderdale County, AL, died 3 Jun 1969, and was buried in St. Florian Catholic Cemetery, Lauderdale County, AL.
+ 2443 M   i.   **Michael Fay Haeger** was born 21 Mar 1946.
+ 2444 F   ii.   **Karen Ann Haeger** was born 5 Apr 1962 in Lauderdale County, AL.

1128. Jack Clayton Lindsey (*Carlos (Bill) Lindsey*[6], *Adron Leonard (Green) Lindsey Jr.*[5], *Adron Leonard Lindsey Sr.*[4], *Frances (Frankie) Sharp*[3], *Charles W. Sr.*[2], *John Sr.*[1]) was born 1 Jan 1935 in Lauderdale County, AL.

Jack married **Creda Ann Dunn**, daughter of **Horace Clinton Dunn** and **Geneva Mae Odom**, 6 Apr 1963 in Lauderdale County, AL. Creda was born 2 Sep 1941 in Franklin County, AL.

1129. William Lindsey McDonald (*Pauline Myran Lindsey*[6], *Adron Leonard (Green) Lindsey Jr.*[5], *Adron Leonard Lindsey Sr.*[4], *Frances (Frankie) Sharp*[3], *Charles W. Sr.*[2], *John Sr.*[1]) was born 7 Jun 1927 in Florence, Lauderdale County, AL.

      General Notes: "William and Dorothy are graduates of Florence State Teachers College, where Dorothy also received her master's degree. Dorothy is a retired teacher of arts and humanities, William is a retired TVA manager, retired Army Reserve Colonel and a retired United Methodist minister... He has been the Florence City Historian for many years..." William McDonald

William married **Dorothy Evelyn Carter**, daughter of **Edward Lacy Carter** and **Alma Thora Hall**, 3 Nov 1945 in Lauderdale County, AL. Dorothy was born 3 Dec 1927 in Lauderdale County, AL.
+ 2445 F   i.   **Nancy Carter McDonald** was born 6 Jun 1947 in Lauderdale County, AL.
+ 2446 F   ii.   **Suzannah Lee McDonald** was born 27 Apr 1955 in Lauderdale County, AL.

1130. Jimmy Joe McDonald (*Pauline Myran Lindsey*[6], *Adron Leonard (Green) Lindsey Jr.*[5], *Adron Leonard Lindsey Sr.*[4], *Frances (Frankie) Sharp*[3], *Charles W. Sr.*[2], *John Sr.*[1]) was born 24 Jul 1929 in Lauderdale County, AL.

Jimmy married **Elizabeth (Betty) Dean Staggs**, daughter of **Lester Daniel Staggs Sr.** and **Carrie Emalene Wylie**, 23 Dec 1948 in Iuka, Tishomingo County, MS. Elizabeth was born 2 Feb 1929 in Lauderdale County, AL.
+ 2447 F   i.   **Constance Jane McDonald** was born 3 Nov 1951 in Lauderdale County, AL.

Jimmy next married **Barbara Ann Brown** 21 Apr 1976. Barbara was born 21 Apr 1934 in Roanoke, Roanoke County, VA.
   2448 F   i.   **Rhonda Grubbs**.
   2449 M   ii.   **Barry Grubbs**.

1131. Marvin McDaniel McDonald (*Pauline Myran Lindsey*[6], *Adron Leonard (Green) Lindsey Jr.*[5], *Adron Leonard Lindsey Sr.*[4], *Frances (Frankie) Sharp*[3], *Charles W. Sr.*[2], *John Sr.*[1]) was born 25 Mar 1931 in Lauderdale County, AL, died 17 Apr 1994, and was buried in Pleasant Hill Cemetery, Lauderdale County, AL.

Marvin married **Helen Josphine Butler**, daughter of **Jesse Butler** and **Waymon Gibson**, in 1951 in Mississippi. Helen was born 19 Apr 1936 in Iron City, Wayne County, TN.
+ 2450 M   i.   **Phillip Dewayne McDonald Sr.** was born 30 Sep 1953 in Lauderdale County, AL.
+ 2451 M   ii.   **John Thomas McDonald** was born 11 Oct 1955 in Lauderdale County, AL.

+ 2452 F   iii.   **Melissa Ann McDonald** was born 31 Mar 1957 in Lauderdale County, AL.
+ 2453 F   iv.   **Paula Annette McDonald** was born 9 Sep 1959 in Lauderdale County, AL.

Marvin next married **Dorothy Ellen Broadfoot**, daughter of **Owen W. Broadfoot** and **Mildred White**, 2 Apr 1971 in Lauderdale County, AL. Dorothy was born 19 Apr 1926 in Lauderdale County, AL and died 30 Jul 1992.

1132. Bobby Jeffrey McDonald (*Pauline Myran Lindsey^6, Adron Leonard (Green) Lindsey Jr.^{5}, Adron Leonard Lindsey Sr.^{4}, Frances (Frankie) Sharp^3, Charles W. Sr.^{2}, John Sr.^{1}*) was born 19 May 1935 in Lauderdale County, AL.

Bobby married **Dorothy Dell Farris**, daughter of **Enlow Franklin Farris** and **Mary Ruth Nowlin**, 24 Oct 1953 in Iuka, Tishomingo County, MS. Dorothy was born 21 Oct 1935 in Collinwood, TN.
+ 2454 M   i.   **Jeffery Steven McDonald** was born 15 Aug 1954 in Lauderdale County, AL.

1133. Virginia Lee McDonald (*Pauline Myran Lindsey^6, Adron Leonard (Green) Lindsey Jr.^{5}, Adron Leonard Lindsey Sr.^{4}, Frances (Frankie) Sharp^3, Charles W. Sr.^{2}, John Sr.^{1}*) was born 18 Sep 1938 in Lauderdale County, AL.

General Notes: "Virginia and her brother, William McDonald came to the Wood Reunion 2005 at the old home place. She and I worked together at Humana Hospital in the 80's...." Sharon Wood

Virginia married **Charles David Lindsey Sr.**, son of **Edgar Bruce Lindsey** and **Thurza Dean**, 25 Apr 1956 in Lauderdale County, AL. Charles was born 25 Apr 1933 in Lauderdale County, AL.
+ 2455 F   i.   **Debra Leigh Lindsey** was born 10 Nov 1957 in Lauderdale County, AL.
+ 2456 M   ii.   **Charles David Lindsey Jr.** was born 5 Dec 1959 in Lauderdale County, AL.
+ 2457 M   iii.   **William Brian Lindsey** was born 26 May 1963 in Lauderdale County, AL.

1134. John Nelson McDonald Sr. (*Pauline Myran Lindsey^6, Adron Leonard (Green) Lindsey Jr.^{5}, Adron Leonard Lindsey Sr.^{4}, Frances (Frankie) Sharp^3, Charles W. Sr.^{2}, John Sr.^{1}*) was born 9 Jul 1943 in Lauderdale County, AL.

John married **Mary Ethel Harrison**, daughter of **Earl Cherry Harrison** and **Mildred Gaither Mills**, 4 Oct 1961 in Lauderdale County, AL. Mary was born 21 Sep 1943 in Lauderdale County, AL.
+ 2458 F   i.   **Marsha Lynn McDonald** was born 1 Mar 1963 in Lauderdale County, AL.
+ 2459 M   ii.   **John Nelson McDonald Jr.** was born 2 Dec 1964 in Lauderdale County, AL.

1135. Thomas Glenn McDonald (*Pauline Myran Lindsey^6, Adron Leonard (Green) Lindsey Jr.^{5}, Adron Leonard Lindsey Sr.^{4}, Frances (Frankie) Sharp^3, Charles W. Sr.^{2}, John Sr.^{1}*) was born 22 Oct 1945 in Lauderdale County, AL.

Thomas married **Margo Delores Wilson**, daughter of **James Earnest Wilson** and **Lucille Johnson**, 1 Sep 1965 in Lauderdale County, AL. Margo was born 17 Sep 1946 in Madison County, AL.
  2460 F   i.   **Amy Morgan McDonald** was born 12 Feb 1969 in Lauderdale County, AL.
+ 2461 M   ii.   **William Thomas McDonald** was born 6 Jan 1972 in Lauderdale County, AL.

1136. Ray Arlen Hall (*Laura Lindsey^6, Adron Leonard (Green) Lindsey Jr.^{5}, Adron Leonard Lindsey Sr.^{4}, Frances (Frankie) Sharp^3, Charles W. Sr.^{2}, John Sr.^{1}*) was born 24 Sep 1930 in Lauderdale County, AL.

Ray married **Jean Marie Morris**, daughter of **Charles F. Morris Sr.** and **Margaret F. Hogan**, 27 Sep 1952 in Quincy, MA. Jean was born 15 Sep 1932 in Quincy, MA.
+ 2462 F   i.   **Maureen Louise Hall** was born 26 Feb 1954 in Quincy, MA.
+ 2463 M   ii.   **James Ray Hall** was born 19 May 1955 in Quincy, MA.
+ 2464 F   iii.   **Donna J. Hall** was born 15 Jul 1957 in Quincy, MA.
+ 2465 M   iv.   **William (Bill) Charles Hall** was born 16 Dec 1959 in Quincy, MA.
+ 2466 F   v.   **Janet Marie Hall** was born 5 Mar 1963 in Quincy, MA.
+ 2467 M   vi.   **Josesph Michael Hall** was born 2 Dec 1964 in Quincy, MA.
  2468 F   vii.   **Joane Eileen Hall** was born 19 Mar 1967 in Quincy, MA.
  2469 F   viii.   **Diane Elizabeth Hall** was born 15 Feb 1970 in Quincy, MA.

1137. James Franklin Hall Jr. (*Laura Lindsey[6], Adron Leonard (Green) Lindsey Jr.[5], Adron Leonard Lindsey Sr.[4], Frances (Frankie) Sharp[3], Charles W. Sr.[2], John Sr.[1]*) was born 4 Apr 1934 in Lauderdale County, AL.

James married **Kathleen Ophelia Robinson**, daughter of **Nelson Robinson** and **Eunice Ophelia Sides**, 6 Sep 1958 in Colbert County, AL. Kathleen was born 30 Nov 1934 in Double Springs, Winston County, AL.
+ 2470 F i. **Lura Kathleen Hall** was born 17 Sep 1962 in Lauderdale County, AL.
+ 2471 F ii. **Stephanie Amanda Hall** was born 2 Jul 1965 in Lauderdale County, AL.
+ 2472 M iii. **David Nelson Hall** was born 12 Oct 1972 in Lauderdale County, AL.

1138. Howard Thomas Hall (*Laura Lindsey[6], Adron Leonard (Green) Lindsey Jr.[5], Adron Leonard Lindsey Sr.[4], Frances (Frankie) Sharp[3], Charles W. Sr.[2], John Sr.[1]*) was born 24 Aug 1936 in Lauderdale County, AL.

Howard married **Francis Louise Cox**, daughter of **Otis Lee Cox** and **Dorothy J. Godsey**, 25 Jun 1959 in Lauderdale County, AL. Francis was born 11 Jun 1941 in Winston County, AL.
2473 M i. **Lindsey Thomas Hall** was born 1 Dec 1960.
2474 M ii. **Howard Godsey Hall** was born 23 Mar 1964.

1139. Mary Nell Lindsey (*Nelson McCaun Lindsey[6], Adron Leonard (Green) Lindsey Jr.[5], Adron Leonard Lindsey Sr.[4], Frances (Frankie) Sharp[3], Charles W. Sr.[2], John Sr.[1]*) was born 10 Aug 1941 in Colbert County, AL.

Mary married **Robert F. Atwell Jr.**, son of **Robert F. Atwell Sr.** and **Hazel Brewer**, 22 Aug 1958 in Lafayette, GA. Robert was born 7 Oct 1940 in Lauderdale County, AL.
+ 2475 F i. **Joanna Kay Atwell** was born 12 Oct 1956 in Colbert County, AL.
+ 2476 F ii. **Selina Marie Atwell** was born 18 May 1959 in Biloxi, MS.
+ 2477 M iii. **Robert F. Atwell III** was born 31 Jan 1961 in Quantico, VA.

1140. Mae Virginia Lindsey (*Nelson McCaun Lindsey[6], Adron Leonard (Green) Lindsey Jr.[5], Adron Leonard Lindsey Sr.[4], Frances (Frankie) Sharp[3], Charles W. Sr.[2], John Sr.[1]*) was born 25 Feb 1946 in Colbert County, AL.

Mae married **James Roland Robbins**. James was born 23 Feb 1945.
+ 2478 F i. **Vera Maelin Robbins** was born 23 Mar 1962.
+ 2479 F ii. **Melissa Ann Robbins** was born 11 Mar 1968.

Mae next married **Bruce Faust**.

1141. Linda Sue Lindsey (*Nelson McCaun Lindsey[6], Adron Leonard (Green) Lindsey Jr.[5], Adron Leonard Lindsey Sr.[4], Frances (Frankie) Sharp[3], Charles W. Sr.[2], John Sr.[1]*) was born 22 Mar 1954 in Colbert County, AL.

Linda married **Vernon Keith Eubanks**, son of **V. L. Eubanks** and **Mary Pauline Crowell**, 24 Aug 1973 in Colbert County, AL. Vernon was born 9 Oct 1954 in Colbert County, AL, died 13 Jan 1980, and was buried in Oakwood Cemetery, Sheffield, Colbert County, AL.

Linda next married **Roger Dale Williamson**. Roger was born 9 Oct 1948.
2480 F i. **Courtney Lindsey Williamson** was born 4 Apr 1979.

1142. Howard Carlos Lindsey (*Howard Shannon Lindsey[6], Adron Leonard (Green) Lindsey Jr.[5], Adron Leonard Lindsey Sr.[4], Frances (Frankie) Sharp[3], Charles W. Sr.[2], John Sr.[1]*) was born 24 Apr 1941 in Columbus, GA.

Howard married **Sandra Toth**.
2481 M i. **James Howard Lindsey** was born 22 Aug 1964.
2482 M ii. **Michael Shannon Lindsey** was born 1 May 1967.

Howard next married **Jane Murtishaw**.

1143. Iris Gail Lindsey (*Howard Shannon Lindsey[6], Adron Leonard (Green) Lindsey Jr.[5], Adron Leonard Lindsey Sr.[4], Frances (Frankie) Sharp[3], Charles W. Sr.[2], John Sr.[1]*) was born 30 Nov 1942 in Columbus, GA.

Iris married **Joseph Herbert Knicely** 6 Jun 1964.

2483 F i. **Kimberly Lynn Knicely** was born 10 Jun 1967 in Melbourne, FL.

Iris next married **Ed A. Damaan**.

1145. Richard G. Lindsey (*Marvin Glenn Lindsey⁶, Adron Leonard (Green) Lindsey Jr.⁵, Adron Leonard Lindsey Sr.⁴, Frances (Frankie) Sharp³, Charles W. Sr.², John Sr.¹*) was born 26 Jan 1947, died 6 Oct 1992, and was buried in Valhalla Memorial Gardens, Huntsville, AL.

Richard married **Linda Maureen Clonts** 29 Aug 1970. Linda was born 6 Oct 1948 in New Market, AL.
2484 M i. **Christopher Glenn Lindsey** was born 4 Feb 1973.
2485 F ii. **Susan Maureen Lindsey** was born 6 Oct 1978.

1146. Andrea Ophelia Ellender Lindsey (*Marvin Glenn Lindsey⁶, Adron Leonard (Green) Lindsey Jr.⁵, Adron Leonard Lindsey Sr.⁴, Frances (Frankie) Sharp³, Charles W. Sr.², John Sr.¹*) was born 16 Aug 1948.

Andrea married **Michael Stewart**. Michael was born 16 Aug 1948.

1147. Brenda Jean Lindsey (*Marvin Glenn Lindsey⁶, Adron Leonard (Green) Lindsey Jr.⁵, Adron Leonard Lindsey Sr.⁴, Frances (Frankie) Sharp³, Charles W. Sr.², John Sr.¹*) was born 16 Apr 1951.

Brenda married **Timothy Alan Ingram**. Timothy was born 23 Jul 1952.

1148. William Richard Lindsey (*Claude Raymond Lindsey Sr.⁶, Adron Leonard (Green) Lindsey Jr.⁵, Adron Leonard Lindsey Sr.⁴, Frances (Frankie) Sharp³, Charles W. Sr.², John Sr.¹*) was born 31 Aug 1939 in Lauderdale County, AL.

General Notes: "Richard was born before Claud entered the Air Force at the beginning of WWII. Richard was a school administrator at Muncie, Indiana, prior to 1974. In September of that year he witnessed a tragic incident involving his fifteen year old son, William, who was attacked and murdered by a black student in the hall at the high school where Richard was principal. Richard and his family moved from Muncie soon afterwards. The last address I had for them was Hueytown, Alabama; this was the location of Richard's mother-in-law, Mrs, Jewel Price..." William McDonald.

William married **Rosalyn Virginia Price**, daughter of **Jess L. Price** and **Jewell Virginia Judd**, 14 Feb 1959 in Lauderdale County, AL. Rosalyn was born 28 Nov 1942 in Birmingham, Jefferson County, AL.
2486 M i. **William Dennis Lindsey** was born 10 Sep 1959, died 15 Sep 1974, and was buried in Tri-Cities Memorial Gardens, Florence, Lauderdale County, AL.
+ 2487 F ii. **Melissa Lindsey** was born 5 Jan 1969.

1149. Patricia Elois Lindsey (*Claude Raymond Lindsey Sr.⁶, Adron Leonard (Green) Lindsey Jr.⁵, Adron Leonard Lindsey Sr.⁴, Frances (Frankie) Sharp³, Charles W. Sr.², John Sr.¹*) was born 5 Sep 1947.

Patricia married **James Harold Kicker** 28 Dec 1972. James was born 23 Feb 1936.
2488 M i. **David Clinton Kicker** was born 2 Feb 1974.

1150. Lucy Claudette Lindsey (*Claude Raymond Lindsey Sr.⁶, Adron Leonard (Green) Lindsey Jr.⁵, Adron Leonard Lindsey Sr.⁴, Frances (Frankie) Sharp³, Charles W. Sr.², John Sr.¹*) was born 3 Jan 1950.

Lucy married **Coy Oscar Nichols** 6 May 1972. Coy was born 18 Mar 1941.
2489 F i. **Anna Suzanne Nichols** was born 13 Nov 1982.
2490 M ii. **Arthur Lindsey Nichols** was born 1 Jun 1986.

1151. Claude Raymond Lindsey Jr. (*Claude Raymond Lindsey Sr.⁶, Adron Leonard (Green) Lindsey Jr.⁵, Adron Leonard Lindsey Sr.⁴, Frances (Frankie) Sharp³, Charles W. Sr.², John Sr.¹*) was born 10 Mar 1953 in Montgomery, AL.

Claude married **Cindy Day**. Cindy was born in Montgomery, AL.
2491 F i. **Autumn Lynn Lindsey**.

Claude next married **Teresa Prater**. Teresa was born in Atlanta, GA.

2492 M i. **Daniel Eugene Prater Lindsey**.

2493 M ii. **Allen Wayne Lindsey** was born 1 Apr 1976.

1152. Judith (Judy) Lynn Lindsey (*Claude Raymond Lindsey Sr.*[6], *Adron Leonard (Green) Lindsey Jr.*[5], *Adron Leonard Lindsey Sr.*[4], *Frances (Frankie) Sharp*[3], *Charles W. Sr.*[2], *John Sr.*[1]) was born 27 May 1955 in Montgomery, AL.

Judith married **David Fields**. David was born in Montgomery, AL.

2494 M i. **Jacob Michael Fields** was born 17 Dec 1979.

2495 M ii. **Charles Harrison Fields** was born 24 Apr 1986.

1155. Jewel Dean Young (*William (Bill) Mack Young*[6], *Eddie Young*[5], *Mary M. (Polly II) Lindsey*[4], *Frances (Frankie) Sharp*[3], *Charles W. Sr.*[2], *John Sr.*[1]) was born 2 Dec 1919 in Lauderdale County, AL, died 2 Jun 2000, and was buried in Tri-Cities Memorial Gardens, Florence, Lauderdale County, AL.

Jewel married **Robert Monroe Chowning**, son of **Arthur E. Chowning** and **Mary Linia Johnson**, 23 Dec 1937 in Lauderdale County, AL. Robert was born 11 Oct 1911 in Martin Mill, TN, died 21 Jul 1980, and was buried in Tri-Cities Memorial Gardens, Florence, Lauderdale County, AL.

+ 2496 F i. **Bobbie Dean Chowning** was born 10 Dec 1940 in Lauderdale County, AL.

1156. Melvin Eugene Young (*William (Bill) Mack Young*[6], *Eddie Young*[5], *Mary M. (Polly II) Lindsey*[4], *Frances (Frankie) Sharp*[3], *Charles W. Sr.*[2], *John Sr.*[1]) was born 15 Mar 1926 in Lauderdale County, AL and was buried in Stutts Road Cemetery, Greenhill, Lauderdale County, AL.

Melvin married **Mable Jewel South**, daughter of **J. W. Fairres** and **Cora Mars**, 3 Feb 1943 in Lauderdale County, AL. Mable was born 19 Jun 1921 in Lauderdale County, AL.

2497 M i. **Melvin Ray Young**.

2498 M ii. **Larry Young** was born 30 May 1946.

2499 M iii. **Gary Young** was born in 1949.

2500 M iv. **David Young** was born in 1950.

2501 F v. **Nancy Young** was born in 1954.

2502 F vi. **Sue Young** was born in 1955.

Melvin next married **Ida Edith South** 1 May 1944 in Lauderdale County, AL.

Melvin next married **Ruth Smith** 2 Mar 1957.

2503 F i. **June Young** was born in 1957.

2504 F ii. **Martha Young** was born in 1959.

2505 F iii. **Angie Young** was born in 1963.

2506 M iv. **Dennis Young** was born in 1964 and died in 1967.

1157. Ruby Dale Young (*William (Bill) Mack Young*[6], *Eddie Young*[5], *Mary M. (Polly II) Lindsey*[4], *Frances (Frankie) Sharp*[3], *Charles W. Sr.*[2], *John Sr.*[1]) was born 11 Nov 1931 in Lauderdale County, AL and was buried in Lauderdale County, AL.

Ruby married **Willard Miles**.

Ruby next married **Samuel Sandock** about 1957 in South Bend, IN.

1158. James Robert Young (*William (Bill) Mack Young*[6], *Eddie Young*[5], *Mary M. (Polly II) Lindsey*[4], *Frances (Frankie) Sharp*[3], *Charles W. Sr.*[2], *John Sr.*[1]) was born 15 Aug 1935 in Lauderdale County, AL.

James married **Bille J. Burns**, daughter of **Marvin A. Burns** and **Waymon England**, 22 Mar 1954 in Iuka, Tishomingo County, MS. Bille was born 7 Mar 1938 in Lauderdale County, AL.

+ 2507 M i. **Richard Dale Young** was born 12 Feb 1955 in Lauderdale County, AL.

+ 2508 F ii. **Karen Delane Young** was born 15 Mar 1958 in Lauderdale County, AL.

+ 2509 F iii. **Sherrie Lynn Young** was born 2 May 1961 in Lauderdale County, AL.

+ 2510 M   iv.   **Kim Russell Young** was born 6 Jun 1962 in Lauderdale County, AL.
+ 2511 F   v.   **Lesa Renee Young** was born 12 Aug 1963 in Lauderdale County, AL.
+ 2512 M   vi.   **Donald Ray Young** was born 22 Oct 1966 in Lauderdale County, AL.

1159. Shirley Ann Young (*William (Bill) Mack Young*[6], *Eddie Young*[5], *Mary M. (Polly II) Lindsey*[4], *Frances (Frankie) Sharp*[3], *Charles W. Sr.*[2], *John Sr.*[1]) was born 11 Feb 1939 in Lauderdale County, AL.

Shirley married **Kenneth Moore Richards**, son of **Pad J. Richards** and **Rosa Mae Rhodes**, 11 Jan 1963 in Lauderdale County, AL. Kenneth was born 20 May 1936 in Lauderdale County, AL.
+ 2513 F   i.   **Shanie Leigh Richards** was born 30 Jul 1969.
+ 2514 F   ii.   **Heather Dawn Richards** was born 2 Apr 1974.

1160. Clara Kay Biggs (*Nellie Bell Young*[6], *Eddie Young*[5], *Mary M. (Polly II) Lindsey*[4], *Frances (Frankie) Sharp*[3], *Charles W. Sr.*[2], *John Sr.*[1]).

Clara married ***Unk Beckett**.

1165. Cecil Lloyd Young (*Earnest Edward Young*[6], *Eddie Young*[5], *Mary M. (Polly II) Lindsey*[4], *Frances (Frankie) Sharp*[3], *Charles W. Sr.*[2], *John Sr.*[1]) was born 22 Dec 1926 in Lauderdale County, AL, died 7 Mar 2002, and was buried in Greenview Memorial Park, Florence, Lauderdale County, AL.

Cecil married **Arline Lee Moody**, daughter of **Ernest Jeremiah Moody** and **Floy Lee Skipworth**, 3 Mar 1947 in Iuka, Tishomingo County, MS. Arline was born 2 Dec 1930 in Lauderdale County, AL.
+ 2515 F   i.   **Wanda Sue Young** was born 28 Jan 1948 in Lauderdale County, AL.
+ 2516 F   ii.   **Teresa Diane Young** was born 19 Nov 1953 in Lauderdale County, AL.

1166. Jay Fred Young (*Earnest Edward Young*[6], *Eddie Young*[5], *Mary M. (Polly II) Lindsey*[4], *Frances (Frankie) Sharp*[3], *Charles W. Sr.*[2], *John Sr.*[1]) was born 28 May 1929 in Lauderdale County, AL.

Jay married **Virginia (Jenny) A. Boswell**, daughter of **Wilbur Boswell** and **Irene Niezgodski**, about 1953 in Mishawaka, St Joseph County, IN. Virginia was born 18 May 1927 in South Bend, IN.
+ 2517 F   i.   **Joyce Fredia Young** was born 19 Feb 1954 in South Bend, IN.
+ 2518 F   ii.   **Brenda Gaye Young** was born 25 Dec 1958 in South Bend, IN.

Jay next married **Flora Marie Wallace**, daughter of **C. W. Wallace** and **Helen *Unk**, 2 Feb 1963 in Mishawaka, St Joseph County, IN. Flora was born 8 Aug 1916 in South Bend, IN, died 20 Dec 1971, and was buried in Mishawaka, St Joseph County, IN.

1167. Doyal Lee Young Sr. (*Earnest Edward Young*[6], *Eddie Young*[5], *Mary M. (Polly II) Lindsey*[4], *Frances (Frankie) Sharp*[3], *Charles W. Sr.*[2], *John Sr.*[1]) was born 28 Aug 1937 in Lauderdale County, AL, died 10 Jan 1994, and was buried in Murphy's Chapel Cemetery, Lauderdale County, AL.

Doyal married **Edith Ann Haddock**, daughter of **Earl Haddock** and **Pearl Joiner**.
+ 2519 M   i.   **Edward (Eddie) Earl Young** was born 12 Dec 1956 in Lauderdale County, AL.
  2520 F   ii.   **Joan Young**.

Doyal next married **Dona Pearl Moss** 16 Feb 1965 in Lauderdale County, AL. Dona was born 7 Jun 1932 in Cherokee County, TX.

Doyal next married **Emma Laverne Price** 16 Oct 1970 in Lauderdale County, AL. Emma was born 3 Jun 1944 in Lauderdale County, AL and died 4 Feb 2001.
  2521 M   i.   **Doyal Lee Young Jr.**

1168. Harold Moore Young (*Earnest Edward Young*[6], *Eddie Young*[5], *Mary M. (Polly II) Lindsey*[4], *Frances (Frankie) Sharp*[3], *Charles W. Sr.*[2], *John Sr.*[1]) was born 27 Oct 1942 in Lauderdale County, AL.

Harold married **Doris Valentine**, daughter of **Herbert W. Valentine** and **Helen Zanof**. Doris was born 17 Sep 1943 in Little Rock, AR.

2522 M i. **Donald Alan Young** was born 6 Nov 1966 in Little Rock, AR.
2523 M ii. **Ronald Wayne Young** was born 6 Feb 1971 in Little Rock, AR.

Harold next married **Tommie Jean Johnson**, daughter of **Jimmy P. Johnson** and **Gladys Shoptaw**, 19 Oct 1990 in Little Rock, AR. Tommie was born 7 Dec 1943 in Little Rock, AR.

1169. Hazel Joyce Young (*Earnest Edward Young*[6], *Eddie Young*[5], *Mary M. (Polly II) Lindsey*[4], *Frances (Frankie) Sharp*[3], *Charles W. Sr.*[2], *John Sr.*[1]) was born 16 Oct 1944 in Lauderdale County, AL.

Hazel married **Floyd Eldridge Keeton**, son of **Andrew Jackson Keeton** and **Nora Mae White**, 10 Sep 1960 in Lauderdale County, AL. Floyd was born 13 Sep 1939 in Lauderdale County, AL.
+ 2524 F i. **Kathy Marie Keeton** was born 23 Jul 1961 in Lawrenceburg, Lawrence County, TN.
+ 2525 M ii. **Ricky Dale Keeton** was born 16 Apr 1963 in Lauderdale County, AL.
+ 2526 M iii. **Randy Lee Keeton** was born 7 Feb 1966 in Lauderdale County, AL.
+ 2527 F iv. **Karen Lynn Keeton** was born 3 Jun 1970 in Lauderdale County, AL.

1170. Elsie Irene Witt (*Willie Leona Young*[6], *Eddie Young*[5], *Mary M. (Polly II) Lindsey*[4], *Frances (Frankie) Sharp*[3], *Charles W. Sr.*[2], *John Sr.*[1]) was born 1 Feb 1936 in Lauderdale County, AL.

Elsie married **Gene Cambel**.

Elsie next married ***Unk Doss**.

1172. Macil Bethrine Young (*Odus Clarence Young Sr.*[6], *Eddie Young*[5], *Mary M. (Polly II) Lindsey*[4], *Frances (Frankie) Sharp*[3], *Charles W. Sr.*[2], *John Sr.*[1]) was born 25 Mar 1928 in Lauderdale County, AL, died 21 Jan 1995, and was buried in Canaan Cemetery, Lauderdale County, AL. Another name for Macil was Macil B. Young.

Macil married **Ralph Roland Gooch**, son of **Homer Clyde Gooch** and **Lizzie Smith Wallace**, 9 Aug 1945 in Lauderdale County, AL. Ralph was born 4 Sep 1923 in Lauderdale County, AL, died 21 Jan 1995, and was buried in Canaan Cemetery, Lauderdale County, AL. Another name for Ralph was Ralph Rowland Gooch.
2528 M i. **Larry Robert Gooch** was born 8 Oct 1946 in Lauderdale County, AL, died in 1959, and was buried in Canaan Cemetery, Lauderdale County, AL.
+ 2529 F ii. **Linda Joyce Gooch** was born 8 Oct 1947 in Lauderdale County, AL.
+ 2530 M iii. **Donnie Lee Gooch** was born 30 Apr 1948 in Lauderdale County, AL.
+ 2531 F iv. **Janet Faye Gooch** was born 16 Nov 1950 in Lauderdale County, AL.
+ 2532 M v. **Jerry Dewayne Gooch** was born 25 Jul 1952 in Lauderdale County, AL.
+ 2533 F vi. **Kathy Ann Gooch** was born 18 Feb 1954 in Lauderdale County, AL.
+ 2534 F vii. **Sharon Jean Gooch** was born 30 Mar 1957 in Florence, Lauderdale County, AL.
+ 2535 M viii. **Timmy Lee Gooch** was born 30 Nov 1958 in Lauderdale County, AL.
+ 2536 F ix. **Marcia Lynn Gooch** was born 7 Aug 1962 in Lauderdale County, AL.
+ 2537 F x. **Marsha Kay Gooch** was born 7 Aug 1962 in Florence, Lauderdale County, AL.
2538 M xi. **Perry Randal Gooch** was born 3 Mar 1963 in Lauderdale County, AL, died 10 Dec 1977, and was buried in Canaan Cemetery, Lauderdale County, AL.

1173. Carlene Vernial Young (*Odus Clarence Young Sr.*[6], *Eddie Young*[5], *Mary M. (Polly II) Lindsey*[4], *Frances (Frankie) Sharp*[3], *Charles W. Sr.*[2], *John Sr.*[1]) was born 31 Mar 1933 in Lauderdale County, AL.

Carlene married **Edgar Phillip Heck** 25 Jun 1949 in Corinth, Alcorn County, MS. Edgar was born 17 Aug 1927 in Hawkins County, TN, died 4 Feb 2001, and was buried in Highland Cemetery, Hawkins County, TN.
+ 2539 F i. **Vicki Ann Heck** was born 2 Aug 1950 in Lauderdale County, AL.
2540 F ii. **Sandra Kay Heck** was born 15 Jan 1956 in Jesup, GA.
2541 M iii. **Eugene Philip Heck** was born 16 Mar 1959 in Jesup, GA.
2542 M iv. **Kenneth Rowland Heck** was born 4 Feb 1964 in Hawkins County, TN.
+ 2543 F v. **Leisa Carol Heck** was born 1 Jun 1967 in Hawkins County, TN.

1174. Clarence William (C. W.) Young (*Odus Clarence Young Sr.*[6], *Eddie Young*[5], *Mary M. (Polly II) Lindsey*[4], *Frances (Frankie) Sharp*[3], *Charles W. Sr.*[2], *John Sr.*[1]) was born 14 Apr 1937 in Lauderdale County, AL and died 15 Jun 1998 in Lauderdale County, AL.

Clarence married **Patricia Ann Dotson** 4 Oct 1958 in St. Joseph County, IN. Patricia was born 14 Aug 1939 in Dyersburg, Dyer County, TN.

+ 2544 M i. **William Mark Young** was born 4 Jan 1961 in St. Joseph County, IN.

  2545 M ii. **Richard Matthew Young** was born 10 Sep 1964 in St. Joseph County, IN.

1175. Melvin Lee Young (*Odus Clarence Young Sr.*[6]*, Eddie Young*[5]*, Mary M. (Polly II) Lindsey*[4]*, Frances (Frankie) Sharp*[3]*, Charles W. Sr.*[2]*, John Sr.*[1]) was born 16 Oct 1939 in Lauderdale County, AL, died 4 Aug 1993, and was buried in McKinney Cemetery, Rogersville, TN.

Melvin married **Beverly Parker**, daughter of **Unknown** and **Unknown**, 9 Oct 1958. Beverly was born 15 Dec 1940 and died 19 Feb 1999 in St. Joseph County, IN.

+ 2546 F i. **Tanya Lynn Young** was born 6 May 1959 in St. Joseph County, IN.

+ 2547 M ii. **Bret Allen Young Sr.** was born 8 Jan 1961 in St. Joseph County, IN.

  2548 F iii. **Kim Lee Young** was born 1 Aug 1963 in St. Joseph County, IN.

+ 2549 M iv. **Troy Lee Young** was born 1 Aug 1963 in St. Joseph County, IN.

+ 2550 F v. **Dawn Marie Young** was born 2 Feb 1971.

1177. Robert Arnold Murphy (*Jessie Bell Dearen*[6]*, Mary Francis (Molly) Young*[5]*, Mary M. (Polly II) Lindsey*[4]*, Frances (Frankie) Sharp*[3]*, Charles W. Sr.*[2]*, John Sr.*[1]) was born 25 Jul 1909 in Lauderdale County, AL, died 13 Aug 1990, and was buried in Greenview Memorial Park, Florence, Lauderdale County, AL.

Robert married **Myrtle Irene Perkins**, daughter of **Will Perkins** and **Hattie A. Howard**, 5 Nov 1928 in Lauderdale County, AL. Myrtle was born 14 Dec 1912 in Lauderdale County, AL, died 30 May 1957, and was buried in Greenview Memorial Park, Florence, Lauderdale County, AL.

+ 2551 M i. **Dewey Arnold Murphy** was born 12 Dec 1929 in Lauderdale County, AL, died 25 Sep 2003, and was buried in Tri-Cities Memorial Gardens, Florence, Lauderdale County, AL.

+ 2552 F ii. **Bobbie Joan Murphy** was born 6 Apr 1932 in Lauderdale County, AL.

+ 2553 F iii. **Margaret Sue Murphy** was born 16 Jul 1936 in Lauderdale County, AL.

Robert next married **Estelle Willis Cobb**.

1179. Doyal Lee Murphy (*Jessie Bell Dearen*[6]*, Mary Francis (Molly) Young*[5]*, Mary M. (Polly II) Lindsey*[4]*, Frances (Frankie) Sharp*[3]*, Charles W. Sr.*[2]*, John Sr.*[1]) was born 24 Sep 1913 in Lauderdale County, AL, died 27 Mar 1948, and was buried in Florence City Cemetery, Florence, Lauderdale County, AL.

Doyal married **Mary Earline Perkins**, daughter of **Foster Edwin Perkins** and **Lillie White**, 5 Dec 1931 in Lauderdale County, AL. Mary was born 7 May 1914 in Loretto, Lawrence County, TN.

+ 2554 M i. **Kenneth Lee Murphy** was born 30 Sep 1936 in Lauderdale County, AL.

+ 2555 F ii. **Elizabeth Ann Murphy** was born 28 Jan 1940 in Lauderdale County, AL.

1180. Jenny Ione Murphy (*Jessie Bell Dearen*[6]*, Mary Francis (Molly) Young*[5]*, Mary M. (Polly II) Lindsey*[4]*, Frances (Frankie) Sharp*[3]*, Charles W. Sr.*[2]*, John Sr.*[1]) was born 22 Feb 1916 in Waco, McLennan County, TX, died 15 Apr 2001, and was buried in Mt. Zion Cemetery, Lauderdale County, AL.

Jenny married **Charles Oshell Goode**, son of **Jess N. Goode** and **Susie Newbern**, 21 Sep 1938 in Lauderdale County, AL. Charles was born 30 Sep 1915 in Lauderdale County, AL, died 20 Apr 1980, and was buried in Mt. Zion Cemetery, Lauderdale County, AL.

+ 2556 M i. **Marshall Elbert Goode** was born 13 Dec 1941 in Lauderdale County, AL.

1181. Karl Jones Murphy (*Jessie Bell Dearen*[6]*, Mary Francis (Molly) Young*[5]*, Mary M. (Polly II) Lindsey*[4]*, Frances (Frankie) Sharp*[3]*, Charles W. Sr.*[2]*, John Sr.*[1]) was born 23 Oct 1917 in Lorena, TX, died 13 Nov 1992, and was buried in Tri-Cities Memorial Gardens, Florence, Lauderdale County, AL.

Karl married **Martha Elizabeth Gatlin**, daughter of **H. Edwin Gatlin** and **Inez Hicks**, 25 Nov 1946 in Lauderdale County, AL. Martha was born 17 Jun 1925 in Lauderdale County, AL, died 10 Jun 1997, and was buried in Tri-Cities Memorial Gardens, Florence, Lauderdale County, AL.

+ 2557 M i. **Gary Carl Murphy** was born 5 Feb 1949 in Colbert County, AL.

  2558 F ii. **Paula Lane Murphy** was born 6 Apr 1950 in Colbert County, AL.

+ 2559 F iii. **Martha Ann Murphy** was born 19 Jun 1951 in Colbert County, AL.

+ 2560 M iv. **Kelley Lee Murphy** was born 15 Jun 1960 in Colbert County, AL.

1182. Ora Kyleene Murphy (*Jessie Bell Dearen*[6], *Mary Francis (Molly) Young*[5], *Mary M. (Polly II) Lindsey*[4], *Frances (Frankie) Sharp*[3], *Charles W. Sr.*[2], *John Sr.*[1]) was born 27 May 1920 in Lauderdale County, AL.

Ora married **Milton Lee Knight**, son of **General Lee Knight** and ***Unk Maples**, 1 Sep 1940 in Lauderdale County, AL. Milton was born 3 Jul 1914 in Lauderdale County, AL, died 28 Nov 1982, and was buried in Sheffield, Colbert County, AL.
+ 2561 F i. **Montez Elaine Knight** was born 18 Jun 1941 in Colbert County, AL.
  2562 F ii. **Melanie Lee Knight** was born 17 Apr 1943 in Colbert County, AL, died 20 Apr 1943, and was buried in Sheffield Cemetery, Sheffield, Colbert County, AL.
+ 2563 F iii. **Tessa Maria Knight** was born 12 May 1947 in Colbert County, AL.

Ora next married **Kermit E. Summerall**.

1183. Hazel Inez Dearen (*William Lee Dearen*[6], *Mary Francis (Molly) Young*[5], *Mary M. (Polly II) Lindsey*[4], *Frances (Frankie) Sharp*[3], *Charles W. Sr.*[2], *John Sr.*[1]) was born 14 Aug 1917 in Waco, McLennan County, TX.

Hazel married **William (Bob) R. Rucker**, son of **Thomas Monroe Rucker** and **Janie Edwards**, 21 Jun 1941 in Waco, McLennan County, TX. William was born 19 Oct 1917 in Denton, TX and died 10 Nov 1991 in Texas.
+ 2564 M i. **William (Bill) Dearen Rucker** was born 21 Jan 1947 in Waco, McLennan County, TX.
+ 2565 F ii. **Cynthia (Cindy) Lynn Rucker** was born 22 Jun 1951 in Houston, Harris County, TX.

1184. Mildred Pauline Dearen (*William Lee Dearen*[6], *Mary Francis (Molly) Young*[5], *Mary M. (Polly II) Lindsey*[4], *Frances (Frankie) Sharp*[3], *Charles W. Sr.*[2], *John Sr.*[1]) was born 29 Sep 1919 in Waco, McLennan County, TX.

Mildred married **Harold M. Harper**, son of **John Wesley Harper** and **Eddie *Unk**, 21 Jul 1941 in Waco, McLennan County, TX. Harold was born 2 Jan 1917 in Waco, McLennan County, TX, died 29 May 1992, and was buried in Rosenthal Cemetery, Waco, McLennon County, TX.
+ 2566 F i. **Donna Sue Harper** was born 5 Oct 1944 in Waco, McLennan County, TX.

1185. Vera Mae Dearen (*William Lee Dearen*[6], *Mary Francis (Molly) Young*[5], *Mary M. (Polly II) Lindsey*[4], *Frances (Frankie) Sharp*[3], *Charles W. Sr.*[2], *John Sr.*[1]) was born 29 Sep 1922 in Waco, McLennan County, TX.

Vera married **Eugene McLaughlin**, son of **Albert McLaughlin** and **Jane *Unk**, 31 Mar 1943 in Waco, McLennan County, TX. Eugene was born 11 Sep 1917 in Detroit, Wayne County, MI, died 10 Dec 1987, and was buried in Restland Memorial Park, Dallas, TX.
  2567 F i. **Sharon Ann McLaughlin** was born 24 Oct 1944 in Waco, McLennan County, TX.
+ 2568 F ii. **Pamela Jean McLaughlin** was born 8 Feb 1953 in Birddrod, England.

1186. Della V. Abilene Sego (*Minnie Pearl Dearen*[6], *Mary Francis (Molly) Young*[5], *Mary M. (Polly II) Lindsey*[4], *Frances (Frankie) Sharp*[3], *Charles W. Sr.*[2], *John Sr.*[1]) was born 14 Mar 1911 in Lauderdale County, AL, died 23 Feb 1997, and was buried in Murphy's Chapel Cemetery, Lauderdale County, AL.

Della married **Virgil Henderson Gean Sr.**, son of **George Wiley Gean** and **Florence Mabel Perkins**, 6 Nov 1927 in Lauderdale County, AL. Virgil was born 15 Nov 1911 in Lauderdale County, AL, died 4 Oct 2004, and was buried in Murphy's Chapel Cemetery, Lauderdale County, AL.
+ 2569 F i. **Mildred Loriene Gean** was born 10 Aug 1931 in Lauderdale County, AL.
+ 2570 F ii. **Geneva Yvonne Gean** was born 4 Aug 1939 in Lauderdale County, AL.
  2571 F iii. **Doris Evelyn Gean** was born 29 Dec 1942 in Lauderdale County, AL, died 14 Jan 1943, and was buried in Williams Chapel Cemetery, Lauderdale County, AL.
+ 2572 F iv. **Mary Kathleen Gean** was born 2 Jun 1944 in Lauderdale County, AL.
+ 2573 M v. **Kenneth Aaron Gean** was born 19 Jul 1946 in Lauderdale County, AL.
  2574 M vi. **Carrol Marion Gean** was born 31 Aug 1948 in Lauderdale County, AL, died 21 Sep 1969, and was buried in Murphy's Chapel Cemetery, Lauderdale County, AL.
+ 2575 F vii. **Sharon Elaine Gean** was born 5 Jan 1952 in Waynesboro, Wayne County, TN.
+ 2576 M viii. **Virgil Henderson Gean Jr.** was born 29 Dec 1953 in Waynesboro, Wayne County, TN.

1187. Mary Alice Sego (*Minnie Pearl Dearen*[6], *Mary Francis (Molly) Young*[5], *Mary M. (Polly II) Lindsey*[4], *Frances (Frankie) Sharp*[3], *Charles W. Sr.*[2], *John Sr.*[1]) was born 19 Jun 1913 in Lauderdale County, AL, died 28 Nov 1994, and was buried in Chapel Hills Memorial Gardens, Mishawaka, IN.

   Mary married **Arthur Thomas Holcombe**, son of **Lanier Holcombe** and **Lou Faulkner**, 11 Jun 1932 in Lauderdale County, AL. Arthur was born 10 Jan 1912 in Lauderdale County, AL, died 6 Mar 1976, and was buried in Chapel Hills Memorial Gardens, Mishawaka, IN.

   + 2577 F   i.   **Doris Geraldine Holcombe** was born 19 Apr 1933 in Lauderdale County, AL.
   + 2578 F   ii.   **Robbie Louellen Holcombe** was born 8 Nov 1934 in Lauderdale County, AL, died 23 Mar 2007, and was buried in Mishawaka, IN.
   + 2579 M   iii. **Thomas Edsel Holcombe** was born 24 Mar 1940 in Waterloo, Lauderdale County, AL.
     2580 F   iv.   **Barbara Faye Holcombe** was born 30 Dec 1948 in Florence, Lauderdale County, AL.
     2581 M   v.   **Gary Boyce Holcombe** was born 24 Dec 1955 in Mishawaka, St Joseph County, IN, died 31 May 1976, and was buried in Niles, MI.

1188. Frances Boyce Sego (*Minnie Pearl Dearen*[6], *Mary Francis (Molly) Young*[5], *Mary M. (Polly II) Lindsey*[4], *Frances (Frankie) Sharp*[3], *Charles W. Sr.*[2], *John Sr.*[1]) was born 1 Mar 1915 in Waterloo, Lauderdale County, AL.

   Frances married **Carl Bedford Williams**, son of **John Williams** and **Liza White**, 30 Mar 1932 in Lauderdale County, AL. Carl was born 26 Jan 1912 in Lauderdale County, AL, died 5 Jun 1996, and was buried in Williams Chapel Cemetery, Lauderdale County, AL.

   + 2582 F   i.   **Sarah Beatrice Williams** was born 3 Jan 1934 in Hardin County, TN, died 17 Nov 1998, and was buried in White's Creek Cemetery, Hardin County, TN.
   + 2583 M   ii.   **Jerry Wayne Williams** was born 28 May 1947 in Lauderdale County, AL.
   + 2584 M   iii. **Larry David Williams** was born 23 Dec 1952 in Mishawaka, St Joseph County, IN.
   + 2585 F   iv.   **Debra Lynn Williams** was born 16 Aug 1954 in Mishawaka, St Joseph County, IN, died 6 Jun 2006, and was buried in Williams Chapel Cemetery, Lauderdale County, AL.

1190. Willie Doyal Sego (*Minnie Pearl Dearen*[6], *Mary Francis (Molly) Young*[5], *Mary M. (Polly II) Lindsey*[4], *Frances (Frankie) Sharp*[3], *Charles W. Sr.*[2], *John Sr.*[1]) was born 25 Mar 1924 in Lauderdale County, AL, died 15 Nov 2002, and was buried in Crestwood Cemetery, Gadsden, AL.

   Willie married **Hazel Ila Lou Hand** 7 May 1949 in Gadsden, Etowah County, AL. Hazel was born 21 Jun 1927 in Atlanta, Cobb County, GA.

   + 2586 M   i.   **Dennis Masterson Sego** was born 11 Jan 1951 in Gadsden, Etowah County, AL.
   + 2587 F   ii.   **Karen Beth Sego** was born 22 Feb 1954 in Gadsden, Etowah County, AL.
   + 2588 F   iii. **Melissa Lou (Lisa) Sego** was born 25 Apr 1958 in Gadsden, AL.

1191. Clara Bell Sego (*Minnie Pearl Dearen*[6], *Mary Francis (Molly) Young*[5], *Mary M. (Polly II) Lindsey*[4], *Frances (Frankie) Sharp*[3], *Charles W. Sr.*[2], *John Sr.*[1]) was born 18 May 1928 in Waterloo, Lauderdale County, AL.

   Clara married **Bartley Andrew White**, son of **Marion Walter White** and **Mary Jane Hubbard**, 28 Sep 1946 in Lauderdale County, AL. Bartley was born 20 Apr 1921 in Hardin County, TN, died 28 Feb 2006, and was buried in Williams Chapel Cemetery, Lauderdale County, AL.

   + 2589 F   i.   **Marilyn Kaye White** was born 13 Aug 1947 in Lauderdale County, AL.
   + 2590 M   ii.   **Warren Lee White** was born 4 Aug 1949 in Lauderdale County, AL.
   + 2591 F   iii. **Glenda Juanita White** was born 21 Jun 1951 in Lauderdale County, AL.
   + 2592 F   iv.   **Lavenia Gail White** was born 26 Jul 1959 in Lauderdale County, AL.
   + 2593 M   v.   **Carlos Walter White** was born 17 Apr 1971 in Lauderdale County, AL.

1193. John Lemuel Dearen (*James Edgar Dearen*[6], *Mary Francis (Molly) Young*[5], *Mary M. (Polly II) Lindsey*[4], *Frances (Frankie) Sharp*[3], *Charles W. Sr.*[2], *John Sr.*[1]) was born 25 Jul 1934 in Waco, McLennan County, TX.

   John married **Jeanette Rice** 25 Jan 1954 in Houston, Harris County, TX. Jeanette was born in 1936.

   + 2594 M   i.   **John Michael Dearen** was born 25 Feb 1956 in Houston, Harris County, TX.
   + 2595 F   ii.   **Shawn Leigh Dearen** was born 4 Jun 1960 in Houston, Harris County, TX.

   John next married **Helen Frances Hamilton** 25 Jan 1975.

1194. Edgar Lee Dearen (*James Edgar Dearen*[6]*, Mary Francis (Molly) Young*[5]*, Mary M. (Polly II) Lindsey*[4]*, Frances (Frankie) Sharp*[3]*, Charles W. Sr.*[2]*, John Sr.*[1]) was born 15 Oct 1936 in Corsicana, Navarro County, TX.

Edgar married **Linda German**.

2596	F	i.	**Janet Leigh Dearen** was born in Corsicana, Navarro County, TX.
2597	M	ii.	**Ronald Gene Dearen** was born in Corsicana, Navarro County, TX.
2598	F	iii.	**Pamela Dearen** was born in Corsicana, Navarro County, TX.

1195. Nancy Ray Dearen (*James Edgar Dearen*[6]*, Mary Francis (Molly) Young*[5]*, Mary M. (Polly II) Lindsey*[4]*, Frances (Frankie) Sharp*[3]*, Charles W. Sr.*[2]*, John Sr.*[1]) was born 15 Sep 1938 in Corsicana, Navarro County, TX.

Nancy married **Jerrel Brewer** 4 Feb 1956 in Corsicana, Navarro County, TX.

2599	M	i.	**Dewayne Brewer** was born in Fort Worth, Tarrant County, TX and died 15 Dec 1995.
2600	M	ii.	**Kenneth Brewer** was born in Fort Worth, Tarrant County, TX.

1196. Martha Dearen (*James Edgar Dearen*[6]*, Mary Francis (Molly) Young*[5]*, Mary M. (Polly II) Lindsey*[4]*, Frances (Frankie) Sharp*[3]*, Charles W. Sr.*[2]*, John Sr.*[1]) was born 31 Dec 1939 in Corsicana, Navarro County, TX and died 22 Oct 1997 in Corsicana, Navarro County, TX.

Martha married **Carlton McManess**.

1199. Rufus Allen South (*Clara Edna Dearen*[6]*, Mary Francis (Molly) Young*[5]*, Mary M. (Polly II) Lindsey*[4]*, Frances (Frankie) Sharp*[3]*, Charles W. Sr.*[2]*, John Sr.*[1]) was born 20 Dec 1933 in Lauderdale County, AL.

Rufus married **Marcella Ann Tucker**, daughter of **Joe Tucker** and **Carrie Wallace**, 19 Dec 1954 in Iuka, Tishomingo County, MS. Marcella was born 8 Mar 1937 in Lauderdale County, AL.

+	2601	M	i.	**Roger Allen South** was born 12 Oct 1955 in Lauderdale County, AL.
+	2602	M	ii.	**James Cecil South** was born 6 Oct 1956 in Lauderdale County, AL.
+	2603	M	iii.	**Randal Keith South** was born 24 Aug 1959 in Lauderdale County, AL.
+	2604	M	iv.	**Ricky Lynn South** was born 23 Sep 1960 in Lauderdale County, AL.
+	2605	M	v.	**Steven Dewayne South** was born 16 Oct 1962 in Lauderdale County, AL.
+	2606	M	vi.	**Phillip Dale South** was born 9 Jan 1964 in Lauderdale County, AL.

1200. Eva Leigh South (*Clara Edna Dearen*[6]*, Mary Francis (Molly) Young*[5]*, Mary M. (Polly II) Lindsey*[4]*, Frances (Frankie) Sharp*[3]*, Charles W. Sr.*[2]*, John Sr.*[1]) was born 2 Feb 1939 in Lauderdale County, AL, died 5 Jul 1972, and was buried in Murphy's Chapel Cemetery, Lauderdale County, AL.

Eva married **Jimmy Daniel Faulkner**, son of **Dewey Faulkner** and **Viva Horton**, in Oct 1957 in Lauderdale County, AL. Jimmy was born 13 Jan 1940 in Lauderdale County, AL.

+	2607	F	i.	**Tamara Faye Faulkner** was born 19 Oct 1958 in Lauderdale County, AL.
+	2608	F	ii.	**Martina Ann Faulkner** was born 23 Aug 1961 in Lauderdale County, AL.

Eva next married **Ron Blankenship**.

1201. William (Doc) Turner Dailey Sr. (*Florence L. Ticer*[6]*, Roxie Leona Young*[5]*, Mary M. (Polly II) Lindsey*[4]*, Frances (Frankie) Sharp*[3]*, Charles W. Sr.*[2]*, John Sr.*[1]) was born 6 Dec 1911 in Lauderdale County, AL, died 7 Sep 1974, and was buried in Cloverdale COC Cemetery, Lauderdale County, AL.

William married **Carrie Ann Young**, daughter of **Hulet Edward Young** and **Lillian Ella Young**, 13 May 1928 in Lauderdale County, AL. Carrie was born 21 May 1909 in Lauderdale County, AL, died 25 May 1984, and was buried in Cloverdale COC Cemetery, Lauderdale County, AL.
(Duplicate Line. See Person 741)

1202. Clarence L. V. Dennis (*Florence L. Ticer*[6]*, Roxie Leona Young*[5]*, Mary M. (Polly II) Lindsey*[4]*, Frances (Frankie) Sharp*[3]*, Charles W. Sr.*[2]*, John Sr.*[1]) was born 20 Sep 1915 in Lauderdale County, AL, died 6 Apr 1990 in Lauderdale County, AL, and was buried in Greenview Memorial Park, Florence, Lauderdale County, AL.

Clarence married **Earsly B. Faulkner** 18 Jun 1933 in Lauderdale County, AL. Earsly was born in 1920 in Waterloo, Lauderdale County, AL, died 6 Mar 1996, and was buried in Greenview Memorial Park, Florence, Lauderdale County, AL.

2609	M	i.	**Clarence W. Dennis**.
2610	M	ii.	**Johnny A. Dennis**.
2611	M	iii.	**Donnie L. Dennis**.
2612	F	iv.	**Shirley H. Dennis**.
2613	F	v.	**Sandra Dennis**.

1203. John Albert Dennis (*Florence L. Ticer*[6], *Roxie Leona Young*[5], *Mary M. (Polly II) Lindsey*[4], *Frances (Frankie) Sharp*[3], *Charles W. Sr.*[2], *John Sr.*[1]) was born in 1917 in Lauderdale County, AL, died 3 Apr 1983, and was buried in Tri-Cities Memorial Gardens, Florence, Lauderdale County, AL.

John married **Alma Rachel Davis**. Alma was born in 1914 in Lauderdale County, AL and was buried in Tri-Cities Memorial Gardens, Florence, Lauderdale County, AL.

2614	M	i.	**Morrie Davis Dennis**.
2615	F	ii.	**Bonnie Sue Dennis**.
+ 2616	M	iii.	**Johnnie Russel Dennis** was born 30 Oct 1938 in Lauderdale County, AL.
+ 2617	M	iv.	**Jerry Dennis** was born 16 Sep 1941 in Lauderdale County, AL.

John next married **Gazell Sizemore**.

1204. Dalton L. Dennis (*Florence L. Ticer*[6], *Roxie Leona Young*[5], *Mary M. (Polly II) Lindsey*[4], *Frances (Frankie) Sharp*[3], *Charles W. Sr.*[2], *John Sr.*[1]) was born 25 Jun 1919 in Lauderdale County, AL.

Dalton married **Ruby L. Murphy**, daughter of **Tom Buford (Tinker) Murphy** and **Mary S. O'Bryan**. Ruby was born 18 Apr 1919 in Lauderdale County, AL and died in May 1992 in Moralcardin, IN.

+ 2618	F	i.	**Mary Dennis**.
+ 2619	F	ii.	**Sue Dennis**.
2620	F	iii.	**Betty Sue Dennis** was born 5 Nov 1938, died 29 Mar 1939, and was buried in Murphy's Chapel Cemetery, Lauderdale County, AL.
+ 2621	M	iv.	**Hugh L. Dennis** was born 18 Feb 1940 in Hardin County, TN.
2622	M	v.	**Donald E. Dennis** was born 5 Sep 1941, died 22 Nov 1956, and was buried in Murphy's Chapel Cemetery, Lauderdale County, AL.
+ 2623	M	vi.	**Herman Dennis** was born 28 Feb 1948.

1205. Christine Dennis (*Florence L. Ticer*[6], *Roxie Leona Young*[5], *Mary M. (Polly II) Lindsey*[4], *Frances (Frankie) Sharp*[3], *Charles W. Sr.*[2], *John Sr.*[1]) was born 16 Jun 1921 in Hardin County, TN.

Christine married **Earnest Reed**. Earnest was born 4 Nov 1917 in Wayne County, TN.

+ 2624	M	i.	**James Fay Reed** was born 25 Mar 1939 in Collinwood, TN.
+ 2625	M	ii.	**Dennis Ray Reed** was born 29 Jan 1941 in Collinwood, TN.
+ 2626	M	iii.	**Robert Earnest Reed** was born 29 Nov 1942 in Collinwood, TN.
+ 2627	M	iv.	**Cleo William Reed** was born 15 Aug 1946 in Collinwood, TN.
+ 2628	M	v.	**Leo Jasper Reed** was born 15 Aug 1946 in Collinwood, TN.
+ 2629	M	vi.	**Roger Dale Reed** was born 28 Sep 1949 in Collinwood, TN.
2630	M	vii.	**Tray Lynn Reed** was born 30 Nov 1951 in Lewis County, TN.

1206. Troy Burlon Dennis (*Florence L. Ticer*[6], *Roxie Leona Young*[5], *Mary M. (Polly II) Lindsey*[4], *Frances (Frankie) Sharp*[3], *Charles W. Sr.*[2], *John Sr.*[1]) was born 18 Jul 1923 in Hardin County, TN, died 5 Jul 1992, and was buried in Tri-Cities Memorial Gardens, Florence, Lauderdale County, AL.

Troy married **Ruria Kathleen White**. Ruria was born 28 Jul 1927 in Lauderdale County, AL.

+ 2631	M	i.	**Troy Wayne Dennis** was born in Aug 1948 in Lauderdale County, AL.
+ 2632	M	ii.	**Wendall Dean Dennis** was born 14 Nov 1953 in Mishawaka, St Joseph County, IN.
+ 2633	F	iii.	**Leigh Ann Dennis** was born 27 Jul 1965 in Lauderdale County, AL.

1207. Curtis Dennis (*Florence L. Ticer*[6], *Roxie Leona Young*[5], *Mary M. (Polly II) Lindsey*[4], *Frances (Frankie) Sharp*[3], *Charles W. Sr.*[2], *John Sr.*[1]) was born 20 Oct 1925 in Waterloo, Lauderdale County, AL.

Curtis married **Betty Stephens**, daughter of **Albert Stephens** and **Julia Davis**. Betty was born 13 Mar 1932 in Pinckney, IL.

+ 2634 F i. **Judith Anne Dennis** was born 7 Jul 1955 in South Bend, IN.
+ 2635 F ii. **Tina Marie Dennis** was born 15 Jan 1958 in Milwauka, WI.

1208. Dorothy W. Dennis (*Florence L. Ticer*[6]*, Roxie Leona Young*[5]*, Mary M. (Polly II) Lindsey*[4]*, Frances (Frankie) Sharp*[3]*, Charles W. Sr.*[2]*, John Sr.*[1]) was born 7 Jul 1933 in Hardin County, TN.

Dorothy married **L. B. Davis** 18 Oct 1953 in Hardin County, TN. L. was born 6 Jul 1930 in Cherokee, Colbert County, AL and died 25 Feb 1993 in Mishawaka, St Joseph County, IN.

+ 2636 F i. **Susan Marie Davis** was born 15 Aug 1954 in Highland Park, IN.
  2637 M ii. **Richard Lee Davis** was born 17 Nov 1959 in South Bend, IN.

1209. Elsie Irene Ticer (*Robert Clark Ticer II*[6]*, Roxie Leona Young*[5]*, Mary M. (Polly II) Lindsey*[4]*, Frances (Frankie) Sharp*[3]*, Charles W. Sr.*[2]*, John Sr.*[1]) was born in Apr 1920 in Waterloo, Lauderdale County, AL, died in Apr 1989, and was buried in Osceola, Elkhart County, IN.

Elsie married **Virgil M. McFall** 10 Dec 1935 in Lauderdale County, AL. Virgil was born 22 Apr 1912 in Wayne County, TN.

1210. Raymond Cecil Ticer Sr. (*Robert Clark Ticer II*[6]*, Roxie Leona Young*[5]*, Mary M. (Polly II) Lindsey*[4]*, Frances (Frankie) Sharp*[3]*, Charles W. Sr.*[2]*, John Sr.*[1]) was born 10 May 1922 in Lauderdale County, AL, died 21 Feb 1989, and was buried in Shady Grove Cemetery, Colbert County, AL.

Raymond married **Mary Evangeline Rhodes**, daughter of **James Norman Rhodes** and **Bessie Irions**, 2 Dec 1958 in Lauderdale County, AL. Mary was born 31 Jan 1927 in Lauderdale County, AL, died 3 Mar 2002, and was buried in Shady Grove Cemetery, Colbert County, AL.

  2638 F i. **Cecilia Ticer**.
  2639 M ii. **Raymond Cecil Ticer Jr.**

1211. James Allen Ticer (*Robert Clark Ticer II*[6]*, Roxie Leona Young*[5]*, Mary M. (Polly II) Lindsey*[4]*, Frances (Frankie) Sharp*[3]*, Charles W. Sr.*[2]*, John Sr.*[1]) was born 4 Jul 1924 in Waterloo, Lauderdale County, AL, died 20 Oct 1998, and was buried in Williams Chapel Cemetery, Lauderdale County, AL.

James married **Frances Sybil Young**, daughter of **Robert Edward (Bunt) Young** and **Estelle Eugene Wood**, 14 Dec 1946 in Lauderdale County, AL. Frances was born 29 Sep 1926 in Hempstead, Nassau County, NY.

+ 2640 M i. **Gary Allen Ticer** was born 10 Jan 1948 in Florence, Lauderdale County, AL.
+ 2641 M ii. **Larry David Ticer** was born 21 May 1949 in Florence, Lauderdale County, AL.
+ 2642 M iii. **Mitchell Wayne Ticer** was born 19 May 1950 in Florence, Lauderdale County, AL.
+ 2643 F iv. **Sandra Gail Ticer** was born 21 Jul 1953 in Florence, Lauderdale County, AL.
+ 2644 F v. **Sally Joyce Ticer** was born 21 Jul 1953 in Florence, Lauderdale County, AL.

1212. Joy M. Ticer (*Robert Clark Ticer II*[6]*, Roxie Leona Young*[5]*, Mary M. (Polly II) Lindsey*[4]*, Frances (Frankie) Sharp*[3]*, Charles W. Sr.*[2]*, John Sr.*[1]) was born 27 Oct 1926 in Waterloo, Lauderdale County, AL.

Joy married **Bill Green**.

1213. Velva Ticer (*Robert Clark Ticer II*[6]*, Roxie Leona Young*[5]*, Mary M. (Polly II) Lindsey*[4]*, Frances (Frankie) Sharp*[3]*, Charles W. Sr.*[2]*, John Sr.*[1]) was born 6 Jan 1928 in Waterloo, Lauderdale County, AL.

Velva married **Almon Simpson**.

1214. Arnold Lee Ticer (*Robert Clark Ticer II*[6]*, Roxie Leona Young*[5]*, Mary M. (Polly II) Lindsey*[4]*, Frances (Frankie) Sharp*[3]*, Charles W. Sr.*[2]*, John Sr.*[1]) was born 5 May 1931 in Waterloo, Lauderdale County, AL.

Arnold married **Betty Faye Rhodes**, daughter of **James Norman Rhodes** and **Bessie Irions**, 13 Oct 1951 in Iuka, Tishomingo County, MS. Betty was born 19 Aug 1934 in Lauderdale County, AL.

+ 2645 M i. **Steven Lee Ticer** was born 30 May 1953 in St. Joseph County, IN, died 12 May 1988, and was buried in Sherrod Valley Cemetery, Lauderdale County, AL.
+ 2646 M ii. **Rayford Arnold Ticer** was born 14 Jul 1954 in Lauderdale County, AL.
+ 2647 F iii. **Angela Faye Ticer** was born 16 Sep 1965 in Lauderdale County, AL.

1215. Doris (Elwee) Ticer (*Robert Clark Ticer II ^{6}, Roxie Leona Young ^{5}, Mary M. (Polly II) Lindsey ^{4}, Frances (Frankie) Sharp ^{3}, Charles W. Sr. ^{2}, John Sr. ^{1}*) was born 19 Oct 1933 in Waterloo, Lauderdale County, AL.

Doris married **J. R. Richardson**, son of **Emmitt Richardson** and **Charity McGee**, 22 Aug 1954 in Iuka, Tishomingo County, MS. J. was born 29 Mar 1930 in Lauderdale County, AL, died in Oct 1985, and was buried in Barnett Cemetery, Lauderdale County, AL.
  2648 M i. **Tony Russell Richardson** was born 7 Jan 1958 in Lauderdale County, AL and died 19 Nov 1998 in Anderdon, AL.
+ 2649 M ii. **Cletis Richardson** was born 9 Jun 1966.

1216. Robert Ernest Ticer (*Robert Clark Ticer II ^{6}, Roxie Leona Young ^{5}, Mary M. (Polly II) Lindsey ^{4}, Frances (Frankie) Sharp ^{3}, Charles W. Sr. ^{2}, John Sr. ^{1}*) was born 3 Feb 1937 in Waterloo, Lauderdale County, AL and was buried in Eudora, AR.

Robert married **Mary Maxine Bradley**, daughter of **Edward Bradley** and **Maude Ray**. Mary was born 11 Jan 1942 in Chicot, AR.
  2650 M i. **Robert Day Ticer** was born 13 Jul 1963 in Laramie, WY.
+ 2651 F ii. **Susan Maxine Ticer** was born 17 Aug 1965.

1217. Virtie Viola Weaver (*Mary Ann Ticer ^{6}, Roxie Leona Young ^{5}, Mary M. (Polly II) Lindsey ^{4}, Frances (Frankie) Sharp ^{3}, Charles W. Sr. ^{2}, John Sr. ^{1}*) was born 5 Jul 1918 in Lauderdale County, AL.

Virtie married **Harold James Weston**, son of **James Hudson Weston** and **Linnie James**, 9 Nov 1937 in Savannah, Hardin County, TN. Harold was born 4 Sep 1918 in Lauderdale County, AL, died 31 Mar 1999, and was buried in Osceola, Elkhart County, IN.
+ 2652 M i. **James Harold Weston** was born 18 Jul 1937 in Lauderdale County, AL.
+ 2653 M ii. **Jack Glen Weston** was born 10 Nov 1942 in Mishawaka, St Joseph County, IN and died 14 May 1986.
+ 2654 M iii. **Jerry Wayne Weston** was born 3 May 1944 in Mishawaka, St Joseph County, IN.
+ 2655 F iv. **Jo Ann Weston** was born 6 Jul 1948 in Mishawaka, St Joseph County, IN.
+ 2656 M v. **Tommy Eugene Weston** was born 13 Apr 1953 in Mishawaka, St Joseph County, IN.

Virtie next married **Ralph Barker**.

1218. Roxie Lucille Weaver (*Mary Ann Ticer ^{6}, Roxie Leona Young ^{5}, Mary M. (Polly II) Lindsey ^{4}, Frances (Frankie) Sharp ^{3}, Charles W. Sr. ^{2}, John Sr. ^{1}*) was born 22 Jun 1921 in Lauderdale County, AL, died 2 Apr 1993, and was buried in Chapel Hills Memorial Gardens, Mishawaka, IN.

Roxie married **Johnny Hall Whitaker**, son of **J. R. Whitaker** and **Lena Faulkner**, 5 Dec 1937 in Lauderdale County, AL. Johnny was born 2 Sep 1916 in Lauderdale County, AL, died 14 May 2006, and was buried in Chapel Hills Memorial Gardens, Mishawaka, IN.
+ 2657 M i. **Ernest (Ernie) Doyle Whitaker** was born 31 Mar 1939 in Waterloo, Lauderdale County, AL.
  2658 M ii. **Herschel Ray Whitaker** was born 18 Apr 1941 in St. Joseph County, IN, died 30 Oct 1950, and was buried in Chapel Hills Memorial Gardens, Mishawaka, IN.
  2659 M iii. **Robert Lee Whitaker** was born 12 Sep 1943 in St. Joseph County, IN, died 14 Feb 1973, and was buried in Chapel Hills Memorial Gardens, Mishawaka, IN.

1219. Clara Oneita Weaver (*Mary Ann Ticer ^{6}, Roxie Leona Young ^{5}, Mary M. (Polly II) Lindsey ^{4}, Frances (Frankie) Sharp ^{3}, Charles W. Sr. ^{2}, John Sr. ^{1}*) was born 17 Aug 1925 in Lauderdale County, AL.

Clara married **Glenn E. Sipress** 2 Aug 1943 in Bartow, FL. Glenn was born 20 Oct 1923 in St. Joseph County, IN, died 4 Dec 1981, and was buried in Chapel Hills Memorial Gardens, Mishawaka, IN.
  2660 M i. **Randall Sipress** was born 1 Nov 1951 in Mishawaka, St Joseph County, IN.

1220. James Paul Weaver (*Mary Ann Ticer*^{6}, *Roxie Leona Young*^{5}, *Mary M. (Polly II) Lindsey*^{4}, *Frances (Frankie) Sharp*^{3}, *Charles W. Sr.*^{2}, *John Sr.*^{1}) was born 8 Nov 1927 in Lauderdale County, AL.

James married **Amanda Willine Higgins**, daughter of **William Higgins** and **Grace Blount**, 13 Jul 1945 in South Bend, IN. Amanda was born 16 Sep 1929 in Waterloo, Lauderdale County, AL.

+ 2661 M i. **James Weaver** was born 19 Oct 1946 in Florence, Lauderdale County, AL.
+ 2662 M ii. **Harry Malcom Weaver** was born 27 Aug 1949 in Florence, Lauderdale County, AL.
  2663 F iii. **Elaine Rena Weaver** was born 9 Oct 1951 in South Bend, IN.
+ 2664 F iv. **Roxanne Weaver** was born 24 Dec 1958 in South Bend, IN.

1221. William Clarence Weaver (*Mary Ann Ticer*^{6}, *Roxie Leona Young*^{5}, *Mary M. (Polly II) Lindsey*^{4}, *Frances (Frankie) Sharp*^{3}, *Charles W. Sr.*^{2}, *John Sr.*^{1}) was born 15 Oct 1931 in Lauderdale County, AL.

William married **Wilma Earline Winsett**, daughter of **John T. Winsett** and **Bertha Wilson**, 4 Jul 1959 in Lauderdale County, AL. Wilma was born 11 Sep 1928 in Hamilton, AL.

1222. Mary June Weaver (*Mary Ann Ticer*^{6}, *Roxie Leona Young*^{5}, *Mary M. (Polly II) Lindsey*^{4}, *Frances (Frankie) Sharp*^{3}, *Charles W. Sr.*^{2}, *John Sr.*^{1}) was born 30 Mar 1934 in Lauderdale County, AL, died 28 Apr 2004, and was buried in Chapel Hills Memorial Gardens, Mishawaka, IN.

Mary married **James Edward Cherry** 6 Jan 1952 in Iuka, Tishomingo County, MS. James was born 9 May 1933 in Waterloo, Lauderdale County, AL.

  2665 M i. **James Steven Cherry** was born 2 Mar 1953 in South Bend, IN.
  2666 F ii. **Carolyn Ann Cherry** was born 7 Apr 1956 in Mishawaka, St Joseph County, IN.
  2667 F iii. **Haili Cherry**.

1223. Bobby Joe Ticer (*David (Dave) Washington Ticer*^{6}, *Roxie Leona Young*^{5}, *Mary M. (Polly II) Lindsey*^{4}, *Frances (Frankie) Sharp*^{3}, *Charles W. Sr.*^{2}, *John Sr.*^{1}) was born 26 Oct 1933 in Saltillo, TN, died 16 Apr 1997, and was buried in Richardson Cemetery, Lauderdale County, AL.

Bobby married **Francis Marie Hinton** 20 Apr 1957 in Lauderdale County, AL. Francis was born 28 Jun 1938.

  2668 F i. **Pamela Ticer**.
  2669 M ii. **Phillip Ticer**.

1224. Montie Wayne Ticer (*David (Dave) Washington Ticer*^{6}, *Roxie Leona Young*^{5}, *Mary M. (Polly II) Lindsey*^{4}, *Frances (Frankie) Sharp*^{3}, *Charles W. Sr.*^{2}, *John Sr.*^{1}) was born 19 Apr 1936 in Lauderdale County, AL, died 16 Nov 1985, and was buried in Richardson Cemetery, Lauderdale County, AL.

Montie married **Barbara Fay Moore**, daughter of **Berlin Moore** and **Quinnie Faulkner**, in Lauderdale County, AL. Barbara was born 6 Jun 1942 in Lauderdale County, AL and died 14 Jun 1993.

+ 2670 F i. **Cheryl Annette Ticer** was born 19 Mar 1958 in Lauderdale County, AL.

1225. Peggy Ann Ticer (*David (Dave) Washington Ticer*^{6}, *Roxie Leona Young*^{5}, *Mary M. (Polly II) Lindsey*^{4}, *Frances (Frankie) Sharp*^{3}, *Charles W. Sr.*^{2}, *John Sr.*^{1}) was born 7 Dec 1938 in Lauderdale County, AL.

Peggy married **Boyce Edward Young**, son of **Arnold Edward (Ed) Young** and **Reba Jean Johnson**, 2 Dec 1958 in Lauderdale County, AL. Boyce was born 21 Oct 1936 in Lauderdale County, AL.

+ 2671 F i. **Jill Michelle Young** was born 29 Mar 1969 in Lauderdale County, AL.
+ 2672 F ii. **Amy Dee Young** was born 31 Aug 1972 in Lauderdale County, AL.
+ 2673 M iii. **Bradley Edward Young** was born 17 Dec 1974 in Lauderdale County, AL.

1226. Deaner Beatrice Goodman (*Myrtle S. Ticer*^{6}, *Roxie Leona Young*^{5}, *Mary M. (Polly II) Lindsey*^{4}, *Frances (Frankie) Sharp*^{3}, *Charles W. Sr.*^{2}, *John Sr.*^{1}) was born 15 Feb 1915.

Deaner married **Gabiel Claudio** 19 Dec 1981 in Cook County, IL.

1230. Earline Inese Goodman (*Myrtle S. Ticer ^{6}, Roxie Leona Young ^{5}, Mary M. (Polly II) Lindsey ^{4}, Frances (Frankie) Sharp ^{3}, Charles W. Sr. ^{2}, John Sr. ^{1}*) was born in Lauderdale County, AL, died in Oct 1951, and was buried in Stoney Point Cemetery, Lauderdale County, AL.

Earline married **Ralph Phillip**.

1232. Gladys Marie Jones (*Lillian T. Ticer ^{6}, Roxie Leona Young ^{5}, Mary M. (Polly II) Lindsey ^{4}, Frances (Frankie) Sharp ^{3}, Charles W. Sr. ^{2}, John Sr. ^{1}*) was born 26 Feb 1927 in Lauderdale County, AL.

Gladys married **Dewey M. Robertson** 18 Aug 1948 in Lauderdale County, AL. Dewey was born 11 Feb 1922 in Lauderdale County, AL, died 28 Mar 2005, and was buried in Wright Cemetery, Wright, Lauderdale County, AL.

1234. James Ellis Jones (*Lillian T. Ticer ^{6}, Roxie Leona Young ^{5}, Mary M. (Polly II) Lindsey ^{4}, Frances (Frankie) Sharp ^{3}, Charles W. Sr. ^{2}, John Sr. ^{1}*) was born 30 May 1931 in Lauderdale County, AL, died 2 Jan 1985, and was buried in Wright Cemetery, Wright, Lauderdale County, AL.

James married **Reeda Mae Sharp**, daughter of **Reeder Earl Sharp** and **Dorothy Betty White**, 20 Jun 1951 in Iuka, Tishomingo County, MS. Reeda was born 9 Mar 1935 in Lauderdale County, AL.
   2674 M   i.   **Jammie David Jones** was born 4 Oct 1953 in Lauderdale County, AL.
+ 2675 M   ii.   **Keith Lynn Jones** was born 6 Oct 1958 in Lauderdale County, AL.

1235. Charles Edward Jones (*Lillian T. Ticer ^{6}, Roxie Leona Young ^{5}, Mary M. (Polly II) Lindsey ^{4}, Frances (Frankie) Sharp ^{3}, Charles W. Sr. ^{2}, John Sr. ^{1}*) was born 16 Sep 1935 in Lauderdale County, AL.

Charles married **Marcella Joiner**.
   2676 F   i.   **Eddie Jones**.
   2677 F   ii.   **Brenda Jones**.

1236. Nina Faye Jones (*Lillian T. Ticer ^{6}, Roxie Leona Young ^{5}, Mary M. (Polly II) Lindsey ^{4}, Frances (Frankie) Sharp ^{3}, Charles W. Sr. ^{2}, John Sr. ^{1}*) was born 6 Oct 1937 in Lauderdale County, AL.

Nina married ***Unk Williams**.

1237. Roy Lynn Jones (*Lillian T. Ticer ^{6}, Roxie Leona Young ^{5}, Mary M. (Polly II) Lindsey ^{4}, Frances (Frankie) Sharp ^{3}, Charles W. Sr. ^{2}, John Sr. ^{1}*) was born 20 Jan 1940 in Lauderdale County, AL.

Roy married **Cathy *Unk**.

1238. Kenneth Ray Jones (*Lillian T. Ticer ^{6}, Roxie Leona Young ^{5}, Mary M. (Polly II) Lindsey ^{4}, Frances (Frankie) Sharp ^{3}, Charles W. Sr. ^{2}, John Sr. ^{1}*) was born 2 Oct 1942 in Lauderdale County, AL, died 7 Mar 1970, and was buried in Wright Cemetery, Wright, Lauderdale County, AL.

Kenneth married **Carolyn Lois Sharp**, daughter of **Loye Arvel Sharp** and **Pearlie Mae Wood**, 21 Dec 1965 in Lauderdale County, AL. Carolyn was born 24 Nov 1944 in Gravely Springs, Lauderdale County, AL.

1239. Jimmie Nell Brown (*Pearl Etta Ticer ^{6}, Roxie Leona Young ^{5}, Mary M. (Polly II) Lindsey ^{4}, Frances (Frankie) Sharp ^{3}, Charles W. Sr. ^{2}, John Sr. ^{1}*) was born 15 Dec 1936 in Lauderdale County, AL.

Jimmie married **Grady Edward Patrick Jr.**, son of **Grady Edward Patrick Sr.** and **Mary Ethel Williams**, 24 Mar 1957 in Lauderdale County, AL. Grady was born 8 Sep 1936 in Lauderdale County, AL.
+ 2678 F   i.   **Kim Renee Patrick** was born 28 Feb 1962 in Japan.
+ 2679 F   ii.   **Tina Denise Patrick** was born 9 Dec 1964 in Huntsville, Madison County, AL.

1240. Benjamin Franklin Brown Jr. (*Pearl Etta Ticer ^{6}, Roxie Leona Young ^{5}, Mary M. (Polly II) Lindsey ^{4}, Frances (Frankie) Sharp ^{3}, Charles W. Sr. ^{2}, John Sr. ^{1}*) was born 21 May 1939 in Lauderdale County, AL.

Benjamin married **Carletta Jackson** 24 Aug 1958 in Colbert County, AL.

1241. Ronnie Lowell Brown (*Pearl Etta Ticer* [6], *Roxie Leona Young* [5], *Mary M. (Polly II) Lindsey* [4], *Frances (Frankie) Sharp* [3], *Charles W. Sr.* [2], *John Sr.* [1]) was born 7 Jun 1941 in Lauderdale County, AL.

Ronnie married **Theresa Juanita McDonald**, daughter of **James T. McDonald** and **June Rose Wilson**, 2 Jun 1959 in Colbert County, AL. Theresa was born 27 Aug 1941 in Colbert County, AL, died 29 Mar 1983, and was buried in Murphy's Chapel Cemetery, Lauderdale County, AL.

+ 2680 M   i.   **Ricky Lowell Brown Sr.** was born 27 Nov 1959 in Colbert County, AL, died 15 Jun 2000, and was buried in Murphy's Chapel Cemetery, Lauderdale County, AL.
+ 2681 M   ii.   **Ralph Lee Brown** was born 13 Jan 1961 in Colbert County, AL.
+ 2682 M   iii.   **Ronald Lynn Brown** was born 26 Feb 1963 in Colbert County, AL.
   2683 M   iv.   **Robbie Lorinan Brown** was born 15 Aug 1964 in Colbert County, AL.
   2684 M   v.   **Roger Lloyd Brown** was born 13 Sep 1968 in Colbert County, AL, died 2 Jan 1994, and was buried in Murphy's Chapel Cemetery, Lauderdale County, AL.

Ronnie next married **Sharon Elaine Gean**, daughter of **Virgil Henderson Gean Sr.** and **Della V. Abilene Sego**, 13 May 1990 in Lauderdale County, AL. Sharon was born 5 Jan 1952 in Waynesboro, Wayne County, TN.

   2685 F   i.   **Rachel Lane Brown** was born 30 May 1992 in Lauderdale County, AL.

1242. Dorothy (Dottie) Norene Brown (*Pearl Etta Ticer* [6], *Roxie Leona Young* [5], *Mary M. (Polly II) Lindsey* [4], *Frances (Frankie) Sharp* [3], *Charles W. Sr.* [2], *John Sr.* [1]) was born 24 Nov 1943 in Lauderdale County, AL.

Dorothy married **Larry Elmer Haataja**, son of **Elmer Matt Haataja** and **Kathleen Spires**, 6 Sep 1964 in Lauderdale County, AL. Larry was born 8 Apr 1944 in Lauderdale County, AL.

+ 2686 M   i.   **Matthew Shannon Haataja** was born 20 Nov 1966 in Lauderdale County, AL.
+ 2687 M   ii.   **Scott Franklin Haataja** was born 12 Feb 1971 in Lauderdale County, AL.

Dorothy next married **Robert Pettus** 18 Aug 1995.

1245. Princess Inez Chambers (*Hettie Milford* [6], *Delia (Dee) Young* [5], *Mary M. (Polly II) Lindsey* [4], *Frances (Frankie) Sharp* [3], *Charles W. Sr.* [2], *John Sr.* [1]).

Princess married ***Unk Ellis**.

1247. Milford Faxon Chambers (*Hettie Milford* [6], *Delia (Dee) Young* [5], *Mary M. (Polly II) Lindsey* [4], *Frances (Frankie) Sharp* [3], *Charles W. Sr.* [2], *John Sr.* [1]).

Milford married **Delorease Blankenship**. Delorease was born 10 Jul 1914.

1249. Woodrow Chambers (*Hettie Milford* [6], *Delia (Dee) Young* [5], *Mary M. (Polly II) Lindsey* [4], *Frances (Frankie) Sharp* [3], *Charles W. Sr.* [2], *John Sr.* [1]) was born in 1917 in Memphis, Shelby County, TN, died 14 Jan 1998, and was buried in Ashland Cemetery, Ashland, MS.

Woodrow married **Mary Helen Roberts**.

   2688 M   i.   **Herbert Russell Chambers**.
   2689 M   ii.   **Milford Harley Chambers**.

1251. Elizabeth Virgina Maupin (*Hettie Milford* [6], *Delia (Dee) Young* [5], *Mary M. (Polly II) Lindsey* [4], *Frances (Frankie) Sharp* [3], *Charles W. Sr.* [2], *John Sr.* [1]) was born 27 Jun 1929 in Memphis, Shelby County, TN.

Elizabeth married **John Leek**.

1252. Jo Anna Maupin (*Hettie Milford* [6], *Delia (Dee) Young* [5], *Mary M. (Polly II) Lindsey* [4], *Frances (Frankie) Sharp* [3], *Charles W. Sr.* [2], *John Sr.* [1]) was born 20 Oct 1934 in Memphis, Shelby County, TN.

Jo married **Charles Benjamin Sanders Sr.**. Charles was born 6 Jan 1935 in Lagrange, TN.

+ 2690 F   i.   **Joanna Faith Sanders**.

2691 M ii. **Charles Benjamin Sanders Jr.**

1253. Elsie Perkins (*Etta Lee Milford^6, Delia (Dee) Young^5, Mary M. (Polly II) Lindsey^4, Frances (Frankie) Sharp^3, Charles W. Sr.^{2}, John Sr.^{1}*) was born 28 Apr 1909 in Tyronza, Poinsett County, AR.

Elsie married **Marcus Avery Spiegel**. Marcus was born 2 Apr 1901 in Ensley, AL and died 14 Apr 1954 in Harrisburg, Poinsett County, AR.

1254. Nancy Delia (Dee) Perkins (*Etta Lee Milford^6, Delia (Dee) Young^5, Mary M. (Polly II) Lindsey^4, Frances (Frankie) Sharp^3, Charles W. Sr.^{2}, John Sr.^{1}*) was born 3 Dec 1910 in Magazine, AR.

Nancy married **Herman Guy Becker** 1 Aug 1926 in Emmons, MO. Herman died 27 Oct 1961 in Elkhart, Elkhart County, IN.
+ 2692 F i. **Sylvia Marie Becker** was born 28 Jul 1927 in Trumann, AR.
+ 2693 F ii. **Sybile Vilena Becker** was born 16 Sep 1928 in Trumann, AR.
  2694 M iii. **Perry Lee Becker** was born 13 Jul 1932 in Trumann, AR and died in Aug 1933 in Trumann, AR.
+ 2695 F iv. **Catherine Doris Becker** was born 22 Dec 1940 in Marked Tree, Poinsett County, AR and died in Eminence, MO.

1255. James Douglas Perkins (*Etta Lee Milford^6, Delia (Dee) Young^5, Mary M. (Polly II) Lindsey^4, Frances (Frankie) Sharp^3, Charles W. Sr.^{2}, John Sr.^{1}*) was born 23 Sep 1912 in Magazine, AR and died 23 Nov 1978 in St. Joseph County, IN.

James married **Annabelle Farmer**. Annabelle was born 7 May 1924 in Kokomo, Howard, IN.

1256. Woodrow Wilson Perkins (*Etta Lee Milford^6, Delia (Dee) Young^5, Mary M. (Polly II) Lindsey^4, Frances (Frankie) Sharp^3, Charles W. Sr.^{2}, John Sr.^{1}*) was born 12 Oct 1914 in Vineyard, Phillips, AR and died in Jul 1975 in Jonesboro, Craighead County, AR.

Woodrow married **Edith Rose Woods** 8 Dec 1935 in Promised Land, AR. Edith was born 24 Nov 1914 in Tyronza, Poinsett County, AR.

1257. Freddie Perkins (*Etta Lee Milford^6, Delia (Dee) Young^5, Mary M. (Polly II) Lindsey^4, Frances (Frankie) Sharp^3, Charles W. Sr.^{2}, John Sr.^{1}*) was born 25 Dec 1917 in Arkansas.

Freddie married **Elmer Clarence Kasinger**. Elmer was born 19 Sep 1914 in Etowah, AR.

1258. Samuel Burton Perkins (*Etta Lee Milford^6, Delia (Dee) Young^5, Mary M. (Polly II) Lindsey^4, Frances (Frankie) Sharp^3, Charles W. Sr.^{2}, John Sr.^{1}*) was born 23 Aug 1919 in Weona, Poinsett County, AR and died 18 Sep 1981 in Indiana.

Samuel married **Margaret Ellen Mitchell** 1 Jan 1949 in Jonesboro, Craighead County, AR. Margaret was born 22 Mar 1927 in Delrose, TN.

1259. Annie Lue Perkins (*Etta Lee Milford^6, Delia (Dee) Young^5, Mary M. (Polly II) Lindsey^4, Frances (Frankie) Sharp^3, Charles W. Sr.^{2}, John Sr.^{1}*) was born 28 Aug 1923 in Weona, Poinsett County, AR, died 22 Dec 2004, and was buried in Chapel Hill Memorial Garden, Osceola, IN.

Annie married **Marion Frances McCaskill** 18 Feb 1939. Marion was born 28 Apr 1915 in Baldwin, MS, died 8 Jun 2004, and was buried in Chapel Hill Memorial Garden, Osceola, IN.
+ 2696 F i. **Anna Lee McCaskill** was born 18 Mar 1940 in Arkansas.
+ 2697 F ii. **Mary Frances McCaskill** was born 31 Mar 1941.
+ 2698 M iii. **Lloyd Donnell McCaskill** was born 16 Feb 1946.
+ 2699 M iv. **Marion F. McCaskill** was born 14 Apr 1947.
+ 2700 F v. **Esther Marie McCaskill** was born 25 Aug 1953.
+ 2701 F vi. **Julie Kay McCaskill** was born 1 Jun 1955.
+ 2702 F vii. **Pamela Jean McCaskill** was born 13 Apr 1957.

2703 F viii. **Debra Jean McCaskill** was born 10 Aug 1965.

1262. Robert Dalton Jones (*Ada Young*[6], *Lou Young*[5], *Mary M. (Polly II) Lindsey*[4], *Frances (Frankie) Sharp*[3], *Charles W. Sr.*[2], *John Sr.*[1]) was born 20 Jun 1916 in Lauderdale County, AL.

Robert married **Mamie Odell Wright**, daughter of **Percy Phillip Wright Sr.** and **Nettie Bama Blackburn**, 9 Jul 1938 in Lauderdale County, AL. Mamie was born 30 May 1917 in Lauderdale County, AL.
+ 2704 M i. **Robert (Bobby) Percy Jones** was born 16 Sep 1940 in Lauderdale County, AL.
+ 2705 M ii. **John Gary Jones** was born 31 May 1947 in Lauderdale County, AL.

1263. Mary Louise Jones (*Ada Young*[6], *Lou Young*[5], *Mary M. (Polly II) Lindsey*[4], *Frances (Frankie) Sharp*[3], *Charles W. Sr.*[2], *John Sr.*[1]) was born 11 Jul 1918 in Lauderdale County, AL, died 7 Dec 2001, and was buried in Greenview Memorial Park, Florence, Lauderdale County, AL.

Mary married **Percey Phillips (Pet) Wright Jr.**, son of **Percy Phillip Wright Sr.** and **Nettie Bama Blackburn**, 16 Oct 1937 in Lauderdale County, AL. Percey was born 7 Sep 1919 in Lauderdale County, AL.
+ 2706 F i. **Jackie Juanita Wright** was born 19 Feb 1940 in Lauderdale County, AL.
+ 2707 F ii. **Elinda Gaye Wright** was born 9 Sep 1943 in Lauderdale County, AL.

1264. Millard Horace Billingsley (*Verna Virella Young*[6], *Lou Young*[5], *Mary M. (Polly II) Lindsey*[4], *Frances (Frankie) Sharp*[3], *Charles W. Sr.*[2], *John Sr.*[1]) was born 7 Feb 1924 in Lauderdale County, AL.

Millard married **Elvia Woodward** 10 Dec 1948.
+ 2708 F i. **Brenda Billingsley** was born 18 Oct 1952.
+ 2709 F ii. **Beverly Billingsley** was born 23 Jun 1954.

1265. James (Pete) Marshall Billingsley (*Verna Virella Young*[6], *Lou Young*[5], *Mary M. (Polly II) Lindsey*[4], *Frances (Frankie) Sharp*[3], *Charles W. Sr.*[2], *John Sr.*[1]) was born 22 Jan 1926 in Lauderdale County, AL, died 22 Aug 1980, and was buried in Mt. Zion Cemetery, Lauderdale County, AL.

James married **Elvira Wengler** in 1950 in Germany.

James next married **Lillie Torres**. Lillie was born in California.

1266. William Eugene Billingsley (*Verna Virella Young*[6], *Lou Young*[5], *Mary M. (Polly II) Lindsey*[4], *Frances (Frankie) Sharp*[3], *Charles W. Sr.*[2], *John Sr.*[1]) was born 1 Apr 1930 in Lauderdale County, AL.

William married **Audry Woodward** 11 May 1957. Audry was born 31 Oct 1928.
+ 2710 F i. **Teresa Estell Billingsley** was born 6 Feb 1958.
+ 2711 F ii. **Elaine Renee Billingsley** was born 13 Mar 1961.
+ 2712 M iii. **Brian Eugene Billingsley** was born 6 Jun 1967.

1267. Grady Earl Billingsley (*Verna Virella Young*[6], *Lou Young*[5], *Mary M. (Polly II) Lindsey*[4], *Frances (Frankie) Sharp*[3], *Charles W. Sr.*[2], *John Sr.*[1]) was born 10 Dec 1931 in Lauderdale County, AL.

Grady married **Bertha Grigsby** 29 Jan 1955. Bertha was born 7 Jan 1936.
+ 2713 F i. **Donna Faye Billingsley** was born 22 Sep 1956.
2714 M ii. **Michael Allen Billingsley**.

1268. Thomas Moore Billingsley (*Verna Virella Young*[6], *Lou Young*[5], *Mary M. (Polly II) Lindsey*[4], *Frances (Frankie) Sharp*[3], *Charles W. Sr.*[2], *John Sr.*[1]) was born 18 Mar 1933 in Lauderdale County, AL.

Thomas married **Margaret Alliene Wright** 12 Mar 1960. Margaret was born 17 Apr 1938.
+ 2715 F i. **Deborah Alliene Billingsley** was born 22 Nov 1962.

1269. Ruth Vernet Witt (*Mary Etta Young*[6], *Lou Young*[5], *Mary M. (Polly II) Lindsey*[4], *Frances (Frankie) Sharp*[3], *Charles W. Sr.*[2], *John Sr.*[1]) was born 11 Jun 1927 in Lauderdale County, AL.

Ruth married **Paul Ellis Grigsby**, son of **Erskin Grigsby** and **Beulah Mae Tidwell**, 4 Sep 1948 in Lauderdale County, AL. Paul was born 13 May 1925 in Lauderdale County, AL.

+ 2716 M i. **Gary Ellis Grigsby** was born 25 Dec 1952 in Lauderdale County, AL.
+ 2717 M ii. **Thomas Keith Grigsby** was born 27 Oct 1955 in Lauderdale County, AL.
+ 2718 F iii. **Cheryl Ann Grigsby** was born 13 Jun 1958 in Lauderdale County, AL.
+ 2719 M iv. **Tony Paul Grigsby** was born 22 Jul 1964 in Lauderdale County, AL.

1270. James Arnold Witt (*Mary Etta Young[6], Lou Young[5], Mary M. (Polly II) Lindsey[4], Frances (Frankie) Sharp[3], Charles W. Sr.[2], John Sr.[1]*) was born 21 Feb 1929 in Lauderdale County, AL.

James married **Dorothy Lee Crowder**, daughter of **Howard Lemay Crowder** and **Wilodean Broadfoot**, in Aug 1951 in Iuka, Tishomingo County, MS. Dorothy was born 19 Oct 1929 in Lauderdale County, AL, died 10 Aug 2005, and was buried in Pleasant Hill Cemetery, Lauderdale County, AL.

+ 2720 F i. **Sandra Dee Witt** was born 12 Nov 1951 in Lauderdale County, AL.
+ 2721 M ii. **James Michael Witt** was born 23 Feb 1953 in Lauderdale County, AL.
+ 2722 F iii. **Sharon Lee Witt** was born 26 Jan 1957 in Lauderdale County, AL.

1271. Virgil David Witt (*Mary Etta Young[6], Lou Young[5], Mary M. (Polly II) Lindsey[4], Frances (Frankie) Sharp[3], Charles W. Sr.[2], John Sr.[1]*) was born 12 Feb 1931 in Lauderdale County, AL, died 14 Jan 1963, and was buried in Greenview Memorial Park, Florence, Lauderdale County, AL.

Virgil married **Joyce Laverne Trousdale**, daughter of **Logan Wallace Trousdale** and **Velma Elizabeth Hamner**. Joyce was born 2 Sep 1933 in Lauderdale County, AL, died 22 Feb 1996, and was buried in Greenview Memorial Park, Florence, Lauderdale County, AL.

+ 2723 F i. **Jennifer Joy Witt** was born 2 Jan 1957 in Lauderdale County, AL.
+ 2724 M ii. **David Lynn Witt** was born 3 Jun 1960 in Lauderdale County, AL.

1272. Ila Jean Witt (*Mary Etta Young[6], Lou Young[5], Mary M. (Polly II) Lindsey[4], Frances (Frankie) Sharp[3], Charles W. Sr.[2], John Sr.[1]*) was born 3 Mar 1933 in Lauderdale County, AL.

Ila married **Dorman Glenn Wallace**, son of **Edward Guy Wallace** and **Willie Mae Wesson**, 9 Jun 1951. Dorman was born 22 May 1925, died 14 Aug 1995, and was buried in Greenview Memorial Park, Florence, Lauderdale County, AL.

+ 2725 F i. **Glenda Jean Wallace** was born 14 Sep 1952.
+ 2726 M ii. **Dorman Richey Wallace** was born 19 Dec 1956.
+ 2727 M iii. **Roger Lance Wallace** was born 5 Jan 1958.

1273. Betty Lou Witt (*Mary Etta Young[6], Lou Young[5], Mary M. (Polly II) Lindsey[4], Frances (Frankie) Sharp[3], Charles W. Sr.[2], John Sr.[1]*) was born 2 Feb 1935 in Lauderdale County, AL.

Betty married **Douglas Gene Olive Sr.**, son of **Cef W. Olive** and **Maggie Weatherby**, 16 Feb 1952 in Iuka, Tishomingo County, MS. Douglas was born 27 Mar 1933 in Lauderdale County, AL, died 11 Oct 2004, and was buried in Greenview Memorial Park, Florence, Lauderdale County, AL.

+ 2728 M i. **Douglas Gene Olive Jr.** was born 4 Oct 1954 in Lauderdale County, AL.
+ 2729 F ii. **Dona Sue Olive** was born 26 Sep 1959 in Lauderdale County, AL.

1274. Carolyn Sue Witt (*Mary Etta Young[6], Lou Young[5], Mary M. (Polly II) Lindsey[4], Frances (Frankie) Sharp[3], Charles W. Sr.[2], John Sr.[1]*) was born 22 Aug 1937 in Lauderdale County, AL.

Carolyn married **Harry Brooks Wallace**, son of **Edward Guy Wallace** and **Willie Mae Wesson**, 7 Jun 1957 in Lauderdale County, AL. Harry was born 15 Jul 1931 in Lauderdale County, AL, died 20 Aug 2000, and was buried in Greenview Memorial Park, Florence, Lauderdale County, AL.

+ 2730 F i. **Karen Anne Wallace** was born 11 Dec 1958.
+ 2731 F ii. **Brenda Brooke Wallace** was born 20 Jan 1961.
  2732 M iii. **Harry Mark Wallace** was born 25 Nov 1962, died 31 Jul 1983, and was buried in Greenview Memorial Park, Florence, Lauderdale County, AL.

1275. Dorothy Jo Witt (*Mary Etta Young* [6], *Lou Young* [5], *Mary M. (Polly II) Lindsey* [4], *Frances (Frankie) Sharp* [3], *Charles W. Sr.* [2], *John Sr.* [1]) was born 12 Nov 1939 in Lauderdale County, AL.

Dorothy married **Ralph Coleman Austin**, son of **Roy B. Austin** and **Willie Mae Chowning**, 20 Apr 1960 in Lauderdale County, AL. Ralph was born 10 Aug 1931 in Lauderdale County, AL.

Dorothy next married **Haggard Franklin Greene** 15 May 1976. Haggard was born 12 May 1925.

1276. Thomas Clyde (T. C.) Witt Jr. (*Mary Etta Young* [6], *Lou Young* [5], *Mary M. (Polly II) Lindsey* [4], *Frances (Frankie) Sharp* [3], *Charles W. Sr.* [2], *John Sr.* [1]) was born 12 Feb 1942 in Lauderdale County, AL.

Thomas married **Betty Mae Montgomery**, daughter of **Buren Allen Montgomery** and **Louise Wallace**, 6 Aug 1966 in Lauderdale County, AL. Betty was born 4 Jun 1946 in Lauderdale County, AL.
+ 2733   F   i.   **Amie Alice Witt** was born 23 May 1971 in Lauderdale County, AL.
+ 2734   F   ii.   **Andrea Jill Witt** was born 11 Jul 1976 in Lauderdale County, AL.

1277. Mary Etta Witt (*Mary Etta Young* [6], *Lou Young* [5], *Mary M. (Polly II) Lindsey* [4], *Frances (Frankie) Sharp* [3], *Charles W. Sr.* [2], *John Sr.* [1]) was born 27 Feb 1944 in Lauderdale County, AL.

Mary married **Cecil Moore Sharp**, son of **James (Little James) Robert Sharp** and **Carrie Lee Brown**, 27 Apr 1962 in Lauderdale County, AL. Cecil was born 11 Jan 1943 in Lauderdale County, AL.
+ 2735   F   i.   **Melinda Lane Sharp** was born 19 Dec 1962 in Lauderdale County, AL.
+ 2736   M   ii.   **Jeffrey Lance Sharp** was born 17 Mar 1966 in Lauderdale County, AL.

1278. Virginia Francine Witt (*Mary Etta Young* [6], *Lou Young* [5], *Mary M. (Polly II) Lindsey* [4], *Frances (Frankie) Sharp* [3], *Charles W. Sr.* [2], *John Sr.* [1]) was born 12 Feb 1947 in Lauderdale County, AL and was buried in Greenview Memorial Park, Florence, Lauderdale County, AL.

Virginia married **Charles (Sonny) Ruben Young II**, son of **Charles Ruben Young I** and **Ruby Mae Wood**, 7 Feb 1963 in Lauderdale County, AL. Charles was born 14 Jun 1946 in Lauderdale County, AL.
+ 2737   M   i.   **Charles Thomas Young** was born 22 Apr 1965 in Lauderdale County, AL.
+ 2738   M   ii.   **James Damon Young** was born 16 Mar 1966 in Lauderdale County, AL.

1279. Danny Price Witt (*Mary Etta Young* [6], *Lou Young* [5], *Mary M. (Polly II) Lindsey* [4], *Frances (Frankie) Sharp* [3], *Charles W. Sr.* [2], *John Sr.* [1]) was born 7 Sep 1950 in Lauderdale County, AL.

Danny married **Sandra Jeanette Stults**, daughter of **Hubert Stults** and **Kathryn Holt**, 22 Sep 1973 in Lauderdale County, AL. Sandra was born 15 Oct 1952 in Loretto, Lawrence County, TN.
+ 2739   M   i.   **Chadwick Todd Witt** was born 2 Jul 1974 in Lauderdale County, AL.
  2740   M   ii.   **Craig Ryan Witt** was born 26 Jul 1975 in Lauderdale County, AL.

1280. Shirley Diane Witt (*Mary Etta Young* [6], *Lou Young* [5], *Mary M. (Polly II) Lindsey* [4], *Frances (Frankie) Sharp* [3], *Charles W. Sr.* [2], *John Sr.* [1]) was born 22 Aug 1952 in Lauderdale County, AL.

Shirley married **Richard Wayne Cypert**, son of **John Thomas Cypert** and **Joy Deloris Barackmra**, 2 Jan 1971 in Lauderdale County, AL. Richard was born 13 Nov 1951 in Castroville, TX.
+ 2741   M   i.   **Jody Aaron Cypert** was born 7 Dec 1972 in Lauderdale County, AL.

1281. Billie Faye Lovelace (*Della Young* [6], *Lou Young* [5], *Mary M. (Polly II) Lindsey* [4], *Frances (Frankie) Sharp* [3], *Charles W. Sr.* [2], *John Sr.* [1]) was born 19 Feb 1938 in Lauderdale County, AL.

Billie married **Elvin George Posey** 4 Aug 1956 in Los Vegas, Clark County, NV. Elvin was born 22 Apr 1933 in Pagosa Spes, Archuleta County, CO.
+ 2742   F   i.   **Jeanna Luanne Posey** was born 4 Oct 1957 in Long Beach, CA.
+ 2743   M   ii.   **George Jeffery Posey** was born 25 Sep 1958 in Long Beach, CA.
+ 2744   F   iii.   **Donna Patience Posey** was born 5 Apr 1960 in Long Beach, CA.

1282. Barbara Jean Lovelace (*Della Young ^{6}, Lou Young ^{5}, Mary M. (Polly II) Lindsey ^{4}, Frances (Frankie) Sharp ^{3}, Charles W. Sr. ^{2}, John Sr. ^{1}*) was born 24 Nov 1939 in Lauderdale County, AL.

Barbara married **David Leon Collum**, son of **Cleburn Collum** and **Pauline Brewer**, 16 Nov 1958 in Lauderdale County, AL. David was born 11 Nov 1939 in Lauderdale County, AL.

+ 2745 F   i.   **Sherry Venetia Collum** was born 18 Dec 1959 in Lauderdale County, AL.
+ 2746 F   ii.   **Cynthia (Cindy) Lynn Collum** was born 17 Feb 1963 in Lauderdale County, AL.

1284. Doyle Parnell (*Alonzo Parnell ^{6}, Dora Lee Young ^{5}, Mary M. (Polly II) Lindsey ^{4}, Frances (Frankie) Sharp ^{3}, Charles W. Sr. ^{2}, John Sr. ^{1}*).

Doyle married ***Unk**.

1292. Sharon Sue Bracken (*Vertia Thora Parnell ^{6}, Dora Lee Young ^{5}, Mary M. (Polly II) Lindsey ^{4}, Frances (Frankie) Sharp ^{3}, Charles W. Sr. ^{2}, John Sr. ^{1}*).

Sharon married ***Unk Klusman**.

1293. Katherine McFall (*Toye R. Young ^{6}, Lee Jackson Young ^{5}, Mary M. (Polly II) Lindsey ^{4}, Frances (Frankie) Sharp ^{3}, Charles W. Sr. ^{2}, John Sr. ^{1}*) was born in Waterloo, Lauderdale County, AL.

Katherine married ***Unk Lee**.
2747 F   i.   **Karen Elaine Lee**.
2748 M   ii.   **John W. Lee**.
2749 M   iii. **Robert Eugene Lee**.
2750 M   iv.   **Kenneth A. Lee**.

1294. Hershel Eugene McFall (*Toye R. Young ^{6}, Lee Jackson Young ^{5}, Mary M. (Polly II) Lindsey ^{4}, Frances (Frankie) Sharp ^{3}, Charles W. Sr. ^{2}, John Sr. ^{1}*).

Hershel married ***Unk**.
2751 F   i.   **Janett D. McFall**.

1295. Virgil Lee Sharp (*Pearl V. Young ^{6}, Lee Jackson Young ^{5}, Mary M. (Polly II) Lindsey ^{4}, Frances (Frankie) Sharp ^{3}, Charles W. Sr. ^{2}, John Sr. ^{1}*) was born 20 Jun 1928 in Mishawaka, St Joseph County, IN.

Virgil married **Jean Harsh Smith**, daughter of **Myron Smith** and **May Harsh**, 6 Jul 1949 in Mishawaka, St Joseph County, IN. Jean was born 29 May 1926 in Georgetown, SC.

+ 2752 F   i.   **Janice Marlene Sharp** was born 15 Sep 1950 in Mishawaka, St Joseph County, IN.
+ 2753 M   ii.   **Dale Dalton Sharp** was born 30 Oct 1951 in Mishawaka, St Joseph County, IN.
+ 2754 F   iii. **Joyce Christine Sharp** was born 10 Mar 1955 in Mishawaka, St Joseph County, IN.
  2755 M   iv.   **Douglas Lee Sharp** was born 4 Dec 1959 in Mishawaka, St Joseph County, IN.

1296. Ronnie Lowell Young (*Hosea Leba Young ^{6}, Lee Jackson Young ^{5}, Mary M. (Polly II) Lindsey ^{4}, Frances (Frankie) Sharp ^{3}, Charles W. Sr. ^{2}, John Sr. ^{1}*) was born 16 Sep 1934 in Mishawaka, St Joseph County, IN, died 20 Sep 2000, and was buried in Williams Chapel Cemetery, Lauderdale County, AL.

Ronnie married **Charlene Darby**.

1297. James Lee Young (*Hosea Leba Young ^{6}, Lee Jackson Young ^{5}, Mary M. (Polly II) Lindsey ^{4}, Frances (Frankie) Sharp ^{3}, Charles W. Sr. ^{2}, John Sr. ^{1}*) was born 28 Nov 1941 in Mishawaka, St Joseph County, IN.

James married **Linda Burch** 4 Jul 1959.

1298. Donnie D. Young (*Hosea Leba Young ^{6}, Lee Jackson Young ^{5}, Mary M. (Polly II) Lindsey ^{4}, Frances (Frankie) Sharp ^{3}, Charles W. Sr. ^{2}, John Sr. ^{1}*) was born 10 Mar 1944 in Mishawaka, St Joseph County, IN.

Donnie married **Fran Bompos**.

1299. Larry T. Young (*Hosea Leba Young*[6], *Lee Jackson Young*[5], *Mary M. (Polly II) Lindsey*[4], *Frances (Frankie) Sharp*[3], *Charles W. Sr.*[2], *John Sr.*[1]) was born 14 May 1947 in Mishawaka, St Joseph County, IN.

Larry married **Judy Kelly**.

1300. Shirley Young (*Hosea Leba Young*[6], *Lee Jackson Young*[5], *Mary M. (Polly II) Lindsey*[4], *Frances (Frankie) Sharp*[3], *Charles W. Sr.*[2], *John Sr.*[1]) was born 4 Nov.

Shirley married **Jack Miller**.

1302. Opal Wood (*John Hampton (Charlie) Wood*[6], *Louisa F. Lindsey*[5], *John S. Lindsey*[4], *Frances (Frankie) Sharp*[3], *Charles W. Sr.*[2], *John Sr.*[1]) was born 24 Oct 1917.

Opal married **Chester Eads** in 1936. Chester was born in 1909 and died in 1973 in Scurry County, TX.

1303. John Franklin Wood (*John Hampton (Charlie) Wood*[6], *Louisa F. Lindsey*[5], *John S. Lindsey*[4], *Frances (Frankie) Sharp*[3], *Charles W. Sr.*[2], *John Sr.*[1]) was born 27 Nov 1928.

John married **Shirley Kinney** in 1952.

1304. Delora May Clanton (*Bertha Mae Wood*[6], *Louisa F. Lindsey*[5], *John S. Lindsey*[4], *Frances (Frankie) Sharp*[3], *Charles W. Sr.*[2], *John Sr.*[1]) was born 27 May 1915 in Griffithville, White County, AR.

Delora married **Leo Scarbrough**.

Delora next married **Roy Kay** 23 Jul 1930 in Big Spring, TX. Roy died 10 Jan 1933 in Big Spring, TX.

Delora next married **E. R. Richardson** 27 Jun 1934 in Big Spring, TX. E. died 16 Apr 1971 in Big Spring, TX.

1305. William Carl Clanton (*Bertha Mae Wood*[6], *Louisa F. Lindsey*[5], *John S. Lindsey*[4], *Frances (Frankie) Sharp*[3], *Charles W. Sr.*[2], *John Sr.*[1]) was born 8 Feb 1917 in Kent County, TX.

William married **Ruby Pearl Graham** 12 May 1936. Ruby was born 28 Dec 1919 in Ackerly, Howard County, TX.

1306. Murrell Wilson Clanton (*Bertha Mae Wood*[6], *Louisa F. Lindsey*[5], *John S. Lindsey*[4], *Frances (Frankie) Sharp*[3], *Charles W. Sr.*[2], *John Sr.*[1]) was born 10 Mar 1919.

Murrell married **Grace Newson** 10 Jul 1939.

1308. Wallace Harold Rinehart (*Ada Evelyn Wood*[6], *Louisa F. Lindsey*[5], *John S. Lindsey*[4], *Frances (Frankie) Sharp*[3], *Charles W. Sr.*[2], *John Sr.*[1]) was born 28 Nov 1934 in Snyder, Scurry County, TX.

Wallace married **Joan Louise Hubbard**, daughter of **John Hamilton Hubbard** and **Louise Hankey**, 25 Apr 1959 in New York City, Kings County, NY. Joan was born 5 Jun 1937 in Creagerstown, MD and died 16 Aug 1991 in Cheverly, MD.
+ 2756 F   i.   **Cara Estelle Rinehart** was born 5 Feb 1965 in Washington, D. C..

1309. William Porter Rinehart (*Ada Evelyn Wood*[6], *Louisa F. Lindsey*[5], *John S. Lindsey*[4], *Frances (Frankie) Sharp*[3], *Charles W. Sr.*[2], *John Sr.*[1]) was born 9 Apr 1941 in Snyder, Scurry County, TX.

William married **Barbara Carol King** 16 Jun 1959 in Snyder, Scurry County, TX. Barbara was born 14 May 1941 in Lubbock, Lubbock County, TX.
+ 2757 F   i.   **Pamela Michelle Rinehart** was born 21 Sep 1961 in Odessa, Ector County, TX.
  2758 M   ii.   **William Scott Rinehart** was born 17 Apr 1965 in Abilene, Taylor County, TX.

+ 2759 M   iii.   **Brian Earl Rinehart** was born 25 Jul 1967 in Snyder, Scurry County, TX.
  2760 M   iv.   **Christopher Lynn Rinehart** was born 13 Nov 1971 in Ft Worth, Tarrant County, TX.

1311. Evelyn May Wood (*Lemuel Carl Wood*[6], *Louisa F. Lindsey*[5], *John S. Lindsey*[4], *Frances (Frankie) Sharp*[3], *Charles W. Sr.*[2], *John Sr.*[1]) was born 4 Mar 1930 in Snyder, Scurry County, TX, died 9 Aug 1987, and was buried in Lubbock, Lubbock County, TX.

Evelyn married **Van Urbin Meador** 3 Jul 1946 in Snyder, Scurry County, TX. Van was born 2 Nov 1921 in Desdemonia, TX, died 13 Jan 2000, and was buried in Dunn Cemetery, Scurry County, TX.
+ 2761 F   i.   **Teresa Kay Meador** was born 19 Aug 1947 in Snyder, Scurry County, TX.
+ 2762 M   ii.   **Michael Van Meador** was born 6 Jul 1949 in Snyder, Scurry County, TX.
+ 2763 F   iii. **Karen Durelle Meador** was born 10 Aug 1950 in Snyder, Scurry County, TX.
+ 2764 M   iv.   **Daryl Wayne Meador** was born 3 Mar 1952 in Snyder, Scurry County, TX.
+ 2765 F   v.   **Daphna Michelle Meador** was born 14 Nov 1954 in Snyder, Scurry County, TX.

1312. Daryl Elmer Wood (*Lemuel Carl Wood*[6], *Louisa F. Lindsey*[5], *John S. Lindsey*[4], *Frances (Frankie) Sharp*[3], *Charles W. Sr.*[2], *John Sr.*[1]) was born 28 Jun 1932 in Snyder, Scurry County, TX.

Daryl married **Doris Wanee Caldwell** 6 Oct 1952 in Lovington, NM. Doris was born 11 May 1935 in Noodle, Taylor County, TX.
+ 2766 M   i.   **David Carl Wood** was born 27 May 1954 in Texas.
  2767 F   ii.   **Tania Jo Wood** was born 30 Nov 1956 in Texas.

1313. Laverne Bruce (*Viney Viola Sharp*[6], *Robert Patton*[5], *James (Jim) Charles Sr.*[4], *Adron (Edwin/Ade) Sr.*[3], *Charles W. Sr.*[2], *John Sr.*[1]) was born 4 Nov 1896 in Lauderdale County, AL, died 20 Nov 1975, and was buried in Elmwood Cemetery, Birmingham, AL.

Laverne married **James Thomas McRae Sr.** 20 Oct 1920. James was born 3 Aug 1900 and died 20 Oct 1968.
+ 2768 M   i.   **James Thomas McRae Jr.** was born 18 Aug 1922.
  2769 M   ii.   **Wallace Bruce McRae** was born 6 May 1925 and died 27 May 1925.
+ 2770 M   iii. **Donald K. McRae.**

1314. Patricia Bruce (*Viney Viola Sharp*[6], *Robert Patton*[5], *James (Jim) Charles Sr.*[4], *Adron (Edwin/Ade) Sr.*[3], *Charles W. Sr.*[2], *John Sr.*[1]) was born 26 Nov 1897 in Lauderdale County, AL, died 24 Mar 1979, and was buried in Birmingham, Jefferson County, AL.

Patricia married **Clifford M. Wesson** 8 May 1919. Clifford was born 4 Jul 1896, died in 1989, and was buried in Birmingham, Jefferson County, AL.
  2771 M   i.   **Lowell Bruce Wesson** was born 22 Oct 1922 in Birmingham, Jefferson County, AL.
+ 2772 M   ii.   **Robert (Bob) C. Wesson** was born 3 Jul 1926 in Birmingham, Jefferson County, AL.

1315. Lewis Bruce (*Viney Viola Sharp*[6], *Robert Patton*[5], *James (Jim) Charles Sr.*[4], *Adron (Edwin/Ade) Sr.*[3], *Charles W. Sr.*[2], *John Sr.*[1]) was born 24 Oct 1901 in Lauderdale County, AL, died 23 May 1974, and was buried in Gravely Springs Cemetery, Lauderdale County, AL.

Lewis married **Lyda Mae Lancaster**, daughter of **Jim Lancaster** and **Nellie Fulmer**, 31 Jul 1922 in Lauderdale County, AL. Lyda was born 12 Jan 1902 in Lauderdale County, AL, died 11 Jul 1980, and was buried in Gravely Springs Cemetery, Lauderdale County, AL.
+ 2773 F   i.   **Mary Sue Bruce** was born 16 Jun 1923 in Lauderdale County, AL.
+ 2774 F   ii.   **Francis Laurene Bruce** was born 10 Apr 1927 in Lauderdale County, AL.

1316. Nellie Mae Pickens (*Carrie Eudora Sharp*[6], *Robert Patton*[5], *James (Jim) Charles Sr.*[4], *Adron (Edwin/Ade) Sr.*[3], *Charles W. Sr.*[2], *John Sr.*[1]) was born 22 Sep 1900 in Lauderdale County, AL.

Nellie married **Glen Allen Malsbury**, son of **William K. Malsbury** and **Harriet Smith**, 26 Aug 1924. Glen was born 4 Jan 1894 in Ashland, NE.
+ 2775 F   i.   **Glenell Malsbury** was born 3 Jan 1930 in Shawnee, OK.

1317. Stella Iown Pickens (*Carrie Eudora Sharp^6, Robert Patton^5, James (Jim) Charles Sr.^{4}, Adron (Edwin/Ade) Sr.^{3}, Charles W. Sr.^{2}, John Sr.^{1}*) was born 16 Jul 1902 in Lauderdale County, AL, died 6 Apr 1975, and was buried in Florence, Lauderdale County, AL.

Stella married **Thomas J. Dugger** 12 Jul 1921 in Pleasant Hill, TN. Thomas was born 13 May 1900 in Pleasant Hill, TN.

+	2776	F	i.	**Margaret Dugger** was born 9 Feb 1922 in Lauderdale County, AL and died 13 Dec 1970.
	2777	F	ii.	**Barbara Claire Dugger** was born 22 Jun 1927 in Cincinnati, OH and died 13 Dec 1931.
+	2778	M	iii.	**Gordon F. Dugger** was born 11 Apr 1930.
	2779	F	iv.	**Jeanette Marion Dugger**.

1318. Era Viola Pickens (*Carrie Eudora Sharp^6, Robert Patton^5, James (Jim) Charles Sr.^{4}, Adron (Edwin/Ade) Sr.^{3}, Charles W. Sr.^{2}, John Sr.^{1}*) was born 31 Oct 1905 in Lauderdale County, AL and died 24 May 1988.

Era married **William Allen Elliott** 27 Dec 1921.

Era next married **Edgar J. Purnell Jr.** 30 May 1940 in Lauderdale County, AL. Edgar was born 12 May 1900 in Mississippi.

1319. Casey Watson Pickens (*Carrie Eudora Sharp^6, Robert Patton^5, James (Jim) Charles Sr.^{4}, Adron (Edwin/Ade) Sr.^{3}, Charles W. Sr.^{2}, John Sr.^{1}*) was born 1 Jan 1908 in Savannah, Hardin County, TN and died 21 Jan 1991.

Casey married **June Austin** 18 Mar 1934.

1320. Cecil Edgar Pickens (*Carrie Eudora Sharp^6, Robert Patton^5, James (Jim) Charles Sr.^{4}, Adron (Edwin/Ade) Sr.^{3}, Charles W. Sr.^{2}, John Sr.^{1}*) was born 12 Mar 1910 in Lauderdale County, AL and died 17 Nov 1973.

Cecil married **Fern Lee Smith** 10 Jun 1943.

1321. Joe Wilson Pickens (*Carrie Eudora Sharp^6, Robert Patton^5, James (Jim) Charles Sr.^{4}, Adron (Edwin/Ade) Sr.^{3}, Charles W. Sr.^{2}, John Sr.^{1}*) was born 11 Nov 1912 in Lauderdale County, AL.

Joe married **Earline Marks** 7 Jun 1935.

1323. Glen Wilson Sharp (*Oscar Eldred^6, Robert Patton^5, James (Jim) Charles Sr.^{4}, Adron (Edwin/Ade) Sr.^{3}, Charles W. Sr.^{2}, John Sr.^{1}*) was born 17 Jul 1918 in Ft Smith, AR and died in 2000.

Glen married **Evelyn Borden**.

1324. Leon Wallace Sharp (*Oscar Eldred^6, Robert Patton^5, James (Jim) Charles Sr.^{4}, Adron (Edwin/Ade) Sr.^{3}, Charles W. Sr.^{2}, John Sr.^{1}*) was born 5 Sep 1926 in Marian, Lee County, AR and died 1 Apr 1983.

Leon married **Margie Russell**.

| 2780 | F | i. | **Margie Ann Sharp** was born 20 Mar 1949. |
| 2781 | F | ii. | **Laura Teresa Sharp** was born in Dec 1953. |

Leon next married **Betty Jan Dean** in 1955.

2782	F	i.	**Jana Lynn Sharp** was born 7 Aug 1956.
2783	M	ii.	**James Glen Sharp** was born 12 Apr 1962.
2784	F	iii.	**Mollie Sharp** was born 11 Feb 1965.
2785	F	iv.	**Mary Jane Sharp** was born 20 Jul 1967.
2786	M	v.	**John Eldred Sharp** was born 5 Feb 1970.

1325. Joseph Patton Sharp (*Oscar Eldred^6, Robert Patton^5, James (Jim) Charles Sr.^{4}, Adron (Edwin/Ade) Sr.^{3}, Charles W. Sr.^{2}, John Sr.^{1}*) was born 26 Aug 1929 in Marian, Lee County, AR, died in 2000, and was buried in Marian, Lee County, AR.

Joseph married **Bernice Ballard** 11 Jan 1955.
+ 2787 F i. **Dona Gail Sharp** was born 8 Feb 1957.
  2788 F ii. **Joyce Ann Sharp** was born 5 Sep 1960.

1327. Thelma Cornelia Sharp (*Robert Marvin Sr.*[6], *Robert Patton*[5], *James (Jim) Charles Sr.*[4], *Adron (Edwin/Ade) Sr.*[3], *Charles W. Sr.*[2], *John Sr.*[1]) was born 24 Oct 1914 in Savannah, Hardin County, TN.

Thelma married **Lorimer Patrick** in Arkansas.

1328. Robert Marvin Sharp Jr. (*Robert Marvin Sr.*[6], *Robert Patton*[5], *James (Jim) Charles Sr.*[4], *Adron (Edwin/Ade) Sr.*[3], *Charles W. Sr.*[2], *John Sr.*[1]) was born 30 Apr 1916 in Savannah, Hardin County, TN.

Robert married **Clytee Scruggs** in Earl, AR.

1329. Freda Rae Sharp (*Robert Marvin Sr.*[6], *Robert Patton*[5], *James (Jim) Charles Sr.*[4], *Adron (Edwin/Ade) Sr.*[3], *Charles W. Sr.*[2], *John Sr.*[1]) was born 30 May 1921 in Tyronza, Poinsett County, AR.

Freda married **Pope Finn** 29 Jul 1939.

1330. James Patton Sharp (*Robert Marvin Sr.*[6], *Robert Patton*[5], *James (Jim) Charles Sr.*[4], *Adron (Edwin/Ade) Sr.*[3], *Charles W. Sr.*[2], *John Sr.*[1]) was born 18 Apr 1925 in Etowah, AR and died 3 Mar 1982.

James married **Peggy Gallagher**.

1331. Thomas Earle (Tommy) Sharp (*Robert Marvin Sr.*[6], *Robert Patton*[5], *James (Jim) Charles Sr.*[4], *Adron (Edwin/Ade) Sr.*[3], *Charles W. Sr.*[2], *John Sr.*[1]) was born 10 Nov 1927.

Thomas married **Mickie Glisson**.

1332. Melverda Sharp (*Robert Marvin Sr.*[6], *Robert Patton*[5], *James (Jim) Charles Sr.*[4], *Adron (Edwin/Ade) Sr.*[3], *Charles W. Sr.*[2], *John Sr.*[1]) was born 18 Sep 1932.

Melverda married **J. C. Scarbrough**.

1333. Irene Handley (*Virgie Lenora Sharp*[6], *Robert Patton*[5], *James (Jim) Charles Sr.*[4], *Adron (Edwin/Ade) Sr.*[3], *Charles W. Sr.*[2], *John Sr.*[1]) was born 17 May 1906.

Irene married **Fred Welch** 17 Apr 1927.

1335. Trula Handley (*Virgie Lenora Sharp*[6], *Robert Patton*[5], *James (Jim) Charles Sr.*[4], *Adron (Edwin/Ade) Sr.*[3], *Charles W. Sr.*[2], *John Sr.*[1]).

Trula married ***Unk Therakeld**.

1336. Fay Ashburn (*Ella Myrtle Sharp*[6], *Robert Patton*[5], *James (Jim) Charles Sr.*[4], *Adron (Edwin/Ade) Sr.*[3], *Charles W. Sr.*[2], *John Sr.*[1]).

Fay married **Evelyn *Unk**.

Fay next married **Patty *Unk**.

1337. Virginia Ashburn (*Ella Myrtle Sharp*[6], *Robert Patton*[5], *James (Jim) Charles Sr.*[4], *Adron (Edwin/Ade) Sr.*[3], *Charles W. Sr.*[2], *John Sr.*[1]).

Virginia married ***Unk Rogers**.

1338. Robert Arthur Gammill (*Lizzie Oneita Sharp*[6], *Robert Patton*[5], *James (Jim) Charles Sr.*[4], *Adron (Edwin/Ade) Sr.*[3], *Charles W. Sr.*[2], *John Sr.*[1]) was born 18 Aug 1918.

Robert married **Clara Louise Bullard** 4 Nov 1938.

1339. Bernis Carl Gammill (*Lizzie Oneita Sharp*[6], *Robert Patton*[5], *James (Jim) Charles Sr.*[4], *Adron (Edwin/Ade) Sr.*[3], *Charles W. Sr.*[2], *John Sr.*[1]) was born 5 Apr 1921 and died 18 Jan 1965.

Bernis married **Mary Elizabeth McLord**.

1340. Ora Elizabeth Gammill (*Lizzie Oneita Sharp*[6], *Robert Patton*[5], *James (Jim) Charles Sr.*[4], *Adron (Edwin/Ade) Sr.*[3], *Charles W. Sr.*[2], *John Sr.*[1]) was born 13 Feb 1925.

Ora married **Robert Jess Heimdale**.

1341. Frank Wilson Waggener Sr. (*Annie Inez Sharp*[6], *Robert Patton*[5], *James (Jim) Charles Sr.*[4], *Adron (Edwin/Ade) Sr.*[3], *Charles W. Sr.*[2], *John Sr.*[1]) was born 23 May 1924 in Memphis, Shelby County, TN.

Frank married **Evelyn Ray** 4 Dec 1943.
  2789 M   i.   **Frank Wilson Waggener Jr.** was born 1 Nov 1946.

1342. Gwendolyn Waggener (*Annie Inez Sharp*[6], *Robert Patton*[5], *James (Jim) Charles Sr.*[4], *Adron (Edwin/Ade) Sr.*[3], *Charles W. Sr.*[2], *John Sr.*[1]) was born 18 Aug 1926.

Gwendolyn married **Robert H. Wilkinson Sr.** 27 Apr 1957.
+ 2790 M   i.   **Robert H. Wilkinson Jr.** was born 3 Oct 1958.
+ 2791 F   ii.   **Mary Ann Wilkinson** was born 28 Oct 1960.
  2792 M   iii. **William Frank Wilkinson** was born 3 Aug 1966.

1343. Barbara Ann Rochelle (*Annie Inez Sharp*[6], *Robert Patton*[5], *James (Jim) Charles Sr.*[4], *Adron (Edwin/Ade) Sr.*[3], *Charles W. Sr.*[2], *John Sr.*[1]) was born 12 Dec 1939 in Memphis, Shelby County, TN.

Barbara married **Robert Harold Cobb**, son of **Herman R. Cobb** and **Mary Louise Roberts**, 6 Dec 1959 in Memphis, Shelby County, TN. Robert was born 28 Oct 1939 in Memphis, Shelby County, TN.
+ 2793 M   i.   **Richard Lewis Cobb** was born 26 Mar 1962 in Memphis, Shelby County, TN.

Barbara next married **Marion Monroe Carden Jr.**, son of **Marion Monroe Carden Sr.** and **Lillie Virginia Roberts**. Marion was born 19 Jan 1929 in Hulbert, AR.

1344. Mary Virginia Givens (*Ida Lois Sharp*[6], *Robert Patton*[5], *James (Jim) Charles Sr.*[4], *Adron (Edwin/Ade) Sr.*[3], *Charles W. Sr.*[2], *John Sr.*[1]) was born 15 Mar 1924 in Florence, Lauderdale County, AL. Another name for Mary is Mary Virginia Givens.

Mary married **Roy Egbert McCorkle Jr.**, son of **Roy Egbert McCorkle Sr.** and **Susan Grace Spurgeon**, 26 Apr 1943. Roy was born 19 Jan 1927 in Colbert County, AL and died 24 Dec 1944 in English Channel, WWII.
+ 2794 M   i.   **Roy Egbert McCorkle III** was born 13 Jun 1944 in Colbert County, AL.

Mary next married **Thomas Jackson (Jack) McCarley**, son of **Thomas McCarley** and **Blanche Guinn**, 24 Apr 1946. Thomas was born 6 Mar 1924, died 4 Apr 1997, and was buried in Greenview Memorial Park, Florence, Lauderdale County, AL.
+ 2795 F   i.   **Mary Thomas (Tommie) McCarley** was born 12 Mar 1947 in Sheffield, Colbert County, AL.
+ 2796 F   ii.   **Jackie Leigh McCarley** was born 8 Nov 1951 in Sheffield, Colbert County, AL.
+ 2797 F   iii. **Kerry Ann McCarley** was born 15 Jun 1961 in Lauderdale County, AL.
+ 2798 M   iv. **Michael Kevin McCarley** was born 15 Jun 1961 in Florence, Lauderdale County, AL.

1345. Robert Orlan Givens Sr. (*Ida Lois Sharp*[6], *Robert Patton*[5], *James (Jim) Charles Sr.*[4], *Adron (Edwin/Ade) Sr.*[3], *Charles W. Sr.*[2], *John Sr.*[1]) was born 5 Sep 1925 in Florence, Lauderdale County, AL, died 18 Dec 1991, and was buried in New Hollywood Cemetery, Elizabeth City, NC.

Robert married **Carolyn Scott** 25 Mar 1944. Carolyn was born 25 Mar 1928 in Elizabeth City, NC, died 25 Jul 1986, and was buried in New Hollywood Cemetery, Elizabeth City, NC.

+ 2799 F i. **Bobbie Carol Givens** was born 28 Mar 1945.
+ 2800 F ii. **Mary Francis Givens** was born 20 Nov 1946.
+ 2801 F iii. **Lois Marie Givens** was born 19 May 1950.
+ 2802 M iv. **Robert (Bobby) Orlon Givens Jr.** was born 28 Jan 1954.
+ 2803 M v. **Scott Patton Givens Sr.** was born 16 Dec 1958.

1346. Thomas Edsel Givens (*Ida Lois Sharp*[6], *Robert Patton*[5], *James (Jim) Charles Sr.*[4], *Adron (Edwin/Ade) Sr.*[3], *Charles W. Sr.*[2], *John Sr.*[1]) was born 14 Nov 1927 in Florence, Lauderdale County, AL.

Thomas married **Melba Glenda Cloud**, daughter of **Allen Cloud** and **Zelda Dean**, 18 Feb 1956. Melba was born 3 Apr 1933 in West Monroe, LA.

+ 2804 F i. **Gina Gail Givens** was born 7 May 1958.
+ 2805 F ii. **Geri Lisa Givens** was born 30 Apr 1962.
+ 2806 M iii. **Thomas Brent Givens** was born 10 Sep 1966.

1347. Francis Ann Givens (*Ida Lois Sharp*[6], *Robert Patton*[5], *James (Jim) Charles Sr.*[4], *Adron (Edwin/Ade) Sr.*[3], *Charles W. Sr.*[2], *John Sr.*[1]) was born 21 Nov 1930 in Memphis, Shelby County, TN.

Francis married **William W. Ashley Sr.**, son of **Alton Dye Ashley** and **Florence Alice Cathcart**, 24 Dec 1949. William was born 19 Sep 1923 in Chattanooga, Cumberland County, TN.

+ 2807 M i. **William W. Ashley Jr.** was born 29 Oct 1952 in Birmingham, Jefferson County, AL.
+ 2808 F ii. **Alice Marie Ashley** was born 24 Dec 1956 in Miami, FL.

1348. Billy Fred Givens (*Ida Lois Sharp*[6], *Robert Patton*[5], *James (Jim) Charles Sr.*[4], *Adron (Edwin/Ade) Sr.*[3], *Charles W. Sr.*[2], *John Sr.*[1]) was born 22 Dec 1932 in Memphis, Shelby County, TN.

Billy married **Joyce Dumas**, daughter of **Jesse Aubrey Dumas** and **Mary Cowan**, 28 Jan 1957. Joyce was born 30 Aug 1935 in West Monroe, LA.

2809 M i. **Matthew Bryant Givens** was born 27 Mar 1960 in Baton Rouge, LA.
+ 2810 F ii. **Joni Leslie Givens** was born 5 Dec 1961 in Baton Rouge, LA.
+ 2811 M iii. **Mark Bradley Givens** was born 7 Jun 1966 in Baton Rouge, LA.

1349. Velma Rogers (*Lillian Anna (Lillie) Sharp*[6], *John Thomas (Tom)*[5], *James (Jim) Charles Sr.*[4], *Adron (Edwin/Ade) Sr.*[3], *Charles W. Sr.*[2], *John Sr.*[1]).

Velma married ***Unk Brooks** about 1925 in Tennessee.

2812 M i. **Charles Brooks.**
2813 M ii. **James Brooks.**
2814 M iii. **Wayne Brooks.**

1350. Emmet P. Rogers (*Lillian Anna (Lillie) Sharp*[6], *John Thomas (Tom)*[5], *James (Jim) Charles Sr.*[4], *Adron (Edwin/Ade) Sr.*[3], *Charles W. Sr.*[2], *John Sr.*[1]) was born 26 Jun 1902 in Lauderdale County, AL and died 23 Jun 1962 in McNairy County, TN.

Emmet married **Lola M. Droke** about 1925 in Tennessee. Lola was born 7 Jun 1903 in Tennessee, died 23 Nov 1979, and was buried in Milledgeville Cemetery, Hardin County, TN.

1352. Edmon (Eddie) Falmer Rogers (*Lillian Anna (Lillie) Sharp*[6], *John Thomas (Tom)*[5], *James (Jim) Charles Sr.*[4], *Adron (Edwin/Ade) Sr.*[3], *Charles W. Sr.*[2], *John Sr.*[1]) was born 26 Sep 1905 in Tennessee and died 8 Oct 1980 in McNairy County, TN.

Edmon married **Ether Pauline Phillips**, daughter of **George Phillips** and **Chester Wilkins**, 4 Dec 1926 in Hardin County, TN. Ether was born 11 Mar 1909 in Hardin County, TN and died 18 Oct 1963 in Hardin County, TN.

+ 2815 F   i.   **Dorothy M. Rogers** was born 14 Nov 1927 in Hardin County, TN.

1353. Claudie Thomas Rogers (*Lillian Anna (Lillie) Sharp^6, John Thomas (Tom)^5, James (Jim) Charles Sr.^{4}, Adron (Edwin/Ade) Sr.^{3}, Charles W. Sr.^{2}, John Sr.^{1}*) was born in 1907 in McNairy County, TN and died in 1987 in Hardin County, TN.

Claudie married **Emmie A. *Unk** about 1930. Emmie was born in 1910 and died in 1990.

1354. Clydie B. Rogers (*Lillian Anna (Lillie) Sharp^6, John Thomas (Tom)^5, James (Jim) Charles Sr.^{4}, Adron (Edwin/Ade) Sr.^{3}, Charles W. Sr.^{2}, John Sr.^{1}*) was born in 1909 in McNairy County, TN and died 4 Sep 1999 in Adamsville, McNairy County, TN.

Clydie married **Evelyn Harris**.

+ 2816 M   i.   **Clyde Norris Rogers Sr.** was born about 1939 in Adamsville, McNairy County, TN and died 4 Sep 1999.
+ 2817 F   ii.   **Minnie Faye Rogers**.

1355. Robert W. Rogers (*Lillian Anna (Lillie) Sharp^6, John Thomas (Tom)^5, James (Jim) Charles Sr.^{4}, Adron (Edwin/Ade) Sr.^{3}, Charles W. Sr.^{2}, John Sr.^{1}*) was born in Hardin County, TN and died 12 Oct 1991 in Hardin County, TN.

Robert married **Eva A. Phillips**.

+ 2818 M   i.   **Bob R. Rogers** was born 29 Sep 1929 in Adamsville, McNairy County, TN.
+ 2819 F   ii.   **Mary Helen Rogers** was born 3 Aug 1932 in Adamsville, McNairy County, TN.
+ 2820 M   iii.   **Phillip David Rogers Sr.** was born 10 Oct 1934 in Adamsville, McNairy County, TN.
+ 2821 F   iv.   **Elizabeth Rogers**.

1357. Ernest Powers Holcombe (*Maggie Sharp^6, John Thomas (Tom)^5, James (Jim) Charles Sr.^{4}, Adron (Edwin/Ade) Sr.^{3}, Charles W. Sr.^{2}, John Sr.^{1}*) was born 9 Oct 1898 in Florence, Lauderdale County, AL, died 5 Jan 1978, and was buried in Williams Chapel Cemetery, Lauderdale County, AL.

Ernest married **Sarah H. Dennis**, daughter of **Jay Dennis** and **Rosie Bryant**, 5 Jun 1920 in Lauderdale County, AL. Sarah was born 2 Nov 1902 in Florence, Lauderdale County, AL, died 12 Oct 1992, and was buried in Williams Chapel Cemetery, Lauderdale County, AL.

    2822 F   i.   **Erlene Holcombe** was born 8 Oct 1921 in Florence, Lauderdale County, AL, died 14 Jan 1922, and was buried in Williams Chapel Cemetery, Lauderdale County, AL.
+ 2823 M   ii.   **Willard Lee Holcombe** was born 21 Apr 1923 in Florence, Lauderdale County, AL.
+ 2824 M   iii.   **James Lee Holcombe** was born 20 Jul 1925 in Florence, Lauderdale County, AL.
+ 2825 F   iv.   **Geneva Bernice Holcombe** was born 25 Jan 1928 in Florence, Lauderdale County, AL.
+ 2826 M   v.   **Arnold Holcombe** was born 16 Feb 1930 in Florence, Lauderdale County, AL.
+ 2827 M   vi.   **Willie Cletus Holcombe** was born 12 Aug 1932 in Florence, Lauderdale County, AL.
+ 2828 M   vii.   **Edwin Ray Holcombe** was born 18 Dec 1936 in Florence, Lauderdale County, AL.
    2829 F viii.   **Nina Ruth Holcombe** was born 12 Oct 1939 in Florence, Lauderdale County, AL, died 17 Mar 1941, and was buried in Williams Chapel Cemetery, Lauderdale County, AL.
+ 2830 M   ix.   **Jimmy Leonard Holcombe** was born 6 Jun 1943 in Florence, Lauderdale County, AL.

1358. Elmer Patford Holcombe (*Maggie Sharp^6, John Thomas (Tom)^5, James (Jim) Charles Sr.^{4}, Adron (Edwin/Ade) Sr.^{3}, Charles W. Sr.^{2}, John Sr.^{1}*) was born 1 Feb 1903 in Florence, Lauderdale County, AL, died 17 Oct 1980, and was buried in Walston Cemetery, Oakland, Lauderdale County, AL.

Elmer married **Lola Pearl Sledge**, daughter of **James Madison Sledge** and **Julia Emma Cox**, 15 Nov 1929 in Lauderdale County, AL. Lola was born 25 Jan 1908 in Lauderdale County, AL, died 17 Sep 1963, and was buried in Walston Cemetery, Oakland, Lauderdale County, AL.

    2831 M   i.   **Allen Jones Holcombe** was born 14 May 1930 in Lauderdale County, AL and died 14 Sep 1939.

+ 2832 F ii. **Hazel Juanita Holcombe** was born 17 Nov 1931 in Lauderdale County, AL, died 13 Mar 2009, and was buried in Pine Hill Cemetery, Lauderdale County, AL.

+ 2833 F iii. **Mable Inez Holcombe** was born 1 Aug 1934 in Lauderdale County, AL, died 10 May 1999, and was buried in Walston Cemetery, Oakland, Lauderdale County, AL.

+ 2834 F iv. **Reba Nell Holcombe** was born 11 Jun 1940 in Lauderdale County, AL.

1359. Hubert Lee Holcombe (*Maggie Sharp*[6], *John Thomas (Tom)*[5], *James (Jim) Charles Sr.*[4], *Adron (Edwin/Ade) Sr.*[3], *Charles W. Sr.*[2], *John Sr.*[1]) was born 21 Aug 1904 in Florence, Lauderdale County, AL, died 30 Jun 1955, and was buried in Williams Chapel Cemetery, Lauderdale County, AL.

Hubert married **Esther Loretta Murphy**, daughter of **Charley B. Murphy** and **Carrie Brown**, 4 Nov 1927 in Lauderdale County, AL. Esther was born 5 Sep 1910 in Lauderdale County, AL, died 3 Feb 1986, and was buried in Williams Chapel Cemetery, Lauderdale County, AL.

+ 2835 M i. **Charles Herschel Holcombe** was born 5 May 1930 in Lauderdale County, AL, died 20 Apr 2001, and was buried in Williams Chapel Cemetery, Lauderdale County, AL.

+ 2836 M ii. **Lawrence O'steen Holcombe** was born 20 Sep 1932 in Lauderdale County, AL.

+ 2837 F iii. **Edith Elizabeth Holcombe** was born 7 May 1936 in Lauderdale County, AL.

+ 2838 F iv. **Helen Lee Holcombe** was born 28 Aug 1942 in Lauderdale County, AL.

1362. Jesse Thomas Sharp Sr. (*Hallie (Hal) B.*[6], *John Thomas (Tom)*[5], *James (Jim) Charles Sr.*[4], *Adron (Edwin/Ade) Sr.*[3], *Charles W. Sr.*[2], *John Sr.*[1]) was born 10 Feb 1901 in Lauderdale County, AL, died 19 Sep 1990, and was buried in Rogersville Civitan Cemetery, Lauderdale County, AL.

Jesse married **Maude Helen Bedingfield**, daughter of **Ira Hobbs Bedingfield** and **Ada Tennessee Greer**, 5 Jun 1921 in Lauderdale County, AL. Maude was born 26 Oct 1904 in Lauderdale County, AL, died 9 Sep 1993, and was buried in Rogersville Civitan Cemetery, Lauderdale County, AL.

+ 2839 F i. **Robbie Nell Sharp** was born 18 Jul 1927 in Rogersville, Lauderdale County, AL.

+ 2840 M ii. **Jesse Thomas Sharp Jr.** was born 4 Jul 1932 in Lauderdale County, AL, died 27 Apr 1998, and was buried in Civitan Cemetery, Lauderdale County, AL.

1363. Vessey David Sharp (*Hallie (Hal) B.*[6], *John Thomas (Tom)*[5], *James (Jim) Charles Sr.*[4], *Adron (Edwin/Ade) Sr.*[3], *Charles W. Sr.*[2], *John Sr.*[1]) was born 4 Dec 1902 in Waterloo, Lauderdale County, AL, died 28 Aug 1953, and was buried in Rogersville Civitan Cemetery, Lauderdale County, AL.

Vessey married **Gladys Fay Foster**, daughter of **Andrew Jackson Foster** and **Callie Ann Gothard**, 9 Apr 1942 in Lauderdale County, AL. Gladys was born 31 Mar 1910 in Lauderdale County, AL, died 1 Jun 1993, and was buried in Rogersville Civitan Cemetery, Lauderdale County, AL.

+ 2841 F i. **Martha Jane Sharp** was born 14 Mar 1943 in Lauderdale County, AL.

+ 2842 F ii. **Margaret Jean Sharp** was born 29 Nov 1945 in Lauderdale County, AL.

1364. Letha Birdie Sharp (*Hallie (Hal) B.*[6], *John Thomas (Tom)*[5], *James (Jim) Charles Sr.*[4], *Adron (Edwin/Ade) Sr.*[3], *Charles W. Sr.*[2], *John Sr.*[1]) was born 28 Jul 1904 in Lauderdale County, AL, died 17 Apr 2003, and was buried in Florence City Cemetery, Florence, Lauderdale County, AL.

Letha married **Dewey G. White** 5 Jun 1937 in Lauderdale County, AL. Dewey was born 10 Apr 1898 in Hardin County, TN, died 17 Dec 1967, and was buried in Florence City Cemetery, Florence, Lauderdale County, AL.

2843 M i. **Infant White** died at birth.

2844 M ii. **Infant White** died at birth.

2845 M iii. **Infant White** died at birth.

2846 F iv. **Freida Nell Reid White**.

1365. Mary Zethayr Sharp (*Hallie (Hal) B.*[6], *John Thomas (Tom)*[5], *James (Jim) Charles Sr.*[4], *Adron (Edwin/Ade) Sr.*[3], *Charles W. Sr.*[2], *John Sr.*[1]) was born 29 Jun 1906 in Waterloo, Lauderdale County, AL, died 5 Apr 1997, and was buried in Rogersville Civitan Cemetery, Lauderdale County, AL.

Mary married **Willie L. Gresham** 28 May 1958 in Lauderdale County, AL. Willie was born 28 Sep 1892 in Lauderdale County, AL, died 8 Mar 1969, and was buried in Rogersville Civitan Cemetery, Lauderdale County, AL.

1366. Fred Noel Sharp Sr. (*Hallie (Hal) B.* [6], *John Thomas (Tom)* [5], *James (Jim) Charles Sr.* [4], *Adron (Edwin/Ade) Sr.* [3], *Charles W. Sr.* [2], *John Sr.* [1]) was born 7 Jun 1909 in Waterloo, Lauderdale County, AL, died 23 May 1973, and was buried in Florence City Cemetery, Florence, Lauderdale County, AL.

Fred married **Virginia Hayes**, daughter of **William Lester Hayes** and **Mary Ellen Coates**, 20 Oct 1949 in Lauderdale County, AL. Virginia was born 25 Sep 1926 in Lauderdale County, AL.

+ 2847 M i. **Fred Noel Sharp Jr.** was born 15 Nov 1950 in Lauderdale County, AL.
+ 2848 F ii. **Sandra Kay Sharp** was born 3 Feb 1952 in Lauderdale County, AL.
+ 2849 F iii. **Susie Mae Sharp** was born 20 Aug 1953 in Lauderdale County, AL.
+ 2850 F iv. **Janice Marie Sharp** was born 19 Oct 1954 in Lauderdale County, AL.
+ 2851 M v. **Jeffrey Allen Sharp I** was born 8 Mar 1966 in Lauderdale County, AL.

1367. Thursa Lou Sharp (*Hallie (Hal) B.* [6], *John Thomas (Tom)* [5], *James (Jim) Charles Sr.* [4], *Adron (Edwin/Ade) Sr.* [3], *Charles W. Sr.* [2], *John Sr.* [1]) was born 5 Jun 1911 in Lauderdale County, AL, died in 1997, and was buried in Rogersville Civitan Cemetery, Lauderdale County, AL.

Thursa married **Ezra Milton Burk**, son of **Lyonel Burk** and **Mollie Cockrell**, 26 Apr 1930 in Lauderdale County, AL. Ezra was born 28 Jul 1904 in Lauderdale County, AL.

+ 2852 M i. **Milton Sharp Burk** was born 12 Apr 1931 in Lauderdale County, AL.
+ 2853 M ii. **Donald Oneal Burk** was born 9 Nov 1934 in Lauderdale County, AL.
+ 2854 M iii. **Jimmy Ray Burk** was born 26 Oct 1936 in Giles County, TN, died 22 Aug 1996, and was buried in Bethel Cemetery, Center Star, Lauderdale County, AL.

1368. Leona May Sharp (*Hallie (Hal) B.* [6], *John Thomas (Tom)* [5], *James (Jim) Charles Sr.* [4], *Adron (Edwin/Ade) Sr.* [3], *Charles W. Sr.* [2], *John Sr.* [1]) was born 27 Jul 1915 in Lauderdale County, AL, died 23 Sep 2003, and was buried in Florence City Cemetery, Florence, Lauderdale County, AL.

Leona married **Don Douglas Littrell**, son of **John Allen Littrell** and **Frances Riddle**, 13 Apr 1936 in Lawrence County, TN. Don was born 11 Apr 1917 in Lawrence County, TN, died 28 May 2003, and was buried in Florence City Cemetery, Florence, Lauderdale County, AL.

+ 2855 F i. **Mary Ann Littrell** was born 14 Jul 1942 in Colbert County, AL.
+ 2856 F ii. **Maude Ellen Littrell** was born 17 Aug 1946 in Colbert County, AL.

1370. John Edward Sharp (*James (Swagger)* [6], *John Thomas (Tom)* [5], *James (Jim) Charles Sr.* [4], *Adron (Edwin/Ade) Sr.* [3], *Charles W. Sr.* [2], *John Sr.* [1]) was born 9 Jan 1910 in Lauderdale County, AL, died 17 Mar 1993, and was buried in St. Joseph Valley Cemetery, Mishawaka, IN.

John married **Marie Powers Robertson**, daughter of **John Wesley Robertson** and **Nettie Eliza Cheek**, 9 Dec 1933 in Lauderdale County, AL. Marie was born 21 May 1914 in Wright, Lauderdale County, AL, died 1 Jan 1994, and was buried in St. Joseph Valley Cemetery, Mishawaka, IN.

+ 2857 F i. **Mary Ann Sharp** was born 21 Sep 1934 in Lauderdale County, AL.
  2858 F ii. **Sarah Joan Sharp** was born 4 Apr 1936 in Lauderdale County, AL and died 4 Apr 1936 in Lauderdale County, AL.

1371. Homer Carroll Sharp (*James (Swagger)* [6], *John Thomas (Tom)* [5], *James (Jim) Charles Sr.* [4], *Adron (Edwin/Ade) Sr.* [3], *Charles W. Sr.* [2], *John Sr.* [1]) was born 18 Jul 1913 in Lauderdale County, AL, died 30 Oct 1992, and was buried in Rose Lawn Cemetery, Decatur, AL.

Homer married **Jewell Melinda Cagle**, daughter of **Martin Luther Cagle** and **Minnie Melinda Smith**, 21 May 1938 in Lauderdale County, AL. Jewell was born 14 Apr 1919 in Lawrence County, AL.

+ 2859 F i. **Melinda Sue Sharp** was born 6 Oct 1950 in Morgan County, AL.
+ 2860 F ii. **Carol Sharp** was born 9 Dec 1955 in Morgan County, AL.
  2861 M iii. **James Luke Sharp** was born 7 Apr 1960 in Morgan County, AL.

1372. Bessie Etoil Sharp (*James (Swagger)* [6], *John Thomas (Tom)* [5], *James (Jim) Charles Sr.* [4], *Adron (Edwin/Ade) Sr.* [3], *Charles W. Sr.* [2], *John Sr.* [1]) was born 9 Sep 1914 in Lauderdale County, AL, died 8 Mar 2002, and was buried in Oak Grove Cemetery, Lauderdale County, AL.

General Notes: Obituary - Times Daily, Florence, Lauderdale County, Alabama

"Bessie Etoyle Sharp Mitchell, 87, Florence, Ala., died Thursday, March 7, 2002, after an extended illness. Visitation will begin at 4 p.m. today at Souls Harbor Apostolic Church. The funeral will be at 2 p.m. Sunday at the church, with burial in Oak Grove Cemetery. Officiating at the funeral will be Pastor Bobby Crosswhite. She was a native and lifelong resident of Lauderdale County.

She is survived by her sons, James 'Buddy' Mitchell and wife, Mary Ann, Thomas Larry Mitchell and wife, Nita; daughters, Martha Lee Webster and husband, Bobby, Judy Crosswhite and husband, Bobby; special nieces, Teresa Griffus and Vicky McMahan; sisters, Rachel Dewberry, Ayleen Sharp; brother, Lowell Sharp; grandchildren, Nena Haigler (Hayne), Michael Neal Gene, Kim Clayton, Terry Mitchell, Eddy Mitchell (Karen), Russ Mitchell (Anna), Sherrie LaBlanc (Lenny), Steve Mitchell (April), Deanna Parker (Daniel), Keith Crosswhite, Kelli Daniel (Greg); 19 great -grandchildren; one great-great-grandchild.

She was preceded in death by her husband, Edward Lee Mitchell; son, Russell Taylor Mitchell; brothers, Edward Sharp and Homer Sharp; sisters, Annie Mae Ragan and Nell Cagle.

Pallbearers will include grandsons. Honorary pallbearers will be Chuck Barrett, Johnny Ray, Bobby Griffus, Tim Hollis, Joe Pitts, Berlon Sharp and Michael Goodwin.

She was a member of the Souls Harbor Apostolic Church.

We give honor to God for our mother and honor to our mother for the beautiful Christian life she lived and for the example she left behind. Some people make the world brighter just by being in it.

Greenview Funeral Home, Florence, is directing."

Bessie married **Edward Lee Mitchell**, son of **James Mason Mitchell** and **Emma Elizabeth Butler**, 29 Jun 1934 in Lauderdale County, AL. Edward was born 23 Sep 1908 in Lauderdale County, AL, died 17 Jun 1966, and was buried in Oak Grove Cemetery, Lauderdale County, AL.

+ 2862 F   i.   **Martha Lee Mitchell** was born 13 Aug 1935 in Rogersville, Lauderdale County, AL.
+ 2863 M   ii. **James Ralph (Buddy) Mitchell** was born 29 Jan 1937 in Rogersville, Lauderdale County, AL.
+ 2864 M   iii. **Russell Taylor Mitchell** was born 18 Aug 1938 in Rogersville, Lauderdale County, AL, died 17 Apr 1965, and was buried in Oak Grove Cemetery, Lauderdale County, AL.
+ 2865 M   iv. **Thomas Larry (Tommy) Mitchell** was born 29 Oct 1941 in Lauderdale County, AL.
+ 2866 F   v.   **Judy Elaine Mitchell** was born 9 Feb 1946 in Lauderdale County, AL.

1373. Annie May Sharp (*James (Swagger)* [6], *John Thomas (Tom)* [5], *James (Jim) Charles Sr.* [4], *Adron (Edwin/Ade) Sr.* [3], *Charles W. Sr.* [2], *John Sr.* [1]) was born 13 Jan 1917 in Alabama.

Annie married **Jessie L. Ragan** 7 Nov 1936 in Lauderdale County, AL. Jessie was born 4 Jul 1915 in Dixon County, TN.

1374. Mollie Nell Sharp (*James (Swagger)* [6], *John Thomas (Tom)* [5], *James (Jim) Charles Sr.* [4], *Adron (Edwin/Ade) Sr.* [3], *Charles W. Sr.* [2], *John Sr.* [1]) was born 19 Jun 1920 in Lauderdale County, AL.

Mollie married **Martin Leonard Cagle**, son of **Martin Luther Cagle** and **Minnie Melinda Smith**, 12 Jun 1937 in Lauderdale County, AL. Martin was born 12 Sep 1916 in Franklin County, AL, died 3 Jan 1993, and was buried in Rose Lawn Cemetery, Decatur, AL.

  2867 M   i.   **Harry Cagle**.
+ 2868 F   ii. **Gwendolyn Cagle**.

1375. Rachel Violet Sharp (*James (Swagger)* [6], *John Thomas (Tom)* [5], *James (Jim) Charles Sr.* [4], *Adron (Edwin/Ade) Sr.* [3], *Charles W. Sr.* [2], *John Sr.* [1]) was born 18 Feb 1923 in Lauderdale County, AL.

Rachel married **Homer Claude Dewberry Jr.**, son of **Homer Claude Dewberry Sr.** and **Sara Edna Vaughn**, 9 Feb 1946. Homer was born 16 Feb 1918 in Lauderdale County, AL, died 21 Jun 2001, and was buried in Walston Cemetery, Oakland, Lauderdale County, AL.

+ 2869 F   i.   **Claudeen Dewberry** was born 21 Mar 1941 in Lauderdale County, AL.
+ 2870 F   ii. **Cheryl Evelyn Dewberry** was born 29 Nov 1946 in Lauderdale County, AL.
+ 2871 F   iii. **Jean Gay Dewberry** was born 18 Jan 1949 in Lauderdale County, AL.
+ 2872 F   iv. **Edna Kaye Dewberry** was born 10 Sep 1951 in Lauderdale County, AL.

1376. James Loyal Sharp (*James (Swagger)* [6], *John Thomas (Tom)* [5], *James (Jim) Charles Sr.* [4], *Adron (Edwin/Ade) Sr.* [3], *Charles W. Sr.* [2], *John Sr.* [1]) was born 12 Jun 1927 in Lauderdale County, AL.

James married **Dicie M. McKee** 16 Oct 1948 in Iuka, Tishomingo County, MS. Dicie was born 24 Aug 1926 in Decatur, Morgan County, AL.

+ 2873 M   i.   **Donnie Dwayne Sharp** was born 12 Nov 1949.
+ 2874 M   ii.   **James Harold Sharp** was born 28 Jun 1952.
+ 2875 M   iii. **Randall Boyd Sharp** was born 16 May 1962.

1377. Aileen Beulah Sharp (*James (Swagger)* [6], *John Thomas (Tom)* [5], *James (Jim) Charles Sr.* [4], *Adron (Edwin/Ade) Sr.* [3], *Charles W. Sr.* [2], *John Sr.* [1]) was born 24 Feb 1927 in Waterloo, Lauderdale County, AL.

Aileen married **Thomas Charles Kelley Sr.**, son of **Sam Kelley** and **Hattie Goins**, 8 Mar 1949 in Lauderdale County, AL. Thomas was born 7 Dec 1927 in Florence, Lauderdale County, AL.

  2876 M   i.   **Thomas (Tommy) Charles Kelley Jr.** was born 13 Feb 1951 in Breckinridge, KY.
+ 2877 M   ii.   **Teddy Steven Kelley** was born 26 Sep 1953 in Lauderdale County, AL.
+ 2878 F   iii. **Teresa Dawn Kelley** was born 13 Sep 1954 in Lauderdale County, AL.
+ 2879 F   iv.   **Vicki Melitha Kelley** was born 25 Mar 1959 in Lauderdale County, AL.

1378. Ellie Berry Sharp Sr. (*Thomas Leslie (Peck)* [6], *John Thomas (Tom)* [5], *James (Jim) Charles Sr.* [4], *Adron (Edwin/Ade) Sr.* [3], *Charles W. Sr.* [2], *John Sr.* [1]) was born 11 Jul 1910 in Lauderdale County, AL, died 26 Feb 1975, and was buried in Wright Cemetery, Wright, Lauderdale County, AL.

Ellie married **Irene Francis Davis**, daughter of **Willie Frank Davis** and **Corene Francis Strange**, 9 Dec 1929 in Iuka, Tishomingo County, MS. Irene was born 7 Jun 1913 in Lauderdale County, AL.

+ 2880 M   i.   **Ellie Berry Sharp Jr.** was born 2 Jun 1930 in Lauderdale County, AL and died 10 Aug 1997.
+ 2881 M   ii.   **Allen Bernard Sharp** was born 3 Aug 1933 in Lauderdale County, AL.
+ 2882 M   iii. **Donald Glenn Sharp** was born 1 Oct 1936 in Lauderdale County, AL.
+ 2883 F   iv.   **Sarah Carrene Sharp** was born 20 Mar 1939 in Lauderdale County, AL.
+ 2884 F   v.   **Sandra Sue Sharp** was born 12 May 1945 in Lauderdale County, AL.
+ 2885 F   vi.   **Barbara Ann Sharp** was born 29 Dec 1947 in Lauderdale County, AL.

1379. Earl Leslie Sharp (*Thomas Leslie (Peck)* [6], *John Thomas (Tom)* [5], *James (Jim) Charles Sr.* [4], *Adron (Edwin/Ade) Sr.* [3], *Charles W. Sr.* [2], *John Sr.* [1]) was born 15 Sep 1912 in Wright, Lauderdale County, AL, died 20 Jan 1999, and was buried in Wright Cemetery, Wright, Lauderdale County, AL.

General Notes: Obituary - Times Daily, Florence, Lauderdale County, Alabama

"Mr. Earl Leslie Sharp, 86, Waterloo, passed away on Wednesday, Jan. 20, 1999 at Hardin County General Hospital, after an extended illness. Visitation was Thursday, Jan. 21, 1999, at Elkins Funeral Home, Florence.
A grave side service will be held at 1 p.m. Friday at Wright's Cemetery in the Wright community, with the Rev. Emory Bailey officiating. Elkins Funeral Home is directing.
Mr. Sharp was born and raised in Waterloo, Ala. He was a self -employed trader and was of the Methodist faith.
He is survived by his wife of 65 years, Mary Nadine White Sharp of Waterloo; daughter, Doris Elizabeth Terrell of Central; sons, Bobby Sharp, Sammy Sharp, Tommy Sharp, Donnie Sharp and Jerry Lynn Sharp, all of Waterloo; seven granddaughters; six great -grandsons.
Pallbearers will include Buddy Terrell, Carl Young, Lewis Young, Ray Higgins, Adam Holcombe and David Holcombe."

Earl married **Mary Nadine White**, daughter of **William (Billy) Edgar White** and **Willie Jewel Robertson**, 7 Dec 1933 in Lauderdale County, AL. Mary was born 16 Dec 1919 in Wright, Lauderdale County, AL, died 19 Jun 2008, and was buried in Wright Cemetery, Wright, Lauderdale County, AL.

+ 2886 F   i.   **Doris Elizabeth Sharp** was born 7 Jul 1935 in Lauderdale County, AL.
+ 2887 M   ii.   **Bobby Elwood Sharp** was born 22 Oct 1943 in Lauderdale County, AL.
+ 2888 M   iii. **Tommy White Sharp** was born 9 Sep 1947 in Lauderdale County, AL.

2889 M iv. **Sammy Earl Sharp** was born 27 Feb 1947 in Lauderdale County, AL, died 12 Dec 2004, and was buried in Wright Cemetery, Wright, Lauderdale County, AL.

+ 2890 M v. **Donnie Murray Sharp** was born 10 Jan 1950 in Lauderdale County, AL.

+ 2891 M vi. **Jerry Lynn Sharp** was born 24 May 1953 in Lauderdale County, AL.

1381. Virgil Sharp (*Thomas Leslie (Peck)* [6], *John Thomas (Tom)* [5], *James (Jim) Charles Sr.* [4], *Adron (Edwin/Ade) Sr.* [3], *Charles W. Sr.* [2], *John Sr.* [1]) was born 12 Feb 1918 in Lauderdale County, AL and died in 1969.

Virgil married **Nancy Brinkley** in 1941.

1382. Wilma Lutell Sharp (*Thomas Leslie (Peck)* [6], *John Thomas (Tom)* [5], *James (Jim) Charles Sr.* [4], *Adron (Edwin/Ade) Sr.* [3], *Charles W. Sr.* [2], *John Sr.* [1]) was born 2 Dec 1920 in Savannah, TN.

Wilma married **Horace Jenson**, son of **Joseph C. Jenson** and **Ada Keppley**, 25 Dec 1942 in Marion, Crittenden County, AR. Horace was born 13 Nov 1925 in Lauderdale County, AL, died 1 Aug 1972 in Nashville, Davidson County, TN, and was buried in Memphis, Shelby County, TN.

+ 2892 M i. **James D. Jenson Sr.** was born 1 Apr 1944 in Memphis, Shelby County, TN.

+ 2893 M ii. **Lawrence K. Jenson** was born 9 Nov 1952 in Memphis, Shelby County, TN.

+ 2894 F iii. **Jan Carol Jenson** was born 8 Jun 1957 in Memphis, Shelby County, TN.

1383. Selbert Sharp (*Thomas Leslie (Peck)* [6], *John Thomas (Tom)* [5], *James (Jim) Charles Sr.* [4], *Adron (Edwin/Ade) Sr.* [3], *Charles W. Sr.* [2], *John Sr.* [1]) was born 28 Apr 1921 in Savannah, TN.

Selbert married **Helen Epps**.

1384. Ray Sharp (*Thomas Leslie (Peck)* [6], *John Thomas (Tom)* [5], *James (Jim) Charles Sr.* [4], *Adron (Edwin/Ade) Sr.* [3], *Charles W. Sr.* [2], *John Sr.* [1]) was born 22 Mar 1924 in Savannah, TN.

Ray married **Janet Lawson** in 1945.

1385. Robert (Bob) Sharp (*Thomas Leslie (Peck)* [6], *John Thomas (Tom)* [5], *James (Jim) Charles Sr.* [4], *Adron (Edwin/Ade) Sr.* [3], *Charles W. Sr.* [2], *John Sr.* [1]) was born 9 Sep 1926 in Savannah, TN and died in 1999 in Memphis, Shelby County, TN.

Robert married **Jane Allen** in 1942.

1386. Murray Sharp (*Thomas Leslie (Peck)* [6], *John Thomas (Tom)* [5], *James (Jim) Charles Sr.* [4], *Adron (Edwin/Ade) Sr.* [3], *Charles W. Sr.* [2], *John Sr.* [1]) was born 18 Jun 1928 in Savannah, TN.

Murray married **Charlotte Strong** in 1950.

1387. Broadus Sharp (*Thomas Leslie (Peck)* [6], *John Thomas (Tom)* [5], *James (Jim) Charles Sr.* [4], *Adron (Edwin/Ade) Sr.* [3], *Charles W. Sr.* [2], *John Sr.* [1]) was born 1 Apr 1930 in Lauderdale County, AL.

Broadus married **Mary Helen Sandridge**.

1390. Brenda Joyce Sharp (*Thomas Leslie (Peck)* [6], *John Thomas (Tom)* [5], *James (Jim) Charles Sr.* [4], *Adron (Edwin/Ade) Sr.* [3], *Charles W. Sr.* [2], *John Sr.* [1]) was born 16 Aug 1941 in Colbert County, AL.

Brenda married **Douglas Pennington**, son of **Henry Pennington** and **Gertrude Balentine**, 23 May 1959 in Lauderdale County, AL. Douglas was born 11 Jun 1937 in Lauderdale County, AL, died 10 Jul 1964, and was buried in Macedonia Cemetery, Lauderdale County, AL.

+ 2895 M i. **Michael Dewayne Pennington** was born 14 Oct 1960 in Lauderdale County, AL.

+ 2896 M ii. **Terry Keith Pennington** was born 27 Jul 1963 in Lauderdale County, AL.

Brenda next married **Bobby Ray Terry**, son of **Robert Coleman Singlemon** and **Willie Franklin Goodwin**. Bobby was born 5 Oct in Hillsboro, AL, died in Sep 1984, and was buried in Colbert Memorial Gardens, Colbert County, AL.

2897 F i. **Kim Dawn Terry** was born 25 Jul 1966 in Colbert County, AL.

1391. Judy Amisonia Sharp (*Thomas Leslie (Peck)* [6], *John Thomas (Tom)* [5], *James (Jim) Charles Sr.* [4], *Adron (Edwin/Ade) Sr.* [3], *Charles W. Sr.* [2], *John Sr.* [1]) was born 26 Mar 1943 in Colbert County, AL.

Judy married **Paul Douglas Fox**, son of **John Lee Fox** and **Lucille Swaner**, 1 Dec 1960 in Lauderdale County, AL. Paul was born 8 Feb 1942 in Colbert County, AL.

+ 2898 F i. **Mitzi Kay Fox** was born 19 Jan 1963 in Lauderdale County, AL.
+ 2899 M ii. **Christopher Alan Fox** was born 30 Aug 1964 in Colbert County, AL.

1393. Terry Lee Sharp (*Edgar Lee* [6], *John Thomas (Tom)* [5], *James (Jim) Charles Sr.* [4], *Adron (Edwin/Ade) Sr.* [3], *Charles W. Sr.* [2], *John Sr.* [1]) was born 13 Sep 1915 in Lauderdale County, AL, died 14 Jan 1994, and was buried in Greenview Memorial Park, Florence, Lauderdale County, AL.

Terry married **Jewel Estelle Young**, daughter of **John Robert Young** and **Callie Fielder**, 23 Dec 1944 in Lauderdale County, AL. Jewel was born 28 Sep 1920 in Lauderdale County, AL, died 4 Dec 2004, and was buried in Greenview Memorial Park, Florence, Lauderdale County, AL.
(Duplicate Line. See Person 895)

1394. Doyle Woodrow Sharp (*Edgar Lee* [6], *John Thomas (Tom)* [5], *James (Jim) Charles Sr.* [4], *Adron (Edwin/Ade) Sr.* [3], *Charles W. Sr.* [2], *John Sr.* [1]) was born 22 Feb 1917 in Lauderdale County, AL, died 15 Nov 1987 in Lauderdale County, AL, and was buried in Greenview Memorial Park, Florence, Lauderdale County, AL.

Doyle married **Hazel Hart**, daughter of **John Leland Hart** and **Delta Marie Biggs**, 23 Dec 1944 in Lauderdale County, AL. Hazel was born 23 Jan 1929 in Lauderdale County, AL.

+ 2900 M i. **Jerry Woodrow Sharp** was born 29 Nov 1948 in Lauderdale County, AL.
+ 2901 F ii. **Joyce Elaine Sharp** was born 15 Jun 1951 in Lauderdale County, AL.

1395. Mary Elizabeth Sharp (*Edgar Lee* [6], *John Thomas (Tom)* [5], *James (Jim) Charles Sr.* [4], *Adron (Edwin/Ade) Sr.* [3], *Charles W. Sr.* [2], *John Sr.* [1]) was born 16 Nov 1918 in Lauderdale County, AL, died 10 Oct 1976, and was buried in Greenview Memorial Park, Florence, Lauderdale County, AL.

Mary married **Roy Robertson**, son of **Mills Berry Robertson** and **Mary Jo Young**, 3 Feb 1940 in Lauderdale County, AL. Roy was born 23 Jan 1914 in Wright, Lauderdale County, AL, died 10 Oct 1979, and was buried in Greenview Memorial Park, Florence, Lauderdale County, AL.

+ 2902 F i. **Joann Robertson** was born 5 Jul 1946 in Lauderdale County, AL.
+ 2903 M ii. **Berry Lee (Buck) Robertson** was born 13 Jun 1949 in Lauderdale County, AL.
+ 2904 F iii. **Charlotte Rose Robertson** was born 31 Jan 1953 in Lauderdale County, AL.
+ 2905 M iv. **Gary Lynn (Peanut) Robertson** was born 11 Sep 1955 in Lauderdale County, AL.

1396. Annie Bell Sharp (*Edgar Lee* [6], *John Thomas (Tom)* [5], *James (Jim) Charles Sr.* [4], *Adron (Edwin/Ade) Sr.* [3], *Charles W. Sr.* [2], *John Sr.* [1]) was born 11 Jun 1920 in Lauderdale County, AL, died 8 Mar 2009, and was buried in Greenview Memorial Park, Florence, Lauderdale County, AL.

Annie married **Joe Leonard Mansell**, son of **Tom Mansell** and **Isabella Parker**, 23 Nov 1943 in Lauderdale County, AL. Joe was born in Lauderdale County, AL, died 18 Jul 1964, and was buried in Greenview Memorial Park, Florence, Lauderdale County, AL.

+ 2906 F i. **Janice Kay Mansell** was born 1 Nov 1946 in Lauderdale County, AL.
+ 2907 M ii. **Jimmy Don Mansell** was born in Mar 1951 in Lauderdale County, AL.
+ 2908 F iii. **Connie Renee Mansell** was born 2 Feb 1958 in Lauderdale County, AL.

1397. Edna Idelle Sharp (*Edgar Lee* [6], *John Thomas (Tom)* [5], *James (Jim) Charles Sr.* [4], *Adron (Edwin/Ade) Sr.* [3], *Charles W. Sr.* [2], *John Sr.* [1]) was born 23 Jun 1922 in Lauderdale County, AL, died 18 Jul 1997, and was buried in Rhodesville Cemetery, Lauderdale County, AL.

Edna married **Joe Lewis Higgins** 22 Nov 1962 in Lauderdale County, AL. Joe was born 26 Aug 1925 in Lauderdale County, AL.

Edna next married **James Godwin Garner**, son of **James Jackson Garner** and **Cora Rhodes**, 9 Dec 1966 in Lauderdale County, AL. James was born 29 Apr 1921 in Lauderdale County, AL, died 2 Oct 2001, and was buried in Rhodesville Cemetery, Lauderdale County, AL.

General Notes: Obituary - Times Daily, Florence, Lauderdale County, Alabama

"James G. Garner, 80, Florence, died Tuesday, Oct. 2, 2001, at his residence. The funeral service will be Thursday, Oct. 4, 2001, at 2 p.m. at Rhodesville Methodist Church. Remains will lie in state at the church one hour before
service time. Terry Willis and Jerry Hastin will officiate. Interment will follow in Rhodesville Cemetery.
He was a lifelong resident of Lauderdale County, retired from Colbert Steam Plant, and member of Rhodesville United Methodist and Carpenters Local No. 109. He enjoyed woodworking.
He was preceded in death by his wife, Edna Idell Sharp Garner in 1997; and a brother, Jimmy Garner.
Survivors include his daughter, Diane Garner Bratcher and her husband, Kenneth L.; brothers, Jack Garner of Florence and Clyde Garner of Killen,; grandchildren, Ken Bratcher and his wife, Sharon, of Killen, Kerri Risner and her husband, Bobby, of Florence; great -grandchildren, Heather, Dustin and Kayla Bratcher and Kagen Risner.
Pallbearers will be Chad Vaden, Bobby Pittman, Carl Counce, Johnny Garner, Horace Rhodes and Tim Rhodes. Honorary pallbearers will be Cecil Perkins, Will Rhodes, Jerry Darby and Rube Hamby.
Memorial donations may be made to the Alzheimer's Association of the Shoals, COAL, P.O. Box 1608, Florence, AL. Spry Funeral Home-Serenity Chapel, Florence, is directing."

+ 2909   F   i.   **Diane Garner**.

1398. Julia Edneta Sharp (*Edgar Lee* [6], *John Thomas (Tom)* [5], *James (Jim) Charles Sr.* [4], *Adron (Edwin/Ade) Sr.* [3], *Charles W. Sr.* [2], *John Sr.* [1]) was born 23 Dec 1924 in Lauderdale County, AL and was buried in Wright Cemetery, Wright, Lauderdale County, AL.

Julia married **Jodie Woodrow Rogers**, son of **Albert G. Rogers** and **Etta Maggie (Etter) Milford**, 12 Jan 1947 in Lauderdale County, AL. Jodie was born 15 Dec 1916 in Gravely Springs, Lauderdale County, AL, died 29 Mar 1964, and was buried in Wright Cemetery, Wright, Lauderdale County, AL.
+ 2910   M   i.   **Kenneth Dale Rogers** was born 17 Apr 1950 in Lauderdale County, AL.
+ 2911   M   ii.   **Stephen Phillip Rogers** was born 4 Mar 1955 in Lauderdale County, AL.

1399. John Thomas Sharp (*Edgar Lee* [6], *John Thomas (Tom)* [5], *James (Jim) Charles Sr.* [4], *Adron (Edwin/Ade) Sr.* [3], *Charles W. Sr.* [2], *John Sr.* [1]) was born 26 Oct 1927 in Lauderdale County, AL, died 7 Mar 2001, and was buried in Greenview Memorial Park, Florence, Lauderdale County, AL.

General Notes: Obituary - Times Daily, Florence, Lauderdale County, Alabama

"John Thomas Sharp, 73, a longtime resident of Florence, died at his residence Wednesday, March 7, 2001, after an extended illness.
Friends and relatives may visit with the family 6 - 8 p.m. today at Greenview Funeral Home. Funeral services will be Saturday, March 10, 2001, at 1 p.m. at Greenview Memorial Chapel, with the Revs. Guy Estave, minister of Forest Hills Baptist Church, and Charlie Thompson officiating. Burial will follow in the Garden of Rest, Greenview Memorial Park.
Mr. Sharp was a retired salesman for Magnum Furniture Co. of Florence and worked recently for Fire and Stone of Muscle Shoals, Ala. He was a charter member and deacon of Forest Hills Baptist Church. He was a veteran of the Korean War.
Survivors include his wife of 49 years, Mary Evelyn Wylie Sharp, Florence; one son, Gregory T. Sharp and wife, Cindy, of Florence; grandchildren, Jennifer Herrmann and Christy Sharp; daughter, Cynthia Gibson and husband, Dennis, of Killen; and grandson, Kyle Gibson; four sisters, Ann Mansell of Florence, Lillian Sharp of Florence, Emogene Womble of Central and Julie Rogers of Florence.

Preceding Mr. Sharp in death were his parents, Lonnie Alberta Glasscock and Edgar Lee Sharp, longtime residents of Lauderdale County; two brothers, Terry Lee Sharp and Doyle Sharp; two sisters, Dale Garner and Mary Elizabeth Robertson.

John was a loving husband, father and grandfather.

Active pallbearers will be Jack Moore, Jim Wells, Chuck Burgess, Mike Harrison, Sam Magnum and John Bishop. Honorary pallbearers will be Dan Peterman, Don Price, John Riley, Paul Curry, Robert Sharp and Sherman Eabes.

Memorials may be made to the building fund of Forrest Hills Baptist Church of Florence.

Greenview Funeral Home, Florence, is directing."

John married **Mary Evelyn Wylie**, daughter of **James Newton Wylie** and **Willie Mae Wesson**, 20 Oct 1951 in Iuka, Tishomingo County, MS. Mary was born 28 Feb 1935 in Lauderdale County, AL, died 4 Nov 2007, and was buried in Greenview Memorial Park, Florence, Lauderdale County, AL.

+ 2912 M   i.   **Gregory Thomas Sharp** was born 1 Jan 1955 in Lauderdale County, AL.
+ 2913 F   ii.   **Cynthia (Cindy) Jo Sharp** was born 3 Jun 1961 in Lauderdale County, AL.

1400. Ellen Emogene Sharp (*Edgar Lee*[6], *John Thomas (Tom)*[5], *James (Jim) Charles Sr.*[4], *Adron (Edwin/Ade) Sr.*[3], *Charles W. Sr.*[2], *John Sr.*[1]) was born 12 Apr 1932 in Lauderdale County, AL.

Ellen married **Leslie Brooks Womble**, son of **Robert Clark Womble** and **Lucile Gladys Gooch**, 8 Apr 1949 in Lauderdale County, AL. Leslie was born 23 Sep 1927 in Lauderdale County, AL, died 15 Jul 1999, and was buried in Wright Cemetery, Wright, Lauderdale County, AL.

General Notes: Obituary - Times Daily, Florence, Lauderdale County, Alabama

"Leslie Brooks "L.B." Womble, 71, of Florence, died Thursday, July 15, 1999 after an extended illness. Visitation was Friday evening at Greenview. The funeral will be Saturday at 2 p.m. at Greenview Funeral Home Chapel with burial in Wright Cemetery. Officiating at the funeral will be the Revs. Mickey Davis and Rowe Wren.

Mr. Womble was a native and lifelong resident of Lauderdale County.

He is survived by his wife, Emogene Sharp Womble, Florence; daughter, Judy Diane Smith, Florence; sisters, Dorothy Woods, Waterloo, Faye Davis, Florence, Ruby Hanback, Florence; brothers, R.C. Womble, Florence, Columbus Womble, Atlanta, Ga., grandsons, Anthony Smith and Craig Smith.

Mr. Womble was preceded in death by his parents, Robert Clark Womble, Sr. and Lucille Gladys Gooch Womble, and a sister, Margaret Isley.

Pallbearers will be Carl Young, Samuel Marks, Joel Brown, Larry Cole, Jimmy Marks, Danny Haddock. Honorary pallbearers will be Gerald Marks, Steve Tune, Donald McDaniel, and employees of the State Highway Department.

Mr. Womble was retired from the State Highway Department as a heavy equipment operator. He was a member of Wright United Methodist Church. Mr. Womble was a U.S. Army veteran of the Korean War and was a member of the Korean War Veterans Association, the American Legion and the Alabama Retired State Employees Association.

Thanks to Hospice of the Shoals. Greenview Funeral Home of Florence is directing."

+ 2914 F   i.   **Judy Diane Womble** was born 25 Aug 1953 in Lauderdale County, AL.

1401. Dorothy Maurita Hairell (*Minor (Mina) Houston Sharp*[6], *John Thomas (Tom)*[5], *James (Jim) Charles Sr.*[4], *Adron (Edwin/Ade) Sr.*[3], *Charles W. Sr.*[2], *John Sr.*[1]) was born 17 Sep 1918 in Waterloo, Lauderdale County, AL.

Dorothy married **Mack Clifton Patton** 4 Aug 1937 in Lauderdale County, AL. Mack was born 18 Nov 1914 in Bono, AR.

1402. Idna Cynthia Hairell (*Minor (Mina) Houston Sharp*[6], *John Thomas (Tom)*[5], *James (Jim) Charles Sr.*[4], *Adron (Edwin/Ade) Sr.*[3], *Charles W. Sr.*[2], *John Sr.*[1]) was born 20 Feb 1922 in Lauderdale County, AL.

Idna married **Raymond Williard Barker**, son of **Floyd Barker** and **Bama Wright**, 21 Dec 1941 in Colbert County, AL. Raymond was born 16 Apr 1921 in Lauderdale County, AL.

+ 2915 M   i.   **Hairel Ray Barker** was born 21 Oct 1942 in Lauderdale County, AL.

+ 2916 F ii. **Linda Gail Barker** was born 8 Jun 1950 in Lauderdale County, AL.
+ 2917 M iii. **Glenn Gary Barker** was born 22 Apr 1954 in Lauderdale County, AL.

1403. Willie Clyde Bruce (*James Pinkney Bruce Sr.*[6], *Matilda Ann Sharp*[5], *James (Jim) Charles Sr.*[4], *Adron (Edwin/Ade) Sr.*[3], *Charles W. Sr.*[2], *John Sr.*[1]) was born about 1901 in Alabama.

Willie married **Annie Della Byrd**, daughter of **Carl Byrd** and **Mildred *Unk**, about 1920. Annie was born about 1901 in Tennessee.
+ 2918 F i. **Mattie Sue Bruce** was born 9 Sep 1922 in Lauderdale County, AL.
+ 2919 M ii. **William Carl Bruce Sr.** was born in Jun 1925 in Lauderdale County, AL.

1404. Pearl I. Bruce (*James Pinkney Bruce Sr.*[6], *Matilda Ann Sharp*[5], *James (Jim) Charles Sr.*[4], *Adron (Edwin/Ade) Sr.*[3], *Charles W. Sr.*[2], *John Sr.*[1]) was born about 1904 in Alabama.

Pearl married **Jessie L. Tucker** 17 Dec 1921 in Lauderdale County, AL.

1405. Jewell Bruce (*James Pinkney Bruce Sr.*[6], *Matilda Ann Sharp*[5], *James (Jim) Charles Sr.*[4], *Adron (Edwin/Ade) Sr.*[3], *Charles W. Sr.*[2], *John Sr.*[1]) was born about 1906 in Alabama.

Jewell married **Turner Jackson** 8 Nov 1927 in Lauderdale County, AL.

1406. James Pinkney Bruce Jr. (*James Pinkney Bruce Sr.*[6], *Matilda Ann Sharp*[5], *James (Jim) Charles Sr.*[4], *Adron (Edwin/Ade) Sr.*[3], *Charles W. Sr.*[2], *John Sr.*[1]) was born 20 Jun 1909 in Lauderdale County, AL.

James married **Lennie Bevis** 19 Jun 1930 in Lauderdale County, AL.

James next married **Zelma Jackson**, daughter of **John Jackson** and **Unknown**, 2 Oct 1945 in Lauderdale County, AL. Zelma was born 24 Sep 1927 in Colbert County, AL.
+ 2920 M i. **John Paul Bruce** was born 21 Dec 1964 in Winnebago, IL.

James next married **Ida Mary Winborn**, daughter of **Dossey W. Winborn Sr.** and **Esther B. Austin**, 7 Jan 1985 in Lauderdale County, AL. Ida was born 4 Apr 1912 in Alabama, died 23 Aug 2003, and was buried in Pisgah Cemetery, Lauderdale County, AL.

1407. Riggle Bruce (*James Pinkney Bruce Sr.*[6], *Matilda Ann Sharp*[5], *James (Jim) Charles Sr.*[4], *Adron (Edwin/Ade) Sr.*[3], *Charles W. Sr.*[2], *John Sr.*[1]) was born 13 Feb 1913 in Lauderdale County, AL and died 14 Aug 1993.

Riggle married **Gracie Tilley** 20 Dec 1934 in Lauderdale County, AL. Gracie was born 30 Jul 1917 in Lutts, Wayne County, TN.
+ 2921 M i. **Granville Ray Bruce** was born 6 Nov 1935 in Lauderdale County, AL and died 20 Jul 1988 in Kennett, MO.
+ 2922 F ii. **Shirley Francis Bruce** was born 16 Sep 1937 in Florence, Lauderdale County, AL and died in May 1999 in Kennett, MO.
+ 2923 F iii. **Gracie Jeanette Bruce** was born 23 Oct 1939.
+ 2924 M iv. **Edwin Dewayne Bruce** was born 4 Oct 1942 in Kennett, MO and died in 1995 in Oxford, Lafayette County, MS.
+ 2925 F v. **Cyndra Kay Bruce** was born 25 Feb 1947 in Kennett, MO and died in Memphis, Shelby County, TN.
+ 2926 M vi. **Jackie Dewayne Bruce** was born 5 Jun 1952 in St. Louis, MO.
+ 2927 F vii. **Pamela June Bruce** was born 28 Nov 1954 in Kennett, MO.

1408. John Gilbert Bruce Sr. (*James Pinkney Bruce Sr.*[6], *Matilda Ann Sharp*[5], *James (Jim) Charles Sr.*[4], *Adron (Edwin/Ade) Sr.*[3], *Charles W. Sr.*[2], *John Sr.*[1]) was born 25 Apr 1915 in Lauderdale County, AL, died 2 Feb 1986, and was buried in Williams Chapel Cemetery, Lauderdale County, AL.

John married **Winnie Lee White**, daughter of **James Calvin (Cal) Reese Lafayette White** and **Margaret Alice (Maggie) Crider**, 14 Dec 1935 in Lauderdale County, AL. Winnie was born 23 Mar 1918 in Lauderdale County, AL, died 21 Sep 1985, and was buried in Williams Chapel Cemetery, Lauderdale County, AL.

+ 2928 M i. **James Millard Bruce Sr.** was born 8 Sep 1937 in Lauderdale County, AL.
+ 2929 M ii. **Reggie Paul Bruce** was born 5 Feb 1939 in Lauderdale County, AL.
+ 2930 M iii. **Harold Sherman Bruce** was born 30 Sep 1941 in Lauderdale County, AL.
+ 2931 M iv. **John Gilbert Bruce Jr.** was born 20 Feb 1943 in Lauderdale County, AL.
+ 2932 F v. **Virginia Alice Bruce** was born 25 Jun 1944 in Lauderdale County, AL.
+ 2933 M vi. **Freddie Lee Bruce Sr.** was born 15 Jan 1946 in Lauderdale County, AL.

1409. Cleona Bruce (*James Pinkney Bruce Sr.*[6], *Matilda Ann Sharp*[5], *James (Jim) Charles Sr.*[4], *Adron (Edwin/Ade) Sr.*[3], *Charles W. Sr.*[2], *John Sr.*[1]) was born in 1918 in Lauderdale County, AL, died in 1997, and was buried in Tri-Cities Memorial Gardens, Florence, Lauderdale County, AL.

Cleona married **Hewitt Cannon**, son of **William P. Cannon** and **Meddie Key**, 14 Jun 1940 in Lauderdale County, AL. Hewitt was born 12 Aug 1915.

1410. Mary Leona Bruce (*James Pinkney Bruce Sr.*[6], *Matilda Ann Sharp*[5], *James (Jim) Charles Sr.*[4], *Adron (Edwin/Ade) Sr.*[3], *Charles W. Sr.*[2], *John Sr.*[1]) was born about 1919 in Alabama.

Mary married **Theodore Roosevelt Smith**, son of **John S. Smith** and **Ora Bell Keith**, 28 Feb 1944 in Lauderdale County, AL. Theodore was born 25 Apr 1920 in Valley Head, AL.

1413. Nettie Bethel Bruce (*Robert William Bruce*[6], *Matilda Ann Sharp*[5], *James (Jim) Charles Sr.*[4], *Adron (Edwin/Ade) Sr.*[3], *Charles W. Sr.*[2], *John Sr.*[1]) was born 26 Jul 1911 in Lauderdale County, AL, died 9 Jan 1998, and was buried in Murphy's Chapel Cemetery, Lauderdale County, AL.

Nettie married **Odus Clarence Young Sr.**, son of **Mack Edward Young** and **Eddie Young**, 30 Oct 1927 in Waynesboro, TN. Odus was born 7 Mar 1909 in Lauderdale County, AL, died 1 Jun 1968, and was buried in Murphy's Chapel Cemetery, Lauderdale County, AL.
(Duplicate Line. See Person 489)

1414. Amos Jerry Bruce Sr. (*Robert William Bruce*[6], *Matilda Ann Sharp*[5], *James (Jim) Charles Sr.*[4], *Adron (Edwin/Ade) Sr.*[3], *Charles W. Sr.*[2], *John Sr.*[1]) was born 17 Dec 1913 in Lauderdale County, AL.

Amos married **Lois Katherine Blakney**, daughter of **W. C. Blakney** and **Alice McCartney**, 10 Feb 1941 in Lauderdale County, AL. Lois was born 27 Mar 1923 in Bessemer, AL.

+ 2934 M i. **Amos Jerry Bruce Jr.** was born 24 Feb 1942 in Rogersville, Lauderdale County, AL.
+ 2935 M ii. **Charles William Bruce** was born 16 Oct 1945 in Florence, Lauderdale County, AL.
+ 2936 F iii. **Evelyn Katherine Bruce** was born 27 Jun 1952 in Lauderdale County, AL.
+ 2937 F iv. **Rachel Annette Bruce** was born 18 Apr 1958 in Lauderdale County, AL.

1415. Naomi Deborah Bruce (*Robert William Bruce*[6], *Matilda Ann Sharp*[5], *James (Jim) Charles Sr.*[4], *Adron (Edwin/Ade) Sr.*[3], *Charles W. Sr.*[2], *John Sr.*[1]) was born 7 Jan 1915 in Lauderdale County, AL.

Naomi married **Louis Mason, Sr.** 1 Sept 1944 in Lauderdale County, AL. Louis was born 1 Nov 1903 in West Point, Lawrence County, TN, died 16 June 1984 and was buried in Cooper Cemetery, Rogersville, AL.

• F i **Elizabeth Ann Mason.** was born 26 April 1949 in Florence, Lauderdale County, AL.

General Notes: "Naomi was stepmother to Erma Nadine, Louis, Jr. and Billy Ray Mason....."Millie Mason"

1416. Paul Byrum Bruce (*Robert William Bruce*[6], *Matilda Ann Sharp*[5], *James (Jim) Charles Sr.*[4], *Adron (Edwin/Ade) Sr.*[3], *Charles W. Sr.*[2], *John Sr.*[1]) was born 24 Nov 1916 in Lauderdale County, AL, died 9 Aug 1980, and was buried in Murphy's Chapel Cemetery, Lauderdale County, AL.

Paul married **Annie Ruth Wood**, daughter of **Floyde Leonard Wood** and **Martha (Mattie) Inez Taylor**, 30 Oct 1947 in Lauderdale County, AL. Annie was born 13 Aug 1927 in Lauderdale County, AL, died 18 Aug 2006, and was buried in Murphy's Chapel Cemetery, Lauderdale County, AL.
(Duplicate Line. See Person 1112)

1417. Reeder Warner Bruce (*Robert William Bruce*[6], *Matilda Ann Sharp*[5], *James (Jim) Charles Sr.*[4], *Adron (Edwin/Ade) Sr.*[3], *Charles W. Sr.*[2], *John Sr.*[1]) was born 9 Sep 1918 in Lauderdale County, AL, died 11 Jan 2008, and was buried in Greenview Memorial Park, Florence, Lauderdale County, AL.

Obituary - Times Daily, Florence, Lauderdale County, Alabama

"Reeder Warner Bruce, age 87, of Florence, died Friday, Jan. 11, 2008, at Glenwood Convalescent Center. Visitation will be Sunday, Jan. 13, from 7 - 9 p.m. at Greenview Funeral Home. The funeral service will be Monday, Jan. 14, at 11 a.m. in Greenview Memorial Park. Officiating at the service will be the Rev. Donnie McDaniel.
Mr. Bruce was a native of Lauderdale County and a member of Underwood Baptist Church. He was retired from the Alabama State Highway Department, where he worked for 33 years. He supported his family by working with his hands. He was a builder, butcher, heavy duty mechanic shop foreman and a farmer. As a veteran of World War II, he served three years in the Air Force and Army working as a food inspector.
He is survived by his son, Lanny Warner Bruce and wife, Joyce, Florence; two daughters, Merita Bruce Newton and husband, Kim, Florence, Mitzi Diane Keys and husband, Dalen, Landerberg, Pa.;brother, John Bruce, Osceola, Ind.; sister, Naomi Mason, Florence; grandchildren, Collin Warner Bruce (Tara), Emily Bruce Waddell (Trey), Kelly Newton Dyer (Jason), Reeda Newton Brewer (Tony),Tiffany Keys Heiger (James), Hannah Keys and Chase Sawyer Keys; great -grandchildren, Nate and Natalie Brewer, Lily and Maggie Dyer.
He was preceded in death by his wife of 63 years, Lois Seaton Bruce; parents, Robert William and Mamie Rogers Bruce; brothers, Amos, Cyrus, Byrum, Abel and Durwood Bruce; sisters, Nettie Young and Viola Melton.
Pallbearers will be Tony Brewer, Collin Bruce, Trey Waddell, Chase Keys, Danny Wylie and Jerry Phillips. Memorials may be made to Underwood Baptist Church Building Fund, 5091 Highway 157, Florence, AL 35633 or to Shoals Praise and Worship Choir, 8390 County Road 6, Florence, AL 35633.
The family will be forever grateful to Dr. Timothy Ashley and staff, Dr. Robert Webb and the administration and staff of Glenwood Convalescent Center for their loving care and support. We know those who are in Christ never see each other for the last time. The Lord is our strength and song.
Arrangements by Greenview Funeral Home

Reeder married **Vertie Lois Seaton**, daughter of **William (Willie) Richard Seaton** and **Carrie Mildred Smith**, 26 Nov 1939 in Lauderdale County, AL. Vertie was born 2 Apr 1921 in Waterloo, Lauderdale County, AL, died 16 Aug 2002, and was buried in Greenview Memorial Park, Florence, Lauderdale County, AL.

+ 2938 F i. **Merita Kay Bruce** was born 17 Mar 1948 in Lauderdale County, AL.
+ 2939 M ii. **Lanny Warner Bruce** was born 20 Mar 1951 in Lauderdale County, AL.
+ 2940 F iii. **Mitzi Diane Bruce** was born 20 Feb 1957 in Lauderdale County, AL.

1418. Robert Cyrus Bruce (*Robert William Bruce*[6], *Matilda Ann Sharp*[5], *James (Jim) Charles Sr.*[4], *Adron (Edwin/Ade) Sr.*[3], *Charles W. Sr.*[2], *John Sr.*[1]) was born 22 Sep 1919 in Lauderdale County, AL, died 5 Aug 1971 in Oak Ridge, TN, and was buried in Solway Church Cemetery, Oak Ridge, TN.

Robert married **Mary Lucille Melton**, daughter of **James Wylie (Jim) Melton** and **Callie Pearl Wood**, 19 Dec 1937 in Lauderdale County, AL. Mary was born 7 Dec 1918 in Lauderdale County, AL.

+ 2941 M i. **Bobby Joel Bruce**.
+ 2942 F ii. **Betty Jane Bruce**.
+ 2943 F iii. **Donna Sue Bruce**.

1419. Harding Abel Bruce (*Robert William Bruce*[6], *Matilda Ann Sharp*[5], *James (Jim) Charles Sr.*[4], *Adron (Edwin/Ade) Sr.*[3], *Charles W. Sr.*[2], *John Sr.*[1]) was born 24 Oct 1922 in Lauderdale County, AL, died 10 May 1997, and was buried in Murphy's Chapel Cemetery, Lauderdale County, AL.

General Notes:

WW II Vet, earned WW II Victory Medal, the European-African Middle Eastern Service Medal and the Good Conduct Medal. Worked for Dodge Manufacturing/Reliance Electric in Mishawaka, Indiana for 33 years...Sharon Wood

Harding married **Beulah Mae Dowdy**, daughter of **Willie M. Dowdy** and **Minnie Ida Witt**, 8 Mar 1942 in Lauderdale County, AL. Beulah was born 21 Jul 1923 in Lauderdale County, AL, died 10 Mar 2006, and was buried in Murphy's Chapel Cemetery, Lauderdale County, AL.

+ 2944 F   i.   **Janice Bruce.**
+ 2945 F   ii. **Sheila Bruce.**
+ 2946 F   iii. **Becky Bruce.**
  2947 F   iv. **Sandra Bruce** was born 5 Oct 1947, died 5 Oct 1947, and was buried in Murphy's Chapel Cemetery, Lauderdale County, AL.

1420. Viola T. Bruce (*Robert William Bruce*[6], *Matilda Ann Sharp*[5], *James (Jim) Charles Sr.*[4], *Adron (Edwin/Ade) Sr.*[3], *Charles W. Sr.*[2], *John Sr.*[1]) was born 8 Dec 1924 in Lauderdale County, AL, died 13 Oct 1995, and was buried in Murphy's Chapel Cemetery, Lauderdale County, AL.

Viola married **Joseph Wheeler (Joe) Melton**, son of **James Wylie (Jim) Melton** and **Callie Pearl Wood**. Joseph was born 30 Mar 1923 in Lauderdale County, AL, died 26 Oct 1986, and was buried in Murphy's Chapel Cemetery, Lauderdale County, AL.

+ 2948 F   i.   **Beverly Jo Melton** was born 27 Dec 1952 in Lauderdale County, AL.
  2949 M   ii. **Timothy (Tim) James Melton** was born 17 Aug 1959 in Lauderdale County, AL.

1422. John C. Bruce (*Robert William Bruce*[6], *Matilda Ann Sharp*[5], *James (Jim) Charles Sr.*[4], *Adron (Edwin/Ade) Sr.*[3], *Charles W. Sr.*[2], *John Sr.*[1]) was born 10 Jul 1932 in Lauderdale County, AL, died 24 Nov 2008, and was buried in Chapel Hill Memorial Garden, Osceola, IN.

General Notes: Obituary - South Bend Tribune, Osceola, Indiana

"John C. Bruce, 76, of Osceola, passed away at 11:30 a. m. Monday, November 24, 2008, in his home. John was born on July 10, 1932, in Florence, AL, to the late Robert and Mamie (Rogers) Bruce. On September 12, 1973, he married Judy Domonkos. He is survived by his loving wife, Judy of Osceola; two children, David (Judy) Chesnutt of Elkhart and Tracy (Matthew) Longfellow of South Bend; and two grandchildren, Justina and Daniel Bass. He is also survived by one sister, Naomi Mason of Florence, AL. He was preceded in death by his parents, sis brothers, Amos, Able, Cyrus, Derwood, Byron and Reeder Bruce, and two sisters, Viola Melton and Nettie Young. John proudly served his country in the U. S. Army and was honorably discharged in 1953. He worked for Dodge Manufacturing for 17 years and Uniroyal for 12 years before his retirement. He also worked for many musical instrument manufactures in Elkhart. He was an avid collector of flags and baseball caps and will be remembered for his love of family and his wonderful sense of humor. Visitation will be held from 2:00 - 6:00 p. m. Sunday, November 30, 2008, in Chapel Hill Funeral Home, 10776 McKinley Highway, Osceola. Funeral services will be held at 10:00 a. m. Monday, December 1, 2008, in the funeral home, with burial to follow in Chapel Hill Memorial Gardens, Osceola. In lieu of flowers, the family requests that memorial donations be made to the Center for Hospice & Palliative Care, Inc., 111 Sunnybrook Court, South Bend, IN 46637. The family would like to thank Dr. Mark Stanish, M.D., Dr. Rafat Ansari, M. D., Dr. Edward Delle Donne, M. D., and all the nurses for their care of John. Online condolences may be sent to the family at www.chapelhillmemorial.com"

John married **Marge *Unk**.
+ 2950 M   i.   **Johnny Bruce Chesnutt.**

John next married **Judy Domonkos**.
+ 2951 F   i.   **Tracy Bruce.**

1423. Turner Cuelell Long (*Lilly Eddie Levie Bruce*[6], *Matilda Ann Sharp*[5], *James (Jim) Charles Sr.*[4], *Adron (Edwin/Ade) Sr.*[3], *Charles W. Sr.*[2], *John Sr.*[1]) was born 2 Aug 1903 in Lauderdale County, AL and died 4 Apr 1984 in Sugar Tree, TN.

Turner married **Elfie Maude Henderson**, daughter of **Andrew Henderson** and **Hattie Barter**, 25 Jul 1925 in Cross County, AR. Elfie was born 9 Nov 1904 in Colt, AR.

2952	F	i.	**Doralene Long** was born 27 Oct 1926 in Stamps, AR and died 24 Oct 1968 in Oswego, NY.
2953	M	ii.	**Howard Cuelell Long** was born 28 Apr 1930 in Camden, AR and died 2 Jun 1968 in Memphis, Shelby County, TN.
2954	M	iii.	**Homer Dee Long** was born 2 Dec 1930 in Lauderdale County, AL.
2955	F	iv.	**Lillian Aileen Long** was born 18 Mar 1932 in Lauderdale County, AL.
2956	F	v.	**Hattie Marie Long** was born 14 Jul 1935 in Lauderdale County, AL.

1424. Magie Estelle Long (*Lilly Eddie Levie Bruce*[6], *Matilda Ann Sharp*[5], *James (Jim) Charles Sr.*[4], *Adron (Edwin/Ade) Sr.*[3], *Charles W. Sr.*[2], *John Sr.*[1]) was born 27 Apr 1905 in Gill, AR and died 20 Mar 1955 in Memphis, Shelby County, TN.

Magie married **Leland Elijah Summers** 22 Oct 1922 in Cross County, AR. Leland was born 10 Nov 1902 in St. Frances County, AR and died in Apr 1964 in Memphis, Shelby County, TN.

2957	M	i.	**Ira Summers** was born 24 Jan 1924 in Memphis, Shelby County, TN and died 24 Jan 1924.
2958	M	ii.	**C. Thomas Summers** was born 24 Nov 1924 in Cross County, AR and died in Oct 1997 in Memphis, Shelby County, TN.
2959	F	iii.	**Lily Marquerite Summers** was born 11 May 1926 in Memphis, Shelby County, TN.
2960	M	iv.	**Virgil Lee Summers** was born in 1929 in Cross County, AR and died in 1931 in Cross County, AR.
2961	F	v.	**Anita Summers** was born in 1931 and died 18 Feb 1986.
2962	F	vi.	**Mary Ann Summers** was born in 1934 in Memphis, Shelby County, TN.
2963	M	vii.	**Robert Bruce Summers** was born in 1936 in Cross County, AR and died in Memphis, Shelby County, TN.
+ 2964	F	viii.	**Rose Marie Summers** was born 10 Mar 1938 in Memphis, Shelby County, TN.
2965	M	ix.	**David Leland Summers** was born in 1940 in Cross County, AR.

1425. Abbie Leona Long (*Lilly Eddie Levie Bruce*[6], *Matilda Ann Sharp*[5], *James (Jim) Charles Sr.*[4], *Adron (Edwin/Ade) Sr.*[3], *Charles W. Sr.*[2], *John Sr.*[1]) was born 7 Jul 1907 in Cross County, AR and died about 1995 in Batesville, MS.

Abbie married **Edward Fred Hadorn** 18 Oct 1925 in Arkansas. Edward was born 26 Feb 1898 and died 20 Mar 1968 in Batesville, MS.

2966	M	i.	**James Edward Hadorn** was born 22 Jul 1927.
2967	M	ii.	**Fred Milton Hadorn** was born 7 Sep 1928.
2968	F	iii.	**Emma Jane Hadorn** was born 30 Dec 1930.
2969	M	iv.	**Frank Raymond Hadorn** was born 14 Jul 1933.
2970	M	v.	**William Eugene Hadorn** was born 10 Feb 1936.
2971	F	vi.	**Gloria Ann Hadorn** was born 28 Feb 1938.
2972	M	vii.	**August David Hadorn** was born 3 May 1941.
2973	M	viii.	**Jessie Ray Hadorn** was born 1 May 1945.
2974	F	ix.	**Grave Levie Hadorn** was born 1 May 1945.

1426. Carrie D. Long (*Lilly Eddie Levie Bruce*[6], *Matilda Ann Sharp*[5], *James (Jim) Charles Sr.*[4], *Adron (Edwin/Ade) Sr.*[3], *Charles W. Sr.*[2], *John Sr.*[1]) was born about 1909 in Cross County, AR.

Carrie married **John Bolger** before 1929.

2975	M	i.	**Earl Bolger** was born circa 1930.
2976	F	ii.	**Ruth Bolger** was born circa 1931.
2977	M	iii.	**Johnny Bolger** was born circa 1932.

Carrie next married **William Jackson** about 1933.

| 2978 | F | i. | **Dorothy Jackson** was born 2 Oct 1934. |
| 2979 | M | ii. | **George Jackson** was born circa 1935. |

1427. Lillian Long (*Lilly Eddie Levie Bruce*[6], *Matilda Ann Sharp*[5], *James (Jim) Charles Sr.*[4], *Adron (Edwin/Ade) Sr.*[3], *Charles W. Sr.*[2], *John Sr.*[1]) was born 25 Dec 1912 in Cross County, AR and died in California.

Lillian married **Tommy Moore** in Memphis, Shelby County, TN. Tommy died in California.

| 2980 | F | i. | **Betty Moore** was born in Memphis, Shelby County, TN. |

| 2981 | F | ii. | **Helen Moore** was born in Memphis, Shelby County, TN. |
| 2982 | F | iii. | **Ernestine Moore** was born in Memphis, Shelby County, TN. |

1428. Virginia Long (*Lilly Eddie Levie Bruce*^{6}, *Matilda Ann Sharp*^{5}, *James (Jim) Charles Sr.*^{4}, *Adron (Edwin/Ade) Sr.*^{3}, *Charles W. Sr.*^{2}, *John Sr.*^{1}) was born 14 Dec 1914 in Cross County, AR.

Virginia married **Robert Lee Jackson Sr.** in Memphis, Shelby County, TN. Robert was born 22 Jan 1909 in Memphis, Shelby County, TN and died in 1976 in Texas.

2983	M	i.	**Robert Lee Jackson Jr.** was born 6 Sep 1935 in Memphis, Shelby County, TN.
2984	F	ii.	**Mildred Jackson** was born 8 Jul 1938 in Memphis, Shelby County, TN.
2985	M	iii.	**Chester Jackson** was born 25 Oct 1942 in Memphis, Shelby County, TN.
2986	M	iv.	**Lawrence Jackson** was born 11 Nov 1950 in Memphis, Shelby County, TN.

Virginia next married **William Jack Jackson** about 1926 in Memphis, Shelby County, TN. William was born about 1912.

| 2987 | M | i. | **William (Billy) Jackson** was born 2 Nov 1927. |
| 2988 | M | ii. | **Thomas Jackson** was born 22 Feb 1929. |

1429. John Long (*Lilly Eddie Levie Bruce*^{6}, *Matilda Ann Sharp*^{5}, *James (Jim) Charles Sr.*^{4}, *Adron (Edwin/Ade) Sr.*^{3}, *Charles W. Sr.*^{2}, *John Sr.*^{1}) was born 18 Nov 1916 in Cross County, AR and died about 1990 in Memphis, Shelby County, TN.

John married **Lucille McHughes**. Lucille was born in Memphis, Shelby County, TN.

2989	M	i.	**Jack Rowland Long**.
2990	M	ii.	**Johnny E. Long**.
2991	F	iii.	**Betty Aileen Long**.
2992	F	iv.	**Lilly Lee Long**.
2993	F	v.	**Barbara Jane Long**.

1430. James Ireis Long (*Lilly Eddie Levie Bruce*^{6}, *Matilda Ann Sharp*^{5}, *James (Jim) Charles Sr.*^{4}, *Adron (Edwin/Ade) Sr.*^{3}, *Charles W. Sr.*^{2}, *John Sr.*^{1}) was born 25 Jan 1919 in Cross County, AR.

James married **Lynnie Mae Clark** 25 Jan 1937 in Memphis, Shelby County, TN.

| 2994 | F | i. | **Joyce Audrey Long** was born 28 Jan 1938. |
| 2995 | F | ii. | **Joyce Ann Long** was born 22 Feb 1940. |

1431. Ernest Steven Long Sr. (*Lilly Eddie Levie Bruce*^{6}, *Matilda Ann Sharp*^{5}, *James (Jim) Charles Sr.*^{4}, *Adron (Edwin/Ade) Sr.*^{3}, *Charles W. Sr.*^{2}, *John Sr.*^{1}) was born about 1920 in Memphis, Shelby County, TN.

Ernest married ***Unk**.

Ernest next married **Katherine Cook** in Memphis, Shelby County, TN.

2996	M	i.	**Ernest Steven Long Jr.** was born circa 1941.
2997	F	ii.	**Katherine Ducky Long** was born circa 1948.
2998	M	iii.	**Ronald Long** was born circa 1950.
2999	M	iv.	**Larry Long** was born 19 Jun 1951.
3000	F	v.	**Patricia Long** was born circa 1952.
3001	M	vi.	**Dennis Long** was born circa 1953.
3002	M	vii.	**Denise Long** was born circa 1962 in Memphis, Shelby County, TN and died in 1991 in Memphis, Shelby County, TN.

1432. Margie Grace Long (*Lilly Eddie Levie Bruce*^{6}, *Matilda Ann Sharp*^{5}, *James (Jim) Charles Sr.*^{4}, *Adron (Edwin/Ade) Sr.*^{3}, *Charles W. Sr.*^{2}, *John Sr.*^{1}) was born 4 May 1923 in Memphis, Shelby County, TN.

Margie married **Raymond Floyd Snell Sr.** about 1942 in Memphis, Shelby County, TN. Raymond was born 5 Mar 1921 in Memphis, Shelby County, TN.

3003	M	i.	**Raymond Floyd Snell Jr.** was born 8 Jan 1943.
3004	M	ii.	**Robert Fay Snell** was born 12 Aug 1946.
3005	F	iii.	**Renaldi Marlene Snell** was born 25 Aug 1947.

1433. Leacia Mae Bruce (*George Owen Bruce*[6]*, Matilda Ann Sharp*[5]*, James (Jim) Charles Sr.*[4]*, Adron (Edwin/Ade) Sr.*[3]*, Charles W. Sr.*[2]*, John Sr.*[1]) was born 25 May 1922 in Lauderdale County, AL.

Leacia married **Edward R. Pitassi**, son of **Antonio Pitassi** and **Jean McHardy**, 8 Sep 1943 in Lauderdale County, AL. Edward was born 19 Feb 1922 in Providence, RI.

1434. Jessie D. Bruce (*George Owen Bruce*[6]*, Matilda Ann Sharp*[5]*, James (Jim) Charles Sr.*[4]*, Adron (Edwin/Ade) Sr.*[3]*, Charles W. Sr.*[2]*, John Sr.*[1]) was born 28 Feb 1928 in Lauderdale County, AL.

Jessie married **Vera Smith**, daughter of **Chester Owen Smith** and **Verna Pearl Milford**, 28 Dec 1946 in Lauderdale County, AL. Vera was born 3 Nov 1927 in Lauderdale County, AL.

1435. Lady Carrie Wood (*Margie Ann (Marjorie) Bruce*[6]*, Matilda Ann Sharp*[5]*, James (Jim) Charles Sr.*[4]*, Adron (Edwin/Ade) Sr.*[3]*, Charles W. Sr.*[2]*, John Sr.*[1]) was born 4 Aug 1913 in Gravely Springs, Lauderdale County, AL, died 22 Sep 1996, and was buried in Oak Grove Cemetery, Lauderdale County, AL.

Lady married **Emmet Lee Phillips**, son of **Emmet Walter Phillips** and **Elizabeth Virginia Jackson**, 28 Nov 1931 in Lauderdale County, AL. Emmet was born 29 Jul 1909 in Florence, Lauderdale County, AL, died 14 Nov 1957 in Little Rock, AR, and was buried in Oak Grove Cemetery, Lauderdale County, AL.
- \+ 3006 F i. **Gracie Mozella Phillips** was born 24 Sep 1934 in Waterloo, Lauderdale County, AL.
- \+ 3007 F ii. **Marcella Vernette Phillips** was born 25 Jul 1936 in Waterloo, Lauderdale County, AL.
- \+ 3008 F iii. **Clista Faye Phillips** was born 8 Feb 1938 in Waterloo, Lauderdale County, AL.
- \+ 3009 F iv. **Mable Rita Phillips** was born 31 May 1939 in Waterloo, Lauderdale County, AL.
- \+ 3010 M v. **Ronald Eugene Phillips** was born 17 May 1941 in Waterloo, Lauderdale County, AL.
- \+ 3011 M vi. **Billy Gerald Phillips** was born 22 Aug 1943 in Waterloo, Lauderdale County, AL.
- \+ 3012 F vii. **Clara Lavon Phillips** was born 16 Apr 1946 in Waterloo, Lauderdale County, AL, died 13 Feb 1976, and was buried in Oak Grove Cemetery, Lauderdale County, AL.
- \+ 3013 M viii. **Milton Dale Phillips Sr.** was born 5 Nov 1947 in Waterloo, Lauderdale County, AL, died 4 Aug 2004, and was buried in Oak Grove Cemetery, Lauderdale County, AL.

1436. Pearlie Mae Wood (*Margie Ann (Marjorie) Bruce*[6]*, Matilda Ann Sharp*[5]*, James (Jim) Charles Sr.*[4]*, Adron (Edwin/Ade) Sr.*[3]*, Charles W. Sr.*[2]*, John Sr.*[1]) was born 1 May 1915 in Gravely Springs, Lauderdale County, AL, died 26 Feb 2003, and was buried in Oak Grove Cemetery, Lauderdale County, AL.

Pearlie married **Loye Arvel Sharp**, son of **Louis (Bud) Wheeler Sharp** and **Ada (Adar) Elizabeth Hill**, 18 Oct 1935 in Lauderdale County, AL. Loye was born 1 Mar 1916 in Gravely Springs, Lauderdale County, AL, died 29 Oct 2004, and was buried in Oak Grove Cemetery, Lauderdale County, AL.
(Duplicate Line. See Person 616)

1437. Claude Ellis Wood Sr. (*Margie Ann (Marjorie) Bruce*[6]*, Matilda Ann Sharp*[5]*, James (Jim) Charles Sr.*[4]*, Adron (Edwin/Ade) Sr.*[3]*, Charles W. Sr.*[2]*, John Sr.*[1]) was born 26 Apr 1917 in Gravely Springs, Lauderdale County, AL, died 30 Jan 2006, and was buried in Oak Grove Cemetery, Lauderdale County, AL.

Claude married **Elizabeth Lee Phillips**, daughter of **Emmet Walter Phillips** and **Elizabeth Virginia Jackson**, 5 Jul 1936 in Lauderdale County, AL. Elizabeth was born 2 May 1920 in Florence, Lauderdale County, AL, died 13 Dec 1972, and was buried in Oak Grove Cemetery, Lauderdale County, AL.
- \+ 3014 M i. **Claude Ellis Wood Jr.** was born 19 Dec 1936 in Florence, Lauderdale County, AL.
- \+ 3015 F ii. **Eva Jean Wood** was born 21 Mar 1939 in Florence, Lauderdale County, AL, died 31 May 2005, and was buried in Oak Grove Cemetery, Lauderdale County, AL.
- \+ 3016 F iii. **Rachel Ann Wood** was born 21 Feb 1942 in Florence, Lauderdale County, AL.
- \+ 3017 M iv. **Larry Ray (Soap) Wood** was born 22 May 1944 in Florence, Lauderdale County, AL, died 22 Oct 1987, and was buried in Oak Grove Cemetery, Lauderdale County, AL.

Claude next married **Azalee Estell Parrish**, daughter of **Varnie William Parrish** and **Ruthie L. Wood**, 9 Mar 1974 in Lauderdale County, AL. Azalee was born 15 Oct 1920 in Lauderdale County, AL, died 8 Sep 1988, and was buried in Oak Grove Cemetery, Lauderdale County, AL.

1438. Leonard Earl Wood (*Margie Ann (Marjorie) Bruce*[6], *Matilda Ann Sharp*[5], *James (Jim) Charles Sr.*[4], *Adron (Edwin/Ade) Sr.*[3], *Charles W. Sr.*[2], *John Sr.*[1]) was born 4 Jun 1919 in Gravely Springs, Lauderdale County, AL, died 30 Oct 2001, and was buried in Oak Grove Cemetery, Lauderdale County, AL.

Leonard married **Beatrice (Be-At) Wood**, daughter of **Hurbert (Herb) Lee Wood** and **Ozella (Ella) Perkins**, 24 Dec 1938 in Lauderdale County, AL. Beatrice was born 1 Jul 1918 in Gravely Springs, Lauderdale County, AL, died 6 Nov 1987, and was buried in Oak Grove Cemetery, Lauderdale County, AL.

+ 3018	M	i.	**Wallace Earl Wood** was born 24 Nov 1939 in Florence, Lauderdale County, AL.
+ 3019	M	ii.	**Thomas Moore Wood** was born 1 Jul 1941 in Florence, Lauderdale County, AL.
+ 3020	F	iii.	**Geraldine (Judy) Wood** was born 27 Dec 1942 in Florence, Lauderdale County, AL.
+ 3021	F	iv.	**Jo Carolyn Wood** was born 16 Jun 1948 in Florence, Lauderdale County, AL.
3022	F	v.	**Phillis Ann Wood** was born 3 Nov 1949 in Lauderdale County, AL, died 5 Apr 1952, and was buried in Oak Grove Cemetery, Lauderdale County, AL.

Leonard next married **Virginia Ophelia Phillips**, daughter of **Emmet Walter Phillips** and **Elizabeth Virginia Jackson**. Virginia was born 11 Nov 1923, died 27 Mar 2005, and was buried in Pine Hill Cemetery, Lauderdale County, AL.

+ 3023	F	i.	**Louise Phillips Reeves** was born about 1943 in Lauderdale County, AL.

1439. Pauline Inez Wood (*Margie Ann (Marjorie) Bruce*[6], *Matilda Ann Sharp*[5], *James (Jim) Charles Sr.*[4], *Adron (Edwin/Ade) Sr.*[3], *Charles W. Sr.*[2], *John Sr.*[1]) was born 1 May 1921 in Gravely Springs, Lauderdale County, AL, died 17 Feb 2007, and was buried in Oak Grove Cemetery, Lauderdale County, AL.

Pauline married **Lawrence (Toby) Eldred Sharp**, son of **Louis (Bud) Wheeler Sharp** and **Ada (Adar) Elizabeth Hill**. Lawrence was born 22 May 1919 in Lauderdale County, AL, died 14 May 1994, and was buried in Oak Grove Cemetery, Lauderdale County, AL.
(Duplicate Line. See Person 617)

1440. Onita Katherine (Neat) Wood (*Margie Ann (Marjorie) Bruce*[6], *Matilda Ann Sharp*[5], *James (Jim) Charles Sr.*[4], *Adron (Edwin/Ade) Sr.*[3], *Charles W. Sr.*[2], *John Sr.*[1]) was born 7 Jul 1924 in Gravely Springs, Lauderdale County, AL.

Onita married **William Turner Allison**, son of **Presley (Press) Harrison Allison** and **Margie (Lady) J. Sharp**, 30 Aug 1943 in Lauderdale County, AL. William was born 3 Jul 1921 in Gravely Springs, Lauderdale County, AL, died 11 Feb 1999, and was buried in Oak Grove Cemetery, Lauderdale County, AL.

(Duplicate Line. See Person 626)

1441. Wallace Ray Wood (*Margie Ann (Marjorie) Bruce*[6], *Matilda Ann Sharp*[5], *James (Jim) Charles Sr.*[4], *Adron (Edwin/Ade) Sr.*[3], *Charles W. Sr.*[2], *John Sr.*[1]) was born 10 May 1929 in Gravely Springs, Lauderdale County, AL, died 1 Mar 1980, and was buried in Oak Grove Cemetery, Lauderdale County, AL.

Wallace had a relationship with **Elsie Smith**.

+ 3024	F	i.	**Peggy Ann Wood** was born 4 Jul 1948.

Wallace married **Mabel Elois (Lady Maude) Gibbs**, daughter of **Dempsy Comer Gibbs** and **Bertha Lutell Scott**, 31 Mar 1957. Mabel was born 18 Apr 1935.

+ 3025	M	i.	**Johnny Ray Wood** was born 15 Jun 1958 in West Memphis, Crittenden County, AR.
+ 3026	M	ii.	**Mark Alan Wood** was born 26 Dec 1964 in Florence, Lauderdale County, AL.
3027	M	iii.	**Tracy David Wood** was born 4 Aug 1967 in Florence, Lauderdale County, AL, died 14 Oct 1993, and was buried in Oak Grove Cemetery, Lauderdale County, AL.

1443. Fannie Birdie Sharp (*Lee Hal*[6], *Owen Bennett (Doc)*[5], *James (Jim) Charles Sr.*[4], *Adron (Edwin/Ade) Sr.*[3], *Charles W. Sr.*[2], *John Sr.*[1]) was born 15 Apr 1910 in Lauderdale County, AL.

Fannie married **Jones Thomas Webb**, son of **James Burt Webb** and **Minnie Parker**, 24 Dec 1930 in Lauderdale County, AL. Jones was born 24 May 1912 in Lauderdale County, AL, died 28 Aug 1998, and was buried in Tri-Cities Memorial Gardens, Florence, Lauderdale County, AL.

+ 3028 M i. **James Burt (J B) Webb** was born 27 Nov 1936 in Lauderdale County, AL.

1444. Reeder Earl Sharp (*Lee Hal*[6]*, Owen Bennett (Doc)*[5]*, James (Jim) Charles Sr.*[4]*, Adron (Edwin/Ade) Sr.*[3]*, Charles W. Sr.*[2]*, John Sr.*[1]) was born 1 Jul 1913 in Lauderdale County, AL, died 4 Dec 1938, and was buried in Wright Cemetery, Wright, Lauderdale County, AL.

Reeder married **Dorothy Betty White**, daughter of **Dempsey Dave White** and **Lucinda Ida Young**, 22 Feb 1935 in Lauderdale County, AL. Dorothy was born 27 Feb 1916 in Lauderdale County, AL, died 8 Dec 1992, and was buried in Wright Cemetery, Wright, Lauderdale County, AL.

+ 3029 F i. **Reeda Mae Sharp** was born 9 Mar 1935 in Lauderdale County, AL.
+ 3030 F ii. **Betty June Sharp** was born 8 Jun 1936 in Lauderdale County, AL.

1445. Grace Leona Sharp (*Lee Hal*[6]*, Owen Bennett (Doc)*[5]*, James (Jim) Charles Sr.*[4]*, Adron (Edwin/Ade) Sr.*[3]*, Charles W. Sr.*[2]*, John Sr.*[1]) was born 8 Jun 1918 in Waterloo, Lauderdale County, AL.

Grace married **Elmer Woodrow Mansell**, son of **Tom Mansell** and **Isabella Parker**, 27 May 1939 in Lauderdale County, AL. Elmer was born 23 Aug 1914 in Waterloo, Lauderdale County, AL, died 3 Jan 1982, and was buried in Greenview Memorial Park, Florence, Lauderdale County, AL.

+ 3031 F i. **Wanda Gail Mansell** was born 17 Mar 1943 in Lauderdale County, AL.
+ 3032 M ii. **Bobby Elmer Mansell** was born 6 Feb 1952 in Lauderdale County, AL.

1446. Ethel Lucille Glasscock (*Ada Irene Sharp*[6]*, Owen Bennett (Doc)*[5]*, James (Jim) Charles Sr.*[4]*, Adron (Edwin/Ade) Sr.*[3]*, Charles W. Sr.*[2]*, John Sr.*[1]) was born 18 Sep 1910 in Lauderdale County, AL, died 8 Jun 1987, and was buried in Greenview Memorial Park, Florence, Lauderdale County, AL.

Ethel married **George Stanley Perkins Sr.**, son of **Noah Josiah Perkins** and **Mary (Mollie) Emily Wesson**, 28 Jan 1938 in Lauderdale County, AL. George was born 13 Oct 1906 in Lauderdale County, AL, died 31 Jul 1998, and was buried in Greenview Memorial Park, Florence, Lauderdale County, AL.

+ 3033 F i. **Irish Virginia Perkins** was born 4 Nov 1938 in Lauderdale County, AL.
+ 3034 F ii. **Mary Elaine Perkins** was born 12 May 1940 in Lauderdale County, AL.
+ 3035 F iii. **Myra Evelyn Perkins** was born 10 Jan 1942 in Lauderdale County, AL.
+ 3036 M iv. **George Stanley Perkins Jr.** was born 17 Sep 1946 in Lauderdale County, AL.

1447. Vivian Veatrice Glasscock (*Ada Irene Sharp*[6]*, Owen Bennett (Doc)*[5]*, James (Jim) Charles Sr.*[4]*, Adron (Edwin/Ade) Sr.*[3]*, Charles W. Sr.*[2]*, John Sr.*[1]) was born 16 May 1913 in Lauderdale County, AL, died 28 Mar 1998 in Lauderdale County, AL, and was buried in Greenview Memorial Park, Florence, Lauderdale County, AL.

Vivian married **Charles Crawford Ross**, son of **Charles Travis Ross** and **Salonia I. Moseley**, 27 May 1964. Charles was born 14 Nov 1897 in South Pittsburgh, TN, died 6 Jan 1986, and was buried in Florence City Cemetery, Florence, Lauderdale County, AL.

1448. Irene Glasscock (*Ada Irene Sharp*[6]*, Owen Bennett (Doc)*[5]*, James (Jim) Charles Sr.*[4]*, Adron (Edwin/Ade) Sr.*[3]*, Charles W. Sr.*[2]*, John Sr.*[1]) was born 21 May 1916 in Lauderdale County, AL, died 23 Dec 1952, and was buried in Greenview Memorial Park, Florence, Lauderdale County, AL.

Irene married **Thomas Owen Holt**, son of **Burt Holt** and **Annie Williams**, 26 Oct 1945 in Lauderdale County, AL. Thomas was born 20 Aug 1917 in Cypress Inn, Wayne County, TN, died 26 Oct 1987, and was buried in Tri-Cities Memorial Gardens, Florence, Lauderdale County, AL.

1450. Fred Glasscock Sr. (*Ada Irene Sharp*[6]*, Owen Bennett (Doc)*[5]*, James (Jim) Charles Sr.*[4]*, Adron (Edwin/Ade) Sr.*[3]*, Charles W. Sr.*[2]*, John Sr.*[1]) was born 11 May 1919 in Lauderdale County, AL, died 9 Jun 1995, and was buried in Greenview Memorial Park, Florence, Lauderdale County, AL.

Fred married **Estella Mary Haygood**, daughter of **Noah E. Haygood** and **Mable Wallace**, 28 Feb 1946 in Lauderdale County, AL. Estella was born 28 Jun 1928 in Tennessee.

+ 3037 F i. **Brenda Glasscock.**
+ 3038 F ii. **Alice Kay Glasscock** was born in Jul 1952.
+ 3039 M iii. **Fred Glasscock Jr.** was born 19 Apr 1956 in Madison County, AL.

1451. James Arnold Glasscock (*Ada Irene Sharp*[6], *Owen Bennett (Doc)*[5], *James (Jim) Charles Sr.*[4], *Adron (Edwin/Ade) Sr.*[3], *Charles W. Sr.*[2], *John Sr.*[1]) was born 31 Oct 1921 in Lauderdale County, AL, died 8 Dec 1992, and was buried in Greenview Memorial Park, Florence, Lauderdale County, AL.

James married **Mary Marguerite Burgess**, daughter of **Theodore R. Burgess** and **Mattie Patterson**, 21 Apr 1946 in Lauderdale County, AL. Mary was born 5 May 1926 in Lauderdale County, AL.
+ 3040 F i. **Cheryl Antoinette Glasscock** was born 11 Feb 1947 in Lauderdale County, AL.

1452. Harold Owen Glasscock (*Ada Irene Sharp*[6], *Owen Bennett (Doc)*[5], *James (Jim) Charles Sr.*[4], *Adron (Edwin/Ade) Sr.*[3], *Charles W. Sr.*[2], *John Sr.*[1]) was born 27 Jul 1924 in Lauderdale County, AL, died 10 Feb 1999, and was buried in Greenview Memorial Park, Florence, Lauderdale County, AL.

Harold married **Marjorie Hudson**, daughter of **Sam Hudson** and **Beatrice Colburn**, 20 Dec 1947 in Colbert County, AL. Marjorie was born 28 Apr 1928 in Colbert County, AL.
+ 3041 M i. **Sam Harold Glasscock** was born 16 Sep 1948 in Lauderdale County, AL.
  3042 F ii. **Elizabeth Anne (Libby) Glasscock** was born 11 Nov 1952 in Lauderdale County, AL.
  3043 M iii. **John Owen Glasscock** was born 7 Oct 1961 in Lauderdale County, AL.

1453. William Boyce Glasscock (*Ada Irene Sharp*[6], *Owen Bennett (Doc)*[5], *James (Jim) Charles Sr.*[4], *Adron (Edwin/Ade) Sr.*[3], *Charles W. Sr.*[2], *John Sr.*[1]) was born 14 Feb 1927 in Lauderdale County, AL, died 13 Sep 1991, and was buried in Greenview Memorial Park, Florence, Lauderdale County, AL.

William married **Lena Mae Behel**, daughter of **Edward Mayfield Behel Sr.** and **Waymon Billingsley**, 15 Jun 1952 in Lauderdale County, AL. Lena was born 27 Aug 1930 in Lauderdale County, AL, died 18 May 1995, and was buried in Greenview Memorial Park, Florence, Lauderdale County, AL.
+ 3044 F i. **Cheri Ann Glasscock** was born 9 Sep 1955 in Lauderdale County, AL.
+ 3045 F ii. **Vicki Lynn Glasscock** was born 28 Oct 1957 in Lauderdale County, AL.

1454. Lois Etoile Sharp (*Harrell Emmett*[6], *Owen Bennett (Doc)*[5], *James (Jim) Charles Sr.*[4], *Adron (Edwin/Ade) Sr.*[3], *Charles W. Sr.*[2], *John Sr.*[1]) was born 19 Dec 1916 in Lauderdale County, AL, died 28 Jul 1990, and was buried in Macedonia Cemetery, Lauderdale County, AL.

Lois married **Lowell Hanback**, son of **Wylie Edward Hanback** and **Letha Emmertian Balentine**, 29 Oct 1938 in Lauderdale County, AL. Lowell was born 14 Mar 1917 in Cloverdale, Lauderdale County, AL, died 12 Feb 1969, and was buried in Macedonia Cemetery, Lauderdale County, AL.
+ 3046 M i. **Joel Dennis Hanback** was born 12 Sep 1940 in Lauderdale County, AL, died 11 Sep 2001, and was buried in Macedonia Cemetery, Lauderdale County, AL.
+ 3047 F ii. **Doris Ann Hanback** was born 25 Sep 1945 in Lauderdale County, AL.

Lois next married **James Thomas Wilson** 16 Oct 1969 in Lauderdale County, AL. James was born 19 Feb 1917 in Lauderdale County, AL.

1455. Mary Helen Sharp (*Harrell Emmett*[6], *Owen Bennett (Doc)*[5], *James (Jim) Charles Sr.*[4], *Adron (Edwin/Ade) Sr.*[3], *Charles W. Sr.*[2], *John Sr.*[1]) was born 7 Sep 1919 in Waterloo, Lauderdale County, AL, died 26 Aug 2003, and was buried in Greenview Memorial Park, Florence, Lauderdale County, AL.

Mary married **Nathan Carroll Roberson**, son of **Nathan Tucker Roberson** and **Tamsey Virginia Barnett**, 2 Oct 1943 in Lauderdale County, AL. Nathan was born 27 Apr 1913 in Wayne County, TN, died 26 May 1977, and was buried in Greenview Memorial Park, Florence, Lauderdale County, AL.
+ 3048 M i. **Nathan Harold Roberson** was born 10 Jun 1945 in Lauderdale County, AL.
  3049 M ii. **Bobby Joe Roberson** was born 4 Jul 1947.
+ 3050 F iii. **Virginia Ann Roberson** was born 8 Jan 1949 in Lauderdale County, AL.
+ 3051 M iv. **David Lynn Roberson** was born 13 Oct 1950 in Lauderdale County, AL.
+ 3052 M v. **Larry Bruce Roberson** was born 1 May 1952 in Lauderdale County, AL.
  3053 M vi. **Timothy Dale Roberson** was born 22 Dec 1953.

+ 3054 F vii.   **Carolyn Faye Roberson** was born 3 Nov 1955 in Lauderdale County, AL.
  3055 M viii.   **Jerry Thomas Roberson** was born 21 Nov 1957, died 16 Mar 1982, and was buried in Greenview Memorial Park, Florence, Lauderdale County, AL.
+ 3056 F ix.   **Martha Sue Roberson** was born 26 Jul 1959 in Lauderdale County, AL.

1460. Curtis (Slick) Wood (*Mildred Sharp*[6]*, Owen Bennett (Doc)*[5]*, James (Jim) Charles Sr.*[4]*, Adron (Edwin/Ade) Sr.*[3]*, Charles W. Sr.*[2]*, John Sr.*[1]) was born 30 Jun 1917 in Lauderdale County, AL, died 17 Feb 2000, and was buried in Oak Grove Cemetery, Lauderdale County, AL.

Curtis married **Sally Cordelia White**, daughter of **Benjamin Franklin (Frank) White** and **Hannah Adeline Davis**, 18 Mar 1939 in Lauderdale County, AL. Sally was born 5 Apr 1914 in Lauderdale County, AL, died 24 Dec 1999, and was buried in Oak Grove Cemetery, Lauderdale County, AL.

+ 3057 F i.   **Jimmie Nell Wood** was born 19 Dec 1939 in Lauderdale County, AL.
+ 3058 M ii.   **Cletus Wood** was born 19 Apr 1941 in Lauderdale County, AL, died 23 Jan 1966, and was buried in Oak Grove Cemetery, Lauderdale County, AL.

1461. Mary Edith (Tootsie) Wood (*Mildred Sharp*[6]*, Owen Bennett (Doc)*[5]*, James (Jim) Charles Sr.*[4]*, Adron (Edwin/Ade) Sr.*[3]*, Charles W. Sr.*[2]*, John Sr.*[1]) was born 31 Jan 1921 in Lauderdale County, AL and died 2 Feb 2007.

Mary married **Glenn Leek Franks**, son of **Lon Franks** and **Nannie Tucker**, 18 Jan 1947 in Lauderdale County, AL. Glenn was born 12 Feb 1917 in Hardin County, TN, died 5 Apr 1994, and was buried in Greenview Memorial Park, Florence, Lauderdale County, AL.

+ 3059 M i.   **Jerry Glenn Franks** was born 28 Nov 1947.
+ 3060 M ii.   **Larry Roland Franks** was born 21 Dec 1951, died 17 Oct 1981, and was buried in Greenview Memorial Park, Florence, Lauderdale County, AL.
+ 3061 F iii.   **Sherron Diane Franks** was born 28 Nov 1954.

1462. Ray Wood (*Mildred Sharp*[6]*, Owen Bennett (Doc)*[5]*, James (Jim) Charles Sr.*[4]*, Adron (Edwin/Ade) Sr.*[3]*, Charles W. Sr.*[2]*, John Sr.*[1]) was born 9 Feb 1921 in Lauderdale County, AL, died 31 Oct 1991, and was buried in Greenview Memorial Park, Florence, Lauderdale County, AL.

Ray married **Clara Estelle Allison**, daughter of **Presley (Press) Harrison Allison** and **Margie (Lady) J. Sharp**, 21 Nov 1942 in Lauderdale County, AL. Clara was born 9 Jul 1924 in Lauderdale County, AL.
(Duplicate Line. See Person 629)

1463. Joseph Wood (*Mildred Sharp*[6]*, Owen Bennett (Doc)*[5]*, James (Jim) Charles Sr.*[4]*, Adron (Edwin/Ade) Sr.*[3]*, Charles W. Sr.*[2]*, John Sr.*[1]) was born 13 Mar 1928 in Lauderdale County, AL and died 25 Jan 1993 in Lauderdale County, AL (cremated).

Joseph married **Laurel Ann Ellithorpe**. Laurel was born in 1933.
  3062 F i.   **Theresa Ann Wood**.
  3063 F ii.   **Shannon Lynn Wood**.
  3064 M iii. **Derrick Lee Wood**.
  3065 M iv.   **Vincent Carl Wood**.
  3066 F v.   **Monica Irene Wood**.

1464. Erlene Wood (*Mildred Sharp*[6]*, Owen Bennett (Doc)*[5]*, James (Jim) Charles Sr.*[4]*, Adron (Edwin/Ade) Sr.*[3]*, Charles W. Sr.*[2]*, John Sr.*[1]) was born 24 Oct 1934 in Lauderdale County, AL.

Erlene married **Ralph Gibson**. Ralph was born 17 Apr 1933 and died in 2001 in Michigan.
+ 3067 F i.   **Carla Jo Gibson** was born 15 Jul 1955.
+ 3068 F ii.   **Lisa Gaye Gibson** was born 9 Jun 1961.

1465. Rassie Wood (*Mildred Sharp*[6]*, Owen Bennett (Doc)*[5]*, James (Jim) Charles Sr.*[4]*, Adron (Edwin/Ade) Sr.*[3]*, Charles W. Sr.*[2]*, John Sr.*[1]) was born 23 Apr 1937 in Lauderdale County, AL, died 7 Jan 1987, and was buried in Oak Grove Cemetery, Lauderdale County, AL.

Rassie married **Luda Zoria Lanier**, daughter of **Willie A. Lanier** and **Bell Thigpen**, 27 Apr 1964 in Lauderdale County, AL. Luda was born 10 Oct 1940 in Lauderdale County, AL.

1466. Mary Frances Cummings (*Lillie May Sharp[6], James Charles Jr.[5], James (Jim) Charles Sr.[4], Adron (Edwin/Ade) Sr.[3], Charles W. Sr.[2], John Sr.[1]*) was born 9 Jul 1919 in Lauderdale County, AL.

Mary married **Sterling Ernest Young**, son of **Wylie Young** and **Melissa Bevis**, 26 Mar 1938 in Lauderdale County, AL. Sterling was born 17 Sep 1913 in Alabama, died 8 Jan 1987, and was buried in Tri-Cities Memorial Gardens, Florence, Lauderdale County, AL.

+ 3069 F i. **Shelby Jean Young** was born 31 Mar 1940 in Lauderdale County, AL, died 20 Mar 1995, and was buried in Tri-Cities Memorial Gardens, Florence, Lauderdale County, AL.
+ 3070 F ii. **Pauline (Polly) Young** was born 26 May 1941 in Lauderdale County, AL.
+ 3071 F iii. **Betty Ruth Young** was born 18 Mar 1943 in Lauderdale County, AL.
+ 3072 M iv. **Donnie Ray Young Sr.** was born 29 Nov 1950 in Lauderdale County, AL, died 29 Jun 2003, and was buried in Greenview Memorial Park, Florence, Lauderdale County, AL.
+ 3073 F v. **Kathy Lynn Young** was born 30 Nov 1955 in Lauderdale County, AL.
+ 3074 M vi. **Ricky Eugene Young** was born 10 Aug 1958 in Lauderdale County, AL.

1467. Lucian Jones (Jay) Cummings I (*Lillie May Sharp[6], James Charles Jr.[5], James (Jim) Charles Sr.[4], Adron (Edwin/Ade) Sr.[3], Charles W. Sr.[2], John Sr.[1]*) was born 8 Jul 1927 in Lauderdale County, AL, died 24 Oct 1990, and was buried in New Hope Cemetery, Lauderdale County, AL.

Lucian married **Dorothy Annett Myrick** in Jul 1950.
+ 3075 F i. **Susan Cheri Cummings** was born 28 Dec 1958 in Lauderdale County, AL.

Lucian next married **Winnie Mae Brandon**, daughter of **Clarence W. Brandon** and **Maebell McDaniel**, 2 May 1965 in Lauderdale County, AL. Winnie was born 6 Mar 1940 in Hardin County, TN.
+ 3076 F i. **Debra Mae Cummings** was born 11 Nov 1966 in Lauderdale County, AL.
3077 M ii. **Lucian (Jay) Jones Cummings II** was born 1 Jan 1969 in Lauderdale County, AL.

1468. Paul Lee Cummings (*Lillie May Sharp[6], James Charles Jr.[5], James (Jim) Charles Sr.[4], Adron (Edwin/Ade) Sr.[3], Charles W. Sr.[2], John Sr.[1]*) was born 25 Aug 1929 in Lauderdale County, AL.

Paul married **Francis Cordelia Clemons**, daughter of **Charles Thomas Clemons** and **Nettie Gilmore**, 3 Jun 1947 in Lauderdale County, AL. Francis was born 14 Dec 1924 in Lauderdale County, AL, died 9 Jul 1986, and was buried in Hill Cemetery, Lauderdale County, AL.
+ 3078 M i. **Harold Lee Cummings** was born 30 Jan 1949 in Lauderdale County, AL.
+ 3079 F ii. **Joyce Dianne Cummings** was born 11 Aug 1950 in Lauderdale County, AL.
+ 3080 F iii. **Patsy Correan Cummings** was born 29 Aug 1951 in Lauderdale County, AL.
+ 3081 F iv. **Betty Carolyn Cummings** was born 16 May 1953 in Lauderdale County, AL and was buried in Hill Cemetery, Lauderdale County, AL.
+ 3082 M v. **Gary Dale Cummings** was born 30 Apr 1958 in Lauderdale County, AL.
+ 3083 M vi. **Gregory Lynn Cummings** was born 23 Oct 1962 in Lauderdale County, AL.

Paul next married **Virginia Mae Weeks**, daughter of **Charlie Weeks** and **Lillie Clara Burns**, 10 Sep 1988 in Lauderdale County, AL. Virginia was born 12 Jan 1931 in Lauderdale County, AL.

1469. Lillie Earline (Jean) Sharp (*Turner Lee[6], James Charles Jr.[5], James (Jim) Charles Sr.[4], Adron (Edwin/Ade) Sr.[3], Charles W. Sr.[2], John Sr.[1]*) was born 21 Sep 1938 in Lauderdale County, AL.

Lillie married **Roy Dee (Pete) Gann**, son of **Floyd Gann** and **Myrtle Smith**. Roy was born 23 Feb 1936 in Lauderdale County, AL, died 10 May 1981, and was buried in Canaan Cemetery, Lauderdale County, AL.
+ 3084 F i. **Donna Carol Gann** was born 8 Nov 1956 in Lauderdale County, AL.
+ 3085 F ii. **Mary Decarla Gann** was born 15 Jan 1966 in Lauderdale County, AL.

Lillie next married **Wilbert Lee Salter**. Wilbert was born 16 Jul 1940.

Lillie next married **William Roland Young**, son of **William (Bill) Young** and **Audry Sharp**, 12 Nov 1996 in Lauderdale County, AL. William was born 19 Nov 1935 in Lauderdale County, AL.

1470. Marvin Lee Sharp (*Turner Lee*[6], *James Charles Jr.*[5], *James (Jim) Charles Sr.*[4], *Adron (Edwin/Ade) Sr.*[3], *Charles W. Sr.*[2], *John Sr.*[1]) was born 13 Jan 1940 in Lauderdale County, AL.

Marvin married **Laura *Unk**.
3086 M i. **Matthew Sharp**.
3087 F ii. **Rebecca Jane Sharp**.
3088 M iii. **Anthony Sharp**.

1471. James Earl Sharp (*Turner Lee*[6], *James Charles Jr.*[5], *James (Jim) Charles Sr.*[4], *Adron (Edwin/Ade) Sr.*[3], *Charles W. Sr.*[2], *John Sr.*[1]) was born 27 Jun 1941 in Lauderdale County, AL.

James married **Imogene Williams**, daughter of **John Frank Williams** and *Unk, 19 Jul 1964 in Lauderdale County, AL. Imogene was born 27 Apr 1944 in Cullman County, AL.
3089 F i. **Angela Sharp**.
3090 M ii. **Robert Sharp**.
3091 M iii. **James Sharp**.
3092 M iv. **William Sharp**.
3093 F v. **Lois Sharp**.

1473. Ernest Frederick Sharp (*Turner Lee*[6], *James Charles Jr.*[5], *James (Jim) Charles Sr.*[4], *Adron (Edwin/Ade) Sr.*[3], *Charles W. Sr.*[2], *John Sr.*[1]) was born 21 Jul 1945 in Lauderdale County, AL.

Ernest married **Clara *Unk**.

1474. Harold Douglas Sharp (*Turner Lee*[6], *James Charles Jr.*[5], *James (Jim) Charles Sr.*[4], *Adron (Edwin/Ade) Sr.*[3], *Charles W. Sr.*[2], *John Sr.*[1]) was born 21 Jan 1946 in Lauderdale County, AL, died 24 Dec 2005, and was buried in Macedonia Cemetery, Lauderdale County, AL.

Harold married **Annette Coleman**, daughter of **Ethridge Coleman** and **Gertrude Grubbs**, 28 Feb 1966 in Lauderdale County, AL. Annette was born 12 Oct 1946 in Bedford County, TN.

1476. Lois Darnell Sharp (*Turner Lee*[6], *James Charles Jr.*[5], *James (Jim) Charles Sr.*[4], *Adron (Edwin/Ade) Sr.*[3], *Charles W. Sr.*[2], *John Sr.*[1]) was born 16 Apr 1953 in Lauderdale County, AL.

Lois married **Charles D. Flippo**.

1477. Clarence Earl Sharp (*James (Little James) Robert*[6], *James Charles Jr.*[5], *James (Jim) Charles Sr.*[4], *Adron (Edwin/Ade) Sr.*[3], *Charles W. Sr.*[2], *John Sr.*[1]) was born 11 Jun 1929 in Lauderdale County, AL, died 24 Feb 1998, and was buried in Greenview Memorial Park, Florence, Lauderdale County, AL.

Clarence married **Hildagard Margarita Kuester**, daughter of **Ernst August Kuester** and **Anna Maria Tiojan**, 13 Oct 1947 in Inning, Germany. Hildagard was born 9 Apr 1924 in Germany.
+ 3094 F i. **Mary Ruth Sharp** was born 3 Oct 1948 in Inning, Germany.

1478. James Loyd Sharp (*James (Little James) Robert*[6], *James Charles Jr.*[5], *James (Jim) Charles Sr.*[4], *Adron (Edwin/Ade) Sr.*[3], *Charles W. Sr.*[2], *John Sr.*[1]) was born 28 Nov 1930 in Lauderdale County, AL, died 5 Aug 2001, and was buried in Woodlawn Cemetery, Woodlawn, TN.

James married **Norma Jean Martin**, daughter of **Darrell Jasper Martin** and **Amy Myrtle Ramsey**, 5 Jun 1957 in Branson, MO. Norma was born 22 Sep 1937 in Newton County, AR.
+ 3095 F i. **Teresa Kay Sharp** was born 27 Jun 1958 in Ft Leonardwood, MO.
+ 3096 F ii. **Jean Lorraine Sharp** was born 11 Nov 1960 in Heidelberg, Germany.

1479. Robert Lee Sharp (*James (Little James) Robert*[6], *James Charles Jr.*[5], *James (Jim) Charles Sr.*[4], *Adron (Edwin/Ade) Sr.*[3], *Charles W. Sr.*[2], *John Sr.*[1]) was born 21 Oct 1932 in Lauderdale County, AL.

Robert married **Glenda Mae Newton**, daughter of **Baxter Paul Newton** and **Ester Laverne James**, 17 May 1957 in Lauderdale County, AL. Glenda was born 18 Jul 1935 in Lauderdale County, AL.

+ 3097 F i. **Tamra (Tammy) Leah Sharp** was born 17 Mar 1958 in Lauderdale County, AL.
+ 3098 F ii. **Rebecca (Becky) Lynne Sharp** was born 9 Feb 1960 in Lauderdale County, AL.
+ 3099 M iii. **Robert (Bobby) Glenn Sharp** was born 23 Jan 1968 in Lauderdale County, AL.

1480. Clyde Ray Sharp (*James (Little James) Robert* [6], *James Charles Jr.* [5], *James (Jim) Charles Sr.* [4], *Adron (Edwin/Ade) Sr.* [3], *Charles W. Sr.* [2], *John Sr.* [1]) was born 11 Apr 1936 in Lauderdale County, AL, died 3 Oct 1998, and was buried in Macedonia Cemetery, Lauderdale County, AL.

Clyde married **Daisy Ruth May**, daughter of **John Tilton May** and **Bertha Wright**, 17 Apr 1954 in Iuka, Tishomingo County, MS. Daisy was born 20 Oct 1933 in Lauderdale County, AL.

+ 3100 M i. **Mitchell Ray Sharp** was born 14 Oct 1960 in Lauderdale County, AL.
+ 3101 M ii. **Roger Dale Sharp** was born 11 Apr 1965 in Lauderdale County, AL.

1481. Pearl Rebecca Sharp (*James (Little James) Robert* [6], *James Charles Jr.* [5], *James (Jim) Charles Sr.* [4], *Adron (Edwin/Ade) Sr.* [3], *Charles W. Sr.* [2], *John Sr.* [1]) was born 18 Feb 1937 in Lauderdale County, AL.

Pearl married **Jack Tilton May Jr.**, son of **Jack Tilton May Sr.** and **Bertha Wright**, 24 Jul 1954 in Iuka, Tishomingo County, MS. Jack was born 27 Apr 1935 in Lauderdale County, AL, died 28 Aug 2000, and was buried in Greenview Memorial Park, Florence, Lauderdale County, AL.

+ 3102 F i. **Patricia (Pam) Ann May** was born 14 Jul 1956 in Lauderdale County, AL.
+ 3103 F ii. **Vickie Lynn May** was born 26 Mar 1957 in Lauderdale County, AL.
+ 3104 F iii. **Deana Leigh May** was born 19 Apr 1964 in Lauderdale County, AL.
+ 3105 M iv. **Sammy Alan May** was born 20 Jul 1971 in Lauderdale County, AL.

1482. Cecil Moore Sharp (*James (Little James) Robert* [6], *James Charles Jr.* [5], *James (Jim) Charles Sr.* [4], *Adron (Edwin/Ade) Sr.* [3], *Charles W. Sr.* [2], *John Sr.* [1]) was born 11 Jan 1943 in Lauderdale County, AL.

Cecil married **Mary Etta Witt**, daughter of **Thomas Clyde (T. C.) Witt Sr.** and **Mary Etta Young**, 27 Apr 1962 in Lauderdale County, AL. Mary was born 27 Feb 1944 in Lauderdale County, AL.
(Duplicate Line. See Person 1277)

1483. Emmy Luetellace (Lou) Cobb (*Minor Lucille Sharp* [6], *James Charles Jr.* [5], *James (Jim) Charles Sr.* [4], *Adron (Edwin/Ade) Sr.* [3], *Charles W. Sr.* [2], *John Sr.* [1]) was born 30 Nov 1930.

Emmy married **Homer Reeder Johnson I** 19 Nov 1949. Homer was born 3 Sep 1922, died 6 Sep 1970, and was buried in Mt. Hope Cemetery, Lutts, TN.

+ 3106 F i. **Jewel Faye Johnson** was born 11 Dec 1951 in Lauderdale County, AL.
+ 3107 M ii. **Homer Reeder Johnson II** was born 9 Mar 1954 in Lauderdale County, AL, died 13 Jul 1977, and was buried in Mt. Hope Cemetery, Lutts, TN.
+ 3108 F iii. **Betty Lou Johnson** was born 16 Jun 1956 in Wayne County, TN, died 18 Nov 1985, and was buried in Mt. Hope Cemetery, Lutts, TN.
+ 3109 M iv. **Billy Gene Johnson I** was born 9 Jan 1962 in Lauderdale County, AL.

1484. Villace Lorene Cobb (*Minor Lucille Sharp* [6], *James Charles Jr.* [5], *James (Jim) Charles Sr.* [4], *Adron (Edwin/Ade) Sr.* [3], *Charles W. Sr.* [2], *John Sr.* [1]) was born 21 Mar 1932.

Villace married **Columbus Ciscoe Carson** 3 Mar 1951.

+ 3110 F i. **Patsy Willodean Carson** was born 4 Feb 1952 in Lauderdale County, AL.
+ 3111 M ii. **James Elmer Carson** was born 21 Jul 1960 in Lauderdale County, AL.
+ 3112 M iii. **Danny Eugene Carson** was born 17 Sep 1961 in Lauderdale County, AL.
  3113 M iv. **Randy Lee Carson** was born 18 Aug 1968 in Lauderdale County, AL.

1485. Julia Loretta Cobb (*Minor Lucille Sharp* [6], *James Charles Jr.* [5], *James (Jim) Charles Sr.* [4], *Adron (Edwin/Ade) Sr.* [3], *Charles W. Sr.* [2], *John Sr.* [1]) was born 4 Dec 1933 in Lauderdale County, AL, died 16 Feb 1993, and was buried in Wesley Chapel Cemetery, Lauderdale County, AL.

Julia married **Bill L. Johnson**. Bill was born 29 Jan 1931, died 29 Aug 1992, and was buried in Hunters Cemetery, Miami, FL.

+ 3114 F i. **Peggy Ann Johnson** was born 22 Dec 1950 in Lauderdale County, AL.
+ 3115 F ii. **Carolyn Sue Johnson** was born 11 Jun 1954 in St. Joseph, TN.
  3116 F iii. **Infant Johnson** was born 23 Mar 1958 in Lauderdale County, AL, died 24 Mar 1958, and was buried in Wesley Chapel Cemetery, Lauderdale County, AL.

Julia next married **Early Dean Jackson** 28 Oct 1954. Early was born 24 Feb 1917, died 29 Jun 1993, and was buried in Wesley Chapel Cemetery, Lauderdale County, AL.

+ 3117 F i. **Bertha Lucille Jackson** was born 3 Jul 1961 in Lauderdale County, AL.

1486. Helen Marie Keel (*Maggie Lorene Sharp⁶, James Charles Jr.⁵, James (Jim) Charles Sr.⁴, Adron (Edwin/Ade) Sr.³, Charles W. Sr.², John Sr.¹*) was born 14 Nov 1938 in Lauderdale County, AL.

Helen married **Robert William Tate Sr.** 16 Dec 1954. Robert was born 9 Mar 1930.

+ 3118 M i. **Robert William Tate Jr.** was born 8 Dec 1955 in Lauderdale County, AL.
+ 3119 F ii. **Lisa Marie Tate** was born 12 Jun 1959 in Lauderdale County, AL.

Helen next married **Perry Lee (Ed) Morris** 1 Apr 1968. Perry was born 30 Sep 1940.

+ 3120 F i. **Melissa Diane Morris** was born 26 Nov 1968 in Memphis, Shelby County, TN.

1487. James Walbert Keel (*Maggie Lorene Sharp⁶, James Charles Jr.⁵, James (Jim) Charles Sr.⁴, Adron (Edwin/Ade) Sr.³, Charles W. Sr.², John Sr.¹*) was born 19 May 1940 in Lauderdale County, AL.

James married **Annie Fay Dial**, daughter of **Walter Yancy Dial** and **Mary Lucille Montgomery**, 13 Sep 1963 in Lauderdale County, AL. Annie was born 28 Dec 1944 in Lauderdale County, AL.

+ 3121 F i. **Teresa Marie Keel** was born 26 Sep 1965 in Lauderdale County, AL.
+ 3122 M ii. **Donald Mark Keel** was born 3 Dec 1968 in Lauderdale County, AL.
  3123 M iii. **Alex Marlowe Keel** was born 28 Aug 1972 in Lauderdale County, AL.

1490. Joyce Lorene Keel (*Maggie Lorene Sharp⁶, James Charles Jr.⁵, James (Jim) Charles Sr.⁴, Adron (Edwin/Ade) Sr.³, Charles W. Sr.², John Sr.¹*) was born 5 Jun 1946 in Lauderdale County, AL.

Joyce married **James (Jimmy) Virgil May**, son of **Virgil Thomas May** and **Daphne Mirl Daniel**, 17 Sep 1961 in Lauderdale County, AL. James was born 24 Oct 1940 in Lauderdale County, AL.

  3124 F i. **Tina Marie May** was born 15 Jul 1962 in Lauderdale County, AL.
  3125 M ii. **Rand Lynn May** was born 20 Aug 1965 in Lauderdale County, AL.

1491. Lois Laverne Keel (*Maggie Lorene Sharp⁶, James Charles Jr.⁵, James (Jim) Charles Sr.⁴, Adron (Edwin/Ade) Sr.³, Charles W. Sr.², John Sr.¹*) was born 20 Oct 1947 in Lauderdale County, AL.

Lois married **Billy Ray Walker**, son of **John Hampton Walker** and **Louetta Lemay**, 15 Feb 1963 in Lauderdale County, AL. Billy was born 29 Mar 1937 in Lauderdale County, AL.

+ 3126 M i. **Marlow Ray Walker** was born 6 Dec 1966 in Lauderdale County, AL.
+ 3127 F ii. **Gena Marie Walker** was born 25 Oct 1967 in Lauderdale County, AL.
+ 3128 F iii. **Wanda Kay Walker** was born 3 Mar 1970 in Lauderdale County, AL.
+ 3129 M iv. **Billy Wayne Walker** was born 14 Nov 1971 in Lauderdale County, AL.

1493. Linda Kay Keel (*Maggie Lorene Sharp⁶, James Charles Jr.⁵, James (Jim) Charles Sr.⁴, Adron (Edwin/Ade) Sr.³, Charles W. Sr.², John Sr.¹*) was born 7 Jul 1950 in Lauderdale County, AL.

Linda married **Arthur Newton Bates Sr.**, son of **Wilburn N. Bates** and **Hazel Walker**, 29 Nov 1970 in Lauderdale County, AL. Arthur was born 13 Feb 1947 in Lauderdale County, AL.

+ 3130 F i. **Sandra Marie Bates** was born 31 Jul 1972 in Lauderdale County, AL.
  3131 M ii. **Arthur Newton Bates Jr.** was born 27 Jun 1975 in Jefferson County, AL.
  3132 F iii. **Valerie Kay Bates** was born 20 Apr 1980 in Jefferson County, AL.

1494. Ruby Pauline Sharp (*Elmer^6, Charles W.^{5}, James (Jim) Charles Sr.^{4}, Adron (Edwin/Ade) Sr.^{3}, Charles W. Sr.^{2}, John Sr.^{1}*) was born 28 Jan 1922 in Lauderdale County, AL, died 24 Mar 2003, and was buried in Greenview Memorial Park, Florence, Lauderdale County, AL.

Ruby married **Willie Marshall Hubbard**, son of **John Washington Hubbard** and **Bertha Scott**, 28 Jan 1940 in Lauderdale County, AL. Willie was born 20 Jan 1916 in Lauderdale County, AL, died 10 Jan 1992, and was buried in Greenview Memorial Park, Florence, Lauderdale County, AL.

+ 3133	M	i.	**Neal Lee Hubbard** was born 20 Dec 1940 in Lauderdale County, AL.
+ 3134	F	ii.	**Clara Evelyn Hubbard** was born 9 Jan 1943 in Florence, Lauderdale County, AL.
+ 3135	M	iii.	**Elmer John (E. J.) Hubbard** was born 22 Apr 1945 in Florence, Lauderdale County, AL.
+ 3136	M	iv.	**Alfred Willie Hubbard** was born 27 Oct 1947 in Florence, Lauderdale County, AL, died 19 Jul 1969, and was buried in Greenview Memorial Park, Florence, Lauderdale County, AL.
3137	M	v.	**Billy Ray Hubbard** was born 6 Mar 1950 in Florence, Lauderdale County, AL, died 30 Aug 2000, and was buried in Greenview Memorial Park, Florence, Lauderdale County, AL.

General Notes: Obituary - Times Daily, Florence, Lauderdale County, Alabama,

"Billy Ray Hubbard, 50, Florence, Ala., died Wednesday, Aug. 30, 2000. Visitation will be 6-9 p.m. today at Greenview. The grave side service will be at 11 a.m. Friday at Greenview Memorial Park. Officiating at the service will be Henry Melton.
Mr. Hubbard was a native and lifelong resident of Lauderdale County.
He is survived by his mother, Pauline Hubbard, Florence, Ala.; sisters, Clara Stricklin and husband, William, Florence, Ala., Mary Nash and husband, Mike, Florence, Ala., Shelia Johnson and husband, Larry, Slidell, La.; brothers, Neal Hubbard and wife, Linda, Killen, Ala., E.J. Hubbard and wife, Betty, Killen, Ala., Dwight Hubbard and wife, Louann, Sheffield, Ala., and Spencer Hubbard, Florence, Ala.
Mr. Hubbard was preceded in death by his father, Willie Marshall Hubbard and a brother, Alfred Hubbard.
Pallbearers will include Chris Blalock, Craig Smith, Brian Davis, Michael Nash, Jr., Steve Jennings, Ronnie Davis. Greenview Funeral Home of Florence directing."

+ 3138	F	vi.	**Mary Ruth Hubbard** was born 31 Aug 1952 in Florence, Lauderdale County, AL.
+ 3139	M	vii.	**Dwight Corbin Hubbard** was born 5 May 1955 in Florence, Lauderdale County, AL.
+ 3140	M	viii.	**Spencer Eugene Hubbard** was born 28 Feb 1958 in Florence, Lauderdale County, AL.
+ 3141	F	ix.	**Sheila Ann Hubbard** was born 18 Jun 1960 in Florence, Lauderdale County, AL.

1495. Mary Madgalene Sharp (*Elmer^6, Charles W.^{5}, James (Jim) Charles Sr.^{4}, Adron (Edwin/Ade) Sr.^{3}, Charles W. Sr.^{2}, John Sr.^{1}*) was born 29 Jul 1926 in Lauderdale County, AL.

Mary married **Shirley F. Mitchell**, son of **W. E. Mitchell** and **Lillie Mae Carder**, 25 Jun 1946 in Lauderdale County, AL. Shirley was born 17 Oct 1923 in Kentucky.

3142	M	i.	**Johnny Mitchell**.
3143	F	ii.	**Phyllis Mitchell**.
3144	M	iii.	**Perry Mitchell**.

1496. William (Bill) Harvel Sharp (*Elmer^6, Charles W.^{5}, James (Jim) Charles Sr.^{4}, Adron (Edwin/Ade) Sr.^{3}, Charles W. Sr.^{2}, John Sr.^{1}*) was born 11 Mar 1927 in Lauderdale County, AL.

William married **Betty Lou McGarrity** 4 Jun 1950 in Mishawaka, St Joseph County, IN. Betty was born 3 Mar 1930 in Mishawaka, St Joseph County, IN.

+ 3145	F	i.	**Sherry Lynn Sharp** was born 7 Apr 1951 in Mishawaka, St Joseph County, IN.
+ 3146	F	ii.	**Pamela Sue Sharp** was born 2 Jan 1953 in Mishawaka, St Joseph County, IN.

1497. Curtis Corbin Sharp (*Elmer^6, Charles W.^{5}, James (Jim) Charles Sr.^{4}, Adron (Edwin/Ade) Sr.^{3}, Charles W. Sr.^{2}, John Sr.^{1}*) was born 15 Nov 1928 in Lauderdale County, AL.

Curtis married **Anne Mae Vliek** 15 Sep 1953 in Decatur, MI. Anne was born 7 Dec 1932 in Decatur, MI.

+ 3147	M	i.	**Steven Alan Sharp** was born 12 Sep 1955 in South Bend, IN.
3148	F	ii.	**Patricia Ann Sharp** was born 23 Jul 1957 in South Bend, IN.

1498. Agnes Geneva Sharp (*Elmer*[6], *Charles W.*[5], *James (Jim) Charles Sr.*[4], *Adron (Edwin/Ade) Sr.*[3], *Charles W. Sr.*[2], *John Sr.*[1]) was born 3 May 1931 in Lauderdale County, AL.

Agnes married **Aaron Cole** 24 Jan 1953 in Mishawaka, St Joseph County, IN. Aaron was born 20 Apr 1928 in Preston, Bath County, KY.

   3149 F   i.   **Linda Gayle Austin** was born 8 Feb 1966.

1499. James Earl Sharp (*Elmer*[6], *Charles W.*[5], *James (Jim) Charles Sr.*[4], *Adron (Edwin/Ade) Sr.*[3], *Charles W. Sr.*[2], *John Sr.*[1]) was born in Aug 1933 in Lauderdale County, AL.

James married **Roseann Kathryn Burbalt** 7 Apr 1956 in Roseland, IN. Roseann was born 4 Jun 1934 in Chicago, IL.

+ 3150 F   i.   **Monica Sharp** was born 24 Jul 1957 in Evergreen Park, IL.
+ 3151 M   ii.   **Michael James Sharp** was born 24 Feb 1959 in Evergreen Park, IL.
   3152 F   iii. **Teresa Ann Sharp** was born 5 Jun 1962 in Evergreen Park, IL.
   3153 M   iv. **Samuel Thomas Sharp** was born 30 Dec 1963 in Evergreen Park, IL.

1501. Vivian Katherine Sharp (*Elmer*[6], *Charles W.*[5], *James (Jim) Charles Sr.*[4], *Adron (Edwin/Ade) Sr.*[3], *Charles W. Sr.*[2], *John Sr.*[1]) was born 30 Jun 1937 in Lauderdale County, AL.

Vivian married **John Eugene Egyed** 19 Nov 1960 in South Bend, IN. John was born 17 May 1934 in South Bend, IN.

   3154 F   i.   **Mary Elizabeth Egyed** was born 8 Apr 1970 in South Bend, IN.

1502. Rachel Ruth Sharp (*Elmer*[6], *Charles W.*[5], *James (Jim) Charles Sr.*[4], *Adron (Edwin/Ade) Sr.*[3], *Charles W. Sr.*[2], *John Sr.*[1]) was born 19 Feb 1942 in Lauderdale County, AL.

Rachel married **James Doyle Hall** 3 Jun 1961 in South Bend, IN. James was born 4 Dec 1940 in Allen, Floyd County, KY.

+ 3155 F   i.   **Michelle Lee Hall** was born 2 Aug 1964 in South Bend, IN.
+ 3156 F   ii.   **Sharon Kay Hall** was born 8 Dec 1965 in Huntsville, Madison County, AL.
   3157 M   iii. **James David Hall** was born 7 Jan 1969 in Huntsville, Madison County, AL.

1503. W. C. Sharp (*William Hubert*[6], *Charles W.*[5], *James (Jim) Charles Sr.*[4], *Adron (Edwin/Ade) Sr.*[3], *Charles W. Sr.*[2], *John Sr.*[1]) was born 9 Sep 1927 in Lauderdale County, AL.

W. married **Clara Delores (Delo) Parrish**, daughter of **Jim Watson (Totch) Parrish** and **Mary Bertha Strawn**, 12 Jun 1948 in Lauderdale County, AL. Clara was born 22 Feb 1932 in Lauderdale County, AL.

+ 3158 M   i.   **Raymond Curtis Sharp** was born 23 Apr 1949 in Lauderdale County, AL.
+ 3159 F   ii.   **Barbara Carol Sharp** was born 5 Apr 1951 in Lauderdale County, AL.
+ 3160 M   iii. **Louis Alton Sharp** was born 30 Oct 1952 in Lauderdale County, AL.
+ 3161 M   iv. **Kenneth Jay Sharp** was born 25 May 1955 in Lauderdale County, AL.
+ 3162 M   v.   **Ricky Wayne Sharp** was born 30 Nov 1957 in Lauderdale County, AL.

1504. Dorothy Virginia Sharp (*William Hubert*[6], *Charles W.*[5], *James (Jim) Charles Sr.*[4], *Adron (Edwin/Ade) Sr.*[3], *Charles W. Sr.*[2], *John Sr.*[1]) was born 17 Aug 1930 in Lauderdale County, AL, died 8 Nov 2007, and was buried in Cloverdale COC Cemetery, Lauderdale County, AL.

Dorothy married **Grafford Eugene Wallace**, son of **Owen Wilburn Wallace** and **Lillie Martin**, 6 Jul 1951 in Iuka, Tishomingo County, MS. Grafford was born 12 Mar 1930 in Lauderdale County, AL, died 1 Sep 2008, and was buried in Cloverdale COC Cemetery, Lauderdale County, AL.

+ 3163 F   i.   **Martha Gean Wallace** was born 2 Mar 1952 in Lauderdale County, AL.
+ 3164 M   ii.   **David Eugene Wallace** was born 16 Oct 1956 in Lauderdale County, AL.
+ 3165 F   iii. **Nancy Sue Wallace** was born 16 Oct 1966.
+ 3166 M   iv. **Tony Keith Wallace** was born 17 Apr 1969 in Lauderdale County, AL.

1505. Gladys Corrine Sharp (*William Hubert⁶, Charles W.⁵, James (Jim) Charles Sr.⁴, Adron (Edwin/Ade) Sr.³, Charles W. Sr.², John Sr.¹*) was born 24 Dec 1934 in Gravely Springs, Lauderdale County, AL, died 8 Mar 1966, and was buried in Murphy's Chapel Cemetery, Lauderdale County, AL.

Gladys married **Thomas Crayton South**, son of **William Floyd South** and **Mary Ann Strange**, about 1954 in Iuka, Tishomingo County, MS. Thomas was born 1 Oct 1938 in Waterloo, Lauderdale County, AL.

+ 3167	M	i.	**William Tommy South** was born 18 Jul 1956 in Lauderdale County, AL.
3168	F	ii.	**Vicki Lynn South** was born 23 Sep 1960 in Lauderdale County, AL, died 27 Oct 1960, and was buried in Murphy's Chapel Cemetery, Lauderdale County, AL.
+ 3169	M	iii.	**Bobby Lance South** was born 12 Jan 1962 in Lauderdale County, AL.
3170	M	iv.	**Jimmy Karl South** was born 16 Nov 1964 in Lauderdale County, AL.

1506. Sarah Ruth Sharp (*William Hubert⁶, Charles W.⁵, James (Jim) Charles Sr.⁴, Adron (Edwin/Ade) Sr.³, Charles W. Sr.², John Sr.¹*) was born 29 Mar 1935 in Lauderdale County, AL.

Sarah married **Comer Jack Askew I.**

+ 3171	F	i.	**Janice Kay Askew** was born 7 Aug 1954 in Lauderdale County, AL.
+ 3172	M	ii.	**Comer Jack Askew II** was born 9 Apr 1956 in Lauderdale County, AL.
+ 3173	F	iii.	**Theresa Kay Askew** was born 17 Feb 1962 in Peoria, IL.

Sarah next married **Stanley Morton Smith.**

1507. Betty May Sharp (*William Hubert⁶, Charles W.⁵, James (Jim) Charles Sr.⁴, Adron (Edwin/Ade) Sr.³, Charles W. Sr.², John Sr.¹*) was born 5 Sep 1937 in Lauderdale County, AL.

Betty married **Buford Eli Arnold Jr.** 27 Jul 1963 in Lauderdale County, AL. Buford was born 24 Oct 1941 in Lauderdale County, AL.

+ 3174	F	i.	**Melissa Diane Arnold** was born 16 Oct 1964 in Peoria, IL.
3175	M	ii.	**Steve Eli Arnold** was born 9 Oct 1965 in Lauderdale County, AL.
+ 3176	F	iii.	**Pamela Regina Arnold** was born 7 Sep 1969 in Lauderdale County, AL.
+ 3177	F	iv.	**Karen Denise Arnold** was born 4 Dec 1971 in Lauderdale County, AL.

1508. Jack Jonah Sharp (*William Hubert⁶, Charles W.⁵, James (Jim) Charles Sr.⁴, Adron (Edwin/Ade) Sr.³, Charles W. Sr.², John Sr.¹*) was born 15 Sep 1938 in Lauderdale County, AL.

Jack married **Mary Elizabeth Staggs**, daughter of **Eddie Staggs** and **Dixie Vandiver**, 12 Mar 1960 in Lauderdale County, AL. Mary was born 16 May 1944 in Lauderdale County, AL.

Jack next married **Patricia Ann Stroup** 4 Sep 1970. Patricia was born 29 Mar 1947 in Peoria, IL.

1509. Billy Joe Sharp (*William Hubert⁶, Charles W.⁵, James (Jim) Charles Sr.⁴, Adron (Edwin/Ade) Sr.³, Charles W. Sr.², John Sr.¹*) was born 9 Dec 1943 in Lauderdale County, AL.

Billy married **Dorothy Jean Hunt** 9 May 1964 in Lauderdale County, AL. Dorothy was born 5 Dec 1946 in Lauderdale County, AL.

+ 3178	M	i.	**Jeffery Scott Sharp** was born 7 Sep 1965 in Peoria, IL.
+ 3179	M	ii.	**Craig Lynn Sharp** was born 21 Sep 1966 in Peoria, IL.

Billy next married **Crystal Knox.**

1510. William Edward (Tiny) Sharp (*William Hubert⁶, Charles W.⁵, James (Jim) Charles Sr.⁴, Adron (Edwin/Ade) Sr.³, Charles W. Sr.², John Sr.¹*) was born 26 Jun 1946 in Lauderdale County, AL.

William married **Judy Ann Melton**, daughter of **Buford Eldred Melton Sr.** and **Annabelle Jeanette (Ann) Unsted**, 10 Oct 1967 in Lauderdale County, AL. Judy was born 17 May 1951 in Mishawaka, St Joseph County, IN.

General Notes: "Don & Judy officially adopted her grandchildren, January, 2009. These were Brian Jr., Bradley and Brittney, children of Brian Sr...." Sharon Wood

+ 3180 M   i.   **James Edward (Buddy) Sharp** was born 30 Oct 1968 in ECM Hospital, Florence, Lauderdale County, AL.
+ 3181 F   ii.   **Vicki June Sharp** was born 3 Dec 1970 in ECM Hospital, Florence, Lauderdale County, AL.
+ 3182 M   iii. **Brian Keith Sharp Sr.** was born 11 Aug 1975 in Lauderdale County, AL.
+ 3183 F   iv.   **Angela Marie Sharp** was born 19 Aug 1976 in Lauderdale County, AL.

1512. Fred Demphis Young (*Aurelia Sharp* [6], *Charles W.* [5], *James (Jim) Charles Sr.* [4], *Adron (Edwin/Ade) Sr.* [3], *Charles W. Sr.* [2], *John Sr.* [1]) was born 8 Feb 1940 in Lauderdale County, AL.

Fred married **Joyce Ann (Joe Ann) Cox**, daughter of **Price Cox** and **Ida Balentine**, 22 Jun 1963 in Lauderdale County, AL. Joyce was born 1 Jul 1944 in Lauderdale County, AL.

1513. Mary Rachel Young (*Aurelia Sharp* [6], *Charles W.* [5], *James (Jim) Charles Sr.* [4], *Adron (Edwin/Ade) Sr.* [3], *Charles W. Sr.* [2], *John Sr.* [1]) was born 24 Oct 1943 in Lauderdale County, AL.

Mary married **Louie Edwin Bevis**, son of **Andrew Griffin Bevis** and **Cora Belle McFall**, 20 Jun 1966 in Wayne County, TN. Louie was born 11 Aug 1944 in Wayne County, TN, died 27 Aug 1978, and was buried in Murphy's Chapel Cemetery, Lauderdale County, AL.

+ 3184 F   i.   **Janet Lou Bevis** was born 4 Aug 1963 in Lauderdale County, AL.
+ 3185 M   ii.   **Edwin Dwayne Bevis** was born 29 May 1967 in Lauderdale County, AL.
+ 3186 M   iii. **Lonnie Ray Bevis** was born 25 Jul 1969 in Lauderdale County, AL.

1514. Robbie Lou Young (*Aurelia Sharp* [6], *Charles W.* [5], *James (Jim) Charles Sr.* [4], *Adron (Edwin/Ade) Sr.* [3], *Charles W. Sr.* [2], *John Sr.* [1]) was born 2 Sep 1946.

Robbie married **Gloyd Strickland**.

1515. William Roland Young (*Audry Sharp* [6], *Charles W.* [5], *James (Jim) Charles Sr.* [4], *Adron (Edwin/Ade) Sr.* [3], *Charles W. Sr.* [2], *John Sr.* [1]) was born 19 Nov 1935 in Lauderdale County, AL.

William married **Audrey Jean Hanback**, daughter of **Jess Hanback** and **Ida Davis**, 6 Nov 1954 in Iuka, Tishomingo County, MS. Audrey was born 19 Aug 1938 in Wayne County, TN, died 27 Sep 1987, and was buried in Brush Creek Cemetery, Lauderdale County, AL.

+ 3187 M   i.   **James Roland Young** was born 15 Jan 1955 in Lauderdale County, AL.
+ 3188 M   ii.   **Billy Gean Young** was born 14 Jan 1957 in Lauderdale County, AL.
+ 3189 F   iii. **Angelia Diane Young** was born 6 Jun 1958 in Florence, Lauderdale County, AL.
+ 3190 M   iv.   **Eric Dwayne Young** was born 28 Apr 1960 in Lauderdale County, AL.
+ 3191 F   v.   **Deborah (Debbie) Aletha Young** was born 26 Sep 1964 in Lauderdale County, AL.

William next married **Lillie Earline (Jean) Sharp**, daughter of **Turner Lee Sharp** and **Minnie Pearl Daniels**, 12 Nov 1996 in Lauderdale County, AL. Lillie was born 21 Sep 1938 in Lauderdale County, AL. **(Duplicate Line. See Person 1469)**

1516. Cletus Dempsey (Skeet) Young (*Audry Sharp* [6], *Charles W.* [5], *James (Jim) Charles Sr.* [4], *Adron (Edwin/Ade) Sr.* [3], *Charles W. Sr.* [2], *John Sr.* [1]) was born 3 Nov 1937 in Lauderdale County, AL.

Cletus married **Eva Jean Wood**, daughter of **Claude Ellis Wood Sr.** and **Elizabeth Lee Phillips**, about 1956 in Iuka, Tishomingo County, MS. Eva was born 21 Mar 1939 in Florence, Lauderdale County, AL, died 31 May 2005, and was buried in Oak Grove Cemetery, Lauderdale County, AL.

+ 3192 M   i.   **Donnie Ray Young** was born 4 Feb 1957 in Florence, Lauderdale County, AL.
+ 3193 F   ii.   **Betty Jean Young** was born 4 Jun 1958 in Lauderdale County, AL.
+ 3194 M   iii. **Travis Cletus Young** was born 21 Jan 1964 in Lauderdale County, AL.

1517. Bonnie Mae Young (*Audry Sharp* [6], *Charles W.* [5], *James (Jim) Charles Sr.* [4], *Adron (Edwin/Ade) Sr.* [3], *Charles W. Sr.* [2], *John Sr.* [1]) was born 4 Aug 1941 in Lauderdale County, AL.

Bonnie married **Willie Dalton Bevis**, son of **Andrew Griffin Bevis** and **Cora Belle McFall**, 9 Sep 1960 in Lauderdale County, AL. Willie was born 26 Sep 1939 in Wayne County, TN.

+ 3195 F   i.   **Brenda Sue Bevis** was born 8 Nov 1964 in Cooksville, TN.

+ 3196 M   ii.   **Terry Lynn Bevis** was born 2 Aug 1971 in Lauderdale County, AL.

1519. Jewel Dean Young (*Audry Sharp*[6], *Charles W.*[5], *James (Jim) Charles Sr.*[4], *Adron (Edwin/Ade) Sr.*[3], *Charles W. Sr.*[2], *John Sr.*[1]) was born 8 Oct 1944 in Lauderdale County, AL, died 2 Jun 2000, and was buried in Tri-Cities Memorial Gardens, Florence, Lauderdale County, AL.

Jewel married **Daniel Scott**, son of **Robert Owen Scott** and **Eula Beatrice Young**, 7 Jun 1963 in Lauderdale County, AL. Daniel was born 6 Jan 1943 in Lauderdale County, AL.

+ 3197 M   i.   **Jeffery Daniel Scott** was born 6 Feb 1964 in Lauderdale County, AL.

+ 3198 M   ii.   **Johnny Wayne Scott** was born 30 Aug 1966 in Lauderdale County, AL.

   3199 M   iii.   **Tommy Dale Scott** was born 3 Nov 1967, died 8 Feb 1987, and was buried in Murphy's Chapel Cemetery, Lauderdale County, AL.

1520. Barbara Sue Young (*Audry Sharp*[6], *Charles W.*[5], *James (Jim) Charles Sr.*[4], *Adron (Edwin/Ade) Sr.*[3], *Charles W. Sr.*[2], *John Sr.*[1]) was born 12 Jun 1947 in Lauderdale County, AL.

Barbara married **Clay Louis Daniels**, son of **Melvin Robert Daniels** and **Mageline Cox**, 24 Nov 1969 in Lauderdale County, AL. Clay was born 17 Dec 1938 in Hardin County, TN, died 27 Nov 2001, and was buried in Oak Grove Cemetery, Lauderdale County, AL.

   3200 M   i.   **Joey Clay Daniels** was born 5 Oct 1970 in Lauderdale County, AL, died 13 Feb 1971, and was buried in Oak Grove Cemetery, Lauderdale County, AL.

+ 3201 M   ii.   **Bobby Louis Daniels** was born 19 Feb 1972 in Lauderdale County, AL.

+ 3202 F   iii.   **Julie Sue Daniels** was born 4 Nov 1973 in Lauderdale County, AL.

   3203 F   iv.   **Amy Joyce Daniels** was born 12 Nov 1981 in Lauderdale County, AL.

1521. James Charles (J. C.) Young (*Eura (Eurie) Sharp*[6], *Charles W.*[5], *James (Jim) Charles Sr.*[4], *Adron (Edwin/Ade) Sr.*[3], *Charles W. Sr.*[2], *John Sr.*[1]) was born 26 Oct 1940 in Florence, Lauderdale County, AL.

James married **Rachel Ann Wood**, daughter of **Claude Ellis Wood Sr.** and **Elizabeth Lee Phillips**, 8 Apr 1961 in Lauderdale County, AL. Rachel was born 21 Feb 1942 in Florence, Lauderdale County, AL.

+ 3204 F   i.   **Tammy Ann Young** was born 8 Sep 1962 in Lauderdale County, AL.

1522. Alice Beulah Young (*Eura (Eurie) Sharp*[6], *Charles W.*[5], *James (Jim) Charles Sr.*[4], *Adron (Edwin/Ade) Sr.*[3], *Charles W. Sr.*[2], *John Sr.*[1]) was born 5 Aug 1942 in Lauderdale County, AL.

Alice married **Charles Hampton Sharp**, son of **William Herbert (Hubbard) Sharp** and **Flora Wood**, 24 Jun 1958 in Booneville, MS. Charles was born 5 Feb 1939 in Lauderdale County, AL.

+ 3205 M   i.   **Charles Dewayne Sharp** was born 16 Jan 1961 in Lauderdale County, AL.

+ 3206 F   ii.   **Phyllis Natalie Sharp** was born 6 Feb 1962 in Lauderdale County, AL.

+ 3207 F   iii.   **Carmen Renea Sharp** was born 10 May 1963 in Lauderdale County, AL.

1523. Agnes Gwindolin Young (*Eura (Eurie) Sharp*[6], *Charles W.*[5], *James (Jim) Charles Sr.*[4], *Adron (Edwin/Ade) Sr.*[3], *Charles W. Sr.*[2], *John Sr.*[1]) was born 9 Apr 1945 in Lauderdale County, AL.

Agnes married ***Unk**.

+ 3208 M   i.   **Michael Wade Young** was born 18 Nov 1973 in Lauderdale County, AL.

Agnes next married **Elton Dewitt Collins**, son of **Edwin Collins** and **Anne Helton**, 27 Dec 1985 in Hardin County, TN. Elton was born 5 Jun 1947 in Jackson, TN.

   3209 F   i.   **Kristina Michelle Collins** was born 15 May 1986.

1524. Donald Kenneth Young (*Eura (Eurie) Sharp*[6], *Charles W.*[5], *James (Jim) Charles Sr.*[4], *Adron (Edwin/Ade) Sr.*[3], *Charles W. Sr.*[2], *John Sr.*[1]) was born 9 Jan 1948 in Lauderdale County, AL.

Donald married **Lois Inez Bevis**, daughter of **Andrew Griffin Bevis** and **Cora Belle McFall**, 10 Oct 1966 in Lauderdale County, AL. Lois was born 7 Mar 1942 in Wayne County, TN.

1525. Dorothy Mae Young (*Eura (Eurie) Sharp*[6], *Charles W.*[5], *James (Jim) Charles Sr.*[4], *Adron (Edwin/Ade) Sr.*[3], *Charles W. Sr.*[2], *John Sr.*[1]) was born 26 May 1949 in Lauderdale County, AL.

Dorothy married **Paul Howard Ezekiel**, son of **James Ezekiel** and **Myrtle Phillips**, 21 Dec 1967 in Lauderdale County, AL. Paul was born 24 Oct 1944 in Lauderdale County, AL.
+ 3210 M i. **Christopher Paul Ezekiel** was born 6 Mar 1972 in Lauderdale County, AL.
  3211 F ii. **Paula Kanisha Ezekiel** was born 6 Feb 1976 in Lauderdale County, AL.

1526. Deborah Sue Young (*Eura (Eurie) Sharp*[6], *Charles W.*[5], *James (Jim) Charles Sr.*[4], *Adron (Edwin/Ade) Sr.*[3], *Charles W. Sr.*[2], *John Sr.*[1]) was born 9 May 1955 in Lauderdale County, AL.

Deborah married **Joseph McKinley Daniels**, son of **Melvin Robert Daniels** and **Mageline Cox**, 19 Aug 1971 in Savannah, TN. Joseph was born 25 Jan 1953 in Memphis, Shelby County, TN.
+ 3212 F i. **Ginger Leigh Daniels** was born 25 Dec 1972 in Lauderdale County, AL.
+ 3213 F ii. **Felicia Dawn Daniels** was born 24 Jan 1977 in Lauderdale County, AL.
+ 3214 F iii. **Heather Nicole Daniels** was born 24 Jan 1982.

1527. Johnny Lynn Young (*Eura (Eurie) Sharp*[6], *Charles W.*[5], *James (Jim) Charles Sr.*[4], *Adron (Edwin/Ade) Sr.*[3], *Charles W. Sr.*[2], *John Sr.*[1]) was born 29 Jul 1957 in Lauderdale County, AL, died 15 Mar 1994, and was buried in Murphy's Chapel Cemetery, Lauderdale County, AL.

Johnny married **Margaret Susan White**, daughter of **Bobby Leon White** and **Lisa Moore Jenkins**, 16 Apr 1976 in Lauderdale County, AL. Margaret was born 14 Jan 1956 in Lauderdale County, AL.
  3215 M i. **Jeremy Lynn Young** was born in Lauderdale County, AL.

1530. Etta Mae Crider (*Marvin Turner Crider*[6], *Elizabeth (Roxie) Belle Sharp*[5], *James (Jim) Charles Sr.*[4], *Adron (Edwin/Ade) Sr.*[3], *Charles W. Sr.*[2], *John Sr.*[1]) was born 14 Jul 1920 in Lauderdale County, AL.

Etta married **Luther Walker**.

1531. Catherine Lorene Crider (*Marvin Turner Crider*[6], *Elizabeth (Roxie) Belle Sharp*[5], *James (Jim) Charles Sr.*[4], *Adron (Edwin/Ade) Sr.*[3], *Charles W. Sr.*[2], *John Sr.*[1]) was born 31 Jul 1925 in Lauderdale County, AL.

Catherine married **Milton Arnold**.

1532. Ruth C. Crider (*Marvin Turner Crider*[6], *Elizabeth (Roxie) Belle Sharp*[5], *James (Jim) Charles Sr.*[4], *Adron (Edwin/Ade) Sr.*[3], *Charles W. Sr.*[2], *John Sr.*[1]) was born 25 Sep 1929 in Lauderdale County, AL.

Ruth married **Lloyd Smith** 4 Oct 1946 in Iuka, Tishomingo County, MS. Lloyd was born 7 Sep 1926 in Colbert County, AL, died 21 Dec 1998, and was buried in Greenview Memorial Park, Florence, Lauderdale County, AL.
+ 3216 M i. **Dannie Lloyd Smith** was born 8 Feb 1948 in Tishomingo, MS.
+ 3217 F ii. **Marsha Lynn Smith** was born 15 Apr 1960 in St. Mary County, MO.
  3218 F iii. **Susan Kay Smith** was born 12 Aug 1961 in Pensacola, Escambia County, FL.

1533. Paul Evertt Crider (*Marvin Turner Crider*[6], *Elizabeth (Roxie) Belle Sharp*[5], *James (Jim) Charles Sr.*[4], *Adron (Edwin/Ade) Sr.*[3], *Charles W. Sr.*[2], *John Sr.*[1]) was born 31 Jul 1935 in Lauderdale County, AL.

Paul married **Lois Streetman**.

1534. Ima Jean Crider (*Marvin Turner Crider*[6], *Elizabeth (Roxie) Belle Sharp*[5], *James (Jim) Charles Sr.*[4], *Adron (Edwin/Ade) Sr.*[3], *Charles W. Sr.*[2], *John Sr.*[1]) was born 9 Apr 1940 in Tishomingo, MS.

Ima married **Louis Lard**.

1535. Paul Douglas Wood Sr. (*Fannie Elizabeth (Sister) Crider ^{6}, Elizabeth (Roxie) Belle Sharp ^{5}, James (Jim) Charles Sr. ^{4}, Adron (Edwin/Ade) Sr. ^{3}, Charles W. Sr. ^{2}, John Sr. ^{1}*) was born 24 Feb 1930 in Lauderdale County, AL, died 2 Oct 1960, and was buried in Oak Grove Cemetery, Lauderdale County, AL.

Paul married **Vita Mae Francis** 16 Aug 1952 in St. Joseph County, IN. Vita was born 4 Sep 1935 in South Bend, IN.

+ 3219	M	i.	**Paul Douglas Wood Jr.** was born 23 Dec 1952 in South Bend, IN.
+ 3220	M	ii.	**Kenneth Dale (K. D.) Wood** was born 25 Nov 1954 in South Bend, IN.
+ 3221	M	iii.	**Jeffrey Samuel (Sam) Wood Sr.** was born 7 Feb 1958 in Lauderdale County, AL.
+ 3222	F	iv.	**Nancy Ann Wood** was born 16 Sep 1959 in South Bend, IN.
+ 3223	F	v.	**Paula Marie Wood** was born 24 Mar 1961 in Lauderdale County, AL.

1536. Rufus Ezra Wood (*Fannie Elizabeth (Sister) Crider ^{6}, Elizabeth (Roxie) Belle Sharp ^{5}, James (Jim) Charles Sr. ^{4}, Adron (Edwin/Ade) Sr. ^{3}, Charles W. Sr. ^{2}, John Sr. ^{1}*) was born 19 Sep 1931 in Lauderdale County, AL, died 19 Dec 2005, and was buried in Milford Cemetery, Lauderdale County, AL.

Rufus married **Alice Elaine Brown**, daughter of **Loyd Orvil Brown** and **Marion Spillman**, 9 Apr 1955 in Iuka, Tishomingo County, MS. Alice was born 3 Jul 1939 in Mishawaka, St Joseph County, IN.

+ 3224	M	i.	**Steven McKinley Wood** was born 25 Oct 1955 in South Bend, IN.
+ 3225	F	ii.	**Pamela Elaine Wood** was born 30 Sep 1956 in South Bend, IN.
3226	F	iii.	**Cynthia Denise Wood** was born 24 Jun 1957 and died 24 Jun 1957.
+ 3227	F	iv.	**Cheryl Elizabeth Wood** was born 4 Jun 1961 in South Bend, IN.
+ 3228	F	v.	**Laurie Lee Wood** was born 16 Jul 1962 in South Bend, IN.

1537. Eldred McKinley Wood (*Fannie Elizabeth (Sister) Crider ^{6}, Elizabeth (Roxie) Belle Sharp ^{5}, James (Jim) Charles Sr. ^{4}, Adron (Edwin/Ade) Sr. ^{3}, Charles W. Sr. ^{2}, John Sr. ^{1}*) was born 25 Aug 1934 in Lauderdale County, AL.

Eldred married **Darlene Arlene Lane**, daughter of **Ora Lane** and **Irene Anderson**, 16 Jul 1965 in South Bend, IN. Darlene was born 22 Jul 1940 in Mishawaka, St Joseph County, IN.

3229	M	i.	**Tracy Allen Wood** was born 28 Mar 1970 in Mishawaka, St Joseph County, IN.

1538. Betty Ann Crider (*John Richard Crider ^{6}, Elizabeth (Roxie) Belle Sharp ^{5}, James (Jim) Charles Sr. ^{4}, Adron (Edwin/Ade) Sr. ^{3}, Charles W. Sr. ^{2}, John Sr. ^{1}*) was born 10 Jul 1956 in Lauderdale County, AL.

Betty married **Eldon Vall Kennamore**, son of **Johnnie Levi Kennamore** and **Robbie Louise Richardson**, 5 Mar 1976 in Lafayette, GA. Eldon was born 31 Jul 1936 in Perry County, TN.

+ 3230	F	i.	**Malissa Diane Kennamore** was born 28 Jun 1975 in Lauderdale County, AL.
3231	M	ii.	**Johnny Eldon Kennamore** was born 4 Nov 1976 in Lauderdale County, AL.
3232	M	iii.	**Gregory Danial Kennamore** was born 11 Feb 1980 in Lauderdale County, AL.

1539. Hazel Irene Wood (*Mary Etta (Virgie) Crider ^{6}, Elizabeth (Roxie) Belle Sharp ^{5}, James (Jim) Charles Sr. ^{4}, Adron (Edwin/Ade) Sr. ^{3}, Charles W. Sr. ^{2}, John Sr. ^{1}*) was born 29 Oct 1925 in Lauderdale County, AL, died 13 Apr 1994, and was buried in Oak Grove Cemetery, Lauderdale County, AL.

Hazel married **Robert James (Bob) Ezekiel**, son of **Jesse James Ezekiel** and **Dewey Leora Wood**, 25 Jul 1942 in Lauderdale County, AL. Robert was born 17 Oct 1920 in Lauderdale County, AL, died 10 Jun 2003, and was buried in Oak Grove Cemetery, Lauderdale County, AL.

+ 3233	F	i.	**Jimmie Nell Ezekiel** was born 8 Aug 1943 in Lauderdale County, AL.
+ 3234	M	ii.	**Jerry Anthony Ezekiel** was born in 1945 in Lauderdale County, AL.
+ 3235	M	iii.	**Colin Earl Ezekiel** was born 25 Aug 1947 in Lauderdale County, AL.
+ 3236	F	iv.	**Linda Faye Ezekiel** was born 18 Feb 1949 in Lauderdale County, AL.
+ 3237	F	v.	**Janice Aileen Ezekiel** was born 14 Apr 1950 in Waterloo, Lauderdale County, AL.
+ 3238	F	vi.	**Christine Ezekiel** was born 7 Jan 1952 in Tyronza, Poinsett County, AR.
+ 3239	M	vii.	**Bobby Gene Ezekiel** was born 27 Jul 1956 in Tyronza, Poinsett County, AR.
+ 3240	F	viii.	**Dorothy Ann Ezekiel** was born 23 Aug 1959 in Tyronza, Poinsett County, AR.
+ 3241	F	ix.	**Barbara Ruth Ezekiel** was born 27 Jul 1962 in Tyronza, Poinsett County, AR.

1540. Charles William Wood (*Mary Etta (Virgie) Crider* ^{6}*, Elizabeth (Roxie) Belle Sharp* ^{5}*, James (Jim) Charles Sr.* ^{4}*, Adron (Edwin/Ade) Sr.* ^{3}*, Charles W. Sr.* ^{2}*, John Sr.* ^{1}) was born 5 Apr 1927 in Lauderdale County, AL, died 21 Nov 1993, and was buried in Oak Grove Cemetery, Lauderdale County, AL.

Charles married **Frances Pearl Balentine**, daughter of **Elmer Clyde Balentine** and **Mattie Sue Stone**, 23 Sep 1950. Frances was born 19 Apr 1934 in Lauderdale County, AL.
+ 3242 M i. **Sherman Daniel Wood** was born 29 Dec 1953 in Tyronza, Poinsett County, AR.
+ 3243 M ii. **Travis Lloyd Wood** was born 16 Jun 1957 in Tyronza, Poinsett County, AR.
+ 3244 F iii. **Freda Marlene Wood** was born 26 Sep 1959 in Tyronza, Poinsett County, AR.

1541. Edith Inez Wood (*Mary Etta (Virgie) Crider* ^{6}*, Elizabeth (Roxie) Belle Sharp* ^{5}*, James (Jim) Charles Sr.* ^{4}*, Adron (Edwin/Ade) Sr.* ^{3}*, Charles W. Sr.* ^{2}*, John Sr.* ^{1}) was born 19 Jan 1929 in Lauderdale County, AL.

Edith married **Bob Lee Brown**, son of **Marvin Brown** and **Laura Elma Parrish**, 2 Aug 1947 in Lauderdale County, AL. Bob was born 2 Feb 1929 in Lauderdale County, AL.
+ 3245 M i. **Glenn Thomas Brown** was born 27 Jul 1948 in Lauderdale County, AL.
+ 3246 M ii. **Bobby Junior Brown** was born 9 May 1950 in Florence, Lauderdale County, AL.
+ 3247 M iii. **Jimmy Turner Brown** was born 24 Jun 1953 in Florence, Lauderdale County, AL.
+ 3248 M iv. **Kenneth Wayne Brown** was born 28 Jun 1957 in Florence, Lauderdale County, AL.

1542. Carl Thomas Wood (*Mary Etta (Virgie) Crider* ^{6}*, Elizabeth (Roxie) Belle Sharp* ^{5}*, James (Jim) Charles Sr.* ^{4}*, Adron (Edwin/Ade) Sr.* ^{3}*, Charles W. Sr.* ^{2}*, John Sr.* ^{1}) was born 8 Oct 1930 in Wright, Lauderdale County, AL.

Carl married **Frances Wilkinson** 11 Mar 1954 in Iuka, Tishomingo County, MS. Frances was born 11 Nov 1934 in Hardin County, TN.
+ 3249 M i. **Charles Wayne Wood** was born 9 Nov 1955 in Tyronza, Poinsett County, AR.
+ 3250 F ii. **Peggy Sue Wood** was born 1 Jan 1958 in South Bend, St Joseph County, IN.
+ 3251 M iii. **Michael Duane Wood** was born 6 Aug 1960 in South Bend, St Joseph County, IN.
+ 3252 M iv. **David Paul Wood** was born 31 Mar 1962 in West Memphis, Crittenden County, AR.

1543. Louis Cola Wood (*Mary Etta (Virgie) Crider* ^{6}*, Elizabeth (Roxie) Belle Sharp* ^{5}*, James (Jim) Charles Sr.* ^{4}*, Adron (Edwin/Ade) Sr.* ^{3}*, Charles W. Sr.* ^{2}*, John Sr.* ^{1}) was born 10 Jun 1935 in Wright, Lauderdale County, AL.

Louis married **Wilma Marcell Ballard**, daughter of **Thomas Crawford (T. C.) Ballard** and **Era Irene Walton**, 18 Aug 1956 in Marked Tree, Poinsett County, AR. Wilma was born 24 Aug 1939.
+ 3253 F i. **Sharon Louise Wood** was born 7 Jun 1957 in Chelford, AR.
+ 3254 M ii. **Ricky Louis Wood** was born 16 Dec 1961 in West Memphis, Crittenden County, AR.
+ 3255 F iii. **Kathryn Lorraine (Lori) Wood** was born 24 Jun 1964 in West Memphis, Crittenden County, AR.
+ 3256 M iv. **Curtis Dwayne Wood** was born 25 May 1968 in West Memphis, Crittenden County, AR.

1544. Betty Sue Wood (*Mary Etta (Virgie) Crider* ^{6}*, Elizabeth (Roxie) Belle Sharp* ^{5}*, James (Jim) Charles Sr.* ^{4}*, Adron (Edwin/Ade) Sr.* ^{3}*, Charles W. Sr.* ^{2}*, John Sr.* ^{1}) was born 21 May 1939 in Wright, Lauderdale County, AL.

Betty married **Bobby Pickens** 19 Apr 1958 in Tyronza, Poinsett County, AR. Bobby was born 19 Mar 1928 in Savannah, Hardin County, TN.
+ 3257 F i. **Jeannie Diane Pickens** was born 1 Nov 1960 in Michigan City, IN.
+ 3258 F ii. **Kathy Ann Pickens** was born 10 Apr 1963 in Michigan City, IN.
+ 3259 M iii. **Robert Joe Pickens** was born 12 Aug 1964 in Jonesboro, Craighead County, AR.
+ 3260 F iv. **Tammy Lynn Pickens** was born 20 Jun 1966 in Michigan City, IN.
+ 3261 F v. **Lisa Renae Pickens** was born 15 Dec 1967 in Michigan City, IN.

1545. Rachel Anna Wood (*Mary Etta (Virgie) Crider* ^{6}*, Elizabeth (Roxie) Belle Sharp* ^{5}*, James (Jim) Charles Sr.* ^{4}*, Adron (Edwin/Ade) Sr.* ^{3}*, Charles W. Sr.* ^{2}*, John Sr.* ^{1}) was born 12 Oct 1945 in Wright, Lauderdale County, AL.

Rachel married **Carl Bing**.

Rachel next married **William Curtis (Bill) Mullins** 19 Jul 1972 in Brownsville, TN. William was born 17 May 1943 in Mississippi.

    3262   F   i.   **Amanda Rachael Mullins** was born 11 Mar 1978 in Memphis, Shelby County, TN.

1548. Edward Joyce (E. J.) Crider (*Edgar Louis (Ed) Crider* [6], *Elizabeth (Roxie) Belle Sharp* [5], *James (Jim) Charles Sr.* [4], *Adron (Edwin/Ade) Sr.* [3], *Charles W. Sr.* [2], *John Sr.* [1]) was born 7 Apr 1941 in Lauderdale County, AL.

Edward married **Sarah Ann Burns**, daughter of **George Luther Burns** and **Opel Earline Smith**, 13 Mar 1964 in Lauderdale County, AL. Sarah was born 9 Jun 1948 in Lauderdale County, AL.

+ 3263   M   i.   **Michael James Crider** was born 20 Oct 1973 in Lauderdale County, AL.
+ 3264   F   ii.   **Tonya Renea Crider** was born 14 Feb 1977 in Lauderdale County, AL.
+ 3265   F   iii.   **Marsha Leeann Crider** was born 18 Sep 1980 in ECM Hospital, Florence, Lauderdale County, AL.

1549. Donald Fay Crider (*Edgar Louis (Ed) Crider* [6], *Elizabeth (Roxie) Belle Sharp* [5], *James (Jim) Charles Sr.* [4], *Adron (Edwin/Ade) Sr.* [3], *Charles W. Sr.* [2], *John Sr.* [1]) was born 24 Sep 1943 in Lauderdale County, AL.

Donald married **Patsy Joyce Clemons**, daughter of **Carroll Eugene Clemons I** and **Elizabeth (Betty) Darby**, 14 Jan 1967 in Lauderdale County, AL. Patsy was born 13 Feb 1947 in Lauderdale County, AL, died 15 Mar 1975, and was buried in Gravely Springs Cemetery, Lauderdale County, AL.

+ 3266   M   i.   **Ricky Donald Crider** was born 30 Jun 1968 in Lauderdale County, AL.
+ 3267   F   ii.   **Vickie Lynn Crider** was born 17 Mar 1970 in Lauderdale County, AL.
+ 3268   M   iii.   **Tony Lee Crider** was born 21 Jan 1974 in Lindsey Grove, Cloverdale, Lauderdale County, AL.

1550. Lois Crider (*James Albert Crider* [6], *Elizabeth (Roxie) Belle Sharp* [5], *James (Jim) Charles Sr.* [4], *Adron (Edwin/Ade) Sr.* [3], *Charles W. Sr.* [2], *John Sr.* [1]) was born in 1939.

Lois married **Willie Huggins**. Willie was born in 1939.

1553. Peggy Crider (*James Albert Crider* [6], *Elizabeth (Roxie) Belle Sharp* [5], *James (Jim) Charles Sr.* [4], *Adron (Edwin/Ade) Sr.* [3], *Charles W. Sr.* [2], *John Sr.* [1]).

Peggy married **Jimmy Daniel Ogletree** circa 1965. Jimmy was born circa 1947, died 6 Oct 2008 in Colbert County, AL, and was buried in Harris Chapel Cemetery, Colbert County, AL.

    3269   M   i.   **Tony Ogletree.**
    3270   M   ii.   **Stephen Ogletree.**
+ 3271   F   iii.   **Shawna Ogletree.**

1555. Bonnie Sue Lambert (*Edith Louise Crider* [6], *Elizabeth (Roxie) Belle Sharp* [5], *James (Jim) Charles Sr.* [4], *Adron (Edwin/Ade) Sr.* [3], *Charles W. Sr.* [2], *John Sr.* [1]).

Bonnie married ***Unk Hamm**.

1556. Shirley Olivia Lambert (*Edith Louise Crider* [6], *Elizabeth (Roxie) Belle Sharp* [5], *James (Jim) Charles Sr.* [4], *Adron (Edwin/Ade) Sr.* [3], *Charles W. Sr.* [2], *John Sr.* [1]).

Shirley married ***Unk Puckett**.

1558. Debra Ann Lambert (*Edith Louise Crider* [6], *Elizabeth (Roxie) Belle Sharp* [5], *James (Jim) Charles Sr.* [4], *Adron (Edwin/Ade) Sr.* [3], *Charles W. Sr.* [2], *John Sr.* [1]).

Debra married ***Unk Wigginton**.

1559. William Dan Lambert (*Edith Louise Crider* [6], *Elizabeth (Roxie) Belle Sharp* [5], *James (Jim) Charles Sr.* [4], *Adron (Edwin/Ade) Sr.* [3], *Charles W. Sr.* [2], *John Sr.* [1]) was born 21 Jun 1954, died 12 Nov 1986, and was buried in Harmony Hill Cemetery, Burnsville, Tishomingo County, MS.

William married **Linda L. *Unk**. Linda was born 1 Nov 1950.

1561. Agnes Lorene Sharp (*William Herbert (Hubbard)* [6], *Louis (Bud) Wheeler* [5], *James (Jim) Charles Sr.* [4], *Adron (Edwin/Ade) Sr.* [3], *Charles W. Sr.* [2], *John Sr.* [1]) was born 30 Jul 1930 in Lauderdale County, AL.

Agnes married **Ray Winiford Hanback**, son of **Obie R. Hanback** and **Annie Marie Brown**, 3 Oct 1953 in Iuka, Tishomingo County, MS. Ray was born 1 Jul 1933 in Lauderdale County, AL.

3272	M	i.	**Donald Ray Hanback** was born 12 Jun 1956 in Lauderdale County, AL, died 8 Apr 1975, and was buried in Macedonia Cemetery, Lauderdale County, AL.
+ 3273	M	ii.	**Thomas Lee Hanback** was born 3 Jun 1957 in Lauderdale County, AL.
+ 3274	M	iii.	**Danny Lynn Hanback** was born 4 Jan 1965 in Lauderdale County, AL.

1562. Ofard William Sharp (*William Herbert (Hubbard)* [6], *Louis (Bud) Wheeler* [5], *James (Jim) Charles Sr.* [4], *Adron (Edwin/Ade) Sr.* [3], *Charles W. Sr.* [2], *John Sr.* [1]) was born 23 Aug 1931 in Lauderdale County, AL, died 7 May 2005, and was buried in Tyronza Cemetery, Tyronza, Poinsett County, AR.

General Notes: "Traveling on Savannah Highway, near the Natchez Trace when a truck that was meeting him, swerved over and hit him head on. The other driver stated that he had a blow out but the trooper told family members that his tires were not blown out. A witness behind him was heard saying that it looked like he was messing with a dog...." Sharon Wood

Ofard married **Mary Lee Parker**.

+ 3275	F	i.	**Retha Sharp**.
+ 3276	F	ii.	**Jane Sharp**.

1563. Hazel Erline Sharp (*William Herbert (Hubbard)* [6], *Louis (Bud) Wheeler* [5], *James (Jim) Charles Sr.* [4], *Adron (Edwin/Ade) Sr.* [3], *Charles W. Sr.* [2], *John Sr.* [1]) was born 4 Jun 1934 in Lauderdale County, AL.

Hazel married **Ellie Jeri Smith**.

Hazel next married ***Unk Lovell**.

1564. Franklin (Duce) Sharp (*William Herbert (Hubbard)* [6], *Louis (Bud) Wheeler* [5], *James (Jim) Charles Sr.* [4], *Adron (Edwin/Ade) Sr.* [3], *Charles W. Sr.* [2], *John Sr.* [1]) was born 8 Sep 1936 in Lauderdale County, AL, died 1 Oct 1999, and was buried in Oak Grove Cemetery, Lauderdale County, AL.

General Notes: Obituary - Times Daily, Florence, Lauderdale County, Alabama

"Franklin 'Duce' Sharp, 63, of Waterloo, Ala., died Friday, Oct. 1, 1999, after an extended illness.
Visitation was Saturday evening at Greenview. The funeral will be Sunday at 2 p.m. at House of Prayer, County Road 60, with burial in Oak Grove Cemetery. Mr. Sharp will be placed in the church one hour before the service. Officiating at the funeral will be the Revs. Larry Burbank and Jim Young.
Mr. Sharp was a native and lifelong resident of Lauderdale County. He is survived by his father, Herbert Sharp, Waterloo, Ala.; sisters, Lorene Hanback, Florence, Ala., and Hazell Lovell, Tyronza, Ark; brothers, Charles Sharp, Waterloo, Ala., Ofard Sharp, Tyronza, Ark., Earl Sharp, Tyronza, Ark.
Mr. Sharp was preceded in death by his wife, Clara Sue Sharp; his mother, Flora Woods Sharp, and a brother, Walter Sharp.
Pallbearers will be Wayne Sharp, Leon Sharp, Eldred Sharp, Steve Wood, Keith Scott, Tommy Hanback, Dewight Wood, Junior Smith. Honorary pallbearer will be Bro. Gerry Duboise.
Greenview Funeral Home of Florence directing."

Franklin married **Clara Sue (Susie) Wood**, daughter of **Lawrence (Toby) Eldred Sharp** and **Pauline Inez Wood**, about 1957 in Iuka, Tishomingo County, MS. Clara was born 12 Feb 1940 in Lauderdale County, AL, died 24 Jan 1994, and was buried in Oak Grove Cemetery, Lauderdale County, AL.

3277	M	i.	**Son Sharp** was born 23 May 1958 in Lauderdale County, AL, died 23 May 1958, and was buried in Oak Grove Cemetery, Lauderdale County, AL.

1565. Charles Hampton Sharp (*William Herbert (Hubbard)* [6] *, Louis (Bud) Wheeler* [5] *, James (Jim) Charles Sr.* [4] *, Adron (Edwin/Ade) Sr.* [3] *, Charles W. Sr.* [2] *, John Sr.* [1]) was born 5 Feb 1939 in Lauderdale County, AL.

Charles married **Alice Beulah Young**, daughter of **Ellie Bert Young** and **Eura (Eurie) Sharp**, 24 Jun 1958 in Booneville, MS. Alice was born 5 Aug 1942 in Lauderdale County, AL.
(Duplicate Line. See Person 1522)

1567. Amos Earl Sharp (*William Herbert (Hubbard)* [6] *, Louis (Bud) Wheeler* [5] *, James (Jim) Charles Sr.* [4] *, Adron (Edwin/Ade) Sr.* [3] *, Charles W. Sr.* [2] *, John Sr.* [1]) was born in Lauderdale County, AL.

Amos married **Barbara Smith**.

1568. Rufus Eldred Sharp (*Loye Arvel* [6] *, Louis (Bud) Wheeler* [5] *, James (Jim) Charles Sr.* [4] *, Adron (Edwin/Ade) Sr.* [3] *, Charles W. Sr.* [2] *, John Sr.* [1]) was born 3 Oct 1936 in Gravely Springs, Lauderdale County, AL.

Rufus married **Polly Ann Witt**, daughter of **Olen L. Witt** and **Bertha Young**, 29 Jan 1956 in Iuka, Tishomingo County, MS. Polly was born 4 Sep 1940 in Lauderdale County, AL, died 13 Aug 1992, and was buried in Murphy's Chapel Cemetery, Lauderdale County, AL.
+ 3278 F i. **Sandra Ann Sharp** was born 22 Jan 1957 in Lauderdale County, AL.
  3279 M ii. **Rufus David (Buddy) Sharp** was born 11 Jul 1958 in Lauderdale County, AL, died 8 Apr 1975, and was buried in Murphy's Chapel Cemetery, Lauderdale County, AL.
+ 3280 M iii. **Jeffrey Keith Sharp** was born 19 Jan 1961 in Lauderdale County, AL.

Rufus next married **Barbara Hubbard Murphy**, daughter of **Herschel Alexander Murphy** and **Letha Mae Hubbard**, 25 Sep 1992 in Lauderdale County, AL. Barbara was born 14 Aug 1946.

1569. Lola Mae Sharp (*Loye Arvel* [6] *, Louis (Bud) Wheeler* [5] *, James (Jim) Charles Sr.* [4] *, Adron (Edwin/Ade) Sr.* [3] *, Charles W. Sr.* [2] *, John Sr.* [1]) was born 16 Mar 1938 in Gravely Springs, Lauderdale County, AL.

Lola married **Jack Norman White**, son of **Will White** and **Margie Balentine**, 25 Jan 1958 in Iuka, Tishomingo County, MS. Jack was born 30 Aug 1938 in Alabama.
+ 3281 M i. **Norman Lynn White** was born 29 Nov 1961 in Lauderdale County, AL.
+ 3282 F ii. **Janet Loletha White** was born 10 Aug 1964 in Hardin County, TN.

1570. Millard Woodrow Sharp (*Loye Arvel* [6] *, Louis (Bud) Wheeler* [5] *, James (Jim) Charles Sr.* [4] *, Adron (Edwin/Ade) Sr.* [3] *, Charles W. Sr.* [2] *, John Sr.* [1]) was born 21 Feb 1940 in Gravely Springs, Lauderdale County, AL.

Millard married **Joyce Elizabeth Nobles**, daughter of **Ernest Nobles Jr.** and **Christine Vernon Hill**, 13 Oct 1962 in Lauderdale County, AL. Joyce was born 26 Nov 1945 in Lauderdale County, AL.
+ 3283 M i. **Timothy (Tim) Woodrow Sharp** was born 31 Jul 1963 in Lauderdale County, AL.
  3284 F ii. **Sherry Joyce Sharp** was born 13 Jul 1964 in Lauderdale County, AL, died 6 Feb 1965, and was buried in Oak Grove Cemetery, Lauderdale County, AL.
+ 3285 F iii. **Kim Rena Sharp** was born 25 Nov 1966 in Lauderdale County, AL.
+ 3286 M iv. **Ernest (Ernie) Lynn Sharp** was born 28 Sep 1976 in Lauderdale County, AL.

Millard next married **Tamara Lynn Lipford**, daughter of **Carl Gene Lipford** and **Peggy Sue Kieter**, 12 Nov 1997 in Lauderdale County, AL. Tamara was born 1 Jan 1958 in Kane County, IL.

1571. Ralph Arvel Sharp (*Loye Arvel* [6] *, Louis (Bud) Wheeler* [5] *, James (Jim) Charles Sr.* [4] *, Adron (Edwin/Ade) Sr.* [3] *, Charles W. Sr.* [2] *, John Sr.* [1]) was born 15 Nov 1942 in Gravely Springs, Lauderdale County, AL.

Ralph married **Dorothy Mozelle Brown**, daughter of **Clarence E. Brown** and **Ruby Mae Geans**, 18 Feb 1961 in Lauderdale County, AL. Dorothy was born 16 Oct 1943 in Lauderdale County, AL.
  3287 M i. **Johnny Wayne Sharp** was born 13 Dec 1961 in Lauderdale County, AL.
+ 3288 F ii. **Sheila Kay Sharp** was born 4 Aug 1963 in Lauderdale County, AL.
+ 3289 F iii. **Karen Denise Sharp** was born 22 Jul 1964 in Lauderdale County, AL.

1572. Carolyn Lois Sharp (*Loye Arvel[6], Louis (Bud) Wheeler[5], James (Jim) Charles Sr.[4], Adron (Edwin/Ade) Sr.[3], Charles W. Sr.[2], John Sr.[1]*) was born 24 Nov 1944 in Gravely Springs, Lauderdale County, AL.

Carolyn married **Kenneth Ray Jones**, son of **Homer Lee Jones** and **Lillian T. Ticer**, 21 Dec 1965 in Lauderdale County, AL. Kenneth was born 2 Oct 1942 in Lauderdale County, AL, died 7 Mar 1970, and was buried in Wright Cemetery, Wright, Lauderdale County, AL.
(Duplicate Line. See Person 1238)

Carolyn next married **Coolidge Clayton (Pete) McCain**, son of **Jesse James McCain** and **Bessie Brown**, 27 Aug 1973 in Lauderdale County, AL. Coolidge was born 8 Apr 1947 in Counce, TN.
+ 3290 M i. **Stephen Coolidge McCain** was born 18 Dec 1974 in ECM Hospital, Florence, Lauderdale County, AL.

1573. Sally Ann (Mavis) Sharp (*Loye Arvel[6], Louis (Bud) Wheeler[5], James (Jim) Charles Sr.[4], Adron (Edwin/Ade) Sr.[3], Charles W. Sr.[2], John Sr.[1]*) was born 27 Oct 1946 in Gravely Springs, Lauderdale County, AL.

Sally married **Larry Bennett Burbank**, son of **John Ethridge Burbank** and **Erma Jane Davis**, 2 Jun 1964 in Lauderdale County, AL. Larry was born 30 May 1946 in Lauderdale County, AL.
+ 3291 F i. **Melissa (Lisa) Ann Burbank** was born 28 Dec 1967 in Lauderdale County, AL.
+ 3292 M ii. **Michael (Mike) Larry Burbank** was born 16 Mar 1971 in Lauderdale County, AL.

1574. Berlon Ray Sharp (*Loye Arvel[6], Louis (Bud) Wheeler[5], James (Jim) Charles Sr.[4], Adron (Edwin/Ade) Sr.[3], Charles W. Sr.[2], John Sr.[1]*) was born 13 Sep 1948 in Gravely Springs, Lauderdale County, AL.

Berlon married **Jo Nell Kelley**, daughter of **Jessie James Kelley** and **Vernette Young**, 27 Mar 1968 in Lauderdale County, AL. Jo was born 3 Jan 1949 in Lauderdale County, AL.
+ 3293 M i. **Terry Ray Sharp** was born 11 Nov 1968 in Lauderdale County, AL.
+ 3294 F ii. **Lola Michelle (Shelly) Sharp** was born 26 Mar 1972 in Lauderdale County, AL.

1576. Clara Sue (Susie) Wood (*Lawrence (Toby) Eldred[6], Louis (Bud) Wheeler[5], James (Jim) Charles Sr.[4], Adron (Edwin/Ade) Sr.[3], Charles W. Sr.[2], John Sr.[1]*) was born 12 Feb 1940 in Lauderdale County, AL, died 24 Jan 1994, and was buried in Oak Grove Cemetery, Lauderdale County, AL.

Clara married **Franklin (Duce) Sharp**, son of **William Herbert (Hubbard) Sharp** and **Flora Wood**, about 1957 in Iuka, Tishomingo County, MS. Franklin was born 8 Sep 1936 in Lauderdale County, AL, died 1 Oct 1999, and was buried in Oak Grove Cemetery, Lauderdale County, AL.
(Duplicate Line. See Person 1564)

1577. Stevie Lawrence Wood (*Lawrence (Toby) Eldred[6], Louis (Bud) Wheeler[5], James (Jim) Charles Sr.[4], Adron (Edwin/Ade) Sr.[3], Charles W. Sr.[2], John Sr.[1]*) was born 13 Jul 1947 in Florence, Lauderdale County, AL.

Stevie married **Lucy Reyes** in 1987.
3295 M i. **Darren Lawrence Wood** was born 19 Jan 1988 in Lauderdale County, AL.
3296 F ii. **Keyle Wood** was born 27 Apr 1998.

Stevie next married **Brenda Joyce Hamilton** 24 Dec 1970 in Lauderdale County, AL. Brenda was born 4 Apr 1950 in Hardin County, TN.
+ 3297 M i. **Dwight Wood** was born 14 Nov 1972.

Stevie next married **Patricia Carolyn Patrick**, daughter of **Joseph Buford Patrick Sr.** and **Virgie Ione Young**, 4 May 1977 in Lauderdale County, AL. Patricia was born 19 Dec 1949 in Lauderdale County, AL.
3298 F i. **Joanie Wood** was born 14 Oct 1975.
3299 M ii. **Kris Wood** was born 13 Mar 1978.

Stevie next married **Glynis Balentine**.
3300 M i. **Michael Balentine Wood** was born 21 Mar 1982.

Stevie next married **Elizabeth Marlene Gargis** 16 Oct 1982 in Lauderdale County, AL. Elizabeth was born 20 Oct 1947 in Colbert County, AL.

1578. Patsy Ann Wood (*Lawrence (Toby) Eldred^6, Louis (Bud) Wheeler^5, James (Jim) Charles Sr.^{4}, Adron (Edwin/Ade) Sr.^{3}, Charles W. Sr.^{2}, John Sr.^{1}*) was born 14 Oct 1949 in Florence, Lauderdale County, AL.

Patsy married **David Scott**, son of **Robert Owen Scott** and **Eula Beatrice Young**, 20 Jul 1966 in Lauderdale County, AL. David was born 6 Jan 1943 in Lauderdale County, AL.
+ 3301 M i. **David Keith (Peanut) Scott** was born 25 Dec 1966.
+ 3302 F ii. **Jennifer Ann Scott** was born 21 Jul 1969.

1579. Ruby Nell Sharp (*Lawrence (Toby) Eldred^6, Louis (Bud) Wheeler^5, James (Jim) Charles Sr.^{4}, Adron (Edwin/Ade) Sr.^{3}, Charles W. Sr.^{2}, John Sr.^{1}*) was born 29 Oct 1941 in Lauderdale County, AL, died 23 Feb 1974 in Mishawaka, St Joseph County, IN, and was buried in Oak Grove Cemetery, Lauderdale County, AL.

Ruby married **Clifford Balentine**, son of **Elmer Clyde Balentine** and **Mattie Sue Stone**, before 1959.
+ 3303 M i. **Rocky Delane Balentine** was born 4 Mar 1959 in Lauderdale County, AL, died 29 Oct 1992, and was buried in Oak Grove Cemetery, Lauderdale County, AL.

Ruby next married **John Edward Harbin Jr.**, son of **John Edward Harbin Sr.** and **Margaret Ellen Woodall**, 8 Apr 1960 in Lauderdale County, AL. John was born 25 Mar 1938 in Florence, Lauderdale County, AL, died 23 Feb 1974, and was buried in Tri-Cities Memorial Gardens, Florence, Lauderdale County, AL.
+ 3304 F i. **Janet Marie Harbin** was born 9 Oct 1962 in Rapid City, SD.

1580. Tony Leon Sharp (*Lawrence (Toby) Eldred^6, Louis (Bud) Wheeler^5, James (Jim) Charles Sr.^{4}, Adron (Edwin/Ade) Sr.^{3}, Charles W. Sr.^{2}, John Sr.^{1}*) was born 28 Jun 1944 in Lauderdale County, AL.

Tony married **Billie Frances Laws**, daughter of **William Lee Laws** and **Mary Eula Wright**, 5 Dec 1966 in Lauderdale County, AL. Billie was born 21 Sep 1942 in Lawrence County, TN.
+ 3305 M i. **Ricky Leon Sharp** was born 19 Aug 1968 in Lauderdale County, AL.

1581. Doris Etoyle Sharp (*Lawrence (Toby) Eldred^6, Louis (Bud) Wheeler^5, James (Jim) Charles Sr.^{4}, Adron (Edwin/Ade) Sr.^{3}, Charles W. Sr.^{2}, John Sr.^{1}*) was born 7 Jul 1946 in Lauderdale County, AL.

Doris married **Bennie LaDon Belcher**, son of **Ben D. Belcher** and **Frankie C. Austin**, 10 Jul 1964 in Lauderdale County, AL. Bennie was born 28 Sep 1943 in Lauderdale County, AL.
+ 3306 F i. **Sherry Denise Belcher** was born 7 Apr 1965 in Lauderdale County, AL.
+ 3307 M ii. **Michael Ladon Belcher** was born 16 Jun 1967 in Lauderdale County, AL.
+ 3308 M iii. **Bennie Datson Belcher** was born 23 Sep 1969 in Lauderdale County, AL.

1582. Alfred Donald Sharp (*Lawrence (Toby) Eldred^6, Louis (Bud) Wheeler^5, James (Jim) Charles Sr.^{4}, Adron (Edwin/Ade) Sr.^{3}, Charles W. Sr.^{2}, John Sr.^{1}*) was born 20 Dec 1947 in Lauderdale County, AL, died 28 Aug 1978, and was buried in Oak Grove Cemetery, Lauderdale County, AL.

Alfred married **Judith Paulette Russell**, daughter of **Drexel Paul (Toad) Russell** and **Audrey Louise Smith**, 20 May 1967 in Niles, MI. Judith was born 1 Jul 1947 in Batesville, AR.
+ 3309 F i. **Lucinda (Cindi) Elizabeth Sharp** was born 23 Aug 1969 in South Bend, St Joseph County, IN.

Alfred next married **Martha June Burgess**.
+ 3310 F i. **Carrie Donyalla (Dana) Nichols** was born 22 Dec 1977 in Florence, Lauderdale County, AL.

1583. Cathy Deloris Sharp (*Lawrence (Toby) Eldred^6, Louis (Bud) Wheeler^5, James (Jim) Charles Sr.^{4}, Adron (Edwin/Ade) Sr.^{3}, Charles W. Sr.^{2}, John Sr.^{1}*) was born 22 Feb 1952 in Lauderdale County, AL.

Cathy married **Dalton Wayne Smith**, son of **Dalton Harmon Smith** and **Vera Adelaide Bevis**, 4 Apr 1969 in Lauderdale County, AL. Dalton was born 12 Feb 1948 in Lauderdale County, AL.
+ 3311 M i. **Mardie Wayne Smith** was born 18 Apr 1974 in Lauderdale County, AL.
+ 3312 F ii. **Amanda Deloris Smith** was born 13 May 1978 in Lauderdale County, AL.

1584. Juston Leveril Sharp (*Lawrence (Toby) Eldred*⁶, *Louis (Bud) Wheeler*⁵, *James (Jim) Charles Sr.*⁴, *Adron (Edwin/Ade) Sr.*³, *Charles W. Sr.*², *John Sr.*¹) was born 19 Nov 1953 in Lauderdale County, AL, died 21 May 1999, and was buried in Oak Grove Cemetery, Lauderdale County, AL.

Juston married **Lana Lynn Taylor**, daughter of **Roy Levell Taylor** and **Katherine Jewell Smith**, 15 May 1980 in Lauderdale County, AL. Lana was born 9 Jul 1960 in South Bend, IN.

+ 3313 F   i.   **Jessica Lynn Sharp** was born 28 Dec 1980 in Loretto, Lawrence County, TN.
+ 3314 M   ii.   **Joshua Paul Sharp** was born 27 Feb 1983 in Loretto, Lawrence County, TN.
   3315 M   iii.   **Jonathan Andrew Sharp** was born 1 Sep 1989 in Lauderdale County, AL.

1585. Danny Wayne Sharp (*Lawrence (Toby) Eldred*⁶, *Louis (Bud) Wheeler*⁵, *James (Jim) Charles Sr.*⁴, *Adron (Edwin/Ade) Sr.*³, *Charles W. Sr.*², *John Sr.*¹) was born 25 Apr 1956 in Lauderdale County, AL, died 20 Dec 1992, and was buried in Oak Grove Cemetery, Lauderdale County, AL.

Danny married **Joan Rae Crosslin**, daughter of **James Leon Crosslin** and **Sarah Edith May**, 21 Feb 1987 in Lauderdale County, AL. Joan was born 9 Oct 1956 in Lauderdale County, AL.

   3316 F   i.   **Melanie Shea Darby Sharp** was born 14 Sep 1974 in Lauderdale County, AL.
   3317 F   ii.   **Sarah Elizabeth Sharp** was born 4 Jul 1981 in Lauderdale County, AL.
+ 3318 F   iii.   **Bonnie Suzanne Sharp** was born 19 Sep 1982 in Lauderdale County, AL.

1586. Melba Rose Sharp (*Lawrence (Toby) Eldred*⁶, *Louis (Bud) Wheeler*⁵, *James (Jim) Charles Sr.*⁴, *Adron (Edwin/Ade) Sr.*³, *Charles W. Sr.*², *John Sr.*¹) was born 13 Mar 1959 in Lauderdale County, AL.

Melba married **Gregory Steven McDougal** 19 Jul 1976 in Lauderdale County, AL.

Melba next married **Danny Howell (Red) Lawrence**, son of **J. Edward Lawrence Sr.** and **Francis Copeland**, 24 Jul 1983 in Lauderdale County, AL. Danny was born 27 May 1956 in Lauderdale County, AL, died 5 Sep 1987, and was buried in Oak Grove Cemetery, Lauderdale County, AL.

   3319 M   i.   **Toby James (T. J.) Lawrence** was born 24 Dec 1984 in Lauderdale County, AL.
   3320 M   ii.   **Shannon Lee Lawrence** was born 24 May 1985 in Lauderdale County, AL.

1587. Tammy Loudean Sharp (*Lawrence (Toby) Eldred*⁶, *Louis (Bud) Wheeler*⁵, *James (Jim) Charles Sr.*⁴, *Adron (Edwin/Ade) Sr.*³, *Charles W. Sr.*², *John Sr.*¹) was born 16 Apr 1962 in Lauderdale County, AL.

Tammy married **Donald Ray Rhodes Sr.**, son of **Arlon Lee Rhodes** and **Bobbie Hall**, 25 May 1979 in Lauderdale County, AL. Donald was born 27 May 1955 in Lauderdale County, AL.

   3321 M   i.   **Donald Ray Rhodes Jr.**
   3322 F   ii.   **April Nicole Rhodes.**
   3323 F   iii.   **Kathelyn Elizabeth Rhodes.**

1588. Carl Robert Young (*Myrtle Lutts*⁶, *Mary Elizabeth Sharp*⁵, *James (Jim) Charles Sr.*⁴, *Adron (Edwin/Ade) Sr.*³, *Charles W. Sr.*², *John Sr.*¹) was born 26 Nov 1937 in Lauderdale County, AL, died 8 Mar 2008 in Lauderdale County, AL, and was buried in Central Heights Community Cemetery, Lauderdale County, AL.

Carl married **Bessie Lou Brown**, daughter of **Clarence E. Brown** and **Ruby Mae Geans**, 14 Jun 1963 in Lauderdale County, AL. Bessie was born 14 Jun 1945 in Lauderdale County, AL.

+ 3324 F   i.   **Lisa Young.**
+ 3325 F   ii.   **Elizabeth Diane Young** was born 2 May 1964 in Lauderdale County, AL.

1589. Laura Young (*Myrtle Lutts*⁶, *Mary Elizabeth Sharp*⁵, *James (Jim) Charles Sr.*⁴, *Adron (Edwin/Ade) Sr.*³, *Charles W. Sr.*², *John Sr.*¹).

Laura married ***Unk Haynes**.

1590. Rita Mae Young (*Myrtle Lutts*⁶, *Mary Elizabeth Sharp*⁵, *James (Jim) Charles Sr.*⁴, *Adron (Edwin/Ade) Sr.*³, *Charles W. Sr.*², *John Sr.*¹).

Rita married ***Unk Narmore**.

1591. June Young (*Myrtle Lutts* [6], *Mary Elizabeth Sharp* [5], *James (Jim) Charles Sr.* [4], *Adron (Edwin/Ade) Sr.* [3], *Charles W. Sr.* [2], *John Sr.* [1]).

June married ***Unk Vaughn**.

1592. Ruby Lucille Allison (*Raymond Andrew Allison* [6], *Margie (Lady) J. Sharp* [5], *James (Jim) Charles Sr.* [4], *Adron (Edwin/Ade) Sr.* [3], *Charles W. Sr.* [2], *John Sr.* [1]) was born 26 Jul 1929 in Lauderdale County, AL.

Ruby married **Ronnie Dale Burbank**, son of **John Ethridge Burbank** and **Erma Jane Davis**, in Sep 1949 in Iuka, Tishomingo County, MS. Ronnie was born 20 Nov 1934 in Lauderdale County, AL.
+ 3326   F   i.   **Karen Sue Burbank** was born 12 Aug 1954 in Lauderdale County, AL.
+ 3327   F   ii.   **Janice Marie Burbank** was born 12 Feb 1956 in Lauderdale County, AL.
+ 3328   M   iii. **Roger Dale Burbank** was born 10 Jul 1958 in Lauderdale County, AL.

Ruby next married **Lonzie Clifford Clemons**, son of **Charles Thomas Clemons** and **Nettie Gilmore**, 15 Mar 1974 in Lauderdale County, AL. Lonzie was born 8 Apr 1930 in Lauderdale County, AL.

1594. Lois Evelyn Allison (*Raymond Andrew Allison* [6], *Margie (Lady) J. Sharp* [5], *James (Jim) Charles Sr.* [4], *Adron (Edwin/Ade) Sr.* [3], *Charles W. Sr.* [2], *John Sr.* [1]) was born 5 Nov 1932 in Lauderdale County, AL.

Lois married **Daniel Maurice Smith**, son of **Emmett Oneal Smith** and **Odella L. Murphy**, 11 Dec 1948 in Iuka, Tishomingo County, MS. Daniel was born 18 Apr 1933 in Lauderdale County, AL, died 5 Mar 1994, and was buried in Oak Grove Cemetery, Lauderdale County, AL.
+ 3329   M   i.   **Billy Rayburn Smith** was born 2 Sep 1950 in Lake County, IL.
+ 3330   F   ii.   **Donna Machele Smith** was born 16 Jun 1955 in St. Joseph County, IN.
+ 3331   M   iii. **Danny Russell Smith** was born 4 Jun 1960 in Lauderdale County, AL.
+ 3332   M   iv.   **Cameron Don Smith** was born 19 Jul 1965 in Lauderdale County, AL.

1595. Elsie Gertrude Allison (*Raymond Andrew Allison* [6], *Margie (Lady) J. Sharp* [5], *James (Jim) Charles Sr.* [4], *Adron (Edwin/Ade) Sr.* [3], *Charles W. Sr.* [2], *John Sr.* [1]) was born 4 Dec 1934 in Lauderdale County, AL.

Elsie married **Alvin Washington Wright**, son of **Henry Washington Wright** and **Ella Penola Montgomery**, 23 Nov 1963 in Lauderdale County, AL. Alvin was born 22 Apr 1920 in Wayne County, TN.
+ 3333   F   i.   **Kathy Renea Wright**.

1596. Harve Harrison Allison (*Raymond Andrew Allison* [6], *Margie (Lady) J. Sharp* [5], *James (Jim) Charles Sr.* [4], *Adron (Edwin/Ade) Sr.* [3], *Charles W. Sr.* [2], *John Sr.* [1]) was born 2 Feb 1936 in Lauderdale County, AL, died 17 Jun 1991, and was buried in Oak Grove Cemetery, Lauderdale County, AL.

Harve married **Tempie Voliun Young**, daughter of **Clarence Roy Young** and **Clara Lorene Seaton**, 6 Sep 1953 in Iuka, Tishomingo County, MS. Tempie was born 22 Dec 1937 in Lauderdale County, AL.
+ 3334   F   i.   **Sherry Elaine Allison** was born 25 Nov 1954 in St. Joseph County, IN.
+ 3335   F   ii.   **Barbara Jean Allison** was born 8 Sep 1957 in South Bend, IN.
+ 3336   F   iii. **Rhonda Carol Allison** was born 3 Jan 1959 in Lauderdale County, AL, died 28 Feb 1996, and was buried in Macedonia Cemetery, Lauderdale County, AL.
+ 3337   F   iv.   **Cindy Ann Allison** was born 17 Apr 1961 in Lauderdale County, AL.
+ 3338   F   v.   **Tammy Laura Allison** was born 25 May 1963 in Lauderdale County, AL.
+ 3339   M   vi.   **Timothy (Tim) Harve Allison** was born 25 May 1963 in Lauderdale County, AL.
+ 3340   F   vii. **Angelina (Angie) Gay Allison** was born 19 Oct 1964 in Lauderdale County, AL.
+ 3341   F viii. **Amanda Dawn Allison** was born 25 Sep 1969 in Lauderdale County, AL.
+ 3342   M   ix.   **Jeffrey Shane Allison** was born 12 Feb 1971 in Lauderdale County, AL.

1597. Marcus Andrew Allison (*Raymond Andrew Allison* [6], *Margie (Lady) J. Sharp* [5], *James (Jim) Charles Sr.* [4], *Adron (Edwin/Ade) Sr.* [3], *Charles W. Sr.* [2], *John Sr.* [1]) was born 7 Sep 1938 in Lauderdale County, AL, died 29 Oct 2005, and was buried in Tri-Cities Memorial Gardens, Florence, Lauderdale County, AL.

Marcus married **Dixie Muriel Putman**, daughter of **Arnold Putman** and **Marie Grisham**, 20 Oct 1962 in Lauderdale County, AL. Dixie was born 14 Feb 1942 in Lauderdale County, AL.

+ 3343 F i. **Lisa Muriel Allison** was born 6 Mar 1964 in Lauderdale County, AL.

1598. Connie Eugene Allison (*Raymond Andrew Allison*[6], *Margie (Lady) J. Sharp*[5], *James (Jim) Charles Sr.*[4], *Adron (Edwin/Ade) Sr.*[3], *Charles W. Sr.*[2], *John Sr.*[1]) was born 28 Dec 1941 in Lauderdale County, AL.

Connie married **Shirley Jean Rideout**, daughter of **Roy Rideout** and **Clara Perry**, 6 Apr 1962 in Lauderdale County, AL. Shirley was born 5 Feb 1944 in Hardin County, TN.

+ 3344 M i. **Gregory Gene Allison** was born 13 Nov 1969 in Lauderdale County, AL.

1599. Vernon Lee Allison (*Raymond Andrew Allison*[6], *Margie (Lady) J. Sharp*[5], *James (Jim) Charles Sr.*[4], *Adron (Edwin/Ade) Sr.*[3], *Charles W. Sr.*[2], *John Sr.*[1]) was born 2 Jan 1943 in Lauderdale County, AL.

Vernon married **Mary Elizabeth (Liz) Carter**, daughter of **Alvin Grady Carter** and **Mary Francis May**, 5 May 1962 in Lauderdale County, AL. Mary was born 12 Mar 1944 in Lauderdale County, AL.

+ 3345 M i. **Rodney Keith Allison** was born 4 Sep 1963 in Lauderdale County, AL.

1601. Rayburn Leon Allison (*Raymond Andrew Allison*[6], *Margie (Lady) J. Sharp*[5], *James (Jim) Charles Sr.*[4], *Adron (Edwin/Ade) Sr.*[3], *Charles W. Sr.*[2], *John Sr.*[1]) was born 13 Jun 1946 in Lauderdale County, AL.

Rayburn married **Jo Carolyn Wood**, daughter of **Leonard Earl Wood** and **Beatrice (Be-At) Wood**, 29 Aug 1964 in Lauderdale County, AL. Jo was born 16 Jun 1948 in Florence, Lauderdale County, AL.

+ 3346 F i. **Vicki Lynn Allison** was born 27 Nov 1965 in Lauderdale County, AL.

1602. Sandra Gail Allison (*Raymond Andrew Allison*[6], *Margie (Lady) J. Sharp*[5], *James (Jim) Charles Sr.*[4], *Adron (Edwin/Ade) Sr.*[3], *Charles W. Sr.*[2], *John Sr.*[1]) was born 4 Jan 1951 in Lauderdale County, AL.

Sandra married **Tommy Lee Baskins**, son of **Walter Amos Baskins** and **Eunice Viola Woods**, 31 May 1969 in Lauderdale County, AL. Tommy was born 22 Apr 1948 in Lauderdale County, AL.

+ 3347 F i. **Kimberly Renee Baskins** was born 24 Apr 1970 in Lauderdale County, AL.

1603. Betty Sue Poole (*Carrie Etta Allison*[6], *Margie (Lady) J. Sharp*[5], *James (Jim) Charles Sr.*[4], *Adron (Edwin/Ade) Sr.*[3], *Charles W. Sr.*[2], *John Sr.*[1]) was born 20 Nov 1942 in Lauderdale County, AL.

Betty married **Paul Kenneth May**, son of **L. C. May** and **Pearl Hanback**, 16 May 1961 in Lauderdale County, AL. Paul was born 30 Nov 1942 in Lauderdale County, AL, died 27 May 1992, and was buried in Pine Hill Cemetery, Lauderdale County, AL.

+ 3348 M i. **Kenneth Eugene May** was born 29 Jun 1961 in Lauderdale County, AL.
+ 3349 M ii. **Roger Lynn May** was born 4 Jun 1963 in Lauderdale County, AL.
+ 3350 M iii. **Timothy (Tim) Wayne May** was born 11 Sep 1967 in Lauderdale County, AL.
  3351 M iv. **Charles Everett May** was born 25 Sep 1973 in Lauderdale County, AL.

1604. Jimmy Carl Poole (*Carrie Etta Allison*[6], *Margie (Lady) J. Sharp*[5], *James (Jim) Charles Sr.*[4], *Adron (Edwin/Ade) Sr.*[3], *Charles W. Sr.*[2], *John Sr.*[1]) was born 6 Aug 1949 in Lauderdale County, AL.

Jimmy married **Rachel Renee Parrish**, daughter of **Thomas Watson Parrish** and **Marjorell Anthony**, 26 Feb 1969 in Lauderdale County, AL. Rachel was born 14 Oct 1951 in Lauderdale County, AL.

+ 3352 M i. **Jimmy Earl Poole** was born 1 Feb 1972 in Lauderdale County, AL.
+ 3353 F ii. **Carrie Leanne Poole** was born 21 Nov 1973 in Lauderdale County, AL.
  3354 F iii. **Corey Anthony Poole** was born 20 Jun 1980.

1605. Virginia Elizabeth Wood (*Lady Jewel Allison*[6], *Margie (Lady) J. Sharp*[5], *James (Jim) Charles Sr.*[4], *Adron (Edwin/Ade) Sr.*[3], *Charles W. Sr.*[2], *John Sr.*[1]) was born 24 Mar 1935 in Waterloo, Lauderdale County, AL.

Virginia married **Cellon Bill Smith**, son of **Jimmy Ottis (Ott) Smith** and **Susie Terry**, 4 Oct 1950 in Iuka, Tishomingo County, MS. Cellon was born 21 Feb 1927 in Lauderdale County, AL.

+ 3355 F i. **Shirley Ann Smith** was born 19 Feb 1952.

+ 3356 F ii. **Mary Katherine Smith** was born 3 Jun 1953.
+ 3357 F iii. **Dorothy Jean Smith** was born 2 Apr 1955.
+ 3358 M iv. **Billy Wayne Smith** was born 31 Dec 1957.
+ 3359 F v. **Carolyn Diane Smith** was born 9 May 1963.

1606. Nettie Louise Wood (*Lady Jewel Allison*[6], *Margie (Lady) J. Sharp*[5], *James (Jim) Charles Sr.*[4], *Adron (Edwin/Ade) Sr.*[3], *Charles W. Sr.*[2], *John Sr.*[1]) was born 1 Jun 1936 in Waterloo, Lauderdale County, AL.

Nettie married **Ray J. Smith**, son of **Jimmy Ottis (Ott) Smith** and **Susie Terry**, 20 Sep 1950 in Iuka, Tishomingo County, MS. Ray was born 25 Jan 1931 in Waterloo, Lauderdale County, AL.
+ 3360 F i. **Margie Louise Smith** was born 23 Aug 1951.
+ 3361 M ii. **Charles Ray Smith** was born 14 Feb 1953.

1607. Rachel Kathrine Wood (*Lady Jewel Allison*[6], *Margie (Lady) J. Sharp*[5], *James (Jim) Charles Sr.*[4], *Adron (Edwin/Ade) Sr.*[3], *Charles W. Sr.*[2], *John Sr.*[1]) was born 29 Jan 1938 in Waterloo, Lauderdale County, AL.

Rachel married **James Edward Gann** 29 Jan 1953 in Turrell, Crittenden County, AR. James was born 16 Jan 1933 in Savannah, TN.
+ 3362 F i. **Judy Ann Gann** was born 12 Jul 1954.
+ 3363 M ii. **Eddie Junior Gann** was born 7 May 1959.

Rachel next married **Joe Cox** after 1959.

1608. Robbie Etoil Wood (*Lady Jewel Allison*[6], *Margie (Lady) J. Sharp*[5], *James (Jim) Charles Sr.*[4], *Adron (Edwin/Ade) Sr.*[3], *Charles W. Sr.*[2], *John Sr.*[1]) was born 23 May 1940 in Waterloo, Lauderdale County, AL.

Robbie married **Rollen Smith**, son of **Jimmy Ottis (Ott) Smith** and **Susie Terry**, 24 Jan 1956 in Arkansas. Rollen was born 12 Sep 1937 in Florence, Lauderdale County, AL.
+ 3364 M i. **Tommy Joe Smith** was born 2 Mar 1957.
+ 3365 F ii. **Jonell Smith** was born 13 Aug 1959.
+ 3366 M iii. **Jerry Wayne Smith** was born 20 Apr 1967.

1609. Thelma Jean Wood (*Lady Jewel Allison*[6], *Margie (Lady) J. Sharp*[5], *James (Jim) Charles Sr.*[4], *Adron (Edwin/Ade) Sr.*[3], *Charles W. Sr.*[2], *John Sr.*[1]) was born 4 Apr 1942 in Waterloo, Lauderdale County, AL.

Thelma married **William Horace Gann** 8 Jun 1959 in Arkansas. William was born 12 Nov 1940 in Tyronza, Poinsett County, AR, died 17 Sep 1994, and was buried in Tyronza Cemetery, Tyronza, Poinsett County, AR.
+ 3367 F i. **Verna Lee (Jenni) Gann** was born 18 Sep 1959.
  3368 F ii. **Janet Lynn Gann** was born 23 Nov 1960 and died 27 Apr 1961.
+ 3369 F iii. **Tina Renea Gann** was born 19 Jun 1962.
+ 3370 F iv. **Francis Louise Gann** was born 14 Nov 1963.
+ 3371 F v. **Carlas Ann Gann** was born 13 Jan 1965.
+ 3372 F vi. **Dona Lynn Gann** was born 7 Jan 1967.
+ 3373 M vii. **Timothy Horace Gann** was born 12 Jan 1968.
+ 3374 M viii. **William Paul Gann** was born 21 Nov 1970.
  3375 M ix. **Preston Wayne Gann** was born 12 Sep 1977.

1610. Nadine Wood (*Lady Jewel Allison*[6], *Margie (Lady) J. Sharp*[5], *James (Jim) Charles Sr.*[4], *Adron (Edwin/Ade) Sr.*[3], *Charles W. Sr.*[2], *John Sr.*[1]) was born 1 Jul 1943 in Waterloo, Lauderdale County, AL.

Nadine married **Walter Edward Greene**, son of **Mansell Greene** and **Unknown**, 18 May 1960 in Tyronza, Poinsett County, AR. Walter was born 28 May 1940 in Waterloo, Lauderdale County, AL.
+ 3376 M i. **Billy Joe Greene Sr.** was born 29 May 1961.
+ 3377 F ii. **Taresa Ann Greene** was born 18 Jul 1963.
+ 3378 F iii. **Sherry Mae Greene** was born 13 Jun 1967.
+ 3379 M iv. **Johnny Walter Greene** was born 26 Jan 1971.

1611. Clara Nell Wood (*Lady Jewel Allison*[6]*, Margie (Lady) J. Sharp*[5]*, James (Jim) Charles Sr.*[4]*, Adron (Edwin/Ade) Sr.*[3]*, Charles W. Sr.*[2]*, John Sr.*[1]) was born 17 Dec 1945 in Waterloo, Lauderdale County, AL.

Clara married **Bedford Ray Greene**, son of **Mansell Greene** and **Unknown**, 12 Sep 1960 in Tyronza, Poinsett County, AR. Bedford was born 24 Apr 1942 in Waterloo, Lauderdale County, AL.
+ 3380 M i. **Bobby Ray Greene Sr.** was born 27 Dec 1961.
+ 3381 M ii. **Roger Dale Greene** was born 27 Jun 1966.
+ 3382 F iii. **Pamela Kay Greene** was born 9 Jul 1969.

1612. Nancy Carolyn Wood (*Lady Jewel Allison*[6]*, Margie (Lady) J. Sharp*[5]*, James (Jim) Charles Sr.*[4]*, Adron (Edwin/Ade) Sr.*[3]*, Charles W. Sr.*[2]*, John Sr.*[1]) was born 5 Oct 1947 in Waterloo, Lauderdale County, AL.

Nancy married **Tommy Oneal McIntyre Sr.** 2 Aug 1970 in Arkansas. Tommy was born 6 Nov 1946 in New Hope, AL.
+ 3383 M i. **Tommy Oneal McIntyre Jr.** was born 15 Apr 1971.

1615. Robert David Wood (*Lady Jewel Allison*[6]*, Margie (Lady) J. Sharp*[5]*, James (Jim) Charles Sr.*[4]*, Adron (Edwin/Ade) Sr.*[3]*, Charles W. Sr.*[2]*, John Sr.*[1]) was born 28 Aug 1956 in Memphis, Shelby County, TN.

Robert married **Bonnie Pendergrass** 25 Mar 1974 in Arkansas.

Robert next married **Donna Duncan** 19 Mar 1983 in Tyronza, Poinsett County, AR. Donna was born 5 Oct 1962.
3384 F i. **Amanda Duncan** was born 10 Apr 1982.
3385 M ii. **Robert Daniel Wood** was born 7 Jul 1987.

1616. Melvin Jack Allison Sr. (*William Turner Allison*[6]*, Margie (Lady) J. Sharp*[5]*, James (Jim) Charles Sr.*[4]*, Adron (Edwin/Ade) Sr.*[3]*, Charles W. Sr.*[2]*, John Sr.*[1]) was born 9 Jun 1943 in Florence, Lauderdale County, AL.

Melvin married **Sheila Marie Young**, daughter of **Reeder Young** and **Marie Pierce**, 18 Oct 1968 in Iuka, Tishomingo County, MS. Sheila was born 8 Jul 1951 in Alabama.
3386 M i. **Melvin Jack Allison Jr.** was born 18 Jul 1970 in Florence, Lauderdale County, AL.
+ 3387 F ii. **Emily Renee Allison** was born 11 Jun 1971 in Florence, Lauderdale County, AL.
3388 F iii. **Bridget Liegh Allison** was born 29 Apr 1976 in Florence, Lauderdale County, AL.

1618. Lonnie Edward Allison (*William Turner Allison*[6]*, Margie (Lady) J. Sharp*[5]*, James (Jim) Charles Sr.*[4]*, Adron (Edwin/Ade) Sr.*[3]*, Charles W. Sr.*[2]*, John Sr.*[1]) was born 20 Aug 1946 in Florence, Lauderdale County, AL.

Lonnie married **Linda Gail Allison**, daughter of **Velty Hoover Allison** and **Ethel Imogene Reeves**, 10 Sep 1970 in Lauderdale County, AL. Linda was born 1 Oct 1950 in Lauderdale County, AL.
3389 F i. **Kala Nichole Allison** was born 23 Mar 1985 in ECM Hospital, Florence, Lauderdale County, AL.

1619. Tony William Allison (*William Turner Allison*[6]*, Margie (Lady) J. Sharp*[5]*, James (Jim) Charles Sr.*[4]*, Adron (Edwin/Ade) Sr.*[3]*, Charles W. Sr.*[2]*, John Sr.*[1]) was born 2 Aug 1948 in Florence, Lauderdale County, AL.

Tony married **Judy Gail Roberson**, daughter of **Arthur H. Roberson** and **Virgie L. Richardson**, 16 Apr 1971 in Lauderdale County, AL. Judy was born 16 Nov 1954 in Lauderdale County, AL.
+ 3390 M i. **Jamie Lynn Allison** was born 12 Dec 1973 in Florence, Lauderdale County, AL.
+ 3391 M ii. **Christopher Heath Allison** was born 16 Sep 1975 in Florence, Lauderdale County, AL.

1620. Clara Jane Allison (*William Turner Allison*[6]*, Margie (Lady) J. Sharp*[5]*, James (Jim) Charles Sr.*[4]*, Adron (Edwin/Ade) Sr.*[3]*, Charles W. Sr.*[2]*, John Sr.*[1]) was born 5 Aug 1957 in Florence, Lauderdale County, AL.

Clara married **Norman Lester Ray**, son of **James Rufus Ray** and **Carrie Virgie Smith**, 5 Mar 1975 in Lauderdale County, AL. Norman was born 20 Jun 1944 in Cleveland, TX.
3392 M i. **David Jonathan Ray** was born 28 Oct 1984 in Loretto, Lawrence County, TN.

3393　M　ii.　**Jarrod Nathaniel Ray** was born 12 Aug 1993 in ECM Hospital, Florence, Lauderdale County, AL.

1621. Evelyn Irene Smith (*Vertie Mae Allison*[6], *Margie (Lady) J. Sharp*[5], *James (Jim) Charles Sr.*[4], *Adron (Edwin/Ade) Sr.*[3], *Charles W. Sr.*[2], *John Sr.*[1]) was born 31 Dec 1939 in Lauderdale County, AL.

Evelyn married **Bobby Gentry**, son of **William Sanford Gentry** and **Viola White**.
+ 3394　M　i.　**Bruce Gentry**.
+ 3395　F　ii.　**Susan Gentry**.
+ 3396　F　iii.　**Karen Gentry**.
　3397　F　iv.　**Julie Gentry** was born 20 Jul 1963.

1622. Charles Leon Smith (*Vertie Mae Allison*[6], *Margie (Lady) J. Sharp*[5], *James (Jim) Charles Sr.*[4], *Adron (Edwin/Ade) Sr.*[3], *Charles W. Sr.*[2], *John Sr.*[1]) was born 27 Jul 1943 in Lauderdale County, AL.

Charles married **Linda Sue Witt**, daughter of **Raymond Witt** and **Annie Lee Martin**, 17 Dec 1961 in Lauderdale County, AL. Linda was born 24 Dec 1943 in Lauderdale County, AL.
　3398　M　i.　**Peanut Smith**.
+ 3399　F　ii.　**Beverly Ann Smith** was born 21 Jan 1966 in Lauderdale County, AL.

1623. Wanda Sue Smith (*Vertie Mae Allison*[6], *Margie (Lady) J. Sharp*[5], *James (Jim) Charles Sr.*[4], *Adron (Edwin/Ade) Sr.*[3], *Charles W. Sr.*[2], *John Sr.*[1]) was born 17 Feb 1946 in Lauderdale County, AL.

Wanda married **Charles (Chuck) Elton Hart**, son of **John Howard Hart** and **Ruby Magdeline Parrish**, 7 Aug 1965 in Lauderdale County, AL. Charles was born 23 Jun 1946 in Lauderdale County, AL.
+ 3400　F　i.　**Jennifer (Jenni) Leigh Hart** was born 8 Oct 1967 in Florence, Lauderdale County, AL.
+ 3401　F　ii.　**Hannah Hart** was born 16 Jan 1970 in Lauderdale County, AL.

1624. Margie Ruth Smith (*Vertie Mae Allison*[6], *Margie (Lady) J. Sharp*[5], *James (Jim) Charles Sr.*[4], *Adron (Edwin/Ade) Sr.*[3], *Charles W. Sr.*[2], *John Sr.*[1]) was born 21 Jul 1948 in Lauderdale County, AL.

Margie married **Eddie Jerry Russell**, son of **Drexel Paul (Toad) Russell** and **Audrey Louise Smith**, 27 Aug 1967 in South Bend, IN. Eddie was born 27 Jan 1949, died 3 Jun 2002, and was buried in Murphy's Chapel Cemetery, Lauderdale County, AL.

+ 3402　F　i.　**Vonda Lynn Russell** was born 6 Jul 1968 in Indiana.

1625. Travis Lynn Smith (*Vertie Mae Allison*[6], *Margie (Lady) J. Sharp*[5], *James (Jim) Charles Sr.*[4], *Adron (Edwin/Ade) Sr.*[3], *Charles W. Sr.*[2], *John Sr.*[1]) was born 23 Aug 1958 in Lauderdale County, AL.

Travis married **Carol Sue Wood**, daughter of **Thomas Moore Wood** and **Lois Inez Bevis**, 1 Jul 1977 in Lauderdale County, AL. Carol was born 29 Aug 1961 in Lauderdale County, AL.
　3403　F　i.　**Catassa Tennille (Tassa) Smith** was born 1 Oct 1981 in Lauderdale County, AL.
　3404　M　ii.　**Dustin Avery (Dusty) Smith** was born 21 Jul 1983 in Lauderdale County, AL.

1626. Vicki Kay Smith (*Vertie Mae Allison*[6], *Margie (Lady) J. Sharp*[5], *James (Jim) Charles Sr.*[4], *Adron (Edwin/Ade) Sr.*[3], *Charles W. Sr.*[2], *John Sr.*[1]) was born 10 Jul 1961 in Lauderdale County, AL.

Vicki married **Ricky Louis Wood**, son of **Louis Cola Wood** and **Wilma Marcell Ballard**, 25 Jul 1980 in Lauderdale County, AL. Ricky was born 16 Dec 1961 in West Memphis, Crittenden County, AR.
+ 3405　F　i.　**Marissa (Rissa) Kay Wood** was born 30 Oct 1981 in ECM Hospital, Florence, Lauderdale County, AL.
+ 3406　M　ii.　**Jason Derek Wood** was born 26 May 1983 in ECM Hospital, Florence, Lauderdale County, AL.

1627. Ricky Dale Smith (*Vertie Mae Allison*[6], *Margie (Lady) J. Sharp*[5], *James (Jim) Charles Sr.*[4], *Adron (Edwin/Ade) Sr.*[3], *Charles W. Sr.*[2], *John Sr.*[1]) was born 15 Jan 1963 in Lauderdale County, AL.

Ricky married **Janet Lou Bevis**, daughter of **Louie Edwin Bevis** and **Mary Rachel Young**, 16 Jul 1982 in Lauderdale County, AL. Janet was born 4 Aug 1963 in Lauderdale County, AL.

1628. Fred Calvin Wood (*Elizabeth Earline Allison*[6], *Margie (Lady) J. Sharp*[5], *James (Jim) Charles Sr.*[4], *Adron (Edwin/Ade) Sr.*[3], *Charles W. Sr.*[2], *John Sr.*[1]) was born 16 Jun 1946 in Lauderdale County, AL.

Fred married **Patricia (Patsy) Ann Baskins**, daughter of **Marshall Baskins** and **Nellie L. Randall**, 2 Mar 1966 in Lauderdale County, AL. Patricia was born 18 Jan 1949 in Lauderdale County, AL.
+ 3407 M   i.   **Calvin Duane Wood** was born 28 Jan 1967 in Lauderdale County, AL.
+ 3408 F   ii.   **Angela Gay Wood** was born 17 Aug 1969 in Lauderdale County, AL.

Fred next married **Judy Burcham** about 1976. Judy was born 15 Mar 1951 in Lauderdale County, AL.
3409 M   i.   **Brian Kyle Wood** was born 23 Jun 1978.
3410 F   ii.   **Amanda Jean Wood** was born 1 Jan 1979.

1629. Jerry Wayne Wood (*Elizabeth Earline Allison*[6], *Margie (Lady) J. Sharp*[5], *James (Jim) Charles Sr.*[4], *Adron (Edwin/Ade) Sr.*[3], *Charles W. Sr.*[2], *John Sr.*[1]) was born 15 Jan 1948 in Lauderdale County, AL.

Jerry married **Janice Gayle Sisson**, daughter of **Sidney Otto Sisson** and **Etta Clark**, 14 Mar 1969 in Lauderdale County, AL. Janice was born 1 Nov 1949 in Winston County, AL.
+ 3411 F   i.   **Nikki Laraine Wood** was born 26 Mar.
+ 3412 F   ii.   **Leigh Ann Wood** was born 3 Dec 1969.

Jerry next married **Melanie Carroll**, daughter of **Orlen William Carroll** and **Patricia Ann Hargett**, 11 Jun 1994 in Lauderdale County, AL. Melanie was born 18 Aug 1964.

1630. Kenneth Carroll Wood (*Elizabeth Earline Allison*[6], *Margie (Lady) J. Sharp*[5], *James (Jim) Charles Sr.*[4], *Adron (Edwin/Ade) Sr.*[3], *Charles W. Sr.*[2], *John Sr.*[1]) was born 10 Jan 1950 in Lauderdale County, AL.

Kenneth married **Cynthia Jean Dupree**, daughter of **Raleigh T. Dupree** and **Ester Sanderson**, 4 Jan 1969 in Lauderdale County, AL. Cynthia was born 4 Nov 1951 in Lauderdale County, AL.
+ 3413 M   i.   **Gregory Lynn Wood** was born 28 Nov 1969 in Alabama.

Kenneth next married ***Unk**.

Kenneth next married **Kathie Jane Peden**, daughter of **Edward J. Peden** and **Ethel Cole**, 28 Jun 1986 in Lauderdale County, AL. Kathie was born 24 Jul 1948 in Lauderdale County, AL.

1631. Gerald Glenn Wood (*Elizabeth Earline Allison*[6], *Margie (Lady) J. Sharp*[5], *James (Jim) Charles Sr.*[4], *Adron (Edwin/Ade) Sr.*[3], *Charles W. Sr.*[2], *John Sr.*[1]) was born 14 Jan 1953 in Lauderdale County, AL.

Gerald married **Rebecca Ann Murphy**, daughter of **Bill Murphy** and **Era Horton**, 10 Jul 1971 in Lauderdale County, AL. Rebecca was born 25 Dec 1950 in Lauderdale County, AL.
+ 3414 F   i.   **Sandra (Sandy) Kay Wood** was born 22 Aug 1972 in Lauderdale County, AL.

Gerald next married **Carole Almeda Thomason**, daughter of **James E. Thomason** and **Virginia Newton**, 3 Aug 1979 in Lauderdale County, AL. Carole was born 9 Apr 1959 in Lauderdale County, AL.

1632. Elizabeth Ann Wood (*Elizabeth Earline Allison*[6], *Margie (Lady) J. Sharp*[5], *James (Jim) Charles Sr.*[4], *Adron (Edwin/Ade) Sr.*[3], *Charles W. Sr.*[2], *John Sr.*[1]) was born 6 Jun 1956 in Lauderdale County, AL.

Elizabeth married **William Ricky Johnson**, son of **B. L. Johnson** and **Chessie Hall**, 4 Nov 1977 in Lauderdale County, AL. William was born 20 Jun 1956 in Lake County, IL.
3415 M   i.   **Richey Johnson** was born in Sep 1979.
3416 M   ii.   **Rodney Allen Johnson** was born 23 Aug 1982.

Elizabeth next married **Johnny Kent** after 1980.
3417 M   i.   **Jordan Kent**.

1633. Lowell Dale Wood (*Elizabeth Earline Allison*[6], *Margie (Lady) J. Sharp*[5], *James (Jim) Charles Sr.*[4], *Adron (Edwin/Ade) Sr.*[3], *Charles W. Sr.*[2], *John Sr.*[1]) was born 1 Nov 1959 in Lauderdale County, AL.

Lowell married **Gail Lorene McDowell**, daughter of **Thomas N. McDowell** and **Joan Owen**, 18 Apr 1979 in Lauderdale County, AL. Gail was born 25 Apr 1959 in Harris County, TX.

Lowell next married **Joan Alice Smith**, daughter of **Sammy O. Smith** and **Betty J. Crittenden**, 23 Dec 1981 in Lauderdale County, AL. Joan was born 17 Aug 1955 in Lauderdale County, AL.

Lowell next married **Juanita Ray (Nita) Carpenter**, daughter of **Cecil W. Carpenter** and **Glenda Winters**, 4 Mar 1983 in Lauderdale County, AL. Juanita was born 18 Sep 1961 in Lauderdale County, AL.
    3418 M   i.   **Christopher Dale Wood** was born 2 Jan 1984.

Lowell next married **Cynthia Bryant**.
    3419 M   i.   **Brandon Wood** was born about 1988.

1634. Ronnie Earl Wood (*Elizabeth Earline Allison*[6], *Margie (Lady) J. Sharp*[5], *James (Jim) Charles Sr.*[4], *Adron (Edwin/Ade) Sr.*[3], *Charles W. Sr.*[2], *John Sr.*[1]) was born 27 Aug 1969 in Lauderdale County, AL.

Ronnie married **Janet Darlene Burnett**, daughter of **Claudie Howard Burnett** and **Lena Virginia Lamar**, 3 Jul 1996 in Lauderdale County, AL. Janet was born 13 May 1963 in Alabama.

1635. Clara Jean (Jeannie) Wood (*Clara Estelle Allison*[6], *Margie (Lady) J. Sharp*[5], *James (Jim) Charles Sr.*[4], *Adron (Edwin/Ade) Sr.*[3], *Charles W. Sr.*[2], *John Sr.*[1]) was born 14 Feb 1947 in Lauderdale County, AL.

Clara married **Eugene Rufus Smith**, son of **Otie Eugene Smith** and **Lorene Springer**, 6 Jun 1964 in Lauderdale County, AL. Eugene was born 18 Oct 1944 in Winston County, AL and died 27 Oct 1998 in Limestone County, AL.
    3420 M   i.   **Douglas Eugene Smith** was born 30 Aug 1967 in Lauderdale County, AL.
+ 3421 M   ii.   **Michael Ray Smith** was born 21 Jan 1972 in Lauderdale County, AL.

1636. Dennis Ray Wood (*Clara Estelle Allison*[6], *Margie (Lady) J. Sharp*[5], *James (Jim) Charles Sr.*[4], *Adron (Edwin/Ade) Sr.*[3], *Charles W. Sr.*[2], *John Sr.*[1]) was born 30 Jan 1948 in Lauderdale County, AL, died 19 Feb 2003, and was buried in Greenview Memorial Park, Florence, Lauderdale County, AL.

Dennis married **Margaret Emory** before 1976.
+ 3422 F   i.   **Tonya Michelle Wood**.
    3423 M   ii.   **Matthew Ray Wood**.

Dennis next married **Deborah Jean Chandler**, daughter of **James E. Chandler** and **Shirley Haygood**, 7 Jun 1976 in Lauderdale County, AL. Deborah was born 29 Mar 1955 in Lawrence County, TN.

Dennis next married **Robbie Moody** after 1976.

1637. Shirley Ann Wood (*Clara Estelle Allison*[6], *Margie (Lady) J. Sharp*[5], *James (Jim) Charles Sr.*[4], *Adron (Edwin/Ade) Sr.*[3], *Charles W. Sr.*[2], *John Sr.*[1]) was born 24 Aug 1949 in Lauderdale County, AL.

Shirley married **James Phillip (Phil) Horton**, son of **James Harlan Horton** and **Ruth Moomaw**, 29 Jul 1966 in Lauderdale County, AL. James was born 17 May 1948 in Lauderdale County, AL, died 23 Mar 1969, and was buried in Community Church Cemetery, Lauderale County, AL.
+ 3424 F   i.   **Jean Ann Horton** was born 6 Jan 1967 in Lauderdale County, AL.

Shirley next married **Cary Allen Taylor**, son of **Elmer C. Taylor** and **Margaret Lewis**, in 1970 in Charleston, IN. Cary was born 20 Mar 1948 in Scottsboro, IN.
+ 3425 M   i.   **Joey Allen Taylor** was born 14 Apr 1972 in Lauderdale County, AL.

Shirley next married **Carlton Elvin Fowler Sr.**, son of **Elvin C. Fowler** and **Margaret Medley**, 3 Mar 1973 in Lauderdale County, AL. Carlton was born 29 Nov 1940 in Lauderdale County, AL.
+ 3426 M   i.   **Carlton (C. J.) Elvin Fowler Jr.** was born 22 Apr 1977 in Lauderdale County, AL.

1638. Martha Jane Wood (*Clara Estelle Allison*⁶, *Margie (Lady) J. Sharp*⁵, *James (Jim) Charles Sr.*⁴, *Adron (Edwin/Ade) Sr.*³, *Charles W. Sr.*², *John Sr.*¹) was born 9 Jul 1952 in Lauderdale County, AL.

Martha married **Jimmy Glyn McCullum Sr.**, son of **Jimmy McCullum** and **Francis Richey**, 12 Jul 1969 in Lauderdale County, AL. Jimmy was born 14 Jul 1951 in Lauderdale County, AL.
+ 3427   F   i.   **Marsha Lynn McCullum** was born 28 Sep 1971 in Florence, Lauderdale County, AL.
+ 3428   F   ii.   **Leigh Ann McCullum** was born 15 Dec 1975 in Florence, Lauderdale County, AL.
   3429   M   iii.   **Jimmy Glenn (Little Jim) McCullum Jr.** was born 10 May 1980 in Florence, Lauderdale County, AL.

1639. Timothy (Tim) Michael Wood (*Clara Estelle Allison*⁶, *Margie (Lady) J. Sharp*⁵, *James (Jim) Charles Sr.*⁴, *Adron (Edwin/Ade) Sr.*³, *Charles W. Sr.*², *John Sr.*¹) was born 22 Mar 1956 in Lauderdale County, AL.

Timothy married **Vivian Marsheila (Sheila) Gilchrist**, daughter of **Vernon H. Gilchrist** and **Willa Mae Brewer**, 28 May 1975 in Lauderdale County, AL. Vivian was born 5 Oct 1957 in Lauderdale County, AL.
+ 3430   M   i.   **Jamie Michael Wood** was born 19 Feb 1976 in Lauderdale County, AL.
+ 3431   F   ii.   **Brandy Nichole Wood** was born 19 Nov 1981 in Lauderdale County, AL.

1640. Linda Gail Allison (*Velty Hoover Allison*⁶, *Margie (Lady) J. Sharp*⁵, *James (Jim) Charles Sr.*⁴, *Adron (Edwin/Ade) Sr.*³, *Charles W. Sr.*², *John Sr.*¹) was born 1 Oct 1950 in Lauderdale County, AL.

Linda married **Lonnie Edward Allison**, son of **William Turner Allison** and **Onita Katherine (Neat) Wood**, 10 Sep 1970 in Lauderdale County, AL. Lonnie was born 20 Aug 1946 in Florence, Lauderdale County, AL. **(Duplicate Line. See Person 1618)**

1641. Earl Steven Allison (*Earl Alvin Allison*⁶, *Margie (Lady) J. Sharp*⁵, *James (Jim) Charles Sr.*⁴, *Adron (Edwin/Ade) Sr.*³, *Charles W. Sr.*², *John Sr.*¹) was born 2 Nov 1950 in South Bend, St Joseph County, IN.

Earl married **Glenda Juanita White**, daughter of **Bartley Andrew White** and **Clara Bell Sego**, 17 Aug 1970 in Lauderdale County, AL. Glenda was born 21 Jun 1951 in Lauderdale County, AL.
+ 3432   M   i.   **Adam Clay Allison** was born 28 Jun 1977 in Lauderdale County, AL.
+ 3433   M   ii.   **Preston Cole Allison** was born 14 Apr 1980 in Lauderdale County, AL.

1642. Rosa Rita Allison (*Earl Alvin Allison*⁶, *Margie (Lady) J. Sharp*⁵, *James (Jim) Charles Sr.*⁴, *Adron (Edwin/Ade) Sr.*³, *Charles W. Sr.*², *John Sr.*¹) was born 18 Jan 1952 in Mishawaka, St Joseph County, IN.

Rosa married **Jimmy Dale White**, son of **George Bethel White** and **Ethel Mattie Kilburn**, 19 Jan 1973 in Lauderdale County, AL. Jimmy was born 18 Nov 1952 in Lauderdale County, AL.
+ 3434   F   i.   **Allison Dawn White** was born 15 Jul 1973 in Lauderdale County, AL.

1644. Foster Woodrow McConnell Sr. (*Jesse Robert McConnell*⁶, *Mary Ann Sharp*⁵, *Charles (Charlie) A.*⁴, *Adron (Edwin/Ade) Sr.*³, *Charles W. Sr.*², *John Sr.*¹) was born 21 Mar 1912 in Booneville, Logan County, AR.

Foster married **Cyril Agnes Swint**, daughter of **Emmitt Monroe Swint** and **Lillian Effie Porter**, 28 Apr 1934 in Booneville, Logan County, AR. Cyril was born 29 Jul 1913 in Booneville, Logan County, AR.
+ 3435   M   i.   **Foster Woodrow McConnell Jr.** was born 2 Aug 1938 in Arkansas.

1648. Hayden D. T. Sharp (*Kelly C.*⁶, *Lil Adron*⁵, *Charles (Charlie) A.*⁴, *Adron (Edwin/Ade) Sr.*³, *Charles W. Sr.*², *John Sr.*¹) was born in Arkansas and died in 1983 in Arkansas.

Hayden married **Stella Mae Sikes**, daughter of **Tobias Sikes** and ***Unk**. Stella was born in Scranton, AR and was buried in Portland, OR.
   3436   F   i.   **Betty Sharp** was born in California and was buried in California.
+ 3437   M   ii.   **Hayden D. Sharp Sr.** was born in California.
   3438   F   iii.   **Dorothy Sharp** was born in California.

1651. Genoa V. Sharp (*Verbie Anter*[6], *Carol (Fuzzy) Louis*[5], *Charles (Charlie) A.*[4], *Adron (Edwin/Ade) Sr.*[3], *Charles W. Sr.*[2], *John Sr.*[1]) was born 16 Aug 1921.

   Genoa married **Calvin Garrett**.

1652. OssaLee Sharp (*Verbie Anter*[6], *Carol (Fuzzy) Louis*[5], *Charles (Charlie) A.*[4], *Adron (Edwin/Ade) Sr.*[3], *Charles W. Sr.*[2], *John Sr.*[1]) was born 8 Aug 1923 and died 2 Jan 2005 in Visalia, Tulare, CA.

   OssaLee married **Wanda Nixon**.

1653. Mirlacoys Sharp (*Verbie Anter*[6], *Carol (Fuzzy) Louis*[5], *Charles (Charlie) A.*[4], *Adron (Edwin/Ade) Sr.*[3], *Charles W. Sr.*[2], *John Sr.*[1]) was born 19 Mar 1926.

   Mirlacoys married **Kenneth Adwan**.

   Mirlacoys next married **Sam McConathy**.

1654. Verbie Anter Sharp Jr. (*Verbie Anter*[6], *Carol (Fuzzy) Louis*[5], *Charles (Charlie) A.*[4], *Adron (Edwin/Ade) Sr.*[3], *Charles W. Sr.*[2], *John Sr.*[1]) was born 11 Apr 1929 and died 4 Jun 2008 in Bakersville, CA.

   Verbie married **Freda Hines**.

1655. Bobby Ray Sharp (*Verbie Anter*[6], *Carol (Fuzzy) Louis*[5], *Charles (Charlie) A.*[4], *Adron (Edwin/Ade) Sr.*[3], *Charles W. Sr.*[2], *John Sr.*[1]) was born 3 Apr 1931 in Hope, Stephens County, OK and died 24 Jan 2002 in Stephens County, OK.

   Bobby married **Audrey Dale Beard** 19 Apr 1951 in Kingsburg, Fresno County, CA.

1686. Jerry Travis White (*Mason Louise Wright*[6], *George Moses (Mode) Wright*[5], *Elizabeth (Lizzie) May Sharp*[4], *John Sr.*[3], *Charles W. Sr.*[2], *John Sr.*[1]) was born 14 Aug 1946 in Lauderdale County, AL, died 15 Feb 1998 in Lauderdale County, AL, and was buried in Greenview Memorial Park, Florence, Lauderdale County, AL.

   Jerry married **Joyce Mae Scott**, daughter of **Homer Franklin Scott** and **Bessie Hodges**, 28 Feb 1965. Joyce was born 1 May 1945 in Lauderdale County, AL.
   + 3439   F   i.   **Sandra (Sandie) Kaye White** was born 18 Jun 1966 in Lauderdale County, AL.

1687. Charles Boyce Hanback (*Etta Buna Wright*[6], *George Moses (Mode) Wright*[5], *Elizabeth (Lizzie) May Sharp*[4], *John Sr.*[3], *Charles W. Sr.*[2], *John Sr.*[1]) was born 14 Dec 1937 in Lauderdale County, AL.

   Charles married **Beatrice Lillie Bennett**, daughter of **William (Bill) Carl Bennett** and **Vera Garrett**, 11 Aug 1959 in Lauderdale County, AL. Beatrice was born 7 Apr 1938 in Lauderdale County, AL.
   + 3440   F   i.   **Dawanda Ann Hanback** was born 27 Feb 1961 in Lauderdale County, AL.
     3441   F   ii.   **Tammula Denise Hanback** was born 26 Mar 1964 in Lauderdale County, AL, died 29 May 1976, and was buried in Tri-Cities Memorial Gardens, Florence, Lauderdale County, AL.
   + 3442   F   iii. **Charlotte Kay Hanback** was born 17 Apr 1968 in Lauderdale County, AL.

1689. Patsy Ann Elliott (*Mattie May Wright*[6], *George Moses (Mode) Wright*[5], *Elizabeth (Lizzie) May Sharp*[4], *John Sr.*[3], *Charles W. Sr.*[2], *John Sr.*[1]) was born 21 Feb 1942 in Colbert County, AL.

   Patsy married **Glenn Warner Stephenson**, son of **M. H. Stephenson** and **Alma Smith**, 27 May 1960 in Colbert County, AL. Glenn was born 31 May 1940.
   + 3443   F   i.   **Beverly Gail Stephenson** was born 27 Oct 1962 in Colbert County, AL.
   + 3444   M   ii.   **Kelvin Martin Stephenson** was born 21 Mar 1976 in Colbert County, AL.

1690. Linda May Elliott (*Mattie May Wright*[6], *George Moses (Mode) Wright*[5], *Elizabeth (Lizzie) May Sharp*[4], *John Sr.*[3], *Charles W. Sr.*[2], *John Sr.*[1]) was born 16 Jan 1948 in Colbert County, AL.

Linda married **James Leonard Berryman Sr.**, son of **Grover Cleveland Berryman** and **Della Mitchell**, 10 Jan 1964 in Colbert County, AL. James was born 6 Jun 1943 in Colbert County, AL.

+ 3445 M i. **James Leonard Berryman Jr.** was born 7 Jul 1964 in Chela, MA.
+ 3446 F ii. **Jeanice Michele Berryman** was born 25 Feb 1966 in Colbert County, AL.
+ 3447 M iii. **Christopher Louis Berryman** was born 21 Oct 1967 in Garden City, MI.

1691. David Ralph Elliott (*Mattie May Wright*[6], *George Moses (Mode) Wright*[5], *Elizabeth (Lizzie) May Sharp*[4], *John Sr.*[3], *Charles W. Sr.*[2], *John Sr.*[1]) was born 14 Apr 1957 in Colbert County, AL.

David married **Bobbie Marlene Young**, daughter of **Robert (Bob) Orman Young** and **Evelyn Lorene White**, 16 Oct 1972 in Lauderdale County, AL. Bobbie was born 9 Jul 1956 in Lauderdale County, AL.

3448 M i. **David Brian Elliott** was born 25 Oct 1973 in Lauderdale County, AL.
3449 M ii. **Bradley Ralph Elliott** was born 13 Oct 1977 in Lauderdale County, AL.
3450 F iii. **Alecia Marlene Elliott** was born 25 Dec 1982 in Lauderdale County, AL.

1692. Thomas (Tommy) Douglas Elliott (*Mattie May Wright*[6], *George Moses (Mode) Wright*[5], *Elizabeth (Lizzie) May Sharp*[4], *John Sr.*[3], *Charles W. Sr.*[2], *John Sr.*[1]) was born 10 Nov 1960 in Colbert County, AL.

Thomas married **Anna Michelle Hillyard**, daughter of **Michael Loyd Hillyard** and **Mavis Lavern Smith**, 28 Feb 1981 in Colbert County, AL. Anna was born 4 Sep 1965 in Reta, Spain.

1693. Robert Carroll Redd (*Edith Louise Wright*[6], *James Phillip Wright*[5], *Elizabeth (Lizzie) May Sharp*[4], *John Sr.*[3], *Charles W. Sr.*[2], *John Sr.*[1]) was born 24 Sep 1946 in Lauderdale County, AL.

Robert married **Nora Josephine Putteet**, daughter of **Alfred Carl Putteet** and **Neva Louise Berg**, 14 Jun 1969 in Lauderdale County, AL. Nora was born 21 Jan 1948 in Auburn, Lee County, AL.

+ 3451 F i. **Catherine Louise Redd** was born 1 Dec 1972 in Lauderdale County, AL.
+ 3452 F ii. **Carroll Josephine Redd** was born 8 Mar 1978 in Lauderdale County, AL.

1694. Jane Anne Williams (*Elizabeth (Lizzie) Inez Wesson*[6], *Martha (Mattie) Jane Wright*[5], *Elizabeth (Lizzie) May Sharp*[4], *John Sr.*[3], *Charles W. Sr.*[2], *John Sr.*[1]) was born in 1929 in Lauderdale County, AL.

Jane married **John Phillip Bruton Wilson**.

1695. Arthur J. Williams Jr. (*Elizabeth (Lizzie) Inez Wesson*[6], *Martha (Mattie) Jane Wright*[5], *Elizabeth (Lizzie) May Sharp*[4], *John Sr.*[3], *Charles W. Sr.*[2], *John Sr.*[1]) was born in 1931 in Lauderdale County, AL.

Arthur married **Margaret Joyce Reed** in 1951.

1696. Donald Arthur Boggess Jr. (*Hazel Wright Wesson*[6], *Martha (Mattie) Jane Wright*[5], *Elizabeth (Lizzie) May Sharp*[4], *John Sr.*[3], *Charles W. Sr.*[2], *John Sr.*[1]) was born in 1928 and died in 1991.

Donald married **Patricia Ruth Barbour**.

1697. Dorothy Ann Boggess (*Hazel Wright Wesson*[6], *Martha (Mattie) Jane Wright*[5], *Elizabeth (Lizzie) May Sharp*[4], *John Sr.*[3], *Charles W. Sr.*[2], *John Sr.*[1]) was born in 1938.

Dorothy married **Harold William Shaffer**.

1698. John Phillip Wesson (*Rawley (Roy) Archibald Wesson*[6], *Martha (Mattie) Jane Wright*[5], *Elizabeth (Lizzie) May Sharp*[4], *John Sr.*[3], *Charles W. Sr.*[2], *John Sr.*[1]) was born 5 Oct 1945 in Lauderdale County, AL.

John married **Joan Louise Christoff**.

1700. Walter Wade Wesson (*Joseph Phillip Wesson*[6], *Martha (Mattie) Jane Wright*[5], *Elizabeth (Lizzie) May Sharp*[4], *John Sr.*[3], *Charles W. Sr.*[2], *John Sr.*[1]) was born in 1934.

Walter married **Elizabeth Ann Moody**.

1701. Phyllis Fay Wesson (*Joseph Phillip Wesson*[6], *Martha (Mattie) Jane Wright*[5], *Elizabeth (Lizzie) May Sharp*[4], *John Sr.*[3], *Charles W. Sr.*[2], *John Sr.*[1]) was born in 1951.

Phyllis married **Robert Ray Jackson**.

1702. Jo Carolyn Sharp (*Ben Faires*[6], *John (Buck) Phillip*[5], *Carroll Ira (Buck)*[4], *John Sr.*[3], *Charles W. Sr.*[2], *John Sr.*[1]) was born 9 Nov 1935 in Lauderdale County, AL.

Jo married **Carl Tom Hudson**.

1703. John Phillip Sharp (*Ben Faires*[6], *John (Buck) Phillip*[5], *Carroll Ira (Buck)*[4], *John Sr.*[3], *Charles W. Sr.*[2], *John Sr.*[1]) was born 30 Apr 1937 in Lauderdale County, AL.

John married **Rebecca Ann Bonner**, daughter of **Willie Lake Bonner** and **Flora Lee Bass**, 22 Aug 1959 in Ethridge, TN. Rebecca was born 28 Jun in Lawrenceburg, Lawrence County, TN.

+	3453	F	i.	**Ginger Ann Sharp** was born 13 Jun 1960 in Lawrenceburg, Lawrence County, TN.
+	3454	F	ii.	**Angela Beth Sharp** was born 19 Sep 1962 in Lawrenceburg, Lawrence County, TN.
+	3455	F	iii.	**Alyson Barbara Sharp** was born 19 Sep 1962.

1704. Ben Travis (Benny) Sharp (*Ben Faires*[6], *John (Buck) Phillip*[5], *Carroll Ira (Buck)*[4], *John Sr.*[3], *Charles W. Sr.*[2], *John Sr.*[1]) was born 1 Dec 1940 in Lauderdale County, AL.

Ben married **Gayle Robinson**, daughter of **James Otis Robinson** and **Ruth Butler**, 24 Nov 1967 in Nashville, Davidson County, TN. Gayle was born 18 Jan 1939 in Pulaski, TN.

  3456 M i.   **Adam Scott Sharp** was born 15 Aug 1963 in Nashville, Davidson County, TN.
  3457 M ii.   **Travis Robinson Sharp** was born 1 Dec 1969 in Nashville, Davidson County, TN.

1706. Mary Frances Sharp (*Lee Howell (Hal)*[6], *John (Buck) Phillip*[5], *Carroll Ira (Buck)*[4], *John Sr.*[3], *Charles W. Sr.*[2], *John Sr.*[1]) was born 28 Jun 1939 in Lawrenceburg, Lawrence County, TN.

Mary married **Douglas Raymond Childress**, son of **Charlie Adron Childress** and **Gussie Taylor**, 29 Jun 1957 in Ethridge, TN. Douglas was born 22 Oct 1937 in Lawrenceburg, Lawrence County, TN.

  + 3458 F i.   **Cynthia Dawn Childress** was born 4 Dec 1958 in Lawrenceburg, Lawrence County, TN.
  + 3459 F ii.   **Laura Lee Childress** was born 16 Jan 1961 in Lawrenceburg, Lawrence County, TN.
  + 3460 M iii. **Christopher Douglas Childress** was born 30 Aug 1966 in Lawrenceburg, Lawrence County, TN.

1707. Nancy Lee Sharp (*Lee Howell (Hal)*[6], *John (Buck) Phillip*[5], *Carroll Ira (Buck)*[4], *John Sr.*[3], *Charles W. Sr.*[2], *John Sr.*[1]) was born 20 Feb 1942 in Lawrenceburg, Lawrence County, TN.

Nancy married **George A. Collin Jr.** 10 Jun 1967. George was born 7 Jul 1937 in Cleveland, OH.

  + 3461 F i.   **Andrea Lee Collin** was born 7 Oct 1968 in Nashville, Davidson County, TN.
    3462 F ii.   **Betsy Lynn Collin** was born 31 Jul 1972 in Charlotte, NC.

1708. Susan Sharp (*Lee Howell (Hal)*[6], *John (Buck) Phillip*[5], *Carroll Ira (Buck)*[4], *John Sr.*[3], *Charles W. Sr.*[2], *John Sr.*[1]) was born 22 Nov 1948 in Lawrenceburg, Lawrence County, TN.

Susan married **John Dale Denardo Jr.**, son of **John Dale Denardo Sr.** and **Josephine Boulie**, 16 Aug 1970 in Ethridge, TN. John was born 8 May 1948 in Monroe, MI.

    3463 F i.   **Emily Carroll Denardo** was born 29 Oct 1976 in Lawrenceburg, Lawrence County, TN.
    3464 F ii.   **Mary Rose Denardo** was born 25 Nov 1981 in Lawrenceburg, Lawrence County, TN.

1709. Marilyn Sharpe Price (*Gladys Lillian Sharp*[6], *John (Buck) Phillip*[5], *Carroll Ira (Buck)*[4], *John Sr.*[3], *Charles W. Sr.*[2], *John Sr.*[1]) was born 25 Mar 1941 in West Palm Beach, FL.

Marilyn married **George Pearson Eubanks**, son of **George Eaton Eubanks** and **Pearl *Unk**, 24 Mar 1962 in Ft Pierce, FL. George was born 6 Jan 1937 in Miami, FL.

+ 3465 F i. **Jennifer Dawn Eubanks** was born 7 Jan 1967 in Orlando, FL.

1710. Clara May Killen (*Minnie Jane Sharp*[6]*, Charlie William*[5]*, William (Candy) Erwin*[4]*, John Sr.*[3]*, Charles W. Sr.*[2]*, John Sr.*[1]) was born 19 Jul 1918 in Lauderdale County, AL.

Clara married **Miley Fulton Haywood**, son of **H. D. Haywood** and **Ida Gist**, 30 Jul 1938 in Lauderdale County, AL. Miley was born 14 Jan 1916 in Lauderdale County, AL.

1711. Ida Odell Killen (*Minnie Jane Sharp*[6]*, Charlie William*[5]*, William (Candy) Erwin*[4]*, John Sr.*[3]*, Charles W. Sr.*[2]*, John Sr.*[1]) was born 2 May 1921 in Lauderdale County, AL.

Ida married **Walter Alvin Dickerson**, son of **Walter Franklin Dickerson** and **Martha Eleytt Shelton**, 21 Dec 1940 in Lauderdale County, AL. Walter was born 16 Sep 1917 in Tuscaloosa, AL.

1712. Mary Dalphine Killen (*Minnie Jane Sharp*[6]*, Charlie William*[5]*, William (Candy) Erwin*[4]*, John Sr.*[3]*, Charles W. Sr.*[2]*, John Sr.*[1]) was born 7 Aug 1926 in Lauderdale County, AL.

Mary married **Joe P. Hines**.

1713. June (Betty) Eleanor Killen (*Minnie Jane Sharp*[6]*, Charlie William*[5]*, William (Candy) Erwin*[4]*, John Sr.*[3]*, Charles W. Sr.*[2]*, John Sr.*[1]) was born 12 Jun 1929 in Lauderdale County, AL.

June married **George Allen Darby**, son of **Joe White Darby** and **Kathy Lou Carroll**, 16 Aug 1946 in Lauderdale County, AL. George was born 2 Oct 1922 in Lauderdale County, AL, died 22 Apr 1988, and was buried in Tri-Cities Memorial Gardens, Florence, Lauderdale County, AL.

+ 3466 F i. **Patsy Ann Darby** was born 23 Oct 1947 in San Diego, CA.
+ 3467 F ii. **Beverly Jane Darby** was born 10 May 1951 in Ft Jackson, SC.
+ 3468 F iii. **Sharon Darby** was born 18 Dec 1953 in Montgomery, AL.
+ 3469 F iv. **Teresa Gail Darby** was born 22 Feb 1956 in Lexington County, Detroit, MI.

June next married **Glen Mann**.

1714. William (Buddy) Doyce Killen (*Minnie Jane Sharp*[6]*, Charlie William*[5]*, William (Candy) Erwin*[4]*, John Sr.*[3]*, Charles W. Sr.*[2]*, John Sr.*[1]) was born 13 Nov 1932 in Lauderdale County, AL.

William married **June Webb** in 1952 in Iuka, Tishomingo County, MS. June was born in Nashville, Davidson County, TN.

3470 F i. **Linda Gayle Killen**.
3471 F ii. **Robin Michelle Killen**.

William next married **Sue Wambles** in 1960.

William next married **Carolyn *Unk** after 1961.

1715. Juanita Joice Killen (*Minnie Jane Sharp*[6]*, Charlie William*[5]*, William (Candy) Erwin*[4]*, John Sr.*[3]*, Charles W. Sr.*[2]*, John Sr.*[1]) was born 13 Nov 1932 in Lauderdale County, AL.

Juanita married **Charles C. (Chick) Sanderson**, son of **J. C. Sanderson** and **Ida Dawson**, 16 Aug 1946 in Lauderdale County, AL. Charles was born 4 Oct 1924 in Lauderdale County, AL and died in Dearborn, MI.

3472 F i. **Dennis Wayne Sanderson**.

Juanita next married **Robert (Boots) Jackson**.

1716. Harold Burt Killen (*Minnie Jane Sharp*[6]*, Charlie William*[5]*, William (Candy) Erwin*[4]*, John Sr.*[3]*, Charles W. Sr.*[2]*, John Sr.*[1]) was born 27 Sep 1934 in Lauderdale County, AL, died 15 Apr 2003, and was buried in Greenview Memorial Park, Florence, Lauderdale County, AL.

Harold married **Martha Jo Cash**, daughter of **Merrill Herschel Cash** and **Zella Danley**, 10 Aug 1954 in Iuka, Tishomingo County, MS. Martha was born 17 Oct 1936 in Lauderdale County, AL.

+ 3473 F   i.   **Deborah Kay Killen** was born 8 Apr 1955 in Lauderdale County, AL.

+ 3474 F   ii.   **Teresa Lynn Killen** was born 10 May 1956 in Lauderdale County, AL.

1718. William Delton Sharp (*Owen Lee*[6], *Charlie William*[5], *William (Candy) Erwin*[4], *John Sr.*[3], *Charles W. Sr.*[2], *John Sr.*[1]) was born 12 Dec 1934 in Lauderdale County, AL and died 24 Mar 2007 in Lauderdale County, AL.

William married **Willa Zoo Cole**, daughter of **Onis M. Cole** and **Otha O. Norwood**, 23 Dec 1960 in Lauderdale County, AL. Willa was born 2 Nov 1938 in Giles County, TN.

3475 F   i.   **Kimberly Lynn Sharp** was born 3 Aug 1961 in Lauderdale County, AL.

3476 M   ii.   **Samuel Todd Sharp** was born 13 Oct 1962 in Lauderdale County, AL.

+ 3477 F   iii. **Leisha Gail Sharp** was born 9 Jan 1964 in Lauderdale County, AL.

1719. Alvie Sharp (*Owen Lee*[6], *Charlie William*[5], *William (Candy) Erwin*[4], *John Sr.*[3], *Charles W. Sr.*[2], *John Sr.*[1]).

Alvie married **Harold Meisenheimer**.

1720. Iatrice Sharp (*Owen Lee*[6], *Charlie William*[5], *William (Candy) Erwin*[4], *John Sr.*[3], *Charles W. Sr.*[2], *John Sr.*[1]).

Iatrice married **Jimmy Myers**.

1721. Robert Earl Sharp (*Donald Edward*[6], *Charlie William*[5], *William (Candy) Erwin*[4], *John Sr.*[3], *Charles W. Sr.*[2], *John Sr.*[1]) was born 12 May 1928 in Lauderdale County, AL, died 24 Dec 1997, and was buried in Center Hill Cemetery, Lauderdale County, AL.

Robert married **Bobbie Sue Michael**, daughter of **John Michael** and **Cecil Allen**, 30 Jul 1954 in Lauderdale County, AL. Bobbie was born 4 Jul 1932 in Lauderdale County, AL.

+ 3478 F   i.   **Robbie Laine Sharp** was born 20 Dec 1955 in Lauderdale County, AL.

+ 3479 M   ii.   **Christopher Michael Sharp** was born 21 Jan 1961 in Lauderdale County, AL, died 10 Jan 2000, and was buried in Center Hill Cemetery, Lauderdale County, AL.

+ 3480 F   iii. **Michelle Suzanne Sharp** was born 30 Nov 1967 in Lauderdale County, AL.

1722. Gloria Eloise Sharp (*Donald Edward*[6], *Charlie William*[5], *William (Candy) Erwin*[4], *John Sr.*[3], *Charles W. Sr.*[2], *John Sr.*[1]) was born 19 Nov 1937 in Lauderdale County, AL.

Gloria married **Charles Earl Snoddy**, son of **James Thomas Snoddy** and **Martha Fern Haraway**, 24 Sep 1955 in Iuka, Tishomingo County, MS. Charles was born 5 Dec 1935 in Elgin, Lauderdale County, AL.

+ 3481 F   i.   **Emily Patricia (Pattie) Snoddy** was born 29 Mar 1959 in Athens, Limestone County, AL.

+ 3482 M   ii.   **Eric Earl Snoddy** was born 5 Feb 1967 in Lauderdale County, AL.

1723. Ethel Austelene Sharp (*Donald Edward*[6], *Charlie William*[5], *William (Candy) Erwin*[4], *John Sr.*[3], *Charles W. Sr.*[2], *John Sr.*[1]) was born 31 Dec 1941 in Lauderdale County, AL.

Ethel married **Dois Melborn Johnston**, son of **Dave Robert Johnston** and **Eula E. Mashburn**, 21 May 1960 in Lauderdale County, AL. Dois was born 6 Aug 1931 in Lauderdale County, AL.

1724. Kennis Coleman Sharp (*Charles Price*[6], *Charlie William*[5], *William (Candy) Erwin*[4], *John Sr.*[3], *Charles W. Sr.*[2], *John Sr.*[1]) was born 4 Jul 1925 in Lexington, Lauderdale County, AL.

Kennis married **Lois Eliese Hammond**, daughter of **Wylie Edward Hammond** and **Thillie Mae McCafferty**, 23 May 1945 in Lauderdale County, AL. Lois was born 28 May 1928 in Alabama.

+ 3483 M   i.   **Ronald Coleman Sharp** was born 15 Feb 1952 in Lawrence County, TN.

+ 3484 F   ii.   **Debra Diane Sharp** was born 7 Feb 1956 in Lawrence County, TN.

1725. Charles Clifford Sharp (*Charles Price*[6], *Charlie William*[5], *William (Candy) Erwin*[4], *John Sr.*[3], *Charles W. Sr.*[2], *John Sr.*[1]) was born 13 Nov 1932 in Lexington, Lauderdale County, AL.

Charles married **Leatha Pearl Oliver**, daughter of **Buford Oliver** and **Annie Laurder**, 3 Feb 1962 in Lauderdale County, AL. Leatha was born 7 Mar 1940 in Lexington, Lauderdale County, AL, died 25 Nov 1999, and was buried in Pettus Cemetery, Lawrenceburg, TN.
+ 3485 M i. **Anthony Clifford Sharp** was born 20 Jun 1964 in Lauderdale County, AL.
+ 3486 M ii. **Rodney Lee Sharp** was born 13 May 1971 in Lauderdale County, AL.
+ 3487 F iii. **April Rotunda Sharp** was born 14 Oct 1978 in Lauderdale County, AL.
+ 3488 F iv. **Rhonda Gail Sharp**.

Charles next married **Gladys Whitney Phillips** 7 Dec 2002 in Lexington, Lauderdale County, AL.

1726. James Kenneth (Moose) Sharp (*Charles Price*[6], *Charlie William*[5], *William (Candy) Erwin*[4], *John Sr.*[3], *Charles W. Sr.*[2], *John Sr.*[1]) was born 4 Jun 1944 in Lexington, Lauderdale County, AL.

James married **Linda Gail Michael**, daughter of **Odis Lee Michael** and **Silvia Elizabeth Davis**, 23 Jul 1965 in Lauderdale County, AL. Linda was born 18 Jul 1947 in Colbert County, AL.
+ 3489 F i. **Teresa Ann Sharp** was born 27 Jan 1967 in Lauderdale County, AL.
+ 3490 M ii. **James Darren Sharp** was born 16 Jul 1969 in Lauderdale County, AL.

1727. Nancy Spence Wilson (*Emily Louise Bounds*[6], *Dollie E. Sharp*[5], *William (Candy) Erwin*[4], *John Sr.*[3], *Charles W. Sr.*[2], *John Sr.*[1]) was born 4 Aug 1947 in Lauderdale County, AL.

Nancy married **James Rollins Sevier Jr.**, son of **James Rollins Sevier Sr.** and **Ilma La Bar**, 16 Mar 1968 in Lauderdale County, AL. James was born 21 May 1946 in Buncombe County, NC.
+ 3491 F i. **Nancy Katherine Sevier** was born 4 Oct 1970 in Lauderdale County, AL.
  3492 M ii. **James Rollin Sevier III** was born 23 May 1973 in Lauderdale County, AL.

1728. Emily Elizabeth Wilson (*Emily Louise Bounds*[6], *Dollie E. Sharp*[5], *William (Candy) Erwin*[4], *John Sr.*[3], *Charles W. Sr.*[2], *John Sr.*[1]) was born 9 Jul 1949 in Lauderdale County, AL.

Emily married **John Seawell Severin**, son of **John Robert Severin** and **Bette Carmen Williams**, 24 Oct 1969 in Auburn, Lee County, AL. John was born 13 May 1948 in Decatur, GA.
+ 3493 F i. **Emily Christian Severin** was born 15 Feb 1970 in Auburn, Lee County, AL.

1729. Patricia Louise Mary Sharp (*Richard Orlando*[6], *Richard Owen*[5], *William (Candy) Erwin*[4], *John Sr.*[3], *Charles W. Sr.*[2], *John Sr.*[1]) was born 25 Mar 1937 in Cuyahoga County, OH.

Patricia married **Eugene Paul Burch** 9 May 1959.

1731. Reta Lambert (*Bessie Virgil Call*[6], *Beulah L. Sharp*[5], *William (Candy) Erwin*[4], *John Sr.*[3], *Charles W. Sr.*[2], *John Sr.*[1]).

Reta married ***Unk Parnell**.

1734. Elbert Turner Cox Sr. (*Ida Mae Call*[6], *Beulah L. Sharp*[5], *William (Candy) Erwin*[4], *John Sr.*[3], *Charles W. Sr.*[2], *John Sr.*[1]) was born 13 Oct 1924 in Lauderdale County, AL, died 25 Aug 1994, and was buried in Tri-Cities Memorial Gardens, Florence, Lauderdale County, AL.

Elbert married **Marie Anne Hoernig**, daughter of **Burno Cornelius Hoernig** and **Annie Lobeck**, 29 Jul 1950 in Lauderdale County, AL. Marie was born 9 Dec 1929 in Lawrenceburg, Lawrence County, TN, died 23 Dec 1964, and was buried in Mt. Olive Cemetery, Troy, MI.
+ 3494 M i. **Elbert Turner Cox Jr.** was born 20 Apr 1951 in Detroit, Wayne County, MI.
  3495 F ii. **Martha Ann Cox** was born 16 Jan 1953 in Detroit, Wayne County, MI, died 19 Oct 1964, and was buried in Mt. Olive Cemetery, Troy, MI.
+ 3496 M iii. **Frank Lee Cox** was born 2 Aug 1954 in Detroit, Wayne County, MI.
+ 3497 M iv. **Thomas Wayne Cox** was born 5 Jan 1956 in Detroit, Wayne County, MI.

3498	F	v.	**Mary Joe Cox** was born 12 Jun 1957 in Detroit, Wayne County, MI, died 19 Dec 1964, and was buried in Mt. Olive Cemetery, Troy, MI.
3499	M	vi.	**John Cox** was born 22 Nov 1958 in Detroit, Wayne County, MI, died 19 Dec 1964, and was buried in Mt. Olive Cemetery, Troy, MI.
3500	F	vii.	**Diane Cox** was born 8 May 1960 in Detroit, Wayne County, MI, died 19 Dec 1964, and was buried in Mt. Olive Cemetery, Troy, MI.
3501	M	viii.	**James (Jimmy) Cox** was born 28 Aug 1961 in Detroit, Wayne County, MI, died 19 Dec 1964, and was buried in Mt. Olive Cemetery, Troy, MI.
3502	M	ix.	**Charles Cox** was born 2 Apr 1962 in Detroit, Wayne County, MI, died 19 Dec 1964, and was buried in Macedonia Cemetery, Lauderdale County, AL.

Elbert next married **Sarah Frances Mosley** 23 Nov 1973 in Lauderdale County, AL. Sarah was born 17 Nov 1924 in Giles County, TN.

Elbert next married **Augusta Rhodes**, daughter of **William Mack Rhodes** and **Jessie Augusta Carroll**, 10 Jul 1993 in Lauderdale County, AL. Augusta was born 15 Jun 1923.

1735. Lee Douglas Cox (*Ida Mae Call ^{6}, Beulah L. Sharp ^{5}, William (Candy) Erwin ^{4}, John Sr. ^{3}, Charles W. Sr. ^{2}, John Sr. ^{1}*) was born 16 Dec 1925 in Lauderdale County, AL, died 31 Oct 1985, and was buried in Tri-Cities Memorial Gardens, Florence, Lauderdale County, AL.

Lee married **Betty Adaline Hayes**, daughter of **Taylor Randolph Hayes** and **N. May De Lones**, 7 Oct 1949 in Iuka, Tishomingo County, MS. Betty was born 15 Mar 1930 in Lauderdale County, AL.

+	3503	F	i.	**Glenda Carolyn Cox** was born 25 Jul 1950 in Lauderdale County, AL.
+	3504	M	ii.	**Andre Douglas Cox** was born 13 Apr 1958 in Lauderdale County, AL.

1737. Johnny Winston Rice (*Daisy Ruth Call ^{6}, Beulah L. Sharp ^{5}, William (Candy) Erwin ^{4}, John Sr. ^{3}, Charles W. Sr. ^{2}, John Sr. ^{1}*) was born in Lauderdale County, AL.

Johnny married **Jo Ann Haynes** 10 Jun 1967.

	3505	F	i.	**Jennifer Rice**.

1738. David Lee Call (*Roy Lee Call ^{6}, Beulah L. Sharp ^{5}, William (Candy) Erwin ^{4}, John Sr. ^{3}, Charles W. Sr. ^{2}, John Sr. ^{1}*) was born 18 Feb 1941 in Lauderdale County, AL.

David married **Linda Kay Cobb**, daughter of ***Unk Cobb** and **Estelle Dill**, 31 Aug 1968 in Lauderdale County, AL.

+	3506	F	i.	**Laura Call** was born 28 Apr 1971.
	3507	F	ii.	**Lisa Call** was born 5 Oct 1974.
	3508	F	iii.	**Dana Call** was born 14 Oct 1976.

1739. Linda Call (*Roy Lee Call ^{6}, Beulah L. Sharp ^{5}, William (Candy) Erwin ^{4}, John Sr. ^{3}, Charles W. Sr. ^{2}, John Sr. ^{1}*) was born 4 May 1946 in Lauderdale County, AL.

Linda married **Thomas E. Boone**.

+	3509	F	i.	**Kim Boone** was born 20 Apr 1961.

1740. Connie Lynn Call (*Roy Lee Call ^{6}, Beulah L. Sharp ^{5}, William (Candy) Erwin ^{4}, John Sr. ^{3}, Charles W. Sr. ^{2}, John Sr. ^{1}*) was born 19 Nov 1950 in Lauderdale County, AL.

Connie married **Michael Lee Raffield**, son of **Horace Arthur Raffield** and **Betty Burns**, 3 Feb 1972 in Lauderdale County, AL. Michael was born 17 Sep 1950 in Bedford County, TN.

	3510	M	i.	**Corbett (Cory) Raffield** was born 3 Aug 1973.

1741. Dennis Howard Call (*Roy Lee Call ^{6}, Beulah L. Sharp ^{5}, William (Candy) Erwin ^{4}, John Sr. ^{3}, Charles W. Sr. ^{2}, John Sr. ^{1}*) was born 30 Nov 1953 in Lauderdale County, AL.

Dennis married **Raynea Donanne Muckey**, daughter of **Dale D. Muckey** and **Donna *Unk**, in California. Raynea was born 12 Oct 1954 in Nebraska.

+ 3511 F i. **Heather Michelle Call**.
  3512 F ii. **Megan Call**.

1742. Greta Call (*Ervin Howard Call ^{6}, Beulah L. Sharp ^{5}, William (Candy) Erwin ^{4}, John Sr. ^{3}, Charles W. Sr. ^{2}, John Sr. ^{1}*).

Greta married **Les Holliman**.

1743. Penelope Anne Sharp (*Dalton ^{6}, Charner Leander Sr. ^{5}, William (Candy) Erwin ^{4}, John Sr. ^{3}, Charles W. Sr. ^{2}, John Sr. ^{1}*) was born 16 Dec 1948.

Penelope married **Joseph Cowaski**.
3513 M i. **Paul Cowaski** was born 10 Jan 1969.
3514 F ii. **Cherise Cowaski** was born 13 Jan 1970.
3515 M iii. **David Cowaski** was born 23 Apr 1971.

1744. James Howard Grigsby Jr. (*Verna Lorena Sharp ^{6}, Charner Leander Sr. ^{5}, William (Candy) Erwin ^{4}, John Sr. ^{3}, Charles W. Sr. ^{2}, John Sr. ^{1}*) was born 19 Mar 1957 in Tuscan, AZ.

James married **Nancy Anna Waddle**, daughter of **Ralph David Waddle Jr.** and **Dorothy Sue Vaughn**. Nancy was born in Bitbird, Germany.
3516 M i. **Bryan David Grigsby** was born 21 Jan 1982.
3517 F ii. **Ann Elizabeth Grigsby** was born 11 Jul 1983.
3518 F iii. **Emily Ruth Grigsby** was born 9 Apr 1986.

1745. Michael Owen Grigsby (*Verna Lorena Sharp ^{6}, Charner Leander Sr. ^{5}, William (Candy) Erwin ^{4}, John Sr. ^{3}, Charles W. Sr. ^{2}, John Sr. ^{1}*) was born 16 Apr 1958 in Selma, AL.

Michael married **Mary Louise Qualls**.
3519 F i. **Amanda Michelle Grigsby** was born 18 Aug 1982 in Spokane, WA.

Michael next married **Rebecca Elaine Walker**, daughter of **Ronald Gene Walker** and **Barbara Ann Meador**, 13 Jul 1985 in Spokane, WA. Rebecca was born 28 Mar 1959 in Fort Worth, TX.
3520 M i. **Andrew Taylor Grigsby** was born 23 Jun 1986 in Spokane, WA.

1746. Elisa Lynn Walker (*Virginia Mae Sharp ^{6}, Charner Leander Sr. ^{5}, William (Candy) Erwin ^{4}, John Sr. ^{3}, Charles W. Sr. ^{2}, John Sr. ^{1}*) was born 8 Dec 1959 in Lauderdale County, AL.

Elisa married **Herbert Lee Fields Jr.**, son of **Herbert Lee Fields Sr.** and **Margaret Collins**, 2 Jun 1978 in Lauderdale County, AL. Herbert was born 20 Oct 1958 in Lauderdale County, AL.
3521 F i. **Heather Lynn Fields** was born 18 Feb 1979 in Lauderdale County, AL.

1748. Susanne Marie Sharp (*Charner Leander Jr. ^{6}, Charner Leander Sr. ^{5}, William (Candy) Erwin ^{4}, John Sr. ^{3}, Charles W. Sr. ^{2}, John Sr. ^{1}*) was born 29 Aug 1971 in Lauderdale County, AL.

Susanne married **Michael *Unk**.
3522 M i. **Casey *Unk**.
3523 M ii. **McKaloy *Unk**.

1749. Kathleen Sharp (*William (Billy) Brevard ^{6}, Burt Hilliard Sr. ^{5}, William (Candy) Erwin ^{4}, John Sr. ^{3}, Charles W. Sr. ^{2}, John Sr. ^{1}*) was born 29 Jul 1942 in Lackwana, NY.

Kathleen married ***Unk Boggs**.
3524 M i. **Shawn Boggs** was born 5 Mar 1970 in Wheeling, WV.
3525 F ii. **Kelly Boggs** was born 14 May 1973 in Weirton, WV.

1750. William Daniel Sharp (*William (Billy) Brevard*^{6}, *Burt Hilliard Sr.*^{5}, *William (Candy) Erwin*^{4}, *John Sr.*^{3}, *Charles W. Sr.*^{2}, *John Sr.*^{1}) was born 21 Dec 1947 in Steubenville, Jefferson County, OH.

William married ***Unk**.
+ 3526 F i. **Melissa Sharp** was born 29 Jan 1972 in Weirton, WV.
  3527 F ii. **Amanda Sharp** was born 30 Jun 1974 in Weirton, WV.
  3528 F iii. **Sara Sharp** was born 23 Jul 1980 in Weirton, WV.

1751. Pamela Sharp (*William (Billy) Brevard*^{6}, *Burt Hilliard Sr.*^{5}, *William (Candy) Erwin*^{4}, *John Sr.*^{3}, *Charles W. Sr.*^{2}, *John Sr.*^{1}) was born 29 Jul 1949 in Steubenville, OH.

Pamela married ***Unk Okey**.
  3529 M i. **Ryan Okey** was born 25 Oct 1996 in Weirton, WV.

1752. Shelly Sharp (*Thomas Milton*^{6}, *Burt Hilliard Sr.*^{5}, *William (Candy) Erwin*^{4}, *John Sr.*^{3}, *Charles W. Sr.*^{2}, *John Sr.*^{1}) was born 19 Oct 1957.

Shelly married **Joe Starcher** in Jun 1982.

1753. Kathy Sharp (*Thomas Milton*^{6}, *Burt Hilliard Sr.*^{5}, *William (Candy) Erwin*^{4}, *John Sr.*^{3}, *Charles W. Sr.*^{2}, *John Sr.*^{1}) was born 13 Jan 1962.

Kathy married **Joe Kainock** in Sep 1983.

1754. Cynthia L. Fabian (*Pauline (Polly) Elaine Sharp*^{6}, *Burt Hilliard Sr.*^{5}, *William (Candy) Erwin*^{4}, *John Sr.*^{3}, *Charles W. Sr.*^{2}, *John Sr.*^{1}) was born 11 Jun 1952 in Steubenville, OH.

Cynthia married **Ronald Northedge**.
  3530 M i. **Jason Northedge** was born 22 May 1974 in Weirton, WV.

Cynthia next married **Jon W. Thompson**, son of **William Thompson** and **Lorraine McFadden**, 21 Aug 1987. Jon was born 21 Dec 1951 in Steubenville, OH.
  3531 M i. **Jon Michael Thompson** was born 1 May 1987 in Steubenville, OH.

1755. Donald N. Fabian (*Pauline (Polly) Elaine Sharp*^{6}, *Burt Hilliard Sr.*^{5}, *William (Candy) Erwin*^{4}, *John Sr.*^{3}, *Charles W. Sr.*^{2}, *John Sr.*^{1}) was born 11 Jun 1953 in Steubenville, OH.

Donald married **Terri Jones**, daughter of **Charles Jones** and **Alice Campbell**, 26 May 1973 in Weirton, WV. Terri was born 6 Apr 1954 in Weirton, WV.
  3532 F i. **Kerri Fabian** was born 21 Sep 1978 in Weirton, WV.

1761. Johnny Ray Witt (*Mae Belle Young*^{6}, *James Wylie (Jim) Young*^{5}, *Julia Ann Young*^{4}, *Mary E. Sharp*^{3}, *Charles W. Sr.*^{2}, *John Sr.*^{1}) was born 8 Jun 1930 in Lauderdale County, AL, died 7 Jan 2005, and was buried in Murphy's Chapel Cemetery, Lauderdale County, AL.

Johnny married **Mary Esther Holloway**, daughter of **William Anderson Holloway** and **Gertrude (Gertie) Odell Dean**, 23 Mar 1954 in Iuka, Tishomingo County, MS. Mary was born 14 Oct 1935 in Lauderdale County, AL.
+ 3533 M i. **Danny Ray Witt** was born 17 Jan 1955 in Lauderdale County, AL.
  3534 M ii. **Ricky Dale Witt** was born in 1956 in Lauderdale County, AL, died in 1956, and was buried in Murphy's Chapel Cemetery, Lauderdale County, AL.
+ 3535 F iii. **Cathy Ann Witt** was born 2 Jan 1959 in Mishawaka, St Joseph County, IN.
+ 3536 M iv. **Randy Lee Witt Sr.** was born 9 Nov 1964 in St. Joseph County, IN.

1762. Letha Helen Witt (*Mae Belle Young*^{6}, *James Wylie (Jim) Young*^{5}, *Julia Ann Young*^{4}, *Mary E. Sharp*^{3}, *Charles W. Sr.*^{2}, *John Sr.*^{1}) was born 19 Jan 1935 in Lauderdale County, AL, died 9 Oct 2005, and was buried in Murphy's Chapel Cemetery, Lauderdale County, AL.

Letha married **Noah (Sonny) L. V. Smith**, son of **Butler Oscar Smith** and **Edna Mae Huffman**, 15 Nov 1952. Noah was born 21 Jul 1932 in Lauderdale County, AL, died 8 Apr 1967, and was buried in Murphy's Chapel Cemetery, Lauderdale County, AL.

3537	M	i.	**Gaylon E. Smith** was born 19 Jul 1953 in Lauderdale County, AL, died 12 May 1972, and was buried in Murphy's Chapel Cemetery, Lauderdale County, AL.
+ 3538	M	ii.	**Lonnie Nolan Smith** was born 13 Oct 1955 in Lauderdale County, AL, died 18 Aug 1973, and was buried in Murphy's Chapel Cemetery, Lauderdale County, AL.
+ 3539	F	iii.	**Laura Kay Smith** was born 7 Feb 1957.
+ 3540	M	iv.	**Jesse Lynn Smith** was born 4 Nov 1959.
+ 3541	F	v.	**Jennifer Gay Smith** was born 12 Oct 1960.

1763. Eva Witt (*Mae Belle Young*[6], *James Wylie (Jim) Young*[5], *Julia Ann Young*[4], *Mary E. Sharp*[3], *Charles W. Sr.*[2], *John Sr.*[1]) was born 25 Oct 1937 in Lauderdale County, AL.

Eva married **Claude Ellis Wood Jr.**, son of **Claude Ellis Wood Sr.** and **Elizabeth Lee Phillips**, 1 Nov 1953 in Iuka, Tishomingo County, MS. Claude was born 19 Dec 1936 in Florence, Lauderdale County, AL.

+ 3542	M	i.	**David Wayne Wood** was born 20 Dec 1955 in Lauderdale County, AL.
+ 3543	F	ii.	**Nancy Mae Wood** was born 9 Oct 1958 in Lauderdale County, AL.

1764. Rachel Lee Witt (*Mae Belle Young*[6], *James Wylie (Jim) Young*[5], *Julia Ann Young*[4], *Mary E. Sharp*[3], *Charles W. Sr.*[2], *John Sr.*[1]) was born 2 Apr 1942 in Lauderdale County, AL, died 3 Nov 2000, and was buried in Murphy's Chapel Cemetery, Lauderdale County, AL.

Rachel married **Hassell Lee Smith** 24 Dec 1960 in Savannah, TN. Hassell was born 15 Nov 1940 in Hardin County, TN.

+ 3544	M	i.	**Wendell Gene Smith** was born 8 May 1964 in Lauderdale County, AL.
+ 3545	M	ii.	**Tracy Kyle Smith** was born 1 Apr 1968 in Lauderdale County, AL.

1766. Gladys Marie Smith (*Nomer Marie Young*[6], *James Wylie (Jim) Young*[5], *Julia Ann Young*[4], *Mary E. Sharp*[3], *Charles W. Sr.*[2], *John Sr.*[1]) was born 19 Mar 1930 in Lauderdale County, AL.

Gladys married **Benjamin Franklin (BF) White**, son of **Benjamin Franklin (Frank) White** and **Hannah Adeline Davis**, 21 Dec 1946 in Lauderdale County, AL. Benjamin was born 23 May 1928 in Lauderdale County, AL, died 8 Aug 1988, and was buried in Chapel Hill Memorial Garden, Osceola, IN.

+ 3546	M	i.	**Jimmy Dale (JD) White Sr.** was born 21 Oct 1947.
+ 3547	F	ii.	**Janice Sue White** was born 11 Nov 1949.
+ 3548	F	iii.	**Sandra Joyce White** was born 25 Sep 1951.
+ 3549	F	iv.	**Jeannie Ruth White** was born 12 Sep 1953.
+ 3550	M	v.	**Jeff Steven White** was born 9 Aug 1955.
+ 3551	M	vi.	**Jackie Ladd White** was born 28 Mar 1957.
+ 3552	F	vii.	**Jill Annette White** was born 15 May 1959.

Gladys next married **John Boyd White** 20 Jul 1996 in Osceola, Elkhart County, IN. John was born 25 Feb 1931 in Lauderdale County, AL.

1767. Randle Arnold Smith (*Nomer Marie Young*[6], *James Wylie (Jim) Young*[5], *Julia Ann Young*[4], *Mary E. Sharp*[3], *Charles W. Sr.*[2], *John Sr.*[1]) was born 14 Jun 1932 in Lauderdale County, AL, died 8 Apr 2001, and was buried in Murphy's Chapel Cemetery, Lauderdale County, AL.

Randle married **Mary Frances Smith** in Sep 1950. Mary was born 19 Feb 1933, died 27 May 2008, and was buried in Murphy's Chapel Cemetery, Lauderdale County, AL.

+ 3553	M	i.	**Ronnie (Red) Arnold Smith** was born 29 Dec 1955.
+ 3554	M	ii.	**Donnie Ray Smith** was born 7 Mar 1957.
3555	M	iii.	**Johnny Dale Smith** was born 31 Jan 1959, died 17 Mar 1984, and was buried in Murphy's Chapel Cemetery, Lauderdale County, AL.
+ 3556	M	iv.	**Lonnie Wayne (Boo) Smith** was born 21 Jan 1962 in Lauderdale County, AL.
3557	M	v.	**Junior Ray Smith** was buried in Murphy's Chapel Cemetery, Lauderdale County, AL.
3558	M	vi.	**Rodney Lee Smith** was born 7 Jan 1972.

1768. Jimmy Lester (JL) Smith (*Nomer Marie Young^6, James Wylie (Jim) Young^5, Julia Ann Young^4, Mary E. Sharp^3, Charles W. Sr.^{2}, John Sr.^{1}*) was born 20 Feb 1935 in Lauderdale County, AL, died 10 Feb 2006, and was buried in Murphy's Chapel Cemetery, Lauderdale County, AL.

Jimmy married **Dorothy Mae White** in Jul 1953. Dorothy died in 1976 and was buried in Murphy's Chapel Cemetery, Lauderdale County, AL.

+ 3559	F	i.	**Carolyn Estelle Smith** was born 31 May 1954, died 8 Mar 1995, and was buried in Chapel Hill Memorial Garden, Osceola, IN.
+ 3560	M	ii.	**Jessie Lynn Smith** was born 21 Apr 1955.
+ 3561	F	iii.	**Kathy Jo Smith** was born 11 Jun 1956.
+ 3562	F	iv.	**Christine Elaine Smith** was born 9 Jun 1957.

Jimmy next married **DeAnn Smith** 24 Jun 1967. DeAnn was born 7 Mar 1946.

1769. Ruth Lucille Smith (*Nomer Marie Young^6, James Wylie (Jim) Young^5, Julia Ann Young^4, Mary E. Sharp^3, Charles W. Sr.^{2}, John Sr.^{1}*) was born 12 Sep 1937 in Lauderdale County, AL, died 24 May 2000, and was buried in Murphy's Chapel Cemetery, Lauderdale County, AL.

Ruth married **James Anderson Holloway**, son of **William Anderson Holloway** and **Gertrude (Gertie) Odell Dean**, 1 Apr 1953 in Iuka, Tishomingo County, MS. James was born 4 Apr 1937 in Lauderdale County, AL, died 13 Sep 2002, and was buried in Murphy's Chapel Cemetery, Lauderdale County, AL.

+ 3563	M	i.	**Roger William Holloway** was born 5 Sep 1954.
+ 3564	F	ii.	**Julia May Holloway** was born 12 Apr 1957.
+ 3565	M	iii.	**James (Jim) Elbert Holloway** was born 8 Dec 1963.

Ruth next married **James (Jim) Sanders**.

+ 3566	F	i.	**Judith (Judy) Sanders**.
+ 3567	F	ii.	**Janell Sanders**.

Ruth next married **Charles Emery (Chuck) Denman Sr.**. Charles was born 18 Apr 1932, died 1 May 2002, and was buried in Murphy's Chapel Cemetery, Lauderdale County, AL.

1770. Beulah Estelle Smith (*Nomer Marie Young^6, James Wylie (Jim) Young^5, Julia Ann Young^4, Mary E. Sharp^3, Charles W. Sr.^{2}, John Sr.^{1}*) was born 21 Mar 1941 in Alabama.

Beulah married **Wallace Earl Wood**, son of **Leonard Earl Wood** and **Beatrice (Be-At) Wood**, 24 Jun 1958 in Booneville, MS. Wallace was born 24 Nov 1939 in Florence, Lauderdale County, AL.

+ 3568	M	i.	**Joey Lee Wood** was born 15 Feb 1960 in Florence, Lauderdale County, AL.
+ 3569	M	ii.	**Keith Deran Wood** was born 1 Apr 1962 in Lauderdale County, AL.
+ 3570	M	iii.	**Gregory Dale Wood** was born 17 Oct 1968 in Lauderdale County, AL.
+ 3571	F	iv.	**Rhonda Sherae Wood** was born 10 Aug 1972 in Lauderdale County, AL.
+ 3572	M	v.	**Jonathan Elbert Wood** was born 12 May 1974 in Lauderdale County, AL.
+ 3573	F	vi.	**Beth Elaine Wood** was born 25 Jul 1979 in ECM Hospital, Florence, Lauderdale County, AL.

1771. Grady Elbert Smith (*Nomer Marie Young^6, James Wylie (Jim) Young^5, Julia Ann Young^4, Mary E. Sharp^3, Charles W. Sr.^{2}, John Sr.^{1}*) was born 4 Jan 1945 in Lauderdale County, AL.

Grady married **Linda Gail Bevis**, daughter of **James Bevis** and **Mildred Holloman**, 11 Sep 1964 in Lauderdale County, AL. Linda was born 4 Dec 1944 in Lauderdale County, AL.

+ 3574	M	i.	**Darin Dwaine Smith** was born 25 Aug 1965 in Lauderdale County, AL.
3575	F	ii.	**Tracy Michelle Smith** was born 22 Nov 1969 in Lauderdale County, AL.

1772. Edwin Smith (*Mozella Young^6, James Wylie (Jim) Young^5, Julia Ann Young^4, Mary E. Sharp^3, Charles W. Sr.^{2}, John Sr.^{1}*) was born 31 Oct 1929.

Edwin married **Betty Maye Scott**, daughter of **Clarence S. Scott** and **Gertie Maye Sego**, 31 Dec 1948 in Iuka, Tishomingo County, MS. Betty was born 17 Apr 1931 in Waterloo, Lauderdale County, AL.

| 3576 | F | i. | **Mellisa Fay Smith** was born 15 Mar 1950. |

3576 F i. **Mellisa Fay Smith** was born 15 Mar 1950.
3577 M ii. **Dannie Ray Smith** was born 8 Dec 1948 in Waterloo, Lauderdale County, AL and died 11 May 1991.
3578 M iii. **Kenneth David Smith** was born 4 Aug 1954 in Mishawaka, St Joseph County, IN.
+ 3579 M iv. **James Allen Smith** was born 15 Apr 1959 in Mishawaka, St Joseph County, IN.

1774. Lavada (Slick) Smith (*Mozella Young^6, James Wylie (Jim) Young^5, Julia Ann Young^4, Mary E. Sharp^3, Charles W. Sr.^{2}, John Sr.^{1}*) was born 22 Jul 1932.

Lavada married **Ed Szymczak**.
3580 F i. **Donna Szymczak**.
3581 M ii. **Edwin Szymczak**.
3582 F iii. **Barbara Szymczak**.

1775. Eulalia (Curly) Smith (*Mozella Young^6, James Wylie (Jim) Young^5, Julia Ann Young^4, Mary E. Sharp^3, Charles W. Sr.^{2}, John Sr.^{1}*) was born 22 Jul 1932 in Lauderdale County, AL, died 3 Sep 1995, and was buried in South Bend, St Joseph County, IN.

Eulalia married **D. C. Smith**, son of **Clyde E. Smith** and **Ollie B. Smith**. D. was born 10 Aug 1934 in Lauderdale County, AL, died 24 Jun 1962, and was buried in Oak Grove Cemetery, Lauderdale County, AL.

Eulalia next married **Owen White**, son of **Benjamin Franklin (Frank) White** and **Hannah Adeline Davis**. Owen was born 28 Apr 1924 in Lauderdale County, AL, died 16 Feb 1999, and was buried in Murphy's Chapel Cemetery, Lauderdale County, AL.
3583 M i. **Ricky White**.
3584 M ii. **James Edwin White**.
3585 M iii. **Calvin White**.
3586 M iv. **Lonnie White**.

1776. Joseph Wheeler Smith (*Mozella Young^6, James Wylie (Jim) Young^5, Julia Ann Young^4, Mary E. Sharp^3, Charles W. Sr.^{2}, John Sr.^{1}*) was born 28 Nov 1937 in Lauderdale County, AL.

Joseph married **Betty Jane Young**, daughter of **Robert Edward (Bunt) Young** and **Estelle Eugene Wood**, 6 Oct 1953 in Iuka, Tishomingo County, MS. Betty was born 2 Sep 1937 in Lauderdale County, AL.
+ 3587 F i. **Catherine Ann (Cathy) Smith** was born 6 Apr 1956 in Indiana.
+ 3588 F ii. **Cindy Jo Smith** was born 19 Mar 1957 in Indiana.
+ 3589 M iii. **Jack Wheeler Smith** was born 12 Apr 1961 in Lauderdale County, AL, died 27 Jun 1998, and was buried in Murphy's Chapel Cemetery, Lauderdale County, AL.

1777. Margaret Young (*Paul Mansel Young^6, James Wylie (Jim) Young^5, Julia Ann Young^4, Mary E. Sharp^3, Charles W. Sr.^{2}, John Sr.^{1}*).

Margaret married **Albert Ledford**.

1778. Christine Young (*Paul Mansel Young^6, James Wylie (Jim) Young^5, Julia Ann Young^4, Mary E. Sharp^3, Charles W. Sr.^{2}, John Sr.^{1}*).

Christine married **Gene Autry Holt**. Gene was born in 1933 in Wayne County, TN, died 22 Feb 2002, and was buried in Cloverdale COC Cemetery, Lauderdale County, AL.
+ 3590 M i. **Wayne Holt**.
+ 3591 M ii. **Kenny Holt**.
3592 M iii. **Ronnie Holt**.
+ 3593 F iv. **Regina Holt**.

1779. Loretta Young (*Paul Mansel Young^6, James Wylie (Jim) Young^5, Julia Ann Young^4, Mary E. Sharp^3, Charles W. Sr.^{2}, John Sr.^{1}*) was born 6 Oct 1954 in Lauderdale County, AL.

Loretta married **Kenneth Russell**, son of **M. C. Russell** and **Martha Vaughn**, 9 May 1975 in Lauderdale County, AL. Kenneth was born 28 Jan 1951 in Shelby County, TN.

3594 F   i.   **Alisa Ray Russell**.

3595 F   ii.   **Lindsey Allison Russell**.

1780. Paulette Young (*Paul Mansel Young^6, James Wylie (Jim) Young^5, Julia Ann Young^4, Mary E. Sharp^3, Charles W. Sr.^{2}, John Sr.^{1}*) was born 1 Nov 1955 in Lauderdale County, AL.

Paulette married **Gordon Wade Russell**, son of **M. C. Russell** and **Martha Vaughn**, 31 May 1978 in Lauderdale County, AL. Gordon was born 29 Mar 1954 in Memphis, Shelby County, TN.

+ 3596 F   i.   **Kimberly Ann Russell** was born 11 Feb 1981 in Lauderdale County, AL.

3597 M   ii.   **Samuel Wayne Russell** was born 4 Aug 1986 in Lauderdale County, AL.

1781. Barbara Lynn Young (*Paul Mansel Young^6, James Wylie (Jim) Young^5, Julia Ann Young^4, Mary E. Sharp^3, Charles W. Sr.^{2}, John Sr.^{1}*) was born 4 Nov 1957 in Lauderdale County, AL.

Barbara married **Ronald Lee Cook**, son of **Willie L. Cook** and **Martha Carroll**, 26 Jun 1980 in Lauderdale County, AL. Ronald was born 29 Jan 1951 in Lauderdale County, AL.

1782. Cathy Young (*Paul Mansel Young^6, James Wylie (Jim) Young^5, Julia Ann Young^4, Mary E. Sharp^3, Charles W. Sr.^{2}, John Sr.^{1}*).

Cathy married **Ron Inman**.

3598 M   i.   **Blake Inman**.

1783. Elsie Sue Young (*Paul Mansel Young^6, James Wylie (Jim) Young^5, Julia Ann Young^4, Mary E. Sharp^3, Charles W. Sr.^{2}, John Sr.^{1}*) was born 23 Apr 1963 in Lauderdale County, AL, died in Apr 2002, and was buried in Florence City Cemetery, Florence, Lauderdale County, AL.

Elsie married **Wendell Wilke Pitts**, son of **Cecil Orbie (Coon) Pitts** and **Mary Omie Parrish**, 19 Jul 1993 in Lauderdale County, AL. Wendell was born 24 Aug 1943 in Lauderdale County, AL.

3599 M   i.   **Steven Nicholas Pitts** was born in 1994 in Lauderdale County, AL.

1786. Betty Lou Jones (*Hazel Inez Young^6, James Wylie (Jim) Young^5, Julia Ann Young^4, Mary E. Sharp^3, Charles W. Sr.^{2}, John Sr.^{1}*).

Betty married **James Olive**.

1787. Jim Robert Jones (*Hazel Inez Young^6, James Wylie (Jim) Young^5, Julia Ann Young^4, Mary E. Sharp^3, Charles W. Sr.^{2}, John Sr.^{1}*).

Jim married **Cathy Cossey**.

1788. Larry Steven McKelvey (*Irene Beulah Young^6, James Wylie (Jim) Young^5, Julia Ann Young^4, Mary E. Sharp^3, Charles W. Sr.^{2}, John Sr.^{1}*) was born 4 Jan 1948 in Lauderdale County, AL.

Larry married **Judy Miles**, daughter of **John Dalton Miles** and **Hazel Wooten**, 2 Sep 1967 in Lauderdale County, AL. Judy was born 28 Nov 1950 in Lauderdale County, AL.

+ 3600 F   i.   **Angelia Kay McKelvey** was born 24 Jan 1967 in Lauderdale County, AL.

+ 3601 F   ii.   **Donna Jean McKelvey** was born 20 Apr 1970 in Lauderdale County, AL.

+ 3602 F   iii.   **Tina Ann McKelvey** was born 27 Aug 1972 in Lauderdale County, AL.

1790. Bobby Moore Scott (*Eula Beatrice Young^6, Hulet Edward Young^5, Julia Ann Young^4, Mary E. Sharp^3, Charles W. Sr.^{2}, John Sr.^{1}*) was born 16 Jun 1937.

Bobby married **Mary *Unk**.

1791. Gary Lance Scott (*Eula Beatrice Young^6, Hulet Edward Young^5, Julia Ann Young^4, Mary E. Sharp^3, Charles W. Sr.^{2}, John Sr.^{1}*) was born 5 Nov 1939.

Gary married **Bobbie Jo Qualls**.
+ 3603 F   i.   **Karen Elaine Scott** was born 14 Oct 1971 in Lauderdale County, AL.
+ 3604 F   ii.   **Pamela Gail Scott**.
+ 3605 M iii. **Gregory (Greg) Lance Scott** was born 15 Nov 1975 in ECM Hospital, Florence, Lauderdale County, AL.

1792. Daniel Scott (*Eula Beatrice Young^6, Hulet Edward Young^5, Julia Ann Young^4, Mary E. Sharp^3, Charles W. Sr.^{2}, John Sr.^{1}*) was born 6 Jan 1943 in Lauderdale County, AL.

Daniel married **Jewel Dean Young**, daughter of **William (Bill) Young** and **Audry Sharp**, 7 Jun 1963 in Lauderdale County, AL. Jewel was born 8 Oct 1944 in Lauderdale County, AL, died 2 Jun 2000, and was buried in Tri-Cities Memorial Gardens, Florence, Lauderdale County, AL.
(Duplicate Line. See Person 1519)

1793. David Scott (*Eula Beatrice Young^6, Hulet Edward Young^5, Julia Ann Young^4, Mary E. Sharp^3, Charles W. Sr.^{2}, John Sr.^{1}*) was born 6 Jan 1943 in Lauderdale County, AL.

David married **Patsy Ann Wood**, daughter of **Lawrence (Toby) Eldred Sharp** and **Pauline Inez Wood**, 20 Jul 1966 in Lauderdale County, AL. Patsy was born 14 Oct 1949 in Florence, Lauderdale County, AL.
(Duplicate Line. See Person 1578)

1794. Peggy Jo Scott (*Eula Beatrice Young^6, Hulet Edward Young^5, Julia Ann Young^4, Mary E. Sharp^3, Charles W. Sr.^{2}, John Sr.^{1}*) was born 19 Nov 1944 in Lauderdale County, AL.

Peggy married **Larry Ray (Soap) Wood**, son of **Claude Ellis Wood Sr.** and **Elizabeth Lee Phillips**, 11 Sep 1961 in Lauderdale County, AL. Larry was born 22 May 1944 in Florence, Lauderdale County, AL, died 22 Oct 1987, and was buried in Oak Grove Cemetery, Lauderdale County, AL.
+ 3606 M   i.   **Dennis Ray Wood** was born 31 Aug 1962 in Lauderdale County, AL.

Peggy next married **Raymond Benson**.

1795. James Owen Scott (*Eula Beatrice Young^6, Hulet Edward Young^5, Julia Ann Young^4, Mary E. Sharp^3, Charles W. Sr.^{2}, John Sr.^{1}*) was born 22 Jul 1946.

James married **Joyce *Unk**.

1796. Julia Earline Scott (*Eula Beatrice Young^6, Hulet Edward Young^5, Julia Ann Young^4, Mary E. Sharp^3, Charles W. Sr.^{2}, John Sr.^{1}*) was born 20 May 1948 in Lauderdale County, AL.

Julia married **Freddie Harold McFall**, son of **Robert Lee McFall** and **Odie Holt**, 24 Jun 1967 in Lauderdale County, AL. Freddie was born 4 May 1936 in Wayne County, TN.
+ 3607 M   i.   **Terry Lynn McFall**.
  3608 F   ii.   **Laura Jo McFall**.
+ 3609 M iii. **Rodney McFall**.

1797. James (Jim) Allen Scott (*Eula Beatrice Young^6, Hulet Edward Young^5, Julia Ann Young^4, Mary E. Sharp^3, Charles W. Sr.^{2}, John Sr.^{1}*) was born 8 Sep 1949 in Lauderdale County, AL.

James married **Grace Young**, daughter of ***Unk** and **Daisy Evelyn Young**. Grace was born in Lauderdale County, AL.
  3610 M   i.   **Mitchell Scott**.
  3611 F   ii.   **Ginger Scott**.

1799. Josephine Oneada Dailey (*Carrie Ann Young[6], Hulet Edward Young[5], Julia Ann Young[4], Mary E. Sharp[3], Charles W. Sr.[2], John Sr.[1]*) was born 25 May 1929 in Lauderdale County, AL, died 19 May 2004, and was buried in Cloverdale COC Cemetery, Lauderdale County, AL.

Josephine married **Hobert Darby**.
3612　M　i.　**Jack Darby.**

Josephine next married **Henry Clinton Sharp**, son of **Columbus Frank Sharp** and **Maggie Stanford**, 17 Jul 1971 in Lauderdale County, AL. Henry was born 25 Jun 1939 in Russell County, Richmond, VA, died 21 Nov 1994, and was buried in Cloverdale COC Cemetery, Lauderdale County, AL.

Josephine next married **Homer Allen Gilchrist**, son of **Christopher Columbus Gilchrist** and **Flora Gillis**. Homer was born 23 Oct 1915 in Wayne County, TN, died 10 Apr 1971, and was buried in Cloverdale COC Cemetery, Lauderdale County, AL.
3613　M　i.　**Ira Joe Darby.**
3614　M　ii.　**Danny Lynn Rainey.**

1800. Margaret Louise Dailey (*Carrie Ann Young[6], Hulet Edward Young[5], Julia Ann Young[4], Mary E. Sharp[3], Charles W. Sr.[2], John Sr.[1]*) was born 10 Dec 1932 in Lauderdale County, AL, died 28 Nov 1995, and was buried in Memorial Cemetery, Savannah, Hardin County, TN.

Margaret married **James Gloyd Gean**, son of **Clifford Dalton Gean** and **Glydia Steely**. James was born 19 Oct 1929 in Lauderdale County, AL, died 9 Mar 1999, and was buried in Memorial Cemetery, Savannah, Hardin County, TN.
+　3615　M　i.　**James Rickey Gean** was born 25 Sep 1945 in Hardin County, TN.
+　3616　M　ii.　**Dannie Lee Gean** was born 18 Sep 1950 in Hardin County, TN.
+　3617　M　iii.　**Thomas Steven Gean** was born 16 Oct 1952 in Hardin County, TN.
+　3618　M　iv.　**Donnie Lynn Gean** was born 22 Mar 1954 in Hardin County, TN.
+　3619　M　v.　**Raymond Dale Gean** was born 13 Sep 1955 in Hardin County, TN.
+　3620　M　vi.　**Mackie Alan Gean** was born 12 Nov 1956 in Hardin County, TN.

1801. William Turner Dailey Jr. (*Carrie Ann Young[6], Hulet Edward Young[5], Julia Ann Young[4], Mary E. Sharp[3], Charles W. Sr.[2], John Sr.[1]*) was born 25 Jan 1939 in Lauderdale County, AL, died 24 Apr 2008, and was buried in Cloverdale COC Cemetery, Lauderdale County, AL.

William married **Margaret Ellen Murphy**, daughter of **Elbert Murphy** and **Cora Sego**, 21 Jul 1957 in Lauderdale County, AL. Margaret was born 22 Jan 1939 in Lauderdale County, AL.
+　3621　M　i.　**Jeffery Lynn Dailey Sr.** was born 13 Jul 1960 in Lauderdale County, AL.
+　3622　F　ii.　**Kimberly Diane Dailey** was born 30 Aug 1966 in Lauderdale County, AL.

1804. James Leon Balentine (*Myrtle Lena Young[6], Hulet Edward Young[5], Julia Ann Young[4], Mary E. Sharp[3], Charles W. Sr.[2], John Sr.[1]*) was born 26 Apr 1940 in Lauderdale County, AL, died 31 Aug 2004, and was buried in Greenview Memorial Park, Florence, Lauderdale County, AL.

James married **Darl-Lynne Jilinski**.
+　3623　M　i.　**Duane Balentine.**
　　3624　M　ii.　**Douglas Balentine.**
+　3625　F　iii.　**Deborah Balentine.**

1807. Dorothy (Dot) Gloria Balentine (*Myrtle Lena Young[6], Hulet Edward Young[5], Julia Ann Young[4], Mary E. Sharp[3], Charles W. Sr.[2], John Sr.[1]*) was born 21 Apr 1945 in Lauderdale County, AL.

Dorothy married **Edgar M. Green Jr.**, son of **Edgar M. Green Sr.** and **Annie Terry**, 6 Nov 1964 in Lauderdale County, AL. Edgar was born 23 Jan 1934 in Hardin County, TN.
+　3626　M　i.　**Barry Green.**
+　3627　M　ii.　**Tim Green.**
+　3628　M　iii.　**Donald Green.**
+　3629　M　iv.　**Michael Green.**

1808. Janice June Balentine (*Myrtle Lena Young*⁶, *Hulet Edward Young*⁵, *Julia Ann Young*⁴, *Mary E. Sharp*³, *Charles W. Sr.*², *John Sr.*¹) was born 17 Jun 1947 in Lauderdale County, AL.

Janice married **Jimmy Dale Holt**, son of **Basil Donald Holt** and **Bertha Guyse**, 27 Jun 1964 in Lauderdale County, AL. Jimmy was born 22 Oct 1940 in Lauderdale County, AL.
+ 3630 M i. **Brian Keith Holt** was born 21 Mar 1968 in Lauderdale County, AL.
+ 3631 M ii. **Bradly Kane Holt** was born 30 Oct 1969 in Lauderdale County, AL.
+ 3632 M iii. **Bart Kenneth Holt** was born 13 Jul 1974 in Lauderdale County, AL.

1809. Boyce Edward Young (*Arnold Edward (Ed) Young*⁶, *Hulet Edward Young*⁵, *Julia Ann Young*⁴, *Mary E. Sharp*³, *Charles W. Sr.*², *John Sr.*¹) was born 21 Oct 1936 in Lauderdale County, AL.

Boyce married **Peggy Ann Ticer**, daughter of **David (Dave) Washington Ticer** and **Erma Lillian Smith**, 2 Dec 1958 in Lauderdale County, AL. Peggy was born 7 Dec 1938 in Lauderdale County, AL.
(Duplicate Line. See Person 1225)

1811. Polly Ann Witt (*Bertha Young*⁶, *Hulet Edward Young*⁵, *Julia Ann Young*⁴, *Mary E. Sharp*³, *Charles W. Sr.*², *John Sr.*¹) was born 4 Sep 1940 in Lauderdale County, AL, died 13 Aug 1992, and was buried in Murphy's Chapel Cemetery, Lauderdale County, AL.

Polly married **Rufus Eldred Sharp**, son of **Loye Arvel Sharp** and **Pearlie Mae Wood**, 29 Jan 1956 in Iuka, Tishomingo County, MS. Rufus was born 3 Oct 1936 in Gravely Springs, Lauderdale County, AL.
(Duplicate Line. See Person 1568)

1814. Randy Harris White (*Rachel Nell Young*⁶, *Hulet Edward Young*⁵, *Julia Ann Young*⁴, *Mary E. Sharp*³, *Charles W. Sr.*², *John Sr.*¹) was born 3 Jul 1953 in Lauderdale County, AL.

Randy married **Patricia Ann McGee**, daughter of **Harland McGee** and **Annie Ruth Creasy**, 29 Oct 1971 in Lauderdale County, AL. Patricia was born 10 Jan 1955 in Lauderdale County, AL.
3633 M i. **Brandon Lee White** was born 4 Jan 1978 in Lauderdale County, AL.

Randy next married **Elaine Goss**, daughter of **Eddie F. Goss** and **Jessie Clara Sledge**, 14 Jun 1990 in Lauderdale County, AL. Elaine was born 16 Jan 1946.

1815. Robbie White (*Rachel Nell Young*⁶, *Hulet Edward Young*⁵, *Julia Ann Young*⁴, *Mary E. Sharp*³, *Charles W. Sr.*², *John Sr.*¹).

Robbie married **Richard Wylie**.
3634 F i. **Robyn Wylie**.
3635 F ii. **Beth Wylie**.

1816. Nancy White (*Rachel Nell Young*⁶, *Hulet Edward Young*⁵, *Julia Ann Young*⁴, *Mary E. Sharp*³, *Charles W. Sr.*², *John Sr.*¹).

Nancy married ***Unk Thornton**.
3636 M i. **Blair Thornton**.

1817. Larry Joe Young (*Joe L. Young*⁶, *Hulet Edward Young*⁵, *Julia Ann Young*⁴, *Mary E. Sharp*³, *Charles W. Sr.*², *John Sr.*¹) was born 26 Jan 1951 in Lauderdale County, AL.

Larry married **Theresa Lynn Hayes**, daughter of **Fred Joel Hayes** and **Pauline Irons**, 13 Mar 1971 in Lauderdale County, AL. Theresa was born 30 Sep 1951 in Lauderdale County, AL.
+ 3637 F i. **Millicent (Millie) Lynn Young** was born 16 Sep 1973 in Lauderdale County, AL.
+ 3638 M ii. **Whitley Joel Young** was born 27 May 1977 in Lauderdale County, AL.

1818. Ronnie Dale Young (*Joe L. Young*⁶, *Hulet Edward Young*⁵, *Julia Ann Young*⁴, *Mary E. Sharp*³, *Charles W. Sr.*², *John Sr.*¹) was born 24 May 1953 in Lauderdale County, AL.

Ronnie married **Connie Marie Killin**, daughter of **Odas Killin** and **Francis Springer**, 2 Sep 1978 in Lauderdale County, AL. Connie was born 18 Oct 1957 in Lauderdale County, AL.

+ 3639 F   i.   **Chasity Dawn Young** was born 21 May 1980 in Lauderdale County, AL.

  3640 M   ii.   **Dusty Joe Young** was born 17 Apr 1984 in Lauderdale County, AL.

1819. Deborah Young (*Grady L. Young*^{6}, *Hulet Edward Young*^{5}, *Julia Ann Young*^{4}, *Mary E. Sharp*^{3}, *Charles W. Sr.*^{2}, *John Sr.*^{1}).

Deborah married ***Unk Richards**.

1826. Betsy (Bessie Bob) Anderson (*Virgie Ione Young*^{6}, *Turner Andrew Young*^{5}, *Julia Ann Young*^{4}, *Mary E. Sharp*^{3}, *Charles W. Sr.*^{2}, *John Sr.*^{1}) was born 23 Jan 1934.

Betsy married **Robert Stripling**.

1829. Patricia Carolyn Patrick (*Virgie Ione Young*^{6}, *Turner Andrew Young*^{5}, *Julia Ann Young*^{4}, *Mary E. Sharp*^{3}, *Charles W. Sr.*^{2}, *John Sr.*^{1}) was born 19 Dec 1949 in Lauderdale County, AL.

Patricia married **Stevie Lawrence Wood**, son of **Lawrence (Toby) Eldred Sharp** and **Pauline Inez Wood**, 4 May 1977 in Lauderdale County, AL. Stevie was born 13 Jul 1947 in Florence, Lauderdale County, AL. **(Duplicate Line. See Person 1577)**

1833. Joyce Holt (*Myrtle Mae Young*^{6}, *Turner Andrew Young*^{5}, *Julia Ann Young*^{4}, *Mary E. Sharp*^{3}, *Charles W. Sr.*^{2}, *John Sr.*^{1}).

Joyce married ***Unk Hinson**.

1835. Mary Ann Holt (*Myrtle Mae Young*^{6}, *Turner Andrew Young*^{5}, *Julia Ann Young*^{4}, *Mary E. Sharp*^{3}, *Charles W. Sr.*^{2}, *John Sr.*^{1}).

Mary married ***Unk Wisdom**.

1836. Nancy Holt (*Myrtle Mae Young*^{6}, *Turner Andrew Young*^{5}, *Julia Ann Young*^{4}, *Mary E. Sharp*^{3}, *Charles W. Sr.*^{2}, *John Sr.*^{1}).

Nancy married **Harold Stanfield**.

+ 3641 M   i.   **Michael Harold Stanfield Sr.**

+ 3642 M   ii.   **Stacy Shawn Stanfield.**

+ 3643 F   iii.   **Angela Michelle Stanfield** was born in 1968 in Lauderdale County, AL and died 14 Sep 2006 in Lauderdale County, AL.

1837. Bobbie Holt (*Myrtle Mae Young*^{6}, *Turner Andrew Young*^{5}, *Julia Ann Young*^{4}, *Mary E. Sharp*^{3}, *Charles W. Sr.*^{2}, *John Sr.*^{1}).

Bobbie married ***Unk Brogden**.

1839. Penny Holt (*Myrtle Mae Young*^{6}, *Turner Andrew Young*^{5}, *Julia Ann Young*^{4}, *Mary E. Sharp*^{3}, *Charles W. Sr.*^{2}, *John Sr.*^{1}).

Penny married ***Unk Phillips**.

1840. Joe Benny Cooper (*Gladys Lee Young*^{6}, *Turner Andrew Young*^{5}, *Julia Ann Young*^{4}, *Mary E. Sharp*^{3}, *Charles W. Sr.*^{2}, *John Sr.*^{1}) was born in 1940 in Lauderdale County, AL.

Joe married **Jane Scott**.

+ 3644 F   i.   **Terri Kay Cooper** was born in 1963.

+ 3645 M   ii.   **Michael Joe Cooper** was born in 1965.

1841. James Steven (Steve) Cooper (*Gladys Lee Young[6], Turner Andrew Young[5], Julia Ann Young[4], Mary E. Sharp[3], Charles W. Sr.[2], John Sr.[1]*) was born 4 Jul 1951 in Lauderdale County, AL.

James married **Jancie Kay (Peggy) Wesson**, daughter of **Thomas Wesson** and **Virgie Horton**, 12 Mar 1973 in Lauderdale County, AL. Jancie was born 4 Mar 1955 in Lauderdale County, AL.
+ 3646 M   i.   **Joshua Steven Cooper** was born 12 Jan 1976 in Lauderdale County, AL.
+ 3647 M   ii.   **Zachary Ryan Cooper** was born 4 Jan 1980 in Lauderdale County, AL.

1842. Donny Joe Young (*Noah Sewell Young[6], Turner Andrew Young[5], Julia Ann Young[4], Mary E. Sharp[3], Charles W. Sr.[2], John Sr.[1]*).

Donny married **Linda *Unk**.
3648 M   i.   **Dustin Young**.

1848. Charles Dennis Miles (*Clara Belle Young[6], Cleave Homer Young[5], Julia Ann Young[4], Mary E. Sharp[3], Charles W. Sr.[2], John Sr.[1]*) was born 10 Apr 1941 in Indiana and died 29 Aug 2005 in Muncie, Delaware County, IN.

Charles married **Cathy Pruitt** in Indiana. Cathy was born 19 Apr 1948.
+ 3649 M   i.   **Brett Allen Miles Sr.** was born 19 Nov 1967 in Indiana.
+ 3650 F   ii.   **Denise Renae Miles** was born 21 Dec 1971 in Indiana.

1849. Mary Francis Miles (*Clara Belle Young[6], Cleave Homer Young[5], Julia Ann Young[4], Mary E. Sharp[3], Charles W. Sr.[2], John Sr.[1]*) was born 21 Apr 1943 in Indiana.

Mary married ***Unk Hatfield**.
+ 3651 F   i.   **Shawna Kay Hatfield**.

1850. Billy Ray Miles (*Clara Belle Young[6], Cleave Homer Young[5], Julia Ann Young[4], Mary E. Sharp[3], Charles W. Sr.[2], John Sr.[1]*) was born 12 Feb 1948 in Indiana.

Billy married **Elizabeth Jean Corell**. Elizabeth was born 30 Apr 1953.
3652 M   i.   **Joshua Aaron Miles** was born 18 Nov 1976 in Indiana.
3653 F   ii.   **Hannah Elizabeth Miles** was born 3 Mar 1985 in Indiana.
3654 M   iii.   **Lucas John Miles** was born 3 Nov 1989 in Indiana.

1851. Sandra Kay Miles (*Clara Belle Young[6], Cleave Homer Young[5], Julia Ann Young[4], Mary E. Sharp[3], Charles W. Sr.[2], John Sr.[1]*) was born 22 Oct 1949 in California.

Sandra married ***Unk Martin**.
3655 M   i.   **Dax Cannon Martin** was born 5 Jan 1971.
3656 M   ii.   **Nicholas John Martin** was born 6 May 1973.

1852. Bonnie Fay Miles (*Clara Belle Young[6], Cleave Homer Young[5], Julia Ann Young[4], Mary E. Sharp[3], Charles W. Sr.[2], John Sr.[1]*) was born 19 Dec 1952 in California.

Bonnie married **John David Kamp**. John was born in 1953.
3657 F   i.   **Gretchen Ann Kamp** was born 8 Nov 1987.

1855. Melissa Young (*Larry Joe Young[6], Cleave Homer Young[5], Julia Ann Young[4], Mary E. Sharp[3], Charles W. Sr.[2], John Sr.[1]*).

Melissa married ***Unk Aidgard**.

1856. Michael Young Sr. (*Kerry W. Young*[6], *Wheeler Young*[5], *Julia Ann Young*[4], *Mary E. Sharp*[3], *Charles W. Sr.*[2], *John Sr.*[1]).

    Michael married **Carol Delee**.
+ 3658 M   i.   **Michael Young Jr.**
  3659 F   ii.   **Tammy Young**.

1857. Ronald Young (*Kerry W. Young*[6], *Wheeler Young*[5], *Julia Ann Young*[4], *Mary E. Sharp*[3], *Charles W. Sr.*[2], *John Sr.*[1]) was born 18 Jul 1946 in Mishawaka, St Joseph County, IN and died 13 May 1992 in Mishawaka, St Joseph County, IN.

    Ronald married **Pat Kanouse** 5 Jun 1971 in St. Joseph County, IN. Pat was born in 1948.
  3660 M   i.   **Christopher Young**.
  3661 M   ii.   **Mark Young** was born in 1973.
  3662 M   iii. **Matthew Young** was born in 1973.

1859. Daniel Oneal Stutts Jr. (*Daniel Oneal Stutts Sr.*[6], *Mollie Jo Sharp*[5], *Berry Nolan*[4], *Joseph (Joe)*[3], *Charles W. Sr.*[2], *John Sr.*[1]) was born 17 Jan 1934 in Colbert County, AL.

    Daniel married **Dara Mae Willis** 20 Apr 1968 in Colbert County, AL.

1860. Dolly Jane Stutts (*Daniel Oneal Stutts Sr.*[6], *Mollie Jo Sharp*[5], *Berry Nolan*[4], *Joseph (Joe)*[3], *Charles W. Sr.*[2], *John Sr.*[1]) was born 21 Apr 1936 in Colbert County, AL.

    Dolly married **James Curtis Gargis**, son of **Parke Gargis** and **Ludie B. Myhan**, 18 Dec 1953 in Colbert County, AL. James was born 7 Jul 1931 in Colbert County, AL.

1861. James Alvin Sharp Sr. (*James Wesley*[6], *James David*[5], *Berry Nolan*[4], *Joseph (Joe)*[3], *Charles W. Sr.*[2], *John Sr.*[1]) was born 27 Apr 1948 in Lauderdale County, AL.

    James married **Claudia Ann Flaherty**, daughter of **William Henry Flaherty** and **Mary Francis Hill**, 5 May 1972 in Lauderdale County, AL. Claudia was born 6 Jun 1949 in Lauderdale County, AL.
  3663 M   i.   **James Alvin Sharp Jr.** was born 19 Feb 1975 in Scottsboro, AL.
  3664 F   ii.   **Amy Francis Sharp** was born 28 May 1977 in Scottsboro, AL.

1862. Wanda Marie Sharp (*James Wesley*[6], *James David*[5], *Berry Nolan*[4], *Joseph (Joe)*[3], *Charles W. Sr.*[2], *John Sr.*[1]) was born 11 Aug 1949 in Lauderdale County, AL.

    Wanda married **James Larry Kiser**, son of **David Lamar Kiser** and **Mary Denise Chamers**, 7 Jul 1972 in Lauderdale County, AL. James was born 10 Oct 1949 in Colbert County, AL.
  3665 M   i.   **Jason Larry Kiser** was born 13 Sep 1976 in Colbert County, AL.
+ 3666 F   ii.   **Jamie Marie Kiser** was born 11 Oct 1977 in Colbert County, AL.
  3667 F   iii. **Jennifer Wanda Kiser** was born 16 Mar 1980 in Colbert County, AL.

1863. Roger Wayne Sharp (*James Wesley*[6], *James David*[5], *Berry Nolan*[4], *Joseph (Joe)*[3], *Charles W. Sr.*[2], *John Sr.*[1]) was born 19 Nov 1951 in Lauderdale County, AL.

    Roger married **Paula Jane Shippey**, daughter of **David J. Shippey** and **Claudell *Unk**, 11 Jul 1981 in Huntsville, Madison County, AL. Paula was born 2 Mar 1954 in Huntsville, Madison County, AL.

1864. Sandra Louise Sharp (*James Wesley*[6], *James David*[5], *Berry Nolan*[4], *Joseph (Joe)*[3], *Charles W. Sr.*[2], *John Sr.*[1]) was born 11 Sep 1953 in Lauderdale County, AL.

    Sandra married **Cecil T. Pounders Jr.**, son of **Cecil T. Pounders Sr.** and **Frances Headley**, 10 Jun 1978 in Lauderdale County, AL. Cecil was born 10 Dec 1950 in Red Bay, Franklin County, AL.
  3668 M   i.   **Ilex Cecil Pounders** was born 29 Jun 1983 in Decatur, Morgan County, AL.
  3669 F   ii.   **Holley Rose Pounders** was born 25 Sep 1985 in Decatur, Morgan County, AL.

1865. Albert Leon Sharp (*James Wesley* [6], *James David* [5], *Berry Nolan* [4], *Joseph (Joe)* [3], *Charles W. Sr.* [2], *John Sr.* [1]) was born 11 Sep 1955 in Lauderdale County, AL.

Albert married **Connie Elizabeth Harlan**, daughter of **Thomas Leon Harlan** and **Maxine Cox**, 1 May 1981 in Lauderdale County, AL. Connie was born 25 Nov 1952 in Lauderdale County, AL.

+ 3670   M   i.   **Wesley Leon Sharp** was born 6 Feb 1984 in Lauderdale County, AL.
   3671   M   ii.   **William Daniel Sharp** was born 15 Jan 1987 in Lauderdale County, AL.

1866. David Lynn Sharp (*Clyde Joel (Link)* [6], *James David* [5], *Berry Nolan* [4], *Joseph (Joe)* [3], *Charles W. Sr.* [2], *John Sr.* [1]) was born 18 Mar 1941 in Lauderdale County, AL.

David married **Deloris Marilyn Taylor**, daughter of **Marion Albert Taylor** and **Mary Francis Graves**, 15 Jul 1963 in Lauderdale County, AL. Deloris was born 14 Dec 1946 in Lauderdale County, AL.

+ 3672   M   i.   **Timothy Lynn Sharp** was born 13 Jun 1966 in Lauderdale County, AL.

1867. Robert Owen Sharp (*Clyde Joel (Link)* [6], *James David* [5], *Berry Nolan* [4], *Joseph (Joe)* [3], *Charles W. Sr.* [2], *John Sr.* [1]) was born 14 Feb 1942 in Lauderdale County, AL.

Robert married **Linda Askew**.

   3673   M   i.   **Shannon Sharp**.

1868. James Kenneth Sharp (*Clyde Joel (Link)* [6], *James David* [5], *Berry Nolan* [4], *Joseph (Joe)* [3], *Charles W. Sr.* [2], *John Sr.* [1]) was born 19 Dec 1944 in Lauderdale County, AL.

James married **Wanda Faye Hicks**, daughter of **Dewey Lee Hicks** and **Flora Belle Thompson**, 3 May 1975 in Charlottesville, Albemarle County, VA. Wanda was born 18 Sep 1952 in Whiteville, Columbus County, NC.

1869. Betty Lou Turbyfill (*Velma Nadine Sharp* [6], *James David* [5], *Berry Nolan* [4], *Joseph (Joe)* [3], *Charles W. Sr.* [2], *John Sr.* [1]) was born 16 Dec 1941 in Russellville, Franklin County, AL.

Betty married **Dudley Guy Elmore II**, son of **Dudley Guy Elmore I** and ***Unk**, in Maryland. Dudley was born 3 Jun 1936 in Indiana.

+ 3674   F   i.   **Tina Marie Elmore** was born 31 Oct 1959 in Ft Meade, MD.
+ 3675   M   ii.   **Dudley Guy Elmore III** was born 28 Dec 1960 in Camp Fujinobi, Japan.

1870. Donald Eugene Turbyfill (*Velma Nadine Sharp* [6], *James David* [5], *Berry Nolan* [4], *Joseph (Joe)* [3], *Charles W. Sr.* [2], *John Sr.* [1]) was born 26 Sep 1943 in Lauderdale County, AL.

Donald married **Wanda Sue Prichard** 31 May 1965 in Texarkana, Bowie County, TX. Wanda was born 1 Feb 1947 in Little Rock, Saline County, AR.

+ 3676   F   i.   **Margo Luree Turbyfill** was born 17 May 1966 in Beale AFB, Yuba County, CA.
   3677   M   ii.   **Daniel Eugene Turbyfill** was born 3 Oct 1972 in Airforce Academy, Denver, CO.

1871. Clara Dean Turbyfill (*Velma Nadine Sharp* [6], *James David* [5], *Berry Nolan* [4], *Joseph (Joe)* [3], *Charles W. Sr.* [2], *John Sr.* [1]) was born 3 Apr 1944 in Lauderdale County, AL.

Clara married **Larry Lester Johnston**, son of **Lester Lee Johnston Sr.** and **Delphia Alice Hellums**, in Lauderdale County, AL.

+ 3678   M   i.   **Bradley Scott Johnston** was born 14 Oct 1964 in Florence, Lauderdale County, AL.
   3679   M   ii.   **William Joel Johnston** was born 16 Dec 1967.
+ 3680   F   iii.   **Angela Michelle Johnston** was born 19 Feb 1970.

1872. Thomas (Tommy) Ray Turbyfill (*Velma Nadine Sharp* [6], *James David* [5], *Berry Nolan* [4], *Joseph (Joe)* [3], *Charles W. Sr.* [2], *John Sr.* [1]) was born 14 Sep 1947 in Lauderdale County, AL.

Thomas married **Kathy Lou Grigsby**, daughter of **William Lloyd Grigsby** and **Frankie Mae Ross**, 30 Jan 1970 in Lauderdale County, AL. Kathy was born 19 Sep 1950 in Lauderdale County, AL.

+ 3681 F   i.   **Heather Nicole Turbyfill** was born 26 Oct 1973 in Lauderdale County, AL.

1873. Charles Robert Turbyfill (*Velma Nadine Sharp*[6], *James David*[5], *Berry Nolan*[4], *Joseph (Joe)*[3], *Charles W. Sr.*[2], *John Sr.*[1]) was born 18 Jun 1949 in Lauderdale County, AL, died 25 Oct 2000, and was buried in Stoney Point Cemetery, Lauderdale County, AL.

Charles married **Sandra Nadine Lewis**, daughter of **Charles E. Lewis** and **Edith L. Mays**, 25 Dec 1970 in Lauderdale County, AL. Sandra was born 1 Nov 1952 in Lauderdale County, AL.

+ 3682 M   i.   **Christopher Lee Turbyfill** was born 8 Sep 1972 in Lauderdale County, AL.
   3683 M   ii.   **Shannon Lewis Turbyfill** was born 11 Sep 1974 in Lauderdale County, AL.

Charles next married **Martina Ann Faulkner**, daughter of **Jimmy Daniel Faulkner** and **Eva Leigh South**, 15 Jun 1987 in Lauderdale County, AL. Martina was born 23 Aug 1961 in Lauderdale County, AL.

   3684 M   i.   **Robert Dustin Turbyfill** was born 2 Jan 1989 in Lauderdale County, AL.

1874. Mary Nell Turbyfill (*Velma Nadine Sharp*[6], *James David*[5], *Berry Nolan*[4], *Joseph (Joe)*[3], *Charles W. Sr.*[2], *John Sr.*[1]) was born 17 Mar 1951 in Lauderdale County, AL.

Mary married **Jerry Dennis Hall**, son of **L. E. Hall** and **Avie Lona Gladney**, 29 May 1971 in Lauderdale County, AL. Jerry was born 19 Mar 1951 in Colbert County, AL.

   3685 F   i.   **Dana Maria Hall** was born 11 Mar 1976 in Clarksville, Montgomery County, TN.
   3686 F   ii.   **Amy Denise Hall** was born 19 Apr 1978 in Hattiesburg, Perry County, MS.

Mary next married **Dan Clement**.

1875. Jerry Lynn Turbyfill (*Velma Nadine Sharp*[6], *James David*[5], *Berry Nolan*[4], *Joseph (Joe)*[3], *Charles W. Sr.*[2], *John Sr.*[1]) was born 6 Jan 1953 in Lauderdale County, AL, died 15 Aug 2003 in Shreveport, LA, and was buried in Stoney Point Cemetery, Lauderdale County, AL.

Jerry married **Shelia Ann Brown**, daughter of **Charles E. Brown** and **Christine Thornton**, 31 Aug 1974 in Lauderdale County, AL. Shelia was born 16 Dec 1956 in Lauderdale County, AL.

+ 3687 F   i.   **Christy Ann Turbyfill** was born 14 Sep 1975 in Lauderdale County, AL.
   3688 M   ii.   **Jayson Lynn Turbyfill** was born 12 Oct 1979 in Lauderdale County, AL.

1879. Paul Edward Sharp Jr. (*Paul Edward Sr.*[6], *James David*[5], *Berry Nolan*[4], *Joseph (Joe)*[3], *Charles W. Sr.*[2], *John Sr.*[1]) was born 10 Sep 1958 in Lauderdale County, AL.

Paul married **Phyllis *Unk**.

1880. James Briggs Sharp (*Paul Edward Sr.*[6], *James David*[5], *Berry Nolan*[4], *Joseph (Joe)*[3], *Charles W. Sr.*[2], *John Sr.*[1]) was born 9 Dec 1963 in Lauderdale County, AL.

James married **Jody Baptist**, daughter of **Dwight Baptist** and **Bette Leckrooe**, 27 Jul 1987 in Birmingham, Jefferson County, AL. Jody was born 27 Jul 1963 in Springfield, Morgan County, IL.

   3689 M   i.   **Carter Briggs Sharp** was born 1 Jun 1992 in Birmingham, Jefferson County, AL.

James next married **Kerry Ann McCarley**, daughter of **Thomas Jackson (Jack) McCarley** and **Mary Virginia Givens**, 27 Sep 1997 in Birmingham, Jefferson County, AL. Kerry was born 15 Jun 1961 in Lauderdale County, AL.

   3690 F   i.   **Carley Ann Sharp** was born 19 Jun 2000 in Birmingham, Jefferson County, AL.

1884. Robert Steven Lansdell (*Kathryn Etoil Sharp*[6], *James David*[5], *Berry Nolan*[4], *Joseph (Joe)*[3], *Charles W. Sr.*[2], *John Sr.*[1]) was born 17 Mar 1953 in Lauderdale County, AL.

Robert married **Nancy King Townsend**, daughter of **Williard Townsend** and **Ina Maye King**, 5 Apr 1982 in Memphis, Shelby County, TN. Nancy was born 20 Feb 1956 in Lauderdale County, AL.

3691 F i. **Caroline Diana Lansdell** was born 3 Jan 1983 in Nashville, Davidson County, TN.

3692 M ii. **Jason Robert King Lansdell** was born 14 Feb 1985 in Nashville, Davidson County, TN.

1885. Michael Lee Lansdell (*Kathryn Etoil Sharp* [6], *James David* [5], *Berry Nolan* [4], *Joseph (Joe)* [3], *Charles W. Sr.* [2], *John Sr.* [1]) was born 3 Jul 1956 in Lauderdale County, AL.

Michael married **Lynne Carol Bishop**, daughter of **James O. Bishop** and **Doris Isbell**, 16 Aug 1986 in Colbert County, AL. Lynne was born 29 Jun 1957 in Leighton, Colbert County, AL.

3693 F i. **Emily Beth Lansdell** was born 29 Jul 1989 in Birmingham, Jefferson County, AL.

3694 M ii. **Andrew Michael Lansdell** was born 14 Jul 1992 in Birmingham, Jefferson County, AL.

1886. Kathy Diane Lansdell (*Kathryn Etoil Sharp* [6], *James David* [5], *Berry Nolan* [4], *Joseph (Joe)* [3], *Charles W. Sr.* [2], *John Sr.* [1]) was born 15 Dec 1958 in Lauderdale County, AL.

Kathy married **Scott Edward Ludwig**, son of **David W. Ludwig** and **Kathryn Scofield**, 28 May 1993 in Lauderdale County, AL. Scott was born 9 Mar 1958 in Pittsburg, PA.

3695 M i. **Charles (Chase) Robert Ludwig** was born 15 Nov 1989 in Huntsville, Madison County, AL.

1887. James Riley Wilkes (*James Chambers Wilkes* [6], *Eula Elizabeth Sharp* [5], *Berry Nolan* [4], *Joseph (Joe)* [3], *Charles W. Sr.* [2], *John Sr.* [1]) was born 20 Jan 1930 in Colbert County, AL.

James married **Thelma Janice DeLony**, daughter of **Preston DeLony** and **Laura Hurley**, 30 May 1950 in Iuka, Tishomingo County, MS. Thelma was born 12 Jan 1932 in Colbert County, AL, died 19 Sep 1994, and was buried in Colbert Memorial Gardens, Colbert County, AL.

+ 3696 F i. **Laura Kaye Wilkes** was born 25 Feb 1952 in Colbert County, AL.

1888. Shirley Jean Wilkes (*James Chambers Wilkes* [6], *Eula Elizabeth Sharp* [5], *Berry Nolan* [4], *Joseph (Joe)* [3], *Charles W. Sr.* [2], *John Sr.* [1]) was born 1 Sep 1935 in Colbert County, AL.

Shirley married **Darwall Denton White**, son of **Claude White** and **Jewell Ayers**, 8 Mar 1951 in Iuka, Tishomingo County, MS. Darwall was born 16 Mar 1934 in Lawrence County, AL.

+ 3697 M i. **Darwall James White I** was born 17 Jan 1952 in Lauderdale County, AL.

3698 M ii. **Claudie Benton White** was born 1 Aug 1957, died in 1989, and was buried in Colbert Memorial Gardens, Colbert County, AL.

3699 M iii. **Michael Shane White** was born 2 Mar 1961 in Colbert County, AL, died 27 May 1982, and was buried in Colbert Memorial Gardens, Colbert County, AL.

1890. Annie Mae Wilkes (*Elting Wilkes* [6], *Eula Elizabeth Sharp* [5], *Berry Nolan* [4], *Joseph (Joe)* [3], *Charles W. Sr.* [2], *John Sr.* [1]) was born 23 Feb 1934 in Lauderdale County, AL.

Annie married **Joe Dewitt Jennings**. Joe was born 22 Sep 1931.

+ 3700 M i. **Gary Dewitt Jennings** was born 17 May 1957.

+ 3701 M ii. **Joe Keith Jennings** was born 25 Sep 1962.

1891. Jimmy Carroll Wilkes (*Elting Wilkes* [6], *Eula Elizabeth Sharp* [5], *Berry Nolan* [4], *Joseph (Joe)* [3], *Charles W. Sr.* [2], *John Sr.* [1]) was born 25 Oct 1938 in Lauderdale County, AL.

Jimmy married **Rebecca Johnson**. Rebecca was born 13 May 1938.

+ 3702 M i. **Jeffrey Bruce Wilkes** was born 26 Dec 1961.

+ 3703 M ii. **Jimmy Kevin Wilkes** was born 31 Aug 1964.

1892. Patsy Lee Wilkes (*Elting Wilkes* [6], *Eula Elizabeth Sharp* [5], *Berry Nolan* [4], *Joseph (Joe)* [3], *Charles W. Sr.* [2], *John Sr.* [1]) was born 30 Apr 1944 in Lauderdale County, AL.

Patsy married **Jerry Dee Thompson**, son of **Sheilds Thompson** and **Ida Jane Rich**, 15 Sep 1962 in Lauderdale County, AL. Jerry was born 10 Dec 1942 in Wayne County, TN.

+ 3704 F i. **Kathy Lynn Thompson** was born 10 Dec 1963.

3705 F ii. **Kimberly Ann Thompson** was born 6 Oct 1966, died 6 Oct 1966, and was buried in Stoney Point Cemetery, Lauderdale County, AL.

+ 3706 M iii. **Brian Lee Thompson** was born 19 Nov 1968.

1893. Joe Wheeler Wilkes (*Elting Wilkes*^{6}, *Eula Elizabeth Sharp*^{5}, *Berry Nolan*^{4}, *Joseph (Joe)*^{3}, *Charles W. Sr.*^{2}, *John Sr.*^{1}) was born 29 Jan 1949 in Lauderdale County, AL.

Joe married **Dawn Alicia Nicholson**. Dawn was born 5 May 1953.

+ 3707 M i. **Anthony Charles Wilkes** was born 20 Nov 1976.

+ 3708 F ii. **Nicole Elizabeth Wilkes** was born 29 Apr 1979.

3709 M iii. **Nathan Elting Wilkes** was born 4 Aug 1980.

1894. Aubrey Neal Wilkes (*Levi (Lee) Grant Wilkes II*^{6}, *Eula Elizabeth Sharp*^{5}, *Berry Nolan*^{4}, *Joseph (Joe)*^{3}, *Charles W. Sr.*^{2}, *John Sr.*^{1}) was born 2 Oct 1938 in Lauderdale County, AL.

Aubrey married **Jennie Faye Aday**, daughter of **Herbert Aday** and **Carrie Mae Nichols**, 13 Apr 1963 in Lauderdale County, AL. Jennie was born 7 Apr 1947 in Colbert County, AL.

3710 M i. **Ross Phillip Wilkes** was born 7 May 1970 in Colbert County, AL.

3711 F ii. **Mandy DeAnne Wilkes** was born 19 Nov 1974 in St. Petersburg, FL.

3712 F iii. **Stefane Dawn Wilkes** was born 4 Dec 1991 in Lauderdale County, AL.

1895. Mary Lee Wilkes (*Levi (Lee) Grant Wilkes II*^{6}, *Eula Elizabeth Sharp*^{5}, *Berry Nolan*^{4}, *Joseph (Joe)*^{3}, *Charles W. Sr.*^{2}, *John Sr.*^{1}) was born 18 May 1940 in Lauderdale County, AL.

Mary married **Arthur Calvin Berryman** in 1954 in Iuka, Tishomingo County, MS.

+ 3713 F i. **Paula Louise Berryman** was born 1 Feb 1955 in Colbert County, AL.

Mary next married **James Phillip Nichols**, son of **Marvin Laverne Nichols** and **Edith Irene McAnally**, 13 Apr 1957 in Iuka, Tishomingo County, MS. James was born 1 Feb 1937 in Colbert County, AL.

+ 3714 M i. **Tony Philip Nichols** was born 12 Sep 1957 in Colbert County, AL.

+ 3715 M ii. **Jerome Clay Nichols** was born 26 Oct 1962 in Colbert County, AL.

1896. Levi Grant Wilkes III (*Levi (Lee) Grant Wilkes II*^{6}, *Eula Elizabeth Sharp*^{5}, *Berry Nolan*^{4}, *Joseph (Joe)*^{3}, *Charles W. Sr.*^{2}, *John Sr.*^{1}) was born 4 Jul 1943 in Lauderdale County, AL.

Levi married **Angela Louise Hale**, daughter of **Jospeh Hale** and **Ellene Irene Walker**, 9 Sep 1971 in Colbert County, AL. Angela was born 2 Mar 1947 in Colbert County, AL.

+ 3716 F i. **Debra Lynne Wilkes** was born 23 Dec 1966 in Rapids Parish, LA.

1898. Bonnie Faye Wilkes (*Earl Berry Wilkes*^{6}, *Eula Elizabeth Sharp*^{5}, *Berry Nolan*^{4}, *Joseph (Joe)*^{3}, *Charles W. Sr.*^{2}, *John Sr.*^{1}) was born 6 Jun 1942 in Lauderdale County, AL.

Bonnie married **William David Walker**, son of **Curtis D. Walker** and **Lucille Webb**, 6 Jun 1961 in Lauderdale County, AL. William was born 21 May 1939 in Colbert County, AL.

+ 3717 M i. **Kenneth David Walker** was born 28 Jul 1963.

+ 3718 M ii. **Mark David Walker** was born 7 Aug 1965.

1900. Charles Ashley Wilkes Sr. (*Earl Berry Wilkes*^{6}, *Eula Elizabeth Sharp*^{5}, *Berry Nolan*^{4}, *Joseph (Joe)*^{3}, *Charles W. Sr.*^{2}, *John Sr.*^{1}) was born 3 Nov 1948 in Lauderdale County, AL.

Charles married **Charlotte Ann Hughen**, daughter of **James F. Hughen** and **Callie Nations**, 8 Jun 1974 in Lauderdale County, AL. Charlotte was born 13 Dec 1948 in Montgomery County, AL.

3719 F i. **Callie Ann Wilkes** was born in Hendersonville, TN.

3720 M ii. **Charles Ashley Wilkes Jr.** was born in Hendersonville, TN.

1901. John Jackson Wilkes Sr. (*Rufus Jackson Wilkes*^{6}, *Eula Elizabeth Sharp*^{5}, *Berry Nolan*^{4}, *Joseph (Joe)*^{3}, *Charles W. Sr.*^{2}, *John Sr.*^{1}) was born 10 Oct 1942 in Lauderdale County, AL.

John married **Francis Elizabeth Burns**, daughter of **Ben Turner Burns** and **Pauline (Polly) Vaughn**, 26 Oct 1961 in Lauderdale County, AL. Francis was born 24 Apr 1944 in Lauderdale County, AL.

 3721 M i. **John Jackson Wilkes Jr.** was born 15 Aug 1962 in Lauderdale County, AL.
+ 3722 F ii. **Donna Elizabeth Wilkes** was born 5 May 1964 in Lauderdale County, AL.
+ 3723 F iii. **Paula Christine Wilkes** was born 4 Dec 1965 in Lauderdale County, AL.

John next married **Annie Ruth Forsythe** 26 Jan 1979 in Lauderdale County, AL. Annie was born 4 Oct 1939 in Lauderdale County, AL.

1902. Rufus Grant Wilkes (*Rufus Jackson Wilkes*[6], *Eula Elizabeth Sharp*[5], *Berry Nolan*[4], *Joseph (Joe)*[3], *Charles W. Sr.*[2], *John Sr.*[1]) was born 8 May 1944 in Lauderdale County, AL.

Rufus married **Patricia Kay Johnson**, daughter of **Denny Johnson** and **Francis Rutland**, 6 Feb 1964 in Lauderdale County, AL. Patricia was born 11 Nov 1946 in Lauderdale County, AL, died 28 May 1968, and was buried in Greenview Memorial Park, Florence, Lauderdale County, AL.

 3724 M i. **David Grant Wilkes** was born 26 Oct 1965 in Lauderdale County, AL.

Rufus next married **Patricia Diane Blackstock**, daughter of **Clifford H. Blackstock** and **Dorothy Linville**, 8 Aug 1969 in Lauderdale County, AL.

+ 3725 M i. **Jason McKinley Wilkes** was born 16 Dec 1971 in Lauderdale County, AL.
+ 3726 F ii. **Lya Janeen Wilkes** was born 4 Nov 1972 in Lauderdale County, AL.

1903. Robert Norman Sharp (*Charles Roy*[6], *Charles Robert*[5], *Berry Nolan*[4], *Joseph (Joe)*[3], *Charles W. Sr.*[2], *John Sr.*[1]) was born 23 Feb 1940 in Lauderdale County, AL, died 20 Feb 1988, and was buried in Stoney Point Cemetery, Lauderdale County, AL.

Robert married **Naomi Sue Logan**, daughter of **Maurice Robert Logan** and **Minnie Mae Young**, 9 Aug 1963 in Lauderdale County, AL. Naomi was born 11 Aug 1940 in Lauderdale County, AL.

+ 3727 F i. **Jennifer Suzanne Sharp** was born 17 Oct 1976 in Lauderdale County, AL.
+ 3728 M ii. **Robert Bentley Sharp** was born 29 Sep 1981 in Lauderdale County, AL.

1904. Jerry Clayton Sharp (*Charles Roy*[6], *Charles Robert*[5], *Berry Nolan*[4], *Joseph (Joe)*[3], *Charles W. Sr.*[2], *John Sr.*[1]) was born 31 Jan 1941 in Lauderdale County, AL.

Jerry married **Patricia Ann Lindsey**, daughter of **Edgar Bruce Lindsey** and **Thurza Dean**, 20 Apr 1962 in Lauderdale County, AL. Patricia was born 20 Apr 1944 in Lauderdale County, AL.

 3729 F i. **Katherine Paige Sharp** was born 26 Sep 1965 in Lauderdale County, AL.

1905. Charles Timothy Sharp (*Charles Roy*[6], *Charles Robert*[5], *Berry Nolan*[4], *Joseph (Joe)*[3], *Charles W. Sr.*[2], *John Sr.*[1]) was born 12 Mar 1941 in Lauderdale County, AL.

Charles married **Judy Fanning**, daughter of **Roye Lowe Fanning** and **Ruby Prosser**, 11 Aug 1969 in Lauderdale County, AL. Judy was born 9 Aug 1948 in Madison County, AL.

Charles next married **Patricia Wallace**, daughter of **William Shelby Wallace** and **Roxie Mae Gooch**, 16 Jan 2000 in Lauderdale County, AL. Patricia was born 3 Dec 1946.

1906. Candace Marie Sharp (*Charles Roy*[6], *Charles Robert*[5], *Berry Nolan*[4], *Joseph (Joe)*[3], *Charles W. Sr.*[2], *John Sr.*[1]) was born 5 Jan 1958 in Lauderdale County, AL, died 24 Apr 2004, and was buried in Stoney Point Cemetery, Lauderdale County, AL.

Candace married **Dennis Dale Kelly**, son of **Orbie Oakley Kelly** and **Mary Louise Berry**, 13 Sep 1990 in Lauderdale County, AL. Dennis was born 11 Aug 1953 in Michigan.

1907. Jimmy Howard Dodd (*Elizabeth Sharp*[6], *Charles Robert*[5], *Berry Nolan*[4], *Joseph (Joe)*[3], *Charles W. Sr.*[2], *John Sr.*[1]) was born 2 Jul 1947 in Lauderdale County, AL.

Jimmy married **Alice Faye Montgomery**, daughter of **Herschel Vernon Montgomery** and **Annie Ruth Whitten**, 4 Aug 1967 in Lauderdale County, AL. Alice was born 30 Jul 1947 in Lauderdale County, AL.

+ 3730 M i. **Jody Lynn Dodd** was born 20 Oct 1972 in Lauderdale County, AL.
+ 3731 F ii. **Stacy Michelle Dodd** was born 1 Sep 1975 in Lauderdale County, AL.

1908. Danny Rae Dodd (*Elizabeth Sharp*[6], *Charles Robert*[5], *Berry Nolan*[4], *Joseph (Joe)*[3], *Charles W. Sr.*[2], *John Sr.*[1]) was born 30 Mar 1949 in Lauderdale County, AL.

Danny married **Sheron Kay Huckaba**, daughter of **William B. Huckaba** and **Betty L. Stantz**, 4 Jun 1971 in Lauderdale County, AL. Sheron was born 14 Apr 1951 in Riley County, KS.

3732 M i. **Brandon Shane Dodd** was born 24 Nov 1974 in Lauderdale County, AL.
3733 F ii. **Jill Suzanne Dodd** was born 27 Sep 1976 in Lauderdale County, AL.

Danny next married **Teresa Ann Moore**, daughter of **Bobby Ray Moore** and **Grace Tucker**, 10 Feb 1989 in Gatlinburg, TN. Teresa was born 2 Nov 1952 in Lauderdale County, AL.

1909. Roger Anthony Dodd (*Elizabeth Sharp*[6], *Charles Robert*[5], *Berry Nolan*[4], *Joseph (Joe)*[3], *Charles W. Sr.*[2], *John Sr.*[1]) was born 22 Aug 1954 in Lauderdale County, AL.

Roger married **Debbie Lee Butler**, daughter of **Elvin Butler** and **Erma Ruth Balentine**, 18 Jan 1974 in Lauderdale County, AL. Debbie was born 23 Aug 1955 in Lauderdale County, AL.

3734 F i. **Christine (Christa) Lee Dodd** was born 27 Jul 1974 in Lauderdale County, AL.
+ 3735 F ii. **Kathy Lynn Dodd** was born 3 Jul 1976 in Lauderdale County, AL.
3736 F iii. **Karen Elizabeth Dodd** was born 2 Apr 1978 in Lauderdale County, AL.

1910. Robert (Bobby) Michael Sharp (*Berry Robert*[6], *Charles Robert*[5], *Berry Nolan*[4], *Joseph (Joe)*[3], *Charles W. Sr.*[2], *John Sr.*[1]) was born 25 Oct 1955 in Lauderdale County, AL.

Robert married **Patricia Lynn Helton**, daughter of **Leonard David Helton** and **Wanda Ealine Beavers**, 22 Dec 1977 in Lauderdale County, AL. Patricia was born 20 Aug 1960 in Lauderdale County, AL.

3737 M i. **Michael Daniel Sharp** was born 18 Jun 1985 in Lauderdale County, AL.
3738 M ii. **Adam Tyler Sharp** was born 29 Sep 1989 in Lauderdale County, AL.

1911. Johnny Phillip Sharp (*Berry Robert*[6], *Charles Robert*[5], *Berry Nolan*[4], *Joseph (Joe)*[3], *Charles W. Sr.*[2], *John Sr.*[1]) was born 13 Feb 1959 in Lauderdale County, AL.

Johnny married **Susan Honey**, daughter of **Leonard Honey** and **Helen Askew**, 22 Dec 1984 in Colbert County, AL. Susan was born 1 Dec 1957 in Colbert County, AL.

3739 M i. **Joseph Philip Sharp** was born 20 Jun 1985 in Lauderdale County, AL.

Johnny next married **Janice Lanetta Wimpee**, daughter of **Martio Russell Wimpee Sr.** and **Mary Catherine *Unk**, in Lauderdale County, AL. Janice was born 9 May 1964 in Lauderdale County, AL.

3740 F i. **Kayla Michele Wimpee Sharp** was born 9 Mar 1987.
3741 M ii. **Brandon Berry Sharp** was born 14 Nov 1989 in Lauderdale County, AL.

1912. Sandra Dee Gibbs (*Deedie P. Sharp*[6], *Charles Robert*[5], *Berry Nolan*[4], *Joseph (Joe)*[3], *Charles W. Sr.*[2], *John Sr.*[1]) was born 7 Feb 1961 in Murfreesboro, TN.

Sandra married **Mark Anthony Crowden**, son of **Gary William Crowden** and **Mary Sue Reatheford**, 28 Aug 1987 in Lauderdale County, AL. Mark was born 5 Jan 1964 in Lauderdale County, AL.

3742 F i. **Sara Margaret Crowden** was born 28 Mar 1986 in Lauderdale County, AL.
3743 F ii. **Tara Michelle Crowden** was born 5 Dec 1992 in Lauderdale County, AL.

1913. Jeffrey Brown Gibbs (*Deedie P. Sharp*[6], *Charles Robert*[5], *Berry Nolan*[4], *Joseph (Joe)*[3], *Charles W. Sr.*[2], *John Sr.*[1]) was born 25 Sep 1964 in Lauderdale County, AL.

Jeffrey married **Vanessa Diane White**, daughter of **Raymond D. White** and **Margie Talley**, 19 Oct 1985 in Lauderdale County, AL. Vanessa was born 10 Apr 1965 in Lauderdale County, AL.

3744 M   i.   **Jeffrey Todd Gibbs** was born 20 Apr 1986 in Lauderdale County, AL.
3745 F   ii.   **Lindsi Nicole Gibbs** was born 8 Jan 1988 in Lauderdale County, AL.

1914. Charles (Chuck) Ray Sharp (*Billy Eugene*[6], *Charles Robert*[5], *Berry Nolan*[4], *Joseph (Joe)*[3], *Charles W. Sr.*[2], *John Sr.*[1]) was born 5 Sep 1955 in Jefferson County, AL.

Charles married **Sheran Wilkerson**.

1917. Robert Michael Statom (*Ollie Mitchell Statom II*[6], *Lovie Francis Sharp*[5], *Berry Nolan*[4], *Joseph (Joe)*[3], *Charles W. Sr.*[2], *John Sr.*[1]) was born 31 Dec 1949 in Lauderdale County, AL.

Robert married **Rose Marie Booten**, daughter of **George Russell Booten** and **Lola Mildred Lindberg**, 28 Jul 1973 in Tuscan, AZ. Rose was born 24 May 1951 in Tuscan, AZ.
3746 M   i.   **Ryan Michael Statom** was born 8 May 1983 in Tuscan, AZ.
3747 M   ii.   **Jonathan Mark Statom** was born 23 Jan 1987 in Tuscan, AZ.

1918. Martha Ann Statom (*Nolan Sharp Statom*[6], *Muncie Venetta Sharp*[5], *Berry Nolan*[4], *Joseph (Joe)*[3], *Charles W. Sr.*[2], *John Sr.*[1]) was born 18 Jan 1942 in Lauderdale County, AL.

Martha married **James Hamilton (Punkin) Hill**. James died 3 Feb 1998 and was buried in Greenview Memorial Park, Florence, Lauderdale County, AL.

Martha next married **Bobby Joe Stults Sr.**, son of **Raymond Stults** and **Bessie Chambers**, 7 Jul 1967 in Moulton, AL. Bobby was born 2 Feb 1940 in Wayne County, TN, died 9 Jun 1978, and was buried in Greenview Memorial Park, Florence, Lauderdale County, AL.
+ 3748 M   i.   **Bobby Joey Stults Jr.** was born 11 Jan 1968 in Lauderdale County, AL.

1919. Frances Kay Statom (*Nolan Sharp Statom*[6], *Muncie Venetta Sharp*[5], *Berry Nolan*[4], *Joseph (Joe)*[3], *Charles W. Sr.*[2], *John Sr.*[1]) was born 17 Dec 1943 in Lauderdale County, AL.

Frances married **David Lloyd Townsley**, son of **Lloyd Lambert Townsley** and **Dorothy Lucille Brethrick**, 10 Aug 1962 in Lauderdale County, AL. David was born 20 Jul 1942 in Lauderdale County, AL.
+ 3749 F   i.   **Tonith Townsley** was born 19 Mar 1965 in Lauderdale County, AL.
  3750 F   ii.   **Tyra Townsley** was born 20 Mar 1968, died 6 Sep 1975, and was buried in Greenview Memorial Park, Florence, Lauderdale County, AL.
+ 3751 F   iii.   **Trella Townsley** was born 21 Sep 1979 in Lauderdale County, AL.

Frances next married **Bobby Robbins**.

1920. Roy Wade Hodges (*Lois Katherine Statom*[6], *Muncie Venetta Sharp*[5], *Berry Nolan*[4], *Joseph (Joe)*[3], *Charles W. Sr.*[2], *John Sr.*[1]) was born 6 Sep 1940 in Lauderdale County, AL.

Roy married **Pamela Faye Mays**, daughter of **Walter Earl Mays** and **Lucille Warren**, 26 Oct 1958 in Lauderdale County, AL. Pamela was born 10 Feb 1942 in Lauderdale County, AL.
+ 3752 F   i.   **Rhonda Lynn Hodges** was born about 1960.
+ 3753 M   ii.   **Gregory Wade Hodges** was born 11 Feb 1961 in Lauderdale County, AL.
+ 3754 M   iii.   **Victor Wayne Hodges** was born 25 Aug 1968 in Lauderdale County, AL.
  3755 M   iv.   **Walter Warren Hodges**.

Roy next married **Patti Fusrno**.
3756 M   i.   **Glenn Hodges** was born 20 Dec 1972 in California.

1921. Larry Joe Hodges (*Lois Katherine Statom*[6], *Muncie Venetta Sharp*[5], *Berry Nolan*[4], *Joseph (Joe)*[3], *Charles W. Sr.*[2], *John Sr.*[1]) was born 30 Jun 1942 in Lauderdale County, AL.

Larry married **Vonda Lannette Thrasher**, daughter of **Lonnie M. Thrasher** and **Lois M. Berryman**, 23 Oct 1964 in Lauderdale County, AL. Vonda was born 23 Jun 1945 in Lawrence County, AL.
+ 3757 M   i.   **Jody Marion Hodges** was born 4 Oct 1965 in Lauderdale County, AL.

+ 3758   M   ii.   **Jason Larry Hodges** was born 13 Apr 1971 in Lauderdale County, AL.

1922. Johnny Dale Hodges (*Lois Katherine Statom*[6], *Muncie Venetta Sharp*[5], *Berry Nolan*[4], *Joseph (Joe)*[3], *Charles W. Sr.*[2], *John Sr.*[1]) was born 22 Aug 1947 in Lauderdale County, AL.

Johnny married **Beverlia Mavline Davis**, daughter of **Cortez Davis** and **Earline Green**, 1 Aug 1978 in Lauderdale County, AL. Beverlia was born 12 May 1951 in Lauderdale County, AL.

1923. Earl Douglas Zahnd II (*Hilda Mae Statom*[6], *Muncie Venetta Sharp*[5], *Berry Nolan*[4], *Joseph (Joe)*[3], *Charles W. Sr.*[2], *John Sr.*[1]) was born 26 Jul 1943 in Lauderdale County, AL, died 26 Apr 1999, and was buried in Greenview Memorial Park, Florence, Lauderdale County, AL.

Earl married **Rebecca Susan Mitchell** in May 1960 in Athens, Limestone County, AL.
+ 3759   M   i.   **Jeffrey Todd Zahnd** was born 7 Jul 1962 in Lauderdale County, AL.
+ 3760   M   ii.   **Earl Douglas Zahnd III** was born 26 Dec 1994 in Lauderdale County, AL.

Earl next married **Glenda Fields**.

1924. Philip Gene Zahnd Sr. (*Hilda Mae Statom*[6], *Muncie Venetta Sharp*[5], *Berry Nolan*[4], *Joseph (Joe)*[3], *Charles W. Sr.*[2], *John Sr.*[1]) was born 3 Mar 1947 in Lauderdale County, AL.

Philip married **Judith Diane Montgomery**, daughter of **James Hershel Montgomery** and **Mary Magdalene Pounders**, 3 Apr 1970 in Lauderdale County, AL. Judith was born 7 Dec 1948 in Lauderdale County, AL.
+ 3761   M   i.   **Philip Gene (Gino) Zahnd Jr.** was born 28 Jun 1974 in Montgomery, AL.
  3762   F   ii.   **Ashley Nikole Zahnd** was born 6 Jan 1978 in Atlanta, Fulton County, GA.
  3763   F   iii. **Aubrey M. Zahnd** was born 4 Dec 1982 in Merritta, GA.
  3764   M   iv.   **Elliot Price Zahnd** was born 4 Dec 1982 in Merritta, GA.

1925. James Ervin Hickman Jr. (*Dolly Francis Statom*[6], *Muncie Venetta Sharp*[5], *Berry Nolan*[4], *Joseph (Joe)*[3], *Charles W. Sr.*[2], *John Sr.*[1]) was born 28 Jun 1952 in Lauderdale County, AL.

James married **Martha Blake Timberlake**, daughter of **Lewis Romph Timberlake** and **Martha Blake**, 18 May 1980 in Colbert County, AL. Martha was born 5 May 1958 in Colbert County, AL.
  3765   F   i.   **Martha Francis Hickman** was born 26 Nov 1986 in Lauderdale County, AL.

1929. Sterling Josh Statom (*John Price Statom Jr.*[6], *Muncie Venetta Sharp*[5], *Berry Nolan*[4], *Joseph (Joe)*[3], *Charles W. Sr.*[2], *John Sr.*[1]) was born 4 Nov 1964 in Lauderdale County, AL.

Sterling married **Tracy Carol Burcham**, daughter of **Walter J. Burcham Jr.** and **Jo Carneg**, 18 May 1996 in Lauderdale County, AL. Tracy was born 25 Oct 1966 in Lauderdale County, AL.
  3766   F   i.   **Megan Lynn Statom** was born 25 May 1997 in Lauderdale County, AL.
  3767   F   ii.   **Morgan Leigh Statom** was born 23 Sep 1998 in Lauderdale County, AL.

1930. Patricia Gail Berkey (*Mattie Jo Statom*[6], *Muncie Venetta Sharp*[5], *Berry Nolan*[4], *Joseph (Joe)*[3], *Charles W. Sr.*[2], *John Sr.*[1]) was born 24 Mar 1949 in Lauderdale County, AL.

Patricia married **Douglas Wesley Hendon Jr.**, son of **Douglas Wesley Hendon Sr.** and **Martha Louise Harris**, 11 Nov 1967 in Lauderdale County, AL. Douglas was born 20 Jul 1948 in Lauderdale County, AL.
+ 3768   F   i.   **Lisa Michelle Hendon** was born 31 Mar 1968 in Lauderdale County, AL.
  3769   M   ii.   **Chad Wesley Hendon** was born 11 May 1982 in Lauderdale County, AL.

1932. Denise Lynne Berkey (*Mattie Jo Statom*[6], *Muncie Venetta Sharp*[5], *Berry Nolan*[4], *Joseph (Joe)*[3], *Charles W. Sr.*[2], *John Sr.*[1]) was born 24 Aug 1957 in Lauderdale County, AL.

Denise married **Steve William Herbert**, son of **Herbert T. Herbert** and **Jessie Stewart**, 10 Jun 1977 in Lauderdale County, AL. Steve was born 19 Jul 1951 in Charleston, Charleston County, SC.
  3770   F   i.   **Kelly Lynne Herbert** was born 6 Aug 1981 in Lauderdale County, AL.
  3771   M   ii.   **Jacob Andrew Herbert** was born 27 Sep 1983 in Lauderdale County, AL.

1933. Jennifer Leigh James (*Betty Ruth Statom*[6], *Muncie Venetta Sharp*[5], *Berry Nolan*[4], *Joseph (Joe)*[3], *Charles W. Sr.*[2], *John Sr.*[1]) was born 20 Jul 1956 in Lauderdale County, AL.

Jennifer married **Douglas Edward Richardson**, son of **W. P. Richardson** and **Ruby Mangum**, 27 Aug 1978 in Lauderdale County, AL. Douglas was born 27 Feb 1943 in Hardin County, TN.

3772	F	i.	**Jacquelyn Richardson** was born 24 Dec 1982 in Lauderdale County, AL.
3773	F	ii.	**Julie Renee Richardson** was born 30 Apr 1988 in Lauderdale County, AL.

1935. Jerry Glynn James (*Betty Ruth Statom*[6], *Muncie Venetta Sharp*[5], *Berry Nolan*[4], *Joseph (Joe)*[3], *Charles W. Sr.*[2], *John Sr.*[1]) was born 20 Apr 1962 in Lauderdale County, AL.

Jerry married **Ella Finn Bennett**, daughter of **Charles Bennett** and **Jerry Hudson**, 30 Jul 1994 in Birmingham, Jefferson County, AL. Ella was born 27 Jun 1970 in Jasper, Walker County, AL.

1936. Joey Kynn James (*Betty Ruth Statom*[6], *Muncie Venetta Sharp*[5], *Berry Nolan*[4], *Joseph (Joe)*[3], *Charles W. Sr.*[2], *John Sr.*[1]) was born 20 Apr 1962 in Lauderdale County, AL.

Joey married **Andrea Florence Williams**, daughter of **David Charles Williams** and **Ruth Lucille Lowe**, 10 Sep 1988 in Lauderdale County, AL. Andrea was born 13 Apr 1964 in Jefferson City, CA.

3774	F	i.	**Hillary Taylor James** was born 26 Jan 1989 in Lauderdale County, AL.

1937. Harry Lee Sharp (*James Dalton*[6], *James Leander*[5], *Benjamin Franklin*[4], *Joseph (Joe)*[3], *Charles W. Sr.*[2], *John Sr.*[1]) was born 6 Mar 1929 in Lauderdale County, AL and died 15 Sep 1988 in South Bend, IN (cremated).

Harry married **Elinora Glyn Marks**, daughter of **Emmit J. Marks** and **Pauline O'Bryant**, 13 Aug 1949 in Iuka, Tishomingo County, MS. Elinora was born 2 May 1931 in Lauderdale County, AL.

+ 3775	M	i.	**Randell Lee Sharp** was born 24 Oct 1950 in Lauderdale County, AL.
+ 3776	F	ii.	**Jenna Lynn Sharp** was born 8 Jan 1953 in South Bend, IN.
+ 3777	M	iii.	**Mark Adrian Sharp** was born 13 Dec 1954 in Mishawaka, St Joseph County, IN.

1939. Helen Elizabeth Sharp (*James Dalton*[6], *James Leander*[5], *Benjamin Franklin*[4], *Joseph (Joe)*[3], *Charles W. Sr.*[2], *John Sr.*[1]) was born 22 Jul 1934 in Lauderdale County, AL.

Helen married **Glen David Austin Sr.**, son of **Bryan Austin** and **Chester Fulmer**, 10 Oct 1952 in Lauderdale County, AL. Glen was born 28 Mar 1933 in Lauderdale County, AL.

+ 3778	M	i.	**Glen David Austin Jr.** was born 14 Aug 1957 in Lauderdale County, AL, died 19 Mar 2004, and was buried in Greenview Memorial Park, Florence, Lauderdale County, AL.
+ 3779	M	ii.	**James Bryan Austin** was born 13 Aug 1960 in Lauderdale County, AL.

1940. Bobby Montgomery Sharp (*James Dalton*[6], *James Leander*[5], *Benjamin Franklin*[4], *Joseph (Joe)*[3], *Charles W. Sr.*[2], *John Sr.*[1]) was born 25 Feb 1937 in Lauderdale County, AL.

Bobby married **Ressie Lenora Hubbard**, daughter of **Charlie Hubbard** and **Bobbie Louise Garrison**. Ressie was born 26 Mar 1939 in West Brockton, AL.

+ 3780	M	i.	**Patrick Shawn Sharp** was born 24 Sep 1962 in Birmingham, Jefferson County, AL.
+ 3781	F	ii.	**Virginia Dawn Sharp** was born 12 Jan 1964 in Lemoor, CA.
+ 3782	M	iii.	**Todd Montgomery Sharp** was born 2 Jul 1968 in Lauderdale County, AL.

1941. Martha Wilhelminia Sharp (*James Dalton*[6], *James Leander*[5], *Benjamin Franklin*[4], *Joseph (Joe)*[3], *Charles W. Sr.*[2], *John Sr.*[1]) was born 7 Oct 1939 in Lauderdale County, AL.

Martha married **Johnny L. Simmons**, son of **William Robert Simmons** and **Iris Paulk**, 22 Jun 1957 in Iuka, Tishomingo County, MS. Johnny was born 11 Aug 1938 in Lauderdale County, AL.

+ 3783	F	i.	**Tina Marlee Simmons** was born 7 May 1962 in Lauderdale County, AL.
+ 3784	F	ii.	**Kimberly Paige Simmons** was born 3 Jul 1965 in Lauderdale County, AL.
+ 3785	M	iii.	**Bradley Robert Simmons** was born 12 May 1968 in Lauderdale County, AL.
+ 3786	M	iv.	**John Eric Simmons** was born 18 Mar 1970 in Lauderdale County, AL.

1942. Richard Lynn (Rick) Sharp (*James Dalton*[6], *James Leander*[5], *Benjamin Franklin*[4], *Joseph (Joe)*[3], *Charles W. Sr.*[2], *John Sr.*[1]) was born 25 Jan 1953 in Lauderdale County, AL.

Richard married **Judy Lynn West**, daughter of **Pat West** and **Marion Goad**, 5 Aug 1983 in Springfield, TN. Judy was born 17 Oct 1951 in Carthage, TN.

        General Notes: "Two children from first marriage, adopted by Richard Lynn Sharp..." Sharon Wood

+ 3787 M   i.   **Jason Allen Russell Sharp** was born 8 May 1975 in Sumner County, TN.
+ 3788 F   ii.   **Jessica (Jessie) Nicole Russell Sharp** was born 20 Sep 1979 in Lauderdale County, AL.

1943. Audrey Ruth Dixon (*Thelma Mae Sharp*[6], *James Leander*[5], *Benjamin Franklin*[4], *Joseph (Joe)*[3], *Charles W. Sr.*[2], *John Sr.*[1]) was born 2 Nov 1938 in Lawrenceburg, Lawrence County, TN.

Audrey married **Manuel Lloyd May**, son of **Carver Swinea May** and **Mary Lee Olive**, 28 Feb 1953 in Iuka, Tishomingo County, MS. Manuel was born 9 Sep 1926 in Lauderdale County, AL.

+ 3789 M   i.   **Manuel Dale May** was born 21 Jan 1954 in Lauderdale County, AL.
+ 3790 F   ii.   **Audrey Rebecca May** was born 14 Mar 1955 in Lauderdale County, AL.
+ 3791 M   iii.   **Wymon Lance May** was born 15 Dec 1960 in Lauderdale County, AL.
+ 3792 F   iv.   **Deborah Diane May** was born 2 Sep 1962 in Lauderdale County, AL.

1944. Robert Dale Dixon (*Thelma Mae Sharp*[6], *James Leander*[5], *Benjamin Franklin*[4], *Joseph (Joe)*[3], *Charles W. Sr.*[2], *John Sr.*[1]) was born 30 Mar 1947 in Lawrenceburg, Lawrence County, TN.

Robert married **Linda Sue Hannah**, daughter of ***Unk Hannah** and **Pauline Purser**. Linda was born 28 Dec 1946 in Lawrence County, TN.

+ 3793 F   i.   **Paula Dixon** was born 28 Dec 1966 in Lawrence County, TN.

1945. Samuel (Sammie) Coy Smith (*Mary Katherine Thrasher*[6], *Nora E. Sharp*[5], *Benjamin Franklin*[4], *Joseph (Joe)*[3], *Charles W. Sr.*[2], *John Sr.*[1]) was born 10 Apr 1942 in Lauderdale County, AL.

Samuel married **Jamie Lynn Tate**, daughter of **Aulton H. Tate** and **Vera Pettigrew**, 2 Jun 1961 in Lauderdale County, AL. Jamie was born 23 May 1943 in Colbert County, AL, died in 1967, and was buried in Florence City Cemetery, Florence, Lauderdale County, AL.

+ 3794 F   i.   **Emily Suzanne Smith** was born 16 May 1974 in Lauderdale County, AL.

1946. Debora Louise Smith (*Mary Katherine Thrasher*[6], *Nora E. Sharp*[5], *Benjamin Franklin*[4], *Joseph (Joe)*[3], *Charles W. Sr.*[2], *John Sr.*[1]) was born 1 Oct 1952 in Lauderdale County, AL.

Debora married **Bedford Franklin Tuten Jr.**, son of **Bedford Franklin Tuten Sr.** and **Helen Goode**, 23 Dec 1973 in Lauderdale County, AL. Bedford was born 23 Jan 1953 in Colbert County, AL.

3795 F   i.   **Jennifer Michelle Tuten**.
3796 M   ii.   **David Franklin Tuten**.

1947. Brenda Sharp (*Edwin Robert*[6], *Berry Robert*[5], *Benjamin Franklin*[4], *Joseph (Joe)*[3], *Charles W. Sr.*[2], *John Sr.*[1]).

Brenda married **James Stone**.

        General Notes: "Lives in Richmond, Virginia..." David Sharp

1948. Myra Sharp (*Edwin Robert*[6], *Berry Robert*[5], *Benjamin Franklin*[4], *Joseph (Joe)*[3], *Charles W. Sr.*[2], *John Sr.*[1]).

Myra married **Robert Sherrod**.

General Notes: "Lives in Decatur, Alabama..." David Sharp

1949. Wanda Sharp (*Edwin Robert*[6], *Berry Robert*[5], *Benjamin Franklin*[4], *Joseph (Joe)*[3], *Charles W. Sr.*[2], *John Sr.*[1]).

Wanda married **Howard Cox**.

1950. William David Sharp (*Edwin Robert*[6], *Berry Robert*[5], *Benjamin Franklin*[4], *Joseph (Joe)*[3], *Charles W. Sr.*[2], *John Sr.*[1]) was born 28 Jul 1940 in Lauderdale County, AL.

General Notes: "Lives in Florence, Alabama..." David Sharp

William married **Nancy Rebecca McClure**, daughter of **Robert Foster McClure** and **Elizabeth Marie Davis**, 5 Nov 1960 in Lauderdale County, AL. Nancy was born 7 Jul 1941 in Colbert County, AL.
+ 3797 F   i.   **Mary Elizabeth (Beth) Sharp** was born 29 Aug 1961 in Lauderdale County, AL.
   3798 F   ii.   **Haley Rebecca Sharp** was born 31 Oct 1977 in Lauderdale County, AL.

1951. James Robert Sharp Sr. (*Edwin Robert*[6], *Berry Robert*[5], *Benjamin Franklin*[4], *Joseph (Joe)*[3], *Charles W. Sr.*[2], *John Sr.*[1]) was born 25 Dec 1944 in Lauderdale County, AL.

General Notes: "Lives in Florence, Alabama..." Sharon Wood

James married **Sandra Gail Gallien**, daughter of **Archie Hayes Gallien** and **Elizabeth Julia Roberts**, 18 Jun 1964 in Lauderdale County, AL. Sandra was born 29 Nov 1947 in Lauderdale County, AL.
+ 3799 M   i.   **James Robert Sharp Jr.** was born 13 Aug 1965 in Lauderdale County, AL.
+ 3800 F   ii.   **Tambriana Dee Sharp** was born 5 Sep 1968 in Lauderdale County, AL.
+ 3801 F   iii.   **Jeri Khristy Sharp** was born 11 Oct 1971 in Lauderdale County, AL.
+ 3802 M   iv.   **David Hayes Sharp** was born 29 Feb 1980 in Colbert County, AL.

1952. Linda Ann Sharp (*William Frank*[6], *Berry Robert*[5], *Benjamin Franklin*[4], *Joseph (Joe)*[3], *Charles W. Sr.*[2], *John Sr.*[1]) was born 9 Sep 1944 in Lauderdale County, AL.

Linda married **Kenneth Byra Posey**, son of **George F. Posey** and **Mary E. Bryan**, 6 Jun 1964 in Lauderdale County, AL. Kenneth was born 25 Nov 1941 in Lawrence County, TN.
+ 3803 F   i.   **Lesley Lynn Posey** was born 14 Nov 1965 in Madison County, AL.
   3804 M   ii.   **Kenneth Lee Posey** was born 30 Jul 1968 in Madison County, AL.

Linda next married **Vance Persall**, son of **Harry Vance Persall** and **Lucille H. Grantham**, 12 Aug 1978 in Huntsville, Madison County, AL. Vance was born 3 Nov 1938 in Crisp County, GA.

1954. James Edward Lard (*Beatrice E. Cagle*[6], *Ethel Belle Sharp*[5], *Benjamin Franklin*[4], *Joseph (Joe)*[3], *Charles W. Sr.*[2], *John Sr.*[1]) was born 22 Mar 1938 in Lauderdale County, AL, died 14 Jul 1991, and was buried in Mt. Tabor Cemetery, Lauderdale County, AL.

James married **Patricia Ernestine Kinberg** before 1970.
   3805 F   i.   **Eldena Raye Lard**.
   3806 M   ii.   **Mark Stuart Lard**.
   3807 M   iii.   **James Ernest Lard** was buried in Connecticut.
   3808 F   iv.   **Susan Dale Lard**.
   3809 F   v.   **Beth Lard**.

James next married **Rebecca Louise South**, daughter of **Alonzo Allen South** and **Dorothy Louise Aday**, 30 Mar 1970 in Colbert County, AL. Rebecca was born 12 Apr 1953 in Iuka, Tishomingo County, MS.
   3810 F   i.   **Jennifer Rebecca Lard** was born 14 Nov 1971 in Colbert County, AL.
   3811 M   ii.   **Edward Ray Lard** was born 5 Jan 1973 in Colbert County, AL.

1955. Myra Elyne Lard (*Beatrice E. Cagle*[6], *Ethel Belle Sharp*[5], *Benjamin Franklin*[4], *Joseph (Joe)*[3], *Charles W. Sr.*[2], *John Sr.*[1]) was born 28 Sep 1939 in Lauderdale County, AL.

Myra married **Billy Eugene Young**, son of **Homer David Young** and **Callie Lou Wesson**, 5 May 1957 in Lauderdale County, AL. Billy was born 4 Oct 1929 in Lauderdale County, AL.

+ 3812 M i. **Anthony Todd Young** was born 13 Dec 1962 in Lauderdale County, AL.
+ 3813 F ii. **Amanda Layne Young** was born 28 Aug 1963 in Lauderdale County, AL.

1956. Jackie Leon Lard (*Beatrice E. Cagle*[6], *Ethel Belle Sharp*[5], *Benjamin Franklin*[4], *Joseph (Joe)*[3], *Charles W. Sr.*[2], *John Sr.*[1]) was born 15 Feb 1942 in Lauderdale County, AL.

Jackie married **Jackie Mae Prince**, daughter of **Jessie Mack Prince** and **Mary Effie Danley**, 28 Sep 1963 in Lauderdale County, AL. Jackie was born 3 Nov 1946 in Lawrence County, AL.

3814 F i. **Stacey Renee Lard** was born 20 Apr 1968 in Columbia, SC.

1957. Lynda Gale Lard (*Beatrice E. Cagle*[6], *Ethel Belle Sharp*[5], *Benjamin Franklin*[4], *Joseph (Joe)*[3], *Charles W. Sr.*[2], *John Sr.*[1]) was born 13 Nov 1944 in Lauderdale County, AL.

Lynda married **Leonard O. Waldrep**, son of **Willlie Albert Lard** and **Beatrice Collum**, 19 Oct 1966 in Mobile, AL. Leonard was born 30 Aug 1945 in Colbert County, AL, died 8 Jan 2004, and was buried in Tri-Cities Memorial Gardens, Florence, Lauderdale County, AL.

+ 3815 M i. **Lyndell Shawn Waldrep** was born 19 Oct 1968 in Colbert County, AL.
+ 3816 F ii. **Ladonice Waldrep** was born 19 Oct 1968.

Lynda next married **Wayne L. Lawson**, son of **Reeder Lawson** and **Martha *Unk**.

1958. Vivi Don Lard (*Beatrice E. Cagle*[6], *Ethel Belle Sharp*[5], *Benjamin Franklin*[4], *Joseph (Joe)*[3], *Charles W. Sr.*[2], *John Sr.*[1]) was born 25 Jan 1946 in Lauderdale County, AL.

Vivi married **Gonzalo Penya**, son of **Victor Pena Cortes** and **Sixta T. Vargas**, 18 Mar 1967. Gonzalo was born 6 Apr 1945 in Bogota, Columbia, South America.

+ 3817 M i. **Gregory Ernest Pena Penya** was born 2 May 1968 in Atlanta, Fulton County, GA.
+ 3818 M ii. **Eric Ranier Penya** was born 10 Nov 1970 in Atlanta, Fulton County, GA.

1960. Odis (Dale) Lard (*Beatrice E. Cagle*[6], *Ethel Belle Sharp*[5], *Benjamin Franklin*[4], *Joseph (Joe)*[3], *Charles W. Sr.*[2], *John Sr.*[1]) was born 11 Sep 1951 in Lauderdale County, AL.

Odis married **Sandra Kaye Leek**, daughter of **Alton Landrell Leek** and **Fannie Pearl Dixon**, 23 Aug 1991 in Lauderdale County, AL. Sandra was born 24 Dec 1944 in Lauderdale County, AL.

1961. Lindon Loyd Cagle (*Lloyd Brooke Cagle*[6], *Ethel Belle Sharp*[5], *Benjamin Franklin*[4], *Joseph (Joe)*[3], *Charles W. Sr.*[2], *John Sr.*[1]) was born 26 Nov 1944 in Lauderdale County, AL.

Lindon married **Carol Sue Edward**, daughter of **Lawrence Edward Jr.** and **Mae Marie *Unk**, 1 Aug 1963 in Peoria, IL. Carol was born 22 Dec 1945 in Marion, IL.

+ 3819 M i. **Robbie Linn Cagle** was born 22 Jul 1965 in Peoria, IL.
+ 3820 F ii. **Leisa Joann Cagle** was born 23 Aug 1967 in Peoria, IL.

1962. Shirley Ann Russell (*Evelyn Clara Cagle*[6], *Ethel Belle Sharp*[5], *Benjamin Franklin*[4], *Joseph (Joe)*[3], *Charles W. Sr.*[2], *John Sr.*[1]) was born 25 Oct 1943 in Lauderdale County, AL.

Shirley married **Cleatus Ray Reaves Sr.**, son of **Williard E. Reaves** and **Mable Holt**, 23 Jan 1962 in Lauderdale County, AL. Cleatus was born 3 Jul 1941 in Wayne County, TN.

3821 M i. **Cleatus Ray Reaves Jr.** was born 30 Jan 1963 in Lauderdale County, AL.
3822 F ii. **Carol Dawn Reaves** was born 8 Jun 1966 in Lauderdale County, AL.

1963. Rebecca Russell (*Evelyn Clara Cagle*[6], *Ethel Belle Sharp*[5], *Benjamin Franklin*[4], *Joseph (Joe)*[3], *Charles W. Sr.*[2], *John Sr.*[1]) was born in Lauderdale County, AL.

Rebecca married **William Michael O'Kelley**, son of **W. M. O'Kelley** and **Ruby Lee Price**. William was born 27 Feb 1957 in Lauderdale County, AL.

3823 F i. **De Nita O'Kelley**.
3824 M ii. **Christopher Michael O'Kelley**.

1964. Kathy Russell (*Evelyn Clara Cagle* ^{6}, *Ethel Belle Sharp* ^{5}, *Benjamin Franklin* ^{4}, *Joseph (Joe)* ^{3}, *Charles W. Sr.* ^{2}, *John Sr.* ^{1}) was born in Lauderdale County, AL.

Kathy married ***Unk Jackson**.

1966. James Albert Russell Sr. (*Evelyn Clara Cagle* ^{6}, *Ethel Belle Sharp* ^{5}, *Benjamin Franklin* ^{4}, *Joseph (Joe)* ^{3}, *Charles W. Sr.* ^{2}, *John Sr.* ^{1}) was born 14 Oct 1950 in Lauderdale County, AL.

James married **Wanda Faye Riley**, daughter of **James N. Riley** and **Myrtle Skipworth**, 24 Apr 1970 in Lauderdale County, AL. Wanda was born 16 Mar 1952 in Lauderdale County, AL.

3825 F i. **Kimberly Michelle Russell** was born 10 Feb 1971.
3826 M ii. **James Albert Russell Jr.** was born in Jan 1974.
3827 M iii. **Stewart Edward Russell** was born in Jan 1974.
3828 M iv. **Nathan Carroll Russell** was born 25 Nov 1983.

1967. Myra Lynn Lard (*Francis Jeanette Cagle* ^{6}, *Ethel Belle Sharp* ^{5}, *Benjamin Franklin* ^{4}, *Joseph (Joe)* ^{3}, *Charles W. Sr.* ^{2}, *John Sr.* ^{1}) was born 26 Jun 1957 in Lauderdale County, AL.

Myra married **Charles McGuire** in 1985 in Lauderdale County, AL.

1968. Harold Ray Cagle (*William Edward Cagle Jr.* ^{6}, *Ethel Belle Sharp* ^{5}, *Benjamin Franklin* ^{4}, *Joseph (Joe)* ^{3}, *Charles W. Sr.* ^{2}, *John Sr.* ^{1}) was born 28 Jul 1951 in Lauderdale County, AL.

Harold married **Melinda Ann Morgan**, daughter of **Arnold C. Morgan** and **Vera Vickery**, 4 May 1984 in Lauderdale County, AL. Melinda was born 16 Feb 1963 in Lauderdale County, AL.

3829 F i. **Heather Ann Cagle** was born 16 May 1986 in Lauderdale County, AL.

1969. Mary Diane Cagle (*William Edward Cagle Jr.* ^{6}, *Ethel Belle Sharp* ^{5}, *Benjamin Franklin* ^{4}, *Joseph (Joe)* ^{3}, *Charles W. Sr.* ^{2}, *John Sr.* ^{1}) was born 6 Oct 1952 in Lauderdale County, AL.

Mary married **Billy Floyd Hinton**, son of **Floyd V. Hinton** and **Edna Austin**, 7 Jul 1970 in Lauderdale County, AL. Billy was born 21 Jul 1946 in Lauderdale County, AL.

+ 3830 F i. **Christy Louise Hinton** was born 2 Jul 1971 in Lauderdale County, AL.
3831 M ii. **Bradley Dewayne Hinton** was born 4 May 1974.

Mary next married **Larry Dean Holden**, son of **Arnold G. Holden** and **Francis Dean**, 18 Jul 1980 in Lauderdale County, AL. Larry was born 26 Oct 1951 in Colbert County, AL.

3832 M i. **Jeremy Ross Holden** was born 30 Jun 1981 in Lauderdale County, AL.
3833 F ii. **Jessica Leann Holden** was born 3 Aug 1983 in Lauderdale County, AL.

1970. Teresa Yvonne Cagle (*William Edward Cagle Jr.* ^{6}, *Ethel Belle Sharp* ^{5}, *Benjamin Franklin* ^{4}, *Joseph (Joe)* ^{3}, *Charles W. Sr.* ^{2}, *John Sr.* ^{1}) was born 20 Jun 1955 in Peoria, IL.

Teresa married **Gary Edward Hayes**, son of **Lloyd Thomas Hayes** and **Vera Inez Balentine**, 12 Jun 1970 in Lauderdale County, AL. Gary was born 15 Oct 1951 in Lauderdale County, AL.

+ 3834 F i. **Jennifer Yvonne Hayes** was born 20 Aug 1972 in Lauderdale County, AL.
3835 M ii. **Jamie Edward Hayes** was born 29 Mar 1975 in Lauderdale County, AL.

Teresa next married **Richard Lee Nelson**, son of **Turner Nelson** and **Ila M. Williams**, 7 Mar 1980 in Lauderdale County, AL. Richard was born 8 Jul 1951 in Colbert County, AL.

3836 F i. **LaDonna Mae Nelson** was born 3 Nov 1980 in Lauderdale County, AL.

1971. Melissa Rene Cagle (*William Edward Cagle Jr.*[6], *Ethel Belle Sharp*[5], *Benjamin Franklin*[4], *Joseph (Joe)*[3], *Charles W. Sr.*[2], *John Sr.*[1]) was born 22 Aug 1959 in Peoria, IL.

Melissa married **James Roland Young**, son of **William Roland Young** and **Audrey Jean Hanback**, before 1975. James was born 15 Jan 1955 in Lauderdale County, AL.
| 3837 | M | i. | **Jason Bradon Young** was born 19 Jun 1975 in Lauderdale County, AL. |
| 3838 | M | ii. | **Kirk Nickalos Young** was born 27 Jun 1980 in Lauderdale County, AL. |

Melissa next married **Jerry Lynn Phillips**, son of **Sidney Phillips** and **Lorena Balentine**, 3 Feb 1987 in Lauderdale County, AL. Jerry was born 16 Jul 1963 in Lauderdale County, AL.

Melissa next married **Kenneth Ray Cantrell** after 1987.

1973. Delora Jean Cagle (*William Edward Cagle Jr.*[6], *Ethel Belle Sharp*[5], *Benjamin Franklin*[4], *Joseph (Joe)*[3], *Charles W. Sr.*[2], *John Sr.*[1]) was born 11 Sep 1964 in Peoria, IL.

Delora married **Roland Lee Parrish Jr.**, son of **Roland Lee Parrish Sr.** and **Shirley Louise Beasley**, 2 Mar 1979 in Lauderdale County, AL. Roland was born 11 Sep 1960 in Lauderdale County, AL.
| 3839 | M | i. | **Michael Lee Parrish** was born 12 Mar 1980 in Peoria, IL. |

1974. Denise Lynn Cagle (*William Edward Cagle Jr.*[6], *Ethel Belle Sharp*[5], *Benjamin Franklin*[4], *Joseph (Joe)*[3], *Charles W. Sr.*[2], *John Sr.*[1]) was born 11 Sep 1964 in Peoria, IL.

Denise married **Roger Dale Rhodes**, son of **Arlon Lee Rhodes** and **Bobbie Hall**, 28 May 1986 in Lauderdale County, AL. Roger was born 14 Jun 1954 in Lauderdale County, AL.
| 3840 | M | i. | **Alexander Blair Rhodes** was born 30 Oct 1987 in Lauderdale County, AL. |
| 3841 | M | ii. | **Greg Nelson Rhodes** was born 1 Nov 1990 in Lauderdale County, AL. |

1975. Charles William Lawson (*Fayna (Faye) Cagle*[6], *Ethel Belle Sharp*[5], *Benjamin Franklin*[4], *Joseph (Joe)*[3], *Charles W. Sr.*[2], *John Sr.*[1]) was born 17 Jan 1952 in Lauderdale County, AL.

Charles married **Gayla Sue Fair**, daughter of **James A. Fair** and **Jewel A. Coleman**, 7 Oct 1972 in Lauderdale County, AL. Gayla was born 11 Dec 1950 in Dallas County, AR.

1976. Cathy Sue Lawson (*Fayna (Faye) Cagle*[6], *Ethel Belle Sharp*[5], *Benjamin Franklin*[4], *Joseph (Joe)*[3], *Charles W. Sr.*[2], *John Sr.*[1]) was born 7 May 1954 in Lauderdale County, AL.

Cathy married **Johnny William Riley**, son of **Homer Lee Riley** and **Birdie Glover**, 16 Jul 1970 in Iuka, Tishomingo County, MS. Johnny was born 4 Nov 1951 in Lauderdale County, AL.
| + 3842 | M | i. | **Gregory Lee Riley** was born 30 Oct 1970. |
| 3843 | F | ii. | **Kerry Alicia Riley** was born 28 Oct 1982 in Lauderdale County, AL, died 26 Mar 2001, and was buried in Mt. Zion Cemetery, Lauderdale County, AL. |

1977. Larry Steven Lawson (*Fayna (Faye) Cagle*[6], *Ethel Belle Sharp*[5], *Benjamin Franklin*[4], *Joseph (Joe)*[3], *Charles W. Sr.*[2], *John Sr.*[1]) was born 25 Jul 1959 in Lauderdale County, AL.

Larry married **Cathy Sue Hodges**, daughter of **Chester Hall Hodges** and **Mary Katryn O'Kelley**, 6 Sep 1980 in Lauderdale County, AL. Cathy was born 24 Mar 1957 in Lauderdale County, AL.
3844	M	i.	**Derrick Brown Lawson** was born 10 Jan 1979 in Lauderdale County, AL.
3845	F	ii.	**Emily Michelle Lawson** was born 13 Jun 1983 in Lauderdale County, AL.
3846	F	iii.	**Jennifer Diane Lawson** was born 20 Sep 1985 in Lauderdale County, AL.
3847	M	iv.	**Jeremy Daryal Lawson** was born 20 Sep 1985 in Lauderdale County, AL.

1981. Melvin Douglas Hill (*Donald J. Hill*[6], *Maggie Leona Sharp*[5], *Benjamin Franklin*[4], *Joseph (Joe)*[3], *Charles W. Sr.*[2], *John Sr.*[1]) was born 17 Nov 1948 in Lauderdale County, AL.

Melvin married **Linda Faye Richardson**, daughter of **Joe M. Richardson** and **Willodean Swinea**, 24 Sep 1971 in Lauderdale County, AL. Linda was born 21 Mar 1952 in Lauderdale County, AL.

3848 M i. **Bradley Christopher Hill** was born 1 Dec 1971 in Lauderdale County, AL.

3849 F ii. **Rachel Lindsey Hill** was born 11 Apr 1976 in Lauderdale County, AL.

1983. Paul Eugene Kelley (*Mary Opel Hill*[6], *Maggie Leona Sharp*[5], *Benjamin Franklin*[4], *Joseph (Joe)*[3], *Charles W. Sr.*[2], *John Sr.*[1]) was born 6 Apr 1949 in Lauderdale County, AL.

Paul married **Linda L. Henson**, daughter of **Walter Lee Henson** and **Pauline Stults**, 16 Dec 1967 in Lauderdale County, AL. Linda was born 22 Jul 1949 in Wayne County, TN.

1984. Joyce Lynn Kelley (*Mary Opel Hill*[6], *Maggie Leona Sharp*[5], *Benjamin Franklin*[4], *Joseph (Joe)*[3], *Charles W. Sr.*[2], *John Sr.*[1]) was born 10 Oct 1954 in Lauderdale County, AL.

Joyce married **Herbert Truman Richardson**, son of **Bradley Richardson** and **Lillian Evelyn Wilson**, 22 Oct 1971 in Wayne County, TN. Herbert was born 11 Jul 1949 in Lauderdale County, AL.

+ 3850 M i. **Michael Erick Richardson** was born 18 Mar 1982 in Colbert County, AL.

Joyce next married **Raymond Henry Alstadt**, son of **Harold E. Alstadt** and **Ruby Dallas**, 21 May 1982 in Lauderdale County, AL. Raymond was born 9 Jul 1948 in Reaves County, PA.

3851 F i. **Brittany Rae Alstadt** was born 4 Feb 1985 in Colbert County, AL.

1987. Turner L. Sharp Jr. (*Turner L. Sr.*[6], *Charles Edward (Eddie)*[5], *John Levi*[4], *Charles W. II*[3], *Charles W. Sr.*[2], *John Sr.*[1]) died about 1995.

Turner married **Jane *Unk**.

3852 F i. **Susan Sharp**.

3853 M ii. **Chris Sharp**.

1988. Vernon Howard Sharp (*Turner L. Sr.*[6], *Charles Edward (Eddie)*[5], *John Levi*[4], *Charles W. II*[3], *Charles W. Sr.*[2], *John Sr.*[1]) was born 2 Jan 1929 in Mishawaka, St Joseph County, IN, died 15 Jan 1996, and was buried in Memory Gardens, Savannah, Hardin County, TN.

Vernon married **Frances Lovella Haggard**, daughter of **J. W. Haggard** and **Mary Jane Bell**, 25 Dec 1947 in Hardin County, TN. Frances was born 11 Feb 1928 in Hardin County, TN.

+ 3854 F i. **Stacy Jane Sharp** was born 28 Sep 1968 in Savannah, Hardin County, TN.

1989. Charles Henry Hill Jr. (*Charles Henry Hill Sr.*[6], *Alice Maxwell Sharp*[5], *John Levi*[4], *Charles W. II*[3], *Charles W. Sr.*[2], *John Sr.*[1]) was born 26 Nov 1957 in Long Beach, Los Angeles, CA.

Charles married **Devoron Kathleen Davis** 14 Aug 1982 in Carmel, Monterey, CA. Devoron was born in 1955.

3855 M i. **Grant Robert Hill** was born 31 May 1988 in California.

1990. Paula Elaine Hill (*Charles Henry Hill Sr.*[6], *Alice Maxwell Sharp*[5], *John Levi*[4], *Charles W. II*[3], *Charles W. Sr.*[2], *John Sr.*[1]) was born 10 Aug 1960 in Long Beach, Los Angeles, CA.

Paula married **Michael Lee Slayton Sr.** 10 Jan 1981 in Palmdale, Los Angeles, CA. Michael was born 20 Dec 1956 in Gardena, Los Angeles, CA.

3856 M i. **Michael Lee Slayton Jr.** was born 22 Oct 1983 in Panarama City, CA.

1992. David Craig Greene I (*Rita Faye Hill*[6], *Alice Maxwell Sharp*[5], *John Levi*[4], *Charles W. II*[3], *Charles W. Sr.*[2], *John Sr.*[1]) was born 20 Apr 1957 in Los Angeles, CA.

David married **Michelle Renee Kapfer** 9 Jan 1977 in Palmdale, Los Angeles, CA. Michelle was born 12 Feb 1960 in Los Angeles, CA.

+ 3857 F i. **Mandi Eilee Greene** was born 3 Aug 1979 in Apple Valley, CA.

3858 M ii. **David Craig Greene II** was born 27 Jan 1982 in Apple Valley, CA.

1993. Clell Marker Greene Jr. (*Rita Faye Hill [6], Alice Maxwell Sharp [5], John Levi [4], Charles W. II [3], Charles W. Sr. [2], John Sr. [1]*) was born 26 Apr 1962 in Redondo Beach, Los Angeles, CA.

Clell married **Kimberly Marie Alviso** 20 Oct 1990 in Moreno Valley, Riverside, CA. Kimberly was born 25 Feb 1960 in Compton, CA.

1996. Charles Everett Blackburn (*Willie Carmen Box [6], James (Jim) W. Box [5], Amanda Jane Sharp [4], Charles W. II [3], Charles W. Sr. [2], John Sr. [1]*) was born 17 Apr 1942 in Lauderdale County, AL, died 7 Nov 1999, and was buried in New Hope Cemetery, Lauderdale County, AL.

Charles married **Laurel Jane Heid**, daughter of **Harry Herbert Heid** and **Maxine Simmers**, 18 Feb 1966 in Lauderdale County, AL. Laurel was born 11 Apr 1942 in Dover, Tuscarawas County, OH.
+ 3859 F i. **Angela Carmon Blackburn** was born 18 Jan 1970 in Spartanburg County, SC.
 3860 M ii. **John David (J. D.) Blackburn** was born 12 Feb 1975.

1997. Ruby Louise Box (*John Carroll (J. C.) Box Sr. [6], James (Jim) W. Box [5], Amanda Jane Sharp [4], Charles W. II [3], Charles W. Sr. [2], John Sr. [1]*) was born 15 Feb 1933.

Ruby married **James E. Kelley** 22 Nov 1947.

1998. Thomas Carroll Box (*John Carroll (J. C.) Box Sr. [6], James (Jim) W. Box [5], Amanda Jane Sharp [4], Charles W. II [3], Charles W. Sr. [2], John Sr. [1]*) was born 4 Aug 1934 in Lauderdale County, AL.

Thomas married **Carolyn Sue Harrison**, daughter of **Ross Harrison** and **Deedie Wesson**, 14 Aug 1954 in Iuka, Tishomingo County, MS. Carolyn was born 16 Oct 1934 in Lauderdale County, AL.
+ 3861 M i. **Gregory (Greg) Thomas Box** was born 3 Jun 1956 in Lauderdale County, AL.
+ 3862 M ii. **James Windell Box** was born 15 May 1959 in Lauderdale County, AL.

1999. Donald Andrew Box (*John Carroll (J. C.) Box Sr. [6], James (Jim) W. Box [5], Amanda Jane Sharp [4], Charles W. II [3], Charles W. Sr. [2], John Sr. [1]*) was born 28 Nov 1935 in Lauderdale County, AL.

Donald married **Judy Ann Mason**, daughter of **James E. Mason** and **Annie B. Dean**, 6 Aug 1960 in Lauderdale County, AL. Judy was born 31 Jan 1940 in Rogersville, Lauderdale County, AL.
+ 3863 F i. **Donna Jo Box** was born 27 Mar 1961 in Lauderdale County, AL.
+ 3864 F ii. **Teresa Ann Box** was born 14 Oct 1962 in Lauderdale County, AL.
+ 3865 F iii. **Judy Darlene Box** was born 19 Dec 1963.

2000. Rose Mary Box (*John Carroll (J. C.) Box Sr. [6], James (Jim) W. Box [5], Amanda Jane Sharp [4], Charles W. II [3], Charles W. Sr. [2], John Sr. [1]*) was born 9 May 1949.

Rose married **David Ray Dover** 9 Jul 1965.

2001. Clara Ruth Anderson (*Herschel D. Anderson [6], Charles David Anderson Sr. [5], Mary Elizabeth (Molly) Sharp [4], Charles W. II [3], Charles W. Sr. [2], John Sr. [1]*).

Clara married ***Unk Grant.**
 3866 M i. **Mike Grant.**
 3867 F ii. **Michelle Grant.**

2002. John Hines Gray (*Vera Anderson [6], Charles David Anderson Sr. [5], Mary Elizabeth (Molly) Sharp [4], Charles W. II [3], Charles W. Sr. [2], John Sr. [1]*) was born 27 May 1939 in Lauderdale County, AL.

John married **Billie Sue Hughes** in 1956 in Iuka, Tishomingo County, MS.
 3868 F i. **Kay Elizabeth Gray** was born 5 Oct 1957 in Lauderdale County, AL.
+ 3869 F ii. **Donna Jean Gray** was born 9 May 1959 in Lauderdale County, AL.

2003. Charles Leon Gray (*Vera Anderson* [6], *Charles David Anderson Sr.* [5], *Mary Elizabeth (Molly) Sharp* [4], *Charles W. II* [3], *Charles W. Sr.* [2], *John Sr.* [1]) was born 2 May 1943 in Lauderdale County, AL.

Charles married **Patsy Kaye Jeffreys**, daughter of **Melvin Jeffreys** and **Donna S. Hill**, 26 Sep 1973 in Lauderdale County, AL. Patsy was born 30 Oct 1950 in Colbert County, AL.
3870 M i. **Christopher Matthews Gray** was born 5 Sep 1975 in Lauderdale County, AL.
3871 F ii. **Miranda Gray** was born 28 Sep 1978 in Lauderdale County, AL.

2004. David Eugene Anderson Sr. (*John William Anderson* [6], *Charles David Anderson Sr.* [5], *Mary Elizabeth (Molly) Sharp* [4], *Charles W. II* [3], *Charles W. Sr.* [2], *John Sr.* [1]) was born 21 Feb 1942 in Nashville, Davidson County, TN.

David married **Jacqueline Balentine**, daughter of **John W. Balentine** and **Myrtle Rogers**, 20 Apr 1969 in Lauderdale County, AL.
3872 M i. **David Eugene Anderson Jr.** was born 18 Jul 1974.

2013. Inesse Joyner (*Christine Anderson* [6], *Charles David Anderson Sr.* [5], *Mary Elizabeth (Molly) Sharp* [4], *Charles W. II* [3], *Charles W. Sr.* [2], *John Sr.* [1]).

Inesse married **Leo Penrose**.
3873 M i. **Allen Penrose**.
3874 F ii. **Susan Penrose**.

2014. Gerald Joyner (*Christine Anderson* [6], *Charles David Anderson Sr.* [5], *Mary Elizabeth (Molly) Sharp* [4], *Charles W. II* [3], *Charles W. Sr.* [2], *John Sr.* [1]).

Gerald married ***Unk**.
3875 M i. **Jim Joyner**.

2019. Martha Treviso (*Geneva Anderson* [6], *Charles David Anderson Sr.* [5], *Mary Elizabeth (Molly) Sharp* [4], *Charles W. II* [3], *Charles W. Sr.* [2], *John Sr.* [1]).

Martha married **Bill Clyne**.

2021. Larry David Gean (*Ruby Anderson* [6], *Charles David Anderson Sr.* [5], *Mary Elizabeth (Molly) Sharp* [4], *Charles W. II* [3], *Charles W. Sr.* [2], *John Sr.* [1]) was born 9 Aug 1946 in South Bend, St Joseph County, IN.

Larry married **Pat Howard** 3 Apr 1970.
3876 F i. **Amy Leigh Gean** was born 17 Jun 1972.

2022. Cheryl Darline Gean (*Ruby Anderson* [6], *Charles David Anderson Sr.* [5], *Mary Elizabeth (Molly) Sharp* [4], *Charles W. II* [3], *Charles W. Sr.* [2], *John Sr.* [1]) was born 7 Dec 1949 in South Bend, St Joseph County, IN.

Cheryl married **Donald M. Harrison** 11 Dec 1973.
3877 F i. **Alicia Dawn Harrison** was born 15 May 1972.

2023. Kenneth Edward Gean (*Ruby Anderson* [6], *Charles David Anderson Sr.* [5], *Mary Elizabeth (Molly) Sharp* [4], *Charles W. II* [3], *Charles W. Sr.* [2], *John Sr.* [1]) was born 8 Sep 1951 in South Bend, St Joseph County, IN.

Kenneth married **Melissa Ann Powell** 7 Jan 1972.
3878 M i. **Russell Thomas Gean** was born 28 Oct 1972.

2024. Wanda Gail Gean (*Ruby Anderson* [6], *Charles David Anderson Sr.* [5], *Mary Elizabeth (Molly) Sharp* [4], *Charles W. II* [3], *Charles W. Sr.* [2], *John Sr.* [1]) was born 8 Nov 1957 in South Bend, St Joseph County, IN.

Wanda married **Marty E. Pruitt** 21 Jul 1974.

2025. Katherine Jean Balentine (*Lucille Anderson*[6]*, Charles David Anderson Sr.*[5]*, Mary Elizabeth (Molly) Sharp*[4]*, Charles W. II*[3]*, Charles W. Sr.*[2]*, John Sr.*[1]) was born in Feb 1945 in Lauderdale County, AL.

Katherine married **Robert Bristo**.

2026. Carolyn Joan Balentine (*Lucille Anderson*[6]*, Charles David Anderson Sr.*[5]*, Mary Elizabeth (Molly) Sharp*[4]*, Charles W. II*[3]*, Charles W. Sr.*[2]*, John Sr.*[1]) was born 2 May 1949 in Lauderdale County, AL.

Carolyn married **John Henry Brown**, son of **Emmitt Louis Brown** and **Edna Palmer**, 5 May 1967 in Colbert County, AL. John was born 13 Apr 1947 in Lauderdale County, AL.
+ 3879 M i. **Robert Lance Brown** was born 12 Jul 1971 in Lauderdale County, AL.
  3880 F ii. **Rebecca Leigh Brown** was born 10 Oct 1976 in Lauderdale County, AL.

2027. Marilyn Jo Balentine (*Lucille Anderson*[6]*, Charles David Anderson Sr.*[5]*, Mary Elizabeth (Molly) Sharp*[4]*, Charles W. II*[3]*, Charles W. Sr.*[2]*, John Sr.*[1]) was born 8 Apr 1954 in Lauderdale County, AL.

Marilyn married **Michael Allen Kendrick**.
3881 M i. **Jason Lucian Kendrick**.

2028. Martha Lee Balentine (*Lucille Anderson*[6]*, Charles David Anderson Sr.*[5]*, Mary Elizabeth (Molly) Sharp*[4]*, Charles W. II*[3]*, Charles W. Sr.*[2]*, John Sr.*[1]) was born 14 Mar 1956 in Lauderdale County, AL.

Martha married **Vernon Dennis Neal**.

2032. Charlotte Earl Romine (*Maxine Anderson*[6]*, Robert (Bud) Henry Anderson*[5]*, Mary Elizabeth (Molly) Sharp*[4]*, Charles W. II*[3]*, Charles W. Sr.*[2]*, John Sr.*[1]) was born 7 Jan 1945 in Lauderdale County, AL.

Charlotte married **John Charles Winchester**, son of **Joseph Fred Winchester** and **Vivian Carter**, 31 May 1969. John was born 26 Jul 1942 in Russellville, Franklin County, AL, died 13 Feb 1997, and was buried in Greenview Memorial Park, Florence, Lauderdale County, AL.
3882 F i. **Laura Ellen Winchester** was born 26 Jun 1972 in Lauderdale County, AL and died 3 Mar 1985.
3883 F ii. **Erin Winchester**.

2034. James Larry Winter (*Mary Alice Anderson*[6]*, Robert (Bud) Henry Anderson*[5]*, Mary Elizabeth (Molly) Sharp*[4]*, Charles W. II*[3]*, Charles W. Sr.*[2]*, John Sr.*[1]) was born 15 Mar 1943 in Nashville, Davidson County, TN.

James married **Patricia Harriet Anderson**. Patricia was born 10 Apr 1944 in Nashville, Davidson County, TN.
3884 M i. **Patrick William Winter** was born 14 Jan 1975 in Nashville, Davidson County, TN.
3885 M ii. **Bengamin Eastman Winter** was born 21 Dec 1975 in Nashville, Davidson County, TN.

2035. Kenneth Gene Womble (*Francis Geraldine Anderson*[6]*, Robert (Bud) Henry Anderson*[5]*, Mary Elizabeth (Molly) Sharp*[4]*, Charles W. II*[3]*, Charles W. Sr.*[2]*, John Sr.*[1]) was born 20 May 1940.

Kenneth married **Marlyn Bevers** 6 Oct 1970. Marlyn was born 24 Nov 1944.

2037. James Robert Anderson (*Robert (Bob) Fulmer Anderson*[6]*, Robert (Bud) Henry Anderson*[5]*, Mary Elizabeth (Molly) Sharp*[4]*, Charles W. II*[3]*, Charles W. Sr.*[2]*, John Sr.*[1]) was born 5 Jan 1947 in Lauderdale County, AL.

James married **Thalia Danley** 7 Jun 1969.

2038. Phillip Edward Anderson (*Robert (Bob) Fulmer Anderson*[6]*, Robert (Bud) Henry Anderson*[5]*, Mary Elizabeth (Molly) Sharp*[4]*, Charles W. II*[3]*, Charles W. Sr.*[2]*, John Sr.*[1]) was born 15 Oct 1949 in Lauderdale County, AL.

Phillip married **Phyllis Mullins** 21 Dec 1970.

2039. Stephen Gary Anderson (*Robert (Bob) Fulmer Anderson^6, Robert (Bud) Henry Anderson^5, Mary Elizabeth (Molly) Sharp^4, Charles W. II^3, Charles W. Sr.^{2}, John Sr.^{1}*) was born 27 May 1951 in Lauderdale County, AL.

Stephen married **Paula Tolbert** 31 Dec 1970.

2040. Timothy Milton Anderson (*Robert (Bob) Fulmer Anderson^6, Robert (Bud) Henry Anderson^5, Mary Elizabeth (Molly) Sharp^4, Charles W. II^3, Charles W. Sr.^{2}, John Sr.^{1}*) was born 11 Oct 1958 in Lauderdale County, AL.

Timothy married **Kathy Phillips**.

2041. Mary Ann Anderson (*Robert (Bob) Fulmer Anderson^6, Robert (Bud) Henry Anderson^5, Mary Elizabeth (Molly) Sharp^4, Charles W. II^3, Charles W. Sr.^{2}, John Sr.^{1}*) was born 28 Jan 1960 in Lauderdale County, AL.

Mary married **Mark Christopher Stults** in Lauderdale County, AL.

2042. Mark Van Anderson (*Robert (Bob) Fulmer Anderson^6, Robert (Bud) Henry Anderson^5, Mary Elizabeth (Molly) Sharp^4, Charles W. II^3, Charles W. Sr.^{2}, John Sr.^{1}*) was born 28 Jan 1960 in Lauderdale County, AL.

Mark married **Tammy Haynes** in Lauderdale County, AL.

2043. David Claude Anderson (*Robert (Bob) Fulmer Anderson^6, Robert (Bud) Henry Anderson^5, Mary Elizabeth (Molly) Sharp^4, Charles W. II^3, Charles W. Sr.^{2}, John Sr.^{1}*) was born 5 Sep 1961 in Lauderdale County, AL.

David married **Myra Dixon** in Lauderdale County, AL.

2044. Shelia Dianne Anderson (*Gene Tunney Anderson Sr.^{6}, Robert (Bud) Henry Anderson^5, Mary Elizabeth (Molly) Sharp^4, Charles W. II^3, Charles W. Sr.^{2}, John Sr.^{1}*) was born 23 Jan 1954 in Lauderdale County, AL.

Shelia married **Bob Bullock**.

2048. Mary Adeline Saxton (*Jess Lloyd Saxton Sr.^{6}, Mary Adeline (Addie) Anderson^5, Mary Elizabeth (Molly) Sharp^4, Charles W. II^3, Charles W. Sr.^{2}, John Sr.^{1}*).

Mary married **Donald Mitchel Wirington**.

Mary next married **Thomas Emil Hirth**.

2049. Jess Lloyd Saxton Jr. (*Jess Lloyd Saxton Sr.^{6}, Mary Adeline (Addie) Anderson^5, Mary Elizabeth (Molly) Sharp^4, Charles W. II^3, Charles W. Sr.^{2}, John Sr.^{1}*).

Jess married **Diane McGuire** 2 Dec 1962.
3886	F	i.	**Kimberly Ann Saxton** was born in 1963.
3887	M	ii.	**Jess Scott Saxton** was born in 1964.
3888	M	iii.	**Keith Michele Saxton** was born in 1967.
3889	M	iv.	**David Joseph Saxton** was born in 1969.

2051. Scott Lee Sharp (*Charles William^6, William Lee^5, Charles Franklin^4, Charles W. II^3, Charles W. Sr.^{2}, John Sr.^{1}*) was born 13 Aug 1945 in Paris, Lamar County, TX.

Scott married **Alice Marie Rice** in Aug 1975 in Amarillo, TX.
| 3890 | M | i. | **Charles Edward Sharp** was born 3 Aug 1980. |

2052. Susan Sharp (*Charles William^6, William Lee^5, Charles Franklin^4, Charles W. II^3, Charles W. Sr.^{2}, John Sr.^{1}*) was born 12 Dec 1954 in Paris, Lamar County, TX.

Susan married **Nathaniel Hall Jones** in May 1972 in Amarillo, TX.
3891 M i. **Jason Nathaniel Jones** was born 21 Sep 1972.
3892 F ii. **Shona Jane Jones** was born 7 Mar 1977.

2053. Victor Barney Hutto (*Virginia Lee Sharp* [6], *William Lee* [5], *Charles Franklin* [4], *Charles W. II* [3], *Charles W. Sr.* [2], *John Sr.* [1]).

Victor married **Jennifer *Unk**.
3893 F i. **Chelsie Hutto**.

2054. Bruce Hutto (*Virginia Lee Sharp* [6], *William Lee* [5], *Charles Franklin* [4], *Charles W. II* [3], *Charles W. Sr.* [2], *John Sr.* [1]).

Bruce married **Cindy *Unk**.

2055. Jerry Wade Wright (*Clora Ovrille Dowdy* [6], *Hosea (Hozie) Durille Dowdy* [5], *Rachel Ann (Babe) Sharp* [4], *Charles W. II* [3], *Charles W. Sr.* [2], *John Sr.* [1]) was born 9 Nov 1940 in Lauderdale County, AL.

Jerry married **Darris Mae Boothe**, daughter of **Myers Luther Boothe** and **Cecile Faulkner**, 12 Nov 1960 in Colbert County, AL. Darris was born 23 Feb 1941 in Tishomingo, MS.
+ 3894 M i. **Christopher Shannon Wright** was born 14 Apr 1969 in Colbert County, AL.
3895 M ii. **Danny Wade Wright** was born 25 Oct 1971 in Colbert County, AL.

2056. Timothy Elliot Wright (*Clora Ovrille Dowdy* [6], *Hosea (Hozie) Durille Dowdy* [5], *Rachel Ann (Babe) Sharp* [4], *Charles W. II* [3], *Charles W. Sr.* [2], *John Sr.* [1]) was born 5 Sep 1943 in Lauderdale County, AL.

Timothy married **Janice Kathleen Rickard**, daughter of **Claude Rickard** and **Olive Kathleen Clemmons**, 17 May 1963 in Lauderdale County, AL. Janice was born 31 Jan 1943 in Lauderdale County, AL.
+ 3896 F i. **Cynthia (Cindy) Lea Wright** was born 22 Jan 1965 in Lauderdale County, AL.
+ 3897 F ii. **Candace (Candi) Lynn Wright** was born 20 Jan 1968 in Lauderdale County, AL.
+ 3898 M iii. **Ethan Elliot Wright** was born 9 Jan 1972 in Lauderdale County, AL.

2057. Horace Lanny Wright (*Clora Ovrille Dowdy* [6], *Hosea (Hozie) Durille Dowdy* [5], *Rachel Ann (Babe) Sharp* [4], *Charles W. II* [3], *Charles W. Sr.* [2], *John Sr.* [1]) was born 20 Oct 1947 in Lauderdale County, AL.

Horace married **Hilda Sue Canerdy**, daughter of **Arthur Lee Canerdy** and **Beulah Lucille Miles**, 12 Aug 1967 in Lauderdale County, AL. Hilda was born 19 Oct 1948 in Lauderdale County, AL.
+ 3899 M i. **Matthew Wayne Wright** was born 11 Oct 1970 in Lauderdale County, AL.
3900 M ii. **Dustin Andrew Wright** was born 3 Feb 1975 in Lauderdale County, AL.
3901 M iii. **Scott Anthony Wright** was born 31 Jul 1983 in Lauderdale County, AL.

2058. James Floyd Dowdy Jr. (*James Floyd Dowdy Sr.* [6], *Hosea (Hozie) Durille Dowdy* [5], *Rachel Ann (Babe) Sharp* [4], *Charles W. II* [3], *Charles W. Sr.* [2], *John Sr.* [1]) was born 9 Aug 1948 in Denver, CO.

James married **Rachel Margaret Formby** in May.

2059. Dorlea Francis Dowdy (*James Floyd Dowdy Sr.* [6], *Hosea (Hozie) Durille Dowdy* [5], *Rachel Ann (Babe) Sharp* [4], *Charles W. II* [3], *Charles W. Sr.* [2], *John Sr.* [1]) was born 26 Mar 1950 in Denver, CO.

Dorlea married **Wilber Glenn Rikard**, son of **Henry Wilber Rikard** and **Lula Mae Tidwell**, 12 Jun 1970 in Huntsville, Madison County, AL. Wilber was born 13 Oct 1943 in Colbert County, AL.
3902 M i. **Gabriel Rikard** was born 1 Jul 1973 in Colbert County, AL.
3903 F ii. **Megan Elizabeth Rikard** was born 13 Mar 1976 in Colbert County, AL.
3904 F iii. **Kiley Ellen Rikard** was born 28 Mar 1978 in Colbert County, AL.

2060. Kenneth Herschel Dowdy (*James Floyd Dowdy Sr.* [6], *Hosea (Hozie) Durille Dowdy* [5], *Rachel Ann (Babe) Sharp* [4], *Charles W. II* [3], *Charles W. Sr.* [2], *John Sr.* [1]) was born 8 Dec 1952 in Denver, CO.

Kenneth married **Beverly Choate**.

2062. Michael Robin Slaughter (*Juanita Ventelle Dowdy*[6], *Hosea (Hozie) Durille Dowdy*[5], *Rachel Ann (Babe) Sharp*[4], *Charles W. II*[3], *Charles W. Sr.*[2], *John Sr.*[1]) was born 30 Mar 1959 in Lauderdale County, AL.

Michael married **Tammy King**, daughter of **Joseph King** and **Mary Louise Walters**, 30 Oct 1982 in Pensacola, Escambia County, FL. Tammy was born 26 Nov 1959 in Pensacola, Escambia County, FL.
  3905 M   i.   **Garet Michael Slaughter** was born 9 Sep 1985 in Decatur, Morgan County, AL.
  3906 F   ii.   **Miranda Leigh Slaughter** was born 2 Oct 1987 in Decatur, Morgan County, AL.
  3907 M   iii. **Conner Joseph Slaughter** was born 13 Jul 1991 in Decatur, Morgan County, AL.

2063. John Stewart Hanback (*Addye Faye Dowdy*[6], *Hosea (Hozie) Durille Dowdy*[5], *Rachel Ann (Babe) Sharp*[4], *Charles W. II*[3], *Charles W. Sr.*[2], *John Sr.*[1]) was born 7 Nov 1958 in Huntsville, Madison County, AL.

John married **Leigh Ann Hester**.

2064. Barry Lee Hanback (*Addye Faye Dowdy*[6], *Hosea (Hozie) Durille Dowdy*[5], *Rachel Ann (Babe) Sharp*[4], *Charles W. II*[3], *Charles W. Sr.*[2], *John Sr.*[1]) was born 22 Sep 1961 in Huntsville, Madison County, AL.

Barry married **Beverly Payne** in May 1985.

2065. Omi Jean Watkins (*Mary Louise Stults*[6], *Linnie Mae Sharp*[5], *Thomas (Tom) Erwin*[4], *Charles W. II*[3], *Charles W. Sr.*[2], *John Sr.*[1]) was born 16 Nov 1935 in Lauderdale County, AL.

Omi married **Donell Theodore Pollard Sr.**, son of **Ernest LeRoy Pollard** and **Esther L. Dowdy**, 10 Apr 1955 in Lauderdale County, AL. Donell was born 9 Jan 1930 in Flint, MI.
  + 3908 F   i.   **Pamela Jean Pollard** was born 11 Feb 1959 in Lauderdale County, AL.
  + 3909 M   ii.   **Donell Theodore Pollard Jr.** was born 10 Nov 1960 in Lauderdale County, AL.
  + 3910 F   iii. **Teresa Anne Pollard** was born 26 Jan 1969 in Lauderdale County, AL.

2066. Earline Watkins (*Mary Louise Stults*[6], *Linnie Mae Sharp*[5], *Thomas (Tom) Erwin*[4], *Charles W. II*[3], *Charles W. Sr.*[2], *John Sr.*[1]) was born 2 Nov 1938 in Lauderdale County, AL.

Earline married **Daniel Irving Pollard Sr.**, son of **Ernest Leroy Pollard** and **Esther L. Dowdy**, 19 Aug 1956 in Lauderdale County, AL. Daniel was born 20 Dec 1936 in Colbert County, AL.
  + 3911 M   i.   **Daniel Irving Pollard Jr.** was born 26 Aug 1959 in Opelika, Lee County, AL.
  + 3912 M   ii.   **Anthony K. Pollard** was born 20 Sep 1961 in Huntsville, Madison County, AL.
  + 3913 M   iii. **Tracy L. Pollard** was born 2 Mar 1963 in Huntsville, Madison County, AL.
  + 3914 F   iv.   **Kimberly D. Pollard** was born 11 Jan 1966 in Huntsville, Madison County, AL.

2067. Bobbie Sue Watkins (*Mary Louise Stults*[6], *Linnie Mae Sharp*[5], *Thomas (Tom) Erwin*[4], *Charles W. II*[3], *Charles W. Sr.*[2], *John Sr.*[1]) was born 5 Jul 1942 in Lauderdale County, AL, died 23 Sep 2000, and was buried in Greenview Memorial Park, Florence, Lauderdale County, AL.

Bobbie married **Robert Earl Thompson Sr.**, son of **William Kelsie Thompson** and **Monella Pauline Dial**, 6 Nov 1959 in Lauderdale County, AL. Robert was born 14 Jul 1938 in Gunnison, MS.
  + 3915 F   i.   **Angie Kaye Thompson** was born 21 Oct 1960 in Lauderdale County, AL.
  3916 M   ii.   **Robert Earl Thompson** was born 1 Dec 1963 in Lauderdale County, AL.
  + 3917 F   iii. **Mary Paula Thompson** was born 4 Apr 1966 in Lauderdale County, AL.

2068. Charles Lee Watkins (*Mary Louise Stults*[6], *Linnie Mae Sharp*[5], *Thomas (Tom) Erwin*[4], *Charles W. II*[3], *Charles W. Sr.*[2], *John Sr.*[1]) was born 2 Feb 1948 in Lauderdale County, AL.

Charles married **Bobbie Sherry Willis**, daughter of **Robert Emmit Willis** and **Dorothy Marie Irons**, 14 Mar 1971 in Lauderdale County, AL. Bobbie was born 14 Jan 1948 in Lauderdale County, AL.
  + 3918 F   i.   **Jana Lynn Watkins** was born 30 Dec 1971 in Lauderdale County, AL.
  3919 F   ii.   **Ashley Danean Watkins** was born 8 Jun 1974 in Lauderdale County, AL.

2069. Tommie Jo Stults (*Thomas Joel Stults [6], Linnie Mae Sharp [5], Thomas (Tom) Erwin [4], Charles W. II [3], Charles W. Sr. [2], John Sr. [1]*) was born 16 Feb 1942 in Lauderdale County, AL, died 16 Feb 1984, and was buried in Mt. Zion Cemetery, Wayne City, TN.

    Tommie married **Albert Grady Peden**, son of **George Peden** and **Georgie Clemmons**, 21 Jul 1975 in Lauderdale County, AL. Albert was born 25 Jun 1936 in Lauderdale County, AL.
+ 3920 F   i.   **Cynthia Ann Peden** was born 10 Apr 1961 in Lauderdale County, AL.
+ 3921 F   ii.   **Ella Reenea Peden** was born 1 Sep 1962 in Lauderdale County, AL.
+ 3922 F   iii. **Sandra Olean Peden** was born 6 Nov 1964.

2070. Sammy Carter Stults Sr. (*Thomas Joel Stults [6], Linnie Mae Sharp [5], Thomas (Tom) Erwin [4], Charles W. II [3], Charles W. Sr. [2], John Sr. [1]*) was born 20 Jan 1944 in Lauderdale County, AL.

    Sammy married **Betty Ann Wright**, daughter of **Alvin Washington Wright** and **Margaret Lorene Vickery**, 10 May 1963 in Lauderdale County, AL. Betty was born 30 Nov 1944 in Lauderdale County, AL.
+ 3923 M   i.   **Sammy Carter Stults Jr.** was born 16 Aug 1965 in Lauderdale County, AL.
+ 3924 F   ii.   **Ponda Lynn Stults** was born 18 Jan 1969 in Lauderdale County, AL.

    Sammy next married **Barbara Joyce Coats**, daughter of **Willie O. Coats** and **Avery Kuyrendall**, 10 Oct 1979 in Lauderdale County, AL. Barbara was born 22 Jun 1955 in Franklin County, AL.

2071. Horace Calvin Stults Sr. (*Thomas Joel Stults [6], Linnie Mae Sharp [5], Thomas (Tom) Erwin [4], Charles W. II [3], Charles W. Sr. [2], John Sr. [1]*) was born 5 Jul 1949 in Lauderdale County, AL.

    Horace married **Carolyn Huckaba**, daughter of **William Boyd Huckaba** and **Betty Lou Startz**, 15 Sep 1967 in Moulton, AL. Carolyn was born 14 Apr 1952 in Russellville, Franklin County, AL.
3925 M   i.   **Horace Calvin Stults Jr.** was born 19 Feb 1971 in Lauderdale County, AL.
3926 M   ii.   **Clint Jarrod Stults** was born 15 Dec 1976 in Lauderdale County, AL.

2072. Judith Ann (Judy) Stults (*Thomas Joel Stults [6], Linnie Mae Sharp [5], Thomas (Tom) Erwin [4], Charles W. II [3], Charles W. Sr. [2], John Sr. [1]*) was born 1 Sep 1953 in Lauderdale County, AL, died 25 Jan 2003, and was buried in Mt. Zion Cemetery, Wayne City, TN.

    Judith married **Lawrence Madden Branyon**, son of **Thomas Aaron Branyon** and **Edna Madden**, 10 Jan 1969 in Lauderdale County, AL. Lawrence was born 15 Oct 1949 in Fayette City, AL.
+ 3927 F   i.   **Laura Madden Branyon** was born 25 Apr 1970 in Lauderdale County, AL.

    Judith next married ***Unk** in Lauderdale County, AL.

2073. Teresa Jean Stults (*John Bobby Stults [6], Linnie Mae Sharp [5], Thomas (Tom) Erwin [4], Charles W. II [3], Charles W. Sr. [2], John Sr. [1]*) was born 6 Apr 1953 in Lauderdale County, AL.

    Teresa married **Mickey Smith**, son of **John Leldon Smith** and **Mary Smith**. Mickey was born 16 Apr 1952 in Huntsville, Madison County, AL.
3928 F   i.   **Jessica Lynn Smith** was born 21 Aug 1981 in Birmingham, Jefferson County, AL.

2074. Debra Lynn Stults (*John Bobby Stults [6], Linnie Mae Sharp [5], Thomas (Tom) Erwin [4], Charles W. II [3], Charles W. Sr. [2], John Sr. [1]*) was born 12 Apr 1956 in Lauderdale County, AL.

    Debra married **James Tyndal Davis Jr.**, son of **James Tyndal Davis Sr.** and **Beverly Jean Rutherford**, 29 Jul 1979. James was born 10 Apr 1951 in Union, MS.
3929 F   i.   **Sara Elizabeth Davis** was born 29 Aug 1981 in Lauderdale County, AL.
3930 M   ii.   **James Tyndal (Ty) Davis III** was born 21 Feb 1984 in Lauderdale County, AL.

2075. Janice Faye Stults (*John Bobby Stults [6], Linnie Mae Sharp [5], Thomas (Tom) Erwin [4], Charles W. II [3], Charles W. Sr. [2], John Sr. [1]*) was born 9 Mar 1957 in Lauderdale County, AL.

Janice married **Donald Burt Goldstein Jr.**, son of **Donald Burt Goldstein Sr.** and **Mitz Berner**, in Birmingham, Jefferson County, AL. Donald was born in Birmingham, Jefferson County, AL.

   3931 M   i.   **Donald Burt Goldstein III** was born 14 Apr 1982 in Birmingham, Jefferson County, AL.

   3932 F   ii.   **Julie Trey Goldstein** was born 21 Nov 1985 in Birmingham, Jefferson County, AL.

2076. Patsy Marie Sharp (*David Guy*[6], *Guy Thomas*[5], *Thomas (Tom) Erwin*[4], *Charles W. II*[3], *Charles W. Sr.*[2], *John Sr.*[1]) was born 24 Jan 1952 in Lauderdale County, AL.

Patsy married **Larry Angus Waldrep**, son of **Roy Angus Waldrep** and **Stella Kathryn Thompson**, 21 Oct 1969 in Lauderdale County, AL. Larry was born 29 Mar 1946 in Colbert County, AL, died 4 Jun 2005, and was buried in Cherokee, Colbert County, AL.

+ 3933 F   i.   **Holly Lee Waldrep** was born 7 Dec 1970 in Colbert County, AL.

+ 3934 F   ii.   **Nikky Marie Waldrep** was born 13 Jun 1975 in Colbert County, AL, died 22 Jul 2003, and was buried in Cherokee Memorial Park, Colbert County, AL.

2077. Robbie Dawn Sharp (*Tommy Gerald*[6], *Guy Thomas*[5], *Thomas (Tom) Erwin*[4], *Charles W. II*[3], *Charles W. Sr.*[2], *John Sr.*[1]) was born 15 Sep 1965 in Pensacola, Escambia County, FL.

       General Notes: "July 11, 1996 - Around 3:00 p.m. an F14 Air force Jet crashed into their home, Sean was first listed as missing but was burned. Robbie was burned, taken to Mobile Burn Center..." David Sharp

Robbie married **Robert Scott Cannon**, son of **James B. Cannon Sr.** and **Wanda Zorn**, 26 Oct 1991 in Pensacola, Escambia County, FL. Robert was born 23 Sep 1963 in Pensacola, Escambia County, FL.

   3935 M   i.   **Sean Thomas Cannon** was born 8 Apr 1992 in Pensacola, Escambia County, FL, died 11 Jul 1996, and was buried in Eastern Gate Memorial Gardens, Pensacola, FL.

           General Notes: "Marine Air Force F.16 Jet crashed into Robin's house, killing son..." David Sharp

2078. Angelia Leigh Murphy (*Nancy Kay Sharp*[6], *Guy Thomas*[5], *Thomas (Tom) Erwin*[4], *Charles W. II*[3], *Charles W. Sr.*[2], *John Sr.*[1]) was born 9 Sep 1965 in Lauderdale County, AL.

Angelia married **Eric Jame Foster Sr.**, son of **Alvin Eli Foster** and **Colleen Ann Kurilo**, 17 Feb 1985 in Summerville, SC. Eric was born 15 Aug 1965 in Summerville, Dorchester County, SC.

   3936 F   i.   **Tabatha Jenne' Foster** was born 23 Sep 1985 in Charleston, Dorchester County, SC.

   3937 M   ii.   **Eric Jame Foster Jr.** was born 4 Oct 1988 in Giessen, Germany.

2081. Cindy Ann Sharp (*Walter Eugene*[6], *Ellis Eugene*[5], *Thomas (Tom) Erwin*[4], *Charles W. II*[3], *Charles W. Sr.*[2], *John Sr.*[1]) was born 20 Apr 1958 in Lauderdale County, AL.

Cindy married **Robert Lee Youngblood**, son of **George Robert Youngblood** and **Lenora Cook**, 25 Jun 1981 in Albany, GA. Robert was born 8 Jul 1957 in Albany, GA.

   3938 F   i.   **Elizabeth Ashley Youngblood** was born 2 Sep 1983 in Albany, GA.

   3939 F   ii.   **Ivy Leigh Youngblood** was born 10 Jun 1985 in Albany, GA.

   3940 M   iii. **Robert (Bobby) Eugene Youngblood** was born 21 Aug 1986 in Albany, GA.

2082. James Donald (Donnie) Vinson (*Donna Joyce Sharp*[6], *Ellis Eugene*[5], *Thomas (Tom) Erwin*[4], *Charles W. II*[3], *Charles W. Sr.*[2], *John Sr.*[1]) was born 23 Oct 1959 in Florence, Lauderdale County, AL.

James married **Barbara Ann Little**, daughter of **Albert Frank Little** and **Virginia Holcombe**, 6 Jun 1981 in Colbert County, AL. Barbara was born 2 Sep 1962 in Decatur, Morgan County, AL.

   3941 F   i.   **Rachel Ann Vinson** was born 24 Dec 1994 in Covington, GA.

2083. Andrea Jean Vinson (*Donna Joyce Sharp*[6], *Ellis Eugene*[5], *Thomas (Tom) Erwin*[4], *Charles W. II*[3], *Charles W. Sr.*[2], *John Sr.*[1]) was born 30 Oct 1961 in Florence, Lauderdale County, AL.

Andrea married **Paul Brian Stanton**, son of **Walter G. Stanton** and **Marilyn L. Taylor**, 17 Jan 1987 in Colbert County, AL. Paul was born 11 Apr 1962 in Buffalo, NY.

   3942 F   i.   **Kaitlin Lindsey Stanton** was born 20 Jun 1990 in Canton, OH.

3943 M ii. **Jospeh Brian Stanton** was born 2 Apr 1992 in Canton, OH.
3944 F iii. **Erin Nicole Stanton** was born 9 Jan 1995 in Canton, OH.

2084. Melanie Lynne Vinson (*Donna Joyce Sharp*[6], *Ellis Eugene*[5], *Thomas (Tom) Erwin*[4], *Charles W. II*[3], *Charles W. Sr.*[2], *John Sr.*[1]) was born 5 Feb 1963 in Florence, Lauderdale County, AL.

Melanie married **Andrew Ignatius Solis**, son of **Manvel Maurice Solis** and **Martha Fernandez**, 11 Jul 1987 in Colbert County, AL. Andrew was born 31 Jul 1963 in Lakeland, FL.
3945 F i. **Danielle (Dani) Wesley Solis** was born 2 Dec 1992 in Tallahassee, FL.
3946 M ii. **Jack Andrew Solis** was born 18 Dec 1998 in Naples, FL.

2087. Charles Sowders (*Ella Mae Young*[6], *William C. Young*[5], *Matilda Ann White*[4], *Eliza Jane Sharp*[3], *Charles W. Sr.*[2], *John Sr.*[1]).

Charles married **Dorothy Herron**.

2089. James Hoyt Boatright Sr. (*Lady Goldie Saddler*[6], *Cora Young*[5], *Matilda Ann White*[4], *Eliza Jane Sharp*[3], *Charles W. Sr.*[2], *John Sr.*[1]) was born 26 Jul 1920 in Wright, Lauderdale County, AL.

James married **Bessie A. Mitchell**, daughter of **Robert D. Mitchell** and **Pearl Watson**, 29 Sep 1945 in Lauderdale County, AL. Bessie was born 9 Sep 1922 in Colbert County, AL, died 16 Jan 1988, and was buried in Richardson Cemetery, Lauderdale County, AL.
+ 3947 M i. **James Hoyt Boatright Jr.** was born 27 Jul 1946 in Lauderdale County, AL.
3948 M ii. **Richard Boatright**.
3949 M iii. **John Boatright**.
+ 3950 M iv. **Steven Mitchell Boatright Sr.** was born 4 Mar 1955 in Lauderdale County, AL.

2090. Wernita Elizabeth Boatright (*Lady Goldie Saddler*[6], *Cora Young*[5], *Matilda Ann White*[4], *Eliza Jane Sharp*[3], *Charles W. Sr.*[2], *John Sr.*[1]) was born 3 Nov 1922 in Lauderdale County, AL.

Wernita married **Phillip Nolan Robinson**, son of **Alonzo D. Robinson** and **Velma Phillips**, 6 Jun 1941 in Lauderdale County, AL. Phillip was born 7 Dec 1917 in Lauderdale County, AL, died 1 May 1989, and was buried in Walston Cemetery, Oakland, Lauderdale County, AL.
+ 3951 F i. **Brenda Sue Robinson** was born 15 Oct 1943 in Lauderdale County, AL.
+ 3952 M ii. **Jackie Dale Robinson** was born 25 Oct 1946 in Lauderdale County, AL.

2091. Donald Douglas Boatright (*Lady Goldie Saddler*[6], *Cora Young*[5], *Matilda Ann White*[4], *Eliza Jane Sharp*[3], *Charles W. Sr.*[2], *John Sr.*[1]) was born 16 Jan 1930 in Lauderdale County, AL.

Donald married **Mary Ann McCorkle**, daughter of **Joe W. McCorkle** and **Myrtie Haynes**, 3 Sep 1948 in Lauderdale County, AL. Mary was born 28 Jul 1930 in Lauderdale County, AL, died in Nov 1987, and was buried in Richardson Cemetery, Lauderdale County, AL.
+ 3953 F i. **Shawn Boatright**.
3954 M ii. **Shane Boatright**.

2092. Wanda Joy Pruitt (*Vera Alean Saddler*[6], *Cora Young*[5], *Matilda Ann White*[4], *Eliza Jane Sharp*[3], *Charles W. Sr.*[2], *John Sr.*[1]).

Wanda married **Charles Whitelaw**.

2093. James Lewis Saddler (*James Louie Saddler*[6], *Cora Young*[5], *Matilda Ann White*[4], *Eliza Jane Sharp*[3], *Charles W. Sr.*[2], *John Sr.*[1]) was born 6 Jul 1932 in Lauderdale County, AL.

James married **Marilyn Bryant**, daughter of **Harry Bryant** and **Virginia Morrison**, 14 Feb.

2094. Larry Dennis Sharp (*Jewel Estelle Young*[6], *John Robert Young*[5], *Matilda Ann White*[4], *Eliza Jane Sharp*[3], *Charles W. Sr.*[2], *John Sr.*[1]) was born 17 Sep 1945 in Lauderdale County, AL.

Larry married **Sandra Kay Green**, daughter of **John Robert Green** and **Norma Ailee McLendon**, 4 Dec 1976 in Sardis, MS. Sandra was born 20 Aug 1949 in Sardis, MS.

    3955 F   i.   **Jennifer Lee Sharp** was born 29 Jul 1979 in Jackson, MS.

    3956 F   ii.   **Julie Kathryn Sharp** was born 28 Oct 1982 in Jackson, MS.

2095. Roberta Nathalie Sharp (*Jewel Estelle Young^6, John Robert Young^5, Matilda Ann White^4, Eliza Jane Sharp^3, Charles W. Sr.^{2}, John Sr.^{1}*) was born 21 Aug 1951 in Lauderdale County, AL.

Roberta married **William Neal Hayes Jr.**, son of **William Neal Hayes Sr.** and **Dorothy McGehee**, 8 Oct 1979 in Lauderdale County, AL. William was born 28 Apr 1952 in Pike County, MS.

+ 3957 F   i.   **Lindsey Ann Hayes** was born 22 Aug 1982 in Lauderdale County, AL.

2098. Linda Arnalla Young (*Arnold Andrew Young^6, Andrew Cleveland Young^5, Matilda Ann White^4, Eliza Jane Sharp^3, Charles W. Sr.^{2}, John Sr.^{1}*) was born 8 Jul 1947 in Athens, Limestone County, AL.

Linda married **Phillip Orton Street**, son of **Orton W. Street** and **Evelyn Poorman**, 23 Jun 1973 in Lauderdale County, AL. Phillip was born 11 Feb 1942 in Cuyahoga County, OH.

    3958 M   i.   **Mark Phillip Street** was born 15 May 1974 in Lauderdale County, AL.

+ 3959 M   ii.   **Eric Andrew Street** was born 8 Sep 1977 in Lauderdale County, AL.

2103. Tempie Voliun Young (*Clarence Roy Young^6, Clarence W. Young^5, Matilda Ann White^4, Eliza Jane Sharp^3, Charles W. Sr.^{2}, John Sr.^{1}*) was born 22 Dec 1937 in Lauderdale County, AL.

Tempie married **Harve Harrison Allison**, son of **Raymond Andrew Allison** and **Bama Inez Ingram**, 6 Sep 1953 in Iuka, Tishomingo County, MS. Harve was born 2 Feb 1936 in Lauderdale County, AL, died 17 Jun 1991, and was buried in Oak Grove Cemetery, Lauderdale County, AL.
(Duplicate Line. See Person 1596)

2104. Roy Lewis Young (*Clarence Roy Young^6, Clarence W. Young^5, Matilda Ann White^4, Eliza Jane Sharp^3, Charles W. Sr.^{2}, John Sr.^{1}*) was born 9 Aug 1943 in Lauderdale County, AL.

Roy married **Linda Sue Taylor** 22 Aug 1964 in Savannah, TN.

2105. Phillip Dale Young (*Clarence Roy Young^6, Clarence W. Young^5, Matilda Ann White^4, Eliza Jane Sharp^3, Charles W. Sr.^{2}, John Sr.^{1}*) was born 11 Mar 1950 in Lauderdale County, AL.

Phillip married **Barbara Jean Mangrum**, daughter of **James E. Mangrum** and **Jessie Mitchell**, 5 Mar 1971 in Lauderdale County, AL. Barbara was born 29 Aug 1950 in Colbert County, AL.

2106. Judith Ann Young (*John David Young^6, Clarence W. Young^5, Matilda Ann White^4, Eliza Jane Sharp^3, Charles W. Sr.^{2}, John Sr.^{1}*) was born 5 Jan 1947 in Lauderdale County, AL, died 21 Jan 1993, and was buried in Mishawaka, St Joseph County, IN.

Judith married **Tom Raymond Williams** in 1962 in St. Joseph County, IN. Tom was born 29 Aug 1942 in Terre Haute, IN.

+ 3960 F   i.   **Tammie Kaye Williams** was born 29 Dec 1962 in Mishawaka, St Joseph County, IN.

+ 3961 M   ii.   **James Eugene Williams** was born 6 Jan 1965 in Mishawaka, St Joseph County, IN.

2107. Glenda Sue Young (*John David Young^6, Clarence W. Young^5, Matilda Ann White^4, Eliza Jane Sharp^3, Charles W. Sr.^{2}, John Sr.^{1}*) was born 23 Jul 1949 in Lauderdale County, AL.

Glenda married **John Bentley** 6 Apr 1968 in South Bend, IN. John was born 19 Aug 1947 in Seco, Letcher County, KY.

+ 3962 M   i.   **David Michael Bentley** was born 21 Oct 1967 in South Bend, IN.

+ 3963 F   ii.   **Tracie Marie Bentley** was born 20 May 1972 in South Bend, IN.

    3964 M   iii.   **John Kevin Bentley** was born 27 Jul 1973 in South Bend, IN.

2108. Reba Kay Young (*John David Young⁶, Clarence W. Young⁵, Matilda Ann White⁴, Eliza Jane Sharp³, Charles W. Sr.², John Sr.¹*) was born 3 Dec 1952 in Mishawaka, St Joseph County, IN.

Reba married **Jerry Polleck**.
+ 3965 F i. **Kimberly Ann Polleck** was born 13 Apr 1971 in Mishawaka, St Joseph County, IN.

Reba next married **Norman Vincent Koziatek** 31 Mar 1979. Norman was born 25 Jan 1955 in Mishawaka, St Joseph County, IN.
3966 M i. **Michael N. Koziatek** was born 29 Feb 1980 in Mishawaka, St Joseph County, IN.
3967 M ii. **Brian K. Koziatek** was born 12 Jan 1984 in Elkhart, Elkhart County, IN.

2109. Rose Marie Young (*John David Young⁶, Clarence W. Young⁵, Matilda Ann White⁴, Eliza Jane Sharp³, Charles W. Sr.², John Sr.¹*) was born 11 Aug 1954 in Mishawaka, St Joseph County, IN.

Rose married **Randy Leon Verspett**. Randy was born 4 Oct 1952 in Mishawaka, St Joseph County, IN.
3968 F i. **Jennifer Lynn Verspett** was born 3 Apr 1973 in South Bend, IN.
3969 M ii. **Joseph Ryan Verspett** was born 1 Oct 1977 in Mishawaka, St Joseph County, IN.
3970 M iii. **Phillip Michael Verspett** was born 3 Nov 1980 in Mishawaka, St Joseph County, IN.

2110. Patsy Hawkins (*Marie Mae Young⁶, Edna G. (Birdie) Young⁵, Matilda Ann White⁴, Eliza Jane Sharp³, Charles W. Sr.², John Sr.¹*).

Patsy married **Brady Holderead**.

2112. Bonnie Iness Teer (*Florence Golden⁶, Rosa Hinton⁵, Martha Jane White⁴, Eliza Jane Sharp³, Charles W. Sr.², John Sr.¹*).

Bonnie married **Myron Melvin Lee**.

2115. Martha Janice Golden (*John Golden⁶, Rosa Hinton⁵, Martha Jane White⁴, Eliza Jane Sharp³, Charles W. Sr.², John Sr.¹*) was born in 1953.

Martha married ***Unk Ruther**.

2117. Larry Carlton Hinton (*Jones Carlton Hinton⁶, Jones Henry Hinton⁵, Martha Jane White⁴, Eliza Jane Sharp³, Charles W. Sr.², John Sr.¹*) was born in 1944.

Larry married **Linda Dugan**.
+ 3971 F i. **Krista Marie Hinton**.
3972 M ii. **Scott Ryan Hinton** was born in 1968.

2118. Anita Louise Hinton (*Jones Carlton Hinton⁶, Jones Henry Hinton⁵, Martha Jane White⁴, Eliza Jane Sharp³, Charles W. Sr.², John Sr.¹*) was born in 1947.

Anita married **James Ruffato**.

2119. James Arnold Hinton (*Jones Carlton Hinton⁶, Jones Henry Hinton⁵, Martha Jane White⁴, Eliza Jane Sharp³, Charles W. Sr.², John Sr.¹*) was born in 1948.

James married **Millicent Costello**.
3973 F i. **Amber Nicole Hinton** was born in 1976.

James next married **Nancy Martinez**.
3974 F i. **Michele Lee Hinton** was born in 1978.

2120. Curtis Melvin Hinton Jr. (*Curtis Melvin Hinton Sr.⁶, Jones Henry Hinton⁵, Martha Jane White⁴, Eliza Jane Sharp³, Charles W. Sr.², John Sr.¹*) was born in 1947.

Curtis married **Nancy Upchurch**.

3975 F i. **Nancy Michele Hinton** was born in 1968.
3976 M ii. **Michael Hinton** was born in 1968.

2121. Cynthia Ann Hinton (*Curtis Melvin Hinton Sr.*^{6}, *Jones Henry Hinton*^{5}, *Martha Jane White*^{4}, *Eliza Jane Sharp*^{3}, *Charles W. Sr.*^{2}, *John Sr.*^{1}) was born in 1952.

Cynthia married **Richard Gaylon Hamilton**.

3977 F i. **Ashley Hamilton** was born in 1972.
3978 M ii. **Blake Hamilton** was born in 1981.
3979 M iii. **Caine Hamilton** was born in 1982.

2123. Candy Jones Hinton (*Curtis Melvin Hinton Sr.*^{6}, *Jones Henry Hinton*^{5}, *Martha Jane White*^{4}, *Eliza Jane Sharp*^{3}, *Charles W. Sr.*^{2}, *John Sr.*^{1}) was born in 1958.

Candy married **Willard Warren Woolfolk**.

3980 F i. **Virginia Leigh Woolfolk** was born in 1982.
3981 M ii. **Curtis Warren Woolfolk** was born in 1983.

2124. Wendy Estelle Hinton (*Curtis Melvin Hinton Sr.*^{6}, *Jones Henry Hinton*^{5}, *Martha Jane White*^{4}, *Eliza Jane Sharp*^{3}, *Charles W. Sr.*^{2}, *John Sr.*^{1}) was born in 1965.

Wendy married **Jeffrey Allen Houston**.

3982 F i. **Annalee Grace Houston** was born in 1992.
3983 F ii. **Sara Rebekah Houston** was born in 1994.

2125. Hubert Jeffrey Burson Jr. (*Vernon Juanita Hinton*^{6}, *Jones Henry Hinton*^{5}, *Martha Jane White*^{4}, *Eliza Jane Sharp*^{3}, *Charles W. Sr.*^{2}, *John Sr.*^{1}) was born in 1943.

Hubert married **Marilyn Bryant**.

+ 3984 M i. **Jefferson Dean Burson** was born in 1964.
+ 3985 M ii. **Francis Paul Burson** was born in 1965.
+ 3986 M iii. **Christopher Evan Burson** was born in 1966.

2126. Linda Kay Burson (*Vernon Juanita Hinton*^{6}, *Jones Henry Hinton*^{5}, *Martha Jane White*^{4}, *Eliza Jane Sharp*^{3}, *Charles W. Sr.*^{2}, *John Sr.*^{1}) was born in 1944.

Linda married **Michael Lawrence Padron**.

+ 3987 M i. **Lawrence Jefferson Padron** was born in 1965.
+ 3988 F ii. **Susanna Marie Padron** was born in 1966.
  3989 M iii. **Dennis Padron** was born in 1968.
+ 3990 F iv. **Valeria Lynn Padron** was born in 1970.

2127. Gloria Jean Burson (*Vernon Juanita Hinton*^{6}, *Jones Henry Hinton*^{5}, *Martha Jane White*^{4}, *Eliza Jane Sharp*^{3}, *Charles W. Sr.*^{2}, *John Sr.*^{1}) was born in 1946.

Gloria married **Eddie Paul Merrill**.

3991 M i. **Damon Ashley Merrill** was born in 1968.
3992 M ii. **Daniel Burson Merrill** was born in 1987.

2128. Roslyn Darleen Burson (*Vernon Juanita Hinton*^{6}, *Jones Henry Hinton*^{5}, *Martha Jane White*^{4}, *Eliza Jane Sharp*^{3}, *Charles W. Sr.*^{2}, *John Sr.*^{1}) was born in 1947.

Roslyn married **Thomas Reilly**.

Roslyn next married **Grant Hall**.

+ 3993 F i. **Shannon Hall** was born in 1969.

+ 3994 F ii. **Monica Hall** was born in 1971.

3995 F iii. **Dana Shay Hall** was born in 1974.

2129. Joseph Norman Hearin III (*Gloria Mae Hinton^6, Jones Henry Hinton^5, Martha Jane White^4, Eliza Jane Sharp^3, Charles W. Sr.^{2}, John Sr.^{1}*) was born in 1947.

Joseph married **Christine *Unk**.

3996 M i. **Joseph Norman Hearin IV** was born in 1970.

Joseph next married **Karen Taylor**.

3997 M i. **Thomas Taylor Hearin** was born in 1989.

3998 M ii. **Elijah David Hearin** was born in 1995.

2130. Norma Susan Hinton (*Lloyd Thurston Hinton Sr.^{6}, Jones Henry Hinton^5, Martha Jane White^4, Eliza Jane Sharp^3, Charles W. Sr.^{2}, John Sr.^{1}*) was born in 1949.

Norma married **Al Johnson**.

Norma next married **Jessie Strickland**.

+ 3999 F i. **Sandy Michelle Strickland** was born in 1969.

4000 M ii. **Tracy Strickland** was born in 1975.

2131. Lloyd Thurston Hinton Jr. (*Lloyd Thurston Hinton Sr.^{6}, Jones Henry Hinton^5, Martha Jane White^4, Eliza Jane Sharp^3, Charles W. Sr.^{2}, John Sr.^{1}*) was born in 1951.

Lloyd married **Kim *Unk**.

4001 F i. **Brooks Hinton** was born in 1981.

4002 F ii. **Carley Young Hinton** was born in 1983.

2132. Richard George Hinton (*Lloyd Thurston Hinton Sr.^{6}, Jones Henry Hinton^5, Martha Jane White^4, Eliza Jane Sharp^3, Charles W. Sr.^{2}, John Sr.^{1}*) was born in 1952.

Richard married **Sherry Ray *Unk**.

+ 4003 F i. **Christy Lee Hinton** was born in 1976.

4004 M ii. **Richard Hinton** was born in 1979.

2133. Britt Hinton (*Lloyd Thurston Hinton Sr.^{6}, Jones Henry Hinton^5, Martha Jane White^4, Eliza Jane Sharp^3, Charles W. Sr.^{2}, John Sr.^{1}*) was born in 1955.

Britt married **Elizabeth Pichard**.

4005 M i. **Bradley William Hinton** was born in 1985.

4006 F ii. **Sarah Elizabeth Hinton** was born in 1990.

2134. Rita Charlotte Johnson (*Ola Roselyn Hinton^6, Jones Henry Hinton^5, Martha Jane White^4, Eliza Jane Sharp^3, Charles W. Sr.^{2}, John Sr.^{1}*) was born in 1953.

Rita married **William Gary Lowman Sr.**.

4007 M i. **William Gary Lowman Jr.** was born in 1979.

4008 M ii. **Clinton Hooper Lowman** was born in 1981.

2135. Vernon Annette Wilkerson (*Charles B. Wilkerson^6, Vernon L. B. Hinton^5, Martha Jane White^4, Eliza Jane Sharp^3, Charles W. Sr.^{2}, John Sr.^{1}*) was born in 1940.

Vernon married **Dallas Freeman Carroll Jr.**.

2141. Paul Ray Young II (*Paul Ray Young I^6, Charles Westbrook Young Sr.^{5}, Ella Prooterwill White^4, Eliza Jane Sharp^3, Charles W. Sr.^{2}, John Sr.^{1}*) was born 15 Dec 1952 in Lauderdale County, AL and died 15 Dec 2006 in Lauderdale County, AL.

Paul married **Da Ron Cottrell** 22 Sep 1970 in Lauderdale County, AL. Da was born 5 Mar 1955 in Quarry County, NM.

2147. Jim I. Young Jr. (*Joseph Inloe Young I^6, Charles Westbrook Young Sr.^{5}, Ella Prooterwill White^4, Eliza Jane Sharp^3, Charles W. Sr.^{2}, John Sr.^{1}*) was born 12 Jul 1956 in Indiana.

Jim married **Tammy Alene Boatright**, daughter of **James Hoyt Boatright Jr.** and **Betty Ruth Vickers**, 8 Jun 1988 in Lauderdale County, AL. Tammy was born 4 May 1970 in Lauderdale County, AL.
4009 M i. **Catlin Gregory Young** was born in 1987.

2148. Joseph (Jody) Inloe Young II (*Joseph Inloe Young I^6, Charles Westbrook Young Sr.^{5}, Ella Prooterwill White^4, Eliza Jane Sharp^3, Charles W. Sr.^{2}, John Sr.^{1}*) was born 22 Dec 1967 in Lauderdale County, AL.

Joseph married **Michelle Anne Collins**, daughter of **Bernie James Collins** and **Mary Kathleen Gean**, 9 Feb 1989 in Lauderdale County, AL. Michelle was born 26 Jan 1970 in Evansville, Vanderburgh County, IN. Another name for Michelle is Michelle Anne Collins.
4010 F i. **Megan Veronica Young** was born 19 Dec 1989 in Lauderdale County, AL.
4011 F ii. **Felicia Lynn Young** was born 24 Jun 1992 in Lauderdale County, AL.

Joseph next married **Chloe Witt** after 1990.

2149. Sarah Duffy Sharp (*Edgar Chisholm Jr.^{6}, Edgar Chisholm Sr.^{5}, William (Bill) Edgar^4, David Allen^3, Charles W. Sr.^{2}, John Sr.^{1}*) was born 18 Feb 1957 in Houston, TX.

Sarah married **Charles Edward Hurley** 16 Dec 1984. Charles was born 13 Aug 1946 in Maryland.
4012 M i. **Jason Michael Hurley** was born 26 May in Houston, TX.

2150. Edgar Chisholm Sharp III (*Edgar Chisholm Jr.^{6}, Edgar Chisholm Sr.^{5}, William (Bill) Edgar^4, David Allen^3, Charles W. Sr.^{2}, John Sr.^{1}*) was born 7 Jun 1960 in Houston, TX.

Edgar married **Margarita Zuniza** 10 Jul 1993 in Austin, TX. Margarita was born 12 Aug 1959 in California.

2151. Melinda Ann Killen (*Milton Stribling Killen Jr.^{6}, Minnie Louise Sharp^5, William (Bill) Edgar^4, David Allen^3, Charles W. Sr.^{2}, John Sr.^{1}*) was born 31 Dec 1953 in Lauderdale County, AL.

Melinda married **John Jesse Corlew III** in May 1979. John died in May 1980 and was buried in Murfreesboro, TN.
4013 F i. **Jesse Anna Catherine Corlew** was born 4 Sep 1980 in Memphis, Shelby County, TN.

Melinda next married **Harry A. Haines** 2 Jan 1982. Harry was born 22 May 1926.
4014 F i. **Jesse Anna Catherine Corlew** was born 4 Sep 1980 in Memphis, Shelby County, TN.

2152. Milton Reid Killen (*Milton Stribling Killen Jr.^{6}, Minnie Louise Sharp^5, William (Bill) Edgar^4, David Allen^3, Charles W. Sr.^{2}, John Sr.^{1}*) was born 31 Jan 1958 in Toledo, OH.

Milton married **Karleen Joan Orosch**, daughter of **John Joseph Orosch** and **Lucienne Henriette Vermeulen**, 17 Feb 1990 in Falls Church, VA. Karleen was born 13 Jul 1957.
4015 M i. **Andrew Milton Reid Killen** was born 8 Aug 1993 in Dale City, CA.

2153. Elyse Carpenter Killen (*Milton Stribling Killen Jr.^{6}, Minnie Louise Sharp^5, William (Bill) Edgar^4, David Allen^3, Charles W. Sr.^{2}, John Sr.^{1}*) was born 3 Oct 1961 in Verdun, France.

Elyse married **Charles Kevin Hall**, son of **Dr. Charles Ray Hall** and **Martha Ann Bean**, 26 May 1985 in Huntsville, Madison County, AL. Charles was born 9 Oct 1960 in Memphis, Shelby County, TN.

    4016 M   i.   **Charles Parker Hall** was born 13 May 1991 in Huntsville, Madison County, AL.

2155. Laura Kathleen Killen (*William (Billy) Sharp Killen*[6], *Minnie Louise Sharp*[5], *William (Bill) Edgar*[4], *David Allen*[3], *Charles W. Sr.*[2], *John Sr.*[1]) was born 8 Oct 1953 in Lauderdale County, AL.

Laura married **David Ray**.

2157. Jenny Louise Killen (*William (Billy) Sharp Killen*[6], *Minnie Louise Sharp*[5], *William (Bill) Edgar*[4], *David Allen*[3], *Charles W. Sr.*[2], *John Sr.*[1]) was born 24 Aug 1958 in Athens, Limestone County, AL.

Jenny married **Felton Hutto**.

2161. Billy Eugene Killen (*Jimmy Eugene Killen*[6], *Minnie Louise Sharp*[5], *William (Bill) Edgar*[4], *David Allen*[3], *Charles W. Sr.*[2], *John Sr.*[1]) was born 17 Jan 1953 in Athens, Limestone County, AL.

Billy married **Karen Allen**, daughter of **James Allen** and **Dorothy Eaves**, 23 May 1975 in Athens, Limestone County, AL. Karen was born 20 Jul 1953 in Athens, Limestone County, AL.

    4017 F   i.   **Alysha Eva Killen** was born 12 Sep 1979 in Decatur, Morgan County, AL.
    4018 F   ii.   **Haley Dawn Killen** was born 7 Sep 1983 in Decatur, Morgan County, AL.

2162. Brenda Maxine Killen (*Jimmy Eugene Killen*[6], *Minnie Louise Sharp*[5], *William (Bill) Edgar*[4], *David Allen*[3], *Charles W. Sr.*[2], *John Sr.*[1]) was born 20 Jun 1954 in Athens, Limestone County, AL.

Brenda married **Harris Toney Mitchell Jr.**, son of **Harris Toney Mitchell Sr.** and **Ann *Unk**, 20 Jan 1979. Harris was born 20 Dec 1954 in Huntsville, Madison County, AL.

    4019 M   i.   **Harris Toney Mitchell III** was born 8 Jun 1987 in Huntsville, Madison County, AL.

2163. Debra Killen (*Don Sherron Killen*[6], *Minnie Louise Sharp*[5], *William (Bill) Edgar*[4], *David Allen*[3], *Charles W. Sr.*[2], *John Sr.*[1]) was born 2 Oct 1952 in Athens, Limestone County, AL.

Debra married **Mike Ezell**, son of **Herbert E. Ezell** and **Jean Hardaway**, 13 Feb 1971 in Athens, Limestone County, AL. Mike was born 8 Oct 1951.

+ 4020 M   i.   **Brett Ezell** was born 16 Mar 1972 in Shreveport, LA.
    4021 M   ii.   **Keith Ezell** was born 26 Jul 1974 in Shreveport, LA.

2166. William Paul Sharp (*James Buford Jr.*[6], *James Buford Sr.*[5], *James (Jim) Hulet*[4], *David Allen*[3], *Charles W. Sr.*[2], *John Sr.*[1]) was born 11 Nov 1951 in Colbert County, AL.

William married **Laura Evelina Struzick**, daughter of **Edward H. Struzick** and **Evelyn Childress**, 12 Jun 1973 in Lauderdale County, AL. Laura was born 13 Aug 1952 in Jefferson County, AL.

William next married **Rita Sue Lamb**, daughter of **Marlie Monroe Lamb** and **Ethel Mae Grigsby**, 14 Dec 1989 in Colbert County, AL. Rita was born 25 May 1953, died 22 Apr 2000, and was buried in Greenview Memorial Park, Florence, Lauderdale County, AL.

    4022 M   i.   **Braden Paul Sharp** was born 17 Aug 1989 in Colbert County, AL.

2168. Linda Gay Sharp (*James Buford Jr.*[6], *James Buford Sr.*[5], *James (Jim) Hulet*[4], *David Allen*[3], *Charles W. Sr.*[2], *John Sr.*[1]) was born 31 Aug 1956 in Colbert County, AL.

Linda married **Kendall Allen Norris**, son of **James T. Norris Sr.** and **Myra E. Hester**, 29 Jul 1973 in Lauderdale County, AL. Kendall was born 4 Nov 1954 in Salinas, KS.

Linda next married **William Joseph (Joey) McDonnell Jr.**, son of **William Joseph McDonnell Sr.** and **Ester Walker**, 4 Jun 1978 in Lauderdale County, AL. William was born 16 Mar 1948 in Seoul, Korea.

    4023 M   i.   **Samuel Braden McDonnell** was born 24 Jan 1979 in Colbert County, AL.

2169. Nancy Lynn Sharp (*James Buford Jr.*[6], *James Buford Sr.*[5], *James (Jim) Hulet*[4], *David Allen*[3], *Charles W. Sr.*[2], *John Sr.*[1]) was born 20 Apr 1961 in Lauderdale County, AL.

    Nancy married **Gayle Hoyt (Snuffy) Smith** 4 Jun 1984.
    4024 F   i.   **Laura Gail Smith** was born 21 Feb 1988 in Colbert County, AL.

2170. Melanie Jane Sharp (*Joseph (Joe) Dickson*[6], *James Buford Sr.*[5], *James (Jim) Hulet*[4], *David Allen*[3], *Charles W. Sr.*[2], *John Sr.*[1]) was born 4 Jul 1964 in Lauderdale County, AL.

    Melanie married **Randle Wayne Perkins**, son of **Henry Clayton Perkins** and **Cheryl Darlene Adams**, 28 Aug 1988 in Lauderdale County, AL. Randle was born 3 Feb 1965 in Lauderdale County, AL.
    4025 M   i.   **Ryan Matthew Perkins** was born 28 Jul 1990 in Lauderdale County, AL.
    4026 F   ii.   **Rachel Marie Perkins** was born 15 Sep 1995 in Lauderdale County, AL.

2171. Jo Lynn Sharp (*Joseph (Joe) Dickson*[6], *James Buford Sr.*[5], *James (Jim) Hulet*[4], *David Allen*[3], *Charles W. Sr.*[2], *John Sr.*[1]) was born 28 Feb 1971 in Lauderdale County, AL.

    Jo married **Michael Shawn McClure**, son of **Charles Lowell McClure** and **Judy Belle Mitchell**, 23 May 1992 in Lauderdale County, AL. Michael was born 18 Aug 1968 in Lauderdale County, AL.
    4027 F   i.   **Sarah Grace McClure** was born 18 Feb 1996 in Lauderdale County, AL.
    4028 F   ii.   **Hannah Marie McClure** was born 1 Apr 1999 in Lauderdale County, AL.
    4029 F   iii.   **Katherine Lynn McClure** was born 17 Dec 2001 in Lauderdale County, AL.

2172. Susanne Sharp (*John Alvin Sr.*[6], *James Buford Sr.*[5], *James (Jim) Hulet*[4], *David Allen*[3], *Charles W. Sr.*[2], *John Sr.*[1]) was born 25 Feb 1962 in Lauderdale County, AL.

    Susanne married **Jimmy Hatcher**.
    4030 M   i.   **Troy Hatcher**.

2173. John Alvin Sharp Jr. (*John Alvin Sr.*[6], *James Buford Sr.*[5], *James (Jim) Hulet*[4], *David Allen*[3], *Charles W. Sr.*[2], *John Sr.*[1]) was born 26 Jun 1973 in Lauderdale County, AL.

    John married **Rhonda *Unk**.
    4031 F   i.   **Jaylee Sharp**.

2174. Robert Denson Akers (*Mallie Denson Stewart*[6], *Cynthia Emmanola Sharp*[5], *Joseph (Joe) Powers Sr.*[4], *David Allen*[3], *Charles W. Sr.*[2], *John Sr.*[1]) was born 22 Aug 1952 in Lauderdale County, AL.

    Robert married **Karen Ann Kilar**, daughter of **Marion Frank Kilar** and **Audrey Martin Smith**, 22 Dec 1975 in Pensacola, Escambia County, FL. Karen was born 29 Jan 1954 in Chicago, IL.
    4032 F   i.   **Ashley Lianne Akers** was born 20 Mar 1981 in Pensacola, Escambia County, FL.

2175. Ellen Louise Akers (*Mallie Denson Stewart*[6], *Cynthia Emmanola Sharp*[5], *Joseph (Joe) Powers Sr.*[4], *David Allen*[3], *Charles W. Sr.*[2], *John Sr.*[1]) was born 6 Dec 1954 in Jacksonville, FL.

    Ellen married **Steve Keath Woodfin**, son of **James Thomas Woodfin** and **Lorine Rolin**, 22 Jun 1973 in Pensacola, Escambia County, FL. Steve was born 24 May 1949 in Athens, Limestone County, AL.
    4033 M   i.   **Christopher (Chris) Woodfin** was born 25 Sep 1975 in Decatur, Morgan County, AL.
    4034 M   ii.   **James (Jamie) Woodfin** was born 25 Feb 1979 in Pensacola, Escambia County, FL.

2176. Peggy Leigh Akers (*Mallie Denson Stewart*[6], *Cynthia Emmanola Sharp*[5], *Joseph (Joe) Powers Sr.*[4], *David Allen*[3], *Charles W. Sr.*[2], *John Sr.*[1]) was born 3 May 1956 in San Diego, CA.

    Peggy married **Dewitt Anthony Brown**, son of **Bernard Axle Brown** and **Jane Milstead**, 14 Aug 1987 in Pensacola, Escambia County, FL. Dewitt was born 21 Aug 1962 in Pensacola, Escambia County, FL.
    4035 M   i.   **Cody William Brown** was born 11 Apr 1989 in Covington, LA.
    4036 F   ii.   **Sarah Jane Brown** was born 16 Nov 2000 in Pensacola, Escambia County, FL.

2177. Theresa Ann Akers (*Mallie Denson Stewart^6, Cynthia Emmanola Sharp^5, Joseph (Joe) Powers Sr.^{4}, David Allen^3, Charles W. Sr.^{2}, John Sr.^{1}*) was born 15 Jun 1957 in San Diego, CA.

Theresa married ***Unk Champaign**.

4037 M   i.   **Eddie Champaign** was born in Jan 1981.
4038 F   ii.   **Peri Leigh Champaign** was born in 1986.
4039 M   iii.   **Macon Champaign**.

2178. Joyelyn Holland Hale (*William Holland Hale^6, Mayro Sharp^5, Joseph (Joe) Powers Sr.^{4}, David Allen^3, Charles W. Sr.^{2}, John Sr.^{1}*) was born 17 Aug 1955 in Lauderdale County, AL.

Joyelyn married **Kevin Warren Jangaard**, son of **Arnt L. Jangaard** and **Lucille Ziegler**, 21 Jan 1982 in Lauderdale County, AL. Kevin was born 2 Jan 1949 in Richmond City, NY.

4040 M   i.   **William (Will) Hale Jangaard** was born 14 Mar 1986 in Salem, MA.

2179. Debra Arlene Sharp (*Ralph Morrow^6, Joseph Powers (J. P.) Jr.^{5}, Joseph (Joe) Powers Sr.^{4}, David Allen^3, Charles W. Sr.^{2}, John Sr.^{1}*) was born 17 Sep 1956 in Lauderdale County, AL.

Debra married **Hernon Randolph Peters**, son of **Hernon D. Peters** and **Joyce Arthur**, 5 Dec 1973 in Lauderdale County, AL. Hernon was born 19 Nov 1953 in Wills County, IL.

4041 M   i.   **David Michael Peters** was born 9 Feb 1974 in Tampa, FL.

2180. Eddie D. Sharp (*Ralph Morrow^6, Joseph Powers (J. P.) Jr.^{5}, Joseph (Joe) Powers Sr.^{4}, David Allen^3, Charles W. Sr.^{2}, John Sr.^{1}*) was born 18 Aug 1957 in Lauderdale County, AL.

Eddie married **Jane Redman**. Jane was born 5 May 1962 in St. Joseph County, IN.

4042 M   i.   **Matthew D. Sharp** was born 29 Mar 1983 in St. Joseph County, IN.
4043 F   ii.   **Carrie L. Sharp** was born 19 Jul 1984 in St. Joseph County, IN.

2182. Ralph David Sharp (*Ralph Morrow^6, Joseph Powers (J. P.) Jr.^{5}, Joseph (Joe) Powers Sr.^{4}, David Allen^3, Charles W. Sr.^{2}, John Sr.^{1}*) was born 26 Aug 1968 in St. Joseph County, IN.

Ralph married **Kimberly Sue Fertick**.

4044 F   i.   **Andrea L. Sharp** was born in Sep 1993 in Tampa, FL.

2183. Tina Kaye Sharp (*Billy Joe^6, Joseph Powers (J. P.) Jr.^{5}, Joseph (Joe) Powers Sr.^{4}, David Allen^3, Charles W. Sr.^{2}, John Sr.^{1}*) was born 30 Jan 1964 in Lauderdale County, AL.

Tina married **Stephen Jay Broadfoot**, son of **Lee S. Broadfoot** and **Gloria Vernon**, 5 Dec 1986 in Lauderdale County, AL. Stephen was born 19 Jan 1964 in Lauderdale County, AL.

4045 F   i.   **Jordan Leigh Broadfoot** was born 7 Nov 1989 in El Paso, El Paso County, TX.
4046 F   ii.   **Stephanie Paige Broadfoot** was born 7 Nov 1993 in Lauderdale County, AL.

2184. Pamela Diane Sharp (*Billy Joe^6, Joseph Powers (J. P.) Jr.^{5}, Joseph (Joe) Powers Sr.^{4}, David Allen^3, Charles W. Sr.^{2}, John Sr.^{1}*) was born 4 Oct 1965 in Lauderdale County, AL.

Pamela married **Steven Craig Peppers**, son of **Earnest G. Peppers** and **Charlotte McGuire**, 5 Dec 1986 in Lauderdale County, AL. Steven was born 7 Jan 1965 in Jefferson County, AL.

4047 F   i.   **Brittney Nicole Peppers** was born 27 May 1988 in Lauderdale County, AL.
4048 F   ii.   **Makensie Peppers** was born 22 Feb 1992 in Birmingham, Jefferson County, AL.

2185. Vicky Robin Sharp (*Billy Joe^6, Joseph Powers (J. P.) Jr.^{5}, Joseph (Joe) Powers Sr.^{4}, David Allen^3, Charles W. Sr.^{2}, John Sr.^{1}*) was born 11 Jun 1967 in Lauderdale County, AL.

Vicky married **Kevin Wade Putman**, son of **Jerry Spencer Putman** and **Mary Francis Garrison**, 12 Mar 1988 in Lauderdale County, AL. Kevin was born 27 May 1965 in Lauderdale County, AL.

4049   M   i.   **Brandon Wade Putman** was born 29 Aug 1994 in Lauderdale County, AL.

2186. Natasha Jo Sharp (*Billy Joe ^{6}, Joseph Powers (J. P.) Jr. ^{5}, Joseph (Joe) Powers Sr. ^{4}, David Allen ^{3}, Charles W. Sr. ^{2}, John Sr. ^{1}*) was born 21 Aug 1977 in Lauderdale County, AL.

Natasha married **Kristin Brady Walker**, son of **Eckard Walker** and **Barbara Peck**, 30 Jun 2001 in Lauderdale County, AL. Kristin was born 23 May 1974 in Lauderdale County, AL.

2187. Cynthia (Cindy) Robyn Sharp (*Daniel C. ^{6}, Joseph Powers (J. P.) Jr. ^{5}, Joseph (Joe) Powers Sr. ^{4}, David Allen ^{3}, Charles W. Sr. ^{2}, John Sr. ^{1}*) was born 2 May 1961 in Lauderdale County, AL.

Cynthia married **Bobby Lee Rickard Jr.**, son of **Bobby Lee Rickard Sr.** and **Norma Smith**, 27 Jan 1984 in Lauderdale County, AL. Bobby was born 27 Aug 1956 in Lauderdale County, AL.
4050   F   i.   **Whitney Leigh Rickard** was born 4 Nov 1987 in Lauderdale County, AL.

2188. Kelli Layne Sharp (*Daniel C. ^{6}, Joseph Powers (J. P.) Jr. ^{5}, Joseph (Joe) Powers Sr. ^{4}, David Allen ^{3}, Charles W. Sr. ^{2}, John Sr. ^{1}*) was born 22 May 1969 in Lauderdale County, AL.

Kelli married **Dunnavan Glenn Arnold**, son of **Steve Steele Arnold** and **Phyllis Sue Vann**, 14 Feb 1998 in Pigeon Forge, TN. Dunnavan was born 13 Jul 1967 in Decatur, Morgan County, AL.

2189. Mary Jacqueline (Jackie) Sharp (*Ronald Gene ^{6}, David (Big David) Roderick ^{5}, Joseph (Joe) Powers Sr. ^{4}, David Allen ^{3}, Charles W. Sr. ^{2}, John Sr. ^{1}*) was born 29 Nov 1964 in Lauderdale County, AL.

Mary married **Stanley Keith Holt**, son of **Jimmy E. Holt** and **Margie Cummings**, 26 Jun 1981 in Lauderdale County, AL. Stanley was born 1 Dec 1961 in Lauderdale County, AL.
4051   F   i.   **Heather Marie Holt** was born 1 Jul 1983 in Lauderdale County, AL.
4052   F   ii.   **Whitney Brooke Holt** was born 27 Oct 1991 in Lauderdale County, AL.

2190. Amy Janice Sharp (*Ronald Gene ^{6}, David (Big David) Roderick ^{5}, Joseph (Joe) Powers Sr. ^{4}, David Allen ^{3}, Charles W. Sr. ^{2}, John Sr. ^{1}*) was born 25 Mar 1977 in Lauderdale County, AL.

Amy married **David McKay Key**, son of **Joe M. Key** and **Susan Diane Banks**, 10 Jun 2000 in Gatlinburg, TN. David was born 12 Apr 1972 in Apple Valley, CA.

2192. Julie Deann Peters (*Angelia Gail Sharp ^{6}, David (Big David) Roderick ^{5}, Joseph (Joe) Powers Sr. ^{4}, David Allen ^{3}, Charles W. Sr. ^{2}, John Sr. ^{1}*) was born 16 Jul 1974 in Lauderdale County, AL.

Julie married **Charles Christopher Blalock**, son of **Charles Clifford Blalock** and **Clara Evelyn Hubbard**, 17 May 1991 in Lauderdale County, AL. Charles was born 25 Aug 1974 in Lauderdale County, AL.
4053   M   i.   **Charles Luke Blalock** was born 5 Oct 1991 in Lauderdale County, AL.

Julie next married **David Eugene Holland**, son of **Eugene E. Holland** and **Shelia *Unk**, 1 Dec 1995 in Lauderdale County, AL. David was born 29 Sep 1973 in Colbert County, AL.
4054   M   i.   **Jonathan William Holland** was born 1 Jan 1997 in Lauderdale County, AL.

2193. Lyda Kathleen Tate (*Betty Jane Sharp ^{6}, Lyda Mae Sharp ^{5}, Andrew Jefferson Sr. ^{4}, David Allen ^{3}, Charles W. Sr. ^{2}, John Sr. ^{1}*) was born 5 Dec 1957.

Lyda married **Richard Alexander Kassum** 1 Sep 1974. Richard was born 15 Jan 1958.
4055   M   i.   **Richard Brian Kassum** was born 2 Apr 1983.
4056   M   ii.   **Drew Benbrook Kassum** was born 3 Sep 1985.
4057   F   iii.   **Chelsa Leigh Kassum** was born 10 Jun 1987.

2194. Marie Lynn Tate (*Betty Jane Sharp ^{6}, Lyda Mae Sharp ^{5}, Andrew Jefferson Sr. ^{4}, David Allen ^{3}, Charles W. Sr. ^{2}, John Sr. ^{1}*) was born 18 May 1959.

Marie married **James David Lambert** 1 Sep 1974. James was born 13 Sep 1954.

4058	M	i.	**Jamie Lynn Lambert** was born 23 Jan 1975.
4059	F	ii.	**Lisa Marie Lambert** was born 4 Sep 1981.
4060	F	iii.	**Trisha Ann Lambert** was born 20 Nov 1984.

2195. Stacy Leigh Tate (*Betty Jane Sharp*[6], *Lyda Mae Sharp*[5], *Andrew Jefferson Sr.*[4], *David Allen*[3], *Charles W. Sr.*[2], *John Sr.*[1]) was born 24 Feb 1967.

Stacy married **James Hugh Pendergrast** 15 Sep 1990. James was born 1 Feb 1966.

2196. Linda Sharp (*John David Sharp*[6], *Lyda Mae Sharp*[5], *Andrew Jefferson Sr.*[4], *David Allen*[3], *Charles W. Sr.*[2], *John Sr.*[1]).

Linda married **Daniel Sarenana**.

4061	F	i.	**Taylor Sarenana**.
4062	F	ii.	**Natalie Sarenana**.

2197. Donald Sharp (*John David Sharp*[6], *Lyda Mae Sharp*[5], *Andrew Jefferson Sr.*[4], *David Allen*[3], *Charles W. Sr.*[2], *John Sr.*[1]).

Donald married **Loretta *Unk**.

4063	F	i.	**Rebecca Sharp**.

2198. Karen Diana Sharp (*John David Sharp*[6], *Lyda Mae Sharp*[5], *Andrew Jefferson Sr.*[4], *David Allen*[3], *Charles W. Sr.*[2], *John Sr.*[1]).

Karen married **Roger Smith**.

4064	F	i.	**Casi Smith**.
4065	F	ii.	**Paige Smith**.
4066	M	iii.	**Micah Smith**.

2199. Paul David Sharp (*John David Sharp*[6], *Lyda Mae Sharp*[5], *Andrew Jefferson Sr.*[4], *David Allen*[3], *Charles W. Sr.*[2], *John Sr.*[1]).

Paul married **Dawn *Unk**.

4067	F	i.	**Jessica Sharp**.
4068	M	ii.	**Shea Paul Sharp**.

Paul next married **Crystal *Unk**.

4069	F	i.	**Savannah Sharp**.
4070	M	ii.	**Eric Sharp**.

2205. Lisa Lauguter (*Kathleen Margaret Watson*[6], *Evelyn Marie (Verna) Sharp*[5], *Andrew Jefferson Sr.*[4], *David Allen*[3], *Charles W. Sr.*[2], *John Sr.*[1]).

Lisa married ***Unk**.

2206. Rhonda Lauguter (*Kathleen Margaret Watson*[6], *Evelyn Marie (Verna) Sharp*[5], *Andrew Jefferson Sr.*[4], *David Allen*[3], *Charles W. Sr.*[2], *John Sr.*[1]).

Rhonda married ***Unk**.

2211. Gary Allen Simmons (*John William Paton Simmons*[6], *Helen Margaret Sharp*[5], *Andrew Jefferson Sr.*[4], *David Allen*[3], *Charles W. Sr.*[2], *John Sr.*[1]) was born 3 Jun 1964.

Gary married **Debbie Distafine** in Apr 1995.

Seventh Generation

2213. George William Lindsey (*Marvin Elmer Lindsey[7], George W. Lindsey[6], John Phillip Lindsey II[5], Caleb (Calip) Lindsey[4], Frances (Frankie) Sharp[3], Charles W. Sr.[2], John Sr.[1]*) was born 1 Jul 1935 in Lauderdale County, AL.

George married **Glenda Maxine Craft**, daughter of **Leo M. Craft** and **Ida Killen**, 18 Jun 1957 in Colbert County, AL. Glenda was born 28 Jan 1938 in Colbert County, AL.
    4071 M   i.   **Jason Craft Lindsey** was born 25 Feb 1974 in Huntsville, Madison County, AL.

2214. Mary Elizabeth Lindsey (*Marvin Elmer Lindsey[7], George W. Lindsey[6], John Phillip Lindsey II[5], Caleb (Calip) Lindsey[4], Frances (Frankie) Sharp[3], Charles W. Sr.[2], John Sr.[1]*) was born 30 Oct 1940 in Lauderdale County, AL.

Mary married **Archie Pride Burton**, son of **James Smith Burton** and **Mae Louise Gibson**, 9 Feb 1962. Archie was born 22 May 1939 in Colbert County, AL.
    4072 F   i.   **Kimberly Elizabeth Burton** was born 10 Dec 1963 in Madison County, AL.

2215. Robbie Lee Lindsey (*Marvin Elmer Lindsey[7], George W. Lindsey[6], John Phillip Lindsey II[5], Caleb (Calip) Lindsey[4], Frances (Frankie) Sharp[3], Charles W. Sr.[2], John Sr.[1]*) was born 19 Oct 1945 in Lauderdale County, AL.

Robbie married **Freddie Lee Wylie**, son of **Odias Avon Wylie** and **Cecile H. Hearn**, 30 Nov 1962 in Lauderdale County, AL. Freddie was born 18 Dec 1942 in Lauderdale County, AL.
+ 4073 F   i.   **Sharon Arlene Wylie** was born 7 May 1967 in Lauderdale County, AL.
+ 4074 M   ii.   **Scott Fredrick Wylie** was born 27 Jun 1971 in Lauderdale County, AL.

2216. Rachel June Lindsey (*Katen Lewis Lindsey[7], J. Lewis Lindsey[6], Joseph A. Lindsey[5], Caleb (Calip) Lindsey[4], Frances (Frankie) Sharp[3], Charles W. Sr.[2], John Sr.[1]*).

Rachel married ***Unk**.
    4075 M   i.   ***Unk.**
    4076 M   ii.   ***Unk.**

2217. Shirley Ann Hall (*Lester Lawrence Hall Sr.[7], Ada Bell Lindsey[6], Joseph A. Lindsey[5], Caleb (Calip) Lindsey[4], Frances (Frankie) Sharp[3], Charles W. Sr.[2], John Sr.[1]*) was born 16 Jun 1944 in Lauderdale County, AL.

Shirley married **Herbert Calvin Hayes Jr.**, son of **Herbert Calvin Hayes Sr.** and **Adar Mae Hamilton**, 4 Jul 1960 in Colbert County, AL. Herbert was born 11 Jun 1941 in Colbert County, AL.
+ 4077 M   i.   **Herbert Calvin Hayes III** was born 3 May 1962 in Colbert County, AL.

2219. Lester Lawrence Hall Jr. (*Lester Lawrence Hall Sr.[7], Ada Bell Lindsey[6], Joseph A. Lindsey[5], Caleb (Calip) Lindsey[4], Frances (Frankie) Sharp[3], Charles W. Sr.[2], John Sr.[1]*) was born 5 Jun 1948 in Lauderdale County, AL.

Lester married **Donna Faye Terrell**, daughter of **Edgar E. Terrell** and **Ila Mae Liles**, 19 Nov 1966 in Lauderdale County, AL. Donna was born 18 Jul 1950 in Lauderdale County, AL.
+ 4078 F   i.   **Melissa Gail Hall** was born 13 Nov 1967 in Lauderdale County, AL.

Lester next married **Jo Ann Carter**, daughter of **Glenn Carter** and **Comadell Elder**, 14 Sep 1973 in Lauderdale County, AL. Jo was born 19 Dec in Orange County, FL.
+ 4079 F   i.   **Leslie Ann Hall** was born 19 Nov 1975 in Lauderdale County, AL.
+ 4080 F   ii.   **Miranda Kaye Hall** was born 6 Apr 1979 in Lauderdale County, AL.

2220. Dovie Leigh Hall (*Lester Lawrence Hall Sr.[7], Ada Bell Lindsey[6], Joseph A. Lindsey[5], Caleb (Calip) Lindsey[4], Frances (Frankie) Sharp[3], Charles W. Sr.[2], John Sr.[1]*) was born 13 Aug 1949 in Lauderdale County, AL.

Dovie married **Ralph E. Jackson**, son of **Floyd Jackson** and **Easter Morris**, 20 Dec 1967 in Lauderdale County, AL. Ralph was born 20 Oct 1945 in Lauderdale County, AL.

    4081 F   i.   **Kimberly Dawn Jackson** was born 26 Jul 1971 in Lauderdale County, AL.

    4082 M   ii.   **Jason Kyle Jackson** was born 9 Apr 1974 in Lauderdale County, AL.

2221. Johnny Houston Hall (*Lester Lawrence Hall Sr.^{7}, Ada Bell Lindsey^6, Joseph A. Lindsey^5, Caleb (Calip) Lindsey^4, Frances (Frankie) Sharp^3, Charles W. Sr.^{2}, John Sr.^{1}*) was born 14 Feb 1951 in Lauderdale County, AL.

Johnny married **Frances Kaye Kirby**, daughter of **Millard L. Kirby** and **Lorene Risner**, 19 Mar 1971 in Lauderdale County, AL. Frances was born 4 Mar 1954 in Lauderdale County, AL.

    4083 F   i.   **Capothia Lynn Hall** was born 26 Mar 1973 in Memphis, Shelby County, TN.

    4084 F   ii.   **Amanda Dawn Hall** was born 8 Nov 1979 in Colbert County, AL.

2222. Robin Michele Hall (*Lester Lawrence Hall Sr.^{7}, Ada Bell Lindsey^6, Joseph A. Lindsey^5, Caleb (Calip) Lindsey^4, Frances (Frankie) Sharp^3, Charles W. Sr.^{2}, John Sr.^{1}*) was born 22 Jan 1953 in Lauderdale County, AL.

Robin married **Jacky Wayne Moore**, son of **Robert D. Moore** and **Pearline Murks**, in Lauderdale County, AL. Jacky was born 4 Feb 1947 in Lauderdale County, AL.

+ 4085 F   i.   **Jacqueline Michele Moore** was born 10 Dec 1969 in Lauderdale County, AL.

    4086 F   ii.   **Tara Jacinda Moore** was born 3 Jun 1979 in Lauderdale County, AL.

2223. Carlene Hall (*Lester Lawrence Hall Sr.^{7}, Ada Bell Lindsey^6, Joseph A. Lindsey^5, Caleb (Calip) Lindsey^4, Frances (Frankie) Sharp^3, Charles W. Sr.^{2}, John Sr.^{1}*) was born 28 Mar 1955 in Ann Harber, MI.

Carlene married **Ronnie Dale Keeton**, son of **Virgil H. Keeton** and **Rosie Nobles**, in Lauderdale County, AL. Ronnie was born 13 Oct 1953 in Lauderdale County, AL.

+ 4087 M   i.   **Christopher Dale Keeton** was born 21 Aug 1971 in Lauderdale County, AL.

+ 4088 F   ii.   **Tracey Leigh Keeton** was born 4 Sep 1976 in Lauderdale County, AL.

2225. Floyd Edward Hall Jr. (*Floyd Edward Hall Sr.^{7}, Ada Bell Lindsey^6, Joseph A. Lindsey^5, Caleb (Calip) Lindsey^4, Frances (Frankie) Sharp^3, Charles W. Sr.^{2}, John Sr.^{1}*) was born 5 Sep 1940 in Lauderdale County, AL.

Floyd married **Deloris Maxine Higdon**, daughter of **James Andrew Higdon** and **Myrtle Alflene Tuder**, 25 Oct 1958 in Mobile, AL. Deloris was born 21 Oct 1942 in Colbert County, AL.

+ 4089 F   i.   **Tonia Dee Hall** was born 19 Oct 1959 in Lauderdale County, AL.

+ 4090 F   ii.   **Twila Gail Hall** was born 19 Oct 1962 in Augusta County, GA.

+ 4091 M iii. **Barry Alan Hall** was born 31 May 1964 in Lauderdale County, AL.

Floyd next married **Margaret Lou Harrison**, daughter of **Herby Giles Harrison Sr.** and **Minnie Viola Cobb**, 27 Oct 1974 in Lauderdale County, AL. Margaret was born 8 Oct 1944 in Lauderdale County, AL.

2226. Clara Mae Hall (*Floyd Edward Hall Sr.^{7}, Ada Bell Lindsey^6, Joseph A. Lindsey^5, Caleb (Calip) Lindsey^4, Frances (Frankie) Sharp^3, Charles W. Sr.^{2}, John Sr.^{1}*) was born 11 Sep 1942 in Lauderdale County, AL.

Clara married **Doyle Augustus Chambers**, son of **George Chambers** and **Goldie Clemmons**, 21 Feb 1959 in Lauderdale County, AL. Doyle was born 6 Jul 1939 in Lauderdale County, AL.

+ 4092 M   i.   **Richard Doyle Chambers** was born 10 Dec 1959 in Lauderdale County, AL.

+ 4093 F   ii.   **Rhonda Lynn Chambers** was born 26 Sep 1960 in Lauderdale County, AL.

+ 4094 F iii. **Sheila Dianne Chambers** was born 4 Sep 1961 in Lauderdale County, AL.

+ 4095 F   iv. **Cindy Gail Chambers** was born 21 Sep 1963 in Lauderdale County, AL.

+ 4096 F   v.   **Brenda Lee Chambers** was born 17 Mar 1966 in Lauderdale County, AL.

+ 4097 F   vi. **Donna Marie Chambers** was born 22 Jan 1969 in Lauderdale County, AL.

+ 4098 F vii. **Melisa Kaye Chambers** was born 1 Dec 1974 in Lauderdale County, AL.

2227. Sara Jane Hall (*Floyd Edward Hall Sr.^{7}, Ada Bell Lindsey^6, Joseph A. Lindsey^5, Caleb (Calip) Lindsey^4, Frances (Frankie) Sharp^3, Charles W. Sr.^{2}, John Sr.^{1}*) was born 24 Aug 1944 in Lauderdale County, AL.

Sara married **James Doyle Adams**, son of **James Marvin Adams** and **Lilly Bryant**, 12 Oct 1959 in Lauderdale County, AL. James was born 23 Apr 1938 in Jackson County, AL.

+ 4099 M i. **James Anthony Adams** was born 22 Sep 1960 in Lauderdale County, AL.

 4100 M ii. **Michael Douglas Adams** was born 5 Jul 1962 in Lauderdale County, AL, died 24 Apr 1979, and was buried in Greenview Memorial Park, Florence, Lauderdale County, AL.

+ 4101 F iii. **Bonnie Sue Adams** was born 20 Jun 1965 in Lauderdale County, AL.

+ 4102 F iv. **Edna Jane Adams** was born 26 Apr 1964 in Lauderdale County, AL.

+ 4103 F v. **Sharon Kay Adams** was born 25 Dec 1966 in Lauderdale County, AL.

Sara next married **Charles E. Poole** 3 Mar 1973 in Lauderdale County, AL. Charles was born 12 Nov 1950 in Shelby County, TN.

2228. Wayne Joseph Hall (*Floyd Edward Hall Sr.^{7}, Ada Bell Lindsey^6, Joseph A. Lindsey^5, Caleb (Calip) Lindsey^4, Frances (Frankie) Sharp^3, Charles W. Sr.^{2}, John Sr.^{1}*) was born 26 Feb 1949 in Lauderdale County, AL.

Wayne married **Mary Ellen Stumpe**, daughter of **Raymon Henry Stumpe** and **Catherine Jolly**, 14 Jan 1972 in Lauderdale County, AL. Mary was born 24 Oct 1948 in Lauderdale County, AL.

 4104 F i. **Jamie DeAnna Hall** was born 27 Dec 1979 in Lauderdale County, AL.

2229. Barbara Kaye Hall (*Floyd Edward Hall Sr.^{7}, Ada Bell Lindsey^6, Joseph A. Lindsey^5, Caleb (Calip) Lindsey^4, Frances (Frankie) Sharp^3, Charles W. Sr.^{2}, John Sr.^{1}*) was born 8 Jul 1952 in Lauderdale County, AL.

Barbara married **Ralph Edward McMurtrey**, son of **Arthur Spencer McMurtrey** and **Nadine Harris**, 12 Aug 1973 in Lauderdale County, AL. Ralph was born 11 Nov 1946 in Lauderdale County, AL.

+ 4105 F i. **Regina Lynn McMurtrey** was born 11 Sep 1974 in Lauderdale County, AL.

2230. Jerry Michael Hall (*Floyd Edward Hall Sr.^{7}, Ada Bell Lindsey^6, Joseph A. Lindsey^5, Caleb (Calip) Lindsey^4, Frances (Frankie) Sharp^3, Charles W. Sr.^{2}, John Sr.^{1}*) was born 9 Mar 1955 in Lauderdale County, AL.

Jerry married **Brenda Sue Whitlock**, daughter of **Charlie Whitlock** and **Mary V. Sudden**. Brenda was born 30 Sep 1949 in Franklin County, AL.

 4106 F i. **Dianna Michele Hall** was born 9 Jan 1977 in Lauderdale County, AL, died 17 Jan 1977, and was buried in Greenview Memorial Park, Florence, Lauderdale County, AL.

 4107 F ii. **Cristy Michele Hall** was born 26 Oct 1978 in Lauderdale County, AL.

Jerry next married **Dona Renea Whitehead**, daughter of **Charles E. Whitehead** and **Mary Lawson**, 7 Oct 1983 in Lauderdale County, AL. Dona was born 26 Mar 1957 in Lauderdale County, AL.

2232. Judy Jane Lindsey (*Herschel Lee Lindsey^7, Lee Willie Lindsey^6, Joseph A. Lindsey^5, Caleb (Calip) Lindsey^4, Frances (Frankie) Sharp^3, Charles W. Sr.^{2}, John Sr.^{1}*).

Judy married **Jerry Prince**.

2235. Jewell Virgie Garrett (*Ethel M. Lindsey^7, Albert Curtis Lindsey^6, David A. Lindsey^5, Caleb (Calip) Lindsey^4, Frances (Frankie) Sharp^3, Charles W. Sr.^{2}, John Sr.^{1}*) was born 23 Dec 1922 in Lauderdale County, AL.

Jewell married **Leonard Wilson Brown Sr.**, son of **Marvin Francis Brown** and **Clara South**, in 1953 in Colbert County, AL. Leonard was born 4 Nov 1921 in Lauderdale County, AL, died 6 May 2001, and was buried in Tri-Cities Memorial Gardens, Florence, Lauderdale County, AL.

General Notes: Was found dead in home with son...from David Sharp notes

 4108 M i. **Leonard Wilson Brown Jr.** was born 13 Aug 1959 in Lauderdale County, AL, died 6 May 2001, and was buried in Tri-Cities Memorial Gardens, Florence, Lauderdale County, AL.

General Notes: Was found dead in home with father...from David Sharp notes

 4109 M ii. ***Unk Brown.**

2236. Edna Juanita Lindsey (*Charles Edward Lindsey^7, Albert Curtis Lindsey^6, David A. Lindsey^5, Caleb (Calip) Lindsey^4, Frances (Frankie) Sharp^3, Charles W. Sr.^{2}, John Sr.^{1}*) was born 19 Sep 1924 in Lauderdale County, AL.

Edna married **William B. McCormick**, son of **Willie McCormick** and **Rosa Lee Kennedy**, 21 Aug 1943 in Lauderdale County, AL. William was born 28 Aug 1925 in Lauderdale County, AL, died 8 May 1975, and was buried in Center Star Cemetery, Lauderdale County, AL.

| 4110 | M | i. | **Charles William McCormick**. |
| 4111 | F | ii. | **Betty Doris McCormick**. |

2237. Gentry Aaron Lindsey (*Charles Edward Lindsey^7, Albert Curtis Lindsey^6, David A. Lindsey^5, Caleb (Calip) Lindsey^4, Frances (Frankie) Sharp^3, Charles W. Sr.^{2}, John Sr.^{1}*) was born 2 Feb 1927 in Lauderdale County, AL.

Gentry married **Francis Lucille Jaynes**, daughter of **Thomas Willard Jaynes** and **Maudie Hale**, 20 Oct 1945 in Lauderdale County, AL. Francis was born 1 Oct 1927 in Lauderdale County, AL.

+	4112	F	i.	**Shirley Jean Lindsey** was born 1 Feb 1948 in Lauderdale County, AL.
+	4113	M	ii.	**Larry Wayne Lindsey** was born 5 Sep 1949 in Lauderdale County, AL.
+	4114	F	iii.	**Sandra Gail Lindsey** was born 2 Aug 1951 in Lauderdale County, AL.
+	4115	F	iv.	**Susan Denise Lindsey** was born 20 Mar 1969 in Lauderdale County, AL.

2238. Mable Lindsey (*Charles Edward Lindsey^7, Albert Curtis Lindsey^6, David A. Lindsey^5, Caleb (Calip) Lindsey^4, Frances (Frankie) Sharp^3, Charles W. Sr.^{2}, John Sr.^{1}*) was born 16 Oct 1930 in Lauderdale County, AL.

Mable married **James S. Melton**, son of **Boyd Melton** and **Jessie Stockard**, 28 Mar 1947 in Lauderdale County, AL. James was born 10 Jun 1927 in Wayne County, TN, died 15 Jan 1993, and was buried in Tri-Cities Memorial Gardens, Florence, Lauderdale County, AL.

2239. Margaret Marie Lindsey (*Charles Edward Lindsey^7, Albert Curtis Lindsey^6, David A. Lindsey^5, Caleb (Calip) Lindsey^4, Frances (Frankie) Sharp^3, Charles W. Sr.^{2}, John Sr.^{1}*) was born 23 Jan 1933 in Lauderdale County, AL.

Margaret married **Jessie Clifford Pigg**, son of **Jessie James Pigg** and **Mary Elizabeth Putman**, 28 Mar 1947 in Iuka, Tishomingo County, MS. Jessie was born 2 Apr 1926 in Lauderdale County, AL.

+	4116	F	i.	**Linda Faye Pigg** was born 27 Aug 1948 in Lauderdale County, AL.
+	4117	F	ii.	**Patricia Gail Pigg** was born 25 May 1958 in Lauderdale County, AL.
+	4118	M	iii.	**Ronald Clifford Pigg** was born 22 Mar 1965 in Lauderdale County, AL.
+	4119	F	iv.	**Paula Marie Pigg** was born 6 Jan 1968 in Lauderdale County, AL.
+	4120	F	v.	**Pamela Renee Pigg** was born 6 Jan 1968 in Lauderdale County, AL.

2240. Sarah Melissa Lindsey (*Charles Edward Lindsey^7, Albert Curtis Lindsey^6, David A. Lindsey^5, Caleb (Calip) Lindsey^4, Frances (Frankie) Sharp^3, Charles W. Sr.^{2}, John Sr.^{1}*) was born in Lauderdale County, AL.

Sarah married **Gene Hamm**.

4121	F	i.	***Unk Hamm**.
4122	F	ii.	***Unk Hamm**.
4123	F	iii.	***Unk Hamm**.

2241. Charles Roberta Lindsey (*Charles Edward Lindsey^7, Albert Curtis Lindsey^6, David A. Lindsey^5, Caleb (Calip) Lindsey^4, Frances (Frankie) Sharp^3, Charles W. Sr.^{2}, John Sr.^{1}*) was born 19 Jul 1942 in Lauderdale County, AL.

Charles married **James Waddell**, son of **John Pearl Waddell** and **Rosie Mable Mashman**, 21 Aug 1953 in Lauderdale County, AL.

4124	M	i.	**Charles Edward Waddell** was born 31 Jan 1960 in Chicago, IL.
4125	M	ii.	**Calvin Lee Waddell** was born 24 Dec 1960 in Chicago, IL.
4126	F	iii.	**Linda Jeanette Waddell** was born 25 Aug 1964 in Chicago, IL.
4127	F	iv.	**Tammy Lou Waddell** was born 18 Nov 1965 in High Point, NC.
4128	M	v.	**Gentry James Waddell** was born 11 Jul 1967 in High Point, NC.

4129 M vi.   **Kenneth Lynn Waddell** was born 29 Dec 1969 in Ashboro, NC.

2242. Helen Louise Lindsey (*Dalton Allen Lindsey[7], Albert Curtis Lindsey[6], David A. Lindsey[5], Caleb (Calip) Lindsey[4], Frances (Frankie) Sharp[3], Charles W. Sr.[2], John Sr.[1]*) was born 10 Oct 1932 in Lauderdale County, AL.

    Helen married **Johnny B. Thornton** 14 Oct 1950.
+ 4130 F i.   **Deborah Janice Thornton** was born 24 Aug 1951.
+ 4131 F ii.   **Kimberly Celeste Thornton** was born 18 Sep 1964.

2243. Carl Dewey Lindsey (*Dalton Allen Lindsey[7], Albert Curtis Lindsey[6], David A. Lindsey[5], Caleb (Calip) Lindsey[4], Frances (Frankie) Sharp[3], Charles W. Sr.[2], John Sr.[1]*) was born 3 Apr 1937 in Lauderdale County, AL.

    Carl married **Rebecca Ann Williams**, daughter of **Thomas Sanford Williams** and **Lillie Rebecca Smith**, 15 Jun 1957 in Lauderdale County, AL. Rebecca was born 24 Jul 1938 in Lauderdale County, AL.
    4132 M i.   **Timothy Allen Lindsey** was born 11 Mar 1958.
    4133 M ii.   **Carl David Lindsey** was born 8 Oct 1962.
    4134 F iii.   **Rebecca Lindsey** was born 14 Aug 1966.

2244. Cheryl Dianne Gables Lindsey (*Clifton D. Lindsey[7], Edward (Ed) Price Lindsey[6], David A. Lindsey[5], Caleb (Calip) Lindsey[4], Frances (Frankie) Sharp[3], Charles W. Sr.[2], John Sr.[1]*) was born 15 Apr 1952 in Jasper, Walker County, AL.

    Cheryl married **John Terry Wylie**, son of **William P. Wylie** and **Mary C. Garner**, 12 Aug 1972 in Lauderdale County, AL. John was born 15 Dec 1951 in Lauderdale County, AL.
    4135 M i.   **Michael Andrew Wylie** was born 27 May 1977 in Lauderdale County, AL.
    4136 M ii.   **Adam Barrett Wylie** was born 7 Dec 1978 in Lauderdale County, AL.

    Cheryl next married ***Unk Selman**.

2245. Debra Kaye Lindsey (*Clifton D. Lindsey[7], Edward (Ed) Price Lindsey[6], David A. Lindsey[5], Caleb (Calip) Lindsey[4], Frances (Frankie) Sharp[3], Charles W. Sr.[2], John Sr.[1]*) was born 2 Aug 1957 in Lauderdale County, AL.

    Debra married **Stanley Price Fergerson**, son of **Price T. Fergerson** and **Evelyn King**, 30 Jun 1982 in Lauderdale County, AL. Stanley was born 9 Jul 1958 in Franklin County, AL.
    4137 M i.   **Phillip Travis Fergerson** was born 4 Aug 1987 in Lauderdale County, AL.

2246. Susan Renee Lindsey (*Clifton D. Lindsey[7], Edward (Ed) Price Lindsey[6], David A. Lindsey[5], Caleb (Calip) Lindsey[4], Frances (Frankie) Sharp[3], Charles W. Sr.[2], John Sr.[1]*) was born 13 May 1959 in Lauderdale County, AL.

    Susan married **James Hilton Parnell**, son of **Joseph Hilton Parnell Sr.** and **Sarah Ann Bell**, 7 Jul 1978 in Lauderdale County, AL. James was born 3 Mar 1956 in Arkadelphia, Clark County, AR.
    4138 M i.   **Joseph Heath Parnell** was born 27 Mar 1981 in Lauderdale County, AL.
    4139 M ii.   **Stephen Barrett Parnell** was born 11 Dec 1990 in Lauderdale County, AL.

2249. Kathleen Ann Suggs (*Carolyn Virginia Eagle[7], Mary Mable Bennett[6], Mollie Elizabeth Lindsey[5], Caleb (Calip) Lindsey[4], Frances (Frankie) Sharp[3], Charles W. Sr.[2], John Sr.[1]*).

    Kathleen married **Shayne Roland**.
    4140 F i.   **Sarah Bethany Roland**.
    4141 F ii.   **Ashley Lauren Roland**.
    4142 F iii.   **Chessie Diane Roland**.

2250. Sandra Lee Suggs (*Carolyn Virginia Eagle[7], Mary Mable Bennett[6], Mollie Elizabeth Lindsey[5], Caleb (Calip) Lindsey[4], Frances (Frankie) Sharp[3], Charles W. Sr.[2], John Sr.[1]*).

    Sandra married **Malcolm B. Volentine**.

2251. Mary Louise Suggs (*Carolyn Virginia Eagle*[7], *Mary Mable Bennett*[6], *Mollie Elizabeth Lindsey*[5], *Caleb (Calip) Lindsey*[4], *Frances (Frankie) Sharp*[3], *Charles W. Sr.*[2], *John Sr.*[1]).

Mary married **Owen (Cotton) Sandy**.

2254. Michael T. Pepper (*Carolyn Virginia Eagle*[7], *Mary Mable Bennett*[6], *Mollie Elizabeth Lindsey*[5], *Caleb (Calip) Lindsey*[4], *Frances (Frankie) Sharp*[3], *Charles W. Sr.*[2], *John Sr.*[1]).

Michael married **Yong *Unk**.

2255. Patrick D. Pepper (*Carolyn Virginia Eagle*[7], *Mary Mable Bennett*[6], *Mollie Elizabeth Lindsey*[5], *Caleb (Calip) Lindsey*[4], *Frances (Frankie) Sharp*[3], *Charles W. Sr.*[2], *John Sr.*[1]).

Patrick married **Sharman *Unk**.

2257. Linda Faye Romine (*Howard James Romine*[7], *Nellie Mitchum*[6], *America Lindsey*[5], *Caleb (Calip) Lindsey*[4], *Frances (Frankie) Sharp*[3], *Charles W. Sr.*[2], *John Sr.*[1]) was born 4 Apr 1946 in Lauderdale County, AL.

Linda married **Kelley W. Allen**, son of **E. Winfield Allen** and **Marion Boesiger**, 29 Dec 1984 in Lauderdale County, AL. Kelley was born 17 Jul 1948 in Lauderdale County, AL.

2258. Donna Diane Romine (*Howard James Romine*[7], *Nellie Mitchum*[6], *America Lindsey*[5], *Caleb (Calip) Lindsey*[4], *Frances (Frankie) Sharp*[3], *Charles W. Sr.*[2], *John Sr.*[1]) was born 28 Aug 1947 in Lauderdale County, AL.

Donna married **James Douglas Hartley**, son of **Buford Hartley** and **Gearldine Sanderson**, 16 Dec 1972 in Lauderdale County, AL. James was born 25 Jun 1947 in Lauderdale County, AL.

2260. Susan Marie Romine (*Richard Leland Romine*[7], *Nellie Mitchum*[6], *America Lindsey*[5], *Caleb (Calip) Lindsey*[4], *Frances (Frankie) Sharp*[3], *Charles W. Sr.*[2], *John Sr.*[1]) was born 22 Sep 1945 in Colbert County, AL.

Susan married **Brad George Hunter**, son of **Aldon Leon Hunter** and **Emma Gertrude Wright**, 22 Sep 1963 in Colbert County, AL. Brad was born 14 Nov 1940 in Colbert County, AL.
| 4143 | M | i. | **Gregory Scott Hunter** was born 14 Oct 1969 in Lauderdale County, AL. |
| 4144 | F | ii. | **Andrea Lynn Hunter** was born 15 Apr 1971 in Lauderdale County, AL. |

2261. Richard Morris Romine (*Richard Leland Romine*[7], *Nellie Mitchum*[6], *America Lindsey*[5], *Caleb (Calip) Lindsey*[4], *Frances (Frankie) Sharp*[3], *Charles W. Sr.*[2], *John Sr.*[1]) was born 8 Aug 1948 in Lauderdale County, AL.

Richard married **Phyllis Lee Emmons**, daughter of **Gillus Emmons** and **Florence Jones**, 29 Feb 1980 in Birmingham, Jefferson County, AL. Phyllis was born 7 Mar 1950 in Corpus Cristi, Nueces County, TX.
| + 4145 | F | i. | **Rachel Kimberly Romine** was born 20 Mar 1973 in Lauderdale County, AL. |
| 4146 | M | ii. | **Richard Emmons Romine** was born 11 Oct 1981 in Birmingham, Jefferson County, AL. |

2263. William Dean Romine (*Richard Leland Romine*[7], *Nellie Mitchum*[6], *America Lindsey*[5], *Caleb (Calip) Lindsey*[4], *Frances (Frankie) Sharp*[3], *Charles W. Sr.*[2], *John Sr.*[1]) was born 6 Sep 1954 in Lauderdale County, AL.

William married **Nancy Ann Welchert** in 1980.

2264. Jerry Trapp Crowell Jr. (*Barbara B. Mitchum*[7], *Bufford Lee Mitchum*[6], *America Lindsey*[5], *Caleb (Calip) Lindsey*[4], *Frances (Frankie) Sharp*[3], *Charles W. Sr.*[2], *John Sr.*[1]) was born 23 Dec 1956 in Lauderdale County, AL.

Jerry married **Susan Elaine Hibbett**, daughter of **Lester Lee Hibbett** and **Kathryn Elaine Williams**, 11 Jun 1982 in Lauderdale County, AL. Susan was born 22 Jun 1954 in Jefferson County, AL.
| 4147 | M | i. | **Jerry Trapp Crowell III** was born 10 Oct 1984 in Lauderdale County, AL. |
| 4148 | M | ii. | **Jason Lee Crowell** was born 1 Apr 1987 in Lauderdale County, AL. |

2265. Marilyn Leigh Crowell (*Barbara B. Mitchum* [7], *Bufford Lee Mitchum* [6], *America Lindsey* [5], *Caleb (Calip) Lindsey* [4], *Frances (Frankie) Sharp* [3], *Charles W. Sr.* [2], *John Sr.* [1]) was born 15 Jul 1960 in Lauderdale County, AL.

Marilyn married **Cecil Ingram** 30 Jun 1990 in Lauderdale County, AL.
4149 M i. **Wayne Ingram**.
4150 F ii. **Allison Ingram**.

2266. Donald Edward Lindsey III (*Donald Edward Lindsey Jr.* [7], *Donald Edward Lindsey Sr.* [6], *Robert Andrew Lindsey* [5], *Caleb (Calip) Lindsey* [4], *Frances (Frankie) Sharp* [3], *Charles W. Sr.* [2], *John Sr.* [1]) was born 1 Sep 1956 in Lauderdale County, AL.

Donald married **Kathy Fletcher** in Texas. Kathy was born in Texas.
4151 M i. **Justin Lindsey**.
4152 F ii. **Amanda Lindsey**.

2267. Robert Russell Lindsey (*Donald Edward Lindsey Jr.* [7], *Donald Edward Lindsey Sr.* [6], *Robert Andrew Lindsey* [5], *Caleb (Calip) Lindsey* [4], *Frances (Frankie) Sharp* [3], *Charles W. Sr.* [2], *John Sr.* [1]) was born 22 Sep 1958 in Lauderdale County, AL.

Robert married **Mary Ann Moore**, daughter of **James C. Moore** and **Myrtle Rice**, 28 Nov 1981 in Lauderdale County, AL. Mary was born 16 Dec 1955 in Lauderdale County, AL.
4153 F i. **Jamie Dianna Lindsey** was born 21 Apr 1982 in Lauderdale County, AL.

2268. Laurel Lee Lindsey (*Donald Edward Lindsey Jr.* [7], *Donald Edward Lindsey Sr.* [6], *Robert Andrew Lindsey* [5], *Caleb (Calip) Lindsey* [4], *Frances (Frankie) Sharp* [3], *Charles W. Sr.* [2], *John Sr.* [1]) was born 1 Jul 1963 in Lauderdale County, AL.

Laurel married **Leslie Paul Holt**, son of **Edsel Holt** and **Inez Hill**, 31 Aug 1990 in Lauderdale County, AL. Leslie was born 10 Sep 1963 in Lauderdale County, AL.
4154 M i. **Wesley Dale Holt** was born in Jul 2002 in Lauderdale County, AL.

2269. Beth May Cofield (*Rebecca Ann Lindsey* [7], *Donald Edward Lindsey Sr.* [6], *Robert Andrew Lindsey* [5], *Caleb (Calip) Lindsey* [4], *Frances (Frankie) Sharp* [3], *Charles W. Sr.* [2], *John Sr.* [1]) was born 14 Apr 1962 in Lauderdale County, AL.

Beth married **Eddie Wayne Tayes**, son of **Edison A. Tayes** and **Mary Pettus**, 22 Mar 1985 in Lauderdale County, AL. Eddie was born 24 Feb 1956 in Lauderdale County, AL.

2270. Crystal Alese Cofield (*Rebecca Ann Lindsey* [7], *Donald Edward Lindsey Sr.* [6], *Robert Andrew Lindsey* [5], *Caleb (Calip) Lindsey* [4], *Frances (Frankie) Sharp* [3], *Charles W. Sr.* [2], *John Sr.* [1]) was born 5 Sep 1963 in Lauderdale County, AL.

Crystal married **Mark Glenn Watkins**, son of **James Wilber Watkins** and **Claudie Clayton Glover**, 3 Oct 1981 in Lauderdale County, AL. Mark was born 23 Apr 1952 in Lauderdale County, AL.
4155 M i. **Nicklos Clay Watkins** was born 12 Aug 1987 in Langley AFB, VA.
4156 F ii. **Celsie Leiden Watkins** was born 7 Oct 1990 in Leiden, Netherlands.
4157 M iii. **Joshua Tracy Watkins** was born 24 May 1992 in Roderdam, Netherlands.

2271. Lee Ann Cofield (*Rebecca Ann Lindsey* [7], *Donald Edward Lindsey Sr.* [6], *Robert Andrew Lindsey* [5], *Caleb (Calip) Lindsey* [4], *Frances (Frankie) Sharp* [3], *Charles W. Sr.* [2], *John Sr.* [1]) was born 18 Nov 1965 in Lauderdale County, AL.

Lee married **David Allen Post**, son of **Billy J. Post** and **Lorene Givers**, 13 Jun 1986 in Lauderdale County, AL. David was born 11 Mar 1960 in Comanche County, AL.
4158 F i. **Micha Nicole Post** was born 30 Nov 1987 in Langley AFB, VA.

2272. William Ricky (Ric) Wilson (*Carolyn Lindsey* [7], *Chester B. Lindsey* [6], *Alonzo Brown Lindsey* [5], *Caleb (Calip) Lindsey* [4], *Frances (Frankie) Sharp* [3], *Charles W. Sr.* [2], *John Sr.* [1]) was born 20 Jul 1953 in Lauderdale County, AL.

William married **Dannyle James**. Dannyle was born in 1953 in Goodway, AL.
4159 F i. **Lindsey Shay Wilson** was born 22 Jun 1980.
4160 M ii. **William (Will) Richard Wilson** was born 22 Jun 1980.

William next married **Brenda *Unk**.

2281. Ronald Joseph Lindsey (*Ronald Gregg Lindsey* [7], *Thomas Arnett Lindsey* [6], *Alonzo Brown Lindsey* [5], *Caleb (Calip) Lindsey* [4], *Frances (Frankie) Sharp* [3], *Charles W. Sr.* [2], *John Sr.* [1]) was born 29 Aug in Fitsgerald, GA.

Ronald married **Sharon *Unk**.
4161 M i. **Rian Caleb Lindsey**.

2285. Anthony Shane Lindsey Pope (*Angelia Dee Lindsey* [7], *Thomas Arnett Lindsey* [6], *Alonzo Brown Lindsey* [5], *Caleb (Calip) Lindsey* [4], *Frances (Frankie) Sharp* [3], *Charles W. Sr.* [2], *John Sr.* [1]) was born 25 Apr 1972 in Macon, GA.

Anthony married **Kate McCall**. Kate was born 6 Dec 1971 in Wheeling, WV.
4162 F i. **Myra Lindsey Pope** was born 16 Apr 1992 in Macon, GA.

2290. James William May Sr. (*Lilly Mae Lindsey* [7], *Millard Lindsey* [6], *Maraday (Merry Dee) Lindsey* [5], *Andrew Jackson Lindsey* [4], *Frances (Frankie) Sharp* [3], *Charles W. Sr.* [2], *John Sr.* [1]) was born 5 Oct 1926 in Franklin County, AL, died 25 Nov 1985, and was buried in Union Hill Cemetery, Franklin County, AL.

James married **Crodelia Ergle** 12 May 1946. Crodelia was born 20 Nov 1929.
+ 4163 M i. **Benjamin Franklin May** was born 27 Jan 1948, died 21 Jul 1997, and was buried in Blue Springs Cemetery, Franklin County, AL.
+ 4164 M ii. **Winford Dale May** was born 12 May 1950.
+ 4165 F iii. **Kathy Diane May** was born 12 Nov 1951.

James next married **Doris M. Stewart** 22 Feb 1954. Doris was born 27 Nov 1932.
+ 4166 F i. **Sherry Lynn May** was born 19 Sep 1958 in Russellville, Franklin County, AL.
4167 M ii. **James William May Jr.** was born 26 Jan 1962, died 27 Jan 1962, and was buried in Union Hill Cemetery, Franklin County, AL.

2292. Virginia Nell Wood (*Viola Beatrice Lindsey* [7], *Millard Lindsey* [6], *Maraday (Merry Dee) Lindsey* [5], *Andrew Jackson Lindsey* [4], *Frances (Frankie) Sharp* [3], *Charles W. Sr.* [2], *John Sr.* [1]) was born 22 Mar 1933 in Cherokee, Colbert County, AL, died 29 Mar 1991, and was buried in Barton Cemetery, Colbert County, AL.

Virginia married **Aaron Andis**. Aaron was born in Arkansas.
+ 4168 M i. **Winfred Dale Andis**.
+ 4169 M ii. **Allen Wayne Andis** died in 1994.
+ 4170 F iii. **Dottie Lou Andis** was born 13 Nov 1955 in Flint, MI.
+ 4171 F iv. **Patricia Gail Andis** was born 28 May 1957 in Flint, MI.
+ 4172 F v. **Helen Marie Andis** was born in Jan 1964.

2293. Sarah Elizabeth (Lib) Wood (*Viola Beatrice Lindsey* [7], *Millard Lindsey* [6], *Maraday (Merry Dee) Lindsey* [5], *Andrew Jackson Lindsey* [4], *Frances (Frankie) Sharp* [3], *Charles W. Sr.* [2], *John Sr.* [1]) was born 8 Sep 1934 in Cherokee, Colbert County, AL, died 6 May 2005, and was buried in Barton Cemetery, Colbert County, AL.

Sarah married **Robert Thompson** about 1956.
+ 4173 M i. **Bobby Lenard Thompson** was born 13 Sep 1957 in Methodist Hospital, Memphis, Shelby County, TN.

Sarah next married **William Archie Ezekiel**, son of **Jesse James Ezekiel** and **Dewey Leora Wood**, about 1959. William was born 2 Feb 1928 in Wright, Lauderdale County, AL, died 26 Dec 1995, and was buried in Oak Grove Cemetery, Lauderdale County, AL.

+ 4174   M   i.   **Billy Gene Ezekiel Sr.** was born 31 Mar 1960 in Florence, Lauderdale County, AL.

2294. Shirley Jean Wood (*Viola Beatrice Lindsey*^{7}, *Millard Lindsey*^{6}, *Maraday (Merry Dee) Lindsey*^{5}, *Andrew Jackson Lindsey*^{4}, *Frances (Frankie) Sharp*^{3}, *Charles W. Sr.*^{2}, *John Sr.*^{1}) was born 19 Jul 1936 in Cherokee, Colbert County, AL, died 13 Dec 1998, and was buried in Barton Cemetery, Colbert County, AL.

Shirley married **James Edward Cossey**, son of **George Lewis Cossey** and **Mary Catherine Michael**, 1 Jan 1955 in Iuka, Tishomingo County, MS. James was born 19 May 1935 in Hardin County, TN.

+ 4175   F   i.   **Donna Kay Cossey** was born 6 Apr 1956 in Turrell, Crittenden County, AR.
+ 4176   F   ii.   **Deborah (Debbie) Faye Cossey** was born 4 Jul 1957 in West Memphis, Crittenden County, AR.
+ 4177   M   iii.   **James Daniel (Danny) Cossey** was born 24 Jul 1958 in Caraway Methodist Hospital, Birmingham, Jefferson County, AL.
+ 4178   M   iv.   **Dennis Ray Cossey** was born 30 Jan 1963 in Caraway Methodist Hospital, Birmingham, Jefferson County, AL.
  4179   M   v.   **David Leon Cossey** was born 16 Jun 1966 in Birmingham, Jefferson County, AL, died 18 Jun 1966, and was buried in Barton Cemetery, Colbert County, AL.

Shirley next married **Larry Rice Popejoy** about 1969.

Shirley next married **William (Bill) Featherston** about 1970.

Shirley next married **Walter William Wright** about 1971.

2295. Beatrice Marie Wood (*Viola Beatrice Lindsey*^{7}, *Millard Lindsey*^{6}, *Maraday (Merry Dee) Lindsey*^{5}, *Andrew Jackson Lindsey*^{4}, *Frances (Frankie) Sharp*^{3}, *Charles W. Sr.*^{2}, *John Sr.*^{1}) was born 15 Sep 1937 in Cherokee, Colbert County, AL.

Beatrice married **Paul Albert Capooth** 24 May 1958 in Corinth, Alcorn County, MS. Paul was born 4 Feb 1930 in Guys, TN.

+ 4180   M   i.   **Roger Dale Capooth** was born 23 Aug 1959 in Selmer, McNairy County, TN.

Beatrice next married **Randiff Jerell Mills** 20 Dec 1984. Randiff was born in Cherokee, Colbert County, AL.

2296. Jack Leon Wood (*Viola Beatrice Lindsey*^{7}, *Millard Lindsey*^{6}, *Maraday (Merry Dee) Lindsey*^{5}, *Andrew Jackson Lindsey*^{4}, *Frances (Frankie) Sharp*^{3}, *Charles W. Sr.*^{2}, *John Sr.*^{1}) was born 20 Oct 1939 in Cherokee, Colbert County, AL.

Jack married **Josie Hamm** before 1969.

Jack next married **Barbara Ann Bordon** 24 Dec 1969. Barbara was born in 1952.

+ 4181   F   i.   **Patricia Ann (Lucy) Borden** was born 25 Jul 1970 in Colbert County, AL.
  4182   F   ii.   **Katherine Viola (Susie) Wood** was born 20 Aug 1972 in Colbert County, AL.

2297. Patsy Faye Wood (*Viola Beatrice Lindsey*^{7}, *Millard Lindsey*^{6}, *Maraday (Merry Dee) Lindsey*^{5}, *Andrew Jackson Lindsey*^{4}, *Frances (Frankie) Sharp*^{3}, *Charles W. Sr.*^{2}, *John Sr.*^{1}) was born 30 Apr 1941 in Cherokee, Colbert County, AL.

Patsy married **Robert Lee Campbell** 23 Nov 1958 in Hayti, MO.

+ 4183   F   i.   **Cathy Marlene Campbell** was born 14 Oct 1959 in Pernscott County, MO.
+ 4184   F   ii.   **Sharon Lee Campbell** was born 7 Jan 1962 in Sheffield, Colbert County, AL.

Patsy next married **G. W. (Dub) Phillips** 2 Jul 1966 in Sheffield, Colbert County, AL.

+ 4185   F   i.   **Cheryl Renee Campbell** was born 11 Aug 1964 in Vislia, CA.
+ 4186   M   ii.   **Gary Wayne Phillips** was born 8 Feb 1968.

4187 F iii. **Barbara Lynn Phillips** was born 23 Nov 1969 in Decatur General Hospital, Decatur, Morgan County, AL.

4188 F iv. **Kristy Elizabeth Phillips** was born 27 Jun 1976 in Decatur General Hospital, Decatur, Morgan County, AL, died 19 Aug 1983, and was buried in Barton Cemetery, Colbert County, AL.

2300. Barbara Gail (Cookie) Wood (*Viola Beatrice Lindsey*[7], *Millard Lindsey*[6], *Maraday (Merry Dee) Lindsey*[5], *Andrew Jackson Lindsey*[4], *Frances (Frankie) Sharp*[3], *Charles W. Sr.*[2], *John Sr.*[1]) was born 14 Sep 1945 in Cherokee, Colbert County, AL.

Barbara married **Luther Burton Williams** 16 Apr 1966.

Barbara next married **Travis Wayne Dixon** 2 Sep 1979 in Lauderdale County, AL.

4189 F i. **Melissa Gail (Missy) Dixon** was born 2 Sep 1979 in Selmer, McNairy County, TN.

General Notes: "She is sister to Kristy Elizabeth Phillips and has a sister that G.W. Phillips' sister adopted..." Debbie Wasserburger

2303. David Leon Wood Worsham (*Viola Beatrice Lindsey*[7], *Millard Lindsey*[6], *Maraday (Merry Dee) Lindsey*[5], *Andrew Jackson Lindsey*[4], *Frances (Frankie) Sharp*[3], *Charles W. Sr.*[2], *John Sr.*[1]) was born 11 Aug 1971 in Colbert County, AL, died 6 Feb 1999, and was buried in Barton Cemetery, Colbert County, AL.

David married **Otonya *Unk**.

4190 M i. **Dakota Leon Worsham**.

2305. Geraldine Burns (*Ola Mae Lindsey*[7], *Millard Lindsey*[6], *Maraday (Merry Dee) Lindsey*[5], *Andrew Jackson Lindsey*[4], *Frances (Frankie) Sharp*[3], *Charles W. Sr.*[2], *John Sr.*[1]).

Geraldine married **Robert Staricks**.

2310. Evaline Morgan (*Bessie Lee Lindsey*[7], *Millard Lindsey*[6], *Maraday (Merry Dee) Lindsey*[5], *Andrew Jackson Lindsey*[4], *Frances (Frankie) Sharp*[3], *Charles W. Sr.*[2], *John Sr.*[1]).

Evaline married **Garland Wood**.

2311. Dorothy Lorraine Morgan (*Bessie Lee Lindsey*[7], *Millard Lindsey*[6], *Maraday (Merry Dee) Lindsey*[5], *Andrew Jackson Lindsey*[4], *Frances (Frankie) Sharp*[3], *Charles W. Sr.*[2], *John Sr.*[1]).

Dorothy married **Philip McClean**.

2312. Sue Morgan (*Bessie Lee Lindsey*[7], *Millard Lindsey*[6], *Maraday (Merry Dee) Lindsey*[5], *Andrew Jackson Lindsey*[4], *Frances (Frankie) Sharp*[3], *Charles W. Sr.*[2], *John Sr.*[1]).

Sue married **Joe Sims**.

2313. Peggy Morgan (*Bessie Lee Lindsey*[7], *Millard Lindsey*[6], *Maraday (Merry Dee) Lindsey*[5], *Andrew Jackson Lindsey*[4], *Frances (Frankie) Sharp*[3], *Charles W. Sr.*[2], *John Sr.*[1]).

Peggy married **Buford Mask**.

2315. Betty Jo Morgan (*Bessie Lee Lindsey*[7], *Millard Lindsey*[6], *Maraday (Merry Dee) Lindsey*[5], *Andrew Jackson Lindsey*[4], *Frances (Frankie) Sharp*[3], *Charles W. Sr.*[2], *John Sr.*[1]).

Betty married **Joe Cooksey**.

4191 F i. **Shannon Renee Cooksey**.

4192 M ii. **Joseph Christopher Cooksey**.

4193 M iii. **Seth Michael Cooksey**.

2318. Charles Edward Morgan (*Bessie Lee Lindsey*[7], *Millard Lindsey*[6], *Maraday (Merry Dee) Lindsey*[5], *Andrew Jackson Lindsey*[4], *Frances (Frankie) Sharp*[3], *Charles W. Sr.*[2], *John Sr.*[1]) was born 27 May 1951 in Turrell, Crittenden County, AR.

Charles married **Beverly Jane Harris** 10 Feb 1979 in Lauderdale County, AL. Beverly was born 2 Aug 1958 in Corinth, Alcorn County, MS.

| 4194 | M | i. | **Charlie Daniel Morgan** was born 30 Aug 1982 in Tupelo, MS. |
| 4195 | F | ii. | **Kelly Lee Ann Morgan** was born 18 Dec 1987 in Corinth, Alcorn County, MS. |

2331. Kathyleen Lindsey (*Coleman Edison Lindsey*[7], *Kerom William Lindsey*[6], *Greenberry Lee Lindsey Sr.*[5], *Sylvester (Sill) B. Lindsey*[4], *Frances (Frankie) Sharp*[3], *Charles W. Sr.*[2], *John Sr.*[1]) was born 2 Feb 1937 in Lauderdale County, AL.

Kathyleen married **Charles Daniel Dowdy**, son of **Homer Lee Dowdy** and **Ada S. Moore**, in May 1954 in Iuka, Tishomingo County, MS. Charles was born 28 Jan 1932 in Lauderdale County, AL.

+ 4196	M	i.	**Gregory Allen Dowdy** was born 18 Mar 1956 in Lauderdale County, AL.
+ 4197	F	ii.	**Nancy Ruth Dowdy** was born 3 Sep 1957 in Lauderdale County, AL.
+ 4198	M	iii.	**Jeffrey Wade Dowdy** was born 28 Aug 1962 in Lauderdale County, AL.
+ 4199	F	iv.	**Cynthia (Cindy) Lyn Dowdy** was born 19 Mar 1965 in Lauderdale County, AL.

2332. Owen Wayne Lindsey (*Coleman Edison Lindsey*[7], *Kerom William Lindsey*[6], *Greenberry Lee Lindsey Sr.*[5], *Sylvester (Sill) B. Lindsey*[4], *Frances (Frankie) Sharp*[3], *Charles W. Sr.*[2], *John Sr.*[1]) was born 16 Aug 1941 in Lauderdale County, AL.

Owen married **Betty Jo Vaden**, daughter of **Noble Delaney Vaden** and **Myrtle McAfee**, 18 May 1961 in Lauderdale County, AL. Betty was born 10 Dec 1941 in Lauderdale County, AL.

| + 4200 | M | i. | **Anthony Wayne Lindsey** was born 13 Mar 1963 in Aiken, SC. |
| + 4201 | M | ii. | **Brian Mitchell Lindsey** was born 11 Feb 1964 in Lauderdale County, AL. |

2334. Lynwood Clyde Lindsey (*Clyde Roosevelt Lindsey*[7], *Samuel S. Lindsey*[6], *Greenberry Lee Lindsey Sr.*[5], *Sylvester (Sill) B. Lindsey*[4], *Frances (Frankie) Sharp*[3], *Charles W. Sr.*[2], *John Sr.*[1]) was born 5 May 1928 in Lauderdale County, AL, died 19 May 1967, and was buried in Wright Cemetery, Wright, Lauderdale County, AL.

Lynwood married **Clara Estelle Young**, daughter of **Colonel Carl Young** and **Ethel Bevis**, 8 May 1955 in Iuka, Tishomingo County, MS. Clara was born 5 Jan 1927 in Lauderdale County, AL, died 28 Dec 1998, and was buried in Wright Cemetery, Wright, Lauderdale County, AL.

2336. Wallace Wilbur Joiner (*Georgia Mae Lindsey*[7], *John David Lindsey*[6], *Greenberry Lee Lindsey Sr.*[5], *Sylvester (Sill) B. Lindsey*[4], *Frances (Frankie) Sharp*[3], *Charles W. Sr.*[2], *John Sr.*[1]) was born 27 Jan 1935.

Wallace married **Clara Jean Bevins** 17 Jun 1954. Clara was born 15 May 1935.

+ 4202	M	i.	**Bruce Elliot Joiner** was born 10 Oct 1956.
+ 4203	F	ii.	**Sharon Kay Joiner** was born 3 Aug 1958.
+ 4204	F	iii.	**Cathy Lynn Joiner** was born 24 Aug 1962.

2337. June Jenette Joiner (*Georgia Mae Lindsey*[7], *John David Lindsey*[6], *Greenberry Lee Lindsey Sr.*[5], *Sylvester (Sill) B. Lindsey*[4], *Frances (Frankie) Sharp*[3], *Charles W. Sr.*[2], *John Sr.*[1]) was born 11 Oct 1937.

June married **John Louis Tubbs** 4 Jun 1955. John was born 24 Dec 1933.

| + 4205 | M | i. | **Steven Louis Tubbs** was born 22 Apr 1959. |

June next married **Leslie Dale Ames** 21 Jul 1962. Leslie was born 13 Jul 1935 and died 21 Jan 1973.

| + 4206 | F | i. | **Sandra Jo Ames** was born 27 Aug 1967. |

2339. Charles David Lindsey Sr. (*Edgar Bruce Lindsey*[7], *John David Lindsey*[6], *Greenberry Lee Lindsey Sr.*[5], *Sylvester (Sill) B. Lindsey*[4], *Frances (Frankie) Sharp*[3], *Charles W. Sr.*[2], *John Sr.*[1]) was born 25 Apr 1933 in Lauderdale County, AL.

Charles married **Virginia Lee McDonald**, daughter of **William Ervin McDonald** and **Pauline Myran Lindsey**, 25 Apr 1956 in Lauderdale County, AL. Virginia was born 18 Sep 1938 in Lauderdale County, AL. **(Duplicate Line. See Person 1133)**

2340. **Raymond Oneal Lindsey** (*Edgar Bruce Lindsey^7, John David Lindsey^6, Greenberry Lee Lindsey Sr.^{5}, Sylvester (Sill) B. Lindsey^4, Frances (Frankie) Sharp^3, Charles W. Sr.^{2}, John Sr.^{1}*) was born 18 Jul 1936 in Lauderdale County, AL.

Raymond married **Geraldine Nash**, daughter of **Plum Smiley Nash** and **Erma Lee Liegg**, 24 Aug 1957 in Lauderdale County, AL. Geraldine was born 17 Jul 1939 in Limestone County, AL.
+ 4207 M i. **Neal Lindsey**.
+ 4208 M ii. **Craig Lindsey**.
+ 4209 M iii. **Todd Lindsey**.

2341. **Patricia Ann Lindsey** (*Edgar Bruce Lindsey^7, John David Lindsey^6, Greenberry Lee Lindsey Sr.^{5}, Sylvester (Sill) B. Lindsey^4, Frances (Frankie) Sharp^3, Charles W. Sr.^{2}, John Sr.^{1}*) was born 20 Apr 1944 in Lauderdale County, AL.

Patricia married **Jerry Clayton Sharp**, son of **Charles Roy Sharp** and **Gladys Marie Wallace**, 20 Apr 1962 in Lauderdale County, AL. Jerry was born 31 Jan 1941 in Lauderdale County, AL. **(Duplicate Line. See Person 1904)**

2342. **James Bruce Lindsey** (*Edgar Bruce Lindsey^7, John David Lindsey^6, Greenberry Lee Lindsey Sr.^{5}, Sylvester (Sill) B. Lindsey^4, Frances (Frankie) Sharp^3, Charles W. Sr.^{2}, John Sr.^{1}*) was born 11 May 1951 in Chicago, IL.

James married **Therese Ann Nands** 27 Sep 1975. Therese was born 8 May 1953 in Chicago, IL.
+ 4210 M i. **Jason James Lindsey** was born 1 May 1976 in Melrose Park, IL.

2343. **Louise Lindsey** (*Donald Lindsey^7, John David Lindsey^6, Greenberry Lee Lindsey Sr.^{5}, Sylvester (Sill) B. Lindsey^4, Frances (Frankie) Sharp^3, Charles W. Sr.^{2}, John Sr.^{1}*).

Louise married ***Unk Heintz**.

2350. **Wanda Gail Johnson** (*James Edward Johnson^7, Pearlie Ann Milford^6, Julie (Julia) Lindsey^5, Sylvester (Sill) B. Lindsey^4, Frances (Frankie) Sharp^3, Charles W. Sr.^{2}, John Sr.^{1}*).

Wanda married ***Unk Wilkerson**.

2356. **Rebecca Ann Johnston** (*Susie Belle Pierce^7, Amy Gertrude Lindsey^6, Adron (Little Ade) Lindsey^5, Sylvester (Sill) B. Lindsey^4, Frances (Frankie) Sharp^3, Charles W. Sr.^{2}, John Sr.^{1}*) was born 13 Oct 1948 in Colbert County, AL.

Rebecca married **James Edward O'Kelley**, son of **James R. O'Kelley** and **Julia C. Doonley**, 8 Apr 1976. James was born 15 Nov 1947 in Lauderdale County, AL.
4211 M i. **Jeffery O'Kelley**.
4212 M ii. **Josh O'Kelley**.

2357. **William (Bill) Ross Johnston** (*Susie Belle Pierce^7, Amy Gertrude Lindsey^6, Adron (Little Ade) Lindsey^5, Sylvester (Sill) B. Lindsey^4, Frances (Frankie) Sharp^3, Charles W. Sr.^{2}, John Sr.^{1}*) was born 3 Jan 1952 in Colbert County, AL.

William married **Connie Sue Cole**, daughter of **Clifton L. Cole** and **Mary Russell**, 7 Nov 1983 in Lauderdale County, AL. Connie was born 9 Dec 1958 in Giles County, TN.
4213 F i. **Siera Sue Johnston**.

2358. James Maurice Johnston (*Susie Belle Pierce*[7], *Amy Gertrude Lindsey*[6], *Adron (Little Ade) Lindsey*[5], *Sylvester (Sill) B. Lindsey*[4], *Frances (Frankie) Sharp*[3], *Charles W. Sr.*[2], *John Sr.*[1]) was born 3 Mar 1961 in Lauderdale County, AL.

James married **Rhonda Charline Wanner**, daughter of **Bobby A. Wanner** and **Patsy Wilson**, 11 Sep 1981 in Lauderdale County, AL. Rhonda was born 27 Jun 1961 in Lauderdale County, AL.
 4214 M i. **Juston Lee Johnston.**
 4215 F ii. **Brandy Nicole Johnston.**

2361. Betty Dean Pigg (*Mildred Lucille Pierce*[7], *Amy Gertrude Lindsey*[6], *Adron (Little Ade) Lindsey*[5], *Sylvester (Sill) B. Lindsey*[4], *Frances (Frankie) Sharp*[3], *Charles W. Sr.*[2], *John Sr.*[1]).

Betty married **Jessie McCoy.**

2366. Karen Anne Perkins (*Bobbie Lee Pierce*[7], *Amy Gertrude Lindsey*[6], *Adron (Little Ade) Lindsey*[5], *Sylvester (Sill) B. Lindsey*[4], *Frances (Frankie) Sharp*[3], *Charles W. Sr.*[2], *John Sr.*[1]) was born 8 Jan 1947 in Lawrence County, TN.

Karen married **Ronald Eugene Lowery** 1 May 1964.
 + 4216 M i. **Kenneth Eugene Lowery** was born 8 Apr 1965 in Lawrence County, TN.
 + 4217 M ii. **Anthony Wayne Lowery** was born 5 Nov 1966 in Lawrence County, TN.
 + 4218 M iii. **Shoan Lee Lowery** was born 14 Feb 1969 in Lawrence County, TN.

Karen next married **Robert Neal Rice** 23 May 1979.

2367. Connie Lee Perkins (*Bobbie Lee Pierce*[7], *Amy Gertrude Lindsey*[6], *Adron (Little Ade) Lindsey*[5], *Sylvester (Sill) B. Lindsey*[4], *Frances (Frankie) Sharp*[3], *Charles W. Sr.*[2], *John Sr.*[1]) was born 23 Jul 1949 in Lawrence County, TN.

Connie married **Larry Gene Massey.**
 + 4219 M i. **Larry Bret Massey** was born 24 Aug 1969 in Lawrence County, TN.
 + 4220 M ii. **Chad Pierce Massey** was born 29 Jun 1971 in Lawrence County, TN.

Connie next married **Jim Cain.**
 4221 M i. **Chase Garrison Cain** was born 14 May 1993 in Columbia, Maury County, TN.

Connie next married **William Burks** in 1973.
 + 4222 M i. **Gregory Gains Burks** was born 23 Jun 1975 in Lawrence County, TN.

2368. Dianna Lynn Perkins (*Bobbie Lee Pierce*[7], *Amy Gertrude Lindsey*[6], *Adron (Little Ade) Lindsey*[5], *Sylvester (Sill) B. Lindsey*[4], *Frances (Frankie) Sharp*[3], *Charles W. Sr.*[2], *John Sr.*[1]) was born 10 Apr 1951 in Muncie, Delaware County, IN.

Dianna married **Robert Thomas (Tommy) Story** 29 Mar 1971 in Lawrence County, TN. Robert was born 20 Sep 1949 in Lawrence County, TN.
 + 4223 F i. **Kesha Annette Story** was born 5 Dec 1973 in Columbia, Maury County, TN.
 + 4224 F ii. **Tiffani LeNea (Tippi) Story** was born 3 Nov 1975 in Columbia, Maury County, TN.

2369. Homer Clyde Perkins III (*Bobbie Lee Pierce*[7], *Amy Gertrude Lindsey*[6], *Adron (Little Ade) Lindsey*[5], *Sylvester (Sill) B. Lindsey*[4], *Frances (Frankie) Sharp*[3], *Charles W. Sr.*[2], *John Sr.*[1]) was born 27 Oct 1953 in Muncie, Delaware County, IN.

Homer married **Martha Faye Richardson** 1 Apr 1980 in Pulaski, Giles County, TN.
 4225 M i. **Phillip Dewayne Perkins** was born 7 Oct 1980 in Columbia, Maury County, TN.
 + 4226 M ii. **Michael Blake Perkins** was born 13 Aug 1983 in Columbia, Maury County, TN.

2370. Pamela Sue Perkins (*Bobbie Lee Pierce^7, Amy Gertrude Lindsey^6, Adron (Little Ade) Lindsey^5, Sylvester (Sill) B. Lindsey^4, Frances (Frankie) Sharp^3, Charles W. Sr.^{2}, John Sr.^{1}*) was born 27 Oct 1955 in Muncie, Delaware County, IN.

   Pamela married **Doug Holden**.
   4227 F i. **Jennifer Holden** was born 21 Oct 1977 in Columbia, Maury County, TN.

   Pamela next married **Ronnie Leighton**.
   4228 F i. **Pammie Cherie Leighton** was born 2 Mar 1972 in Columbia, Maury County, TN.

2374. Betty Smith (*Evelyn Bills^7, Viola Lindsey^6, Adron (Little Ade) Lindsey^5, Sylvester (Sill) B. Lindsey^4, Frances (Frankie) Sharp^3, Charles W. Sr.^{2}, John Sr.^{1}*).

   Betty married **Larry Clemmons**.

2375. Dollie Smith (*Evelyn Bills^7, Viola Lindsey^6, Adron (Little Ade) Lindsey^5, Sylvester (Sill) B. Lindsey^4, Frances (Frankie) Sharp^3, Charles W. Sr.^{2}, John Sr.^{1}*).

   Dollie married **Donald Dick**.
   4229 F i.   **Donna Dick**.
   4230 F ii.   **Diana Dick**.
   4231 F iii. **Denise Dick**.

2380. Mary Ann Barrier (*Henry Olen Barrier^7, Josie Etta Haynes^6, Lucretia (Lula) Lindsey^5, Adron Leonard Lindsey Sr.^{4}, Frances (Frankie) Sharp^3, Charles W. Sr.^{2}, John Sr.^{1}*).

   Mary married ***Unk Arnold**.

2381. Donna Sue Barrier (*Henry Olen Barrier^7, Josie Etta Haynes^6, Lucretia (Lula) Lindsey^5, Adron Leonard Lindsey Sr.^{4}, Frances (Frankie) Sharp^3, Charles W. Sr.^{2}, John Sr.^{1}*) was born 27 Mar 1948 in Lauderdale County, AL.

   Donna married **Tommy White Sharp**, son of **Earl Leslie Sharp** and **Mary Nadine White**, 8 Jul 1967 in Lauderdale County, AL. Tommy was born 9 Sep 1947 in Lauderdale County, AL.
   + 4232 F i.   **Terri Lynn Sharp** was born 19 Nov 1971 in Lauderdale County, AL.
   + 4233 F ii. **Jami Suzanne Sharp** was born 11 May 1983 in Lauderdale County, AL.

2382. Harry Wilbern Odum Sr. (*Carmel Inez Haynes^7, Clarence Haynes^6, Lucretia (Lula) Lindsey^5, Adron Leonard Lindsey Sr.^{4}, Frances (Frankie) Sharp^3, Charles W. Sr.^{2}, John Sr.^{1}*) was born 26 Oct 1931 in Tyronza, Poinsett County, AR.

   Harry married **Betty Jo Pinion**. Betty was born 26 Apr 1933 in Obion County, TN.
   + 4234 F i.   **Deborah Diane Odum** was born 1 Jun 1952 in Memphis, Shelby County, TN.
   + 4235 M ii.   **Harry Wilbern Odum Jr.** was born 4 Oct 1953 in Memphis, Shelby County, TN.
   + 4236 F iii. **Cheryl Annette Odum** was born 24 Apr 1961 in Memphis, Shelby County, TN.

2384. Joyce Ann Haynes (*Edwin Lenard Haynes^7, Clarence Haynes^6, Lucretia (Lula) Lindsey^5, Adron Leonard Lindsey Sr.^{4}, Frances (Frankie) Sharp^3, Charles W. Sr.^{2}, John Sr.^{1}*) was born in Tyronza, Poinsett County, AR.

   Joyce married **Paul Green** 17 Apr 1982. Paul was born 16 May 1931.

2386. Gary Doyle Haynes (*Doyle Odell Haynes^7, Clarence Haynes^6, Lucretia (Lula) Lindsey^5, Adron Leonard Lindsey Sr.^{4}, Frances (Frankie) Sharp^3, Charles W. Sr.^{2}, John Sr.^{1}*) was born 12 Dec 1950 in Memphis, Shelby County, TN.

   Gary married **Margarette Darolyne Woods**. Margarette was born 1 Oct 1952 in Craighead County, AR.
   4237 M i. **Stewart Odell Haynes** was born 12 Jun 1984 in Crittenden County, AR.

4238 M ii. **Caleb Lee Haynes** was born 18 Dec 1985 in Crittenden County, AR.

2387. Linda Sue Haynes (*Weldon Lewis Haynes*[7]*, Clarence Haynes*[6]*, Lucretia (Lula) Lindsey*[5]*, Adron Leonard Lindsey Sr.*[4]*, Frances (Frankie) Sharp*[3]*, Charles W. Sr.*[2]*, John Sr.*[1]) was born 31 Mar 1943 in Craighead County, AR.

Linda married **Alan Poole**.
4239 F i. **Margaret Michelle Poole** was born 5 Jul 1969 in Crittenden County, AR.
4240 F ii. **Penny Lynn Poole** was born 17 Feb 1975 in Crittenden County, AR.
4241 F iii. **Jenny Lou Poole** was born 17 Feb 1975 in Crittenden County, AR.

2388. Phyllis Kay Haynes (*Weldon Lewis Haynes*[7]*, Clarence Haynes*[6]*, Lucretia (Lula) Lindsey*[5]*, Adron Leonard Lindsey Sr.*[4]*, Frances (Frankie) Sharp*[3]*, Charles W. Sr.*[2]*, John Sr.*[1]) was born 6 Mar 1946 in California.

Phyllis married **Berlon Wayne Wilson**. Berlon was born 23 Aug 1946 in Pulaski County, AR.
4242 F i. **Carrie Lynn Wilson** was born 30 Nov 1970 in Arkansas.
4243 F ii. **Kellie Rebecca Wilson** was born 9 Oct 1973 in Arkansas.
4244 F iii. **Nikkie Melissa Wilson** was born 9 Nov 1973 in Arkansas.
4245 F iv. **LEslie Allison Wilson** was born 14 Jan 1975 in Arkansas.

2392. Mary Lou Faye Harmon (*Dora Inez Tacker*[7]*, Lou Tishie Haynes*[6]*, Lucretia (Lula) Lindsey*[5]*, Adron Leonard Lindsey Sr.*[4]*, Frances (Frankie) Sharp*[3]*, Charles W. Sr.*[2]*, John Sr.*[1]) was born 16 Sep 1926.

Mary married **Raymond Lee Perry** 15 Mar 1947. Raymond was born 26 Jul 1920 and died 3 Mar 2003.
4246 F i. **Rana Lynn Perry**.
4247 F ii. **Ardra Gwen Perry**.
4248 F iii. **Marta Annette Perry**.

2393. Gradie Marguerite Harmon (*Dora Inez Tacker*[7]*, Lou Tishie Haynes*[6]*, Lucretia (Lula) Lindsey*[5]*, Adron Leonard Lindsey Sr.*[4]*, Frances (Frankie) Sharp*[3]*, Charles W. Sr.*[2]*, John Sr.*[1]) was born 9 Nov 1929.

Gradie married **Joe Omby McKnight** 23 Dec 1952. Joe was born 23 Aug 1923 and died 17 Jan 1991.
4249 M i. **Joey Donald McKnight**.

2394. Billy Thomas Harmon Sr. (*Dora Inez Tacker*[7]*, Lou Tishie Haynes*[6]*, Lucretia (Lula) Lindsey*[5]*, Adron Leonard Lindsey Sr.*[4]*, Frances (Frankie) Sharp*[3]*, Charles W. Sr.*[2]*, John Sr.*[1]) was born 7 Dec 1933 and died 21 Jun 2001.

Billy married **Nora Minton** 6 Feb 1953. Nora was born 15 May 1931.
4250 F i. **Patricia Harmon**.
4251 F ii. **Anne Harmon**.
4252 M iii. **Billy Harmon Jr.**
4253 F iv. **Phyllis Harmon**.

2396. Odie Jack Harmon (*Dora Inez Tacker*[7]*, Lou Tishie Haynes*[6]*, Lucretia (Lula) Lindsey*[5]*, Adron Leonard Lindsey Sr.*[4]*, Frances (Frankie) Sharp*[3]*, Charles W. Sr.*[2]*, John Sr.*[1]) was born 25 Jul 1941.

Odie married **Edana L. Decker** 27 Jun 1961. Edana was born 10 Nov 1945.
4254 M i. **Alan Jack Harmon**.
4255 F ii. **Andrea Kay Harmon**.
4256 M iii. **Grady Evan Harmon**.
4257 M iv. **Stephen Lyle Harmon**.

2397. Harold Mack Harmon (*Dora Inez Tacker*[7]*, Lou Tishie Haynes*[6]*, Lucretia (Lula) Lindsey*[5]*, Adron Leonard Lindsey Sr.*[4]*, Frances (Frankie) Sharp*[3]*, Charles W. Sr.*[2]*, John Sr.*[1]) was born 22 Mar 1944.

Harold married **Diane Myrick** 18 Jan 1964.
4258 F i. **Michelle Harmon**.

4259 M ii. **Ronald Harmon**.
4260 F iii. **Trina Harmon**.

2398. Norma Jean Harmon (*Dora Inez Tacker*[7]*, Lou Tishie Haynes*[6]*, Lucretia (Lula) Lindsey*[5]*, Adron Leonard Lindsey Sr.*[4]*, Frances (Frankie) Sharp*[3]*, Charles W. Sr.*[2]*, John Sr.*[1]) was born 5 Jan 1948.

Norma married **Donald Huggins** 14 Oct 1965.
4261 F i. **Tracie Huggins**.
4262 F ii. **Stacie Huggins**.

2410. Glenda Gayle Winborn (*Ruby Mae Wood*[7]*, Martha (Mattie) Inez Taylor*[6]*, Lucretia (Lula) Lindsey*[5]*, Adron Leonard Lindsey Sr.*[4]*, Frances (Frankie) Sharp*[3]*, Charles W. Sr.*[2]*, John Sr.*[1]) was born in Lauderdale County, AL.

Glenda married ***Unk Phillips**.

2411. Wanda Sue Winborn (*Ruby Mae Wood*[7]*, Martha (Mattie) Inez Taylor*[6]*, Lucretia (Lula) Lindsey*[5]*, Adron Leonard Lindsey Sr.*[4]*, Frances (Frankie) Sharp*[3]*, Charles W. Sr.*[2]*, John Sr.*[1]) was born in Lauderdale County, AL.

Wanda married **Ron Langford**.

2413. Willard Leon (Pete) Winborn (*Ruby Mae Wood*[7]*, Martha (Mattie) Inez Taylor*[6]*, Lucretia (Lula) Lindsey*[5]*, Adron Leonard Lindsey Sr.*[4]*, Frances (Frankie) Sharp*[3]*, Charles W. Sr.*[2]*, John Sr.*[1]) was born 27 Nov 1946 in Lauderdale County, AL.

Willard married **Connie Lorene Fleming**. Connie was born 26 Jun 1946.
4263 M i. **Ricky Leo Winborn** was born 9 Aug 1970.
4264 M ii. **Michael Wayne Winborn** was born 6 Jun 1973.

2414. Douglas Ray Winborn (*Ruby Mae Wood*[7]*, Martha (Mattie) Inez Taylor*[6]*, Lucretia (Lula) Lindsey*[5]*, Adron Leonard Lindsey Sr.*[4]*, Frances (Frankie) Sharp*[3]*, Charles W. Sr.*[2]*, John Sr.*[1]) was born 16 Jul 1948 in Lauderdale County, AL.

Douglas married **Teresa Dawn Kelley**, daughter of **Thomas Charles Kelley Sr.** and **Aileen Beulah Sharp**, 3 Apr 1970 in Lauderdale County, AL. Teresa was born 13 Sep 1954 in Lauderdale County, AL.
+ 4265 F i. **Michelle Dawn Winborn** was born 22 Sep 1971 in Lauderdale County, AL.

Douglas next married **Theresa Maxine Sharpston**, daughter of **Robert (R. J.) Sharpston Sr.** and **Mable Rita Phillips**. Theresa was born 8 May 1961 in Florida.
4266 F i. **Theresha Winborn**.
4267 M ii. **Bubba Winborn**.
4268 F iii. **Kasey Winborn**.
4269 M iv. **Gregory Winborn**.
4270 F v. **Kala Winborn**.

2415. Martha Faye Winborn (*Ruby Mae Wood*[7]*, Martha (Mattie) Inez Taylor*[6]*, Lucretia (Lula) Lindsey*[5]*, Adron Leonard Lindsey Sr.*[4]*, Frances (Frankie) Sharp*[3]*, Charles W. Sr.*[2]*, John Sr.*[1]) was born 9 Jun 1953 in Lauderdale County, AL.

Martha married **William Jerry Vickery**.

Martha next married ***Unk Johnson**.

2418. Sandra (Sandy) Jean Wood (*Floyde Virgil Wood*[7]*, Martha (Mattie) Inez Taylor*[6]*, Lucretia (Lula) Lindsey*[5]*, Adron Leonard Lindsey Sr.*[4]*, Frances (Frankie) Sharp*[3]*, Charles W. Sr.*[2]*, John Sr.*[1]) was born 22 Dec 1954.

Sandra married **Michael Rzepka** 1 Dec 1984. Michael was born 13 Nov 1951.

2419. Patricia (Pat) Wood (*Floyde Virgil Wood*[7], *Martha (Mattie) Inez Taylor*[6], *Lucretia (Lula) Lindsey*[5], *Adron Leonard Lindsey Sr.*[4], *Frances (Frankie) Sharp*[3], *Charles W. Sr.*[2], *John Sr.*[1]) was born 21 Mar 1959.

Patricia married **Jack Endicott**.

+ 4271 F   i.   **Casey Endicott** was born 29 Mar 1979.
+ 4272 M   ii.   **Timothy Endicott** was born 9 Sep 1984.

2420. Brenda Ruth Bruce (*Annie Ruth Wood*[7], *Martha (Mattie) Inez Taylor*[6], *Lucretia (Lula) Lindsey*[5], *Adron Leonard Lindsey Sr.*[4], *Frances (Frankie) Sharp*[3], *Charles W. Sr.*[2], *John Sr.*[1]) was born 19 Nov 1948 in Lauderdale County, AL.

Brenda married **David Daniels**, son of **Melvin Robert Daniels** and **Mageline Cox**. David was born 4 Feb 1948.

+ 4273 M   i.   **Derek Robert Daniels** was born 17 Feb 1970.
+ 4274 F   ii.   **Vickie Denise Daniels** was born 5 Feb 1972.

Brenda next married ***Unk Blake**.

2421. Michael Wayne Bruce (*Annie Ruth Wood*[7], *Martha (Mattie) Inez Taylor*[6], *Lucretia (Lula) Lindsey*[5], *Adron Leonard Lindsey Sr.*[4], *Frances (Frankie) Sharp*[3], *Charles W. Sr.*[2], *John Sr.*[1]) was born 30 May 1951 in Lauderdale County, AL.

Michael married **Sharon Antoinette Boyd**, daughter of **Rolland Norman Boyd** and **Nettie Sue Harvey**, 15 Aug 1974 in Lauderdale County, AL. Sharon was born 28 Jun 1953 in Lauderdale County, AL.

2422. Barbara Sue Bruce (*Annie Ruth Wood*[7], *Martha (Mattie) Inez Taylor*[6], *Lucretia (Lula) Lindsey*[5], *Adron Leonard Lindsey Sr.*[4], *Frances (Frankie) Sharp*[3], *Charles W. Sr.*[2], *John Sr.*[1]) was born 30 Oct 1954 in Lauderdale County, AL.

Barbara married **Danny Alan Barrier**, son of **John Henry Barrier** and **Eri Evelyn Williams**, 28 Nov 1968 in Lauderdale County, AL. Danny was born 15 Feb 1951 in Hardin County, TN.

+ 4275 M   i.   **John Paul Barrier** was born 22 Sep 1970 in Lauderdale County, AL.
+ 4276 F   ii.   **Joannie Lee Barrier** was born 6 Sep 1976 in Lauderdale County, AL.
   4277 M   iii.   **Benjamin Alan Barrier** was born 12 Jul 1982 in Lewis County, TN.

2423. John Daniel Bruce (*Annie Ruth Wood*[7], *Martha (Mattie) Inez Taylor*[6], *Lucretia (Lula) Lindsey*[5], *Adron Leonard Lindsey Sr.*[4], *Frances (Frankie) Sharp*[3], *Charles W. Sr.*[2], *John Sr.*[1]) was born 23 Jun 1958 in Lauderdale County, AL.

John married **Kimberly *Unk**.

   4278 M   i.   **Daniel Wayne Bruce** was born in Oct 1994.

2424. David Paul Bruce (*Annie Ruth Wood*[7], *Martha (Mattie) Inez Taylor*[6], *Lucretia (Lula) Lindsey*[5], *Adron Leonard Lindsey Sr.*[4], *Frances (Frankie) Sharp*[3], *Charles W. Sr.*[2], *John Sr.*[1]) was born 9 Jul 1961 in Lauderdale County, AL.

David married **Lisa Duke**.

2425. Terry Lynn Bruce (*Annie Ruth Wood*[7], *Martha (Mattie) Inez Taylor*[6], *Lucretia (Lula) Lindsey*[5], *Adron Leonard Lindsey Sr.*[4], *Frances (Frankie) Sharp*[3], *Charles W. Sr.*[2], *John Sr.*[1]) was born 24 Dec 1964 in Lauderdale County, AL.

Terry married **Karon Denise Brown**, daughter of **Dwight Gabriel Brown** and **Gwenda Gale Neill**, 16 Aug 1987 in Lauderdale County, AL. Karon was born 30 Dec 1964 in Hardin County, AL.

   4279 M   i.   **Brandon Dwight Bruce** was born in 1988.

Terry next married **Lisa Barker** before 1991.

   4280 M   i.   **Hunter Cole Bruce** was born 31 Dec 1991.

2426. Becky Lou Bruce (*Annie Ruth Wood[7], Martha (Mattie) Inez Taylor[6], Lucretia (Lula) Lindsey[5], Adron Leonard Lindsey Sr.[4], Frances (Frankie) Sharp[3], Charles W. Sr.[2], John Sr.[1]*) was born 11 Dec 1966 in Lauderdale County, AL.

Becky married **Donald Harry Schmidlkofer**, son of **Donald Howard Schmidlkofer** and **Catherine Agnes Patterson**, 20 Nov 1992 in Lauderdale County, AL. Donald was born 24 Feb 1967 in Lauderdale County, AL.
4281 M i. **Ryan Harry Schmidlkofer** was born 22 May 1998 in Lauderdale County, AL.

2427. Karen Denise Wood (*Glen Wood[7], Martha (Mattie) Inez Taylor[6], Lucretia (Lula) Lindsey[5], Adron Leonard Lindsey Sr.[4], Frances (Frankie) Sharp[3], Charles W. Sr.[2], John Sr.[1]*) was born 24 Sep 1954 in Lauderdale County, AL.

Karen married **Patrick August Eck**, son of **Joseph H. Eck** and **Mary Zierer**, 16 Jun 1976 in Lauderdale County, AL. Patrick was born 11 Jun 1948 in Lauderdale County, AL.
+ 4282 F i. **Holly Lynn Eck** was born 29 Dec 1978.
4283 F ii. **Amy Christine Eck** was born 16 Sep 1981.
4284 F iii. **Christy Lynn Eck** was born 5 Sep 1985.

Karen next married **Larry Charles Cochran** 27 Jan 1994 in Lauderdale County, AL. Larry was born 8 Jan 1952 in Colbert County, AL.
4285 M i. **Charles Blake Cochran** was born 9 Jun 1994.

Karen next married **Tim Barrett** about 1995.

2428. Glenna Joy Wood (*Glen Wood[7], Martha (Mattie) Inez Taylor[6], Lucretia (Lula) Lindsey[5], Adron Leonard Lindsey Sr.[4], Frances (Frankie) Sharp[3], Charles W. Sr.[2], John Sr.[1]*) was born 25 Jan 1956 in Lauderdale County, AL.

Glenna married **Tulon Conrad McRight Jr.**, son of **Tulon Conrad McRight Sr.** and **Hazel Harris**, 19 Sep 1980 in Lauderdale County, AL. Tulon was born 26 Nov 1954 in Lauderdale County, AL.
4286 M i. **Joshua Conrad McRight** was born 5 Oct 1983.
4287 M ii. **Martin Glenn McRight** was born 17 Mar 1986.
4288 F iii. **Emily Joy McRight** was born 12 Sep 1989.

2429. Kent Maurice Wood (*Glen Wood[7], Martha (Mattie) Inez Taylor[6], Lucretia (Lula) Lindsey[5], Adron Leonard Lindsey Sr.[4], Frances (Frankie) Sharp[3], Charles W. Sr.[2], John Sr.[1]*) was born 3 Feb 1958 in Lauderdale County, AL.

Kent married **Connie Robertson**, daughter of **Floyd Robertson** and **Lillie Williams**, before 1992 in Lauderdale County, AL. Connie was born 3 Feb 1957 in Lauderdale County, AL.

Kent next married **Karen Delane Young**, daughter of **James Robert Young** and **Bille J. Burns**, 22 Feb 1992 in Lauderdale County, AL. Karen was born 15 Mar 1958 in Lauderdale County, AL.
4289 M i. **Jarrod Glen Wood** was born 11 May 1990.

2430. Barry Keith Wood (*Glen Wood[7], Martha (Mattie) Inez Taylor[6], Lucretia (Lula) Lindsey[5], Adron Leonard Lindsey Sr.[4], Frances (Frankie) Sharp[3], Charles W. Sr.[2], John Sr.[1]*) was born 14 Jan 1960 in Lauderdale County, AL.

Barry married **Deloris Diane Price**, daughter of **Jimmy Price** and **Lila Smith**, 10 Sep 1982 in Lauderdale County, AL. Deloris was born 16 Oct 1961 in Lawrence County, TN.
4290 M i. **Barry Jason Wood** was born 31 May 1984.
4291 M ii. **Bradley Kent Wood** was born 17 May 1990.
4292 F iii. **Rachel Diane Wood** was born 29 Aug 1997.

2431. Lisa Rene Wood (*Glen Wood[7], Martha (Mattie) Inez Taylor[6], Lucretia (Lula) Lindsey[5], Adron Leonard Lindsey Sr.[4], Frances (Frankie) Sharp[3], Charles W. Sr.[2], John Sr.[1]*) was born 21 Mar 1962 in Lauderdale County, AL.

Lisa married **Alvin Mikel Montgomery**, son of **Alvin E. Montgomery** and **Kathleen M. Montgomery**, 28 Mar 1980 in Lauderdale County, AL. Alvin was born 8 Dec 1959 in Lauderdale County, AL.

4293	F	i.	**Alicia Joy Montgomery** was born 14 Jun 1981 in Lauderdale County, AL.
4294	F	ii.	**Brittany Rene Montgomery** was born 16 May 1985 in Lauderdale County, AL.

2432. Debra Lynn Hipps (*Elza Darlene Wood^7, Martha (Mattie) Inez Taylor^6, Lucretia (Lula) Lindsey^5, Adron Leonard Lindsey Sr.^{4}, Frances (Frankie) Sharp^3, Charles W. Sr.^{2}, John Sr.^{1}*) was born 22 May 1952 in Lauderdale County, AL.

Debra married **Sammy Lee Linville**, son of **Sam M. Linville** and **Oma Taylor**, 5 Oct 1968 in Lauderdale County, AL. Sammy was born 22 Jan 1950 in Lauderdale County, AL.

+ 4295	F	i.	**Krysta Lynn Linville** was born 15 Oct 1969 in Lauderdale County, AL.
4296	M	ii.	**Benjamin Lee Linville** was born 12 Aug 1976 in Lauderdale County, AL.

2433. Jackie Diane Hipps (*Elza Darlene Wood^7, Martha (Mattie) Inez Taylor^6, Lucretia (Lula) Lindsey^5, Adron Leonard Lindsey Sr.^{4}, Frances (Frankie) Sharp^3, Charles W. Sr.^{2}, John Sr.^{1}*) was born 9 Oct 1954 in Lauderdale County, AL.

Jackie married **Thomas (Tommy) Eugene Darby Jr.**, son of **Thomas Eugene Darby Sr.** and **Billie Faye Hill**, 28 Jul 1978 in Lauderdale County, AL. Thomas was born 1 Jul 1953 in Lauderdale County, AL.

+ 4297	M	i.	**Thomas Riley (Ry) Darby** was born 8 Jun 1983 in Lauderdale County, AL.

2434. Nancy Carol Hipps (*Elza Darlene Wood^7, Martha (Mattie) Inez Taylor^6, Lucretia (Lula) Lindsey^5, Adron Leonard Lindsey Sr.^{4}, Frances (Frankie) Sharp^3, Charles W. Sr.^{2}, John Sr.^{1}*) was born 21 Jan 1961 in Lauderdale County, AL.

Nancy married **Nicholas (Nick) French**. Nicholas was born 11 Apr 1959.

+ 4298	F	i.	**Lori Darlene Hipps** was born 29 Jul 1983.

2435. Jesse James (Jamie) Hipps (*Elza Darlene Wood^7, Martha (Mattie) Inez Taylor^6, Lucretia (Lula) Lindsey^5, Adron Leonard Lindsey Sr.^{4}, Frances (Frankie) Sharp^3, Charles W. Sr.^{2}, John Sr.^{1}*) was born 2 May 1965 in Lauderdale County, AL.

Jesse married **Teresa Holcomb**. Teresa was born 9 Jul 1963 in Russellville, Franklin County, AL.

+ 4299	F	i.	**Jessica Danielle Hipps** was born 27 Apr 1983.
4300	F	ii.	**Andrea Marie Hipps** was born 15 Jul 1985.

2436. Danny Joe Cole (*Josephine Wood^7, Martha (Mattie) Inez Taylor^6, Lucretia (Lula) Lindsey^5, Adron Leonard Lindsey Sr.^{4}, Frances (Frankie) Sharp^3, Charles W. Sr.^{2}, John Sr.^{1}*) was born 7 Nov 1955.

Danny married **Sherry Lynn Welco**. Sherry was born 21 Mar 1958.

4301	M	i.	**Matthew Kyle Cole** was born 14 Apr 1988.
4302	M	ii.	**Samuel Gage Cole** was born 1 Apr 1990.

2438. James Gregory Wood (*James Edward Wood^7, Martha (Mattie) Inez Taylor^6, Lucretia (Lula) Lindsey^5, Adron Leonard Lindsey Sr.^{4}, Frances (Frankie) Sharp^3, Charles W. Sr.^{2}, John Sr.^{1}*) was born 6 Mar 1963.

James married **Christy Austin** 13 Mar 1998. Christy was born 18 Oct 1970.

4303	M	i.	**Tydus Austin Stewart** was born 7 Mar 1995.
4304	F	ii.	**Gracie Elizabeth Wood** was born 28 Nov 2001.

2441. Harold Wade Wood (*Harold Taylor Wood^7, Martha (Mattie) Inez Taylor^6, Lucretia (Lula) Lindsey^5, Adron Leonard Lindsey Sr.^{4}, Frances (Frankie) Sharp^3, Charles W. Sr.^{2}, John Sr.^{1}*) was born 20 Jun 1975.

Harold married **Bethany Renea Cox** 15 Jul 2000 in Colbert County, AL.

2443. Michael Fay Haeger (*Dolly Katherine Lindsey*[7], *Carlos (Bill) Lindsey*[6], *Adron Leonard (Green) Lindsey Jr.*[5], *Adron Leonard Lindsey Sr.*[4], *Frances (Frankie) Sharp*[3], *Charles W. Sr.*[2], *John Sr.*[1]) was born 21 Mar 1946.

Michael married **Carolyn Johnson**. Carolyn was born 8 Apr 1950.

| 4305 | M | i. | **Eric Steven Haeger** was born 14 Jun 1964. |
| 4306 | M | ii. | **Michael Todd Haeger** was born 17 Apr 1968. |

2444. Karen Ann Haeger (*Dolly Katherine Lindsey*[7], *Carlos (Bill) Lindsey*[6], *Adron Leonard (Green) Lindsey Jr.*[5], *Adron Leonard Lindsey Sr.*[4], *Frances (Frankie) Sharp*[3], *Charles W. Sr.*[2], *John Sr.*[1]) was born 5 Apr 1962 in Lauderdale County, AL.

Karen married **Michael Allen Muse**, son of **William Thomas Muse** and **Juanita Elizabeth Myrick**, 21 Jul 1980 in Lauderdale County, AL. Michael was born 22 Nov 1956 in Mishawaka, St Joseph County, IN.

| 4307 | F | i. | **Andrea Nicole Muse** was born 22 Jan 1984 in Lauderdale County, AL. |
| 4308 | F | ii. | **Lauren Brittney Muse** was born 20 Jul 1988 in Lauderdale County, AL. |

2445. Nancy Carter McDonald (*William Lindsey McDonald*[7], *Pauline Myran Lindsey*[6], *Adron Leonard (Green) Lindsey Jr.*[5], *Adron Leonard Lindsey Sr.*[4], *Frances (Frankie) Sharp*[3], *Charles W. Sr.*[2], *John Sr.*[1]) was born 6 Jun 1947 in Lauderdale County, AL.

Nancy married **John William Scarbrough**, son of **James W. Scarbrough** and **Ruth Osborn Porter**, 6 Jun 1967 in Lauderdale County, AL. John was born 18 Mar 1946.

Nancy next married **Marvin McDaniel Buttram**, son of **August Daniel Buttram** and **Mary Rebecca Eppes**, 11 Mar 1974. Marvin was born 5 Jul 1947 in Jefferson County, AL.

| | 4311 | M | i. | **Carter McDaniel Buttram** was born 23 Jan 1971. |
| + | 4312 | F | ii. | **Lindsey Katherine Buttram** was born 15 Aug 1973. |

2446. Suzannah Lee McDonald (*William Lindsey McDonald*[7], *Pauline Myran Lindsey*[6], *Adron Leonard (Green) Lindsey Jr.*[5], *Adron Leonard Lindsey Sr.*[4], *Frances (Frankie) Sharp*[3], *Charles W. Sr.*[2], *John Sr.*[1]) was born 27 Apr 1955 in Lauderdale County, AL.

Suzannah married **Mark Carey McClellan** 16 Jul 1977. Mark was born 5 Mar 1957 in Bay County, FL.

| 4313 | M | i. | **Andrew William McClellan** was born 14 Sep 1981. |
| 4314 | F | ii. | **Amanda Suzannah Carey McClellan** was born 25 Jul 1985. |

Suzannah next married **Eric Michael Backensto** 8 Jun 1991. Eric was born 21 Feb 1966 in Glascow, Valley County, MT.

| 4315 | M | i. | **Michael McDonald Backensto** was born 5 Jan 1994. |

2447. Constance Jane McDonald (*Jimmy Joe McDonald*[7], *Pauline Myran Lindsey*[6], *Adron Leonard (Green) Lindsey Jr.*[5], *Adron Leonard Lindsey Sr.*[4], *Frances (Frankie) Sharp*[3], *Charles W. Sr.*[2], *John Sr.*[1]) was born 3 Nov 1951 in Lauderdale County, AL.

Constance married **Kenneth David**.

| 4316 | F | i. | **Carrie Elizabeth David** was born 29 Jun 1974 in Richland, TX. |

2450. Phillip Dewayne McDonald Sr. (*Marvin McDaniel McDonald*[7], *Pauline Myran Lindsey*[6], *Adron Leonard (Green) Lindsey Jr.*[5], *Adron Leonard Lindsey Sr.*[4], *Frances (Frankie) Sharp*[3], *Charles W. Sr.*[2], *John Sr.*[1]) was born 30 Sep 1953 in Lauderdale County, AL.

Phillip married **Rita Faye Davis**, daughter of **Louis L. Davis** and **Catherine Heupel**, 2 Oct 1971 in Lauderdale County, AL. Rita was born 16 Jul 1956 in Lauderdale County, AL.

+	4317	M	i.	**Phillip Dewayne McDonald Jr.** was born 31 Mar 1972 in Lauderdale County, AL.
+	4318	F	ii.	**Samantha Ann McDonald** was born 2 Nov 1974 in Lauderdale County, AL.
	4319	F	iii.	**Jennifer McDonald** was born in Aug 1977 in Lauderdale County, AL.

Phillip next married **Nola Denise Poague**, daughter of **William S. Poague** and **Elois Anders**, 28 Jan 1985 in Lauderdale County, AL. Nola was born 26 Feb 1954 in Colbert County, AL.

2451. John Thomas McDonald (*Marvin McDaniel McDonald*[7], *Pauline Myran Lindsey*[6], *Adron Leonard (Green) Lindsey Jr.*[5], *Adron Leonard Lindsey Sr.*[4], *Frances (Frankie) Sharp*[3], *Charles W. Sr.*[2], *John Sr.*[1]) was born 11 Oct 1955 in Lauderdale County, AL.

John married **Elizabeth (Beth) Arcella Staggs**, daughter of **Writher Odell Staggs** and **Wanda Ann Casteel**, 7 Jul 1991 in Lauderdale County, AL. Elizabeth was born 5 Dec 1961 in Lauderdale County, AL.
4320 M i. **Jessie Odell McDonald** was born 26 Dec 1977 in Lauderdale County, AL.

John next married **Tammy Raceine Churchwell**, daughter of **Larry Leon Churchwell** and **Nella Faye Pounders**, 30 Jul 1993 in Lauderdale County, AL. Tammy was born 25 Jun 1959 in Lauderdale County, AL.
4321 F i. **Sonya Faith McDonald** was born 22 Oct 1975.

2452. Melissa Ann McDonald (*Marvin McDaniel McDonald*[7], *Pauline Myran Lindsey*[6], *Adron Leonard (Green) Lindsey Jr.*[5], *Adron Leonard Lindsey Sr.*[4], *Frances (Frankie) Sharp*[3], *Charles W. Sr.*[2], *John Sr.*[1]) was born 31 Mar 1957 in Lauderdale County, AL.

Melissa married **Michael Allison Hipps**, son of **Clifford Allison Hipps** and **Florence Camilla Luebke**, 6 Jun 1975 in Lauderdale County, AL. Michael was born 13 Jan 1957 in Lauderdale County, AL.
4322 F i. **Mary Elizabeth Hipps** was born 31 Jan 1977 in Lauderdale County, AL.
4323 M ii. **Michael Bradley Hipps** was born 4 Jun 1980 in Lauderdale County, AL.

2453. Paula Annette McDonald (*Marvin McDaniel McDonald*[7], *Pauline Myran Lindsey*[6], *Adron Leonard (Green) Lindsey Jr.*[5], *Adron Leonard Lindsey Sr.*[4], *Frances (Frankie) Sharp*[3], *Charles W. Sr.*[2], *John Sr.*[1]) was born 9 Sep 1959 in Lauderdale County, AL.

Paula married **Dwight Pilkinton**.

Paula next married **Joe Marcus Crews**, son of **Joe Rex Crews** and **Mildred Cain**, 21 May 1993 in Lauderdale County, AL. Joe was born 26 Nov in Selma, AL.

2454. Jeffery Steven McDonald (*Bobby Jeffrey McDonald*[7], *Pauline Myran Lindsey*[6], *Adron Leonard (Green) Lindsey Jr.*[5], *Adron Leonard Lindsey Sr.*[4], *Frances (Frankie) Sharp*[3], *Charles W. Sr.*[2], *John Sr.*[1]) was born 15 Aug 1954 in Lauderdale County, AL.

Jeffery married **Brenda Jeannette Wallace**, daughter of **William Wallace** and **Mary Velma Talley**, 9 Aug 1992 in Colbert County, AL. Brenda was born 3 Nov 1957 in Colbert County, AL.
4324 F i. **Cheyanne Marie Lawana McDonald** was born 9 Mar 1993 in Colbert County, AL.

2455. Debra Leigh Lindsey (*Virginia Lee McDonald*[7], *Pauline Myran Lindsey*[6], *Adron Leonard (Green) Lindsey Jr.*[5], *Adron Leonard Lindsey Sr.*[4], *Frances (Frankie) Sharp*[3], *Charles W. Sr.*[2], *John Sr.*[1]) was born 10 Nov 1957 in Lauderdale County, AL.

Debra married **Dennis Gray Brooks**, son of **William (Bill) D. Brooks** and **Willehmia Gray**, 28 Sep 1974 in Lauderdale County, AL. Dennis was born 30 Oct 1956 in Lauderdale County, AL.
4325 M i. **Brain Matthew Brooks** was born 10 Mar 1980 in Lauderdale County, AL.
4326 F ii. **Leann Elizabeth Brooks** was born 10 Jan 1982 in Lauderdale County, AL.
4327 M iii. **Andrew David Brooks** was born 16 Apr 1985 in Lauderdale County, AL.

2456. Charles David Lindsey Jr. (*Virginia Lee McDonald*[7], *Pauline Myran Lindsey*[6], *Adron Leonard (Green) Lindsey Jr.*[5], *Adron Leonard Lindsey Sr.*[4], *Frances (Frankie) Sharp*[3], *Charles W. Sr.*[2], *John Sr.*[1]) was born 5 Dec 1959 in Lauderdale County, AL.

Charles married **Lisa Ann Danley**, daughter of **Arthur Clyde Danley** and **Gloria Dean Gillis**, 11 Jul 1981 in Lauderdale County, AL. Lisa was born 11 Jan 1961 in Lauderdale County, AL.
4328 F i. **Danille Joy Lindsey** was born 15 Nov 1988 in Davidson County, TN.

2457. William Brian Lindsey (*Virginia Lee McDonald[7], Pauline Myran Lindsey[6], Adron Leonard (Green) Lindsey Jr.[5], Adron Leonard Lindsey Sr.[4], Frances (Frankie) Sharp[3], Charles W. Sr.[2], John Sr.[1]*) was born 26 May 1963 in Lauderdale County, AL.

William married **Lisa Lee Turberville**, daughter of **Travis Albert Turberville** and **Dorothy Alexander**, 11 Aug 1984 in Colbert County, AL. Lisa was born 3 Aug 1961 in Colbert County, AL.

| 4329 | M | i. | **William Travis Lindsey** was born 3 Dec 1985 in Colbert County, AL. |
| 4330 | M | ii. | **Brian Thomas Lindsey** was born 3 Sep 1990 in Lauderdale County, AL. |

2458. Marsha Lynn McDonald (*John Nelson McDonald Sr.[7], Pauline Myran Lindsey[6], Adron Leonard (Green) Lindsey Jr.[5], Adron Leonard Lindsey Sr.[4], Frances (Frankie) Sharp[3], Charles W. Sr.[2], John Sr.[1]*) was born 1 Mar 1963 in Lauderdale County, AL.

Marsha married **Terry Clyde Oakley**, son of **Bill Oakley** and **Hazel Ann May**, 8 Oct 1982 in Lauderdale County, AL. Terry was born 20 Mar 1962 in Lauderdale County, AL.

4331	M	i.	**Jonathan William Oakley** was born 22 Nov 1985 in Lauderdale County, AL.
4332	M	ii.	**Eric Denton Oakley** was born 4 Feb 1989 in Lauderdale County, AL.
4333	M	iii.	**Austen Terry Oakley** was born 24 Oct 1994 in Lauderdale County, AL.

2459. John Nelson McDonald Jr. (*John Nelson McDonald Sr.[7], Pauline Myran Lindsey[6], Adron Leonard (Green) Lindsey Jr.[5], Adron Leonard Lindsey Sr.[4], Frances (Frankie) Sharp[3], Charles W. Sr.[2], John Sr.[1]*) was born 2 Dec 1964 in Lauderdale County, AL.

John married **Kimberly Paige Simmons**, daughter of **Johnny L. Simmons** and **Martha Wilhelminia Sharp**, 18 May 1985 in Lake Mary, FL. Kimberly was born 3 Jul 1965 in Lauderdale County, AL.

4334	M	i.	**John Nicholas McDonald** was born 1 Jun 1987 in Lauderdale County, AL.
4335	M	ii.	**Wess Lee McDonald** was born 10 Dec 1990 in Lauderdale County, AL.
4336	M	iii.	**Caleb Nelson McDonald** was born 8 Aug 1996 in Lauderdale County, AL.

2461. William Thomas McDonald (*Thomas Glenn McDonald[7], Pauline Myran Lindsey[6], Adron Leonard (Green) Lindsey Jr.[5], Adron Leonard Lindsey Sr.[4], Frances (Frankie) Sharp[3], Charles W. Sr.[2], John Sr.[1]*) was born 6 Jan 1972 in Lauderdale County, AL.

William married **Kellie Larette Jeffreys**, daughter of **Larry W. Jeffreys** and **Becky Kelley**, 24 Jun 1994 in Lauderdale County, AL. Kellie was born 12 Aug 1973 in Lauderdale County, AL.

2462. Maureen Louise Hall (*Ray Arlen Hall[7], Laura Lindsey[6], Adron Leonard (Green) Lindsey Jr.[5], Adron Leonard Lindsey Sr.[4], Frances (Frankie) Sharp[3], Charles W. Sr.[2], John Sr.[1]*) was born 26 Feb 1954 in Quincy, MA.

Maureen married **David Michael Hallsen Sr.**, son of **Magnus Hallsen** and **Eleanor Davis**, 27 Aug 1977 in Quincy, MA. David was born 20 Feb 1951 in Quincy, MA.

| 4337 | F | i. | **Erica Leigh Hallsen** was born 12-26-1985q in Quincy, MA. |
| 4338 | M | ii. | **David Michael Hallsen Jr.** was born 22 Jun 1991 in Quincy, MA. |

2463. James Ray Hall (*Ray Arlen Hall[7], Laura Lindsey[6], Adron Leonard (Green) Lindsey Jr.[5], Adron Leonard Lindsey Sr.[4], Frances (Frankie) Sharp[3], Charles W. Sr.[2], John Sr.[1]*) was born 19 May 1955 in Quincy, MA.

James married **Mary Jane Callahan**, daughter of **Robert Callahan** and **Carnella DeNalla**, 12 Oct 1980 in Quincy, MA. Mary was born 15 Dec 1957 in Quincy, MA.

| 4339 | F | i. | **Tricia Amanda Hall** was born 8 Dec 1986 in Boston, MA. |
| 4340 | F | ii. | **Leanne Marie Hall** was born 10 Aug 1990 in Boston, MA. |

2464. Donna J. Hall (*Ray Arlen Hall[7], Laura Lindsey[6], Adron Leonard (Green) Lindsey Jr.[5], Adron Leonard Lindsey Sr.[4], Frances (Frankie) Sharp[3], Charles W. Sr.[2], John Sr.[1]*) was born 15 Jul 1957 in Quincy, MA.

Donna married **Paul W. Scanlan** 17 May 1986. Paul was born 8 Aug 1957 in Boston, MA.

2465. William (Bill) Charles Hall (*Ray Arlen Hall*[7]*, Laura Lindsey*[6]*, Adron Leonard (Green) Lindsey Jr.*[5]*, Adron Leonard Lindsey Sr.*[4]*, Frances (Frankie) Sharp*[3]*, Charles W. Sr.*[2]*, John Sr.*[1]) was born 16 Dec 1959 in Quincy, MA.

William married **Kathleen Helen McManus**, daughter of **George McManus** and **Helen Ray**, 15 Jul 1984 in Quincy, MA. Kathleen was born 1 May 1960 in Boston, MA.

| 4341 | F | i. | **Jennifer H. Hall** was born 27 Oct 1985 in Boston, MA. |
| 4342 | M | ii. | **Daniel W. Hall** was born 7 Jan 1993 in Boston, MA. |

2466. Janet Marie Hall (*Ray Arlen Hall*[7]*, Laura Lindsey*[6]*, Adron Leonard (Green) Lindsey Jr.*[5]*, Adron Leonard Lindsey Sr.*[4]*, Frances (Frankie) Sharp*[3]*, Charles W. Sr.*[2]*, John Sr.*[1]) was born 5 Mar 1963 in Quincy, MA.

Janet married **Scott Thomas Floore** 7 Oct 1984 in Quincy, MA. Scott was born 30 Jan 1961 in Jefferson County, KY.

4343	M	i.	**Kevin James Floore** was born 18 Aug 1987 in Louisville County, KY.
4344	F	ii.	**Elizabeth Ann Floore** was born 22 Apr 1990 in Louisville County, KY.
4345	F	iii.	**Claudia Ray Floore** was born 22 Feb 1992 in Fisher, IN.

2467. Josesph Michael Hall (*Ray Arlen Hall*[7]*, Laura Lindsey*[6]*, Adron Leonard (Green) Lindsey Jr.*[5]*, Adron Leonard Lindsey Sr.*[4]*, Frances (Frankie) Sharp*[3]*, Charles W. Sr.*[2]*, John Sr.*[1]) was born 2 Dec 1964 in Quincy, MA.

Josesph married **Darlene Marie Manning** 27 May 1989 in Quincy, MA. Darlene was born 20 Oct 1964.

4346	F	i.	**Patricia Michelle Hall** was born 24 May 1983 in Boston, MA.
4347	M	ii.	**Christopher Michael Hall** was born 19 Jul 1990 in Boston, MA.
4348	M	iii.	**Stephen M. Hall** was born 12 Dec 1993 in Boston, MA.

2470. Lura Kathleen Hall (*James Franklin Hall Jr.*[7]*, Laura Lindsey*[6]*, Adron Leonard (Green) Lindsey Jr.*[5]*, Adron Leonard Lindsey Sr.*[4]*, Frances (Frankie) Sharp*[3]*, Charles W. Sr.*[2]*, John Sr.*[1]) was born 17 Sep 1962 in Lauderdale County, AL.

Lura married **David Dink Smith**, son of **James E. Smith** and **Mary Grace Millett**, 25 May 1985 in Colbert County, AL. David was born 24 Nov 1960 in Tuscaloosa County, AL.

4349	M	i.	**Wesley Daivd Smith** was born 11 Oct 1985 in Columbus AFB, MS.
4350	F	ii.	**Katherine Lindsey Smith** was born 24 Aug 1990 in Birmingham, Jefferson County, AL.
4351	F	iii.	**Robin Grace Smith** was born 17 May 1992 in Birmingham, Jefferson County, AL.

2471. Stephanie Amanda Hall (*James Franklin Hall Jr.*[7]*, Laura Lindsey*[6]*, Adron Leonard (Green) Lindsey Jr.*[5]*, Adron Leonard Lindsey Sr.*[4]*, Frances (Frankie) Sharp*[3]*, Charles W. Sr.*[2]*, John Sr.*[1]) was born 2 Jul 1965 in Lauderdale County, AL.

Stephanie married **William Howard Broadfoot III**, son of **William Howard Broadfoot II** and **Ruth Rickard**, 11 Jun 1988 in Lauderdale County, AL. William was born 6 Dec 1964 in Madison County, AL.

2472. David Nelson Hall (*James Franklin Hall Jr.*[7]*, Laura Lindsey*[6]*, Adron Leonard (Green) Lindsey Jr.*[5]*, Adron Leonard Lindsey Sr.*[4]*, Frances (Frankie) Sharp*[3]*, Charles W. Sr.*[2]*, John Sr.*[1]) was born 12 Oct 1972 in Lauderdale County, AL.

David married **Margaret Kathryn Richter**, daughter of **Frank J. Richter** and **Susan Harrison**, 14 Jun 1997 in Guntersville, AL. Margaret was born 23 Feb 1973 in Guntersville, AL.

2475. Joanna Kay Atwell (*Mary Nell Lindsey*[7]*, Nelson McCaun Lindsey*[6]*, Adron Leonard (Green) Lindsey Jr.*[5]*, Adron Leonard Lindsey Sr.*[4]*, Frances (Frankie) Sharp*[3]*, Charles W. Sr.*[2]*, John Sr.*[1]) was born 12 Oct 1956 in Colbert County, AL.

Joanna married **James Noel Hardwick**, son of **Jack Carrol Hardwick** and **Martha Jean Kelly**, 29 Apr 1989 in Colbert County, AL. James was born 13 Feb 1962 in Lauderdale County, AL.

| 4352 | M | i. | **James Mason Hardwick** was born 25 Jan 1995 in Colbert County, AL. |
| 4353 | M | ii. | **Matthew McCuin Hardwick** was born 24 Sep 1997 in Colbert County, AL. |

2476. Selina Marie Atwell (*Mary Nell Lindsey*[7], *Nelson McCaun Lindsey*[6], *Adron Leonard (Green) Lindsey Jr.*[5], *Adron Leonard Lindsey Sr.*[4], *Frances (Frankie) Sharp*[3], *Charles W. Sr.*[2], *John Sr.*[1]) was born 18 May 1959 in Biloxi, MS.

Selina married **Kenny M. Pearson**. Kenny was born 28 May 1958.
4354　F　　i.　**Laura Ann Pearson** was born 31 May 1980.
4355　M　　ii.　**David Martin Pearson** was born 26 Jan 1985.

2477. Robert F. Atwell III (*Mary Nell Lindsey*[7], *Nelson McCaun Lindsey*[6], *Adron Leonard (Green) Lindsey Jr.*[5], *Adron Leonard Lindsey Sr.*[4], *Frances (Frankie) Sharp*[3], *Charles W. Sr.*[2], *John Sr.*[1]) was born 31 Jan 1961 in Quantico, VA.

Robert married **Sylvia Ann Stone**, daughter of **William Sanford Stone** and **Vera Pauline Laird**, 11 Jun 1983 in Colbert County, AL. Sylvia was born 13 Feb 1961 in Colbert County, AL.
4356　M　　i.　**Robert F. Atwell IV** was born 26 May 1991.
4357　F　　ii.　**Anna Lea Atwell** was born 26 May 1991.

2478. Vera Maelin Robbins (*Mae Virginia Lindsey*[7], *Nelson McCaun Lindsey*[6], *Adron Leonard (Green) Lindsey Jr.*[5], *Adron Leonard Lindsey Sr.*[4], *Frances (Frankie) Sharp*[3], *Charles W. Sr.*[2], *John Sr.*[1]) was born 23 Mar 1962.

Vera married **Roy Dean Morris**. Roy was born 5 Oct 1959.
4358　F　　i.　**Anna Lindsey Morris** was born 28 Jan 1987.

2479. Melissa Ann Robbins (*Mae Virginia Lindsey*[7], *Nelson McCaun Lindsey*[6], *Adron Leonard (Green) Lindsey Jr.*[5], *Adron Leonard Lindsey Sr.*[4], *Frances (Frankie) Sharp*[3], *Charles W. Sr.*[2], *John Sr.*[1]) was born 11 Mar 1968.

Melissa married **Raymond Andrew Long**. Raymond was born 1 Jan 1965.

2487. Melissa Lindsey (*William Richard Lindsey*[7], *Claude Raymond Lindsey Sr.*[6], *Adron Leonard (Green) Lindsey Jr.*[5], *Adron Leonard Lindsey Sr.*[4], *Frances (Frankie) Sharp*[3], *Charles W. Sr.*[2], *John Sr.*[1]) was born 5 Jan 1969.

Melissa married **Colon Ray Barrentine Jr.**.
4359　F　　i.　**Savannah Rose Barrentine**.

2496. Bobbie Dean Chowning (*Jewel Dean Young*[7], *William (Bill) Mack Young*[6], *Eddie Young*[5], *Mary M. (Polly II) Lindsey*[4], *Frances (Frankie) Sharp*[3], *Charles W. Sr.*[2], *John Sr.*[1]) was born 10 Dec 1940 in Lauderdale County, AL.

Bobbie married **Alan Irwin Weiss** 4 Sep 1958. Alan was born in 1938 in Michigan, died 21 May 1983, and was buried in Tri-Cities Memorial Gardens, Florence, Lauderdale County, AL.
+ 4360　F　　i.　**Debra Lynn Weiss** was born 3 Jun 1959 in Manistee, MI.
4361　M　　ii.　**David Alan Weiss** was born 28 Jun 1963 in Detroit, Wayne County, MI.

2507. Richard Dale Young (*James Robert Young*[7], *William (Bill) Mack Young*[6], *Eddie Young*[5], *Mary M. (Polly II) Lindsey*[4], *Frances (Frankie) Sharp*[3], *Charles W. Sr.*[2], *John Sr.*[1]) was born 12 Feb 1955 in Lauderdale County, AL.

Richard married **Opel Estelle Martin**, daughter of **William J. Martin** and **Annie Lancaster**, 10 May 1975 in Lauderdale County, AL. Opel was born 5 Aug 1956 in Lauderdale County, AL.

2508. Karen Delane Young (*James Robert Young*[7], *William (Bill) Mack Young*[6], *Eddie Young*[5], *Mary M. (Polly II) Lindsey*[4], *Frances (Frankie) Sharp*[3], *Charles W. Sr.*[2], *John Sr.*[1]) was born 15 Mar 1958 in Lauderdale County, AL.

Karen married **Roland Lynn Irons**, son of **Roland O. Irons** and **Lona Rhodes**, 6 May 1977 in Lauderdale County, AL. Roland was born 3 Aug 1958 in Lauderdale County, AL.
+ 4362　F　　i.　**Melissa Beth Irons** was born 20 Nov 1977.

Karen next married **Kent Maurice Wood**, son of **Glen Wood** and **Geneva Arelia Underwood**, 22 Feb 1992 in Lauderdale County, AL. Kent was born 3 Feb 1958 in Lauderdale County, AL.
(Duplicate Line. See Person 2429)

2509. Sherrie Lynn Young (*James Robert Young*^{7}, *William (Bill) Mack Young*^{6}, *Eddie Young*^{5}, *Mary M. (Polly II) Lindsey*^{4}, *Frances (Frankie) Sharp*^{3}, *Charles W. Sr.*^{2}, *John Sr.*^{1}) was born 2 May 1961 in Lauderdale County, AL.

Sherrie married **Jonathan Loyce Davis**, son of **Johnnie R. Davis** and **Wilma Stotts**, 4 Apr 1980 in Lauderdale County, AL. Jonathan was born 28 Jun 1960 in Lauderdale County, AL.

2510. Kim Russell Young (*James Robert Young*^{7}, *William (Bill) Mack Young*^{6}, *Eddie Young*^{5}, *Mary M. (Polly II) Lindsey*^{4}, *Frances (Frankie) Sharp*^{3}, *Charles W. Sr.*^{2}, *John Sr.*^{1}) was born 6 Jun 1962 in Lauderdale County, AL.

Kim married **Judy Irene Murphy**, daughter of **Dewey Arnold Murphy** and **Ester Anna Franks**, 20 Aug 1982 in Lauderdale County, AL. Judy was born 27 Apr 1964 in Norfolk, VA.
    4363 F   i.   **Hayley Anna Young** was born 28 Aug 1987 in Lauderdale County, AL.

2511. Lesa Renee Young (*James Robert Young*^{7}, *William (Bill) Mack Young*^{6}, *Eddie Young*^{5}, *Mary M. (Polly II) Lindsey*^{4}, *Frances (Frankie) Sharp*^{3}, *Charles W. Sr.*^{2}, *John Sr.*^{1}) was born 12 Aug 1963 in Lauderdale County, AL.

Lesa married **Danny Raye Poe**, son of **Edgar D. Poe** and **Janice Bowen**, 2 Apr 1982 in Lauderdale County, AL. Danny was born 4 Apr 1962 in Lauderdale County, AL.

2512. Donald Ray Young (*James Robert Young*^{7}, *William (Bill) Mack Young*^{6}, *Eddie Young*^{5}, *Mary M. (Polly II) Lindsey*^{4}, *Frances (Frankie) Sharp*^{3}, *Charles W. Sr.*^{2}, *John Sr.*^{1}) was born 22 Oct 1966 in Lauderdale County, AL.

Donald married **Nancy Ann Horton**, daughter of **James R. Horton** and **Genevie Rich**, 28 Sep 1977 in Lauderdale County, AL. Nancy was born 19 Nov 1959 in Wayne County, TN.

2513. Shanie Leigh Richards (*Shirley Ann Young*^{7}, *William (Bill) Mack Young*^{6}, *Eddie Young*^{5}, *Mary M. (Polly II) Lindsey*^{4}, *Frances (Frankie) Sharp*^{3}, *Charles W. Sr.*^{2}, *John Sr.*^{1}) was born 30 Jul 1969.

Shanie married **Lawrence Alan Ayers** 24 Mar 1990.

2514. Heather Dawn Richards (*Shirley Ann Young*^{7}, *William (Bill) Mack Young*^{6}, *Eddie Young*^{5}, *Mary M. (Polly II) Lindsey*^{4}, *Frances (Frankie) Sharp*^{3}, *Charles W. Sr.*^{2}, *John Sr.*^{1}) was born 2 Apr 1974.

Heather married **Richard Howard Hale Jr.** 26 Jun 1993.

2515. Wanda Sue Young (*Cecil Lloyd Young*^{7}, *Earnest Edward Young*^{6}, *Eddie Young*^{5}, *Mary M. (Polly II) Lindsey*^{4}, *Frances (Frankie) Sharp*^{3}, *Charles W. Sr.*^{2}, *John Sr.*^{1}) was born 28 Jan 1948 in Lauderdale County, AL.

Wanda married **Robert Holland (Jody) Gamble**, son of **Robert A. Gamble** and **Sarah Kathleen Holland**, 27 Jan 1968 in Lauderdale County, AL. Robert was born 27 May 1947 in Jackson County, AL.
+ 4364 F   i.   **Kerri Beth Gamble** was born 6 Jul 1970 in Lauderdale County, AL.
+ 4365 F   ii.   **Melanie Leigh Gamble** was born 20 May 1974 in Ft Worth, Tarrant County, TX.
   4366 F   iii. **Katherine Mallory Gamble** was born 21 Jun 1987 in Colbert County, AL.

2516. Teresa Diane Young (*Cecil Lloyd Young*^{7}, *Earnest Edward Young*^{6}, *Eddie Young*^{5}, *Mary M. (Polly II) Lindsey*^{4}, *Frances (Frankie) Sharp*^{3}, *Charles W. Sr.*^{2}, *John Sr.*^{1}) was born 19 Nov 1953 in Lauderdale County, AL.

Teresa married **Dennis A. Yerby**, son of **Edward (Dunk) L. Yerby** and **Joyce Brown**, 29 Nov 1975 in Lauderdale County, AL. Dennis was born 15 Dec 1947 in Lauderdale County, AL.
   4367 M   i.   **Ryan Chadwick (Chad) Yerby** was born 22 Mar 1977 in Lauderdale County, AL.
+ 4368 F   ii.   **Shana Nicole Yerby** was born 25 Aug 1978 in Lauderdale County, AL.

Teresa next married **Kenneth Ray Williams**, son of **Ray Williams** and **Mary Lou Holden**. Kenneth was born 13 May 1959 in Lauderdale County, AL.

2517. Joyce Fredia Young (*Jay Fred Young*[7], *Earnest Edward Young*[6], *Eddie Young*[5], *Mary M. (Polly II) Lindsey*[4], *Frances (Frankie) Sharp*[3], *Charles W. Sr.*[2], *John Sr.*[1]) was born 19 Feb 1954 in South Bend, IN.

Joyce married ***Unk Powell**.

2518. Brenda Gaye Young (*Jay Fred Young*[7], *Earnest Edward Young*[6], *Eddie Young*[5], *Mary M. (Polly II) Lindsey*[4], *Frances (Frankie) Sharp*[3], *Charles W. Sr.*[2], *John Sr.*[1]) was born 25 Dec 1958 in South Bend, IN.

Brenda married **Robert Lawson I**, son of **Unknown** and **Unknown**.

4369	M	i.	**Robert Rex Lawson II** was born 19 Nov 1982 in South Bend, IN.
4370	M	ii.	**Jeremy M. Lawson** was born 20 Feb 1984 in South Bend, IN.

2519. Edward (Eddie) Earl Young (*Doyal Lee Young Sr.*[7], *Earnest Edward Young*[6], *Eddie Young*[5], *Mary M. (Polly II) Lindsey*[4], *Frances (Frankie) Sharp*[3], *Charles W. Sr.*[2], *John Sr.*[1]) was born 12 Dec 1956 in Lauderdale County, AL.

Edward married **Judy Nell Lamar**, daughter of **Dalton Lamar** and **Bertha L. Burns**. Judy was born 9 Nov 1961 in Lauderdale County, AL.

2524. Kathy Marie Keeton (*Hazel Joyce Young*[7], *Earnest Edward Young*[6], *Eddie Young*[5], *Mary M. (Polly II) Lindsey*[4], *Frances (Frankie) Sharp*[3], *Charles W. Sr.*[2], *John Sr.*[1]) was born 23 Jul 1961 in Lawrenceburg, Lawrence County, TN.

Kathy married **Bobby Lance Parrish Sr.**, son of **James Roy Parrish** and **Mary Evelyn Ghrigsby**, 23 Nov 1979 in Lauderdale County, AL. Bobby was born 16 Jan 1961 in Lauderdale County, AL.

+ 4371	F	i.	**April Dawn Parrish** was born 6 Oct 1979.
4372	F	ii.	**Cindy Marie Parrish** was born 7 Aug 1981 in Lauderdale County, AL.
4373	M	iii.	**Bobby Lance Parrish Jr.** was born 14 Jul 1986 in Lauderdale County, AL.

2525. Ricky Dale Keeton (*Hazel Joyce Young*[7], *Earnest Edward Young*[6], *Eddie Young*[5], *Mary M. (Polly II) Lindsey*[4], *Frances (Frankie) Sharp*[3], *Charles W. Sr.*[2], *John Sr.*[1]) was born 16 Apr 1963 in Lauderdale County, AL.

Ricky married **Carrie Lynn Hubbert**, daughter of **Paul L. Hubbert** and **Donna Rosdick**, 22 Apr 1983 in Lauderdale County, AL. Carrie was born 16 Dec 1964 in Jefferson County, AL.

4374	M	i.	**Adam Andrew Keeton** was born 22 Apr 1993 in Lauderdale County, AL, died 30 Dec 2007, and was buried in Wesley Chapel Cemetery, Lauderdale County, AL.

2526. Randy Lee Keeton (*Hazel Joyce Young*[7], *Earnest Edward Young*[6], *Eddie Young*[5], *Mary M. (Polly II) Lindsey*[4], *Frances (Frankie) Sharp*[3], *Charles W. Sr.*[2], *John Sr.*[1]) was born 7 Feb 1966 in Lauderdale County, AL.

Randy married **Patricia Rene Barns**, daughter of **Gary L. Barns** and **Beverly Grigsby**, 3 Jun 1986 in Lauderdale County, AL. Patricia was born 28 Apr 1966 in Lauderdale County, AL.

4375	F	i.	**Sharon Renee Keeton** was born 20 Dec 1986 in Lauderdale County, AL.
4376	F	ii.	**Tiffaney Lee Keeton** was born 18 Feb 1988 in Lauderdale County, AL.

2527. Karen Lynn Keeton (*Hazel Joyce Young*[7], *Earnest Edward Young*[6], *Eddie Young*[5], *Mary M. (Polly II) Lindsey*[4], *Frances (Frankie) Sharp*[3], *Charles W. Sr.*[2], *John Sr.*[1]) was born 3 Jun 1970 in Lauderdale County, AL.

Karen married **Alfred Lynn South**, son of **Chester Linbergh South** and **Rachel Eleanor Grigsby**, 14 Feb 1991 in Lauderdale County, AL. Alfred was born 14 Jul 1963 in Lauderdale County, AL.

2529. Linda Joyce Gooch (*Macil Bethrine Young*[7], *Odus Clarence Young Sr.*[6], *Eddie Young*[5], *Mary M. (Polly II) Lindsey*[4], *Frances (Frankie) Sharp*[3], *Charles W. Sr.*[2], *John Sr.*[1]) was born 8 Oct 1947 in Lauderdale County, AL.

Linda married **David Kenneth Skipworth**, son of **Thomas Alvin Skipworth** and **Ellen C. Winborn**, 13 Apr 1964 in Lauderdale County, AL. David was born 11 Jul 1944 in Lauderdale County, AL.

+ 4377 F i. **Tammy Diane Skipworth**.
+ 4378 F ii. **Tina Dinese Skipworth**.
  4379 M iii. **David Kenneth Skipworth Jr.**
+ 4380 F iv. **Tabitha Ann Skipworth**.
+ 4381 F v. **Angela Joyce Skipworth**.

2530. Donnie Lee Gooch (*Macil Bethrine Young*[7], *Odus Clarence Young Sr.*[6], *Eddie Young*[5], *Mary M. (Polly II) Lindsey*[4], *Frances (Frankie) Sharp*[3], *Charles W. Sr.*[2], *John Sr.*[1]) was born 30 Apr 1948 in Lauderdale County, AL.

Donnie married **Sherry Katherine Turner**, daughter of **Raymond P. Turner** and **Doris Ester**, 22 Mar 1971 in Lauderdale County, AL. Sherry was born 26 Jul 1952 in Tishomingo County, MS.

+ 4382 F i. **Sonia Michelle Gooch**.
+ 4383 F ii. **Barbara Green Gooch**.

2531. Janet Faye Gooch (*Macil Bethrine Young*[7], *Odus Clarence Young Sr.*[6], *Eddie Young*[5], *Mary M. (Polly II) Lindsey*[4], *Frances (Frankie) Sharp*[3], *Charles W. Sr.*[2], *John Sr.*[1]) was born 16 Nov 1950 in Lauderdale County, AL.

Janet married **Samuel Earl McIntyre**, son of **Donald D. McIntyre** and **Alice Risner**, 10 May 1966 in Lauderdale County, AL. Samuel was born 25 Jun 1949 in Lauderdale County, AL.

  4384 M i. **Bryan Eric McIntyre** was born 6 Dec 1967.
+ 4385 M ii. **Brad Evan McIntyre** was born 5 Aug 1974.

Janet next married **Doyle Fay Risner**.

2532. Jerry Dewayne Gooch (*Macil Bethrine Young*[7], *Odus Clarence Young Sr.*[6], *Eddie Young*[5], *Mary M. (Polly II) Lindsey*[4], *Frances (Frankie) Sharp*[3], *Charles W. Sr.*[2], *John Sr.*[1]) was born 25 Jul 1952 in Lauderdale County, AL.

Jerry married **Sandra Kay Wright**, daughter of **J. T. Wright** and **Ima J. Price**, 27 Apr 1973 in Lauderdale County, AL. Sandra was born 18 Jun 1956 in Lewis County, TN.

  4386 M i. **Joshua Harnell Gooch**.
  4387 M ii. **Jacob Dannon Gooch**.

2533. Kathy Ann Gooch (*Macil Bethrine Young*[7], *Odus Clarence Young Sr.*[6], *Eddie Young*[5], *Mary M. (Polly II) Lindsey*[4], *Frances (Frankie) Sharp*[3], *Charles W. Sr.*[2], *John Sr.*[1]) was born 18 Feb 1954 in Lauderdale County, AL.

Kathy married **Gary Oneal Smith**, son of **Amos J. P. Smith** and **Lois Holloway**, 30 Apr 1973 in Lauderdale County, AL. Gary was born 10 Aug 1954 in Lauderdale County, AL.

+ 4388 F i. **Stephanie Nicole Smith** was born in 1973.
+ 4389 M ii. **Shannon Nole Smith** was born 29 Aug 1977 in Lauderdale County, AL.

2534. Sharon Jean Gooch (*Macil Bethrine Young*[7], *Odus Clarence Young Sr.*[6], *Eddie Young*[5], *Mary M. (Polly II) Lindsey*[4], *Frances (Frankie) Sharp*[3], *Charles W. Sr.*[2], *John Sr.*[1]) was born 30 Mar 1957 in Florence, Lauderdale County, AL.

Sharon married **Lonnie Nolan Smith**, son of **Noah (Sonny) L. V. Smith** and **Letha Helen Witt**, 20 Apr 1973 in Lauderdale County, AL. Lonnie was born 13 Oct 1955 in Lauderdale County, AL, died 18 Aug 1973, and was buried in Murphy's Chapel Cemetery, Lauderdale County, AL.

+ 4390 F i. **Chastidy Recale Smith** was born 6 Nov 1973.

Sharon next married **Michael Eugene Jones Sr.**, son of **Herschel E. Jones** and **Jeannie Deck**, 23 Nov 1976 in Lauderdale County, AL. Michael was born 3 Aug 1952.

+ 4391 M i. **Michael Eugene Jones Jr.**
+ 4392 M ii. **Troy Christopher Jones**.

Sharon next married **Winfred Lynn Wood**, son of **Almon Wood** and **Evadean Joyce Balentine**, 19 May 2000 in Lauderdale County, AL. Winfred was born 9 Jul 1953 in Lauderdale County, AL, died 5 Oct 2002, and was buried in Pine Hill Cemetery, Lauderdale County, AL. Another name for Winfred was Winford Lynn Wood.

Sharon next married **Jack Norman White**, son of **Will White** and **Margie Balentine**. Jack was born 30 Aug 1938 in Alabama.

2535. Timmy Lee Gooch (*Macil Bethrine Young*⁷, *Odus Clarence Young Sr.*⁶, *Eddie Young*⁵, *Mary M. (Polly II) Lindsey*⁴, *Frances (Frankie) Sharp*³, *Charles W. Sr.*², *John Sr.*¹) was born 30 Nov 1958 in Lauderdale County, AL.

Timmy married **Judy Carol Thigpen**, daughter of **James A. Thigpen** and **Ila R. White**, 14 Mar 1980 in Lauderdale County, AL. Judy was born 16 Apr 1964 in Lauderdale County, AL.
+ 4393 F i. **Jennifer Sherae Gooch**.

2536. Marcia Lynn Gooch (*Macil Bethrine Young*⁷, *Odus Clarence Young Sr.*⁶, *Eddie Young*⁵, *Mary M. (Polly II) Lindsey*⁴, *Frances (Frankie) Sharp*³, *Charles W. Sr.*², *John Sr.*¹) was born 7 Aug 1962 in Lauderdale County, AL.

Marcia married **John Eric (Elwood) Wood**, son of **John (Johnnie) Glenn Wood** and **Lila Jean Berry**. John was born 23 Feb 1963 in Florence, Lauderdale County, AL, died 14 Feb 1986 in Tennessee, and was buried in Oak Grove Cemetery, Lauderdale County, AL.

+ 4394 F i. **Erica Lynn Gooch** was born 13 Feb 1979 in Florence, Lauderdale County, AL.

Marcia next married **Roger Dale Ezekiel** 1 Dec 1987 in Lauderdale County, AL. Roger was born 18 Aug 1961 in Lauderdale County, AL.
+ 4395 M i. **Rodney Dale Ezekiel**.

Marcia next married **Homer Liles**.

2537. Marsha Kay Gooch (*Macil Bethrine Young*⁷, *Odus Clarence Young Sr.*⁶, *Eddie Young*⁵, *Mary M. (Polly II) Lindsey*⁴, *Frances (Frankie) Sharp*³, *Charles W. Sr.*², *John Sr.*¹) was born 7 Aug 1962 in Florence, Lauderdale County, AL.

Marsha married **Ronnie Clemons**, son of **Carroll Eugene Clemons I** and **Elizabeth (Betty) Darby**, 9 Aug 1979 in Lauderdale County, AL. Ronnie was born 24 Feb 1961 in Lauderdale County, AL.
+ 4396 M i. **Ryan Keith Clemons** was born 24 Mar 1980 in Lauderdale County, AL.
  4397 M ii. **Derrick Heath Clemons** was born 29 Mar 1982 in Lauderdale County, AL.
  4398 F iii. **Natasha Beth Clemons** was born 16 Jul 1986 in Lauderdale County, AL.

2539. Vicki Ann Heck (*Carlene Vernial Young*⁷, *Odus Clarence Young Sr.*⁶, *Eddie Young*⁵, *Mary M. (Polly II) Lindsey*⁴, *Frances (Frankie) Sharp*³, *Charles W. Sr.*², *John Sr.*¹) was born 2 Aug 1950 in Lauderdale County, AL.

Vicki married **Patrick William Richards** 6 Jun 1970 in Hawkins County, TN. Patrick was born 13 Dec 1950 in Hawkins County, TN.
+ 4399 M i. **Chris Richards** was born 11 Mar 1972 in Weisbaden, Germany.
+ 4400 F ii. **Carlene M. Richards** was born 15 May 1979 in Knoxville, TN.

2543. Leisa Carol Heck (*Carlene Vernial Young*⁷, *Odus Clarence Young Sr.*⁶, *Eddie Young*⁵, *Mary M. (Polly II) Lindsey*⁴, *Frances (Frankie) Sharp*³, *Charles W. Sr.*², *John Sr.*¹) was born 1 Jun 1967 in Hawkins County, TN.

Leisa married **Tony Ayers**. Tony was born 10 Oct 1967.
  4401 F i. **Kari Ayers** was born 23 Jan 1992.
  4402 M ii. **J. P. Ayers** was born 8 Apr 1995.

2544. William Mark Young (*Clarence William (C. W.) Young*⁷, *Odus Clarence Young Sr.*⁶, *Eddie Young*⁵, *Mary M. (Polly II) Lindsey*⁴, *Frances (Frankie) Sharp*³, *Charles W. Sr.*², *John Sr.*¹) was born 4 Jan 1961 in St. Joseph County, IN.

William married **Lisa Ann (Dean) Young** 9 Jun 1984. Lisa was born 26 Oct 1965 in Hawkins County, TN.

4403 M i. **William Corey Young** was born 10 Sep 1987 in Sullivan County, TN.
He never married and had no children.

4404 M ii. **Joshua Lee Young** was born 1 Nov 1989 in Sullivan County, TN.

4405 F iii. **Jennifer Madison Young** was born 30 Nov 1992 in Hamblen County, TN.

4406 F iv. **Julie Elisabeth Young** was born 15 Oct 1993 in Greene County, TN.

2546. Tanya Lynn Young (*Melvin Lee Young*[7], *Odus Clarence Young Sr.*[6], *Eddie Young*[5], *Mary M. (Polly II) Lindsey*[4], *Frances (Frankie) Sharp*[3], *Charles W. Sr.*[2], *John Sr.*[1]) was born 6 May 1959 in St. Joseph County, IN.

Tanya married **Raymon Michen** 22 Mar 1978. Raymon was born 10 Mar 1949 in England.

4407 M i. **Chad Stefan Michen** was born 25 Apr 1978 in St. Joseph County, IN.

Tanya next married **Richard Emge** 19 Aug 1993. Richard was born 24 Jul 1935.

4408 M i. ***Unk Emge**.

2547. Bret Allen Young Sr. (*Melvin Lee Young*[7], *Odus Clarence Young Sr.*[6], *Eddie Young*[5], *Mary M. (Polly II) Lindsey*[4], *Frances (Frankie) Sharp*[3], *Charles W. Sr.*[2], *John Sr.*[1]) was born 8 Jan 1961 in St. Joseph County, IN.

Bret married someone.

4409 M i. **Bret Allen Young Jr.** was born 6 Apr 1983.

2549. Troy Lee Young (*Melvin Lee Young*[7], *Odus Clarence Young Sr.*[6], *Eddie Young*[5], *Mary M. (Polly II) Lindsey*[4], *Frances (Frankie) Sharp*[3], *Charles W. Sr.*[2], *John Sr.*[1]) was born 1 Aug 1963 in St. Joseph County, IN.

Troy married someone.

4410 F i. **Kara (Key) Young** was born 26 Jan 1987.

2550. Dawn Marie Young (*Melvin Lee Young*[7], *Odus Clarence Young Sr.*[6], *Eddie Young*[5], *Mary M. (Polly II) Lindsey*[4], *Frances (Frankie) Sharp*[3], *Charles W. Sr.*[2], *John Sr.*[1]) was born 2 Feb 1971.

Dawn married **Kurt Kriger** 19 Apr 1991.

4411 M i. **Nicholas Kriger** was born 26 Jan 1991.

2551. Dewey Arnold Murphy (*Robert Arnold Murphy*[7], *Jessie Bell Dearen*[6], *Mary Francis (Molly) Young*[5], *Mary M. (Polly II) Lindsey*[4], *Frances (Frankie) Sharp*[3], *Charles W. Sr.*[2], *John Sr.*[1]) was born 12 Dec 1929 in Lauderdale County, AL, died 25 Sep 2003, and was buried in Tri-Cities Memorial Gardens, Florence, Lauderdale County, AL.

Dewey married **Ester Anna Franks**, daughter of **Edwin Alex Franks** and **Sadie Bell Taylor**, 25 Nov 1950 in Tappahannock, VA. Ester was born 12 Sep 1929 in Shilow, VA.

+ 4412 M i. **Gary Lee Murphy** was born 15 Feb 1952 in Richmond, VA.

+ 4413 F ii. **Joan Denise Murphy** was born 13 Feb 1954 in Lauderdale County, AL.

+ 4414 M iii. **Roger Dale Murphy** was born 4 Mar 1955 in Norfolk, VA.

+ 4415 F iv. **Judy Irene Murphy** was born 27 Apr 1964 in Norfolk, VA.

2552. Bobbie Joan Murphy (*Robert Arnold Murphy*[7], *Jessie Bell Dearen*[6], *Mary Francis (Molly) Young*[5], *Mary M. (Polly II) Lindsey*[4], *Frances (Frankie) Sharp*[3], *Charles W. Sr.*[2], *John Sr.*[1]) was born 6 Apr 1932 in Lauderdale County, AL.

Bobbie married **Ellis Ray Bedford**. Ellis was born in Philadelphia, PA.

4416 M i. **Jonathan David Bedford** was born 13 Jan 1958 in Philadelphia, PA.

4417 F ii. **Tamara Leigh Bedford** was born 24 Jan 1961 in York, NE.

Bobbie next married ***Unk Ballard**.

2553. Margaret Sue Murphy (*Robert Arnold Murphy*[7], *Jessie Bell Dearen*[6], *Mary Francis (Molly) Young*[5], *Mary M. (Polly II) Lindsey*[4], *Frances (Frankie) Sharp*[3], *Charles W. Sr.*[2], *John Sr.*[1]) was born 16 Jul 1936 in Lauderdale County, AL.

Margaret married **Clarence U. Cochran** 3 Oct 1959. Clarence was born 30 Nov 1929 in Lake County, TN.

+ 4418 F   i.   **Tonya Shae Cochran** was born 16 Apr 1961 in Davidson County, TN.

2554. Kenneth Lee Murphy (*Doyal Lee Murphy*[7], *Jessie Bell Dearen*[6], *Mary Francis (Molly) Young*[5], *Mary M. (Polly II) Lindsey*[4], *Frances (Frankie) Sharp*[3], *Charles W. Sr.*[2], *John Sr.*[1]) was born 30 Sep 1936 in Lauderdale County, AL.

Kenneth married **Sara Faye Tirey**, daughter of **Alfred Carroll Tirey** and **Grace Guthrie**, 25 Nov 1959 in Lauderdale County, AL. Sara was born 26 Feb 1937 in Walker County, AL.

+ 4419 F   i.   **Jennifer Robin Murphy** was born 22 Feb 1961 in Lauderdale County, AL.

+ 4420 F   ii.   **Melissa Jill Murphy** was born 12 Nov 1964 in Lauderdale County, AL.

2555. Elizabeth Ann Murphy (*Doyal Lee Murphy*[7], *Jessie Bell Dearen*[6], *Mary Francis (Molly) Young*[5], *Mary M. (Polly II) Lindsey*[4], *Frances (Frankie) Sharp*[3], *Charles W. Sr.*[2], *John Sr.*[1]) was born 28 Jan 1940 in Lauderdale County, AL.

Elizabeth married **Billy Ray Richards**, son of **K. C. Richards** and **Mary Lou Hayes**, 1 Sep 1967 in Lauderdale County, AL. Billy was born 27 Aug 1941 in Lauderdale County, AL.

4421 M   i.   **Gregory Keith Richards** was born 9 May 1969 in Lauderdale County, AL.

2556. Marshall Elbert Goode (*Jenny Ione Murphy*[7], *Jessie Bell Dearen*[6], *Mary Francis (Molly) Young*[5], *Mary M. (Polly II) Lindsey*[4], *Frances (Frankie) Sharp*[3], *Charles W. Sr.*[2], *John Sr.*[1]) was born 13 Dec 1941 in Lauderdale County, AL.

Marshall married **Sybil Ann Clark**, daughter of **Cecil Lamar Clark** and **Sybil Cummings**, 2 Sep 1961 in Lauderdale County, AL. Sybil was born 7 Jun 1942 in Franklin County, AL.

+ 4422 M   i.   **Charles Daniel Goode** was born 9 Jul 1964 in Lauderdale County, AL.

2557. Gary Carl Murphy (*Karl Jones Murphy*[7], *Jessie Bell Dearen*[6], *Mary Francis (Molly) Young*[5], *Mary M. (Polly II) Lindsey*[4], *Frances (Frankie) Sharp*[3], *Charles W. Sr.*[2], *John Sr.*[1]) was born 5 Feb 1949 in Colbert County, AL.

Gary married **Judy Carolyn Holt**, daughter of **Enoch Arden Holt** and **Hazel Rich**, 20 Mar 1972 in Lauderdale County, AL. Judy was born 30 Dec 1949 in Lauderdale County, AL.

+ 4423 F   i.   **Jessia Ann Murphy** was born 22 Oct 1965 in Lauderdale County, AL.

4424 F   ii.   **Rebecca Ashley Murphy** was born 16 Feb 1976.

2559. Martha Ann Murphy (*Karl Jones Murphy*[7], *Jessie Bell Dearen*[6], *Mary Francis (Molly) Young*[5], *Mary M. (Polly II) Lindsey*[4], *Frances (Frankie) Sharp*[3], *Charles W. Sr.*[2], *John Sr.*[1]) was born 19 Jun 1951 in Colbert County, AL.

Martha married **George Dale Nesbitt Jr.**, son of **Earl George Nesbitt II** and **Imogene Redman**, 7 Mar 1975 in Lauderdale County, AL. George was born 10 Jan 1950 in Colbert County, AL.

4425 F   i.   **Erin Elizabeth Nesbitt** was born 3 Dec 1978 in Colbert County, AL.

4426 F   ii.   **Emily Lane Nesbitt** was born 25 Sep 1981 in Colbert County, AL.

2560. Kelley Lee Murphy (*Karl Jones Murphy*[7], *Jessie Bell Dearen*[6], *Mary Francis (Molly) Young*[5], *Mary M. (Polly II) Lindsey*[4], *Frances (Frankie) Sharp*[3], *Charles W. Sr.*[2], *John Sr.*[1]) was born 15 Jun 1960 in Colbert County, AL.

Kelley married **Belevee Gay McFee**, daughter of **Lowell T. McFee** and **Sylvia Davis**, 26 Jul 1980 in Lauderdale County, AL. Belevee was born 31 Oct 1959 in Atlanta, Fulton County, GA.

4427 M   i.   **Juston Lee Murphy** was born 12 Jul 1981 in Colbert County, AL.

4428 M   ii.   **Benjamin Kyle Murphy** was born 22 Sep 1985 in Colbert County, AL.

2561. Montez Elaine Knight (*Ora Kyleene Murphy⁷, Jessie Bell Dearen⁶, Mary Francis (Molly) Young⁵, Mary M. (Polly II) Lindsey⁴, Frances (Frankie) Sharp³, Charles W. Sr.², John Sr.¹*) was born 18 Jun 1941 in Colbert County, AL.

Montez married **John Timothy Sherrod Sr.**, son of **Albert B. Sherrod** and **Tera Thompson**, 6 Jun 1959 in Colbert County, AL. John was born 23 Aug 1938 in Colbert County, AL.

4429	F	i.	**Maria Montez Sherrod** was born 9 Apr 1961 in Colbert County, AL.
4430	F	ii.	**Timra Gay Sherrod** was born 6 Oct 1962 in Colbert County, AL.
4431	M	iii.	**John Timothy Sherrod Jr.** was born 29 Dec 1967 in Colbert County, AL.

2563. Tessa Maria Knight (*Ora Kyleene Murphy⁷, Jessie Bell Dearen⁶, Mary Francis (Molly) Young⁵, Mary M. (Polly II) Lindsey⁴, Frances (Frankie) Sharp³, Charles W. Sr.², John Sr.¹*) was born 12 May 1947 in Colbert County, AL.

Tessa married **George Walter Echols Jr.**, son of **George Walter Echols Sr.** and **Emma Kate Seale**, 1 Jan 1967 in Jefferson County, AL. George was born 15 Jun 1944 in Jefferson County, AL.

+ 4432	M	i.	**William Bryan Echols** was born 19 Apr 1969 in Jefferson County, AL.
+ 4433	F	ii.	**Georgeanna Lee Echols** was born 21 Mar 1970 in Jefferson County, AL.
+ 4434	M	iii.	**Johnny Neal Echols** was born 28 Apr 1976 in Lauderdale County, AL.

2564. William (Bill) Dearen Rucker (*Hazel Inez Dearen⁷, William Lee Dearen⁶, Mary Francis (Molly) Young⁵, Mary M. (Polly II) Lindsey⁴, Frances (Frankie) Sharp³, Charles W. Sr.², John Sr.¹*) was born 21 Jan 1947 in Waco, McLennan County, TX.

William married **Annette Ritchey** 29 Mar 1980 in McKinney, Collin County, TX. Annette was born 25 Jun 1957 in McKinney, Collin County, TX.

4435	F	i.	**Lauren Annette Rucker** was born 16 Nov 1983.
4436	M	ii.	**Brian Dearen Rucker** was born 2 Mar 1987.

2565. Cynthia (Cindy) Lynn Rucker (*Hazel Inez Dearen⁷, William Lee Dearen⁶, Mary Francis (Molly) Young⁵, Mary M. (Polly II) Lindsey⁴, Frances (Frankie) Sharp³, Charles W. Sr.², John Sr.¹*) was born 22 Jun 1951 in Houston, Harris County, TX.

Cynthia married **Marvin Patraw** 19 Apr 1986 in Dallas, Tarrant County, TX. Marvin was born 21 Sep 1940 in Michigan.

2566. Donna Sue Harper (*Mildred Pauline Dearen⁷, William Lee Dearen⁶, Mary Francis (Molly) Young⁵, Mary M. (Polly II) Lindsey⁴, Frances (Frankie) Sharp³, Charles W. Sr.², John Sr.¹*) was born 5 Oct 1944 in Waco, McLennan County, TX.

Donna married **Bill Blahuta** 11 Feb 1964 in Waco, McLennan County, TX.

+ 4437	M	i.	**John Corey Blahuta** was born 29 Apr 1969 in Waco, McLennan County, TX.

2568. Pamela Jean McLaughlin (*Vera Mae Dearen⁷, William Lee Dearen⁶, Mary Francis (Molly) Young⁵, Mary M. (Polly II) Lindsey⁴, Frances (Frankie) Sharp³, Charles W. Sr.², John Sr.¹*) was born 8 Feb 1953 in Birddrod, England.

Pamela married **Steve Pavisen** 11 Jun 1988 in Houston, TX. Steve was buried in Restland Memorial Park, Dallas, TX.

4438	M	i.	**Michael Pavisen.**

2569. Mildred Loriene Gean (*Della V. Abilene Sego⁷, Minnie Pearl Dearen⁶, Mary Francis (Molly) Young⁵, Mary M. (Polly II) Lindsey⁴, Frances (Frankie) Sharp³, Charles W. Sr.², John Sr.¹*) was born 10 Aug 1931 in Lauderdale County, AL.

Mildred married **Billy Ray Mason**, son of **Louis Mason Sr.** and **Lois Ardene Cooper**, 25 Dec 1954 in Iuka, Tishomingo County, MS. Billy was born 31 Aug 1933 in Rogersville, Lauderdale County, AL.

+ 4439	M	i.	**Michael Darrow Mason** was born 13 Oct 1956 in Brunswick, Glynn County, GA.

+ 4440 F ii. **Wanda Lorene Mason** was born 1 Dec 1957 in Lauderdale County, AL.

+ 4441 F iii. **Belinda Lois Mason** was born 30 Dec 1958 in Jacksonville, Duval County, FL.

2570. Geneva Yvonne Gean (*Della V. Abilene Sego*[7], *Minnie Pearl Dearen*[6], *Mary Francis (Molly) Young*[5], *Mary M. (Polly II) Lindsey*[4], *Frances (Frankie) Sharp*[3], *Charles W. Sr.*[2], *John Sr.*[1]) was born 4 Aug 1939 in Lauderdale County, AL.

Geneva married **Billy Ray Hill**, son of **Bob Hill** and **Bertha Merel**, 29 Mar 1959 in Lauderdale County, AL. Billy was born 6 Jul 1939 in Lauderdale County, AL.

+ 4442 M i. **Ronnie Ray Hill** was born 29 Jul 1960 in Lauderdale County, AL.

+ 4443 M ii. **Randal Reed Hill** was born 27 Sep 1962 in Lauderdale County, AL.

+ 4444 F iii. **Roanna Renee Hill** was born 9 Nov 1964 in Loretto, Lawrence County, TN.

2572. Mary Kathleen Gean (*Della V. Abilene Sego*[7], *Minnie Pearl Dearen*[6], *Mary Francis (Molly) Young*[5], *Mary M. (Polly II) Lindsey*[4], *Frances (Frankie) Sharp*[3], *Charles W. Sr.*[2], *John Sr.*[1]) was born 2 Jun 1944 in Lauderdale County, AL. Another name for Mary is Mary Katherine Gean.

Mary married **Bernie James Collins** 8 Oct 1962 in North Carolina. Bernie was born 1 May 1943 in Wayne County, TN.

+ 4445 M i. **David Maurice Collins** was born 22 May 1963 in Lauderdale County, AL.

+ 4446 M ii. **Richard Lee Collins** was born 13 Dec 1964 in Evansville, Vanderburgh County, IN.

+ 4447 F iii. **Michelle Anne Collins** was born 26 Jan 1970 in Evansville, Vanderburgh County, IN.

+ 4448 M iv. **Keith Alan Collins** was born 14 Aug 1971 in Lawrenceburg, Lawrence County, TN.

Mary next married **Travis Martin**.

2573. Kenneth Aaron Gean (*Della V. Abilene Sego*[7], *Minnie Pearl Dearen*[6], *Mary Francis (Molly) Young*[5], *Mary M. (Polly II) Lindsey*[4], *Frances (Frankie) Sharp*[3], *Charles W. Sr.*[2], *John Sr.*[1]) was born 19 Jul 1946 in Lauderdale County, AL.

Kenneth married **Wanda Sue Lard**, daughter of **John Buford Lard Sr.** and **Helen Lorene Odell**, 31 Aug 1967 in Lauderdale County, AL. Wanda was born 22 Nov 1949 in Lauderdale County, AL.

+ 4449 M i. **Michael Aaron Gean** was born 28 Sep 1969 in Lauderdale County, AL.

+ 4450 F ii. **Susan Lorene Gean** was born 1 Aug 1974 in Lauderdale County, AL.

2575. Sharon Elaine Gean (*Della V. Abilene Sego*[7], *Minnie Pearl Dearen*[6], *Mary Francis (Molly) Young*[5], *Mary M. (Polly II) Lindsey*[4], *Frances (Frankie) Sharp*[3], *Charles W. Sr.*[2], *John Sr.*[1]) was born 5 Jan 1952 in Waynesboro, Wayne County, TN.

Sharon married **Robert Jerry Wylie**, son of **Marvin Edison Wylie** and **Ruthie Mae Simpson**, 25 Nov 1973 in Lauderdale County, AL.

Sharon next married **Ronnie Lowell Brown**, son of **Benjamin Franklin Brown Sr.** and **Pearl Etta Ticer**, 13 May 1990 in Lauderdale County, AL. Ronnie was born 7 Jun 1941 in Lauderdale County, AL.
(Duplicate Line. See Person 1241)

2576. Virgil Henderson Gean Jr. (*Della V. Abilene Sego*[7], *Minnie Pearl Dearen*[6], *Mary Francis (Molly) Young*[5], *Mary M. (Polly II) Lindsey*[4], *Frances (Frankie) Sharp*[3], *Charles W. Sr.*[2], *John Sr.*[1]) was born 29 Dec 1953 in Waynesboro, Wayne County, TN.

Virgil married **Deborah Jean Arnold**, daughter of **Buford E. Arnold** and **Alice K. Wilbanks**, 10 Aug 1973 in Lauderdale County, AL. Deborah was born 4 Aug 1955 in Lauderdale County, AL.

+ 4451 F i. **Kisha Leane Gean** was born 3 Jun 1975 in Lauderdale County, AL.

+ 4452 F ii. **Kimberly Dawn Gean** was born 20 Jun 1980 in Lauderdale County, AL.

2577. Doris Geraldine Holcombe (*Mary Alice Sego*[7], *Minnie Pearl Dearen*[6], *Mary Francis (Molly) Young*[5], *Mary M. (Polly II) Lindsey*[4], *Frances (Frankie) Sharp*[3], *Charles W. Sr.*[2], *John Sr.*[1]) was born 19 Apr 1933 in Lauderdale County, AL.

Doris married **Loson Donald Young**, son of **Marvin Young** and **Emma Fisher**, 21 Nov 1951 in Iuka, Tishomingo County, MS.

+ 4453 F   i.   **Judy Loretta Young** was born 29 Nov 1952 in Mishawaka, St Joseph County, IN.
+ 4454 F   ii.   **Vickie Jane Young** was born 3 Nov 1955 in Mishawaka, St Joseph County, IN.

Doris next married **Aghbert James (Ed) Bertrand** in 1976 in Mishawaka, St Joseph County, IN.

2578. Robbie Louellen Holcombe (*Mary Alice Sego*[7], *Minnie Pearl Dearen*[6], *Mary Francis (Molly) Young*[5], *Mary M. (Polly II) Lindsey*[4], *Frances (Frankie) Sharp*[3], *Charles W. Sr.*[2], *John Sr.*[1]) was born 8 Nov 1934 in Lauderdale County, AL, died 23 Mar 2007, and was buried in Mishawaka, IN.

Robbie married **Willard Russell Newland** 21 Dec 1952 in Mishawaka, St Joseph County, IN. Willard was born 6 Jul 1930 in New Carlisle, IN, died 11 Jul 1965, and was buried in Mishawaka, St Joseph County, IN.

+ 4455 F   i.   **Donna Christine Newland** was born 14 Aug 1953 in Mishawaka, St Joseph County, IN.
+ 4456 F   ii.   **Shelly Jean Newland** was born 3 Oct 1955 in Mishawaka, St Joseph County, IN.
+ 4457 M   iii.   **Russell Glen Newland** was born 7 Apr 1961 in Mishawaka, St Joseph County, IN.

Robbie next married **Clinton Harold Webb** 10 Dec 1977 in Mishawaka, St Joseph County, IN.

2579. Thomas Edsel Holcombe (*Mary Alice Sego*[7], *Minnie Pearl Dearen*[6], *Mary Francis (Molly) Young*[5], *Mary M. (Polly II) Lindsey*[4], *Frances (Frankie) Sharp*[3], *Charles W. Sr.*[2], *John Sr.*[1]) was born 24 Mar 1940 in Waterloo, Lauderdale County, AL.

Thomas married **Carol Gressham** 8 Apr 1961 in Dayton, Montgomery County, OH.

Thomas next married **Estella Hahn** 20 Aug 1982 in Dayton, Montgomery County, OH.

2582. Sarah Beatrice Williams (*Frances Boyce Sego*[7], *Minnie Pearl Dearen*[6], *Mary Francis (Molly) Young*[5], *Mary M. (Polly II) Lindsey*[4], *Frances (Frankie) Sharp*[3], *Charles W. Sr.*[2], *John Sr.*[1]) was born 3 Jan 1934 in Hardin County, TN, died 17 Nov 1998, and was buried in White's Creek Cemetery, Hardin County, TN.

Sarah married **Bobby James Stricklin**, son of **Ellis Monk Stricklin** and **Geneva L. Gean**, 29 Oct 1965 in Mishawaka, St Joseph County, IN. Bobby was born 22 Feb 1939 in Mishawaka, St Joseph County, IN, died 4 Nov 1991, and was buried in White's Creek Cemetery, Hardin County, TN.

+ 4458 F   i.   **Tammy Lou Stricklin** was born 6 Sep 1965 in South Bend, IN.
+ 4459 M   ii.   **Thomas (Tommy) James Stricklin** was born 28 Jun 1967 in South Bend, IN.

2583. Jerry Wayne Williams (*Frances Boyce Sego*[7], *Minnie Pearl Dearen*[6], *Mary Francis (Molly) Young*[5], *Mary M. (Polly II) Lindsey*[4], *Frances (Frankie) Sharp*[3], *Charles W. Sr.*[2], *John Sr.*[1]) was born 28 May 1947 in Lauderdale County, AL.

Jerry married **Ruth Ann Benson** 14 Jul 1973 in Mishawaka, St Joseph County, IN. Ruth was born 28 Nov 1947.

2584. Larry David Williams (*Frances Boyce Sego*[7], *Minnie Pearl Dearen*[6], *Mary Francis (Molly) Young*[5], *Mary M. (Polly II) Lindsey*[4], *Frances (Frankie) Sharp*[3], *Charles W. Sr.*[2], *John Sr.*[1]) was born 23 Dec 1952 in Mishawaka, St Joseph County, IN.

Larry married **Mary Ann Bosler**, daughter of **Ed Bosler** and **Joyce *Unk**. Mary was born 24 Mar 1955 in Mishawaka, St Joseph County, IN.

  4460 F   i.   **Tonya Ann Williams** was born 28 Dec 972 in Mishawaka, St Joseph County, IN.
+ 4461 F   ii.   **Carla Lynn Williams** was born 1 Apr 1976 in Mishawaka, St Joseph County, IN.

Larry next married **Marcia Bennett**. Marcia was born 13 Jan 1949.

2585. Debra Lynn Williams (*Frances Boyce Sego*[7], *Minnie Pearl Dearen*[6], *Mary Francis (Molly) Young*[5], *Mary M. (Polly II) Lindsey*[4], *Frances (Frankie) Sharp*[3], *Charles W. Sr.*[2], *John Sr.*[1]) was born 16 Aug 1954 in Mishawaka, St Joseph County, IN, died 6 Jun 2006, and was buried in Williams Chapel Cemetery, Lauderdale County, AL.

Debra married **Carl Edward Chandler**. Carl was born 27 Feb 1951 in Lauderdale County, AL.

4462   M   i.   **Jonathan David Chandler** was born 4 Jun 1980 in Lauderdale County, AL.

Debra next married **Joe Lowry**.

2586. Dennis Masterson Sego (*Willie Doyal Sego*[7], *Minnie Pearl Dearen*[6], *Mary Francis (Molly) Young*[5], *Mary M. (Polly II) Lindsey*[4], *Frances (Frankie) Sharp*[3], *Charles W. Sr.*[2], *John Sr.*[1]) was born 11 Jan 1951 in Gadsden, Etowah County, AL.

Dennis married **Deborah Lynn Clark**. Deborah was born 9 Jun 1956.

4463   F   i.   **Jennifer Elizabeth Sego** was born 23 Aug 1977.

4464   M   ii.   **David Sego** was born in Jul 1979.

2587. Karen Beth Sego (*Willie Doyal Sego*[7], *Minnie Pearl Dearen*[6], *Mary Francis (Molly) Young*[5], *Mary M. (Polly II) Lindsey*[4], *Frances (Frankie) Sharp*[3], *Charles W. Sr.*[2], *John Sr.*[1]) was born 22 Feb 1954 in Gadsden, Etowah County, AL.

Karen married **Lenly Loran Smith** in Gadsden, Etowah County, AL. Lenly was born 25 Jan 1949.

4465   M   i.   **Justin Duane Smith** was born 9 May 1973 in Gadsden, Etowah County, AL, died 4 Mar 2000, and was buried in Crestwood Cemetery, Gadsden, AL.

2588. Melissa Lou (Lisa) Sego (*Willie Doyal Sego*[7], *Minnie Pearl Dearen*[6], *Mary Francis (Molly) Young*[5], *Mary M. (Polly II) Lindsey*[4], *Frances (Frankie) Sharp*[3], *Charles W. Sr.*[2], *John Sr.*[1]) was born 25 Apr 1958 in Gadsden, AL.

Melissa married **Lew Brian Breeden**. Lew was born 29 May 1959.

4466   F   i.   **Deanna Lee Breeden** was born 13 Feb 1979.

Melissa next married **James Mark Stephens Sr.** 22 Dec 1984 in Gadsden, Etowah County, AL. James was born 20 Mar 1960 in Gadsden, Etowah County, AL.

4467   M   i.   **James Mark Stephens Jr.** was born 3 Aug 1987.

2589. Marilyn Kaye White (*Clara Bell Sego*[7], *Minnie Pearl Dearen*[6], *Mary Francis (Molly) Young*[5], *Mary M. (Polly II) Lindsey*[4], *Frances (Frankie) Sharp*[3], *Charles W. Sr.*[2], *John Sr.*[1]) was born 13 Aug 1947 in Lauderdale County, AL.

Marilyn married **James Edward Weatherington**, son of **M. O. Weatherington** and **Pauline Austin**, 23 Aug 1968 in Lauderdale County, AL. James was born 21 May 1946 in Oakland, County, MI.

2590. Warren Lee White (*Clara Bell Sego*[7], *Minnie Pearl Dearen*[6], *Mary Francis (Molly) Young*[5], *Mary M. (Polly II) Lindsey*[4], *Frances (Frankie) Sharp*[3], *Charles W. Sr.*[2], *John Sr.*[1]) was born 4 Aug 1949 in Lauderdale County, AL.

Warren married **Judy Johnson** about 1965 in Lauderdale County, AL.

4468   F   i.   **Shannon Lee White** was born 18 Jun 1974.

Warren next married **Peggy Leah Ezell** 6 Feb 2002 in Lauderdale County, AL. Peggy was born 19 May 1959 in Lauderdale County, AL.

2591. Glenda Juanita White (*Clara Bell Sego*[7], *Minnie Pearl Dearen*[6], *Mary Francis (Molly) Young*[5], *Mary M. (Polly II) Lindsey*[4], *Frances (Frankie) Sharp*[3], *Charles W. Sr.*[2], *John Sr.*[1]) was born 21 Jun 1951 in Lauderdale County, AL.

Glenda married **Earl Steven Allison**, son of **Earl Alvin Allison** and **Darnell Eunice Burbank**, 17 Aug 1970 in Lauderdale County, AL. Earl was born 2 Nov 1950 in South Bend, St Joseph County, IN.
(Duplicate Line. See Person 1641)

2592. Lavenia Gail White (*Clara Bell Sego⁷, Minnie Pearl Dearen⁶, Mary Francis (Molly) Young⁵, Mary M. (Polly II) Lindsey⁴, Frances (Frankie) Sharp³, Charles W. Sr.², John Sr.¹*) was born 26 Jul 1959 in Lauderdale County, AL.

Lavenia married **Bobby Joe White**, son of **George Bethel White** and **Ethel Mattie Kilburn**, 28 Oct 1976 in Lauderdale County, AL. Bobby was born 8 Sep 1956 in Lauderdale County, AL.

+ 4469 F   i.   **Mandy Lynn White** was born 17 Feb 1977 in Lauderdale County, AL.

2593. Carlos Walter White (*Clara Bell Sego⁷, Minnie Pearl Dearen⁶, Mary Francis (Molly) Young⁵, Mary M. (Polly II) Lindsey⁴, Frances (Frankie) Sharp³, Charles W. Sr.², John Sr.¹*) was born 17 Apr 1971 in Lauderdale County, AL.

Carlos married **Linda Renee Myhan**, daughter of **Larry Dwight Myhan** and **Shelby Jean South**, 18 Sep 1992 in Lauderdale County, AL. Linda was born 20 Apr 1973 in Lauderdale County, AL.

4470 F   i.   **Katelyn Dannielle White** was born 3 Apr 1995 in Lauderdale County, AL.
4471 M   ii.   **Noah Andrew White** was born 5 Feb 2003 in Lauderdale County, AL.

2594. John Michael Dearen (*John Lemuel Dearen⁷, James Edgar Dearen⁶, Mary Francis (Molly) Young⁵, Mary M. (Polly II) Lindsey⁴, Frances (Frankie) Sharp³, Charles W. Sr.², John Sr.¹*) was born 25 Feb 1956 in Houston, Harris County, TX.

John married **Lynn *Unk**.
4472 F   i.   **Jeannette Rosiland Dearen** was born 28 Apr 1987 in Houston, Harris County, TX.

2595. Shawn Leigh Dearen (*John Lemuel Dearen⁷, James Edgar Dearen⁶, Mary Francis (Molly) Young⁵, Mary M. (Polly II) Lindsey⁴, Frances (Frankie) Sharp³, Charles W. Sr.², John Sr.¹*) was born 4 Jun 1960 in Houston, Harris County, TX.

Shawn married **Kenneth Pennick Jr.**.
4473 F   i.   **Jessica Ashley Pennick** was born 24 Jun 1985 in Houston, Harris County, TX.
4474 M   ii.   **Brandon Paul Pennick** was born 26 Jun 1987 in Houston, Harris County, TX.
4475 F   iii.   **Brittney Ann Pennick** was born 12 Jun 1990 in Houston, Harris County, TX.

Shawn next married **Mark Neen**.

2601. Roger Allen South (*Rufus Allen South⁷, Clara Edna Dearen⁶, Mary Francis (Molly) Young⁵, Mary M. (Polly II) Lindsey⁴, Frances (Frankie) Sharp³, Charles W. Sr.², John Sr.¹*) was born 12 Oct 1955 in Lauderdale County, AL.

Roger married **Regina Anettea Jones**, daughter of **William H. Jones** and **Francis E. Lee**, 19 Sep 1974 in Lauderdale County, AL. Regina was born 8 May 1959 in Lauderdale County, AL.

+ 4476 F   i.   **Amanda Kay South** was born 16 Nov 1976 in Lauderdale County, AL.
+ 4477 F   ii.   **Brandy Annette South** was born 25 Sep 1979 in Dallas, TX.
+ 4478 M   iii.   **Christopher Allen South** was born 19 Jun 1981 in Lauderdale County, AL.

2602. James Cecil South (*Rufus Allen South⁷, Clara Edna Dearen⁶, Mary Francis (Molly) Young⁵, Mary M. (Polly II) Lindsey⁴, Frances (Frankie) Sharp³, Charles W. Sr.², John Sr.¹*) was born 6 Oct 1956 in Lauderdale County, AL.

James married **Pamela Faye Young**, daughter of **Arthur D. Young** and **Mary Katheryn Cherry**, 1 Jul 1987 in Lauderdale County, AL. Pamela was born 9 Aug 1958 in Lauderdale County, AL.

+ 4479 M   i.   **Jeremy Clay South** was born 24 Dec 1981 in Lauderdale County, AL.

2603. Randal Keith South (*Rufus Allen South⁷, Clara Edna Dearen⁶, Mary Francis (Molly) Young⁵, Mary M. (Polly II) Lindsey⁴, Frances (Frankie) Sharp³, Charles W. Sr.², John Sr.¹*) was born 24 Aug 1959 in Lauderdale County, AL.

Randal married **Debra Lynn Jones**, daughter of **William H. Jones** and **Francis E. Lee**, 29 Jun 1979 in Lauderdale County, AL. Debra was born 20 Jun 1962 in Dallas, TX.

  + 4480 F   i.   **Tisha Latonya South** was born 9 Apr 1981 in Lauderdale County, AL.

  + 4481 F   ii.   **Randi Marie South** was born in Jul 1982 in Lauderdale County, AL.

Randal next married **Cheryl Annette Ticer**, daughter of **Montie Wayne Ticer** and **Barbara Fay Moore**. Cheryl was born 19 Mar 1958 in Lauderdale County, AL.

2604. Ricky Lynn South (*Rufus Allen South*[7], *Clara Edna Dearen*[6], *Mary Francis (Molly) Young*[5], *Mary M. (Polly II) Lindsey*[4], *Frances (Frankie) Sharp*[3], *Charles W. Sr.*[2], *John Sr.*[1]) was born 23 Sep 1960 in Lauderdale County, AL.

Ricky married **Teresa Ann Hipps**, daughter of **Billy Hipps Sr.** and **Mildred Beasley**, 5 Jun 1982 in Lauderdale County, AL. Teresa was born 8 Jan 1965 in Lauderdale County, AL.

  4482 M   i.   **Michael Allen South** was born 27 May 1986 in Lauderdale County, AL.

  4483 M   ii.   **Matthew Lynn South** was born 29 Aug 1988 in Lauderdale County, AL.

2605. Steven Dewayne South (*Rufus Allen South*[7], *Clara Edna Dearen*[6], *Mary Francis (Molly) Young*[5], *Mary M. (Polly II) Lindsey*[4], *Frances (Frankie) Sharp*[3], *Charles W. Sr.*[2], *John Sr.*[1]) was born 16 Oct 1962 in Lauderdale County, AL.

Steven married **Stacy Lee Neher**, daughter of **Joseph William Neher** and **Joyce Ann Howard**, 17 Jun 1995 in Lauderdale County, AL. Stacy was born 30 Nov 1961.

  4484 F   i.   **Carrie LeeAnn South** was born 24 Jan 1997 in Lauderdale County, AL.

2606. Phillip Dale South (*Rufus Allen South*[7], *Clara Edna Dearen*[6], *Mary Francis (Molly) Young*[5], *Mary M. (Polly II) Lindsey*[4], *Frances (Frankie) Sharp*[3], *Charles W. Sr.*[2], *John Sr.*[1]) was born 9 Jan 1964 in Lauderdale County, AL.

Phillip married **Alicia Nicole McGill**, daughter of **James Ted McGill** and **Patricia Gale Fleming**, 27 Apr 1991 in Lauderdale County, AL. Alicia was born 20 Nov 1970 in Alabama.

  4485 M   i.   **Wesley Tyler South** was born 4 May 1993 in Lauderdale County, AL.

  4486 F   ii.   **Kasi Nichole South** was born 26 Oct 1995 in Lauderdale County, AL.

2607. Tamara Faye Faulkner (*Eva Leigh South*[7], *Clara Edna Dearen*[6], *Mary Francis (Molly) Young*[5], *Mary M. (Polly II) Lindsey*[4], *Frances (Frankie) Sharp*[3], *Charles W. Sr.*[2], *John Sr.*[1]) was born 19 Oct 1958 in Lauderdale County, AL.

Tamara married **Terry Melvin Hart**, son of **James Melvin Hart** and **Lola Murphy**, 7 Oct 1974 in Iuka, Tishomingo County, MS. Terry was born 25 Feb 1957 in Dearborn, MI, died 3 Jun 1986, and was buried in Murphy's Chapel Cemetery, Lauderdale County, AL.

  + 4487 M   i.   **Adrian Lee Hart** was born 13 Nov 1976 in Lauderdale County, AL.

  + 4488 F   ii.   **Christina Ann Hart** was born 1 May 1982 in Lauderdale County, AL.

2608. Martina Ann Faulkner (*Eva Leigh South*[7], *Clara Edna Dearen*[6], *Mary Francis (Molly) Young*[5], *Mary M. (Polly II) Lindsey*[4], *Frances (Frankie) Sharp*[3], *Charles W. Sr.*[2], *John Sr.*[1]) was born 23 Aug 1961 in Lauderdale County, AL.

Martina married **Marvin Andrew Croy Sr.**, son of **William T. Croy** and **Sarah Hall**, 3 May 1979 in Lauderdale County, AL. Marvin was born 26 Dec 1955 in Colbert County, AL.

  4489 M   i.   **Marvin Andrew Croy Jr.** was born 13 Oct 1980 in Christian County, KY.

Martina next married **Charles Robert Turbyfill**, son of **William Oscar Turbyfill** and **Velma Nadine Sharp**, 15 Jun 1987 in Lauderdale County, AL. Charles was born 18 Jun 1949 in Lauderdale County, AL, died 25 Oct 2000, and was buried in Stoney Point Cemetery, Lauderdale County, AL.

(Duplicate Line. See Person 1873)

2616. Johnnie Russel Dennis (*John Albert Dennis^7, Florence L. Ticer^6, Roxie Leona Young^5, Mary M. (Polly II) Lindsey^4, Frances (Frankie) Sharp^3, Charles W. Sr.^{2}, John Sr.^{1}*) was born 30 Oct 1938 in Lauderdale County, AL.

Johnnie married **Hannah *Unk**.

2617. Jerry Dennis (*John Albert Dennis^7, Florence L. Ticer^6, Roxie Leona Young^5, Mary M. (Polly II) Lindsey^4, Frances (Frankie) Sharp^3, Charles W. Sr.^{2}, John Sr.^{1}*) was born 16 Sep 1941 in Lauderdale County, AL.

Jerry married **Becky *Unk**.

2618. Mary Dennis (*Dalton L. Dennis^7, Florence L. Ticer^6, Roxie Leona Young^5, Mary M. (Polly II) Lindsey^4, Frances (Frankie) Sharp^3, Charles W. Sr.^{2}, John Sr.^{1}*).

Mary married **Larry Suver**.

2619. Sue Dennis (*Dalton L. Dennis^7, Florence L. Ticer^6, Roxie Leona Young^5, Mary M. (Polly II) Lindsey^4, Frances (Frankie) Sharp^3, Charles W. Sr.^{2}, John Sr.^{1}*).

Sue married **Larry Suver**.
+ 4490 F i. **Terri Suver**.
+ 4491 F ii. **Tina Suver** was born in 1962.

2621. Hugh L. Dennis (*Dalton L. Dennis^7, Florence L. Ticer^6, Roxie Leona Young^5, Mary M. (Polly II) Lindsey^4, Frances (Frankie) Sharp^3, Charles W. Sr.^{2}, John Sr.^{1}*) was born 18 Feb 1940 in Hardin County, TN.

Hugh married **Archie Maruiel Franks**.
+ 4492 F i. **Sherry Dennis**.
4493 M ii. **Greg Dennis**.

2623. Herman Dennis (*Dalton L. Dennis^7, Florence L. Ticer^6, Roxie Leona Young^5, Mary M. (Polly II) Lindsey^4, Frances (Frankie) Sharp^3, Charles W. Sr.^{2}, John Sr.^{1}*) was born 28 Feb 1948.

Herman married **Kathy *Unk**.
4494 M i. **Shawn Dennis**.
4495 M ii. **Ryan Dennis**.

2624. James Fay Reed (*Christine Dennis^7, Florence L. Ticer^6, Roxie Leona Young^5, Mary M. (Polly II) Lindsey^4, Frances (Frankie) Sharp^3, Charles W. Sr.^{2}, John Sr.^{1}*) was born 25 Mar 1939 in Collinwood, TN.

James married **Joyce Marie Wayland**.

2625. Dennis Ray Reed (*Christine Dennis^7, Florence L. Ticer^6, Roxie Leona Young^5, Mary M. (Polly II) Lindsey^4, Frances (Frankie) Sharp^3, Charles W. Sr.^{2}, John Sr.^{1}*) was born 29 Jan 1941 in Collinwood, TN.

Dennis married **Ora Faye Reaves**.

2626. Robert Earnest Reed (*Christine Dennis^7, Florence L. Ticer^6, Roxie Leona Young^5, Mary M. (Polly II) Lindsey^4, Frances (Frankie) Sharp^3, Charles W. Sr.^{2}, John Sr.^{1}*) was born 29 Nov 1942 in Collinwood, TN.

Robert married **Bernita Sue Brown**.

2627. Cleo William Reed (*Christine Dennis^7, Florence L. Ticer^6, Roxie Leona Young^5, Mary M. (Polly II) Lindsey^4, Frances (Frankie) Sharp^3, Charles W. Sr.^{2}, John Sr.^{1}*) was born 15 Aug 1946 in Collinwood, TN.

Cleo married **Brenda Joyce Dial**.

2628. Leo Jasper Reed (*Christine Dennis*[7]*, Florence L. Ticer*[6]*, Roxie Leona Young*[5]*, Mary M. (Polly II) Lindsey*[4]*, Frances (Frankie) Sharp*[3]*, Charles W. Sr.*[2]*, John Sr.*[1]) was born 15 Aug 1946 in Collinwood, TN.

Leo married **Mayren Jean Keeton**.

2629. Roger Dale Reed (*Christine Dennis*[7]*, Florence L. Ticer*[6]*, Roxie Leona Young*[5]*, Mary M. (Polly II) Lindsey*[4]*, Frances (Frankie) Sharp*[3]*, Charles W. Sr.*[2]*, John Sr.*[1]) was born 28 Sep 1949 in Collinwood, TN.

Roger married **Arleen Joyce Williams**.

2631. Troy Wayne Dennis (*Troy Burlon Dennis*[7]*, Florence L. Ticer*[6]*, Roxie Leona Young*[5]*, Mary M. (Polly II) Lindsey*[4]*, Frances (Frankie) Sharp*[3]*, Charles W. Sr.*[2]*, John Sr.*[1]) was born in Aug 1948 in Lauderdale County, AL.

Troy married **Nyla Jane Haynes**.

2632. Wendall Dean Dennis (*Troy Burlon Dennis*[7]*, Florence L. Ticer*[6]*, Roxie Leona Young*[5]*, Mary M. (Polly II) Lindsey*[4]*, Frances (Frankie) Sharp*[3]*, Charles W. Sr.*[2]*, John Sr.*[1]) was born 14 Nov 1953 in Mishawaka, St Joseph County, IN.

Wendall married **Patsy Jane Benson** 4 Sep 1971 in Lauderdale County, AL.

2633. Leigh Ann Dennis (*Troy Burlon Dennis*[7]*, Florence L. Ticer*[6]*, Roxie Leona Young*[5]*, Mary M. (Polly II) Lindsey*[4]*, Frances (Frankie) Sharp*[3]*, Charles W. Sr.*[2]*, John Sr.*[1]) was born 27 Jul 1965 in Lauderdale County, AL.

Leigh married **Roger D. Balentine**.
+ 4496 F   i.   **Brittany Denise Balentine**.

2634. Judith Anne Dennis (*Curtis Dennis*[7]*, Florence L. Ticer*[6]*, Roxie Leona Young*[5]*, Mary M. (Polly II) Lindsey*[4]*, Frances (Frankie) Sharp*[3]*, Charles W. Sr.*[2]*, John Sr.*[1]) was born 7 Jul 1955 in South Bend, IN.

Judith married **Paul Madala**.

2635. Tina Marie Dennis (*Curtis Dennis*[7]*, Florence L. Ticer*[6]*, Roxie Leona Young*[5]*, Mary M. (Polly II) Lindsey*[4]*, Frances (Frankie) Sharp*[3]*, Charles W. Sr.*[2]*, John Sr.*[1]) was born 15 Jan 1958 in Milwauka, WI.

Tina married **Skip Murphy**.

2636. Susan Marie Davis (*Dorothy W. Dennis*[7]*, Florence L. Ticer*[6]*, Roxie Leona Young*[5]*, Mary M. (Polly II) Lindsey*[4]*, Frances (Frankie) Sharp*[3]*, Charles W. Sr.*[2]*, John Sr.*[1]) was born 15 Aug 1954 in Highland Park, IN.

Susan married **Greg F. Edwards**.

2640. Gary Allen Ticer (*James Allen Ticer*[7]*, Robert Clark Ticer II*[6]*, Roxie Leona Young*[5]*, Mary M. (Polly II) Lindsey*[4]*, Frances (Frankie) Sharp*[3]*, Charles W. Sr.*[2]*, John Sr.*[1]) was born 10 Jan 1948 in Florence, Lauderdale County, AL.

Gary married **Elgena Covington**.

Gary next married **Deborah Elizabeth (Debbi) Tune**, daughter of **John D. Tune** and **Wanda Perkins**, 15 Feb 1975 in Lauderdale County, AL. Deborah was born 26 Nov 1955 in Hardin County, TN.

Gary next married **Elgena Brewer** in 1978. Elgena was born in Nov 1938 in Greenhill, Lauderdale County, AL.

2641. Larry David Ticer (*James Allen Ticer*[7]*, Robert Clark Ticer II*[6]*, Roxie Leona Young*[5]*, Mary M. (Polly II) Lindsey*[4]*, Frances (Frankie) Sharp*[3]*, Charles W. Sr.*[2]*, John Sr.*[1]) was born 21 May 1949 in Florence, Lauderdale County, AL.

Larry married **Patrica Ann Putt**, daughter of **Dan W. Putt** and **Wanda Pickens**, 21 Jul 1975 in Lauderdale County, AL. Patrica was born 7 Feb 1958 in Fort Fairfield, ME.

4497 F i. **Rachel Ticer**.

4498 F ii. **April Dawn Ticer**.

Larry next married **Nora Ann Parks** 6 May 1985 in Lauderdale County, AL. Nora was born 14 Mar 1950 in Madison County, AL.

2642. Mitchell Wayne Ticer (*James Allen Ticer*[7], *Robert Clark Ticer II*[6], *Roxie Leona Young*[5], *Mary M. (Polly II) Lindsey*[4], *Frances (Frankie) Sharp*[3], *Charles W. Sr.*[2], *John Sr.*[1]) was born 19 May 1950 in Florence, Lauderdale County, AL.

Mitchell married **Sharon Jean (Jeanie) Solomon**, daughter of **Jack L. Solomon** and **Dorothy Thompson**, 23 Mar 1971 in Lauderdale County, AL. Sharon was born 2 Jun 1950 in Lauderdale County, AL.

4499 F i. **Jamie Renee Ticer**.

2643. Sandra Gail Ticer (*James Allen Ticer*[7], *Robert Clark Ticer II*[6], *Roxie Leona Young*[5], *Mary M. (Polly II) Lindsey*[4], *Frances (Frankie) Sharp*[3], *Charles W. Sr.*[2], *John Sr.*[1]) was born 21 Jul 1953 in Florence, Lauderdale County, AL.

Sandra married **Randy Wayne Weatherington**, son of **M. O. Weatherington** and **Pauline Austin**, 18 Mar 1972 in Lauderdale County, AL. Randy was born 8 Jan 1951 in Lauderdale County, AL.

2644. Sally Joyce Ticer (*James Allen Ticer*[7], *Robert Clark Ticer II*[6], *Roxie Leona Young*[5], *Mary M. (Polly II) Lindsey*[4], *Frances (Frankie) Sharp*[3], *Charles W. Sr.*[2], *John Sr.*[1]) was born 21 Jul 1953 in Florence, Lauderdale County, AL.

Sally married **Danny William Murphy**, son of **Lloyd E. Murphy** and **Helen C. Brewer**, 18 Mar 1972 in Lauderdale County, AL. Danny was born 18 Sep 1950 in Lauderdale County, AL.

2645. Steven Lee Ticer (*Arnold Lee Ticer*[7], *Robert Clark Ticer II*[6], *Roxie Leona Young*[5], *Mary M. (Polly II) Lindsey*[4], *Frances (Frankie) Sharp*[3], *Charles W. Sr.*[2], *John Sr.*[1]) was born 30 May 1953 in St. Joseph County, IN, died 12 May 1988, and was buried in Sherrod Valley Cemetery, Lauderdale County, AL.

Steven married **Brenda Luanna Lamar**, daughter of **Melvin H. Lamar** and **Joyce Davenport**, 17 Sep 1971 in Lauderdale County, AL. Brenda was born 16 Oct 1954 in Colbert County, AL.

+ 4500 M i. **Christopher (Chris) Ticer** was born 22 Mar 1972 in Lauderdale County, AL.

2646. Rayford Arnold Ticer (*Arnold Lee Ticer*[7], *Robert Clark Ticer II*[6], *Roxie Leona Young*[5], *Mary M. (Polly II) Lindsey*[4], *Frances (Frankie) Sharp*[3], *Charles W. Sr.*[2], *John Sr.*[1]) was born 14 Jul 1954 in Lauderdale County, AL.

Rayford married **Lawanna Lee Coleman**, daughter of **Aden J. Coleman** and **Laura J. Lovelace**, 5 Jan 1973 in Lauderdale County, AL.

+ 4501 F i. **Lorie Lee Ticer** was born 29 Jul 1973 in Lauderdale County, AL.

Rayford next married **Shelia Elizabeth Shores**, daughter of **William G. Shores** and **Elizabeth McFall**, 2 Aug 1980 in Lauderdale County, AL. Shelia was born 17 Aug 1957 in Goosebay, Labrador.

Rayford next married **Cheri Lynn Brown**, daughter of **Louis A. Brown** and **Ellen McIntyre**, 18 Nov 1983 in Lauderdale County, AL. Cheri was born 22 Sep 1924 in Lauderdale County, AL.

2647. Angela Faye Ticer (*Arnold Lee Ticer*[7], *Robert Clark Ticer II*[6], *Roxie Leona Young*[5], *Mary M. (Polly II) Lindsey*[4], *Frances (Frankie) Sharp*[3], *Charles W. Sr.*[2], *John Sr.*[1]) was born 16 Sep 1965 in Lauderdale County, AL.

Angela married **Jon Stacy Haddock**, son of **Gertha C. Haddock** and **Margaret Hyde**, 18 Nov 1983 in Lauderdale County, AL. Jon was born 17 May 1962 in Lauderdale County, AL.

2649. Cletis Richardson (*Doris (Elwee) Ticer*[7], *Robert Clark Ticer II*[6], *Roxie Leona Young*[5], *Mary M. (Polly II) Lindsey*[4], *Frances (Frankie) Sharp*[3], *Charles W. Sr.*[2], *John Sr.*[1]) was born 9 Jun 1966.

Cletis married **Kimberly *Unk**.

2651. Susan Maxine Ticer (*Robert Ernest Ticer*[7], *Robert Clark Ticer II*[6], *Roxie Leona Young*[5], *Mary M. (Polly II) Lindsey*[4], *Frances (Frankie) Sharp*[3], *Charles W. Sr.*[2], *John Sr.*[1]) was born 17 Aug 1965.

Susan married **Dale Shipman Charles**.

2652. James Harold Weston (*Virtie Viola Weaver*[7], *Mary Ann Ticer*[6], *Roxie Leona Young*[5], *Mary M. (Polly II) Lindsey*[4], *Frances (Frankie) Sharp*[3], *Charles W. Sr.*[2], *John Sr.*[1]) was born 18 Jul 1937 in Lauderdale County, AL.

James married **Lillie Mae White** 29 Jun 1957 in Mishawaka, St Joseph County, IN.

2653. Jack Glen Weston (*Virtie Viola Weaver*[7], *Mary Ann Ticer*[6], *Roxie Leona Young*[5], *Mary M. (Polly II) Lindsey*[4], *Frances (Frankie) Sharp*[3], *Charles W. Sr.*[2], *John Sr.*[1]) was born 10 Nov 1942 in Mishawaka, St Joseph County, IN and died 14 May 1986.

Jack married **Eileen Whitaker** 10 Nov 1967 in Mishawaka, St Joseph County, IN.

2654. Jerry Wayne Weston (*Virtie Viola Weaver*[7], *Mary Ann Ticer*[6], *Roxie Leona Young*[5], *Mary M. (Polly II) Lindsey*[4], *Frances (Frankie) Sharp*[3], *Charles W. Sr.*[2], *John Sr.*[1]) was born 3 May 1944 in Mishawaka, St Joseph County, IN.

Jerry married **Linda Nyeres** 18 Apr 1964 in Mishawaka, St Joseph County, IN.

2655. Jo Ann Weston (*Virtie Viola Weaver*[7], *Mary Ann Ticer*[6], *Roxie Leona Young*[5], *Mary M. (Polly II) Lindsey*[4], *Frances (Frankie) Sharp*[3], *Charles W. Sr.*[2], *John Sr.*[1]) was born 6 Jul 1948 in Mishawaka, St Joseph County, IN.

Jo married **Dempsey Gross** 5 Jun 1965 in Mishawaka, St Joseph County, IN.

2656. Tommy Eugene Weston (*Virtie Viola Weaver*[7], *Mary Ann Ticer*[6], *Roxie Leona Young*[5], *Mary M. (Polly II) Lindsey*[4], *Frances (Frankie) Sharp*[3], *Charles W. Sr.*[2], *John Sr.*[1]) was born 13 Apr 1953 in Mishawaka, St Joseph County, IN.

Tommy married **Sharon Laughman** 16 Aug 1975 in Mishawaka, St Joseph County, IN.

2657. Ernest (Ernie) Doyle Whitaker (*Roxie Lucille Weaver*[7], *Mary Ann Ticer*[6], *Roxie Leona Young*[5], *Mary M. (Polly II) Lindsey*[4], *Frances (Frankie) Sharp*[3], *Charles W. Sr.*[2], *John Sr.*[1]) was born 31 Mar 1939 in Waterloo, Lauderdale County, AL.

Ernest married **Joan *Unk**.

2661. James Weaver (*James Paul Weaver*[7], *Mary Ann Ticer*[6], *Roxie Leona Young*[5], *Mary M. (Polly II) Lindsey*[4], *Frances (Frankie) Sharp*[3], *Charles W. Sr.*[2], *John Sr.*[1]) was born 19 Oct 1946 in Florence, Lauderdale County, AL.

James married **Ann Leach** 27 Nov 1965 in Indiana.

2662. Harry Malcom Weaver (*James Paul Weaver*[7], *Mary Ann Ticer*[6], *Roxie Leona Young*[5], *Mary M. (Polly II) Lindsey*[4], *Frances (Frankie) Sharp*[3], *Charles W. Sr.*[2], *John Sr.*[1]) was born 27 Aug 1949 in Florence, Lauderdale County, AL.

Harry married **Kandy Kay McLemore** 12 Apr 1971 in South Bend, IN.

2664. Roxanne Weaver (*James Paul Weaver*[7], *Mary Ann Ticer*[6], *Roxie Leona Young*[5], *Mary M. (Polly II) Lindsey*[4], *Frances (Frankie) Sharp*[3], *Charles W. Sr.*[2], *John Sr.*[1]) was born 24 Dec 1958 in South Bend, IN.

Roxanne married **Dennis Hess** 17 Dec 1977 in Mishawaka, St Joseph County, IN.

2670. Cheryl Annette Ticer (*Montie Wayne Ticer*[7], *David (Dave) Washington Ticer*[6], *Roxie Leona Young*[5], *Mary M. (Polly II) Lindsey*[4], *Frances (Frankie) Sharp*[3], *Charles W. Sr.*[2], *John Sr.*[1]) was born 19 Mar 1958 in Lauderdale County, AL.

Cheryl married **Lloyd Robert Smith**, son of **Lloyd Smith** and **Shirley Benson**, 15 Apr 1978 in Lauderdale County, AL. Lloyd was born 6 Sep 1957 in Florence, Lauderdale County, AL.
    4502   M   i.   **Scott Alan Smith** was born 8 Nov 1979 in Florence, Lauderdale County, AL.

Cheryl next married **Randal Keith South**, son of **Rufus Allen South** and **Marcella Ann Tucker**. Randal was born 24 Aug 1959 in Lauderdale County, AL.
(Duplicate Line. See Person 2603)

2671. Jill Michelle Young (*Peggy Ann Ticer*[7], *David (Dave) Washington Ticer*[6], *Roxie Leona Young*[5], *Mary M. (Polly II) Lindsey*[4], *Frances (Frankie) Sharp*[3], *Charles W. Sr.*[2], *John Sr.*[1]) was born 29 Mar 1969 in Lauderdale County, AL.

Jill married **Robert Daniel Brooks**, son of **Donald Ray Brooks** and **Barbara Patricia Bennett**, 3 Aug 1992 in Lauderdale County, AL. Robert was born 3 Dec 1964 in Arkansas.

2672. Amy Dee Young (*Peggy Ann Ticer*[7], *David (Dave) Washington Ticer*[6], *Roxie Leona Young*[5], *Mary M. (Polly II) Lindsey*[4], *Frances (Frankie) Sharp*[3], *Charles W. Sr.*[2], *John Sr.*[1]) was born 31 Aug 1972 in Lauderdale County, AL.

Amy married **Trey Jayson LeCory**, son of **Ralph Clinton LeCory** and **Lucky Jean Nelson**, 29 Mar 1997 in Lauderdale County, AL. Trey was born 30 Dec 1974.

2673. Bradley Edward Young (*Peggy Ann Ticer*[7], *David (Dave) Washington Ticer*[6], *Roxie Leona Young*[5], *Mary M. (Polly II) Lindsey*[4], *Frances (Frankie) Sharp*[3], *Charles W. Sr.*[2], *John Sr.*[1]) was born 17 Dec 1974 in Lauderdale County, AL.

Bradley married **Jennifer Dawn Herring** 8 Apr 2006 in Russellville, Franklin County, AL.

2675. Keith Lynn Jones (*James Ellis Jones*[7], *Lillian T. Ticer*[6], *Roxie Leona Young*[5], *Mary M. (Polly II) Lindsey*[4], *Frances (Frankie) Sharp*[3], *Charles W. Sr.*[2], *John Sr.*[1]) was born 6 Oct 1958 in Lauderdale County, AL.

Keith married **Angelia Lenae Hanvey**, daughter of **Alfred Hanvey** and **Barbara Jean Hanback**. Angelia was born 28 Jun 1970 in Lauderdale County, AL.
    4503   M   i.   **Kolbie Lynn Jones** was born 11 Mar 1991 in Lauderdale County, AL.
    4504   M   ii.   **Kyle Lee Jones** was born 26 Oct 1992 in Lauderdale County, AL.

2678. Kim Renee Patrick (*Jimmie Nell Brown*[7], *Pearl Etta Ticer*[6], *Roxie Leona Young*[5], *Mary M. (Polly II) Lindsey*[4], *Frances (Frankie) Sharp*[3], *Charles W. Sr.*[2], *John Sr.*[1]) was born 28 Feb 1962 in Japan.

Kim married **Eddie Letson**.

2679. Tina Denise Patrick (*Jimmie Nell Brown*[7], *Pearl Etta Ticer*[6], *Roxie Leona Young*[5], *Mary M. (Polly II) Lindsey*[4], *Frances (Frankie) Sharp*[3], *Charles W. Sr.*[2], *John Sr.*[1]) was born 9 Dec 1964 in Huntsville, Madison County, AL.

Tina married **D. B. Broadway**.

2680. Ricky Lowell Brown Sr. (*Ronnie Lowell Brown[7], Pearl Etta Ticer[6], Roxie Leona Young[5], Mary M. (Polly II) Lindsey[4], Frances (Frankie) Sharp[3], Charles W. Sr.[2], John Sr.[1]*) was born 27 Nov 1959 in Colbert County, AL, died 15 Jun 2000, and was buried in Murphy's Chapel Cemetery, Lauderdale County, AL.

Ricky married **Donna Kaye Warren**, daughter of **Jack Gwynn Warren** and **Linda Gail Bordon**, 26 Jan 1990 in Lauderdale County, AL. Donna was born 12 Sep 1967 in Colbert County, AL.

4505	M	i.	**Robert Corey Maxwell** was born 3 Dec 1987 in Colbert County, AL.
4506	M	ii.	**Ricky Lowell Brown II** was born 18 Oct 1990 in Lauderdale County, AL, died 18 Oct 1990, and was buried in Murphy's Chapel Cemetery, Lauderdale County, AL.
4507	M	iii.	**Dustin Drew Brown** was born 31 Aug 1993 in Lauderdale County, AL.
4508	M	iv.	**Ronnie Matthew Brown** was born 10 Jul 1996 in Lauderdale County, AL.

2681. Ralph Lee Brown (*Ronnie Lowell Brown[7], Pearl Etta Ticer[6], Roxie Leona Young[5], Mary M. (Polly II) Lindsey[4], Frances (Frankie) Sharp[3], Charles W. Sr.[2], John Sr.[1]*) was born 13 Jan 1961 in Colbert County, AL.

Ralph married **Selina Gail Mitchell**, daughter of **James David Mitchell** and **Linda Faye Haddock**, 20 Jun 1980 in Lauderdale County, AL. Selina was born 6 Jun 1962 in Lauderdale County, AL.

4509	F	i.	**Theresa Gail Brown** was born 30 Oct 1984 in Lauderdale County, AL.
4510	F	ii.	**Elisha Faye Brown** was born 27 Feb 1986 in Lauderdale County, AL.

2682. Ronald Lynn Brown (*Ronnie Lowell Brown[7], Pearl Etta Ticer[6], Roxie Leona Young[5], Mary M. (Polly II) Lindsey[4], Frances (Frankie) Sharp[3], Charles W. Sr.[2], John Sr.[1]*) was born 26 Feb 1963 in Colbert County, AL.

Ronald married **Wanda Darlene O'Kelley**, daughter of **James Wesley O'Kelley** and **Dorothy Marie Chambers**, 17 Jul 1982 in Lauderdale County, AL. Wanda was born 1 May 1960 in Lauderdale County, AL.

4511	F	i.	**Ashley Nicole Brown** was born 22 Mar 1982 in Lauderdale County, AL.
4512	F	ii.	**Tiffany Darlene Brown** was born 17 Jan 1984 in Lauderdale County, AL.

2686. Matthew Shannon Haataja (*Dorothy (Dottie) Norene Brown[7], Pearl Etta Ticer[6], Roxie Leona Young[5], Mary M. (Polly II) Lindsey[4], Frances (Frankie) Sharp[3], Charles W. Sr.[2], John Sr.[1]*) was born 20 Nov 1966 in Lauderdale County, AL.

Matthew married **Deanne Fay Maples**, daughter of **Earl Wesley Maples** and **Katherine Fay Medley**, 31 Aug 1991 in Lauderdale County, AL. Deanne was born 2 Mar 1967 in Alabama.

4513	M	i.	**Austin Matthew Haataja** was born 10 Nov 1993 in Huntsville, Madison County, AL.

2687. Scott Franklin Haataja (*Dorothy (Dottie) Norene Brown[7], Pearl Etta Ticer[6], Roxie Leona Young[5], Mary M. (Polly II) Lindsey[4], Frances (Frankie) Sharp[3], Charles W. Sr.[2], John Sr.[1]*) was born 12 Feb 1971 in Lauderdale County, AL.

Scott married **Alisha Shay Conner**, daughter of **Steven Eldon Conner** and **Teresa Gaye Hanback**, 1 Dec 1990 in Lauderdale County, AL. Alisha was born 10 Jul 1971 in Lauderdale County, AL.

4514	M	i.	**Evan Drake Haataja** was born 3 May 1990 in Lauderdale County, AL.

2690. Joanna Faith Sanders (*Jo Anna Maupin[7], Hettie Milford[6], Delia (Dee) Young[5], Mary M. (Polly II) Lindsey[4], Frances (Frankie) Sharp[3], Charles W. Sr.[2], John Sr.[1]*).

Joanna married **Brian Thompson**.

2692. Sylvia Marie Becker (*Nancy Delia (Dee) Perkins[7], Etta Lee Milford[6], Delia (Dee) Young[5], Mary M. (Polly II) Lindsey[4], Frances (Frankie) Sharp[3], Charles W. Sr.[2], John Sr.[1]*) was born 28 Jul 1927 in Trumann, AR.

Sylvia married **Thomas Franklin Monroe**. Thomas was born 4 Feb 1920 in Corinth, Alcorn County, MS.

2693. Sybile Vilena Becker (*Nancy Delia (Dee) Perkins[7], Etta Lee Milford[6], Delia (Dee) Young[5], Mary M. (Polly II) Lindsey[4], Frances (Frankie) Sharp[3], Charles W. Sr.[2], John Sr.[1]*) was born 16 Sep 1928 in Trumann, AR.

Sybile married **Andrew M. Glick** 19 Sep 1952 in Elkhart, Elkhart County, IN. Andrew was born 16 Sep 1922 in Holmes County, OH.

2695. Catherine Doris Becker (*Nancy Delia (Dee) Perkins[7], Etta Lee Milford[6], Delia (Dee) Young[5], Mary M. (Polly II) Lindsey[4], Frances (Frankie) Sharp[3], Charles W. Sr.[2], John Sr.[1]*) was born 22 Dec 1940 in Marked Tree, Poinsett County, AR and died in Eminence, MO.

Catherine married ***Unk McGlocklin**.

2696. Anna Lee McCaskill (*Annie Lue Perkins[7], Etta Lee Milford[6], Delia (Dee) Young[5], Mary M. (Polly II) Lindsey[4], Frances (Frankie) Sharp[3], Charles W. Sr.[2], John Sr.[1]*) was born 18 Mar 1940 in Arkansas.

Anna married **Kenny Beard**.

2697. Mary Frances McCaskill (*Annie Lue Perkins[7], Etta Lee Milford[6], Delia (Dee) Young[5], Mary M. (Polly II) Lindsey[4], Frances (Frankie) Sharp[3], Charles W. Sr.[2], John Sr.[1]*) was born 31 Mar 1941.

Mary married **Robert Drew**.

2698. Lloyd Donnell McCaskill (*Annie Lue Perkins[7], Etta Lee Milford[6], Delia (Dee) Young[5], Mary M. (Polly II) Lindsey[4], Frances (Frankie) Sharp[3], Charles W. Sr.[2], John Sr.[1]*) was born 16 Feb 1946.

General Notes: "Baptist Minister...Elijah Young Book..." Sharon Wood

Lloyd married **Sandra Oakley**.

2699. Marion F. McCaskill (*Annie Lue Perkins[7], Etta Lee Milford[6], Delia (Dee) Young[5], Mary M. (Polly II) Lindsey[4], Frances (Frankie) Sharp[3], Charles W. Sr.[2], John Sr.[1]*) was born 14 Apr 1947.

Marion married **Louise Fell**.

2700. Esther Marie McCaskill (*Annie Lue Perkins[7], Etta Lee Milford[6], Delia (Dee) Young[5], Mary M. (Polly II) Lindsey[4], Frances (Frankie) Sharp[3], Charles W. Sr.[2], John Sr.[1]*) was born 25 Aug 1953.

Esther married **Michael Poole**.

General Notes: "Baptist Minister... Elijah Young Book..." Sharon Wood

2701. Julie Kay McCaskill (*Annie Lue Perkins[7], Etta Lee Milford[6], Delia (Dee) Young[5], Mary M. (Polly II) Lindsey[4], Frances (Frankie) Sharp[3], Charles W. Sr.[2], John Sr.[1]*) was born 1 Jun 1955.

Julie married **Richard Woody**.

General Notes: Baptist Minister...Elijah Young Book...sw

2702. Pamela Jean McCaskill (*Annie Lue Perkins[7], Etta Lee Milford[6], Delia (Dee) Young[5], Mary M. (Polly II) Lindsey[4], Frances (Frankie) Sharp[3], Charles W. Sr.[2], John Sr.[1]*) was born 13 Apr 1957.

Pamela married **Kevin Kennedy**.

General Notes: "Baptist Minister...Elijah Young Book..." Sharon Wood

2704. Robert (Bobby) Percy Jones (*Robert Dalton Jones[7], Ada Young[6], Lou Young[5], Mary M. (Polly II) Lindsey[4], Frances (Frankie) Sharp[3], Charles W. Sr.[2], John Sr.[1]*) was born 16 Sep 1940 in Lauderdale County, AL.

Robert married **Nancy Carolyn Balentine**, daughter of **John W. Balentine** and **Myrtle Rogers**, 8 Oct 1961. Nancy was born 15 Dec 1942.

4515	F	i.	**Jennifer Lynn Jones** was born 20 Jul 1964.
+ 4516	F	ii.	**Molly Elizabeth Jones** was born 22 Apr 1970 in Lauderdale County, AL and died 2 Jun 2006 in Lauderdale County, AL.

2705. John Gary Jones (*Robert Dalton Jones[7], Ada Young[6], Lou Young[5], Mary M. (Polly II) Lindsey[4], Frances (Frankie) Sharp[3], Charles W. Sr.[2], John Sr.[1]*) was born 31 May 1947 in Lauderdale County, AL.

John married **Lynn Hendon**.

4517	M	i.	**Garith Brett Jones** was born 22 Jul 1975.
4518	F	ii.	**Brooke Jones** was born 31 Jan 1978.

2706. Jackie Juanita Wright (*Mary Louise Jones[7], Ada Young[6], Lou Young[5], Mary M. (Polly II) Lindsey[4], Frances (Frankie) Sharp[3], Charles W. Sr.[2], John Sr.[1]*) was born 19 Feb 1940 in Lauderdale County, AL.

Jackie married **Harry Hughes (Jitterbug) Thomas**, son of **Robert M. Thomas Sr.** and **Ruby Minor**, 18 Nov 1960 in Lauderdale County, AL. Harry was born 10 Jan 1940 in Lauderdale County, AL, died 7 Aug 1989, and was buried in Greenview Memorial Park, Florence, Lauderdale County, AL.

+ 4519	M	i.	**Percy Hugh Thomas** was born 23 Sep 1961.
4520	M	ii.	**Harry Joel Thomas** was born 1 Nov 1962.
4521	M	iii.	**Robert Jason Thomas** was born 4 Aug 1973.
4522	M	iv.	**John Malcolm Thomas** was born 15 May 1977.

2707. Elinda Gaye Wright (*Mary Louise Jones[7], Ada Young[6], Lou Young[5], Mary M. (Polly II) Lindsey[4], Frances (Frankie) Sharp[3], Charles W. Sr.[2], John Sr.[1]*) was born 9 Sep 1943 in Lauderdale County, AL.

Elinda married **Jerry Lynn Bevis**, son of **Jessie Andrew Bevis II** and **Goldie Sunshine Young**, 23 Dec 1962 in Lauderdale County, AL. Jerry was born 19 Oct 1942 in Lauderdale County, AL.

4523	F	i.	**Christie Lynn Bevis** was born 14 Jun 1966 in Lauderdale County, AL.
+ 4524	F	ii.	**Stacey LeAnn Bevis** was born 24 Jan 1970 in Lauderdale County, AL.

Elinda next married **Paul Robert Austin** 7 Oct 1989 in Lauderdale County, AL. Paul was born 14 Oct 1943 in Lauderdale County, AL.

2708. Brenda Billingsley (*Millard Horace Billingsley[7], Verna Virella Young[6], Lou Young[5], Mary M. (Polly II) Lindsey[4], Frances (Frankie) Sharp[3], Charles W. Sr.[2], John Sr.[1]*) was born 18 Oct 1952.

Brenda married **William Terry Boston** 15 Nov 1975. William was born 27 Jul 1950.

4525	F	i.	**Rachel E. Boston** was born 9 May 1982.
4526	M	ii.	**William Andrew Boston** was born 23 Dec 1984.
4527	M	iii.	**Brian B. Boston** was born 26 Mar 1988.

2709. Beverly Billingsley (*Millard Horace Billingsley[7], Verna Virella Young[6], Lou Young[5], Mary M. (Polly II) Lindsey[4], Frances (Frankie) Sharp[3], Charles W. Sr.[2], John Sr.[1]*) was born 23 Jun 1954.

Beverly married **James H. Powers** 24 Jul 1976. James was born 12 Mar 1947.

4528	M	i.	**Evan James Powers** was born 15 Nov 1981.

2710. Teresa Estell Billingsley (*William Eugene Billingsley[7], Verna Virella Young[6], Lou Young[5], Mary M. (Polly II) Lindsey[4], Frances (Frankie) Sharp[3], Charles W. Sr.[2], John Sr.[1]*) was born 6 Feb 1958.

Teresa married **Edison Traveleterd** in Apr 1986.

4529	M	i.	**Willian Dane Traveleterd** was born 4 Jun 1991.

2711. Elaine Renee Billingsley (*William Eugene Billingsley[7], Verna Virella Young[6], Lou Young[5], Mary M. (Polly II) Lindsey[4], Frances (Frankie) Sharp[3], Charles W. Sr.[2], John Sr.[1]*) was born 13 Mar 1961.

Elaine married **Phillip Summers** in 1983.

+ 4530	F	i.	**Shelly Summers** was born 13 May 1984.

Elaine next married **Mark Forrest** in 1987.

2712. Brian Eugene Billingsley (*William Eugene Billingsley*[7]*, Verna Virella Young*[6]*, Lou Young*[5]*, Mary M. (Polly II) Lindsey*[4]*, Frances (Frankie) Sharp*[3]*, Charles W. Sr.*[2]*, John Sr.*[1]) was born 6 Jun 1967.

Brian married **Bridget Knoll** in Nov 1992.
4531 M   i.   **William Marshall Billingsley** was born in Nov 1994.
4532 F   ii.   **Catherine Marie Billingsley** was born 28 Jan 1996.

2713. Donna Faye Billingsley (*Grady Earl Billingsley*[7]*, Verna Virella Young*[6]*, Lou Young*[5]*, Mary M. (Polly II) Lindsey*[4]*, Frances (Frankie) Sharp*[3]*, Charles W. Sr.*[2]*, John Sr.*[1]) was born 22 Sep 1956.

Donna married **Victor Edward Philippi** 26 Dec 1975. Victor was born 17 Jun 1955.
4533 M   i.   **Victor Grady Philippi** was born 22 Feb 1980.
4534 M   ii.   **Justin Edward (Tiger) Philippi** was born 20 Mar 1981.

2715. Deborah Alliene Billingsley (*Thomas Moore Billingsley*[7]*, Verna Virella Young*[6]*, Lou Young*[5]*, Mary M. (Polly II) Lindsey*[4]*, Frances (Frankie) Sharp*[3]*, Charles W. Sr.*[2]*, John Sr.*[1]) was born 22 Nov 1962.

Deborah married **Ross Cornelius Jr.** 20 Sep 1986. Ross was born 11 Jan 1954.

2716. Gary Ellis Grigsby (*Ruth Vernet Witt*[7]*, Mary Etta Young*[6]*, Lou Young*[5]*, Mary M. (Polly II) Lindsey*[4]*, Frances (Frankie) Sharp*[3]*, Charles W. Sr.*[2]*, John Sr.*[1]) was born 25 Dec 1952 in Lauderdale County, AL.

Gary married **Linda Elaine Wilkinson**, daughter of **Robert L. Wilkinson** and **Mable Robertson**, 1 Dec 1976 in Lauderdale County, AL. Linda was born 10 Jun 1955 in Lauderdale County, AL.

2717. Thomas Keith Grigsby (*Ruth Vernet Witt*[7]*, Mary Etta Young*[6]*, Lou Young*[5]*, Mary M. (Polly II) Lindsey*[4]*, Frances (Frankie) Sharp*[3]*, Charles W. Sr.*[2]*, John Sr.*[1]) was born 27 Oct 1955 in Lauderdale County, AL.

Thomas married **Vickey Sue Johns** 22 Aug 1980. Vickey was born 2 Jul 1957.
4535 F   i.   **Lindsey Beth Grigsby** was born 6 Jan 1984 in Lauderdale County, AL.
4536 M   ii.   **Jarred Paul Grigsby** was born 20 Mar 1987 in Lauderdale County, AL.

2718. Cheryl Ann Grigsby (*Ruth Vernet Witt*[7]*, Mary Etta Young*[6]*, Lou Young*[5]*, Mary M. (Polly II) Lindsey*[4]*, Frances (Frankie) Sharp*[3]*, Charles W. Sr.*[2]*, John Sr.*[1]) was born 13 Jun 1958 in Lauderdale County, AL.

Cheryl married **Wade Linville Austin** 12 Jun 1987. Wade was born 19 Jan 1957.
4537 F   i.   **Ambrey Michelle Austin** was born 22 Oct 1988 in Lauderdale County, AL.
4538 F   ii.   **Allison Brooke Austin** was born 13 Jun 1991 in Lauderdale County, AL.

2719. Tony Paul Grigsby (*Ruth Vernet Witt*[7]*, Mary Etta Young*[6]*, Lou Young*[5]*, Mary M. (Polly II) Lindsey*[4]*, Frances (Frankie) Sharp*[3]*, Charles W. Sr.*[2]*, John Sr.*[1]) was born 22 Jul 1964 in Lauderdale County, AL.

Tony married **Lori Deanna Ledbetter** 22 Jan 1994. Lori was born 10 Mar 1967.

2720. Sandra Dee Witt (*James Arnold Witt*[7]*, Mary Etta Young*[6]*, Lou Young*[5]*, Mary M. (Polly II) Lindsey*[4]*, Frances (Frankie) Sharp*[3]*, Charles W. Sr.*[2]*, John Sr.*[1]) was born 12 Nov 1951 in Lauderdale County, AL.

Sandra married **Roy Lee Baskins**, son of **Oscar Edward Baskins** and **Elsie Mae Arnold**, 2 Sep 1972 in Lauderdale County, AL. Roy was born 18 Jul 1952 in Lauderdale County, AL.
4539 M   i.   **Jason Roy Baskins** was born 8 Mar 1976 in Lauderdale County, AL.
4540 M   ii.   **Justin Dean Baskins** was born 5 Dec 1978 in Lauderdale County, AL.
4541 M   iii.   **Jordan Lee Baskins** was born 23 Jan 1981 in Lauderdale County, AL.

2721. James Michael Witt (*James Arnold Witt*[7], *Mary Etta Young*[6], *Lou Young*[5], *Mary M. (Polly II) Lindsey*[4], *Frances (Frankie) Sharp*[3], *Charles W. Sr.*[2], *John Sr.*[1]) was born 23 Feb 1953 in Lauderdale County, AL.

James married **Terrye Lynn McGee** 27 Jul 1973 in Lauderdale County, AL. Terrye was born 15 Feb 1953 in Lauderdale County, AL.

James next married **Judy Ann Lawrence**, daughter of **Larken Glasto Lawrence** and **Dawanda Lou Wynn**, 28 May 1999 in Savannah, TN. Judy was born 5 Oct 1955 in Chicago, IL.

2722. Sharon Lee Witt (*James Arnold Witt*[7], *Mary Etta Young*[6], *Lou Young*[5], *Mary M. (Polly II) Lindsey*[4], *Frances (Frankie) Sharp*[3], *Charles W. Sr.*[2], *John Sr.*[1]) was born 26 Jan 1957 in Lauderdale County, AL.

Sharon married **Cecil Gerald Crunk Jr.**, son of **Cecil Gerald Crunk Sr.** and **Lorene Williams**, 11 Jul 1975 in Lauderdale County, AL. Cecil was born 11 Nov 1956 in Lauderdale County, AL.
4542 F i. **Amanda (Mandy) Lee Crunk** was born 16 Feb 1976.

Sharon next married **Melvin James Burns** 21 Jul 1982. Melvin was born 8 Apr 1945.

2723. Jennifer Joy Witt (*Virgil David Witt*[7], *Mary Etta Young*[6], *Lou Young*[5], *Mary M. (Polly II) Lindsey*[4], *Frances (Frankie) Sharp*[3], *Charles W. Sr.*[2], *John Sr.*[1]) was born 2 Jan 1957 in Lauderdale County, AL.

Jennifer married **Robert Archie McCarley Jr.**, son of **Robert Archie McCarley Sr.** and **Olive Slaton**, 30 Jun 1975 in Lauderdale County, AL. Robert was born 27 May 1955 in Lauderdale County, AL.

Jennifer next married **Barry Wayne Quillen**, son of **Alfred H. Quillen** and **Marjorie Burks**, 30 Mar 1978 in Lauderdale County, AL. Barry was born 4 Aug 1956 in Lauderdale County, AL.

Jennifer next married **John Warren Nichols** 9 Jun 1987. John was born 10 Apr 1959.
4543 F i. **Haley Elizabeth Nichols** was born 16 Oct 1983.
4544 M ii. **John Austin Nichols** was born 18 Jun 1994.

2724. David Lynn Witt (*Virgil David Witt*[7], *Mary Etta Young*[6], *Lou Young*[5], *Mary M. (Polly II) Lindsey*[4], *Frances (Frankie) Sharp*[3], *Charles W. Sr.*[2], *John Sr.*[1]) was born 3 Jun 1960 in Lauderdale County, AL.

David married **Tracey Leigh Babock**, daughter of **Roger L. Babock** and **Paula *Unk**, 16 Jun 1985. Tracey was born 9 Sep 1963 in Lauderdale County, AL, died 11 May 2004, and was buried in Tri-Cities Memorial Gardens, Florence, Lauderdale County, AL.
4545 M i. **David Lee Witt** was born 7 Jul 1988.
4546 F ii. **Rachel Lynn Witt** was born 28 Apr 1991.
4547 M iii. **Andrew Michael Witt** was born 5 Jan 1993.

2725. Glenda Jean Wallace (*Ila Jean Witt*[7], *Mary Etta Young*[6], *Lou Young*[5], *Mary M. (Polly II) Lindsey*[4], *Frances (Frankie) Sharp*[3], *Charles W. Sr.*[2], *John Sr.*[1]) was born 14 Sep 1952.

Glenda married **Thomas Dewey Crossno** 23 Aug 1986.
4548 F i. **Rachel Amanda Crossno** was born 30 Jun 1987.
4549 F ii. **Kimberly Kaylee Crossno** was born 27 May 1989.
4550 F iii. **Melanie Erin Crossno** was born 29 Sep 1990.

2726. Dorman Richey Wallace (*Ila Jean Witt*[7], *Mary Etta Young*[6], *Lou Young*[5], *Mary M. (Polly II) Lindsey*[4], *Frances (Frankie) Sharp*[3], *Charles W. Sr.*[2], *John Sr.*[1]) was born 19 Dec 1956.

Dorman married **Theresa Renee Gates** 17 Feb 1978. Theresa was born 17 Sep 1959.
4551 F i. **Victoria Leigh Wallace** was born 25 Oct 1978.
4552 M ii. **Andrew Gates Wallace** was born 4 Sep 1981.
4553 F iii. **Elizabeth Marie Wallace** was born 15 Dec 1982.

Dorman next married **Kim Marie Schlafer** 2 Aug 1993. Kim was born 4 Aug 1961.

2727. Roger Lance Wallace (*Ila Jean Witt*[7], *Mary Etta Young*[6], *Lou Young*[5], *Mary M. (Polly II) Lindsey*[4], *Frances (Frankie) Sharp*[3], *Charles W. Sr.*[2], *John Sr.*[1]) was born 5 Jan 1958.

Roger married **Suzanne Ray Robertson** 26 Oct 1990. Suzanne was born 25 Jun 1965.
4554 M i. **Clinton Glenn Wallace** was born 23 Jan 1992.
4555 M ii. **Jacob Robert Wallace** was born 9 Sep 1995.

2728. Douglas Gene Olive Jr. (*Betty Lou Witt*[7], *Mary Etta Young*[6], *Lou Young*[5], *Mary M. (Polly II) Lindsey*[4], *Frances (Frankie) Sharp*[3], *Charles W. Sr.*[2], *John Sr.*[1]) was born 4 Oct 1954 in Lauderdale County, AL.

Douglas married **Mary Howard**, daughter of **Jimmy Dale Howard I** and **Mary Jo Campbell**, 5 Dec 1972 in Lauderdale County, AL. Mary was born 28 Nov 1954 in Knox County, TN.
+ 4556 F i. **Mary Lou (Bonnie) Olive** was born 11 Jul 1973 in Lauderdale County, AL.
4557 M ii. **Brett Seaf Olive** was born 31 Aug 1982 in Lauderdale County, AL.

2729. Dona Sue Olive (*Betty Lou Witt*[7], *Mary Etta Young*[6], *Lou Young*[5], *Mary M. (Polly II) Lindsey*[4], *Frances (Frankie) Sharp*[3], *Charles W. Sr.*[2], *John Sr.*[1]) was born 26 Sep 1959 in Lauderdale County, AL.

Dona married **Terry Wade Wright**, son of **Olin E. Wright** and **Effie Holt**, 29 Oct 1973 in Lauderdale County, AL. Terry was born 16 Mar 1956 in Lauderdale County, AL.
4558 F i. **Lauren Casey Wright** was born 10 Oct 1982.
4559 M ii. **Chase Wade Wright** was born 24 Jul 1984.

2730. Karen Anne Wallace (*Carolyn Sue Witt*[7], *Mary Etta Young*[6], *Lou Young*[5], *Mary M. (Polly II) Lindsey*[4], *Frances (Frankie) Sharp*[3], *Charles W. Sr.*[2], *John Sr.*[1]) was born 11 Dec 1958.

Karen married **William Jay Kilburn** 22 Apr 1976. William was born 19 Mar 1956.
4560 M i. **William Gregory (Greg) Kilburn** was born 11 Dec 1977.
4561 M ii. **Joshua (Josh) Wallace Kilburn** was born 22 Jul 1980.
4562 M iii. **Dustin Jay Kilburn** was born 6 Sep 1982.

Karen next married **Gary Melvin Addison** 14 Feb 1990. Gary was born 22 Jul 1950.
4563 M i. **Shane Thomas Witt Addison** was born 15 Mar 1992.

2731. Brenda Brooke Wallace (*Carolyn Sue Witt*[7], *Mary Etta Young*[6], *Lou Young*[5], *Mary M. (Polly II) Lindsey*[4], *Frances (Frankie) Sharp*[3], *Charles W. Sr.*[2], *John Sr.*[1]) was born 20 Jan 1961.

Brenda married **Eric Douglas Metz** 3 Sep 1983. Eric was born 5 Mar 1959.
4564 M i. **Derek Mark Metz** was born 23 Nov 1985.
4565 M ii. **Jeremy Tyler Metz** was born 19 Sep 1992.

2733. Amie Alice Witt (*Thomas Clyde (T. C.) Witt Jr.*[7], *Mary Etta Young*[6], *Lou Young*[5], *Mary M. (Polly II) Lindsey*[4], *Frances (Frankie) Sharp*[3], *Charles W. Sr.*[2], *John Sr.*[1]) was born 23 May 1971 in Lauderdale County, AL.

Amie married **Jeff Thompson** in Birmingham, Jefferson County, AL.

2734. Andrea Jill Witt (*Thomas Clyde (T. C.) Witt Jr.*[7], *Mary Etta Young*[6], *Lou Young*[5], *Mary M. (Polly II) Lindsey*[4], *Frances (Frankie) Sharp*[3], *Charles W. Sr.*[2], *John Sr.*[1]) was born 11 Jul 1976 in Lauderdale County, AL.

Andrea married **Robert Eric Jones**, son of **Glover L. Jones Jr.** and **Carolyn Gordy**, 2 Sep 2000 in Birmingham, Jefferson County, AL. Robert was born 30 Aug 1972 in Fort Oglethorpe, GA.

2735. Melinda Lane Sharp (*Mary Etta Witt*[7], *Mary Etta Young*[6], *Lou Young*[5], *Mary M. (Polly II) Lindsey*[4], *Frances (Frankie) Sharp*[3], *Charles W. Sr.*[2], *John Sr.*[1]) was born 19 Dec 1962 in Lauderdale County, AL.

Melinda married **James Christopher Daniel**, son of **Charles A. Daniel** and **Jonel Isom**, 31 May 1986 in Lauderdale County, AL. James was born 17 Mar 1963 in Jefferson County, AL.

2736. Jeffrey Lance Sharp (*Mary Etta Witt⁷, Mary Etta Young⁶, Lou Young⁵, Mary M. (Polly II) Lindsey⁴, Frances (Frankie) Sharp³, Charles W. Sr.², John Sr.¹*) was born 17 Mar 1966 in Lauderdale County, AL.

Jeffrey married **Tracey Ann Cromwell**, daughter of **Robert W. Cromwell** and **Dianna Smith**, 16 Jan 1986 in Lauderdale County, AL. Tracey was born 1 Dec 1967 in St. Louis, MO.

Jeffrey next married **Tamela Green**, daughter of **Earl Green** and **Arnelle Parrish**, 29 Aug 1997. Tamela was born 13 Aug 1969 in Lauderdale County, AL.

4566 M   i.   **Dylan Lance Sharp** was born 11 May 2000.
4567 M   ii.   **Dedan Lee Sharp** was born 17 Sep 2004.

2737. Charles Thomas Young (*Virginia Francine Witt⁷, Mary Etta Young⁶, Lou Young⁵, Mary M. (Polly II) Lindsey⁴, Frances (Frankie) Sharp³, Charles W. Sr.², John Sr.¹*) was born 22 Apr 1965 in Lauderdale County, AL.

Charles married **Mary Paige Williams** 9 Aug 1991. Mary was born 3 Feb 1968.

2738. James Damon Young (*Virginia Francine Witt⁷, Mary Etta Young⁶, Lou Young⁵, Mary M. (Polly II) Lindsey⁴, Frances (Frankie) Sharp³, Charles W. Sr.², John Sr.¹*) was born 16 Mar 1966 in Lauderdale County, AL.

James married **Angie Tobias**, daughter of **James Tobias** and **Billie Jean**, 15 Sep 1990 in Memphis, Shelby County, TN. Angie was born 23 Apr 1965 in Memphis, Shelby County, TN.

4568 M   i.   **Colton Will Young** was born 22 Apr 1995 in Cartersville, TN.
4569 M   ii.   **Grayson Tobias Young** was born 31 Jan 1998 in Cartersville, TN.

2739. Chadwick Todd Witt (*Danny Price Witt⁷, Mary Etta Young⁶, Lou Young⁵, Mary M. (Polly II) Lindsey⁴, Frances (Frankie) Sharp³, Charles W. Sr.², John Sr.¹*) was born 2 Jul 1974 in Lauderdale County, AL.

Chadwick married **Amanda Marie Purser**, daughter of **Wayne Purser** and **Christina Karl**, 26 May 2001 in Lauderdale County, AL. Amanda was born 28 Feb 1980 in Lauderdale County, AL.

2741. Jody Aaron Cypert (*Shirley Diane Witt⁷, Mary Etta Young⁶, Lou Young⁵, Mary M. (Polly II) Lindsey⁴, Frances (Frankie) Sharp³, Charles W. Sr.², John Sr.¹*) was born 7 Dec 1972 in Lauderdale County, AL.

Jody married **Andrea Stults** in Lauderdale County, AL.

2742. Jeanna Luanne Posey (*Billie Faye Lovelace⁷, Della Young⁶, Lou Young⁵, Mary M. (Polly II) Lindsey⁴, Frances (Frankie) Sharp³, Charles W. Sr.², John Sr.¹*) was born 4 Oct 1957 in Long Beach, CA.

Jeanna married **Peter (Pete) John Opsteph** 20 Aug 1978 in Riverside, CA. Peter was born 5 Oct 1950 in Dortrectch, Holland.

4570 M   i.   **Michael Ryan Opsteph** was born 13 Jan 1980.
4571 M   ii.   **Paul Matthew Opsteph** was born 27 Sep 1985.

Jeanna next married **Dr. Edwin Edillion**.
4572 M   i.   **Eric Edwin Edillion** was born 31 Oct 1991.

2743. George Jeffery Posey (*Billie Faye Lovelace⁷, Della Young⁶, Lou Young⁵, Mary M. (Polly II) Lindsey⁴, Frances (Frankie) Sharp³, Charles W. Sr.², John Sr.¹*) was born 25 Sep 1958 in Long Beach, CA.

George married **Christina Ann Hughes** 20 Jul 1985 in Walnut, CA. Christina was born 1 Sep 1959.
4573 M   i.   **Davis Posey**.

2744. Donna Patience Posey (*Billie Faye Lovelace⁷, Della Young⁶, Lou Young⁵, Mary M. (Polly II) Lindsey⁴, Frances (Frankie) Sharp³, Charles W. Sr.², John Sr.¹*) was born 5 Apr 1960 in Long Beach, CA.

Donna married **James DeBoor** 19 Sep 1981 in Placentia, Orange County, CA. James was born 24 Jul 1961 in Westwood, Los Angeles County, CA.

4574 F i. **Chelyse Danielle DeBoor** was born 25 Sep 1989 in Anaheim, CA.
4575 F ii. **Breanne Justine DeBoor** was born 28 Jun 1991 in Anaheim, CA.

Donna next married **Robert Nichols**. Robert was born in California.

2745. Sherry Venetia Collum (*Barbara Jean Lovelace[7], Della Young[6], Lou Young[5], Mary M. (Polly II) Lindsey[4], Frances (Frankie) Sharp[3], Charles W. Sr.[2], John Sr.[1]*) was born 18 Dec 1959 in Lauderdale County, AL.

Sherry married **Robert Wesley Butler**, son of **William Gilbert Butler** and **Winifred Lee Thompson**, 20 May 1989 in Lauderdale County, AL. Robert was born 18 Nov 1958 in Lauderdale County, AL.

4576 F i. **Jean Thompson Butler** was born 4 Oct 1996 in Montgomery County, AL.

2746. Cynthia (Cindy) Lynn Collum (*Barbara Jean Lovelace[7], Della Young[6], Lou Young[5], Mary M. (Polly II) Lindsey[4], Frances (Frankie) Sharp[3], Charles W. Sr.[2], John Sr.[1]*) was born 17 Feb 1963 in Lauderdale County, AL.

Cynthia married **Steven Douglas White**, son of **Robert Vassaders** and **Dora Connie White**, 13 Nov 1993 in Lauderdale County, AL. Steven was born 26 Sep 1961 in Choctow County, AL.

4577 M i. **James Edward White** was born 11 Mar 1986 in Mobile, AL.
4578 M ii. **Andrew Robert White** was born 26 Feb 1988 in Mobile, AL.
4579 F iii. **Stephanie Jane White** was born 14 Apr 1998 in Lauderdale County, AL.

2752. Janice Marlene Sharp (*Virgil Lee Sharp[7], Pearl V. Young[6], Lee Jackson Young[5], Mary M. (Polly II) Lindsey[4], Frances (Frankie) Sharp[3], Charles W. Sr.[2], John Sr.[1]*) was born 15 Sep 1950 in Mishawaka, St Joseph County, IN.

Janice married **William Lynn Taylor** 10 Oct 1980 in Mishawaka, St Joseph County, IN. William was born 31 Oct 1948 in Delaware.

4580 M i. **Christopher (Chris) Lee Taylor** was born 20 Aug 1981 in Oregon.
4581 M ii. **Andy Timothy Taylor** was born 8 Jun 1988 in Oregon.

2753. Dale Dalton Sharp (*Virgil Lee Sharp[7], Pearl V. Young[6], Lee Jackson Young[5], Mary M. (Polly II) Lindsey[4], Frances (Frankie) Sharp[3], Charles W. Sr.[2], John Sr.[1]*) was born 30 Oct 1951 in Mishawaka, St Joseph County, IN.

Dale married **Malinda *Unk**.

4582 M i. **Jerome Dale Sharp** was born 6 May 1971.
4583 F ii. **Jamie Christine Sharp** was born 22 Nov 1974.
4584 M iii. **Joshua David Sharp** was born 13 May 1977.

2754. Joyce Christine Sharp (*Virgil Lee Sharp[7], Pearl V. Young[6], Lee Jackson Young[5], Mary M. (Polly II) Lindsey[4], Frances (Frankie) Sharp[3], Charles W. Sr.[2], John Sr.[1]*) was born 10 Mar 1955 in Mishawaka, St Joseph County, IN.

Joyce married **Dennis Olsen** 24 Aug 1984 in Mishawaka, St Joseph County, IN. Dennis was born 5 Jun 1948.

4585 F i. **Lindsey Ann Olsen** was born 6 Nov 1981.
4586 F ii. **Lacey Kristil Olsen** was born 8 Dec 1988.
4587 F iii. **Kelsey Leigh Olsen** was born 3 Oct 1989.

2756. Cara Estelle Rinehart (*Wallace Harold Rinehart[7], Ada Evelyn Wood[6], Louisa F. Lindsey[5], John S. Lindsey[4], Frances (Frankie) Sharp[3], Charles W. Sr.[2], John Sr.[1]*) was born 5 Feb 1965 in Washington, D. C..

Cara married **Raymond Douglas Sampson Jr.** 27 Mar 1983 in College Park, MD.

4588 F i. **Candace April Sampson** was born in 1983.
4589 M ii. **Randall Earl Sampson** was born in 1987.

Cara next married **Wayne Joseph Strianese** about 1994. Wayne was born in 1965.

4590 M i. **Ryan Wayne Strianese** was born in 1995.

2757. Pamela Michelle Rinehart (*William Porter Rinehart*[7]*, Ada Evelyn Wood*[6]*, Louisa F. Lindsey*[5]*, John S. Lindsey*[4]*, Frances (Frankie) Sharp*[3]*, Charles W. Sr.*[2]*, John Sr.*[1]) was born 21 Sep 1961 in Odessa, Ector County, TX.

Pamela married **David Todd White** 22 May 1982.
4591 M i. **David Black White**.
4592 M ii. **Drew Grayson White**.

2759. Brian Earl Rinehart (*William Porter Rinehart*[7]*, Ada Evelyn Wood*[6]*, Louisa F. Lindsey*[5]*, John S. Lindsey*[4]*, Frances (Frankie) Sharp*[3]*, Charles W. Sr.*[2]*, John Sr.*[1]) was born 25 Jul 1967 in Snyder, Scurry County, TX.

Brian married **Tracie Rene Axelson**.
4593 M i. **Brian Keith Rinehart**.
4594 F ii. **Tayler Denea Rinehart**.

2761. Teresa Kay Meador (*Evelyn May Wood*[7]*, Lemuel Carl Wood*[6]*, Louisa F. Lindsey*[5]*, John S. Lindsey*[4]*, Frances (Frankie) Sharp*[3]*, Charles W. Sr.*[2]*, John Sr.*[1]) was born 19 Aug 1947 in Snyder, Scurry County, TX.

Teresa married **Gaylen Wayne Dabbs** 3 Aug 1969.
4595 M i. **Damon Wayne Dabbs** was born 16 Apr 1967.
4596 F ii. **Andrea Gayle Dabbs** was born 19 Aug 1970.

2762. Michael Van Meador (*Evelyn May Wood*[7]*, Lemuel Carl Wood*[6]*, Louisa F. Lindsey*[5]*, John S. Lindsey*[4]*, Frances (Frankie) Sharp*[3]*, Charles W. Sr.*[2]*, John Sr.*[1]) was born 6 Jul 1949 in Snyder, Scurry County, TX.

Michael married **Shirley Jeanette Graham** 6 Aug 1974.
4597 F i. **Melissa Shawn Meador** was born 21 Jul 1975 in Ruidoso, NM.
4598 M ii. **Michael Shane Meador** was born 28 May 1978 in Roswell, NM.

2763. Karen Durelle Meador (*Evelyn May Wood*[7]*, Lemuel Carl Wood*[6]*, Louisa F. Lindsey*[5]*, John S. Lindsey*[4]*, Frances (Frankie) Sharp*[3]*, Charles W. Sr.*[2]*, John Sr.*[1]) was born 10 Aug 1950 in Snyder, Scurry County, TX.

Karen married **Francis Jean Chapman** 12 Nov 1966.
4599 F i. **Barbara Michelle Chapman** was born 30 Jun 1970 in Landsthul, Germany.
4600 M ii. **Jason Carl Chapman** was born 26 Feb 1974 in El Paso, El Paso County, TX.

2764. Daryl Wayne Meador (*Evelyn May Wood*[7]*, Lemuel Carl Wood*[6]*, Louisa F. Lindsey*[5]*, John S. Lindsey*[4]*, Frances (Frankie) Sharp*[3]*, Charles W. Sr.*[2]*, John Sr.*[1]) was born 3 Mar 1952 in Snyder, Scurry County, TX.

Daryl married **Sharon Kay Dollins** 1 Mar 1974.
4601 M i. **Christopher Bryan Meador** was born 1 Jul 1975 in Snyder, Scurry County, TX.
4602 F ii. **Stephanie Kay Meador** was born 15 Nov 1976 in Snyder, Scurry County, TX.

2765. Daphna Michelle Meador (*Evelyn May Wood*[7]*, Lemuel Carl Wood*[6]*, Louisa F. Lindsey*[5]*, John S. Lindsey*[4]*, Frances (Frankie) Sharp*[3]*, Charles W. Sr.*[2]*, John Sr.*[1]) was born 14 Nov 1954 in Snyder, Scurry County, TX.

Daphna married **David Allen Dillaka** 5 Feb 1975.
4603 M i. **Jonathon Van Burton** was born 11 Sep 1971 in Colorado City, TX.

2766. David Carl Wood (*Daryl Elmer Wood*[7]*, Lemuel Carl Wood*[6]*, Louisa F. Lindsey*[5]*, John S. Lindsey*[4]*, Frances (Frankie) Sharp*[3]*, Charles W. Sr.*[2]*, John Sr.*[1]) was born 27 May 1954 in Texas.

David married **Zena Elaine Johnson** 25 Jul 1975.

2768. James Thomas McRae Jr. (*Laverne Bruce[7], Viney Viola Sharp[6], Robert Patton[5], James (Jim) Charles Sr.[4], Adron (Edwin/Ade) Sr.[3], Charles W. Sr.[2], John Sr.[1]*) was born 18 Aug 1922.

James married **Thelma Jean White**, daughter of **Merrill Cantrell White** and **Lela Mae Dacus**, 12 Jul 1948 in Birmingham, Jefferson County, AL. Thelma was born 31 May 1928 in York, AL.
+ 4604 M i. **James Robert McRae** was born 22 May 1949 in Birmingham, Jefferson County, AL.
+ 4605 F ii. **Gail Jeane McRae** was born 15 Nov 1950 in Birmingham, Jefferson County, AL.
+ 4606 F iii. **Marsha Laurene McRae** was born 25 May 1955 in Birmingham, Jefferson County, AL.
+ 4607 M iv. **William Merrill McRae** was born 10 Apr 1959 in Fairfield, AL.

2770. Donald K. McRae (*Laverne Bruce[7], Viney Viola Sharp[6], Robert Patton[5], James (Jim) Charles Sr.[4], Adron (Edwin/Ade) Sr.[3], Charles W. Sr.[2], John Sr.[1]*).

Donald married **Carol Johnson** 14 Jun 1956.

2772. Robert (Bob) C. Wesson (*Patricia Bruce[7], Viney Viola Sharp[6], Robert Patton[5], James (Jim) Charles Sr.[4], Adron (Edwin/Ade) Sr.[3], Charles W. Sr.[2], John Sr.[1]*) was born 3 Jul 1926 in Birmingham, Jefferson County, AL.

Robert married **Betty Jane Bonner** 15 Mar 1947.

2773. Mary Sue Bruce (*Lewis Bruce[7], Viney Viola Sharp[6], Robert Patton[5], James (Jim) Charles Sr.[4], Adron (Edwin/Ade) Sr.[3], Charles W. Sr.[2], John Sr.[1]*) was born 16 Jun 1923 in Lauderdale County, AL.

Mary married **James Thomas Darby**, son of **Joe White Darby** and **Kathy Lou Carroll**, 21 Jun 1946. James was born 13 Dec 1920 in Lauderdale County, AL.
+ 4608 F i. **Susan Rebecca Darby** was born 2 Oct 1953 in Lauderdale County, AL.
+ 4609 M ii. **James Bruce Darby** was born 27 Dec 1956 in Lauderdale County, AL.

2774. Francis Laurene Bruce (*Lewis Bruce[7], Viney Viola Sharp[6], Robert Patton[5], James (Jim) Charles Sr.[4], Adron (Edwin/Ade) Sr.[3], Charles W. Sr.[2], John Sr.[1]*) was born 10 Apr 1927 in Lauderdale County, AL.

Francis married **James W. Wallace Sr.**, son of **Martin W. Wallace** and **Mary Jane Blair**, 21 Dec 1946 in Lauderdale County, AL. James was born 2 Aug 1926 in Lauderdale County, AL.
+ 4610 M i. **James W. Wallace Jr.** was born 28 Aug 1951 in Lauderdale County, AL.

2775. Glenell Malsbury (*Nellie Mae Pickens[7], Carrie Eudora Sharp[6], Robert Patton[5], James (Jim) Charles Sr.[4], Adron (Edwin/Ade) Sr.[3], Charles W. Sr.[2], John Sr.[1]*) was born 3 Jan 1930 in Shawnee, OK.

Glenell married **Joe Dare Owens** 10 Aug 1949.
+ 4611 F i. **Susan Owens** was born 4 Dec 1951 in Inglewood, CA.
+ 4612 F ii. **Julia Owens** was born 2 Apr 1954 in Bartsville, OK.

2776. Margaret Dugger (*Stella Iown Pickens[7], Carrie Eudora Sharp[6], Robert Patton[5], James (Jim) Charles Sr.[4], Adron (Edwin/Ade) Sr.[3], Charles W. Sr.[2], John Sr.[1]*) was born 9 Feb 1922 in Lauderdale County, AL and died 13 Dec 1970.

Margaret married **Paul F. Coker** 1 Sep 1956.

2778. Gordon F. Dugger (*Stella Iown Pickens[7], Carrie Eudora Sharp[6], Robert Patton[5], James (Jim) Charles Sr.[4], Adron (Edwin/Ade) Sr.[3], Charles W. Sr.[2], John Sr.[1]*) was born 11 Apr 1930.

Gordon married **Carol Jean Morrison** 28 Sep 1949.
+ 4613 F i. **Mary Sue Dugger** was born 13 Mar 1955 in Cincinnati, OH.

2787. Dona Gail Sharp (*Joseph Patton[7], Oscar Eldred[6], Robert Patton[5], James (Jim) Charles Sr.[4], Adron (Edwin/Ade) Sr.[3], Charles W. Sr.[2], John Sr.[1]*) was born 8 Feb 1957.

Dona married **Andy Wooten** 23 Apr 1976.

4614 M i. **Drew Wooten** was born 8 Feb 1979.

4615 F ii. **Natalie Jo Wooten** was born 24 Mar 1982.

2790. Robert H. Wilkinson Jr. (*Gwendolyn Waggener*[7], *Annie Inez Sharp*[6], *Robert Patton*[5], *James (Jim) Charles Sr.*[4], *Adron (Edwin/Ade) Sr.*[3], *Charles W. Sr.*[2], *John Sr.*[1]) was born 3 Oct 1958.

Robert married **Alice Jean French**. Alice was born 28 Aug 1960.

2791. Mary Ann Wilkinson (*Gwendolyn Waggener*[7], *Annie Inez Sharp*[6], *Robert Patton*[5], *James (Jim) Charles Sr.*[4], *Adron (Edwin/Ade) Sr.*[3], *Charles W. Sr.*[2], *John Sr.*[1]) was born 28 Oct 1960.

Mary married **Kenneth Clark**.

4616 F i. **Ashley Michele Clark** was born 3 Feb 1980.

Mary next married **Stanley Pendley**.

2793. Richard Lewis Cobb (*Barbara Ann Rochelle*[7], *Annie Inez Sharp*[6], *Robert Patton*[5], *James (Jim) Charles Sr.*[4], *Adron (Edwin/Ade) Sr.*[3], *Charles W. Sr.*[2], *John Sr.*[1]) was born 26 Mar 1962 in Memphis, Shelby County, TN.

Richard married **Tami Lynn Kemp** 12 Sep 1987.

2794. Roy Egbert McCorkle III (*Mary Virginia Givens*[7], *Ida Lois Sharp*[6], *Robert Patton*[5], *James (Jim) Charles Sr.*[4], *Adron (Edwin/Ade) Sr.*[3], *Charles W. Sr.*[2], *John Sr.*[1]) was born 13 Jun 1944 in Colbert County, AL.

Roy married **Marilyn Stevenson** 30 Aug 1969. Marilyn was born 24 Apr 1947.

4617 F i. **Allison Miller McCorkle** was born 4 Apr 1972.

4618 F ii. **Courtney Ann McCorkle** was born 18 Apr 1974.

2795. Mary Thomas (Tommie) McCarley (*Mary Virginia Givens*[7], *Ida Lois Sharp*[6], *Robert Patton*[5], *James (Jim) Charles Sr.*[4], *Adron (Edwin/Ade) Sr.*[3], *Charles W. Sr.*[2], *John Sr.*[1]) was born 12 Mar 1947 in Sheffield, Colbert County, AL.

Mary married **William Eugene Farmer Sr.**, son of **Joseph Eugene Farmer** and **Addie Lou Williams**, 29 Jan 1966. William was born 16 May 1945 in Colbert County, AL.

+ 4619 F i. **Mary Francis Farmer** was born 1 Sep 1966 in Florence, Lauderdale County, AL.

+ 4620 F ii. **Cheri Lynn Farmer** was born 27 May 1968 in Lauderdale County, AL.

4621 M iii. **William Eugene Farmer Jr.** was born 23 Jan 1974.

Mary next married **Robert E. Imhoff** 19 Jun 1981.

2796. Jackie Leigh McCarley (*Mary Virginia Givens*[7], *Ida Lois Sharp*[6], *Robert Patton*[5], *James (Jim) Charles Sr.*[4], *Adron (Edwin/Ade) Sr.*[3], *Charles W. Sr.*[2], *John Sr.*[1]) was born 8 Nov 1951 in Sheffield, Colbert County, AL.

Jackie married **Jack Leory Grissom**, son of **Dexter Grissom** and **Nancy *Unk**, 6 Jun 1970 in Colbert County, AL. Jack was born 9 May 1946 in Franklin County, AL.

4622 F i. **Mary Leigh Grissom** was born 27 Sep 1973.

4623 F ii. **Anna Kathryn Grissom** was born 13 Jun 1977.

4624 M iii. **Jacob Grissom** was born 16 Mar 1979.

2797. Kerry Ann McCarley (*Mary Virginia Givens*[7], *Ida Lois Sharp*[6], *Robert Patton*[5], *James (Jim) Charles Sr.*[4], *Adron (Edwin/Ade) Sr.*[3], *Charles W. Sr.*[2], *John Sr.*[1]) was born 15 Jun 1961 in Lauderdale County, AL.

Kerry married **Bernard Ross Michaud**, son of **Marc R. Michaud** and **Huguette La-Croir**, 16 Sep 1987 in Lauderdale County, AL. Bernard was born 22 Sep 1961 in New Haven County, CT.

4625 M i. **Marc Ross Michaud** was born 19 Apr 1988 in Huntsville, Madison County, AL.

Kerry next married **David Cassady** 16 Nov 1991. David was born 25 Jul 1955.

Kerry next married **James Briggs Sharp**, son of **Paul Edward Sharp Sr.** and **Fay Wilcoxson**, 27 Sep 1997 in Birmingham, Jefferson County, AL. James was born 9 Dec 1963 in Lauderdale County, AL. **(Duplicate Line. See Person 1880)**

2798. Michael Kevin McCarley (*Mary Virginia Givens^{7}, Ida Lois Sharp^{6}, Robert Patton^{5}, James (Jim) Charles Sr.^{4}, Adron (Edwin/Ade) Sr.^{3}, Charles W. Sr.^{2}, John Sr.^{1}*) was born 15 Jun 1961 in Florence, Lauderdale County, AL.

Michael married **Hillary Ann Buckley**, daughter of **Charles Richard Buckley** and **Janet Ann Brown**, 20 Aug 1994 in Lauderdale County, AL. Hillary was born 20 Aug 1961 in Hamilton, IN.

2799. Bobbie Carol Givens (*Robert Orlan Givens Sr.^{7}, Ida Lois Sharp^{6}, Robert Patton^{5}, James (Jim) Charles Sr.^{4}, Adron (Edwin/Ade) Sr.^{3}, Charles W. Sr.^{2}, John Sr.^{1}*) was born 28 Mar 1945.

Bobbie married **Donnie Paul Harris** 12 Apr 1963.
+ 4626　M　i.　**Miles Orlan Harris** was born 19 Jun 1965.

Bobbie next married **Jasper Norman Moore** 24 Jun 1977.

2800. Mary Francis Givens (*Robert Orlan Givens Sr.^{7}, Ida Lois Sharp^{6}, Robert Patton^{5}, James (Jim) Charles Sr.^{4}, Adron (Edwin/Ade) Sr.^{3}, Charles W. Sr.^{2}, John Sr.^{1}*) was born 20 Nov 1946.

Mary married **Wilford Sylvester Dail Jr.** 18 Jul 1965.
+ 4627　F　i.　**Denise Danielle Dail** was born 24 May 1967.

Mary next married **Julian Paul Lane Sr.** 5 Dec 1975.
4628　M　i.　**Julian Paul (J. P.) Lane Jr.** was born 1 Jan 1977.

2801. Lois Marie Givens (*Robert Orlan Givens Sr.^{7}, Ida Lois Sharp^{6}, Robert Patton^{5}, James (Jim) Charles Sr.^{4}, Adron (Edwin/Ade) Sr.^{3}, Charles W. Sr.^{2}, John Sr.^{1}*) was born 19 May 1950.

Lois married **Allen Randall Brown Sr.** 11 Jan 1970.
4629　F　i.　**Allison Darnell Brown** was born 24 Jan 1971.
4630　M　ii.　**Allen Randall Brown Jr.** was born 16 Jun 1972.

2802. Robert (Bobby) Orlon Givens Jr. (*Robert Orlan Givens Sr.^{7}, Ida Lois Sharp^{6}, Robert Patton^{5}, James (Jim) Charles Sr.^{4}, Adron (Edwin/Ade) Sr.^{3}, Charles W. Sr.^{2}, John Sr.^{1}*) was born 28 Jan 1954.

Robert married **Carol Jean Medyette** 5 Aug 1972.
4631　F　i.　**Millicent Louise Givens** was born 5 Oct 1975, died 5 Oct 1975, and was buried in New Hollywood Cemetery, Elizabeth City, NC.
4632　M　ii.　**Robert Orlon Givens III** was born 11 Nov 1976.

2803. Scott Patton Givens Sr. (*Robert Orlan Givens Sr.^{7}, Ida Lois Sharp^{6}, Robert Patton^{5}, James (Jim) Charles Sr.^{4}, Adron (Edwin/Ade) Sr.^{3}, Charles W. Sr.^{2}, John Sr.^{1}*) was born 16 Dec 1958.

Scott married **Lynda Cheryl Long** 29 Jun 1975.
4633　M　i.　**Scott Patton Givens Jr.** was born 2 Oct 1975.
4634　F　ii.　**Tabatha Ann Givens** was born 31 May 1983.

Scott next married **Kathleen Clifton** 2 May 1992.

2804. Gina Gail Givens (*Thomas Edsel Givens^{7}, Ida Lois Sharp^{6}, Robert Patton^{5}, James (Jim) Charles Sr.^{4}, Adron (Edwin/Ade) Sr.^{3}, Charles W. Sr.^{2}, John Sr.^{1}*) was born 7 May 1958.

Gina married **Joseph Charles Zimmerman** 22 May 1982. Joseph was born 6 Aug 1957.
4635　M　i.　**Joseph Parker Zimmerman** was born 23 Aug 1989.

4636 M ii. **Thomas Neil Zimmerman** was born 2 Jan 1992.

2805. Geri Lisa Givens (*Thomas Edsel Givens*[7], *Ida Lois Sharp*[6], *Robert Patton*[5], *James (Jim) Charles Sr.*[4], *Adron (Edwin/Ade) Sr.*[3], *Charles W. Sr.*[2], *John Sr.*[1]) was born 30 Apr 1962.

Geri married **Philip Neil Taylor**. Philip was born 23 Aug 1964.

2806. Thomas Brent Givens (*Thomas Edsel Givens*[7], *Ida Lois Sharp*[6], *Robert Patton*[5], *James (Jim) Charles Sr.*[4], *Adron (Edwin/Ade) Sr.*[3], *Charles W. Sr.*[2], *John Sr.*[1]) was born 10 Sep 1966.

Thomas married **Claire Elaine Kilpatrick** 28 Sep 1991. Claire was born 6 May 1966.

2807. William W. Ashley Jr. (*Francis Ann Givens*[7], *Ida Lois Sharp*[6], *Robert Patton*[5], *James (Jim) Charles Sr.*[4], *Adron (Edwin/Ade) Sr.*[3], *Charles W. Sr.*[2], *John Sr.*[1]) was born 29 Oct 1952 in Birmingham, Jefferson County, AL.

William married **Della Stauber** 22 Sep 1979. Della was born 27 May 1959.
4637 M i. **William W. Ashley III** was born 12 Aug 1982.
4638 F ii. **Rachel Ann Ashley** was born 22 Aug 1986.

2808. Alice Marie Ashley (*Francis Ann Givens*[7], *Ida Lois Sharp*[6], *Robert Patton*[5], *James (Jim) Charles Sr.*[4], *Adron (Edwin/Ade) Sr.*[3], *Charles W. Sr.*[2], *John Sr.*[1]) was born 24 Dec 1956 in Miami, FL.

Alice married **Steven Douglas Hall** 5 May 1984. Steven was born 18 Jul 1954.

2810. Joni Leslie Givens (*Billy Fred Givens*[7], *Ida Lois Sharp*[6], *Robert Patton*[5], *James (Jim) Charles Sr.*[4], *Adron (Edwin/Ade) Sr.*[3], *Charles W. Sr.*[2], *John Sr.*[1]) was born 5 Dec 1961 in Baton Rouge, LA.

Joni married **Derrick Bell** 13 Feb 1993. Derrick was born 27 May 1960.

2811. Mark Bradley Givens (*Billy Fred Givens*[7], *Ida Lois Sharp*[6], *Robert Patton*[5], *James (Jim) Charles Sr.*[4], *Adron (Edwin/Ade) Sr.*[3], *Charles W. Sr.*[2], *John Sr.*[1]) was born 7 Jun 1966 in Baton Rouge, LA.

Mark married **Lori Roberson** 23 Jul 1988. Lori was born 23 Nov 1969.
4639 M i. **Zachery Craig Givens** was born 15 Jun 1990.

2815. Dorothy M. Rogers (*Edmon (Eddie) Falmer Rogers*[7], *Lillian Anna (Lillie) Sharp*[6], *John Thomas (Tom)*[5], *James (Jim) Charles Sr.*[4], *Adron (Edwin/Ade) Sr.*[3], *Charles W. Sr.*[2], *John Sr.*[1]) was born 14 Nov 1927 in Hardin County, TN.

Dorothy married **Albert Morron Durham**, son of **James Durham** and **Virginia Shelby**, 21 Apr 1945 in Corinth, Alcorn County, MS. Albert was born 12 Sep 1918 in Forrest, NM.
+ 4640 M i. **Leonard E. Durham** was born 20 Oct 1947 in Adamsville, McNairy County, TN.
4641 F ii. **Betty Durham**.

2816. Clyde Norris Rogers Sr. (*Clydie B. Rogers*[7], *Lillian Anna (Lillie) Sharp*[6], *John Thomas (Tom)*[5], *James (Jim) Charles Sr.*[4], *Adron (Edwin/Ade) Sr.*[3], *Charles W. Sr.*[2], *John Sr.*[1]) was born about 1939 in Adamsville, McNairy County, TN and died 4 Sep 1999.

Clyde married **Jean *Unk** 5 Aug 1968 in Atlanta, Fulton County, GA. Jean was born in 1945 in Hayden, KY.
4642 M i. **Clyde Norris Rogers Jr.** was born 2 May 1969.
4643 F ii. **Audrey Regina Rogers** was born 31 Aug 1971.

2817. Minnie Faye Rogers (*Clydie B. Rogers*[7], *Lillian Anna (Lillie) Sharp*[6], *John Thomas (Tom)*[5], *James (Jim) Charles Sr.*[4], *Adron (Edwin/Ade) Sr.*[3], *Charles W. Sr.*[2], *John Sr.*[1]).

Minnie married **Charles Goff**.
4644 F i. **Sharon Goff**.

2818. Bob R. Rogers (*Robert W. Rogers* [7], *Lillian Anna (Lillie) Sharp* [6], *John Thomas (Tom)* [5], *James (Jim) Charles Sr.* [4], *Adron (Edwin/Ade) Sr.* [3], *Charles W. Sr.* [2], *John Sr.* [1]) was born 29 Sep 1929 in Adamsville, McNairy County, TN.

Bob married **Rowanna Jolliff**, daughter of **Richard Jolliff** and **Elois Pankey**, 5 Dec 1959 in Lafayette, GA. Rowanna was born 12 Apr 1936 in Manila, Mississippi County, AR.

    4645 F   i.   **Sarah Lynn Rogers** was born 12 Dec 1960 in Chattanooga, Cumberland County, TN.
+ 4646 F   ii.   **Rebecca Ann Rogers** was born 25 Feb 1963 in Memphis, Shelby County, TN.
    4647 M   iii. **Robert Wymon Rogers** was born 21 Nov 1972 in Memphis, Shelby County, TN.

2819. Mary Helen Rogers (*Robert W. Rogers* [7], *Lillian Anna (Lillie) Sharp* [6], *John Thomas (Tom)* [5], *James (Jim) Charles Sr.* [4], *Adron (Edwin/Ade) Sr.* [3], *Charles W. Sr.* [2], *John Sr.* [1]) was born 3 Aug 1932 in Adamsville, McNairy County, TN.

Mary married **Lloyd Mack Elrod Sr.**, son of **Samuel Elrod** and **Zora *Unk**, 1 May 1954 in Memphis, Shelby County, TN. Lloyd was born 8 Jan 1930 in Arkansas.

+ 4648 F   i.   **Deborah A. Elrod** was born 16 Sep 1957 in Memphis, Shelby County, TN.
+ 4649 M   ii.   **Lloyd Mack Elrod Jr.** was born 10 May 1961 in Memphis, Shelby County, TN.

2820. Phillip David Rogers Sr. (*Robert W. Rogers* [7], *Lillian Anna (Lillie) Sharp* [6], *John Thomas (Tom)* [5], *James (Jim) Charles Sr.* [4], *Adron (Edwin/Ade) Sr.* [3], *Charles W. Sr.* [2], *John Sr.* [1]) was born 10 Oct 1934 in Adamsville, McNairy County, TN.

Phillip married **Diane McCullum**, daughter of **Charles McCullum** and **Hazel Carrier**, 22 Nov 1967 in Memphis, Shelby County, TN. Diane was born 1 Mar 1938 in Brinkley, AR.

+ 4650 M   i.   **Phillip David Rogers Jr.** was born 1 Mar 1970.
    4651 M   ii.   **Christopher Steven Rogers** was born 30 Aug 1974.

2821. Elizabeth Rogers (*Robert W. Rogers* [7], *Lillian Anna (Lillie) Sharp* [6], *John Thomas (Tom)* [5], *James (Jim) Charles Sr.* [4], *Adron (Edwin/Ade) Sr.* [3], *Charles W. Sr.* [2], *John Sr.* [1]).

Elizabeth married **Harrell Conaway**.

+ 4652 F   i.   **Monica Conaway** was born 26 Apr 1970 in Selmer, McNairy County, TN.
    4653 M   ii.   **Joey Conaway**.

2823. Willard Lee Holcombe (*Ernest Powers Holcombe* [7], *Maggie Sharp* [6], *John Thomas (Tom)* [5], *James (Jim) Charles Sr.* [4], *Adron (Edwin/Ade) Sr.* [3], *Charles W. Sr.* [2], *John Sr.* [1]) was born 21 Apr 1923 in Florence, Lauderdale County, AL.

Willard married **Mary Delise Bevis**, daughter of **George Bevis** and **Sarah Austin**, 20 Dec 1946 in Lauderdale County, AL. Mary was born 27 Jan 1924 in Savannah, Hardin County, TN.

+ 4654 F   i.   **Doris Jean Holcombe** was born 6 Dec 1947 in Lauderdale County, AL.
+ 4655 M   ii.   **Anthony Lee Holcombe** was born 17 May 1955 in Florence, Lauderdale County, AL.

2824. James Lee Holcombe (*Ernest Powers Holcombe* [7], *Maggie Sharp* [6], *John Thomas (Tom)* [5], *James (Jim) Charles Sr.* [4], *Adron (Edwin/Ade) Sr.* [3], *Charles W. Sr.* [2], *John Sr.* [1]) was born 20 Jul 1925 in Florence, Lauderdale County, AL.

James married **Fannie Ursula McCurry**, daughter of **Robert Loyd McCurry** and **Mary Ella Holt**, 24 Dec 1947 in Lauderdale County, AL. Fannie was born 11 Dec 1927 in Wayne County, TN.

+ 4656 M   i.   **Daniel Leon Holcombe** was born 30 May 1950 in Hardin County, TN.
+ 4657 M   ii.   **Steven Lee Holcombe** was born 13 Jul 1951 in Hardin County, TN.
+ 4658 M   iii. **Grady Allen Holcombe** was born 11 May 1953 in Hardin County, TN.
+ 4659 M   iv. **Timothy Wayne Holcombe** was born 3 Jun 1957 in Hardin County, TN.
+ 4660 F   v.   **Geneva Gwen Holcombe** was born 24 Nov 1961 in Savannah, Hardin County, TN.

2825. Geneva Bernice Holcombe (*Ernest Powers Holcombe*[7], *Maggie Sharp*[6], *John Thomas (Tom)*[5], *James (Jim) Charles Sr.*[4], *Adron (Edwin/Ade) Sr.*[3], *Charles W. Sr.*[2], *John Sr.*[1]) was born 25 Jan 1928 in Florence, Lauderdale County, AL.

Geneva married **Thomas Lee Bennett Jr.**, son of **Thomas Lee Bennett Sr.** and **Mary Belle Moore**, 29 Jun 1972 in Lauderdale County, AL. Thomas was born 9 Aug 1902 in Davis County, KY and was buried in Florence City Cemetery, Florence, Lauderdale County, AL.

2826. Arnold Holcombe (*Ernest Powers Holcombe*[7], *Maggie Sharp*[6], *John Thomas (Tom)*[5], *James (Jim) Charles Sr.*[4], *Adron (Edwin/Ade) Sr.*[3], *Charles W. Sr.*[2], *John Sr.*[1]) was born 16 Feb 1930 in Florence, Lauderdale County, AL.

Arnold married **Patsy Carolyn Austin**, daughter of **Eldridge Allen Austin** and **Emily Lee Patterson**, 30 Jul 1955 in Iuka, Tishomingo County, MS. Patsy was born 8 Mar 1939 in Savannah, Hardin County, TN.
+ 4661 M   i.   **Ricky Lynn Holcombe** was born 9 Jan 1957 in Savannah, Hardin County, TN.
+ 4662 F   ii.   **Alicia Carol Holcombe** was born 6 Jul 1968 in Jackson, TN.

2827. Willie Cletus Holcombe (*Ernest Powers Holcombe*[7], *Maggie Sharp*[6], *John Thomas (Tom)*[5], *James (Jim) Charles Sr.*[4], *Adron (Edwin/Ade) Sr.*[3], *Charles W. Sr.*[2], *John Sr.*[1]) was born 12 Aug 1932 in Florence, Lauderdale County, AL.

Willie married **Anna Faye Stricklin**, daughter of **William T. Stricklin** and **Mollie Franks**, 16 Feb 1956 in Iuka, Tishomingo County, MS. Anna was born 26 Jan 1936 in Hardin County, TN.
+ 4663 M   i.   **Garry Phillip Holcombe** was born 25 Sep 1957 in Hardin County, TN.
+ 4664 F   ii.   **Carla Diane Holcombe** was born 12 Oct 1959 in Florence, Lauderdale County, AL.
  4665 M   iii.   **Mark Allen Holcombe** was born 29 Oct 1968 in Florence, Lauderdale County, AL.

2828. Edwin Ray Holcombe (*Ernest Powers Holcombe*[7], *Maggie Sharp*[6], *John Thomas (Tom)*[5], *James (Jim) Charles Sr.*[4], *Adron (Edwin/Ade) Sr.*[3], *Charles W. Sr.*[2], *John Sr.*[1]) was born 18 Dec 1936 in Florence, Lauderdale County, AL.

Edwin married **Mildred Elaine Blackwell**, daughter of **Jack Martin Blackwell** and **Mildred Newport**, 7 May 1960 in Colbert County, AL. Mildred was born 13 May 1936 in Knox County, TN.

2830. Jimmy Leonard Holcombe (*Ernest Powers Holcombe*[7], *Maggie Sharp*[6], *John Thomas (Tom)*[5], *James (Jim) Charles Sr.*[4], *Adron (Edwin/Ade) Sr.*[3], *Charles W. Sr.*[2], *John Sr.*[1]) was born 6 Jun 1943 in Florence, Lauderdale County, AL.

Jimmy married **Frances Ganelle McKee**, daughter of **Joe Virgil McKee** and **Annie Roberta Henry**, 15 Feb 1964 in Lauderdale County, AL. Frances was born 2 Jan 1943 in Chambers County, AL.
+ 4666 M   i.   **Tracy Lyn Holcombe** was born 4 Dec 1967 in Florence, Lauderdale County, AL.
+ 4667 M   ii.   **Jimmy Keith Holcombe** was born 15 Dec 1972 in Florence, Lauderdale County, AL.

2832. Hazel Juanita Holcombe (*Elmer Patford Holcombe*[7], *Maggie Sharp*[6], *John Thomas (Tom)*[5], *James (Jim) Charles Sr.*[4], *Adron (Edwin/Ade) Sr.*[3], *Charles W. Sr.*[2], *John Sr.*[1]) was born 17 Nov 1931 in Lauderdale County, AL, died 13 Mar 2009, and was buried in Pine Hill Cemetery, Lauderdale County, AL.

General Notes: Obituary - Times Daily, Florence, Lauderdale County, AL
March 19, 2009

"Mrs. Hazel J. Hipps, 77, of Brighton, Mich., formerly of Florence, passed away Friday, March 13, 2009, at West Hickory Haven, Milford. She was born Nov. 17, 1931, in Waterloo, Ala., the daughter of Elmer Patford and Lola Pearl (Sledge) Holcombe. On July 23, 1947, she was married to William H. Hipps. Mrs. Hipps was a member of Brighton Church of Christ. Before her retirement , Hazel had been an admitting supervisor for Oakwood Hospital for 20 years.
Visitation will be from 4 - 8 p.m. Friday, March 20, 2009, at Greenview Funeral Home. Funeral services will be at 11 a.m. Saturday, March 21, 2009, at Pine Hill Church of Christ, with burial in the adjoining

cemetery, Officiating will be James Farris. The body will be placed in the church one hour before the service.

Mrs. Hipps was preceded in death by her husband, William H. Hipps, and two sisters, Inez Chandler and Reba Melton.

Surviving are her children, Cathy (John) Gomes, of Brighton, Douglas (Beth) Hipps, of Milford, Shelia Phipps, of Brighton, and Susan (Don) Lindgren, of Farmington Hills; eight grandchildren; eight great - grandchildren; and several nieces and nephews. Pallbearers will be family and friends.

Memorial contributions in Hazel's name are suggested to the American Diabetes Association or to the American Heart Association. Arrangements by Greenview Funeral Home."

Hazel married **William Howard Hipps**, son of **William Reeder Hipps** and **Hattie Bevis**, 23 Jul 1947 in Corinth, Alcorn County, MS. William was born 9 Oct 1924 in Lutts, Wayne County, TN.

+ 4668 F i. **Cathy Rouna Hipps** was born 19 Jul 1949 in Lauderdale County, AL.
+ 4669 M ii. **Wilford Douglas Hipps** was born 3 Dec 1952 in Wayne County, MI.
+ 4670 F iii. **Shelia Diane Hipps** was born 17 Jan 1956 in Wayne County, MI.
+ 4671 F iv. **Susan Michelle Hipps** was born 20 May 1957 in Wayne County, MI.

2833. Mable Inez Holcombe (*Elmer Patford Holcombe*[7]*, Maggie Sharp*[6]*, John Thomas (Tom)*[5]*, James (Jim) Charles Sr.*[4]*, Adron (Edwin/Ade) Sr.*[3]*, Charles W. Sr.*[2]*, John Sr.*[1]) was born 1 Aug 1934 in Lauderdale County, AL, died 10 May 1999, and was buried in Walston Cemetery, Oakland, Lauderdale County, AL.

Mable married **Thomas Clifton Chandler**, son of **Joe James Chandler** and **Bommer Gertrude Richardson**, 1 Aug 1953 in Iuka, Tishomingo County, MS. Thomas was born 16 Apr 1930 in Lauderdale County, AL.

+ 4672 M i. **Jerry Wayne Chandler** was born 9 Aug 1955 in Lauderdale County, AL.
+ 4673 F ii. **Teresa Kaye Chandler** was born 28 Mar 1958 in Lauderdale County, AL.

2834. Reba Nell Holcombe (*Elmer Patford Holcombe*[7]*, Maggie Sharp*[6]*, John Thomas (Tom)*[5]*, James (Jim) Charles Sr.*[4]*, Adron (Edwin/Ade) Sr.*[3]*, Charles W. Sr.*[2]*, John Sr.*[1]) was born 11 Jun 1940 in Lauderdale County, AL.

Reba married **Lloyd Hardiman Melton**, son of **Leonard S. Melton** and **Bessie Lard**, 21 Dec 1961 in Lauderdale County, AL. Lloyd was born 11 Apr 1927 in Lauderdale County, AL.

2835. Charles Herschel Holcombe (*Hubert Lee Holcombe*[7]*, Maggie Sharp*[6]*, John Thomas (Tom)*[5]*, James (Jim) Charles Sr.*[4]*, Adron (Edwin/Ade) Sr.*[3]*, Charles W. Sr.*[2]*, John Sr.*[1]) was born 5 May 1930 in Lauderdale County, AL, died 20 Apr 2001, and was buried in Williams Chapel Cemetery, Lauderdale County, AL.

Charles married **Ethel Ivadell Hinton**, daughter of **Marvin Lindsey Hinton** and **Estelle McFall**, 20 Apr 1957 in Corinth, Alcorn County, MS. Ethel was born 6 Jul 1934 in Wayne County, TN.

+ 4674 M i. **Terry Hubert Holcombe** was born 18 Sep 1958 in Lauderdale County, AL.
+ 4675 M ii. **Dwayne Charles Holcombe** was born 3 Sep 1961 in Lauderdale County, AL.
+ 4676 M iii. **Bryan Lindsey Holcombe** was born 9 Oct 1967 in Lauderdale County, AL.

2836. Lawrence O'steen Holcombe (*Hubert Lee Holcombe*[7]*, Maggie Sharp*[6]*, John Thomas (Tom)*[5]*, James (Jim) Charles Sr.*[4]*, Adron (Edwin/Ade) Sr.*[3]*, Charles W. Sr.*[2]*, John Sr.*[1]) was born 20 Sep 1932 in Lauderdale County, AL.

Lawrence married **Mary Earline Tune**, daughter of **Hamp Tune** and **Hilda Austin**, 19 Nov 1955 in Lauderdale County, AL. Mary was born 13 Dec 1936 in Hardin County, TN, died 19 Mar 1993, and was buried in Williams Chapel Cemetery, Lauderdale County, AL.

+ 4677 M i. **David Lawrence Holcombe** was born 5 Jul 1957 in Lauderdale County, AL.
+ 4678 F ii. **Rhonda Sue Holcombe** was born 3 Sep 1960 in Lauderdale County, AL.

2837. Edith Elizabeth Holcombe (*Hubert Lee Holcombe*[7]*, Maggie Sharp*[6]*, John Thomas (Tom)*[5]*, James (Jim) Charles Sr.*[4]*, Adron (Edwin/Ade) Sr.*[3]*, Charles W. Sr.*[2]*, John Sr.*[1]) was born 7 May 1936 in Lauderdale County, AL.

Edith married **Jack Eugene Hart**, son of **John Leland Hart** and **Delta Marie Biggs**, 12 Sep 1953 in Corinth, Alcorn County, MS. Jack was born 29 Aug 1934 in Lauderdale County, AL.

+ 4679 M   i.   **Donald Eugene Hart** was born 20 Dec 1954 in Lauderdale County, AL.
+ 4680 F   ii.   **Shirley Ann Hart** was born 29 Nov 1957 in Lauderdale County, AL.

2838. Helen Lee Holcombe (*Hubert Lee Holcombe*[7], *Maggie Sharp*[6], *John Thomas (Tom)*[5], *James (Jim) Charles Sr.*[4], *Adron (Edwin/Ade) Sr.*[3], *Charles W. Sr.*[2], *John Sr.*[1]) was born 28 Aug 1942 in Lauderdale County, AL.

Helen married **Charles Edward Parker**, son of **Edward O. Parker** and **Odessie Turpin**, 17 Mar 1962 in Lauderdale County, AL. Charles was born 17 Mar 1941 in Lauderdale County, AL.
  4681 F   i.   **Vicki Charlene Parker** was born 18 Aug 1963 in Lauderdale County, AL, died 6 Mar 1975, and was buried in Williams Chapel Cemetery, Lauderdale County, AL.
+ 4682 M   ii.   **Nelson Edward Parker** was born 14 Aug 1967 in Lauderdale County, AL.
  4683 F   iii. **Lora Leigh Parker** was born 4 Apr 1973 in Lauderdale County, AL.

2839. Robbie Nell Sharp (*Jesse Thomas Sr.*[7], *Hallie (Hal) B.*[6], *John Thomas (Tom)*[5], *James (Jim) Charles Sr.*[4], *Adron (Edwin/Ade) Sr.*[3], *Charles W. Sr.*[2], *John Sr.*[1]) was born 18 Jul 1927 in Rogersville, Lauderdale County, AL.

Robbie married **William Ray Goode**, son of **Orville Goode** and **Alma May Owens**, 26 Nov 1947 in Lauderdale County, AL. William was born 3 Dec 1926 in Rogersville, Lauderdale County, AL.
+ 4684 F   i.   **Connie Faye Goode** was born 2 Dec 1949 in Puerto Rico.
+ 4685 M   ii.   **Michael Ray Goode** was born 30 Apr 1952 in Lauderdale County, AL.
+ 4686 M   iii. **Phillip Glenn Goode** was born 24 Mar 1954 in Dade, FL.

2840. Jesse Thomas Sharp Jr. (*Jesse Thomas Sr.*[7], *Hallie (Hal) B.*[6], *John Thomas (Tom)*[5], *James (Jim) Charles Sr.*[4], *Adron (Edwin/Ade) Sr.*[3], *Charles W. Sr.*[2], *John Sr.*[1]) was born 4 Jul 1932 in Lauderdale County, AL, died 27 Apr 1998, and was buried in Civitan Cemetery, Lauderdale County, AL.

Jesse married **Betty Muriel Holden**, daughter of **Luther Holden** and **Elizabeth Williams**, 9 Feb 1960 in Lauderdale County, AL. Betty was born 22 Jan 1937 in Lauderdale County, AL.
  4687 F   i.   **Kristie Denise Sharp** was born 28 Jan 1969 in Limestone County, AL.
  4688 F   ii.   **Windy Sharp** was born 21 Apr 1971 in Limestone County, AL.

2841. Martha Jane Sharp (*Vessey David*[7], *Hallie (Hal) B.*[6], *John Thomas (Tom)*[5], *James (Jim) Charles Sr.*[4], *Adron (Edwin/Ade) Sr.*[3], *Charles W. Sr.*[2], *John Sr.*[1]) was born 14 Mar 1943 in Lauderdale County, AL.

Martha married **James Ray Eady Sr.**, son of **George C. Eady** and **Amy Mae Simmons**, 30 Jun 1962 in Lauderdale County, AL. James was born 30 Mar 1937 in St. Clair County, AL.
+ 4689 M   i.   **James Ray Eady II** was born 7 Aug 1964 in Lauderdale County, AL.
+ 4690 F   ii.   **Margaret Elizabeth Eady** was born 4 May 1967 in Lauderdale County, AL.
+ 4691 F   iii. **Callie Suzanne Eady** was born 1 Jul 1973 in Lauderdale County, AL.

2842. Margaret Jean Sharp (*Vessey David*[7], *Hallie (Hal) B.*[6], *John Thomas (Tom)*[5], *James (Jim) Charles Sr.*[4], *Adron (Edwin/Ade) Sr.*[3], *Charles W. Sr.*[2], *John Sr.*[1]) was born 29 Nov 1945 in Lauderdale County, AL.

Margaret married **Bobby Gerald Clemons**, son of **Ben C. Clemons** and **Nellie Robertson**, 22 Jun 1979 in Lauderdale County, AL. Bobby was born 11 Jun 1942 in Lauderdale County, AL, died 11 Oct 1981, and was buried in Rogersville Civitan Cemetery, Lauderdale County, AL.

2847. Fred Noel Sharp Jr. (*Fred Noel Sr.*[7], *Hallie (Hal) B.*[6], *John Thomas (Tom)*[5], *James (Jim) Charles Sr.*[4], *Adron (Edwin/Ade) Sr.*[3], *Charles W. Sr.*[2], *John Sr.*[1]) was born 15 Nov 1950 in Lauderdale County, AL.

Fred married **Nong Kaphon** before 1981. Nong was born 23 Mar 1953 in Khorrt, Thailand.
  4692 F   i.   **Diane Lyn Sharp** was born 13 Mar 1974 in Ft Benning, GA.

Fred next married **Christine Kruep** 20 Feb 1981 in Honolulu, HI. Christine was born 23 Jun 1956 in Illinois.
  4693 M   i.   **Patrick Noel Sharp** was born 19 Nov 1981 in Honolulu, HI.

2848. Sandra Kay Sharp (*Fred Noel Sr.*[7], *Hallie (Hal) B.*[6], *John Thomas (Tom)*[5], *James (Jim) Charles Sr.*[4], *Adron (Edwin/Ade) Sr.*[3], *Charles W. Sr.*[2], *John Sr.*[1]) was born 3 Feb 1952 in Lauderdale County, AL.

Sandra married **George Elliot Carpenter**, son of **Oscar Carpenter** and **Mable Elliot**, 5 Aug 1972 in Lauderdale County, AL. George was born 8 May 1951 in Colbert County, AL.

+ 4694 M   i.   **Andrew Elliot Carpenter** was born 9 Mar 1974 in Birmingham, Jefferson County, AL.
   4695 F   ii.   **Anna Noelle Carpenter** was born 19 Nov 1976 in Lauderdale County, AL.

2849. Susie Mae Sharp (*Fred Noel Sr.*[7]*, Hallie (Hal) B.*[6]*, John Thomas (Tom)*[5]*, James (Jim) Charles Sr.*[4]*, Adron (Edwin/Ade) Sr.*[3]*, Charles W. Sr.*[2]*, John Sr.*[1]) was born 20 Aug 1953 in Lauderdale County, AL.

Susie married **James Henry Carter Jr.** 26 Nov 1977 in Lauderdale County, AL. James was born 12 Nov 1952 in Lauderdale County, AL.

Susie next married **James Winston Martin**, son of **Woodrow Wilson Martin** and **Mary Lucille Thompson**, 2 Nov 1979 in Limestone County, AL. James was born 27 Feb 1945 in Lauderdale County, AL.

+ 4696 M   i.   **Jeremy Winn Martin** was born 23 Jun 1980 in Limestone County, AL.

Susie next married **Murphy D. Heird** after 1979.

2850. Janice Marie Sharp (*Fred Noel Sr.*[7]*, Hallie (Hal) B.*[6]*, John Thomas (Tom)*[5]*, James (Jim) Charles Sr.*[4]*, Adron (Edwin/Ade) Sr.*[3]*, Charles W. Sr.*[2]*, John Sr.*[1]) was born 19 Oct 1954 in Lauderdale County, AL.

Janice married **Guy Clifton McCombs III**, son of **Guy Clifton McCombs II** and **Imogene Williamson**, 17 Jun 1978 in Lauderdale County, AL. Guy was born 24 Aug 1952 in Baton Rouge, LA.

   4697 F   i.   **Kristen Marie McCombs** was born 27 Jul 1983 in Lauderdale County, AL.
   4698 M   ii.   **Guy Clifton McCombs IV** was born 17 Jan 1986 in Lauderdale County, AL, died 4 Apr 1986, and was buried in Florence City Cemetery, Florence, Lauderdale County, AL.
   4699 F   iii.   **Mary Katherine McCombs** was born 15 Jul 1990 in Lauderdale County, AL.

2851. Jeffrey Allen Sharp I (*Fred Noel Sr.*[7]*, Hallie (Hal) B.*[6]*, John Thomas (Tom)*[5]*, James (Jim) Charles Sr.*[4]*, Adron (Edwin/Ade) Sr.*[3]*, Charles W. Sr.*[2]*, John Sr.*[1]) was born 8 Mar 1966 in Lauderdale County, AL.

Jeffrey married **Shirley Renee Bevis**, daughter of **Billy Daniel Bevis** and **Mary Boyd Weaver**, 17 Jul 1990 in Colbert County, AL. Shirley was born 16 Jan 1961 in Colbert County, AL.

   4700 M   i.   **Jeffrey Allen Sharp II** was born 9 Oct 1991 in Colbert County, AL.

2852. Milton Sharp Burk (*Thursa Lou Sharp*[7]*, Hallie (Hal) B.*[6]*, John Thomas (Tom)*[5]*, James (Jim) Charles Sr.*[4]*, Adron (Edwin/Ade) Sr.*[3]*, Charles W. Sr.*[2]*, John Sr.*[1]) was born 12 Apr 1931 in Lauderdale County, AL.

Milton married **Mary Anna Kieff**, daughter of **Earl Kieff** and **Reba Pugh**, 7 Oct 1951. Mary was born 9 May 1931 in Limestone County, AL.

+ 4701 M   i.   **Charles Milton Burk** was born 11 Jan 1958 in Summit, OH.

2853. Donald Oneal Burk (*Thursa Lou Sharp*[7]*, Hallie (Hal) B.*[6]*, John Thomas (Tom)*[5]*, James (Jim) Charles Sr.*[4]*, Adron (Edwin/Ade) Sr.*[3]*, Charles W. Sr.*[2]*, John Sr.*[1]) was born 9 Nov 1934 in Lauderdale County, AL.

Donald married **Dorothy Irene Worted** 3 Sep 1951. Dorothy was born 13 Nov 1932 in Montgomery County, OH.

+ 4702 F   i.   **Linda Sue Burk** was born 1 Sep 1954 in Montgomery County, OH.
+ 4703 F   ii.   **Melissa Burk** was born 4 Jul 1961 in Montgomery County, OH.

2854. Jimmy Ray Burk (*Thursa Lou Sharp*[7]*, Hallie (Hal) B.*[6]*, John Thomas (Tom)*[5]*, James (Jim) Charles Sr.*[4]*, Adron (Edwin/Ade) Sr.*[3]*, Charles W. Sr.*[2]*, John Sr.*[1]) was born 26 Oct 1936 in Giles County, TN, died 22 Aug 1996, and was buried in Bethel Cemetery, Center Star, Lauderdale County, AL.

Jimmy married **Bobbi Adkins** 13 Jul.

+ 4704 F   i.   **Lisa Lou Burk** was born 8 Aug 1958 in Giles County, TN.

2855. Mary Ann Littrell (*Leona May Sharp*[7], *Hallie (Hal) B.*[6], *John Thomas (Tom)*[5], *James (Jim) Charles Sr.*[4], *Adron (Edwin/Ade) Sr.*[3], *Charles W. Sr.*[2], *John Sr.*[1]) was born 14 Jul 1942 in Colbert County, AL.

Mary married **James Anderson (Andy) Weaver Jr.**, son of **James Anderson Weaver Sr.** and **Elizabeth Warrenfells**, 20 Oct 1962 in Lauderdale County, AL. James was born 1 Apr 1937 in Walker County, GA.

+ 4705 M   i.   **James Anderson (Jim) Weaver III** was born 4 Jul 1964 in Bibb County, GA.
+ 4706 F   ii.   **Donna Douglas Weaver** was born 9 Nov 1970 in Bibb County, GA.

2856. Maude Ellen Littrell (*Leona May Sharp*[7], *Hallie (Hal) B.*[6], *John Thomas (Tom)*[5], *James (Jim) Charles Sr.*[4], *Adron (Edwin/Ade) Sr.*[3], *Charles W. Sr.*[2], *John Sr.*[1]) was born 17 Aug 1946 in Colbert County, AL.

Maude married **Ronald Moore Ayers**, son of **C. G. Ayers** and **Clara Ballard**, 9 Mar 1968 in Lauderdale County, AL. Ronald was born 28 Dec 1943.

+ 4707 M   i.   **Shannon Lee Ayers** was born 1 Dec 1968 in Colbert County, AL.
+ 4708 F   ii.   **Amanda Lane Ayers** was born 16 Jan 1972 in Colbert County, AL.

2857. Mary Ann Sharp (*John Edward*[7], *James (Swagger)*[6], *John Thomas (Tom)*[5], *James (Jim) Charles Sr.*[4], *Adron (Edwin/Ade) Sr.*[3], *Charles W. Sr.*[2], *John Sr.*[1]) was born 21 Sep 1934 in Lauderdale County, AL.

Mary married **Robert James Cira** in South Bend, IN.

+ 4709 M   i.   **Timothy James Cira** was born 17 Sep 1956.
   4710 F   ii.   **Deborah Ann Cira** was born 28 Feb 1958.
+ 4711 M   iii. **Brian Robert Cira** was born 24 May 1961.
+ 4712 F   iv. **Dana Michelle Cira** was born 30 Apr 1968.

2859. Melinda Sue Sharp (*Homer Carroll*[7], *James (Swagger)*[6], *John Thomas (Tom)*[5], *James (Jim) Charles Sr.*[4], *Adron (Edwin/Ade) Sr.*[3], *Charles W. Sr.*[2], *John Sr.*[1]) was born 6 Oct 1950 in Morgan County, AL.

Melinda married **Jerry Gilbert Kelso**, son of **James Gilbert Kelso** and **Audean Carter**, 11 Dec 1976 in Lauderdale County, AL. Jerry was born 21 Aug 1954 in Lawrence County, AL.

   4713 M   i.   **Eric Nielson Kelso** was born 21 May 1982 in Lauderdale County, AL.
   4714 M   ii.   **Jon Nicholas Kelso** was born 21 Jan 1986 in Lauderdale County, AL.

2860. Carol Sharp (*Homer Carroll*[7], *James (Swagger)*[6], *John Thomas (Tom)*[5], *James (Jim) Charles Sr.*[4], *Adron (Edwin/Ade) Sr.*[3], *Charles W. Sr.*[2], *John Sr.*[1]) was born 9 Dec 1955 in Morgan County, AL.

Carol married ***Unk Collier**.

2862. Martha Lee Mitchell (*Bessie Etoil Sharp*[7], *James (Swagger)*[6], *John Thomas (Tom)*[5], *James (Jim) Charles Sr.*[4], *Adron (Edwin/Ade) Sr.*[3], *Charles W. Sr.*[2], *John Sr.*[1]) was born 13 Aug 1935 in Rogersville, Lauderdale County, AL.

Martha married **Eddo Neal Gean**, son of **Henry Letherd Gean** and **Ida Florence Vinson**, 28 Feb 1959 in Colbert County, AL. Eddo was born 29 Jun 1926 in Lauderdale County, AL, died 3 Dec 1997, and was buried in Greenview Memorial Park, Florence, Lauderdale County, AL.

+ 4715 F   i.   **Nena Lee Gean** was born 28 Mar 1960 in Longbrook, CA.
+ 4716 M   ii.   **Michael Neal Gean** was born 23 Dec 1961 in Lauderdale County, AL.

2863. James Ralph (Buddy) Mitchell (*Bessie Etoil Sharp*[7], *James (Swagger)*[6], *John Thomas (Tom)*[5], *James (Jim) Charles Sr.*[4], *Adron (Edwin/Ade) Sr.*[3], *Charles W. Sr.*[2], *John Sr.*[1]) was born 29 Jan 1937 in Rogersville, Lauderdale County, AL.

James married **Mary Ann Smith**, daughter of **Emmett Oneal Smith** and **Odella L. Murphy**, 16 Jan 1960 in Lauderdale County, AL. Mary was born 3 Jun 1942 in Lauderdale County, AL.

+ 4717 F   i.   **Kimberly (Kim) Mitchell** was born 24 Nov 1960.
+ 4718 M   ii.   **Jeffrey Terrell (Terry) Mitchell** was born 24 Feb 1964 in Lauderdale County, AL.
+ 4719 M   iii. **Eddie Kyle Mitchell** was born 14 Dec 1968 in Lauderdale County, AL.

2864. Russell Taylor Mitchell (*Bessie Etoil Sharp ^{7}, James (Swagger) ^{6}, John Thomas (Tom) ^{5}, James (Jim) Charles Sr. ^{4}, Adron (Edwin/Ade) Sr. ^{3}, Charles W. Sr. ^{2}, John Sr. ^{1}*) was born 18 Aug 1938 in Rogersville, Lauderdale County, AL, died 17 Apr 1965, and was buried in Oak Grove Cemetery, Lauderdale County, AL.

Russell married **Katie Joan Lane**, daughter of **Coleman Lane** and **Ruby Lee Risner**, 9 Sep 1958 in Lauderdale County, AL. Katie was born 27 Jan 1939 in Lauderdale County, AL.
+ 4720 M   i.   **Russell Edward Mitchell** was born 30 Sep 1959 in Lauderdale County, AL.
+ 4721 F   ii.   **Sherrie Alane Mitchell** was born 15 Feb 1960 in Lauderdale County, AL.

2865. Thomas Larry (Tommy) Mitchell (*Bessie Etoil Sharp ^{7}, James (Swagger) ^{6}, John Thomas (Tom) ^{5}, James (Jim) Charles Sr. ^{4}, Adron (Edwin/Ade) Sr. ^{3}, Charles W. Sr. ^{2}, John Sr. ^{1}*) was born 29 Oct 1941 in Lauderdale County, AL.

Thomas married **Reba Juanita Gray**, daughter of **Thomas L. Gray** and **Laura Belle Smith**, 22 Jul 1967 in Lauderdale County, AL. Reba was born 27 Aug 1948 in Lauderdale County, AL.
+ 4722 M   i.   **Larry Steven Mitchell** was born 26 May 1968 in Lauderdale County, AL.
+ 4723 F   ii.   **Deanna Lynn Mitchell** was born 19 Mar 1970 in Lauderdale County, AL.

2866. Judy Elaine Mitchell (*Bessie Etoil Sharp ^{7}, James (Swagger) ^{6}, John Thomas (Tom) ^{5}, James (Jim) Charles Sr. ^{4}, Adron (Edwin/Ade) Sr. ^{3}, Charles W. Sr. ^{2}, John Sr. ^{1}*) was born 9 Feb 1946 in Lauderdale County, AL.

Judy married **Bobby Glen Crosswhite**, son of **James Fox Crosswhite** and **Thelma Ramsey**, 22 May 1965 in Waukegan, IL. Bobby was born 28 Jan 1942 in Colbert County, AL.
+ 4724 M   i.   **Keith Glenn Crosswhite** was born 15 Aug 1966 in Lauderdale County, AL.
+ 4725 F   ii.   **Kelli Cheree Crosswhite** was born 9 Mar 1970 in Lauderdale County, AL.

2868. Gwendolyn Cagle (*Mollie Nell Sharp ^{7}, James (Swagger) ^{6}, John Thomas (Tom) ^{5}, James (Jim) Charles Sr. ^{4}, Adron (Edwin/Ade) Sr. ^{3}, Charles W. Sr. ^{2}, John Sr. ^{1}*).

Gwendolyn married someone.
4726 M   i.   **Jimmy *Unk**.
4727 F   ii.   **Rhonda *Unk**.

2869. Claudeen Dewberry (*Rachel Violet Sharp ^{7}, James (Swagger) ^{6}, John Thomas (Tom) ^{5}, James (Jim) Charles Sr. ^{4}, Adron (Edwin/Ade) Sr. ^{3}, Charles W. Sr. ^{2}, John Sr. ^{1}*) was born 21 Mar 1941 in Lauderdale County, AL.

Claudeen married **James Dale Springer**, son of **James Lenon Springer** and **Betty Ines Whitehead**, 16 Apr 1958 in Lauderdale County, AL. James was born 31 Dec 1938 in Lauderdale County, AL.
+ 4728 F   i.   **Suzanne Springer** was born 22 May 1961 in Lauderdale County, AL.
+ 4729 F   ii.   **Sherrie Shelane Springer** was born 16 Oct 1963 in Lauderdale County, AL.

Claudeen next married **Hugh Bell**.
+ 4730 F   i.   **Debra Kaye Bell** was born 17 Jul 1966 in Tuscaloosa, AL.

2870. Cheryl Evelyn Dewberry (*Rachel Violet Sharp ^{7}, James (Swagger) ^{6}, John Thomas (Tom) ^{5}, James (Jim) Charles Sr. ^{4}, Adron (Edwin/Ade) Sr. ^{3}, Charles W. Sr. ^{2}, John Sr. ^{1}*) was born 29 Nov 1946 in Lauderdale County, AL.

Cheryl married **Virgil Grigsby**.
+ 4731 M   i.   **Mark Anthony Grigsby** was born 10 Dec 1969 in Lauderdale County, AL.

Cheryl next married **Gary Smallwood**.

2871. Jean Gay Dewberry (*Rachel Violet Sharp ^{7}, James (Swagger) ^{6}, John Thomas (Tom) ^{5}, James (Jim) Charles Sr. ^{4}, Adron (Edwin/Ade) Sr. ^{3}, Charles W. Sr. ^{2}, John Sr. ^{1}*) was born 18 Jan 1949 in Lauderdale County, AL.

Jean married **Roy Wayne Seay**, son of **Roy William Seay** and **Lewell Dockey**. Roy was born 16 Mar 1945 in Tuscaloosa County, AL.

4732 F i. **Ashley Nicole Seay** was born 5 Jan 1982 in Huntsville, Madison County, AL.

2872. Edna Kaye Dewberry (*Rachel Violet Sharp*[7], *James (Swagger)*[6], *John Thomas (Tom)*[5], *James (Jim) Charles Sr.*[4], *Adron (Edwin/Ade) Sr.*[3], *Charles W. Sr.*[2], *John Sr.*[1]) was born 10 Sep 1951 in Lauderdale County, AL.

Edna married **William Jimmy Behel**, son of **Earl E. Behel** and **Georgia Clemmons**, 26 Jun 1971 in Lauderdale County, AL. William was born 3 Jan 1945 in Lauderdale County, AL.
4733 F i. **Amanda Summer Behel** was born 23 Nov 1977 in Hermitage, TN.

2873. Donnie Dwayne Sharp (*James Loyal*[7], *James (Swagger)*[6], *John Thomas (Tom)*[5], *James (Jim) Charles Sr.*[4], *Adron (Edwin/Ade) Sr.*[3], *Charles W. Sr.*[2], *John Sr.*[1]) was born 12 Nov 1949.

Donnie married **Deborah Kay Norman**. Deborah was born 3 Sep 1954.
4734 F i. **Tracey Michelle Sharp** was born 6 Jul 1979.

2874. James Harold Sharp (*James Loyal*[7], *James (Swagger)*[6], *John Thomas (Tom)*[5], *James (Jim) Charles Sr.*[4], *Adron (Edwin/Ade) Sr.*[3], *Charles W. Sr.*[2], *John Sr.*[1]) was born 28 Jun 1952.

James married **Brenda Gail Lacey**. Brenda was born 7 Mar 1952.
4735 F i. **Christy Nicole Sharp** was born 1 Aug 1976.

2875. Randall Boyd Sharp (*James Loyal*[7], *James (Swagger)*[6], *John Thomas (Tom)*[5], *James (Jim) Charles Sr.*[4], *Adron (Edwin/Ade) Sr.*[3], *Charles W. Sr.*[2], *John Sr.*[1]) was born 16 May 1962.

Randall married **Regina Gail Turpen**, daughter of **Oneal Turpen** and **Unknown**. Regina was born 29 Dec 1964.

2877. Teddy Steven Kelley (*Aileen Beulah Sharp*[7], *James (Swagger)*[6], *John Thomas (Tom)*[5], *James (Jim) Charles Sr.*[4], *Adron (Edwin/Ade) Sr.*[3], *Charles W. Sr.*[2], *John Sr.*[1]) was born 26 Sep 1953 in Lauderdale County, AL.

Teddy married **Glenda Gail Hinton**, daughter of **Floyd V. Hinton** and **Edna Austin**, 29 Nov 1974 in Lauderdale County, AL.
+ 4736 M i. **Brian Keith Kelley** was born 30 Jul 1973 in Lauderdale County, AL.
  4737 M ii. **Darrell Steven Kelley** was born 20 Jan 1976 in Lauderdale County, AL.

Teddy next married **Misty Dawn Myrick**, daughter of **John Edward Myrick** and **Debra Kay Hamm**, 9 Dec 2000 in Lauderdale County, AL. Misty was born 22 Feb 1977.

2878. Teresa Dawn Kelley (*Aileen Beulah Sharp*[7], *James (Swagger)*[6], *John Thomas (Tom)*[5], *James (Jim) Charles Sr.*[4], *Adron (Edwin/Ade) Sr.*[3], *Charles W. Sr.*[2], *John Sr.*[1]) was born 13 Sep 1954 in Lauderdale County, AL.

Teresa married **Douglas Ray Winborn**, son of **James Leo Winborn** and **Ruby Mae Wood**, 3 Apr 1970 in Lauderdale County, AL. Douglas was born 16 Jul 1948 in Lauderdale County, AL.
(Duplicate Line. See Person 2414)

2879. Vicki Melitha Kelley (*Aileen Beulah Sharp*[7], *James (Swagger)*[6], *John Thomas (Tom)*[5], *James (Jim) Charles Sr.*[4], *Adron (Edwin/Ade) Sr.*[3], *Charles W. Sr.*[2], *John Sr.*[1]) was born 25 Mar 1959 in Lauderdale County, AL.

Vicki married **Royce Earl McMahan**, son of **Danley L. McMahan** and **Ruthie Pearline Rogers**, 25 May 1984 in Lauderdale County, AL. Royce was born 22 Jun 1950 in Athens, Limestone County, AL.
4738 M i. **Zackary Dane McMahan** was born 13 Mar 1985 in Lauderdale County, AL.
4739 M ii. **Zane Nathaniel McMahan** was born 11 Jun 1987 in Lauderdale County, AL.
4740 M iii. **Casey Dewayne McMahan** was born 23 Jan 1990 in Lauderdale County, AL.

2880. Ellie Berry Sharp Jr. (*Ellie Berry Sr.*[7], *Thomas Leslie (Peck)*[6], *John Thomas (Tom)*[5], *James (Jim) Charles Sr.*[4], *Adron (Edwin/Ade) Sr.*[3], *Charles W. Sr.*[2], *John Sr.*[1]) was born 2 Jun 1930 in Lauderdale County, AL and died 10 Aug 1997.

Ellie married **Patricia Ann Bolger**, daughter of **Bobby Kirk** and **Evelyn *Unk**, in Sep 1950 in Liverpool, England. Patricia was born 9 Jul 1931 in Liverpool, England.

4741	M	i.	**Glenn Sharp** was born 11 Nov 1951 in Liverpool, England.
4742	M	ii.	**Anthony Sharp** was born 26 Dec 1954 in Liverpool, England.

2881. Allen Bernard Sharp (*Ellie Berry Sr.* [7], *Thomas Leslie (Peck)* [6], *John Thomas (Tom)* [5], *James (Jim) Charles Sr.* [4], *Adron (Edwin/Ade) Sr.* [3], *Charles W. Sr.* [2], *John Sr.* [1]) was born 3 Aug 1933 in Lauderdale County, AL.

Allen married **Lola Jean Wallace**, daughter of **Bruner Edward Wallace** and **Anne Davis Hayes**, 24 Dec 1953 in Lauderdale County, AL. Lola was born 17 Nov 1934 in Lauderdale County, AL.

4743	F	i.	**Pamela Ann Sharp** was born 18 Jun 1957 in Lauderdale County, AL.
4744	M	ii.	**Mark Allen Sharp** was born 28 Jun 1962 in Lauderdale County, AL.

2882. Donald Glenn Sharp (*Ellie Berry Sr.* [7], *Thomas Leslie (Peck)* [6], *John Thomas (Tom)* [5], *James (Jim) Charles Sr.* [4], *Adron (Edwin/Ade) Sr.* [3], *Charles W. Sr.* [2], *John Sr.* [1]) was born 1 Oct 1936 in Lauderdale County, AL.

Donald married **Betty Jean Smith**, daughter of **Clarence Smith** and **Inez Kimbrough**, 15 Nov 1958 in Lauderdale County, AL. Betty was born 16 Aug 1942 in Lauderdale County, AL.

4745	M	i.	**Barry Eugene Sharp**.
+ 4746	F	ii.	**Martha Sue Sharp** was born 5 Mar 1960 in Lauderdale County, AL.
+ 4747	M	iii.	**Donald (Donnie) Ray Sharp** was born 9 Feb 1963 in Lauderdale County, AL.
+ 4748	M	iv.	**Daniel (Danny) Glen Sharp** was born 3 Dec 1964 in Lauderdale County, AL.

2883. Sarah Carrene Sharp (*Ellie Berry Sr.* [7], *Thomas Leslie (Peck)* [6], *John Thomas (Tom)* [5], *James (Jim) Charles Sr.* [4], *Adron (Edwin/Ade) Sr.* [3], *Charles W. Sr.* [2], *John Sr.* [1]) was born 20 Mar 1939 in Lauderdale County, AL.

Sarah married **Fletcher Leon Gray**, son of **Eirt Benton Gray** and **Tina Shaw**, 3 Jun 1956 in Lauderdale County, AL. Fletcher was born 18 May 1937 in Lauderdale County, AL.

Sarah next married **Bob Downey** 21 May 1988 in Gatlinburg, TN.

2884. Sandra Sue Sharp (*Ellie Berry Sr.* [7], *Thomas Leslie (Peck)* [6], *John Thomas (Tom)* [5], *James (Jim) Charles Sr.* [4], *Adron (Edwin/Ade) Sr.* [3], *Charles W. Sr.* [2], *John Sr.* [1]) was born 12 May 1945 in Lauderdale County, AL.

Sandra married **Billy Ray Lawler**, son of **Hulon Lawler** and **Beulah Shirley**, 26 Dec 1964 in Lauderdale County, AL. Billy was born 3 Aug 1942 in Franklin County, AL.

+ 4749	F	i.	**Anessa Michelle Lawler** was born 2 Jan 1968 in Lauderdale County, AL.
+ 4750	M	ii.	**Lesley (Les) Lamoine Lawler** was born 20 Feb 1972 in Lauderdale County, AL.

2885. Barbara Ann Sharp (*Ellie Berry Sr.* [7], *Thomas Leslie (Peck)* [6], *John Thomas (Tom)* [5], *James (Jim) Charles Sr.* [4], *Adron (Edwin/Ade) Sr.* [3], *Charles W. Sr.* [2], *John Sr.* [1]) was born 29 Dec 1947 in Lauderdale County, AL.

Barbara married **Marvin Eugene Gann**, son of **Melvin C. Gann** and **Ida Dell Cheek**, 18 Jun 1966 in Lauderdale County, AL. Marvin was born 18 Sep 1946 in Colbert County, AL.

4751	M	i.	**Shannon (Shane) Eugene Gann** was born 25 Feb 1970 in Lauderdale County, AL.
4752	M	ii.	**Jeromey Emil Gann** was born 4 Jun 1973 in Lauderdale County, AL.

2886. Doris Elizabeth Sharp (*Earl Leslie* [7], *Thomas Leslie (Peck)* [6], *John Thomas (Tom)* [5], *James (Jim) Charles Sr.* [4], *Adron (Edwin/Ade) Sr.* [3], *Charles W. Sr.* [2], *John Sr.* [1]) was born 7 Jul 1935 in Lauderdale County, AL.

Doris married **William Howard Terrell**, son of **Homer Terrell** and **Myrtle Smith**, 15 Apr 1956 in Iuka, Tishomingo County, MS. William was born 24 Jun 1934 in Lauderdale County, AL.

+ 4753	F	i.	**Cheryl Denise Terrell** was born 24 Jun 1964 in Lauderdale County, AL.

2887. Bobby Elwood Sharp (*Earl Leslie* [7], *Thomas Leslie (Peck)* [6], *John Thomas (Tom)* [5], *James (Jim) Charles Sr.* [4], *Adron (Edwin/Ade) Sr.* [3], *Charles W. Sr.* [2], *John Sr.* [1]) was born 22 Oct 1943 in Lauderdale County, AL.

Bobby married **Francis Willadean Morris**, daughter of **James Walter Morris** and **Effie Lee Steely**, 12 Nov 1960. Francis was born 16 Jan 1940 in Hardin County, TN.

4754 F i. **Rita Sharp.**

4755 F ii. **Reginia Sharp.**

2888. Tommy White Sharp (*Earl Leslie*[7], *Thomas Leslie (Peck)*[6], *John Thomas (Tom)*[5], *James (Jim) Charles Sr.*[4], *Adron (Edwin/Ade) Sr.*[3], *Charles W. Sr.*[2], *John Sr.*[1]) was born 9 Sep 1947 in Lauderdale County, AL.

Tommy married **Donna Sue Barrier**, daughter of **Henry Olen Barrier** and **Lady Maude Wesson**, 8 Jul 1967 in Lauderdale County, AL. Donna was born 27 Mar 1948 in Lauderdale County, AL. **(Duplicate Line. See Person 2381)**

2890. Donnie Murray Sharp (*Earl Leslie*[7], *Thomas Leslie (Peck)*[6], *John Thomas (Tom)*[5], *James (Jim) Charles Sr.*[4], *Adron (Edwin/Ade) Sr.*[3], *Charles W. Sr.*[2], *John Sr.*[1]) was born 10 Jan 1950 in Lauderdale County, AL.

Donnie married **Elizabeth Ann (Penny) Kelley**, daughter of **Earl Kelley** and **Bessie James**, 20 Mar 1979 in Lauderdale County, AL. Elizabeth was born 4 Aug 1948 in Lauderdale County, AL.

+ 4756 F i. **Jennifer Michelle Sharp** was born 31 Jan 1982 in Lauderdale County, AL.

2891. Jerry Lynn Sharp (*Earl Leslie*[7], *Thomas Leslie (Peck)*[6], *John Thomas (Tom)*[5], *James (Jim) Charles Sr.*[4], *Adron (Edwin/Ade) Sr.*[3], *Charles W. Sr.*[2], *John Sr.*[1]) was born 24 May 1953 in Lauderdale County, AL.

Jerry married **Sandra Gail Clemons**, daughter of **Robert P. Clemons III** and **Lelia Gertrude White**, 1 Dec 1972 in Lauderdale County, AL. Sandra was born 21 Sep 1952 in Lauderdale County, AL.

+ 4757 F i. **Misty Dawn Sharp** was born 19 Apr 1976 in Lauderdale County, AL.

2892. James D. Jenson Sr. (*Wilma Lutell Sharp*[7], *Thomas Leslie (Peck)*[6], *John Thomas (Tom)*[5], *James (Jim) Charles Sr.*[4], *Adron (Edwin/Ade) Sr.*[3], *Charles W. Sr.*[2], *John Sr.*[1]) was born 1 Apr 1944 in Memphis, Shelby County, TN.

James married **Sandra Patty** 1 Jun 1965.

4758 M i. **James D. Jenson Jr.** was born 14 Mar 1969 in Memphis, Shelby County, TN.

4759 M ii. **Joseph C. Jenson** was born 15 Aug 1971 in Memphis, Shelby County, TN.

2893. Lawrence K. Jenson (*Wilma Lutell Sharp*[7], *Thomas Leslie (Peck)*[6], *John Thomas (Tom)*[5], *James (Jim) Charles Sr.*[4], *Adron (Edwin/Ade) Sr.*[3], *Charles W. Sr.*[2], *John Sr.*[1]) was born 9 Nov 1952 in Memphis, Shelby County, TN.

Lawrence married **Leesa Bland** 6 Oct 1965.

4760 F i. **Leesa Grace Jenson** was born 1 Aug 1986 in Memphis, Shelby County, TN.

4761 M ii. **Lawrence (Luke) K. Jenson Jr.** was born 15 Oct 1988 in Memphis, Shelby County, TN.

4762 F iii. **Mary Bland Jenson** was born 17 Feb 1992 in Memphis, Shelby County, TN.

2894. Jan Carol Jenson (*Wilma Lutell Sharp*[7], *Thomas Leslie (Peck)*[6], *John Thomas (Tom)*[5], *James (Jim) Charles Sr.*[4], *Adron (Edwin/Ade) Sr.*[3], *Charles W. Sr.*[2], *John Sr.*[1]) was born 8 Jun 1957 in Memphis, Shelby County, TN.

Jan married **Robert F. Rice**, son of **Dan Rice** and **Evelyn Henson**.

2895. Michael Dewayne Pennington (*Brenda Joyce Sharp*[7], *Thomas Leslie (Peck)*[6], *John Thomas (Tom)*[5], *James (Jim) Charles Sr.*[4], *Adron (Edwin/Ade) Sr.*[3], *Charles W. Sr.*[2], *John Sr.*[1]) was born 14 Oct 1960 in Lauderdale County, AL.

Michael married **Teresa Arlene Pitts**, daughter of **Eddie Roy Pitts** and **Martha Ann Balentine**. Teresa was born 28 Mar 1963 in Lauderdale County, AL.

4763 F i. **Amy Nicole Pennington** was born 25 Mar 1983 in Lauderdale County, AL.

4764 F ii. **Heather Michelle Pennington** was born 11 Sep 1987 in Lauderdale County, AL.

2896. Terry Keith Pennington (*Brenda Joyce Sharp*[7], *Thomas Leslie (Peck)*[6], *John Thomas (Tom)*[5], *James (Jim) Charles Sr.*[4], *Adron (Edwin/Ade) Sr.*[3], *Charles W. Sr.*[2], *John Sr.*[1]) was born 27 Jul 1963 in Lauderdale County, AL.

Terry married **Melissa Gaye Burbank**, daughter of **Berl Reed Burbank** and **Anita Joyce Bourdon**, 23 May in Lauderdale County, AL. Melissa was born 25 Mar 1964 in Lauderdale County, AL.

4765 M i. **Douglas Reed Pennington** was born 11 Aug 1985 in Lauderdale County, AL.

2898. Mitzi Kay Fox (*Judy Amisonia Sharp*[7], *Thomas Leslie (Peck)*[6], *John Thomas (Tom)*[5], *James (Jim) Charles Sr.*[4], *Adron (Edwin/Ade) Sr.*[3], *Charles W. Sr.*[2], *John Sr.*[1]) was born 19 Jan 1963 in Lauderdale County, AL.

Mitzi married **James Anthony (Tony) Hollingsworth**, son of **James R. Hollingsworth** and **Lerlene Draper**, 18 Jul 1981 in Lauderdale County, AL. James was born 13 Oct 1958 in Lauderdale County, AL.

4766 M i. **Nicholas Keith Hollingsworth** was born 25 Jan 1981 in Lauderdale County, AL.

Mitzi next married **William Royal McCall** 2 Jul 1993 in Mobile, AL.

4767 M i. **Zachary Collins McCall** was born 13 Jan 1993 in Mobile, AL.
4768 M ii. **Mark Evans McCall** was born 24 Mar 1997 in Mobile, AL.

2899. Christopher Alan Fox (*Judy Amisonia Sharp*[7], *Thomas Leslie (Peck)*[6], *John Thomas (Tom)*[5], *James (Jim) Charles Sr.*[4], *Adron (Edwin/Ade) Sr.*[3], *Charles W. Sr.*[2], *John Sr.*[1]) was born 30 Aug 1964 in Colbert County, AL.

Christopher married **Malissa Sleugh**, daughter of **Ted Sleugh** and **Carol *Unk**, in Sep 1990 in Mobile, AL.

4769 M i. **Benjamin Paul Fox** was born 21 Feb 1991 in Mobile, AL.
4770 M ii. **Matthew Thomas Fox** was born 8 Jun 1992 in Mobile, AL.

2900. Jerry Woodrow Sharp (*Doyle Woodrow*[7], *Edgar Lee*[6], *John Thomas (Tom)*[5], *James (Jim) Charles Sr.*[4], *Adron (Edwin/Ade) Sr.*[3], *Charles W. Sr.*[2], *John Sr.*[1]) was born 29 Nov 1948 in Lauderdale County, AL.

Jerry married **Pamela Rose Holcombe**, daughter of **William Clyde (Willie) Holcombe** and **Cora Blanch Rogers**, 25 Sep 1970 in Lauderdale County, AL. Pamela was born 17 May 1951 in Lauderdale County, AL.

4771 F i. **Erica Dawn Sharp** was born 31 Jul 1974 in Kenitria, Morocco.

2901. Joyce Elaine Sharp (*Doyle Woodrow*[7], *Edgar Lee*[6], *John Thomas (Tom)*[5], *James (Jim) Charles Sr.*[4], *Adron (Edwin/Ade) Sr.*[3], *Charles W. Sr.*[2], *John Sr.*[1]) was born 15 Jun 1951 in Lauderdale County, AL.

Joyce married **David Emerson Dunn Sr.**, son of **Emerson Dunn** and **Charlotte L. Blythe**. David was born 6 Jun 1949 in Scott County, KY.

4772 M i. **David Emerson Dunn Jr.** was born 24 Feb 1973 in Lauderdale County, AL.

2902. Joann Robertson (*Mary Elizabeth Sharp*[7], *Edgar Lee*[6], *John Thomas (Tom)*[5], *James (Jim) Charles Sr.*[4], *Adron (Edwin/Ade) Sr.*[3], *Charles W. Sr.*[2], *John Sr.*[1]) was born 5 Jul 1946 in Lauderdale County, AL.

Joann married **Andrew Terry Hager**, son of **Andrew Lewis Hager** and **Daisy M. Keeton**, 25 Feb 1977 in Lauderdale County, AL. Andrew was born 10 Jul 1942 in Lauderdale County, AL.

4773 M i. **Christopher Andrew Hager** was born 20 Jul 1979 in Lauderdale County, AL.

2903. Berry Lee (Buck) Robertson (*Mary Elizabeth Sharp*[7], *Edgar Lee*[6], *John Thomas (Tom)*[5], *James (Jim) Charles Sr.*[4], *Adron (Edwin/Ade) Sr.*[3], *Charles W. Sr.*[2], *John Sr.*[1]) was born 13 Jun 1949 in Lauderdale County, AL.

Berry married **Wanda Elizabeth Stricklin**, daughter of **Henry Ellis Stricklin** and **Violet Beatrice Gean**, 19 Aug 1992 in Lauderdale County, AL. Wanda was born 13 Jan 1951 in Hardin County, TN.

+ 4774 M i. **Daniel Scott Robertson** was born 29 Aug 1970 in Lauderdale County, AL.
4775 M ii. **Mitchell Joshua Robertson** was born 29 Aug 1973 in Lauderdale County, AL.

2904. Charlotte Rose Robertson (*Mary Elizabeth Sharp*[7], *Edgar Lee*[6], *John Thomas (Tom)*[5], *James (Jim) Charles Sr.*[4], *Adron (Edwin/Ade) Sr.*[3], *Charles W. Sr.*[2], *John Sr.*[1]) was born 31 Jan 1953 in Lauderdale County, AL.

Charlotte married **Donald Dane McDaniel**, son of **George Milton McDaniel** and **Pearl Olene Shook**, 2 Jan 1969 in Lauderdale County, AL. Donald was born 21 May 1949 in Lauderdale County, AL.

+ 4776 F i. **Kimberly Renee McDaniel** was born 17 Aug 1969 in Lauderdale County, AL.

2905. Gary Lynn (Peanut) Robertson (*Mary Elizabeth Sharp ^{7}, Edgar Lee ^{6}, John Thomas (Tom) ^{5}, James (Jim) Charles Sr. ^{4}, Adron (Edwin/Ade) Sr. ^{3}, Charles W. Sr. ^{2}, John Sr. ^{1}*) was born 11 Sep 1955 in Lauderdale County, AL.

Gary married **Vina Mae Ray**, daughter of **Thomas Wilson Ray** and **Lillie Belle Morgan**, 15 Jan 1975 in Lauderdale County, AL. Vina was born 13 Feb 1958 in New Caney, TX.

4777 M i. **Roy Lynn Robertson** was born 18 Jul 1979 in Lauderdale County, AL.
4778 M ii. **Thomas Berry Robertson** was born 22 Apr 1982 in Lauderdale County, AL.

2906. Janice Kay Mansell (*Annie Bell Sharp ^{7}, Edgar Lee ^{6}, John Thomas (Tom) ^{5}, James (Jim) Charles Sr. ^{4}, Adron (Edwin/Ade) Sr. ^{3}, Charles W. Sr. ^{2}, John Sr. ^{1}*) was born 1 Nov 1946 in Lauderdale County, AL.

Janice married **Donnie Dodd Arnold**, son of **Leo Arnold** and **Blanche Dodd**, 12 Aug 1965 in Lauderdale County, AL. Donnie was born 8 Jun 1945 in Lauderdale County, AL.

+ 4779 F i. **Kelly Leanne Arnold** was born 30 Sep 1975 in Lauderdale County, AL.

2907. Jimmy Don Mansell (*Annie Bell Sharp ^{7}, Edgar Lee ^{6}, John Thomas (Tom) ^{5}, James (Jim) Charles Sr. ^{4}, Adron (Edwin/Ade) Sr. ^{3}, Charles W. Sr. ^{2}, John Sr. ^{1}*) was born in Mar 1951 in Lauderdale County, AL.

Jimmy married **Patricia Ann Turner**, daughter of **George Hampton Turner** and **Mary Hardeman**, 4 Aug 1973 in Lauderdale County, AL. Patricia was born 22 Aug 1952 in Lauderdale County, AL.

+ 4780 M i. **Christopher Britt Mansell** was born 27 Oct 1977 in Lauderdale County, AL.

2908. Connie Renee Mansell (*Annie Bell Sharp ^{7}, Edgar Lee ^{6}, John Thomas (Tom) ^{5}, James (Jim) Charles Sr. ^{4}, Adron (Edwin/Ade) Sr. ^{3}, Charles W. Sr. ^{2}, John Sr. ^{1}*) was born 2 Feb 1958 in Lauderdale County, AL.

Connie married **David Ricky Brewer**, son of **Collier B. Brewer** and **Elsie Moss**, 16 Nov 1979 in Lauderdale County, AL. David was born 9 Oct 1952 in Lauderdale County, AL.

4781 M i. **Juston David Brewer** was born 31 Aug 1982 in Lauderdale County, AL.
4782 M ii. **Jarred Scott Brewer** was born 25 Apr 1986 in Lauderdale County, AL.

2909. Diane Garner (*Edna Idelle Sharp ^{7}, Edgar Lee ^{6}, John Thomas (Tom) ^{5}, James (Jim) Charles Sr. ^{4}, Adron (Edwin/Ade) Sr. ^{3}, Charles W. Sr. ^{2}, John Sr. ^{1}*).

Diane married **Kenneth L. Bratcher**.

+ 4783 M i. **Ken Bratcher**.
+ 4784 F ii. **Kerri Bratcher**.

2910. Kenneth Dale Rogers (*Julia Edneta Sharp ^{7}, Edgar Lee ^{6}, John Thomas (Tom) ^{5}, James (Jim) Charles Sr. ^{4}, Adron (Edwin/Ade) Sr. ^{3}, Charles W. Sr. ^{2}, John Sr. ^{1}*) was born 17 Apr 1950 in Lauderdale County, AL.

Kenneth married **Donna Suzan Haynes**, daughter of **Thomas Edward Haynes** and **Mrytle Eugene Hughes**, 26 May 1972 in Lauderdale County, AL. Donna was born 28 Sep 1952 in Lauderdale County, AL.

4785 F i. **Amy Melissa Rogers** was born 6 Feb 1975 in Lauderdale County, AL.
4786 M ii. **Brian Kenneth Rogers** was born 15 Aug 1977 in Lauderdale County, AL.
4787 M iii. **Christopher Thomas Rogers** was born 11 Jun 1979 in Lauderdale County, AL.

2911. Stephen Phillip Rogers (*Julia Edneta Sharp ^{7}, Edgar Lee ^{6}, John Thomas (Tom) ^{5}, James (Jim) Charles Sr. ^{4}, Adron (Edwin/Ade) Sr. ^{3}, Charles W. Sr. ^{2}, John Sr. ^{1}*) was born 4 Mar 1955 in Lauderdale County, AL.

Stephen married **Teresa Morris** in Jan 1975 in Hardin County, TN.

4788 M i. **Jody Boyd Rogers** was born 16 Nov 1978 in Lauderdale County, AL.
4789 F ii. **Stephanie Michelle Rogers** was born 13 Mar 1982 in Lauderdale County, AL.

2912. Gregory Thomas Sharp (*John Thomas[7], Edgar Lee[6], John Thomas (Tom)[5], James (Jim) Charles Sr.[4], Adron (Edwin/Ade) Sr.[3], Charles W. Sr.[2], John Sr.[1]*) was born 1 Jan 1955 in Lauderdale County, AL.

Gregory married **Cynthia (Cindy) Elizabeth Buttrum**, daughter of **Wilburn D. Buttrum** and **Patricia A. Smitherom**, 19 Jul 1974 in Lauderdale County, AL. Cynthia was born 6 Aug 1957 in Lauderdale County, AL.
+ 4790 F   i.   **Jennifer Sheree Sharp** was born 20 Apr 1977 in Lauderdale County, AL.
  4791 F   ii. **Christy Leigh Sharp** was born 19 Jul 1980 in Lauderdale County, AL.

2913. Cynthia (Cindy) Jo Sharp (*John Thomas[7], Edgar Lee[6], John Thomas (Tom)[5], James (Jim) Charles Sr.[4], Adron (Edwin/Ade) Sr.[3], Charles W. Sr.[2], John Sr.[1]*) was born 3 Jun 1961 in Lauderdale County, AL.

Cynthia married **Dennis Lee Gibson**, son of **Glenn T. Gibson** and **Gerda Krasson**, 25 Sep 1987 in Lauderdale County, AL. Dennis was born 24 May 1957 in Douglas County, NE.
  4792 M   i.   **Kyle Gibson**.

2914. Judy Diane Womble (*Ellen Emogene Sharp[7], Edgar Lee[6], John Thomas (Tom)[5], James (Jim) Charles Sr.[4], Adron (Edwin/Ade) Sr.[3], Charles W. Sr.[2], John Sr.[1]*) was born 25 Aug 1953 in Lauderdale County, AL.

Judy married **Jerald Wayne Smith**, son of **John Wesley Smith** and **Nellie Sue Norris,** 17 Jul 1973 in Lauderdale County, AL. Jerald was born 21 Feb 1955 in South Bend, St Joseph County, IN.
+ 4793 M   i.   **Anthony Derrick Smith** was born 29 Jun 1977 in Lauderdale County, AL.
  4794 M   ii. **Matthew Craig Smith** was born 20 Mar 1988 in Lauderdale County, AL.

2915. Hairel Ray Barker (*Idna Cynthia Hairell[7], Minor (Mina) Houston Sharp[6], John Thomas (Tom)[5], James (Jim) Charles Sr.[4], Adron (Edwin/Ade) Sr.[3], Charles W. Sr.[2], John Sr.[1]*) was born 21 Oct 1942 in Lauderdale County, AL.

Hairel married **Wanda Helene Southerland**, daughter of **Luther Southerland** and **Ola Mae Cooper**. Wanda was born 1 Sep 1942 in Colbert County, AL.
+ 4795 M   i.   **Brian Ray Barker** was born 31 Oct 1969 in Jefferson County, AL.
+ 4796 F   ii. **Michelle Leigh Barker** was born 3 Dec 1972.

2916. Linda Gail Barker (*Idna Cynthia Hairell[7], Minor (Mina) Houston Sharp[6], John Thomas (Tom)[5], James (Jim) Charles Sr.[4], Adron (Edwin/Ade) Sr.[3], Charles W. Sr.[2], John Sr.[1]*) was born 8 Jun 1950 in Lauderdale County, AL.

Linda married **Lanier Thomas Holcombe**, son of **William Clyde (Willie) Holcombe** and **Cora Blanch Rogers**, 17 Oct 1969 in Lauderdale County, AL. Lanier was born 28 May 1949.
  4797 F   i.   **Diona Lynn Holcombe** was born 3 Jun 1970 in Lauderdale County, AL.
  4798 M   ii. **Jsaon Todd Holcombe** was born 24 Jun 1974 in Lauderdale County, AL.

2917. Glenn Gary Barker (*Idna Cynthia Hairell[7], Minor (Mina) Houston Sharp[6], John Thomas (Tom)[5], James (Jim) Charles Sr.[4], Adron (Edwin/Ade) Sr.[3], Charles W. Sr.[2], John Sr.[1]*) was born 22 Apr 1954 in Lauderdale County, AL.

Glenn married **Kay Ford** 4 Jan 1975 in Lauderdale County, AL.
  4799 F   i.   **Malissa Dawn Barker** was born 24 Jan 1979 in Lauderdale County, AL.
  4800 M   ii. **Bradford Glenn Barker** was born 26 Sep 1986 in Lauderdale County, AL.

2918. Mattie Sue Bruce (*Willie Clyde Bruce[7], James Pinkney Bruce Sr.[6], Matilda Ann Sharp[5], James (Jim) Charles Sr.[4], Adron (Edwin/Ade) Sr.[3], Charles W. Sr.[2], John Sr.[1]*) was born 9 Sep 1922 in Lauderdale County, AL.

Mattie married **Joseph Frank Mattiace**, son of **Frank Joseph Mattiace** and **Mary Riccil**, 11 Sep 1942 in Lauderdale County, AL. Joseph was born 6 Jun 1922 in Greenwich, RI.

2919. William Carl Bruce Sr. (*Willie Clyde Bruce[7], James Pinkney Bruce Sr.[6], Matilda Ann Sharp[5], James (Jim) Charles Sr.[4], Adron (Edwin/Ade) Sr.[3], Charles W. Sr.[2], John Sr.[1]*) was born in Jun 1925 in Lauderdale County, AL.

William married **Mildred S. Stewart**, daughter of **Oscar Stewart** and **Gladys Richardson**, 28 Nov 1946 in Lauderdale County, AL. Mildred was born 30 Apr 1927 in Lauderdale County, AL.

+ 4801 M i. **William Carl Bruce Jr.** was born 14 Nov 1952 in Lauderdale County, AL.
+ 4802 F ii. **Mildred Diane Bruce** was born 5 Oct 1955 in Lauderdale County, AL.

2920. John Paul Bruce (*James Pinkney Bruce Jr.*[7], *James Pinkney Bruce Sr.*[6], *Matilda Ann Sharp*[5], *James (Jim) Charles Sr.*[4], *Adron (Edwin/Ade) Sr.*[3], *Charles W. Sr.*[2], *John Sr.*[1]) was born 21 Dec 1964 in Winnebago, IL.

John married **Kathryn Reginia England**, daughter of **Ralph England** and **Mary Smith**, 27 Dec 1985 in Lauderdale County, AL. Kathryn was born 22 Mar 1965 in Lauderdale County, AL.

2921. Granville Ray Bruce (*Riggle Bruce*[7], *James Pinkney Bruce Sr.*[6], *Matilda Ann Sharp*[5], *James (Jim) Charles Sr.*[4], *Adron (Edwin/Ade) Sr.*[3], *Charles W. Sr.*[2], *John Sr.*[1]) was born 6 Nov 1935 in Lauderdale County, AL and died 20 Jul 1988 in Kennett, MO.

Granville married **Bonnie Faye Cayson** 20 Feb 1959 in Dunklin County, MO.

2922. Shirley Francis Bruce (*Riggle Bruce*[7], *James Pinkney Bruce Sr.*[6], *Matilda Ann Sharp*[5], *James (Jim) Charles Sr.*[4], *Adron (Edwin/Ade) Sr.*[3], *Charles W. Sr.*[2], *John Sr.*[1]) was born 16 Sep 1937 in Florence, Lauderdale County, AL and died in May 1999 in Kennett, MO.

Shirley married **Carlos Ray Smith** 26 Jul 1957 in Chicago, IL.

2923. Gracie Jeanette Bruce (*Riggle Bruce*[7], *James Pinkney Bruce Sr.*[6], *Matilda Ann Sharp*[5], *James (Jim) Charles Sr.*[4], *Adron (Edwin/Ade) Sr.*[3], *Charles W. Sr.*[2], *John Sr.*[1]) was born 23 Oct 1939.

Gracie married **Francis Lynn Campbell** 7 Oct 1961.

2924. Edwin Dewayne Bruce (*Riggle Bruce*[7], *James Pinkney Bruce Sr.*[6], *Matilda Ann Sharp*[5], *James (Jim) Charles Sr.*[4], *Adron (Edwin/Ade) Sr.*[3], *Charles W. Sr.*[2], *John Sr.*[1]) was born 4 Oct 1942 in Kennett, MO and died in 1995 in Oxford, Lafayette County, MS.

Edwin married **Doris Ann Jones** 18 May 1963.

2925. Cyndra Kay Bruce (*Riggle Bruce*[7], *James Pinkney Bruce Sr.*[6], *Matilda Ann Sharp*[5], *James (Jim) Charles Sr.*[4], *Adron (Edwin/Ade) Sr.*[3], *Charles W. Sr.*[2], *John Sr.*[1]) was born 25 Feb 1947 in Kennett, MO and died in Memphis, Shelby County, TN.

Cyndra married **Jimmie Lee Smith** 6 Apr 1963 in Kennett, MO.

2926. Jackie Dewayne Bruce (*Riggle Bruce*[7], *James Pinkney Bruce Sr.*[6], *Matilda Ann Sharp*[5], *James (Jim) Charles Sr.*[4], *Adron (Edwin/Ade) Sr.*[3], *Charles W. Sr.*[2], *John Sr.*[1]) was born 5 Jun 1952 in St. Louis, MO.

Jackie married **Mary Ballard** 30 Oct 1974.

2927. Pamela June Bruce (*Riggle Bruce*[7], *James Pinkney Bruce Sr.*[6], *Matilda Ann Sharp*[5], *James (Jim) Charles Sr.*[4], *Adron (Edwin/Ade) Sr.*[3], *Charles W. Sr.*[2], *John Sr.*[1]) was born 28 Nov 1954 in Kennett, MO.

Pamela married **Eugene Stidham** 3 Dec 1971.

2928. James Millard Bruce Sr. (*John Gilbert Bruce Sr.*[7], *James Pinkney Bruce Sr.*[6], *Matilda Ann Sharp*[5], *James (Jim) Charles Sr.*[4], *Adron (Edwin/Ade) Sr.*[3], *Charles W. Sr.*[2], *John Sr.*[1]) was born 8 Sep 1937 in Lauderdale County, AL.

James married **Martha Jane Hargrave** 27 Jan 1961 in Genesse County, MI.

+ 4803 M i. **John Terry Bruce** was born 25 Oct 1961 in Genesse County, MI.

4804 M ii. **James Millard Bruce Jr.** was born 10 Mar 1964 in Genesse County, MI.

2929. Reggie Paul Bruce (*John Gilbert Bruce Sr.*[7], *James Pinkney Bruce Sr.*[6], *Matilda Ann Sharp*[5], *James (Jim) Charles Sr.*[4], *Adron (Edwin/Ade) Sr.*[3], *Charles W. Sr.*[2], *John Sr.*[1]) was born 5 Feb 1939 in Lauderdale County, AL.

Reggie married **Lana Jane Thornton**, daughter of **W. G. Thornton** and **Eliza Mae Dean**, 24 Dec 1958 in Lauderdale County, AL. Lana was born 22 Feb 1942 in Lauderdale County, AL.
+ 4805 F i. **Pamela Jane Bruce** was born 15 Mar 1961 in Lauderdale County, AL.
+ 4806 F ii. **Paula Malin Bruce** was born 3 Sep 1962 in Lauderdale County, AL.
+ 4807 F iii. **Kimberly Jan Bruce** was born 7 Dec 1965 in Lauderdale County, AL.

2930. Harold Sherman Bruce (*John Gilbert Bruce Sr.*[7], *James Pinkney Bruce Sr.*[6], *Matilda Ann Sharp*[5], *James (Jim) Charles Sr.*[4], *Adron (Edwin/Ade) Sr.*[3], *Charles W. Sr.*[2], *John Sr.*[1]) was born 30 Sep 1941 in Lauderdale County, AL.

Harold married **Carolyn Jean Allen**, daughter of **Henry Nelson Allen** and **Emma Odell Springer**, 30 Apr 1964 in Lauderdale County, AL. Carolyn was born 19 Aug 1943 in Lauderdale County, AL.
+ 4808 M i. **Quennon Chancey Bruce** was born 19 Oct 1969 in Lauderdale County, AL.
+ 4809 F ii. **Zabrina Camilla Bruce** was born 26 May 1973 in Lauderdale County, AL.

2931. John Gilbert Bruce Jr. (*John Gilbert Bruce Sr.*[7], *James Pinkney Bruce Sr.*[6], *Matilda Ann Sharp*[5], *James (Jim) Charles Sr.*[4], *Adron (Edwin/Ade) Sr.*[3], *Charles W. Sr.*[2], *John Sr.*[1]) was born 20 Feb 1943 in Lauderdale County, AL.

John married **Susan Gail Risner**, daughter of **William Thomas Risner** and **Edith Olean Phillips**, 9 Jan 1993 in Lauderdale County, AL. Susan was born 24 Nov 1952 in Lauderdale County, AL.
4810 M i. **Joseph (Joey) Paul Bruce.**
+ 4811 F ii. **Sherri Lynn Bruce** was born 24 Dec 1966 in Lauderdale County, AL.
+ 4812 F iii. **Virginia Suzanene Bruce** was born 26 Mar 1969 in Lauderdale County, AL.
4813 F iv. **July Jacqueline Bruce.**

John next married **Dale *Unk**.

2932. Virginia Alice Bruce (*John Gilbert Bruce Sr.*[7], *James Pinkney Bruce Sr.*[6], *Matilda Ann Sharp*[5], *James (Jim) Charles Sr.*[4], *Adron (Edwin/Ade) Sr.*[3], *Charles W. Sr.*[2], *John Sr.*[1]) was born 25 Jun 1944 in Lauderdale County, AL.

Virginia married **Charles Thomas Risner**, son of **William Thomas Risner** and **Edith Olean Phillips**, 19 Nov 1960 in Ringgold, GA. Charles was born in 1943 in Lauderdale County, AL, died 14 Jun 2001, and was buried in Sherrod Valley Cemetery, Lauderdale County, AL.
+ 4814 F i. **Tina Louise Risner** was born 2 Feb 1962 in Lauderdale County, AL.
4815 M ii. **Zachary Lane Risner** was born 20 Mar 1964 in Lauderdale County, AL.

2933. Freddie Lee Bruce Sr. (*John Gilbert Bruce Sr.*[7], *James Pinkney Bruce Sr.*[6], *Matilda Ann Sharp*[5], *James (Jim) Charles Sr.*[4], *Adron (Edwin/Ade) Sr.*[3], *Charles W. Sr.*[2], *John Sr.*[1]) was born 15 Jan 1946 in Lauderdale County, AL.

Freddie married **Pamela Jo Von Linsowe**, daughter of **Martin John Von Linsowe** and **Wilma M. Fields**, 17 Jan 1970 in Flint, MI. Pamela was born 15 Jan 1951 in Lexington, KY.
4816 F i. **Amy Bruce** was born 8 Jan 1977 in Flint, MI.
4817 M ii. **Freddie Lee Bruce Jr.** was born 12 Jan 1979 in Flint, MI.

2934. Amos Jerry Bruce Jr. (*Amos Jerry Bruce Sr.*[7], *Robert William Bruce*[6], *Matilda Ann Sharp*[5], *James (Jim) Charles Sr.*[4], *Adron (Edwin/Ade) Sr.*[3], *Charles W. Sr.*[2], *John Sr.*[1]) was born 24 Feb 1942 in Rogersville, Lauderdale County, AL.

Amos married **Betty Ruth Bryant**, daughter of **Charles Kyle Bryant** and **Alta Stella Simmons**, 24 Jun 1963 in Noblesville, Hamilton County, IN. Betty was born 20 Jun 1943 in Fair Oak, AR.
+ 4818 M i. **Gregory Alan Bruce** was born 23 Sep 1964 in Anderson, IN.

+ 4819 M   ii.   **Scott Blakney Bruce** was born 14 Oct 1969 in Athens, GA.

2935. Charles William Bruce (*Amos Jerry Bruce Sr.*[7], *Robert William Bruce*[6], *Matilda Ann Sharp*[5], *James (Jim) Charles Sr.*[4], *Adron (Edwin/Ade) Sr.*[3], *Charles W. Sr.*[2], *John Sr.*[1]) was born 16 Oct 1945 in Florence, Lauderdale County, AL.

Charles married **Susan Mitchell Adams**, daughter of **Frederick Adams** and **Everette Mitchell**, 3 Aug 1968 in Tuscumbia, Colbert County, AL. Susan was born 6 Aug 1946 in Colbert County, AL.
+ 4820 F   i.   **Shannon Kelly Bruce** was born 2 Feb 1971 in Lownes County, GA.
+ 4821 M   ii.   **Chad Adam Bruce** was born 20 Oct 1977 in Opelika, Lee County, AL.

2936. Evelyn Katherine Bruce (*Amos Jerry Bruce Sr.*[7], *Robert William Bruce*[6], *Matilda Ann Sharp*[5], *James (Jim) Charles Sr.*[4], *Adron (Edwin/Ade) Sr.*[3], *Charles W. Sr.*[2], *John Sr.*[1]) was born 27 Jun 1952 in Lauderdale County, AL.

Evelyn married **Michael Eroy Bradford**, son of **Joe B. Bradford** and **Marlene Byrd**, 16 Apr 1971 in Lauderdale County, AL. Michael was born 27 Aug 1952 in Lauderdale County, AL.

Evelyn next married **Terry Don Horton** 30 Oct 1980 in Lauderdale County, AL. Terry was born 15 Oct 1947 in Lauderdale County, AL.

Evelyn next married **Jerry Weedman** 16 Aug 1982.

2937. Rachel Annette Bruce (*Amos Jerry Bruce Sr.*[7], *Robert William Bruce*[6], *Matilda Ann Sharp*[5], *James (Jim) Charles Sr.*[4], *Adron (Edwin/Ade) Sr.*[3], *Charles W. Sr.*[2], *John Sr.*[1]) was born 18 Apr 1958 in Lauderdale County, AL.

Rachel married **Danny Thomas Hollander**, son of **Donald Thomas Hollander** and **Unknown**, 2 Apr 1977 in Tuscumbia, Colbert County, AL. Danny was born 20 Apr 1958 in Lauderdale County, AL.
+ 4822 M   i.   **Drew Nathaniel Hollander** was born 4 Oct 1981 in Lauderdale County, AL.
  4823 F   ii.   **Callie Michelle Hollander** was born 9 May 1985 in Lauderdale County, AL.

• **Elizabeth Ann Mason** was born 26 April 1949 in Florence, Lauderale County, AL.

Elizabeth married **Dwight Lamar Evans**, son of **William (Bill) Buster Evans** and **Vera Morrow** 19 Dec 1971 in Florence, Lauderdale County, AL. Dwight was born 27 Oct 1951 in Walker County, AL.
    M   i   **Kristopher Dwight Evans** was born 21 Aug 1976 in Decatur, AL. See page 505.
    F   ii   **Lori Ann Evans** was born 29 Nov 1979, Decatur, AL. See page 505.

2938. Merita Kay Bruce (*Reeder Warner Bruce*[7], *Robert William Bruce*[6], *Matilda Ann Sharp*[5], *James (Jim) Charles Sr.*[4], *Adron (Edwin/Ade) Sr.*[3], *Charles W. Sr.*[2], *John Sr.*[1]) was born 17 Mar 1948 in Lauderdale County, AL.

Merita married **William Kimberly (Kim) Newton**, son of **William D. Newton** and **Dorothy J. Beddingfield**, 7 Aug 1970 in Lauderdale County, AL. William was born 7 Jul 1949 in Limestone County, AL.
+ 4824 F   i.   **Kelly Newton**.
+ 4825 F   ii.   **Reeda Newton**.

2939. Lanny Warner Bruce (*Reeder Warner Bruce*[7], *Robert William Bruce*[6], *Matilda Ann Sharp*[5], *James (Jim) Charles Sr.*[4], *Adron (Edwin/Ade) Sr.*[3], *Charles W. Sr.*[2], *John Sr.*[1]) was born 20 Mar 1951 in Lauderdale County, AL.

Lanny married **Joyce Elaine Davis**, daughter of **Lloyd G. Davis** and **Jewell Haddock**, 23 Sep 1972 in Lauderdale County, AL. Joyce was born 23 Jan 1952 in Lauderdale County, AL.
+ 4826 M   i.   **Collin Warner Bruce**.
+ 4827 F   ii.   **Emily Bruce**.
+ 4828 F   iii.   **Kelly Bruce**.
+ 4829 F   iv.   **Reeda Bruce**.

2940. Mitzi Diane Bruce (*Reeder Warner Bruce* ^{7}, *Robert William Bruce* ^{6}, *Matilda Ann Sharp* ^{5}, *James (Jim) Charles Sr.* ^{4}, *Adron (Edwin/Ade) Sr.* ^{3}, *Charles W. Sr.* ^{2}, *John Sr.* ^{1}) was born 20 Feb 1957 in Lauderdale County, AL.

Mitzi married **Dalen Eugene Keys**, son of **Charles E. Keys** and **L. Juanita Stevens**, 31 Dec 1975 in Lauderdale County, AL. Dalen was born 9 Apr 1957 in Monroe County, NY.

+ 4830 F i. **Tiffany Keys**.
  4831 F ii. **Hannah Keys**.
  4832 M iii. **Chase Sawyer Keys**.

2941. Bobby Joel Bruce (*Robert Cyrus Bruce* ^{7}, *Robert William Bruce* ^{6}, *Matilda Ann Sharp* ^{5}, *James (Jim) Charles Sr.* ^{4}, *Adron (Edwin/Ade) Sr.* ^{3}, *Charles W. Sr.* ^{2}, *John Sr.* ^{1}).

Bobby married **Glois *Unk**.
  4833 M i. **David Joey Bruce**.

2942. Betty Jane Bruce (*Robert Cyrus Bruce* ^{7}, *Robert William Bruce* ^{6}, *Matilda Ann Sharp* ^{5}, *James (Jim) Charles Sr.* ^{4}, *Adron (Edwin/Ade) Sr.* ^{3}, *Charles W. Sr.* ^{2}, *John Sr.* ^{1}).

Betty married **Ray *Unk**.

2943. Donna Sue Bruce (*Robert Cyrus Bruce* ^{7}, *Robert William Bruce* ^{6}, *Matilda Ann Sharp* ^{5}, *James (Jim) Charles Sr.* ^{4}, *Adron (Edwin/Ade) Sr.* ^{3}, *Charles W. Sr.* ^{2}, *John Sr.* ^{1}).

Donna married **Tim *Unk**.

2944. Janice Bruce (*Harding Abel Bruce* ^{7}, *Robert William Bruce* ^{6}, *Matilda Ann Sharp* ^{5}, *James (Jim) Charles Sr.* ^{4}, *Adron (Edwin/Ade) Sr.* ^{3}, *Charles W. Sr.* ^{2}, *John Sr.* ^{1}).

Janice married ***Unk Coffman**.

2945. Sheila Bruce (*Harding Abel Bruce* ^{7}, *Robert William Bruce* ^{6}, *Matilda Ann Sharp* ^{5}, *James (Jim) Charles Sr.* ^{4}, *Adron (Edwin/Ade) Sr.* ^{3}, *Charles W. Sr.* ^{2}, *John Sr.* ^{1}).

Sheila married ***Unk Houser**.

2946. Becky Bruce (*Harding Abel Bruce* ^{7}, *Robert William Bruce* ^{6}, *Matilda Ann Sharp* ^{5}, *James (Jim) Charles Sr.* ^{4}, *Adron (Edwin/Ade) Sr.* ^{3}, *Charles W. Sr.* ^{2}, *John Sr.* ^{1}).

Becky married ***Unk Wegner**.

2948. Beverly Jo Melton (*Viola T. Bruce* ^{7}, *Robert William Bruce* ^{6}, *Matilda Ann Sharp* ^{5}, *James (Jim) Charles Sr.* ^{4}, *Adron (Edwin/Ade) Sr.* ^{3}, *Charles W. Sr.* ^{2}, *John Sr.* ^{1}) was born 27 Dec 1952 in Lauderdale County, AL.

Beverly married **Sam Barton**.
  4834 M i. **Nicholas James Barton** was born 28 Oct 1985.

2950. Johnny Bruce Chesnutt (*John C. Bruce* ^{7}, *Robert William Bruce* ^{6}, *Matilda Ann Sharp* ^{5}, *James (Jim) Charles Sr.* ^{4}, *Adron (Edwin/Ade) Sr.* ^{3}, *Charles W. Sr.* ^{2}, *John Sr.* ^{1}).

Johnny married **Judy *Unk**.

2951. Tracy Bruce (*John C. Bruce* ^{7}, *Robert William Bruce* ^{6}, *Matilda Ann Sharp* ^{5}, *James (Jim) Charles Sr.* ^{4}, *Adron (Edwin/Ade) Sr.* ^{3}, *Charles W. Sr.* ^{2}, *John Sr.* ^{1}).

Tracy married **Tracy Longfellow**.

2964. Rose Marie Summers (*Magie Estelle Long^7, Lilly Eddie Levie Bruce^6, Matilda Ann Sharp^5, James (Jim) Charles Sr.^{4}, Adron (Edwin/Ade) Sr.^{3}, Charles W. Sr.^{2}, John Sr.^{1}*) was born 10 Mar 1938 in Memphis, Shelby County, TN.

Rose married **Henry Edward Miller** 2 Mar 1957 in San Diego, CA. Henry was born 1 May 1931 in Harvard, NE.

3006. Gracie Mozella Phillips (*Lady Carrie Wood^7, Margie Ann (Marjorie) Bruce^6, Matilda Ann Sharp^5, James (Jim) Charles Sr.^{4}, Adron (Edwin/Ade) Sr.^{3}, Charles W. Sr.^{2}, John Sr.^{1}*) was born 24 Sep 1934 in Waterloo, Lauderdale County, AL.

Gracie married **Edward Earl Mitchell** 22 Dec 1951. Edward was born 12 Nov 1925 in Waterloo, Lauderdale County, AL.
+ 4835 M   i.   **Steven Earl Mitchell** was born 26 Oct 1952 in Harrisburg, Poinsett County, AR.
+ 4836 M   ii. **Kevin Bruce Mitchell** was born 7 Nov 1960.

3007. Marcella Vernette Phillips (*Lady Carrie Wood^7, Margie Ann (Marjorie) Bruce^6, Matilda Ann Sharp^5, James (Jim) Charles Sr.^{4}, Adron (Edwin/Ade) Sr.^{3}, Charles W. Sr.^{2}, John Sr.^{1}*) was born 25 Jul 1936 in Waterloo, Lauderdale County, AL.

Marcella married **Oliver Dewey Carter** 23 Oct 1954. Oliver was born 27 Dec 1932.
+ 4837 F   i.   **Shirley Ann Carter** was born 27 Aug 1959.
+ 4838 F   ii.   **Sue Carter** was born 26 Jan 1961.
+ 4839 F   iii. **Norma Jean Carter**.

3008. Clista Faye Phillips (*Lady Carrie Wood^7, Margie Ann (Marjorie) Bruce^6, Matilda Ann Sharp^5, James (Jim) Charles Sr.^{4}, Adron (Edwin/Ade) Sr.^{3}, Charles W. Sr.^{2}, John Sr.^{1}*) was born 8 Feb 1938 in Waterloo, Lauderdale County, AL.

Clista married **Herman Ray Scott** 10 Apr 1956. Herman was born 9 Sep 1934 in Alabama.
  4840 M   i.   **Danny Ray Scott** was born 27 Aug 1958, died 21 Jul 1986, and was buried in Bumpus Creek Cemetery, Lauderdale County, AL.
+ 4841 F   ii.   **Deborah Faye (Debbie) Scott** was born 31 Oct 1970 in Lauderdale County, AL.
+ 4842 M   iii. **David Mark Scott** was born 4 Oct 1974.
  4843 M   iv.   **Gary Dewayne Scott** was born 21 Oct 1980.

3009. Mable Rita Phillips (*Lady Carrie Wood^7, Margie Ann (Marjorie) Bruce^6, Matilda Ann Sharp^5, James (Jim) Charles Sr.^{4}, Adron (Edwin/Ade) Sr.^{3}, Charles W. Sr.^{2}, John Sr.^{1}*) was born 31 May 1939 in Waterloo, Lauderdale County, AL.

Mable married **Robert (R. J.) Sharpston Sr.** 23 Jul 1956 in Lauderdale County, AL. Robert was born 28 Jan 1935.
  4844 F   i.   **Dora Lynn Sharpston** was born 30 Oct 1957 in Tyronza, Poinsett County, AR, died 30 Oct 1957, and was buried in Tyronza Cemetery, Tyronza, Poinsett County, AR.
+ 4845 M   ii.   **Bennie Erin Sharpston** was born 19 Mar 1959 in Crittenden County, AR.
+ 4846 F   iii. **Theresa Maxine Sharpston** was born 8 May 1961 in Florida.
+ 4847 M   iv.   **Robert (R. J.) Sharpston Jr.** was born 1 Mar 1962 in Florida.
+ 4848 F   v.   **Lisa Diane Sharpston** was born 8 Jan 1969 in Alabama.
+ 4849 M   vi.   **Timothy Waylon Sharpston** was born 2 Apr 1974 in Alabama.

3010. Ronald Eugene Phillips (*Lady Carrie Wood^7, Margie Ann (Marjorie) Bruce^6, Matilda Ann Sharp^5, James (Jim) Charles Sr.^{4}, Adron (Edwin/Ade) Sr.^{3}, Charles W. Sr.^{2}, John Sr.^{1}*) was born 17 May 1941 in Waterloo, Lauderdale County, AL.

Ronald married **Florine Kelley**, daughter of **William Colonel (Cornel) Kelley** and **Elizabeth (Lizzie) Young**, 7 Mar 1960 in Lauderdale County, AL. Florine was born 5 Feb 1940 in Lauderdale County, AL, died 24 Apr 2005, and was buried in Oak Grove Cemetery, Lauderdale County, AL.

+ 4850 F i. **Laura Jane Phillips** was born 6 Mar 1961 in Lauderdale County, AL.

  4851 M ii. **Randy Lee Phillips** was born 11 Jul 1963 in Lauderdale County, AL, died 10 Jul 1982, and was buried in Oak Grove Cemetery, Lauderdale County, AL.

  General Notes: "see notes under brother Roger Gene..." Sharon Wood

  4852 M iii. **Roger Gene Phillips** was born 7 Aug 1965 in Lauderdale County, AL, died 10 Jul 1982, and was buried in Oak Grove Cemetery, Lauderdale County, AL.

  General Notes: "Died in a drowning accident while swimming with his brother and three others at Oneal Bridge, Florence, Alabama. The Times Daily stated that the boys had been swimming about one and one- half hours when an undertow current occurred and pulled three of the boys under. Roger, his brother, Randy, and a cousin, Randy Kelley, all were drowned. They are all buried at Oak Grove Cemetery...." Sharon Wood

  4853 F iv. **Rhonda Kaye Phillips** was born 13 Jan 1968 in Lauderdale County, AL, died 3 Feb 1968, and was buried in Oak Grove Cemetery, Lauderdale County, AL.

+ 4854 F v. **Sherry Ann Phillips** was born 17 Apr 1969.

+ 4855 F vi. **Patricia Diane Phillips** was born 14 Mar 1970.

+ 4856 M vii. **Gaylon Ronald Phillips** was born 2 Sep 1972 in Lauderdale County, AL.

3011. Billy Gerald Phillips (*Lady Carrie Wood*[7], *Margie Ann (Marjorie) Bruce*[6], *Matilda Ann Sharp*[5], *James (Jim) Charles Sr.*[4], *Adron (Edwin/Ade) Sr.*[3], *Charles W. Sr.*[2], *John Sr.*[1]) was born 22 Aug 1943 in Waterloo, Lauderdale County, AL.

Billy married **Thelma Chambers** in 1979.

3012. Clara Lavon Phillips (*Lady Carrie Wood*[7], *Margie Ann (Marjorie) Bruce*[6], *Matilda Ann Sharp*[5], *James (Jim) Charles Sr.*[4], *Adron (Edwin/Ade) Sr.*[3], *Charles W. Sr.*[2], *John Sr.*[1]) was born 16 Apr 1946 in Waterloo, Lauderdale County, AL, died 13 Feb 1976, and was buried in Oak Grove Cemetery, Lauderdale County, AL.

Clara married **Bobby Shearil Burney**, son of **Jim Burney** and **Susie Joiner**, 28 Feb 1966 in Lauderdale County, AL. Bobby was born 15 Feb 1942 in Lauderdale County, AL.

  4857 F i. **Melissa Faye Burney**.

  4858 F ii. **Michelle Burney**.

3013. Milton Dale Phillips Sr. (*Lady Carrie Wood*[7], *Margie Ann (Marjorie) Bruce*[6], *Matilda Ann Sharp*[5], *James (Jim) Charles Sr.*[4], *Adron (Edwin/Ade) Sr.*[3], *Charles W. Sr.*[2], *John Sr.*[1]) was born 5 Nov 1947 in Waterloo, Lauderdale County, AL, died 4 Aug 2004, and was buried in Oak Grove Cemetery, Lauderdale County, AL.

Milton married **Pamela Gail Barnett**, daughter of **Hollis Turner Barnett** and **Dorothy Christine Miller**, 1 Nov 1969 in Lauderdale County, AL. Pamela was born 26 Aug 1951, died 13 Mar 1998, and was buried in Oak Grove Cemetery, Lauderdale County, AL.

+ 4859 F i. **Tina Phillips** was born about 1970.

+ 4860 F ii. **Tammy Phillips** was born about 1971.

+ 4861 M iii. **Milton Dale Phillips Jr.** was born about 1972.

+ 4862 F iv. **Tamesa Phillips** was born about 1976.

+ 4863 F v. **Tara Phillips** was born 8 Aug 1979.

Milton next married **Sherry Barnett**.

3014. Claude Ellis Wood Jr. (*Claude Ellis Wood Sr.*[7], *Margie Ann (Marjorie) Bruce*[6], *Matilda Ann Sharp*[5], *James (Jim) Charles Sr.*[4], *Adron (Edwin/Ade) Sr.*[3], *Charles W. Sr.*[2], *John Sr.*[1]) was born 19 Dec 1936 in Florence, Lauderdale County, AL.

Claude married **Eva Witt**, daughter of **Homer Lee Witt** and **Mae Belle Young**, 1 Nov 1953 in Iuka, Tishomingo County, MS. Eva was born 25 Oct 1937 in Lauderdale County, AL.
(Duplicate Line. See Person 1763)

3015. Eva Jean Wood (*Claude Ellis Wood Sr.*[7], *Margie Ann (Marjorie) Bruce*[6], *Matilda Ann Sharp*[5], *James (Jim) Charles Sr.*[4], *Adron (Edwin/Ade) Sr.*[3], *Charles W. Sr.*[2], *John Sr.*[1]) was born 21 Mar 1939 in Florence, Lauderdale County, AL, died 31 May 2005, and was buried in Oak Grove Cemetery, Lauderdale County, AL.

Eva married **Cletus Dempsey (Skeet) Young**, son of **William (Bill) Young** and **Audry Sharp**, about 1956 in Iuka, Tishomingo County, MS. Cletus was born 3 Nov 1937 in Lauderdale County, AL.
(Duplicate Line. See Person 1516)

3016. Rachel Ann Wood (*Claude Ellis Wood Sr.*[7], *Margie Ann (Marjorie) Bruce*[6], *Matilda Ann Sharp*[5], *James (Jim) Charles Sr.*[4], *Adron (Edwin/Ade) Sr.*[3], *Charles W. Sr.*[2], *John Sr.*[1]) was born 21 Feb 1942 in Florence, Lauderdale County, AL.

Rachel married **James Charles (J. C.) Young**, son of **Ellie Bert Young** and **Eura (Eurie) Sharp**, 8 Apr 1961 in Lauderdale County, AL. James was born 26 Oct 1940 in Florence, Lauderdale County, AL.
(Duplicate Line. See Person 1521)

3017. Larry Ray (Soap) Wood (*Claude Ellis Wood Sr.*[7], *Margie Ann (Marjorie) Bruce*[6], *Matilda Ann Sharp*[5], *James (Jim) Charles Sr.*[4], *Adron (Edwin/Ade) Sr.*[3], *Charles W. Sr.*[2], *John Sr.*[1]) was born 22 May 1944 in Florence, Lauderdale County, AL, died 22 Oct 1987, and was buried in Oak Grove Cemetery, Lauderdale County, AL.

Larry married **Peggy Jo Scott**, daughter of **Robert Owen Scott** and **Eula Beatrice Young**, 11 Sep 1961 in Lauderdale County, AL. Peggy was born 19 Nov 1944 in Lauderdale County, AL.
(Duplicate Line. See Person 1794)

3018. Wallace Earl Wood (*Leonard Earl Wood*[7], *Margie Ann (Marjorie) Bruce*[6], *Matilda Ann Sharp*[5], *James (Jim) Charles Sr.*[4], *Adron (Edwin/Ade) Sr.*[3], *Charles W. Sr.*[2], *John Sr.*[1]) was born 24 Nov 1939 in Florence, Lauderdale County, AL.

Wallace married **Beulah Estelle Smith**, daughter of **Elbert Grady Smith** and **Nomer Marie Young**, 24 Jun 1958 in Booneville, MS. Beulah was born 21 Mar 1941 in Alabama.
(Duplicate Line. See Person 1770)

3019. Thomas Moore Wood (*Leonard Earl Wood*[7], *Margie Ann (Marjorie) Bruce*[6], *Matilda Ann Sharp*[5], *James (Jim) Charles Sr.*[4], *Adron (Edwin/Ade) Sr.*[3], *Charles W. Sr.*[2], *John Sr.*[1]) was born 1 Jul 1941 in Florence, Lauderdale County, AL.

Thomas had a relationship with **Lois Inez Bevis**, daughter of **Andrew Griffin Bevis** and **Cora Belle McFall**. Lois was born 7 Mar 1942 in Wayne County, TN.
+ 4864 F   i.   **Carol Sue Wood** was born 29 Aug 1961 in Lauderdale County, AL.
+ 4865 M   ii.   **Randall Thomas Wood** was born 14 Feb 1964 in Lauderdale County, AL.

Thomas married **Billie Jane Guthrie**, daughter of **Harry Guthrie** and **Amanda Van Housen**, 13 Nov 1972 in Lauderdale County, AL. Billie was born 13 Dec 1933 in Marion County, TN.
+ 4866 M   i.   **Joseph Thomas (Tommy) Wood** was born 29 May 1976 in ECM Hospital, Florence, Lauderdale County, AL.

3020. Geraldine (Judy) Wood (*Leonard Earl Wood*[7], *Margie Ann (Marjorie) Bruce*[6], *Matilda Ann Sharp*[5], *James (Jim) Charles Sr.*[4], *Adron (Edwin/Ade) Sr.*[3], *Charles W. Sr.*[2], *John Sr.*[1]) was born 27 Dec 1942 in Florence, Lauderdale County, AL.

Geraldine married **Ray Brown**, son of **Clarence E. Brown** and **Ruby Mae Geans**, 10 Feb 1959 in Lauderdale County, AL. Ray was born 17 Nov 1941 in Lauderdale County, AL.
+ 4867 F   i.   **Teresa Jo Brown** was born 20 Dec 1959 in Lauderdale County, AL.
+ 4868 M   ii.   **Travis Ray Brown** was born 30 Oct 1961 in Florence, Lauderdale County, AL.

+ 4869 M iii.   **Terry Richard Brown** was born 27 May 1968 in Florence, Lauderdale County, AL.

3021. Jo Carolyn Wood (*Leonard Earl Wood*[7], *Margie Ann (Marjorie) Bruce*[6], *Matilda Ann Sharp*[5], *James (Jim) Charles Sr.*[4], *Adron (Edwin/Ade) Sr.*[3], *Charles W. Sr.*[2], *John Sr.*[1]) was born 16 Jun 1948 in Florence, Lauderdale County, AL.

Jo married **Rayburn Leon Allison**, son of **Raymond Andrew Allison** and **Bama Inez Ingram**, 29 Aug 1964 in Lauderdale County, AL. Rayburn was born 13 Jun 1946 in Lauderdale County, AL.
(Duplicate Line. See Person 1601)

3023. Louise Phillips Reeves (*Leonard Earl Wood*[7], *Margie Ann (Marjorie) Bruce*[6], *Matilda Ann Sharp*[5], *James (Jim) Charles Sr.*[4], *Adron (Edwin/Ade) Sr.*[3], *Charles W. Sr.*[2], *John Sr.*[1]) was born about 1943 in Lauderdale County, AL.

Louise married **Harvey Ross Young**, son of **Robert Edward (Bunt) Young** and **Estelle Eugene Wood**, in Lauderdale County, AL. Harvey was born 22 Aug 1935 in Lauderdale County, AL.
4870 M i.   **Raymond Young**.
4871 M ii.   **Edward Young**.

3024. Peggy Ann Wood (*Wallace Ray Wood*[7], *Margie Ann (Marjorie) Bruce*[6], *Matilda Ann Sharp*[5], *James (Jim) Charles Sr.*[4], *Adron (Edwin/Ade) Sr.*[3], *Charles W. Sr.*[2], *John Sr.*[1]) was born 4 Jul 1948.

Peggy married ***Unk Eldridge**.

3025. Johnny Ray Wood (*Wallace Ray Wood*[7], *Margie Ann (Marjorie) Bruce*[6], *Matilda Ann Sharp*[5], *James (Jim) Charles Sr.*[4], *Adron (Edwin/Ade) Sr.*[3], *Charles W. Sr.*[2], *John Sr.*[1]) was born 15 Jun 1958 in West Memphis, Crittenden County, AR.

Johnny married **Nancy Lynn Melton**, daughter of **Buford Eldred Melton Sr.** and **Annabelle Jeanette (Ann) Unsted**, 12 Jun 1978 in Lauderdale County, AL. Nancy was born 12 Jun 1962 in Lauderdale County, AL.
+ 4872 M i.   **Jason Ray Wood** was born 10 May 1984 in ECM Hospital, Florence, Lauderdale County, AL.
4873 M ii.   **Jeremy Lynn Wood** was born 18 Feb 1988 in ECM Hospital, Florence, Lauderdale County, AL.

3026. Mark Alan Wood (*Wallace Ray Wood*[7], *Margie Ann (Marjorie) Bruce*[6], *Matilda Ann Sharp*[5], *James (Jim) Charles Sr.*[4], *Adron (Edwin/Ade) Sr.*[3], *Charles W. Sr.*[2], *John Sr.*[1]) was born 26 Dec 1964 in Florence, Lauderdale County, AL.

Mark married **Amy Sue Zimmerman** 12 Oct 2002 in Lauderdale County, AL. Amy was born in Baraboo, WI.

3028. James Burt (J B) Webb (*Fannie Birdie Sharp*[7], *Lee Hal*[6], *Owen Bennett (Doc)*[5], *James (Jim) Charles Sr.*[4], *Adron (Edwin/Ade) Sr.*[3], *Charles W. Sr.*[2], *John Sr.*[1]) was born 27 Nov 1936 in Lauderdale County, AL.

James married **Nancy Fay Taylor**, daughter of **Lyle Edward Taylor** and **Mary Ethel Garett**, 27 Nov 1959 in Lauderdale County, AL. Nancy was born 12 Jun 1936 in Corinth, Alcorn County, MS.
+ 4874 M i.   **Burt Taylor Webb** was born 8 Jul 1962 in Lauderdale County, AL.
4875 F ii.   **Anna Kathryn Webb** was born 18 May 1968 in Lauderdale County, AL.

3029. Reeda Mae Sharp (*Reeder Earl*[7], *Lee Hal*[6], *Owen Bennett (Doc)*[5], *James (Jim) Charles Sr.*[4], *Adron (Edwin/Ade) Sr.*[3], *Charles W. Sr.*[2], *John Sr.*[1]) was born 9 Mar 1935 in Lauderdale County, AL.

Reeda married **James Ellis Jones**, son of **Homer Lee Jones** and **Lillian T. Ticer**, 20 Jun 1951 in Iuka, Tishomingo County, MS. James was born 30 May 1931 in Lauderdale County, AL, died 2 Jan 1985, and was buried in Wright Cemetery, Wright, Lauderdale County, AL.
(Duplicate Line. See Person 1234)

Reeda next married **David Narimore**.

3030. Betty June Sharp (*Reeder Earl*[7], *Lee Hal*[6], *Owen Bennett (Doc)*[5], *James (Jim) Charles Sr.*[4], *Adron (Edwin/Ade) Sr.*[3], *Charles W. Sr.*[2], *John Sr.*[1]) was born 8 Jun 1936 in Lauderdale County, AL.

Betty married **Thomas Roger Vaughn Jr.**, son of **Thomas Roger Vaughn Sr.** and **Gladys Dean Wallace**, 21 Jul 1952 in Iuka, Tishomingo County, MS. Thomas was born 4 Apr 1933 in Corinth, Alcorn County, MS, died 26 Aug 1992, and was buried in Walston Cemetery, Oakland, Lauderdale County, AL.

+ 4876	F	i.	**Connie Faye Vaughn** was born 21 Apr 1953 in Lauderdale County, AL.
+ 4877	M	ii.	**Anthony (Tony) Reed Vaughn** was born 21 Nov 1956 in Lauderdale County, AL, died 18 May 1989, and was buried in Walston Cemetery, Oakland, Lauderdale County, AL.
4878	M	iii.	**Joey Jay Vaughn** was born 25 Aug 1961 in Lauderdale County, AL.
+ 4879	M	iv.	**Eric Jerome Vaughn** was born 7 Jun 1963 in Lauderdale County, AL.
4880	M	v.	**Mitchell Cline Vaughn** was born 23 Jun 1964 in Lauderdale County, AL.

3031. Wanda Gail Mansell (*Grace Leona Sharp*[7], *Lee Hal*[6], *Owen Bennett (Doc)*[5], *James (Jim) Charles Sr.*[4], *Adron (Edwin/Ade) Sr.*[3], *Charles W. Sr.*[2], *John Sr.*[1]) was born 17 Mar 1943 in Lauderdale County, AL.

Wanda married **Roger Stephen Mann**, son of **Cleburn L. Mann** and **Mary Sandy**, 3 May 1985 in Lauderdale County, AL. Roger was born 29 Mar 1948 in Benton City, TN.

3032. Bobby Elmer Mansell (*Grace Leona Sharp*[7], *Lee Hal*[6], *Owen Bennett (Doc)*[5], *James (Jim) Charles Sr.*[4], *Adron (Edwin/Ade) Sr.*[3], *Charles W. Sr.*[2], *John Sr.*[1]) was born 6 Feb 1952 in Lauderdale County, AL.

Bobby married **Janice Marie Burbank**, daughter of **Ronnie Dale Burbank** and **Ruby Lucille Allison**, 29 Oct 1971 in Lauderdale County, AL. Janice was born 12 Feb 1956 in Lauderdale County, AL.

4881	M	i.	**Tracy Wade Mansell** was born 21 Apr 1972 in Lauderdale County, AL.

3033. Irish Virginia Perkins (*Ethel Lucille Glasscock*[7], *Ada Irene Sharp*[6], *Owen Bennett (Doc)*[5], *James (Jim) Charles Sr.*[4], *Adron (Edwin/Ade) Sr.*[3], *Charles W. Sr.*[2], *John Sr.*[1]) was born 4 Nov 1938 in Lauderdale County, AL.

Irish married **Henry Shannon Phillips Sr.**, son of **Henry Coburn Phillips** and **Doris McPeters**, 1 Jun 1958 in Lauderdale County, AL. Henry was born 19 Oct 1937 in Fernandina Beach, Nassau County, FL.

+ 4882	F	i.	**Pamela Denise Phillips** was born 14 Apr 1959 in Lauderdale County, AL.
4883	M	ii.	**Henry Shannon Phillips Jr.** was born 2 May 1960 in Lauderdale County, AL.
+ 4884	M	iii.	**Kevin Patrick Phillips** was born 31 Oct 1961 in Lauderdale County, AL.
+ 4885	F	iv.	**Dana Colleen Phillips** was born 16 Jan 1963 in Hartselle, AL.
+ 4886	M	v.	**Gwendolyn Carmel Phillips** was born 11 Jun 1967 in Athens, Limestone County, AL.

3034. Mary Elaine Perkins (*Ethel Lucille Glasscock*[7], *Ada Irene Sharp*[6], *Owen Bennett (Doc)*[5], *James (Jim) Charles Sr.*[4], *Adron (Edwin/Ade) Sr.*[3], *Charles W. Sr.*[2], *John Sr.*[1]) was born 12 May 1940 in Lauderdale County, AL.

Mary married **Buddy Gene Poorman**, son of **Merhl Poorman** and **Verla Brown**, 14 Jun 1971 in Lauderdale County, AL. Buddy was born 12 Dec 1939 in Hutchinson, Reno, KS.

4887	M	i.	**Joy Lee Poorman** was born 11 Aug 1974.

3035. Myra Evelyn Perkins (*Ethel Lucille Glasscock*[7], *Ada Irene Sharp*[6], *Owen Bennett (Doc)*[5], *James (Jim) Charles Sr.*[4], *Adron (Edwin/Ade) Sr.*[3], *Charles W. Sr.*[2], *John Sr.*[1]) was born 10 Jan 1942 in Lauderdale County, AL.

Myra married **William (Billy) Aaron Smith Jr.**, son of **William Aaron Smith Sr.** and **Christine Llewellyn**, 17 Jul 1960 in Lauderdale County, AL. William was born 20 Feb 1941 in Lauderdale County, AL.

4888	F	i.	**Natalie Suzanne Smith** was born 12 Sep 1961.

Myra next married **Jim Brown**.

3036. George Stanley Perkins Jr. (*Ethel Lucille Glasscock*[7], *Ada Irene Sharp*[6], *Owen Bennett (Doc)*[5], *James (Jim) Charles Sr.*[4], *Adron (Edwin/Ade) Sr.*[3], *Charles W. Sr.*[2], *John Sr.*[1]) was born 17 Sep 1946 in Lauderdale County, AL.

George married **Ann Burdette** 30 May 1993 in Nachitoches, LA.

    4889 F   i.   **Leah Renee Perkins**.

3037. Brenda Glasscock (*Fred Glasscock Sr.* [7], *Ada Irene Sharp* [6], *Owen Bennett (Doc)* [5], *James (Jim) Charles Sr.* [4], *Adron (Edwin/Ade) Sr.* [3], *Charles W. Sr.* [2], *John Sr.* [1]).

Brenda married ***Unk Olson**.

3038. Alice Kay Glasscock (*Fred Glasscock Sr.* [7], *Ada Irene Sharp* [6], *Owen Bennett (Doc)* [5], *James (Jim) Charles Sr.* [4], *Adron (Edwin/Ade) Sr.* [3], *Charles W. Sr.* [2], *John Sr.* [1]) was born in Jul 1952.

Alice married **David L. McNair Sr.**, son of **Bobby McNair** and **Unknown**, in Lauderdale County, AL.

  + 4890 F   i.   **Keely Leann McNair** was born 17 Feb 1978 in Lauderdale County, AL.
    4891 M   ii.   **David Lee McNair Jr.**
  + 4892 F   iii.   **Dawn McNair**.
  + 4893 F   iv.   **Dana McNair**.

3039. Fred Glasscock Jr. (*Fred Glasscock Sr.* [7], *Ada Irene Sharp* [6], *Owen Bennett (Doc)* [5], *James (Jim) Charles Sr.* [4], *Adron (Edwin/Ade) Sr.* [3], *Charles W. Sr.* [2], *John Sr.* [1]) was born 19 Apr 1956 in Madison County, AL.

Fred married **Gloria Darlene Dawson**, daughter of **Willard Dawson** and **Mary Hood**, 7 Jun 1975 in Lauderdale County, AL. Gloria was born 21 May 1958 in Boeington County, FL.

    4894 M   i.   **Quentin Glasscock**.
  + 4895 M   ii.   **Bryan Mitchell Glasscock** was born 15 Jul 1978.

3040. Cheryl Antoinette Glasscock (*James Arnold Glasscock* [7], *Ada Irene Sharp* [6], *Owen Bennett (Doc)* [5], *James (Jim) Charles Sr.* [4], *Adron (Edwin/Ade) Sr.* [3], *Charles W. Sr.* [2], *John Sr.* [1]) was born 11 Feb 1947 in Lauderdale County, AL.

Cheryl married **Samuel Tolbert Murphy**, son of **Eugene Whitfield Murphy Jr.** and **Essie Mae Carroll**, 18 Mar 1967 in Barton, FL. Samuel was born 6 Oct 1945 in Petersburg, VA.

    4896 F   i.   **Melody Anne Murphy** was born 5 Jul 1976 in Polk County, FL.

3041. Sam Harold Glasscock (*Harold Owen Glasscock* [7], *Ada Irene Sharp* [6], *Owen Bennett (Doc)* [5], *James (Jim) Charles Sr.* [4], *Adron (Edwin/Ade) Sr.* [3], *Charles W. Sr.* [2], *John Sr.* [1]) was born 16 Sep 1948 in Lauderdale County, AL.

Sam married **Larraine Elizabeth Glock**, daughter of **Charles A. Glock** and **Ruth Morris**, 13 Jun 1970 in Lauderdale County, AL. Larraine was born 12 Jun 1950 in Lauderdale County, AL.

  + 4897 F   i.   **Leigh Marie Glasscock** was born 11 Aug 1973 in Opelika County, AL.
    4898 F   ii.   **Krista Kathryn Glasscock** was born 24 Feb 1976 in Lauderdale County, AL.

3044. Cheri Ann Glasscock (*William Boyce Glasscock* [7], *Ada Irene Sharp* [6], *Owen Bennett (Doc)* [5], *James (Jim) Charles Sr.* [4], *Adron (Edwin/Ade) Sr.* [3], *Charles W. Sr.* [2], *John Sr.* [1]) was born 9 Sep 1955 in Lauderdale County, AL.

Cheri married **Rich Allen Wingo**, son of **Joe H. Wingo Jr.** and **Norma Roll**, 12 Jan 1980 in Lauderdale County, AL. Rich was born 16 Jul 1956 in Tuscaloosa, AL.

    4899 M   i.   **Jacob Joe Wingo** was born 18 Feb 1986 in Tuscaloosa, AL.
    4900 M   ii.   **William Luke Wingo** was born 7 Mar 1994 in Tuscaloosa, AL.

3045. Vicki Lynn Glasscock (*William Boyce Glasscock* [7], *Ada Irene Sharp* [6], *Owen Bennett (Doc)* [5], *James (Jim) Charles Sr.* [4], *Adron (Edwin/Ade) Sr.* [3], *Charles W. Sr.* [2], *John Sr.* [1]) was born 28 Oct 1957 in Lauderdale County, AL.

Vicki married **Allen Cox Jones**, son of **Jasper Allen Jones** and **Francis Cox**, 16 Aug 1980 in Lauderdale County, AL. Allen was born 31 Mar 1955 in Pike County, AL.

    4901 M   i.   **William Allen Jones** was born 11 Nov 1983 in Troy, AL.
    4902 M   ii.   **Benjamin Cox Jones** was born 3 Apr 1987 in Troy, AL.

4903 M iii. **Samuel Jones** was born 19 Apr 1990 in Troy, AL.

3046. Joel Dennis Hanback (*Lois Etoile Sharp*[7], *Harrell Emmett*[6], *Owen Bennett (Doc)*[5], *James (Jim) Charles Sr.*[4], *Adron (Edwin/Ade) Sr.*[3], *Charles W. Sr.*[2], *John Sr.*[1]) was born 12 Sep 1940 in Lauderdale County, AL, died 11 Sep 2001, and was buried in Macedonia Cemetery, Lauderdale County, AL.

Joel married **Doris June Haataja**, daughter of **Elmer Matt Haataja** and **Kathleen Spires**, 16 Apr 1960 in Lauderdale County, AL. Doris was born 26 Nov 1940 in Lauderdale County, AL.

+ 4904 F i. **Deena Lynn Hanback** was born 30 May 1962 in Lapoite County, IN.
+ 4905 F ii. **Charlotte June Hanback** was born 3 Apr 1966 in Lauderdale County, AL.
  4906 M iii. **Phillip Wayne Hanback** was born 23 Nov 1968.

3047. Doris Ann Hanback (*Lois Etoile Sharp*[7], *Harrell Emmett*[6], *Owen Bennett (Doc)*[5], *James (Jim) Charles Sr.*[4], *Adron (Edwin/Ade) Sr.*[3], *Charles W. Sr.*[2], *John Sr.*[1]) was born 25 Sep 1945 in Lauderdale County, AL.

Doris married **Charles Ross May**, son of **Joe Belue May** and **Ann Pauline Haataja**, 30 Oct 1965 in Lauderdale County, AL. Charles was born 25 Mar 1940 in Lauderdale County, AL.

+ 4907 F i. **Stephanie Ann May** was born 19 Mar 1970 in Lauderdale County, AL.
  4908 M ii. **Kevin Ross May** was born 22 Jul 1974 in Lauderdale County, AL.
+ 4909 F iii. **Lynette Carol May** was born 17 Jan 1980 in Lauderdale County, AL.

3048. Nathan Harold Roberson (*Mary Helen Sharp*[7], *Harrell Emmett*[6], *Owen Bennett (Doc)*[5], *James (Jim) Charles Sr.*[4], *Adron (Edwin/Ade) Sr.*[3], *Charles W. Sr.*[2], *John Sr.*[1]) was born 10 Jun 1945 in Lauderdale County, AL.

Nathan married **Amanda Eloise Darby**, daughter of **Ross E. Darby** and **Ruth Young**, 7 Sep 1968 in Lauderdale County, AL. Amanda was born 10 Oct 1947 in Lauderdale County, AL, died 27 May 2000, and was buried in Greenview Memorial Park, Florence, Lauderdale County, AL.

+ 4910 M i. **Paul Nathan Roberson** was born 8 Nov 1972 in Lauderdale County, AL.

3050. Virginia Ann Roberson (*Mary Helen Sharp*[7], *Harrell Emmett*[6], *Owen Bennett (Doc)*[5], *James (Jim) Charles Sr.*[4], *Adron (Edwin/Ade) Sr.*[3], *Charles W. Sr.*[2], *John Sr.*[1]) was born 8 Jan 1949 in Lauderdale County, AL.

Virginia married **Evan LeRoy (Roy) Kelsey**, son of **Evans C. Kelsey** and **Ruth Birdsong**, 21 Jan 1967 in Lauderdale County, AL. Evan was born 31 May 1945 in Giles County, TN.

+ 4911 M i. **Randall Lee (Randy) Kelsey** was born 1 Jan 1969 in Lauderdale County, AL.
+ 4912 M ii. **Robert (Robbie) Michael Kelsey** was born 10 Aug 1971 in Lauderdale County, AL.

Virginia next married **Glenn Arlis Posey**, son of **Harold Vestor Posey** and **Grace *Unk**, about 1978. Glenn was born 9 Jan 1932 in Colbert County, AL.

  4913 F i. **Carolyn Suzanne Posey** was born 21 Jan 1979 in Lauderdale County, AL.

Virginia next married **Glenn Potts** after 1978.

Virginia next married **Billy Smith**.

3051. David Lynn Roberson (*Mary Helen Sharp*[7], *Harrell Emmett*[6], *Owen Bennett (Doc)*[5], *James (Jim) Charles Sr.*[4], *Adron (Edwin/Ade) Sr.*[3], *Charles W. Sr.*[2], *John Sr.*[1]) was born 13 Oct 1950 in Lauderdale County, AL.

David married **Jo Ann Dean** 8 Jun 1974. Jo was born 8 Aug 1951.

  4914 M i. **David Hilton Roberson** was born 4 May 1980 in Montgomery, AL.
  4915 M ii. **John Sherman Roberson** was born 15 Jul 1986.
  4916 F iii. **Mary Nix Roberson** was born 20 Nov 1995.

3052. Larry Bruce Roberson (*Mary Helen Sharp*[7], *Harrell Emmett*[6], *Owen Bennett (Doc)*[5], *James (Jim) Charles Sr.*[4], *Adron (Edwin/Ade) Sr.*[3], *Charles W. Sr.*[2], *John Sr.*[1]) was born 1 May 1952 in Lauderdale County, AL.

Larry married **Teresa Diane McGee**, daughter of **Elvis C. McGee** and **Sarah Cody**, 7 Jun 1976 in Lauderdale County, AL. Teresa was born 2 Aug 1956 in Lauderdale County, AL.

4917 M i. **Larry Ryan Roberson** was born 1 Mar 1981 in Lauderdale County, AL.

4918 M ii. **Lenny Rhet Roberson** was born 8 Aug 1992 in Lauderdale County, AL.

3054. Carolyn Faye Roberson (*Mary Helen Sharp^7, Harrell Emmett^6, Owen Bennett (Doc)^5, James (Jim) Charles Sr.^{4}, Adron (Edwin/Ade) Sr.^{3}, Charles W. Sr.^{2}, John Sr.^{1}*) was born 3 Nov 1955 in Lauderdale County, AL.

Carolyn married **Thomas Randall Crittenden**, son of **Clarence C. Crittenden** and **Rana Balch**, 22 Nov 1975 in Lauderdale County, AL. Thomas was born 16 Apr 1955 in Wayne County, MI.

4919 F i. **Katie Beth Crittenden** was born 23 Nov 1980 in McMinville, TN.

4920 F ii. **Karen Brooke Crittenden** was born 23 Nov 1980 in McMinville, TN.

4921 M iii. **Thomas Wade Crittenden** was born 12 Feb 1985 in McMinville, TN.

3056. Martha Sue Roberson (*Mary Helen Sharp^7, Harrell Emmett^6, Owen Bennett (Doc)^5, James (Jim) Charles Sr.^{4}, Adron (Edwin/Ade) Sr.^{3}, Charles W. Sr.^{2}, John Sr.^{1}*) was born 26 Jul 1959 in Lauderdale County, AL.

Martha married **Bobby Wayne Malone**, son of **John A. Malone** and **Wilma Lee Mitchell**, 3 Sep 1982 in Lauderdale County, AL. Bobby was born 29 Mar 1953 in Colbert County, AL.

3057. Jimmie Nell Wood (*Curtis (Slick) Wood^7, Mildred Sharp^6, Owen Bennett (Doc)^5, James (Jim) Charles Sr.^{4}, Adron (Edwin/Ade) Sr.^{3}, Charles W. Sr.^{2}, John Sr.^{1}*) was born 19 Dec 1939 in Lauderdale County, AL.

Jimmie married **Clarence Murphy** before 1963.

Jimmie next married **Leonard Fred (Bucky) Jacobs**, son of **Thomas E. Jacobs** and **Maggie Lee Weldon**, 30 Jan 1963 in Lauderdale County, AL. Leonard was born 18 Mar 1941 in Lauderdale County, AL.

+ 4922 F i. **Kimberlie Jacobs** was born 19 May 1967.

Jimmie next married **Ralph Webb** after Feb 1963.

3058. Cletus Wood (*Curtis (Slick) Wood^7, Mildred Sharp^6, Owen Bennett (Doc)^5, James (Jim) Charles Sr.^{4}, Adron (Edwin/Ade) Sr.^{3}, Charles W. Sr.^{2}, John Sr.^{1}*) was born 19 Apr 1941 in Lauderdale County, AL, died 23 Jan 1966, and was buried in Oak Grove Cemetery, Lauderdale County, AL.

Cletus married **Marjorie (Margie) Jenkins**, daughter of **Charlie Jenkins** and **Mary Stutts**, 14 Apr 1962 in Lauderdale County, AL. Marjorie was born 31 Jan 1937 in Lawrence County, AL.

+ 4923 F i. **Teresa Anna Wood** was born 14 Jun 1965 in Lauderdale County, AL.

3059. Jerry Glenn Franks (*Mary Edith (Tootsie) Wood^7, Mildred Sharp^6, Owen Bennett (Doc)^5, James (Jim) Charles Sr.^{4}, Adron (Edwin/Ade) Sr.^{3}, Charles W. Sr.^{2}, John Sr.^{1}*) was born 28 Nov 1947.

Jerry married **Rose Marie Shook**, daughter of **Claude Washington Shook** and **Rosella Coggins**, 9 Oct 1965 in Lauderdale County, AL. Rose was born 1 Aug 1947 in Colbert County, AL.

Jerry next married **Marjorie (Margie) Jenkins**, daughter of **Charlie Jenkins** and **Mary Stutts**. Marjorie was born 31 Jan 1937 in Lawrence County, AL.

3060. Larry Roland Franks (*Mary Edith (Tootsie) Wood^7, Mildred Sharp^6, Owen Bennett (Doc)^5, James (Jim) Charles Sr.^{4}, Adron (Edwin/Ade) Sr.^{3}, Charles W. Sr.^{2}, John Sr.^{1}*) was born 21 Dec 1951, died 17 Oct 1981, and was buried in Greenview Memorial Park, Florence, Lauderdale County, AL.

Larry married **Gaynell Nappier**.

4924 M i. **Scott Thomas (Scottie) Jordan**.

4925 F ii. **Jennifer Ann Jordan**.

3061. Sherron Diane Franks (*Mary Edith (Tootsie) Wood^7, Mildred Sharp^6, Owen Bennett (Doc)^5, James (Jim) Charles Sr.^{4}, Adron (Edwin/Ade) Sr.^{3}, Charles W. Sr.^{2}, John Sr.^{1}*) was born 28 Nov 1954.

Sherron married **Kenny Byars**. Kenny was born in Tupelo, MS.

3067. Carla Jo Gibson (*Erlene Wood*^{7}, *Mildred Sharp*^{6}, *Owen Bennett (Doc)*^{5}, *James (Jim) Charles Sr.*^{4}, *Adron (Edwin/Ade) Sr.*^{3}, *Charles W. Sr.*^{2}, *John Sr.*^{1}) was born 15 Jul 1955.

Carla married **Randy James Irvin**. Randy was born 16 Jan 1954.
4926 M i. **Joseph Gibson Irvin** was born 21 Nov 1981.
4927 F ii. **Laura Jane Irvin** was born 8 Dec 1986.

3068. Lisa Gaye Gibson (*Erlene Wood*^{7}, *Mildred Sharp*^{6}, *Owen Bennett (Doc)*^{5}, *James (Jim) Charles Sr.*^{4}, *Adron (Edwin/Ade) Sr.*^{3}, *Charles W. Sr.*^{2}, *John Sr.*^{1}) was born 9 Jun 1961.

Lisa married **Michael Richard Kaczynski**. Michael was born 14 Jul 1961.
4928 F i. **Rebecca Lee Kaczynski** was born 13 Dec 1989.

3069. Shelby Jean Young (*Mary Frances Cummings*^{7}, *Lillie May Sharp*^{6}, *James Charles Jr.*^{5}, *James (Jim) Charles Sr.*^{4}, *Adron (Edwin/Ade) Sr.*^{3}, *Charles W. Sr.*^{2}, *John Sr.*^{1}) was born 31 Mar 1940 in Lauderdale County, AL, died 20 Mar 1995, and was buried in Tri-Cities Memorial Gardens, Florence, Lauderdale County, AL.

Shelby married **Billy Joe Crosslin**, son of **Joe Crosslin** and **Elizabeth Price**, 1 Sep 1956. Billy was born 2 Feb 1939 in Lauderdale County, AL and died 22 Apr 1979.
4929 F i. **Freda Karen Crosslin** was born 12 Dec 1957 in Lauderdale County, AL.
+ 4930 F ii. **Cammie Jo Crosslin** was born 12 Jul 1966 in Zion, IL.

Shelby next married **James Hershel Miles** 4 Mar 1977. James was born 4 Mar 1977.

3070. Pauline (Polly) Young (*Mary Frances Cummings*^{7}, *Lillie May Sharp*^{6}, *James Charles Jr.*^{5}, *James (Jim) Charles Sr.*^{4}, *Adron (Edwin/Ade) Sr.*^{3}, *Charles W. Sr.*^{2}, *John Sr.*^{1}) was born 26 May 1941 in Lauderdale County, AL.

Pauline married **Billy Levon Barnett**, son of **James Ovus Barnett** and **Bessie Mae McClanahan**, 22 Sep 1956 in Iuka, Tishomingo County, MS. Billy was born 30 Mar 1938 in Lauderdale County, AL, died 9 Jun 1976, and was buried in Center Hill Cemetery, Lauderdale County, AL.
+ 4931 M i. **Tony Levon Barnett** was born 2 Aug 1959 in Lauderdale County, AL.
+ 4932 M ii. **Tommy Leron Barnett** was born 29 Apr 1963 in Lauderdale County, AL.

Pauline next married **Lawrence Parham** 4 Nov 1958.

3071. Betty Ruth Young (*Mary Frances Cummings*^{7}, *Lillie May Sharp*^{6}, *James Charles Jr.*^{5}, *James (Jim) Charles Sr.*^{4}, *Adron (Edwin/Ade) Sr.*^{3}, *Charles W. Sr.*^{2}, *John Sr.*^{1}) was born 18 Mar 1943 in Lauderdale County, AL.

Betty married **Charles Edwin Gray Sr.**, son of **Otis Gray** and **Ruth Evelyn Davis**, 4 Nov 1958 in Lauderdale County, AL. Charles was born 11 Jun 1941 in Lauderdale County, AL.
+ 4933 F i. **LaDonna Kay Gray** was born 22 Jul 1960 in Lauderdale County, AL.
+ 4934 M ii. **Charles Edwin Gray Jr.** was born 19 Oct 1962 in Lauderdale County, AL.

3072. Donnie Ray Young Sr. (*Mary Frances Cummings*^{7}, *Lillie May Sharp*^{6}, *James Charles Jr.*^{5}, *James (Jim) Charles Sr.*^{4}, *Adron (Edwin/Ade) Sr.*^{3}, *Charles W. Sr.*^{2}, *John Sr.*^{1}) was born 29 Nov 1950 in Lauderdale County, AL, died 29 Jun 2003, and was buried in Greenview Memorial Park, Florence, Lauderdale County, AL.

Donnie married **Myra Sue Rideout**, daughter of **Grady Lee Rideout** and **Irene J. Wright**, 13 Sep 1969 in Lauderdale County, AL. Myra was born 25 Jun 1954 in Lauderdale County, AL.
+ 4935 F i. **Wendy Dawn Young** was born 20 Jul 1973 in Lauderdale County, AL.
+ 4936 M ii. **Donnie Ray Young Jr.** was born 30 Oct 1981 in Lauderdale County, AL.

3073. Kathy Lynn Young (*Mary Frances Cummings*^{7}, *Lillie May Sharp*^{6}, *James Charles Jr.*^{5}, *James (Jim) Charles Sr.*^{4}, *Adron (Edwin/Ade) Sr.*^{3}, *Charles W. Sr.*^{2}, *John Sr.*^{1}) was born 30 Nov 1955 in Lauderdale County, AL.

Kathy married **Eddie Steven King** 26 Aug 1972.

4937 M   i.   **Shane Steven King** was born 28 Mar 1973.

4938 M   ii.   **Robby Douglas King** was born 12 Jan 1977.

Kathy next married **Timothy Lane Jones** 2 May 1983.

4939 F   i.   **Kelli Savannah Jones** was born 11 Jun 1986.

3074. Ricky Eugene Young (*Mary Frances Cummings^7, Lillie May Sharp^6, James Charles Jr.^{5}, James (Jim) Charles Sr.^{4}, Adron (Edwin/Ade) Sr.^{3}, Charles W. Sr.^{2}, John Sr.^{1}*) was born 10 Aug 1958 in Lauderdale County, AL.

Ricky married **Aubrey Elaine Brockwell**, daughter of **E. W. Brockwell Jr.** and **Patsy Mason**, 16 Apr 1979 in Lauderdale County, AL. Aubrey was born 14 Apr 1961 in Lauderdale County, AL.

4940 M   i.   **Christopher David Young** was born 31 Aug 1983.

3075. Susan Cheri Cummings (*Lucian Jones (Jay) Cummings I^7, Lillie May Sharp^6, James Charles Jr.^{5}, James (Jim) Charles Sr.^{4}, Adron (Edwin/Ade) Sr.^{3}, Charles W. Sr.^{2}, John Sr.^{1}*) was born 28 Dec 1958 in Lauderdale County, AL.

Susan married **John David Moseley**, son of **Jack Moseley** and **Billie Burch**, 9 Dec 1983. John was born 12 Dec 1952 in Lauderdale County, AL.

4941 M   i.   **John Michael Moseley** was born 22 Feb 1990 in Lauderdale County, AL.

3076. Debra Mae Cummings (*Lucian Jones (Jay) Cummings I^7, Lillie May Sharp^6, James Charles Jr.^{5}, James (Jim) Charles Sr.^{4}, Adron (Edwin/Ade) Sr.^{3}, Charles W. Sr.^{2}, John Sr.^{1}*) was born 11 Nov 1966 in Lauderdale County, AL.

Debra married **Walton Randall (Randy) Risner**, son of **William T. Risner** and **Edith Phillips**, 30 Aug 1985 in Lauderdale County, AL. Walton was born 14 Jul 1955 in Lauderdale County, AL.

4942 F   i.   **Stephanie Roxanne Risner** was born 24 Feb 1987 in Lauderdale County, AL.

3078. Harold Lee Cummings (*Paul Lee Cummings^7, Lillie May Sharp^6, James Charles Jr.^{5}, James (Jim) Charles Sr.^{4}, Adron (Edwin/Ade) Sr.^{3}, Charles W. Sr.^{2}, John Sr.^{1}*) was born 30 Jan 1949 in Lauderdale County, AL.

Harold married **Mary Jeanette Muns**, daughter of **Luther W. Muns** and **Lillie B. Gray**, 23 Nov 1968 in Lauderdale County, AL. Mary was born 4 Mar 1949 in Lauderdale County, AL.

+ 4943 F   i.   **Tammy Leigh Cummings** was born 5 Sep 1970.

Harold next married **Brenda Gail Staggs**, daughter of **Roy Bennett Staggs** and **Annie Ruth Chambers**, 9 Aug 1993 in Lauderdale County, AL. Brenda was born 9 Apr 1965.

3079. Joyce Dianne Cummings (*Paul Lee Cummings^7, Lillie May Sharp^6, James Charles Jr.^{5}, James (Jim) Charles Sr.^{4}, Adron (Edwin/Ade) Sr.^{3}, Charles W. Sr.^{2}, John Sr.^{1}*) was born 11 Aug 1950 in Lauderdale County, AL.

Joyce married **Daniel Reyna Vargas** 14 Apr 1972. Daniel was born 9 Dec 1948 in Waukegan, IL.

4944 M   i.   **Daniel Reyna Vargas** was born 12 Aug 1976 in Waukegan, IL.

4945 F   ii.   **Shelia Dianne Vargas** was born 20 Sep 1979 in Waukegan, IL.

3080. Patsy Correan Cummings (*Paul Lee Cummings^7, Lillie May Sharp^6, James Charles Jr.^{5}, James (Jim) Charles Sr.^{4}, Adron (Edwin/Ade) Sr.^{3}, Charles W. Sr.^{2}, John Sr.^{1}*) was born 29 Aug 1951 in Lauderdale County, AL.

Patsy married **Anthony Paul Indelicato Sr.**, son of **Salvador Anthony Indelicato** and **Pauline Ruhlander**, 27 Aug 1971 in Duqvion, IL. Anthony was born 24 Sep 1949 in Litchfield, IL.

4946 M   i.   **Anthony Paul Indelicato Jr.** was born 3 May 1975 in Lauderdale County, AL.

4947 M   ii.   **Michael Lee Indelicato** was born 25 Jun 1979 in Lauderdale County, AL.

Patsy next married **Robert John Mager**, son of **John Robert Mager** and **Marilyn Herston**, 6 Jul 1985 in Lauderdale County, AL. Robert was born 18 Sep 1949.

4948　F　i.　**Katie Michelle Mager** was born 30 Aug 1993 in Lauderdale County, AL.

3081. Betty Carolyn Cummings (*Paul Lee Cummings[7], Lillie May Sharp[6], James Charles Jr.[5], James (Jim) Charles Sr.[4], Adron (Edwin/Ade) Sr.[3], Charles W. Sr.[2], John Sr.[1]*) was born 16 May 1953 in Lauderdale County, AL and was buried in Hill Cemetery, Lauderdale County, AL.

Betty married **John Barry Myers** 16 Feb 1980.

3082. Gary Dale Cummings (*Paul Lee Cummings[7], Lillie May Sharp[6], James Charles Jr.[5], James (Jim) Charles Sr.[4], Adron (Edwin/Ade) Sr.[3], Charles W. Sr.[2], John Sr.[1]*) was born 30 Apr 1958 in Lauderdale County, AL.

Gary married **Debbie Lee Eisman**, daughter of **Wallace J. Eisman** and **Christa Stenzet**, 17 Oct 1981 in Las Cruces, NM. Debbie was born 26 Apr 1961 in El Paso, El Paso County, TX.

4949　F　i.　**April Marie Cummings** was born 19 Feb 1994 in Lauderdale County, AL.

3083. Gregory Lynn Cummings (*Paul Lee Cummings[7], Lillie May Sharp[6], James Charles Jr.[5], James (Jim) Charles Sr.[4], Adron (Edwin/Ade) Sr.[3], Charles W. Sr.[2], John Sr.[1]*) was born 23 Oct 1962 in Lauderdale County, AL.

Gregory married **Liza Leanne Segars**, daughter of **John Segars** and **Nancy Jane Peck**, 17 Jun 1990 in Las Cruces, NM. Liza was born 15 Feb 1972 in Lauderdale County, AL.

4950　F　i.　**Bethany Grace Cummings** was born 6 Jun 1994 in Lauderdale County, AL.

3084. Donna Carol Gann (*Lillie Earline (Jean) Sharp[7], Turner Lee[6], James Charles Jr.[5], James (Jim) Charles Sr.[4], Adron (Edwin/Ade) Sr.[3], Charles W. Sr.[2], John Sr.[1]*) was born 8 Nov 1956 in Lauderdale County, AL.

Donna married **Johnny Wayne Lawson**, son of **Martin L. Lawson** and **Martha Collins**, 23 Dec 1983 in Lauderdale County, AL. Johnny was born 3 Oct 1958 in Lauderdale County, AL.

4951　M　i.　**Adam G. Lawson** was born 19 May 1988 in Lauderdale County, AL.
4952　M　ii.　**Jonathan E. Lawson** was born 21 Jan 1995 in Lauderdale County, AL.

3085. Mary Decarla Gann (*Lillie Earline (Jean) Sharp[7], Turner Lee[6], James Charles Jr.[5], James (Jim) Charles Sr.[4], Adron (Edwin/Ade) Sr.[3], Charles W. Sr.[2], John Sr.[1]*) was born 15 Jan 1966 in Lauderdale County, AL.

Mary married **Eric Keith Killen**, son of **Derrick E. Killen** and **Rebecca Kennedy**, 3 Sep 1983 in Lauderdale County, AL. Eric was born 29 Aug 1965 in Lauderdale County, AL.

4953　M　i.　**Tyler James Killen** was born 26 Mar 1986 in Lauderdale County, AL.
4954　F　ii.　**Molly Noel Killen** was born 27 Jun 1993 in Lauderdale County, AL.

3094. Mary Ruth Sharp (*Clarence Earl[7], James (Little James) Robert[6], James Charles Jr.[5], James (Jim) Charles Sr.[4], Adron (Edwin/Ade) Sr.[3], Charles W. Sr.[2], John Sr.[1]*) was born 3 Oct 1948 in Inning, Germany.

Mary married **Phillip Scritchfield** in 1973.
4955　M　i.　**Craig Christopher Scritchfield** was born 8 May 1976.
4956　F　ii.　**Crystal Ann Scritchfield** was born 30 Mar 1979.

3095. Teresa Kay Sharp (*James Loyd[7], James (Little James) Robert[6], James Charles Jr.[5], James (Jim) Charles Sr.[4], Adron (Edwin/Ade) Sr.[3], Charles W. Sr.[2], John Sr.[1]*) was born 27 Jun 1958 in Ft Leonardwood, MO.

Teresa married **Douglas Henry Owens**, son of **Billy Henry Owens** and **Myrtle Corena Akin**, 7 Jun 1980 in Clarksville, Montgomery County, TN. Douglas was born 10 Sep 1957 in Colorado Springs, CO.

4957　M　i.　**John Douglas Owens** was born 24 Sep 1981 in Lackland AFB, TX.
4958　M　ii.　**Michael Scott Owens** was born 3 Aug 1983 in Columbus AFB, MS.

3096. Jean Lorraine Sharp (*James Loyd[7], James (Little James) Robert[6], James Charles Jr.[5], James (Jim) Charles Sr.[4], Adron (Edwin/Ade) Sr.[3], Charles W. Sr.[2], John Sr.[1]*) was born 11 Nov 1960 in Heidelberg, Germany.

Jean married **Michael Lee Johnson Sr.**, son of **Gerald Lee Johnson** and **Lillian Emeline Hurley**, 30 Dec 1983. Michael was born 4 Oct 1955 in Gibson City, TN.

4959 M i. **Michael Lee Johnson Jr.** was born 24 Oct 1985 in Ft Campbell, TN.
4960 F ii. **Amy Caroline Johnson** was born 5 Jan 1987 in Ft Campbell, TN.

3097. Tamra (Tammy) Leah Sharp (*Robert Lee* [7], *James (Little James) Robert* [6], *James Charles Jr.* [5], *James (Jim) Charles Sr.* [4], *Adron (Edwin/Ade) Sr.* [3], *Charles W. Sr.* [2], *John Sr.* [1]) was born 17 Mar 1958 in Lauderdale County, AL. Another name for Tamra is Tamara Leah Sharp.

Tamra married **Gregory Paul Risner**, son of **James Paul Risner** and **Nellie Joann Gilbert**, 19 Dec 1982 in Florence, Lauderdale County, AL. Gregory was born 6 Jul 1959 in Dallas County, AL.

4961 F i. **Lane Katherine Risner** was born 19 Mar 1994 in Tampa, FL.

3098. Rebecca (Becky) Lynne Sharp (*Robert Lee* [7], *James (Little James) Robert* [6], *James Charles Jr.* [5], *James (Jim) Charles Sr.* [4], *Adron (Edwin/Ade) Sr.* [3], *Charles W. Sr.* [2], *John Sr.* [1]) was born 9 Feb 1960 in Lauderdale County, AL.

Rebecca married **Vance Scott McCune**, son of **Donald McCune** and **Jean Clever**, 15 Aug 1981 in Lauderdale County, AL. Vance was born 2 Feb 1953 in Layfette, IN.

4962 F i. **Julie Elizabeth McCune** was born 14 Oct 1985 in Tuscaloosa, AL.

3099. Robert (Bobby) Glenn Sharp (*Robert Lee* [7], *James (Little James) Robert* [6], *James Charles Jr.* [5], *James (Jim) Charles Sr.* [4], *Adron (Edwin/Ade) Sr.* [3], *Charles W. Sr.* [2], *John Sr.* [1]) was born 23 Jan 1968 in Lauderdale County, AL.

Robert married **Sonia Meshell Ezell**, daughter of **Hollis Lee Ezell** and **Stella Ann Clemons**, 4 Jun 1994 in Lauderdale County, AL. Sonia was born 10 Nov 1970 in Lauderdale County, AL.

4963 F i. **Anna Grace Sharp** was born 13 Feb 1999 in Athens, Limestone County, AL.
4964 M ii. **Brandon Lee Sharp** was born 20 Nov 2004 in Athens, Limestone County, AL, died 20 Nov 2004, and was buried in Roselawn Cemetery, Athens, AL.

3100. Mitchell Ray Sharp (*Clyde Ray* [7], *James (Little James) Robert* [6], *James Charles Jr.* [5], *James (Jim) Charles Sr.* [4], *Adron (Edwin/Ade) Sr.* [3], *Charles W. Sr.* [2], *John Sr.* [1]) was born 14 Oct 1960 in Lauderdale County, AL.

Mitchell married **Judy Cromwell**, daughter of **Robert W. Cromwell** and **Dianna Smith**, 31 May 1980 in Lauderdale County, AL. Judy was born 4 Oct 1962 in Mishawaka, IL.

4965 M i. **Matthew Ray Sharp** was born 25 Jul 1987.
4966 M ii. **Tyler Blake Sharp** was born 5 Jan 1989.

3101. Roger Dale Sharp (*Clyde Ray* [7], *James (Little James) Robert* [6], *James Charles Jr.* [5], *James (Jim) Charles Sr.* [4], *Adron (Edwin/Ade) Sr.* [3], *Charles W. Sr.* [2], *John Sr.* [1]) was born 11 Apr 1965 in Lauderdale County, AL.

Roger married **Cindy Renee Cromwell**, daughter of **Robert W. Cromwell** and **Dianna Smith**, 20 Aug 1983 in Lauderdale County, AL. Cindy was born 11 Jun 1965 in Lauderdale County, AL.

4967 F i. **Lindsey Rennea Sharp** was born 31 Aug 1985 in Lauderdale County, AL.
4968 M ii. **Daniel Kyle Sharp** was born 20 Apr 1989 in Lauderdale County, AL.

Roger next married **Deborah Fowler Smith**, daughter of **Charles Edward Fowler** and **Mattie Ruth Rutherford**, 28 Jun 1996 in Lauderdale County, AL.

+ 4969 F i. **Leah Nicole Smith**.

3102. Patricia (Pam) Ann May (*Pearl Rebecca Sharp* [7], *James (Little James) Robert* [6], *James Charles Jr.* [5], *James (Jim) Charles Sr.* [4], *Adron (Edwin/Ade) Sr.* [3], *Charles W. Sr.* [2], *John Sr.* [1]) was born 14 Jul 1956 in Lauderdale County, AL.

Patricia married **Garon (Skipper) Coy Thomas**, son of **Garon (Tommy) F. Thomas** and **Connie Birdwell**, 11 Jan 1974 in Lauderdale County, AL. Garon was born 16 Apr 1952 in Morgan City, AL.

+ 4970 F i. **Kristie Dawn Thomas** was born 29 Apr 1977 in Colbert County, AL.

4971 F ii. **Tonya Michelle Thomas** was born 17 Aug 1982.

3103. Vickie Lynn May (*Pearl Rebecca Sharp*[7]*, James (Little James) Robert*[6]*, James Charles Jr.*[5]*, James (Jim) Charles Sr.*[4]*, Adron (Edwin/Ade) Sr.*[3]*, Charles W. Sr.*[2]*, John Sr.*[1]) was born 26 Mar 1957 in Lauderdale County, AL.

Vickie married **Franklin Wayne Willard**, son of **Ned R. Willard** and **Ruth Clemons**, 20 Dec 1975 in Lauderdale County, AL. Franklin was born 27 Feb 1954 in Lauderdale County, AL.
+ 4972 F i. **Sabrena Rebecca Willard** was born 11 Nov 1980 in Lauderdale County, AL.
  4973 F ii. **Sophia Diana Willard** was born 21 Apr 1983 in Lauderdale County, AL.

3104. Deana Leigh May (*Pearl Rebecca Sharp*[7]*, James (Little James) Robert*[6]*, James Charles Jr.*[5]*, James (Jim) Charles Sr.*[4]*, Adron (Edwin/Ade) Sr.*[3]*, Charles W. Sr.*[2]*, John Sr.*[1]) was born 19 Apr 1964 in Lauderdale County, AL.

Deana married **Richard Loyd Johnson**, son of **Richard Johnson** and **Patsy Annette Croley**, 8 Aug 1992 in Lauderdale County, AL. Richard was born 4 May 1966 in Lauderdale County, AL.
  4974 F i. **Carrie Elizabeth Johnson** was born 13 Mar 1996 in Athens, Limestone County, AL.
  4975 F ii. **Mallory Mae Johnson** was born 3 Oct 2000 in Athens, Limestone County, AL.

3105. Sammy Alan May (*Pearl Rebecca Sharp*[7]*, James (Little James) Robert*[6]*, James Charles Jr.*[5]*, James (Jim) Charles Sr.*[4]*, Adron (Edwin/Ade) Sr.*[3]*, Charles W. Sr.*[2]*, John Sr.*[1]) was born 20 Jul 1971 in Lauderdale County, AL.

Sammy married **Lisa Reae Graves**, daughter of **L. C. Graves** and **Alberta Lopp**, 15 Apr 1995 in Lauderdale County, AL. Lisa was born 25 Nov 1972 in Lauderdale County, AL.
  4976 F i. **Rachel Ann May** was born 17 Apr 1997 in Colbert County, AL.
  4977 M ii. **Riley Morgan May** was born 10 Sep 1999 in Colbert County, AL.

3106. Jewel Faye Johnson (*Emmy Luetellace (Lou) Cobb*[7]*, Minor Lucille Sharp*[6]*, James Charles Jr.*[5]*, James (Jim) Charles Sr.*[4]*, Adron (Edwin/Ade) Sr.*[3]*, Charles W. Sr.*[2]*, John Sr.*[1]) was born 11 Dec 1951 in Lauderdale County, AL.

Jewel married **Bobby Joe Harrison Sr.**, son of **Leonard Harrison** and **Vadean Jackson**, 2 Jul 1970 in Lauderdale County, AL. Bobby was born 10 Apr 1950 in Lauderdale County, AL.
  4978 M i. **Bobby Joe Harrison Jr.** was born 5 Jan 1971 in Lauderdale County, AL.
+ 4979 M ii. **Joey Wayne Harrison** was born 20 Dec in Lauderdale County, AL.

3107. Homer Reeder Johnson II (*Emmy Luetellace (Lou) Cobb*[7]*, Minor Lucille Sharp*[6]*, James Charles Jr.*[5]*, James (Jim) Charles Sr.*[4]*, Adron (Edwin/Ade) Sr.*[3]*, Charles W. Sr.*[2]*, John Sr.*[1]) was born 9 Mar 1954 in Lauderdale County, AL, died 13 Jul 1977, and was buried in Mt. Hope Cemetery, Lutts, TN.

Homer married **Janice Faye Futrell**, daughter of **Thomas L. Futrell** and **Nadine Prince**, 20 Apr 1973 in Lauderdale County, AL. Janice was born 19 Apr 1959 in Dade County, FL.
  4980 F i. **Julie Annette Johnson** was born 25 Jan 1974.
  4981 M ii. **Reeder Jason Johnson** was born 23 Dec 1977.

3108. Betty Lou Johnson (*Emmy Luetellace (Lou) Cobb*[7]*, Minor Lucille Sharp*[6]*, James Charles Jr.*[5]*, James (Jim) Charles Sr.*[4]*, Adron (Edwin/Ade) Sr.*[3]*, Charles W. Sr.*[2]*, John Sr.*[1]) was born 16 Jun 1956 in Wayne County, TN, died 18 Nov 1985, and was buried in Mt. Hope Cemetery, Lutts, TN.

Betty married **James Dalton (J. D.) Lamar Jr.**, son of **James Dalton Lamar Sr.** and **Bertha Lee Burns**, 29 Aug 1977. James was born 22 Oct 1956 in Lauderdale County, AL.
+ 4982 F i. **Angela Hope Lamar** was born 22 Dec 1977.

3109. Billy Gene Johnson I (*Emmy Luetellace (Lou) Cobb*[7]*, Minor Lucille Sharp*[6]*, James Charles Jr.*[5]*, James (Jim) Charles Sr.*[4]*, Adron (Edwin/Ade) Sr.*[3]*, Charles W. Sr.*[2]*, John Sr.*[1]) was born 9 Jan 1962 in Lauderdale County, AL.

Billy married **Katy Sue Williams**, daughter of **Ronald C. Williams** and **Margaret Parrish**, 19 Nov 1983 in Lauderdale County, AL. Katy was born 29 May 1966 in Lauderdale County, AL.

4983 M i. **Billy Gene Johnson II** was born 3 Jul 1986.
4984 M ii. **Brian Thomas Johnson** was born 23 Mar 1989.
4985 F iii. **Kailey Louise Johnson** was born 27 Jan 1991.

3110. Patsy Willodean Carson (*Villace Lorene Cobb[7], Minor Lucille Sharp[6], James Charles Jr.[5], James (Jim) Charles Sr.[4], Adron (Edwin/Ade) Sr.[3], Charles W. Sr.[2], John Sr.[1]*) was born 4 Feb 1952 in Lauderdale County, AL.

Patsy married **Waylon Jackson Crosslin**, son of **Jack J. Crosslin** and **Geneva Ida Whitten**, 8 Jul 1985 in Lauderdale County, AL. Waylon was born 3 Mar 1951 in Lauderdale County, AL.

3111. James Elmer Carson (*Villace Lorene Cobb[7], Minor Lucille Sharp[6], James Charles Jr.[5], James (Jim) Charles Sr.[4], Adron (Edwin/Ade) Sr.[3], Charles W. Sr.[2], John Sr.[1]*) was born 21 Jul 1960 in Lauderdale County, AL.

James married **Diane Marie Clowdus**, daughter of **William L. Clowdus** and **Billie Shell**, 24 Apr 1979 in Lauderdale County, AL. Diane was born 5 Dec 1956 in Lauderdale County, AL.

4986 M i. **James David Carson** was born 16 Apr 1979 in Lauderdale County, AL.
4987 M ii. **Danny Lee Carson** was born 9 Sep 1980 in Lauderdale County, AL.

3112. Danny Eugene Carson (*Villace Lorene Cobb[7], Minor Lucille Sharp[6], James Charles Jr.[5], James (Jim) Charles Sr.[4], Adron (Edwin/Ade) Sr.[3], Charles W. Sr.[2], John Sr.[1]*) was born 17 Sep 1961 in Lauderdale County, AL.

Danny married **Lori Renee Wachter**, daughter of **George Thomas Wachter** and **Lillie Ollene Sparks**, 25 Jul 1992 in Lauderdale County, AL. Lori was born 2 Oct 1966.

3114. Peggy Ann Johnson (*Julia Loretta Cobb[7], Minor Lucille Sharp[6], James Charles Jr.[5], James (Jim) Charles Sr.[4], Adron (Edwin/Ade) Sr.[3], Charles W. Sr.[2], John Sr.[1]*) was born 22 Dec 1950 in Lauderdale County, AL.

Peggy married **Luther Lee Simpson Sr.**, son of **Luther Timothy Simpson** and **Mary Kelley**, 24 Dec 1966 in Lauderdale County, AL. Luther was born 27 Jul 1949 in Lauderdale County, AL.

4988 M i. **Luther Lee Simpson Jr.** was born 9 Jan 1972.
4989 M ii. **Mark Anthony Simpson** was born 6 Nov 1973.

3115. Carolyn Sue Johnson (*Julia Loretta Cobb[7], Minor Lucille Sharp[6], James Charles Jr.[5], James (Jim) Charles Sr.[4], Adron (Edwin/Ade) Sr.[3], Charles W. Sr.[2], John Sr.[1]*) was born 11 Jun 1954 in St. Joseph, TN.

Carolyn married **Roger Dwight Quillen Sr.**, son of **Frankie E. Quillen** and **Eva Scott**, 20 Sep 1969 in Lauderdale County, AL. Roger was born 8 Jun 1945 in Lauderdale County, AL.

+ 4990 M i. **Roger Dwight Quillen Jr.** was born 9 Jan 1972 in Lauderdale County, AL.
+ 4991 M ii. **Rex Dwayne Quillen** was born 18 May 1972 in Lauderdale County, AL.
4992 M iii. **Rory Daniel Quillen** was born 5 Sep 1973 in Lauderdale County, AL.

3117. Bertha Lucille Jackson (*Julia Loretta Cobb[7], Minor Lucille Sharp[6], James Charles Jr.[5], James (Jim) Charles Sr.[4], Adron (Edwin/Ade) Sr.[3], Charles W. Sr.[2], John Sr.[1]*) was born 3 Jul 1961 in Lauderdale County, AL.

Bertha married **Ricky Lynn English I**, son of **Allen E. English** and **Eunise Barnell**, 10 Sep 1976 in Lauderdale County, AL. Ricky was born 10 Jul 1954 in Lauderdale County, AL.

4993 M i. **Ricky Lynn English II** was born 31 Jul 1978.

Bertha next married **William Ricky Johnson**, son of **B. L. Johnson** and **Chessie Hall**, 16 Mar 1984 in Lauderdale County, AL. William was born 20 Jun 1951 in Lake County, IL.

4994 M i. **Christopher Ryann Johnson** was born 12 Sep 1984.

Bertha next married **James David House**, son of **Bud House** and **Irene Burgress**, 16 Apr 1993 in Lauderdale County, AL. James was born 14 Jun 1954 in Lauderdale County, AL.

3118. Robert William Tate Jr. (*Helen Marie Keel^7, Maggie Lorene Sharp^6, James Charles Jr.^{5}, James (Jim) Charles Sr.^{4}, Adron (Edwin/Ade) Sr.^{3}, Charles W. Sr.^{2}, John Sr.^{1}*) was born 8 Dec 1955 in Lauderdale County, AL.

Robert married **Julie Carrol Hornsbery** 27 Jun 1974. Julie was born 27 Jun 1957.

4995	M	i.	**Robert William Tate III** was born 14 Sep 1976.
4996	M	ii.	**Eric Gerard Tate** was born 12 Aug 1980.
4997	M	iii.	**Nichelous Ryan Tate** was born 30 Dec 1982.

3119. Lisa Marie Tate (*Helen Marie Keel^7, Maggie Lorene Sharp^6, James Charles Jr.^{5}, James (Jim) Charles Sr.^{4}, Adron (Edwin/Ade) Sr.^{3}, Charles W. Sr.^{2}, John Sr.^{1}*) was born 12 Jun 1959 in Lauderdale County, AL.

Lisa married **Joseph Farrel Bolton** 14 Jul 1985. Joseph was born 21 Sep 1954.

3120. Melissa Diane Morris (*Helen Marie Keel^7, Maggie Lorene Sharp^6, James Charles Jr.^{5}, James (Jim) Charles Sr.^{4}, Adron (Edwin/Ade) Sr.^{3}, Charles W. Sr.^{2}, John Sr.^{1}*) was born 26 Nov 1968 in Memphis, Shelby County, TN.

Melissa married **Rand Dwayne Coleman** 9 Jun 1990. Rand was born 8 Oct 1964.

| 4998 | M | i. | **Tyler Dwayne Coleman** was born 26 Feb 1992 in Memphis, Shelby County, TN. |

3121. Teresa Marie Keel (*James Walbert Keel^7, Maggie Lorene Sharp^6, James Charles Jr.^{5}, James (Jim) Charles Sr.^{4}, Adron (Edwin/Ade) Sr.^{3}, Charles W. Sr.^{2}, John Sr.^{1}*) was born 26 Sep 1965 in Lauderdale County, AL.

Teresa married **David Nolan Mitchell**, son of **David Raymond Mitchell** and **Bobbie Lee Phelps**, 27 Mar 1991 in Lauderdale County, AL. David was born 30 Sep 1963 in Lauderdale County, AL.

| 4999 | M | i. | **Zachary Nolan Mitchell** was born 6 Jun 1992. |

3122. Donald Mark Keel (*James Walbert Keel^7, Maggie Lorene Sharp^6, James Charles Jr.^{5}, James (Jim) Charles Sr.^{4}, Adron (Edwin/Ade) Sr.^{3}, Charles W. Sr.^{2}, John Sr.^{1}*) was born 3 Dec 1968 in Lauderdale County, AL.

Donald married **Lisa Renee Stump** 8 Oct 1989 in Marshall County, IN. Lisa was born 6 Jan 1970 in Marshall County, IN.

| 5000 | F | i. | **Alaina Marie Keel** was born 8 Sep 1990 in Marshall County, IN. |
| 5001 | F | ii. | **Jessica Lynn Keel** was born 4 Sep 1996 in Lauderdale County, AL. |

3126. Marlow Ray Walker (*Lois Laverne Keel^7, Maggie Lorene Sharp^6, James Charles Jr.^{5}, James (Jim) Charles Sr.^{4}, Adron (Edwin/Ade) Sr.^{3}, Charles W. Sr.^{2}, John Sr.^{1}*) was born 6 Dec 1966 in Lauderdale County, AL.

Marlow married **Donna Marie Creasy**, daughter of **Daniel A. Creasy** and **Brenda Hayes**, 12 Oct 1991 in Lauderdale County, AL. Donna was born 9 Jan 1967 in Lauderdale County, AL.

| 5002 | F | i. | **Brittany Morgan Walker** was born 5 Aug 1992. |

3127. Gena Marie Walker (*Lois Laverne Keel^7, Maggie Lorene Sharp^6, James Charles Jr.^{5}, James (Jim) Charles Sr.^{4}, Adron (Edwin/Ade) Sr.^{3}, Charles W. Sr.^{2}, John Sr.^{1}*) was born 25 Oct 1967 in Lauderdale County, AL.

Gena married **James Earl Abernathy**, son of **Willie Earl Abernathy** and **Anne Bell Walker**, 12 Jan 1991 in Lauderdale County, AL. James was born 27 Dec 1963 in Lauderdale County, AL.

| 5003 | M | i. | **Nocona Colt Abernathy** was born 24 Aug 1991. |
| 5004 | M | ii. | **Elam Teal Abernathy** was born 12 Apr 1993. |

3128. Wanda Kay Walker (*Lois Laverne Keel^7, Maggie Lorene Sharp^6, James Charles Jr.^{5}, James (Jim) Charles Sr.^{4}, Adron (Edwin/Ade) Sr.^{3}, Charles W. Sr.^{2}, John Sr.^{1}*) was born 3 Mar 1970 in Lauderdale County, AL.

Wanda married **Stephen Douglas Harbin**, son of **Emerald C. Harbin** and **Laura Francis Hannah**, 29 Jun 1990 in Lauderdale County, AL. Stephen was born 17 Jan 1966 in Lauderdale County, AL.

| 5005 | M | i. | **Ryan Douglas Harbin** was born 25 Sep 1994 in Lauderdale County, AL. |

3129. Billy Wayne Walker (*Lois Laverne Keel[7], Maggie Lorene Sharp[6], James Charles Jr.[5], James (Jim) Charles Sr.[4], Adron (Edwin/Ade) Sr.[3], Charles W. Sr.[2], John Sr.[1]*) was born 14 Nov 1971 in Lauderdale County, AL.

Billy married **Christina Nicole Reed**, daughter of **William David Reed** and **Betty Ruth Heupel**, 8 Feb 1993 in Lauderdale County, AL. Christina was born 7 Sep 1976 in Lauderdale County, AL.

3130. Sandra Marie Bates (*Linda Kay Keel[7], Maggie Lorene Sharp[6], James Charles Jr.[5], James (Jim) Charles Sr.[4], Adron (Edwin/Ade) Sr.[3], Charles W. Sr.[2], John Sr.[1]*) was born 31 Jul 1972 in Lauderdale County, AL.

Sandra married **Chris Allen McGuire**, son of **Donald Eugene McGuire** and **Remona Bottomle**, 24 Nov 1990 in Marshall County, AL. Chris was born 19 Nov 1969 in Blount County, AL.
5006 F i. **Megan Marie McGuire** was born 27 Feb 1997 in Marshall County, AL.

Sandra next married **Prisciliano Hernandez**.
5007 M i. **David Alexander Hernandez** was born 11 Jan 2004 in Marshall County, AL.

3133. Neal Lee Hubbard (*Ruby Pauline Sharp[7], Elmer[6], Charles W.[5], James (Jim) Charles Sr.[4], Adron (Edwin/Ade) Sr.[3], Charles W. Sr.[2], John Sr.[1]*) was born 20 Dec 1940 in Lauderdale County, AL.

Neal married **Linda Mae Pickens**, daughter of **William Perrie Pickens** and **Gracie Elizabeth Liles**, 17 Sep 1960 in Lauderdale County, AL. Linda was born 15 Sep 1942 in Lauderdale County, AL.
+ 5008 F i. **Mae Leigh Hubbard** was born 12 Jul 1971 in Lauderdale County, AL.

3134. Clara Evelyn Hubbard (*Ruby Pauline Sharp[7], Elmer[6], Charles W.[5], James (Jim) Charles Sr.[4], Adron (Edwin/Ade) Sr.[3], Charles W. Sr.[2], John Sr.[1]*) was born 9 Jan 1943 in Florence, Lauderdale County, AL.

Clara married **Kenneth White**, son of **Roy C. White** and **Ruth Evelyn Heard**, 10 Aug 1962 in Lauderdale County, AL. Kenneth was born 1 Nov 1940 in Prentis County, MS.
+ 5009 F i. **Amanda Lynne White** was born 13 Jul 1963 in Lauderdale County, AL.

Clara next married **Charles Clifford Blalock**, son of **Noble Blalock** and **Alfreada Hinson**, 21 May 1971 in Lauderdale County, AL. Charles was born 17 Sep 1948 in Florence, Lauderdale County, AL.
5010 F i. **Amelia Dawn Blalock** was born 26 Aug 1973.
+ 5011 M ii. **Charles Christopher Blalock** was born 25 Aug 1974 in Lauderdale County, AL.

Clara next married **William Stricklin** 6 Dec 1997 in Lauderdale County, AL. William was born 22 Jan 1937.

3135. Elmer John (E. J.) Hubbard (*Ruby Pauline Sharp[7], Elmer[6], Charles W.[5], James (Jim) Charles Sr.[4], Adron (Edwin/Ade) Sr.[3], Charles W. Sr.[2], John Sr.[1]*) was born 22 Apr 1945 in Florence, Lauderdale County, AL.

Elmer married **Betty Sue Michael**, daughter of **Taylor N. Michael** and **Alma B. Kilpatrick**, 8 Aug 1964 in Lauderdale County, AL. Betty was born 27 Mar 1947 in Florence, Lauderdale County, AL.
+ 5012 F i. **Jeanette Faye Hubbard** was born 7 Mar 1966 in Lauderdale County, AL.
+ 5013 F ii. **Janette Gaye Hubbard** was born 7 Mar 1966 in Lauderdale County, AL.
+ 5014 F iii. **Jennifer Kaye Hubbard** was born 10 Aug 1967 in Lauderdale County, AL.
+ 5015 F iv. **Jannice Maye Hubbard** was born 22 Oct 1972 in Lauderdale County, AL.

3136. Alfred Willie Hubbard (*Ruby Pauline Sharp[7], Elmer[6], Charles W.[5], James (Jim) Charles Sr.[4], Adron (Edwin/Ade) Sr.[3], Charles W. Sr.[2], John Sr.[1]*) was born 27 Oct 1947 in Florence, Lauderdale County, AL, died 19 Jul 1969, and was buried in Greenview Memorial Park, Florence, Lauderdale County, AL.

General Notes: "Died in Vietnam..." David Sharp

Alfred married **Sandra Kay Owens**, daughter of **Oscar B. Owens** and **Ina C. Murks**, 17 May 1968 in Lauderdale County, AL. Sandra was born 25 Dec 1950 in Lawrenceburg, Lawrence County, TN.
+ 5016 F i. **Sandy Alphelia Hubbard** was born 1 Aug 1969 in Lauderdale County, AL.

3138. Mary Ruth Hubbard (*Ruby Pauline Sharp⁷, Elmer⁶, Charles W.⁵, James (Jim) Charles Sr.⁴, Adron (Edwin/Ade) Sr.³, Charles W. Sr.², John Sr.¹*) was born 31 Aug 1952 in Florence, Lauderdale County, AL.

Mary married **Michael (Mike) Edward Nash Sr.**, son of **Norme E. Nash** and **Geraldine Buck**, 5 Aug 1971 in Lauderdale County, AL. Michael was born 12 Apr 1950 in Morgan County, AL.
+ 5017 M   i.   **Michael Edward Nash Jr.** was born 30 Mar 1972 in Morgan County, AL.
+ 5018 F   ii.   **Melanie Renee Nash** was born 13 Apr 1974 in Morgan County, AL.

3139. Dwight Corbin Hubbard (*Ruby Pauline Sharp⁷, Elmer⁶, Charles W.⁵, James (Jim) Charles Sr.⁴, Adron (Edwin/Ade) Sr.³, Charles W. Sr.², John Sr.¹*) was born 5 May 1955 in Florence, Lauderdale County, AL.

Dwight married **Loretta Suzanne Guthrie** in Lauderdale County, AL. Loretta was born 28 Oct 1960 in Florence, Lauderdale County, AL.

Dwight next married **Lou Ann Lindsey**, daughter of **James Harrell Lindsey** and **Mary Elizabeth Rhoden**, in Colbert County, AL. Lou was born 16 Sep 1965 in Lauderdale County, AL.
+ 5019 F   i.   **Elizabeth Cathryn Hubbard** was born 20 Apr 1979 in Lauderdale County, AL.
  5020 F   ii.   **Rebecca Anne Hubbard** was born 30 Jun 1980 in Lauderdale County, AL.

3140. Spencer Eugene Hubbard (*Ruby Pauline Sharp⁷, Elmer⁶, Charles W.⁵, James (Jim) Charles Sr.⁴, Adron (Edwin/Ade) Sr.³, Charles W. Sr.², John Sr.¹*) was born 28 Feb 1958 in Florence, Lauderdale County, AL.

Spencer married **Melissa Kay Watkins**, daughter of **Buford Delmer Watkins** and **Irene Butler**, 14 Mar 1980 in Lauderdale County, AL. Melissa was born 27 Sep 1962 in Florence, Lauderdale County, AL.
  5021 F   i.   **Malissa Jean Hubbard** was born 29 May 1981 in Lauderdale County, AL.
  5022 F   ii.   **Brittney Dawn Hubbard** was born 7 Jun 1985 in Lauderdale County, AL.

3141. Sheila Ann Hubbard (*Ruby Pauline Sharp⁷, Elmer⁶, Charles W.⁵, James (Jim) Charles Sr.⁴, Adron (Edwin/Ade) Sr.³, Charles W. Sr.², John Sr.¹*) was born 18 Jun 1960 in Florence, Lauderdale County, AL.

Sheila married **Larry Johnson**.

Sheila next married **Danny Wade Kelley**, son of **Rufus H. Kelley** and **Lillie Parrish**, 22 Apr 1978 in Lauderdale County, AL. Danny was born 25 Feb 1954 in Florence, Lauderdale County, AL.

3145. Sherry Lynn Sharp (*William (Bill) Harvel⁷, Elmer⁶, Charles W.⁵, James (Jim) Charles Sr.⁴, Adron (Edwin/Ade) Sr.³, Charles W. Sr.², John Sr.¹*) was born 7 Apr 1951 in Mishawaka, St Joseph County, IN.

Sherry married **David Alexander Tokarski**.

3146. Pamela Sue Sharp (*William (Bill) Harvel⁷, Elmer⁶, Charles W.⁵, James (Jim) Charles Sr.⁴, Adron (Edwin/Ade) Sr.³, Charles W. Sr.², John Sr.¹*) was born 2 Jan 1953 in Mishawaka, St Joseph County, IN.

Pamela married **Ralph Jaronick** 13 Feb 1976.

3147. Steven Alan Sharp (*Curtis Corbin⁷, Elmer⁶, Charles W.⁵, James (Jim) Charles Sr.⁴, Adron (Edwin/Ade) Sr.³, Charles W. Sr.², John Sr.¹*) was born 12 Sep 1955 in South Bend, IN.

Steven married **Marcia Ellen Halasi** 18 Oct 1980. Marcia was born 27 Oct 1953 in South Bend, IN.

3150. Monica Sharp (*James Earl⁷, Elmer⁶, Charles W.⁵, James (Jim) Charles Sr.⁴, Adron (Edwin/Ade) Sr.³, Charles W. Sr.², John Sr.¹*) was born 24 Jul 1957 in Evergreen Park, IL.

Monica married **James Wayne Summers** 3 Jul 1981. James was born 18 Oct 1954 in Houston, TX.

3151. Michael James Sharp (*James Earl⁷, Elmer⁶, Charles W.⁵, James (Jim) Charles Sr.⁴, Adron (Edwin/Ade) Sr.³, Charles W. Sr.², John Sr.¹*) was born 24 Feb 1959 in Evergreen Park, IL.

Michael married **Lois Morris** 28 Jan 1983. Lois was born 17 Oct 1955 in Toney, AL.

3155. Michelle Lee Hall (*Rachel Ruth Sharp* ^{7}, *Elmer* ^{6}, *Charles W.* ^{5}, *James (Jim) Charles Sr.* ^{4}, *Adron (Edwin/Ade) Sr.* ^{3}, *Charles W. Sr.* ^{2}, *John Sr.* ^{1}) was born 2 Aug 1964 in South Bend, IN.

Michelle married **Julio Raul Gonzalez** 21 Aug 1982. Julio was born 17 Aug 1964 in Acuno, Mexico.

3156. Sharon Kay Hall (*Rachel Ruth Sharp* ^{7}, *Elmer* ^{6}, *Charles W.* ^{5}, *James (Jim) Charles Sr.* ^{4}, *Adron (Edwin/Ade) Sr.* ^{3}, *Charles W. Sr.* ^{2}, *John Sr.* ^{1}) was born 8 Dec 1965 in Huntsville, Madison County, AL.

Sharon married **Michael Clay Taylor** 22 Dec 1983. Michael was born 5 Aug 1965 in Fayetteville, TN.

3158. Raymond Curtis Sharp (*W. C.* ^{7}, *William Hubert* ^{6}, *Charles W.* ^{5}, *James (Jim) Charles Sr.* ^{4}, *Adron (Edwin/Ade) Sr.* ^{3}, *Charles W. Sr.* ^{2}, *John Sr.* ^{1}) was born 23 Apr 1949 in Lauderdale County, AL.

Raymond married **Valerie Kay Bell**, daughter of **Raymond Bell** and **Lovie Todd**, 25 Jul 1971 in Collinwood, TN. Valerie was born 1 Sep 1946 in Wayne County, TN.
+ 5023 M i. **Adam Logan Sharp** was born 10 Nov 1979 in Lauderdale County, AL.

3159. Barbara Carol Sharp (*W. C.* ^{7}, *William Hubert* ^{6}, *Charles W.* ^{5}, *James (Jim) Charles Sr.* ^{4}, *Adron (Edwin/Ade) Sr.* ^{3}, *Charles W. Sr.* ^{2}, *John Sr.* ^{1}) was born 5 Apr 1951 in Lauderdale County, AL.

Barbara married **Dennis Almon Wood**, son of **Almon Wood** and **Evadean Joyce Balentine**, 21 Nov 1969 in Lauderdale County, AL. Dennis was born 29 Mar 1951 in Lauderdale County, AL.
+ 5024 M i. **Eric Wayne Wood** was born 29 Sep 1971 in Lauderdale County, AL.
  5025 M ii. **Matthew Dennis Wood** was born 9 Nov 1975, died 11 Nov 1975, and was buried in Oak Grove Cemetery, Lauderdale County, AL.

Barbara next married **John David Parrish**, son of **David Franklin Parrish** and **Helen Faye Wood**, 2 Sep 1977 in Lauderdale County, AL. John was born 23 Sep 1946 in Lauderdale County, AL.
+ 5026 M i. **David Morgan Parrish** was born 7 Mar 1980 in Lauderdale County, AL.

3160. Louis Alton Sharp (*W. C.* ^{7}, *William Hubert* ^{6}, *Charles W.* ^{5}, *James (Jim) Charles Sr.* ^{4}, *Adron (Edwin/Ade) Sr.* ^{3}, *Charles W. Sr.* ^{2}, *John Sr.* ^{1}) was born 30 Oct 1952 in Lauderdale County, AL.

Louis married **Deborah Ann Mathenia**, daughter of **James Mathenia** and **Virginia Stater**, 11 Aug 1972 in Peoria, IL. Deborah was born 14 Apr 1953 in Peoria, IL.
  5027 M i. **Christopher Alton Sharp** was born 24 Jun 1973 in Lauderdale County, AL.
+ 5028 M ii. **James (Jamie) Marion Sharp** was born 11 Jan 1975 in Peoria, IL.
  5029 F iii. **Angelique Evon Sharp** was born 4 May 1977 in Peoria, IL.

Louis next married **Kelly Daneen Ward**, daughter of **Belvie H. Ward Jr.** and **Peggy Hill**, 6 Sep 1983 in Lauderdale County, AL. Kelly was born 8 Mar 1965 in Marion County, IN.
+ 5030 F i. **Chambra Dawn Sharp** was born 18 Jan 1984 in Tishomingo, MS.

3161. Kenneth Jay Sharp (*W. C.* ^{7}, *William Hubert* ^{6}, *Charles W.* ^{5}, *James (Jim) Charles Sr.* ^{4}, *Adron (Edwin/Ade) Sr.* ^{3}, *Charles W. Sr.* ^{2}, *John Sr.* ^{1}) was born 25 May 1955 in Lauderdale County, AL.

Kenneth married **Martha Ann McDaniel**, daughter of **George Milton McDaniel** and **Pearl Olene Shook**, 30 May 1975 in Lauderdale County, AL. Martha was born 29 Jul 1657 in Elkhart, Elkhart County, IN.

3162. Ricky Wayne Sharp (*W. C.* ^{7}, *William Hubert* ^{6}, *Charles W.* ^{5}, *James (Jim) Charles Sr.* ^{4}, *Adron (Edwin/Ade) Sr.* ^{3}, *Charles W. Sr.* ^{2}, *John Sr.* ^{1}) was born 30 Nov 1957 in Lauderdale County, AL.

Ricky married **Diedre Suzanne Lott**, daughter of **Ray T. Lott** and **Charlene Vada Hinton**, 18 Dec 1982 in Lauderdale County, AL. Diedre was born 7 Jun 1954 in Lauderdale County, AL.

3163. Martha Gean Wallace (*Dorothy Virginia Sharp*[7], *William Hubert*[6], *Charles W.*[5], *James (Jim) Charles Sr.*[4], *Adron (Edwin/Ade) Sr.*[3], *Charles W. Sr.*[2], *John Sr.*[1]) was born 2 Mar 1952 in Lauderdale County, AL.

Martha married **Jacky Lee Johnson**, son of **James Arnold Johnson** and **Margaret Sego**, 7 Dec 1974 in Wayne County, TN. Jacky was born 4 Apr 1955 in Lauderdale County, AL.
5031 M i. **James Wesley Heath Johnson** was born 19 Feb 1980 in Lauderdale County, AL.
5032 M ii. **Tyler Owen Johnson** was born 26 Nov 1982 in Lauderdale County, AL.

3164. David Eugene Wallace (*Dorothy Virginia Sharp*[7], *William Hubert*[6], *Charles W.*[5], *James (Jim) Charles Sr.*[4], *Adron (Edwin/Ade) Sr.*[3], *Charles W. Sr.*[2], *John Sr.*[1]) was born 16 Oct 1956 in Lauderdale County, AL.

David married **Joye Darlene Butler**, daughter of **Thomas M. Butler** and **Era Murphy**, 8 Oct 1983 in Lauderdale County, AL. Joye was born 19 Aug 1959 in Lauderdale County, AL.
5033 M i. **Bradley Shane Wallace** was born 1 Aug 1987 in Lauderdale County, AL.
5034 F ii. **Ashley Erin Wallace** was born 24 Feb 1990 in Lauderdale County, AL.

3165. Nancy Sue Wallace (*Dorothy Virginia Sharp*[7], *William Hubert*[6], *Charles W.*[5], *James (Jim) Charles Sr.*[4], *Adron (Edwin/Ade) Sr.*[3], *Charles W. Sr.*[2], *John Sr.*[1]) was born 16 Oct 1966.

Nancy married **Damian Randolph Webb**, son of **Roland C. Webb** and **Margie Earnest Dickerson**, 30 Jun 1990 in Lauderdale County, AL. Damian was born 15 Mar 1965 in Sheboygan, WI.

3166. Tony Keith Wallace (*Dorothy Virginia Sharp*[7], *William Hubert*[6], *Charles W.*[5], *James (Jim) Charles Sr.*[4], *Adron (Edwin/Ade) Sr.*[3], *Charles W. Sr.*[2], *John Sr.*[1]) was born 17 Apr 1969 in Lauderdale County, AL.

Tony married **Laura *Unk**.

3167. William Tommy South (*Gladys Corrine Sharp*[7], *William Hubert*[6], *Charles W.*[5], *James (Jim) Charles Sr.*[4], *Adron (Edwin/Ade) Sr.*[3], *Charles W. Sr.*[2], *John Sr.*[1]) was born 18 Jul 1956 in Lauderdale County, AL.

William married **Sandra Smith**.

3169. Bobby Lance South (*Gladys Corrine Sharp*[7], *William Hubert*[6], *Charles W.*[5], *James (Jim) Charles Sr.*[4], *Adron (Edwin/Ade) Sr.*[3], *Charles W. Sr.*[2], *John Sr.*[1]) was born 12 Jan 1962 in Lauderdale County, AL.

Bobby married **Toni Marie Caddell**, daughter of **Marion C. Caddell** and **Mildred Smith**, 18 Dec 1982 in Lauderdale County, AL. Toni was born 15 Nov 1959 in Jefferson County, AL.

3171. Janice Kay Askew (*Sarah Ruth Sharp*[7], *William Hubert*[6], *Charles W.*[5], *James (Jim) Charles Sr.*[4], *Adron (Edwin/Ade) Sr.*[3], *Charles W. Sr.*[2], *John Sr.*[1]) was born 7 Aug 1954 in Lauderdale County, AL.

Janice married **Larry Alton Lawrence**.
5035 M i. **Clint Alton Lawrence** was born 29 Nov 1975 in Roanoke, Roanoke County, VA.
+ 5036 M ii. **Aaron Kyle Lawrence** was born 11 Jul 1981 in Roanoke, Roanoke County, VA.

3172. Comer Jack Askew II (*Sarah Ruth Sharp*[7], *William Hubert*[6], *Charles W.*[5], *James (Jim) Charles Sr.*[4], *Adron (Edwin/Ade) Sr.*[3], *Charles W. Sr.*[2], *John Sr.*[1]) was born 9 Apr 1956 in Lauderdale County, AL.

Comer married **Patricia Ann Beakey** 10 Aug 1974.
+ 5037 M i. **Chris Jason Askew** was born 14 May 1977 in Goshen, IN.
5038 F ii. **Jessica Ann Askew** was born 17 Nov 1983 in Roanoke, Roanoke County, VA.

3173. Theresa Kay Askew (*Sarah Ruth Sharp*[7], *William Hubert*[6], *Charles W.*[5], *James (Jim) Charles Sr.*[4], *Adron (Edwin/Ade) Sr.*[3], *Charles W. Sr.*[2], *John Sr.*[1]) was born 17 Feb 1962 in Peoria, IL.

Theresa married **Timothy R. Smith** 12 Jun 1982.
5039 M i. **Collin Christopher Smith** was born 28 Nov 1987 in Roanoke, Roanoke County, VA.

3174. Melissa Diane Arnold (*Betty May Sharp*[7], *William Hubert*[6], *Charles W.*[5], *James (Jim) Charles Sr.*[4], *Adron (Edwin/Ade) Sr.*[3], *Charles W. Sr.*[2], *John Sr.*[1]) was born 16 Oct 1964 in Peoria, IL.

Melissa married **Amos Jerome Stout**, son of **David H. Stout** and **Flora Bostick**, 10 Oct 1984 in Lauderdale County, AL. Amos was born 16 Sep 1961 in Colbert County, AL, died 13 Nov 2001, and was buried in Isbell Chapel Cemetery.

General Notes: Obituary - Times Daily, Florence, Lauderdale County, Alabama

"Amos Jerome Stout, 40, Tuscumbia, Ala., died Tuesday, Nov. 13, 2001. Visitation will be 6 - 8 p.m. Thursday. Nov. 15, 2001, at Morrison Funeral Home, Tuscumbia. The funeral will be at 2 p.m. Friday, Nov. 16, 2001, at Morrison Funeral Home chapel, Tuscumbia, with burial in Isbell Chapel Cemetery. Morrison Funeral Home, Tuscumbia, is directing. Officiating will be Mike Sams and Charles Pace.

Mr. Stout was a native of Colbert County and a member of Colbert Heights Baptist Church. He enjoyed hunting, motorcycle riding and bow shooting with his daughters.

He is survived by his wife, Diane Arnold Stout, Tuscumbia, Ala.; mother, Flora Mae Stout, Tuscumbia, Ala.; daughters, Becky Stout and Erica Stout, both of Tuscumbia, Ala.; brothers, Daniel Stout, Tuscumbia, Doug Stout and Charlie Stout, both of Muscle Shoals, Kenneth Stout, Decatur.

Pallbearers will be Roy Knight, John Kreglow, Danny Joe Jeffers, Buddy Graves, Kenny Vandiver and Bobby Eugene Montgomery. Honorary pallbearers will be Steve Arnold, Brandon Harrison, Danny Pounders and Buddy Montgomery."

5040	F	i.	**Rebecca Dianna Stout** was born 1 Jun 1985 in Lauderdale County, AL.

3176. Pamela Regina Arnold (*Betty May Sharp*[7], *William Hubert*[6], *Charles W.*[5], *James (Jim) Charles Sr.*[4], *Adron (Edwin/Ade) Sr.*[3], *Charles W. Sr.*[2], *John Sr.*[1]) was born 7 Sep 1969 in Lauderdale County, AL.

Pamela married **Tommy McArthur Pruitt Jr.**, son of **Tommy McArthur Pruitt Sr.** and **Helen Marie**, 5 Jun 1990 in Lauderdale County, AL. Tommy was born 16 Feb 1971 in Lauderdale County, AL.

5041	M	i.	**Tommy McArthur Pruitt III** was born 1 Nov 1991 in Lauderdale County, AL.

3177. Karen Denise Arnold (*Betty May Sharp*[7], *William Hubert*[6], *Charles W.*[5], *James (Jim) Charles Sr.*[4], *Adron (Edwin/Ade) Sr.*[3], *Charles W. Sr.*[2], *John Sr.*[1]) was born 4 Dec 1971 in Lauderdale County, AL.

Karen married **Christopher (Kim) Pruitt**, son of **Earl Ray Pruitt** and **Alba Faye Roberson**, 24 Jun 1991 in Lauderdale County, AL. Christopher was born 1 Nov 1966 in Lauderdale County, AL.

5042	F	i.	**Melanie Corrine Pruitt** was born 22 Jan 1993.

3178. Jeffery Scott Sharp (*Billy Joe*[7], *William Hubert*[6], *Charles W.*[5], *James (Jim) Charles Sr.*[4], *Adron (Edwin/Ade) Sr.*[3], *Charles W. Sr.*[2], *John Sr.*[1]) was born 7 Sep 1965 in Peoria, IL.

Jeffery married **Tammy Krause**, daughter of **Roland Krause** and **Valery Bart**, 30 Sep 1989 in Peoria, IL. Tammy was born 4 Jan in California.

5043	M	i.	**Ryan Sharp** was born 4 Jan 1998 in California.
5044	M	ii.	**Aaron Sharp** was born 4 Jan 1998 in California.

3179. Craig Lynn Sharp (*Billy Joe*[7], *William Hubert*[6], *Charles W.*[5], *James (Jim) Charles Sr.*[4], *Adron (Edwin/Ade) Sr.*[3], *Charles W. Sr.*[2], *John Sr.*[1]) was born 21 Sep 1966 in Peoria, IL.

Craig married **Jennifer Smith**, daughter of **Ronald Smith** and **Judy Hayworth**, 30 Sep 1989 in Peoria, IL. Jennifer was born 12 Nov 1971 in Peoria, IL.

5045	F	i.	**Sarah Sharp** was born 20 Feb 1990 in Peoria, IL.
5046	M	ii.	**Madison Sharp** was born 4 Jun 1996 in Peoria, IL.
5047	F	iii.	**Ronee Sharp** was born 28 Sep 1997 in Peoria, IL.

3180. James Edward (Buddy) Sharp (*William Edward (Tiny)* [7], *William Hubert* [6], *Charles W.* [5], *James (Jim) Charles Sr.* [4], *Adron (Edwin/Ade) Sr.* [3], *Charles W. Sr.* [2], *John Sr.* [1]) was born 30 Oct 1968 in ECM Hospital, Florence, Lauderdale County, AL.

James married **Kathryn Lorraine (Lori) Wood**, daughter of **Louis Cola Wood** and **Wilma Marcell Ballard**, 21 Nov 1986 in Lauderdale County, AL. Kathryn was born 24 Jun 1964 in West Memphis, Crittenden County, AR.

5048	M	i.	**Tyler James Sharp** was born 2 Jan 1989 in ECM Hospital, Florence, Lauderdale County, AL.
5049	F	ii.	**Ashley Kathryn Sharp** was born 2 Jan 1994 in ECM Hospital, Florence, Lauderdale County, AL.

3181. Vicki June Sharp (*William Edward (Tiny)* [7], *William Hubert* [6], *Charles W.* [5], *James (Jim) Charles Sr.* [4], *Adron (Edwin/Ade) Sr.* [3], *Charles W. Sr.* [2], *John Sr.* [1]) was born 3 Dec 1970 in ECM Hospital, Florence, Lauderdale County, AL.

Vicki married **Larry Simpson Baxter Jr.**, son of **Larry Simpson Baxter Sr.** and **Lois Virginia Johnson**, 17 Nov 1989 in Lauderdale County, AL. Larry was born 5 Feb 1970 in Tennessee.

5050	M	i.	**Luke Cody Baxter** was born 15 Nov 1991 in Columbia, TN.
5051	F	ii.	**Savannah Danielle Baxter** was born 16 Sep 1994 in Columbia, TN.
5052	F	iii.	**Jasmyn Summer Baxter** was born 16 Apr 1996 in Columbia, TN.

3182. Brian Keith Sharp Sr. (*William Edward (Tiny)* [7], *William Hubert* [6], *Charles W.* [5], *James (Jim) Charles Sr.* [4], *Adron (Edwin/Ade) Sr.* [3], *Charles W. Sr.* [2], *John Sr.* [1]) was born 11 Aug 1975 in Lauderdale County, AL.

Brian married **Jodie Marie Pritts**, daughter of **James Pritts** and **Unknown**.

5053	M	i.	**Brian Keith Sharp Jr.** was born 11 Mar 1999.
5054	M	ii.	**Bradley James Sharp** was born 24 Dec 1999.
5055	F	iii.	**Brittney Sharp** was born in Jul 2001.

3183. Angela Marie Sharp (*William Edward (Tiny)* [7], *William Hubert* [6], *Charles W.* [5], *James (Jim) Charles Sr.* [4], *Adron (Edwin/Ade) Sr.* [3], *Charles W. Sr.* [2], *John Sr.* [1]) was born 19 Aug 1976 in Lauderdale County, AL.

Angela married **Brian Keith Kelley**, son of **Teddy Steven Kelley** and **Glenda Gail Hinton**, 9 May 1998 in Lauderdale County, AL. Brian was born 30 Jul 1973 in Lauderdale County, AL.

5056	M	i.	**Trevor Donovan Kelley** was born 28 Dec 1997 in ECM Hospital, Florence, Lauderdale County, AL.
5057	M	ii.	**Trenton Blain Kelley** was born 12 Sep 1999 in ECM Hospital, Florence, Lauderdale County, AL.

3184. Janet Lou Bevis (*Mary Rachel Young* [7], *Aurelia Sharp* [6], *Charles W.* [5], *James (Jim) Charles Sr.* [4], *Adron (Edwin/Ade) Sr.* [3], *Charles W. Sr.* [2], *John Sr.* [1]) was born 4 Aug 1963 in Lauderdale County, AL.

Janet married **Ricky Dale Smith**, son of **Arthur Lee (Dick) Smith** and **Vertie Mae Allison**, 16 Jul 1982 in Lauderdale County, AL. Ricky was born 15 Jan 1963 in Lauderdale County, AL.
(Duplicate Line. See Person 1627)

3185. Edwin Dwayne Bevis (*Mary Rachel Young* [7], *Aurelia Sharp* [6], *Charles W.* [5], *James (Jim) Charles Sr.* [4], *Adron (Edwin/Ade) Sr.* [3], *Charles W. Sr.* [2], *John Sr.* [1]) was born 29 May 1967 in Lauderdale County, AL.

Edwin married **Vonda Lynn Russell**, daughter of **Eddie Jerry Russell** and **Margie Ruth Smith**, 4 Nov 1988 in Lauderdale County, AL. Vonda was born 6 Jul 1968 in Indiana.

5058	F	i.	**Miceala Faith (KK) Bevis** was born 20 Oct 1994 in Lauderdale County, AL.
5059	M	ii.	**Jarred Paul Bevis** was born 16 Jan 1996 in Lauderdale County, AL.
5060	M	iii.	**Kristopher Edwin Bevis** was born 16 Jan 1996 in Lauderdale County, AL.

3186. Lonnie Ray Bevis (*Mary Rachel Young* [7], *Aurelia Sharp* [6], *Charles W.* [5], *James (Jim) Charles Sr.* [4], *Adron (Edwin/Ade) Sr.* [3], *Charles W. Sr.* [2], *John Sr.* [1]) was born 25 Jul 1969 in Lauderdale County, AL.

Lonnie married **Tina Rose Benson**, daughter of **Raymond Benson** and **Mackie Bell White**, 14 Sep 1991 in Lauderdale County, AL. Tina was born 8 Nov 1969 in Lauderdale County, AL.

5061	M	i.	**Nathaniel Wade Bevis** was born 26 Sep 1989 in Lauderdale County, AL.
5062	M	ii.	**Louie Andrew Bevis** was born 12 Aug 1993 in Lauderdale County, AL.
5063	M	iii.	**Lonie Blake Bevis** was born 29 Aug 1994 in Lauderdale County, AL.

3187. James Roland Young (*William Roland Young* [7], *Audry Sharp* [6], *Charles W.* [5], *James (Jim) Charles Sr.* [4], *Adron (Edwin/Ade) Sr.* [3], *Charles W. Sr.* [2], *John Sr.* [1]) was born 15 Jan 1955 in Lauderdale County, AL.

James married **Melissa Rene Cagle**, daughter of **William Edward Cagle Jr.** and **Nellie Jane Kelley**, before 1975. Melissa was born 22 Aug 1959 in Peoria, IL.
(Duplicate Line. See Person 1971)

James next married **Ann *Unk**.

3188. Billy Gean Young (*William Roland Young* [7], *Audry Sharp* [6], *Charles W.* [5], *James (Jim) Charles Sr.* [4], *Adron (Edwin/Ade) Sr.* [3], *Charles W. Sr.* [2], *John Sr.* [1]) was born 14 Jan 1957 in Lauderdale County, AL.

Billy married **Mary Janice Burton**, daughter of **Leonard Burton** and **Mildred Aline Franks**, 29 Jun 1979 in Colbert County, AL. Mary was born 24 Apr 1955 in Colbert County, AL.

| 5064 | M | i. | **Jesse Paul Young** was born 29 Jul 1981 in Lauderdale County, AL. |
| 5065 | M | ii. | **Joshua Bartley Young** was born 7 Sep 1989 in Lauderdale County, AL. |

3189. Angelia Diane Young (*William Roland Young* [7], *Audry Sharp* [6], *Charles W.* [5], *James (Jim) Charles Sr.* [4], *Adron (Edwin/Ade) Sr.* [3], *Charles W. Sr.* [2], *John Sr.* [1]) was born 6 Jun 1958 in Florence, Lauderdale County, AL.

Angelia married **Travis Lloyd Wood**, son of **Charles William Wood** and **Frances Pearl Balentine**, 16 Jul 1976 in Lauderdale County, AL. Travis was born 16 Jun 1957 in Tyronza, Poinsett County, AR.

| + 5066 | F | i. | **Emily Selena Wood** was born 14 Feb 1979 in ECM Hospital, Florence, Lauderdale County, AL. |
| 5067 | M | ii. | **Cassidy Travis Wood** was born 2 Apr 1983 in ECM Hospital, Florence, Lauderdale County, AL. |

3190. Eric Dwayne Young (*William Roland Young* [7], *Audry Sharp* [6], *Charles W.* [5], *James (Jim) Charles Sr.* [4], *Adron (Edwin/Ade) Sr.* [3], *Charles W. Sr.* [2], *John Sr.* [1]) was born 28 Apr 1960 in Lauderdale County, AL.

Eric married **Donnie Jean Roden**, daughter of **Claude Roden** and **Edna *Unk**, 2 Oct 1981 in Lauderdale County, AL. Donnie was born 25 Apr 1943 in Colbert County, AL.

3191. Deborah (Debbie) Aletha Young (*William Roland Young* [7], *Audry Sharp* [6], *Charles W.* [5], *James (Jim) Charles Sr.* [4], *Adron (Edwin/Ade) Sr.* [3], *Charles W. Sr.* [2], *John Sr.* [1]) was born 26 Sep 1964 in Lauderdale County, AL.

Deborah married **Kevin Lee Smith**, son of **John Wesley Smith** and **Nellie Sue Norris**, 11 Jun 1992 in Lauderdale County, AL. Kevin was born 26 Jun 1964 in South Bend, IN.

| 5068 | M | i. | **Colt Seaver Smith** was born 29 Feb 1988 in Lauderdale County, AL. |
| 5069 | F | ii. | **Lacey Danielle Smith** was born 7 Apr 1992 in Lauderdale County, AL. |

3192. Donnie Ray Young (*Cletus Dempsey (Skeet) Young* [7], *Audry Sharp* [6], *Charles W.* [5], *James (Jim) Charles Sr.* [4], *Adron (Edwin/Ade) Sr.* [3], *Charles W. Sr.* [2], *John Sr.* [1]) was born 4 Feb 1957 in Florence, Lauderdale County, AL.

Donnie married **Wanda Delores Arnold**, daughter of **Henry Arnold** and **Martha Ray**, 28 Nov 1975 in Lauderdale County, AL. Wanda was born 30 May 1957 in Houston, TX.

| + 5070 | F | i. | **Shana Nicole Young** was born 28 Apr 1976 in Lauderdale County, AL. |
| 5071 | M | ii. | **Ryan Mitchell Young** was born 1 Jan 1983 in ECM Hospital, Florence, Lauderdale County, AL. |

Donnie next married **Jean Ann Paris** 25 May 1996 in Lauderdale County, AL. Jean was born 20 Sep 1957.

5072   F   i.   **Brianna Nicole Young** was born 24 Oct 1996 in ECM Hospital, Florence, Lauderdale County, AL.

3193. Betty Jean Young (*Cletus Dempsey (Skeet) Young ^{7}, Audry Sharp ^{6}, Charles W. ^{5}, James (Jim) Charles Sr. ^{4}, Adron (Edwin/Ade) Sr. ^{3}, Charles W. Sr. ^{2}, John Sr. ^{1}*) was born 4 Jun 1958 in Lauderdale County, AL.

Betty married **Steven Ray Gilchrist**, son of **Robert Stephen Gilchrist** and **Ressie Jean Winborn**, 4 Jun 1976 in Mississippi. Steven was born 27 Sep 1956 in Lauderdale County, AL.

+ 5073   M   i.   **Kenneth Lee Gilchrist** was born 16 Mar 1977 in Lauderdale County, AL.

3194. Travis Cletus Young (*Cletus Dempsey (Skeet) Young ^{7}, Audry Sharp ^{6}, Charles W. ^{5}, James (Jim) Charles Sr. ^{4}, Adron (Edwin/Ade) Sr. ^{3}, Charles W. Sr. ^{2}, John Sr. ^{1}*) was born 21 Jan 1964 in Lauderdale County, AL.

Travis married **Deena Lynn Hanback**, daughter of **Joel Dennis Hanback** and **Doris June Haataja**, 7 Nov 1987 in Lauderdale County, AL. Deena was born 30 May 1962 in Lapoite County, IN.

5074   M   i.   **Tyler Matt Young** was born 27 Sep 1990 in ECM Hospital, Florence, Lauderdale County, AL.

5075   M   ii.   **Trevor Clint Young** was born 18 Jan 1992 in ECM Hospital, Florence, Lauderdale County, AL, died 18 Jan 1992, and was buried in Murphy's Chapel Cemetery, Lauderdale County, AL.

5076   M   iii.   **Infant Son Young** was born 21 Jan 1994 in ECM Hospital, Florence, Lauderdale County, AL, died 21 Jan 1994, and was buried in Murphy's Chapel Cemetery, Lauderdale County, AL.

5077   F   iv.   **Kaylee Rose Young** was born 6 May 1996 in Birmingham, Jefferson County, AL.

3195. Brenda Sue Bevis (*Bonnie Mae Young ^{7}, Audry Sharp ^{6}, Charles W. ^{5}, James (Jim) Charles Sr. ^{4}, Adron (Edwin/Ade) Sr. ^{3}, Charles W. Sr. ^{2}, John Sr. ^{1}*) was born 8 Nov 1964 in Cooksville, TN.

Brenda married **Timothy (Tim) Woodrow Sharp**, son of **Millard Woodrow Sharp** and **Joyce Elizabeth Nobles**, 8 May 1981 in Lauderdale County, AL. Timothy was born 31 Jul 1963 in Lauderdale County, AL.

+ 5078   M   i.   **Brandon Craig Sharp** was born 3 Oct 1981 in Lauderdale County, AL.

5079   F   ii.   **Brandi Shree Sharp** was born 6 Apr 1990 in Lauderdale County, AL.

3196. Terry Lynn Bevis (*Bonnie Mae Young ^{7}, Audry Sharp ^{6}, Charles W. ^{5}, James (Jim) Charles Sr. ^{4}, Adron (Edwin/Ade) Sr. ^{3}, Charles W. Sr. ^{2}, John Sr. ^{1}*) was born 2 Aug 1971 in Lauderdale County, AL.

Terry married **Crystal Leann Friend**, daughter of **Ronald Nelson Friend** and **Patricia Joann Grisham**, 22 Dec 1990 in Lauderdale County, AL. Crystal was born 14 Jul 1971.

3197. Jeffery Daniel Scott (*Jewel Dean Young ^{7}, Audry Sharp ^{6}, Charles W. ^{5}, James (Jim) Charles Sr. ^{4}, Adron (Edwin/Ade) Sr. ^{3}, Charles W. Sr. ^{2}, John Sr. ^{1}*) was born 6 Feb 1964 in Lauderdale County, AL.

Jeffery married **Tina Jo Glasgow** 15 Feb in Lauderdale County, AL.

3198. Johnny Wayne Scott (*Jewel Dean Young ^{7}, Audry Sharp ^{6}, Charles W. ^{5}, James (Jim) Charles Sr. ^{4}, Adron (Edwin/Ade) Sr. ^{3}, Charles W. Sr. ^{2}, John Sr. ^{1}*) was born 30 Aug 1966 in Lauderdale County, AL.

Johnny married **Maria Gay Thompson**, daughter of **Jackie M. Thompson** and **Patricia Burbank**, 2 Nov 1985 in Lauderdale County, AL. Maria was born 6 Jul 1965 in Dallas County, TX.

5080   M   i.   **Jonathan Blake Scott** was born 25 Feb 1987 in Lauderdale County, AL.

5081   M   ii.   **Jordan Taylor Scott** was born 28 May 1989 in Lauderdale County, AL.

3201. Bobby Louis Daniels (*Barbara Sue Young ^{7}, Audry Sharp ^{6}, Charles W. ^{5}, James (Jim) Charles Sr. ^{4}, Adron (Edwin/Ade) Sr. ^{3}, Charles W. Sr. ^{2}, John Sr. ^{1}*) was born 19 Feb 1972 in Lauderdale County, AL.

Bobby married **Nicole Lynn Craig**, daughter of **Thomas Bartley Craig** and **Patricia Lea Fell**, 20 May 1995 in Wayne County, TN. Nicole was born 14 Apr 1977 in Lauderdale County, AL.

3202. Julie Sue Daniels (*Barbara Sue Young^7, Audry Sharp^6, Charles W.^{5}, James (Jim) Charles Sr.^{4}, Adron (Edwin/Ade) Sr.^{3}, Charles W. Sr.^{2}, John Sr.^{1}*) was born 4 Nov 1973 in Lauderdale County, AL.

Julie married **James Robert Rhodes**, son of **James Cleveland Rhodes** and **Reba Dell Noble**, 20 Nov 1992 in Hardin County, TN. James was born 12 Jan 1972 in Lauderdale County, AL.

| 5082 | F | i. | **Canadian Rosanna Rhodes** was born 3 Dec 1992 in Lauderdale County, AL. |

3204. Tammy Ann Young (*James Charles (J. C.) Young^7, Eura (Eurie) Sharp^6, Charles W.^{5}, James (Jim) Charles Sr.^{4}, Adron (Edwin/Ade) Sr.^{3}, Charles W. Sr.^{2}, John Sr.^{1}*) was born 8 Sep 1962 in Lauderdale County, AL.

Tammy married **Mickey Kelley**, son of **William Colonel (Cornel) Kelley** and **Elizabeth (Lizzie) Young**, 8 Sep 1978 in Lauderdale County, AL. Mickey was born 10 Aug 1960 in Lauderdale County, AL.

| 5083 | M | i. | **Nicholas Dewayne Kelley** was born 27 Feb 1985 in Lauderdale County, AL. |
| 5084 | F | ii. | **Chelsia Brooke Kelley** was born 8 Jun 1995 in Lauderdale County, AL. |

3205. Charles Dewayne Sharp (*Alice Beulah Young^7, Eura (Eurie) Sharp^6, Charles W.^{5}, James (Jim) Charles Sr.^{4}, Adron (Edwin/Ade) Sr.^{3}, Charles W. Sr.^{2}, John Sr.^{1}*) was born 16 Jan 1961 in Lauderdale County, AL.

Charles married **Elizabeth Anne Benson**, daughter of **Lowell Ralph Benson** and **Elsie Jeanette Winborn**, 8 Jul 1994 in Lauderdale County, AL. Elizabeth was born 30 Aug 1959 in Lauderdale County, AL.

| 5085 | M | i. | **Dylan Wayne Sharp** was born 7 Sep 1992 in Lauderdale County, AL. |

3206. Phyllis Natalie Sharp (*Alice Beulah Young^7, Eura (Eurie) Sharp^6, Charles W.^{5}, James (Jim) Charles Sr.^{4}, Adron (Edwin/Ade) Sr.^{3}, Charles W. Sr.^{2}, John Sr.^{1}*) was born 6 Feb 1962 in Lauderdale County, AL.

Phyllis married **Jamie Sederall Palmer**, son of **James Robert Palmer** and **Linnie Yvonne Vasser**, 11 Jun 1983 in Lauderdale County, AL. Jamie was born 29 Aug 1962 in Lauderdale County, AL.

| 5086 | F | i. | **Andrea Hope Palmer** was born 21 Aug 1988 in Lauderdale County, AL. |
| 5087 | M | ii. | **Chad Nolan Palmer** was born 17 Jul 1992 in Lauderdale County, AL. |

3207. Carmen Renea Sharp (*Alice Beulah Young^7, Eura (Eurie) Sharp^6, Charles W.^{5}, James (Jim) Charles Sr.^{4}, Adron (Edwin/Ade) Sr.^{3}, Charles W. Sr.^{2}, John Sr.^{1}*) was born 10 May 1963 in Lauderdale County, AL.

Carmen married **Jeffery Oneal Gray**, son of **Granville Oneal Gray** and **Dorothy Betty Devaney**, 18 Dec 1981 in Lauderdale County, AL. Jeffery was born 2 Nov 1957 in St. Louis, MO.

5088	F	i.	**Kayla Falawn Gray** was born 15 Oct 1982 in Lauderdale County, AL.
5089	F	ii.	**Ashley Renea Gray** was born 12 Mar 1988 in Lauderdale County, AL.
5090	M	iii.	**Zackary Oneal Gray** was born 30 Nov 1992 in Lauderdale County, AL.

3208. Michael Wade Young (*Agnes Gwindolin Young^7, Eura (Eurie) Sharp^6, Charles W.^{5}, James (Jim) Charles Sr.^{4}, Adron (Edwin/Ade) Sr.^{3}, Charles W. Sr.^{2}, John Sr.^{1}*) was born 18 Nov 1973 in Lauderdale County, AL.

Michael married **Lisa Michelle Young**, daughter of **Roderick Price Young** and **Rosalie Chaney**, 17 Sep 1997 in Lauderdale County, AL. Lisa was born 5 Nov 1975 in Lauderdale County, AL.

| 5091 | F | i. | **Alysa Michelle Young** was born 15 May 1997 in Lauderdale County, AL. |

3210. Christopher Paul Ezekiel (*Dorothy Mae Young^7, Eura (Eurie) Sharp^6, Charles W.^{5}, James (Jim) Charles Sr.^{4}, Adron (Edwin/Ade) Sr.^{3}, Charles W. Sr.^{2}, John Sr.^{1}*) was born 6 Mar 1972 in Lauderdale County, AL.

Christopher married **Shelly Annette Starkey**, daughter of **James Cox Starkey** and **Linda Lou Logan**, 24 Aug 1994 in Lauderdale County, AL. Shelly was born 25 Aug 1970 in Colbert County, AL.

| 5092 | F | i. | **Krista Louise Ezekiel** was born 5 Mar 1995 in Colbert County, AL. |
| 5093 | M | ii. | **James Logan Ezekiel** was born 5 May 1997 in Colbert County, AL. |

3212. Ginger Leigh Daniels (*Deborah Sue Young^7, Eura (Eurie) Sharp^6, Charles W.^{5}, James (Jim) Charles Sr.^{4}, Adron (Edwin/Ade) Sr.^{3}, Charles W. Sr.^{2}, John Sr.^{1}*) was born 25 Dec 1972 in Lauderdale County, AL.

Ginger married **Tony Clyde Balentine**, son of **Danny Eugene Balentine** and **Linda Kay Eaton**, 19 Feb 1994 in Lauderdale County, AL. Tony was born 28 Dec 1972 in Lauderdale County, AL.

   5094 M   i.   **Devin Andrew Balentine** was born 12 Sep 1995.

   5095 F   ii.   **Whitney Balentine**.

3213. Felicia Dawn Daniels (*Deborah Sue Young*^{7}, *Eura (Eurie) Sharp*^{6}, *Charles W.*^{5}, *James (Jim) Charles Sr.*^{4}, *Adron (Edwin/Ade) Sr.*^{3}, *Charles W. Sr.*^{2}, *John Sr.*^{1}) was born 24 Jan 1977 in Lauderdale County, AL.

Felicia married **Stephen Coolidge McCain**, son of **Coolidge Clayton (Pete) McCain** and **Carolyn Lois Sharp**, 13 Jun 1998 in Lauderdale County, AL. Stephen was born 18 Dec 1974 in ECM Hospital, Florence, Lauderdale County, AL.

   5096 M   i.   **Ryan Bennett McCain** was born 3 Jan 2003 in Lauderdale County, AL.

3214. Heather Nicole Daniels (*Deborah Sue Young*^{7}, *Eura (Eurie) Sharp*^{6}, *Charles W.*^{5}, *James (Jim) Charles Sr.*^{4}, *Adron (Edwin/Ade) Sr.*^{3}, *Charles W. Sr.*^{2}, *John Sr.*^{1}) was born 24 Jan 1982.

Heather married **Bennie Reed Franks**, son of **Bennie Earshell Franks** and **Janet Lynn Coats**, 1 Jun 2002 in Lauderdale County, AL. Bennie was born 20 Jul 1971.

   5097 F   i.   **Gracie Franks**.

3216. Dannie Lloyd Smith (*Ruth C. Crider*^{7}, *Marvin Turner Crider*^{6}, *Elizabeth (Roxie) Belle Sharp*^{5}, *James (Jim) Charles Sr.*^{4}, *Adron (Edwin/Ade) Sr.*^{3}, *Charles W. Sr.*^{2}, *John Sr.*^{1}) was born 8 Feb 1948 in Tishomingo, MS.

Dannie married **Rebecca C. Barber**.

3217. Marsha Lynn Smith (*Ruth C. Crider*^{7}, *Marvin Turner Crider*^{6}, *Elizabeth (Roxie) Belle Sharp*^{5}, *James (Jim) Charles Sr.*^{4}, *Adron (Edwin/Ade) Sr.*^{3}, *Charles W. Sr.*^{2}, *John Sr.*^{1}) was born 15 Apr 1960 in St. Mary County, MO.

Marsha married **Sammy Martin**.

3219. Paul Douglas Wood Jr. (*Paul Douglas Wood Sr.*^{7}, *Fannie Elizabeth (Sister) Crider*^{6}, *Elizabeth (Roxie) Belle Sharp*^{5}, *James (Jim) Charles Sr.*^{4}, *Adron (Edwin/Ade) Sr.*^{3}, *Charles W. Sr.*^{2}, *John Sr.*^{1}) was born 23 Dec 1952 in South Bend, IN.

Paul married **Mary Lynn Skipworth**, daughter of **Ellis Monroe Skipworth** and **Lizzie Mae Lanier**, 29 Jun 1973. Mary was born 12 Aug 1955 in Lauderdale County, AL.

 + 5098 F   i.   **Tonya Lynn Wood** was born 18 Dec 1974 in ECM Hospital, Florence, Lauderdale County, AL.

Paul next married **Martha Gail Thigpen**, daughter of **William Maple Thigpen** and **Birdie Mae *Unk**, 29 Dec 1980 in Lauderdale County, AL. Martha was born 25 May 1955 in Lauderdale County, AL.

   5099 F   i.   **Selena Kay Wood** was born 1 May 1977 in Huntsville, Madison County, AL.

   5100 F   ii.   **Roxanna Gail (Roxie) Wood** was born 15 Jan 1982 in Huntsville, Madison County, AL.

3220. Kenneth Dale (K. D.) Wood (*Paul Douglas Wood Sr.*^{7}, *Fannie Elizabeth (Sister) Crider*^{6}, *Elizabeth (Roxie) Belle Sharp*^{5}, *James (Jim) Charles Sr.*^{4}, *Adron (Edwin/Ade) Sr.*^{3}, *Charles W. Sr.*^{2}, *John Sr.*^{1}) was born 25 Nov 1954 in South Bend, IN.

Kenneth married **Rachel Marie Green**, daughter of **Cecil (Red) Green** and **Maggie Marie Moore**, 11 Apr 1977 in Lauderdale County, AL. Rachel was born 5 Jul 1961 in Hillsboro County, FL.

   5101 F   i.   **Kendall Marie Wood** was born 13 Feb 1996 in ECM Hospital, Florence, Lauderdale County, AL.

3221. Jeffrey Samuel (Sam) Wood Sr. (*Paul Douglas Wood Sr.*^{7}, *Fannie Elizabeth (Sister) Crider*^{6}, *Elizabeth (Roxie) Belle Sharp*^{5}, *James (Jim) Charles Sr.*^{4}, *Adron (Edwin/Ade) Sr.*^{3}, *Charles W. Sr.*^{2}, *John Sr.*^{1}) was born 7 Feb 1958 in Lauderdale County, AL.

Jeffrey married **Mary Lynn Skipworth**, daughter of **Ellis Monroe Skipworth** and **Lizzie Mae Lanier**, 17 Jul 1978 in Lauderdale County, AL. Mary was born 12 Aug 1955 in Lauderdale County, AL.

    5102   M   i.   **Jeffrey Samuel Wood Jr.** was born 2 Jun 1979 in Crockett General, Lawrenceburg, Lawrence County, TN.

3222. Nancy Ann Wood (*Paul Douglas Wood Sr.*[7], *Fannie Elizabeth (Sister) Crider*[6], *Elizabeth (Roxie) Belle Sharp*[5], *James (Jim) Charles Sr.*[4], *Adron (Edwin/Ade) Sr.*[3], *Charles W. Sr.*[2], *John Sr.*[1]) was born 16 Sep 1959 in South Bend, IN.

Nancy married **Jimmy Redus Madry**, son of **Redus Madry** and **Jewell Green**, 4 Nov 1981 in Lauderdale County, AL. Jimmy was born 5 Sep 1960 in Limestone County, AL.

    5103   F   i.   **Jenny Marie Madry** was born 28 Sep 1983 in Lauderdale County, AL, died 9 Nov 1983, and was buried in Oak Grove Cemetery, Lauderdale County, AL.

3223. Paula Marie Wood (*Paul Douglas Wood Sr.*[7], *Fannie Elizabeth (Sister) Crider*[6], *Elizabeth (Roxie) Belle Sharp*[5], *James (Jim) Charles Sr.*[4], *Adron (Edwin/Ade) Sr.*[3], *Charles W. Sr.*[2], *John Sr.*[1]) was born 24 Mar 1961 in Lauderdale County, AL.

Paula married **Andrew Monroe Skipworth I**, son of **Ellis Monroe Skipworth** and **Lizzie Mae Lanier**, 15 Mar 1982 in Lauderdale County, AL. Andrew was born 11 Mar 1958 in Lauderdale County, AL.

    5104   F   i.   **Sabrina Lynn Skipworth** was born 3 Sep 1981 in Lauderdale County, AL.
    5105   M   ii.   **Andrew Monroe Skipworth II** was born 22 Jan 1984 in Lauderdale County, AL.
    5106   M   iii.   **Matthew Blake Skipworth** was born 12 Jul 1986 in Lauderdale County, AL.

3224. Steven McKinley Wood (*Rufus Ezra Wood*[7], *Fannie Elizabeth (Sister) Crider*[6], *Elizabeth (Roxie) Belle Sharp*[5], *James (Jim) Charles Sr.*[4], *Adron (Edwin/Ade) Sr.*[3], *Charles W. Sr.*[2], *John Sr.*[1]) was born 25 Oct 1955 in South Bend, IN.

Steven married **Derise Ann Lundsford**, daughter of **Claude Lundsford** and **Shirley Dawson**, 28 Jan 1975 in Iuka, Tishomingo County, MS. Derise was born 26 Dec 1957 in South Bend, IN.

 + 5107   M   i.   **Jason McKinley Wood** was born 11 Nov 1976 in South Bend, IN.
    5108   M   ii.   **Robby Lee Wood** was born 31 Dec 1978 in South Bend, IN.
    5109   M   iii.   **Todd Allen Wood** was born 20 Mar 1981 in South Bend, IN.

3225. Pamela Elaine Wood (*Rufus Ezra Wood*[7], *Fannie Elizabeth (Sister) Crider*[6], *Elizabeth (Roxie) Belle Sharp*[5], *James (Jim) Charles Sr.*[4], *Adron (Edwin/Ade) Sr.*[3], *Charles W. Sr.*[2], *John Sr.*[1]) was born 30 Sep 1956 in South Bend, IN.

Pamela married **Mickey Lewis Clemons**, son of **Carroll Eugene Clemons I** and **Elizabeth (Betty) Darby**, 11 Mar 1972 in Iuka, Tishomingo County, MS. Mickey was born 26 Jun 1952 in Florence, Lauderdale County, AL.

 + 5110   F   i.   **Tammy Lynn Clemons** was born 14 Aug 1972 in Florence, Lauderdale County, AL.
    5111   F   ii.   **Kimberly Dawn Clemons** was born 3 Jan 1977 in Florence, Lauderdale County, AL, died 6 Jun 2003, and was buried in Gravely Springs Cemetery, Lauderdale County, AL.
    5112   M   iii.   **Dusty Wayne Clemons** was born 13 Aug 1980 in Florence, Lauderdale County, AL.

3227. Cheryl Elizabeth Wood (*Rufus Ezra Wood*[7], *Fannie Elizabeth (Sister) Crider*[6], *Elizabeth (Roxie) Belle Sharp*[5], *James (Jim) Charles Sr.*[4], *Adron (Edwin/Ade) Sr.*[3], *Charles W. Sr.*[2], *John Sr.*[1]) was born 4 Jun 1961 in South Bend, IN.

Cheryl married **Boyce Clemons**, son of **Carroll Eugene Clemons I** and **Elizabeth (Betty) Darby**. Boyce was born 14 Sep 1954 in Florence, Lauderdale County, AL.

 + 5113   F   i.   **Christy Lynn Clemons** was born 9 Mar 1977 in South Bend, IN.
    5114   M   ii.   **Shannon Boyce Clemons** was born 6 Nov 1981 in Florence, Lauderdale County, AL, died 8 Jun 2003, and was buried in Gravely Springs Cemetery, Lauderdale County, AL.

3228. Laurie Lee Wood (*Rufus Ezra Wood*[7], *Fannie Elizabeth (Sister) Crider*[6], *Elizabeth (Roxie) Belle Sharp*[5], *James (Jim) Charles Sr.*[4], *Adron (Edwin/Ade) Sr.*[3], *Charles W. Sr.*[2], *John Sr.*[1]) was born 16 Jul 1962 in South Bend, IN.

Laurie married **Michael Ellis**.

5115　F　　i.　　　**Tabitha Leann Wood** was born 31 Aug 1985 in South Bend, IN.

3230. Malissa Diane Kennamore (*Betty Ann Crider*[7], *John Richard Crider*[6], *Elizabeth (Roxie) Belle Sharp*[5], *James (Jim) Charles Sr.*[4], *Adron (Edwin/Ade) Sr.*[3], *Charles W. Sr.*[2], *John Sr.*[1]) was born 28 Jun 1975 in Lauderdale County, AL.

Malissa married **Timothy (Tim) Wayne Horton**, son of **Jerry Wayne Horton** and **Glenda Borden**, 17 Dec 1993 in Colbert County, AL. Timothy was born 7 Oct 1975 in Lauderdale County, AL.

5116　M　　i.　　　**Devon Wayne Horton** was born 3 Jan 1994 in Colbert County, AL.

5117　M　　ii.　　**Kevin Austin Horton** was born 5 Jun 1998 in Colbert County, AL.

3233. Jimmie Nell Ezekiel (*Hazel Irene Wood*[7], *Mary Etta (Virgie) Crider*[6], *Elizabeth (Roxie) Belle Sharp*[5], *James (Jim) Charles Sr.*[4], *Adron (Edwin/Ade) Sr.*[3], *Charles W. Sr.*[2], *John Sr.*[1]) was born 8 Aug 1943 in Lauderdale County, AL.

Jimmie married **Bobby Winders** 6 Jun 1963. Bobby was born 26 Jul 1944.

+ 5118　F　　i.　　　**Audrey Lynn Winders** was born 28 Apr 1964 in West Memphis, Crittenden County, AR.

+ 5119　F　　ii.　　**Lisa Renee Winders** was born 4 Jun 1966 in West Memphis, Crittenden County, AR.

5120　M　　iii.　**Jim Bob Winders** was born 29 Jul 1974 in West Memphis, Crittenden County, AR.

3234. Jerry Anthony Ezekiel (*Hazel Irene Wood*[7], *Mary Etta (Virgie) Crider*[6], *Elizabeth (Roxie) Belle Sharp*[5], *James (Jim) Charles Sr.*[4], *Adron (Edwin/Ade) Sr.*[3], *Charles W. Sr.*[2], *John Sr.*[1]) was born in 1945 in Lauderdale County, AL.

Jerry married **Sue Swink** in 1965. Sue was born 4 Feb 1944.

5121　M　　i.　　　**Michael Anthony Ezekiel** was born 5 Sep 1967 in Blytheville, AR.

3235. Colin Earl Ezekiel (*Hazel Irene Wood*[7], *Mary Etta (Virgie) Crider*[6], *Elizabeth (Roxie) Belle Sharp*[5], *James (Jim) Charles Sr.*[4], *Adron (Edwin/Ade) Sr.*[3], *Charles W. Sr.*[2], *John Sr.*[1]) was born 25 Aug 1947 in Lauderdale County, AL.

Colin married **Rachel McCorkle** 24 Dec 1966. Rachel was born 23 Jan 1947 in Memphis, Shelby County, TN.

+ 5122　M　　i.　　　**Jeffrey Earl Ezekiel** was born 28 Apr 1968 in Biloxi, MS.

3236. Linda Faye Ezekiel (*Hazel Irene Wood*[7], *Mary Etta (Virgie) Crider*[6], *Elizabeth (Roxie) Belle Sharp*[5], *James (Jim) Charles Sr.*[4], *Adron (Edwin/Ade) Sr.*[3], *Charles W. Sr.*[2], *John Sr.*[1]) was born 18 Feb 1949 in Lauderdale County, AL.

Linda married **Vernon Franks** 22 Aug 1974.

5123　M　　i.　　　**Timothy Allen Franks** was born 20 Jan 1976 in Osceola, AR.

5124　M　　ii.　　**Robert Matthew Franks** was born 8 Jul 1982 in Memphis, Shelby County, TN.

3237. Janice Aileen Ezekiel (*Hazel Irene Wood*[7], *Mary Etta (Virgie) Crider*[6], *Elizabeth (Roxie) Belle Sharp*[5], *James (Jim) Charles Sr.*[4], *Adron (Edwin/Ade) Sr.*[3], *Charles W. Sr.*[2], *John Sr.*[1]) was born 14 Apr 1950 in Waterloo, Lauderdale County, AL.

Janice married **Lannie E. Brant** 16 Nov 1970 in Osceola, AR. Lannie was born 22 Jun 1949.

5125　M　　i.　　　**Robert Lannie Brant** was born 8 Feb 1973 in St. Marys, GA.

5126　F　　ii.　　**Rebecca Aileen Brant** was born 15 Oct 1981 in Brunswick, Glynn County, GA.

3238. Christine Ezekiel (*Hazel Irene Wood*[7], *Mary Etta (Virgie) Crider*[6], *Elizabeth (Roxie) Belle Sharp*[5], *James (Jim) Charles Sr.*[4], *Adron (Edwin/Ade) Sr.*[3], *Charles W. Sr.*[2], *John Sr.*[1]) was born 7 Jan 1952 in Tyronza, Poinsett County, AR.

Christine married **Ray Brewington** 8 Jul 1977 in Tyronza, Poinsett County, AR. Ray died 8 Aug 2001.

+ 5127　M　　i.　　　**Tony Wayne Brewington** was born 14 Apr 1975 in Osceola, AR.

5128   M   ii.   **Daniel Joseph Brewington** was born 22 Mar 1979 in Memphis, Shelby County, TN.

Christine next married **Charles Wheeler**.

3239. Bobby Gene Ezekiel (*Hazel Irene Wood*[7], *Mary Etta (Virgie) Crider*[6], *Elizabeth (Roxie) Belle Sharp*[5], *James (Jim) Charles Sr.*[4], *Adron (Edwin/Ade) Sr.*[3], *Charles W. Sr.*[2], *John Sr.*[1]) was born 27 Jul 1956 in Tyronza, Poinsett County, AR.

    Bobby married **Paula Emanus** 12 Jun 1984. Paula was born 27 Mar 1957.
    5129   M   i.   **Christopher Gene Ezekiel** was born 27 Sep 1983 in Killeen, TX.
    5130   F   ii.   **Ashley Marie Ezekiel** was born 23 Feb 1985 in Memphis, Shelby County, TN.
    5131   M   iii.   **Justin Paul Ezekiel** was born 8 Feb 1988 in Memphis, Shelby County, TN.

3240. Dorothy Ann Ezekiel (*Hazel Irene Wood*[7], *Mary Etta (Virgie) Crider*[6], *Elizabeth (Roxie) Belle Sharp*[5], *James (Jim) Charles Sr.*[4], *Adron (Edwin/Ade) Sr.*[3], *Charles W. Sr.*[2], *John Sr.*[1]) was born 23 Aug 1959 in Tyronza, Poinsett County, AR.

    Dorothy married **Wesley Holt** 25 Jul 1977. Wesley died in Sep 1995 and was buried in Tyronza Cemetery, Tyronza, Poinsett County, AR.
+ 5132   F   i.   **Stephanie Diane Holt** was born 14 Feb 1978 in Memphis, Shelby County, TN.
    5133   M   ii.   **Bryan Lee Holt** was born 21 Jul 1979 in Osceola, AR.
    5134   M   iii.   **Steven Mitchell Holt** was born 9 Jun 1983 in Osceola, AR.

    Dorothy next married **Terry Collins**. Terry was born in Arkansas.

3241. Barbara Ruth Ezekiel (*Hazel Irene Wood*[7], *Mary Etta (Virgie) Crider*[6], *Elizabeth (Roxie) Belle Sharp*[5], *James (Jim) Charles Sr.*[4], *Adron (Edwin/Ade) Sr.*[3], *Charles W. Sr.*[2], *John Sr.*[1]) was born 27 Jul 1962 in Tyronza, Poinsett County, AR.

    Barbara married **Danny Oneal** 12 Sep 1980 in Brunswick, Glynn County, GA. Danny was born 19 May 1959.
    5135   M   i.   **Danny Michael Oneal** was born 29 Dec 1980 in Brunswick, Glynn County, GA.

3242. Sherman Daniel Wood (*Charles William Wood*[7], *Mary Etta (Virgie) Crider*[6], *Elizabeth (Roxie) Belle Sharp*[5], *James (Jim) Charles Sr.*[4], *Adron (Edwin/Ade) Sr.*[3], *Charles W. Sr.*[2], *John Sr.*[1]) was born 29 Dec 1953 in Tyronza, Poinsett County, AR.

    Sherman married **Betty Jo Kelley**, daughter of **William Colonel (Cornel) Kelley** and **Elizabeth (Lizzie) Young**, 11 May 1972 in Lauderdale County, AL. Betty was born 27 Apr 1958 in Lauderdale County, AL.
+ 5136   M   i.   **Kenny Daniel Wood** was born 16 Sep 1973 in ECM Hospital, Florence, Lauderdale County, AL.
+ 5137   F   ii.   **Gwendolyn Michelle (Shelly) Wood** was born 28 Aug 1976 in ECM Hospital, Florence, Lauderdale County, AL.
+ 5138   M   iii.   **Gregory Lynn Wood** was born 8 Dec 1977 in Colbert County, AL.

    Sherman next married **Martha McGough** 5 May 1988 in Russellville, Franklin County, AL. Martha was born 6 Nov 1959 in Russellville, Franklin County, AL.
+ 5139   F   i.   **Misty McGough**.

3243. Travis Lloyd Wood (*Charles William Wood*[7], *Mary Etta (Virgie) Crider*[6], *Elizabeth (Roxie) Belle Sharp*[5], *James (Jim) Charles Sr.*[4], *Adron (Edwin/Ade) Sr.*[3], *Charles W. Sr.*[2], *John Sr.*[1]) was born 16 Jun 1957 in Tyronza, Poinsett County, AR.

    Travis married **Angelia Diane Young**, daughter of **William Roland Young** and **Audrey Jean Hanback**, 16 Jul 1976 in Lauderdale County, AL. Angelia was born 6 Jun 1958 in Florence, Lauderdale County, AL.
    (Duplicate Line. See Person 3189)

3244. Freda Marlene Wood (*Charles William Wood*[7], *Mary Etta (Virgie) Crider*[6], *Elizabeth (Roxie) Belle Sharp*[5], *James (Jim) Charles Sr.*[4], *Adron (Edwin/Ade) Sr.*[3], *Charles W. Sr.*[2], *John Sr.*[1]) was born 26 Sep 1959 in Tyronza, Poinsett County, AR.

Freda married **James Lewis Wright I**, son of **Albert Lee Wright Sr.** and **Mary Virginia White**, 19 Oct 1973 in Lauderdale County, AL. James was born 22 May 1955 in Lauderdale County, AL.

| 5140 | M | i. | **James Lewis Wright II** was born 4 Jan 1974 in ECM Hospital, Florence, Lauderdale County, AL, died 18 Sep 1976, and was buried in Evergreen Cemetery, Lauderdale County, AL. |
| 5141 | M | ii. | **William Chad Wright** was born 17 Sep 1982 in ECM Hospital, Florence, Lauderdale County, AL. |

Freda next married **Charles Wesley Porter** 1 Aug 1991 in Lauderdale County, AL. Charles was born 18 Oct 1964 in Florence, Lauderdale County, AL.

| 5142 | F | i. | **Haley Kristen Porter** was born 10 Dec 1992 in ECM Hospital, Florence, Lauderdale County, AL. |

3245. Glenn Thomas Brown (*Edith Inez Wood*[7], *Mary Etta (Virgie) Crider*[6], *Elizabeth (Roxie) Belle Sharp*[5], *James (Jim) Charles Sr.*[4], *Adron (Edwin/Ade) Sr.*[3], *Charles W. Sr.*[2], *John Sr.*[1]) was born 27 Jul 1948 in Lauderdale County, AL.

Glenn married **Mary Jo Schulte**. Mary was born 16 Sep 1934.

| + 5143 | F | i. | **Wanda Lee Tatum**. |
| + 5144 | F | ii. | **Karen Lynn Tatum** was born 30 Oct 1959 in Colbert County, AL. |

3246. Bobby Junior Brown (*Edith Inez Wood*[7], *Mary Etta (Virgie) Crider*[6], *Elizabeth (Roxie) Belle Sharp*[5], *James (Jim) Charles Sr.*[4], *Adron (Edwin/Ade) Sr.*[3], *Charles W. Sr.*[2], *John Sr.*[1]) was born 9 May 1950 in Florence, Lauderdale County, AL.

Bobby married **Cochita Leard** 30 Mar 1972. Cochita was born 12 Jun 1950.

| + 5145 | F | i. | **Talina Shawn Brown** was born 15 Apr 1973 in Memphis, Shelby County, TN. |

3247. Jimmy Turner Brown (*Edith Inez Wood*[7], *Mary Etta (Virgie) Crider*[6], *Elizabeth (Roxie) Belle Sharp*[5], *James (Jim) Charles Sr.*[4], *Adron (Edwin/Ade) Sr.*[3], *Charles W. Sr.*[2], *John Sr.*[1]) was born 24 Jun 1953 in Florence, Lauderdale County, AL.

Jimmy married **Mary Frances (Susan) White** 26 Jul 1974 in Lauderdale County, AL. Mary was born 2 Feb 1957.

+ 5146	F	i.	**Amanda Leann Brown** was born 26 Jun 1979 in ECM Hospital, Florence, Lauderdale County, AL.
5147	M	ii.	**Jeremy Christopher Brown** was born 6 Apr 1982 in ECM Hospital, Florence, Lauderdale County, AL.
5148	M	iii.	**Clinton Jared Brown** was born 16 Feb 1985 in ECM Hospital, Florence, Lauderdale County, AL.

3248. Kenneth Wayne Brown (*Edith Inez Wood*[7], *Mary Etta (Virgie) Crider*[6], *Elizabeth (Roxie) Belle Sharp*[5], *James (Jim) Charles Sr.*[4], *Adron (Edwin/Ade) Sr.*[3], *Charles W. Sr.*[2], *John Sr.*[1]) was born 28 Jun 1957 in Florence, Lauderdale County, AL.

Kenneth married **Karen Lynn Tatum**, daughter of **Tillman Tatum** and **Mary Jo Schulte**, 28 Mar 1980 in Lauderdale County, AL. Karen was born 30 Oct 1959 in Colbert County, AL.

| + 5149 | F | i. | **Yolanda Lynn Brown** was born 28 Jun 1982 in ECM Hospital, Florence, Lauderdale County, AL. |
| 5150 | M | ii. | **Kyle Wayne Brown** was born 6 Jun 1988 in ECM Hospital, Florence, Lauderdale County, AL. |

3249. Charles Wayne Wood (*Carl Thomas Wood [7], Mary Etta (Virgie) Crider [6], Elizabeth (Roxie) Belle Sharp [5], James (Jim) Charles Sr. [4], Adron (Edwin/Ade) Sr. [3], Charles W. Sr. [2], John Sr. [1]*) was born 9 Nov 1955 in Tyronza, Poinsett County, AR.

Charles married **Loretta Stewart** 31 Dec 1976.

3250. Peggy Sue Wood (*Carl Thomas Wood [7], Mary Etta (Virgie) Crider [6], Elizabeth (Roxie) Belle Sharp [5], James (Jim) Charles Sr. [4], Adron (Edwin/Ade) Sr. [3], Charles W. Sr. [2], John Sr. [1]*) was born 1 Jan 1958 in South Bend, St Joseph County, IN.

Peggy married **Anthony Gwynn Moss** 13 Mar 1977 in Middleton, TN. Anthony was born 31 Aug 1957 in Bolivar, TN.

+ 5151 M i. **Joseph Brandon Moss** was born 26 Feb 1979 in Memphis, Shelby County, TN.
  5152 F ii. **Laura Caitlin Moss** was born 1 Jan 1989 in Memphis, Shelby County, TN.

3251. Michael Duane Wood (*Carl Thomas Wood [7], Mary Etta (Virgie) Crider [6], Elizabeth (Roxie) Belle Sharp [5], James (Jim) Charles Sr. [4], Adron (Edwin/Ade) Sr. [3], Charles W. Sr. [2], John Sr. [1]*) was born 6 Aug 1960 in South Bend, St Joseph County, IN.

Michael married **Gloria Pipkin** 15 Jul 1979 in Somerville, TN.

  5153 F i. **Jennifer Lynn Wood** was born 19 Sep 1980 in Bolivar, TN.
  5154 M ii. **Thomas David Wood** was born 31 Jan 1984 in Jackson, TN.
  5155 M iii. **Kevin Duane Wood** was born 2 Jun 1991 in Jackson, TN.

3252. David Paul Wood (*Carl Thomas Wood [7], Mary Etta (Virgie) Crider [6], Elizabeth (Roxie) Belle Sharp [5], James (Jim) Charles Sr. [4], Adron (Edwin/Ade) Sr. [3], Charles W. Sr. [2], John Sr. [1]*) was born 31 Mar 1962 in West Memphis, Crittenden County, AR.

David married **Jeanette Roberts** 24 Feb 1984 in Oakland, TN.

+ 5156 M i. **Anthony Mark Wood** was born 28 May 1982 in Bolivar, TN.
  5157 F ii. **Heather Danielle Wood** was born 5 Jul 1987 in Memphis, Shelby County, TN.

3253. Sharon Louise Wood (*Louis Cola Wood [7], Mary Etta (Virgie) Crider [6], Elizabeth (Roxie) Belle Sharp [5], James (Jim) Charles Sr. [4], Adron (Edwin/Ade) Sr. [3], Charles W. Sr. [2], John Sr. [1]*) was born 7 Jun 1957 in Chelford, AR.

Sharon married **Joey Lee Wood**, son of **Wallace Earl Wood** and **Beulah Estelle Smith**, 24 Dec 1982 in Lauderdale County, AL. Joey was born 15 Feb 1960 in Florence, Lauderdale County, AL.

  5158 M i. **Joshua (Josh) Lee Wood** was born 14 Sep 1990 in ECM Hospital, Florence, Lauderdale County, AL.

3254. Ricky Louis Wood (*Louis Cola Wood [7], Mary Etta (Virgie) Crider [6], Elizabeth (Roxie) Belle Sharp [5], James (Jim) Charles Sr. [4], Adron (Edwin/Ade) Sr. [3], Charles W. Sr. [2], John Sr. [1]*) was born 16 Dec 1961 in West Memphis, Crittenden County, AR.

Ricky married **Vicki Kay Smith**, daughter of **Arthur Lee (Dick) Smith** and **Vertie Mae Allison**, 25 Jul 1980 in Lauderdale County, AL. Vicki was born 10 Jul 1961 in Lauderdale County, AL.
(Duplicate Line. See Person 1626)

3255. Kathryn Lorraine (Lori) Wood (*Louis Cola Wood [7], Mary Etta (Virgie) Crider [6], Elizabeth (Roxie) Belle Sharp [5], James (Jim) Charles Sr. [4], Adron (Edwin/Ade) Sr. [3], Charles W. Sr. [2], John Sr. [1]*) was born 24 Jun 1964 in West Memphis, Crittenden County, AR.

Kathryn married **James Edward (Buddy) Sharp**, son of **William Edward (Tiny) Sharp** and **Judy Ann Melton**, 21 Nov 1986 in Lauderdale County, AL. James was born 30 Oct 1968 in ECM Hospital, Florence, Lauderdale County, AL.
(Duplicate Line. See Person 3180)

3256. Curtis Dwayne Wood (*Louis Cola Wood*[7], *Mary Etta (Virgie) Crider*[6], *Elizabeth (Roxie) Belle Sharp*[5], *James (Jim) Charles Sr.*[4], *Adron (Edwin/Ade) Sr.*[3], *Charles W. Sr.*[2], *John Sr.*[1]) was born 25 May 1968 in West Memphis, Crittenden County, AR.

    Curtis married **Jennifer (Jenni) Leigh Hart**, daughter of **Charles (Chuck) Elton Hart** and **Wanda Sue Smith**, 1 Oct 1993 in Lauderdale County, AL. Jennifer was born 8 Oct 1967 in Florence, Lauderdale County, AL.

 + 5159 M   i.   **Jeffrey Curtis Wood** was born 5 Feb 1988 in ECM Hospital, Florence, Lauderdale County, AL.

   5160 M   ii.   **Dylan Dwayne Wood** was born 8 Mar 1995 in ECM Hospital, Florence, Lauderdale County, AL.

3257. Jeannie Diane Pickens (*Betty Sue Wood*[7], *Mary Etta (Virgie) Crider*[6], *Elizabeth (Roxie) Belle Sharp*[5], *James (Jim) Charles Sr.*[4], *Adron (Edwin/Ade) Sr.*[3], *Charles W. Sr.*[2], *John Sr.*[1]) was born 1 Nov 1960 in Michigan City, IN.

    Jeannie married **Jackie Lynn Armstrong** 14 Mar 1980 in Hickory Withe, TN. Jackie was born 25 Dec 1960 in Memphis, Shelby County, TN.

 + 5161 M   i.   **Eric Jason Armstrong** was born 30 Dec 1981 in Memphis, Shelby County, TN.

   5162 F   ii.   **Jenna Lynn Armstrong** was born 9 Jan 1985 in Memphis, Shelby County, TN.

3258. Kathy Ann Pickens (*Betty Sue Wood*[7], *Mary Etta (Virgie) Crider*[6], *Elizabeth (Roxie) Belle Sharp*[5], *James (Jim) Charles Sr.*[4], *Adron (Edwin/Ade) Sr.*[3], *Charles W. Sr.*[2], *John Sr.*[1]) was born 10 Apr 1963 in Michigan City, IN.

    Kathy married **Norman Sanders** 17 Dec 1983 in Memphis, Shelby County, TN. Norman was born 5 Sep 1960 in Memphis, Shelby County, TN.

 + 5163 F   i.   **Ashley Nicole Sanders** was born 24 Jun 1984 in Memphis, Shelby County, TN.

3259. Robert Joe Pickens (*Betty Sue Wood*[7], *Mary Etta (Virgie) Crider*[6], *Elizabeth (Roxie) Belle Sharp*[5], *James (Jim) Charles Sr.*[4], *Adron (Edwin/Ade) Sr.*[3], *Charles W. Sr.*[2], *John Sr.*[1]) was born 12 Aug 1964 in Jonesboro, Craighead County, AR.

    Robert married **Carol Green** 23 Dec 1984 in Somerville, TN. Carol was born 15 Sep 1967.

   5164 M   i.   **Adam Ray Pickens** was born 30 Mar 1985 in Memphis, Shelby County, TN.

   5165 M   ii.   **Jesse Aaron Pickens** was born 18 Apr 1986 in Memphis, Shelby County, TN.

    Robert next married **Becky Harman** in 2001.

3260. Tammy Lynn Pickens (*Betty Sue Wood*[7], *Mary Etta (Virgie) Crider*[6], *Elizabeth (Roxie) Belle Sharp*[5], *James (Jim) Charles Sr.*[4], *Adron (Edwin/Ade) Sr.*[3], *Charles W. Sr.*[2], *John Sr.*[1]) was born 20 Jun 1966 in Michigan City, IN.

    Tammy married **Alejanerino Montalvo** 8 Feb 1988 in Millington, TN. Alejanerino was born 15 Aug 1967 in Brooklyn, NY.

   5166 M   i.   **Ronald Andrew Pickens** was born 19 Mar 1985 in Tennessee.

   5167 M   ii.   **Alex Daniel Montalvo** was born 12 Jan 1989 in Millington, TN.

   5168 F   iii. **Stephanie Elizabeth Montalvo** was born 20 Apr 1990 in Jacksonville, FL.

3261. Lisa Renae Pickens (*Betty Sue Wood*[7], *Mary Etta (Virgie) Crider*[6], *Elizabeth (Roxie) Belle Sharp*[5], *James (Jim) Charles Sr.*[4], *Adron (Edwin/Ade) Sr.*[3], *Charles W. Sr.*[2], *John Sr.*[1]) was born 15 Dec 1967 in Michigan City, IN.

    Lisa married **Keith Hawkins** 1 Mar 1986 in Somerville, TN. Keith was born 11 Jul 1965 in Somerville, TN.

 + 5169 M   i.   **Corey Ryan Hawkins** was born 14 May 1988 in Memphis, Shelby County, TN.

   5170 F   ii.   **Whitney Hawkins** was born in 1995 in Memphis, Shelby County, TN.

    Lisa next married **Robert Doyle** in 2002.

   5171 F   i.   **Madison Grace Doyle** was born 12 Mar 2003.

3263. Michael James Crider (*Edward Joyce (E. J.) Crider*[7], *Edgar Louis (Ed) Crider*[6], *Elizabeth (Roxie) Belle Sharp*[5], *James (Jim) Charles Sr.*[4], *Adron (Edwin/Ade) Sr.*[3], *Charles W. Sr.*[2], *John Sr.*[1]) was born 20 Oct 1973 in Lauderdale County, AL.

Michael married **Kendra Nichole Hatchett**, daughter of **Charles Keith Hatchett** and **Charlene Fielder**, 21 Oct 1995 in Lauderdale County, AL. Kendra was born 12 Jul 1977 in Wayne County, TN.

5172	F	i.	**Samantha Faith Crider** was born 8 Jul 1999 in ECM Hospital, Florence, Lauderdale County, AL.

3264. Tonya Renea Crider (*Edward Joyce (E. J.) Crider*[7], *Edgar Louis (Ed) Crider*[6], *Elizabeth (Roxie) Belle Sharp*[5], *James (Jim) Charles Sr.*[4], *Adron (Edwin/Ade) Sr.*[3], *Charles W. Sr.*[2], *John Sr.*[1]) was born 14 Feb 1977 in Lauderdale County, AL.

Tonya married **Benjamin Jennings Odom IV**, son of **Benjamin Jennings Odom III** and **Joyce Marie Fortner**, 22 Mar 1996 in Lauderdale County, AL. Benjamin was born 25 Jul 1974 in Lauderdale County, AL.

5173	F	i.	**Morgan Shanelle Odom** was born 30 Apr 1993 in Lauderdale County, AL.
5174	M	ii.	**Bryan Mackenzie Odom** was born 21 Aug 1997 in Lauderdale County, AL.
5175	M	iii.	**James Macquire Odom** was born 8 Dec 1999 in Lauderdale County, AL.
5176	M	iv.	**Meyson Jennings Odom** was born 22 Jan 2004 in Lauderdale County, AL, died 24 Feb 2004, and was buried in Rhodesville Cemetery, Lauderdale County, AL.

3265. Marsha Leeann Crider (*Edward Joyce (E. J.) Crider*[7], *Edgar Louis (Ed) Crider*[6], *Elizabeth (Roxie) Belle Sharp*[5], *James (Jim) Charles Sr.*[4], *Adron (Edwin/Ade) Sr.*[3], *Charles W. Sr.*[2], *John Sr.*[1]) was born 18 Sep 1980 in ECM Hospital, Florence, Lauderdale County, AL.

Marsha married **Gregory (Greg) Lance Scott**, son of **Gary Lance Scott** and **Bobbie Jo Qualls**, 25 Sep 1998 in Lauderdale County, AL. Gregory was born 15 Nov 1975 in ECM Hospital, Florence, Lauderdale County, AL.

5177	M	i.	**Colton J. (C. J.) Scott**.

3266. Ricky Donald Crider (*Donald Fay Crider*[7], *Edgar Louis (Ed) Crider*[6], *Elizabeth (Roxie) Belle Sharp*[5], *James (Jim) Charles Sr.*[4], *Adron (Edwin/Ade) Sr.*[3], *Charles W. Sr.*[2], *John Sr.*[1]) was born 30 Jun 1968 in Lauderdale County, AL.

Ricky married **Stacie Darlene Haddock**, daughter of **Clifford David Haddock** and **Edna Eloise Mitchell**, 24 Nov 1989 in Lauderdale County, AL. Stacie was born 7 Oct 1970 in Alabama.

5178	M	i.	**Zackery Taylor Crider** was born 10 May 1989 in Lauderdale County, AL.
5179	F	ii.	**Megan Brooke Crider** was born 19 Apr 1992 in Lauderdale County, AL.
5180	M	iii.	**Austin Dakota Crider** was born in Mar 2002 in Lauderdale County, AL.

3267. Vickie Lynn Crider (*Donald Fay Crider*[7], *Edgar Louis (Ed) Crider*[6], *Elizabeth (Roxie) Belle Sharp*[5], *James (Jim) Charles Sr.*[4], *Adron (Edwin/Ade) Sr.*[3], *Charles W. Sr.*[2], *John Sr.*[1]) was born 17 Mar 1970 in Lauderdale County, AL.

Vickie married **Timothy Wayne Irons**, son of **Unknown** and **Unknown**.

+ 5181	M	i.	**Donald Wayne Crider** was born 11 Mar 1987 in ECM Hospital, Florence, Lauderdale County, AL.

Vickie next married **Robert Lee (Bobby) Baskins Sr.**, son of **David Doyle Baskins** and **Margaret Lorene Joiner**, 12 Nov 1996 in Lauderdale County, AL. Robert was born 15 Jan 1956 in Indiana.

5182	M	i.	**Robert Lee (B. J.) Baskins Jr.** was born 20 May 1997 in ECM Hospital, Florence, Lauderdale County, AL.

3268. Tony Lee Crider (*Donald Fay Crider*[7], *Edgar Louis (Ed) Crider*[6], *Elizabeth (Roxie) Belle Sharp*[5], *James (Jim) Charles Sr.*[4], *Adron (Edwin/Ade) Sr.*[3], *Charles W. Sr.*[2], *John Sr.*[1]) was born 21 Jan 1974 in Lindsey Grove, Cloverdale, Lauderdale County, AL.

Tony married **April Marie Benson**, daughter of **Billy Carol Benson** and **Brenda Kaye Copeland**, 30 Jun 2001 in Lauderdale County, AL. April was born 21 Jun 1982 in Savannah, TN.

3271. Shawna Ogletree (*Peggy Crider* [7], *James Albert Crider* [6], *Elizabeth (Roxie) Belle Sharp* [5], *James (Jim) Charles Sr.* [4], *Adron (Edwin/Ade) Sr.* [3], *Charles W. Sr.* [2], *John Sr.* [1]).

Shawna married **Matthew Barrier**.

3273. Thomas Lee Hanback (*Agnes Lorene Sharp* [7], *William Herbert (Hubbard)* [6], *Louis (Bud) Wheeler* [5], *James (Jim) Charles Sr.* [4], *Adron (Edwin/Ade) Sr.* [3], *Charles W. Sr.* [2], *John Sr.* [1]) was born 3 Jun 1957 in Lauderdale County, AL.

Thomas married **Sylvia Ann Pitts**, daughter of **Teddy Loyd Pitts** and **Daisy Evelyn Young**, 12 Dec 1975 in Lauderdale County, AL. Sylvia was born 17 Mar 1961 in Lauderdale County, AL.
+ 5183 M i. **Tommy Dewayne Hanback** was born 26 Sep 1976 in Lauderdale County, AL.
+ 5184 M ii. **Teddy Ray Hanback** was born 29 Feb 1980 in Lauderdale County, AL.

3274. Danny Lynn Hanback (*Agnes Lorene Sharp* [7], *William Herbert (Hubbard)* [6], *Louis (Bud) Wheeler* [5], *James (Jim) Charles Sr.* [4], *Adron (Edwin/Ade) Sr.* [3], *Charles W. Sr.* [2], *John Sr.* [1]) was born 4 Jan 1965 in Lauderdale County, AL.

Danny married **Carrie Robinson**.
5185 M i. **Danny Ray Robinson** was born 10 Dec 1989 in Lauderdale County, AL.
5186 M ii. **Roger Dale Robinson** was born 8 Jun 1991 in Lauderdale County, AL.

Danny next married **Brenda Cochran** before 1986.
5187 M i. **Dylan Lane Hanback** was born 6 Aug 1996 in Lauderdale County, AL.
5188 M ii. **Koby Ray Hanback** was born 14 May 1999 in Lauderdale County, AL.

Danny next married **Ladusta Rae Woods** 26 Dec 2004 in Lauderdale County, AL.

3275. Retha Sharp (*Ofard William* [7], *William Herbert (Hubbard)* [6], *Louis (Bud) Wheeler* [5], *James (Jim) Charles Sr.* [4], *Adron (Edwin/Ade) Sr.* [3], *Charles W. Sr.* [2], *John Sr.* [1]).

Retha married ***Unk Ross**.

3276. Jane Sharp (*Ofard William* [7], *William Herbert (Hubbard)* [6], *Louis (Bud) Wheeler* [5], *James (Jim) Charles Sr.* [4], *Adron (Edwin/Ade) Sr.* [3], *Charles W. Sr.* [2], *John Sr.* [1]).

Jane married ***Unk Cavitt**.

3278. Sandra Ann Sharp (*Rufus Eldred* [7], *Loye Arvel* [6], *Louis (Bud) Wheeler* [5], *James (Jim) Charles Sr.* [4], *Adron (Edwin/Ade) Sr.* [3], *Charles W. Sr.* [2], *John Sr.* [1]) was born 22 Jan 1957 in Lauderdale County, AL.

Sandra married **Charles (Chief) Wayne Britnell**, son of **Marion Gilbert Britnell** and **Mary Kevod**, 15 Oct 1973 in Lauderdale County, AL. Charles was born 14 Oct 1955 in Franklin County, AL.
+ 5189 F i. **Crystal (Christy) Dawn Britnell** was born 7 Apr 1974 in Alabama.

3280. Jeffrey Keith Sharp (*Rufus Eldred* [7], *Loye Arvel* [6], *Louis (Bud) Wheeler* [5], *James (Jim) Charles Sr.* [4], *Adron (Edwin/Ade) Sr.* [3], *Charles W. Sr.* [2], *John Sr.* [1]) was born 19 Jan 1961 in Lauderdale County, AL.

Jeffrey married **Sheila Diane Garner**, daughter of **Thomas Garner** and **Carol Joyce Hollins**, 3 Jan 1980 in Mississippi. Sheila was born 31 Dec 1962 in Colbert County, AL.
+ 5190 F i. **Amy Denise Sharp** was born 8 May 1979 in Lauderdale County, AL.
+ 5191 F ii. **Amanda Diane Sharp** was born 5 May 1983 in Lauderdale County, AL.
5192 F iii. **Ashley Nicole Sharp** was born 8 Aug 1990 in Lauderdale County, AL.

3281. Norman Lynn White (*Lola Mae Sharp ^{7}, Loye Arvel ^{6}, Louis (Bud) Wheeler ^{5}, James (Jim) Charles Sr. ^{4}, Adron (Edwin/Ade) Sr. ^{3}, Charles W. Sr. ^{2}, John Sr. ^{1}*) was born 29 Nov 1961 in Lauderdale County, AL.

Norman married **Vicki Lynn Hayes**, daughter of **James N. Hayes** and **Lorene Peden**, 12 Mar 1982 in Lauderdale County, AL. Vicki was born 5 Dec 1964 in Lauderdale County, AL.

   5193 M   i.   **Norman Jeremey White** was born 5 Dec 1982.
+ 5194 F   ii.   **Misty Dawn White** was born 27 Apr 1984.
   5195 M iii. **Christopher Lynn White** was born 4 Aug 1989.

3282. Janet Loletha White (*Lola Mae Sharp ^{7}, Loye Arvel ^{6}, Louis (Bud) Wheeler ^{5}, James (Jim) Charles Sr. ^{4}, Adron (Edwin/Ade) Sr. ^{3}, Charles W. Sr. ^{2}, John Sr. ^{1}*) was born 10 Aug 1964 in Hardin County, TN.

Janet married **Clifford Dean Fessler**, son of **Clifford E. Fessler** and **Margaret Keslen**, 22 May 1987 in Lauderdale County, AL. Clifford was born 25 Feb 1960 in Sedgewick County, KS.

   5196 M   i.   **Cory Todd Fessler** was born 1 Sep 1981.
   5197 M   ii.   **Eric Wade Fessler** was born 15 Nov 1982.
   5198 M iii. **Michael Dean Fessler** was born 27 Sep 1987.

3283. Timothy (Tim) Woodrow Sharp (*Millard Woodrow ^{7}, Loye Arvel ^{6}, Louis (Bud) Wheeler ^{5}, James (Jim) Charles Sr. ^{4}, Adron (Edwin/Ade) Sr. ^{3}, Charles W. Sr. ^{2}, John Sr. ^{1}*) was born 31 Jul 1963 in Lauderdale County, AL.

Timothy married **Brenda Sue Bevis**, daughter of **Willie Dalton Bevis** and **Bonnie Mae Young**, 8 May 1981 in Lauderdale County, AL. Brenda was born 8 Nov 1964 in Cooksville, TN.
(Duplicate Line. See Person 3195)

3285. Kim Rena Sharp (*Millard Woodrow ^{7}, Loye Arvel ^{6}, Louis (Bud) Wheeler ^{5}, James (Jim) Charles Sr. ^{4}, Adron (Edwin/Ade) Sr. ^{3}, Charles W. Sr. ^{2}, John Sr. ^{1}*) was born 25 Nov 1966 in Lauderdale County, AL.

Kim married **David Lee Pennington**, son of **Charles A. Pennington** and **Mary Brannon**, 19 Nov 1984 in Lauderdale County, AL. David was born 19 Dec 1960 in Lauderdale County, AL.

Kim next married **James Allen Mayfield** 4 Feb 1989. James was born 29 Jun 1970.

3286. Ernest (Ernie) Lynn Sharp (*Millard Woodrow ^{7}, Loye Arvel ^{6}, Louis (Bud) Wheeler ^{5}, James (Jim) Charles Sr. ^{4}, Adron (Edwin/Ade) Sr. ^{3}, Charles W. Sr. ^{2}, John Sr. ^{1}*) was born 28 Sep 1976 in Lauderdale County, AL.

Ernest married **Jessica Lynn Sharp**, daughter of **Juston Leveril Sharp** and **Lana Lynn Taylor**, 6 Jun 1998 in Lauderdale County, AL. Jessica was born 28 Dec 1980 in Loretto, Lawrence County, TN.

   5199 F   i.   **Alexandria (Allie) Faith Sharp** was born 7 Dec 2000.
   5200 F   ii.   **Ella Grace Sharp** was born 1 Sep 2005.

3288. Sheila Kay Sharp (*Ralph Arvel ^{7}, Loye Arvel ^{6}, Louis (Bud) Wheeler ^{5}, James (Jim) Charles Sr. ^{4}, Adron (Edwin/Ade) Sr. ^{3}, Charles W. Sr. ^{2}, John Sr. ^{1}*) was born 4 Aug 1963 in Lauderdale County, AL.

Sheila married **Stacy Allen Dodd**, son of **Allen Eugene Dodd** and **Frances Charlene Fielder**, 17 Feb 1989 in Lauderdale County, AL. Stacy was born 17 Apr 1966 in Lauderdale County, AL.

   5201 M   i.   **Jonathan Craig Dodd** was born 19 Dec 1991 in Lauderdale County, AL.
   5202 F   ii.   **Kacey Lashae Dodd** was born 28 Mar 1993 in Lauderdale County, AL.

3289. Karen Denise Sharp (*Ralph Arvel ^{7}, Loye Arvel ^{6}, Louis (Bud) Wheeler ^{5}, James (Jim) Charles Sr. ^{4}, Adron (Edwin/Ade) Sr. ^{3}, Charles W. Sr. ^{2}, John Sr. ^{1}*) was born 22 Jul 1964 in Lauderdale County, AL.

Karen married **Timothy Franklin McKelvey**, son of **Herman McKelvey** and **Ann Fowler**, 21 Dec 1991 in Lauderdale County, AL. Timothy was born 29 May 1963 in Lauderdale County, AL.

   5203 F   i.   **Kala Denise Sharp McKelvey** was born 25 Dec 1986 in Lauderdale County, AL.
   5204 M   ii.   **Bradley Chad Sharp McKelvey** was born 6 Feb 1989 in Lauderdale County, AL.
   5205 F   iii. **Kathlyn Danielle Sharp McKelvey** was born 26 Feb 1991 in Lauderdale County, AL.
   5206 M   iv. **John David McKelvey** was born 13 Apr 1998 in Lauderdale County, AL.

3290. Stephen Coolidge McCain (*Carolyn Lois Sharp*[7], *Loye Arvel*[6], *Louis (Bud) Wheeler*[5], *James (Jim) Charles Sr.*[4], *Adron (Edwin/Ade) Sr.*[3], *Charles W. Sr.*[2], *John Sr.*[1]) was born 18 Dec 1974 in ECM Hospital, Florence, Lauderdale County, AL.

Stephen married **Felicia Dawn Daniels**, daughter of **Joseph McKinley Daniels** and **Deborah Sue Young**, 13 Jun 1998 in Lauderdale County, AL. Felicia was born 24 Jan 1977 in Lauderdale County, AL. **(Duplicate Line. See Person 3213)**

3291. Melissa (Lisa) Ann Burbank (*Sally Ann (Mavis) Sharp*[7], *Loye Arvel*[6], *Louis (Bud) Wheeler*[5], *James (Jim) Charles Sr.*[4], *Adron (Edwin/Ade) Sr.*[3], *Charles W. Sr.*[2], *John Sr.*[1]) was born 28 Dec 1967 in Lauderdale County, AL.

Melissa married **Gaylon Holden**, son of **Jackie R. Holden** and **Annie Stooksberry**, 4 Dec 1987 in Lauderdale County, AL. Gaylon was born 6 Apr 1957 in Lawrence County, TN.
5207 F i. **Brooke Leigh Ann Holden** was born 4 Nov 1990 in Colbert County, AL.

3292. Michael (Mike) Larry Burbank (*Sally Ann (Mavis) Sharp*[7], *Loye Arvel*[6], *Louis (Bud) Wheeler*[5], *James (Jim) Charles Sr.*[4], *Adron (Edwin/Ade) Sr.*[3], *Charles W. Sr.*[2], *John Sr.*[1]) was born 16 Mar 1971 in Lauderdale County, AL.

Michael married **Susan Abernathy**.
5208 M i. **Dillon Brady Abernathy** was born 27 Jan 1995.

Michael next married **Shelly Allison Wood**, daughter of **Jack Wood** and **Betty Joyce Foust**, 14 Aug 1991 in Lauderdale County, AL. Shelly was born 30 Sep 1972 in Lauderdale County, AL.
5209 F i. **Haley Savana Burbank** was born 13 Aug 1992 in Lauderdale County, AL.

Michael had a relationship with **Vanessa Rose Melton**, daughter of **Buford Eldred Melton Jr.** and **Linda Mae Clemons**. Vanessa was born 5 Sep 1980 in Evansville, IN.
5210 F i. **Lindsi Burbank** was born in Aug 2000.
5211 M ii. **Michael Burbank**.
5212 F iii. **Allie Burbank**.

3293. Terry Ray Sharp (*Berlon Ray*[7], *Loye Arvel*[6], *Louis (Bud) Wheeler*[5], *James (Jim) Charles Sr.*[4], *Adron (Edwin/Ade) Sr.*[3], *Charles W. Sr.*[2], *John Sr.*[1]) was born 11 Nov 1968 in Lauderdale County, AL.

Terry married **Amy Elaine Brewer**, daughter of **Thomas Dale Brewer** and **Phyllis Elaine Helton**, 10 Mar 1989 in Colbert County, AL. Amy was born 18 Jul 1970 in Colbert County, AL.

Terry next married **Debra Gail Crosswhite** 6 May 1995 in Lauderdale County, AL. Debra was born 12 Apr 1968.
5213 M i. **Nicholas Ryan Sharp** was born 16 Jun 1996.

3294. Lola Michelle (Shelly) Sharp (*Berlon Ray*[7], *Loye Arvel*[6], *Louis (Bud) Wheeler*[5], *James (Jim) Charles Sr.*[4], *Adron (Edwin/Ade) Sr.*[3], *Charles W. Sr.*[2], *John Sr.*[1]) was born 26 Mar 1972 in Lauderdale County, AL.

Lola married **Gary Wade Wood**, son of **Gary Quinton Wood** and **Donnabell Jeanette Lane**, 30 Aug 1991 in Lauderdale County, AL. Gary was born 3 Mar 1969 in Lauderdale County, AL.
5214 F i. **Tesa Brayde Wood** was born 13 Jul 1991 in Lauderdale County, AL.
5215 F ii. **Tara Kayde Wood** was born 29 Aug 1993 in Lauderdale County, AL.

3297. Dwight Wood (*Stevie Lawrence*[7], *Lawrence (Toby) Eldred*[6], *Louis (Bud) Wheeler*[5], *James (Jim) Charles Sr.*[4], *Adron (Edwin/Ade) Sr.*[3], *Charles W. Sr.*[2], *John Sr.*[1]) was born 14 Nov 1972.

Dwight married ***Unk** about 1990.
5216 M i. **Camron Wood** was born in 1991.
5217 F ii. **Britney Wood** was born in 1993.

3301. David Keith (Peanut) Scott (*Patsy Ann Wood*[7], *Lawrence (Toby) Eldred*[6], *Louis (Bud) Wheeler*[5], *James (Jim) Charles Sr.*[4], *Adron (Edwin/Ade) Sr.*[3], *Charles W. Sr.*[2], *John Sr.*[1]) was born 25 Dec 1966.

David married **Lisa Young**, daughter of **Carl Robert Young** and **Bessie Lou Brown**.

| 5218 | F | i. | **Tia Beth Scott** was born 21 Apr 1988. |
| 5219 | F | ii. | **Carly Ann Scott** was born 25 Sep 1992. |

3302. Jennifer Ann Scott (*Patsy Ann Wood*[7], *Lawrence (Toby) Eldred*[6], *Louis (Bud) Wheeler*[5], *James (Jim) Charles Sr.*[4], *Adron (Edwin/Ade) Sr.*[3], *Charles W. Sr.*[2], *John Sr.*[1]) was born 21 Jul 1969.

Jennifer married **Wesley Chance Threet**. Wesley was born 12 Jan.

| 5220 | M | i. | **Trace Scott Threet** was born 6 Apr 1996. |

3303. Rocky Delane Balentine (*Ruby Nell Sharp*[7], *Lawrence (Toby) Eldred*[6], *Louis (Bud) Wheeler*[5], *James (Jim) Charles Sr.*[4], *Adron (Edwin/Ade) Sr.*[3], *Charles W. Sr.*[2], *John Sr.*[1]) was born 4 Mar 1959 in Lauderdale County, AL, died 29 Oct 1992, and was buried in Oak Grove Cemetery, Lauderdale County, AL.

Rocky married **Tonissi (Tony) Michele Peters**, daughter of **Charles W. Peters** and **June Myrick**, 12 Apr 1985 in Lauderdale County, AL. Tonissi was born 13 Nov 1961 in Lauderdale County, AL.

| 5221 | M | i. | **Matthew Balentine**. |
| 5222 | M | ii. | **Brandon Balentine**. |

3304. Janet Marie Harbin (*Ruby Nell Sharp*[7], *Lawrence (Toby) Eldred*[6], *Louis (Bud) Wheeler*[5], *James (Jim) Charles Sr.*[4], *Adron (Edwin/Ade) Sr.*[3], *Charles W. Sr.*[2], *John Sr.*[1]) was born 9 Oct 1962 in Rapid City, SD.

Janet married **Michael (Mike) Dennis Phillips**, son of **Myron D. Phillips** and **Kaye Smith**, 23 Jun 1984 in Lauderdale County, AL. Michael was born 16 Nov 1962 in Lauderdale County, AL.

| 5223 | F | i. | **Rachel Marie Phillips** was born 8 Feb 2000. |
| 5224 | F | ii. | **Ruby Kaye Phillips** was born 16 May 2003. |

3305. Ricky Leon Sharp (*Tony Leon*[7], *Lawrence (Toby) Eldred*[6], *Louis (Bud) Wheeler*[5], *James (Jim) Charles Sr.*[4], *Adron (Edwin/Ade) Sr.*[3], *Charles W. Sr.*[2], *John Sr.*[1]) was born 19 Aug 1968 in Lauderdale County, AL.

Ricky married **Theresa Lynn Stanfield**, daughter of **Robert Stanfield** and **Laura Jacqueline Keller**, 24 Aug 1992 in Lauderdale County, AL. Theresa was born 11 May 1971 in Lauderdale County, AL.

| + 5225 | F | i. | **Paige Nicole Sharp**. |
| 5226 | M | ii. | **Kyle Sharp**. |

3306. Sherry Denise Belcher (*Doris Etoyle Sharp*[7], *Lawrence (Toby) Eldred*[6], *Louis (Bud) Wheeler*[5], *James (Jim) Charles Sr.*[4], *Adron (Edwin/Ade) Sr.*[3], *Charles W. Sr.*[2], *John Sr.*[1]) was born 7 Apr 1965 in Lauderdale County, AL.

Sherry married **Samuel Matthews** before 1983 in Wayne County, TN.

| 5227 | F | i. | **Angela Denise Matthews** was born 11 Feb 1983 in Loretto, Lawrence County, TN and died 20 Jul 2000. |

Sherry next married **Billy Wayne Pigg**, son of **Joel Howard Pigg** and **Linda Gail Lard**, 17 Sep 1988 in Lauderdale County, AL. Billy was born 19 Dec 1962 in Lauderdale County, AL.

| 5228 | M | i. | **Bennie Wayne Pigg** was born 19 May 1986 in Lauderdale County, AL. |

Sherry next married **John Troy Tays**, son of **John Kenneth Tays** and **Dorothy Lee Holden**, 2 Aug 1991 in Lauderdale County, AL. John was born 11 Jul 1970 in Lauderdale County, AL.

| 5229 | M | i. | **Dustin Troy Tays** was born 15 Dec 1991 in Lauderdale County, AL. |

3307. Michael Ladon Belcher (*Doris Etoyle Sharp*[7], *Lawrence (Toby) Eldred*[6], *Louis (Bud) Wheeler*[5], *James (Jim) Charles Sr.*[4], *Adron (Edwin/Ade) Sr.*[3], *Charles W. Sr.*[2], *John Sr.*[1]) was born 16 Jun 1967 in Lauderdale County, AL.

Michael married **Tonya Faust**, daughter of **Ronnie Foust** and **Janet Kones**, 27 Jun 1992 in Lauderdale County, AL. Tonya was born 30 Jun 1971 in Lauderdale County, AL.

5230 F   i.   **Brodie Shannon Belcher** was born 28 Oct 1996.

3308. Bennie Datson Belcher (*Doris Etoyle Sharp*[7], *Lawrence (Toby) Eldred*[6], *Louis (Bud) Wheeler*[5], *James (Jim) Charles Sr.*[4], *Adron (Edwin/Ade) Sr.*[3], *Charles W. Sr.*[2], *John Sr.*[1]) was born 23 Sep 1969 in Lauderdale County, AL.

Bennie married **Anna Monique Wright** in Lauderdale County, AL. Anna was born 4 May 1971.

5231 F   i.   **Anna Clare Belcher** was born 19 Nov 1996.
5232 M   ii.   **Joseph Benjamin Belcher** was born 23 Jan 1999.

3309. Lucinda (Cindi) Elizabeth Sharp (*Alfred Donald*[7], *Lawrence (Toby) Eldred*[6], *Louis (Bud) Wheeler*[5], *James (Jim) Charles Sr.*[4], *Adron (Edwin/Ade) Sr.*[3], *Charles W. Sr.*[2], *John Sr.*[1]) was born 23 Aug 1969 in South Bend, St Joseph County, IN.

Lucinda married **Gregory Dale Wood**, son of **Wallace Earl Wood** and **Beulah Estelle Smith**, 29 Jul 1988 in Lauderdale County, AL. Gregory was born 17 Oct 1968 in Lauderdale County, AL.

5233 F   i.   **Kelsey Brooke Wood** was born 10 Aug 1993 in ECM Hospital, Florence, Lauderdale County, AL.
5234 M   ii.   **Alex Gregory Wood** was born 5 Nov 1998 in ECM Hospital, Florence, Lauderdale County, AL.

3310. Carrie Donyalla (Dana) Nichols (*Alfred Donald*[7], *Lawrence (Toby) Eldred*[6], *Louis (Bud) Wheeler*[5], *James (Jim) Charles Sr.*[4], *Adron (Edwin/Ade) Sr.*[3], *Charles W. Sr.*[2], *John Sr.*[1]) was born 22 Dec 1977 in Florence, Lauderdale County, AL.

Carrie married **Damon Richard Sherer** 16 Jul 2005 in Colbert County, AL.

3311. Mardie Wayne Smith (*Cathy Deloris Sharp*[7], *Lawrence (Toby) Eldred*[6], *Louis (Bud) Wheeler*[5], *James (Jim) Charles Sr.*[4], *Adron (Edwin/Ade) Sr.*[3], *Charles W. Sr.*[2], *John Sr.*[1]) was born 18 Apr 1974 in Lauderdale County, AL.

Mardie married **Michelle Leigh Thurston**, daughter of **Gerald Lee Thurston** and **Norma Jane Mullen**, 29 Dec 1993 in Lauderdale County, AL. Michelle was born 18 Jan 1975 in Lauderdale County, AL.

5235 M   i.   **Codie Wayne Smith** was born 18 Aug 1992 in Lauderdale County, AL.

Mardie next married **Michelle Moone** in Florida.

5236 F   i.   **Alisha Marie Smith** was born 3 Apr 1998.
5237 M   ii.   **Brett Matthew Smith** was born 19 Sep 2003.
5238 F   iii.   **Dallas Rose Smith** was born 30 Sep 2008.

3312. Amanda Deloris Smith (*Cathy Deloris Sharp*[7], *Lawrence (Toby) Eldred*[6], *Louis (Bud) Wheeler*[5], *James (Jim) Charles Sr.*[4], *Adron (Edwin/Ade) Sr.*[3], *Charles W. Sr.*[2], *John Sr.*[1]) was born 13 May 1978 in Lauderdale County, AL.

Amanda married **Anthony Scott Richey**, son of **Walter Anthony Richey** and **Kimberly Sue Bradford**, in Lauderdale County, AL. Anthony was born 22 Jan 1977.

5239 F   i.   **Cassidy Jean Richey** was born 20 Aug 2000.

3313. Jessica Lynn Sharp (*Juston Leveril*[7], *Lawrence (Toby) Eldred*[6], *Louis (Bud) Wheeler*[5], *James (Jim) Charles Sr.*[4], *Adron (Edwin/Ade) Sr.*[3], *Charles W. Sr.*[2], *John Sr.*[1]) was born 28 Dec 1980 in Loretto, Lawrence County, TN.

Jessica married **Ernest (Ernie) Lynn Sharp**, son of **Millard Woodrow Sharp** and **Joyce Elizabeth Nobles**, 6 Jun 1998 in Lauderdale County, AL. Ernest was born 28 Sep 1976 in Lauderdale County, AL.
(Duplicate Line. See Person 3286)

3314. Joshua Paul Sharp (*Juston Leveril*[7], *Lawrence (Toby) Eldred*[6], *Louis (Bud) Wheeler*[5], *James (Jim) Charles Sr.*[4], *Adron (Edwin/Ade) Sr.*[3], *Charles W. Sr.*[2], *John Sr.*[1]) was born 27 Feb 1983 in Loretto, Lawrence County, TN.

Joshua married **Tarawynoka (Tara) Ruth Shaneyfelt**, daughter of **Tony Edward Shaneyfelt** and **Mary Ann Copeland**, 31 Dec 2005 in Lauderdale County, AL. Tarawynoka was born 9 Sep 1983.

| 5240 | M | i. | **Juston Tyler Sharp** was born 15 Apr 2001. |
| 5241 | M | ii. | **Joshua Brantley Sharp** was born 6 Nov 2004. |

3318. Bonnie Suzanne Sharp (*Danny Wayne*[7], *Lawrence (Toby) Eldred*[6], *Louis (Bud) Wheeler*[5], *James (Jim) Charles Sr.*[4], *Adron (Edwin/Ade) Sr.*[3], *Charles W. Sr.*[2], *John Sr.*[1]) was born 19 Sep 1982 in Lauderdale County, AL.

Bonnie married **Jarrett Ray King**, son of **Tony Curtis King** and **Janet Lee Sotherland**, 31 Aug 2002 in Lauderdale County, AL. Jarrett was born 7 Nov 1980 in Franklin County, AL.

3324. Lisa Young (*Carl Robert Young*[7], *Myrtle Lutts*[6], *Mary Elizabeth Sharp*[5], *James (Jim) Charles Sr.*[4], *Adron (Edwin/Ade) Sr.*[3], *Charles W. Sr.*[2], *John Sr.*[1]).

Lisa married **David Keith (Peanut) Scott**, son of **David Scott** and **Patsy Ann Wood**. David was born 25 Dec 1966.
(Duplicate Line. See Person 3301)

3325. Elizabeth Diane Young (*Carl Robert Young*[7], *Myrtle Lutts*[6], *Mary Elizabeth Sharp*[5], *James (Jim) Charles Sr.*[4], *Adron (Edwin/Ade) Sr.*[3], *Charles W. Sr.*[2], *John Sr.*[1]) was born 2 May 1964 in Lauderdale County, AL.

Elizabeth married **Randall Thomas Wood**, son of **Thomas Moore Wood** and **Lois Inez Bevis**, 27 Nov 1986 in Lauderdale County, AL. Randall was born 14 Feb 1964 in Lauderdale County, AL.

| 5242 | F | i. | **Monica Whitney Wood** was born 14 Mar 1990 in ECM Hospital, Florence, Lauderdale County, AL. |
| 5243 | F | ii. | **Destinee Starr Wood** was born 23 Oct 1994 in ECM Hospital, Florence, Lauderdale County, AL. |

3326. Karen Sue Burbank (*Ruby Lucille Allison*[7], *Raymond Andrew Allison*[6], *Margie (Lady) J. Sharp*[5], *James (Jim) Charles Sr.*[4], *Adron (Edwin/Ade) Sr.*[3], *Charles W. Sr.*[2], *John Sr.*[1]) was born 12 Aug 1954 in Lauderdale County, AL.

Karen married **Max Eugene Hill**, son of **James Hill** and **Mildred L. Wright**, 17 Aug 1978 in Lauderdale County, AL. Max was born 15 Jul 1953 in Lauderdale County, AL.

3327. Janice Marie Burbank (*Ruby Lucille Allison*[7], *Raymond Andrew Allison*[6], *Margie (Lady) J. Sharp*[5], *James (Jim) Charles Sr.*[4], *Adron (Edwin/Ade) Sr.*[3], *Charles W. Sr.*[2], *John Sr.*[1]) was born 12 Feb 1956 in Lauderdale County, AL.

Janice married **Bobby Elmer Mansell**, son of **Elmer Woodrow Mansell** and **Grace Leona Sharp**, 29 Oct 1971 in Lauderdale County, AL. Bobby was born 6 Feb 1952 in Lauderdale County, AL.
(Duplicate Line. See Person 3032)

3328. Roger Dale Burbank (*Ruby Lucille Allison*[7], *Raymond Andrew Allison*[6], *Margie (Lady) J. Sharp*[5], *James (Jim) Charles Sr.*[4], *Adron (Edwin/Ade) Sr.*[3], *Charles W. Sr.*[2], *John Sr.*[1]) was born 10 Jul 1958 in Lauderdale County, AL.

Roger married **Lois Marie Parrish**, daughter of **Grady L. Parrish** and **Sarah Ruth Parrish**, 14 Jul 1977 in Lauderdale County, AL. Lois was born 11 Dec 1958 in Lauderdale County, AL.

| 5244 | F | i. | **Angie Marie Burbank** was born in Mar 1978 in Lauderdale County, AL. |

Roger next married **Beverly Elaine Graves**, daughter of **Granville O. Graves** and **Dorothy Devaney**, 2 Jul 1982 in Lauderdale County, AL. Beverly was born 7 Dec 1962 in St. Louis, MO.

| 5245 | M | i. | **Patrick Ryan Burbank** was born 9 Sep 1987 in Lauderdale County, AL. |

5246 M ii. **Dustin Craig Burbank** was born 7 Sep 1989 in Lauderdale County, AL.

Roger next married **Shirley *Unk**.

3329. Billy Rayburn Smith (*Lois Evelyn Allison*[7]*, Raymond Andrew Allison*[6]*, Margie (Lady) J. Sharp*[5]*, James (Jim) Charles Sr.*[4]*, Adron (Edwin/Ade) Sr.*[3]*, Charles W. Sr.*[2]*, John Sr.*[1]) was born 2 Sep 1950 in Lake County, IL.

Billy married **Pamela Lois Balentine**, daughter of **Elmer Clyde Balentine** and **Mattie Sue Stone**, 4 Apr 1969 in Lauderdale County, AL. Pamela was born 15 Feb 1950 in Lauderdale County, AL.
+ 5247 M i. **Brian Billy Smith** was born 20 Dec 1971 in Lauderdale County, AL.
+ 5248 F ii. **Regina Lynn Smith** was born 11 May 1977 in Lauderdale County, AL.

3330. Donna Machele Smith (*Lois Evelyn Allison*[7]*, Raymond Andrew Allison*[6]*, Margie (Lady) J. Sharp*[5]*, James (Jim) Charles Sr.*[4]*, Adron (Edwin/Ade) Sr.*[3]*, Charles W. Sr.*[2]*, John Sr.*[1]) was born 16 Jun 1955 in St. Joseph County, IN.

Donna married **Bobby David Angel**, son of **Bobby R. Angel** and **Ethel Burbank**, 26 Dec 1973 in Lauderdale County, AL. Bobby was born 3 Oct 1953 in Lauderdale County, AL.
5249 M i. **Brandon Heath Angel** was born 2 Jun 1978 in ECM Hospital, Florence, Lauderdale County, AL, died 1 May 2002, and was buried in Wesley Chapel Cemetery, Lauderdale County, AL.

3331. Danny Russell Smith (*Lois Evelyn Allison*[7]*, Raymond Andrew Allison*[6]*, Margie (Lady) J. Sharp*[5]*, James (Jim) Charles Sr.*[4]*, Adron (Edwin/Ade) Sr.*[3]*, Charles W. Sr.*[2]*, John Sr.*[1]) was born 4 Jun 1960 in Lauderdale County, AL.

Danny married **Janice Kay Hopkins**, daughter of **Robert Hopkins** and **Linda Faye Mitchell**, 4 Nov 1977 in Lexington, TN. Janice was born 28 Oct 1962 in Ohio.
+ 5250 M i. **Mark Anthony Smith** was born 7 Mar 1979 in ECM Hospital, Florence, Lauderdale County, AL.
+ 5251 F ii. **Melanie Joy Smith** was born 6 Aug 1982 in ECM Hospital, Florence, Lauderdale County, AL.

3332. Cameron Don Smith (*Lois Evelyn Allison*[7]*, Raymond Andrew Allison*[6]*, Margie (Lady) J. Sharp*[5]*, James (Jim) Charles Sr.*[4]*, Adron (Edwin/Ade) Sr.*[3]*, Charles W. Sr.*[2]*, John Sr.*[1]) was born 19 Jul 1965 in Lauderdale County, AL.

Cameron married **Annabelle Jeanette Melton**, daughter of **Buford Eldred Melton Sr.** and **Annabelle Jeanette (Ann) Unsted**, 1 Jun 1982 in Lauderdale County, AL. Annabelle was born 6 Dec 1965 in Lauderdale County, AL.
5252 F i. **Shaloe Amber Smith** was born 20 Jul 1985 in ECM Hospital, Florence, Lauderdale County, AL.
+ 5253 M ii. **Isaac Don Smith** was born 31 May 1988 in ECM Hospital, Florence, Lauderdale County, AL.
5254 F iii. **Adrian Shalaine Smith** was born 3 Jun 1992 in ECM Hospital, Florence, Lauderdale County, AL.
5255 F iv. **Bethany Smith** was born in 2000.
5256 M v. **David Smith** was born in 2003.

3333. Kathy Renea Wright (*Elsie Gertrude Allison*[7]*, Raymond Andrew Allison*[6]*, Margie (Lady) J. Sharp*[5]*, James (Jim) Charles Sr.*[4]*, Adron (Edwin/Ade) Sr.*[3]*, Charles W. Sr.*[2]*, John Sr.*[1]).

Kathy married **Donnie Kelly**.
5257 F i. **Kala Kelly**.

Kathy next married **Mark Russell**.

3334. Sherry Elaine Allison (*Harve Harrison Allison[7], Raymond Andrew Allison[6], Margie (Lady) J. Sharp[5], James (Jim) Charles Sr.[4], Adron (Edwin/Ade) Sr.[3], Charles W. Sr.[2], John Sr.[1]*) was born 25 Nov 1954 in St. Joseph County, IN.

Sherry married **Daniel Alvin Holcombe**, son of **Ruben L. Holcombe** and **Phyllis Glaysher**, 15 Dec 1973 in Lauderdale County, AL. Daniel was born 16 Apr 1954 in St. Joseph County, IN and was buried in Pine Hill Cemetery, Lauderdale County, AL.
+ 5258 M i. **Daniel Eric Holcombe** was born 26 Jan 1976 in Lauderdale County, AL.

3335. Barbara Jean Allison (*Harve Harrison Allison[7], Raymond Andrew Allison[6], Margie (Lady) J. Sharp[5], James (Jim) Charles Sr.[4], Adron (Edwin/Ade) Sr.[3], Charles W. Sr.[2], John Sr.[1]*) was born 8 Sep 1957 in South Bend, IN.

Barbara married **Charles Beve Adams Jr.**, son of **Charles Beve Adams Sr.** and **Marie Lovelace**, 30 Mar 1979 in Lauderdale County, AL. Charles was born 2 Nov 1953 in Lauderdale County, AL.

3336. Rhonda Carol Allison (*Harve Harrison Allison[7], Raymond Andrew Allison[6], Margie (Lady) J. Sharp[5], James (Jim) Charles Sr.[4], Adron (Edwin/Ade) Sr.[3], Charles W. Sr.[2], John Sr.[1]*) was born 3 Jan 1959 in Lauderdale County, AL, died 28 Feb 1996, and was buried in Macedonia Cemetery, Lauderdale County, AL.

Rhonda married **Ralph Garland Hensley**, son of **Shelby R. Hensley** and **Arlene Adams**, 8 Jun 1977 in Lauderdale County, AL. Ralph was born 16 Dec 1950 in Wayne County, TN, died 2 Nov 2000, and was buried in Macedonia Cemetery, Lauderdale County, AL.
5259 F i. **Brittany Hensley**.

3337. Cindy Ann Allison (*Harve Harrison Allison[7], Raymond Andrew Allison[6], Margie (Lady) J. Sharp[5], James (Jim) Charles Sr.[4], Adron (Edwin/Ade) Sr.[3], Charles W. Sr.[2], John Sr.[1]*) was born 17 Apr 1961 in Lauderdale County, AL.

Cindy married **Jerry Wayne Pigg**, son of **Unknown** and **Ruby Haithcoat**, in Colbert County, AL. Jerry was born in Cypress Inn, Wayne County, TN.
5260 M i. **Christopher Wayne Pigg** was born 11 Nov 1983 in Lauderdale County, AL.
5261 F ii. **April Dawn Pigg**.

3338. Tammy Laura Allison (*Harve Harrison Allison[7], Raymond Andrew Allison[6], Margie (Lady) J. Sharp[5], James (Jim) Charles Sr.[4], Adron (Edwin/Ade) Sr.[3], Charles W. Sr.[2], John Sr.[1]*) was born 25 May 1963 in Lauderdale County, AL.

Tammy married **Terry Lee Foster**, son of **Ted I. Foster** and **Hazel Lois Gober**, 13 May 1996 in Lauderdale County, AL. Terry was born 21 Dec 1944.

3339. Timothy (Tim) Harve Allison (*Harve Harrison Allison[7], Raymond Andrew Allison[6], Margie (Lady) J. Sharp[5], James (Jim) Charles Sr.[4], Adron (Edwin/Ade) Sr.[3], Charles W. Sr.[2], John Sr.[1]*) was born 25 May 1963 in Lauderdale County, AL.

Timothy married **Connie Jo McDaniel**, daughter of **Gilbert Lee McDaniel** and **Viola M. Jones**, 20 Feb 1998 in Lauderdale County, AL. Connie was born 17 Jul 1969 in Colbert County, AL.

3340. Angelina (Angie) Gay Allison (*Harve Harrison Allison[7], Raymond Andrew Allison[6], Margie (Lady) J. Sharp[5], James (Jim) Charles Sr.[4], Adron (Edwin/Ade) Sr.[3], Charles W. Sr.[2], John Sr.[1]*) was born 19 Oct 1964 in Lauderdale County, AL.

Angelina married **Gregory Allen Phillips**, son of **Allen W. Phillips** and **Grace V. Peden**, 22 Oct 1982 in Lauderdale County, AL. Gregory was born 25 Dec 1958 in Lauderdale County, AL.

3341. Amanda Dawn Allison (*Harve Harrison Allison ^{7}, Raymond Andrew Allison ^{6}, Margie (Lady) J. Sharp ^{5}, James (Jim) Charles Sr. ^{4}, Adron (Edwin/Ade) Sr. ^{3}, Charles W. Sr. ^{2}, John Sr. ^{1}*) was born 25 Sep 1969 in Lauderdale County, AL.

Amanda married **Terry Dwayne Smith**, son of **Delmer Smith** and **Mary Lucille Bevis**, 4 Dec 1987 in Lauderdale County, AL. Terry was born 30 Sep 1966 in Lauderdale County, AL.
5262 F   i.   **Whitney Blake Smith** was born 24 May 1988 in Lauderdale County, AL.
5263 M   ii.   **Tyler Dewayne Smith** was born 11 Oct 1990 in Lauderdale County, AL.

Amanda next married **Russell Von Nash**, son of **Millard Filmore Nash** and **Brenda Joyce Gressham**, 3 Jul 1997 in Lauderdale County, AL. Russell was born 21 Jan 1966 in Mississippi.

3342. Jeffrey Shane Allison (*Harve Harrison Allison ^{7}, Raymond Andrew Allison ^{6}, Margie (Lady) J. Sharp ^{5}, James (Jim) Charles Sr. ^{4}, Adron (Edwin/Ade) Sr. ^{3}, Charles W. Sr. ^{2}, John Sr. ^{1}*) was born 12 Feb 1971 in Lauderdale County, AL.

Jeffrey married **Kimberly Marlene Benson**, daughter of **Danny Wayne Benson** and **Patsy Marlene Cossey**, 31 Aug 1990 in Lauderdale County, AL. Kimberly was born 13 Mar 1972 in Lauderdale County, AL.

3343. Lisa Muriel Allison (*Marcus Andrew Allison ^{7}, Raymond Andrew Allison ^{6}, Margie (Lady) J. Sharp ^{5}, James (Jim) Charles Sr. ^{4}, Adron (Edwin/Ade) Sr. ^{3}, Charles W. Sr. ^{2}, John Sr. ^{1}*) was born 6 Mar 1964 in Lauderdale County, AL.

Lisa married **Rex Hayden Childs Jr.**, son of **Rex Hayden Childs Sr.** and **Shelby Mock**, 12 Aug 1983 in Lauderdale County, AL. Rex was born 31 Oct 1962 in Corinth, Alcorn County, MS.
5264 F   i.   **Allison Brooke Childs**.

3344. Gregory Gene Allison (*Connie Eugene Allison ^{7}, Raymond Andrew Allison ^{6}, Margie (Lady) J. Sharp ^{5}, James (Jim) Charles Sr. ^{4}, Adron (Edwin/Ade) Sr. ^{3}, Charles W. Sr. ^{2}, John Sr. ^{1}*) was born 13 Nov 1969 in Lauderdale County, AL.

Gregory married **Connie Darlene Montgomery**, daughter of **Freddie C. Montgomery** and **Mildred West**, 27 Nov 1987 in Lauderdale County, AL. Connie was born 9 Dec 1968 in Lauderdale County, AL.

3345. Rodney Keith Allison (*Vernon Lee Allison ^{7}, Raymond Andrew Allison ^{6}, Margie (Lady) J. Sharp ^{5}, James (Jim) Charles Sr. ^{4}, Adron (Edwin/Ade) Sr. ^{3}, Charles W. Sr. ^{2}, John Sr. ^{1}*) was born 4 Sep 1963 in Lauderdale County, AL.

Rodney married **Amanda Dawn Jaynes**, daughter of **Thomas O. Jaynes** and **Frances Canerday**, 10 Sep 1982 in Lauderdale County, AL. Amanda was born 21 Jul 1964 in Lauderdale County, AL.
+ 5265 F   i.   **Brittney Michelle Allison** was born 29 Aug 1985 in Lauderdale County, AL.

3346. Vicki Lynn Allison (*Rayburn Leon Allison ^{7}, Raymond Andrew Allison ^{6}, Margie (Lady) J. Sharp ^{5}, James (Jim) Charles Sr. ^{4}, Adron (Edwin/Ade) Sr. ^{3}, Charles W. Sr. ^{2}, John Sr. ^{1}*) was born 27 Nov 1965 in Lauderdale County, AL.

Vicki married **Shawn Paul Overholser**, son of **Phillip Lamar Overholser** and **Deborah (Deb) Sue Johnson**, 13 Feb 1993 in Lauderdale County, AL. Shawn was born 30 Apr 1972 in Elkhart, Elkhart County, IN.
5266 F   i.   **Meagan Allison Overholser** was born 24 May 1994 in South Bend, St Joseph County, IN.
5267 M   ii.   **Madison Grant Overholser** was born 29 Apr 1998 in ECM Hospital, Florence, Lauderdale County, AL.
5268 M   iii.   **A'Rheonna Barrett (adopting)** was born 23 May 2008 in ECM Hospital, Florence, Lauderdale County, AL.

3347. Kimberly Renee Baskins (*Sandra Gail Allison ^{7}, Raymond Andrew Allison ^{6}, Margie (Lady) J. Sharp ^{5}, James (Jim) Charles Sr. ^{4}, Adron (Edwin/Ade) Sr. ^{3}, Charles W. Sr. ^{2}, John Sr. ^{1}*) was born 24 Apr 1970 in Lauderdale County, AL.

Kimberly married **Warren Dewayne Lane**, son of **Tulrie Wayne Lane** and **Wanda Gail Lane**, 8 Sep 1984 in Lauderdale County, AL. Warren was born 29 Sep 1968 in Lauderdale County, AL.

Kimberly next married **Jerry Cliff Condrey**, son of **Clifford D. Condrey** and **Tara Elease Milligan**, 2 Jul 1993 in Lauderdale County, AL. Jerry was born 8 Nov 1956 in Lauderdale County, AL.

3348. Kenneth Eugene May (*Betty Sue Poole^7, Carrie Etta Allison^6, Margie (Lady) J. Sharp^5, James (Jim) Charles Sr.^{4}, Adron (Edwin/Ade) Sr.^{3}, Charles W. Sr.^{2}, John Sr.^{1}*) was born 29 Jun 1961 in Lauderdale County, AL.

Kenneth married **Linda Putman** 25 Jun 1993 in Lauderdale County, AL.

3349. Roger Lynn May (*Betty Sue Poole^7, Carrie Etta Allison^6, Margie (Lady) J. Sharp^5, James (Jim) Charles Sr.^{4}, Adron (Edwin/Ade) Sr.^{3}, Charles W. Sr.^{2}, John Sr.^{1}*) was born 4 Jun 1963 in Lauderdale County, AL.

Roger married **Rhonda Denise Lindsey**, daughter of **Cleadus Harrel Lindsey** and **Wanda June Butler**, 8 Jan 1982 in Lauderdale County, AL. Rhonda was born 16 Mar 1963 in Lauderdale County, AL.
5269 M i. **Timothy Eugene May** was born 1 Aug 1985 in Lauderdale County, AL.

3350. Timothy (Tim) Wayne May (*Betty Sue Poole^7, Carrie Etta Allison^6, Margie (Lady) J. Sharp^5, James (Jim) Charles Sr.^{4}, Adron (Edwin/Ade) Sr.^{3}, Charles W. Sr.^{2}, John Sr.^{1}*) was born 11 Sep 1967 in Lauderdale County, AL.

Timothy married **Lanita Karola Lewis**, daughter of **Grady Eugene Lewis** and **Opel Bernice Williams**, 10 Sep 1987 in Lauderdale County, AL. Lanita was born 4 Oct 1966 in Lauderdale County, AL.
5270 M i. **Justin Wayne May** was born 10 Dec 1988 in Lauderdale County, AL.
5271 M ii. **Conner James May** was born 8 Apr 1997 in Lauderdale County, AL.

Timothy next married **Teresa Hood** 11 Apr 1997.

3352. Jimmy Earl Poole (*Jimmy Carl Poole^7, Carrie Etta Allison^6, Margie (Lady) J. Sharp^5, James (Jim) Charles Sr.^{4}, Adron (Edwin/Ade) Sr.^{3}, Charles W. Sr.^{2}, John Sr.^{1}*) was born 1 Feb 1972 in Lauderdale County, AL.

Jimmy married **Teresa Ann Reeves**, daughter of **Jerry Ray Reeves** and **Ruth Ann Burch**, 8 Mar 1991 in Lauderdale County, AL. Teresa was born 9 Nov 1971 in Lauderdale County, AL.
5272 F i. **Andrea Brooke Poole** was born 25 Sep 1994.
5273 F ii. **Ashley Brianna Poole** was born 27 Dec 1997.

3353. Carrie Leanne Poole (*Jimmy Carl Poole^7, Carrie Etta Allison^6, Margie (Lady) J. Sharp^5, James (Jim) Charles Sr.^{4}, Adron (Edwin/Ade) Sr.^{3}, Charles W. Sr.^{2}, John Sr.^{1}*) was born 21 Nov 1973 in Lauderdale County, AL.

Carrie married **Timothy Mason Richardson**, son of **Jerry Mason Richardson** and **Dorothy Jean Jackson**, 14 Feb 1997 in Lauderdale County, AL. Timothy was born 12 Jul 1965 in Alabama.
5274 M i. **Brent Richardson**.
5275 F ii. **Braily Richardson** was born in 2008.

3355. Shirley Ann Smith (*Virginia Elizabeth Wood^7, Lady Jewel Allison^6, Margie (Lady) J. Sharp^5, James (Jim) Charles Sr.^{4}, Adron (Edwin/Ade) Sr.^{3}, Charles W. Sr.^{2}, John Sr.^{1}*) was born 19 Feb 1952.

Shirley married **Donnie Taylor** 19 May 1972.
5276 F i. **Jennifer Sue Taylor** was born 15 Oct 1973.
5277 M ii. **Donnie Allen Taylor** was born 26 Jul 1975.
5278 M iii. **Christopher Thomas Taylor** was born 13 May 1980.

3356. Mary Katherine Smith (*Virginia Elizabeth Wood^7, Lady Jewel Allison^6, Margie (Lady) J. Sharp^5, James (Jim) Charles Sr.^{4}, Adron (Edwin/Ade) Sr.^{3}, Charles W. Sr.^{2}, John Sr.^{1}*) was born 3 Jun 1953.

Mary married **Jimmy Dale Welsh** 12 Nov 1971.

5279 F i. **Angie Janay Welsh** was born 16 Feb 1973.
5280 M ii. **Shawn Dale Welsh** was born 4 Jun 1974.
5281 F iii. **Kimberley Gail Welsh** was born 5 Aug 1977.
5282 M iv. **Brian Steven Welsh** was born 1 Oct 1978.

3357. Dorothy Jean Smith (*Virginia Elizabeth Wood*[7], *Lady Jewel Allison*[6], *Margie (Lady) J. Sharp*[5], *James (Jim) Charles Sr.*[4], *Adron (Edwin/Ade) Sr.*[3], *Charles W. Sr.*[2], *John Sr.*[1]) was born 2 Apr 1955.

Dorothy married **Phillip Lawry** 26 May 1972.
5283 F i. **Stephanie Virginia Lawry** was born 13 Mar 1974.
5284 M ii. **Charles Phillip Lawry** was born 2 Nov 1979.

3358. Billy Wayne Smith (*Virginia Elizabeth Wood*[7], *Lady Jewel Allison*[6], *Margie (Lady) J. Sharp*[5], *James (Jim) Charles Sr.*[4], *Adron (Edwin/Ade) Sr.*[3], *Charles W. Sr.*[2], *John Sr.*[1]) was born 31 Dec 1957.

Billy married **Sharon Delores Hosman** 27 Jun 1981.
5285 M i. **Bradley Alan Smith** was born 29 Aug 1982.
5286 F ii. **Leslie Amber Smith** was born 26 Apr 1985.

3359. Carolyn Diane Smith (*Virginia Elizabeth Wood*[7], *Lady Jewel Allison*[6], *Margie (Lady) J. Sharp*[5], *James (Jim) Charles Sr.*[4], *Adron (Edwin/Ade) Sr.*[3], *Charles W. Sr.*[2], *John Sr.*[1]) was born 9 May 1963.

Carolyn married **Jerry Organ** 6 Jun 1983.

3360. Margie Louise Smith (*Nettie Louise Wood*[7], *Lady Jewel Allison*[6], *Margie (Lady) J. Sharp*[5], *James (Jim) Charles Sr.*[4], *Adron (Edwin/Ade) Sr.*[3], *Charles W. Sr.*[2], *John Sr.*[1]) was born 23 Aug 1951.

Margie married **Thomas Walker Lawson Sr.** 17 Dec 1971.
5287 F i. **Malisa Machell Lawson** was born 1 Aug 1974.
5288 F ii. **Elizabeth Ewin Lawson** was born 23 Jun 1982.
5289 M iii. **Thomas Walker Lawson Jr.** was born 8 Dec 1986.

3361. Charles Ray Smith (*Nettie Louise Wood*[7], *Lady Jewel Allison*[6], *Margie (Lady) J. Sharp*[5], *James (Jim) Charles Sr.*[4], *Adron (Edwin/Ade) Sr.*[3], *Charles W. Sr.*[2], *John Sr.*[1]) was born 14 Feb 1953.

Charles married **Pamela Sue Gean**, daughter of **Cleo Gean** and **Era Smith**, 2 Jun 1982.
5290 M i. **Jeremy Ray Smith** was born 10 Apr 1975.
5291 F ii. **Amanda Lynn Smith** was born 31 Dec 1979.

3362. Judy Ann Gann (*Rachel Kathrine Wood*[7], *Lady Jewel Allison*[6], *Margie (Lady) J. Sharp*[5], *James (Jim) Charles Sr.*[4], *Adron (Edwin/Ade) Sr.*[3], *Charles W. Sr.*[2], *John Sr.*[1]) was born 12 Jul 1954.

Judy married **Ronald Barton Hood** 7 Jan 1972.
5292 M i. **Ronald Edward Hood** was born 30 Aug 1972.
5293 M ii. **James Robert Hood** was born 2 Jul 1975.
5294 M iii. **Jeffery Paul Hood** was born 17 Jun 1977.

3363. Eddie Junior Gann (*Rachel Kathrine Wood*[7], *Lady Jewel Allison*[6], *Margie (Lady) J. Sharp*[5], *James (Jim) Charles Sr.*[4], *Adron (Edwin/Ade) Sr.*[3], *Charles W. Sr.*[2], *John Sr.*[1]) was born 7 May 1959.

Eddie married **Shirley Eaves** 6 Jun 1980.

Eddie next married **Robin Dell Vanhoozer** 5 Jul 1985.
5295 F i. **Kathrin Nicole Gann** was born 22 Aug 1986.

3364. Tommy Joe Smith (*Robbie Etoil Wood*[7], *Lady Jewel Allison*[6], *Margie (Lady) J. Sharp*[5], *James (Jim) Charles Sr.*[4], *Adron (Edwin/Ade) Sr.*[3], *Charles W. Sr.*[2], *John Sr.*[1]) was born 2 Mar 1957.

Tommy married **Crystal Sweeny**.

3365. Jonell Smith (*Robbie Etoil Wood*[7], *Lady Jewel Allison*[6], *Margie (Lady) J. Sharp*[5], *James (Jim) Charles Sr.*[4], *Adron (Edwin/Ade) Sr.*[3], *Charles W. Sr.*[2], *John Sr.*[1]) was born 13 Aug 1959.

    Jonell married **Terry Glenn Ballard**, son of **Wilford Luvert Ballard** and **Rena Mae Miller**, 12 Apr 1980 in Lepanto, Poinsett County, AR. Terry was born 7 Oct 1961 in Tyronza, Poinsett County, AR.
+ 5296 F   i.   **April Michelle Ballard** was born 1 Nov 1982 in West Memphis, Crittenden County, AR.
+ 5297 F   ii.   **Amy Nicole Ballard** was born 17 Feb 1986 in West Memphis, Crittenden County, AR.

3366. Jerry Wayne Smith (*Robbie Etoil Wood*[7], *Lady Jewel Allison*[6], *Margie (Lady) J. Sharp*[5], *James (Jim) Charles Sr.*[4], *Adron (Edwin/Ade) Sr.*[3], *Charles W. Sr.*[2], *John Sr.*[1]) was born 20 Apr 1967.

    Jerry married **Cindy Lou Hosman** in 1992.
5298 M   i.   **Preston Brian Neal** was born 20 Apr 1987.

    Jerry next married **Ann Denise Jones** in 1987.
5299 F   i.   **Jessica Ann Smith** was born 9 Mar 1989.

3367. Verna Lee (Jenni) Gann (*Thelma Jean Wood*[7], *Lady Jewel Allison*[6], *Margie (Lady) J. Sharp*[5], *James (Jim) Charles Sr.*[4], *Adron (Edwin/Ade) Sr.*[3], *Charles W. Sr.*[2], *John Sr.*[1]) was born 18 Sep 1959.

    Verna married **Donald Ray Busby** 1 Jan 1981.
5300 M   i.   **Raymond George Busby** was born 21 Jul 1983.
5301 F   ii.   **Lesa Michelle Busby** was born 28 Sep 1992.

3369. Tina Renea Gann (*Thelma Jean Wood*[7], *Lady Jewel Allison*[6], *Margie (Lady) J. Sharp*[5], *James (Jim) Charles Sr.*[4], *Adron (Edwin/Ade) Sr.*[3], *Charles W. Sr.*[2], *John Sr.*[1]) was born 19 Jun 1962.

    Tina married **Scotty Wayne Stone** 10 Aug 1979.
5302 M   i.   **Jason Wayne Stone** was born 18 Sep 1980.
5303 F   ii.   **Tanya Renea Stone** was born 15 Aug 1983.

3370. Francis Louise Gann (*Thelma Jean Wood*[7], *Lady Jewel Allison*[6], *Margie (Lady) J. Sharp*[5], *James (Jim) Charles Sr.*[4], *Adron (Edwin/Ade) Sr.*[3], *Charles W. Sr.*[2], *John Sr.*[1]) was born 14 Nov 1963.

    Francis married **Hubert Lee Busby** 3 Feb 1981.
5304 M   i.   **Delbert Lee Busby** was born 7 Jan 1982.
5305 F   ii.   **Sara Louise Busby** was born 23 Sep 1983.

3371. Carlas Ann Gann (*Thelma Jean Wood*[7], *Lady Jewel Allison*[6], *Margie (Lady) J. Sharp*[5], *James (Jim) Charles Sr.*[4], *Adron (Edwin/Ade) Sr.*[3], *Charles W. Sr.*[2], *John Sr.*[1]) was born 13 Jan 1965.

    Carlas married **Thomas Rollan** 24 Apr 1981.
5306 M   i.   **Trinity Lee Rollan** was born 6 Jan 1988.
5307 M   ii.   **Travis Dean Rollan** was born 23 Oct 1989.

3372. Dona Lynn Gann (*Thelma Jean Wood*[7], *Lady Jewel Allison*[6], *Margie (Lady) J. Sharp*[5], *James (Jim) Charles Sr.*[4], *Adron (Edwin/Ade) Sr.*[3], *Charles W. Sr.*[2], *John Sr.*[1]) was born 7 Jan 1967.

    Dona married **James Taylor Thomas** 8 Feb 1985.
5308 M   i.   **James Christopher Thomas** was born 24 Aug 1985.
5309 M   ii.   **Anthony Taylor Thomas** was born 5 Jun 1989.
5310 M   iii.   **Austin Allen Thomas** was born 1 Jan 1994.

3373. Timothy Horace Gann (*Thelma Jean Wood^7, Lady Jewel Allison^6, Margie (Lady) J. Sharp^5, James (Jim) Charles Sr.^{4}, Adron (Edwin/Ade) Sr.^{3}, Charles W. Sr.^{2}, John Sr.^{1}*) was born 12 Jan 1968.

Timothy married **Lorie Mae Jenkins** 11 Jun 1987.
5311 M   i.   **Timothy Bret Wayne Gann** was born 27 Dec 1989.

3374. William Paul Gann (*Thelma Jean Wood^7, Lady Jewel Allison^6, Margie (Lady) J. Sharp^5, James (Jim) Charles Sr.^{4}, Adron (Edwin/Ade) Sr.^{3}, Charles W. Sr.^{2}, John Sr.^{1}*) was born 21 Nov 1970.

William married **Angela Smith**.
5312 M   i.   **William Blake Gann**.
5313 M   ii.   **Eathon Tyler Gann**.
5314 F   iii.   **Haley Breanna Gann**.

3376. Billy Joe Greene Sr. (*Nadine Wood^7, Lady Jewel Allison^6, Margie (Lady) J. Sharp^5, James (Jim) Charles Sr.^{4}, Adron (Edwin/Ade) Sr.^{3}, Charles W. Sr.^{2}, John Sr.^{1}*) was born 29 May 1961.

Billy married **Linda Sue Hood** 9 Feb 1979.
5315 M   i.   **Billy Joe Greene Jr.** was born 10 Apr 1982.
5316 F   ii.   **Breanna Nicole Greene** was born 30 Jul 1985.

Billy next married **Robin Aches** after 1985.

3377. Taresa Ann Greene (*Nadine Wood^7, Lady Jewel Allison^6, Margie (Lady) J. Sharp^5, James (Jim) Charles Sr.^{4}, Adron (Edwin/Ade) Sr.^{3}, Charles W. Sr.^{2}, John Sr.^{1}*) was born 18 Jul 1963.

Taresa married **Jimmy D. Walling** 24 Jul 1981.
5317 M   i.   **Heath Dewayne Walling** was born 9 Mar 1982.
5318 M   ii.   **Jonathan Daniel Walling** was born 12 Feb 1985.
5319 F   iii.   **Whitney Paige Walling** was born 21 Feb 1994.

3378. Sherry Mae Greene (*Nadine Wood^7, Lady Jewel Allison^6, Margie (Lady) J. Sharp^5, James (Jim) Charles Sr.^{4}, Adron (Edwin/Ade) Sr.^{3}, Charles W. Sr.^{2}, John Sr.^{1}*) was born 13 Jun 1967.

Sherry married **William H. Stone** 2 Aug 1986.
5320 F   i.   **Maranda Ann Stone** was born 30 Jan 1987.
5321 F   ii.   **Lindsey Nicole Stone** was born 4 Dec 1989.
5322 F   iii.   **Leslie Ann Stone** was born 4 Dec 1989, died 4 Dec 1989, and was buried in Tyronza Cemetery, Tyronza, Poinsett County, AR.

Sherry next married **David Lee Cruthis** after 1989.

3379. Johnny Walter Greene (*Nadine Wood^7, Lady Jewel Allison^6, Margie (Lady) J. Sharp^5, James (Jim) Charles Sr.^{4}, Adron (Edwin/Ade) Sr.^{3}, Charles W. Sr.^{2}, John Sr.^{1}*) was born 26 Jan 1971.

Johnny married **Jill Neal**.
5323 M   i.   **Anthony Mansfield Greene** was born in Dec 1988.
5324 F   ii.   **Salena Jewel Greene** was born 1 Jan 1995.

3380. Bobby Ray Greene Sr. (*Clara Nell Wood^7, Lady Jewel Allison^6, Margie (Lady) J. Sharp^5, James (Jim) Charles Sr.^{4}, Adron (Edwin/Ade) Sr.^{3}, Charles W. Sr.^{2}, John Sr.^{1}*) was born 27 Dec 1961.

Bobby married **Mary Lynn Lard** 3 Jul 1983.
5325 F   i.   **Ashley Beth Greene** was born 11 Jun 1983.
5326 M   ii.   **Bobby Ray Greene Jr.** was born 28 Apr 1984.

3381. Roger Dale Greene (*Clara Nell Wood*[7], *Lady Jewel Allison*[6], *Margie (Lady) J. Sharp*[5], *James (Jim) Charles Sr.*[4], *Adron (Edwin/Ade) Sr.*[3], *Charles W. Sr.*[2], *John Sr.*[1]) was born 27 Jun 1966.

Roger married **Angie Kirk** 5 Sep 1987.

Roger next married **Cheryl Lynn Blansett** before 1990.
5327 M i. **Dustin Seth Greene** was born 28 Jul 1990.

3382. Pamela Kay Greene (*Clara Nell Wood*[7], *Lady Jewel Allison*[6], *Margie (Lady) J. Sharp*[5], *James (Jim) Charles Sr.*[4], *Adron (Edwin/Ade) Sr.*[3], *Charles W. Sr.*[2], *John Sr.*[1]) was born 9 Jul 1969.

Pamela married **Tim Bone'e**.
5328 F i. **April Diane Bone'e** was born 26 Apr 1988.
5329 M ii. **Brandon Kyle Bone'e** was born 10 Oct 1990.

3383. Tommy Oneal McIntyre Jr. (*Nancy Carolyn Wood*[7], *Lady Jewel Allison*[6], *Margie (Lady) J. Sharp*[5], *James (Jim) Charles Sr.*[4], *Adron (Edwin/Ade) Sr.*[3], *Charles W. Sr.*[2], *John Sr.*[1]) was born 15 Apr 1971.

Tommy married **Carla Parrish** 10 Feb.

3387. Emily Renee Allison (*Melvin Jack Allison Sr.*[7], *William Turner Allison*[6], *Margie (Lady) J. Sharp*[5], *James (Jim) Charles Sr.*[4], *Adron (Edwin/Ade) Sr.*[3], *Charles W. Sr.*[2], *John Sr.*[1]) was born 11 Jun 1971 in Florence, Lauderdale County, AL.

Emily married **Raymon Vazquez Vega**, son of **Ramon Vazquez Crespo** and **Maria Vega Rosado**, 6 Oct 1989 in Lauderdale County, AL. Raymon was born 12 Dec 1963 in Puerto Rico.
5330 F i. **Christina Renee Vazquez** was born 4 Mar 1994 in ECM Hospital, Florence, Lauderdale County, AL.

3390. Jamie Lynn Allison (*Tony William Allison*[7], *William Turner Allison*[6], *Margie (Lady) J. Sharp*[5], *James (Jim) Charles Sr.*[4], *Adron (Edwin/Ade) Sr.*[3], *Charles W. Sr.*[2], *John Sr.*[1]) was born 12 Dec 1973 in Florence, Lauderdale County, AL.

Jamie married **Jennifer Gayle Hoagland**, daughter of **Royce Edward Hoagland** and **Vickie Kay Castleman**, 11 Feb 1995 in Lauderdale County, AL. Jennifer was born 3 Jan 1977 in Texas.

3391. Christopher Heath Allison (*Tony William Allison*[7], *William Turner Allison*[6], *Margie (Lady) J. Sharp*[5], *James (Jim) Charles Sr.*[4], *Adron (Edwin/Ade) Sr.*[3], *Charles W. Sr.*[2], *John Sr.*[1]) was born 16 Sep 1975 in Florence, Lauderdale County, AL.

Christopher married **Jeanie Corrina McWilliams**, daughter of **Jerry Fair McWilliams** and **Carol Ann Matthews**, 3 May 1995 in Lauderdale County, AL. Jeanie was born 9 Feb 1978 in Alabama.
5331 M i. **Son Allison** was born in 2000.
5332 M ii. **Son Allison** was born in 2004.

3394. Bruce Gentry (*Evelyn Irene Smith*[7], *Vertie Mae Allison*[6], *Margie (Lady) J. Sharp*[5], *James (Jim) Charles Sr.*[4], *Adron (Edwin/Ade) Sr.*[3], *Charles W. Sr.*[2], *John Sr.*[1]).

Bruce married **Kit *Unk**.
5333 F i. **Mandy Gentry**.
5334 M ii. **Brett Gentry**.

3395. Susan Gentry (*Evelyn Irene Smith*[7], *Vertie Mae Allison*[6], *Margie (Lady) J. Sharp*[5], *James (Jim) Charles Sr.*[4], *Adron (Edwin/Ade) Sr.*[3], *Charles W. Sr.*[2], *John Sr.*[1]).

Susan married **David Galarza**.
5335 M i. **Juan-Samuel David Galarza** was born in Sep 2003.

3396. Karen Gentry (*Evelyn Irene Smith[7], Vertie Mae Allison[6], Margie (Lady) J. Sharp[5], James (Jim) Charles Sr. [4], Adron (Edwin/Ade) Sr. [3], Charles W. Sr. [2], John Sr. [1]*).

> Karen married **Tim Hale**.
>
> + 5336 F i. **Andrea Hale**.
>   5337 M ii. **Blair Hale**.
>   5338 M iii. **Mason Hale** was born in 1999.

3399. Beverly Ann Smith (*Charles Leon Smith[7], Vertie Mae Allison[6], Margie (Lady) J. Sharp[5], James (Jim) Charles Sr. [4], Adron (Edwin/Ade) Sr. [3], Charles W. Sr. [2], John Sr. [1]*) was born 21 Jan 1966 in Lauderdale County, AL.

> Beverly married **Lonnie Wayne (Boo) Smith**, son of **Randle Arnold Smith** and **Mary Frances Smith**, 1 Mar 1982 in Lauderdale County, AL. Lonnie was born 21 Jan 1962 in Lauderdale County, AL.
>
> 5339 M i. **Michael Smith** was born in Sep 1981.
> 5340 M ii. **Dusty Lyne Smith** was born in 1984.
>
> Beverly next married **David Maury Coburn** 31 Jul 1992 in Lauderdale County, AL. David was born 4 Feb 1955.

3400. Jennifer (Jenni) Leigh Hart (*Wanda Sue Smith[7], Vertie Mae Allison[6], Margie (Lady) J. Sharp[5], James (Jim) Charles Sr. [4], Adron (Edwin/Ade) Sr. [3], Charles W. Sr. [2], John Sr. [1]*) was born 8 Oct 1967 in Florence, Lauderdale County, AL.

> Jennifer married **Curtis Dwayne Wood**, son of **Louis Cola Wood** and **Wilma Marcell Ballard**, 1 Oct 1993 in Lauderdale County, AL. Curtis was born 25 May 1968 in West Memphis, Crittenden County, AR.
> **(Duplicate Line. See Person 3256)**

3401. Hannah Hart (*Wanda Sue Smith[7], Vertie Mae Allison[6], Margie (Lady) J. Sharp[5], James (Jim) Charles Sr. [4], Adron (Edwin/Ade) Sr. [3], Charles W. Sr. [2], John Sr. [1]*) was born 16 Jan 1970 in Lauderdale County, AL.

> Hannah married ***Unk**.
> 5341 M i. **Jordan Wade Hart** was born 24 Dec 1987.

3402. Vonda Lynn Russell (*Margie Ruth Smith[7], Vertie Mae Allison[6], Margie (Lady) J. Sharp[5], James (Jim) Charles Sr. [4], Adron (Edwin/Ade) Sr. [3], Charles W. Sr. [2], John Sr. [1]*) was born 6 Jul 1968 in Indiana.

> Vonda married **Edwin Dwayne Bevis**, son of **Louie Edwin Bevis** and **Mary Rachel Young**, 4 Nov 1988 in Lauderdale County, AL. Edwin was born 29 May 1967 in Lauderdale County, AL.
> **(Duplicate Line. See Person 3185)**

3405. Marissa (Rissa) Kay Wood (*Vicki Kay Smith[7], Vertie Mae Allison[6], Margie (Lady) J. Sharp[5], James (Jim) Charles Sr. [4], Adron (Edwin/Ade) Sr. [3], Charles W. Sr. [2], John Sr. [1]*) was born 30 Oct 1981 in ECM Hospital, Florence, Lauderdale County, AL.

> Marissa married **Perry Howard Inman III**, son of **Perry Howard Inman II** and **Cynthia (Cindy) *Unk**, 20 Dec 2003 in Lauderdale County, AL. Perry was born 31 Jul 1983.

3406. Jason Derek Wood (*Vicki Kay Smith[7], Vertie Mae Allison[6], Margie (Lady) J. Sharp[5], James (Jim) Charles Sr. [4], Adron (Edwin/Ade) Sr. [3], Charles W. Sr. [2], John Sr. [1]*) was born 26 May 1983 in ECM Hospital, Florence, Lauderdale County, AL.

> Jason married **Brittany Helm**, daughter of **Alan Hutto** and **Lisa Helm**, 3 May 2008 in Trinity, Lawrence County, AL. Brittany was born 21 Jun 1985 in Missouri.

3407. Calvin Duane Wood (*Fred Calvin Wood[7], Elizabeth Earline Allison[6], Margie (Lady) J. Sharp[5], James (Jim) Charles Sr. [4], Adron (Edwin/Ade) Sr. [3], Charles W. Sr. [2], John Sr. [1]*) was born 28 Jan 1967 in Lauderdale County, AL.

Calvin married **Glenda Nell Wilkerson**, daughter of **Elgin Ervin Wilkerson** and **Nellie Nell Guthrie**, 28 Jun 1989 in Lauderdale County, AL. Glenda was born 6 Jul 1959 in Alabama.

Calvin next married **Ladonna Larraine Gautney** 9 May 1994 in Lauderdale County, AL. Ladonna was born 7 Jan 1965.

5342 F i. **Mary Elizabeth Wood** was born 31 Aug 1995 in Lauderdale County, AL.

3408. Angela Gay Wood (*Fred Calvin Wood*[7], *Elizabeth Earline Allison*[6], *Margie (Lady) J. Sharp*[5], *James (Jim) Charles Sr.*[4], *Adron (Edwin/Ade) Sr.*[3], *Charles W. Sr.*[2], *John Sr.*[1]) was born 17 Aug 1969 in Lauderdale County, AL.

Angela married **Michael Lynn Gatlin**, son of **Verlon O. Gatlin** and **Carol A. Tate**, 5 Jul 1996 in Lauderdale County, AL. Michael was born 8 Feb 1968 in Lauderdale County, AL.

3411. Nikki Laraine Wood (*Jerry Wayne Wood*[7], *Elizabeth Earline Allison*[6], *Margie (Lady) J. Sharp*[5], *James (Jim) Charles Sr.*[4], *Adron (Edwin/Ade) Sr.*[3], *Charles W. Sr.*[2], *John Sr.*[1]) was born 26 Mar.

Nikki married **John Leonard Fulmer**, son of **Robert Fulmer** and **Brenda *Unk**, 23 Oct 2004 in Gatlinburg, TN.

3412. Leigh Ann Wood (*Jerry Wayne Wood*[7], *Elizabeth Earline Allison*[6], *Margie (Lady) J. Sharp*[5], *James (Jim) Charles Sr.*[4], *Adron (Edwin/Ade) Sr.*[3], *Charles W. Sr.*[2], *John Sr.*[1]) was born 3 Dec 1969.

Leigh married **Darin Martin Doucette**, son of **Lionel Joseph Doucette** and **Colleen Ann Dobeck**, 17 Oct 1998 in Lauderdale County, AL. Darin was born 17 Apr 1971.

3413. Gregory Lynn Wood (*Kenneth Carroll Wood*[7], *Elizabeth Earline Allison*[6], *Margie (Lady) J. Sharp*[5], *James (Jim) Charles Sr.*[4], *Adron (Edwin/Ade) Sr.*[3], *Charles W. Sr.*[2], *John Sr.*[1]) was born 28 Nov 1969 in Alabama.

Gregory married **Amy Camille Calvert** 3 Aug 1989 in Lauderdale County, AL. Amy was born 16 Nov 1969 in Mississippi.

5343 F i. **Tamra Wood**.
5344 M ii. **Zackery Lynn Wood** was born 25 Jun 1991 in ECM Hospital, Florence, Lauderdale County, AL.

3414. Sandra (Sandy) Kay Wood (*Gerald Glenn Wood*[7], *Elizabeth Earline Allison*[6], *Margie (Lady) J. Sharp*[5], *James (Jim) Charles Sr.*[4], *Adron (Edwin/Ade) Sr.*[3], *Charles W. Sr.*[2], *John Sr.*[1]) was born 22 Aug 1972 in Lauderdale County, AL.

Sandra married **Michael Lynn Young**, son of **Donald L. Young** and **Shirly Ann Cochran**, 26 Oct 1995 in Lauderdale County, AL. Michael was born 3 Jul 1972 in Lauderdale County, AL.

3421. Michael Ray Smith (*Clara Jean (Jeannie) Wood*[7], *Clara Estelle Allison*[6], *Margie (Lady) J. Sharp*[5], *James (Jim) Charles Sr.*[4], *Adron (Edwin/Ade) Sr.*[3], *Charles W. Sr.*[2], *John Sr.*[1]) was born 21 Jan 1972 in Lauderdale County, AL.

Michael married **April Dawn Conner**, daughter of **Curtis Michael Conner** and **Norma Marvell Clemmons**, 14 Jan 1995 in Lauderdale County, AL. April was born 5 Oct 1975.

5345 F i. **Marissa Michele Smith** was born 15 Apr 1994 in Lauderdale County, AL.
5346 F ii. **Crystal Grace Smith** was born 16 Jun 1997 in Lauderdale County, AL.
5347 F iii. **Delaina Brooke Smith** was born 12 Jun 1999 in Lauderdale County, AL.

3422. Tonya Michelle Wood (*Dennis Ray Wood*[7], *Clara Estelle Allison*[6], *Margie (Lady) J. Sharp*[5], *James (Jim) Charles Sr.*[4], *Adron (Edwin/Ade) Sr.*[3], *Charles W. Sr.*[2], *John Sr.*[1]).

Tonya married ***Unk Flewallen**.

3424. Jean Ann Horton (*Shirley Ann Wood[7], Clara Estelle Allison[6], Margie (Lady) J. Sharp[5], James (Jim) Charles Sr.[4], Adron (Edwin/Ade) Sr.[3], Charles W. Sr.[2], John Sr.[1]*) was born 6 Jan 1967 in Lauderdale County, AL.

Jean married **Jamie Kimbrough**.
5348 F i. **Amanda Dawn Kimbrough** was born 6 May 1983 in Lauderdale County, AL.

Jean next married **Jerry Payton Jr.**, son of **Jerry Payton Sr.** and **Unknown**.
5349 F i. **Ashley Ann Payton** was born 14 Jan 1987 in Lauderdale County, AL.

Jean next married **Christopher Willis**.
5350 F i. **Haley Nicole Willis** was born 13 Mar 1996 in Colbert County, AL.

3425. Joey Allen Taylor (*Shirley Ann Wood[7], Clara Estelle Allison[6], Margie (Lady) J. Sharp[5], James (Jim) Charles Sr.[4], Adron (Edwin/Ade) Sr.[3], Charles W. Sr.[2], John Sr.[1]*) was born 14 Apr 1972 in Lauderdale County, AL.

Joey married **Emily M. Gullett**, daughter of **Jimmy Lloyd Gullett** and **Grace Smith**, 15 Apr 2000 in Colbert County, AL. Emily was born 31 Oct.

3426. Carlton (C. J.) Elvin Fowler Jr. (*Shirley Ann Wood[7], Clara Estelle Allison[6], Margie (Lady) J. Sharp[5], James (Jim) Charles Sr.[4], Adron (Edwin/Ade) Sr.[3], Charles W. Sr.[2], John Sr.[1]*) was born 22 Apr 1977 in Lauderdale County, AL.

Carlton married **Christie Lynn Borden** 28 Jul 1998 in Colbert County, AL.

Carlton next married **Heather Dawn Parker** 12 May 2001 in Killen, AL.

3427. Marsha Lynn McCullum (*Martha Jane Wood[7], Clara Estelle Allison[6], Margie (Lady) J. Sharp[5], James (Jim) Charles Sr.[4], Adron (Edwin/Ade) Sr.[3], Charles W. Sr.[2], John Sr.[1]*) was born 28 Sep 1971 in Florence, Lauderdale County, AL.

Marsha married **Patrick Brian Terry**, son of **John Stanley Terry** and **Joyce Ann Hubbard**, 21 Sep 1991 in Lauderdale County, AL. Patrick was born 11 Aug 1970.
5351 M i. **Morgan Lane Terry** was born 21 Jan 1991 in Lauderdale County, AL.
5352 F ii. **Meagan LeAnne Terry** was born 21 Jan 1991 in Lauderdale County, AL.

Marsha next married **Wallace Wade Thorp**, son of **Charles Minton Thorp** and **Loretta Marie Hester**, 21 May 1995 in Lauderdale County, AL. Wallace was born 26 Aug 1965.
5353 M i. **Hunter Wade Thorp** was born 29 Oct 1994 in Lauderdale County, AL.

3428. Leigh Ann McCullum (*Martha Jane Wood[7], Clara Estelle Allison[6], Margie (Lady) J. Sharp[5], James (Jim) Charles Sr.[4], Adron (Edwin/Ade) Sr.[3], Charles W. Sr.[2], John Sr.[1]*) was born 15 Dec 1975 in Florence, Lauderdale County, AL.

Leigh married **David Logan Manion**, son of **Charles Roderick Manion** and **Norma Sue Grace**, 23 Aug 1997 in Lauderdale County, AL. David was born 25 Jul 1974 in West Memphis, Crittenden County, AR.

3430. Jamie Michael Wood (*Timothy (Tim) Michael Wood[7], Clara Estelle Allison[6], Margie (Lady) J. Sharp[5], James (Jim) Charles Sr.[4], Adron (Edwin/Ade) Sr.[3], Charles W. Sr.[2], John Sr.[1]*) was born 19 Feb 1976 in Lauderdale County, AL.

Jamie married **Audrey Kay Burnett**, daughter of **Stephen Ralph Burnett** and **Debra Lynn Leopard**, 4 Aug 2001 in Lauderdale County, AL. Audrey was born 10 Nov 1981.

3431. Brandy Nichole Wood (*Timothy (Tim) Michael Wood[7], Clara Estelle Allison[6], Margie (Lady) J. Sharp[5], James (Jim) Charles Sr.[4], Adron (Edwin/Ade) Sr.[3], Charles W. Sr.[2], John Sr.[1]*) was born 19 Nov 1981 in Lauderdale County, AL.

Brandy married **John William Patrick**, son of **Roy Patrick** and **Teresa Blenkisopp**, 18 Sep 2004 in Colbert County, AL. John was born 17 Sep 1979 in Huntsville, Madison County, AL.

3432. Adam Clay Allison (*Earl Steven Allison*[7], *Earl Alvin Allison*[6], *Margie (Lady) J. Sharp*[5], *James (Jim) Charles Sr.*[4], *Adron (Edwin/Ade) Sr.*[3], *Charles W. Sr.*[2], *John Sr.*[1]) was born 28 Jun 1977 in Lauderdale County, AL.

Adam married **Jonna Leeann Hill**, daughter of **Leon Hill** and **Melanie *Unk**, 23 Aug 2003 in Lauderdale County, AL. Jonna was born 12 Feb 1983 in Lauderdale County, AL.
5354 F i.   **Katie Ann Allison** was born 9 Aug 2004 in Lauderdale County, AL.

3433. Preston Cole Allison (*Earl Steven Allison*[7], *Earl Alvin Allison*[6], *Margie (Lady) J. Sharp*[5], *James (Jim) Charles Sr.*[4], *Adron (Edwin/Ade) Sr.*[3], *Charles W. Sr.*[2], *John Sr.*[1]) was born 14 Apr 1980 in Lauderdale County, AL.

Preston married **Lori Beth Cole**, daughter of **Billy Ray Cole** and **Teresa Ann Hill**, 15 Feb 2003 in Lauderdale County, AL. Lori was born 20 Mar 1981 in Lauderdale County, AL.
5355 M i.   **Brandon Cole Allison** was born 16 Sep 2003 in Lauderdale County, AL.

3434. Allison Dawn White (*Rosa Rita Allison*[7], *Earl Alvin Allison*[6], *Margie (Lady) J. Sharp*[5], *James (Jim) Charles Sr.*[4], *Adron (Edwin/Ade) Sr.*[3], *Charles W. Sr.*[2], *John Sr.*[1]) was born 15 Jul 1973 in Lauderdale County, AL.

Allison married **George Seaton Cook**, son of **Jimmy Linman Cook** and **Jean Carolyn Seaton**, 9 Apr 1993 in Lauderdale County, AL. George was born 13 Jul 1970.

3435. Foster Woodrow McConnell Jr. (*Foster Woodrow McConnell Sr.*[7], *Jesse Robert McConnell*[6], *Mary Ann Sharp*[5], *Charles (Charlie) A.*[4], *Adron (Edwin/Ade) Sr.*[3], *Charles W. Sr.*[2], *John Sr.*[1]) was born 2 Aug 1938 in Arkansas.

Foster married **Shirley Ann Bolick** 15 May 1971. Shirley was born 22 Jan 1943.

3437. Hayden D. Sharp Sr. (*Hayden D. T.*[7], *Kelly C.*[6], *Lil Adron*[5], *Charles (Charlie) A.*[4], *Adron (Edwin/Ade) Sr.*[3], *Charles W. Sr.*[2], *John Sr.*[1]) was born in California.

Hayden married **Bonnie K. Johnson**, daughter of **Glenn Johnson** and **Joyce Lane**, in California.
+ 5356 M i.   **Hayden D. Sharp Jr.** was born in 1972 in California.
  5357 M ii.   **Andrew Sharp** was born in 1975 in California.
  5358 F iii. **Mike Sharp** was born in 1983 in California.

3439. Sandra (Sandie) Kaye White (*Jerry Travis White*[7], *Mason Louise Wright*[6], *George Moses (Mode) Wright*[5], *Elizabeth (Lizzie) May Sharp*[4], *John Sr.*[3], *Charles W. Sr.*[2], *John Sr.*[1]) was born 18 Jun 1966 in Lauderdale County, AL.

Sandra married **David Anthony Tubbs**, son of **John Laddell Tubbs** and **Margaret Evelyn Stanfield**, 27 May 1989 in Lauderdale County, AL. David was born 10 Jul 1964 in Lauderdale County, AL.
5359 F i.   **Lauren Nicole Tubbs** was born 19 Aug 1991 in Lauderdale County, AL.

3440. Dawanda Ann Hanback (*Charles Boyce Hanback*[7], *Etta Buna Wright*[6], *George Moses (Mode) Wright*[5], *Elizabeth (Lizzie) May Sharp*[4], *John Sr.*[3], *Charles W. Sr.*[2], *John Sr.*[1]) was born 27 Feb 1961 in Lauderdale County, AL.

Dawanda married **James Ronald Carbine**, son of **Eugene R. Carbine** and **Barbara Herston**, 11 Aug 1984 in Lauderdale County, AL. James was born 17 Dec 1959 in Lauderdale County, AL.
5360 F i.   **Elizabeth Ann Carbine** was born 7 Jul 1988 in Franklin, TN.
5361 F ii.   **Kristan Renee Carbine** was born 13 Aug 1989 in Franklin, TN.

3442. Charlotte Kay Hanback (*Charles Boyce Hanback[7], Etta Buna Wright[6], George Moses (Mode) Wright[5], Elizabeth (Lizzie) May Sharp[4], John Sr.[3], Charles W. Sr.[2], John Sr.[1]*) was born 17 Apr 1968 in Lauderdale County, AL.

Charlotte married **Richard Bryan Hare** 20 Aug 1994 in Lauderdale County, AL. Richard was born in Montgomery, AL.

3443. Beverly Gail Stephenson (*Patsy Ann Elliott[7], Mattie May Wright[6], George Moses (Mode) Wright[5], Elizabeth (Lizzie) May Sharp[4], John Sr.[3], Charles W. Sr.[2], John Sr.[1]*) was born 27 Oct 1962 in Colbert County, AL.

Beverly married **James Paul Tolbert**, son of **James Joseph Tolbert** and **Lena Pearl Smith**, 2 Dec 1981 in Colbert County, AL. James was born 31 Oct 1960 in Colbert County, AL.
5362 M   i.   **Joseph Lee Tolbert** was born 13 Apr 1982 in Colbert County, AL.

3444. Kelvin Martin Stephenson (*Patsy Ann Elliott[7], Mattie May Wright[6], George Moses (Mode) Wright[5], Elizabeth (Lizzie) May Sharp[4], John Sr.[3], Charles W. Sr.[2], John Sr.[1]*) was born 21 Mar 1976 in Colbert County, AL.

Kelvin married **Cynthia Leigh Jacobs**, daughter of **William Thomas Stephenson** and **Carolyn Rogers**, 27 Mar 1999 in Colbert County, AL. Cynthia was born 10 Oct 1974.

3445. James Leonard Berryman Jr. (*Linda May Elliott[7], Mattie May Wright[6], George Moses (Mode) Wright[5], Elizabeth (Lizzie) May Sharp[4], John Sr.[3], Charles W. Sr.[2], John Sr.[1]*) was born 7 Jul 1964 in Chela, MA.

James married **Tina Michelle Mansell**, daughter of **Buford Mansell** and **Billie Sue Fleming**, 1 Oct 1988 in Colbert County, AL. Tina was born 13 May 1965 in Colbert County, AL.
5363 M   i.   **Samuel James Berryman** was born 12 Nov 1998 in Colbert County, AL.

3446. Jeanice Michele Berryman (*Linda May Elliott[7], Mattie May Wright[6], George Moses (Mode) Wright[5], Elizabeth (Lizzie) May Sharp[4], John Sr.[3], Charles W. Sr.[2], John Sr.[1]*) was born 25 Feb 1966 in Colbert County, AL.

Jeanice married **Norman Owen Farris**, son of **Grady Owen Farris** and **Jewell Faye Allen**, 8 Jun 1991 in Colbert County, AL. Norman was born 17 May 1954 in Loretto, Lawrence County, TN.
5364 M   i.   **Tyler Colby Farris** was born 19 Mar 1992 in Lauderdale County, AL.
5365 F   ii.   **Rachel Marie Farris** was born 1 May 1996 in Lauderdale County, AL.

3447. Christopher Louis Berryman (*Linda May Elliott[7], Mattie May Wright[6], George Moses (Mode) Wright[5], Elizabeth (Lizzie) May Sharp[4], John Sr.[3], Charles W. Sr.[2], John Sr.[1]*) was born 21 Oct 1967 in Garden City, MI.

Christopher married **Tamara (Tammy) Anne Borden**, daughter of **Anthony Delorse** and **Judith Ann Salasa**, 19 Aug 1988 in Colbert County, AL. Tamara was born 22 Jul 1968 in Chicago, IL.
5366 M   i.   **Douglas Greg Berryman** was born 29 Jun 1985 in Colbert County, AL.
5367 F   ii.   **Marisa Shae Berryman** was born 6 Mar 1989 in Colbert County, AL.
5368 F   iii. **Ether Leigh Berryman** was born 22 Jul 1991 in Colbert County, AL.

3451. Catherine Louise Redd (*Robert Carroll Redd[7], Edith Louise Wright[6], James Phillip Wright[5], Elizabeth (Lizzie) May Sharp[4], John Sr.[3], Charles W. Sr.[2], John Sr.[1]*) was born 1 Dec 1972 in Lauderdale County, AL.

Catherine married **Alex O'Briant** 21 Jun 1997 in Lauderdale County, AL.

3452. Carroll Josephine Redd (*Robert Carroll Redd[7], Edith Louise Wright[6], James Phillip Wright[5], Elizabeth (Lizzie) May Sharp[4], John Sr.[3], Charles W. Sr.[2], John Sr.[1]*) was born 8 Mar 1978 in Lauderdale County, AL.

Carroll married **Robert Jeremy Stephens** 27 Oct 2001 in Lauderdale County, AL.

3453. Ginger Ann Sharp (*John Phillip[7], Ben Faires[6], John (Buck) Phillip[5], Carroll Ira (Buck)[4], John Sr.[3], Charles W. Sr.[2], John Sr.[1]*) was born 13 Jun 1960 in Lawrenceburg, Lawrence County, TN.

Ginger married **Terry Brown** 19 Sep 1992.

3454. Angela Beth Sharp (*John Phillip* [7], *Ben Faires* [6], *John (Buck) Phillip* [5], *Carroll Ira (Buck)* [4], *John Sr.* [3], *Charles W. Sr.* [2], *John Sr.* [1]) was born 19 Sep 1962 in Lawrenceburg, Lawrence County, TN.

Angela married **Frankie Lavon Adkins** 20 Aug 1982.

3455. Alyson Barbara Sharp (*John Phillip* [7], *Ben Faires* [6], *John (Buck) Phillip* [5], *Carroll Ira (Buck)* [4], *John Sr.* [3], *Charles W. Sr.* [2], *John Sr.* [1]) was born 19 Sep 1962.

Alyson married **John David Schwall** 11 Sep 1993.

3458. Cynthia Dawn Childress (*Mary Frances Sharp* [7], *Lee Howell (Hal)* [6], *John (Buck) Phillip* [5], *Carroll Ira (Buck)* [4], *John Sr.* [3], *Charles W. Sr.* [2], *John Sr.* [1]) was born 4 Dec 1958 in Lawrenceburg, Lawrence County, TN.

Cynthia married **Dan Winfree** 10 Jul 1991.
   5369 M   i.   **Brandon Kyle Romer Winfree** was born 31 Mar 1982 in St. Louis, MO.

3459. Laura Lee Childress (*Mary Frances Sharp* [7], *Lee Howell (Hal)* [6], *John (Buck) Phillip* [5], *Carroll Ira (Buck)* [4], *John Sr.* [3], *Charles W. Sr.* [2], *John Sr.* [1]) was born 16 Jan 1961 in Lawrenceburg, Lawrence County, TN.

Laura married **Eddie Haygood** 5 Mar 1984.
   5370 F   i.   **Brittany Lee Haygood** was born 8 Feb 1986 in Columbia, TN.
   5371 M   ii.   **Justin Caleb Haygood** was born 22 Jul 1988 in Columbia, TN.

3460. Christopher Douglas Childress (*Mary Frances Sharp* [7], *Lee Howell (Hal)* [6], *John (Buck) Phillip* [5], *Carroll Ira (Buck)* [4], *John Sr.* [3], *Charles W. Sr.* [2], *John Sr.* [1]) was born 30 Aug 1966 in Lawrenceburg, Lawrence County, TN.

Christopher married **Stacie Cobb** 7 Jun 1991.

3461. Andrea Lee Collin (*Nancy Lee Sharp* [7], *Lee Howell (Hal)* [6], *John (Buck) Phillip* [5], *Carroll Ira (Buck)* [4], *John Sr.* [3], *Charles W. Sr.* [2], *John Sr.* [1]) was born 7 Oct 1968 in Nashville, Davidson County, TN.

Andrea married **Timothy McCarty** 12 Feb 1995.

3465. Jennifer Dawn Eubanks (*Marilyn Sharpe Price* [7], *Gladys Lillian Sharp* [6], *John (Buck) Phillip* [5], *Carroll Ira (Buck)* [4], *John Sr.* [3], *Charles W. Sr.* [2], *John Sr.* [1]) was born 7 Jan 1967 in Orlando, FL.

Jennifer married **David Edmund Toon** 25 Oct 1988.

3466. Patsy Ann Darby (*June (Betty) Eleanor Killen* [7], *Minnie Jane Sharp* [6], *Charlie William* [5], *William (Candy) Erwin* [4], *John Sr.* [3], *Charles W. Sr.* [2], *John Sr.* [1]) was born 23 Oct 1947 in San Diego, CA.

Patsy married **Shelby Jackson Gargis**, son of **Claude Gargis** and **Mae Patterson**, 7 Jun 1981 in Lauderdale County, AL. Shelby was born 23 Oct 1947 in Benton, KY.
+ 5372 M   i.   **Samuel Jackson Gargis**.
   5373 F   ii.   **Jennifer Lynn Gargis** was born 15 Jun.

3467. Beverly Jane Darby (*June (Betty) Eleanor Killen* [7], *Minnie Jane Sharp* [6], *Charlie William* [5], *William (Candy) Erwin* [4], *John Sr.* [3], *Charles W. Sr.* [2], *John Sr.* [1]) was born 10 May 1951 in Ft Jackson, SC.

Beverly married **Howard Clayton Kelley**, son of *Unk and **Ollie F. Kelley**, 27 Sep 1970 in Lauderdale County, AL. Howard was born 13 Feb 1949 in Colbert County, AL.

3468. Sharon Darby (*June (Betty) Eleanor Killen* [7], *Minnie Jane Sharp* [6], *Charlie William* [5], *William (Candy) Erwin* [4], *John Sr.* [3], *Charles W. Sr.* [2], *John Sr.* [1]) was born 18 Dec 1953 in Montgomery, AL.

Sharon married **Jackson Bradley**.

5374	M	i.	**William Dustin Bradley.**
5375	F	ii.	**Sharon Rebecca Bradley.**
5376	M	iii.	**Allen Clayton Bradley.**
5377	M	iv.	**Jonathan Craig Bradley.**

Sharon next married **William Joseph Head Jr.** 22 Nov 1974 in Lauderdale County, AL. William was born 3 May 1953 in Lawrence County, TN.

3469. Teresa Gail Darby (*June (Betty) Eleanor Killen*[7]*, Minnie Jane Sharp*[6]*, Charlie William*[5]*, William (Candy) Erwin*[4]*, John Sr.*[3]*, Charles W. Sr.*[2]*, John Sr.*[1]) was born 22 Feb 1956 in Lexington County, Detroit, MI.

Teresa married **John Richard Garner**, son of **Clyde E. Garner Sr.** and **Nancy Richardson**, 6 Dec 1974 in Lauderdale County, AL. John was born 26 Aug 1956 in Lauderdale County, AL.

| 5378 | M | i. | **John Richard Garner Jr.** |
| 5379 | M | ii. | **Christopher Lee Garner.** |

Teresa next married **Jimmy Smith**.

| 5380 | M | i. | **James Robert Smith.** |

3473. Deborah Kay Killen (*Harold Burt Killen*[7]*, Minnie Jane Sharp*[6]*, Charlie William*[5]*, William (Candy) Erwin*[4]*, John Sr.*[3]*, Charles W. Sr.*[2]*, John Sr.*[1]) was born 8 Apr 1955 in Lauderdale County, AL.

Deborah married **Bob Edward Linville**, son of **Cawer Linville** and **Gladys Whitten**, 7 Jul 1979 in Lauderdale County, AL. Bob was born 3 Jan 1954 in Elkhart, Elkhart County, IN.

5381	F	i.	**Tiffany Joy Linville** was born 25 Sep 1981 in Lauderdale County, AL.
5382	F	ii.	**Brittany Noelle Linville** was born 3 Apr 1987 in Lauderdale County, AL.
5383	M	iii.	**Jon Michael Linville** was born 23 Sep 1989 in Lauderdale County, AL.

3474. Teresa Lynn Killen (*Harold Burt Killen*[7]*, Minnie Jane Sharp*[6]*, Charlie William*[5]*, William (Candy) Erwin*[4]*, John Sr.*[3]*, Charles W. Sr.*[2]*, John Sr.*[1]) was born 10 May 1956 in Lauderdale County, AL.

Teresa married **James Mack Patterson**, son of **James A. Patterson** and **Lou Eva Korte**, 28 Jun 1974 in Lauderdale County, AL. James was born 9 Apr 1956 in Lauderdale County, AL.

	5384	F	i.	**Michelle Patterson** was born 1 Dec 1974 in Lauderdale County, AL.
+	5385	F	ii.	**Melanie Patterson** was born 7 Sep 1978 in Lauderdale County, AL.
	5386	F	iii.	**Meredith Patterson** was born 26 Feb 1982 in Lauderdale County, AL.

3477. Leisha Gail Sharp (*William Delton*[7]*, Owen Lee*[6]*, Charlie William*[5]*, William (Candy) Erwin*[4]*, John Sr.*[3]*, Charles W. Sr.*[2]*, John Sr.*[1]) was born 9 Jan 1964 in Lauderdale County, AL.

Leisha married **Donald Wayne Voss**, son of **Rayford Delane Voss** and **Ella Jean Ezell**, 30 Apr 1992 in Lauderdale County, AL. Donald was born 28 May 1965 in Columbia, TN.

| 5387 | M | i. | **Caleb Cole Voss** was born 9 May 1995 in Lauderdale County, AL. |
| 5388 | F | ii. | **Tessa Jean Voss** was born 16 Jul 1996 in Lauderdale County, AL. |

3478. Robbie Laine Sharp (*Robert Earl*[7]*, Donald Edward*[6]*, Charlie William*[5]*, William (Candy) Erwin*[4]*, John Sr.*[3]*, Charles W. Sr.*[2]*, John Sr.*[1]) was born 20 Dec 1955 in Lauderdale County, AL.

Robbie married **Terry Lee Goodman**, son of **Louis H. Goodwin** and **Iva Mae Palmer**, 3 Sep 1976 in Colbert County, AL. Terry was born 6 Jun 1955 in Shelby County, TN.

5389	F	i.	**Leigh Goodman.**
5390	M	ii.	**Drew Goodman.**
5391	F	iii.	**Tiffany Goodman.**

3479. Christopher Michael Sharp (*Robert Earl*[7], *Donald Edward*[6], *Charlie William*[5], *William (Candy) Erwin*[4], *John Sr.*[3], *Charles W. Sr.*[2], *John Sr.*[1]) was born 21 Jan 1961 in Lauderdale County, AL, died 10 Jan 2000, and was buried in Center Hill Cemetery, Lauderdale County, AL.

Christopher married **Janice Melissa House**, daughter of **Grady Alexander House** and **Mary Alice Terrell**, 3 Nov 1994 in Lauderdale County, AL. Janice was born 22 Jun 1957 in Lauderdale County, AL.

3480. Michelle Suzanne Sharp (*Robert Earl*[7], *Donald Edward*[6], *Charlie William*[5], *William (Candy) Erwin*[4], *John Sr.*[3], *Charles W. Sr.*[2], *John Sr.*[1]) was born 30 Nov 1967 in Lauderdale County, AL.

Michelle married **Jeffrey Lee Ensey**, son of **Richard L. Ensey** and **Wanda Carmack**, 2 Jul 1987 in Lauderdale County, AL. Jeffrey was born 26 Mar 1966 in Colbert County, AL.
5392 F i. **Kayla M. Ensey** was born 2 Apr 1988 in Lauderdale County, AL and died 2 Apr 1988.
5393 M ii. **Jeffrey Tyler Ensey** was born 20 Mar 1989 in Lauderdale County, AL.
5394 F iii. **Hayley K. Ensey** was born 12 Jun 1993 in Lauderdale County, AL.

3481. Emily Patricia (Pattie) Snoddy (*Gloria Eloise Sharp*[7], *Donald Edward*[6], *Charlie William*[5], *William (Candy) Erwin*[4], *John Sr.*[3], *Charles W. Sr.*[2], *John Sr.*[1]) was born 29 Mar 1959 in Athens, Limestone County, AL.

Emily married **Steven James Hinkle**, son of **William J. Hinkle** and **Wildena Stewart**, 28 Mar 1981 in Lauderdale County, AL. Steven was born 31 Oct 1955.
5395 F i. **Holly Elizabeth Hinkle** was born 5 Jan 1984 in Atlanta, Fulton County, GA.
5396 M ii. **William Charles Hinkle** was born 15 Apr 1989 in Atlanta, Fulton County, GA.

3482. Eric Earl Snoddy (*Gloria Eloise Sharp*[7], *Donald Edward*[6], *Charlie William*[5], *William (Candy) Erwin*[4], *John Sr.*[3], *Charles W. Sr.*[2], *John Sr.*[1]) was born 5 Feb 1967 in Lauderdale County, AL.

Eric married **Stacy Renee Simmons**, daughter of **Floyd Simmons** and **Janet Howington**, 17 Sep 1994 in Gadsden, AL. Stacy was born 7 Oct in Gadsden, AL.

3483. Ronald Coleman Sharp (*Kennis Coleman*[7], *Charles Price*[6], *Charlie William*[5], *William (Candy) Erwin*[4], *John Sr.*[3], *Charles W. Sr.*[2], *John Sr.*[1]) was born 15 Feb 1952 in Lawrence County, TN.

Ronald married **Sara June Johns**, daughter of **Hollis Edward Johns** and **Sara Ileen Grigsby**, 22 Jun 1973 in Lauderdale County, AL. Sara was born 10 Mar 1957 in Lawrence County, TN.
+ 5397 F i. **Kristy Michelle Sharp** was born 6 Nov 1975 in Lauderdale County, AL.
5398 M ii. **Christopher Sharp**.

3484. Debra Diane Sharp (*Kennis Coleman*[7], *Charles Price*[6], *Charlie William*[5], *William (Candy) Erwin*[4], *John Sr.*[3], *Charles W. Sr.*[2], *John Sr.*[1]) was born 7 Feb 1956 in Lawrence County, TN.

Debra married **Carl Ricky Behel**, son of **Hearil Ray Behel** and **Lucy Feltner**, 11 Dec 1974 in Lauderdale County, AL. Carl was born 10 Dec 1953 in Lauderdale County, AL.
5399 F i. **Carla Dauphane Behel** was born 4 Oct 1976 in Lauderdale County, AL, died 3 Apr 2003, and was buried in Shiloh COC Cemetery, Killen, AL.
+ 5400 F ii. **Cortney Lane Behel** was born 4 Nov 1980 in Lauderdale County, AL.

3485. Anthony Clifford Sharp (*Charles Clifford*[7], *Charles Price*[6], *Charlie William*[5], *William (Candy) Erwin*[4], *John Sr.*[3], *Charles W. Sr.*[2], *John Sr.*[1]) was born 20 Jun 1964 in Lauderdale County, AL.

Anthony married **Carei Ann Thomas**, daughter of **Russell A. Thomas Jr.** and **Gwendolyn Jenkins**, 29 Jun 1985 in Lauderdale County, AL. Carei was born 17 Feb 1968 in Cuyahoga County, OH.

3486. Rodney Lee Sharp (*Charles Clifford*[7], *Charles Price*[6], *Charlie William*[5], *William (Candy) Erwin*[4], *John Sr.*[3], *Charles W. Sr.*[2], *John Sr.*[1]) was born 13 May 1971 in Lauderdale County, AL.

Rodney married **Benji Rena Gooch**, daughter of **Grady Benjamin Franklin Gooch** and **Gerlda Rena Varnell**, 2 Aug 1996 in Lauderdale County, AL.

3487. April Rotunda Sharp (*Charles Clifford*[7], *Charles Price*[6], *Charlie William*[5], *William (Candy) Erwin*[4], *John Sr.*[3], *Charles W. Sr.*[2], *John Sr.*[1]) was born 14 Oct 1978 in Lauderdale County, AL.

April married **Mickey Lawton Allen**, son of **Henry Lawton Allen** and **Glenda Kay Gray**, 20 May 2000 in Lauderdale County, AL. Mickey was born 23 Feb 1974 in Lauderdale County, AL.

3488. Rhonda Gail Sharp (*Charles Clifford*[7], *Charles Price*[6], *Charlie William*[5], *William (Candy) Erwin*[4], *John Sr.*[3], *Charles W. Sr.*[2], *John Sr.*[1]).

Rhonda married ***Unk Butler**.

3489. Teresa Ann Sharp (*James Kenneth (Moose)*[7], *Charles Price*[6], *Charlie William*[5], *William (Candy) Erwin*[4], *John Sr.*[3], *Charles W. Sr.*[2], *John Sr.*[1]) was born 27 Jan 1967 in Lauderdale County, AL.

Teresa married **John Gregory Thigpen**, son of **John D. Thigpen** and **Carroll Shelton**, 24 Oct 1987 in Lauderdale County, AL. John was born 3 Jan 1963.
5401 M i. **Nathan Thigpen**.
5402 M ii. **Zachery Thigpen**.

3490. James Darren Sharp (*James Kenneth (Moose)*[7], *Charles Price*[6], *Charlie William*[5], *William (Candy) Erwin*[4], *John Sr.*[3], *Charles W. Sr.*[2], *John Sr.*[1]) was born 16 Jul 1969 in Lauderdale County, AL.

James married **Tracy Ellen Barksdale**, daughter of **Jaimy Barksdale** and **Leslie Ellen Moryan**, 27 Feb 1998 in Colbert County, AL. Tracy was born 28 Jul 1965 in Naples, FL.
5403 M i. **Wesley Duane Killen Sharp** was born 15 Dec 1988 in Lauderdale County, AL.
5404 M ii. **Trenton Daniel Sharp** was born 12 Sep 1998 in Lauderdale County, AL.

3491. Nancy Katherine Sevier (*Nancy Spence Wilson*[7], *Emily Louise Bounds*[6], *Dollie E. Sharp*[5], *William (Candy) Erwin*[4], *John Sr.*[3], *Charles W. Sr.*[2], *John Sr.*[1]) was born 4 Oct 1970 in Lauderdale County, AL.

Nancy married **Kevin Phillips** 15 Aug 1998 in Franklin, TN.

3493. Emily Christian Severin (*Emily Elizabeth Wilson*[7], *Emily Louise Bounds*[6], *Dollie E. Sharp*[5], *William (Candy) Erwin*[4], *John Sr.*[3], *Charles W. Sr.*[2], *John Sr.*[1]) was born 15 Feb 1970 in Auburn, Lee County, AL.

Emily married **Jason Watson**.
5405 F i. **Taylor Ann Watson** was born 14 Nov 1997 in Orlando, FL.

3494. Elbert Turner Cox Jr. (*Elbert Turner Cox Sr.*[7], *Ida Mae Call*[6], *Beulah L. Sharp*[5], *William (Candy) Erwin*[4], *John Sr.*[3], *Charles W. Sr.*[2], *John Sr.*[1]) was born 20 Apr 1951 in Detroit, Wayne County, MI.

Elbert married **Debra Rozell**.
5406 F i. **Ruth Ann Cox**.
5407 M ii. **Bryant Cox**.

3496. Frank Lee Cox (*Elbert Turner Cox Sr.*[7], *Ida Mae Call*[6], *Beulah L. Sharp*[5], *William (Candy) Erwin*[4], *John Sr.*[3], *Charles W. Sr.*[2], *John Sr.*[1]) was born 2 Aug 1954 in Detroit, Wayne County, MI.

Frank married **Cheryl Ann McGinty**, daughter of **James Chandler McGinty** and **Grace Lee Henry**, 21 Jan 1974 in Leesville, LA. Cheryl was born 5 Sep 1955 in Houston, TX.
+ 5408 F i. **Charla Marie Cox** was born 17 Jul 1974 in Houston, TX.
+ 5409 F ii. **Angelia Lee Cox** was born 14 Jan 1976 in Houston, TX.

3497. Thomas Wayne Cox (*Elbert Turner Cox Sr.*[7], *Ida Mae Call*[6], *Beulah L. Sharp*[5], *William (Candy) Erwin*[4], *John Sr.*[3], *Charles W. Sr.*[2], *John Sr.*[1]) was born 5 Jan 1956 in Detroit, Wayne County, MI.

Thomas married **Susan *Unk** in 1983 in Troy, MI.
   5410 M   i.   **Andrew Cox** was born in Sep 1984 in Troy, MI.

3503. Glenda Carolyn Cox (*Lee Douglas Cox*[7], *Ida Mae Call*[6], *Beulah L. Sharp*[5], *William (Candy) Erwin*[4], *John Sr.*[3], *Charles W. Sr.*[2], *John Sr.*[1]) was born 25 Jul 1950 in Lauderdale County, AL.

Glenda married **Howard Stuart Chappell**, son of **Howard Chappell** and **Edith M. Hyde**, 2 Jul 1972 in Lapeer, MI. Howard was born 22 Jul 1946 in Colbert County, AL.

3504. Andre Douglas Cox (*Lee Douglas Cox*[7], *Ida Mae Call*[6], *Beulah L. Sharp*[5], *William (Candy) Erwin*[4], *John Sr.*[3], *Charles W. Sr.*[2], *John Sr.*[1]) was born 13 Apr 1958 in Lauderdale County, AL.

Andre married **Patricia Ann Moore**, daughter of **Robert E. Moore** and **Ivadale Darby**, 4 Sep 1986 in Lapeer, MI. Patricia was born 3 Jul 1953 in Lauderdale County, AL.

3506. Laura Call (*David Lee Call*[7], *Roy Lee Call*[6], *Beulah L. Sharp*[5], *William (Candy) Erwin*[4], *John Sr.*[3], *Charles W. Sr.*[2], *John Sr.*[1]) was born 28 Apr 1971.

Laura married **Steve Ford**.

3509. Kim Boone (*Linda Call*[7], *Roy Lee Call*[6], *Beulah L. Sharp*[5], *William (Candy) Erwin*[4], *John Sr.*[3], *Charles W. Sr.*[2], *John Sr.*[1]) was born 20 Apr 1961.

Kim married **David Bourgeois**.

3511. Heather Michelle Call (*Dennis Howard Call*[7], *Roy Lee Call*[6], *Beulah L. Sharp*[5], *William (Candy) Erwin*[4], *John Sr.*[3], *Charles W. Sr.*[2], *John Sr.*[1]).

Heather married **Joshua Potts** 8 Sep 1996 in Lauderdale County, AL.

3526. Melissa Sharp (*William Daniel*[7], *William (Billy) Brevard*[6], *Burt Hilliard Sr.*[5], *William (Candy) Erwin*[4], *John Sr.*[3], *Charles W. Sr.*[2], *John Sr.*[1]) was born 29 Jan 1972 in Weirton, WV.

Melissa married ***Unk Miser**.

3533. Danny Ray Witt (*Johnny Ray Witt*[7], *Mae Belle Young*[6], *James Wylie (Jim) Young*[5], *Julia Ann Young*[4], *Mary E. Sharp*[3], *Charles W. Sr.*[2], *John Sr.*[1]) was born 17 Jan 1955 in Lauderdale County, AL.

Danny married **Jacqueline Sue (Jackie) White**, daughter of **Joe White** and **Joyce Marvin**, 8 Jan 1972. Jacqueline was born 22 Sep 1955 in South Bend, St Joseph County, IN. Another name for Jacqueline is Jacqueline Sue White.
+ 5411 F   i.   **Kimberly Jean Witt** was born 2 Apr 1972 in South Bend, IN.
  5412 F   ii.   **Jennifer Lynn Witt** was born 26 Dec 1974 in South Bend, St Joseph County, IN.
+ 5413 M iii. **Joshua Daniel Witt** was born 27 Apr 1979 in South Bend, St Joseph County, IN.
  5414 F   iv. **Kara Loraine Mary Witt** was born 17 Apr 1986 in South Bend, St Joseph County, IN.

3535. Cathy Ann Witt (*Johnny Ray Witt*[7], *Mae Belle Young*[6], *James Wylie (Jim) Young*[5], *Julia Ann Young*[4], *Mary E. Sharp*[3], *Charles W. Sr.*[2], *John Sr.*[1]) was born 2 Jan 1959 in Mishawaka, St Joseph County, IN.

Cathy married **Ricky Dale Wood**, son of **Doyle Lee Wood** and **Daisy Marie Wood**, 29 Dec 1981 in Lauderdale County, AL. Ricky was born 19 Jun 1953 in Florence, Lauderdale County, AL.
  5415 F   i.   **Christina Ann Wood** was born 15 Aug 1982, died 16 Aug 1982, and was buried in Murphy's Chapel Cemetery, Lauderdale County, AL.

5416 M ii. **Brandon Dale Wood** was born 30 Jan 1985 in ECM Hospital, Florence, Lauderdale County, AL.

3536. Randy Lee Witt Sr. (*Johnny Ray Witt ^{7}, Mae Belle Young ^{6}, James Wylie (Jim) Young ^{5}, Julia Ann Young ^{4}, Mary E. Sharp ^{3}, Charles W. Sr. ^{2}, John Sr. ^{1}*) was born 9 Nov 1964 in St. Joseph County, IN.

Randy married **Cathy Allison Thomas**, daughter of **Lewis E. Thomas** and **Windolon Hale**, 19 Oct 1983 in Lauderdale County, AL. Cathy was born 16 Feb 1965 in Lauderdale County, AL.
5417 M i. **Randy Lee Witt Jr.** was born 15 Aug 1984.
5418 F ii. **Megan Celeste Witt** was born 4 Jan 1989.
5419 F iii. **Hannah Victoria Witt** was born 9 Apr 1992.

3538. Lonnie Nolan Smith (*Letha Helen Witt ^{7}, Mae Belle Young ^{6}, James Wylie (Jim) Young ^{5}, Julia Ann Young ^{4}, Mary E. Sharp ^{3}, Charles W. Sr. ^{2}, John Sr. ^{1}*) was born 13 Oct 1955 in Lauderdale County, AL, died 18 Aug 1973, and was buried in Murphy's Chapel Cemetery, Lauderdale County, AL.

Lonnie married **Sharon Jean Gooch**, daughter of **Ralph Roland Gooch** and **Macil Bethrine Young**, 20 Apr 1973 in Lauderdale County, AL. Sharon was born 30 Mar 1957 in Florence, Lauderdale County, AL.
(Duplicate Line. See Person 2534)

3539. Laura Kay Smith (*Letha Helen Witt ^{7}, Mae Belle Young ^{6}, James Wylie (Jim) Young ^{5}, Julia Ann Young ^{4}, Mary E. Sharp ^{3}, Charles W. Sr. ^{2}, John Sr. ^{1}*) was born 7 Feb 1957.

Laura married **Mark Thompson** 13 Aug. Mark was born 13 Mar 1958.
5420 M i. **Stacey Thompson** was born 23 Oct 1986.

3540. Jesse Lynn Smith (*Letha Helen Witt ^{7}, Mae Belle Young ^{6}, James Wylie (Jim) Young ^{5}, Julia Ann Young ^{4}, Mary E. Sharp ^{3}, Charles W. Sr. ^{2}, John Sr. ^{1}*) was born 4 Nov 1959.

Jesse married **Frances Melvina Shook**, daughter of **Robert Clayton Shook** and **Hyson Pearline Parrish**, 20 Aug 2004 in Lauderdale County, AL. Frances was born 8 Aug 1961 in Lapoite County, IN.

3541. Jennifer Gay Smith (*Letha Helen Witt ^{7}, Mae Belle Young ^{6}, James Wylie (Jim) Young ^{5}, Julia Ann Young ^{4}, Mary E. Sharp ^{3}, Charles W. Sr. ^{2}, John Sr. ^{1}*) was born 12 Oct 1960.

Jennifer married **Roger Dale Wesson**, son of **Fred Wesson** and **Vella Mae Wood**. Roger was born 29 Oct 1957.
+ 5421 F i. **Shalanda Lavon Wesson** was born 4 Oct 1977 in Lauderdale County, AL.

Jennifer next married **Tommy Gean** in May 1998. Tommy was born 14 Apr 1971.

3542. David Wayne Wood (*Eva Witt ^{7}, Mae Belle Young ^{6}, James Wylie (Jim) Young ^{5}, Julia Ann Young ^{4}, Mary E. Sharp ^{3}, Charles W. Sr. ^{2}, John Sr. ^{1}*) was born 20 Dec 1955 in Lauderdale County, AL.

David married **Patty Ann Williams**, daughter of **Willis M. Williams** and **Peggy Irons**, 4 Apr 1973 in Lauderdale County, AL. Patty was born 8 Sep 1955 in Cleveland, OH.
5422 M i. **David Shane Wood** was born 2 Oct 1973.
5423 M ii. **Heath Nathan Ellis Wood** was born 8 Sep 1976.
+ 5424 M iii. **Joshua Kyle Wood** was born 22 Mar 1980.

3543. Nancy Mae Wood (*Eva Witt ^{7}, Mae Belle Young ^{6}, James Wylie (Jim) Young ^{5}, Julia Ann Young ^{4}, Mary E. Sharp ^{3}, Charles W. Sr. ^{2}, John Sr. ^{1}*) was born 9 Oct 1958 in Lauderdale County, AL.

Nancy married **Billy Dewayne Oakley**, son of **Bill Oakley** and **Hazel Ann May**, 20 Oct 1977 in Lauderdale County, AL. Billy was born 18 Apr 1959 in Lauderdale County, AL.
5425 M i. **Chadrick Dewayne Oakley** was born 7 Dec 1979 in Lauderdale County, AL.
5426 F ii. **Tara Lashelle Oakley** was born 4 Apr 1985 in Lauderdale County, AL.
5427 M iii. **Colby Lee Oakley** was born 23 Jul 1997 in Lauderdale County, AL.

3544. Wendell Gene Smith (*Rachel Lee Witt^7, Mae Belle Young^6, James Wylie (Jim) Young^5, Julia Ann Young^4, Mary E. Sharp^3, Charles W. Sr.^{2}, John Sr.^{1}*) was born 8 May 1964 in Lauderdale County, AL.

Wendell married **Melissa Ann Barkley**, daughter of **Jerry L. Barkley** and **Bessie Jackson**, 14 Jul 1984 in Lauderdale County, AL. Melissa was born 11 Oct 1965 in Lauderdale County, AL.

5428	F	i.	**Girl Smith**.
5429	F	ii.	**Girl Smith**.

3545. Tracy Kyle Smith (*Rachel Lee Witt^7, Mae Belle Young^6, James Wylie (Jim) Young^5, Julia Ann Young^4, Mary E. Sharp^3, Charles W. Sr.^{2}, John Sr.^{1}*) was born 1 Apr 1968 in Lauderdale County, AL.

Tracy married ***Unk.**

5430	M	i.	**Boy Smith**.

3546. Jimmy Dale (JD) White Sr. (*Gladys Marie Smith^7, Nomer Marie Young^6, James Wylie (Jim) Young^5, Julia Ann Young^4, Mary E. Sharp^3, Charles W. Sr.^{2}, John Sr.^{1}*) was born 21 Oct 1947.

Jimmy married **Ruby Jordan** in Feb 1967.

+ 5431	M	i.	**Jimmy Dale White Jr.** was born in Feb 1968.

Jimmy next married **Sue L. Ragan** in Aug 1970.

+ 5432	F	i.	**Traci L. White** was born in May 1968.
+ 5433	F	ii.	**Kim S. White** was born in Jul 1972.

Jimmy next married **Barbara Noe** in Dec 1984.

Jimmy next married **Debbie L. Webber** in Nov 1995. Debbie was born 20 Oct 1953.

3547. Janice Sue White (*Gladys Marie Smith^7, Nomer Marie Young^6, James Wylie (Jim) Young^5, Julia Ann Young^4, Mary E. Sharp^3, Charles W. Sr.^{2}, John Sr.^{1}*) was born 11 Nov 1949.

Janice married **Lawrence Lee Kidder**. Lawrence was born 31 Aug 1944.

+ 5434	F	i.	**Lori Ann Kidder** was born 30 Apr 1970.
+ 5435	F	ii.	**Holly Lynn Kidder** was born 26 May 1979.

3548. Sandra Joyce White (*Gladys Marie Smith^7, Nomer Marie Young^6, James Wylie (Jim) Young^5, Julia Ann Young^4, Mary E. Sharp^3, Charles W. Sr.^{2}, John Sr.^{1}*) was born 25 Sep 1951.

Sandra married **Danny Perry**. Danny was born 19 Feb 1947, died in Sep 2001, and was buried in Chapel Hill Memorial Garden, Osceola, IN.

+ 5436	F	i.	**Melissa Ann (Missy) Perry** was born 25 Jan 1969.

3549. Jeannie Ruth White (*Gladys Marie Smith^7, Nomer Marie Young^6, James Wylie (Jim) Young^5, Julia Ann Young^4, Mary E. Sharp^3, Charles W. Sr.^{2}, John Sr.^{1}*) was born 12 Sep 1953.

Jeannie married **William (Bill) Denny Coleman**. William was born 16 Apr 1953.

5437	M	i.	**Brett Franklin Coleman** was born 28 Mar 1973.
+ 5438	F	ii.	**Jennifer Dawn Coleman** was born 27 Jun 1974.

3550. Jeff Steven White (*Gladys Marie Smith^7, Nomer Marie Young^6, James Wylie (Jim) Young^5, Julia Ann Young^4, Mary E. Sharp^3, Charles W. Sr.^{2}, John Sr.^{1}*) was born 9 Aug 1955.

Jeff married **Kathy *Unk.**

+ 5439	M	i.	**Daniel Steven White** was born 1 Jan 1980.

Jeff next married **Carla Jean White**. Carla was born 4 Dec 1962.

5440	F	i.	**Amanda Marie White** was born 1 Jul 1986.
5441	M	ii.	**Clayton Michael White** was born 4 Sep 1993.

3551. Jackie Ladd White (*Gladys Marie Smith^7, Nomer Marie Young^6, James Wylie (Jim) Young^5, Julia Ann Young^4, Mary E. Sharp^3, Charles W. Sr.^{2}, John Sr.^{1}*) was born 28 Mar 1957.

Jackie married **Doris Jean Jones** 9 Aug 1975. Doris was born 25 Mar 1956.
+ 5442 F   i.   **Kristi Ann White** was born 6 Nov 1976.
+ 5443 F   ii.   **Carrie Lei White** was born 20 Jun 1980.

Jackie next married **Nancy *Unk.**
+ 5444 F   i.   **Jessica Lee White** was born 30 Oct 1981.

Jackie next married **Cindy Kay Shrock** in Oct 1995. Cindy was born 4 Aug 1963.
  5445 M   i.   **Carson Daniel White** was born 26 Oct 2004.

3552. Jill Annette White (*Gladys Marie Smith^7, Nomer Marie Young^6, James Wylie (Jim) Young^5, Julia Ann Young^4, Mary E. Sharp^3, Charles W. Sr.^{2}, John Sr.^{1}*) was born 15 May 1959.

Jill married **Floyd Kenneth (Kenny) Carter** 1 May 1987 in Mishawaka, St Joseph County, IN. Floyd was born 7 Oct 1957.
+ 5446 F   i.   **Jordan Marie Carter** was born 16 Mar 1988.
  5447 M   ii.   **Kenneth Benjamin (Ben) Carter** was born 27 Feb 1993.

3553. Ronnie (Red) Arnold Smith (*Randle Arnold Smith^7, Nomer Marie Young^6, James Wylie (Jim) Young^5, Julia Ann Young^4, Mary E. Sharp^3, Charles W. Sr.^{2}, John Sr.^{1}*) was born 29 Dec 1955.

Ronnie married **Sharon White** 4 Apr 1975. Sharon was born 8 Aug 1954.
+ 5448 F   i.   **Sherry Smith** was born 22 Apr 1977.
  5449 M   ii.   **Nathan Smith** was born 30 Aug 1979.

3554. Donnie Ray Smith (*Randle Arnold Smith^7, Nomer Marie Young^6, James Wylie (Jim) Young^5, Julia Ann Young^4, Mary E. Sharp^3, Charles W. Sr.^{2}, John Sr.^{1}*) was born 7 Mar 1957.

Donnie married **Karen White** 30 May 1977. Karen was born 10 Dec 1958.
+ 5450 M   i.   **Michael Dewayne Smith** was born 16 Sep 1977.
  5451 M   ii.   **Rusty Evan Smith** was born 22 Feb 1981.

3556. Lonnie Wayne (Boo) Smith (*Randle Arnold Smith^7, Nomer Marie Young^6, James Wylie (Jim) Young^5, Julia Ann Young^4, Mary E. Sharp^3, Charles W. Sr.^{2}, John Sr.^{1}*) was born 21 Jan 1962 in Lauderdale County, AL.

Lonnie married **Beverly Ann Smith**, daughter of **Charles Leon Smith** and **Linda Sue Witt**, 1 Mar 1982 in Lauderdale County, AL. Beverly was born 21 Jan 1966 in Lauderdale County, AL.
(Duplicate Line. See Person 3399)

3559. Carolyn Estelle Smith (*Jimmy Lester (JL) Smith^7, Nomer Marie Young^6, James Wylie (Jim) Young^5, Julia Ann Young^4, Mary E. Sharp^3, Charles W. Sr.^{2}, John Sr.^{1}*) was born 31 May 1954, died 8 Mar 1995, and was buried in Chapel Hill Memorial Garden, Osceola, IN.

Carolyn married **Clarence Krager Sr.**.
+ 5452 M   i.   **Clarence Krager Jr.** was born in 1975.
  5453 M   ii.   **Buddy Krager** was born in 1984.

3560. Jessie Lynn Smith (*Jimmy Lester (JL) Smith^7, Nomer Marie Young^6, James Wylie (Jim) Young^5, Julia Ann Young^4, Mary E. Sharp^3, Charles W. Sr.^{2}, John Sr.^{1}*) was born 21 Apr 1955.

Jessie married **Paulette Smith**.

Jessie next married **Betty Davison** 25 Sep 2004 in Niles, MI.

3561. Kathy Jo Smith (*Jimmy Lester (JL) Smith[7], Nomer Marie Young[6], James Wylie (Jim) Young[5], Julia Ann Young[4], Mary E. Sharp[3], Charles W. Sr.[2], John Sr.[1]*) was born 11 Jun 1956.

Kathy married **Richard Decerra Sr.**.

5454	M	i.	**Richard Decerra Jr.**
5455	F	ii.	**Sherry Lynn Decerra.**
5456	F	iii.	**Mary Jo Decerra.**
5457	M	iv.	**James Daniel Decerra.**

Kathy next married **Larry Springman**. Larry died in 2007 and was buried in Indiana.

3562. Christine Elaine Smith (*Jimmy Lester (JL) Smith[7], Nomer Marie Young[6], James Wylie (Jim) Young[5], Julia Ann Young[4], Mary E. Sharp[3], Charles W. Sr.[2], John Sr.[1]*) was born 9 Jun 1957.

Christine married **Frederick Culp**. Frederick was born 20 Oct 1954.

+	5458	F	i.	**Denise Culp** was born 17 Mar 1974.
+	5459	F	ii.	**Carey Culp** was born 14 May 1975.
	5460	F	iii.	**Whitney Culp** was born 12 Jul 1976.

Christine next married ***Unk**.

5461	F	i.	**Ashley Culp** was born in 1990.

3563. Roger William Holloway (*Ruth Lucille Smith[7], Nomer Marie Young[6], James Wylie (Jim) Young[5], Julia Ann Young[4], Mary E. Sharp[3], Charles W. Sr.[2], John Sr.[1]*) was born 5 Sep 1954.

Roger married ***Unk Talbot**.

5462	M	i.	**Larry Talbot.**

Roger next married **Margie Midday**.

5463	M	i.	**Troy Holloway.**
5464	F	ii.	**Heather Holloway.**
5465	M	iii.	**Derek Holloway.**
5466	F	iv.	**Pamela Holloway.**
5467	M	v.	**Blaze Holloway.**
5468	F	vi.	**Margaret Holloway.**
5469	F	vii.	**Mary Holloway.**

Roger next married **Deborah *Unk** in 2006.

3564. Julia May Holloway (*Ruth Lucille Smith[7], Nomer Marie Young[6], James Wylie (Jim) Young[5], Julia Ann Young[4], Mary E. Sharp[3], Charles W. Sr.[2], John Sr.[1]*) was born 12 Apr 1957.

Julia married **Sonny Bell**.

	5470	F	i.	**Aprel Marie Bell** was born 2 Jul 1981.
+	5471	M	ii.	**Jared Joseph Bell** was born 20 Nov 1983.
	5472	M	iii.	**James Anderson (Andy) Bell** was born 16 Nov 1986, died 19 Aug 1991, and was buried in Murphy's Chapel Cemetery, Lauderdale County, AL.

Julia next married ***Unk Decker**.

5473	F	i.	**Terri Ann Decker** was born in 1987.

Julia next married ***Unk**.

5474	F	i.	**Samantha Mahshell Holloway** was born 1 Oct 1991.
5475	F	ii.	**Sandra Rickaya Holloway** was born 20 Apr 1993.

3565. James (Jim) Elbert Holloway (*Ruth Lucille Smith[7], Nomer Marie Young[6], James Wylie (Jim) Young[5], Julia Ann Young[4], Mary E. Sharp[3], Charles W. Sr.[2], John Sr.[1]*) was born 8 Dec 1963.

James married **Barbara *Unk**.

James next married **Vanessa *Unk** 2007 ?.

3566. Judith (Judy) Sanders (*Ruth Lucille Smith*[7], *Nomer Marie Young*[6], *James Wylie (Jim) Young*[5], *Julia Ann Young*[4], *Mary E. Sharp*[3], *Charles W. Sr.*[2], *John Sr.*[1]).

Judith married ***Unk Carroll**.
5476 F   i.   **Stephanie Darcin Carroll** was born in 1986.

3567. Janell Sanders (*Ruth Lucille Smith*[7], *Nomer Marie Young*[6], *James Wylie (Jim) Young*[5], *Julia Ann Young*[4], *Mary E. Sharp*[3], *Charles W. Sr.*[2], *John Sr.*[1]).

Janell married ***Unk**.
5477 F   i.   **Kendra *Unk** was born circa 1990.

3568. Joey Lee Wood (*Beulah Estelle Smith*[7], *Nomer Marie Young*[6], *James Wylie (Jim) Young*[5], *Julia Ann Young*[4], *Mary E. Sharp*[3], *Charles W. Sr.*[2], *John Sr.*[1]) was born 15 Feb 1960 in Florence, Lauderdale County, AL.

Joey married **Sharon Louise Wood**, daughter of **Louis Cola Wood** and **Wilma Marcell Ballard**, 24 Dec 1982 in Lauderdale County, AL. Sharon was born 7 Jun 1957 in Chelford, AR.
(Duplicate Line. See Person 3253)

3569. Keith Deran Wood (*Beulah Estelle Smith*[7], *Nomer Marie Young*[6], *James Wylie (Jim) Young*[5], *Julia Ann Young*[4], *Mary E. Sharp*[3], *Charles W. Sr.*[2], *John Sr.*[1]) was born 1 Apr 1962 in Lauderdale County, AL.

Keith married **Mollie Jane Thornton**, daughter of **David Anthony Thornton** and **Biddy Blessing Broadfoot**, 15 Jul 1988 in Lauderdale County, AL. Mollie was born 24 May 1969 in Lauderdale County, AL.
5478 F   i.   **Anna Katelyn Wood** was born 16 Jul 1990 in ECM Hospital, Florence, Lauderdale County, AL.
5479 M   ii.   **Mason Reed Wood** was born 15 Mar 1993 in ECM Hospital, Florence, Lauderdale County, AL.

3570. Gregory Dale Wood (*Beulah Estelle Smith*[7], *Nomer Marie Young*[6], *James Wylie (Jim) Young*[5], *Julia Ann Young*[4], *Mary E. Sharp*[3], *Charles W. Sr.*[2], *John Sr.*[1]) was born 17 Oct 1968 in Lauderdale County, AL.

Gregory married **Lucinda (Cindi) Elizabeth Sharp**, daughter of **Alfred Donald Sharp** and **Judith Paulette Russell**, 29 Jul 1988 in Lauderdale County, AL. Lucinda was born 23 Aug 1969 in South Bend, St Joseph County, IN.
(Duplicate Line. See Person 3309)

3571. Rhonda Sherae Wood (*Beulah Estelle Smith*[7], *Nomer Marie Young*[6], *James Wylie (Jim) Young*[5], *Julia Ann Young*[4], *Mary E. Sharp*[3], *Charles W. Sr.*[2], *John Sr.*[1]) was born 10 Aug 1972 in Lauderdale County, AL.

Rhonda married **Daniel Lynn Holloway**, son of **David Lee Holloway Sr.** and **Brenda Marie Hart**, 22 Mar 1991 in Lauderdale County, AL. Daniel was born 17 Jul 1970 in Florence, Lauderdale County, AL.
5480 M   i.   **Benjamin Dakota Holloway** was born 15 Aug 1997 in ECM Hospital, Florence, Lauderdale County, AL.
5481 M   ii.   **Levi Daniel Holloway** was born 18 Jun 2004 in ECM Hospital, Florence, Lauderdale County, AL.
5482 F   iii.   **Carissa LaShae Holloway** was born 11 Jun 2008 in ECM Hospital, Florence, Lauderdale County, AL.

3572. Jonathan Elbert Wood (*Beulah Estelle Smith*[7], *Nomer Marie Young*[6], *James Wylie (Jim) Young*[5], *Julia Ann Young*[4], *Mary E. Sharp*[3], *Charles W. Sr.*[2], *John Sr.*[1]) was born 12 May 1974 in Lauderdale County, AL.

Jonathan married **Susan Renee Hopkins**, daughter of **Robert Hopkins** and **Linda Faye Mitchell**, 3 Jun 1994 in Lauderdale County, AL. Susan was born 9 Nov 1976 in Tennessee.

<table>
<tr><td>5483</td><td>M</td><td>i.</td><td>Kendall Allan Wood was born 4 Jul 1997 in ECM Hospital, Florence, Lauderdale County, AL.</td></tr>
<tr><td>5484</td><td>F</td><td>ii.</td><td>Lauren Elizabeth Wood was born 14 Jul 2002 in Helen Keller Hospital, Sheffield, Colbert County, AL.</td></tr>
</table>

3573. Beth Elaine Wood (*Beulah Estelle Smith*[7], *Nomer Marie Young*[6], *James Wylie (Jim) Young*[5], *Julia Ann Young*[4], *Mary E. Sharp*[3], *Charles W. Sr.*[2], *John Sr.*[1]) was born 25 Jul 1979 in ECM Hospital, Florence, Lauderdale County, AL.

Beth married **Carlton Lee Montgomery**, son of **Tony Ajill Montgomery** and **Mary Elaine (Sissy) Lanier**, 28 Jun 2002 in Lauderdale County, AL. Carlton was born 29 Aug 1977.

5485	M	i.	**Aaron Conner Montgomery** was born 5 Oct 2005 in ECM Hospital, Florence, Lauderdale County, AL.

3574. Darin Dwaine Smith (*Grady Elbert Smith*[7], *Nomer Marie Young*[6], *James Wylie (Jim) Young*[5], *Julia Ann Young*[4], *Mary E. Sharp*[3], *Charles W. Sr.*[2], *John Sr.*[1]) was born 25 Aug 1965 in Lauderdale County, AL.

Darin married **Tracey Barber**, daughter of **Calvin E. Barber** and **Rose Mary Conn**, 25 Aug 1983 in Lauderdale County, AL. Tracey was born 19 Jan 1966 in Lauderdale County, AL.

5486	F	i.	**Whitney Leigh Smith** was born 17 Jan 1984.
5487	M	ii.	**Chase Cameron Smith** was born 26 Jul 1988.
5488	F	iii.	**Victoria (Tori) Faith Smith** was born 28 Sep 1994.

3579. James Allen Smith (*Edwin Smith*[7], *Mozella Young*[6], *James Wylie (Jim) Young*[5], *Julia Ann Young*[4], *Mary E. Sharp*[3], *Charles W. Sr.*[2], *John Sr.*[1]) was born 15 Apr 1959 in Mishawaka, St Joseph County, IN.

James married **Michelle Montague**.

+ 5489	M	i.	**Matthew Smith** was born in St. Joseph County, IN.
5490	F	ii.	**Jenny Smith**.
5491	F	iii.	**Julie Smith**.

3587. Catherine Ann (Cathy) Smith (*Joseph Wheeler Smith*[7], *Mozella Young*[6], *James Wylie (Jim) Young*[5], *Julia Ann Young*[4], *Mary E. Sharp*[3], *Charles W. Sr.*[2], *John Sr.*[1]) was born 6 Apr 1956 in Indiana.

Catherine married **Billy Gene Clemons**, son of **E. J. Clemmons** and ***Unk**.

+ 5492	F	i.	**Christy Dawn Clemons** was born 11 Jul 1976.
5493	M	ii.	**Billy Kevin Clemons** was born 27 Aug 1978.

3588. Cindy Jo Smith (*Joseph Wheeler Smith*[7], *Mozella Young*[6], *James Wylie (Jim) Young*[5], *Julia Ann Young*[4], *Mary E. Sharp*[3], *Charles W. Sr.*[2], *John Sr.*[1]) was born 19 Mar 1957 in Indiana.

Cindy married **Bobby Irons**, son of **R. C. Irons** and ***Unk**, in Wayne County, TN.

5494	F	i.	**Pamela Gail Irons** was born 30 Mar 1972.

Cindy next married **Charles South**, son of **Chester L. South** and **Rachel Grigsby**, 14 Nov 1975 in Lauderdale County, AL. Charles was born 19 Aug 1953 in Lauderdale County, AL.

5495	M	i.	**Chad South** was born 8 Feb 1976.

3589. Jack Wheeler Smith (*Joseph Wheeler Smith*[7], *Mozella Young*[6], *James Wylie (Jim) Young*[5], *Julia Ann Young*[4], *Mary E. Sharp*[3], *Charles W. Sr.*[2], *John Sr.*[1]) was born 12 Apr 1961 in Lauderdale County, AL, died 27 Jun 1998, and was buried in Murphy's Chapel Cemetery, Lauderdale County, AL.

Jack married **Debra (Debbie) Gail Wright**, daughter of **Sidney H. Wright** and **Annie R. Rich**, 8 Sep 1980 in Lauderdale County, AL. Debra was born 16 Mar 1960 in Lauderdale County, AL.

5496	F	i.	**Brandi Gail Smith** was born 12 Apr 1981.

3590. Wayne Holt (*Christine Young*[7], *Paul Mansel Young*[6], *James Wylie (Jim) Young*[5], *Julia Ann Young*[4], *Mary E. Sharp*[3], *Charles W. Sr.*[2], *John Sr.*[1]).

Wayne married **Jean *Unk**.

5497 F i. **Britney Holt**.

5498 F ii. **Keoni Holt**.

3591. Kenny Holt (*Christine Young* [7], *Paul Mansel Young* [6], *James Wylie (Jim) Young* [5], *Julia Ann Young* [4], *Mary E. Sharp* [3], *Charles W. Sr.* [2], *John Sr.* [1]).

Kenny married **Regetta *Unk**.

3593. Regina Holt (*Christine Young* [7], *Paul Mansel Young* [6], *James Wylie (Jim) Young* [5], *Julia Ann Young* [4], *Mary E. Sharp* [3], *Charles W. Sr.* [2], *John Sr.* [1]).

Regina married **Philip Risner**.

5499 M i. **Wesley Risner**.

5500 M ii. **Tyler Risner**.

3596. Kimberly Ann Russell (*Paulette Young* [7], *Paul Mansel Young* [6], *James Wylie (Jim) Young* [5], *Julia Ann Young* [4], *Mary E. Sharp* [3], *Charles W. Sr.* [2], *John Sr.* [1]) was born 11 Feb 1981 in Lauderdale County, AL.

Kimberly married **Erick Dale Barnett** 18 Aug 2000 in Lauderdale County, AL.

3600. Angelia Kay McKelvey (*Larry Steven McKelvey* [7], *Irene Beulah Young* [6], *James Wylie (Jim) Young* [5], *Julia Ann Young* [4], *Mary E. Sharp* [3], *Charles W. Sr.* [2], *John Sr.* [1]) was born 24 Jan 1967 in Lauderdale County, AL.

Angelia married **Timothy Ray Bogus**, son of **Bobby Ray Bogus** and **Helen Sue Balentine**, 9 Sep 1988 in Wayne County, TN. Timothy was born 16 Jan 1965 in Lauderdale County, AL.

5501 M i. **Cody Steven Bogus** was born 3 Nov 1988 in Lauderdale County, AL.

5502 M ii. **Justin Ray Bogus** was born 3 Nov 1988 in Lauderdale County, AL.

3601. Donna Jean McKelvey (*Larry Steven McKelvey* [7], *Irene Beulah Young* [6], *James Wylie (Jim) Young* [5], *Julia Ann Young* [4], *Mary E. Sharp* [3], *Charles W. Sr.* [2], *John Sr.* [1]) was born 20 Apr 1970 in Lauderdale County, AL.

Donna married **John Eric Montgomery**, son of **Jimmy Ray Montgomery** and **Gertie Marie Robinette**, 9 Aug 1985 in Lauderdale County, AL. John was born 1 Nov 1966 in Lauderdale County, AL.

3602. Tina Ann McKelvey (*Larry Steven McKelvey* [7], *Irene Beulah Young* [6], *James Wylie (Jim) Young* [5], *Julia Ann Young* [4], *Mary E. Sharp* [3], *Charles W. Sr.* [2], *John Sr.* [1]) was born 27 Aug 1972 in Lauderdale County, AL.

Tina married **Toney McDonald**, son of **Bobby McDonald** and **Elaine Lewis**. Toney was born 30 Sep 1972 in Lauderdale County, AL.

5503 F i. **Brittney Nicole McKelvey** was born 24 Nov 1990 in Lauderdale County, AL.

3603. Karen Elaine Scott (*Gary Lance Scott* [7], *Eula Beatrice Young* [6], *Hulet Edward Young* [5], *Julia Ann Young* [4], *Mary E. Sharp* [3], *Charles W. Sr.* [2], *John Sr.* [1]) was born 14 Oct 1971 in Lauderdale County, AL.

Karen married **Eddie Kyle Mitchell**, son of **James Ralph (Buddy) Mitchell** and **Mary Ann Smith**, 30 Jun 1990 in Lauderdale County, AL. Eddie was born 14 Dec 1968 in Lauderdale County, AL.

5504 F i. **Brylee Celaine Mitchell** was born 2 Jan 1994 in Lauderdale County, AL.

5505 M ii. **Braden Kyle Mitchell** was born 5 Jun 1997.

5506 F iii. **Bryndall Celeste Mitchell** was born 25 Jun 2002.

3604. Pamela Gail Scott (*Gary Lance Scott* [7], *Eula Beatrice Young* [6], *Hulet Edward Young* [5], *Julia Ann Young* [4], *Mary E. Sharp* [3], *Charles W. Sr.* [2], *John Sr.* [1]).

Pamela married **Gerald Thomas (Tommy) Butler** 27 Feb 1981 in Lauderdale County, AL.

+ 5507 F i. **Nicole Butler**.

5508 M ii. **Cody Butler**.

3605. Gregory (Greg) Lance Scott (*Gary Lance Scott⁷, Eula Beatrice Young⁶, Hulet Edward Young⁵, Julia Ann Young⁴, Mary E. Sharp³, Charles W. Sr.², John Sr.¹*) was born 15 Nov 1975 in ECM Hospital, Florence, Lauderdale County, AL.

Gregory married **Marsha Leeann Crider**, daughter of **Edward Joyce (E. J.) Crider** and **Sarah Ann Burns**, 25 Sep 1998 in Lauderdale County, AL. Marsha was born 18 Sep 1980 in ECM Hospital, Florence, Lauderdale County, AL.
(Duplicate Line. See Person 3265)

3606. Dennis Ray Wood (*Peggy Jo Scott⁷, Eula Beatrice Young⁶, Hulet Edward Young⁵, Julia Ann Young⁴, Mary E. Sharp³, Charles W. Sr.², John Sr.¹*) was born 31 Aug 1962 in Lauderdale County, AL.

Dennis married **Deborah Lynn Mathis**, daughter of **Charles Mathis** and **Patricia Parker**, 30 Mar 1984 in Lauderdale County, AL. Deborah was born 5 Apr 1962 in Los Angeles, CA.
5509 F i. **Beth Wood**.

3607. Terry Lynn McFall (*Julia Earline Scott⁷, Eula Beatrice Young⁶, Hulet Edward Young⁵, Julia Ann Young⁴, Mary E. Sharp³, Charles W. Sr.², John Sr.¹*).

Terry married **Mary Lewis Belcher**, daughter of **Floyd Belcher** and **Wanda Putman**, 2 Jun 2007 in Lauderdale County, AL.

3609. Rodney McFall (*Julia Earline Scott⁷, Eula Beatrice Young⁶, Hulet Edward Young⁵, Julia Ann Young⁴, Mary E. Sharp³, Charles W. Sr.², John Sr.¹*).

Rodney married **Rachel *Unk**.

3615. James Rickey Gean (*Margaret Louise Dailey⁷, Carrie Ann Young⁶, Hulet Edward Young⁵, Julia Ann Young⁴, Mary E. Sharp³, Charles W. Sr.², John Sr.¹*) was born 25 Sep 1945 in Hardin County, TN.

James married **Susan Nan Lotte** 22 Dec 1959.

3616. Dannie Lee Gean (*Margaret Louise Dailey⁷, Carrie Ann Young⁶, Hulet Edward Young⁵, Julia Ann Young⁴, Mary E. Sharp³, Charles W. Sr.², John Sr.¹*) was born 18 Sep 1950 in Hardin County, TN.

Dannie married **Mary Ann Ward**, daughter of **Ross Ward** and **Maxine McClusky**, 9 Jun 1972 in Lauderdale County, AL. Mary was born 4 Jul 1952 in Lauderdale County, AL.
5510 M i. **James Lee Gean** was born 27 May 1978 in Lauderdale County, AL.
5511 M ii. **Timothy Daniel Gean** was born 17 Feb 1980 in Lauderdale County, AL and died 1 Oct 1996 in Memory Gardens, Savannah, Hardin County, TN.
5512 F iii. **Dona Suzanne Gean** was born 28 Jun 1982 in Lauderdale County, AL.

3617. Thomas Steven Gean (*Margaret Louise Dailey⁷, Carrie Ann Young⁶, Hulet Edward Young⁵, Julia Ann Young⁴, Mary E. Sharp³, Charles W. Sr.², John Sr.¹*) was born 16 Oct 1952 in Hardin County, TN.

Thomas married **Susan Elizabeth Miles**, daughter of **Arvil L. Miles** and **Hazel Somers**, 23 Jun 1978 in Lauderdale County, AL. Susan was born 26 Feb 1958 in Lauderdale County, AL.
+ 5513 F i. **Rachel Elizabeth Gean** was born 19 Aug 1979 in Lauderdale County, AL.
5514 M ii. **Steven Miles Gean** was born 7 Oct 1982 in Memphis, Shelby County, TN.
5515 M iii. **Tyler Ryan Gean** was born 2 Apr 1986 in Memphis, Shelby County, TN.

3618. Donnie Lynn Gean (*Margaret Louise Dailey⁷, Carrie Ann Young⁶, Hulet Edward Young⁵, Julia Ann Young⁴, Mary E. Sharp³, Charles W. Sr.², John Sr.¹*) was born 22 Mar 1954 in Hardin County, TN.

Donnie married **Shelia Marie Henry**, daughter of **Eulas P. Henry** and **Elsie Marie Pounders**, 24 Mar 1978 in Alabama. Shelia was born 3 Oct 1954 in Colbert County, AL.

5516	F	i.	**Andrea Marie Gean** was born 17 Sep 1980 in McNairy County, TN.
5517	M	ii.	**Robert Andrew Gean**.
5518	M	iii.	**Bradley Alan Gean** was born 23 Nov 1988 in McNairy County, TN.

3619. Raymond Dale Gean (*Margaret Louise Dailey^7, Carrie Ann Young^6, Hulet Edward Young^5, Julia Ann Young^4, Mary E. Sharp^3, Charles W. Sr.^{2}, John Sr.^{1}*) was born 13 Sep 1955 in Hardin County, TN.

Raymond married **Jeanette Maurene Fulmer**, daughter of **Sidney J. Fulmer** and **Volien Faires**, 27 Aug 1976 in Lauderdale County, AL. Jeanette was born 7 Apr 1953 in Lauderdale County, AL.

+ 5519	F	i.	**Tracy Maurene Gean** was born 14 Jun 1981 in Lauderdale County, AL.
+ 5520	M	ii.	**Michael Dale Gean** was born 19 Nov 1977 in Lauderdale County, AL.

3620. Mackie Alan Gean (*Margaret Louise Dailey^7, Carrie Ann Young^6, Hulet Edward Young^5, Julia Ann Young^4, Mary E. Sharp^3, Charles W. Sr.^{2}, John Sr.^{1}*) was born 12 Nov 1956 in Hardin County, TN.

Mackie married **Linda Sue Watkins**, daughter of **Bennie L. Watkins** and **Margaret Goad**, 12 Jun 1976 in Lauderdale County, AL. Linda was born 23 Oct 1953 in Lauderdale County, AL.

5521	M	i.	**Benjamin Gloyd Gean** was born 24 Dec 1980 in Lauderdale County, AL.
5522	F	ii.	**Tabitha Lynn Gean** was born 10 Apr 1982 in Lauderdale County, AL, died 23 Sep 1999, and was buried in Memorial Gardens, Savannah, TN.

3621. Jeffery Lynn Dailey Sr. (*William Turner Dailey Jr.^{7}, Carrie Ann Young^6, Hulet Edward Young^5, Julia Ann Young^4, Mary E. Sharp^3, Charles W. Sr.^{2}, John Sr.^{1}*) was born 13 Jul 1960 in Lauderdale County, AL.

Jeffery married **Tammie Renae Harris**, daughter of **Paul Willis Harris** and **Carolyn Henson**, 16 Mar 1978 in Lauderdale County, AL. Tammie was born 10 Jun 1960 in Lauderdale County, AL.

5523	F	i.	**Jennifer Lynn Dailey** was born 18 May 1980.
5524	F	ii.	**Ashley Renee Dailey** was born 18 Apr.

Jeffery next married **Teresa Diane Heathcoat**, daughter of **Thomas Leroy Heathcoat** and **Mary Ann Ladner**, 4 Oct 1989 in Lauderdale County, AL. Teresa was born 15 Dec 1963.

5525	M	i.	**Jeffery Lynn Dailey Jr.** was born 9 Jul.

3622. Kimberly Diane Dailey (*William Turner Dailey Jr.^{7}, Carrie Ann Young^6, Hulet Edward Young^5, Julia Ann Young^4, Mary E. Sharp^3, Charles W. Sr.^{2}, John Sr.^{1}*) was born 30 Aug 1966 in Lauderdale County, AL.

Kimberly married **Donald Lawson Herd**, son of **Ernest Doyle Herd** and **Bertha Rose Davenport**, 4 Jun 1994 in Lauderdale County, AL. Donald was born 28 Sep 1950.

3623. Duane Balentine (*James Leon Balentine^7, Myrtle Lena Young^6, Hulet Edward Young^5, Julia Ann Young^4, Mary E. Sharp^3, Charles W. Sr.^{2}, John Sr.^{1}*).

Duane married **Jennifer *Unk**.

3625. Deborah Balentine (*James Leon Balentine^7, Myrtle Lena Young^6, Hulet Edward Young^5, Julia Ann Young^4, Mary E. Sharp^3, Charles W. Sr.^{2}, John Sr.^{1}*).

Deborah married **Jeffrey Hensley**.

5526	F	i.	**Victoria Hensley**.
5527	F	ii.	**Emmaleigh Hensley**.

3626. Barry Green (*Dorothy (Dot) Gloria Balentine^7, Myrtle Lena Young^6, Hulet Edward Young^5, Julia Ann Young^4, Mary E. Sharp^3, Charles W. Sr.^{2}, John Sr.^{1}*).

Barry married **Laura *Unk**.

3627. Tim Green (*Dorothy (Dot) Gloria Balentine^7, Myrtle Lena Young^6, Hulet Edward Young^5, Julia Ann Young^4, Mary E. Sharp^3, Charles W. Sr.^{2}, John Sr.^{1}*).

Tim married **Sandra *Unk**.

3628. Donald Green (*Dorothy (Dot) Gloria Balentine^7, Myrtle Lena Young^6, Hulet Edward Young^5, Julia Ann Young^4, Mary E. Sharp^3, Charles W. Sr.^{2}, John Sr.^{1}*).

Donald married **June *Unk**.

3629. Michael Green (*Dorothy (Dot) Gloria Balentine^7, Myrtle Lena Young^6, Hulet Edward Young^5, Julia Ann Young^4, Mary E. Sharp^3, Charles W. Sr.^{2}, John Sr.^{1}*).

Michael married **Jayne *Unk**.

3630. Brian Keith Holt (*Janice June Balentine^7, Myrtle Lena Young^6, Hulet Edward Young^5, Julia Ann Young^4, Mary E. Sharp^3, Charles W. Sr.^{2}, John Sr.^{1}*) was born 21 Mar 1968 in Lauderdale County, AL.

Brian married **Tina Stricklin** 10 Oct 1992 in Lauderdale County, AL.

3631. Bradly Kane Holt (*Janice June Balentine^7, Myrtle Lena Young^6, Hulet Edward Young^5, Julia Ann Young^4, Mary E. Sharp^3, Charles W. Sr.^{2}, John Sr.^{1}*) was born 30 Oct 1969 in Lauderdale County, AL.

Bradly married **Cherie Green** in 1997 in Mobile, AL.

3632. Bart Kenneth Holt (*Janice June Balentine^7, Myrtle Lena Young^6, Hulet Edward Young^5, Julia Ann Young^4, Mary E. Sharp^3, Charles W. Sr.^{2}, John Sr.^{1}*) was born 13 Jul 1974 in Lauderdale County, AL.

Bart married **Dana Newton** 5 Feb 1993 in Lauderdale County, AL.

3637. Millicent (Millie) Lynn Young (*Larry Joe Young^7, Joe L. Young^6, Hulet Edward Young^5, Julia Ann Young^4, Mary E. Sharp^3, Charles W. Sr.^{2}, John Sr.^{1}*) was born 16 Sep 1973 in Lauderdale County, AL.

Millicent married **Dewey Scott Basdon**, son of **Dewey Edward Baston** and **Cynthia Dyanne Little**, 6 Jan 1996 in Lauderdale County, AL. Dewey was born 16 May 1972.
5528 M i. **Walker Joe Basdon** was born 20 Dec 1999 in Lauderdale County, AL.

3638. Whitley Joel Young (*Larry Joe Young^7, Joe L. Young^6, Hulet Edward Young^5, Julia Ann Young^4, Mary E. Sharp^3, Charles W. Sr.^{2}, John Sr.^{1}*) was born 27 May 1977 in Lauderdale County, AL.

Whitley married **Mary Concetta Traglia** 16 Mar 2000.

3639. Chasity Dawn Young (*Ronnie Dale Young^7, Joe L. Young^6, Hulet Edward Young^5, Julia Ann Young^4, Mary E. Sharp^3, Charles W. Sr.^{2}, John Sr.^{1}*) was born 21 May 1980 in Lauderdale County, AL.

Chasity married **Bobby Joe (B. J.) Price**, son of **Harry Kenneth Price** and **Kim Debra Wright**, 8 Jan 2005 in Lauderdale County, AL. Bobby was born 4 Dec 1979.

3641. Michael Harold Stanfield Sr. (*Nancy Holt^7, Myrtle Mae Young^6, Turner Andrew Young^5, Julia Ann Young^4, Mary E. Sharp^3, Charles W. Sr.^{2}, John Sr.^{1}*).

Michael married **Amy *Unk**.
5529 M i. **Michael Harold Stanfield Jr.**
5530 M ii. **Jacob Daniel Stanfield.**

3642. Stacy Shawn Stanfield (*Nancy Holt* [7], *Myrtle Mae Young* [6], *Turner Andrew Young* [5], *Julia Ann Young* [4], *Mary E. Sharp* [3], *Charles W. Sr.* [2], *John Sr.* [1]).

Stacy married **Stephanie *Unk**.
5531 F i. **Kaylee Grace Stanfield.**
5532 F ii. **Riley Gail Stanfield.**

3643. Angela Michelle Stanfield (*Nancy Holt* [7], *Myrtle Mae Young* [6], *Turner Andrew Young* [5], *Julia Ann Young* [4], *Mary E. Sharp* [3], *Charles W. Sr.* [2], *John Sr.* [1]) was born in 1968 in Lauderdale County, AL and died 14 Sep 2006 in Lauderdale County, AL.

Angela married **Michael House.**
5533 F i. **Ashley Michelle House.**
5534 F ii. **Hailey Ann House.**
5535 F iii. **Kylee Brooke House.**
5536 M iv. **Tyler Michael House.**

3644. Terri Kay Cooper (*Joe Benny Cooper* [7], *Gladys Lee Young* [6], *Turner Andrew Young* [5], *Julia Ann Young* [4], *Mary E. Sharp* [3], *Charles W. Sr.* [2], *John Sr.* [1]) was born in 1963.

Terri married **Jeff Lavender.**

3645. Michael Joe Cooper (*Joe Benny Cooper* [7], *Gladys Lee Young* [6], *Turner Andrew Young* [5], *Julia Ann Young* [4], *Mary E. Sharp* [3], *Charles W. Sr.* [2], *John Sr.* [1]) was born in 1965.

Michael married **Dolly Hudson.**
5537 M i. **Rusty Hudson Cooper.**

3646. Joshua Steven Cooper (*James Steven (Steve) Cooper* [7], *Gladys Lee Young* [6], *Turner Andrew Young* [5], *Julia Ann Young* [4], *Mary E. Sharp* [3], *Charles W. Sr.* [2], *John Sr.* [1]) was born 12 Jan 1976 in Lauderdale County, AL.

Joshua married **Jennifer Nicole Neal** 29 May 1999 in Lauderdale County, AL. Jennifer was born 15 Feb 1978 in Lauderdale County, AL.
5538 F i. **Emma Elizabeth Cooper** was born 12 Nov 2003 in Lauderdale County, AL.
5539 F ii. **Claire Katherine Cooper** was born 3 Nov 2006 in Lauderdale County, AL.

3647. Zachary Ryan Cooper (*James Steven (Steve) Cooper* [7], *Gladys Lee Young* [6], *Turner Andrew Young* [5], *Julia Ann Young* [4], *Mary E. Sharp* [3], *Charles W. Sr.* [2], *John Sr.* [1]) was born 4 Jan 1980 in Lauderdale County, AL.

Zachary married **Kandi Mitchell.**
5540 M i. **Mackenlee Rian Cooper** was born 4 May 2005.

3649. Brett Allen Miles Sr. (*Charles Dennis Miles* [7], *Clara Belle Young* [6], *Cleave Homer Young* [5], *Julia Ann Young* [4], *Mary E. Sharp* [3], *Charles W. Sr.* [2], *John Sr.* [1]) was born 19 Nov 1967 in Indiana.

Brett married **Theresa *Unk**.
5541 F i. **Amanda Lynn Miles** was born 19 Nov 1986 in Indiana.
5542 M ii. **Brett Allen Miles Jr.** was born 6 May 1988 in Indiana.

3650. Denise Renae Miles (*Charles Dennis Miles* [7], *Clara Belle Young* [6], *Cleave Homer Young* [5], *Julia Ann Young* [4], *Mary E. Sharp* [3], *Charles W. Sr.* [2], *John Sr.* [1]) was born 21 Dec 1971 in Indiana.

Denise married **Scott Guimberts.**
5543 F i. **Brook Laura Guimberts.**

3651. Shawna Kay Hatfield (*Mary Francis Miles* [7], *Clara Belle Young* [6], *Cleave Homer Young* [5], *Julia Ann Young* [4], *Mary E. Sharp* [3], *Charles W. Sr.* [2], *John Sr.* [1]).

Shawna married **Lance Adkins**.
5544 F   i.   **Kileah Adkins** was born 30 May 1989 in Kentucky.

3658. Michael Young Jr. (*Michael Young Sr.*[7], *Kerry W. Young*[6], *Wheeler Young*[5], *Julia Ann Young*[4], *Mary E. Sharp*[3], *Charles W. Sr.*[2], *John Sr.*[1]).

Michael married **Lisa Gillean**.
5545 M   i.   **Kade Young**.
5546 M   ii.   **Kaelin Young**.
5547 M   iii. **Kary Mitchell Young** was born 10 Feb 1996 in St. Joseph County, IN and died 14 Aug 2002 in St. Joseph County, IN.

3666. Jamie Marie Kiser (*Wanda Marie Sharp*[7], *James Wesley*[6], *James David*[5], *Berry Nolan*[4], *Joseph (Joe)*[3], *Charles W. Sr.*[2], *John Sr.*[1]) was born 11 Oct 1977 in Colbert County, AL.

Jamie married **John Benjamin Drake**, son of **Tommy Drake** and **Lana Forness**, in Colbert County, AL. John was born 27 Apr 1976 in Memphis, Shelby County, TN.
5548 F   i.   **Haley Lexis Drake** was born 17 Jul 1999 in Lauderdale County, AL.

3670. Wesley Leon Sharp (*Albert Leon*[7], *James Wesley*[6], *James David*[5], *Berry Nolan*[4], *Joseph (Joe)*[3], *Charles W. Sr.*[2], *John Sr.*[1]) was born 6 Feb 1984 in Lauderdale County, AL.

Wesley married **Brittany Denise Balentine**, daughter of **Roger D. Balentine** and **Leigh Ann Dennis**, 14 Mar 2009 in Lauderdale County, AL.

3672. Timothy Lynn Sharp (*David Lynn*[7], *Clyde Joel (Link)*[6], *James David*[5], *Berry Nolan*[4], *Joseph (Joe)*[3], *Charles W. Sr.*[2], *John Sr.*[1]) was born 13 Jun 1966 in Lauderdale County, AL.

Timothy married **Rebecca Ruth Shelby**, daughter of **Glen Earl Shelby** and **Betty Jo Crowell**, 26 Aug 1989 in Waynesboro, Wayne County, MS. Rebecca was born 29 Oct 1965 in Nashville, Davidson County, TN.
5549 M   i.   **Brandon Lynn Sharp** was born 15 Oct 1992 in Pensacola. Escambia County, FL.

3674. Tina Marie Elmore (*Betty Lou Turbyfill*[7], *Velma Nadine Sharp*[6], *James David*[5], *Berry Nolan*[4], *Joseph (Joe)*[3], *Charles W. Sr.*[2], *John Sr.*[1]) was born 31 Oct 1959 in Ft Meade, MD.

Tina married **John Michael Ratcliff** 15 Nov 1986 in Carlsbad, Orange County, CA. John was born 3 Sep 1957 in Oceanside, San Diego County, CA.
5550 M   i.   **John Christian Ratcliff** was born 26 Apr 1998 in Wildomar, CA.

3675. Dudley Guy Elmore III (*Betty Lou Turbyfill*[7], *Velma Nadine Sharp*[6], *James David*[5], *Berry Nolan*[4], *Joseph (Joe)*[3], *Charles W. Sr.*[2], *John Sr.*[1]) was born 28 Dec 1960 in Camp Fujinobi, Japan.

Dudley married **Kim Marcotte** 8 Aug 1992 in Carlsbad, Orange County, CA. Kim was born 11 Feb 1962 in Long Beach, CA.
5551 F   i.   **Hilary Lanea Elmore** was born 7 Jun 1985 in Chico, Butte County, CA.
5552 M   ii.   **Austin Elmore** was born 22 Jun 1995 in San Bernardino, CA.

3676. Margo Luree Turbyfill (*Donald Eugene Turbyfill*[7], *Velma Nadine Sharp*[6], *James David*[5], *Berry Nolan*[4], *Joseph (Joe)*[3], *Charles W. Sr.*[2], *John Sr.*[1]) was born 17 May 1966 in Beale AFB, Yuba County, CA.

Margo married **Craig Richard Nash** 8 Nov 1985 in Phoenix, Maricopa County, AZ.

3678. Bradley Scott Johnston (*Clara Dean Turbyfill*[7], *Velma Nadine Sharp*[6], *James David*[5], *Berry Nolan*[4], *Joseph (Joe)*[3], *Charles W. Sr.*[2], *John Sr.*[1]) was born 14 Oct 1964 in Florence, Lauderdale County, AL.

Bradley married **Jennifer Fiske**, daughter of **Gordon Fiske** and **Ann Williams**, 6 Jul 1984 in Lauderdale County, AL. Jennifer was born 6 Jun 1964 in Oregon.

3680. Angela Michelle Johnston (*Clara Dean Turbyfill*[7], *Velma Nadine Sharp*[6], *James David*[5], *Berry Nolan*[4], *Joseph (Joe)*[3], *Charles W. Sr.*[2], *John Sr.*[1]) was born 19 Feb 1970.

Angela married **Tracey Allen White**, son of **Milas Greenberry White** and **Heather Ruth Young**. Tracey was born 16 Apr 1968 in Lauderdale County, AL, died 15 Apr 1988, and was buried in Milford Cemetery, Lauderdale County, AL.
5553 M   i.   **Joshua Allen White** was born 15 Nov 1985.

3681. Heather Nicole Turbyfill (*Thomas (Tommy) Ray Turbyfill*[7], *Velma Nadine Sharp*[6], *James David*[5], *Berry Nolan*[4], *Joseph (Joe)*[3], *Charles W. Sr.*[2], *John Sr.*[1]) was born 26 Oct 1973 in Lauderdale County, AL.

Heather married **Christopher David Lawson**, son of **Archie David Lawson** and **Judy Ann Reynolds**, 27 Nov 1993 in Lauderdale County, AL. Christopher was born 10 Sep 1972 in Lauderdale County, AL.

3682. Christopher Lee Turbyfill (*Charles Robert Turbyfill*[7], *Velma Nadine Sharp*[6], *James David*[5], *Berry Nolan*[4], *Joseph (Joe)*[3], *Charles W. Sr.*[2], *John Sr.*[1]) was born 8 Sep 1972 in Lauderdale County, AL.

Christopher married **Molly Darlene Blackwell**, daughter of **Robert Lane Blackwell** and **Carolyn Sue Flint**, 11 Oct 1997 in Lauderdale County, AL. Molly was born 31 Dec 1974.

3687. Christy Ann Turbyfill (*Jerry Lynn Turbyfill*[7], *Velma Nadine Sharp*[6], *James David*[5], *Berry Nolan*[4], *Joseph (Joe)*[3], *Charles W. Sr.*[2], *John Sr.*[1]) was born 14 Sep 1975 in Lauderdale County, AL.

Christy married ***Unk Malone**.

3696. Laura Kaye Wilkes (*James Riley Wilkes*[7], *James Chambers Wilkes*[6], *Eula Elizabeth Sharp*[5], *Berry Nolan*[4], *Joseph (Joe)*[3], *Charles W. Sr.*[2], *John Sr.*[1]) was born 25 Feb 1952 in Colbert County, AL.

Laura married **Buford Wayne Cassel**, son of **Lonnie Eugene Cassel** and **Hester Zills**, in 1968 in Moulton, AL. Buford was born 20 Apr 1949 in Colbert County, AL.
+ 5554 F   i.   **Ronda Kay Cassel** was born 29 Oct 1969 in Colbert County, AL.
5555 F   ii.   **Angelia Leigh Cassel** was born 29 Sep 1970 in Colbert County, AL.

Laura next married **Tony Gary Holland**, son of **Louis E. Holland** and **Marie Willingham**, 28 May 1976 in Lauderdale County, AL. Tony was born 21 Nov 1946 in Colbert County, AL.
+ 5556 F   i.   **Toni Beth Holland** was born 21 Apr 1977 in Colbert County, AL.
5557 F   ii.   **Sallie Ann Holland** was born 12 Apr 1980 in Colbert County, AL.

Laura next married **Terry Cobb**.

3697. Darwall James White I (*Shirley Jean Wilkes*[7], *James Chambers Wilkes*[6], *Eula Elizabeth Sharp*[5], *Berry Nolan*[4], *Joseph (Joe)*[3], *Charles W. Sr.*[2], *John Sr.*[1]) was born 17 Jan 1952 in Lauderdale County, AL.

Darwall married **Patricia H. Housman**, daughter of **Bob Housman** and **Mary Billings**, 20 Apr 1973. Patricia was born 12 Oct 1952 in Lauderdale County, AL.
5558 F   i.   **Anna Marie White** was born 15 Feb 1977 in Colbert County, AL.
5559 M   ii.   **Darwall James White II** was born 19 Jan 1980 in Colbert County, AL.

3700. Gary Dewitt Jennings (*Annie Mae Wilkes*[7], *Elting Wilkes*[6], *Eula Elizabeth Sharp*[5], *Berry Nolan*[4], *Joseph (Joe)*[3], *Charles W. Sr.*[2], *John Sr.*[1]) was born 17 May 1957.

Gary married **Tammy Sue Wall**. Tammy was born 17 Dec 1966.
5560 M   i.   **Justin Dewitt Jennings** was born 21 Mar 1988.
5561 F   ii.   **Brandi Lee Ann Jennings** was born 23 Jan 1991.

3701. Joe Keith Jennings (*Annie Mae Wilkes* [7], *Elting Wilkes* [6], *Eula Elizabeth Sharp* [5], *Berry Nolan* [4], *Joseph (Joe)* [3], *Charles W. Sr.* [2], *John Sr.* [1]) was born 25 Sep 1962.

   Joe married **Tammy Melissa Choate**. Tammy was born 24 Sep 1964.
   5562 M   i.   **Corey Blake Jennings** was born 3 Sep 1988.

3702. Jeffrey Bruce Wilkes (*Jimmy Carroll Wilkes* [7], *Elting Wilkes* [6], *Eula Elizabeth Sharp* [5], *Berry Nolan* [4], *Joseph (Joe)* [3], *Charles W. Sr.* [2], *John Sr.* [1]) was born 26 Dec 1961.

   Jeffrey married **Michelle Lynn Kennedy**. Michelle was born 3 Sep 1971.
   5563 F   i.   **Sarah Kennedy Wilkes** was born 4 Aug 1998.

3703. Jimmy Kevin Wilkes (*Jimmy Carroll Wilkes* [7], *Elting Wilkes* [6], *Eula Elizabeth Sharp* [5], *Berry Nolan* [4], *Joseph (Joe)* [3], *Charles W. Sr.* [2], *John Sr.* [1]) was born 31 Aug 1964.

   Jimmy married **Donna Gail Paulk**. Donna was born 16 Jul 1966.
   5564 F   i.   **Bethany Leigh Wilkes** was born 23 Feb 1992.
   5565 F   ii.   **Jennah Kathryn Wilkes** was born 4 May 1996.

3704. Kathy Lynn Thompson (*Patsy Lee Wilkes* [7], *Elting Wilkes* [6], *Eula Elizabeth Sharp* [5], *Berry Nolan* [4], *Joseph (Joe)* [3], *Charles W. Sr.* [2], *John Sr.* [1]) was born 10 Dec 1963.

   Kathy married **Rodney Warren Gifford**. Rodney was born 28 Nov 1961.
   5566 M   i.   **Jacob Warren Gifford** was born 30 Mar 1990.
   5567 M   ii.   **Jessie Wheeler Gifford** was born 12 May 1995.

3706. Brian Lee Thompson (*Patsy Lee Wilkes* [7], *Elting Wilkes* [6], *Eula Elizabeth Sharp* [5], *Berry Nolan* [4], *Joseph (Joe)* [3], *Charles W. Sr.* [2], *John Sr.* [1]) was born 19 Nov 1968.

   Brian married **Robin Ashley McDonald**. Robin was born 25 Jun 1973.

3707. Anthony Charles Wilkes (*Joe Wheeler Wilkes* [7], *Elting Wilkes* [6], *Eula Elizabeth Sharp* [5], *Berry Nolan* [4], *Joseph (Joe)* [3], *Charles W. Sr.* [2], *John Sr.* [1]) was born 20 Nov 1976.

   Anthony married **Amanda Dawn Denton**. Amanda was born 30 Aug 1978.

3708. Nicole Elizabeth Wilkes (*Joe Wheeler Wilkes* [7], *Elting Wilkes* [6], *Eula Elizabeth Sharp* [5], *Berry Nolan* [4], *Joseph (Joe)* [3], *Charles W. Sr.* [2], *John Sr.* [1]) was born 29 Apr 1979.

   Nicole married **Greg Alan Blackman**. Greg was born 4 Jul 1977.

3713. Paula Louise Berryman (*Mary Lee Wilkes* [7], *Levi (Lee) Grant Wilkes II* [6], *Eula Elizabeth Sharp* [5], *Berry Nolan* [4], *Joseph (Joe)* [3], *Charles W. Sr.* [2], *John Sr.* [1]) was born 1 Feb 1955 in Colbert County, AL.

   Paula married **Dovie Clifford Zills Sr.**, son of **James W. Zills** and **Christine Spires**, 5 Aug 1972 in Colbert County, AL. Dovie was born 31 Dec 1953 in Colbert County, AL.
   + 5568 M   i.   **Donnie Clifford Zills Jr.** was born 11 Nov 1974 in Colbert County, AL.
     5569 F   ii.   **Tayna Nicole Zills** was born 15 Apr 1977 in Colbert County, AL.

3714. Tony Philip Nichols (*Mary Lee Wilkes* [7], *Levi (Lee) Grant Wilkes II* [6], *Eula Elizabeth Sharp* [5], *Berry Nolan* [4], *Joseph (Joe)* [3], *Charles W. Sr.* [2], *John Sr.* [1]) was born 12 Sep 1957 in Colbert County, AL.

   Tony married **Nancy Ann Nicholson**, daughter of **James Allen Nicholson** and **Lois Caroline Cooper**. Nancy was born 8 Jun 1958 in Birmingham, Jefferson County, AL.
   5570 F   i.   **Christy Leann Nichols** was born 22 Feb 1979 in Lauderdale County, AL.

3715. Jerome Clay Nichols (*Mary Lee Wilkes[7], Levi (Lee) Grant Wilkes II[6], Eula Elizabeth Sharp[5], Berry Nolan[4], Joseph (Joe)[3], Charles W. Sr.[2], John Sr.[1]*) was born 26 Oct 1962 in Colbert County, AL.

Jerome married **Sharon Denise Gregory**, daughter of **Charles Lacey Gregory** and **Marie Willard Phillips**, 8 Mar 1982 in Colbert County, AL. Sharon was born 16 Sep 1961 in Colbert County, AL.
5571 F   i.   **Brittany Denise Nichols** was born 4 Oct 1987 in Colbert County, AL.

3716. Debra Lynne Wilkes (*Levi Grant Wilkes III[7], Levi (Lee) Grant Wilkes II[6], Eula Elizabeth Sharp[5], Berry Nolan[4], Joseph (Joe)[3], Charles W. Sr.[2], John Sr.[1]*) was born 23 Dec 1966 in Rapids Parish, LA.

Debra married **Roy Glenn Tidwell**, son of **R. C. Tidwell** and **Helen Lovelady**, 23 Feb 1983 in Lauderdale County, AL. Roy was born 22 Apr 1963 in Lauderdale County, AL.

Debra next married **Ronald Eugene Wilbanks**, son of **Mac E. Wilbanks** and **Margaret Baskins**, 29 Aug 1985 in Lauderdale County, AL. Ronald was born 7 Nov 1956 in Lauderdale County, AL.

3717. Kenneth David Walker (*Bonnie Faye Wilkes[7], Earl Berry Wilkes[6], Eula Elizabeth Sharp[5], Berry Nolan[4], Joseph (Joe)[3], Charles W. Sr.[2], John Sr.[1]*) was born 28 Jul 1963.

Kenneth married **Shawn Elizabeth Willingham** in Hendersonville, TN.

3718. Mark David Walker (*Bonnie Faye Wilkes[7], Earl Berry Wilkes[6], Eula Elizabeth Sharp[5], Berry Nolan[4], Joseph (Joe)[3], Charles W. Sr.[2], John Sr.[1]*) was born 7 Aug 1965.

Mark married **Kristi Owen** in Colbert County, AL.

3722. Donna Elizabeth Wilkes (*John Jackson Wilkes Sr.[7], Rufus Jackson Wilkes[6], Eula Elizabeth Sharp[5], Berry Nolan[4], Joseph (Joe)[3], Charles W. Sr.[2], John Sr.[1]*) was born 5 May 1964 in Lauderdale County, AL.

Donna married **Rolando Brogan**, son of **Antonio Brogan** and **Wanda Madden**, 6 Sep 1987 in Lauderdale County, AL. Rolando was born 21 Aug 1958 in Sanpedro Sula, Honduras.
5572 M   i.   **Rolando Sean Brogan** was born 15 Feb 1992 in Jefferson County, AL.

3723. Paula Christine Wilkes (*John Jackson Wilkes Sr.[7], Rufus Jackson Wilkes[6], Eula Elizabeth Sharp[5], Berry Nolan[4], Joseph (Joe)[3], Charles W. Sr.[2], John Sr.[1]*) was born 4 Dec 1965 in Lauderdale County, AL.

Paula married **Matthew Hiram Fuller**, son of **Franklin Fuller** and **Jennie Lee Sellers**, 17 Sep 1988 in Lauderdale County, AL. Matthew was born 28 Dec 1963 in Waynesville, NC.
5573 F   i.   **Morgan Katherine Fuller** was born 1 May 1992 in Colbert County, AL.

3725. Jason McKinley Wilkes (*Rufus Grant Wilkes[7], Rufus Jackson Wilkes[6], Eula Elizabeth Sharp[5], Berry Nolan[4], Joseph (Joe)[3], Charles W. Sr.[2], John Sr.[1]*) was born 16 Dec 1971 in Lauderdale County, AL.

Jason married **Paula Renee Rasch**, daughter of **Paul E. Rasch** and **Shelia Buttrum**, 13 Sep 1997 in Lauderdale County, AL.
5574 F   i.   **Claire Wilkes**.

3726. Lya Janeen Wilkes (*Rufus Grant Wilkes[7], Rufus Jackson Wilkes[6], Eula Elizabeth Sharp[5], Berry Nolan[4], Joseph (Joe)[3], Charles W. Sr.[2], John Sr.[1]*) was born 4 Nov 1972 in Lauderdale County, AL.

Lya married **Kelvin Arthur Chowning**, son of **John Coleman Chowning** and **Lois Mae Lewis**, 13 Mar 1992 in Lauderdale County, AL. Kelvin was born 7 Nov 1968 in Lauderdale County, AL.

3727. Jennifer Suzanne Sharp (*Robert Norman[7], Charles Roy[6], Charles Robert[5], Berry Nolan[4], Joseph (Joe)[3], Charles W. Sr.[2], John Sr.[1]*) was born 17 Oct 1976 in Lauderdale County, AL.

Jennifer married **Matthew Ryan Alexander**, son of **Michael G. Alexander** and **Donna Marie Creel**, 22 Jul 2000 in Lauderdale County, AL. Matthew was born 20 Nov 1976 in Lauderdale County, AL.

3728. Robert Bentley Sharp (*Robert Norman[7], Charles Roy[6], Charles Robert[5], Berry Nolan[4], Joseph (Joe)[3], Charles W. Sr.[2], John Sr.[1]*) was born 29 Sep 1981 in Lauderdale County, AL.

Robert married **Amy Earline Hutto**, daughter of **James W. Hutto** and **Marilyn D. Hollander**, 16 Jun 2001 in Lauderdale County, AL. Amy was born in Lauderdale County, AL.

3730. Jody Lynn Dodd (*Jimmy Howard Dodd[7], Elizabeth Sharp[6], Charles Robert[5], Berry Nolan[4], Joseph (Joe)[3], Charles W. Sr.[2], John Sr.[1]*) was born 20 Oct 1972 in Lauderdale County, AL.

Jody married **Erica Lynn Fanning**, daughter of **Kendall Lynn Fanning** and **Teresa Louise Simpson**, 22 Jul 2000 in Huntsville, Madison County, AL. Erica was born 26 Jun 1978 in Huntsville, Madison County, AL.
5575 M i. **Gavin Payne Dodd** was born 17 Apr 2003 in Huntsville, Madison County, AL.

3731. Stacy Michelle Dodd (*Jimmy Howard Dodd[7], Elizabeth Sharp[6], Charles Robert[5], Berry Nolan[4], Joseph (Joe)[3], Charles W. Sr.[2], John Sr.[1]*) was born 1 Sep 1975 in Lauderdale County, AL.

Stacy married **Nathan Quinn Allen**, son of **Jody Allen** and **Ruby Jean James**, 13 Mar 1998 in Lauderdale County, AL. Nathan was born 10 Nov 1968.
5576 F i. **Rayton Faith Allen** was born 16 Dec 1999 in Colbert County, AL.
5577 F ii. **Chloe Hope Allen** was born 3 Aug 2001 in Colbert County, AL.

3735. Kathy Lynn Dodd (*Roger Anthony Dodd[7], Elizabeth Sharp[6], Charles Robert[5], Berry Nolan[4], Joseph (Joe)[3], Charles W. Sr.[2], John Sr.[1]*) was born 3 Jul 1976 in Lauderdale County, AL.

Kathy married **Michale Wilbanks** 27 Dec 1997 in Lauderdale County, AL.

3748. Bobby Joey Stults Jr. (*Martha Ann Statom[7], Nolan Sharp Statom[6], Muncie Venetta Sharp[5], Berry Nolan[4], Joseph (Joe)[3], Charles W. Sr.[2], John Sr.[1]*) was born 11 Jan 1968 in Lauderdale County, AL.

Bobby married **Carol Butler** 29 Mar 1991. Carol was born 19 Aug 1973 in Wayne County, TN.

3749. Tonith Townsley (*Frances Kay Statom[7], Nolan Sharp Statom[6], Muncie Venetta Sharp[5], Berry Nolan[4], Joseph (Joe)[3], Charles W. Sr.[2], John Sr.[1]*) was born 19 Mar 1965 in Lauderdale County, AL.

Tonith married **James Kevin Roberson**, son of **James Terry Roberson** and **Linda Louise Blasingame**, 2 Jul 1988 in Lauderdale County, AL. James was born 29 Jan 1967 in Lauderdale County, AL.
5578 M i. **Hunter Drake Roberson** was born 19 Jan 1994 in Lauderdale County, AL.

3751. Trella Townsley (*Frances Kay Statom[7], Nolan Sharp Statom[6], Muncie Venetta Sharp[5], Berry Nolan[4], Joseph (Joe)[3], Charles W. Sr.[2], John Sr.[1]*) was born 21 Sep 1979 in Lauderdale County, AL.

Trella married ***Unk Patterson**.

3752. Rhonda Lynn Hodges (*Roy Wade Hodges[7], Lois Katherine Statom[6], Muncie Venetta Sharp[5], Berry Nolan[4], Joseph (Joe)[3], Charles W. Sr.[2], John Sr.[1]*) was born about 1960.

Rhonda married **Jimmy Whann**.
5579 M i. **Todd Whann**.
5580 M ii. **Glenn Whann**.

3753. Gregory Wade Hodges (*Roy Wade Hodges[7], Lois Katherine Statom[6], Muncie Venetta Sharp[5], Berry Nolan[4], Joseph (Joe)[3], Charles W. Sr.[2], John Sr.[1]*) was born 11 Feb 1961 in Lauderdale County, AL.

Gregory married **Glenda Dale Brown**, daughter of **Leo F. Lester** and **Pearl Messer**, 23 Sep 1985 in Lauderdale County, AL. Glenda was born 5 Jan 1947.

3754. Victor Wayne Hodges (*Roy Wade Hodges*[7], *Lois Katherine Statom*[6], *Muncie Venetta Sharp*[5], *Berry Nolan*[4], *Joseph (Joe)*[3], *Charles W. Sr.*[2], *John Sr.*[1]) was born 25 Aug 1968 in Lauderdale County, AL.

Victor married **Kelly Faye Richardson**, daughter of **John David Richardson** and **Glenda Faye Butler**, 12 Feb 1993 in Lauderdale County, AL. Kelly was born 14 Jan 1969.

3757. Jody Marion Hodges (*Larry Joe Hodges*[7], *Lois Katherine Statom*[6], *Muncie Venetta Sharp*[5], *Berry Nolan*[4], *Joseph (Joe)*[3], *Charles W. Sr.*[2], *John Sr.*[1]) was born 4 Oct 1965 in Lauderdale County, AL.

Jody married **Patricia Fooshie** 15 Oct 1988.
5581 F   i.   **Ballie Rhea Hodges** was born 19 Sep 1992 in Charlotte, NC.

3758. Jason Larry Hodges (*Larry Joe Hodges*[7], *Lois Katherine Statom*[6], *Muncie Venetta Sharp*[5], *Berry Nolan*[4], *Joseph (Joe)*[3], *Charles W. Sr.*[2], *John Sr.*[1]) was born 13 Apr 1971 in Lauderdale County, AL.

Jason married **Melissa Kay Bevis**, daughter of **Loyal Thomas Bevis** and **Mary Jane Goodwin**, 1 Sep 1990 in Lauderdale County, AL. Melissa was born 17 Jun 1966 in Lauderdale County, AL.
5582 F   i.   **Kayla Breanne Hodges** was born 5 Mar 1991 in Lauderdale County, AL.
5583 M   ii.   **Casey Jay Hodges** was born 29 Jul 1992 in Lauderdale County, AL.

3759. Jeffrey Todd Zahnd (*Earl Douglas Zahnd II*[7], *Hilda Mae Statom*[6], *Muncie Venetta Sharp*[5], *Berry Nolan*[4], *Joseph (Joe)*[3], *Charles W. Sr.*[2], *John Sr.*[1]) was born 7 Jul 1962 in Lauderdale County, AL.

Jeffrey married **Kelly Lynn Haverkamp**, daughter of **William Haverkamp** and **Marilyn Brown**, 29 Nov 1982 in Lauderdale County, AL. Kelly was born 28 Feb 1964 in Landsthul, Germany.

3760. Earl Douglas Zahnd III (*Earl Douglas Zahnd II*[7], *Hilda Mae Statom*[6], *Muncie Venetta Sharp*[5], *Berry Nolan*[4], *Joseph (Joe)*[3], *Charles W. Sr.*[2], *John Sr.*[1]) was born 26 Dec 1994 in Lauderdale County, AL.

Earl married **Donna Sue Sheppard**, daughter of **Talmadge Lee Sheppard** and **Marcella Clemons**, 21 Oct 1994 in Lauderdale County, AL. Donna was born 28 Jun 1971.
5584 M   i.   **Travis (Taz) Arthur Zahnd** was born 24 Nov 1994.

3761. Philip Gene (Gino) Zahnd Jr. (*Philip Gene Zahnd Sr.*[7], *Hilda Mae Statom*[6], *Muncie Venetta Sharp*[5], *Berry Nolan*[4], *Joseph (Joe)*[3], *Charles W. Sr.*[2], *John Sr.*[1]) was born 28 Jun 1974 in Montgomery, AL.

Philip married **Claire Thompson Galp**.

3768. Lisa Michelle Hendon (*Patricia Gail Berkey*[7], *Mattie Jo Statom*[6], *Muncie Venetta Sharp*[5], *Berry Nolan*[4], *Joseph (Joe)*[3], *Charles W. Sr.*[2], *John Sr.*[1]) was born 31 Mar 1968 in Lauderdale County, AL.

Lisa married **Jeffrey Louis Bevis**, son of **Steven Ray Bevis** and **Susan Lucille Cook**, 27 Nov 1993. Jeffrey was born 4 Jun 1969 in Lauderdale County, AL.

3775. Randell Lee Sharp (*Harry Lee*[7], *James Dalton*[6], *James Leander*[5], *Benjamin Franklin*[4], *Joseph (Joe)*[3], *Charles W. Sr.*[2], *John Sr.*[1]) was born 24 Oct 1950 in Lauderdale County, AL.

Randell married **Kathy Jo Doty** 7 May 1973. Kathy was born 23 Feb 1953 in South Bend, IN.
5585 M   i.   **Daniel Lee Sharp** was born 7 Apr 1971 in South Bend, IN.

Randell next married **Janella Marie Yarbrough**. Janella was born 6 Jun 1963 in South Bend, IN.

3776. Jenna Lynn Sharp (*Harry Lee*[7], *James Dalton*[6], *James Leander*[5], *Benjamin Franklin*[4], *Joseph (Joe)*[3], *Charles W. Sr.*[2], *John Sr.*[1]) was born 8 Jan 1953 in South Bend, IN.

Jenna married **Marshall Leroy Steele Sr.** 12 Jun 1971 in South Bend, IN. Marshall was born 9 Mar 1951 in Mishawaka, St Joseph County, IN.

5586	F	i.	**Lanora Lynn Steele** was born 29 Mar 1972 in South Bend, IN, died 5 Apr 1972, and was buried in South Bend, IN.
5587	M	ii.	**Marshall Leroy Steele** was born 1 Sep 1973 in South Bend, IN.
5588	F	iii.	**Melinda Anne Steele** was born 11 Nov 1976 in South Bend, IN.

3777. Mark Adrian Sharp (*Harry Lee^7, James Dalton^6, James Leander^5, Benjamin Franklin^4, Joseph (Joe)^3, Charles W. Sr.^{2}, John Sr.^{1}*) was born 13 Dec 1954 in Mishawaka, St Joseph County, IN.

Mark married **Vera Amanda Bone**, daughter of **Homer Oliver Bone Sr.** and **Louise Elizabeth Day**, 17 Jun 1983 in Lauderdale County, AL. Vera was born 4 Sep 1961 in Lauderdale County, AL.

5589	M	i.	**Joshua Mark Sharp** was born 20 Jul 1984 in Lauderdale County, AL.
5590	F	ii.	**Jennifer Louise Sharp** was born 17 Sep 1985 in Lauderdale County, AL.
5591	F	iii.	**Abigail Grace Sharp** was born 18 Jun 1992 in Lauderdale County, AL.

3778. Glen David Austin Jr. (*Helen Elizabeth Sharp^7, James Dalton^6, James Leander^5, Benjamin Franklin^4, Joseph (Joe)^3, Charles W. Sr.^{2}, John Sr.^{1}*) was born 14 Aug 1957 in Lauderdale County, AL, died 19 Mar 2004, and was buried in Greenview Memorial Park, Florence, Lauderdale County, AL.

Glen married **Susan McKay**, daughter of **Clarence McKay** and **Jane Gregory**, 20 Oct 1978 in Lauderdale County, AL. Susan was born 14 Nov 1959 in Dallas, TX.

5592	M	i.	**Bradley David Austin** was born 15 Dec 1980 in Lauderdale County, AL.
5593	F	ii.	**Katherine (Katie) Austin** was born 2 Sep 1985 in Lauderdale County, AL.
5594	M	iii.	**Michael Bryan Austin** was born 3 Jul 1988 in Lauderdale County, AL.

3779. James Bryan Austin (*Helen Elizabeth Sharp^7, James Dalton^6, James Leander^5, Benjamin Franklin^4, Joseph (Joe)^3, Charles W. Sr.^{2}, John Sr.^{1}*) was born 13 Aug 1960 in Lauderdale County, AL.

James married **Marsha Lynn Dees**, daughter of **Lodis Roosevelt Dees** and **Louise Hardy**, 15 May 1987 in Lauderdale County, AL. Marsha was born 11 Apr 1961 in Saraland, AL.

| 5595 | F | i. | **Ashlee Marie Austin** was born 18 Nov 1985 in Lauderdale County, AL. |
| 5596 | F | ii. | **Anna Elizabeth Austin** was born 18 Dec 1987 in Lauderdale County, AL. |

3780. Patrick Shawn Sharp (*Bobby Montgomery^7, James Dalton^6, James Leander^5, Benjamin Franklin^4, Joseph (Joe)^3, Charles W. Sr.^{2}, John Sr.^{1}*) was born 24 Sep 1962 in Birmingham, Jefferson County, AL.

Patrick married **Chris Ann Plunkett**, daughter of **David Plunkett** and ***Unk Vogel**, 14 Feb 1982 in Longwood, FL. Chris was born 29 Dec 1961 in New York.

| 5597 | M | i. | **Patrick David Sharp** was born 29 Jan 1983 in Orange County, CA. |
| 5598 | M | ii. | **Matthew Shawn Sharp** was born 12 Mar 1985 in Orange County, CA. |

Patrick next married **Anita Smith**, daughter of **Hollis Carter Smith** and **Elizabeth Gail Bergin**, 22 Aug 1992 in Lauderdale County, AL. Anita was born 18 Jun 1967 in Lauderdale County, AL.

3781. Virginia Dawn Sharp (*Bobby Montgomery^7, James Dalton^6, James Leander^5, Benjamin Franklin^4, Joseph (Joe)^3, Charles W. Sr.^{2}, John Sr.^{1}*) was born 12 Jan 1964 in Lemoor, CA.

Virginia married **Phillip Flanagan Machules**, son of **Philip Thomas Machules** and **Ilene *Unk**, 14 Oct 1991 in Lake Mary, FL. Phillip was born 2 Aug 1964 in Staten Island, NY.

| 5599 | M | i. | **Evan Bernard Machules** was born 2 Dec 1994 in Orlando, FL. |
| 5600 | F | ii. | **Brendan Wilhelmina Machules** was born 2 Dec 1994 in Orlando, FL. |

3782. Todd Montgomery Sharp (*Bobby Montgomery^7, James Dalton^6, James Leander^5, Benjamin Franklin^4, Joseph (Joe)^3, Charles W. Sr.^{2}, John Sr.^{1}*) was born 2 Jul 1968 in Lauderdale County, AL.

Todd married **Torey Elizabeth Upham**, daughter of **Troy Lynn Upham** and **Francis Lea Baker**, 24 Nov 1993 in Colbert County, AL. Torey was born 12 Feb 1971 in Wichita Falls, TX.

5601 M i. **Braxton Adam Darby Sharp** was born 21 Feb 1993 in Colbert County, AL.

5602 F ii. **Allison Lea Marie Sharp** was born 28 Oct 1994 in Lauderdale County, AL.

3783. Tina Marlee Simmons (*Martha Wilhelminia Sharp*[7], *James Dalton*[6], *James Leander*[5], *Benjamin Franklin*[4], *Joseph (Joe)*[3], *Charles W. Sr.*[2], *John Sr.*[1]) was born 7 May 1962 in Lauderdale County, AL.

Tina married **James Bryan Martin**, son of **James Roco Martin Jr.** and **Glenda Morris**, 15 Jun 1990. James was born 26 Jan 1963 in Beaufort, SC.

5603 F i. **Abby Elizabeth Martin** was born 18 Mar 1993 in Huntsville, Madison County, AL.

5604 M ii. **William James Martin** was born 5 Jul 1995 in Huntsville, Madison County, AL.

3784. Kimberly Paige Simmons (*Martha Wilhelminia Sharp*[7], *James Dalton*[6], *James Leander*[5], *Benjamin Franklin*[4], *Joseph (Joe)*[3], *Charles W. Sr.*[2], *John Sr.*[1]) was born 3 Jul 1965 in Lauderdale County, AL.

Kimberly married **John Nelson McDonald Jr.**, son of **John Nelson McDonald Sr.** and **Mary Ethel Harrison**, 18 May 1985 in Lake Mary, FL. John was born 2 Dec 1964 in Lauderdale County, AL.
(Duplicate Line. See Person 2459)

3785. Bradley Robert Simmons (*Martha Wilhelminia Sharp*[7], *James Dalton*[6], *James Leander*[5], *Benjamin Franklin*[4], *Joseph (Joe)*[3], *Charles W. Sr.*[2], *John Sr.*[1]) was born 12 May 1968 in Lauderdale County, AL.

Bradley married **Tracie Lynn Robinson**, daughter of **Bobby William Robinson** and **Ann Kay May**, 12 Jun 1992 in Lauderdale County, AL.

3786. John Eric Simmons (*Martha Wilhelminia Sharp*[7], *James Dalton*[6], *James Leander*[5], *Benjamin Franklin*[4], *Joseph (Joe)*[3], *Charles W. Sr.*[2], *John Sr.*[1]) was born 18 Mar 1970 in Lauderdale County, AL.

John married **Tina Diane McCluskey**, daughter of **Larry McCluskey** and **Linda Lanier**, 26 Mar 1994 in Lauderdale County, AL. Tina was born 23 Jul 1969 in Lauderdale County, AL.

5605 F i. **Victoria Noel Simmons** was born 20 Dec 1995 in Lauderdale County, AL.

3787. Jason Allen Russell Sharp (*Richard Lynn (Rick)*[7], *James Dalton*[6], *James Leander*[5], *Benjamin Franklin*[4], *Joseph (Joe)*[3], *Charles W. Sr.*[2], *John Sr.*[1]) was born 8 May 1975 in Sumner County, TN.

General Notes: "Child by Mother's first husband, adopted by Richard Lynn Sharp..." Sharon Wood

Jason married **Shelly Mae Wiedemeyer**, daughter of **James Dale Wiedemeyer** and **Clara Louise Allen**, 18 Aug 1995 in Colbert County, AL. Shelly was born 8 Feb 1976 in Jefferson County, AL.

3788. Jessica (Jessie) Nicole Russell Sharp (*Richard Lynn (Rick)*[7], *James Dalton*[6], *James Leander*[5], *Benjamin Franklin*[4], *Joseph (Joe)*[3], *Charles W. Sr.*[2], *John Sr.*[1]) was born 20 Sep 1979 in Lauderdale County, AL.

General Notes: "Child by Mother's first husband, adopted by Richard Lynn Sharp..." Sharon Wood

Jessica married **Ronald Gene Morris**, son of **Larry Morris** and **Shirley Haynes**, 29 Dec 2000 in Lauderdale County, AL. Ronald was born 6 Nov 1974 in Lauderdale County, AL.

3789. Manuel Dale May (*Audrey Ruth Dixon*[7], *Thelma Mae Sharp*[6], *James Leander*[5], *Benjamin Franklin*[4], *Joseph (Joe)*[3], *Charles W. Sr.*[2], *John Sr.*[1]) was born 21 Jan 1954 in Lauderdale County, AL.

Manuel married **Deborah Estella Simpson** 4 Jan 1975 in Wayne County, TN.

+ 5606 F i. **Lasondra May** was born 21 Dec 1972 in Lauderdale County, AL.

5607 M ii. **Richard Dale May** was born 9 Nov 1975 in Lauderdale County, AL.

Manuel next married **Vickie *Unk**.

3790. Audrey Rebecca May (*Audrey Ruth Dixon^7, Thelma Mae Sharp^6, James Leander^5, Benjamin Franklin^4, Joseph (Joe)^3, Charles W. Sr.^{2}, John Sr.^{1}*) was born 14 Mar 1955 in Lauderdale County, AL.

Audrey married **Eugene Walden**, son of **Unknown** and **Modene Mayes**.
5608 M i. **Corey Eugene Walden** was born in Lauderdale County, AL.
5609 F ii. **Jennifer Leigh Walden** was born in Lauderdale County, AL.

3791. Wymon Lance May (*Audrey Ruth Dixon^7, Thelma Mae Sharp^6, James Leander^5, Benjamin Franklin^4, Joseph (Joe)^3, Charles W. Sr.^{2}, John Sr.^{1}*) was born 15 Dec 1960 in Lauderdale County, AL.

Wymon married **Susan Dale Fink**, daughter of **Earl L. Fink** and **Mary L. Momow**, 26 May 1981 in Wayne County, TN. Susan was born 24 May 1961 in Rockham County, VA.

3792. Deborah Diane May (*Audrey Ruth Dixon^7, Thelma Mae Sharp^6, James Leander^5, Benjamin Franklin^4, Joseph (Joe)^3, Charles W. Sr.^{2}, John Sr.^{1}*) was born 2 Sep 1962 in Lauderdale County, AL.

Deborah married **Ronnie Lawson**, son of **Bill Lawson** and **Rossie Hawks**.
5610 M i. **Ronnie Lynn Lawson** was born 27 Jan 1976 in Dyersburg, Dyer County, TN.
5611 F ii. **Starla Diannell Lawson** was born 26 Aug 1979 in Dyersburg, Dyer County, TN.

Deborah next married **Tomath (Tim) Litrel**.
5612 F i. **Tabena Litrel** was born 19 Nov 1987 in Lauderdale County, AL.
5613 M ii. **Joshaway Mark Litrel** was born 21 Sep 1994 in Lauderdale County, AL.

3793. Paula Dixon (*Robert Dale Dixon^7, Thelma Mae Sharp^6, James Leander^5, Benjamin Franklin^4, Joseph (Joe)^3, Charles W. Sr.^{2}, John Sr.^{1}*) was born 28 Dec 1966 in Lawrence County, TN.

Paula married **Clay Quillen**. Clay was born 7 Sep 1963 in Lawrence County, TN.
5614 M i. **Blake Quillen** was born 27 Nov 1983 in Lawrence County, TN.

3794. Emily Suzanne Smith (*Samuel (Sammie) Coy Smith^7, Mary Katherine Thrasher^6, Nora E. Sharp^5, Benjamin Franklin^4, Joseph (Joe)^3, Charles W. Sr.^{2}, John Sr.^{1}*) was born 16 May 1974 in Lauderdale County, AL.

Emily married **Matthew Norton Wilbanks**, son of **Don Warren Wilbanks** and **Brenda Norton**, 28 Dec 1996 in Lauderdale County, AL. Matthew was born 7 Nov 1970 in Germany.

3797. Mary Elizabeth (Beth) Sharp (*William David^7, Edwin Robert^6, Berry Robert^5, Benjamin Franklin^4, Joseph (Joe)^3, Charles W. Sr.^{2}, John Sr.^{1}*) was born 29 Aug 1961 in Lauderdale County, AL.

Mary married **Gregory Jones Harrison**, son of **Reece Mills Harrison** and **Mary Kathryn Jones**, 27 Apr 1984 in Lauderdale County, AL. Gregory was born 14 Sep 1962 in Lauderdale County, AL.
5615 M i. **Matthew Bryant Harrison** was born 16 Apr 1987 in Lauderdale County, AL.
5616 F ii. **Ashleigh Elizabeth Harrison** was born 28 Jun 1990 in Lauderdale County, AL.
5617 F iii. **Carley Marie Harrison** was born 26 Mar 1996 in Lauderdale County, AL.

3799. James Robert Sharp Jr. (*James Robert Sr.^{7}, Edwin Robert^6, Berry Robert^5, Benjamin Franklin^4, Joseph (Joe)^3, Charles W. Sr.^{2}, John Sr.^{1}*) was born 13 Aug 1965 in Lauderdale County, AL.

James married **Emily Zane Sommer**, daughter of **Jerry Lynn Sommer** and **Linda Kaye Townsley**, 14 Jun 1985 in Lauderdale County, AL. Emily was born 6 Nov 1965 in Lauderdale County, AL.
5618 F i. **Molly Marie Sharp** was born 29 Jun 1987 in Lauderdale County, AL.
5619 F ii. **Maggie Mae Sharp** was born 25 Dec 1995 in Lauderdale County, AL.

3800. Tambriana Dee Sharp (*James Robert Sr.^{7}, Edwin Robert^6, Berry Robert^5, Benjamin Franklin^4, Joseph (Joe)^3, Charles W. Sr.^{2}, John Sr.^{1}*) was born 5 Sep 1968 in Lauderdale County, AL.

Tambriana married **Jeffrey Taylor Haase**, son of **Jerry Haase** and **Marsha *Unk**, in Dec 1991 in Virginia. Jeffrey was born 8 Nov 1966 in Missouri.

5620 F   i.   **Julia Alexandria Haase** was born 24 Feb 1987 in Lauderdale County, AL.

Tambriana next married **Robert Dale Sherrod II**, son of **Robert Dale Sherrod I** and **Myra Grimes**, in Nov 1994 in Tennessee.

5621 F   i.   **Mary Jordon Sherrod** was born 24 Mar 1993 in Lauderdale County, AL.
5622 F   ii.   **Tori Caitlin Sherrod** was born 9 Feb 1995 in Colbert County, AL.
5623 M iii. **Robert Dale Sherrod III** was born 11 Mar 1997 in Lauderdale County, AL.

3801. Jeri Khristy Sharp (*James Robert Sr.*[7], *Edwin Robert*[6], *Berry Robert*[5], *Benjamin Franklin*[4], *Joseph (Joe)*[3], *Charles W. Sr.*[2], *John Sr.*[1]) was born 11 Oct 1971 in Lauderdale County, AL.

Jeri married **Marty K. Wilkinson**, son of **Kevin Wilkinson** and **Ronda McAllister**, 15 Mar 1997 in St. George, UT. Marty was born 19 Jul 1976 in Utah.

5624 M   i.   **Son Wilkerson** was born in Oct 1998 in Colbert County, AL.

3802. David Hayes Sharp (*James Robert Sr.*[7], *Edwin Robert*[6], *Berry Robert*[5], *Benjamin Franklin*[4], *Joseph (Joe)*[3], *Charles W. Sr.*[2], *John Sr.*[1]) was born 29 Feb 1980 in Colbert County, AL.

David married **Elizabeth Reece Graves**, daughter of **Rodney Graves** and **Carol *Unk**, 19 May 2001 in Lauderdale County, AL. Elizabeth was born in Oct 1979 in Lauderdale County, AL.

5625 M   i.   **Reece Adair Sharp** was born 23 Nov 2001 in Lauderdale County, AL.

3803. Lesley Lynn Posey (*Linda Ann Sharp*[7], *William Frank*[6], *Berry Robert*[5], *Benjamin Franklin*[4], *Joseph (Joe)*[3], *Charles W. Sr.*[2], *John Sr.*[1]) was born 14 Nov 1965 in Madison County, AL.

Lesley married **Darryl Wendell Burnette Sr.**, son of **Johnny Burnette** and **Faye Hayes**, 20 May 1989 in Huntsville, Madison County, AL. Darryl was born 5 Aug 1965 in Chilton County, AL.

5626 M   i.   **John Wendell Burnette Jr.** was born 12 Jun 1995 in Huntsville, Madison County, AL.
5627 F   ii.   **Kathryn May Burnette** was born 28 Jun 2001 in Huntsville, Madison County, AL.

3812. Anthony Todd Young (*Myra Elyne Lard*[7], *Beatrice E. Cagle*[6], *Ethel Belle Sharp*[5], *Benjamin Franklin*[4], *Joseph (Joe)*[3], *Charles W. Sr.*[2], *John Sr.*[1]) was born 13 Dec 1962 in Lauderdale County, AL.

Anthony married **Sherry Lynn Mullins**, daughter of **Bobby Mullins** and **Patricia Baily**, 4 Oct 1986 in Beuford, SC. Sherry was born 15 Oct 1959 in Jacksonville, NC.

5628 F   i.   **Ashley Nicole Young** was born 6 Jul 1987 in Altamonte Springs, FL.
5629 F   ii.   **Sumantha Ann Young** was born 19 Mar 1992 in Altamonte Springs, FL.
5630 F   iii. **Savannah Elyne Young** was born 19 Mar 1992 in Altamonte Springs, FL.

3813. Amanda Layne Young (*Myra Elyne Lard*[7], *Beatrice E. Cagle*[6], *Ethel Belle Sharp*[5], *Benjamin Franklin*[4], *Joseph (Joe)*[3], *Charles W. Sr.*[2], *John Sr.*[1]) was born 28 Aug 1963 in Lauderdale County, AL.

Amanda married **David Dwayne Rumble**, son of **Victor N. Rumble** and **Doris Moore**, 19 Oct 1985 in Lauderdale County, AL. David was born 13 Jun 1961 in Colbert County, AL.

5631 M   i.   **Cody Rumble**.
5632 F   ii.   **Deanna Rumble**.
5633 F   iii. **Magan Rumble**.

3815. Lyndell Shawn Waldrep (*Lynda Gale Lard*[7], *Beatrice E. Cagle*[6], *Ethel Belle Sharp*[5], *Benjamin Franklin*[4], *Joseph (Joe)*[3], *Charles W. Sr.*[2], *John Sr.*[1]) was born 19 Oct 1968 in Colbert County, AL.

Lyndell married **Heather Leigh Hanback**, daughter of **David Lynn Hanback** and **Janice Wyonell Sandlin**, 21 Sep 1996 in Lauderdale County, AL. Heather was born 20 Apr 1972 in Lauderdale County, AL.

3816. Ladonice Waldrep (*Lynda Gale Lard*[7], *Beatrice E. Cagle*[6], *Ethel Belle Sharp*[5], *Benjamin Franklin*[4], *Joseph (Joe)*[3], *Charles W. Sr.*[2], *John Sr.*[1]) was born 19 Oct 1968.

Ladonice married **Stefan Neamtu**.

3817. Gregory Ernest Pena Penya (*Vivi Don Lard*[7], *Beatrice E. Cagle*[6], *Ethel Belle Sharp*[5], *Benjamin Franklin*[4], *Joseph (Joe)*[3], *Charles W. Sr.*[2], *John Sr.*[1]) was born 2 May 1968 in Atlanta, Fulton County, GA.

Gregory married **Gina Ann Hale**, daughter of **Gene Hale** and **Dorothy *Unk**, 10 Dec 1988 in Kings Mountain, NC. Gina was born 3 Dec 1969 in Cleveland County, NC.

| 5634 | M | i. | **Victor Scott Pena Penya** was born 28 Oct 1996 in Gastonia, NC. |

3818. Eric Ranier Penya (*Vivi Don Lard*[7], *Beatrice E. Cagle*[6], *Ethel Belle Sharp*[5], *Benjamin Franklin*[4], *Joseph (Joe)*[3], *Charles W. Sr.*[2], *John Sr.*[1]) was born 10 Nov 1970 in Atlanta, Fulton County, GA.

Eric married **Margaret Michelle Hassel**, daughter of **Robert Hassel** and **Gretchen *Unk**, 16 Sep 1995 in Richmond, VA. Margaret was born 5 Nov 1970 in Richmond, VA.

3819. Robbie Linn Cagle (*Lindon Loyd Cagle*[7], *Lloyd Brooke Cagle*[6], *Ethel Belle Sharp*[5], *Benjamin Franklin*[4], *Joseph (Joe)*[3], *Charles W. Sr.*[2], *John Sr.*[1]) was born 22 Jul 1965 in Peoria, IL.

Robbie married **Jill Pollman**.

5635	F	i.	**Adrienne Linn Cagle** was born 29 Jan 1990 in Denver, CO.
5636	F	ii.	**Kierstyn Sarah Cagle** was born 29 Jun 1992 in Pekin, IL.
5637	F	iii.	**Brieanna Pollman Cagle** was born 16 May 1994(?) in Pekin, IL.

3820. Leisa Joann Cagle (*Lindon Loyd Cagle*[7], *Lloyd Brooke Cagle*[6], *Ethel Belle Sharp*[5], *Benjamin Franklin*[4], *Joseph (Joe)*[3], *Charles W. Sr.*[2], *John Sr.*[1]) was born 23 Aug 1967 in Peoria, IL.

Leisa married **Brad Foiles**.

5638	F	i.	**Kayla Nicole Foiles** was born 2 Oct 1987 in Peoria, IL.
5639	M	ii.	**Beau Bradley Foiles** was born 9 Sep 1989 in Peoria, IL.
5640	M	iii.	**Mackenzie Jordan Foiles** was born 12 Jan 1991 in Peoria, IL.
5641	F	iv.	**Ryelee Mae Morgan Foiles** was born 22 Oct 1994 in Peoria, IL.

3830. Christy Louise Hinton (*Mary Diane Cagle*[7], *William Edward Cagle Jr.*[6], *Ethel Belle Sharp*[5], *Benjamin Franklin*[4], *Joseph (Joe)*[3], *Charles W. Sr.*[2], *John Sr.*[1]) was born 2 Jul 1971 in Lauderdale County, AL.

Christy married **Jerry Lynn Tingle**, son of **Jerry M. Tingle** and **Glenda Scott**, 30 Oct 1987 in Lauderdale County, AL. Jerry was born 20 Mar 1970 in Lauderdale County, AL.

3834. Jennifer Yvonne Hayes (*Teresa Yvonne Cagle*[7], *William Edward Cagle Jr.*[6], *Ethel Belle Sharp*[5], *Benjamin Franklin*[4], *Joseph (Joe)*[3], *Charles W. Sr.*[2], *John Sr.*[1]) was born 20 Aug 1972 in Lauderdale County, AL.

Jennifer married **Bryan Keith Liles**, son of **William Lee Liles** and **Deborah Diane White**, 25 Jan 1992 in Lauderdale County, AL. Bryan was born 31 Oct 1970 in Alabama.

| 5642 | M | i. | **Michael Keith Liles** was born 19 Dec 1992 in Lauderdale County, AL. |
| 5643 | M | ii. | **Timothy Liles** was born in Lauderdale County, AL. |

3842. Gregory Lee Riley (*Cathy Sue Lawson*[7], *Fayna (Faye) Cagle*[6], *Ethel Belle Sharp*[5], *Benjamin Franklin*[4], *Joseph (Joe)*[3], *Charles W. Sr.*[2], *John Sr.*[1]) was born 30 Oct 1970.

Gregory married **Rania Davis**.

3850. Michael Erick Richardson (*Joyce Lynn Kelley*[7], *Mary Opel Hill*[6], *Maggie Leona Sharp*[5], *Benjamin Franklin*[4], *Joseph (Joe)*[3], *Charles W. Sr.*[2], *John Sr.*[1]) was born 18 Mar 1982 in Colbert County, AL.

Michael married **Letha Rose McKinney**, daughter of **Robert (Bobby) W. McKinney** and **Unknown**, 2 Oct 1994 in Colbert County, AL.

5644 M i. **Seth Bradford Richardson** was born 15 Jul 1997 in Huntsville, Madison County, AL.

3854. Stacy Jane Sharp (*Vernon Howard^7, Turner L. Sr.^{6}, Charles Edward (Eddie)^5, John Levi^4, Charles W. II^3, Charles W. Sr.^{2}, John Sr.^{1}*) was born 28 Sep 1968 in Savannah, Hardin County, TN.

Stacy married **Dewey J. Smith** 25 Jul 1992 in Savannah, Hardin County, TN.

3857. Mandi Eilee Greene (*David Craig Greene I^7, Rita Faye Hill^6, Alice Maxwell Sharp^5, John Levi^4, Charles W. II^3, Charles W. Sr.^{2}, John Sr.^{1}*) was born 3 Aug 1979 in Apple Valley, CA.

Mandi married ***Unk Guerra**.
5645 M i. **David Paul Guerra** was born 16 Nov 1997 in Apple Valley, CA.

3859. Angela Carmon Blackburn (*Charles Everett Blackburn^7, Willie Carmen Box^6, James (Jim) W. Box^5, Amanda Jane Sharp^4, Charles W. II^3, Charles W. Sr.^{2}, John Sr.^{1}*) was born 18 Jan 1970 in Spartanburg County, SC.

Angela married **David Lee Hunt**, son of **Travis Lynn Hunt** and **Betty Bostick**, 22 Oct 1994 in Tyler, Smith County, TX. David was born 8 Feb 1968 in Fort Worth, TX.
5646 M i. **Austin Hunt**.
5647 M ii. **Jonah Hunt**.

3861. Gregory (Greg) Thomas Box (*Thomas Carroll Box^7, John Carroll (J. C.) Box Sr.^{6}, James (Jim) W. Box^5, Amanda Jane Sharp^4, Charles W. II^3, Charles W. Sr.^{2}, John Sr.^{1}*) was born 3 Jun 1956 in Lauderdale County, AL.

Gregory married **Sherry Denise Winborn**, daughter of **William C. Winborn** and **Sonola L. Bell**, 30 Apr 1976. Sherry was born 29 Mar 1956 in Lauderdale County, AL.
+ 5648 F i. **Erica Faith Box** was born 24 Dec.
5649 F ii. **Jessica Lynn Box**.
5650 M iii. **Jared Box**.

3862. James Windell Box (*Thomas Carroll Box^7, John Carroll (J. C.) Box Sr.^{6}, James (Jim) W. Box^5, Amanda Jane Sharp^4, Charles W. II^3, Charles W. Sr.^{2}, John Sr.^{1}*) was born 15 May 1959 in Lauderdale County, AL.

James married **Sarah Smallwood**.

3863. Donna Jo Box (*Donald Andrew Box^7, John Carroll (J. C.) Box Sr.^{6}, James (Jim) W. Box^5, Amanda Jane Sharp^4, Charles W. II^3, Charles W. Sr.^{2}, John Sr.^{1}*) was born 27 Mar 1961 in Lauderdale County, AL.

Donna married **Terry David Richardson**, son of **David L. Richardson** and **Wanda Brockwell**, 29 Jun 1981 in Lauderdale County, AL. Terry was born 11 Sep 1960 in Lauderdale County, AL.

3864. Teresa Ann Box (*Donald Andrew Box^7, John Carroll (J. C.) Box Sr.^{6}, James (Jim) W. Box^5, Amanda Jane Sharp^4, Charles W. II^3, Charles W. Sr.^{2}, John Sr.^{1}*) was born 14 Oct 1962 in Lauderdale County, AL.

Teresa married **Kenneth Russell Lawler**, son of **Glenn R. Lawler** and **Leatrice Cooper**, 11 Nov 1983 in Lauderdale County, AL. Kenneth was born 5 May 1962 in Russellville, Franklin County, AL.
5651 F i. **Erin Grace Lawler** was born 11 Jun 1988 in Lauderdale County, AL.
5652 M ii. **Caleb Andrew Lawler** was born 27 Jun 1991 in Lauderdale County, AL.

3865. Judy Darlene Box (*Donald Andrew Box^7, John Carroll (J. C.) Box Sr.^{6}, James (Jim) W. Box^5, Amanda Jane Sharp^4, Charles W. II^3, Charles W. Sr.^{2}, John Sr.^{1}*) was born 19 Dec 1963.

Judy married **Tyron Wayne Duncan**, son of **Richard L. Duncan** and **Evelyn Kelly**, 11 Mar 1983. Tyron was born 2 Jun 1962 in Lauderdale County, AL.

Judy next married **Anthony Dena** in 1990.

3869. Donna Jean Gray (*John Hines Gray[7], Vera Anderson[6], Charles David Anderson Sr.[5], Mary Elizabeth (Molly) Sharp[4], Charles W. II[3], Charles W. Sr.[2], John Sr.[1]*) was born 9 May 1959 in Lauderdale County, AL.

Donna married ***Unk Miller**.

3879. Robert Lance Brown (*Carolyn Joan Balentine[7], Lucille Anderson[6], Charles David Anderson Sr.[5], Mary Elizabeth (Molly) Sharp[4], Charles W. II[3], Charles W. Sr.[2], John Sr.[1]*) was born 12 Jul 1971 in Lauderdale County, AL.

Robert married **Mary Lynn Walden** 16 Dec 1989 in Lauderdale County, AL.
5653 M i. **Cody Lance Brown** was born 15 May 1990 in Lauderdale County, AL.

3894. Christopher Shannon Wright (*Jerry Wade Wright[7], Clora Ovrille Dowdy[6], Hosea (Hozie) Durille Dowdy[5], Rachel Ann (Babe) Sharp[4], Charles W. II[3], Charles W. Sr.[2], John Sr.[1]*) was born 14 Apr 1969 in Colbert County, AL.

Christopher married **Tabitha Suzanne Whitehead**, daughter of **Fred Raymond Whitehead** and **Imogene Phillips**, 23 May 1995 in Lauderdale County, AL. Tabitha was born 15 Mar 1964 in Colbert County, AL.
5654 M i. **Shane Thomas Wright** was born 4 Aug 2000 in Lauderdale County, AL.

3896. Cynthia (Cindy) Lea Wright (*Timothy Elliot Wright[7], Clora Ovrille Dowdy[6], Hosea (Hozie) Durille Dowdy[5], Rachel Ann (Babe) Sharp[4], Charles W. II[3], Charles W. Sr.[2], John Sr.[1]*) was born 22 Jan 1965 in Lauderdale County, AL.

Cynthia married **Neal B. Rhodes**, son of **Delbert Coy Rhodes Sr.** and **Eliane Rich**, 15 Oct 1983 in Lauderdale County, AL. Neal was born 1 Oct 1965 in Lauderdale County, AL.
5655 M i. **Wesley Adam Rhodes** was born 8 Mar 1988 in Lauderdale County, AL.
5656 M ii. **Will Evan Rhodes** was born 1 Dec 1990 in Liberty County, GA.

3897. Candace (Candi) Lynn Wright (*Timothy Elliot Wright[7], Clora Ovrille Dowdy[6], Hosea (Hozie) Durille Dowdy[5], Rachel Ann (Babe) Sharp[4], Charles W. II[3], Charles W. Sr.[2], John Sr.[1]*) was born 20 Jan 1968 in Lauderdale County, AL.

Candace married **Micah Allen**, son of **Morris Allen** and **Faye Wesson**, 17 Jul 1987 in Lauderdale County, AL. Micah was born 4 Jul 1967 in Lauderdale County, AL.
5657 M i. **Seth Tyler Allen** was born 4 Jul 1992 in Lauderdale County, AL.
5658 F ii. **Chloe Denise Allen** was born 1 Oct 1995 in Lauderdale County, AL.

3898. Ethan Elliot Wright (*Timothy Elliot Wright[7], Clora Ovrille Dowdy[6], Hosea (Hozie) Durille Dowdy[5], Rachel Ann (Babe) Sharp[4], Charles W. II[3], Charles W. Sr.[2], John Sr.[1]*) was born 9 Jan 1972 in Lauderdale County, AL.

Ethan married **Nikky Marie Waldrep**, daughter of **Larry Angus Waldrep** and **Patsy Marie Sharp**, 25 Feb 1994 in Lauderdale County, AL. Nikky was born 13 Jun 1975 in Colbert County, AL, died 22 Jul 2003, and was buried in Cherokee Memorial Park, Colbert County, AL.

3899. Matthew Wayne Wright (*Horace Lanny Wright[7], Clora Ovrille Dowdy[6], Hosea (Hozie) Durille Dowdy[5], Rachel Ann (Babe) Sharp[4], Charles W. II[3], Charles W. Sr.[2], John Sr.[1]*) was born 11 Oct 1970 in Lauderdale County, AL.

Matthew married **Monica Leigh Nichols**, daughter of **Ronald Elroy Nichols** and **Imogene Irons**, 24 Jul 1994 in Lauderdale County, AL. Monica was born 17 Sep 1971 in Colbert County, AL.
5659 M i. **Dalton Alex Wright** was born 15 Apr 1997 in Colbert County, AL.

3908. Pamela Jean Pollard (*Omi Jean Watkins[7], Mary Louise Stults[6], Linnie Mae Sharp[5], Thomas (Tom) Erwin[4], Charles W. II[3], Charles W. Sr.[2], John Sr.[1]*) was born 11 Feb 1959 in Lauderdale County, AL.

Pamela married **John Clark Burns**, son of **Charles C. Burns** and **Joyce Sanderson**, 2 Feb 1982 in Lauderdale County, AL. John was born 20 Nov 1957 in Odessa, FL and died 26 Jun 1992.

5660	F	i.	**Pamela Rachel Burns** was born 24 Jan 1985 in Lauderdale County, AL.
5661	M	ii.	**John Clark Burns** was born 30 Jul 1988 in Lauderdale County, AL.
5662	M	iii.	**Daniel Gregory Burns** was born 7 Feb 1990 in Lauderdale County, AL.

3909. Donell Theodore Pollard Jr. (*Omi Jean Watkins*^{7}, *Mary Louise Stults*^{6}, *Linnie Mae Sharp*^{5}, *Thomas (Tom) Erwin*^{4}, *Charles W. II*^{3}, *Charles W. Sr.*^{2}, *John Sr.*^{1}) was born 10 Nov 1960 in Lauderdale County, AL.

Donell married **Sherrie Lynn Woods**, daughter of **Dale G. Woods** and **Sherrin Deitz**, 1 Mar 1981 in Lauderdale County, AL. Sherrie was born 26 Dec 1960 in Lauderdale County, AL.

+ 5663 F   i.   **Michelle Lynn Pollard** was born 5 Apr 1982 in Lauderdale County, AL.

3910. Teresa Anne Pollard (*Omi Jean Watkins*^{7}, *Mary Louise Stults*^{6}, *Linnie Mae Sharp*^{5}, *Thomas (Tom) Erwin*^{4}, *Charles W. II*^{3}, *Charles W. Sr.*^{2}, *John Sr.*^{1}) was born 26 Jan 1969 in Lauderdale County, AL.

Teresa married **Harold Lee Smith**. Harold was born in Sep.

5664	M	i.	**Samuel Lee Smith** was born 2 May.
5665	F	ii.	**Olivia Anne Smith**.

3911. Daniel Irving Pollard Jr. (*Earline Watkins*^{7}, *Mary Louise Stults*^{6}, *Linnie Mae Sharp*^{5}, *Thomas (Tom) Erwin*^{4}, *Charles W. II*^{3}, *Charles W. Sr.*^{2}, *John Sr.*^{1}) was born 26 Aug 1959 in Opelika, Lee County, AL.

Daniel married **Susan Scofield** 24 Nov 1984.

3912. Anthony K. Pollard (*Earline Watkins*^{7}, *Mary Louise Stults*^{6}, *Linnie Mae Sharp*^{5}, *Thomas (Tom) Erwin*^{4}, *Charles W. II*^{3}, *Charles W. Sr.*^{2}, *John Sr.*^{1}) was born 20 Sep 1961 in Huntsville, Madison County, AL.

Anthony married **Elaine Katos** 11 Jun 1988.

3913. Tracy L. Pollard (*Earline Watkins*^{7}, *Mary Louise Stults*^{6}, *Linnie Mae Sharp*^{5}, *Thomas (Tom) Erwin*^{4}, *Charles W. II*^{3}, *Charles W. Sr.*^{2}, *John Sr.*^{1}) was born 2 Mar 1963 in Huntsville, Madison County, AL.

Tracy married **Annah Humphrey** 4 Oct 1986.

3914. Kimberly D. Pollard (*Earline Watkins*^{7}, *Mary Louise Stults*^{6}, *Linnie Mae Sharp*^{5}, *Thomas (Tom) Erwin*^{4}, *Charles W. II*^{3}, *Charles W. Sr.*^{2}, *John Sr.*^{1}) was born 11 Jan 1966 in Huntsville, Madison County, AL.

Kimberly married **John Terrell** 28 Sep 1991.

3915. Angie Kaye Thompson (*Bobbie Sue Watkins*^{7}, *Mary Louise Stults*^{6}, *Linnie Mae Sharp*^{5}, *Thomas (Tom) Erwin*^{4}, *Charles W. II*^{3}, *Charles W. Sr.*^{2}, *John Sr.*^{1}) was born 21 Oct 1960 in Lauderdale County, AL.

Angie married **Brentley Alan Tyra**, son of **Floyd Tyra** and **Betty Tittle**, 21 Aug 1982 in Colbert County, AL. Brentley was born 23 Sep 1960.

5666	F	i.	**Morgan Elizabeth Tyra** was born 2 Jan 1986 in Birmingham, Jefferson County, AL.
5667	F	ii.	**Hannah Catherine Tyra** was born 15 Apr 1991 in Birmingham, Jefferson County, AL.
5668	M	iii.	**Carter Alan Tyra** was born 26 Jul 1993 in Birmingham, Jefferson County, AL.

3917. Mary Paula Thompson (*Bobbie Sue Watkins*^{7}, *Mary Louise Stults*^{6}, *Linnie Mae Sharp*^{5}, *Thomas (Tom) Erwin*^{4}, *Charles W. II*^{3}, *Charles W. Sr.*^{2}, *John Sr.*^{1}) was born 4 Apr 1966 in Lauderdale County, AL.

Mary married **Howard Dewayne Spurlock**, son of **Howard Earl Spurlock** and **Linda *Unk**, 15 Jun 1995 in Gatlinburg, TN.

5669 F   i.   **Mallory Danille Spurlock** was born 17 Jan 1996 in Lauderdale County, AL.

3918. Jana Lynn Watkins (*Charles Lee Watkins*[7]*, Mary Louise Stults*[6]*, Linnie Mae Sharp*[5]*, Thomas (Tom) Erwin*[4]*, Charles W. II*[3]*, Charles W. Sr.*[2]*, John Sr.*[1]) was born 30 Dec 1971 in Lauderdale County, AL.

Jana married **Richard Scott Kruse**, son of **David Kruse** and **Jeanett Nebel**, 3 Mar 2001 in Chattanooga, Cumberland County, TN. Richard was born 22 Oct 1970 in Cyrstal Lake, IL.

3920. Cynthia Ann Peden (*Tommie Jo Stults*[7]*, Thomas Joel Stults*[6]*, Linnie Mae Sharp*[5]*, Thomas (Tom) Erwin*[4]*, Charles W. II*[3]*, Charles W. Sr.*[2]*, John Sr.*[1]) was born 10 Apr 1961 in Lauderdale County, AL.

Cynthia married **Charles Leon Cromwell Jr.**, son of **Charles Leon Cromwell Sr.** and **Edith Faye Roberson**, 16 Dec 1978 in Lauderdale County, AL. Charles was born 16 Nov 1958 in Lauderdale County, AL.
5670 M i. **Daniel Joseph Cromwell** was born 28 Apr 1984 in Lauderdale County, AL.

Cynthia next married **Vincent Farris Burney**, son of **Farris Weldon Burney** and **Mavis Arlene Morris**. Vincent was born 7 Dec 1965 in Lauderdale County, AL.
5671 F i. **Rebekah Cromwell Burney** was born 30 Apr 1985 in Lauderdale County, AL.

3921. Ella Reenea Peden (*Tommie Jo Stults*[7]*, Thomas Joel Stults*[6]*, Linnie Mae Sharp*[5]*, Thomas (Tom) Erwin*[4]*, Charles W. II*[3]*, Charles W. Sr.*[2]*, John Sr.*[1]) was born 1 Sep 1962 in Lauderdale County, AL.

Ella married **David Glenn Newberry Sr.**, son of **Glenn Dale Newberry** and **Lura Dean Vaughn**, 8 Jun 1989 in Lauderdale County, AL. David was born 23 Aug 1960 in Lauderdale County, AL.
5672 M i. **David Glenn Newberry Jr.** was born 21 Nov 1997 in Colbert County, AL.

3922. Sandra Olean Peden (*Tommie Jo Stults*[7]*, Thomas Joel Stults*[6]*, Linnie Mae Sharp*[5]*, Thomas (Tom) Erwin*[4]*, Charles W. II*[3]*, Charles W. Sr.*[2]*, John Sr.*[1]) was born 6 Nov 1964.

Sandra married ***Unk White**.
5673 F i. **Ronica Joline White** was born in Colbert County, AL.

3923. Sammy Carter Stults Jr. (*Sammy Carter Stults Sr.*[7]*, Thomas Joel Stults*[6]*, Linnie Mae Sharp*[5]*, Thomas (Tom) Erwin*[4]*, Charles W. II*[3]*, Charles W. Sr.*[2]*, John Sr.*[1]) was born 16 Aug 1965 in Lauderdale County, AL.

Sammy married **Melanie James**, daughter of **Charles James** and **Phyliss Nolan**, 24 Jun 1983. Melanie was born 1 Apr 1966 in Lauderdale County, AL.
5674 M i. **William Carter Stults** was born 24 Sep 1983 in Lauderdale County, AL.
5675 M ii. **Catlin Bryant Stults** was born 6 Oct 1985 in Idaho Falls, ID.
5676 F iii. **Maddine Rose Stults** was born 16 Feb 1996 in Auburn, NE.

3924. Ponda Lynn Stults (*Sammy Carter Stults Sr.*[7]*, Thomas Joel Stults*[6]*, Linnie Mae Sharp*[5]*, Thomas (Tom) Erwin*[4]*, Charles W. II*[3]*, Charles W. Sr.*[2]*, John Sr.*[1]) was born 18 Jan 1969 in Lauderdale County, AL.

Ponda married **Charles Elliote Gordon**, son of **Charles Eugene Gordon** and **Ann Blackstock**, 31 Aug 1991 in Franklin County, AL. Charles was born 15 Aug 1970 in Atlanta, Fulton County, GA.
5677 F i. **Catelynn Elaine Gordon** was born 25 May 1995 in Franklin County, AL.
5678 M ii. **Charles Samuel Gordon** was born 15 Sep 1998 in Franklin County, AL.

3927. Laura Madden Branyon (*Judith Ann (Judy) Stults*[7]*, Thomas Joel Stults*[6]*, Linnie Mae Sharp*[5]*, Thomas (Tom) Erwin*[4]*, Charles W. II*[3]*, Charles W. Sr.*[2]*, John Sr.*[1]) was born 25 Apr 1970 in Lauderdale County, AL.

Laura married **Mike Carter** in Mar 1989 in Orlando, FL. Mike was born in Orlando, FL.
5679 F i. **Rebecca LeAnn Carter** was born 2 Aug 1991 in Orlando, FL.
5680 M ii. **Joshua Carter** was born in Orlando, FL.

3933. Holly Lee Waldrep (*Patsy Marie Sharp[7], David Guy[6], Guy Thomas[5], Thomas (Tom) Erwin[4], Charles W. II[3], Charles W. Sr.[2], John Sr.[1]*) was born 7 Dec 1970 in Colbert County, AL.

Holly married **Michael Anthony Morrison**, son of **Joseph Morrison Jr.** and **Brenda Sue Richardson**, 23 Mar 1990 in Colbert County, AL. Michael was born 13 Dec 1969 in Lauderdale County, AL.

Back: Alexander "Alex" and Rhett Morrison
Front: Michael, Holly Waldrep and Braden Morrison

5681	M	i.	**Michael Alexander (Alex) Morrison** was born 29 Dec 1991 in Nashville, Davidson County, TN.
5682	M	ii.	**Rhett Gannon Morrison** was born 1 Jan 1997 in Colbert County, AL.
5683	M	iii.	**Braden Jacob Morrison** was born 11 Nov 1998 in Colbert County, AL.

3934. Nikky Marie Waldrep (*Patsy Marie Sharp[7], David Guy[6], Guy Thomas[5], Thomas (Tom) Erwin[4], Charles W. II[3], Charles W. Sr.[2], John Sr.[1]*) was born 13 Jun 1975 in Colbert County, AL, died 22 Jul 2003, and was buried in Cherokee Memorial Park, Colbert County, AL.

General Notes: Obituary, Times Daily, July 24, 2003, Florence, Lauderdale County, Alabama

"Nikky Waldrep, 28, of Muscle Shoals, died July, 22, 2003. Visitation will be Friday, July 25, 2003, from noon until 2 p.m. at Morrison Funeral Home, Cherokee. Her funeral service will immediately follow in the funeral home chapel. Interment will be in Cherokee Memorial Park.
Nikky was a Colbert County native, member of Oakland Church of Christ and was employed by Circle Five Outfit. She was preceded in death by her grandparents, Angus and Stella Waldrep.
Survivors include her parents, Larry and Patsy Waldrep; and sister, Holly Morrison, all of Muscle Shoals; grandparents, David and Cordelia Sharp of Florence.
Pallbearers are Tim Waldrep, Tim Trousdale, Jimmy King, Mickey Vess, David Smith and Glenn Murphy. Honorary pallbearers are her special nephews, Alex, Rhett and Braden Morrison.
In lieu of flowers, memorials may be made to St. Jude Children's Research Hospital or Helping Hands. Morrison Funeral Home, Cherokee, is directing."

Nikky married **Ethan Elliot Wright**, son of **Timothy Elliot Wright** and **Janice Kathleen Rickard**, 25 Feb 1994 in Lauderdale County, AL. Ethan was born 9 Jan 1972 in Lauderdale County, AL.
(Duplicate Line. See Person 3898)

3947. James Hoyt Boatright Jr. (*James Hoyt Boatright Sr.[7], Lady Goldie Saddler[6], Cora Young[5], Matilda Ann White[4], Eliza Jane Sharp[3], Charles W. Sr.[2], John Sr.[1]*) was born 27 Jul 1946 in Lauderdale County, AL.

James married **Betty Ruth Vickers**, daughter of **Benjamin F. Vickers** and **Lamander Whitlock**, 1 Sep 1967 in Lauderdale County, AL. Betty was born 21 Feb 1949 in Colbert County, AL.

| + 5684 | F | i. | **Tammy Alene Boatright** was born 4 May 1970 in Lauderdale County, AL. |

3950. Steven Mitchell Boatright Sr. (*James Hoyt Boatright Sr.[7], Lady Goldie Saddler[6], Cora Young[5], Matilda Ann White[4], Eliza Jane Sharp[3], Charles W. Sr.[2], John Sr.[1]*) was born 4 Mar 1955 in Lauderdale County, AL.

Steven married **Joan Marie Fox**, daughter of **Cecil Alexander Fox** and **Lou Jean Higgins**, 24 Jul 1975 in Savannah, TN. Joan was born 24 Jul 1955 in Hardin County, TN.

| 5685 | M | i. | **Steven Mitchell Boatright Jr.** was born 8 Jul 1978 in Lauderdale County, AL. |
| 5686 | M | ii. | **Jonathan Michael Boatright** was born 4 Jul 1982 in Lauderdale County, AL. |

3951. Brenda Sue Robinson (*Wernita Elizabeth Boatright*[7], *Lady Goldie Saddler*[6], *Cora Young*[5], *Matilda Ann White*[4], *Eliza Jane Sharp*[3], *Charles W. Sr.*[2], *John Sr.*[1]) was born 15 Oct 1943 in Lauderdale County, AL.

Brenda married **Franklin Paul Delano**, son of **Paul Leonard Delano** and **Nellie Price**, 17 Mar 1962 in Lauderdale County, AL. Franklin was born 3 Apr 1943 in Lauderdale County, AL.
+ 5687 F   i.   **Sonora Elizabeth Delano** was born 11 Mar 1964 in Lauderdale County, AL.

3952. Jackie Dale Robinson (*Wernita Elizabeth Boatright*[7], *Lady Goldie Saddler*[6], *Cora Young*[5], *Matilda Ann White*[4], *Eliza Jane Sharp*[3], *Charles W. Sr.*[2], *John Sr.*[1]) was born 25 Oct 1946 in Lauderdale County, AL.

Jackie married **Judy Yvonne Ladner**, daughter of **Herbert C. Ladner** and **Mary E. Lee**, 31 Jan 1978 in Lauderdale County, AL. Judy was born 15 Sep 1945 in Colbert County, AL.
+ 5688 F   i.   **Nikkie Dale Robinson** was born 22 Oct 1984 in Lauderdale County, AL.

3953. Shawn Boatright (*Donald Douglas Boatright*[7], *Lady Goldie Saddler*[6], *Cora Young*[5], *Matilda Ann White*[4], *Eliza Jane Sharp*[3], *Charles W. Sr.*[2], *John Sr.*[1]).

Shawn married **Blake Donaldson**.

3957. Lindsey Ann Hayes (*Roberta Nathalie Sharp*[7], *Jewel Estelle Young*[6], *John Robert Young*[5], *Matilda Ann White*[4], *Eliza Jane Sharp*[3], *Charles W. Sr.*[2], *John Sr.*[1]) was born 22 Aug 1982 in Lauderdale County, AL.

Lindsey married **Jeffrey Neil Dunnavant**, son of **Ronald Glenn Dunnavant** and **Patti Ann Bass**, 30 Jun 2007 in Lauderdale County, AL. Jeffrey was born 9 Apr 1982 in Jonesboro, GA.

3959. Eric Andrew Street (*Linda Arnalla Young*[7], *Arnold Andrew Young*[6], *Andrew Cleveland Young*[5], *Matilda Ann White*[4], *Eliza Jane Sharp*[3], *Charles W. Sr.*[2], *John Sr.*[1]) was born 8 Sep 1977 in Lauderdale County, AL.

Eric married **Kristy Leanne Ivey**, daughter of **Gary Wayne Ivey** and **Donna Nell Richardson**, 16 Aug 1997 in Lauderdale County, AL. Kristy was born 14 Jan 1979 in Lauderdale County, AL.
5689 F   i.   **Erica Kaitlyn Street** was born 17 Dec 1997 in Lauderdale County, AL.
5690 M   ii.   **Kameron Andrew Street**.

3960. Tammie Kaye Williams (*Judith Ann Young*[7], *John David Young*[6], *Clarence W. Young*[5], *Matilda Ann White*[4], *Eliza Jane Sharp*[3], *Charles W. Sr.*[2], *John Sr.*[1]) was born 29 Dec 1962 in Mishawaka, St Joseph County, IN.

Tammie married **Paul Gene Overhulser**, son of **Paul Overhulser** and **Ruth Hoover**. Paul was born 21 May 1969 in Mishawaka, St Joseph County, IN.
5691 M   i.   **Zachary Overhulser** was born 12 Nov 1990 in Mishawaka, St Joseph County, IN.
5692 F   ii.   **Abagail Overhulser** was born 3 Feb 1993 in Mishawaka, St Joseph County, IN.

3961. James Eugene Williams (*Judith Ann Young*[7], *John David Young*[6], *Clarence W. Young*[5], *Matilda Ann White*[4], *Eliza Jane Sharp*[3], *Charles W. Sr.*[2], *John Sr.*[1]) was born 6 Jan 1965 in Mishawaka, St Joseph County, IN.

James married **Tina Louise Paff**, daughter of **Leonard Paff** and **Stella Holderman**. Tina was born 29 Dec 1962 in Elkhart, Elkhart County, IN.
5693 M   i.   **Thomas James Williams** was born 3 Jul 1990 in Elkhart, Elkhart County, IN.

3962. David Michael Bentley (*Glenda Sue Young*[7], *John David Young*[6], *Clarence W. Young*[5], *Matilda Ann White*[4], *Eliza Jane Sharp*[3], *Charles W. Sr.*[2], *John Sr.*[1]) was born 21 Oct 1967 in South Bend, IN.

David married **Dawn Noell Bradford**, daughter of **Earl Bradford** and **Susan Montel**, 9 Oct 1988 in Mishawaka, St Joseph County, IN. Dawn was born 22 Dec 1966 in South Bend, IN.
5694 M   i.   **Shawn Michael Bentley** was born 31 Mar 1990 in South Bend, IN.
5695 M   ii.   **Mitchell Eric Bentley** was born 17 Apr 1991 in South Bend, IN.

3963. Tracie Marie Bentley (*Glenda Sue Young^7, John David Young^6, Clarence W. Young^5, Matilda Ann White^4, Eliza Jane Sharp^3, Charles W. Sr.^{2}, John Sr.^{1}*) was born 20 May 1972 in South Bend, IN.

Tracie married someone.

5696 F i. **Billie Rae Bentley**.

3965. Kimberly Ann Polleck (*Reba Kay Young^7, John David Young^6, Clarence W. Young^5, Matilda Ann White^4, Eliza Jane Sharp^3, Charles W. Sr.^{2}, John Sr.^{1}*) was born 13 Apr 1971 in Mishawaka, St Joseph County, IN.

Kimberly married **Michael Shane Kelly** 11 Jul 1992 in Mishawaka, St Joseph County, IN. Michael was born 5 Jun 1968 in Elkhart County, AL.

5697 M i. **Nathen Michael Kelly** was born 7 Oct 1993 in Elkhart County, AL.

3971. Krista Marie Hinton (*Larry Carlton Hinton^7, Jones Carlton Hinton^6, Jones Henry Hinton^5, Martha Jane White^4, Eliza Jane Sharp^3, Charles W. Sr.^{2}, John Sr.^{1}*).

Krista married **Jose Barajas**.

3984. Jefferson Dean Burson (*Hubert Jeffrey Burson Jr.^{7}, Vernon Juanita Hinton^6, Jones Henry Hinton^5, Martha Jane White^4, Eliza Jane Sharp^3, Charles W. Sr.^{2}, John Sr.^{1}*) was born in 1964.

Jefferson married **Susan Irene *Unk**.

3985. Francis Paul Burson (*Hubert Jeffrey Burson Jr.^{7}, Vernon Juanita Hinton^6, Jones Henry Hinton^5, Martha Jane White^4, Eliza Jane Sharp^3, Charles W. Sr.^{2}, John Sr.^{1}*) was born in 1965.

Francis married **Deanna Carole *Unk**.

3986. Christopher Evan Burson (*Hubert Jeffrey Burson Jr.^{7}, Vernon Juanita Hinton^6, Jones Henry Hinton^5, Martha Jane White^4, Eliza Jane Sharp^3, Charles W. Sr.^{2}, John Sr.^{1}*) was born in 1966.

Christopher married **Patricia Lynn *Unk**.

3987. Lawrence Jefferson Padron (*Linda Kay Burson^7, Vernon Juanita Hinton^6, Jones Henry Hinton^5, Martha Jane White^4, Eliza Jane Sharp^3, Charles W. Sr.^{2}, John Sr.^{1}*) was born in 1965.

Lawrence married **Michelle *Unk**.

3988. Susanna Marie Padron (*Linda Kay Burson^7, Vernon Juanita Hinton^6, Jones Henry Hinton^5, Martha Jane White^4, Eliza Jane Sharp^3, Charles W. Sr.^{2}, John Sr.^{1}*) was born in 1966.

Susanna married **Todd Greacher**.

3990. Valeria Lynn Padron (*Linda Kay Burson^7, Vernon Juanita Hinton^6, Jones Henry Hinton^5, Martha Jane White^4, Eliza Jane Sharp^3, Charles W. Sr.^{2}, John Sr.^{1}*) was born in 1970.

Valeria married **Jimmy Martin**.

3993. Shannon Hall (*Roslyn Darleen Burson^7, Vernon Juanita Hinton^6, Jones Henry Hinton^5, Martha Jane White^4, Eliza Jane Sharp^3, Charles W. Sr.^{2}, John Sr.^{1}*) was born in 1969.

Shannon married **David Myrick**.

3994. Monica Hall (*Roslyn Darleen Burson^7, Vernon Juanita Hinton^6, Jones Henry Hinton^5, Martha Jane White^4, Eliza Jane Sharp^3, Charles W. Sr.^{2}, John Sr.^{1}*) was born in 1971.

Monica married **Johnny Martin**.

3999. Sandy Michelle Strickland (*Norma Susan Hinton*[7], *Lloyd Thurston Hinton Sr.*[6], *Jones Henry Hinton*[5], *Martha Jane White*[4], *Eliza Jane Sharp*[3], *Charles W. Sr.*[2], *John Sr.*[1]) was born in 1969.

Sandy married **Thomas Charles Starr Jr.**.

4003. Christy Lee Hinton (*Richard George Hinton*[7], *Lloyd Thurston Hinton Sr.*[6], *Jones Henry Hinton*[5], *Martha Jane White*[4], *Eliza Jane Sharp*[3], *Charles W. Sr.*[2], *John Sr.*[1]) was born in 1976.

Christy married **Charles Gary Davidson**.

4020. Brett Ezell (*Debra Killen*[7], *Don Sherron Killen*[6], *Minnie Louise Sharp*[5], *William (Bill) Edgar*[4], *David Allen*[3], *Charles W. Sr.*[2], *John Sr.*[1]) was born 16 Mar 1972 in Shreveport, LA.

Brett married **Beth Thompson** 20 Jun 1992 in Athens, Limestone County, AL. Beth was born 21 Sep 1972 in Athens, Limestone County, AL.

5698	F	i.	**Elizabeth Bailey Ezell** was born 9 Jan 1991 in Athens, Limestone County, AL.
5699	F	ii.	**Brooks Emerald Ezell** was born 30 Jan 1994 in Huntsville, Madison County, AL.

Eight Generation

4073. Sharon Arlene Wylie (*Robbie Lee Lindsey*[8], *Marvin Elmer Lindsey*[7], *George W. Lindsey*[6], *John Phillip Lindsey II*[5], *Caleb (Calip) Lindsey*[4], *Frances (Frankie) Sharp*[3], *Charles W. Sr.*[2], *John Sr.*[1]) was born 7 May 1967 in Lauderdale County, AL.

Sharon married **Kenneth (Hud) Marshall Bailey** 9 Jan 1993. Kenneth was born 19 Jun 1964 in Arkansas.

4074. Scott Fredrick Wylie (*Robbie Lee Lindsey*[8], *Marvin Elmer Lindsey*[7], *George W. Lindsey*[6], *John Phillip Lindsey II*[5], *Caleb (Calip) Lindsey*[4], *Frances (Frankie) Sharp*[3], *Charles W. Sr.*[2], *John Sr.*[1]) was born 27 Jun 1971 in Lauderdale County, AL.

Scott married **Molly Michelle Matthews**, daughter of **William David Matthews** and **Sondra Kaye Anthony**, 21 Jan 1995 in Jackson, Madison County, TN. Molly was born 8 Oct 1971 in Jackson, Madison County, TN.

4077. Herbert Calvin Hayes III (*Shirley Ann Hall*[8], *Lester Lawrence Hall Sr.*[7], *Ada Bell Lindsey*[6], *Joseph A. Lindsey*[5], *Caleb (Calip) Lindsey*[4], *Frances (Frankie) Sharp*[3], *Charles W. Sr.*[2], *John Sr.*[1]) was born 3 May 1962 in Colbert County, AL.

Herbert married **Jonie Leigh Medford**, daughter of **James Allen Medford** and **Jessie Peterson**, 7 Jul 1994 in McNairy County, TN. Jonie was born 15 May 1959 in Tishomingo, MS.

4078. Melissa Gail Hall (*Lester Lawrence Hall Jr.*[8], *Lester Lawrence Hall Sr.*[7], *Ada Bell Lindsey*[6], *Joseph A. Lindsey*[5], *Caleb (Calip) Lindsey*[4], *Frances (Frankie) Sharp*[3], *Charles W. Sr.*[2], *John Sr.*[1]) was born 13 Nov 1967 in Lauderdale County, AL.

Melissa married **Richard Bryant Martin**, son of **Virgil Bryant Martin** and **Evelyn Virginia Wright**, 7 Jul 1989 in Lauderdale County, AL. Richard was born 23 Feb 1967 in Indiana.

5700	F	i.	**Cassandra Ann Martin**.
5701	F	ii.	**Blair Le Ann Martin**.

4079. Leslie Ann Hall (*Lester Lawrence Hall Jr.*[8], *Lester Lawrence Hall Sr.*[7], *Ada Bell Lindsey*[6], *Joseph A. Lindsey*[5], *Caleb (Calip) Lindsey*[4], *Frances (Frankie) Sharp*[3], *Charles W. Sr.*[2], *John Sr.*[1]) was born 19 Nov 1975 in Lauderdale County, AL.

Leslie married **William Anthony Skelton**, son of **John William Skelton** and **Joyce Marie Balentine**, 16 Sep 1995 in Lauderdale County, AL. William was born 15 Sep 1971 in Lauderdale County, AL.

4080. Miranda Kaye Hall (*Lester Lawrence Hall Jr.* [8], *Lester Lawrence Hall Sr.* [7], *Ada Bell Lindsey* [6], *Joseph A. Lindsey* [5], *Caleb (Calip) Lindsey* [4], *Frances (Frankie) Sharp* [3], *Charles W. Sr.* [2], *John Sr.* [1]) was born 6 Apr 1979 in Lauderdale County, AL.

Miranda married **Leslie Shawn Hill**, son of **Gilbert Roland Hill Jr.** and **Gwin Ann Clemons**, 3 Jun 2000 in Lauderdale County, AL. Leslie was born 17 Apr 1978 in Lauderdale County, AL.

4085. Jacqueline Michele Moore (*Robin Michele Hall* [8], *Lester Lawrence Hall Sr.* [7], *Ada Bell Lindsey* [6], *Joseph A. Lindsey* [5], *Caleb (Calip) Lindsey* [4], *Frances (Frankie) Sharp* [3], *Charles W. Sr.* [2], *John Sr.* [1]) was born 10 Dec 1969 in Lauderdale County, AL.

Jacqueline married **Jack Gwinn Hice Jr.**, son of **Jack Gwinn Hice Sr.** and **Geneva Faye Creekmore**, 15 Jun 1991 in Lauderdale County, AL. Jack was born 12 Sep 1966 in Pascagoula, MS.
5702 M i. **Chandler Jackson Hice** was born 10 Jan 1996 in Colbert County, AL.

4087. Christopher Dale Keeton (*Carlene Hall* [8], *Lester Lawrence Hall Sr.* [7], *Ada Bell Lindsey* [6], *Joseph A. Lindsey* [5], *Caleb (Calip) Lindsey* [4], *Frances (Frankie) Sharp* [3], *Charles W. Sr.* [2], *John Sr.* [1]) was born 21 Aug 1971 in Lauderdale County, AL.

Christopher married **Rhonda Gail White**, daughter of **Ronald Ray White** and **Katherine Gail Murks**, in Lauderdale County, AL. Rhonda was born 3 Feb 1971 in Alabama.
5703 M i. **Duston Ray Keeton** was born 4 May 1989 in Lauderdale County, AL.
5704 M ii. **Bradley Shane Keeton** was born 22 Oct 1991 in Lauderdale County, AL.

4088. Tracey Leigh Keeton (*Carlene Hall* [8], *Lester Lawrence Hall Sr.* [7], *Ada Bell Lindsey* [6], *Joseph A. Lindsey* [5], *Caleb (Calip) Lindsey* [4], *Frances (Frankie) Sharp* [3], *Charles W. Sr.* [2], *John Sr.* [1]) was born 4 Sep 1976 in Lauderdale County, AL.

Tracey married **Johnny Waylon May**, son of **Johnny Roy May** and **Shirley June Herston**, 29 Mar 1995 in Lauderdale County, AL. Johnny was born 4 Sep 1976 in Lauderdale County, AL.

4089. Tonia Dee Hall (*Floyd Edward Hall Jr.* [8], *Floyd Edward Hall Sr.* [7], *Ada Bell Lindsey* [6], *Joseph A. Lindsey* [5], *Caleb (Calip) Lindsey* [4], *Frances (Frankie) Sharp* [3], *Charles W. Sr.* [2], *John Sr.* [1]) was born 19 Oct 1959 in Lauderdale County, AL.

Tonia married **Timothy Hilton Glover**, son of **Dee Glover** and **Alma Ruth Wallace**, 1 Oct 1977 in Lauderdale County, AL. Timothy was born 8 Mar 1957 in Lauderdale County, AL.
5705 F i. **Brittney Rene'e Glover** was born 3 Feb 1979 in Colbert County, AL.
5706 M ii. **Sean Dee Glover** was born 16 Nov 1981 in Colbert County, AL.

4090. Twila Gail Hall (*Floyd Edward Hall Jr.* [8], *Floyd Edward Hall Sr.* [7], *Ada Bell Lindsey* [6], *Joseph A. Lindsey* [5], *Caleb (Calip) Lindsey* [4], *Frances (Frankie) Sharp* [3], *Charles W. Sr.* [2], *John Sr.* [1]) was born 19 Oct 1962 in Augusta County, GA.

Twila married **Daniel Alan Montgomery**, son of **Grayford E. Montgomery** and **Delphie Williams**, 21 Sep 1984 in Lauderdale County, AL. Daniel was born 23 Mar 1956 in Lauderdale County, AL.
5707 F i. **Ashley Danyelle Montgomery** was born 6 Jan 1986 in Lauderdale County, AL.

Twila next married **Gary Rich** 16 Jan 1996 in Wayne County, TN.

4091. Barry Alan Hall (*Floyd Edward Hall Jr.* [8], *Floyd Edward Hall Sr.* [7], *Ada Bell Lindsey* [6], *Joseph A. Lindsey* [5], *Caleb (Calip) Lindsey* [4], *Frances (Frankie) Sharp* [3], *Charles W. Sr.* [2], *John Sr.* [1]) was born 31 May 1964 in Lauderdale County, AL.

Barry married **Deborah Louise Rickard**, daughter of **James Edgar Rickard** and **Dorothy Clay**, 14 Jan 1985 in Lauderdale County, AL. Deborah was born 8 Aug 1964 in Wayne County, TN.

 5708 M i. **Ryan Heath Hall** was born 25 May 1985 in Colbert County, AL.

4092. Richard Doyle Chambers (*Clara Mae Hall*[8], *Floyd Edward Hall Sr.*[7], *Ada Bell Lindsey*[6], *Joseph A. Lindsey*[5], *Caleb (Calip) Lindsey*[4], *Frances (Frankie) Sharp*[3], *Charles W. Sr.*[2], *John Sr.*[1]) was born 10 Dec 1959 in Lauderdale County, AL.

Richard married **Rebecca Lynn Moore**, daughter of **William Moore** and **Betty Coats**, 20 Nov 1981 in Lauderdale County, AL. Rebecca was born 22 Jul 1963 in Wilson County, AR.

 5709 F i. **Erica Michelle Chambers** was born 14 Jun 1983 in Lauderdale County, AL.

4093. Rhonda Lynn Chambers (*Clara Mae Hall*[8], *Floyd Edward Hall Sr.*[7], *Ada Bell Lindsey*[6], *Joseph A. Lindsey*[5], *Caleb (Calip) Lindsey*[4], *Frances (Frankie) Sharp*[3], *Charles W. Sr.*[2], *John Sr.*[1]) was born 26 Sep 1960 in Lauderdale County, AL.

Rhonda married **Oscar David Brown**, son of **Lucky David Brown** and **Anna L. Pendergrass**, 1 May 1993 in Colbert County, AL. Oscar was born 6 Feb 1959 in Tullahoma, TN.

 5710 M i. **Aaron David Brown** was born 31 Jul 1995 in Colbert County, AL.

4094. Sheila Dianne Chambers (*Clara Mae Hall*[8], *Floyd Edward Hall Sr.*[7], *Ada Bell Lindsey*[6], *Joseph A. Lindsey*[5], *Caleb (Calip) Lindsey*[4], *Frances (Frankie) Sharp*[3], *Charles W. Sr.*[2], *John Sr.*[1]) was born 4 Sep 1961 in Lauderdale County, AL.

Sheila married **Robert Lee Hayes**, son of **William Edgar Hayes** and **Mary Haddock**, 20 Sep 1978 in Lauderdale County, AL. Robert was born 22 Dec 1955 in Cook County, IL.

 5711 M i. **Greogry Lee Hayes** was born 3 Feb 1979 in Lauderdale County, AL.
 5712 M ii. **Jason Dwayne Hayes** was born 5 Dec 1983 in Lauderdale County, AL.

4095. Cindy Gail Chambers (*Clara Mae Hall*[8], *Floyd Edward Hall Sr.*[7], *Ada Bell Lindsey*[6], *Joseph A. Lindsey*[5], *Caleb (Calip) Lindsey*[4], *Frances (Frankie) Sharp*[3], *Charles W. Sr.*[2], *John Sr.*[1]) was born 21 Sep 1963 in Lauderdale County, AL.

Cindy married **Bradley Wade Terry**, son of **Anthony Wayne Terry** and **Peggy Ann Austin**, 18 Apr 1986 in Lauderdale County, AL. Bradley was born 14 Aug 1963 in Colbert County, AL.

 5713 F i. **Peggy Ann Terry** was born 23 Nov 1986 in Lauderdale County, AL.

4096. Brenda Lee Chambers (*Clara Mae Hall*[8], *Floyd Edward Hall Sr.*[7], *Ada Bell Lindsey*[6], *Joseph A. Lindsey*[5], *Caleb (Calip) Lindsey*[4], *Frances (Frankie) Sharp*[3], *Charles W. Sr.*[2], *John Sr.*[1]) was born 17 Mar 1966 in Lauderdale County, AL.

Brenda married **William Brent Barkley**, son of **Billy G. Barkley** and **Linda Faye Walker**, 16 Jul 1988 in Lauderdale County, AL. William was born 6 Feb 1966 in Lauderdale County, AL.

 5714 M i. **William Chance Barkley** was born 2 Aug 1991 in Lauderdale County, AL.
 5715 F ii. **Victoria Starr Barkley** was born 11 Nov 1995 in Lauderdale County, AL.

4097. Donna Marie Chambers (*Clara Mae Hall*[8], *Floyd Edward Hall Sr.*[7], *Ada Bell Lindsey*[6], *Joseph A. Lindsey*[5], *Caleb (Calip) Lindsey*[4], *Frances (Frankie) Sharp*[3], *Charles W. Sr.*[2], *John Sr.*[1]) was born 22 Jan 1969 in Lauderdale County, AL.

Donna married **David Lee Eddy**, son of **Royce L. Eddy** and **Martha Faye Watson**, 12 May 1990 in Colbert County, AL. David was born 24 Aug 1963 in Hammond, IN.

 5716 M i. **Christopher Blake Eddy** was born 20 Nov 1986 in Lauderdale County, AL.
 5717 M ii. **Jordan Lee Eddy** was born 26 Mar 1994 in Lauderdale County, AL.

4098. Melisa Kaye Chambers (*Clara Mae Hall*[8], *Floyd Edward Hall Sr.*[7], *Ada Bell Lindsey*[6], *Joseph A. Lindsey*[5], *Caleb (Calip) Lindsey*[4], *Frances (Frankie) Sharp*[3], *Charles W. Sr.*[2], *John Sr.*[1]) was born 1 Dec 1974 in Lauderdale County, AL.

Melisa married **James Shannon Brown**, son of **James Houston Brown** and **Judy Elaine Davis**, 14 Dec 1992 in Lauderdale County, AL. James was born 21 Sep 1973 in Colbert County, AL.

5718　M　i.　**Shannon Chase Brown** was born 3 Feb 1993 in Lauderdale County, AL.

4099. James Anthony Adams (*Sara Jane Hall*[8]*, Floyd Edward Hall Sr.*[7]*, Ada Bell Lindsey*[6]*, Joseph A. Lindsey*[5]*, Caleb (Calip) Lindsey*[4]*, Frances (Frankie) Sharp*[3]*, Charles W. Sr.*[2]*, John Sr.*[1]) was born 22 Sep 1960 in Lauderdale County, AL.

James married **Rose Marie Roder** in Texas. Rose was born 3 Jun 1960 in Texas.

5719　M　i.　**James Anthony Adams II** was born 16 Oct 1982 in Texas.
5720　F　ii.　**Lacie Marie Adams** was born 4 Jul 1987 in Texas.

4101. Bonnie Sue Adams (*Sara Jane Hall*[8]*, Floyd Edward Hall Sr.*[7]*, Ada Bell Lindsey*[6]*, Joseph A. Lindsey*[5]*, Caleb (Calip) Lindsey*[4]*, Frances (Frankie) Sharp*[3]*, Charles W. Sr.*[2]*, John Sr.*[1]) was born 20 Jun 1965 in Lauderdale County, AL.

Bonnie married **Clint Michael** in Lauderdale County, AL.

5721　F　i.　**Maranda Kaye Michael** was born 16 Mar 1984 in Lauderdale County, AL.
5722　M　ii.　**Travis Chase Michael** was born 5 Nov 1992 in Lauderdale County, AL.

4102. Edna Jane Adams (*Sara Jane Hall*[8]*, Floyd Edward Hall Sr.*[7]*, Ada Bell Lindsey*[6]*, Joseph A. Lindsey*[5]*, Caleb (Calip) Lindsey*[4]*, Frances (Frankie) Sharp*[3]*, Charles W. Sr.*[2]*, John Sr.*[1]) was born 26 Apr 1964 in Lauderdale County, AL.

Edna married **Billy Ray Bevis**, son of **Pride T. Bevis** and **Evia E. Hunt**, 9 Jun 1982 in Lauderdale County, AL. Billy was born 27 Nov 1960 in Lauderdale County, AL.

5723　M　i.　**Justin Ross Bevis** was born 12 Aug 1982 in Lauderdale County, AL.

Edna next married **Tommy Michael Roberson**.

5724　M　i.　**Jonathan Michael Roberson** was born 5 Dec 1986 in Lauderdale County, AL.
5725　F　ii.　**Magen Jane Roberson** was born 6 Jun 1992 in Lauderdale County, AL.

4103. Sharon Kay Adams (*Sara Jane Hall*[8]*, Floyd Edward Hall Sr.*[7]*, Ada Bell Lindsey*[6]*, Joseph A. Lindsey*[5]*, Caleb (Calip) Lindsey*[4]*, Frances (Frankie) Sharp*[3]*, Charles W. Sr.*[2]*, John Sr.*[1]) was born 25 Dec 1966 in Lauderdale County, AL.

Sharon married **Robert Dwayne Taylor**, son of **Robert Oneal Taylor** and **Julia Ann Murphy**, 24 Jul 1993 in Lauderdale County, AL. Robert was born 27 Nov 1968 in Lauderdale County, AL.

5726　F　i.　**Montana Brooke Taylor** was born 13 Nov 1995 in Lauderdale County, AL.

4105. Regina Lynn McMurtrey (*Barbara Kaye Hall*[8]*, Floyd Edward Hall Sr.*[7]*, Ada Bell Lindsey*[6]*, Joseph A. Lindsey*[5]*, Caleb (Calip) Lindsey*[4]*, Frances (Frankie) Sharp*[3]*, Charles W. Sr.*[2]*, John Sr.*[1]) was born 11 Sep 1974 in Lauderdale County, AL.

Regina married **Jerry Daniel Urban**, son of **Jimmy Daniel Urban** and **Wanda Faye High**, 13 Nov 1990 in Lauderdale County, AL. Jerry was born 18 Nov 1972 in Lauderdale County, AL.

5727　M　i.　**Chase Daniel Urban** was born 24 Aug 1995 in Lauderdale County, AL.
5728　F　ii.　**Jessica Lynn Urban** was born 8 Apr 1998 in Lauderdale County, AL.

4112. Shirley Jean Lindsey (*Gentry Aaron Lindsey*[8]*, Charles Edward Lindsey*[7]*, Albert Curtis Lindsey*[6]*, David A. Lindsey*[5]*, Caleb (Calip) Lindsey*[4]*, Frances (Frankie) Sharp*[3]*, Charles W. Sr.*[2]*, John Sr.*[1]) was born 1 Feb 1948 in Lauderdale County, AL.

Shirley married **James Henry Wallace**, son of **Henry T. Wallace** and **Mable C. Hendrix**, 22 Dec 1966 in Lauderdale County, AL. James was born 9 Sep 1948 in Lauderdale County, AL.

+ 5729　M　i.　**James David Wallace** was born 10 Aug 1967 in Lauderdale County, AL.
+ 5730　M　ii.　**Thomas (Tommy) Wayne Wallace** was born 9 Oct 1969 in Athens, Limestone County, AL.

+ 5731   F   iii.   **Martha Jean Wallace** was born 13 Nov 1975 in Lauderdale County, AL.

4113. Larry Wayne Lindsey (*Gentry Aaron Lindsey*[8], *Charles Edward Lindsey*[7], *Albert Curtis Lindsey*[6], *David A. Lindsey*[5], *Caleb (Calip) Lindsey*[4], *Frances (Frankie) Sharp*[3], *Charles W. Sr.*[2], *John Sr.*[1]) was born 5 Sep 1949 in Lauderdale County, AL.

Larry married **Kathy Sue Stewart**, daughter of **Loncie Dunkin Stewart** and **Bertha Hill**, 18 Dec 1965 in Lawrenceburg, Lawrence County, TN. Kathy was born 1 Aug 1951 in Lauderdale County, AL.

5732   F   i.   **Sabrina Renee Lindsey** was born 4 Oct 1981 in Colbert County, AL.

4114. Sandra Gail Lindsey (*Gentry Aaron Lindsey*[8], *Charles Edward Lindsey*[7], *Albert Curtis Lindsey*[6], *David A. Lindsey*[5], *Caleb (Calip) Lindsey*[4], *Frances (Frankie) Sharp*[3], *Charles W. Sr.*[2], *John Sr.*[1]) was born 2 Aug 1951 in Lauderdale County, AL.

Sandra married **Michael Leonard Collins**, son of **Calvin L. Collins** and **Ruthell Bright**, 28 Jul 1972 in Lauderdale County, AL. Michael was born 21 Nov 1951 in Marshall County, AL.

5733   F   i.   **Amanda Michelle Collins** was born 14 May 1977 in Colbert County, AL.

4115. Susan Denise Lindsey (*Gentry Aaron Lindsey*[8], *Charles Edward Lindsey*[7], *Albert Curtis Lindsey*[6], *David A. Lindsey*[5], *Caleb (Calip) Lindsey*[4], *Frances (Frankie) Sharp*[3], *Charles W. Sr.*[2], *John Sr.*[1]) was born 20 Mar 1969 in Lauderdale County, AL.

Susan married **James Eldon Balentine**, son of **Tollie Balentine** and **Betty Burch**, 5 Dec 1987 in Lauderdale County, AL. James was born 14 Aug 1963 in Lauderdale County, AL.

5734   M   i.   **Justin Aaron Balentine** was born 17 Sep 1990 in Lauderdale County, AL.
5735   M   ii.   **Jeffrey Wayne Balentine** was born 19 Mar 1993 in Lauderdale County, AL.

4116. Linda Faye Pigg (*Margaret Marie Lindsey*[8], *Charles Edward Lindsey*[7], *Albert Curtis Lindsey*[6], *David A. Lindsey*[5], *Caleb (Calip) Lindsey*[4], *Frances (Frankie) Sharp*[3], *Charles W. Sr.*[2], *John Sr.*[1]) was born 27 Aug 1948 in Lauderdale County, AL.

Linda married **William (Bill) Robert Jones**, son of **Robert P. Jones** and **Evelyn Holt**, 28 Aug 1966 in Lauderdale County, AL. William was born 20 Mar 1946 in Lauderdale County, AL.

+ 5736   F   i.   **Michele LeAnn Jones** was born 4 Jan 1971 in Lauderdale County, AL.
5737   F   ii.   **Amber Marie Jones** was born 25 Nov 1977 in Lauderdale County, AL.

Linda next married **Roland E. Rogers Jr.**, son of **Roland E. Rogers Sr.** and **Edna Richardson**, 20 Sep 1985 in Lauderdale County, AL. Roland was born 20 Mar 1946 in Lauderdale County, AL.

4117. Patricia Gail Pigg (*Margaret Marie Lindsey*[8], *Charles Edward Lindsey*[7], *Albert Curtis Lindsey*[6], *David A. Lindsey*[5], *Caleb (Calip) Lindsey*[4], *Frances (Frankie) Sharp*[3], *Charles W. Sr.*[2], *John Sr.*[1]) was born 25 May 1958 in Lauderdale County, AL.

Patricia married **David Harland Lovelace**, son of **Grady H. Lovelace** and **Geraldine Berdett**, 2 Jun 1989 in Huntsville, Madison County, AL. David was born 29 Mar 1962 in Lauderdale County, AL.

5738   F   i.   **Brittany Nicole Lovelace** was born 29 Apr 1993 in Lauderdale County, AL.

4118. Ronald Clifford Pigg (*Margaret Marie Lindsey*[8], *Charles Edward Lindsey*[7], *Albert Curtis Lindsey*[6], *David A. Lindsey*[5], *Caleb (Calip) Lindsey*[4], *Frances (Frankie) Sharp*[3], *Charles W. Sr.*[2], *John Sr.*[1]) was born 22 Mar 1965 in Lauderdale County, AL.

Ronald married **Pamela Gaye Holt**, daughter of **Granville W. Holt** and **Sue Spain**, 22 Jun 1984 in Lauderdale County, AL. Pamela was born 28 Jul 1965 in Lauderdale County, AL.

5739   M   i.   **Christophee Ryan Pigg** was born 27 Jan 1986 in Lauderdale County, AL.

Ronald next married **Shanna Thompson**. Shanna was born in Sheffield, Colbert County, AL.

4119. Paula Marie Pigg (*Margaret Marie Lindsey*[8], *Charles Edward Lindsey*[7], *Albert Curtis Lindsey*[6], *David A. Lindsey*[5], *Caleb (Calip) Lindsey*[4], *Frances (Frankie) Sharp*[3], *Charles W. Sr.*[2], *John Sr.*[1]) was born 6 Jan 1968 in Lauderdale County, AL.

Paula married **William Delane Brewer**, son of **William T. Brewer** and **Deloris Talley**, 15 Jun 1987 in Lauderdale County, AL. William was born 7 Nov 1965 in Lauderdale County, AL.

| 5740 | F | i. | **Alexia Chailey Brewer** was born 27 May 1993 in Lauderdale County, AL. |
| 5741 | F | ii. | **Kelly Ashlane Brewer** was born 10 Mar 1995 in Lauderdale County, AL. |

4120. Pamela Renee Pigg (*Margaret Marie Lindsey*[8], *Charles Edward Lindsey*[7], *Albert Curtis Lindsey*[6], *David A. Lindsey*[5], *Caleb (Calip) Lindsey*[4], *Frances (Frankie) Sharp*[3], *Charles W. Sr.*[2], *John Sr.*[1]) was born 6 Jan 1968 in Lauderdale County, AL.

Pamela married **Shannon Lynn Barrett**, son of **Bobby J. Barrett** and **Diane Scaton**, 30 Aug 1986 in Lauderdale County, AL. Shannon was born 27 Jul 1967 in Lauderdale County, AL.

| 5742 | F | i. | **Jessica Lynn Barrett** was born 1 Apr 1993 in Lauderdale County, AL. |

4130. Deborah Janice Thornton (*Helen Louise Lindsey*[8], *Dalton Allen Lindsey*[7], *Albert Curtis Lindsey*[6], *David A. Lindsey*[5], *Caleb (Calip) Lindsey*[4], *Frances (Frankie) Sharp*[3], *Charles W. Sr.*[2], *John Sr.*[1]) was born 24 Aug 1951.

Deborah married **Ralph O. Moore**, son of **Herbert F. Moore** and **Anna Patricia Summers**, 28 Nov 1968 in Lauderdale County, AL. Ralph was born 4 Jul 1949 in Colbert County, AL.

| 5743 | M | i. | **William Franklin Moore** was born 17 May 1970 in Lauderdale County, AL. |

4131. Kimberly Celeste Thornton (*Helen Louise Lindsey*[8], *Dalton Allen Lindsey*[7], *Albert Curtis Lindsey*[6], *David A. Lindsey*[5], *Caleb (Calip) Lindsey*[4], *Frances (Frankie) Sharp*[3], *Charles W. Sr.*[2], *John Sr.*[1]) was born 18 Sep 1964.

Kimberly married ***Unk Peck** about 1981.

| 5744 | M | i. | **Elipah Bradford Peck** was born 19 Jan 1982. |

Kimberly next married **Ronald Edwin Holt**, son of **Harold E. Holt** and **Stella Marie Blackhulen**, 9 Oct 1985 in Lauderdale County, AL. Ronald was born 16 Jun 1960 in Lauderdale County, AL.

| 5745 | M | i. | **Joshua Seth Holt** was born 1 May 1986. |

Kimberly next married ***Unk Mills** about 1987.

| 5746 | F | i. | **Jessica Courtney Mills** was born 20 Dec 1987. |
| 5747 | F | ii. | **Jennifer Lindsey Mills** was born 29 May 1990. |

4145. Rachel Kimberly Romine (*Richard Morris Romine*[8], *Richard Leland Romine*[7], *Nellie Mitchum*[6], *America Lindsey*[5], *Caleb (Calip) Lindsey*[4], *Frances (Frankie) Sharp*[3], *Charles W. Sr.*[2], *John Sr.*[1]) was born 20 Mar 1973 in Lauderdale County, AL.

Rachel married **Chris Walter**.

4163. Benjamin Franklin May (*James William May Sr.*[8], *Lilly Mae Lindsey*[7], *Millard Lindsey*[6], *Maraday (Merry Dee) Lindsey*[5], *Andrew Jackson Lindsey*[4], *Frances (Frankie) Sharp*[3], *Charles W. Sr.*[2], *John Sr.*[1]) was born 27 Jan 1948, died 21 Jul 1997, and was buried in Blue Springs Cemetery, Franklin County, AL.

Benjamin married **Mildred Charlotte Long**. Mildred was born 20 May 1947.

| + 5748 | F | i. | **Michelle Lee May** was born 19 Jul 1970. |

Benjamin next married **Betty Moles**.

| 5749 | F | i. | **Brandi Jo May** was born 24 Jan 1982. |

4164. Winford Dale May (*James William May Sr.*[8], *Lilly Mae Lindsey*[7], *Millard Lindsey*[6], *Maraday (Merry Dee) Lindsey*[5], *Andrew Jackson Lindsey*[4], *Frances (Frankie) Sharp*[3], *Charles W. Sr.*[2], *John Sr.*[1]) was born 12 May 1950.

Winford married **Phyllis Cothrum** 7 Jun 1974. Phyllis was born 21 Jul 1955.

5750 F i. **Joanie Leray May** was born 4 May 1977.

4165. Kathy Diane May (*James William May Sr.^{8}, Lilly Mae Lindsey^7, Millard Lindsey^6, Maraday (Merry Dee) Lindsey^5, Andrew Jackson Lindsey^4, Frances (Frankie) Sharp^3, Charles W. Sr.^{2}, John Sr.^{1}*) was born 12 Nov 1951.

Kathy married **Harold Dean Smith** 3 Jul 1969. Harold was born 24 Apr 1951.
+ 5751 F i. **Lisa Diane Smith** was born 28 Oct 1969.
+ 5752 M ii. **Gregory Wayne Smith** was born 26 Dec 1971.

Kathy next married **Michael (Mickey) Blevins** 6 May 1983. Michael was born 16 Jun 1959.

4166. Sherry Lynn May (*James William May Sr.^{8}, Lilly Mae Lindsey^7, Millard Lindsey^6, Maraday (Merry Dee) Lindsey^5, Andrew Jackson Lindsey^4, Frances (Frankie) Sharp^3, Charles W. Sr.^{2}, John Sr.^{1}*) was born 19 Sep 1958 in Russellville, Franklin County, AL.

Sherry married **James Wayne (Jimmy) Lindsey** 3 Jun 1978. James was born 4 Jul 1953.
+ 5753 F i. **Kelly Leann Lindsey** was born 29 Feb 1980.
5754 F ii. **Heather Leshae Lindsey** was born 5 Dec 1983.

Sherry next married **Thomas Garvin Baldy** 22 May 1992. Thomas was born 8 Oct 1947.
5755 M i. **Justin William May Baldy** was born 10 Dec 1987.

4168. Winfred Dale Andis (*Virginia Nell Wood^8, Viola Beatrice Lindsey^7, Millard Lindsey^6, Maraday (Merry Dee) Lindsey^5, Andrew Jackson Lindsey^4, Frances (Frankie) Sharp^3, Charles W. Sr.^{2}, John Sr.^{1}*).

Winfred married **Denise *Unk**.

4169. Allen Wayne Andis (*Virginia Nell Wood^8, Viola Beatrice Lindsey^7, Millard Lindsey^6, Maraday (Merry Dee) Lindsey^5, Andrew Jackson Lindsey^4, Frances (Frankie) Sharp^3, Charles W. Sr.^{2}, John Sr.^{1}*) died in 1994.

Allen married **Anne *Unk**.

4170. Dottie Lou Andis (*Virginia Nell Wood^8, Viola Beatrice Lindsey^7, Millard Lindsey^6, Maraday (Merry Dee) Lindsey^5, Andrew Jackson Lindsey^4, Frances (Frankie) Sharp^3, Charles W. Sr.^{2}, John Sr.^{1}*) was born 13 Nov 1955 in Flint, MI.

Dottie married **Joe Thomas Sr.**.
5756 M i. **Joe Thomas Jr.**

4171. Patricia Gail Andis (*Virginia Nell Wood^8, Viola Beatrice Lindsey^7, Millard Lindsey^6, Maraday (Merry Dee) Lindsey^5, Andrew Jackson Lindsey^4, Frances (Frankie) Sharp^3, Charles W. Sr.^{2}, John Sr.^{1}*) was born 28 May 1957 in Flint, MI.

Patricia married **Bruce Forbes Sr.**.
+ 5757 M i. **Bruce Forbes Jr.**
5758 M ii. **Sammy Forbes**.
5759 M iii. **Timothy Forbes**.

4172. Helen Marie Andis (*Virginia Nell Wood^8, Viola Beatrice Lindsey^7, Millard Lindsey^6, Maraday (Merry Dee) Lindsey^5, Andrew Jackson Lindsey^4, Frances (Frankie) Sharp^3, Charles W. Sr.^{2}, John Sr.^{1}*) was born in Jan 1964.

Helen married ***Unk Ross**.

4173. Bobby Lenard Thompson (*Sarah Elizabeth (Lib) Wood^8, Viola Beatrice Lindsey^7, Millard Lindsey^6, Maraday (Merry Dee) Lindsey^5, Andrew Jackson Lindsey^4, Frances (Frankie) Sharp^3, Charles W. Sr.^{2}, John Sr.^{1}*) was born 13 Sep 1957 in Methodist Hospital, Memphis, Shelby County, TN.

Bobby married someone.
5760 M   i.   **Christopher Thompson.**

4174. Billy Gene Ezekiel Sr. (*Sarah Elizabeth (Lib) Wood*[8]*, Viola Beatrice Lindsey*[7]*, Millard Lindsey*[6]*, Maraday (Merry Dee) Lindsey*[5]*, Andrew Jackson Lindsey*[4]*, Frances (Frankie) Sharp*[3]*, Charles W. Sr.*[2]*, John Sr.*[1]*)* was born 31 Mar 1960 in Florence, Lauderdale County, AL.

Billy married **Connie Joyce Jackson** 26 Feb 1978 in Lauderdale County, AL. Connie was born 16 Jan 1961.
+ 5761 F   i.   **Samantha Dawn Ezekiel** was born 13 Aug 1979.
5762 M   ii. **Christopher Lee Ezekiel** was born 1 Feb 1980.
5763 M   iii. **Billy Gene Ezekiel Jr.** was born 24 Mar 1984.

Billy next married **Cathy Lynn Rideout** 24 Jul 1987 in Lauderdale County, AL. Cathy was born 22 Jul 1952.

4175. Donna Kay Cossey (*Shirley Jean Wood*[8]*, Viola Beatrice Lindsey*[7]*, Millard Lindsey*[6]*, Maraday (Merry Dee) Lindsey*[5]*, Andrew Jackson Lindsey*[4]*, Frances (Frankie) Sharp*[3]*, Charles W. Sr.*[2]*, John Sr.*[1]*)* was born 6 Apr 1956 in Turrell, Crittenden County, AR.

Donna married **Phillip Webb** 20 Oct 1978 in Huntsville, Madison County, AL. Phillip was born 7 Dec 1955 in Gardendale, Jefferson County, AL and died in Sep 1998 in Georgia.
5764 M   i.   **John Matthew Webb** was born 15 Aug 1980 in Birmingham, Jefferson County, AL.

Donna next married **Terry Thompson** between 1978 and 1991.

Donna next married **Glen Allen Moffett** 10 Dec 1991 in Pulaski, Giles County, TN. Glen was born 28 Apr 1966 in Lynch, NE.
5765 M   i.   **Patrick Allen Moffett** was born 16 Jul 1991 in Heidelberg, Germany.

4176. Deborah (Debbie) Faye Cossey (*Shirley Jean Wood*[8]*, Viola Beatrice Lindsey*[7]*, Millard Lindsey*[6]*, Maraday (Merry Dee) Lindsey*[5]*, Andrew Jackson Lindsey*[4]*, Frances (Frankie) Sharp*[3]*, Charles W. Sr.*[2]*, John Sr.*[1]*)* was born 4 Jul 1957 in West Memphis, Crittenden County, AR.

Deborah married **Richard Duane Wasserburger** 2 Dec 1974 in Huntsville, Madison County, AL. Richard was born 28 Dec 1949 in Chadron Municipal Hospital, Dawes County, NE.
5766 F   i.   **Christy Ann Wasserburger** was born 20 Apr 1975 in Huntsville, Madison County, AL.
+ 5767 M   ii. **Jesse Duane Wasserburger** was born 17 May 1977 in Frankfurt Am Main, Hesson, Germany.

4177. James Daniel (Danny) Cossey (*Shirley Jean Wood*[8]*, Viola Beatrice Lindsey*[7]*, Millard Lindsey*[6]*, Maraday (Merry Dee) Lindsey*[5]*, Andrew Jackson Lindsey*[4]*, Frances (Frankie) Sharp*[3]*, Charles W. Sr.*[2]*, John Sr.*[1]*)* was born 24 Jul 1958 in Caraway Methodist Hospital, Birmingham, Jefferson County, AL.

James married **Rhonda Denise Braden**, daughter of **Robert Braden** and **Audrey *Unk**, 29 Dec 1975. Rhonda was born 24 Nov 1958.
5768 M   i.   **James Braden Cossey** was born 15 Dec 1980 in Huntsville, Madison County, AL.
5769 F   ii. **Lisa Danielle Cossey** was born 1 Oct 1983 in Huntsville, Madison County, AL.

4178. Dennis Ray Cossey (*Shirley Jean Wood*[8]*, Viola Beatrice Lindsey*[7]*, Millard Lindsey*[6]*, Maraday (Merry Dee) Lindsey*[5]*, Andrew Jackson Lindsey*[4]*, Frances (Frankie) Sharp*[3]*, Charles W. Sr.*[2]*, John Sr.*[1]*)* was born 30 Jan 1963 in Caraway Methodist Hospital, Birmingham, Jefferson County, AL.

Dennis married **Peggy Sue Heatherly**. Peggy was born in Dec 1967 in Alabama.
5770 F   i.   **Cassandra Lynn Cossey** was born 21 Dec 1986 in Huntsville, Madison County, AL.

Dennis next married **Missy *Unk** about 1979.

4180. Roger Dale Capooth (*Beatrice Marie Wood^8, Viola Beatrice Lindsey^7, Millard Lindsey^6, Maraday (Merry Dee) Lindsey^5, Andrew Jackson Lindsey^4, Frances (Frankie) Sharp^3, Charles W. Sr.^{2}, John Sr.^{1}*) was born 23 Aug 1959 in Selmer, McNairy County, TN.

Roger married **Kimberly Hughes** 14 Feb 1987 in Mitchie, TN. Kimberly was born 3 Feb.

4181. Patricia Ann (Lucy) Borden (*Jack Leon Wood^8, Viola Beatrice Lindsey^7, Millard Lindsey^6, Maraday (Merry Dee) Lindsey^5, Andrew Jackson Lindsey^4, Frances (Frankie) Sharp^3, Charles W. Sr.^{2}, John Sr.^{1}*) was born 25 Jul 1970 in Colbert County, AL.

Patricia married **Glen Hamm**.
5771   F   i.   **Whitney Dawn Hamm** was born 5 Aug 1989.

4183. Cathy Marlene Campbell (*Patsy Faye Wood^8, Viola Beatrice Lindsey^7, Millard Lindsey^6, Maraday (Merry Dee) Lindsey^5, Andrew Jackson Lindsey^4, Frances (Frankie) Sharp^3, Charles W. Sr.^{2}, John Sr.^{1}*) was born 14 Oct 1959 in Pernscott County, MO.

Cathy married **Benford Allen (Buddy) Johnson** before 1978.
5772   M   i.   **Buddy Wayne Johnson** was born 22 Sep 1978.

Cathy next married ***Unk**.
5773   M   i.   **Eric Scott Campbell** was born 26 Jun 1986 in Decatur General Hospital, Decatur, Morgan County, AL.

Cathy next married ***Unk Coan** before 1989.
5774   M   i.   **Joseph Adam Coan** was born 6 Jun 1989.

4184. Sharon Lee Campbell (*Patsy Faye Wood^8, Viola Beatrice Lindsey^7, Millard Lindsey^6, Maraday (Merry Dee) Lindsey^5, Andrew Jackson Lindsey^4, Frances (Frankie) Sharp^3, Charles W. Sr.^{2}, John Sr.^{1}*) was born 7 Jan 1962 in Sheffield, Colbert County, AL.

Sharon married **Stephen Shirley** before 1981.
5775   M   i.   **Douglas Heath Shirley** was born 20 Nov 1981 in Decatur General Hospital, Decatur, Morgan County, AL.

Sharon next married **Gordon Goodwin** before 1984.
5776   F   i.   **Laura Beth (Shirley) Goodwin** was born 20 Aug 1984 in Decatur General Hospital, Decatur, Morgan County, AL.

4185. Cheryl Renee Campbell (*Patsy Faye Wood^8, Viola Beatrice Lindsey^7, Millard Lindsey^6, Maraday (Merry Dee) Lindsey^5, Andrew Jackson Lindsey^4, Frances (Frankie) Sharp^3, Charles W. Sr.^{2}, John Sr.^{1}*) was born 11 Aug 1964 in Vislia, CA.

Cheryl married **Roger Lynn Carver**.
5777   M   i.   **Rusty Lynn Carver** was born 26 Mar 1985 in Decatur General Hospital, Decatur, Morgan County, AL.

4186. Gary Wayne Phillips (*Patsy Faye Wood^8, Viola Beatrice Lindsey^7, Millard Lindsey^6, Maraday (Merry Dee) Lindsey^5, Andrew Jackson Lindsey^4, Frances (Frankie) Sharp^3, Charles W. Sr.^{2}, John Sr.^{1}*) was born 8 Feb 1968.

Gary married ***Unk** before 1987.
5778   F   i.   **Ashley Brook Phillips** was born 15 May 1987.

Gary next married **Rebecca Putman** before 1993.
5779   M   i.   **Jacob Wayne Phillips** was born 3 Feb 1993.

4196. Gregory Allen Dowdy (*Kathyleen Lindsey*[8], *Coleman Edison Lindsey*[7], *Kerom William Lindsey*[6], *Greenberry Lee Lindsey Sr.*[5], *Sylvester (Sill) B. Lindsey*[4], *Frances (Frankie) Sharp*[3], *Charles W. Sr.*[2], *John Sr.*[1]) was born 18 Mar 1956 in Lauderdale County, AL.

    Gregory married **Judy Lynn Shook**, daughter of **Kennan Shook** and **Barbara Lard**, 16 Sep 1978 in Lauderdale County, AL. Judy was born 25 Apr 1959 in Lauderdale County, AL.

| 5780 | F | i. | **Summer Brook Dowdy** was born 14 Jul 1983 in Lauderdale County, AL. |
| 5781 | M | ii. | **Jamin Allen Dowdy** was born 21 Jan 1990 in Lauderdale County, AL. |

4197. Nancy Ruth Dowdy (*Kathyleen Lindsey*[8], *Coleman Edison Lindsey*[7], *Kerom William Lindsey*[6], *Greenberry Lee Lindsey Sr.*[5], *Sylvester (Sill) B. Lindsey*[4], *Frances (Frankie) Sharp*[3], *Charles W. Sr.*[2], *John Sr.*[1]) was born 3 Sep 1957 in Lauderdale County, AL.

    Nancy married **Kenneth Ray Robison**, son of **William A. Robison** and **Peggy Patterson**, 9 Sep 1979 in Lauderdale County, AL. Kenneth was born 6 Oct 1957 in Lauderdale County, AL.

| 5782 | M | i. | **Corey Wade Robison** was born 6 Jul 1983 in Lauderdale County, AL. |
| 5783 | F | ii. | **Lindsey Michele Robison** was born 24 Jan 1986 in Lauderdale County, AL. |

    Nancy next married **Eddie Roberts**.

4198. Jeffrey Wade Dowdy (*Kathyleen Lindsey*[8], *Coleman Edison Lindsey*[7], *Kerom William Lindsey*[6], *Greenberry Lee Lindsey Sr.*[5], *Sylvester (Sill) B. Lindsey*[4], *Frances (Frankie) Sharp*[3], *Charles W. Sr.*[2], *John Sr.*[1]) was born 28 Aug 1962 in Lauderdale County, AL.

    Jeffrey married **Jill Denise Stewart**, daughter of **Jack Stewart** and **Shirley Jean**, 18 Aug 1990. Jill was born 29 Aug 1967 in San Antonio, TX.

| 5784 | F | i. | **Clarke Elise Dowdy** was born 7 Aug 1995 in Monterey, CA. |

4199. Cynthia (Cindy) Lyn Dowdy (*Kathyleen Lindsey*[8], *Coleman Edison Lindsey*[7], *Kerom William Lindsey*[6], *Greenberry Lee Lindsey Sr.*[5], *Sylvester (Sill) B. Lindsey*[4], *Frances (Frankie) Sharp*[3], *Charles W. Sr.*[2], *John Sr.*[1]) was born 19 Mar 1965 in Lauderdale County, AL.

    Cynthia married **Roger Dale Hubbert Jr.**, son of **Roger Dale Hubbert Sr.** and **Pat Spiceland**, 30 Dec 1984 in Lauderdale County, AL. Roger was born 14 Oct 1961 in Guin, AL.

5785	F	i.	**Katy Danell Hubbert** was born 11 Jun 1986 in Lauderdale County, AL.
5786	M	ii.	**Wesley Dale Hubbert** was born 26 Jan 1989 in Lauderdale County, AL.
5787	F	iii.	**Julie Elizabeth Hubbert** was born 19 Mar 1991 in Lauderdale County, AL.

4200. Anthony Wayne Lindsey (*Owen Wayne Lindsey*[8], *Coleman Edison Lindsey*[7], *Kerom William Lindsey*[6], *Greenberry Lee Lindsey Sr.*[5], *Sylvester (Sill) B. Lindsey*[4], *Frances (Frankie) Sharp*[3], *Charles W. Sr.*[2], *John Sr.*[1]) was born 13 Mar 1963 in Aiken, SC.

    Anthony married **Peggy Genice Scott**, daughter of **Bobby Joe Scott** and **Josie Jones**, 13 Nov 1981 in Lauderdale County, AL. Peggy was born 21 Sep 1963 in Lauderdale County, AL.

| 5788 | M | i. | **James Tyler Lindsey** was born 28 Aug 1986 in Lauderdale County, AL. |

4201. Brian Mitchell Lindsey (*Owen Wayne Lindsey*[8], *Coleman Edison Lindsey*[7], *Kerom William Lindsey*[6], *Greenberry Lee Lindsey Sr.*[5], *Sylvester (Sill) B. Lindsey*[4], *Frances (Frankie) Sharp*[3], *Charles W. Sr.*[2], *John Sr.*[1]) was born 11 Feb 1964 in Lauderdale County, AL.

    Brian married **Francis Elizabeth Holloway**, daughter of **Robert Daniel Holloway** and **Georganne Roley Jacob**, 13 Nov 1991 in Colbert County, AL. Francis was born 12 Mar 1963 in Lauderdale County, AL.

| 5789 | F | i. | **Sarah Georganne Elizabeth Lindsey** was born 6 Jan 1995 in Lauderdale County, AL, died 23 Oct 1996, and was buried in Greenview Memorial Park, Florence, Lauderdale County, AL. |

4202. Bruce Elliot Joiner (*Wallace Wilbur Joiner* [8], *Georgia Mae Lindsey* [7], *John David Lindsey* [6], *Greenberry Lee Lindsey Sr.* [5], *Sylvester (Sill) B. Lindsey* [4], *Frances (Frankie) Sharp* [3], *Charles W. Sr.* [2], *John Sr.* [1]) was born 10 Oct 1956.

Bruce married **Brenda Jo Wells** 6 Dec 1980. Brenda was born 30 Nov 1957.
5790 M   i.   **Reid Elliot Joiner** was born 4 Jul 1982.
5791 F   ii.   **Leah Jo Joiner** was born 25 Feb 1985.

4203. Sharon Kay Joiner (*Wallace Wilbur Joiner* [8], *Georgia Mae Lindsey* [7], *John David Lindsey* [6], *Greenberry Lee Lindsey Sr.* [5], *Sylvester (Sill) B. Lindsey* [4], *Frances (Frankie) Sharp* [3], *Charles W. Sr.* [2], *John Sr.* [1]) was born 3 Aug 1958.

Sharon married ***Unk Cuellar** in 1976.
5792 F   i.   **Beth Ann Cuellar** was born 18 Jul 1977.
5793 M   ii.   **Christopher Allan Cuellar** was born in Dec 1981.

4204. Cathy Lynn Joiner (*Wallace Wilbur Joiner* [8], *Georgia Mae Lindsey* [7], *John David Lindsey* [6], *Greenberry Lee Lindsey Sr.* [5], *Sylvester (Sill) B. Lindsey* [4], *Frances (Frankie) Sharp* [3], *Charles W. Sr.* [2], *John Sr.* [1]) was born 24 Aug 1962.

Cathy married **Anthony Ray Bell** 10 Jun 1983.
5794 F   i.   **Lindsey Allison Bell** was born 9 Jun 1988.

4205. Steven Louis Tubbs (*June Jenette Joiner* [8], *Georgia Mae Lindsey* [7], *John David Lindsey* [6], *Greenberry Lee Lindsey Sr.* [5], *Sylvester (Sill) B. Lindsey* [4], *Frances (Frankie) Sharp* [3], *Charles W. Sr.* [2], *John Sr.* [1]) was born 22 Apr 1959.

Steven married **Katrina Marie Boyle** 18 Jun 1994. Katrina was born 7 Sep 1964.

4206. Sandra Jo Ames (*June Jenette Joiner* [8], *Georgia Mae Lindsey* [7], *John David Lindsey* [6], *Greenberry Lee Lindsey Sr.* [5], *Sylvester (Sill) B. Lindsey* [4], *Frances (Frankie) Sharp* [3], *Charles W. Sr.* [2], *John Sr.* [1]) was born 27 Aug 1967.

Sandra married **Jerry D. Karleski** 25 Jun 1993. Jerry was born 20 Dec 1961.
5795 M   i.   **Nathan Reid Karleski** was born 10 Feb 1995.

4207. Neal Lindsey (*Raymond Oneal Lindsey* [8], *Edgar Bruce Lindsey* [7], *John David Lindsey* [6], *Greenberry Lee Lindsey Sr.* [5], *Sylvester (Sill) B. Lindsey* [4], *Frances (Frankie) Sharp* [3], *Charles W. Sr.* [2], *John Sr.* [1]).

Neal married ***Unk**.
5796 M   i.   **Christopher Lindsey**.

4208. Craig Lindsey (*Raymond Oneal Lindsey* [8], *Edgar Bruce Lindsey* [7], *John David Lindsey* [6], *Greenberry Lee Lindsey Sr.* [5], *Sylvester (Sill) B. Lindsey* [4], *Frances (Frankie) Sharp* [3], *Charles W. Sr.* [2], *John Sr.* [1]).

Craig married ***Unk**.
5797 M   i.   **Jason Lindsey**.

4209. Todd Lindsey (*Raymond Oneal Lindsey* [8], *Edgar Bruce Lindsey* [7], *John David Lindsey* [6], *Greenberry Lee Lindsey Sr.* [5], *Sylvester (Sill) B. Lindsey* [4], *Frances (Frankie) Sharp* [3], *Charles W. Sr.* [2], *John Sr.* [1]).

Todd married ***Unk**.
5798 M   i.   **Son Lindsey**.
5799 M   ii.   **Son Lindsey**.

4210. Jason James Lindsey (*James Bruce Lindsey*[8], *Edgar Bruce Lindsey*[7], *John David Lindsey*[6], *Greenberry Lee Lindsey Sr.*[5], *Sylvester (Sill) B. Lindsey*[4], *Frances (Frankie) Sharp*[3], *Charles W. Sr.*[2], *John Sr.*[1]) was born 1 May 1976 in Melrose Park, IL.

   Jason married **Jacqueline (Jaki) *Unk**.
   5800   M   i.   **Dalton Lindsey**.

4216. Kenneth Eugene Lowery (*Karen Anne Perkins*[8], *Bobbie Lee Pierce*[7], *Amy Gertrude Lindsey*[6], *Adron (Little Ade) Lindsey*[5], *Sylvester (Sill) B. Lindsey*[4], *Frances (Frankie) Sharp*[3], *Charles W. Sr.*[2], *John Sr.*[1]) was born 8 Apr 1965 in Lawrence County, TN.

   Kenneth married **Lilliam Gail (Pebbles) Walmer** 7 Apr 1990 in Longview, WA. Lilliam was born 29 Nov 1963.
   5801   F   i.   **Brianna Mae Lowery** was born 8 Sep 1994 in Longview, WA.
   5802   M   ii.   **Nolan Conner Lowery** was born 22 Aug 2002 in Longview, WA.

4217. Anthony Wayne Lowery (*Karen Anne Perkins*[8], *Bobbie Lee Pierce*[7], *Amy Gertrude Lindsey*[6], *Adron (Little Ade) Lindsey*[5], *Sylvester (Sill) B. Lindsey*[4], *Frances (Frankie) Sharp*[3], *Charles W. Sr.*[2], *John Sr.*[1]) was born 5 Nov 1966 in Lawrence County, TN.

   Anthony married ***Unk**.
   5803   M   i.   **Michael Seth Lowery** was born 31 Jul 1995 in Lawrence County, TN.

4218. Shoan Lee Lowery (*Karen Anne Perkins*[8], *Bobbie Lee Pierce*[7], *Amy Gertrude Lindsey*[6], *Adron (Little Ade) Lindsey*[5], *Sylvester (Sill) B. Lindsey*[4], *Frances (Frankie) Sharp*[3], *Charles W. Sr.*[2], *John Sr.*[1]) was born 14 Feb 1969 in Lawrence County, TN.

   Shoan married **Mary Bedingfield**, daughter of **Ida Bedingfield** and **Ada Tennessee Greer**.

4219. Larry Bret Massey (*Connie Lee Perkins*[8], *Bobbie Lee Pierce*[7], *Amy Gertrude Lindsey*[6], *Adron (Little Ade) Lindsey*[5], *Sylvester (Sill) B. Lindsey*[4], *Frances (Frankie) Sharp*[3], *Charles W. Sr.*[2], *John Sr.*[1]) was born 24 Aug 1969 in Lawrence County, TN.

   Larry married **Kelly Renee' Hopkins** 14 Dec 1996 in Jamaica.
   5804   M   i.   **Jacob Cade Massey** was born 18 May 2000 in Colorado.
   5805   F   ii.   **Hannah Renee Massey** was born 31 Dec 2003 in Tennessee.
   5806   M   iii.   **Peyton Lee Massey** was born 4 Jan 2005 in Colorado.

4220. Chad Pierce Massey (*Connie Lee Perkins*[8], *Bobbie Lee Pierce*[7], *Amy Gertrude Lindsey*[6], *Adron (Little Ade) Lindsey*[5], *Sylvester (Sill) B. Lindsey*[4], *Frances (Frankie) Sharp*[3], *Charles W. Sr.*[2], *John Sr.*[1]) was born 29 Jun 1971 in Lawrence County, TN.

   Chad married **Shannon Boston**.
   5807   F   i.   **Rachel Ann Massey** was born 2 Sep 1993.
   5808   F   ii.   **Carli Elizabeth Massey** was born 27 Dec 2001.

   Chad next married **Elizabeth McCullon** 12 Jan 2000 in Lawrence County, TN.
   5809   M   i.   **Chad Massey** was born 30 Oct 2000.
   5810   F   ii.   **Carley Elizabeth Massey** was born 30 Dec 2002.

4222. Gregory Gains Burks (*Connie Lee Perkins*[8], *Bobbie Lee Pierce*[7], *Amy Gertrude Lindsey*[6], *Adron (Little Ade) Lindsey*[5], *Sylvester (Sill) B. Lindsey*[4], *Frances (Frankie) Sharp*[3], *Charles W. Sr.*[2], *John Sr.*[1]) was born 23 Jun 1975 in Lawrence County, TN.

   Gregory married **Eden Luise Kroeger** 15 Feb 2003.

4223. Kesha Annette Story (*Dianna Lynn Perkins*[8]*, Bobbie Lee Pierce*[7]*, Amy Gertrude Lindsey*[6]*, Adron (Little Ade) Lindsey*[5]*, Sylvester (Sill) B. Lindsey*[4]*, Frances (Frankie) Sharp*[3]*, Charles W. Sr.*[2]*, John Sr.*[1]) was born 5 Dec 1973 in Columbia, Maury County, TN.

Kesha married **Donald Sandy Williams** 7 Jul 1994. Donald was born 21 Apr 1968 in Lawrence County, TN.

5811	M	i.	**Kaleb Hunter Williams** was born 18 May 2000 in Columbia, Maury County, TN.
5812	F	ii.	**Katelyn Hannah Williams** was born 29 Apr 2002 in Columbia, Maury County, TN.

4224. Tiffani LeNea (Tippi) Story (*Dianna Lynn Perkins*[8]*, Bobbie Lee Pierce*[7]*, Amy Gertrude Lindsey*[6]*, Adron (Little Ade) Lindsey*[5]*, Sylvester (Sill) B. Lindsey*[4]*, Frances (Frankie) Sharp*[3]*, Charles W. Sr.*[2]*, John Sr.*[1]) was born 3 Nov 1975 in Columbia, Maury County, TN.

Tiffani married **Keith Ray Brazier** 29 Jan 1999 in Ethridge, TN. Keith was born 13 Aug 1973 in Lawrence County, TN.

5813	M	i.	**Treyton Kade Brazier** was born 26 Aug 1999 in Columbia, Maury County, TN.
5814	F	ii.	**Tatum Keauna Brazier** was born 3 Jul 2002 in Columbia, Maury County, TN.

4226. Michael Blake Perkins (*Homer Clyde Perkins III*[8]*, Bobbie Lee Pierce*[7]*, Amy Gertrude Lindsey*[6]*, Adron (Little Ade) Lindsey*[5]*, Sylvester (Sill) B. Lindsey*[4]*, Frances (Frankie) Sharp*[3]*, Charles W. Sr.*[2]*, John Sr.*[1]) was born 13 Aug 1983 in Columbia, Maury County, TN.

Michael married **Brittany Lane Wellington** 20 Sep 2003.

5815	F	i.	**Chole Lane Perkins** was born 29 Mar 2004.

4232. Terri Lynn Sharp (*Donna Sue Barrier*[8]*, Henry Olen Barrier*[7]*, Josie Etta Haynes*[6]*, Lucretia (Lula) Lindsey*[5]*, Adron Leonard Lindsey Sr.*[4]*, Frances (Frankie) Sharp*[3]*, Charles W. Sr.*[2]*, John Sr.*[1]) was born 19 Nov 1971 in Lauderdale County, AL.

Terri married **Fred Rayburn Higgins Jr.**, son of **Fred Rayburn Higgins Sr.** and **Geraldine McIntyre**, 28 Jan 1995 in Lauderdale County, AL. Fred was born 24 Aug 1954 in Lauderdale County, AL.

5816	M	i.	**Jeremy Higgins** was born in 1996.

4233. Jami Suzanne Sharp (*Donna Sue Barrier*[8]*, Henry Olen Barrier*[7]*, Josie Etta Haynes*[6]*, Lucretia (Lula) Lindsey*[5]*, Adron Leonard Lindsey Sr.*[4]*, Frances (Frankie) Sharp*[3]*, Charles W. Sr.*[2]*, John Sr.*[1]) was born 11 May 1983 in Lauderdale County, AL.

Jami married **Regie Leon Wood Jr.**, son of **Regie Leon (Buck) Wood Sr.** and **Nancy Mae Skipworth**, 3 May 2003 in Lauderdale County, AL. Regie was born 28 Feb 1976 in Lauderdale County, AL.

5817	F	i.	**Abigail Wood.**
5818	M	ii.	**Emily Suzanne Wood.**

4234. Deborah Diane Odum (*Harry Wilbern Odum Sr.*[8]*, Carmel Inez Haynes*[7]*, Clarence Haynes*[6]*, Lucretia (Lula) Lindsey*[5]*, Adron Leonard Lindsey Sr.*[4]*, Frances (Frankie) Sharp*[3]*, Charles W. Sr.*[2]*, John Sr.*[1]) was born 1 Jun 1952 in Memphis, Shelby County, TN.

Deborah married **Joe David Graves** 4 Aug 1972. Joe was born in Gibson County, TN.

5819	M	i.	**Rhett David Graves** was born 3 Sep 1977 in Monroe County, TN.

4235. Harry Wilbern Odum Jr. (*Harry Wilbern Odum Sr.*[8]*, Carmel Inez Haynes*[7]*, Clarence Haynes*[6]*, Lucretia (Lula) Lindsey*[5]*, Adron Leonard Lindsey Sr.*[4]*, Frances (Frankie) Sharp*[3]*, Charles W. Sr.*[2]*, John Sr.*[1]) was born 4 Oct 1953 in Memphis, Shelby County, TN.

Harry married **Dale Love** 13 Apr 1983. Dale was born 16 Dec.

5820	F	i.	**Stell Odum** was born 3 Oct 1984 in Los Angeles County, CA.

4236. Cheryl Annette Odum (*Harry Wilbern Odum Sr.*[8], *Carmel Inez Haynes*[7], *Clarence Haynes*[6], *Lucretia (Lula) Lindsey*[5], *Adron Leonard Lindsey Sr.*[4], *Frances (Frankie) Sharp*[3], *Charles W. Sr.*[2], *John Sr.*[1]) was born 24 Apr 1961 in Memphis, Shelby County, TN.

Cheryl married **Michael Dale Stevenson** 19 Sep 1980.
5821 M i. **Ryan Michael Stevenson** was born 18 Jul 1986 in Memphis, Shelby County, TN.
5822 M ii. **Tyler Dale Stevenson** was born 16 Jun 1988 in Memphis, Shelby County, TN.

4265. Michelle Dawn Winborn (*Douglas Ray Winborn*[8], *Ruby Mae Wood*[7], *Martha (Mattie) Inez Taylor*[6], *Lucretia (Lula) Lindsey*[5], *Adron Leonard Lindsey Sr.*[4], *Frances (Frankie) Sharp*[3], *Charles W. Sr.*[2], *John Sr.*[1]) was born 22 Sep 1971 in Lauderdale County, AL.

Michelle married **Shawn Edward Whitworth**, son of **Steve Randy Whitworth** and **Norma Lynnett Taylor**, 19 Aug 1994 in Lauderdale County, AL. Shawn was born 6 Dec 1971.
5823 M i. **Shane Logan Whitworth** was born 27 Oct 1994 in Lauderdale County, AL.

4271. Casey Endicott (*Patricia (Pat) Wood*[8], *Floyde Virgil Wood*[7], *Martha (Mattie) Inez Taylor*[6], *Lucretia (Lula) Lindsey*[5], *Adron Leonard Lindsey Sr.*[4], *Frances (Frankie) Sharp*[3], *Charles W. Sr.*[2], *John Sr.*[1]) was born 29 Mar 1979.

Casey married **Paul Grove** 4 Jun 2006. Paul was born 4 Jan 1981.
5824 M i. **Kevin Grove** was born 4 Aug 2003.
5825 M ii. **Preston Grove** was born 6 Nov 2007.

4272. Timothy Endicott (*Patricia (Pat) Wood*[8], *Floyde Virgil Wood*[7], *Martha (Mattie) Inez Taylor*[6], *Lucretia (Lula) Lindsey*[5], *Adron Leonard Lindsey Sr.*[4], *Frances (Frankie) Sharp*[3], *Charles W. Sr.*[2], *John Sr.*[1]) was born 9 Sep 1984.

Timothy married **Blair Decker** 9 Aug 2008. Blair was born 13 Sep 1984.

4273. Derek Robert Daniels (*Brenda Ruth Bruce*[8], *Annie Ruth Wood*[7], *Martha (Mattie) Inez Taylor*[6], *Lucretia (Lula) Lindsey*[5], *Adron Leonard Lindsey Sr.*[4], *Frances (Frankie) Sharp*[3], *Charles W. Sr.*[2], *John Sr.*[1]) was born 17 Feb 1970.

Derek married **Lori Nicholle West** 3 Oct 1999 in Colbert County, AL.

4274. Vickie Denise Daniels (*Brenda Ruth Bruce*[8], *Annie Ruth Wood*[7], *Martha (Mattie) Inez Taylor*[6], *Lucretia (Lula) Lindsey*[5], *Adron Leonard Lindsey Sr.*[4], *Frances (Frankie) Sharp*[3], *Charles W. Sr.*[2], *John Sr.*[1]) was born 5 Feb 1972.

Vickie married **Jackie Reeves**. Jackie was born 2 Aug 1971.
5826 M i. **Tyler Wayne Reeves** was born 22 Mar 1993.
5827 F ii. **Maggie Danielle Reeves** was born 3 Apr 1996.

4275. John Paul Barrier (*Barbara Sue Bruce*[8], *Annie Ruth Wood*[7], *Martha (Mattie) Inez Taylor*[6], *Lucretia (Lula) Lindsey*[5], *Adron Leonard Lindsey Sr.*[4], *Frances (Frankie) Sharp*[3], *Charles W. Sr.*[2], *John Sr.*[1]) was born 22 Sep 1970 in Lauderdale County, AL.

John married **Tammy Annette Stephens** 8 May 1992. Tammy was born 2 Aug 1967 in Lewis County, TN.
5828 F i. **Haley Brooke Barrier** was born 16 Dec 1992 in Maury County, TN.

4276. Joannie Lee Barrier (*Barbara Sue Bruce*[8], *Annie Ruth Wood*[7], *Martha (Mattie) Inez Taylor*[6], *Lucretia (Lula) Lindsey*[5], *Adron Leonard Lindsey Sr.*[4], *Frances (Frankie) Sharp*[3], *Charles W. Sr.*[2], *John Sr.*[1]) was born 6 Sep 1976 in Lauderdale County, AL.

Joannie married **Joe Dayton Duncan** 24 May 1992. Joe was born 26 Mar 1971 in Maury County, TN.
5829 F i. **Amber Lynn Turner Duncan** was born 8 Sep 1991 in Maury County, TN.

4282. Holly Lynn Eck (*Karen Denise Wood^8, Glen Wood^7, Martha (Mattie) Inez Taylor^6, Lucretia (Lula) Lindsey^5, Adron Leonard Lindsey Sr.^{4}, Frances (Frankie) Sharp^3, Charles W. Sr.^{2}, John Sr.^{1}*) was born 29 Dec 1978.

Holly married **Robert (Robbie) Michael Kelsey**, son of **Evan LeRoy (Roy) Kelsey** and **Virginia Ann Roberson**, in Dec 1994. Robert was born 10 Aug 1971 in Lauderdale County, AL.
5830 M i. **Nicholas Patrick Kelsey**.

4295. Krysta Lynn Linville (*Debra Lynn Hipps^8, Elza Darlene Wood^7, Martha (Mattie) Inez Taylor^6, Lucretia (Lula) Lindsey^5, Adron Leonard Lindsey Sr.^{4}, Frances (Frankie) Sharp^3, Charles W. Sr.^{2}, John Sr.^{1}*) was born 15 Oct 1969 in Lauderdale County, AL.

Krysta married **Michael Stover**.
5831 M i. **Jacob Brodie Stover** was born 2 Mar 1993.
5832 F ii. **Mallorie Hope Stover** was born 13 Sep 1994.

4297. Thomas Riley (Ry) Darby (*Jackie Diane Hipps^8, Elza Darlene Wood^7, Martha (Mattie) Inez Taylor^6, Lucretia (Lula) Lindsey^5, Adron Leonard Lindsey Sr.^{4}, Frances (Frankie) Sharp^3, Charles W. Sr.^{2}, John Sr.^{1}*) was born 8 Jun 1983 in Lauderdale County, AL.

Thomas married **Itsumi *Unk**.

4298. Lori Darlene Hipps (*Nancy Carol Hipps^8, Elza Darlene Wood^7, Martha (Mattie) Inez Taylor^6, Lucretia (Lula) Lindsey^5, Adron Leonard Lindsey Sr.^{4}, Frances (Frankie) Sharp^3, Charles W. Sr.^{2}, John Sr.^{1}*) was born 29 Jul 1983.

Lori married **Michael Hall**.

4299. Jessica Danielle Hipps (*Jesse James (Jamie) Hipps^8, Elza Darlene Wood^7, Martha (Mattie) Inez Taylor^6, Lucretia (Lula) Lindsey^5, Adron Leonard Lindsey Sr.^{4}, Frances (Frankie) Sharp^3, Charles W. Sr.^{2}, John Sr.^{1}*) was born 27 Apr 1983.

Jessica married **Michael Baker**.
5833 F i. **Jesslee Baker**.

4312. Lindsey Katherine Buttram (*Nancy Carter McDonald^8, William Lindsey McDonald^7, Pauline Myran Lindsey^6, Adron Leonard (Green) Lindsey Jr.^{5}, Adron Leonard Lindsey Sr.^{4}, Frances (Frankie) Sharp^3, Charles W. Sr.^{2}, John Sr.^{1}*) was born 15 Aug 1973.

Lindsey married **Gerald Scott Middleton** 24 Sep 1994.

4317. Phillip Dewayne McDonald Jr. (*Phillip Dewayne McDonald Sr.^{8}, Marvin McDaniel McDonald^7, Pauline Myran Lindsey^6, Adron Leonard (Green) Lindsey Jr.^{5}, Adron Leonard Lindsey Sr.^{4}, Frances (Frankie) Sharp^3, Charles W. Sr.^{2}, John Sr.^{1}*) was born 31 Mar 1972 in Lauderdale County, AL.

Phillip married **Sandra Faye Roush**, daughter of **Albert Wesley Roush** and **Shirley Faye King**, 28 May 1992 in Lauderdale County, AL. Sandra was born 20 Dec 1971 in Alabama.

4318. Samantha Ann McDonald (*Phillip Dewayne McDonald Sr.^{8}, Marvin McDaniel McDonald^7, Pauline Myran Lindsey^6, Adron Leonard (Green) Lindsey Jr.^{5}, Adron Leonard Lindsey Sr.^{4}, Frances (Frankie) Sharp^3, Charles W. Sr.^{2}, John Sr.^{1}*) was born 2 Nov 1974 in Lauderdale County, AL.

Samantha married **Lloyd Thomas Davis**, son of **Thomas Glenn Davis** and **Mildred Jeannette Pounders**, 1 Jun 1993 in Lauderdale County, AL. Lloyd was born 25 Jul 1973 in Lauderdale County, AL.
5834 F i. **Rita Danielle Davis**.

4360. Debra Lynn Weiss (*Bobbie Dean Chowning*[8], *Jewel Dean Young*[7], *William (Bill) Mack Young*[6], *Eddie Young*[5], *Mary M. (Polly II) Lindsey*[4], *Frances (Frankie) Sharp*[3], *Charles W. Sr.*[2], *John Sr.*[1]) was born 3 Jun 1959 in Manistee, MI.

Debra married **Mark William Manning**, son of **Billy Dewitt Manning** and **Martha Ruth Easley**, 20 Oct 1990 in Lauderdale County, AL. Mark was born 31 Dec 1956 in Alabama.

4362. Melissa Beth Irons (*Karen Delane Young*[8], *James Robert Young*[7], *William (Bill) Mack Young*[6], *Eddie Young*[5], *Mary M. (Polly II) Lindsey*[4], *Frances (Frankie) Sharp*[3], *Charles W. Sr.*[2], *John Sr.*[1]) was born 20 Nov 1977.

Melissa married **Joshua Daniel Witt**, son of **Danny Ray Witt** and **Jacqueline Sue (Jackie) White**, 12 Apr 2003 in Lauderdale County, AL. Joshua was born 27 Apr 1979 in South Bend, St Joseph County, IN.

4364. Kerri Beth Gamble (*Wanda Sue Young*[8], *Cecil Lloyd Young*[7], *Earnest Edward Young*[6], *Eddie Young*[5], *Mary M. (Polly II) Lindsey*[4], *Frances (Frankie) Sharp*[3], *Charles W. Sr.*[2], *John Sr.*[1]) was born 6 Jul 1970 in Lauderdale County, AL.

Kerri married **Eric Lee Richardson**, son of **Grandville Richardson** and **Margaret Ophelia McLaughlin**, 1 Jul 1988 in Colbert County, AL. Eric was born 12 Jan 1971 in Colbert County, AL.
5835 M i. **Lee Alexander Richardson** was born 23 Jan 1989 in Colbert County, AL.

Kerri next married **Andy White** 23 Nov 1996.
5836 F i. **Hannah Grace White** was born 5 Nov 1998 in Columbia, Maury County, TN.

4365. Melanie Leigh Gamble (*Wanda Sue Young*[8], *Cecil Lloyd Young*[7], *Earnest Edward Young*[6], *Eddie Young*[5], *Mary M. (Polly II) Lindsey*[4], *Frances (Frankie) Sharp*[3], *Charles W. Sr.*[2], *John Sr.*[1]) was born 20 May 1974 in Ft Worth, Tarrant County, TX.

Melanie married **Michael Allen Fell** 22 Jun 1996 in Chaton, AL.
5837 F i. **Morgan Alexis Fell** was born 19 Jul 2000 in Columbia, AL.

4368. Shana Nicole Yerby (*Teresa Diane Young*[8], *Cecil Lloyd Young*[7], *Earnest Edward Young*[6], *Eddie Young*[5], *Mary M. (Polly II) Lindsey*[4], *Frances (Frankie) Sharp*[3], *Charles W. Sr.*[2], *John Sr.*[1]) was born 25 Aug 1978 in Lauderdale County, AL.

Shana married **Brian Keith Balch**, son of **Keith Balch** and **Brenda Hurn**, 25 Oct 2003 in Lauderdale County, AL.

4371. April Dawn Parrish (*Kathy Marie Keeton*[8], *Hazel Joyce Young*[7], *Earnest Edward Young*[6], *Eddie Young*[5], *Mary M. (Polly II) Lindsey*[4], *Frances (Frankie) Sharp*[3], *Charles W. Sr.*[2], *John Sr.*[1]) was born 6 Oct 1979.

April married **Thomas Edward Harrison**, son of **Jim Horrison** and **Mary M. Byrd**, 27 Sep 1999 in Lauderdale County, AL. Thomas was born 15 Mar 1975.
5838 M i. **Carmelo Keith Harrison**.

4377. Tammy Diane Skipworth (*Linda Joyce Gooch*[8], *Macil Bethrine Young*[7], *Odus Clarence Young Sr.*[6], *Eddie Young*[5], *Mary M. (Polly II) Lindsey*[4], *Frances (Frankie) Sharp*[3], *Charles W. Sr.*[2], *John Sr.*[1]).

Tammy married **Stanley Shotts**.
5839 M i. **Stanley Shotts Jr.**
5840 M ii. **Seth Shotts**.
5841 M iii. **Sawyer Shotts**.

4378. Tina Dinese Skipworth (*Linda Joyce Gooch*[8], *Macil Bethrine Young*[7], *Odus Clarence Young Sr.*[6], *Eddie Young*[5], *Mary M. (Polly II) Lindsey*[4], *Frances (Frankie) Sharp*[3], *Charles W. Sr.*[2], *John Sr.*[1]).

Tina married **Robert Dye**.
5842 F i. **Jessica Dye**.
5843 F ii. **Clarissa Joyce Dye**.
5844 M iii. **Anthony Dye**.

4380. Tabitha Ann Skipworth (*Linda Joyce Gooch^8, Macil Bethrine Young^7, Odus Clarence Young Sr.^{6}, Eddie Young^5, Mary M. (Polly II) Lindsey^4, Frances (Frankie) Sharp^3, Charles W. Sr.^{2}, John Sr.^{1}*).

Tabitha married **Brandon Christopher Culver**.
5845 F i. **Rebecca Culver**.
5846 M ii. **Brandon C. Culver**.
5847 F iii. **Robin Culver**.

4381. Angela Joyce Skipworth (*Linda Joyce Gooch^8, Macil Bethrine Young^7, Odus Clarence Young Sr.^{6}, Eddie Young^5, Mary M. (Polly II) Lindsey^4, Frances (Frankie) Sharp^3, Charles W. Sr.^{2}, John Sr.^{1}*).

Angela married **Chris Jones**.

4382. Sonia Michelle Gooch (*Donnie Lee Gooch^8, Macil Bethrine Young^7, Odus Clarence Young Sr.^{6}, Eddie Young^5, Mary M. (Polly II) Lindsey^4, Frances (Frankie) Sharp^3, Charles W. Sr.^{2}, John Sr.^{1}*).

Sonia married **Brandon Tittle**.
5848 M i. **Coty Ray Tittle**.
5849 M ii. **Brandon Cole Tittle**.
+ 5850 M iii. **Michael Pounders**.

4383. Barbara Green Gooch (*Donnie Lee Gooch^8, Macil Bethrine Young^7, Odus Clarence Young Sr.^{6}, Eddie Young^5, Mary M. (Polly II) Lindsey^4, Frances (Frankie) Sharp^3, Charles W. Sr.^{2}, John Sr.^{1}*).

Barbara married **Kevin Denton**.
5851 M i. **Trevor Denton**.

4385. Brad Evan McIntyre (*Janet Faye Gooch^8, Macil Bethrine Young^7, Odus Clarence Young Sr.^{6}, Eddie Young^5, Mary M. (Polly II) Lindsey^4, Frances (Frankie) Sharp^3, Charles W. Sr.^{2}, John Sr.^{1}*) was born 5 Aug 1974.

Brad married **Kimberly Thompson**, daughter of **Wriley Thompson** and **Mary *Unk**.
5852 F i. **Tiffany McIntyre**.
5853 F ii. **Bradlyn McIntyre**.
5854 M iii. **Caden McIntyre**.

4388. Stephanie Nicole Smith (*Kathy Ann Gooch^8, Macil Bethrine Young^7, Odus Clarence Young Sr.^{6}, Eddie Young^5, Mary M. (Polly II) Lindsey^4, Frances (Frankie) Sharp^3, Charles W. Sr.^{2}, John Sr.^{1}*) was born in 1973.

Stephanie married **John Friend**. John was born in 1970.
5855 M i. **Aaron Joseph Friend** was born in 1995.
5856 F ii. **Angelica Beth Friend** was born 6 Jun 1996, died 6 Jun 1996, and was buried in Murphy's Chapel Cemetery, Lauderdale County, AL.
5857 M iii. **David Friend** was born in 1998.
5858 M iv. **Evan Friend** was born in 2001.
5859 M v. **Nolan Friend** was born in 2007.

4389. Shannon Nole Smith (*Kathy Ann Gooch^8, Macil Bethrine Young^7, Odus Clarence Young Sr.^{6}, Eddie Young^5, Mary M. (Polly II) Lindsey^4, Frances (Frankie) Sharp^3, Charles W. Sr.^{2}, John Sr.^{1}*) was born 29 Aug 1977 in Lauderdale County, AL.

Shannon married **Amanda Faye Lawson** 15 May 2004 in Lauderdale County, AL.
5860 F i. **Layla Smith**.

4390. Chastidy Recale Smith (*Sharon Jean Gooch* ^{8}, *Macil Bethrine Young* ^{7}, *Odus Clarence Young Sr.* ^{6}, *Eddie Young* ^{5}, *Mary M. (Polly II) Lindsey* ^{4}, *Frances (Frankie) Sharp* ^{3}, *Charles W. Sr.* ^{2}, *John Sr.* ^{1}) was born 6 Nov 1973.

Chastidy married **Eric Allen Creighton** 14 Feb 1994. Eric was born 18 Mar 1975.
5861 M   i.   **Alex Logan Creighton** was born in 1994.

Chastidy next married **Leonard Casey Jones**, son of **Leonard Ray Jones** and **Connie Sue Wood**. Leonard was born 5 Oct 1974 in Lauderdale County, AL, died 15 Nov 2008, and was buried in Canaan Cemetery, Lauderdale County, AL.

5862 M   i.   **Corbin Casey Jones** was born 26 Aug 1999.

4391. Michael Eugene Jones Jr. (*Sharon Jean Gooch* ^{8}, *Macil Bethrine Young* ^{7}, *Odus Clarence Young Sr.* ^{6}, *Eddie Young* ^{5}, *Mary M. (Polly II) Lindsey* ^{4}, *Frances (Frankie) Sharp* ^{3}, *Charles W. Sr.* ^{2}, *John Sr.* ^{1}).

Michael married **Tara Nico Christopher**.
5863 M   i.   **Michael Eugene Jones III**.
5864 M   ii.   **Matthew Thomas Jones**.
5865 M   iii.   **Mark Christopher Jones**.

4392. Troy Christopher Jones (*Sharon Jean Gooch* ^{8}, *Macil Bethrine Young* ^{7}, *Odus Clarence Young Sr.* ^{6}, *Eddie Young* ^{5}, *Mary M. (Polly II) Lindsey* ^{4}, *Frances (Frankie) Sharp* ^{3}, *Charles W. Sr.* ^{2}, *John Sr.* ^{1}).

Troy married **Christina Ann Hart**, daughter of **Terry Melvin Hart** and **Tamara Faye Faulkner**. Christina was born 1 May 1982 in Lauderdale County, AL.
5866 F   i.   **Lola Elise Jones**.

4393. Jennifer Sherae Gooch (*Timmy Lee Gooch* ^{8}, *Macil Bethrine Young* ^{7}, *Odus Clarence Young Sr.* ^{6}, *Eddie Young* ^{5}, *Mary M. (Polly II) Lindsey* ^{4}, *Frances (Frankie) Sharp* ^{3}, *Charles W. Sr.* ^{2}, *John Sr.* ^{1}).

Jennifer married **Matthew Watson**.
5867 F   i.   **Brianna Nicole Watson**.
5868 M   ii.   **Andrew Tyler Watson**.

4394. Erica Lynn Gooch (*Marcia Lynn Gooch* ^{8}, *Macil Bethrine Young* ^{7}, *Odus Clarence Young Sr.* ^{6}, *Eddie Young* ^{5}, *Mary M. (Polly II) Lindsey* ^{4}, *Frances (Frankie) Sharp* ^{3}, *Charles W. Sr.* ^{2}, *John Sr.* ^{1}) was born 13 Feb 1979 in Florence, Lauderdale County, AL.

Erica married **Adrian Lee Hart**, son of **Terry Melvin Hart** and **Tamara Faye Faulkner**, 26 Jan 1995 in Lauderdale County, AL. Adrian was born 13 Nov 1976 in Lauderdale County, AL.
5869 F   i.   **Shanna Lynn Hart** was born 6 Jun 1995 in Lauderdale County, AL.

Erica next married **Adam Birch**.
5870 M   i.   **Nathan Birch**.
5871 M   ii.   **Ethan Birch**.

4395. Rodney Dale Ezekiel (*Marcia Lynn Gooch* ^{8}, *Macil Bethrine Young* ^{7}, *Odus Clarence Young Sr.* ^{6}, *Eddie Young* ^{5}, *Mary M. (Polly II) Lindsey* ^{4}, *Frances (Frankie) Sharp* ^{3}, *Charles W. Sr.* ^{2}, *John Sr.* ^{1}).

Rodney married **Selina Leann White** 8 May 2004 in Lauderdale County, AL.

4396. Ryan Keith Clemons (*Marsha Kay Gooch* ^{8}, *Macil Bethrine Young* ^{7}, *Odus Clarence Young Sr.* ^{6}, *Eddie Young* ^{5}, *Mary M. (Polly II) Lindsey* ^{4}, *Frances (Frankie) Sharp* ^{3}, *Charles W. Sr.* ^{2}, *John Sr.* ^{1}) was born 24 Mar 1980 in Lauderdale County, AL.

Ryan married ***Unk**.
5872 M   i.   **Jerod Clemons**.
5873 M   ii.   **Sawyer Clemons**.

4399. Chris Richards (*Vicki Ann Heck[8], Carlene Vernial Young[7], Odus Clarence Young Sr.[6], Eddie Young[5], Mary M. (Polly II) Lindsey[4], Frances (Frankie) Sharp[3], Charles W. Sr.[2], John Sr.[1]*) was born 11 Mar 1972 in Weisbaden, Germany.

Chris married **Virginia Katie McHugh** 23 May 1998 in Greenwood, SC. Virginia was born from Sep 224 to 1974.

4400. Carlene M. Richards (*Vicki Ann Heck[8], Carlene Vernial Young[7], Odus Clarence Young Sr.[6], Eddie Young[5], Mary M. (Polly II) Lindsey[4], Frances (Frankie) Sharp[3], Charles W. Sr.[2], John Sr.[1]*) was born 15 May 1979 in Knoxville, TN.

Carlene married **Daniel Stanton** 1 Jan 2001 in Washington County, TN. Daniel was born 19 Jan 1979.
5874 M   i.   **Aaron Moree Stanton** was born 7 Feb 2002.
5875 M   ii. **Patrick Roy Stanton** was born 15 Jan 2005.

4412. Gary Lee Murphy (*Dewey Arnold Murphy[8], Robert Arnold Murphy[7], Jessie Bell Dearen[6], Mary Francis (Molly) Young[5], Mary M. (Polly II) Lindsey[4], Frances (Frankie) Sharp[3], Charles W. Sr.[2], John Sr.[1]*) was born 15 Feb 1952 in Richmond, VA.

Gary married **Paula Ann Lovelady**, daughter of **Paul T. Lovelady** and **Verrin Loosier**, 10 Mar 1972 in Colbert County, AL. Paula was born 1 Dec 1950 in Colbert County, AL.
5876 F   i.   **Aundrea Leeann Murphy** was born 8 Feb 1974 in Tuscumbia, Colbert County, AL.
5877 F   ii. **Luelus Peyton Murphy** was born 4 Aug 1977 in Lauderdale County, AL.

4413. Joan Denise Murphy (*Dewey Arnold Murphy[8], Robert Arnold Murphy[7], Jessie Bell Dearen[6], Mary Francis (Molly) Young[5], Mary M. (Polly II) Lindsey[4], Frances (Frankie) Sharp[3], Charles W. Sr.[2], John Sr.[1]*) was born 13 Feb 1954 in Lauderdale County, AL.

Joan married **Charles Phillip Burton**, son of **Oscar Burton** and **Mary Francis Schonwetter**, 28 Mar 1980 in Boxdale, LA. Charles was born 25 Nov 1955 in Baltimore, MD.
5878 M   i.   **Michael Alexander Burton** was born 4 Oct 1984 in Lauderdale County, AL.
5879 M   ii. **Kyle David Burton** was born 29 Apr 1986 in Denver, CO.

4414. Roger Dale Murphy (*Dewey Arnold Murphy[8], Robert Arnold Murphy[7], Jessie Bell Dearen[6], Mary Francis (Molly) Young[5], Mary M. (Polly II) Lindsey[4], Frances (Frankie) Sharp[3], Charles W. Sr.[2], John Sr.[1]*) was born 4 Mar 1955 in Norfolk, VA.

Roger married **Martha Jean Floyd**, daughter of **Joseph L. Floyd** and **Alice Borden**, 11 Feb 1978 in Lauderdale County, AL. Martha was born 30 Oct 1954 in Corinth, Alcorn County, MS.
5880 M   i.   **Joshua Dale Murphy** was born 28 Oct 1981 in Corinth, Alcorn County, MS.
5881 F   ii. **Mirandey Jean Murphy** was born 22 May 1988 in Norfolk, VA.

4415. Judy Irene Murphy (*Dewey Arnold Murphy[8], Robert Arnold Murphy[7], Jessie Bell Dearen[6], Mary Francis (Molly) Young[5], Mary M. (Polly II) Lindsey[4], Frances (Frankie) Sharp[3], Charles W. Sr.[2], John Sr.[1]*) was born 27 Apr 1964 in Norfolk, VA.

Judy married **Kim Russell Young**, son of **James Robert Young** and **Bille J. Burns**, 20 Aug 1982 in Lauderdale County, AL. Kim was born 6 Jun 1962 in Lauderdale County, AL.
(Duplicate Line. See Person 2510)

4418. Tonya Shae Cochran (*Margaret Sue Murphy[8], Robert Arnold Murphy[7], Jessie Bell Dearen[6], Mary Francis (Molly) Young[5], Mary M. (Polly II) Lindsey[4], Frances (Frankie) Sharp[3], Charles W. Sr.[2], John Sr.[1]*) was born 16 Apr 1961 in Davidson County, TN.

Tonya married **William Stephen Jackson** 25 Sep 1991 in Tennessee.

4419. Jennifer Robin Murphy (*Kenneth Lee Murphy^8, Doyal Lee Murphy^7, Jessie Bell Dearen^6, Mary Francis (Molly) Young^5, Mary M. (Polly II) Lindsey^4, Frances (Frankie) Sharp^3, Charles W. Sr.^{2}, John Sr.^{1}*) was born 22 Feb 1961 in Lauderdale County, AL.

Jennifer married **Robert Davis** 9 May 1987 in Mobile, AL.
5882 M i. **Daniel Murphy Davis** was born 4 May 1988.
5883 F ii. **Sarah Elizabeth Davis** was born 29 Dec 1990.

4420. Melissa Jill Murphy (*Kenneth Lee Murphy^8, Doyal Lee Murphy^7, Jessie Bell Dearen^6, Mary Francis (Molly) Young^5, Mary M. (Polly II) Lindsey^4, Frances (Frankie) Sharp^3, Charles W. Sr.^{2}, John Sr.^{1}*) was born 12 Nov 1964 in Lauderdale County, AL.

Melissa married **Robert Perallta** 4 Sep 1993 in Mobile, AL. Robert was born 27 Aug 1964.

4422. Charles Daniel Goode (*Marshall Elbert Goode^8, Jenny Ione Murphy^7, Jessie Bell Dearen^6, Mary Francis (Molly) Young^5, Mary M. (Polly II) Lindsey^4, Frances (Frankie) Sharp^3, Charles W. Sr.^{2}, John Sr.^{1}*) was born 9 Jul 1964 in Lauderdale County, AL.

Charles married **Sonya Renee Griffin**.

4423. Jessia Ann Murphy (*Gary Carl Murphy^8, Karl Jones Murphy^7, Jessie Bell Dearen^6, Mary Francis (Molly) Young^5, Mary M. (Polly II) Lindsey^4, Frances (Frankie) Sharp^3, Charles W. Sr.^{2}, John Sr.^{1}*) was born 22 Oct 1965 in Lauderdale County, AL.

Jessia married **Frankie Alan Richardson**, son of **Jerry Ivon Richardson** and **Gwendale Gail James**, 21 Jun 1990 in Lauderdale County, AL. Frankie was born 15 Jun 1970 in Alabama.

4432. William Bryan Echols (*Tessa Maria Knight^8, Ora Kyleene Murphy^7, Jessie Bell Dearen^6, Mary Francis (Molly) Young^5, Mary M. (Polly II) Lindsey^4, Frances (Frankie) Sharp^3, Charles W. Sr.^{2}, John Sr.^{1}*) was born 19 Apr 1969 in Jefferson County, AL.

William married **Patricia Ann Scott**, daughter of **Dalton James Scott** and **Patricia Ann Campbell**, 11 Jul 1992 in Lauderdale County, AL. Patricia was born 16 May 1969.
5884 M i. **Patrick Bryan Echols** was born 17 Mar 1993 in Colbert County, AL.

4433. Georgeanna Lee Echols (*Tessa Maria Knight^8, Ora Kyleene Murphy^7, Jessie Bell Dearen^6, Mary Francis (Molly) Young^5, Mary M. (Polly II) Lindsey^4, Frances (Frankie) Sharp^3, Charles W. Sr.^{2}, John Sr.^{1}*) was born 21 Mar 1970 in Jefferson County, AL.

Georgeanna married **Donald Scott Rickard II**, son of **William Hubert Rickard** and **Penny Lee Duffy**, 11 Aug 1990 in Lauderdale County, AL. Donald was born 22 Jan 1969.
5885 M i. **Hunter Lee Rickard** was born 9 Apr 1998 in Lauderdale County, AL.
5886 M ii. **Chandler Scott Rickard** was born 8 May 1999 in Lauderdale County, AL.

4434. Johnny Neal Echols (*Tessa Maria Knight^8, Ora Kyleene Murphy^7, Jessie Bell Dearen^6, Mary Francis (Molly) Young^5, Mary M. (Polly II) Lindsey^4, Frances (Frankie) Sharp^3, Charles W. Sr.^{2}, John Sr.^{1}*) was born 28 Apr 1976 in Lauderdale County, AL.

Johnny married **Jala Leigh Thompson**, daughter of **Freddie Darryl Thompson** and **Martha Elizabeth Flippo**, 16 Dec 2000 in Lauderdale County, AL. Jala was born 12 Apr 1978.

4437. John Corey Blahuta (*Donna Sue Harper^8, Mildred Pauline Dearen^7, William Lee Dearen^6, Mary Francis (Molly) Young^5, Mary M. (Polly II) Lindsey^4, Frances (Frankie) Sharp^3, Charles W. Sr.^{2}, John Sr.^{1}*) was born 29 Apr 1969 in Waco, McLennan County, TX.

John married **Misty Harrison** 6 Jul 1996 in Waco, McLennan County, TX.
5887 F i. **Emma Grace Blahuta** was born 17 May 1999.

4439. Michael Darrow Mason (*Mildred Loriene Gean*[8], *Della V. Abilene Sego*[7], *Minnie Pearl Dearen*[6], *Mary Francis (Molly) Young*[5], *Mary M. (Polly II) Lindsey*[4], *Frances (Frankie) Sharp*[3], *Charles W. Sr.*[2], *John Sr.*[1]) was born 13 Oct 1956 in Brunswick, Glynn County, GA.

Michael married **Lana Gaye Thrailkill**, daughter of **Arthur Thrailkill** and **Evelyn Conway**, 1 Jun 1982 in Portland, San Patricio County, TX. Lana was born 27 Mar 1957 in Corpus Cristi, Nueces County, TX, died 2 Jul 2006, and was buried in Memory Hill Gardens, Bartlett, TN.

| 5888 | M | i. | **Curtis Michael Mason** was born 14 Jul 1983 in Newbern, Craven County, NC. |
| 5889 | M | ii. | **Patrick Louis Mason** was born 13 Apr 1986 in Newbern, Craven County, NC. |

4440. Wanda Lorene Mason (*Mildred Loriene Gean*[8], *Della V. Abilene Sego*[7], *Minnie Pearl Dearen*[6], *Mary Francis (Molly) Young*[5], *Mary M. (Polly II) Lindsey*[4], *Frances (Frankie) Sharp*[3], *Charles W. Sr.*[2], *John Sr.*[1]) was born 1 Dec 1957 in Lauderdale County, AL.

Wanda married **Alan Martin Conner**, son of **Billy Conner** and **Judy Hunt**, 31 Jul 1976 in Lauderdale County, AL. Alan was born 17 Sep 1957 in Lauderdale County, AL.

Wanda next married **Ricky Wayne Legg**, son of **Hollis Legg** and **Geraldine Gully**, 15 Sep 1984 in Lauderdale County, AL. Ricky was born 9 Dec 1960 in Cleveland, Cuyahoga County, OH.

| 5890 | M | i. | **Aron Wayne Legg** was born 22 Mar 1986 in Florence, Lauderdale County, AL. |

Wanda next married **Eddie Wayne (Pete) Clemons**, son of **Benny Clemons** and **Dorothy Canerday**, 14 Feb 1990 in Lauderdale County, AL. Eddie was born 2 Jan 1957 in Lauderdale County, AL.

4441. Belinda Lois Mason (*Mildred Loriene Gean*[8], *Della V. Abilene Sego*[7], *Minnie Pearl Dearen*[6], *Mary Francis (Molly) Young*[5], *Mary M. (Polly II) Lindsey*[4], *Frances (Frankie) Sharp*[3], *Charles W. Sr.*[2], *John Sr.*[1]) was born 30 Dec 1958 in Jacksonville, Duval County, FL.

Belinda married **William Gary Ray**, son of **William C. Ray** and **Mary McDonald**, 28 Oct 1977 in Lauderdale County, AL. William was born 9 Nov 1956 in Smyrna, Rutherford County, TN.

| + 5891 | M | i. | **Jeremy Michael Ray** was born 9 May 1980 in Lauderdale County, AL. |
| + 5892 | F | ii. | **Brittany Belinda Ray** was born 2 Oct 1985 in Florence, Lauderdale County, AL. |

4442. Ronnie Ray Hill (*Geneva Yvonne Gean*[8], *Della V. Abilene Sego*[7], *Minnie Pearl Dearen*[6], *Mary Francis (Molly) Young*[5], *Mary M. (Polly II) Lindsey*[4], *Frances (Frankie) Sharp*[3], *Charles W. Sr.*[2], *John Sr.*[1]) was born 29 Jul 1960 in Lauderdale County, AL.

Ronnie married **Joyce Leigh Rourke** 3 Apr 1993 in Savannah, TN. Joyce was born 31 Oct 1955 in Miami, FL, died 9 Feb 1995, and was buried in Spartan Cemetery, Ocala, FL.

Ronnie next married **Norma *Unk**.

4443. Randal Reed Hill (*Geneva Yvonne Gean*[8], *Della V. Abilene Sego*[7], *Minnie Pearl Dearen*[6], *Mary Francis (Molly) Young*[5], *Mary M. (Polly II) Lindsey*[4], *Frances (Frankie) Sharp*[3], *Charles W. Sr.*[2], *John Sr.*[1]) was born 27 Sep 1962 in Lauderdale County, AL.

Randal married **Natalie Gail Threet** 5 May 1989 in Lauderdale County, AL. Natalie was born 4 Jul 1969 in Lauderdale County, AL.

Randal next married **Doris Ann Willis**, daughter of **James Willis** and **Clara Bass**, 28 Feb 1995 in Savannah, TN. Doris was born 26 Oct 1966 in Lauderdale County, AL.

| 5893 | M | i. | **Kyler Blake Hill** was born 30 Apr 1996 in Lauderdale County, AL. |

4444. Roanna Renee Hill (*Geneva Yvonne Gean*[8], *Della V. Abilene Sego*[7], *Minnie Pearl Dearen*[6], *Mary Francis (Molly) Young*[5], *Mary M. (Polly II) Lindsey*[4], *Frances (Frankie) Sharp*[3], *Charles W. Sr.*[2], *John Sr.*[1]) was born 9 Nov 1964 in Loretto, Lawrence County, TN.

Roanna married **Gene Borden**.

Roanna next married **James William Daniel Jr.** 3 Jun 1989 in Wayne County, TN. James was born 11 Feb 1959 in Wayne County, TN.

Roanna next married **David Russell Kilpatrick**. David was born in Florence, Lauderdale County, AL.

4445. David Maurice Collins (*Mary Kathleen Gean*[8], *Della V. Abilene Sego*[7], *Minnie Pearl Dearen*[6], *Mary Francis (Molly) Young*[5], *Mary M. (Polly II) Lindsey*[4], *Frances (Frankie) Sharp*[3], *Charles W. Sr.*[2], *John Sr.*[1]) was born 22 May 1963 in Lauderdale County, AL.

David married **Sandra Marie Cox**, daughter of **Jimmie L. Cox** and **Martha Ray**, 30 Mar 1984 in Lauderdale County, AL. Sandra was born 30 Apr 1963 in Montgomery County, TX.

5894	M	i.	**Nathan Tyler Collins** was born 18 Sep 1990 in Lauderdale County, AL.
5895	F	ii.	**Amber Faith Collins** was born 1 Sep 1992 in Lauderdale County, AL.

4446. Richard Lee Collins (*Mary Kathleen Gean*[8], *Della V. Abilene Sego*[7], *Minnie Pearl Dearen*[6], *Mary Francis (Molly) Young*[5], *Mary M. (Polly II) Lindsey*[4], *Frances (Frankie) Sharp*[3], *Charles W. Sr.*[2], *John Sr.*[1]) was born 13 Dec 1964 in Evansville, Vanderburgh County, IN.

Richard married **Jolene Marie Schafer** 18 Sep 1983 in Texas. Jolene was born 18 Sep 1965 in Liebenthal County, KS.

5896	F	i.	**Kiesha Marie Collins** was born 26 Jan 1989 in El Paso, El Paso County, TX.
5897	M	ii.	**Jospeh Allen Collins** was born 6 May 1994 in El Paso, El Paso County, TX.

4447. Michelle Anne Collins (*Mary Kathleen Gean*[8], *Della V. Abilene Sego*[7], *Minnie Pearl Dearen*[6], *Mary Francis (Molly) Young*[5], *Mary M. (Polly II) Lindsey*[4], *Frances (Frankie) Sharp*[3], *Charles W. Sr.*[2], *John Sr.*[1]) was born 26 Jan 1970 in Evansville, Vanderburgh County, IN. Another name for Michelle is Michelle Anne Collins.

Michelle married **Robert Trenton Allen** 7 Mar 1987 in Lauderdale County, AL. Robert was born 2 Feb 1969 in Lauderdale County, AL.

+ 5898	M	i.	**Joshua Shae Allen** was born 24 Mar 1988 in ECM Hospital, Florence, Lauderdale County, AL.

Michelle next married **Joseph (Jody) Inloe Young II**, son of **Joseph Inloe Young I** and **Madeline V. Thomas**, 9 Feb 1989 in Lauderdale County, AL. Joseph was born 22 Dec 1967 in Lauderdale County, AL. **(Duplicate Line. See Person 2148)**

Michelle next married **Eric Richardson** 1 Oct 1993.

Michelle next married **Randy Sneed** in Mar 1995 in Giles County, TN.

Michelle next married **Michael Strait** 14 Jun 1996 in Wayne County, TN.

Michelle next married **Jeremy Neal Staggs** 24 Aug 2001 in Gatlinburg, TN.

4448. Keith Alan Collins (*Mary Kathleen Gean*[8], *Della V. Abilene Sego*[7], *Minnie Pearl Dearen*[6], *Mary Francis (Molly) Young*[5], *Mary M. (Polly II) Lindsey*[4], *Frances (Frankie) Sharp*[3], *Charles W. Sr.*[2], *John Sr.*[1]) was born 14 Aug 1971 in Lawrenceburg, Lawrence County, TN.

Keith married **Kristy Marie Spencer**, daughter of **Frank Allen Spencer** and **Myra Jeanette Smith**, 19 Dec 1989 in Lauderdale County, AL. Kristy was born 2 Oct 1973 in Birmingham, Jefferson County, AL.

5899	F	i.	**Ashley Nicole Collins** was born 10 Aug 1994 in Colbert County, AL.
5900	F	ii.	**Halley Collins** was born 26 Feb 1999 in Colbert County, AL.

4449. Michael Aaron Gean (*Kenneth Aaron Gean*[8], *Della V. Abilene Sego*[7], *Minnie Pearl Dearen*[6], *Mary Francis (Molly) Young*[5], *Mary M. (Polly II) Lindsey*[4], *Frances (Frankie) Sharp*[3], *Charles W. Sr.*[2], *John Sr.*[1]) was born 28 Sep 1969 in Lauderdale County, AL.

Michael married **Stephanie Laura Broadfoot**, daughter of **Buck Broadfoot** and **Anna Frye**, in Nov 2000 in Lauderdale County, AL.

4450. Susan Lorene Gean (*Kenneth Aaron Gean*[8], *Della V. Abilene Sego*[7], *Minnie Pearl Dearen*[6], *Mary Francis (Molly) Young*[5], *Mary M. (Polly II) Lindsey*[4], *Frances (Frankie) Sharp*[3], *Charles W. Sr.*[2], *John Sr.*[1]) was born 1 Aug 1974 in Lauderdale County, AL.

Susan married **Darrel Lee Parrish**, son of **Jimmy L. Parrish** and **Brenda Darlene Smith**, 26 Sep 1996 in Lauderdale County, AL. Darrel was born 1 Aug 1973 in Lauderdale County, AL.
5901 M   i.   **Dustin Aaron Gean** was born 9 Aug 1994 in Lauderdale County, AL.
5902 F   ii.   **Samantha Jewel Parrish** was born 9 Dec 1997 in Florence, Lauderdale County, AL.

Susan next married **David Clifton Painter**, son of **Don Painter** and **Wayne Key**.

4451. Kisha Leane Gean (*Virgil Henderson Gean Jr.*[8], *Della V. Abilene Sego*[7], *Minnie Pearl Dearen*[6], *Mary Francis (Molly) Young*[5], *Mary M. (Polly II) Lindsey*[4], *Frances (Frankie) Sharp*[3], *Charles W. Sr.*[2], *John Sr.*[1]) was born 3 Jun 1975 in Lauderdale County, AL.

Kisha married **Keven Lee Tidwell**, son of **Paul Tidwell** and **Beverly Holcombe**, 12 Feb 1993 in Lauderdale County, AL. Keven was born 22 Oct 1973 in Lauderdale County, AL.
5903 F   i.   **Kelsey Leanne Gean** was born 3 Sep 1991 in Lauderdale County, AL.
5904 F   ii.   **Kaitlin Leigh Tidwell** was born 10 Aug 1993 in Lauderdale County, AL, died 15 Feb 2000, and was buried in Rhodesville Cemetery, Lauderdale County, AL.
5905 M   iii.   **Koby Henderson Gean** was born 10 Nov 1996.

Kisha next married **Billy Dewayne Kelsoe** 10 Nov 1998 in Florence, Lauderdale County, AL. Billy was born 24 Apr 1975.

4452. Kimberly Dawn Gean (*Virgil Henderson Gean Jr.*[8], *Della V. Abilene Sego*[7], *Minnie Pearl Dearen*[6], *Mary Francis (Molly) Young*[5], *Mary M. (Polly II) Lindsey*[4], *Frances (Frankie) Sharp*[3], *Charles W. Sr.*[2], *John Sr.*[1]) was born 20 Jun 1980 in Lauderdale County, AL.

Kimberly married **Brad Lawson** 4 Nov 2006 in Destin, Okaloosa County, FL.

4453. Judy Loretta Young (*Doris Geraldine Holcombe*[8], *Mary Alice Sego*[7], *Minnie Pearl Dearen*[6], *Mary Francis (Molly) Young*[5], *Mary M. (Polly II) Lindsey*[4], *Frances (Frankie) Sharp*[3], *Charles W. Sr.*[2], *John Sr.*[1]) was born 29 Nov 1952 in Mishawaka, St Joseph County, IN.

Judy married **Charles Edward Wood**, son of **Audrey Chambers Wood** and **Lillie Mae Sylverius Meziere**, 26 Jun 1971 in Mishawaka, St Joseph County, IN. Charles was born 15 Dec 1949 in Mishawaka, St Joseph County, IN.
5906 F   i.   **Amy Marie Wood** was born 9 May 1973 in Mishawaka, St Joseph County, IN.
5907 F   ii.   **Beth Rene Wood** was born 27 Jul 1976 in Mishawaka, St Joseph County, IN.

4454. Vickie Jane Young (*Doris Geraldine Holcombe*[8], *Mary Alice Sego*[7], *Minnie Pearl Dearen*[6], *Mary Francis (Molly) Young*[5], *Mary M. (Polly II) Lindsey*[4], *Frances (Frankie) Sharp*[3], *Charles W. Sr.*[2], *John Sr.*[1]) was born 3 Nov 1955 in Mishawaka, St Joseph County, IN.

Vickie married **Rickie Andrew Johnson**, son of **D. A. Johnson** and **Clara Ruth Goins**, 25 Sep 1976 in Mishawaka, St Joseph County, IN. Rickie was born 6 Mar 1954 in Mishawaka, St Joseph County, IN.
5908 M   i.   **Matthew Young Johnson** was born 16 Sep 1984.
5909 M   ii.   **Dane Andrew Johnson** was born 9 Dec 1986.

4455. Donna Christine Newland (*Robbie Louellen Holcombe*[8], *Mary Alice Sego*[7], *Minnie Pearl Dearen*[6], *Mary Francis (Molly) Young*[5], *Mary M. (Polly II) Lindsey*[4], *Frances (Frankie) Sharp*[3], *Charles W. Sr.*[2], *John Sr.*[1]) was born 14 Aug 1953 in Mishawaka, St Joseph County, IN.

Donna married **John Lee Joyal Sr.** 3 Nov 1973 in Mishawaka, St Joseph County, IN. John was born 7 Jun 1950 in Mishawaka, St Joseph County, IN.

| 5910 | F | i. | **Angela Lynn Joyal** was born 26 Jul 1973 in Mishawaka, St Joseph County, IN. |
| 5911 | M | ii. | **John Lee Joyal Jr.** was born 12 Nov 1976 in Mishawaka, St Joseph County, IN. |

4456. Shelly Jean Newland (*Robbie Louellen Holcombe^8, Mary Alice Sego^7, Minnie Pearl Dearen^6, Mary Francis (Molly) Young^5, Mary M. (Polly II) Lindsey^4, Frances (Frankie) Sharp^3, Charles W. Sr.^{2}, John Sr.^{1}*) was born 3 Oct 1955 in Mishawaka, St Joseph County, IN.

Shelly married **Jerry Felts**, son of **Frank Meredith Felts** and **Lillian Blanche**, 10 Nov 1973 in Mishawaka, St Joseph County, IN.

| 5912 | F | i. | **Kimberly Janine Felts**. |

Shelly next married **Sam Miller** 16 Feb 1979 in Mishawaka, St Joseph County, IN.

Shelly next married **Ralph Donald Hoyt** 22 Aug 1981.

4457. Russell Glen Newland (*Robbie Louellen Holcombe^8, Mary Alice Sego^7, Minnie Pearl Dearen^6, Mary Francis (Molly) Young^5, Mary M. (Polly II) Lindsey^4, Frances (Frankie) Sharp^3, Charles W. Sr.^{2}, John Sr.^{1}*) was born 7 Apr 1961 in Mishawaka, St Joseph County, IN.

Russell married **Penny Johnston**.

Russell had a relationship with **Linda Johnston**.

| 5913 | F | i. | **Amanda Lynn Newland**. |

4458. Tammy Lou Stricklin (*Sarah Beatrice Williams^8, Frances Boyce Sego^7, Minnie Pearl Dearen^6, Mary Francis (Molly) Young^5, Mary M. (Polly II) Lindsey^4, Frances (Frankie) Sharp^3, Charles W. Sr.^{2}, John Sr.^{1}*) was born 6 Sep 1965 in South Bend, IN.

Tammy married **Stephen Gene Stricklin**, son of **Earl Stricklin** and **Inez Tidwell**, 16 Jul 1983 in Savannah, Hardin County, TN. Stephen was born 1 Oct 1961 in Savannah, Hardin County, TN.

| 5914 | M | i. | **Jermiah Stephen Stricklin** was born 28 Oct 1989 in Florence, Lauderdale County, AL. |

4459. Thomas (Tommy) James Stricklin (*Sarah Beatrice Williams^8, Frances Boyce Sego^7, Minnie Pearl Dearen^6, Mary Francis (Molly) Young^5, Mary M. (Polly II) Lindsey^4, Frances (Frankie) Sharp^3, Charles W. Sr.^{2}, John Sr.^{1}*) was born 28 Jun 1967 in South Bend, IN.

Thomas married **Sharlene Williams**, daughter of **Doyal Williams** and **Helen Christine Benson**, 1 May 1987 in Waterloo, Lauderdale County, AL. Sharlene was born 30 Jan 1966 in Lauderdale County, AL.

| 5915 | F | i. | **Samantha Dawn Stricklin** was born 26 Feb 1991 in Florence, Lauderdale County, AL. |
| 5916 | F | ii. | **Shelby Lynn Stricklin** was born 7 Aug 1992 in Florence, Lauderdale County, AL. |

4461. Carla Lynn Williams (*Larry David Williams^8, Frances Boyce Sego^7, Minnie Pearl Dearen^6, Mary Francis (Molly) Young^5, Mary M. (Polly II) Lindsey^4, Frances (Frankie) Sharp^3, Charles W. Sr.^{2}, John Sr.^{1}*) was born 1 Apr 1976 in Mishawaka, St Joseph County, IN.

Carla married **Chris Stanfield**.

| 5917 | M | i. | **Ethan Dean Reed** was born in Georgia. |

4469. Mandy Lynn White (*Lavenia Gail White^8, Clara Bell Sego^7, Minnie Pearl Dearen^6, Mary Francis (Molly) Young^5, Mary M. (Polly II) Lindsey^4, Frances (Frankie) Sharp^3, Charles W. Sr.^{2}, John Sr.^{1}*) was born 17 Feb 1977 in Lauderdale County, AL.

Mandy married **Norman Glenn Morris** 12 Oct 1997 in Lauderdale County, AL. Norman was born 2 Nov 1974 in Lauderdale County, AL.

| 5918 | F | i. | **Abby Grace Morris** was born 19 May 2000 in Lauderdale County, AL. |
| 5919 | F | ii. | **Emma Cate Morris** was born 2 Sep 2003 in Lauderdale County, AL. |

4476. Amanda Kay South (*Roger Allen South[8], Rufus Allen South[7], Clara Edna Dearen[6], Mary Francis (Molly) Young[5], Mary M. (Polly II) Lindsey[4], Frances (Frankie) Sharp[3], Charles W. Sr.[2], John Sr.[1]*) was born 16 Nov 1976 in Lauderdale County, AL.

Amanda married **Roger Walker Pate Jr.**, son of **Roger Walker Pate Sr.** and **Denise Hill**, 23 Jan 1994 in Lauderdale County, AL. Roger was born 13 Dec 1973 in Colbert County, AL.

5920 F   i.   **Cheyenne Kay Pate** was born 31 Jan 2001 in Lauderdale County, AL.
5921 F   ii.   **Savannah Grace Pate** was born 29 Oct 2002 in Lauderdale County, AL.

4477. Brandy Annette South (*Roger Allen South[8], Rufus Allen South[7], Clara Edna Dearen[6], Mary Francis (Molly) Young[5], Mary M. (Polly II) Lindsey[4], Frances (Frankie) Sharp[3], Charles W. Sr.[2], John Sr.[1]*) was born 25 Sep 1979 in Dallas, TX.

Brandy married **Randall Pounders** 4 Nov 2001 in Lauderdale County, AL.

5922 M   i.   **Justin Lane Pounders** was born 12 Nov 1996 in Lauderdale County, AL.
5923 M   ii.   **Adam Lee Pounders** was born 3 Aug 2004 in Lauderdale County, AL.
5924 M   iii. **Allen Brady Pounders** was born 3 Aug 2004 in Lauderdale County, AL.

4478. Christopher Allen South (*Roger Allen South[8], Rufus Allen South[7], Clara Edna Dearen[6], Mary Francis (Molly) Young[5], Mary M. (Polly II) Lindsey[4], Frances (Frankie) Sharp[3], Charles W. Sr.[2], John Sr.[1]*) was born 19 Jun 1981 in Lauderdale County, AL.

Christopher married **Tasha Angel**, daughter of **Mickie Angel** and **Unknown**, 17 Feb 2001 in Lauderdale County, AL. Tasha was born 2 Mar 1983.

5925 M   i.   **Hunter Ray South** was born 18 Jul 2001 in Lauderdale County, AL.

4479. Jeremy Clay South (*James Cecil South[8], Rufus Allen South[7], Clara Edna Dearen[6], Mary Francis (Molly) Young[5], Mary M. (Polly II) Lindsey[4], Frances (Frankie) Sharp[3], Charles W. Sr.[2], John Sr.[1]*) was born 24 Dec 1981 in Lauderdale County, AL.

Jeremy married **Annie Ogletree** 8 Oct 2005 in Lauderdale County, AL. Annie was born 23 May 1983 in Lauderdale County, AL.

4480. Tisha Latonya South (*Randal Keith South[8], Rufus Allen South[7], Clara Edna Dearen[6], Mary Francis (Molly) Young[5], Mary M. (Polly II) Lindsey[4], Frances (Frankie) Sharp[3], Charles W. Sr.[2], John Sr.[1]*) was born 9 Apr 1981 in Lauderdale County, AL.

Tisha married someone.

5926 F   i.   **Baylee Nicole South** was born 19 Apr 1999 in Lauderdale County, AL.
5927 M   ii.   **Hayen Lee South** was born 17 Jul 2003 in Lauderdale County, AL.

4481. Randi Marie South (*Randal Keith South[8], Rufus Allen South[7], Clara Edna Dearen[6], Mary Francis (Molly) Young[5], Mary M. (Polly II) Lindsey[4], Frances (Frankie) Sharp[3], Charles W. Sr.[2], John Sr.[1]*) was born in Jul 1982 in Lauderdale County, AL.

Randi married **James Lynn Creasy** 11 Sep 1999 in Lauderdale County, AL. James was born 23 Feb 1980.

5928 M   i.   **James Austin Creasy** was born 16 Mar 2000 in Lauderdale County, AL.
5929 M   ii.   **Jacob Alexander Creasy** was born 8 Apr 2002 in Lauderdale County, AL.
5930 M   iii. **Jared Alexander Creasy** was born 23 Dec 2003 in Lauderdale County, AL.

4487. Adrian Lee Hart (*Tamara Faye Faulkner[8], Eva Leigh South[7], Clara Edna Dearen[6], Mary Francis (Molly) Young[5], Mary M. (Polly II) Lindsey[4], Frances (Frankie) Sharp[3], Charles W. Sr.[2], John Sr.[1]*) was born 13 Nov 1976 in Lauderdale County, AL.

Adrian married **Erica Lynn Gooch**, daughter of **John Eric (Elwood) Wood** and **Marcia Lynn Gooch**, 26 Jan 1995 in Lauderdale County, AL. Erica was born 13 Feb 1979 in Florence, Lauderdale County, AL.
(Duplicate Line. See Person 4394)

Adrian next married **Kristen Barrett**, daughter of **Chuck Beauton Barrett Sr.** and **Tamera (Tammy) Dilynn Sharp**.

5931 F   i.   **Halle Hart.**

4488. Christina Ann Hart (*Tamara Faye Faulkner* [8], *Eva Leigh South* [7], *Clara Edna Dearen* [6], *Mary Francis (Molly) Young* [5], *Mary M. (Polly II) Lindsey* [4], *Frances (Frankie) Sharp* [3], *Charles W. Sr.* [2], *John Sr.* [1]) was born 1 May 1982 in Lauderdale County, AL.

Christina married **Troy Christopher Jones**, son of **Michael Eugene Jones Sr.** and **Sharon Jean Gooch**. **(Duplicate Line. See Person 4392)**

4490. Terri Suver (*Sue Dennis* [8], *Dalton L. Dennis* [7], *Florence L. Ticer* [6], *Roxie Leona Young* [5], *Mary M. (Polly II) Lindsey* [4], *Frances (Frankie) Sharp* [3], *Charles W. Sr.* [2], *John Sr.* [1]).

Terri married **Brian Maes**.

5932 F   i.   **Justine Maes.**

4491. Tina Suver (*Sue Dennis* [8], *Dalton L. Dennis* [7], *Florence L. Ticer* [6], *Roxie Leona Young* [5], *Mary M. (Polly II) Lindsey* [4], *Frances (Frankie) Sharp* [3], *Charles W. Sr.* [2], *John Sr.* [1]) was born in 1962.

Tina married ***Unk Kreye**.

5933 M   i.   **Cory Lee Kreye.**

4492. Sherry Dennis (*Hugh L. Dennis* [8], *Dalton L. Dennis* [7], *Florence L. Ticer* [6], *Roxie Leona Young* [5], *Mary M. (Polly II) Lindsey* [4], *Frances (Frankie) Sharp* [3], *Charles W. Sr.* [2], *John Sr.* [1]).

Sherry married someone.

5934 M   i.   **Brandon Dennis.**

4496. Brittany Denise Balentine (*Leigh Ann Dennis* [8], *Troy Burlon Dennis* [7], *Florence L. Ticer* [6], *Roxie Leona Young* [5], *Mary M. (Polly II) Lindsey* [4], *Frances (Frankie) Sharp* [3], *Charles W. Sr.* [2], *John Sr.* [1]).

Brittany married **Wesley Leon Sharp**, son of **Albert Leon Sharp** and **Connie Elizabeth Harlan**, 14 Mar 2009 in Lauderdale County, AL. Wesley was born 6 Feb 1984 in Lauderdale County, AL. **(Duplicate Line. See Person 3670)**

4500. Christopher (Chris) Ticer (*Steven Lee Ticer* [8], *Arnold Lee Ticer* [7], *Robert Clark Ticer II* [6], *Roxie Leona Young* [5], *Mary M. (Polly II) Lindsey* [4], *Frances (Frankie) Sharp* [3], *Charles W. Sr.* [2], *John Sr.* [1]) was born 22 Mar 1972 in Lauderdale County, AL.

Christopher married **Christina Marie Sanderson**, daughter of **Paul Richard Sanderson** and **Carol Francis Long**, 2 Sep 1995 in Lauderdale County, AL. Christina was born 18 Mar 1973 in Lauderdale County, AL.

5935 M   i.   **Carson Lee Ticer.**
5936 M   ii.   **Cody Ticer.**

4501. Lorie Lee Ticer (*Rayford Arnold Ticer* [8], *Arnold Lee Ticer* [7], *Robert Clark Ticer II* [6], *Roxie Leona Young* [5], *Mary M. (Polly II) Lindsey* [4], *Frances (Frankie) Sharp* [3], *Charles W. Sr.* [2], *John Sr.* [1]) was born 29 Jul 1973 in Lauderdale County, AL.

Lorie married **Charles Thomas Condrey Jr.**, son of **Charles Thomas Condrey Sr.** and **Rebecca Sue Trousdale**, 27 Mar 1992 in Lauderdale County, AL. Charles was born 4 Aug 1970 in Lauderdale County, AL.

4516. Molly Elizabeth Jones (*Robert (Bobby) Percy Jones* [8], *Robert Dalton Jones* [7], *Ada Young* [6], *Lou Young* [5], *Mary M. (Polly II) Lindsey* [4], *Frances (Frankie) Sharp* [3], *Charles W. Sr.* [2], *John Sr.* [1]) was born 22 Apr 1970 in Lauderdale County, AL and died 2 Jun 2006 in Lauderdale County, AL.

Molly married *Unk Watkins.
5937 M i. **Robert William Watkins**.

Molly next married **Michael Smith**.

4519. Percy Hugh Thomas (*Jackie Juanita Wright*[8]*, Mary Louise Jones*[7]*, Ada Young*[6]*, Lou Young*[5]*, Mary M. (Polly II) Lindsey*[4]*, Frances (Frankie) Sharp*[3]*, Charles W. Sr.*[2]*, John Sr.*[1]) was born 23 Sep 1961.

Percy married **Michelle Renee Dennis** 25 May 1985 in Lauderdale County, AL. Michelle was born 3 Aug 1962.
5938 M i. **Mitchem Hugh Thomas** was born 13 Jun 1987.
5939 F ii. **Mary Kathryn Thomas** was born 6 Dec 1989.
5940 M iii. **Benjamin Walker Thomas** was born 7 Jun 1994.

4524. Stacey LeAnn Bevis (*Elinda Gaye Wright*[8]*, Mary Louise Jones*[7]*, Ada Young*[6]*, Lou Young*[5]*, Mary M. (Polly II) Lindsey*[4]*, Frances (Frankie) Sharp*[3]*, Charles W. Sr.*[2]*, John Sr.*[1]) was born 24 Jan 1970 in Lauderdale County, AL.

Stacey married **James William (Bill) Hogue** 22 May 1994. James was born 9 Oct 1969.

4530. Shelly Summers (*Elaine Renee Billingsley*[8]*, William Eugene Billingsley*[7]*, Verna Virella Young*[6]*, Lou Young*[5]*, Mary M. (Polly II) Lindsey*[4]*, Frances (Frankie) Sharp*[3]*, Charles W. Sr.*[2]*, John Sr.*[1]) was born 13 May 1984.

Shelly married **Mark Forrest**.

4556. Mary Lou (Bonnie) Olive (*Douglas Gene Olive Jr.*[8]*, Betty Lou Witt*[7]*, Mary Etta Young*[6]*, Lou Young*[5]*, Mary M. (Polly II) Lindsey*[4]*, Frances (Frankie) Sharp*[3]*, Charles W. Sr.*[2]*, John Sr.*[1]) was born 11 Jul 1973 in Lauderdale County, AL.

Mary married **Kelvon Dwaine Black**, son of **William Larry Black** and **Norma Jean Wright**, 25 May 1991 in Lauderdale County, AL. Kelvon was born 22 Jan 1970 in Lauderdale County, AL.
5941 M i. **Kyle Black** was born 2 Oct 1991.

4604. James Robert McRae (*James Thomas McRae Jr.*[8]*, Laverne Bruce*[7]*, Viney Viola Sharp*[6]*, Robert Patton*[5]*, James (Jim) Charles Sr.*[4]*, Adron (Edwin/Ade) Sr.*[3]*, Charles W. Sr.*[2]*, John Sr.*[1]) was born 22 May 1949 in Birmingham, Jefferson County, AL.

James married **Judith Pope**, daughter of **Stanley John Pope** and **Lee *Unk**, 21 Jan 1971 in Vancouver, British Columbia, Canada. Judith was born 7 Apr 1950 in Canada.
5942 M i. **Jason Neville McRae** was born 28 May 1970 in Vancouver, British Columbia, Canada.
5943 M ii. **Jacob Hamilton McRae** was born 23 Apr 1972 in Vancouver, British Columbia, Canada.

James next married **Vickie Lynn Ward** 24 Feb 1990 in Houston, TX.

4605. Gail Jeane McRae (*James Thomas McRae Jr.*[8]*, Laverne Bruce*[7]*, Viney Viola Sharp*[6]*, Robert Patton*[5]*, James (Jim) Charles Sr.*[4]*, Adron (Edwin/Ade) Sr.*[3]*, Charles W. Sr.*[2]*, John Sr.*[1]) was born 15 Nov 1950 in Birmingham, Jefferson County, AL.

Gail married **Robert Alan Leslie**, son of **Gordon Charles Leslie** and **Emily Stanwich**, 19 Aug 1975 in Galena Park, TX. Robert was born 11 Feb 1950 in Niagara Falls, NY.
5944 M i. **Andrew Neal Leslie** was born 17 Sep 1978 in Houston, TX.
5945 M ii. **Patrick Ryan Leslie** was born 15 Aug 1981 in Houston, TX.

4606. Marsha Laurene McRae (*James Thomas McRae Jr.*[8]*, Laverne Bruce*[7]*, Viney Viola Sharp*[6]*, Robert Patton*[5]*, James (Jim) Charles Sr.*[4]*, Adron (Edwin/Ade) Sr.*[3]*, Charles W. Sr.*[2]*, John Sr.*[1]) was born 25 May 1955 in Birmingham, Jefferson County, AL.

Marsha married **Richard Eugene Hawkins**, son of **Vernon Eugene Hawkins II** and **Madalyn Wallace**, 31 May 1975. Richard was born 5 Aug 1952 in Bay City, TX.

| 5946 | M | i. | **Matthew Richard Hawkins** was born 17 Sep 1978 in Houston, TX. |
| 5947 | F | ii. | **Melissa Lauren Hawkins** was born 30 Apr 1980 in Houston, TX. |

Marsha next married **Kent Robert Wells** 30 Sep 1991. Kent was born 4 Sep 1964 in Houston, TX.

4607. William Merrill McRae (*James Thomas McRae Jr.*[8], *Laverne Bruce*[7], *Viney Viola Sharp*[6], *Robert Patton*[5], *James (Jim) Charles Sr.*[4], *Adron (Edwin/Ade) Sr.*[3], *Charles W. Sr.*[2], *John Sr.*[1]) was born 10 Apr 1959 in Fairfield, AL.

William married **Donna Lyn White**, daughter of **Edwin O. Brown** and **Stella Alice Marie Waddington**, 14 Feb 1981. Donna was born 6 Mar 1947 in Denver, CO.

| 5948 | M | i. | **James William Chance McRae** was born 23 Jan 1989 in Denver, CO. |

4608. Susan Rebecca Darby (*Mary Sue Bruce*[8], *Lewis Bruce*[7], *Viney Viola Sharp*[6], *Robert Patton*[5], *James (Jim) Charles Sr.*[4], *Adron (Edwin/Ade) Sr.*[3], *Charles W. Sr.*[2], *John Sr.*[1]) was born 2 Oct 1953 in Lauderdale County, AL.

Susan married **Bradford Stanley Hall**, son of **Dewey W. Hall** and **Faye McCullough**, 9 Jul 1977 in Lauderdale County, AL. Bradford was born 9 Aug 1954 in Lauderdale County, AL.

| 5949 | M | i. | **Bradford Alan Hall** was born 8 Apr 1981 in Lauderdale County, AL. |
| 5950 | M | ii. | **Andrew David Hall** was born 19 Sep 1985 in Lauderdale County, AL. |

4609. James Bruce Darby (*Mary Sue Bruce*[8], *Lewis Bruce*[7], *Viney Viola Sharp*[6], *Robert Patton*[5], *James (Jim) Charles Sr.*[4], *Adron (Edwin/Ade) Sr.*[3], *Charles W. Sr.*[2], *John Sr.*[1]) was born 27 Dec 1956 in Lauderdale County, AL.

James married **Wendy Agnes Keezer**, daughter of **William A. Keezer** and **Sara Fosier**, 21 Mar 1987 in Lauderdale County, AL. Wendy was born 13 Sep 1959 in Hartford County, CT.

| 5951 | M | i. | **William Ethan Darby** was born 3 Oct 1990 in Lauderdale County, AL. |

4610. James W. Wallace Jr. (*Francis Laurene Bruce*[8], *Lewis Bruce*[7], *Viney Viola Sharp*[6], *Robert Patton*[5], *James (Jim) Charles Sr.*[4], *Adron (Edwin/Ade) Sr.*[3], *Charles W. Sr.*[2], *John Sr.*[1]) was born 28 Aug 1951 in Lauderdale County, AL.

James married **Margaret Louise (Peggy) Brink**, daughter of **William Lawrence Brink** and **Betty Gibbons**, 15 Apr 1977 in Lauderdale County, AL. Margaret was born 3 Jan 1953 in Lauderdale County, AL.

4611. Susan Owens (*Glenell Malsbury*[8], *Nellie Mae Pickens*[7], *Carrie Eudora Sharp*[6], *Robert Patton*[5], *James (Jim) Charles Sr.*[4], *Adron (Edwin/Ade) Sr.*[3], *Charles W. Sr.*[2], *John Sr.*[1]) was born 4 Dec 1951 in Inglewood, CA.

Susan married **John Melvin Allen** 25 May 1974.

4612. Julia Owens (*Glenell Malsbury*[8], *Nellie Mae Pickens*[7], *Carrie Eudora Sharp*[6], *Robert Patton*[5], *James (Jim) Charles Sr.*[4], *Adron (Edwin/Ade) Sr.*[3], *Charles W. Sr.*[2], *John Sr.*[1]) was born 2 Apr 1954 in Bartsville, OK.

Julia married **Donald Gene Bevers** 28 Feb 1987.

4613. Mary Sue Dugger (*Gordon F. Dugger*[8], *Stella Iown Pickens*[7], *Carrie Eudora Sharp*[6], *Robert Patton*[5], *James (Jim) Charles Sr.*[4], *Adron (Edwin/Ade) Sr.*[3], *Charles W. Sr.*[2], *John Sr.*[1]) was born 13 Mar 1955 in Cincinnati, OH.

Mary married **Billy Jennings**.

5952	F	i.	**Michelle Jennings**.
5953	F	ii.	**Rosemond Jennings**.
5954	F	iii.	**Stella Marie Jennings**.

4619. Mary Francis Farmer (*Mary Thomas (Tommie) McCarley*[8], *Mary Virginia Givens*[7], *Ida Lois Sharp*[6], *Robert Patton*[5], *James (Jim) Charles Sr.*[4], *Adron (Edwin/Ade) Sr.*[3], *Charles W. Sr.*[2], *John Sr.*[1]) was born 1 Sep 1966 in Florence, Lauderdale County, AL.

Mary married **Keith Ray McGee**, son of **Berlon Ray McGee** and **Ivadean Joyce Myhan**, 5 Apr 1989 in Lauderdale County, AL. Keith was born 5 Jan 1968 in Florence, Lauderdale County, AL.
5955 M i. **Mitchell Keith McGee** was born 19 Apr 1990.

4620. Cheri Lynn Farmer (*Mary Thomas (Tommie) McCarley*[8], *Mary Virginia Givens*[7], *Ida Lois Sharp*[6], *Robert Patton*[5], *James (Jim) Charles Sr.*[4], *Adron (Edwin/Ade) Sr.*[3], *Charles W. Sr.*[2], *John Sr.*[1]) was born 27 May 1968 in Lauderdale County, AL.

Cheri married **Gilbert Porterfield Self**, son of **Henry Harold Self** and **Shirley McBride Williams**, 23 Apr 1994 in Lauderdale County, AL. Gilbert was born 25 Jan 1963 in Florence, Lauderdale County, AL.

4626. Miles Orlan Harris (*Bobbie Carol Givens*[8], *Robert Orlan Givens Sr.*[7], *Ida Lois Sharp*[6], *Robert Patton*[5], *James (Jim) Charles Sr.*[4], *Adron (Edwin/Ade) Sr.*[3], *Charles W. Sr.*[2], *John Sr.*[1]) was born 19 Jun 1965.

Miles married **Lynnessia Ann Bundy** 14 Aug 1988.

4627. Denise Danielle Dail (*Mary Francis Givens*[8], *Robert Orlan Givens Sr.*[7], *Ida Lois Sharp*[6], *Robert Patton*[5], *James (Jim) Charles Sr.*[4], *Adron (Edwin/Ade) Sr.*[3], *Charles W. Sr.*[2], *John Sr.*[1]) was born 24 May 1967.

Denise married **Robert Wayne Fletcher Jr.**.
5956 F i. **Amanda Louise Fletcher** was born 28 Feb 1990.

4640. Leonard E. Durham (*Dorothy M. Rogers*[8], *Edmon (Eddie) Falmer Rogers*[7], *Lillian Anna (Lillie) Sharp*[6], *John Thomas (Tom)*[5], *James (Jim) Charles Sr.*[4], *Adron (Edwin/Ade) Sr.*[3], *Charles W. Sr.*[2], *John Sr.*[1]) was born 20 Oct 1947 in Adamsville, McNairy County, TN.

Leonard married **Bonnie Mae Drummond** 15 Jan 1972 in Hohenwald, TN. Bonnie was born 2 Mar 1951 in Ridgely, TN.

4646. Rebecca Ann Rogers (*Bob R. Rogers*[8], *Robert W. Rogers*[7], *Lillian Anna (Lillie) Sharp*[6], *John Thomas (Tom)*[5], *James (Jim) Charles Sr.*[4], *Adron (Edwin/Ade) Sr.*[3], *Charles W. Sr.*[2], *John Sr.*[1]) was born 25 Feb 1963 in Memphis, Shelby County, TN.

Rebecca married **Scott Deatherage** 31 Aug 1985 in Memphis, Shelby County, TN.

4648. Deborah A. Elrod (*Mary Helen Rogers*[8], *Robert W. Rogers*[7], *Lillian Anna (Lillie) Sharp*[6], *John Thomas (Tom)*[5], *James (Jim) Charles Sr.*[4], *Adron (Edwin/Ade) Sr.*[3], *Charles W. Sr.*[2], *John Sr.*[1]) was born 16 Sep 1957 in Memphis, Shelby County, TN.

Deborah married ***Unk Patterson** 7 Aug 1991 in Memphis, Shelby County, TN.

4649. Lloyd Mack Elrod Jr. (*Mary Helen Rogers*[8], *Robert W. Rogers*[7], *Lillian Anna (Lillie) Sharp*[6], *John Thomas (Tom)*[5], *James (Jim) Charles Sr.*[4], *Adron (Edwin/Ade) Sr.*[3], *Charles W. Sr.*[2], *John Sr.*[1]) was born 10 May 1961 in Memphis, Shelby County, TN.

Lloyd married **Marla Jo Johnson**, daughter of **Marlon Johnson** and **Eva *Unk**, 25 Aug 1984 in Memphis, Shelby County, TN. Marla was born 16 Dec 1961 in Memphis, Shelby County, TN.
5957 M i. **Matthew Elrod** was born 11 Jul 1995 in Memphis, Shelby County, TN.

4650. Phillip David Rogers Jr. (*Phillip David Rogers Sr.*[8], *Robert W. Rogers*[7], *Lillian Anna (Lillie) Sharp*[6], *John Thomas (Tom)*[5], *James (Jim) Charles Sr.*[4], *Adron (Edwin/Ade) Sr.*[3], *Charles W. Sr.*[2], *John Sr.*[1]) was born 1 Mar 1970.

Phillip married **Kelly Casey** 17 May 1994 in Bartlett, TN. Kelly was born 16 Jan 1970 in Ojkaloosa, ID.

4652. Monica Conaway (*Elizabeth Rogers[8], Robert W. Rogers[7], Lillian Anna (Lillie) Sharp[6], John Thomas (Tom)[5], James (Jim) Charles Sr.[4], Adron (Edwin/Ade) Sr.[3], Charles W. Sr.[2], John Sr.[1]*) was born 26 Apr 1970 in Selmer, McNairy County, TN.

Monica married **John C. Gordon** 7 Mar in Adamsville, McNairy County, TN. John was born 24 May 1966 in Romulus, MI.

4654. Doris Jean Holcombe (*Willard Lee Holcombe[8], Ernest Powers Holcombe[7], Maggie Sharp[6], John Thomas (Tom)[5], James (Jim) Charles Sr.[4], Adron (Edwin/Ade) Sr.[3], Charles W. Sr.[2], John Sr.[1]*) was born 6 Dec 1947 in Lauderdale County, AL.

Doris married **Jimmy Carl Wood**, son of **J. C. Wood Sr.** and **Edith Evelyn Irons**, 22 Oct 1966 in Lauderdale County, AL. Jimmy was born 19 Jan 1947 in Lauderdale County, AL.
+ 5958   M   i.   **Christopher Lee Wood** was born 24 Mar 1971 in Florence, Lauderdale County, AL, died 12 Jun 1993, and was buried in Williams Chapel Cemetery, Lauderdale County, AL.

4655. Anthony Lee Holcombe (*Willard Lee Holcombe[8], Ernest Powers Holcombe[7], Maggie Sharp[6], John Thomas (Tom)[5], James (Jim) Charles Sr.[4], Adron (Edwin/Ade) Sr.[3], Charles W. Sr.[2], John Sr.[1]*) was born 17 May 1955 in Florence, Lauderdale County, AL.

Anthony married **Sherry Harvell**, daughter of **J. D. Harvell** and **Lillie Mae Humphrey**, 9 Feb 1979 in Hardin County, TN. Sherry was born 23 Aug 1960 in Savannah, Hardin County, TN.
5959   M   i.   **Joshua Lee Holcombe** was born 7 Sep 1979 in Florence, Lauderdale County, AL.

4656. Daniel Leon Holcombe (*James Lee Holcombe[8], Ernest Powers Holcombe[7], Maggie Sharp[6], John Thomas (Tom)[5], James (Jim) Charles Sr.[4], Adron (Edwin/Ade) Sr.[3], Charles W. Sr.[2], John Sr.[1]*) was born 30 May 1950 in Hardin County, TN.

Daniel married **Wanda Carolyn Young**, daughter of **L. V. Young** and **Juanita Crotts**, 25 Apr 1972 in Hardin County, TN. Wanda was born 5 Jul 1952 in Hardin County, TN.
5960   M   i.   **Shane Dale Holcombe** was born 1 Sep 1974 in Florence, Lauderdale County, AL.
5961   M   ii.   **Brian Keith Holcombe** was born 22 Sep 1975 in Corinth, Alcorn County, MS.

4657. Steven Lee Holcombe (*James Lee Holcombe[8], Ernest Powers Holcombe[7], Maggie Sharp[6], John Thomas (Tom)[5], James (Jim) Charles Sr.[4], Adron (Edwin/Ade) Sr.[3], Charles W. Sr.[2], John Sr.[1]*) was born 13 Jul 1951 in Hardin County, TN.

Steven married **Diannah Lynn Phillips**, daughter of **Willie Eugene Phillips** and **Lena Earline Sheppard**, 10 Jan 1972 in Savannah, TN. Diannah was born 22 Oct 1950 in Dyce Colony, AR.

4658. Grady Allen Holcombe (*James Lee Holcombe[8], Ernest Powers Holcombe[7], Maggie Sharp[6], John Thomas (Tom)[5], James (Jim) Charles Sr.[4], Adron (Edwin/Ade) Sr.[3], Charles W. Sr.[2], John Sr.[1]*) was born 11 May 1953 in Hardin County, TN.

Grady married **Marjorie Ann Wright**, daughter of **Fred White** and **Willie Reed**, 19 Aug 1972 in Lauderdale County, AL. Marjorie was born 30 Aug 1950 in Morgan County, AL.
5962   M   i.   **Derrick Allen Holcombe** was born 30 Aug 1974.

4659. Timothy Wayne Holcombe (*James Lee Holcombe[8], Ernest Powers Holcombe[7], Maggie Sharp[6], John Thomas (Tom)[5], James (Jim) Charles Sr.[4], Adron (Edwin/Ade) Sr.[3], Charles W. Sr.[2], John Sr.[1]*) was born 3 Jun 1957 in Hardin County, TN.

Timothy married **Anita Gay Delano**, daughter of **Charles Austin Delano** and **Frances Bell Vasser**, 2 Sep 1978 in Lauderdale County, AL. Anita was born 20 Apr 1959 in Florence, Lauderdale County, AL.

4660. Geneva Gwen Holcombe (*James Lee Holcombe*[8]*, Ernest Powers Holcombe*[7]*, Maggie Sharp*[6]*, John Thomas (Tom)*[5]*, James (Jim) Charles Sr.*[4]*, Adron (Edwin/Ade) Sr.*[3]*, Charles W. Sr.*[2]*, John Sr.*[1]) was born 24 Nov 1961 in Savannah, Hardin County, TN.

 Geneva married **Earl Dwayne Rich**.
   5963 M   i.   **Casey Dwayne Rich** was born 11 Jul 1985 in Florence, Lauderdale County, AL.
 + 5964 F   ii.   **Candace Delynn Rich** was born 29 Jun 1987 in Florence, Lauderdale County, AL.

4661. Ricky Lynn Holcombe (*Arnold Holcombe*[8]*, Ernest Powers Holcombe*[7]*, Maggie Sharp*[6]*, John Thomas (Tom)*[5]*, James (Jim) Charles Sr.*[4]*, Adron (Edwin/Ade) Sr.*[3]*, Charles W. Sr.*[2]*, John Sr.*[1]) was born 9 Jan 1957 in Savannah, Hardin County, TN.

 Ricky married **Sherri Sue Barnett**, daughter of **Charles Reid Barnett** and **Sue Dobbins**, 19 Jun 1976 in Corinth, Alcorn County, MS.
   5965 M   i.   **Adam Reid Holcombe** was born 16 Jun 1983 in Corinth, Alcorn County, MS.
   5966 M   ii.   **Kyle Austin Holcombe** was born 19 Aug 1988 in Corinth, Alcorn County, MS.

4662. Alicia Carol Holcombe (*Arnold Holcombe*[8]*, Ernest Powers Holcombe*[7]*, Maggie Sharp*[6]*, John Thomas (Tom)*[5]*, James (Jim) Charles Sr.*[4]*, Adron (Edwin/Ade) Sr.*[3]*, Charles W. Sr.*[2]*, John Sr.*[1]) was born 6 Jul 1968 in Jackson, TN.

 Alicia married **Keith McKinny** 18 Aug 1988.

4663. Garry Phillip Holcombe (*Willie Cletus Holcombe*[8]*, Ernest Powers Holcombe*[7]*, Maggie Sharp*[6]*, John Thomas (Tom)*[5]*, James (Jim) Charles Sr.*[4]*, Adron (Edwin/Ade) Sr.*[3]*, Charles W. Sr.*[2]*, John Sr.*[1]) was born 25 Sep 1957 in Hardin County, TN.

 Garry married **Carol Lee Judd**, daughter of **Allen Lee Judd** and **Nellie M. Williams**, 31 Oct 1978 in Lauderdale County, AL. Carol was born 5 Oct 1957 in La Parte County, IN.
   5967 M   i.   **Phillip Lee Holcombe** was born 10 Nov 1979 in Lauderdale County, AL.

 Garry next married **Rhonda Hendrix**, daughter of **Charlie H. Hendrix** and **Mary L. Gist**, 15 Mar 1984 in Lauderdale County, AL. Rhonda was born 5 Oct 1957 in Lake County, IN.
   5968 M   i.   **Gary Andrew Holcombe** was born 6 Apr 1987 in Lauderdale County, AL.

4664. Carla Diane Holcombe (*Willie Cletus Holcombe*[8]*, Ernest Powers Holcombe*[7]*, Maggie Sharp*[6]*, John Thomas (Tom)*[5]*, James (Jim) Charles Sr.*[4]*, Adron (Edwin/Ade) Sr.*[3]*, Charles W. Sr.*[2]*, John Sr.*[1]) was born 12 Oct 1959 in Florence, Lauderdale County, AL.

 Carla married **Gary Michael Engle**, son of **Clarence A. Engle** and **Peggy Robinson**, 2 Nov 1979 in Lauderdale County, AL. Gary was born 24 Jun 1956 in Lawrence County, AL.
   5969 F   i.   **Jana Michelle Engle** was born 21 Jan 1982 in Starksville, MS.
   5970 F   ii.   **Lora Ashley Engle** was born 2 May 1985 in Starksville, MS.
   5971 M   iii.   **Trey Michael Engle** was born 2 Oct 1987 in Starksville, MS.

4666. Tracy Lyn Holcombe (*Jimmy Leonard Holcombe*[8]*, Ernest Powers Holcombe*[7]*, Maggie Sharp*[6]*, John Thomas (Tom)*[5]*, James (Jim) Charles Sr.*[4]*, Adron (Edwin/Ade) Sr.*[3]*, Charles W. Sr.*[2]*, John Sr.*[1]) was born 4 Dec 1967 in Florence, Lauderdale County, AL.

 Tracy married **Sandra (Sandy) Darlene Hellums**, daughter of **Sidney L. Hellums** and **Peggy Ann Trousdale**, 20 Mar 1993 in Lauderdale County, AL. Sandra was born 16 May 1970 in Colbert County, AL.

4667. Jimmy Keith Holcombe (*Jimmy Leonard Holcombe*[8]*, Ernest Powers Holcombe*[7]*, Maggie Sharp*[6]*, John Thomas (Tom)*[5]*, James (Jim) Charles Sr.*[4]*, Adron (Edwin/Ade) Sr.*[3]*, Charles W. Sr.*[2]*, John Sr.*[1]) was born 15 Dec 1972 in Florence, Lauderdale County, AL.

 Jimmy married **Kimberly Renaee Kruithoff**, daughter of **Sam Kruithoff** and **Kathy Parker**, 31 Aug 1996 in Colbert County, AL. Kimberly was born 3 Jun 1971 in Florence, Lauderdale County, AL.

4668. Cathy Rouna Hipps (*Hazel Juanita Holcombe*[8], *Elmer Patford Holcombe*[7], *Maggie Sharp*[6], *John Thomas (Tom)*[5], *James (Jim) Charles Sr.*[4], *Adron (Edwin/Ade) Sr.*[3], *Charles W. Sr.*[2], *John Sr.*[1]) was born 19 Jul 1949 in Lauderdale County, AL.

Cathy married **Johannes Hendrik Gomes**, son of **Johannes Gomes** and **Johanna Kneppers**, 10 Nov 1967 in Wayne County, MI. Johannes was born 27 Sep 1946 in Ymuiden, Netherlands.

+ 5972 M   i.   **Stephen William Gomes** was born 6 Jan 1970.
+ 5973 F   ii.   **Nicole Renee Gomes** was born 7 Jun 1972.

4669. Wilford Douglas Hipps (*Hazel Juanita Holcombe*[8], *Elmer Patford Holcombe*[7], *Maggie Sharp*[6], *John Thomas (Tom)*[5], *James (Jim) Charles Sr.*[4], *Adron (Edwin/Ade) Sr.*[3], *Charles W. Sr.*[2], *John Sr.*[1]) was born 3 Dec 1952 in Wayne County, MI.

Wilford married **Beth Rose Diehl** 9 Sep 1978 in Wayne County, MI. Beth was born 14 Oct 1956 in Wayne County, MI.

5974 F   i.   **Jennifer Rose Hipps** was born 17 Feb 1983 in Wayne County, MI.
5975 F   ii.   **Laurie Elizabeth Hipps** was born 23 Feb 1986 in Wayne County, MI.

4670. Shelia Diane Hipps (*Hazel Juanita Holcombe*[8], *Elmer Patford Holcombe*[7], *Maggie Sharp*[6], *John Thomas (Tom)*[5], *James (Jim) Charles Sr.*[4], *Adron (Edwin/Ade) Sr.*[3], *Charles W. Sr.*[2], *John Sr.*[1]) was born 17 Jan 1956 in Wayne County, MI.

Shelia married **Byron Phillips** 18 Oct. Byron was born 3 Feb 1960.

5976 F   i.   **Sarah Juanita Phillips** was born 12 Dec 1978.
5977 M   ii.   **Jason William Phillips** was born 6 May 1980.

4671. Susan Michelle Hipps (*Hazel Juanita Holcombe*[8], *Elmer Patford Holcombe*[7], *Maggie Sharp*[6], *John Thomas (Tom)*[5], *James (Jim) Charles Sr.*[4], *Adron (Edwin/Ade) Sr.*[3], *Charles W. Sr.*[2], *John Sr.*[1]) was born 20 May 1957 in Wayne County, MI.

Susan married **William Raymond Sweeney II** 14 May 1979 in Wayne County, MI. William was born 7 Mar 1957.

5978 M   i.   **William Raymond Sweeney III** was born 19 Jun 1979.
5979 M   ii.   **Scott Matthew Sweeney** was born 30 Aug 1983.

Susan next married **William Walker** 16 Aug 1994 in Las Vegas, NV. William was born 14 Feb 1945 in Indianapolis, Marion County, IN.

Susan next married **Don Lindgren**.

4672. Jerry Wayne Chandler (*Mable Inez Holcombe*[8], *Elmer Patford Holcombe*[7], *Maggie Sharp*[6], *John Thomas (Tom)*[5], *James (Jim) Charles Sr.*[4], *Adron (Edwin/Ade) Sr.*[3], *Charles W. Sr.*[2], *John Sr.*[1]) was born 9 Aug 1955 in Lauderdale County, AL.

Jerry married **Delilah Charlene Gibson**, daughter of **Thomas J. Gibson** and **Maxine Malone**, 2 Jun 1975 in Lauderdale County, AL. Delilah was born 11 Dec 1958 in Cook County, IL.

5980 M   i.   **Gregory Wayne Chandler** was born 16 Mar 1977 in Lauderdale County, AL.
5981 M   ii.   **Jeffery Craig Chandler** was born 18 Mar 1979 in Lauderdale County, AL.

4673. Teresa Kaye Chandler (*Mable Inez Holcombe*[8], *Elmer Patford Holcombe*[7], *Maggie Sharp*[6], *John Thomas (Tom)*[5], *James (Jim) Charles Sr.*[4], *Adron (Edwin/Ade) Sr.*[3], *Charles W. Sr.*[2], *John Sr.*[1]) was born 28 Mar 1958 in Lauderdale County, AL.

Teresa married **Gregory Steven Riggs**, son of **Noal Wesley Riggs Sr.** and **Helen Joyce Gray**, 10 Mar 1983 in Lauderdale County, AL. Gregory was born 17 Dec 1958 in Lauderdale County, AL.

5982 M   i.   **Shawn Nicholas Riggs** was born 6 Jun 1986 in Lauderdale County, AL.
5983 M   ii.   **Derrick Cody Riggs** was born 18 Nov 1990 in Lauderdale County, AL.

4674. Terry Hubert Holcombe (*Charles Herschel Holcombe*[8], *Hubert Lee Holcombe*[7], *Maggie Sharp*[6], *John Thomas (Tom)*[5], *James (Jim) Charles Sr.*[4], *Adron (Edwin/Ade) Sr.*[3], *Charles W. Sr.*[2], *John Sr.*[1]) was born 18 Sep 1958 in Lauderdale County, AL.

Terry married **Sarah Faye McDaniel**, daughter of **Milton McDaniel** and **Olene Shook**, 16 Jun 1979 in Lauderdale County, AL. Sarah was born 1 Mar 1960 in Lauderdale County, AL.

5984	M	i.	**Terrence Kyle Holcombe** was born 14 Aug 1984 in Vicksburg, MS.
5985	M	ii.	**Daniel Peter Holcombe** was born 25 Jul 1990 in Vicksburg, MS.

4675. Dwayne Charles Holcombe (*Charles Herschel Holcombe*[8], *Hubert Lee Holcombe*[7], *Maggie Sharp*[6], *John Thomas (Tom)*[5], *James (Jim) Charles Sr.*[4], *Adron (Edwin/Ade) Sr.*[3], *Charles W. Sr.*[2], *John Sr.*[1]) was born 3 Sep 1961 in Lauderdale County, AL.

Dwayne married **Lisha Anne Reed**, daughter of **Parker Roger Reed** and **Betty Ann Smith**, 3 Sep 1983 in Lauderdale County, AL. Lisha was born 27 Nov 1959 in Savannah, Hardin County, TN.

+ 5986	F	i.	**Mary Beth Holcombe** was born 8 Apr 1984 in Lauderdale County, AL.

4676. Bryan Lindsey Holcombe (*Charles Herschel Holcombe*[8], *Hubert Lee Holcombe*[7], *Maggie Sharp*[6], *John Thomas (Tom)*[5], *James (Jim) Charles Sr.*[4], *Adron (Edwin/Ade) Sr.*[3], *Charles W. Sr.*[2], *John Sr.*[1]) was born 9 Oct 1967 in Lauderdale County, AL.

Bryan married **Ginger Elizabeth Hellums**, daughter of **Sidney L. Hellums** and **Peggy Ann Trousdale**, 24 Oct 1989 in Lauderdale County, AL. Ginger was born 19 Dec 1967 in Colbert County, AL.

5987	M	i.	**Chase Lindsey Holcombe** was born 20 Jul 1998 in Lauderdale County, AL.

4677. David Lawrence Holcombe (*Lawrence O'steen Holcombe*[8], *Hubert Lee Holcombe*[7], *Maggie Sharp*[6], *John Thomas (Tom)*[5], *James (Jim) Charles Sr.*[4], *Adron (Edwin/Ade) Sr.*[3], *Charles W. Sr.*[2], *John Sr.*[1]) was born 5 Jul 1957 in Lauderdale County, AL.

David married **Cheryl Denise Terrell**, daughter of **William Howard Terrell** and **Doris Elizabeth Sharp**, 14 Feb 1981 in Lauderdale County, AL. Cheryl was born 24 Jun 1964 in Lauderdale County, AL.

5988	M	i.	**Adam David Holcombe** was born 14 Jul 1984 in Lauderdale County, AL.
5989	M	ii.	**Drew Terrell Holcombe** was born 11 Dec 1990 in Lauderdale County, AL.

4678. Rhonda Sue Holcombe (*Lawrence O'steen Holcombe*[8], *Hubert Lee Holcombe*[7], *Maggie Sharp*[6], *John Thomas (Tom)*[5], *James (Jim) Charles Sr.*[4], *Adron (Edwin/Ade) Sr.*[3], *Charles W. Sr.*[2], *John Sr.*[1]) was born 3 Sep 1960 in Lauderdale County, AL.

Rhonda married **Jackie Wayne Barnett**, son of **Arthur Barnett** and **Willadean Dalphine Gladney**, 19 May 1984 in Lauderdale County, AL. Jackie was born 11 Jan 1958 in Lauderdale County, AL.

5990	F	i.	**Holly Marie Barnett** was born 13 Jul 1990 in Lauderdale County, AL.
5991	F	ii.	**Mary Meagan Barnett** was born 13 Jul 1993 in Lauderdale County, AL.

4679. Donald Eugene Hart (*Edith Elizabeth Holcombe*[8], *Hubert Lee Holcombe*[7], *Maggie Sharp*[6], *John Thomas (Tom)*[5], *James (Jim) Charles Sr.*[4], *Adron (Edwin/Ade) Sr.*[3], *Charles W. Sr.*[2], *John Sr.*[1]) was born 20 Dec 1954 in Lauderdale County, AL.

Donald married **Janet Marie Jeffreys**, daughter of **Billy Harlow Jeffreys** and **Betty Jean Moore**, 6 Feb 1978 in Lauderdale County, AL. Janet was born 4 Mar 1960 in Lauderdale County, AL.

5992	M	i.	**Michael Ray Hart** was born 30 Oct 1981 in Lauderdale County, AL.
5993	M	ii.	**Robert Wayne Hart** was born 18 Jul 1985 in Lauderdale County, AL.

4680. Shirley Ann Hart (*Edith Elizabeth Holcombe*[8], *Hubert Lee Holcombe*[7], *Maggie Sharp*[6], *John Thomas (Tom)*[5], *James (Jim) Charles Sr.*[4], *Adron (Edwin/Ade) Sr.*[3], *Charles W. Sr.*[2], *John Sr.*[1]) was born 29 Nov 1957 in Lauderdale County, AL.

Shirley married **Frederick Albert Sudhoff**, son of **Frederick W. Sudhoff** and **Mary Mothler**, 27 Nov 1982 in Lauderdale County, AL. Frederick was born 16 Jan 1952 in Hamilton County, OH.

   5994 F   i.   **Christal Nova Sudhoff** was born 9 Jun 1980 in Lauderdale County, AL.

   5995 F   ii.   **Michelle Lee Sudhoff** was born 31 Oct 1984 in Lauderdale County, AL.

4682. Nelson Edward Parker (*Helen Lee Holcombe*[8], *Hubert Lee Holcombe*[7], *Maggie Sharp*[6], *John Thomas (Tom)*[5], *James (Jim) Charles Sr.*[4], *Adron (Edwin/Ade) Sr.*[3], *Charles W. Sr.*[2], *John Sr.*[1]) was born 14 Aug 1967 in Lauderdale County, AL.

Nelson married **Ivan Paige Little**, daughter of **George Little** and **Frieda Lewis**, 1 Jun 1996 in Townson, TN. Ivan was born 4 Jun 1974 in Jackson County, AL.

4684. Connie Faye Goode (*Robbie Nell Sharp*[8], *Jesse Thomas Sr.*[7], *Hallie (Hal) B.*[6], *John Thomas (Tom)*[5], *James (Jim) Charles Sr.*[4], *Adron (Edwin/Ade) Sr.*[3], *Charles W. Sr.*[2], *John Sr.*[1]) was born 2 Dec 1949 in Puerto Rico.

Connie married **James Lott**. James was born 14 Apr 1950.

   5996 F   i.   **Carrie Heather Lott** was born 17 Sep 1972 in Travis, TX.

4685. Michael Ray Goode (*Robbie Nell Sharp*[8], *Jesse Thomas Sr.*[7], *Hallie (Hal) B.*[6], *John Thomas (Tom)*[5], *James (Jim) Charles Sr.*[4], *Adron (Edwin/Ade) Sr.*[3], *Charles W. Sr.*[2], *John Sr.*[1]) was born 30 Apr 1952 in Lauderdale County, AL.

Michael married **Mary Margaret Prosperi**. Mary was born 14 Jan 1947 in Tarrent, TX.

   5997 F   i.   **Megan Elizabeth Goode** was born 11 Mar 1984 in Midland, TX.

   5998 M   ii.   **McKenzie William Goode** was born 2 Apr 1992 in Midland, TX.

4686. Phillip Glenn Goode (*Robbie Nell Sharp*[8], *Jesse Thomas Sr.*[7], *Hallie (Hal) B.*[6], *John Thomas (Tom)*[5], *James (Jim) Charles Sr.*[4], *Adron (Edwin/Ade) Sr.*[3], *Charles W. Sr.*[2], *John Sr.*[1]) was born 24 Mar 1954 in Dade, FL.

Phillip married **Beverly J. Hayes**. Beverly was born in Brownsville, Cameron, TX.

   5999 F   i.   **Lauren Nicole Goode** was born 14 Oct 1982 in Dallas, TX.

4689. James Ray Eady II (*Martha Jane Sharp*[8], *Vessey David*[7], *Hallie (Hal) B.*[6], *John Thomas (Tom)*[5], *James (Jim) Charles Sr.*[4], *Adron (Edwin/Ade) Sr.*[3], *Charles W. Sr.*[2], *John Sr.*[1]) was born 7 Aug 1964 in Lauderdale County, AL.

James married **Crystal Ann Mills**, daughter of **Woodrow W. Mills Jr.** and **Connie Pagniozzi**, 18 Jan 1997 in Birmingham, Jefferson County, AL. Crystal was born 17 Jan 1971 in Hollywood, FL.

4690. Margaret Elizabeth Eady (*Martha Jane Sharp*[8], *Vessey David*[7], *Hallie (Hal) B.*[6], *John Thomas (Tom)*[5], *James (Jim) Charles Sr.*[4], *Adron (Edwin/Ade) Sr.*[3], *Charles W. Sr.*[2], *John Sr.*[1]) was born 4 May 1967 in Lauderdale County, AL.

Margaret married **John Michael Gregory**, son of **John Robert Gregory** and **Garnetta Smith**, 31 Mar 1988 in Nashville, Davidson County, TN. John was born 20 Jan 1966 in Huntsville, Madison County, AL.

   6000 M   i.   **John Andrew Gregory** was born 11 Nov 1989.

4691. Callie Suzanne Eady (*Martha Jane Sharp*[8], *Vessey David*[7], *Hallie (Hal) B.*[6], *John Thomas (Tom)*[5], *James (Jim) Charles Sr.*[4], *Adron (Edwin/Ade) Sr.*[3], *Charles W. Sr.*[2], *John Sr.*[1]) was born 1 Jul 1973 in Lauderdale County, AL.

Callie married **Alexander Le Dizon**, son of **Andy T. Dizon** and **Unknown**, 13 Dec 1997 in Lauderdale County, AL.

4694. Andrew Elliot Carpenter (*Sandra Kay Sharp*[8], *Fred Noel Sr.*[7], *Hallie (Hal) B.*[6], *John Thomas (Tom)*[5], *James (Jim) Charles Sr.*[4], *Adron (Edwin/Ade) Sr.*[3], *Charles W. Sr.*[2], *John Sr.*[1]) was born 9 Mar 1974 in Birmingham, Jefferson County, AL.

Andrew married **Lauren Constance Mitchell**, daughter of **Charles Kimball Mitchell** and **Grace Elizabeth *Unk**, 4 Aug 2001 in Lexington, VA. Lauren was born 28 Apr 1981 in Lauderdale County, AL.

4696. Jeremy Winn Martin (*Susie Mae Sharp*[8], *Fred Noel Sr.*[7], *Hallie (Hal) B.*[6], *John Thomas (Tom)*[5], *James (Jim) Charles Sr.*[4], *Adron (Edwin/Ade) Sr.*[3], *Charles W. Sr.*[2], *John Sr.*[1]) was born 23 Jun 1980 in Limestone County, AL.

Jeremy married **Jamie Christine Decker**, daughter of **James Decker** and **Diane *Unk**, 12 Oct 2002 in Greenwood, MO.

4701. Charles Milton Burk (*Milton Sharp Burk*[8], *Thursa Lou Sharp*[7], *Hallie (Hal) B.*[6], *John Thomas (Tom)*[5], *James (Jim) Charles Sr.*[4], *Adron (Edwin/Ade) Sr.*[3], *Charles W. Sr.*[2], *John Sr.*[1]) was born 11 Jan 1958 in Summit, OH.

Charles married **Teresa Rae Beasley** 31 Jul 1982 in Franklin County, AL. Teresa was born 15 May 1962 in Franklin County, AL.

6001	M	i.	**Bradley Kyle Burk** was born 18 Jan 1984 in Beauregard County, LA.
6002	F	ii.	**Beth Nicole Burk** was born 18 Feb 1987 in Lauderdale County, TN.

4702. Linda Sue Burk (*Donald Oneal Burk*[8], *Thursa Lou Sharp*[7], *Hallie (Hal) B.*[6], *John Thomas (Tom)*[5], *James (Jim) Charles Sr.*[4], *Adron (Edwin/Ade) Sr.*[3], *Charles W. Sr.*[2], *John Sr.*[1]) was born 1 Sep 1954 in Montgomery County, OH.

Linda married **Don Martin**.

6003	F	i.	**Renae Martin** was born 27 Oct 1977 in Seattle, WA.

4703. Melissa Burk (*Donald Oneal Burk*[8], *Thursa Lou Sharp*[7], *Hallie (Hal) B.*[6], *John Thomas (Tom)*[5], *James (Jim) Charles Sr.*[4], *Adron (Edwin/Ade) Sr.*[3], *Charles W. Sr.*[2], *John Sr.*[1]) was born 4 Jul 1961 in Montgomery County, OH.

Melissa married **Robert Campbell**. Robert was born 13 Feb 1951 in Cook County, IL.

6004	F	i.	**Stephanie Campbell** was born 25 Jul 1981 in Lonoke, Lonoke County, AR.
6005	M	ii.	**Jason Campbell** was born 18 Dec 1982 in Lonoke, Lonoke County, AR.
6006	F	iii.	**Michael Campbell** was born 6 Mar 1986 in Stangcadom, Germany.
6007	M	iv.	**Robert Campbell** was born 28 Jun 1992 in Marcupa, AZ.

4704. Lisa Lou Burk (*Jimmy Ray Burk*[8], *Thursa Lou Sharp*[7], *Hallie (Hal) B.*[6], *John Thomas (Tom)*[5], *James (Jim) Charles Sr.*[4], *Adron (Edwin/Ade) Sr.*[3], *Charles W. Sr.*[2], *John Sr.*[1]) was born 8 Aug 1958 in Giles County, TN.

Lisa married **Billy Wilson Townsend** 9 Sep 1973. Billy was born 5 Sep 1953 in Giles County, TN.

+ 6008	M	i.	**Michael Chad Townsend** was born 10 Aug 1974 in Lauderdale County, AL.
+ 6009	F	ii.	**Sabrina Ann Townsend** was born 31 Aug 1976 in Giles County, TN.

Lisa next married **Joe Pierce**, son of **Joe Wayne Pierce** and **Linda Brown Foster**, 5 Jun 1999 in Lauderdale County, AL. Joe was born 24 Jul 1965.

4705. James Anderson (Jim) Weaver III (*Mary Ann Littrell*[8], *Leona May Sharp*[7], *Hallie (Hal) B.*[6], *John Thomas (Tom)*[5], *James (Jim) Charles Sr.*[4], *Adron (Edwin/Ade) Sr.*[3], *Charles W. Sr.*[2], *John Sr.*[1]) was born 4 Jul 1964 in Bibb County, GA.

James married **Tosha Patterson** 21 Dec 1989. Tosha was born 18 Mar 1966.

6010	F	i.	**Kasey Reigh Weaver** was born 2 Sep 1992 in Bibb County, GA.

4706. Donna Douglas Weaver (*Mary Ann Littrell*[8], *Leona May Sharp*[7], *Hallie (Hal) B.*[6], *John Thomas (Tom)*[5], *James (Jim) Charles Sr.*[4], *Adron (Edwin/Ade) Sr.*[3], *Charles W. Sr.*[2], *John Sr.*[1]) was born 9 Nov 1970 in Bibb County, GA.

Donna married **Jimmy Shuford**.

4707. Shannon Lee Ayers (*Maude Ellen Littrell*[8], *Leona May Sharp*[7], *Hallie (Hal) B.*[6], *John Thomas (Tom)*[5], *James (Jim) Charles Sr.*[4], *Adron (Edwin/Ade) Sr.*[3], *Charles W. Sr.*[2], *John Sr.*[1]) was born 1 Dec 1968 in Colbert County, AL.

Shannon married **Kimberly Stephens** 27 Mar 1992.

4708. Amanda Lane Ayers (*Maude Ellen Littrell*[8], *Leona May Sharp*[7], *Hallie (Hal) B.*[6], *John Thomas (Tom)*[5], *James (Jim) Charles Sr.*[4], *Adron (Edwin/Ade) Sr.*[3], *Charles W. Sr.*[2], *John Sr.*[1]) was born 16 Jan 1972 in Colbert County, AL.

Amanda married **Jason Alan Mackey**, son of **Freddy Ray Mackey** and **Patricia Ann Coburn**, 18 May 1996 in Colbert County, AL. Jason was born 14 Jan 1975 in Colbert County, AL.

4709. Timothy James Cira (*Mary Ann Sharp*[8], *John Edward*[7], *James (Swagger)*[6], *John Thomas (Tom)*[5], *James (Jim) Charles Sr.*[4], *Adron (Edwin/Ade) Sr.*[3], *Charles W. Sr.*[2], *John Sr.*[1]) was born 17 Sep 1956.

Timothy married **Robin *Unk**.

4711. Brian Robert Cira (*Mary Ann Sharp*[8], *John Edward*[7], *James (Swagger)*[6], *John Thomas (Tom)*[5], *James (Jim) Charles Sr.*[4], *Adron (Edwin/Ade) Sr.*[3], *Charles W. Sr.*[2], *John Sr.*[1]) was born 24 May 1961.

Brian married **Jennifer *Unk**.

4712. Dana Michelle Cira (*Mary Ann Sharp*[8], *John Edward*[7], *James (Swagger)*[6], *John Thomas (Tom)*[5], *James (Jim) Charles Sr.*[4], *Adron (Edwin/Ade) Sr.*[3], *Charles W. Sr.*[2], *John Sr.*[1]) was born 30 Apr 1968.

Dana married **Roger Martin**.

4715. Nena Lee Gean (*Martha Lee Mitchell*[8], *Bessie Etoil Sharp*[7], *James (Swagger)*[6], *John Thomas (Tom)*[5], *James (Jim) Charles Sr.*[4], *Adron (Edwin/Ade) Sr.*[3], *Charles W. Sr.*[2], *John Sr.*[1]) was born 28 Mar 1960 in Longbrook, CA.

Nena married **Alvin Hayne Haigler Jr.**, son of **Alvin Hayne Haigler Sr.** and **Loretta Herlong**, 11 Apr 1992 in Lagrange, GA. Alvin was born 12 Apr 1962.
  6011 F   i.   **Brooke Lauren Haigler** was born 23 Nov 1993 in Lagrange, GA.

4716. Michael Neal Gean (*Martha Lee Mitchell*[8], *Bessie Etoil Sharp*[7], *James (Swagger)*[6], *John Thomas (Tom)*[5], *James (Jim) Charles Sr.*[4], *Adron (Edwin/Ade) Sr.*[3], *Charles W. Sr.*[2], *John Sr.*[1]) was born 23 Dec 1961 in Lauderdale County, AL.

Michael married **Kim Clayton**.

4717. Kimberly (Kim) Mitchell (*James Ralph (Buddy) Mitchell*[8], *Bessie Etoil Sharp*[7], *James (Swagger)*[6], *John Thomas (Tom)*[5], *James (Jim) Charles Sr.*[4], *Adron (Edwin/Ade) Sr.*[3], *Charles W. Sr.*[2], *John Sr.*[1]) was born 24 Nov 1960.

Kimberly married **Cherokee Bedwell**.
+ 6012 M   i.   **Shane Bedwell** was born 23 May 198 ?.

Kimberly next married **George Clayton**.
  6013 F   i.   **Jessica Leigh Clayton** was born 13 Feb 1993.
  6014 F   ii.   **Jennifer Morgan Clayton** was born 11 Sep 1996.

4718. Jeffrey Terrell (Terry) Mitchell (*James Ralph (Buddy) Mitchell* [8], *Bessie Etoil Sharp* [7], *James (Swagger)* [6], *John Thomas (Tom)* [5], *James (Jim) Charles Sr.* [4], *Adron (Edwin/Ade) Sr.* [3], *Charles W. Sr.* [2], *John Sr.* [1]) was born 24 Feb 1964 in Lauderdale County, AL.

Jeffrey married **Wanda Gail Evans**, daughter of **Herbert E. Evans** and **Jean C. Crowell**, 10 Sep 1982 in Colbert County, AL. Wanda was born 12 May 1965 in Colbert County, AL.

+ 6015 F   i.   **Trista Paige Mitchell** was born 26 May 1984 in Lauderdale County, AL.
  6016 M   ii.   **Aaron Lee Mitchell** was born 10 Feb 1988 in Lauderdale County, AL.

4719. Eddie Kyle Mitchell (*James Ralph (Buddy) Mitchell* [8], *Bessie Etoil Sharp* [7], *James (Swagger)* [6], *John Thomas (Tom)* [5], *James (Jim) Charles Sr.* [4], *Adron (Edwin/Ade) Sr.* [3], *Charles W. Sr.* [2], *John Sr.* [1]) was born 14 Dec 1968 in Lauderdale County, AL.

Eddie married **Karen Elaine Scott**, daughter of **Gary Lance Scott** and **Bobbie Jo Qualls**, 30 Jun 1990 in Lauderdale County, AL. Karen was born 14 Oct 1971 in Lauderdale County, AL.
(Duplicate Line. See Person 3603)

4720. Russell Edward Mitchell (*Russell Taylor Mitchell* [8], *Bessie Etoil Sharp* [7], *James (Swagger)* [6], *John Thomas (Tom)* [5], *James (Jim) Charles Sr.* [4], *Adron (Edwin/Ade) Sr.* [3], *Charles W. Sr.* [2], *John Sr.* [1]) was born 30 Sep 1959 in Lauderdale County, AL.

Russell married **Anna Marie Scofield**, daughter of **James Scofield** and **Kathrine McDaniel**, 21 Oct 1983 in Lauderdale County, AL. Anna was born 11 Jun 1963 in Los Angeles, CA.

4721. Sherrie Alane Mitchell (*Russell Taylor Mitchell* [8], *Bessie Etoil Sharp* [7], *James (Swagger)* [6], *John Thomas (Tom)* [5], *James (Jim) Charles Sr.* [4], *Adron (Edwin/Ade) Sr.* [3], *Charles W. Sr.* [2], *John Sr.* [1]) was born 15 Feb 1960 in Lauderdale County, AL.

Sherrie married **Leonard (Lenny) Joseph Leblanc**, son of **Zoel Leblanc** and **Unknown**, 28 May 1982 in Lauderdale County, AL. Leonard was born 17 Jun 1951 in Massachusetts.

  6017 F   i.   **Hannah Marie Leblanc** was born 4 Nov 1986 in Lauderdale County, AL.

4722. Larry Steven Mitchell (*Thomas Larry (Tommy) Mitchell* [8], *Bessie Etoil Sharp* [7], *James (Swagger)* [6], *John Thomas (Tom)* [5], *James (Jim) Charles Sr.* [4], *Adron (Edwin/Ade) Sr.* [3], *Charles W. Sr.* [2], *John Sr.* [1]) was born 26 May 1968 in Lauderdale County, AL.

Larry married **April Louise Wooten**, daughter of **James Orville Wooten** and **Mary Magdalene McBride**, 5 Feb 1989 in Lauderdale County, AL. April was born 7 Apr 1970 in Colbert County, AL.

4723. Deanna Lynn Mitchell (*Thomas Larry (Tommy) Mitchell* [8], *Bessie Etoil Sharp* [7], *James (Swagger)* [6], *John Thomas (Tom)* [5], *James (Jim) Charles Sr.* [4], *Adron (Edwin/Ade) Sr.* [3], *Charles W. Sr.* [2], *John Sr.* [1]) was born 19 Mar 1970 in Lauderdale County, AL.

Deanna married **Daniel Glenn Parker**, son of **David Oscar Parker** and **Bobby Elizabeth Gooch**, 1 Nov 1992 in Lauderdale County, AL. Daniel was born 20 Jul 1965 in Lauderdale County, AL.

4724. Keith Glenn Crosswhite (*Judy Elaine Mitchell* [8], *Bessie Etoil Sharp* [7], *James (Swagger)* [6], *John Thomas (Tom)* [5], *James (Jim) Charles Sr.* [4], *Adron (Edwin/Ade) Sr.* [3], *Charles W. Sr.* [2], *John Sr.* [1]) was born 15 Aug 1966 in Lauderdale County, AL.

Keith married **Samantha Gail Davis**, daughter of **Gerold Ray Davis** and **Carolyn Lucille Watson**, 24 Aug 1990 in Lauderdale County, AL.

Keith next married **Melissa Carol Angel**, daughter of **Robert Ray Angel** and **Carolyn Moomaw**, 3 Jul 1999 in Lauderdale County, AL. Melissa was born 17 Mar 1974.

4725. Kelli Cheree Crosswhite (*Judy Elaine Mitchell*[8], *Bessie Etoil Sharp*[7], *James (Swagger)*[6], *John Thomas (Tom)*[5], *James (Jim) Charles Sr.*[4], *Adron (Edwin/Ade) Sr.*[3], *Charles W. Sr.*[2], *John Sr.*[1]) was born 9 Mar 1970 in Lauderdale County, AL.

  Kelli married **Gregory Eugene Daniel**, son of **Horace Olen Daniel** and **Margaret Sue Clemons**, 14 Jun 1991 in Lauderdale County, AL. Gregory was born 26 Jul 1968 in Florence, Lauderdale County, AL.

  6018 F i.   **Mykell Tatiana Daniel** was born 5 Apr 1997 in ECM Hospital, Florence, Lauderdale County, AL.
  6019 M ii.   **Kaden Gregory Daniel** was born 22 Oct 2000 in ECM Hospital, Florence, Lauderdale County, AL.
  6020 M iii. **Kylan Glenn Daniel** was born 5 Jan 2006 in ECM Hospital, Florence, Lauderdale County, AL.

4728. Suzanne Springer (*Claudeen Dewberry*[8], *Rachel Violet Sharp*[7], *James (Swagger)*[6], *John Thomas (Tom)*[5], *James (Jim) Charles Sr.*[4], *Adron (Edwin/Ade) Sr.*[3], *Charles W. Sr.*[2], *John Sr.*[1]) was born 22 May 1961 in Lauderdale County, AL.

  Suzanne married ***Unk Shelton**.

4729. Sherrie Shelane Springer (*Claudeen Dewberry*[8], *Rachel Violet Sharp*[7], *James (Swagger)*[6], *John Thomas (Tom)*[5], *James (Jim) Charles Sr.*[4], *Adron (Edwin/Ade) Sr.*[3], *Charles W. Sr.*[2], *John Sr.*[1]) was born 16 Oct 1963 in Lauderdale County, AL.

  Sherrie married ***Unk Pate**.

4730. Debra Kaye Bell (*Claudeen Dewberry*[8], *Rachel Violet Sharp*[7], *James (Swagger)*[6], *John Thomas (Tom)*[5], *James (Jim) Charles Sr.*[4], *Adron (Edwin/Ade) Sr.*[3], *Charles W. Sr.*[2], *John Sr.*[1]) was born 17 Jul 1966 in Tuscaloosa, AL.

  Debra married ***Unk Sprouse**.

4731. Mark Anthony Grigsby (*Cheryl Evelyn Dewberry*[8], *Rachel Violet Sharp*[7], *James (Swagger)*[6], *John Thomas (Tom)*[5], *James (Jim) Charles Sr.*[4], *Adron (Edwin/Ade) Sr.*[3], *Charles W. Sr.*[2], *John Sr.*[1]) was born 10 Dec 1969 in Lauderdale County, AL.

  Mark married **Jana Lynn Dial**, daughter of **Kenneth Earl Dial** and **Patricia Ann Trotti**, 22 Aug 1992 in Lauderdale County, AL. Jana was born 8 May 1971 in Mobile, AL.

  6021 M i.   **Joshua Nathaniel Grigsby** was born 19 Sep 1994 in Lauderdale County, AL.

4736. Brian Keith Kelley (*Teddy Steven Kelley*[8], *Aileen Beulah Sharp*[7], *James (Swagger)*[6], *John Thomas (Tom)*[5], *James (Jim) Charles Sr.*[4], *Adron (Edwin/Ade) Sr.*[3], *Charles W. Sr.*[2], *John Sr.*[1]) was born 30 Jul 1973 in Lauderdale County, AL.

  Brian married **Angela Marie Sharp**, daughter of **William Edward (Tiny) Sharp** and **Judy Ann Melton**, 9 May 1998 in Lauderdale County, AL. Angela was born 19 Aug 1976 in Lauderdale County, AL.
  (Duplicate Line. See Person 3183)

4746. Martha Sue Sharp (*Donald Glenn*[8], *Ellie Berry Sr.*[7], *Thomas Leslie (Peck)*[6], *John Thomas (Tom)*[5], *James (Jim) Charles Sr.*[4], *Adron (Edwin/Ade) Sr.*[3], *Charles W. Sr.*[2], *John Sr.*[1]) was born 5 Mar 1960 in Lauderdale County, AL.

  Martha married **Dennis Eugene Davis**, son of **Ernest Harden Davis** and **Bertha Marie Spires**, 12 Mar 1977. Dennis was born 5 Mar 1957 in Lauderdale County, AL.

4747. Donald (Donnie) Ray Sharp (*Donald Glenn*[8], *Ellie Berry Sr.*[7], *Thomas Leslie (Peck)*[6], *John Thomas (Tom)*[5], *James (Jim) Charles Sr.*[4], *Adron (Edwin/Ade) Sr.*[3], *Charles W. Sr.*[2], *John Sr.*[1]) was born 9 Feb 1963 in Lauderdale County, AL.

Donald married **Susie Ann Thigpen**, daughter of **Buford C. L. Thigpen** and **Jimmie S. Brewer**, 2 May 1981. Susie was born 30 Jun 1957 in Lauderdale County, AL.

4748. Daniel (Danny) Glen Sharp (*Donald Glenn*[8], *Ellie Berry Sr.*[7], *Thomas Leslie (Peck)*[6], *John Thomas (Tom)*[5], *James (Jim) Charles Sr.*[4], *Adron (Edwin/Ade) Sr.*[3], *Charles W. Sr.*[2], *John Sr.*[1]) was born 3 Dec 1964 in Lauderdale County, AL.

Daniel married **Laura Ann Borden**, daughter of **Roger Lee Borden** and **Mary Elizabeth Wallace**, 8 Jun 1985 in Lauderdale County, AL. Laura was born 9 May 1964 in Colbert County, AL.
6022 F i. **Christy Leighann Sharp** was born 30 Jul 1985 in Lauderdale County, AL.
6023 F ii. **April Noel Sharp** was born 8 Mar 1988 in Lauderdale County, AL.
6024 M iii. **Matthew Quenton Sharp** was born 27 Jan 1990 in Lauderdale County, AL.

4749. Anessa Michelle Lawler (*Sandra Sue Sharp*[8], *Ellie Berry Sr.*[7], *Thomas Leslie (Peck)*[6], *John Thomas (Tom)*[5], *James (Jim) Charles Sr.*[4], *Adron (Edwin/Ade) Sr.*[3], *Charles W. Sr.*[2], *John Sr.*[1]) was born 2 Jan 1968 in Lauderdale County, AL.

Anessa married **Scott David Dorrah**, son of **James W. Dorrah** and **Amanda Beckeet**, 22 May 1987 in Lauderdale County, AL. Scott was born 19 Oct 1966 in Beaver City, PA.
6025 M i. **Justin Scott Dorrah** was born 26 Oct 1988 in Terracon AFB, Spain.
6026 F ii. **Amberly Michelle Dorrah** was born 21 Sep 1992 in Lauderdale County, AL.

4750. Lesley (Les) Lamoine Lawler (*Sandra Sue Sharp*[8], *Ellie Berry Sr.*[7], *Thomas Leslie (Peck)*[6], *John Thomas (Tom)*[5], *James (Jim) Charles Sr.*[4], *Adron (Edwin/Ade) Sr.*[3], *Charles W. Sr.*[2], *John Sr.*[1]) was born 20 Feb 1972 in Lauderdale County, AL.

Lesley married **Susan Dean Gambrell**, daughter of **Edward Gambrell** and **Drucilla Sharp**, 4 Aug 1944 in Lauderdale County, AL. Susan was born 6 Apr 1977 in Lauderdale County, AL.

Lesley next married **Deana M. Rahn**, daughter of **Norman Rahn** and **Unknown**, 14 Jul 2001 in Piedmont, AL.

4753. Cheryl Denise Terrell (*Doris Elizabeth Sharp*[8], *Earl Leslie*[7], *Thomas Leslie (Peck)*[6], *John Thomas (Tom)*[5], *James (Jim) Charles Sr.*[4], *Adron (Edwin/Ade) Sr.*[3], *Charles W. Sr.*[2], *John Sr.*[1]) was born 24 Jun 1964 in Lauderdale County, AL.

Cheryl married **David Lawrence Holcombe**, son of **Lawrence O'steen Holcombe** and **Mary Earline Tune**, 14 Feb 1981 in Lauderdale County, AL. David was born 5 Jul 1957 in Lauderdale County, AL.
(Duplicate Line. See Person 4677)

4756. Jennifer Michelle Sharp (*Donnie Murray*[8], *Earl Leslie*[7], *Thomas Leslie (Peck)*[6], *John Thomas (Tom)*[5], *James (Jim) Charles Sr.*[4], *Adron (Edwin/Ade) Sr.*[3], *Charles W. Sr.*[2], *John Sr.*[1]) was born 31 Jan 1982 in Lauderdale County, AL.

Jennifer married **Michael Lee Price**, son of **Roger Lee Price** and **Ruby Mae Highland**, 31 Dec 2005 in Lauderdale County, AL. Michael was born 22 Feb 1975 in Alabama.

4757. Misty Dawn Sharp (*Jerry Lynn*[8], *Earl Leslie*[7], *Thomas Leslie (Peck)*[6], *John Thomas (Tom)*[5], *James (Jim) Charles Sr.*[4], *Adron (Edwin/Ade) Sr.*[3], *Charles W. Sr.*[2], *John Sr.*[1]) was born 19 Apr 1976 in Lauderdale County, AL.

Misty married **Samuel Tyrus Watson**, son of **William Gregory Watson** and **Beverly Jean Beadle**, 6 Dec 1998 in Lauderdale County, AL. Samuel was born 21 Jul 1973 in Lauderdale County, AL.
6027 M i. **Jackson Call Watson** was born 28 Jun 2001 in Lauderdale County, AL.
6028 M ii. **Cody Lynn Watson** was born 7 Jul 2003 in Lauderdale County, AL.

4774. Daniel Scott Robertson (*Berry Lee (Buck) Robertson^8, Mary Elizabeth Sharp^7, Edgar Lee^6, John Thomas (Tom)^5, James (Jim) Charles Sr.^{4}, Adron (Edwin/Ade) Sr.^{3}, Charles W. Sr.^{2}, John Sr.^{1}*) was born 29 Aug 1970 in Lauderdale County, AL.

Daniel married **Lea May Holt**, daughter of **John Emerald Holt** and **Jacqueline Ann Rolston**, 18 Dec 1992 in Lauderdale County, AL. Lea was born 12 Sep 1970.

4776. Kimberly Renee McDaniel (*Charlotte Rose Robertson^8, Mary Elizabeth Sharp^7, Edgar Lee^6, John Thomas (Tom)^5, James (Jim) Charles Sr.^{4}, Adron (Edwin/Ade) Sr.^{3}, Charles W. Sr.^{2}, John Sr.^{1}*) was born 17 Aug 1969 in Lauderdale County, AL.

Kimberly married **Lorin Chad Payne**, son of **Lovin Lucky Payne** and **Judy Capley**, 6 Jul 1991 in Lauderdale County, AL. Lorin was born 16 Jun 1972 in Lauderdale County, AL.

4779. Kelly Leanne Arnold (*Janice Kay Mansell^8, Annie Bell Sharp^7, Edgar Lee^6, John Thomas (Tom)^5, James (Jim) Charles Sr.^{4}, Adron (Edwin/Ade) Sr.^{3}, Charles W. Sr.^{2}, John Sr.^{1}*) was born 30 Sep 1975 in Lauderdale County, AL.

Kelly married **Bob Jones**.
6029 F   i.   **Emma Jones**.

4780. Christopher Britt Mansell (*Jimmy Don Mansell^8, Annie Bell Sharp^7, Edgar Lee^6, John Thomas (Tom)^5, James (Jim) Charles Sr.^{4}, Adron (Edwin/Ade) Sr.^{3}, Charles W. Sr.^{2}, John Sr.^{1}*) was born 27 Oct 1977 in Lauderdale County, AL.

Christopher married **Kristin *Unk**.
6030 F   i.   **Madison Mansell**.
6031 M   ii.   **Mason Mansell**.

4783. Ken Bratcher (*Diane Garner^8, Edna Idelle Sharp^7, Edgar Lee^6, John Thomas (Tom)^5, James (Jim) Charles Sr.^{4}, Adron (Edwin/Ade) Sr.^{3}, Charles W. Sr.^{2}, John Sr.^{1}*).

Ken married **Sharon *Unk**.
6032 F   i.   **Kayla Bratcher**.
6033 M   ii.   **Dustin Bratcher**.
6034 F   iii. **Heather Bratcher**.

4784. Kerri Bratcher (*Diane Garner^8, Edna Idelle Sharp^7, Edgar Lee^6, John Thomas (Tom)^5, James (Jim) Charles Sr.^{4}, Adron (Edwin/Ade) Sr.^{3}, Charles W. Sr.^{2}, John Sr.^{1}*).

Kerri married **Bobby Myron Risner**, son of **Bobby Gene Risner** and **Evelyn Vaden**, 2 Jul 1994. Bobby was born 15 Jul 1963.
6035 M   i.   **Kagen Risner**.

4790. Jennifer Sheree Sharp (*Gregory Thomas^8, John Thomas^7, Edgar Lee^6, John Thomas (Tom)^5, James (Jim) Charles Sr.^{4}, Adron (Edwin/Ade) Sr.^{3}, Charles W. Sr.^{2}, John Sr.^{1}*) was born 20 Apr 1977 in Lauderdale County, AL.

Jennifer married **Michael Shane Herrmann**, son of **Michael Clark Herrmann** and **Brenda Faye Smith**, 22 Jul 2000 in Lauderdale County, AL. Michael was born 7 Dec 1974.

4793. Anthony Derrick Smith (*Judy Diane Womble^8, Ellen Emogene Sharp^7, Edgar Lee^6, John Thomas (Tom)^5, James (Jim) Charles Sr.^{4}, Adron (Edwin/Ade) Sr.^{3}, Charles W. Sr.^{2}, John Sr.^{1}*) was born 29 Jun 1977 in Lauderdale County, AL.

Anthony married **Lisa *Unk**.
6036 F   i.   **Leslie Brooke Smith** was born in 2000.

4795. Brian Ray Barker (*Hairel Ray Barker*[8], *Idna Cynthia Hairell*[7], *Minor (Mina) Houston Sharp*[6], *John Thomas (Tom)*[5], *James (Jim) Charles Sr.*[4], *Adron (Edwin/Ade) Sr.*[3], *Charles W. Sr.*[2], *John Sr.*[1]) was born 31 Oct 1969 in Jefferson County, AL.

Brian married **Susie Holt Riley** 10 Nov 1990 in Colbert County, AL.

4796. Michelle Leigh Barker (*Hairel Ray Barker*[8], *Idna Cynthia Hairell*[7], *Minor (Mina) Houston Sharp*[6], *John Thomas (Tom)*[5], *James (Jim) Charles Sr.*[4], *Adron (Edwin/Ade) Sr.*[3], *Charles W. Sr.*[2], *John Sr.*[1]) was born 3 Dec 1972.

Michelle married **Christopher Ivan McKinney**, son of **Leslie William McKinney** and **Bobbie Sue Garner**, 21 May 1994 in Lauderdale County, AL. Christopher was born 11 Apr 1972.

4801. William Carl Bruce Jr. (*William Carl Bruce Sr.*[8], *Willie Clyde Bruce*[7], *James Pinkney Bruce Sr.*[6], *Matilda Ann Sharp*[5], *James (Jim) Charles Sr.*[4], *Adron (Edwin/Ade) Sr.*[3], *Charles W. Sr.*[2], *John Sr.*[1]) was born 14 Nov 1952 in Lauderdale County, AL.

William married **Sandra Kaye Ledgewood**, daughter of **Ottie V. Ledgewood** and **Naomi Almond**, 1 Nov 1980 in Lauderdale County, AL. Sandra was born 16 Nov 1955 in Lauderdale County, AL.

4802. Mildred Diane Bruce (*William Carl Bruce Sr.*[8], *Willie Clyde Bruce*[7], *James Pinkney Bruce Sr.*[6], *Matilda Ann Sharp*[5], *James (Jim) Charles Sr.*[4], *Adron (Edwin/Ade) Sr.*[3], *Charles W. Sr.*[2], *John Sr.*[1]) was born 5 Oct 1955 in Lauderdale County, AL.

Mildred married **Donald Keith Robinson**, son of **Charles B. Robinson** and **Aileen McGee**, 30 May 1980 in Lauderdale County, AL. Donald was born 20 Sep 1957 in Colbert County, AL.
6037	F	i.	**Sara Diane Robinson** was born in 1984 in Lauderdale County, AL.
6038	M	ii.	**Daniel Keith Robinson** was born in 1985 in Lauderdale County, AL.
6039	F	iii.	**Katherine Ann Robinson** was born in 1992 in Lauderdale County, AL.
6040	M	iv.	**Benjamin Wade Robinson** was born in 1994 in Lauderdale County, AL.

4803. John Terry Bruce (*James Millard Bruce Sr.*[8], *John Gilbert Bruce Sr.*[7], *James Pinkney Bruce Sr.*[6], *Matilda Ann Sharp*[5], *James (Jim) Charles Sr.*[4], *Adron (Edwin/Ade) Sr.*[3], *Charles W. Sr.*[2], *John Sr.*[1]) was born 25 Oct 1961 in Genesse County, MI.

John married **Susan *Unk**.

4805. Pamela Jane Bruce (*Reggie Paul Bruce*[8], *John Gilbert Bruce Sr.*[7], *James Pinkney Bruce Sr.*[6], *Matilda Ann Sharp*[5], *James (Jim) Charles Sr.*[4], *Adron (Edwin/Ade) Sr.*[3], *Charles W. Sr.*[2], *John Sr.*[1]) was born 15 Mar 1961 in Lauderdale County, AL.

Pamela married **Warren Thomas Carrigan Jr.**, son of **Warren Thomas Carrigan Sr.** and **Ila M. Ham**, 27 Mar 1981 in Lauderdale County, AL. Warren was born 19 Aug 1958 in Lauderdale County, AL.
| 6041 | M | i. | **Warren Thomas Carrigan** was born 1 Apr 1985 in Lauderdale County, AL. |
| 6042 | M | ii. | **Ryan Paul Carrigan** was born 5 Apr 1986 in Lauderdale County, AL. |

4806. Paula Malin Bruce (*Reggie Paul Bruce*[8], *John Gilbert Bruce Sr.*[7], *James Pinkney Bruce Sr.*[6], *Matilda Ann Sharp*[5], *James (Jim) Charles Sr.*[4], *Adron (Edwin/Ade) Sr.*[3], *Charles W. Sr.*[2], *John Sr.*[1]) was born 3 Sep 1962 in Lauderdale County, AL.

Paula married **Stephen Blair Smith**, son of **Ronald E. Smith** and **Barbara Holt**, 6 Aug 1983 in Lauderdale County, AL. Stephen was born 20 Aug 1922 in Lauderdale County, AL.
| 6043 | M | i. | **Evan Smith**. |
| 6044 | M | ii. | **Jacob Bruce Smith**. |

4807. Kimberly Jan Bruce (*Reggie Paul Bruce^8, John Gilbert Bruce Sr.^{7}, James Pinkney Bruce Sr.^{6}, Matilda Ann Sharp^5, James (Jim) Charles Sr.^{4}, Adron (Edwin/Ade) Sr.^{3}, Charles W. Sr.^{2}, John Sr.^{1}*) was born 7 Dec 1965 in Lauderdale County, AL.

Kimberly married **Danny Wayne Cromwell**, son of **Danny Allen Cromwell** and **Shelia Sue Turnbow**, 15 Apr 1989 in Lauderdale County, AL. Danny was born 18 Feb 1967 in Lauderdale County, AL.

| 6045 | F | i. | **Lana Elizabeth Cromwell** was born 16 Mar 1998 in Lauderdale County, AL. |
| 6046 | M | ii. | **Jackson Paul Cromwell** was born 28 Sep 1999 in Lauderdale County, AL. |

Kimberly next married **Warren Bradley Harrison**, son of **Jack Denton Harrison** and **Janet Ann McAlister**, 12 Oct 1996 in Lauderdale County, AL. Warren was born 2 Nov 1967.

4808. Quennon Chancey Bruce (*Harold Sherman Bruce^8, John Gilbert Bruce Sr.^{7}, James Pinkney Bruce Sr.^{6}, Matilda Ann Sharp^5, James (Jim) Charles Sr.^{4}, Adron (Edwin/Ade) Sr.^{3}, Charles W. Sr.^{2}, John Sr.^{1}*) was born 19 Oct 1969 in Lauderdale County, AL.

Quennon married **Moria Kathleen Camfield**, daughter of **Kieron Wallace Camfield** and **Elaine Louise Lockwood**, 16 Nov 1989 in Lauderdale County, AL. Moria was born 15 Feb 1970 in New York.

| 6047 | F | i. | **Elizabeth Irene Bruce** was born 11 Feb 1992 in Lauderdale County, AL. |
| 6048 | M | ii. | **Allen Wayne Bruce** was born 1 Sep 1995 in Lauderdale County, AL. |

4809. Zabrina Camilla Bruce (*Harold Sherman Bruce^8, John Gilbert Bruce Sr.^{7}, James Pinkney Bruce Sr.^{6}, Matilda Ann Sharp^5, James (Jim) Charles Sr.^{4}, Adron (Edwin/Ade) Sr.^{3}, Charles W. Sr.^{2}, John Sr.^{1}*) was born 26 May 1973 in Lauderdale County, AL.

Zabrina married **Anthony Henson**.

| 6049 | F | i. | **Vermillion Mercedes Henson** was born 22 Dec 1995 in Lauderdale County, AL. |

Zabrina next married **Brett Thacker**.

| 6050 | F | i. | **Ash'lee Darretanan Thacker** was born 19 Apr 1998 in Lauderdale County, AL. |

4811. Sherri Lynn Bruce (*John Gilbert Bruce Jr.^{8}, John Gilbert Bruce Sr.^{7}, James Pinkney Bruce Sr.^{6}, Matilda Ann Sharp^5, James (Jim) Charles Sr.^{4}, Adron (Edwin/Ade) Sr.^{3}, Charles W. Sr.^{2}, John Sr.^{1}*) was born 24 Dec 1966 in Lauderdale County, AL.

Sherri married **John Samuel Crandell**, son of **Truman K. Crandell** and **Patricia Kenner**, 13 Sep 1980 in Lauderdale County, AL.

4812. Virginia Suzanene Bruce (*John Gilbert Bruce Jr.^{8}, John Gilbert Bruce Sr.^{7}, James Pinkney Bruce Sr.^{6}, Matilda Ann Sharp^5, James (Jim) Charles Sr.^{4}, Adron (Edwin/Ade) Sr.^{3}, Charles W. Sr.^{2}, John Sr.^{1}*) was born 26 Mar 1969 in Lauderdale County, AL.

Virginia married **David Wayne Muraloski**, son of **Alexander Jospeh Muraloski** and **Virginia Lee Everhart**, 14 Apr 1989 in Lauderdale County, AL.

4814. Tina Louise Risner (*Virginia Alice Bruce^8, John Gilbert Bruce Sr.^{7}, James Pinkney Bruce Sr.^{6}, Matilda Ann Sharp^5, James (Jim) Charles Sr.^{4}, Adron (Edwin/Ade) Sr.^{3}, Charles W. Sr.^{2}, John Sr.^{1}*) was born 2 Feb 1962 in Lauderdale County, AL.

Tina married **William E. Miller Jr.**, son of **William E. Miller Sr.** and **Unknown**, 16 May 1981.

| 6051 | F | i. | **Lori Elizabeth Miller** was born 23 May 1982 in Maryland. |

4818. Gregory Alan Bruce (*Amos Jerry Bruce Jr.^{8}, Amos Jerry Bruce Sr.^{7}, Robert William Bruce^6, Matilda Ann Sharp^5, James (Jim) Charles Sr.^{4}, Adron (Edwin/Ade) Sr.^{3}, Charles W. Sr.^{2}, John Sr.^{1}*) was born 23 Sep 1964 in Anderson, IN.

Gregory married **De Anna Rogers**, daughter of **Jim Rogers** and **Joyce *Unk**. De was born 10 Aug 1969 in Texas.

6052 M i. **Bryant Kyle Bruce** was born 11 Aug 1991 in Houston, Harris County, TX.

4819. Scott Blakney Bruce (*Amos Jerry Bruce Jr.*[8], *Amos Jerry Bruce Sr.*[7], *Robert William Bruce*[6], *Matilda Ann Sharp*[5], *James (Jim) Charles Sr.*[4], *Adron (Edwin/Ade) Sr.*[3], *Charles W. Sr.*[2], *John Sr.*[1]) was born 14 Oct 1969 in Athens, GA.

Scott married **Imelda Bratton** 23 Aug 1990 in Huntsville, TX.
6053 M i. **Tyler Bruce**.
6054 F ii. **Kimberly Bruce**.

Scott next married **Virginia Gonzales**.
6055 F i. **Natalie Bruce** was born 10 Dec 2004.

4820. Shannon Kelly Bruce (*Charles William Bruce*[8], *Amos Jerry Bruce Sr.*[7], *Robert William Bruce*[6], *Matilda Ann Sharp*[5], *James (Jim) Charles Sr.*[4], *Adron (Edwin/Ade) Sr.*[3], *Charles W. Sr.*[2], *John Sr.*[1]) was born 2 Feb 1971 in Lownes County, GA.

Shannon married **Adam Ray Crews**, son of **Ray Crews** and **Gayle Boyette**, 23 Sep 1995 in Opelika, Lee County, AL. Adam was born 23 Aug 1972 in Lee County, AL.
6056 F i. **Hannah Kelly Crews** was born 27 Mar 1998 in Solano County, CA.
6057 M ii. **Hunter Gray Crews** was born 27 Sep 2006 in Lee County, AL.

4821. Chad Adam Bruce (*Charles William Bruce*[8], *Amos Jerry Bruce Sr.*[7], *Robert William Bruce*[6], *Matilda Ann Sharp*[5], *James (Jim) Charles Sr.*[4], *Adron (Edwin/Ade) Sr.*[3], *Charles W. Sr.*[2], *John Sr.*[1]) was born 20 Oct 1977 in Opelika, Lee County, AL.

Chad married **Suzanne Elizabeth Sawyer** 17 Nov 2007 in Dothan, AL. Suzanne was born 9 Oct 1982 in Dothan, AL.

4822. Drew Nathaniel Hollander (*Rachel Annette Bruce*[8], *Amos Jerry Bruce Sr.*[7], *Robert William Bruce*[6], *Matilda Ann Sharp*[5], *James (Jim) Charles Sr.*[4], *Adron (Edwin/Ade) Sr.*[3], *Charles W. Sr.*[2], *John Sr.*[1]) was born 4 Oct 1981 in Lauderdale County, AL.

Drew married **Brie *Unk**.

- **Kristopher Dwight Evans** was born 21 Aug 1976 in Decatur, AL. Son of Elizabeth Ann Mason and Dwight Lamar Evans. See page 376.

   Kristopher married **Julie Ann Schwiethale**, daughter of **Arthur Ernest Schwiethale** and **Marla Jean Skiles,** 17 Aug 1996 in Wichita, Sedgewick, Kansas.
   F   i   **Chloe Reed Evans** born 27 Oct 2001 in Austin, Williamson County, TX.
   F   ii   **Lily Ryan Evans** born 1 July 2004 in Abilene, TX.
   F   iii   **Emma Rayne Evans** born 20 April 2007in Abilene, TX.

- **Lori Ann Evans** was born 29 Nov 1979 in Decatur, AL. Daughter of Elizabeth Ann Mason and Dwight Lamar Evans. See page 376.

   Lori married **Stacy Ryan Dow**, son of **Bobby Dow** and **Judy Ellis** 13 July 2002, Austin, TX. Stacy was born 16 May 1979.
   F   i   **Faith Ellisabeth Dow** born 10 Oct 2006 in Fort Worth, TX.
   F   ii   **Sophia Grace Dow** born 28 July 2008 in Abilene, TX.

4824. Kelly Newton (*Merita Kay Bruce*[8], *Reeder Warner Bruce*[7], *Robert William Bruce*[6], *Matilda Ann Sharp*[5], *James (Jim) Charles Sr.*[4], *Adron (Edwin/Ade) Sr.*[3], *Charles W. Sr.*[2], *John Sr.*[1]).

Kelly married **Jason Dyer**.
6058 F i. **Lily Dyer**.

6059 F ii. **Maggie Dyer**.

4825. Reeda Newton (*Merita Kay Bruce*[8], *Reeder Warner Bruce*[7], *Robert William Bruce*[6], *Matilda Ann Sharp*[5], *James (Jim) Charles Sr.*[4], *Adron (Edwin/Ade) Sr.*[3], *Charles W. Sr.*[2], *John Sr.*[1]).

Reeda married **Tony Brewer**.
6060 M i. **Nate Brewer**.
6061 F ii. **Natalie Brewer**.

4826. Collin Warner Bruce (*Lanny Warner Bruce*[8], *Reeder Warner Bruce*[7], *Robert William Bruce*[6], *Matilda Ann Sharp*[5], *James (Jim) Charles Sr.*[4], *Adron (Edwin/Ade) Sr.*[3], *Charles W. Sr.*[2], *John Sr.*[1]).

Collin married **Tara Shae Galbreath**, daughter of **Richard Galbreath** and **Patsy Lynn Childers**, 10 Aug 2002 in Lauderdale County, AL. Tara was born 12 Oct 1975.

4827. Emily Bruce (*Lanny Warner Bruce*[8], *Reeder Warner Bruce*[7], *Robert William Bruce*[6], *Matilda Ann Sharp*[5], *James (Jim) Charles Sr.*[4], *Adron (Edwin/Ade) Sr.*[3], *Charles W. Sr.*[2], *John Sr.*[1]).

Emily married **Trey Waddell**.

4828. Kelly Bruce (*Lanny Warner Bruce*[8], *Reeder Warner Bruce*[7], *Robert William Bruce*[6], *Matilda Ann Sharp*[5], *James (Jim) Charles Sr.*[4], *Adron (Edwin/Ade) Sr.*[3], *Charles W. Sr.*[2], *John Sr.*[1]).

Kelly married **Jason Dyer**.

4829. Reeda Bruce (*Lanny Warner Bruce*[8], *Reeder Warner Bruce*[7], *Robert William Bruce*[6], *Matilda Ann Sharp*[5], *James (Jim) Charles Sr.*[4], *Adron (Edwin/Ade) Sr.*[3], *Charles W. Sr.*[2], *John Sr.*[1]).

Reeda married **Tony Brewer**.

4830. Tiffany Keys (*Mitzi Diane Bruce*[8], *Reeder Warner Bruce*[7], *Robert William Bruce*[6], *Matilda Ann Sharp*[5], *James (Jim) Charles Sr.*[4], *Adron (Edwin/Ade) Sr.*[3], *Charles W. Sr.*[2], *John Sr.*[1]).

Tiffany married **James Heiger**.

4835. Steven Earl Mitchell (*Gracie Mozella Phillips*[8], *Lady Carrie Wood*[7], *Margie Ann (Marjorie) Bruce*[6], *Matilda Ann Sharp*[5], *James (Jim) Charles Sr.*[4], *Adron (Edwin/Ade) Sr.*[3], *Charles W. Sr.*[2], *John Sr.*[1]) was born 26 Oct 1952 in Harrisburg, Poinsett County, AR.

Steven married **Mary Beth Aue**. Mary was born 28 Dec 1959.
6062 M i. **Benton Thomas Mitchell** was born 24 May 1996 in Arkansas.

4836. Kevin Bruce Mitchell (*Gracie Mozella Phillips*[8], *Lady Carrie Wood*[7], *Margie Ann (Marjorie) Bruce*[6], *Matilda Ann Sharp*[5], *James (Jim) Charles Sr.*[4], *Adron (Edwin/Ade) Sr.*[3], *Charles W. Sr.*[2], *John Sr.*[1]) was born 7 Nov 1960.

Kevin married **Trena Richardson**. Trena was born 1 Feb 1960.
6063 M i. **Christopher Chase Mitchell** was born 31 Mar 1989 in Arkansas.

4837. Shirley Ann Carter (*Marcella Vernette Phillips*[8], *Lady Carrie Wood*[7], *Margie Ann (Marjorie) Bruce*[6], *Matilda Ann Sharp*[5], *James (Jim) Charles Sr.*[4], *Adron (Edwin/Ade) Sr.*[3], *Charles W. Sr.*[2], *John Sr.*[1]) was born 27 Aug 1959.

Shirley married **Terry Randall Cromwell** before 1978.
6064 M i. **Randall Lee Cromwell** was born 17 Sep 1978.
6065 M ii. **Terry Leroy Cromwell** was born 24 Apr 1980.

Shirley next married **Edwin Dwayne Wear** 14 Feb 1992.
6066 F i. **Shalane McKay Wear** was born 17 Feb 1993.
6067 F ii. **Selena Nicole Wear** was born 16 Mar 1995.

4838. Sue Carter (*Marcella Vernette Phillips*[8], *Lady Carrie Wood*[7], *Margie Ann (Marjorie) Bruce*[6], *Matilda Ann Sharp*[5], *James (Jim) Charles Sr.*[4], *Adron (Edwin/Ade) Sr.*[3], *Charles W. Sr.*[2], *John Sr.*[1]) was born 26 Jan 1961.

Sue married **Steven Eugene Hart**.
6068 M i. **Steven Hart**.

Sue next married **Mark Ledford**.
6069 M i. **Brandon Ledford**.
6070 M ii. **Joshua Ledford**.

4839. Norma Jean Carter (*Marcella Vernette Phillips*[8], *Lady Carrie Wood*[7], *Margie Ann (Marjorie) Bruce*[6], *Matilda Ann Sharp*[5], *James (Jim) Charles Sr.*[4], *Adron (Edwin/Ade) Sr.*[3], *Charles W. Sr.*[2], *John Sr.*[1]).

Norma married **Dennis Ray Scott**.
6071 F i. **Vanessa Leann Scott**.
6072 M ii. **Tony Scott**.

4841. Deborah Faye (Debbie) Scott (*Clista Faye Phillips*[8], *Lady Carrie Wood*[7], *Margie Ann (Marjorie) Bruce*[6], *Matilda Ann Sharp*[5], *James (Jim) Charles Sr.*[4], *Adron (Edwin/Ade) Sr.*[3], *Charles W. Sr.*[2], *John Sr.*[1]) was born 31 Oct 1970 in Lauderdale County, AL.

Deborah married **Freddie Wayne Wood**, son of **William Clyde Wood** and **Barbara Dodd**. Freddie was born 16 Aug 1965.
6073 M i. **Dustin Ray Wood**.
6074 M ii. **William Derek Wood**.

4842. David Mark Scott (*Clista Faye Phillips*[8], *Lady Carrie Wood*[7], *Margie Ann (Marjorie) Bruce*[6], *Matilda Ann Sharp*[5], *James (Jim) Charles Sr.*[4], *Adron (Edwin/Ade) Sr.*[3], *Charles W. Sr.*[2], *John Sr.*[1]) was born 4 Oct 1974.

David married **Jessie Coleman**.

4845. Bennie Erin Sharpston (*Mable Rita Phillips*[8], *Lady Carrie Wood*[7], *Margie Ann (Marjorie) Bruce*[6], *Matilda Ann Sharp*[5], *James (Jim) Charles Sr.*[4], *Adron (Edwin/Ade) Sr.*[3], *Charles W. Sr.*[2], *John Sr.*[1]) was born 19 Mar 1959 in Crittenden County, AR.

Bennie married **Donna Audrey Crosslin**, daughter of **Carl L. Crosslin** and **Helen Murks**, 11 Jun 1976 in Lauderdale County, AL. Donna was born 8 Feb 1961 in Cook County, AR.
6075 M i. **Jason Sharpston** was born 5 Jul 1977.
+ 6076 M ii. **Jamie Sharpston** was born 9 Apr 1979.
6077 M iii. **Josh Sharpston** was born 24 Feb 1992.

4846. Theresa Maxine Sharpston (*Mable Rita Phillips*[8], *Lady Carrie Wood*[7], *Margie Ann (Marjorie) Bruce*[6], *Matilda Ann Sharp*[5], *James (Jim) Charles Sr.*[4], *Adron (Edwin/Ade) Sr.*[3], *Charles W. Sr.*[2], *John Sr.*[1]) was born 8 May 1961 in Florida.

Theresa married **Douglas Ray Winborn**, son of **James Leo Winborn** and **Ruby Mae Wood**. Douglas was born 16 Jul 1948 in Lauderdale County, AL.
(Duplicate Line. See Person 2414)

4847. Robert (R. J.) Sharpston Jr. (*Mable Rita Phillips*[8], *Lady Carrie Wood*[7], *Margie Ann (Marjorie) Bruce*[6], *Matilda Ann Sharp*[5], *James (Jim) Charles Sr.*[4], *Adron (Edwin/Ade) Sr.*[3], *Charles W. Sr.*[2], *John Sr.*[1]) was born 1 Mar 1962 in Florida.

Robert married **Charlotte Terry**.

6078 F i. **Shelly Sharpston** was born about 1988.
6079 F ii. **Stephanie Sharpston** was born about 1989.

Robert next married **Kelly *Unk** after 1989.

4848. Lisa Diane Sharpston (*Mable Rita Phillips*^{8}, *Lady Carrie Wood*^{7}, *Margie Ann (Marjorie) Bruce*^{6}, *Matilda Ann Sharp*^{5}, *James (Jim) Charles Sr.*^{4}, *Adron (Edwin/Ade) Sr.*^{3}, *Charles W. Sr.*^{2}, *John Sr.*^{1}) was born 8 Jan 1969 in Alabama.

Lisa married ***Unk Smith** before 1994.
6080 M i. **Skyler Waylon Smith** was born 15 Aug 1994.
6081 M ii. **Brandon Corey Smith** was born about 1996.

Lisa next married **Tim Pearl** after 1996.

4849. Timothy Waylon Sharpston (*Mable Rita Phillips*^{8}, *Lady Carrie Wood*^{7}, *Margie Ann (Marjorie) Bruce*^{6}, *Matilda Ann Sharp*^{5}, *James (Jim) Charles Sr.*^{4}, *Adron (Edwin/Ade) Sr.*^{3}, *Charles W. Sr.*^{2}, *John Sr.*^{1}) was born 2 Apr 1974 in Alabama.

Timothy married **Angel Higginbotham**.
6082 M i. **Andrew Sharpston** was born about 1992.
6083 M ii. **Wesley Sharpston** was born 22 Jul 1998.

4850. Laura Jane Phillips (*Ronald Eugene Phillips*^{8}, *Lady Carrie Wood*^{7}, *Margie Ann (Marjorie) Bruce*^{6}, *Matilda Ann Sharp*^{5}, *James (Jim) Charles Sr.*^{4}, *Adron (Edwin/Ade) Sr.*^{3}, *Charles W. Sr.*^{2}, *John Sr.*^{1}) was born 6 Mar 1961 in Lauderdale County, AL.

Laura married **Jim Calvin Young Jr.**, son of **Jim (JC) Calvin Young Sr.** and **Bernice Wood**. Jim was born 15 Mar 1955 in Lauderdale County, AL.
+ 6084 M i. **Jim Calvin Young III** was born 23 Dec 1982 in Lauderdale County, AL, died 8 Dec 2007, and was buried in Oak Grove Cemetery, Lauderdale County, AL.
6085 M ii. **Jessie Roland Young** was born 26 Mar 1984.

4854. Sherry Ann Phillips (*Ronald Eugene Phillips*^{8}, *Lady Carrie Wood*^{7}, *Margie Ann (Marjorie) Bruce*^{6}, *Matilda Ann Sharp*^{5}, *James (Jim) Charles Sr.*^{4}, *Adron (Edwin/Ade) Sr.*^{3}, *Charles W. Sr.*^{2}, *John Sr.*^{1}) was born 17 Apr 1969.

Sherry married **Timothy Lee (Tim) Adams**, son of **Ross Adams Jr.** and **Tammy Jean Holloway**. Timothy was born 30 Oct 1970.

4855. Patricia Diane Phillips (*Ronald Eugene Phillips*^{8}, *Lady Carrie Wood*^{7}, *Margie Ann (Marjorie) Bruce*^{6}, *Matilda Ann Sharp*^{5}, *James (Jim) Charles Sr.*^{4}, *Adron (Edwin/Ade) Sr.*^{3}, *Charles W. Sr.*^{2}, *John Sr.*^{1}) was born 14 Mar 1970.

Patricia married **Duane Stapleton**.
6086 M i. **Brandon Duane Stapleton** was born in Jan 1999.

4856. Gaylon Ronald Phillips (*Ronald Eugene Phillips*^{8}, *Lady Carrie Wood*^{7}, *Margie Ann (Marjorie) Bruce*^{6}, *Matilda Ann Sharp*^{5}, *James (Jim) Charles Sr.*^{4}, *Adron (Edwin/Ade) Sr.*^{3}, *Charles W. Sr.*^{2}, *John Sr.*^{1}) was born 2 Sep 1972 in Lauderdale County, AL.

Gaylon married **Regina Faye Wood**, daughter of **Grover Wood** and **Aquilla Faye Holloway**, 28 Jun 1992 in Lauderdale County, AL. Regina was born 27 Sep 1974 in Lauderdale County, AL.

4859. Tina Phillips (*Milton Dale Phillips Sr.*^{8}, *Lady Carrie Wood*^{7}, *Margie Ann (Marjorie) Bruce*^{6}, *Matilda Ann Sharp*^{5}, *James (Jim) Charles Sr.*^{4}, *Adron (Edwin/Ade) Sr.*^{3}, *Charles W. Sr.*^{2}, *John Sr.*^{1}) was born about 1970.

Tina married **Stanley Hollander**.
6087 F i. **Ashley Hollander**.

6088   F   ii.   **Samantha Hollander**.

Tina next married **Jason Vaughn**.

4860. Tammy Phillips (*Milton Dale Phillips Sr.^{8}, Lady Carrie Wood^7, Margie Ann (Marjorie) Bruce^6, Matilda Ann Sharp^5, James (Jim) Charles Sr.^{4}, Adron (Edwin/Ade) Sr.^{3}, Charles W. Sr.^{2}, John Sr.^{1}*) was born about 1971.

Tammy married **Tommy Miller**.
6089   F   i.   **Lydia Miller**.
6090   F   ii.   **Madison Miller**.

4861. Milton Dale Phillips Jr. (*Milton Dale Phillips Sr.^{8}, Lady Carrie Wood^7, Margie Ann (Marjorie) Bruce^6, Matilda Ann Sharp^5, James (Jim) Charles Sr.^{4}, Adron (Edwin/Ade) Sr.^{3}, Charles W. Sr.^{2}, John Sr.^{1}*) was born about 1972.

Milton married **Donna Rhodes**.
6091   F   i.   **Lisa Phillips**.
6092   M   ii.   **Milton Dale Phillips III**.

4862. Tamesa Phillips (*Milton Dale Phillips Sr.^{8}, Lady Carrie Wood^7, Margie Ann (Marjorie) Bruce^6, Matilda Ann Sharp^5, James (Jim) Charles Sr.^{4}, Adron (Edwin/Ade) Sr.^{3}, Charles W. Sr.^{2}, John Sr.^{1}*) was born about 1976.

Tamesa married **Danny Carmack**.
6093   M   i.   **Lee Carmack**.
6094   M   ii.   **Michael Carmack**.

Tamesa next married **Steve Whipple**.
6095   M   i.   **Tyler Whipple**.

4863. Tara Phillips (*Milton Dale Phillips Sr.^{8}, Lady Carrie Wood^7, Margie Ann (Marjorie) Bruce^6, Matilda Ann Sharp^5, James (Jim) Charles Sr.^{4}, Adron (Edwin/Ade) Sr.^{3}, Charles W. Sr.^{2}, John Sr.^{1}*) was born 8 Aug 1979.

Tara married **James Rhodes**.

Tara next married ***Unk Allison**.

4864. Carol Sue Wood (*Thomas Moore Wood^8, Leonard Earl Wood^7, Margie Ann (Marjorie) Bruce^6, Matilda Ann Sharp^5, James (Jim) Charles Sr.^{4}, Adron (Edwin/Ade) Sr.^{3}, Charles W. Sr.^{2}, John Sr.^{1}*) was born 29 Aug 1961 in Lauderdale County, AL.

Carol married **Travis Lynn Smith**, son of **Arthur Lee (Dick) Smith** and **Vertie Mae Allison**, 1 Jul 1977 in Lauderdale County, AL. Travis was born 23 Aug 1958 in Lauderdale County, AL.
(Duplicate Line. See Person 1625)

4865. Randall Thomas Wood (*Thomas Moore Wood^8, Leonard Earl Wood^7, Margie Ann (Marjorie) Bruce^6, Matilda Ann Sharp^5, James (Jim) Charles Sr.^{4}, Adron (Edwin/Ade) Sr.^{3}, Charles W. Sr.^{2}, John Sr.^{1}*) was born 14 Feb 1964 in Lauderdale County, AL.

Randall married **Elizabeth Diane Young**, daughter of **Carl Robert Young** and **Bessie Lou Brown**, 27 Nov 1986 in Lauderdale County, AL. Elizabeth was born 2 May 1964 in Lauderdale County, AL.
(Duplicate Line. See Person 3325)

4866. Joseph Thomas (Tommy) Wood (*Thomas Moore Wood^8, Leonard Earl Wood^7, Margie Ann (Marjorie) Bruce^6, Matilda Ann Sharp^5, James (Jim) Charles Sr.^{4}, Adron (Edwin/Ade) Sr.^{3}, Charles W. Sr.^{2}, John Sr.^{1}*) was born 29 May 1976 in ECM Hospital, Florence, Lauderdale County, AL.

Joseph married **Amy Nicole Barrier**, daughter of **James (Bubba) Edward Barrier** and **Charlotte Marie Stowe**, 21 Apr 2000 in Lauderdale County, AL.

| 6096 | F | i. | **Mollie Joanna Wood** was born 4 Jan 2002. |
| 6097 | M | ii. | **Thomas Jake Wood** was born 23 Jan 2004. |

4867. Teresa Jo Brown (*Geraldine (Judy) Wood[8], Leonard Earl Wood[7], Margie Ann (Marjorie) Bruce[6], Matilda Ann Sharp[5], James (Jim) Charles Sr.[4], Adron (Edwin/Ade) Sr.[3], Charles W. Sr.[2], John Sr.[1]*) was born 20 Dec 1959 in Lauderdale County, AL.

Teresa married **Randy Lee Morris**, son of **Marshal Earl Morris** and **Denice Hinton**, 2 May 1975 in Lauderdale County, AL. Randy was born 7 Jun 1948.

+ 6098	M	i.	**Preston Lee Morris** was born 18 Jun 1979 in ECM Hospital, Florence, Lauderdale County, AL.
+ 6099	F	ii.	**Tiffany Dawn Morris** was born 23 May 1982 in ECM Hospital, Florence, Lauderdale County, AL.
6100	M	iii.	**Derrick Randy Morris** was born 24 Sep 1987 in ECM Hospital, Florence, Lauderdale County, AL.

4868. Travis Ray Brown (*Geraldine (Judy) Wood[8], Leonard Earl Wood[7], Margie Ann (Marjorie) Bruce[6], Matilda Ann Sharp[5], James (Jim) Charles Sr.[4], Adron (Edwin/Ade) Sr.[3], Charles W. Sr.[2], John Sr.[1]*) was born 30 Oct 1961 in Florence, Lauderdale County, AL.

Travis married **Doris Ann Taylor**, daughter of **Jimmy Taylor** and **Billie Frances Laws**, 16 Sep 1981 in Lauderdale County, AL. Doris was born 7 Dec 1959 in Rockford, IL.

| + 6101 | F | i. | **Kristin Leeann Brown** was born 20 Apr 1982 in Loretto, Lawrence County, TN. |

4869. Terry Richard Brown (*Geraldine (Judy) Wood[8], Leonard Earl Wood[7], Margie Ann (Marjorie) Bruce[6], Matilda Ann Sharp[5], James (Jim) Charles Sr.[4], Adron (Edwin/Ade) Sr.[3], Charles W. Sr.[2], John Sr.[1]*) was born 27 May 1968 in Florence, Lauderdale County, AL.

Terry married **Pamela Kaye Thigpen**, daughter of **Gayther Dellen Thigpen** and **Betty Stevenson Corum**, 3 Jun 1988 in Lauderdale County, AL. Pamela was born 12 Dec 1969 in Alabama.

| 6102 | M | i. | **Richard Blake Brown** was born 26 Jun 1990 in ECM Hospital, Florence, Lauderdale County, AL. |
| 6103 | F | ii. | **Chastity Danielle Brown** was born 5 Sep 1992 in ECM Hospital, Florence, Lauderdale County, AL. |

4872. Jason Ray Wood (*Johnny Ray Wood[8], Wallace Ray Wood[7], Margie Ann (Marjorie) Bruce[6], Matilda Ann Sharp[5], James (Jim) Charles Sr.[4], Adron (Edwin/Ade) Sr.[3], Charles W. Sr.[2], John Sr.[1]*) was born 10 May 1984 in ECM Hospital, Florence, Lauderdale County, AL.

Jason married **Bridget Lashawn Pennington**, daughter of **James Otis Pennington** and **Gwendolyn Faye McGee**, 14 Aug 2004 in Lauderdale County, AL. Bridget was born 13 Dec 1984.

| 6104 | F | i. | **Katy Jamys Wood** was born 5 Sep 2007 in ECM Hospital, Florence, Lauderdale County, AL. |

4874. Burt Taylor Webb (*James Burt (J B) Webb[8], Fannie Birdie Sharp[7], Lee Hal[6], Owen Bennett (Doc)[5], James (Jim) Charles Sr.[4], Adron (Edwin/Ade) Sr.[3], Charles W. Sr.[2], John Sr.[1]*) was born 8 Jul 1962 in Lauderdale County, AL.

Burt married **Susan Elizabeth Eck**, daughter of **John David Eck** and **Carolyn Eckl**, 18 Mar 1995 in Lauderdale County, AL. Susan was born 4 Jan 1968 in Lauderdale County, AL.

4876. Connie Faye Vaughn (*Betty June Sharp[8], Reeder Earl[7], Lee Hal[6], Owen Bennett (Doc)[5], James (Jim) Charles Sr.[4], Adron (Edwin/Ade) Sr.[3], Charles W. Sr.[2], John Sr.[1]*) was born 21 Apr 1953 in Lauderdale County, AL.

Connie married **Danny Glen Myhan**, son of **Cecil Coburn Myhan** and **Essie L. Holt**, 24 Apr 1970 in Lauderdale County, AL. Danny was born 6 Jun 1950 in Lauderdale County, AL.

4877. Anthony (Tony) Reed Vaughn (*Betty June Sharp^8, Reeder Earl^7, Lee Hal^6, Owen Bennett (Doc)^5, James (Jim) Charles Sr.^{4}, Adron (Edwin/Ade) Sr.^{3}, Charles W. Sr.^{2}, John Sr.^{1}*) was born 21 Nov 1956 in Lauderdale County, AL, died 18 May 1989, and was buried in Walston Cemetery, Oakland, Lauderdale County, AL.

    Anthony married **Kathy McKissack**.
+ 6105 F   i.   **Kristy Dawn Vaughn** was born 1 Apr ?.

4879. Eric Jerome Vaughn (*Betty June Sharp^8, Reeder Earl^7, Lee Hal^6, Owen Bennett (Doc)^5, James (Jim) Charles Sr.^{4}, Adron (Edwin/Ade) Sr.^{3}, Charles W. Sr.^{2}, John Sr.^{1}*) was born 7 Jun 1963 in Lauderdale County, AL.

    Eric married **Carol Lynn Rich**, daughter of **Bobby Rich** and **Windy Blowers**, 1 Jul 1981 in Lauderdale County, AL. Carol was born 25 Dec 1964 in Chatom County, GA.
6106 M   i.   **Ryan Cole Vaughn** was born 1 Jul 1984 in Lauderdale County, AL.
6107 M   ii.   **Rory Kyle Vaughn** was born 19 Nov 1986 in Lauderdale County, AL.

4882. Pamela Denise Phillips (*Irish Virginia Perkins^8, Ethel Lucille Glasscock^7, Ada Irene Sharp^6, Owen Bennett (Doc)^5, James (Jim) Charles Sr.^{4}, Adron (Edwin/Ade) Sr.^{3}, Charles W. Sr.^{2}, John Sr.^{1}*) was born 14 Apr 1959 in Lauderdale County, AL.

    Pamela married **David William Ely** 5 Jun 1982 in Dallas, TX. David was born 1 Nov 1955 in Wisconsin.
6108 M   i.   **Preston William Ely** was born 11 Apr 1985 in Dallas, TX.
6109 M   ii.   **Matthew Coburn Ely** was born 21 Apr 1987 in Dallas, TX.
6110 M   iii.   **Bryan David Ely** was born 14 Jun 1989 in Dallas, TX.

4884. Kevin Patrick Phillips (*Irish Virginia Perkins^8, Ethel Lucille Glasscock^7, Ada Irene Sharp^6, Owen Bennett (Doc)^5, James (Jim) Charles Sr.^{4}, Adron (Edwin/Ade) Sr.^{3}, Charles W. Sr.^{2}, John Sr.^{1}*) was born 31 Oct 1961 in Lauderdale County, AL.

    Kevin married **Nancy Don Leazer**.
6111 F   i.   **Briley Melinda Phillips** was born 8 Jul 1996.

4885. Dana Colleen Phillips (*Irish Virginia Perkins^8, Ethel Lucille Glasscock^7, Ada Irene Sharp^6, Owen Bennett (Doc)^5, James (Jim) Charles Sr.^{4}, Adron (Edwin/Ade) Sr.^{3}, Charles W. Sr.^{2}, John Sr.^{1}*) was born 16 Jan 1963 in Hartselle, AL.

    Dana married **Neal Hancock**.
6112 M   i.   **Dylan Jacob Hancock** was born 1 Dec 1995.

    Dana next married **Robert Alan Phelps**, son of **Jack Davis Phelps** and **Betty Jo Fishburn**, 24 Nov 1990 in Lauderdale County, AL. Robert was born 21 Sep 1962 in Arkansas.

4886. Gwendolyn Carmel Phillips (*Irish Virginia Perkins^8, Ethel Lucille Glasscock^7, Ada Irene Sharp^6, Owen Bennett (Doc)^5, James (Jim) Charles Sr.^{4}, Adron (Edwin/Ade) Sr.^{3}, Charles W. Sr.^{2}, John Sr.^{1}*) was born 11 Jun 1967 in Athens, Limestone County, AL.

    Gwendolyn married **Kelly Lynn Cheatom** 12 Sep 1992 in Fort Worth, TX.

4890. Keely Leann McNair (*Alice Kay Glasscock^8, Fred Glasscock Sr.^{7}, Ada Irene Sharp^6, Owen Bennett (Doc)^5, James (Jim) Charles Sr.^{4}, Adron (Edwin/Ade) Sr.^{3}, Charles W. Sr.^{2}, John Sr.^{1}*) was born 17 Feb 1978 in Lauderdale County, AL.

    Keely married **Jeremiah Eugene Law**, son of **John Wayne Law** and **Ruth Badillo**, 24 Jan 1998 in Lauderdale County, AL. Jeremiah was born 1 Mar 1976 in California.

4892. Dawn McNair (*Alice Kay Glasscock^8, Fred Glasscock Sr.^{7}, Ada Irene Sharp^6, Owen Bennett (Doc)^5, James (Jim) Charles Sr.^{4}, Adron (Edwin/Ade) Sr.^{3}, Charles W. Sr.^{2}, John Sr.^{1}*).

Dawn married **Eric Carter**.

4893. Dana McNair (*Alice Kay Glasscock^8, Fred Glasscock Sr.^{7}, Ada Irene Sharp^6, Owen Bennett (Doc)^5, James (Jim) Charles Sr.^{4}, Adron (Edwin/Ade) Sr.^{3}, Charles W. Sr.^{2}, John Sr.^{1}*).

Dana married **John Sciacca**.

4895. Bryan Mitchell Glasscock (*Fred Glasscock Jr.^{8}, Fred Glasscock Sr.^{7}, Ada Irene Sharp^6, Owen Bennett (Doc)^5, James (Jim) Charles Sr.^{4}, Adron (Edwin/Ade) Sr.^{3}, Charles W. Sr.^{2}, John Sr.^{1}*) was born 15 Jul 1978.

Bryan married **Jennifer Rene Watson**, daughter of **James Roy Watson** and **Katherine Ann Argaeir**, 24 Jun 1997 in Lauderdale County, AL. Jennifer was born 25 Jul 1978.

4897. Leigh Marie Glasscock (*Sam Harold Glasscock^8, Harold Owen Glasscock^7, Ada Irene Sharp^6, Owen Bennett (Doc)^5, James (Jim) Charles Sr.^{4}, Adron (Edwin/Ade) Sr.^{3}, Charles W. Sr.^{2}, John Sr.^{1}*) was born 11 Aug 1973 in Opelika County, AL.

Leigh married **Jason Patrick Seamon**, son of **Daivd Michael Seamon** and **Cheryl Lee Mann**, 15 May 1999 in Lauderdale County, AL. Jason was born 6 Jun 1991 in Michigan.

4904. Deena Lynn Hanback (*Joel Dennis Hanback^8, Lois Etoile Sharp^7, Harrell Emmett^6, Owen Bennett (Doc)^5, James (Jim) Charles Sr.^{4}, Adron (Edwin/Ade) Sr.^{3}, Charles W. Sr.^{2}, John Sr.^{1}*) was born 30 May 1962 in Lapoite County, IN.

Deena married **Travis Cletus Young**, son of **Cletus Dempsey (Skeet) Young** and **Eva Jean Wood**, 7 Nov 1987 in Lauderdale County, AL. Travis was born 21 Jan 1964 in Lauderdale County, AL.
(Duplicate Line. See Person 3194)

4905. Charlotte June Hanback (*Joel Dennis Hanback^8, Lois Etoile Sharp^7, Harrell Emmett^6, Owen Bennett (Doc)^5, James (Jim) Charles Sr.^{4}, Adron (Edwin/Ade) Sr.^{3}, Charles W. Sr.^{2}, John Sr.^{1}*) was born 3 Apr 1966 in Lauderdale County, AL.

Charlotte married **Jimmy Joel Bartlett**, son of **Jimmy Joe Bartlett** and **Sara Anita Allen**, 25 Apr 1999 in Lauderdale County, AL. Jimmy was born 19 Dec 1962 in Lauderdale County, AL.

4907. Stephanie Ann May (*Doris Ann Hanback^8, Lois Etoile Sharp^7, Harrell Emmett^6, Owen Bennett (Doc)^5, James (Jim) Charles Sr.^{4}, Adron (Edwin/Ade) Sr.^{3}, Charles W. Sr.^{2}, John Sr.^{1}*) was born 19 Mar 1970 in Lauderdale County, AL.

Stephanie married **Michael Dale Byrd**, son of **Jimmy Dale Byrd** and **Ivey Morgan**, 23 Nov 1989 in Colbert County, AL. Michael was born 2 Aug 1968 in Opelika, AL.
  6113 F   i.   **Tiffany Lashea Byrd** was born 3 Jul 1990 in Lauderdale County, AL.

4909. Lynette Carol May (*Doris Ann Hanback^8, Lois Etoile Sharp^7, Harrell Emmett^6, Owen Bennett (Doc)^5, James (Jim) Charles Sr.^{4}, Adron (Edwin/Ade) Sr.^{3}, Charles W. Sr.^{2}, John Sr.^{1}*) was born 17 Jan 1980 in Lauderdale County, AL.

Lynette married ***Unk Hendon**.

4910. Paul Nathan Roberson (*Nathan Harold Roberson^8, Mary Helen Sharp^7, Harrell Emmett^6, Owen Bennett (Doc)^5, James (Jim) Charles Sr.^{4}, Adron (Edwin/Ade) Sr.^{3}, Charles W. Sr.^{2}, John Sr.^{1}*) was born 8 Nov 1972 in Lauderdale County, AL.

Paul married **Tara Sue Hood**, daughter of **Thomas Harold Hood Jr.** and **Mona Sue Owens**, 19 Aug 1995 in Lauderdale County, AL. Tara was born 31 Jul 1973 in Lee County, MS.

4911. Randall Lee (Randy) Kelsey (*Virginia Ann Roberson*[8], *Mary Helen Sharp*[7], *Harrell Emmett*[6], *Owen Bennett (Doc)*[5], *James (Jim) Charles Sr.*[4], *Adron (Edwin/Ade) Sr.*[3], *Charles W. Sr.*[2], *John Sr.*[1]) was born 1 Jan 1969 in Lauderdale County, AL.

Randall married **Pamela Gaye Parrish**, daughter of **Freddie Parrish** and **Rebecca Pigg**, 18 Mar 1993 in Lauderdale County, AL. Pamela was born 29 Sep 1969.

4912. Robert (Robbie) Michael Kelsey (*Virginia Ann Roberson*[8], *Mary Helen Sharp*[7], *Harrell Emmett*[6], *Owen Bennett (Doc)*[5], *James (Jim) Charles Sr.*[4], *Adron (Edwin/Ade) Sr.*[3], *Charles W. Sr.*[2], *John Sr.*[1]) was born 10 Aug 1971 in Lauderdale County, AL.

Robert married **Holly Lynn Eck**, daughter of **Patrick August Eck** and **Karen Denise Wood**, in Dec 1994. Holly was born 29 Dec 1978.
(Duplicate Line. See Person 4282)

Robert next married **Sherry Gowan**.

4922. Kimberlie Jacobs (*Jimmie Nell Wood*[8], *Curtis (Slick) Wood*[7], *Mildred Sharp*[6], *Owen Bennett (Doc)*[5], *James (Jim) Charles Sr.*[4], *Adron (Edwin/Ade) Sr.*[3], *Charles W. Sr.*[2], *John Sr.*[1]) was born 19 May 1967.

Kimberlie married **Barry Joe Rich**, son of **James T. Rich** and **Joyce Horton**, 14 Jun 1985 in Lauderdale County, AL. Barry was born 12 Apr 1966 in Lauderdale County, AL.

Kimberlie next married **George Goodman**. George was born 11 May 1968.

Kimberlie next married **Christopher Brent Davis**, son of **Ernest Timothy Davis** and **Judy Ann Keeton**, 28 Jun 1997 in Lauderdale County, AL. Christopher was born 28 Dec 1972.

4923. Teresa Anna Wood (*Cletus Wood*[8], *Curtis (Slick) Wood*[7], *Mildred Sharp*[6], *Owen Bennett (Doc)*[5], *James (Jim) Charles Sr.*[4], *Adron (Edwin/Ade) Sr.*[3], *Charles W. Sr.*[2], *John Sr.*[1]) was born 14 Jun 1965 in Lauderdale County, AL.

Teresa married **Paul Douglas Thomas**, son of **Paul F. Thomas** and **Ollie Stidham**, 7 Aug 1985 in Lauderdale County, AL. Paul was born 23 May 1953 in Dallas County, AL.

4930. Cammie Jo Crosslin (*Shelby Jean Young*[8], *Mary Frances Cummings*[7], *Lillie May Sharp*[6], *James Charles Jr.*[5], *James (Jim) Charles Sr.*[4], *Adron (Edwin/Ade) Sr.*[3], *Charles W. Sr.*[2], *John Sr.*[1]) was born 12 Jul 1966 in Zion, IL.

Cammie married **Donald Maurice Jones**, son of **Dale D. Jones** and **Peggy Black**, 30 Nov 1984 in Lauderdale County, AL. Donald was born 22 Jul 1964 in Madison County, AL.
6114 F i. **Brittney Nicole Jones** was born 27 Jul 1985.
6115 F ii. **Madison Faith Jones** was born 10 Sep 1991.

4931. Tony Levon Barnett (*Pauline (Polly) Young*[8], *Mary Frances Cummings*[7], *Lillie May Sharp*[6], *James Charles Jr.*[5], *James (Jim) Charles Sr.*[4], *Adron (Edwin/Ade) Sr.*[3], *Charles W. Sr.*[2], *John Sr.*[1]) was born 2 Aug 1959 in Lauderdale County, AL.

Tony married **Cynthia (Cindy) Roberson**, daughter of **Sidney P. Robinson** and **Theresa Ezell**, 3 Jul 1981 in Lauderdale County, AL. Cynthia was born 18 Nov 1956 in Wayne County, MI.
6116 M i. **Brian Sidney Barnett** was born 31 Dec 1982.
6117 M ii. **Chase Levon Barnett** was born 6 Apr 1991.

4932. Tommy Leron Barnett (*Pauline (Polly) Young*[8], *Mary Frances Cummings*[7], *Lillie May Sharp*[6], *James Charles Jr.*[5], *James (Jim) Charles Sr.*[4], *Adron (Edwin/Ade) Sr.*[3], *Charles W. Sr.*[2], *John Sr.*[1]) was born 29 Apr 1963 in Lauderdale County, AL.

Tommy married **Rhonda Colleen Jones**, daughter of **Dallas J. Jones** and **Virginia Koller**, 16 Oct 1986 in Lauderdale County, AL. Rhonda was born 24 Aug 1964 in Lauderdale County, AL.

6118 M i. **Joshua (Josh) Aaron Barnett** was born 24 May 1986 in Lauderdale County, AL.
6119 F ii. **Abby Lane Barnett** was born 4 Apr 1989 in Lauderdale County, AL.
6120 M iii. **Donawanna Nicholas Barnett** was born 16 Apr 1993 in Lauderdale County, AL.

4933. LaDonna Kay Gray (*Betty Ruth Young*[8], *Mary Frances Cummings*[7], *Lillie May Sharp*[6], *James Charles Jr.*[5], *James (Jim) Charles Sr.*[4], *Adron (Edwin/Ade) Sr.*[3], *Charles W. Sr.*[2], *John Sr.*[1]) was born 22 Jul 1960 in Lauderdale County, AL.

LaDonna married **Carl David (C. D.) Arnold**, son of **James Carlton Arnold** and **Christine Sloan**, 2 Feb 1979 in Lauderdale County, AL. Carl was born 15 Dec 1951 in Lauderdale County, AL.
6121 F i. **Camie Lynn Arnold** was born 11 Feb 1980 in Lauderdale County, AL.
6122 F ii. **Christy Dawn Arnold** was born 12 Nov 1981 in Lauderdale County, AL.

4934. Charles Edwin Gray Jr. (*Betty Ruth Young*[8], *Mary Frances Cummings*[7], *Lillie May Sharp*[6], *James Charles Jr.*[5], *James (Jim) Charles Sr.*[4], *Adron (Edwin/Ade) Sr.*[3], *Charles W. Sr.*[2], *John Sr.*[1]) was born 19 Oct 1962 in Lauderdale County, AL.

Charles married **Carol Dawn Littrell**, daughter of **Lawrence Terry Littrell** and **Carolyn Sue Biggers**, 12 Nov 1988 in Lauderdale County, AL. Carol was born 16 Feb 1965 in Lauderdale County, AL.

4935. Wendy Dawn Young (*Donnie Ray Young Sr.*[8], *Mary Frances Cummings*[7], *Lillie May Sharp*[6], *James Charles Jr.*[5], *James (Jim) Charles Sr.*[4], *Adron (Edwin/Ade) Sr.*[3], *Charles W. Sr.*[2], *John Sr.*[1]) was born 20 Jul 1973 in Lauderdale County, AL.

Wendy married **Michael Dale Siemientikowski**, son of **MIchael Dale Siemientikowski Jr.** and **Patsy Ruth Waller**, 18 Jun 1994 in Lauderdale County, AL. Michael was born 2 May 1965.
6123 F i. **McKenzie Siemientikowski**.
6124 F ii. **Alexis Siemientikowski**.

4936. Donnie Ray Young Jr. (*Donnie Ray Young Sr.*[8], *Mary Frances Cummings*[7], *Lillie May Sharp*[6], *James Charles Jr.*[5], *James (Jim) Charles Sr.*[4], *Adron (Edwin/Ade) Sr.*[3], *Charles W. Sr.*[2], *John Sr.*[1]) was born 30 Oct 1981 in Lauderdale County, AL.

Donnie married **Tara *Unk**.

4943. Tammy Leigh Cummings (*Harold Lee Cummings*[8], *Paul Lee Cummings*[7], *Lillie May Sharp*[6], *James Charles Jr.*[5], *James (Jim) Charles Sr.*[4], *Adron (Edwin/Ade) Sr.*[3], *Charles W. Sr.*[2], *John Sr.*[1]) was born 5 Sep 1970.

Tammy married **Howard Kyle Gargis** 25 May 1991.
6125 F i. **Katlin Leanne Gargis** was born 22 Sep 1992.

Tammy next married **Steven Holloway** 13 May 1994.

4969. Leah Nicole Smith (*Roger Dale*[8], *Clyde Ray*[7], *James (Little James) Robert*[6], *James Charles Jr.*[5], *James (Jim) Charles Sr.*[4], *Adron (Edwin/Ade) Sr.*[3], *Charles W. Sr.*[2], *John Sr.*[1]).

Leah married **Chad Dewayne Davis**, son of **Martie Davis** and **Deborah Fowler**, 14 Feb 2003.

4970. Kristie Dawn Thomas (*Patricia (Pam) Ann May*[8], *Pearl Rebecca Sharp*[7], *James (Little James) Robert*[6], *James Charles Jr.*[5], *James (Jim) Charles Sr.*[4], *Adron (Edwin/Ade) Sr.*[3], *Charles W. Sr.*[2], *John Sr.*[1]) was born 29 Apr 1977 in Colbert County, AL.

Kristie married **Thomas (Tommy) Andrew Woodfin**, son of **Charles Micheal Woodfin** and **Wyodolyn Elaine Keen**, 7 Jun 1999 in Lauderdale County, AL. Thomas was born 12 Jan 1978.

4972. Sabrena Rebecca Willard (*Vickie Lynn May ^{8}, Pearl Rebecca Sharp ^{7}, James (Little James) Robert ^{6}, James Charles Jr. ^{5}, James (Jim) Charles Sr. ^{4}, Adron (Edwin/Ade) Sr. ^{3}, Charles W. Sr. ^{2}, John Sr. ^{1}*) was born 11 Nov 1980 in Lauderdale County, AL.

Sabrena married **Gregory Scott McFall** 5 Jun in Lauderdale County, AL.

4979. Joey Wayne Harrison (*Jewel Faye Johnson ^{8}, Emmy Luetellace (Lou) Cobb ^{7}, Minor Lucille Sharp ^{6}, James Charles Jr. ^{5}, James (Jim) Charles Sr. ^{4}, Adron (Edwin/Ade) Sr. ^{3}, Charles W. Sr. ^{2}, John Sr. ^{1}*) was born 20 Dec in Lauderdale County, AL.

Joey married **Charlotte Riley**, daughter of **Johnny Riley** and **Margaret Olive**.
6126 M i. **Justin Wayne Harrison** was born 10 Jul 1994.

4982. Angela Hope Lamar (*Betty Lou Johnson ^{8}, Emmy Luetellace (Lou) Cobb ^{7}, Minor Lucille Sharp ^{6}, James Charles Jr. ^{5}, James (Jim) Charles Sr. ^{4}, Adron (Edwin/Ade) Sr. ^{3}, Charles W. Sr. ^{2}, John Sr. ^{1}*) was born 22 Dec 1977.

Angela married **Nick Lanier**.
6127 F i. **Hope Nicole Lanier**.

4990. Roger Dwight Quillen Jr. (*Carolyn Sue Johnson ^{8}, Julia Loretta Cobb ^{7}, Minor Lucille Sharp ^{6}, James Charles Jr. ^{5}, James (Jim) Charles Sr. ^{4}, Adron (Edwin/Ade) Sr. ^{3}, Charles W. Sr. ^{2}, John Sr. ^{1}*) was born 9 Jan 1972 in Lauderdale County, AL.

Roger married **Julie Elaine Hill**, daughter of **Lester Eugene Hill** and **Francis Louise Vines**, 12 Jun 1992 in Lauderdale County, AL. Julie was born 11 Apr 1973 in Lauderdale County, AL.

4991. Rex Dwayne Quillen (*Carolyn Sue Johnson ^{8}, Julia Loretta Cobb ^{7}, Minor Lucille Sharp ^{6}, James Charles Jr. ^{5}, James (Jim) Charles Sr. ^{4}, Adron (Edwin/Ade) Sr. ^{3}, Charles W. Sr. ^{2}, John Sr. ^{1}*) was born 18 May 1972 in Lauderdale County, AL.

Rex married **Carolyn Ann Gaddy**, daughter of **Arlon N. Gaddy** and **Betty Murl Couch**, 12 Nov 1991 in Lauderdale County, AL. Carolyn was born 28 Nov 1975.

Rex next married **Casey Ann Bradley**, daughter of **Stephan Ray Bradley** and **Shelia Ann Oliver**, 31 Jan 1997 in Lauderdale County, AL. Casey was born 16 Mar 1978.

5008. Mae Leigh Hubbard (*Neal Lee Hubbard ^{8}, Ruby Pauline Sharp ^{7}, Elmer ^{6}, Charles W. ^{5}, James (Jim) Charles Sr. ^{4}, Adron (Edwin/Ade) Sr. ^{3}, Charles W. Sr. ^{2}, John Sr. ^{1}*) was born 12 Jul 1971 in Lauderdale County, AL.

Mae married **Brian Keith Davis**, son of **Bobby Gean Davis** and **Francis Ruth Lash**, 21 Jul 1991 in Lauderdale County, AL. Brian was born 7 Oct 1968 in Alabama.

5009. Amanda Lynne White (*Clara Evelyn Hubbard ^{8}, Ruby Pauline Sharp ^{7}, Elmer ^{6}, Charles W. ^{5}, James (Jim) Charles Sr. ^{4}, Adron (Edwin/Ade) Sr. ^{3}, Charles W. Sr. ^{2}, John Sr. ^{1}*) was born 13 Jul 1963 in Lauderdale County, AL.

Amanda married **Thomas Edgar Nichols Jr.**, son of **Thomas Edgar Nichols Sr.** and **Betty White**, 18 Aug 1979 in Lauderdale County, AL. Thomas was born 18 Jul 1961 in Cook County, IL.
6128 M i. **Thomas Edgar Nichols III** was born 11 Aug 1982 in Lauderdale County, AL.
6129 F ii. **Fallon Michelle Nichols** was born 6 Jun 1984 in Lauderdale County, AL.

5011. Charles Christopher Blalock (*Clara Evelyn Hubbard ^{8}, Ruby Pauline Sharp ^{7}, Elmer ^{6}, Charles W. ^{5}, James (Jim) Charles Sr. ^{4}, Adron (Edwin/Ade) Sr. ^{3}, Charles W. Sr. ^{2}, John Sr. ^{1}*) was born 25 Aug 1974 in Lauderdale County, AL.

Charles married **Julie Deann Peters**, daughter of **John Joe Peters** and **Angelia Gail Sharp**, 17 May 1991 in Lauderdale County, AL. Julie was born 16 Jul 1974 in Lauderdale County, AL.
(Duplicate Line. See Person 2192)

Charles next married **Amy Nicole Whitaker**, daughter of **Bob Whitaker** and **Susie *Unk**, 18 Sep 1998 in Colbert County, AL.

5012. Jeanette Faye Hubbard (*Elmer John (E. J.) Hubbard^8, Ruby Pauline Sharp^7, Elmer^6, Charles W.^{5}, James (Jim) Charles Sr.^{4}, Adron (Edwin/Ade) Sr.^{3}, Charles W. Sr.^{2}, John Sr.^{1}*) was born 7 Mar 1966 in Lauderdale County, AL.

Jeanette married **Stephen Robert Jennings**, son of **Charles R. Jennings** and **Carolyn R. Nivens**, 26 Jul 1986 in Lauderdale County, AL. Stephen was born 24 Feb 1964 in Tuscaloosa, AL.

5013. Janette Gaye Hubbard (*Elmer John (E. J.) Hubbard^8, Ruby Pauline Sharp^7, Elmer^6, Charles W.^{5}, James (Jim) Charles Sr.^{4}, Adron (Edwin/Ade) Sr.^{3}, Charles W. Sr.^{2}, John Sr.^{1}*) was born 7 Mar 1966 in Lauderdale County, AL.

Janette married **Ronald Blane Davis**, son of **Edsel C. Davis** and **Dorothy Laird**, 20 May 1986 in Lauderdale County, AL. Ronald was born 13 Jun 1964 in Lauderdale County, AL.

5014. Jennifer Kaye Hubbard (*Elmer John (E. J.) Hubbard^8, Ruby Pauline Sharp^7, Elmer^6, Charles W.^{5}, James (Jim) Charles Sr.^{4}, Adron (Edwin/Ade) Sr.^{3}, Charles W. Sr.^{2}, John Sr.^{1}*) was born 10 Aug 1967 in Lauderdale County, AL.

Jennifer married **Darwin Scott Jennings**, son of **Charles R. Jennings** and **Carolyn R. Nivens**, 8 Aug 1986 in Lauderdale County, AL. Darwin was born 18 Aug 1965 in Tuscaloosa, AL.

5015. Jannice Maye Hubbard (*Elmer John (E. J.) Hubbard^8, Ruby Pauline Sharp^7, Elmer^6, Charles W.^{5}, James (Jim) Charles Sr.^{4}, Adron (Edwin/Ade) Sr.^{3}, Charles W. Sr.^{2}, John Sr.^{1}*) was born 22 Oct 1972 in Lauderdale County, AL.

Jannice married **Kelvin Thomas Whitehead**, son of **Jesse Thomas Whitehead** and **Joyce Ann Hunt**, 8 Aug 1994 in Lauderdale County, AL. Kelvin was born 15 Sep 1971 in Lauderdale County, AL.

5016. Sandy Alphelia Hubbard (*Alfred Willie Hubbard^8, Ruby Pauline Sharp^7, Elmer^6, Charles W.^{5}, James (Jim) Charles Sr.^{4}, Adron (Edwin/Ade) Sr.^{3}, Charles W. Sr.^{2}, John Sr.^{1}*) was born 1 Aug 1969 in Lauderdale County, AL.

Sandy married **Barry Bock**.
6130 M i. **Bradley Bock**.
6131 M ii. **Barry Bock**.

5017. Michael Edward Nash Jr. (*Mary Ruth Hubbard^8, Ruby Pauline Sharp^7, Elmer^6, Charles W.^{5}, James (Jim) Charles Sr.^{4}, Adron (Edwin/Ade) Sr.^{3}, Charles W. Sr.^{2}, John Sr.^{1}*) was born 30 Mar 1972 in Morgan County, AL.

Michael married **Valerie Elizabeth *Unk** 5 Aug 1995. Valerie was born 11 Sep 1973 in McNairy County, TN.

5018. Melanie Renee Nash (*Mary Ruth Hubbard^8, Ruby Pauline Sharp^7, Elmer^6, Charles W.^{5}, James (Jim) Charles Sr.^{4}, Adron (Edwin/Ade) Sr.^{3}, Charles W. Sr.^{2}, John Sr.^{1}*) was born 13 Apr 1974 in Morgan County, AL.

Melanie married **Jamie Craig Smith**, son of **Jamie Smith** and **Gail Allen**, 17 May 1997. Jamie was born 11 Sep 1973 in Lauderdale County, AL.

5019. Elizabeth Cathryn Hubbard (*Dwight Corbin Hubbard^8, Ruby Pauline Sharp^7, Elmer^6, Charles W.^{5}, James (Jim) Charles Sr.^{4}, Adron (Edwin/Ade) Sr.^{3}, Charles W. Sr.^{2}, John Sr.^{1}*) was born 20 Apr 1979 in Lauderdale County, AL.

Elizabeth married **Kenneth Barns**.

5023. Adam Logan Sharp (*Raymond Curtis[8], W. C.[7], William Hubert[6], Charles W.[5], James (Jim) Charles Sr.[4], Adron (Edwin/Ade) Sr.[3], Charles W. Sr.[2], John Sr.[1]*) was born 10 Nov 1979 in Lauderdale County, AL.

    Adam married **Krista Nicole Behel**, daughter of **Thomas Behel** and **Linda *Unk**, 9 Oct 2004.

5024. Eric Wayne Wood (*Barbara Carol Sharp[8], W. C.[7], William Hubert[6], Charles W.[5], James (Jim) Charles Sr.[4], Adron (Edwin/Ade) Sr.[3], Charles W. Sr.[2], John Sr.[1]*) was born 29 Sep 1971 in Lauderdale County, AL.

    Eric married **Regina Gayle Poole**, daughter of **Ralph Cornelius Poole** and **Anna Rea Rester**, 7 Sep 1989 in Lauderdale County, AL. Regina was born 22 Dec 1970 in Louisiana.

6132	M	i.	**Alexander Matthew Wood** was born 15 Aug 1991 in ECM Hospital, Florence, Lauderdale County, AL.
6133	F	ii.	**Elizabeth Autumn Wood** was born 24 Dec 1997 in ECM Hospital, Florence, Lauderdale County, AL.

5026. David Morgan Parrish (*Barbara Carol Sharp[8], W. C.[7], William Hubert[6], Charles W.[5], James (Jim) Charles Sr.[4], Adron (Edwin/Ade) Sr.[3], Charles W. Sr.[2], John Sr.[1]*) was born 7 Mar 1980 in Lauderdale County, AL.

    David married **Rhonda Michelle Pettus**, daughter of **Felix Jeffrey Pettus** and **Patricia Ann Austin**, 27 Mar 1999 in Lauderdale County, AL. Rhonda was born 24 Apr 1982.

6134   M   i.   **Tyler Parrish**.

5028. James (Jamie) Marion Sharp (*Louis Alton[8], W. C.[7], William Hubert[6], Charles W.[5], James (Jim) Charles Sr.[4], Adron (Edwin/Ade) Sr.[3], Charles W. Sr.[2], John Sr.[1]*) was born 11 Jan 1975 in Peoria, IL.

    James married **Kathy Look**.

6135   F   i.   **Ashley Sharp**.

5030. Chambra Dawn Sharp (*Louis Alton[8], W. C.[7], William Hubert[6], Charles W.[5], James (Jim) Charles Sr.[4], Adron (Edwin/Ade) Sr.[3], Charles W. Sr.[2], John Sr.[1]*) was born 18 Jan 1984 in Tishomingo, MS.

    Chambra married **Terry Dewayne Walker**, son of **Elmore O'Neal Walker** and **Opal Lorraine Wright**, 27 Jul 2007 in Lauderdale County, AL. Terry was born 23 Dec 1966.

6136   M   i.   **Son Walker** was born in 2008.

5036. Aaron Kyle Lawrence (*Janice Kay Askew[8], Sarah Ruth Sharp[7], William Hubert[6], Charles W.[5], James (Jim) Charles Sr.[4], Adron (Edwin/Ade) Sr.[3], Charles W. Sr.[2], John Sr.[1]*) was born 11 Jul 1981 in Roanoke, Roanoke County, VA.

    Aaron married **Amanda Delong** 24 Mar 2001.

5037. Chris Jason Askew (*Comer Jack Askew II[8], Sarah Ruth Sharp[7], William Hubert[6], Charles W.[5], James (Jim) Charles Sr.[4], Adron (Edwin/Ade) Sr.[3], Charles W. Sr.[2], John Sr.[1]*) was born 14 May 1977 in Goshen, IN.

    Chris married **Amy Humphreys** 22 Jul 2000. Amy was born 29 Mar 1977 in St. Louis, MO.

6137   M   i.   **Carson Jose Askew** was born 19 Oct 2001 in Roanoke, Roanoke County, VA.

5066. Emily Selena Wood (*Angelia Diane Young[8], William Roland Young[7], Audry Sharp[6], Charles W.[5], James (Jim) Charles Sr.[4], Adron (Edwin/Ade) Sr.[3], Charles W. Sr.[2], John Sr.[1]*) was born 14 Feb 1979 in ECM Hospital, Florence, Lauderdale County, AL.

    Emily married **Jeremy Michael Dowdy**, son of **Jerry Michael (Mike) Dowdy** and **Sandra (Sandy) Renea Smith**, 23 Jun 2001 in Lauderdale County, AL. Jeremy was born 20 Jul 1979.

6138   F   i.   **Anna Claire Dowdy** was born 6 Jul 2005 in Lauderdale County, AL.

5070. Shana Nicole Young (*Donnie Ray Young[8], Cletus Dempsey (Skeet) Young[7], Audry Sharp[6], Charles W.[5], James (Jim) Charles Sr.[4], Adron (Edwin/Ade) Sr.[3], Charles W. Sr.[2], John Sr.[1]*) was born 28 Apr 1976 in Lauderdale County, AL.

Shana married **Paul Rhodes**, son of **Autry Paul Rhodes** and **Carolyn Baskins**, 18 Mar 1996. Paul was born 3 Oct 1969.

6139 F   i.   **Abigail Grace Rhodes** was born 20 Nov 1996.

5073. Kenneth Lee Gilchrist (*Betty Jean Young[8], Cletus Dempsey (Skeet) Young[7], Audry Sharp[6], Charles W.[5], James (Jim) Charles Sr.[4], Adron (Edwin/Ade) Sr.[3], Charles W. Sr.[2], John Sr.[1]*) was born 16 Mar 1977 in Lauderdale County, AL.

Kenneth married **Amanda Brown**.

5078. Brandon Craig Sharp (*Brenda Sue Bevis[8], Bonnie Mae Young[7], Audry Sharp[6], Charles W.[5], James (Jim) Charles Sr.[4], Adron (Edwin/Ade) Sr.[3], Charles W. Sr.[2], John Sr.[1]*) was born 3 Oct 1981 in Lauderdale County, AL.

Brandon married **Amanda Jean Howard**, daughter of **Elvin Howard** and **Lisa *Unk**, 28 Apr 2001 in Colbert County, AL.

5098. Tonya Lynn Wood (*Paul Douglas Wood Jr.[8], Paul Douglas Wood Sr.[7], Fannie Elizabeth (Sister) Crider[6], Elizabeth (Roxie) Belle Sharp[5], James (Jim) Charles Sr.[4], Adron (Edwin/Ade) Sr.[3], Charles W. Sr.[2], John Sr.[1]*) was born 18 Dec 1974 in ECM Hospital, Florence, Lauderdale County, AL.

Tonya married **Lawton Jeffery Leon Russell**, son of **Buddy Russell** and **Goldie Yvonne Balentine**, 29 Nov 1996 in Lauderdale County, AL. Lawton was born 27 Mar 1970 in Lauderdale County, AL.

6140 M   i.   **Jeffery Aaron Blake Russell** was born 7 Oct 1997 in ECM Hospital, Florence, Lauderdale County, AL.

5107. Jason McKinley Wood (*Steven McKinley Wood[8], Rufus Ezra Wood[7], Fannie Elizabeth (Sister) Crider[6], Elizabeth (Roxie) Belle Sharp[5], James (Jim) Charles Sr.[4], Adron (Edwin/Ade) Sr.[3], Charles W. Sr.[2], John Sr.[1]*) was born 11 Nov 1976 in South Bend, IN.

Jason married **Misty Yvonne Donaldson**, daughter of **Charles Ray Donaldson** and **Debra Yvonne McKissack**, 26 Feb 2001 in Lauderdale County, AL. Misty was born 25 Jan 1981 in Lauderdale County, AL.

5110. Tammy Lynn Clemons (*Pamela Elaine Wood[8], Rufus Ezra Wood[7], Fannie Elizabeth (Sister) Crider[6], Elizabeth (Roxie) Belle Sharp[5], James (Jim) Charles Sr.[4], Adron (Edwin/Ade) Sr.[3], Charles W. Sr.[2], John Sr.[1]*) was born 14 Aug 1972 in Florence, Lauderdale County, AL.

Tammy married **Patrick Terrell White**, son of **Milas Greenberry White** and **Heather Ruth Young**, 26 May 1992 in Lauderdale County, AL. Patrick was born 23 Nov 1970 in Lauderdale County, AL.

6141 F   i.   **Tiffany Nichole Clemmons** was born 10 Aug 1991 in Florence, Lauderdale County, AL.

6142 F   ii.   **Savannah Dawn White** was born 14 Jan 1994 in Florence, Lauderdale County, AL.

5113. Christy Lynn Clemons (*Cheryl Elizabeth Wood[8], Rufus Ezra Wood[7], Fannie Elizabeth (Sister) Crider[6], Elizabeth (Roxie) Belle Sharp[5], James (Jim) Charles Sr.[4], Adron (Edwin/Ade) Sr.[3], Charles W. Sr.[2], John Sr.[1]*) was born 9 Mar 1977 in South Bend, IN.

Christy married **Gilbert Lee Haddock**.

6143 M   i.   **Tyler Lee Haddock** was born 15 Oct 1994 in Florence, Lauderdale County, AL.

Christy next married **Timmy Collins**.

6144 F   i.   **Shaylene Brooke Collins** was born 27 Apr 1998 in Lauderdale County, AL.

5118. Audrey Lynn Winders (*Jimmie Nell Ezekiel[8], Hazel Irene Wood[7], Mary Etta (Virgie) Crider[6], Elizabeth (Roxie) Belle Sharp[5], James (Jim) Charles Sr.[4], Adron (Edwin/Ade) Sr.[3], Charles W. Sr.[2], John Sr.[1]*) was born 28 Apr 1964 in West Memphis, Crittenden County, AR.

Audrey married **Tommy David Guy Sr.**.

6145	M	i.	**Jeremy Lynn Guy** was born 22 Nov 1981.
6146	F	ii.	**Jennifer Marie Guy** was born 12 Jun 1984.
6147	M	iii.	**Tommy David Guy Jr.** was born 2 Dec 1985.

5119. Lisa Renee Winders (*Jimmie Nell Ezekiel[8], Hazel Irene Wood[7], Mary Etta (Virgie) Crider[6], Elizabeth (Roxie) Belle Sharp[5], James (Jim) Charles Sr.[4], Adron (Edwin/Ade) Sr.[3], Charles W. Sr.[2], John Sr.[1]*) was born 4 Jun 1966 in West Memphis, Crittenden County, AR.

Lisa married **Don Carlos Martinez Sr.**.

6148	F	i.	**Alicia Marie Martinez** was born 23 Jan 1987.
6149	M	ii.	**Don Carlos Martinez Jr.** was born 25 Feb 1990.

5122. Jeffrey Earl Ezekiel (*Colin Earl Ezekiel[8], Hazel Irene Wood[7], Mary Etta (Virgie) Crider[6], Elizabeth (Roxie) Belle Sharp[5], James (Jim) Charles Sr.[4], Adron (Edwin/Ade) Sr.[3], Charles W. Sr.[2], John Sr.[1]*) was born 28 Apr 1968 in Biloxi, MS.

Jeffrey married **Stephanie Rogers** in 1994.

5127. Tony Wayne Brewington (*Christine Ezekiel[8], Hazel Irene Wood[7], Mary Etta (Virgie) Crider[6], Elizabeth (Roxie) Belle Sharp[5], James (Jim) Charles Sr.[4], Adron (Edwin/Ade) Sr.[3], Charles W. Sr.[2], John Sr.[1]*) was born 14 Apr 1975 in Osceola, AR.

Tony married **Marti Stroup** in 2001.

6150	F	i.	**Madison Clair Brewington** was born 27 Nov 2002.

5132. Stephanie Diane Holt (*Dorothy Ann Ezekiel[8], Hazel Irene Wood[7], Mary Etta (Virgie) Crider[6], Elizabeth (Roxie) Belle Sharp[5], James (Jim) Charles Sr.[4], Adron (Edwin/Ade) Sr.[3], Charles W. Sr.[2], John Sr.[1]*) was born 14 Feb 1978 in Memphis, Shelby County, TN.

Stephanie married **Tomas Arredondo** 16 Jan 1998 in Arkansas. Tomas was born 9 Apr 1975.

5136. Kenny Daniel Wood (*Sherman Daniel Wood[8], Charles William Wood[7], Mary Etta (Virgie) Crider[6], Elizabeth (Roxie) Belle Sharp[5], James (Jim) Charles Sr.[4], Adron (Edwin/Ade) Sr.[3], Charles W. Sr.[2], John Sr.[1]*) was born 16 Sep 1973 in ECM Hospital, Florence, Lauderdale County, AL.

Kenny married ***Unk**.

6151	M	i.	**Kristin Blair Wood** was born 13 Mar 2001.

5137. Gwendolyn Michelle (Shelly) Wood (*Sherman Daniel Wood[8], Charles William Wood[7], Mary Etta (Virgie) Crider[6], Elizabeth (Roxie) Belle Sharp[5], James (Jim) Charles Sr.[4], Adron (Edwin/Ade) Sr.[3], Charles W. Sr.[2], John Sr.[1]*) was born 28 Aug 1976 in ECM Hospital, Florence, Lauderdale County, AL.

Gwendolyn married **Dustin Zane Dabbs** 14 Jun 1996 in Lauderdale County, AL. Dustin was born 10 May 1975 in Lauderdale County, AL.

6152	M	i.	**Codie Jared Dabbs** was born 28 Jul 1993 in ECM Hospital, Florence, Lauderdale County, AL.
6153	M	ii.	**Donavan Zane Dabbs** was born 5 Nov 2002.
6154	F	iii.	**JulieAna Paige Dabbs** was born 9 Feb 2005.

5138. Gregory Lynn Wood (*Sherman Daniel Wood[8], Charles William Wood[7], Mary Etta (Virgie) Crider[6], Elizabeth (Roxie) Belle Sharp[5], James (Jim) Charles Sr.[4], Adron (Edwin/Ade) Sr.[3], Charles W. Sr.[2], John Sr.[1]*) was born 8 Dec 1977 in Colbert County, AL.

Gregory married **Cynthia Gail Stidham** 3 Jul 1999. Cynthia was born 19 Oct 1982 in Hackleburg, Alabama.

6155 M i. **William Darin Ray Wood** was born 1 Dec 1999 in Florence, Lauderdale County, AL, died 11 Jan 2000, and was buried in Oak Grove Cemetery, Lauderdale County, AL.

6156 F ii. **Elizabeth Audrey Nicole Wood** was born 25 Jan 2001.

5139. Misty McGough (*Sherman Daniel Wood^8, Charles William Wood^7, Mary Etta (Virgie) Crider^6, Elizabeth (Roxie) Belle Sharp^5, James (Jim) Charles Sr.^{4}, Adron (Edwin/Ade) Sr.^{3}, Charles W. Sr.^{2}, John Sr.^{1}*).

Misty married **Paul Ray Trankle** 17 Apr 1998. Paul was born 2 Sep 1972.

6157 M i. **Daniel Gene Trankle** was born 21 Jul 1999.

5143. Wanda Lee Tatum (*Glenn Thomas Brown^8, Edith Inez Wood^7, Mary Etta (Virgie) Crider^6, Elizabeth (Roxie) Belle Sharp^5, James (Jim) Charles Sr.^{4}, Adron (Edwin/Ade) Sr.^{3}, Charles W. Sr.^{2}, John Sr.^{1}*).

Wanda married **Gary E. Clemmons**. Gary was born 23 Feb 1952, died 3 Oct 1980, and was buried in Macedonia Cemetery, Lauderdale County, AL.

+ 6158 F i. **Jennifer Clemmons** was born 12 Sep 1976 in ECM Hospital, Florence, Lauderdale County, AL.

Wanda next married **Mark Hughes**.

6159 M i. **Marcus Allen Hughes** was born 19 May 1988 in ECM Hospital, Florence, Lauderdale County, AL.

5144. Karen Lynn Tatum (*Glenn Thomas Brown^8, Edith Inez Wood^7, Mary Etta (Virgie) Crider^6, Elizabeth (Roxie) Belle Sharp^5, James (Jim) Charles Sr.^{4}, Adron (Edwin/Ade) Sr.^{3}, Charles W. Sr.^{2}, John Sr.^{1}*) was born 30 Oct 1959 in Colbert County, AL.

Karen married **Kenneth Wayne Brown**, son of **Bob Lee Brown** and **Edith Inez Wood**, 28 Mar 1980 in Lauderdale County, AL. Kenneth was born 28 Jun 1957 in Florence, Lauderdale County, AL.
(Duplicate Line. See Person 3248)

5145. Talina Shawn Brown (*Bobby Junior Brown^8, Edith Inez Wood^7, Mary Etta (Virgie) Crider^6, Elizabeth (Roxie) Belle Sharp^5, James (Jim) Charles Sr.^{4}, Adron (Edwin/Ade) Sr.^{3}, Charles W. Sr.^{2}, John Sr.^{1}*) was born 15 Apr 1973 in Memphis, Shelby County, TN.

Talina married **John Spiller** 27 Dec 1993 in Ripley, TN.

6160 M i. **Stephen Lee Spiller** was born 3 Aug 1994 in Memphis, Shelby County, TN and died 22 Oct 1994 in Ripley, TN.

6161 M ii. **Hunter Blake Spiller** was born 14 Nov 1995 in Memphis, Shelby County, TN.

6162 M iii. **Houston Lane Spiller** was born 31 Mar 1998.

6163 M iv. **Jonathan Owens Spiller** was born 16 Dec 1999.

5146. Amanda Leann Brown (*Jimmy Turner Brown^8, Edith Inez Wood^7, Mary Etta (Virgie) Crider^6, Elizabeth (Roxie) Belle Sharp^5, James (Jim) Charles Sr.^{4}, Adron (Edwin/Ade) Sr.^{3}, Charles W. Sr.^{2}, John Sr.^{1}*) was born 26 Jun 1979 in ECM Hospital, Florence, Lauderdale County, AL.

Amanda married ***Unk**.

6164 M i. **Bayle Levi Brown** was born 18 Sep 2000.

6165 F ii. **Harleigh Alexzandrea Mae Brown** was born 3 Sep 2003.

5149. Yolanda Lynn Brown (*Kenneth Wayne Brown^8, Edith Inez Wood^7, Mary Etta (Virgie) Crider^6, Elizabeth (Roxie) Belle Sharp^5, James (Jim) Charles Sr.^{4}, Adron (Edwin/Ade) Sr.^{3}, Charles W. Sr.^{2}, John Sr.^{1}*) was born 28 Jun 1982 in ECM Hospital, Florence, Lauderdale County, AL.

Yolanda married **Joshua *Unk**.

6166 F i. **Emma Christine Brown** was born 2 Feb 2000.

5151. Joseph Brandon Moss (*Peggy Sue Wood[8], Carl Thomas Wood[7], Mary Etta (Virgie) Crider[6], Elizabeth (Roxie) Belle Sharp[5], James (Jim) Charles Sr.[4], Adron (Edwin/Ade) Sr.[3], Charles W. Sr.[2], John Sr.[1]*) was born 26 Feb 1979 in Memphis, Shelby County, TN.

Joseph married **Shannon Green** in 2001.
6167 F i. **Girl Moss** was born in Tennessee.

5156. Anthony Mark Wood (*David Paul Wood[8], Carl Thomas Wood[7], Mary Etta (Virgie) Crider[6], Elizabeth (Roxie) Belle Sharp[5], James (Jim) Charles Sr.[4], Adron (Edwin/Ade) Sr.[3], Charles W. Sr.[2], John Sr.[1]*) was born 28 May 1982 in Bolivar, TN.

Anthony married **Mary Beth Peaveyhouse**.
6168 M i. **Cullin Dawson Wood** was born 29 Jan 2002.

Anthony next married **Michelle King**.
6169 M i. **Andy Wood** was born 15 Mar 2005.

5159. Jeffrey Curtis Wood (*Curtis Dwayne Wood[8], Louis Cola Wood[7], Mary Etta (Virgie) Crider[6], Elizabeth (Roxie) Belle Sharp[5], James (Jim) Charles Sr.[4], Adron (Edwin/Ade) Sr.[3], Charles W. Sr.[2], John Sr.[1]*) was born 5 Feb 1988 in ECM Hospital, Florence, Lauderdale County, AL.

Jeffrey married **Mindy Rachelle Shepherd**, daughter of **Tony Shepherd** and **Paula *Unk**, 27 Sep 2008 in Trinity, Lawrence County, AL. Mindy was born in Feb 1989.

5161. Eric Jason Armstrong (*Jeannie Diane Pickens[8], Betty Sue Wood[7], Mary Etta (Virgie) Crider[6], Elizabeth (Roxie) Belle Sharp[5], James (Jim) Charles Sr.[4], Adron (Edwin/Ade) Sr.[3], Charles W. Sr.[2], John Sr.[1]*) was born 30 Dec 1981 in Memphis, Shelby County, TN.

Eric married **Alyssa Marby** in 2007.
6170 M i. **Brennan Cole Armstrong**.

5163. Ashley Nicole Sanders (*Kathy Ann Pickens[8], Betty Sue Wood[7], Mary Etta (Virgie) Crider[6], Elizabeth (Roxie) Belle Sharp[5], James (Jim) Charles Sr.[4], Adron (Edwin/Ade) Sr.[3], Charles W. Sr.[2], John Sr.[1]*) was born 24 Jun 1984 in Memphis, Shelby County, TN.

Ashley married **George (Trip) Gilchrist III** 11 Aug 2007. George was born 3 Aug 1983.
6171 M i. **Jackson Austin Gilchrist** was born 9 Feb 2008.

5169. Corey Ryan Hawkins (*Lisa Renae Pickens[8], Betty Sue Wood[7], Mary Etta (Virgie) Crider[6], Elizabeth (Roxie) Belle Sharp[5], James (Jim) Charles Sr.[4], Adron (Edwin/Ade) Sr.[3], Charles W. Sr.[2], John Sr.[1]*) was born 14 May 1988 in Memphis, Shelby County, TN.

Corey married **Tiffany Jernigan** in 2007.
6172 F i. **Cheyenne Hawkins** was born in Jul 2007.

5181. Donald Wayne Crider (*Vickie Lynn Crider[8], Donald Fay Crider[7], Edgar Louis (Ed) Crider[6], Elizabeth (Roxie) Belle Sharp[5], James (Jim) Charles Sr.[4], Adron (Edwin/Ade) Sr.[3], Charles W. Sr.[2], John Sr.[1]*) was born 11 Mar 1987 in ECM Hospital, Florence, Lauderdale County, AL.

Donald married **Lindsey Brianne Haddock**, daughter of **Anthony Franklin (Bubba) Haddock** and **Beverly Jean Benson**, 27 Jun 2008 in Gulf Shores, Baldwin County, AL. Lindsey was born 11 May 1988.

5183. Tommy Dewayne Hanback (*Thomas Lee Hanback[8], Agnes Lorene Sharp[7], William Herbert (Hubbard)[6], Louis (Bud) Wheeler[5], James (Jim) Charles Sr.[4], Adron (Edwin/Ade) Sr.[3], Charles W. Sr.[2], John Sr.[1]*) was born 26 Sep 1976 in Lauderdale County, AL.

Tommy married **Tonya Renae Stowe**, daughter of **Herbert Stowe** and **Sandra Gail Lanford**, 20 Dec 1997 in Orlando, FL. Tonya was born 28 Oct 1975 in Lauderdale County, AL.

    6173 M   i.   **Logan Dewayne Hanback** was born 28 Sep 1999 in ECM Hospital, Florence, Lauderdale County, AL.

5184. Teddy Ray Hanback (*Thomas Lee Hanback^8, Agnes Lorene Sharp^7, William Herbert (Hubbard)^6, Louis (Bud) Wheeler^5, James (Jim) Charles Sr.^{4}, Adron (Edwin/Ade) Sr.^{3}, Charles W. Sr.^{2}, John Sr.^{1}*) was born 29 Feb 1980 in Lauderdale County, AL.

Teddy married **Kansas Stutts**.

    6174 M   i.   **Colby Ray Hanback**.
    6175 F   ii.   **Madison Hanback**.

5189. Crystal (Christy) Dawn Britnell (*Sandra Ann Sharp^8, Rufus Eldred^7, Loye Arvel^6, Louis (Bud) Wheeler^5, James (Jim) Charles Sr.^{4}, Adron (Edwin/Ade) Sr.^{3}, Charles W. Sr.^{2}, John Sr.^{1}*) was born 7 Apr 1974 in Alabama.

Crystal married **Jeremy Rourke** 1 May 1993 in Lauderdale County, AL. Jeremy was born 9 Oct 1973.

5190. Amy Denise Sharp (*Jeffrey Keith^8, Rufus Eldred^7, Loye Arvel^6, Louis (Bud) Wheeler^5, James (Jim) Charles Sr.^{4}, Adron (Edwin/Ade) Sr.^{3}, Charles W. Sr.^{2}, John Sr.^{1}*) was born 8 May 1979 in Lauderdale County, AL.

Amy married **Scottie Lee Wright**, son of **Ronnie Dale Wright Sr.** and **Judy Kay Pitts**, 3 Dec 1999 in Lauderdale County, AL. Scottie was born 8 Feb 1978 in Lauderdale County, AL.

5191. Amanda Diane Sharp (*Jeffrey Keith^8, Rufus Eldred^7, Loye Arvel^6, Louis (Bud) Wheeler^5, James (Jim) Charles Sr.^{4}, Adron (Edwin/Ade) Sr.^{3}, Charles W. Sr.^{2}, John Sr.^{1}*) was born 5 May 1983 in Lauderdale County, AL.

Amanda married **Matthew Sean Price**, son of **Bryan Keith Price** and **Kimberly Dawn May**, 4 Sep 2004 in Lauderdale County, AL. Matthew was born 12 Mar 1982.

5194. Misty Dawn White (*Norman Lynn White^8, Lola Mae Sharp^7, Loye Arvel^6, Louis (Bud) Wheeler^5, James (Jim) Charles Sr.^{4}, Adron (Edwin/Ade) Sr.^{3}, Charles W. Sr.^{2}, John Sr.^{1}*) was born 27 Apr 1984.

Misty married **Alex Grant Angel**, son of **Lonnie Wayne Angel** and **Linda Evelyn Pitts**, 19 Jul 2003 in Lauderdale County, AL. Alex was born 4 Oct 1983 in Lauderdale County, AL.

5225. Paige Nicole Sharp (*Ricky Leon^8, Tony Leon^7, Lawrence (Toby) Eldred^6, Louis (Bud) Wheeler^5, James (Jim) Charles Sr.^{4}, Adron (Edwin/Ade) Sr.^{3}, Charles W. Sr.^{2}, John Sr.^{1}*).

Paige married **Joshua Ray Barrett** 31 Jul 2008 in Panama City, FL.

5247. Brian Billy Smith (*Billy Rayburn Smith^8, Lois Evelyn Allison^7, Raymond Andrew Allison^6, Margie (Lady) J. Sharp^5, James (Jim) Charles Sr.^{4}, Adron (Edwin/Ade) Sr.^{3}, Charles W. Sr.^{2}, John Sr.^{1}*) was born 20 Dec 1971 in Lauderdale County, AL.

Brian married **Shawn Leigh Wood**, daughter of **Gary Quinton Wood** and **Donnabell Jeanette Lane**, 16 Dec 1994 in Lauderdale County, AL. Shawn was born 8 Dec 1966 in St. Joseph County, IN.

5248. Regina Lynn Smith (*Billy Rayburn Smith^8, Lois Evelyn Allison^7, Raymond Andrew Allison^6, Margie (Lady) J. Sharp^5, James (Jim) Charles Sr.^{4}, Adron (Edwin/Ade) Sr.^{3}, Charles W. Sr.^{2}, John Sr.^{1}*) was born 11 May 1977 in Lauderdale County, AL.

Regina married **Charles (Chuck) Lawrence Parrish**, son of **Charles Ray Parrish** and **Deborah Ann Lanier**, 28 May 1988 in Lauderdale County, AL. Charles was born 3 Jun 1972 in Lauderdale County, AL.

    6176 M   i.   **Jordan Chase Parrish** was born 22 Nov 1997 in Lauderdale County, AL.
    6177 M   ii.   **Logan Daniel Parrish** was born in 2003.

5250. Mark Anthony Smith (*Danny Russell Smith[8], Lois Evelyn Allison[7], Raymond Andrew Allison[6], Margie (Lady) J. Sharp[5], James (Jim) Charles Sr.[4], Adron (Edwin/Ade) Sr.[3], Charles W. Sr.[2], John Sr.[1]*) was born 7 Mar 1979 in ECM Hospital, Florence, Lauderdale County, AL.

Mark married **Gwendolyn (Gwen) Joy Beck**, daughter of **Garey Leon Beck** and **Patsy Jane Russell**, 29 Aug 1999 in Dayton, OH. Gwendolyn was born 23 Mar 1977.

6178   F   i.   **Aubrie Nicole Smith** was born 22 Sep 2003 in Helen Keller Hospital, Sheffield, Colbert County, AL.

6179   F   ii.   **Alyssa Jane Smith** was born 26 Mar 2009 in ECM Hospital, Florence, Lauderdale County, AL.

5251. Melanie Joy Smith (*Danny Russell Smith[8], Lois Evelyn Allison[7], Raymond Andrew Allison[6], Margie (Lady) J. Sharp[5], James (Jim) Charles Sr.[4], Adron (Edwin/Ade) Sr.[3], Charles W. Sr.[2], John Sr.[1]*) was born 6 Aug 1982 in ECM Hospital, Florence, Lauderdale County, AL.

Melanie married **Adam Jeffreys**.

6180   F   i.   **Mallory Jean Smith** was born 22 Apr 2003 in Lauderdale County, AL.

5253. Isaac Don Smith (*Cameron Don Smith[8], Lois Evelyn Allison[7], Raymond Andrew Allison[6], Margie (Lady) J. Sharp[5], James (Jim) Charles Sr.[4], Adron (Edwin/Ade) Sr.[3], Charles W. Sr.[2], John Sr.[1]*) was born 31 May 1988 in ECM Hospital, Florence, Lauderdale County, AL.

Isaac married **Paige Kyle** in Jun 2006 in Bastrop, LA.

6181   F   i.   **Anna Kate Elizabeth Lewis Smith** was born in 2007.

6182   M   ii.   **Aaron Donovan Smith** was born in 2008.

5258. Daniel Eric Holcombe (*Sherry Elaine Allison[8], Harve Harrison Allison[7], Raymond Andrew Allison[6], Margie (Lady) J. Sharp[5], James (Jim) Charles Sr.[4], Adron (Edwin/Ade) Sr.[3], Charles W. Sr.[2], John Sr.[1]*) was born 26 Jan 1976 in Lauderdale County, AL.

Daniel married **Lisa Marie Ashe** 10 Jul 1999 in Stantonville, TN. Lisa was born 18 Jul.

5265. Brittney Michelle Allison (*Rodney Keith Allison[8], Vernon Lee Allison[7], Raymond Andrew Allison[6], Margie (Lady) J. Sharp[5], James (Jim) Charles Sr.[4], Adron (Edwin/Ade) Sr.[3], Charles W. Sr.[2], John Sr.[1]*) was born 29 Aug 1985 in Lauderdale County, AL.

Brittney married **Jeffery Lee Hamm**, son of **John Bennett Hamm** and **Diana Mary Weber**, 22 Jul 2006 in Lauderdale County, AL. Jeffery was born 7 Feb 1982.

5296. April Michelle Ballard (*Jonell Smith[8], Robbie Etoil Wood[7], Lady Jewel Allison[6], Margie (Lady) J. Sharp[5], James (Jim) Charles Sr.[4], Adron (Edwin/Ade) Sr.[3], Charles W. Sr.[2], John Sr.[1]*) was born 1 Nov 1982 in West Memphis, Crittenden County, AR.

April married **Jonathan Privett** 3 May 2003 in Arkansas.

6183   M   i.   **Matthew Carl Privett** was born 5 Nov 2003.

6184   M   ii.   **Chase Robert Privett** was born 19 Apr 2005.

April next married **Matthew Smith** in 2007 in Arkansas.

5297. Amy Nicole Ballard (*Jonell Smith[8], Robbie Etoil Wood[7], Lady Jewel Allison[6], Margie (Lady) J. Sharp[5], James (Jim) Charles Sr.[4], Adron (Edwin/Ade) Sr.[3], Charles W. Sr.[2], John Sr.[1]*) was born 17 Feb 1986 in West Memphis, Crittenden County, AR.

Amy married **Matthew Davis** in 2007 in Arkansas.

5336. Andrea Hale (*Karen Gentry[8], Evelyn Irene Smith[7], Vertie Mae Allison[6], Margie (Lady) J. Sharp[5], James (Jim) Charles Sr.[4], Adron (Edwin/Ade) Sr.[3], Charles W. Sr.[2], John Sr.[1]*).

Andrea married **Jason Shaw**.

5356. Hayden D. Sharp Jr. (*Hayden D. Sr.*[8], *Hayden D. T.*[7], *Kelly C.*[6], *Lil Adron*[5], *Charles (Charlie) A.*[4], *Adron (Edwin/Ade) Sr.*[3], *Charles W. Sr.*[2], *John Sr.*[1]) was born in 1972 in California.

Hayden married **Brooke Ramirez**, daughter of **William Ramirez** and **Barbara Hill**, in 1995 in California. Brooke was born in 1972 in California.
6185 F i. **Alyssa Sharp** was born in 1999 in California.

5372. Samuel Jackson Gargis (*Patsy Ann Darby*[8], *June (Betty) Eleanor Killen*[7], *Minnie Jane Sharp*[6], *Charlie William*[5], *William (Candy) Erwin*[4], *John Sr.*[3], *Charles W. Sr.*[2], *John Sr.*[1]).

Samuel married ***Unk**.
6186 F i. **Megan Gargis**.

5385. Melanie Patterson (*Teresa Lynn Killen*[8], *Harold Burt Killen*[7], *Minnie Jane Sharp*[6], *Charlie William*[5], *William (Candy) Erwin*[4], *John Sr.*[3], *Charles W. Sr.*[2], *John Sr.*[1]) was born 7 Sep 1978 in Lauderdale County, AL.

Melanie married **Joel Auchly**.
6187 M i. **Zane Auchly**.

5397. Kristy Michelle Sharp (*Ronald Coleman*[8], *Kennis Coleman*[7], *Charles Price*[6], *Charlie William*[5], *William (Candy) Erwin*[4], *John Sr.*[3], *Charles W. Sr.*[2], *John Sr.*[1]) was born 6 Nov 1975 in Lauderdale County, AL.

Kristy married **Rodney Brett Gargis**, son of **Benny Wayne Gargis** and **Dorothy Thomison**, 5 Feb 1993 in Lauderdale County, AL. Rodney was born 4 Dec 1973 in Lauderdale County, AL.

5400. Cortney Lane Behel (*Debra Diane Sharp*[8], *Kennis Coleman*[7], *Charles Price*[6], *Charlie William*[5], *William (Candy) Erwin*[4], *John Sr.*[3], *Charles W. Sr.*[2], *John Sr.*[1]) was born 4 Nov 1980 in Lauderdale County, AL.

Cortney married **Brian Keith Jones**, son of **Brancel Jones** and **Brenda Clemmons**, 12 Jun 1999 in Lauderdale County, AL. Brian was born 23 May 1974 in Lauderdale County, AL.

5408. Charla Marie Cox (*Frank Lee Cox*[8], *Elbert Turner Cox Sr.*[7], *Ida Mae Call*[6], *Beulah L. Sharp*[5], *William (Candy) Erwin*[4], *John Sr.*[3], *Charles W. Sr.*[2], *John Sr.*[1]) was born 17 Jul 1974 in Houston, TX.

Charla married **Patrick John Arnold**, son of **Perry Arnold** and **Kathy Diller**, 3 Sep 1993 in Lapeer, MI. Patrick was born 27 Dec 1970 in Lapeer, MI.
6188 F i. **Elise Arnold** was born 4 Sep 1996 in Lapeer, MI.
6189 F ii. **Kathryn Grace Arnold** was born in Oct 1998 in Lapeer, MI.

5409. Angelia Lee Cox (*Frank Lee Cox*[8], *Elbert Turner Cox Sr.*[7], *Ida Mae Call*[6], *Beulah L. Sharp*[5], *William (Candy) Erwin*[4], *John Sr.*[3], *Charles W. Sr.*[2], *John Sr.*[1]) was born 14 Jan 1976 in Houston, TX.

Angelia married **Vincent Mark Shephard**, son of **Mark Shephard** and **Susan *Unk**, in 1990 in Imlay City, MI. Vincent was born 4 Dec 1971 in Port Huron, MI.
6190 M i. **Kolton Vincent Shephard** was born 4 Oct 1996 in Port Huron, MI.

Angelia next married **Terry James Pudvay**, son of **Lyonel Pudvay** and **Linda Dianne *Unk**, 24 Jul 1998 in Flushing, MI. Terry was born in Flint, MI.
6191 F i. **Kathryn Olivia Pudvay** was born 23 Nov 1998 in Flint, MI.

5411. Kimberly Jean Witt (*Danny Ray Witt*[8], *Johnny Ray Witt*[7], *Mae Belle Young*[6], *James Wylie (Jim) Young*[5], *Julia Ann Young*[4], *Mary E. Sharp*[3], *Charles W. Sr.*[2], *John Sr.*[1]) was born 2 Apr 1972 in South Bend, IN.

Kimberly married **Brandon Douglas Taylor**, son of **Ralph Douglas Taylor** and **Beverly Joan Von Bargel**, 15 Apr 1995 in Lauderdale County, AL. Brandon was born 4 Sep 1973.

6192 F i. **Alexis Brooke Taylor** was born 23 Nov 1997 in ECM Hospital, Florence, Lauderdale County, AL.

Kimberly next married **David Saccoccio Jr.** 26 Jul 2008 in Destin, Okaloosa County, FL.

5413. Joshua Daniel Witt (*Danny Ray Witt*[8], *Johnny Ray Witt*[7], *Mae Belle Young*[6], *James Wylie (Jim) Young*[5], *Julia Ann Young*[4], *Mary E. Sharp*[3], *Charles W. Sr.*[2], *John Sr.*[1]) was born 27 Apr 1979 in South Bend, St Joseph County, IN.

Joshua married **Melissa Beth Irons**, daughter of **Roland Lynn Irons** and **Karen Delane Young**, 12 Apr 2003 in Lauderdale County, AL. Melissa was born 20 Nov 1977.
(Duplicate Line. See Person 4362)

5421. Shalanda Lavon Wesson (*Jennifer Gay Smith*[8], *Letha Helen Witt*[7], *Mae Belle Young*[6], *James Wylie (Jim) Young*[5], *Julia Ann Young*[4], *Mary E. Sharp*[3], *Charles W. Sr.*[2], *John Sr.*[1]) was born 4 Oct 1977 in Lauderdale County, AL.

Shalanda married **Steven Borden**.
6193 M i. **Steven Chance Borden** was born 18 Jun 1997.

Shalanda next married **Wesley McFall**.
6194 F i. **Aubrey McFall** was born 14 Apr 2003.

Shalanda next married **Brian Doss**.
6195 F i. **Ailee Belle Doss** was born 22 Jun 2007.

5424. Joshua Kyle Wood (*David Wayne Wood*[8], *Eva Witt*[7], *Mae Belle Young*[6], *James Wylie (Jim) Young*[5], *Julia Ann Young*[4], *Mary E. Sharp*[3], *Charles W. Sr.*[2], *John Sr.*[1]) was born 22 Mar 1980.

Joshua married **April Lentz**.
6196 F i. **Savana Elizabeth Wood**.
6197 F ii. **Kylie Brooklyn Wood** was born 6 Jan 2001 in Florence, Lauderdale County, AL, died 6 Jan 2001, and was buried in Hendrix Chapel Cemetery, Lauderdale County, AL.

5431. Jimmy Dale White Jr. (*Jimmy Dale (JD) White Sr.*[8], *Gladys Marie Smith*[7], *Nomer Marie Young*[6], *James Wylie (Jim) Young*[5], *Julia Ann Young*[4], *Mary E. Sharp*[3], *Charles W. Sr.*[2], *John Sr.*[1]) was born in Feb 1968.

Jimmy married **Debra Anderson**.
6198 M i. **Darian Anderson** was born in Feb 1994.
6199 M ii. **Kaiden A. White** was born in Jan 1999.
6200 F iii. **Alexa M. White** was born in Aug 2000.

5432. Traci L. White (*Jimmy Dale (JD) White Sr.*[8], *Gladys Marie Smith*[7], *Nomer Marie Young*[6], *James Wylie (Jim) Young*[5], *Julia Ann Young*[4], *Mary E. Sharp*[3], *Charles W. Sr.*[2], *John Sr.*[1]) was born in May 1968.

Traci married someone.
6201 M i. **James E. Nielsen** was born in Mar 1986.
6202 F ii. **Summer N. White** was born in Jul 1988.

5433. Kim S. White (*Jimmy Dale (JD) White Sr.*[8], *Gladys Marie Smith*[7], *Nomer Marie Young*[6], *James Wylie (Jim) Young*[5], *Julia Ann Young*[4], *Mary E. Sharp*[3], *Charles W. Sr.*[2], *John Sr.*[1]) was born in Jul 1972.

Kim married ***Unk Johnson**.
6203 M i. **Nicholas A. Johnson** was born in Dec 1999.

5434. Lori Ann Kidder (*Janice Sue White^8, Gladys Marie Smith^7, Nomer Marie Young^6, James Wylie (Jim) Young^5, Julia Ann Young^4, Mary E. Sharp^3, Charles W. Sr.^{2}, John Sr.^{1}*) was born 30 Apr 1970.

    Lori married **Gary William Osterloo**. Gary was born 8 Sep 1954.

| 6204 | M | i. | **Cole William Lee Osterloo** was born 18 Jul 1991. |
| 6205 | M | ii. | **Blake William Osterloo** was born 8 May 1994, died 30 May 2007, and was buried in Memorial Gardens, IN. |

5435. Holly Lynn Kidder (*Janice Sue White^8, Gladys Marie Smith^7, Nomer Marie Young^6, James Wylie (Jim) Young^5, Julia Ann Young^4, Mary E. Sharp^3, Charles W. Sr.^{2}, John Sr.^{1}*) was born 26 May 1979.

    Holly married **Michael Carl Thomas**.

6206	M	i.	**Logan Michael Thomas** was born 18 Feb 1999.
6207	M	ii.	**Isaac Michael Thomas** was born 23 Jun 2001.
6208	F	iii.	**Brooklyn Laurel Hope Thomas** was born 24 Jul 2003, died 24 Nov 2003, and was buried in Indiana.
6209	M	iv.	**Tanner Michael Thomas** was born 23 Aug 2004.
6210	M	v.	**Camden Michael Thomas** was born 23 Jan 2006.

5436. Melissa Ann (Missy) Perry (*Sandra Joyce White^8, Gladys Marie Smith^7, Nomer Marie Young^6, James Wylie (Jim) Young^5, Julia Ann Young^4, Mary E. Sharp^3, Charles W. Sr.^{2}, John Sr.^{1}*) was born 25 Jan 1969.

    Melissa married **Robert Lee Crapo**. Robert was born 3 Sep 1968.

| 6211 | M | i. | **Tyler Austin Crapo** was born 10 Nov 1995. |

5438. Jennifer Dawn Coleman (*Jeannie Ruth White^8, Gladys Marie Smith^7, Nomer Marie Young^6, James Wylie (Jim) Young^5, Julia Ann Young^4, Mary E. Sharp^3, Charles W. Sr.^{2}, John Sr.^{1}*) was born 27 Jun 1974.

    Jennifer married **Brian Scott Coffman**. Brian was born 3 Feb 1974.

| 6212 | F | i. | **Taylor Marie Coffman** was born 27 Feb 2002. |
| 6213 | F | ii. | **Allison Marie Coffman** was born 16 Nov 2003. |

5439. Daniel Steven White (*Jeff Steven White^8, Gladys Marie Smith^7, Nomer Marie Young^6, James Wylie (Jim) Young^5, Julia Ann Young^4, Mary E. Sharp^3, Charles W. Sr.^{2}, John Sr.^{1}*) was born 1 Jan 1980.

    Daniel married ***Unk**.

| 6214 | M | i. | **Jae Allen White** was born 20 Aug 2003. |

5442. Kristi Ann White (*Jackie Ladd White^8, Gladys Marie Smith^7, Nomer Marie Young^6, James Wylie (Jim) Young^5, Julia Ann Young^4, Mary E. Sharp^3, Charles W. Sr.^{2}, John Sr.^{1}*) was born 6 Nov 1976.

    Kristi married **Brian Albert Baker**. Brian was born 12 Sep 1979.

6215	M	i.	**Evan Marshall Baker** was born 22 Nov 2001.
6216	M	ii.	**Ashton Ladd Baker** was born 11 Jan 2003.
6217	M	iii.	**Kedrick Farrell Baker** was born 19 Dec 2006.

5443. Carrie Lei White (*Jackie Ladd White^8, Gladys Marie Smith^7, Nomer Marie Young^6, James Wylie (Jim) Young^5, Julia Ann Young^4, Mary E. Sharp^3, Charles W. Sr.^{2}, John Sr.^{1}*) was born 20 Jun 1980.

    Carrie married **Mark Allen Lingofelter**. Mark was born 5 Oct 1977.

| 6218 | F | i. | **Kaelei-Lynne Nicole Lingofelter** was born 22 Aug 2001. |
| 6219 | M | ii. | **Ryan Allen Lingofelter** was born 16 Oct 2006. |

5444. Jessica Lee White (*Jackie Ladd White^8, Gladys Marie Smith^7, Nomer Marie Young^6, James Wylie (Jim) Young^5, Julia Ann Young^4, Mary E. Sharp^3, Charles W. Sr.^{2}, John Sr.^{1}*) was born 30 Oct 1981.

    Jessica married **Mathias Wayne Metzger**. Mathias was born 24 Oct 1980.

5446. Jordan Marie Carter (*Jill Annette White*[8], *Gladys Marie Smith*[7], *Nomer Marie Young*[6], *James Wylie (Jim) Young*[5], *Julia Ann Young*[4], *Mary E. Sharp*[3], *Charles W. Sr.*[2], *John Sr.*[1]) was born 16 Mar 1988.

Jordan married someone.
6220 F i. **Marissa Marie Carter** was born 10 Jul 2007.

5448. Sherry Smith (*Ronnie (Red) Arnold Smith*[8], *Randle Arnold Smith*[7], *Nomer Marie Young*[6], *James Wylie (Jim) Young*[5], *Julia Ann Young*[4], *Mary E. Sharp*[3], *Charles W. Sr.*[2], *John Sr.*[1]) was born 22 Apr 1977.

Sherry married **Chris White**.
6221 F i. **Shonara Parrish White** was born in Jan 2006.

5450. Michael Dewayne Smith (*Donnie Ray Smith*[8], *Randle Arnold Smith*[7], *Nomer Marie Young*[6], *James Wylie (Jim) Young*[5], *Julia Ann Young*[4], *Mary E. Sharp*[3], *Charles W. Sr.*[2], *John Sr.*[1]) was born 16 Sep 1977.

Michael married **Jennifer Faun Creasy** 10 Jul 1999 in Opelika, AL.
6222 M i. **Briar Mckenzie Smith** was born 7 Jul 2000.
6223 F ii. **Avery Elise Smith** was born 18 Mar 2002.

5452. Clarence Krager Jr. (*Carolyn Estelle Smith*[8], *Jimmy Lester (JL) Smith*[7], *Nomer Marie Young*[6], *James Wylie (Jim) Young*[5], *Julia Ann Young*[4], *Mary E. Sharp*[3], *Charles W. Sr.*[2], *John Sr.*[1]) was born in 1975.

Clarence married someone.
6224 M i. **William Krager**.
6225 F ii. **Caroline Krager**.
6226 M iii. **Dillon Krager**.

5458. Denise Culp (*Christine Elaine Smith*[8], *Jimmy Lester (JL) Smith*[7], *Nomer Marie Young*[6], *James Wylie (Jim) Young*[5], *Julia Ann Young*[4], *Mary E. Sharp*[3], *Charles W. Sr.*[2], *John Sr.*[1]) was born 17 Mar 1974.

Denise married someone.
6227 M i. **Zachary Culp** was born 17 Dec 1969.

5459. Carey Culp (*Christine Elaine Smith*[8], *Jimmy Lester (JL) Smith*[7], *Nomer Marie Young*[6], *James Wylie (Jim) Young*[5], *Julia Ann Young*[4], *Mary E. Sharp*[3], *Charles W. Sr.*[2], *John Sr.*[1]) was born 14 May 1975.

Carey married **John Weir**. John was born 17 Dec 1969.
6228 M i. **Carlton Weir** was born 30 Oct 1995.
6229 F ii. **Sydni Weir** was born 16 Dec 2003.

5471. Jared Joseph Bell (*Julia May Holloway*[8], *Ruth Lucille Smith*[7], *Nomer Marie Young*[6], *James Wylie (Jim) Young*[5], *Julia Ann Young*[4], *Mary E. Sharp*[3], *Charles W. Sr.*[2], *John Sr.*[1]) was born 20 Nov 1983.

Jared married **Nubia Castillo**.
6230 M i. **Caarver Alexander Bell** was born 20 Feb 2004.
6231 M ii. **Sullivan Arwin Bell** was born 21 Feb 2006.
6232 F iii. **Daughter Bell** was born in Dec 2008.

5489. Matthew Smith (*James Allen Smith*[8], *Edwin Smith*[7], *Mozella Young*[6], *James Wylie (Jim) Young*[5], *Julia Ann Young*[4], *Mary E. Sharp*[3], *Charles W. Sr.*[2], *John Sr.*[1]) was born in St. Joseph County, IN.

Matthew married **Kathrine Marie Wood**, daughter of **Gregory Allen Wood** and **Theresa Marie Richardson**, 28 Dec 2002 in St. Joseph County, IN. Kathrine was born 13 Sep 1976 in South Bend, St Joseph County, IN.
6233 F i. **Kierston Marie Smith** was born 22 Sep 2003 in Indianapolis, Marion County, IN.
6234 M ii. **Patrick Allen Smith** was born 18 Oct 2005 in Indianapolis, Marion County, IN.

5492. Christy Dawn Clemons (*Catherine Ann (Cathy) Smith[8], Joseph Wheeler Smith[7], Mozella Young[6], James Wylie (Jim) Young[5], Julia Ann Young[4], Mary E. Sharp[3], Charles W. Sr.[2], John Sr.[1]*) was born 11 Jul 1976.

Christy married **Edwin Staples Howard III** 27 Jul 2002 in Lauderdale County, AL.

5507. Nicole Butler (*Pamela Gail Scott[8], Gary Lance Scott[7], Eula Beatrice Young[6], Hulet Edward Young[5], Julia Ann Young[4], Mary E. Sharp[3], Charles W. Sr.[2], John Sr.[1]*).

Nicole married **Preston Lee Morris**, son of **Randy Lee Morris** and **Teresa Jo Brown**. Preston was born 18 Jun 1979 in ECM Hospital, Florence, Lauderdale County, AL.
6235 F i. **Nisha Desiree Morris** was born 4 Jan 2001 in ECM Hospital, Florence, Lauderdale County, AL.
6236 F ii. **Chelsea Morris** was born 9 Nov 2001 in ECM Hospital, Florence, Lauderdale County, AL.
6237 M iii. **Preston Dane Morris** was born 13 Oct 2007 in ECM Hospital, Florence, Lauderdale County, AL.

5513. Rachel Elizabeth Gean (*Thomas Steven Gean[8], Margaret Louise Dailey[7], Carrie Ann Young[6], Hulet Edward Young[5], Julia Ann Young[4], Mary E. Sharp[3], Charles W. Sr.[2], John Sr.[1]*) was born 19 Aug 1979 in Lauderdale County, AL.

Rachel married **Jeremy Randal Odom**.
6238 F i. **Danielle Elizabeth Gean** was born 1 Nov 2002 in Lauderdale County, AL.

5519. Tracy Maurene Gean (*Raymond Dale Gean[8], Margaret Louise Dailey[7], Carrie Ann Young[6], Hulet Edward Young[5], Julia Ann Young[4], Mary E. Sharp[3], Charles W. Sr.[2], John Sr.[1]*) was born 14 Jun 1981 in Lauderdale County, AL.

Tracy married **Jamie Dewayne Highland**, son of **David Highland** and **June Burns**, 6 Apr 2002 in Hardin County, AL.

5520. Michael Dale Gean (*Raymond Dale Gean[8], Margaret Louise Dailey[7], Carrie Ann Young[6], Hulet Edward Young[5], Julia Ann Young[4], Mary E. Sharp[3], Charles W. Sr.[2], John Sr.[1]*) was born 19 Nov 1977 in Lauderdale County, AL.

Michael married **Amy *Unk**.

5554. Ronda Kay Cassel (*Laura Kaye Wilkes[8], James Riley Wilkes[7], James Chambers Wilkes[6], Eula Elizabeth Sharp[5], Berry Nolan[4], Joseph (Joe)[3], Charles W. Sr.[2], John Sr.[1]*) was born 29 Oct 1969 in Colbert County, AL.

Ronda married **Terrell Ray Roland**, son of **Junior Roland** and **Libby Ann White**, 18 Feb 1994 in Colbert County, AL. Terrell was born 4 Sep 1971 in Colbert County, AL.
6239 F i. **Isabella Janice Roland** was born 3 Oct 1994 in Lauderdale County, AL.

5556. Toni Beth Holland (*Laura Kaye Wilkes[8], James Riley Wilkes[7], James Chambers Wilkes[6], Eula Elizabeth Sharp[5], Berry Nolan[4], Joseph (Joe)[3], Charles W. Sr.[2], John Sr.[1]*) was born 21 Apr 1977 in Colbert County, AL.

Toni married **Christopher Michaels** in Colbert County, AL.
6240 M i. **Christopher Allen Michaels** was born 31 Jul 1996 in Colbert County, AL.

Toni next married **Jonathan McKinny**.

5568. Donnie Clifford Zills Jr. (*Paula Louise Berryman[8], Mary Lee Wilkes[7], Levi (Lee) Grant Wilkes II[6], Eula Elizabeth Sharp[5], Berry Nolan[4], Joseph (Joe)[3], Charles W. Sr.[2], John Sr.[1]*) was born 11 Nov 1974 in Colbert County, AL.

Donnie married **Stacy Marie Simpson**, daughter of **Ed Gene Simpson** and **Anne Marie Wadkins**, 29 Aug 1996 in Colbert County, AL. Stacy was born 18 Sep 1976 in Colbert County, AL.

| 6241 | M | i. | **Slaton Heath Zills** was born 3 Mar 1994 in Colbert County, AL. |
| 6242 | M | ii. | **Hadlen Ethan Zills** was born 30 Apr 1998 in Colbert County, AL. |

5606. Lasondra May (*Manuel Dale May^8, Audrey Ruth Dixon^7, Thelma Mae Sharp^6, James Leander^5, Benjamin Franklin^4, Joseph (Joe)^3, Charles W. Sr.^{2}, John Sr.^{1}*) was born 21 Dec 1972 in Lauderdale County, AL.

Lasondra married **Mitch Passarella** 29 Dec.

| 6243 | M | i. | **Huston Passarella** was born in Lawrence County, AL. |
| 6244 | M | ii. | **Christon Passarella** was born in Lawrence County, AL. |

5648. Erica Faith Box (*Gregory (Greg) Thomas Box^8, Thomas Carroll Box^7, John Carroll (J. C.) Box Sr.^{6}, James (Jim) W. Box^5, Amanda Jane Sharp^4, Charles W. II^3, Charles W. Sr.^{2}, John Sr.^{1}*) was born 24 Dec.

Erica married **Steven Darby**.

5663. Michelle Lynn Pollard (*Donell Theodore Pollard Jr.^{8}, Omi Jean Watkins^7, Mary Louise Stults^6, Linnie Mae Sharp^5, Thomas (Tom) Erwin^4, Charles W. II^3, Charles W. Sr.^{2}, John Sr.^{1}*) was born 5 Apr 1982 in Lauderdale County, AL.

Michelle married **Richey Calhoun** in Dec 1999.

| 6245 | M | i. | **Tolby Calhoun**. |

5684. Tammy Alene Boatright (*James Hoyt Boatright Jr.^{8}, James Hoyt Boatright Sr.^{7}, Lady Goldie Saddler^6, Cora Young^5, Matilda Ann White^4, Eliza Jane Sharp^3, Charles W. Sr.^{2}, John Sr.^{1}*) was born 4 May 1970 in Lauderdale County, AL.

Tammy married **Jim I. Young Jr.**, son of **Joseph Inloe Young I** and **Ruth Ann Carles**, 8 Jun 1988 in Lauderdale County, AL. Jim was born 12 Jul 1956 in Indiana.
(Duplicate Line. See Person 2147)

Tammy next married **Anthony Mark Couch**, son of **William Mark Couch** and **Dorothy Ann Balentine**, 4 Sep 1992 in Lauderdale County, AL. Anthony was born 2 Nov 1969 in Alabama.

| 6246 | F | i. | **Lindsey Ryann Couch** was born in 1995. |

Tammy next married **Tim Austin**.

5687. Sonora Elizabeth Delano (*Brenda Sue Robinson^8, Wernita Elizabeth Boatright^7, Lady Goldie Saddler^6, Cora Young^5, Matilda Ann White^4, Eliza Jane Sharp^3, Charles W. Sr.^{2}, John Sr.^{1}*) was born 11 Mar 1964 in Lauderdale County, AL.

Sonora married **Charles Edward (Eddie) Matthews**, son of **Charles Matthews** and **Christine Dotson**, 7 Sep 1985 in Gulf Shores, AL. Charles was born 10 Oct 1961 in Maryland.

| 6247 | M | i. | **Edward Paul Matthews** was born 1 May 1986 in Fairhope, AL. |

Sonora next married **James Floyd (Jimmy) Smith Jr.**, son of **James Floyd Smith Sr.** and **Bessie Laverne Howard**, 14 Feb 1996 in Lauderdale County, AL. James was born 10 Sep 1956 in Lauderdale County, AL.

5688. Nikkie Dale Robinson (*Jackie Dale Robinson^8, Wernita Elizabeth Boatright^7, Lady Goldie Saddler^6, Cora Young^5, Matilda Ann White^4, Eliza Jane Sharp^3, Charles W. Sr.^{2}, John Sr.^{1}*) was born 22 Oct 1984 in Lauderdale County, AL.

Nikkie married **Bobby Vaill Inman** 21 Jul 2007 in Lauderdale County, AL.

Ninth Generation

5729. James David Wallace (*Shirley Jean Lindsey*^{9}, *Gentry Aaron Lindsey*^{8}, *Charles Edward Lindsey*^{7}, *Albert Curtis Lindsey*^{6}, *David A. Lindsey*^{5}, *Caleb (Calip) Lindsey*^{4}, *Frances (Frankie) Sharp*^{3}, *Charles W. Sr.*^{2}, *John Sr.*^{1}) was born 10 Aug 1967 in Lauderdale County, AL.

James married **Wendy Jean Mackey**, daughter of **Floyd Eugene Mackey** and **Linda Gail Barringer**, 28 Oct 1987 in Lauderdale County, AL. Wendy was born 7 Nov 1966 in Alabama.

5730. Thomas (Tommy) Wayne Wallace (*Shirley Jean Lindsey*^{9}, *Gentry Aaron Lindsey*^{8}, *Charles Edward Lindsey*^{7}, *Albert Curtis Lindsey*^{6}, *David A. Lindsey*^{5}, *Caleb (Calip) Lindsey*^{4}, *Frances (Frankie) Sharp*^{3}, *Charles W. Sr.*^{2}, *John Sr.*^{1}) was born 9 Oct 1969 in Athens, Limestone County, AL.

Thomas married **Marilyn Louise Smith**, daughter of **John E. Smith** and **Francis Holt**, 24 Apr 1987 in Lauderdale County, AL. Marilyn was born 21 Mar 1969 in Alabama.

5731. Martha Jean Wallace (*Shirley Jean Lindsey*^{9}, *Gentry Aaron Lindsey*^{8}, *Charles Edward Lindsey*^{7}, *Albert Curtis Lindsey*^{6}, *David A. Lindsey*^{5}, *Caleb (Calip) Lindsey*^{4}, *Frances (Frankie) Sharp*^{3}, *Charles W. Sr.*^{2}, *John Sr.*^{1}) was born 13 Nov 1975 in Lauderdale County, AL.

Martha married **Michael Dale**. Michael was born in Columbia, TN.

5736. Michele LeAnn Jones (*Linda Faye Pigg*^{9}, *Margaret Marie Lindsey*^{8}, *Charles Edward Lindsey*^{7}, *Albert Curtis Lindsey*^{6}, *David A. Lindsey*^{5}, *Caleb (Calip) Lindsey*^{4}, *Frances (Frankie) Sharp*^{3}, *Charles W. Sr.*^{2}, *John Sr.*^{1}) was born 4 Jan 1971 in Lauderdale County, AL.

Michele married **Ricky Lorey Hyde**, son of **Raymond Hyde** and **Mary Ruth Barksdale**, 31 Mar 1993 in Colbert County, AL. Ricky was born 12 Jun 1955 in Anniston, AL.
6248 F i. **Alexis Marie Hyde** was born 20 Oct 1994 in Lauderdale County, AL.
6249 F ii. **Kristen Leann Hyde** was born 15 May 1998 in Lauderdale County, AL.

5748. Michelle Lee May (*Benjamin Franklin May*^{9}, *James William May Sr.*^{8}, *Lilly Mae Lindsey*^{7}, *Millard Lindsey*^{6}, *Maraday (Merry Dee) Lindsey*^{5}, *Andrew Jackson Lindsey*^{4}, *Frances (Frankie) Sharp*^{3}, *Charles W. Sr.*^{2}, *John Sr.*^{1}) was born 19 Jul 1970.

Michelle married **Shannon Douglas James** 26 Jul 1989.

Michelle next married **Chris Winsted**. Chris was born 17 Sep 1974.
6250 M i. **Zachery Austin Winsted** was born 8 Feb 1998.

Michelle next married **Barry Lynn Graham** 30 Jun 1992. Barry was born in Sep 1969.
6251 M i. **Joshua Graham** was born 5 Jul 1992.

5751. Lisa Diane Smith (*Kathy Diane May*^{9}, *James William May Sr.*^{8}, *Lilly Mae Lindsey*^{7}, *Millard Lindsey*^{6}, *Maraday (Merry Dee) Lindsey*^{5}, *Andrew Jackson Lindsey*^{4}, *Frances (Frankie) Sharp*^{3}, *Charles W. Sr.*^{2}, *John Sr.*^{1}) was born 28 Oct 1969.

Lisa married **David Baxter** 17 Apr 1989. David was born 9 Dec 1967 in Haleyville, AL.
6252 M i. **Jordan Christopher Baxter** was born 7 May 1995.

5752. Gregory Wayne Smith (*Kathy Diane May*^{9}, *James William May Sr.*^{8}, *Lilly Mae Lindsey*^{7}, *Millard Lindsey*^{6}, *Maraday (Merry Dee) Lindsey*^{5}, *Andrew Jackson Lindsey*^{4}, *Frances (Frankie) Sharp*^{3}, *Charles W. Sr.*^{2}, *John Sr.*^{1}) was born 26 Dec 1971.

Gregory married **Angie Renee Baker** 8 Jun 1992.

5753. Kelly Leann Lindsey (*Sherry Lynn May*^{9}, *James William May Sr.*^{8}, *Lilly Mae Lindsey*^{7}, *Millard Lindsey*^{6}, *Maraday (Merry Dee) Lindsey*^{5}, *Andrew Jackson Lindsey*^{4}, *Frances (Frankie) Sharp*^{3}, *Charles W. Sr.*^{2}, *John Sr.*^{1}) was born 29 Feb 1980.

Kelly married **Eric Franklin Baker**. Eric was born 17 May 1979 in Hayden, AL.

5757. Bruce Forbes Jr. (*Patricia Gail Andis^9, Virginia Nell Wood^8, Viola Beatrice Lindsey^7, Millard Lindsey^6, Maraday (Merry Dee) Lindsey^5, Andrew Jackson Lindsey^4, Frances (Frankie) Sharp^3, Charles W. Sr.^{2}, John Sr.^{1}*).

Bruce married **Amanda *Unk**.
| 6253 | M | i. | **Allen Forbes**. |
| 6254 | F | ii. | ***Unk Forbes** was born 24 Dec 1995 in Helen Keller Hospital, Sheffield, Colbert County, AL. |

5761. Samantha Dawn Ezekiel (*Billy Gene Ezekiel Sr.^{9}, Sarah Elizabeth (Lib) Wood^8, Viola Beatrice Lindsey^7, Millard Lindsey^6, Maraday (Merry Dee) Lindsey^5, Andrew Jackson Lindsey^4, Frances (Frankie) Sharp^3, Charles W. Sr.^{2}, John Sr.^{1}*) was born 13 Aug 1979.

Samantha married **Rusty Depoyster**.

5767. Jesse Duane Wasserburger (*Deborah (Debbie) Faye Cossey^9, Shirley Jean Wood^8, Viola Beatrice Lindsey^7, Millard Lindsey^6, Maraday (Merry Dee) Lindsey^5, Andrew Jackson Lindsey^4, Frances (Frankie) Sharp^3, Charles W. Sr.^{2}, John Sr.^{1}*) was born 17 May 1977 in Frankfurt Am Main, Hesson, Germany.

Jesse married **Katherine Ann Machleit**, daughter of **August Machleit** and **Felicia *Unk**, 21 Jun 1996 in Pulaski, Giles County, TN. Katherine was born 28 Oct 1972 in Mt. Clemens, MS.
| 6255 | M | i. | **Jesse Duane Wasserburger II** was born 26 Jul 1996 in Huntsville, Madison County, AL. |
| 6256 | M | ii. | **Sean Thomas Wasserburger** was born 17 Oct 2000 in Huntsville, Madison County, AL. |

5850. Michael Pounders (*Sonia Michelle Gooch^9, Donnie Lee Gooch^8, Macil Bethrine Young^7, Odus Clarence Young Sr.^{6}, Eddie Young^5, Mary M. (Polly II) Lindsey^4, Frances (Frankie) Sharp^3, Charles W. Sr.^{2}, John Sr.^{1}*).

Michael married someone.
6257	M	i.	**Darren Pounders**.
6258	M	ii.	**Cory Pounders**.
6259	M	iii.	**Matthew Pounders**.

5891. Jeremy Michael Ray (*Belinda Lois Mason^9, Mildred Loriene Gean^8, Della V. Abilene Sego^7, Minnie Pearl Dearen^6, Mary Francis (Molly) Young^5, Mary M. (Polly II) Lindsey^4, Frances (Frankie) Sharp^3, Charles W. Sr.^{2}, John Sr.^{1}*) was born 9 May 1980 in Lauderdale County, AL.

Jeremy married **Lori Leigh Balentine**, daughter of **Lendon Balentine** and **Linda Sue Vickery**, 4 Nov 2000 in Lauderdale County, AL. Lori was born 6 Feb 1979 in Lauderdale County, AL.
| 6260 | F | i. | **Leighana Michelle Ray** was born 22 Oct 2003 in Biloxi, MS. |

5892. Brittany Belinda Ray (*Belinda Lois Mason^9, Mildred Loriene Gean^8, Della V. Abilene Sego^7, Minnie Pearl Dearen^6, Mary Francis (Molly) Young^5, Mary M. (Polly II) Lindsey^4, Frances (Frankie) Sharp^3, Charles W. Sr.^{2}, John Sr.^{1}*) was born 2 Oct 1985 in Florence, Lauderdale County, AL.

Brittany married **Joshua Hammond** 13 Mar 2004 in Rogersville, Lauderdale County, AL. Joshua was born 5 Sep 1978.
| 6261 | F | i. | **Emma Faith Hammond** was born 2 Aug 2006 in Florence, Lauderdale County, AL. |
| 6262 | F | ii. | **BryLeigh Mae Hammond** was born 19 May 2008. |

5898. Joshua Shae Allen (*Michelle Anne Collins^9, Mary Kathleen Gean^8, Della V. Abilene Sego^7, Minnie Pearl Dearen^6, Mary Francis (Molly) Young^5, Mary M. (Polly II) Lindsey^4, Frances (Frankie) Sharp^3, Charles W. Sr.^{2}, John Sr.^{1}*) was born 24 Mar 1988 in ECM Hospital, Florence, Lauderdale County, AL.

Joshua married **Amber Nicole Thrasher** 12 Apr 2008 in Loretto, Lawrence County, TN. Amber was born 5 Jul 1988 in Lawrenceburg, Lawrence County, TN.

6263 F i. **Tessa Leanne Allen** was born 14 Sep 2008 in Lawrenceburg, Lawrence County, TN.

5958. Christopher Lee Wood (*Doris Jean Holcombe[9], Willard Lee Holcombe[8], Ernest Powers Holcombe[7], Maggie Sharp[6], John Thomas (Tom)[5], James (Jim) Charles Sr.[4], Adron (Edwin/Ade) Sr.[3], Charles W. Sr.[2], John Sr.[1]*) was born 24 Mar 1971 in Florence, Lauderdale County, AL, died 12 Jun 1993, and was buried in Williams Chapel Cemetery, Lauderdale County, AL.

Christopher married **Lisa Dawn Scott** 1 Jun 1991 in Lauderdale County, AL. Lisa was born 23 Sep 1971 in Alabama.

5964. Candace Delynn Rich (*Geneva Gwen Holcombe[9], James Lee Holcombe[8], Ernest Powers Holcombe[7], Maggie Sharp[6], John Thomas (Tom)[5], James (Jim) Charles Sr.[4], Adron (Edwin/Ade) Sr.[3], Charles W. Sr.[2], John Sr.[1]*) was born 29 Jun 1987 in Florence, Lauderdale County, AL.

Candace married **Charles Mark Glason** 14 Sep 2002.

5972. Stephen William Gomes (*Cathy Rouna Hipps[9], Hazel Juanita Holcombe[8], Elmer Patford Holcombe[7], Maggie Sharp[6], John Thomas (Tom)[5], James (Jim) Charles Sr.[4], Adron (Edwin/Ade) Sr.[3], Charles W. Sr.[2], John Sr.[1]*) was born 6 Jan 1970.

Stephen married **Darlene Murphy** 7 Aug 1999.

5973. Nicole Renee Gomes (*Cathy Rouna Hipps[9], Hazel Juanita Holcombe[8], Elmer Patford Holcombe[7], Maggie Sharp[6], John Thomas (Tom)[5], James (Jim) Charles Sr.[4], Adron (Edwin/Ade) Sr.[3], Charles W. Sr.[2], John Sr.[1]*) was born 7 Jun 1972.

Nicole married **Dale D. Staley** 2 Oct 1999.

5986. Mary Beth Holcombe (*Dwayne Charles Holcombe[9], Charles Herschel Holcombe[8], Hubert Lee Holcombe[7], Maggie Sharp[6], John Thomas (Tom)[5], James (Jim) Charles Sr.[4], Adron (Edwin/Ade) Sr.[3], Charles W. Sr.[2], John Sr.[1]*) was born 8 Apr 1984 in Lauderdale County, AL.

Mary married **William Andrew Angel**, son of **William Floyd Angel** and **Susan Elizabeth Young**, 9 Jun 2007 in Lauderdale County, AL. William was born 7 Nov 1984.

6008. Michael Chad Townsend (*Lisa Lou Burk[9], Jimmy Ray Burk[8], Thursa Lou Sharp[7], Hallie (Hal) B.[6], John Thomas (Tom)[5], James (Jim) Charles Sr.[4], Adron (Edwin/Ade) Sr.[3], Charles W. Sr.[2], John Sr.[1]*) was born 10 Aug 1974 in Lauderdale County, AL.

Michael married **Katina Sinaird** 23 Aug 1991. Katina was born in Limestone County, AL.
6264 M i. **Caleb Jake Townsend**.

6009. Sabrina Ann Townsend (*Lisa Lou Burk[9], Jimmy Ray Burk[8], Thursa Lou Sharp[7], Hallie (Hal) B.[6], John Thomas (Tom)[5], James (Jim) Charles Sr.[4], Adron (Edwin/Ade) Sr.[3], Charles W. Sr.[2], John Sr.[1]*) was born 31 Aug 1976 in Giles County, TN.

Sabrina married **Darrell *Unk** 18 Oct 1996.

6012. Shane Bedwell (*Kimberly (Kim) Mitchell[9], James Ralph (Buddy) Mitchell[8], Bessie Etoil Sharp[7], James (Swagger)[6], John Thomas (Tom)[5], James (Jim) Charles Sr.[4], Adron (Edwin/Ade) Sr.[3], Charles W. Sr.[2], John Sr.[1]*) was born 23 May 198 ?.

Shane married **Monique *Unk**.
6265 F i. **Saloura Bedwell** was born in 1999.

Shane next married **Michelle *Unk**.

6266 F i. **Alexandria Michelle (Alli) Bedwell** was born 16 Nov 2002.

6015. Trista Paige Mitchell (*Jeffrey Terrell (Terry) Mitchell*[9], *James Ralph (Buddy) Mitchell*[8], *Bessie Etoil Sharp*[7], *James (Swagger)*[6], *John Thomas (Tom)*[5], *James (Jim) Charles Sr.*[4], *Adron (Edwin/Ade) Sr.*[3], *Charles W. Sr.*[2], *John Sr.*[1]) was born 26 May 1984 in Lauderdale County, AL.

Trista had a relationship with **Regie Leon Wood Jr.**, son of **Regie Leon (Buck) Wood Sr.** and **Nancy Mae Skipworth**. Regie was born 28 Feb 1976 in Lauderdale County, AL.
6267 F i. **Allisa Brielle Wood** was born 9 Aug 2002.

6076. Jamie Sharpston (*Bennie Erin Sharpston*[9], *Mable Rita Phillips*[8], *Lady Carrie Wood*[7], *Margie Ann (Marjorie) Bruce*[6], *Matilda Ann Sharp*[5], *James (Jim) Charles Sr.*[4], *Adron (Edwin/Ade) Sr.*[3], *Charles W. Sr.*[2], *John Sr.*[1]) was born 9 Apr 1979.

Jamie married **Jill *Unk**.

6084. Jim Calvin Young III (*Laura Jane Phillips*[9], *Ronald Eugene Phillips*[8], *Lady Carrie Wood*[7], *Margie Ann (Marjorie) Bruce*[6], *Matilda Ann Sharp*[5], *James (Jim) Charles Sr.*[4], *Adron (Edwin/Ade) Sr.*[3], *Charles W. Sr.*[2], *John Sr.*[1]) was born 23 Dec 1982 in Lauderdale County, AL, died 8 Dec 2007, and was buried in Oak Grove Cemetery, Lauderdale County, AL.

Jim married **Samantha *Unk**.
6268 M i. **Son Young**.

6098. Preston Lee Morris (*Teresa Jo Brown*[9], *Geraldine (Judy) Wood*[8], *Leonard Earl Wood*[7], *Margie Ann (Marjorie) Bruce*[6], *Matilda Ann Sharp*[5], *James (Jim) Charles Sr.*[4], *Adron (Edwin/Ade) Sr.*[3], *Charles W. Sr.*[2], *John Sr.*[1]) was born 18 Jun 1979 in ECM Hospital, Florence, Lauderdale County, AL.

Preston married **Nicole Butler**, daughter of **Gerald Thomas (Tommy) Butler** and **Pamela Gail Scott**. **(Duplicate Line. See Person 5507)**

6099. Tiffany Dawn Morris (*Teresa Jo Brown*[9], *Geraldine (Judy) Wood*[8], *Leonard Earl Wood*[7], *Margie Ann (Marjorie) Bruce*[6], *Matilda Ann Sharp*[5], *James (Jim) Charles Sr.*[4], *Adron (Edwin/Ade) Sr.*[3], *Charles W. Sr.*[2], *John Sr.*[1]) was born 23 May 1982 in ECM Hospital, Florence, Lauderdale County, AL.

Tiffany had a relationship with someone.
6269 F i. **Addison Jo Morris** was born 2 Dec 2007 in ECM Hospital, Florence, Lauderdale County, AL.

6101. Kristin Leeann Brown (*Travis Ray Brown*[9], *Geraldine (Judy) Wood*[8], *Leonard Earl Wood*[7], *Margie Ann (Marjorie) Bruce*[6], *Matilda Ann Sharp*[5], *James (Jim) Charles Sr.*[4], *Adron (Edwin/Ade) Sr.*[3], *Charles W. Sr.*[2], *John Sr.*[1]) was born 20 Apr 1982 in Loretto, Lawrence County, TN.

Kristin married **Tommy A. D. Ray**, son of **Thomas Duncan Ray** and **Dorothy Rosenquest**, 7 Apr 2001 in Lauderdale County, AL. Tommy was born about 1972 in Alabama.

Kristin next married **Cory Phillip Covington**, son of **Phillip Oneal Covington** and **Ebba Lou Williams**, 26 Aug 2007 in Orange Beach, FL. Cory was born 22 Apr 1981.
6270 F i. **Hadlee Rayanne Covington** was born 24 Jun 2008 in ECM Hospital, Florence, Lauderdale County, AL.

6105. Kristy Dawn Vaughn (*Anthony (Tony) Reed Vaughn*[9], *Betty June Sharp*[8], *Reeder Earl*[7], *Lee Hal*[6], *Owen Bennett (Doc)*[5], *James (Jim) Charles Sr.*[4], *Adron (Edwin/Ade) Sr.*[3], *Charles W. Sr.*[2], *John Sr.*[1]) was born 1 Apr ?.

Kristy married ***Unk Doan** in 1997.

6158. Jennifer Clemmons (*Wanda Lee Tatum[9], Glenn Thomas Brown[8], Edith Inez Wood[7], Mary Etta (Virgie) Crider[6], Elizabeth (Roxie) Belle Sharp[5], James (Jim) Charles Sr.[4], Adron (Edwin/Ade) Sr.[3], Charles W. Sr.[2], John Sr.[1]*) was born 12 Sep 1976 in ECM Hospital, Florence, Lauderdale County, AL.

Jennifer married **Johnny Harrison** 13 Jun 1995 in Lauderdale County, AL. Johnny was born 19 Aug 1975 in ECM Hospital, Florence, Lauderdale County, AL.

6271　M　i.　**Jordan Thomas Harrison** was born 19 Jun 1995 in ECM Hospital, Florence, Lauderdale County, AL.

6272　F　ii.　**Jacey Lee Harrison** was born 27 Sep 1997 in ECM Hospital, Florence, Lauderdale County, AL.

Name Index

A

Arnold: Buford E., 339; Buford Eli Jr., 235; Camie Lynn, 515; Carl David (C. D.), 515; Christy Dawn, 515; Deborah Jean, 339; Donnie Dodd, 373; Dunnavan Glenn, 306; Elise, 525; Elsie Mae, 352; Henry, 400; James Carlton, 515; Karen Denise, 235, 398; Kathryn Grace, 525; Kelly Leanne, 373, 503; Leo, 373; Melissa Diane, 235, 398; Milton, 238; Pamela Regina, 235, 398; Patrick John, 525; Perry, 525; Steve Eli, 235; Steve Steele, 306; Wanda Delores, 400

Arredondo: Tomas, 520

Arthur: Joyce, 305

Artusi: Ann, 136

Ashburn: Fay, 103, 206; Virginia, 103, 206; William Robert, 102

Ashe: Lisa Marie, 524

Ashley: Alice Marie, 208, 361; Alton Dye, 208; Rachel Ann, 361; William W. III, 361; William W. Jr., 208, 361; William W. Sr., 208

Askew: Carson Jose, 518; Chris Jason, 397, 518; Comer Jack I, 235; Comer Jack II, 235, 397; Helen, 279; Janice Kay, 235, 397; Jessica Ann, 397; Linda, 274; Theresa Kay, 235, 397

Atkinson: Alberta, 85, 174; Fred, 85, 174; Hubert, 174; Larry, 174; Ronald, 174

Atwell: Anna Lea, 331; Joanna Kay, 183, 330; Robert F. III, 183, 331; Robert F. IV, 331; Robert F. Jr., 183; Robert F. Sr., 183; Selina Marie, 183, 331

Auchly: Joel, 525; Zane, 525

Aue: Mary Beth, 507

Ault: Arsen, 165

Austin: Allison Brooke, 352; Ambrey Michelle, 352; Anna Elizabeth, 452; Ashlee Marie, 452; Bradley David, 452; Bryan, 282; Christy, 326; Edna, 286, 369; Eldridge Allen, 363; Esther B., 218; Frankie C., 245; Glen David Jr., 282, 452; Glen David Sr., 282; Helen, 149; Hilda, 364; James Bryan, 282, 452; James Robert, 174; June, 205; Katherine (Katie), 452; Linda Gail, 174; Linda Gayle, 234; Michael Bryan, 452; Minnie, 141; Patricia Ann, 518; Patsy Carolyn, 363; Paul Robert, 351; Pauline, 341, 346; Peggy Ann, 466; Ralph Coleman, 201; Robert Arnold, 174; Robert Kevin, 174; Rosie Lee, 166; Roy B., 201; Sarah, 362; Tim, 530; Wade Linville, 352

Axelson: Tracie Rene, 357

Ayers: Amanda Lane, 367, 499; C. G., 367; J. P., 335; Jewell, 276; Kari, 335; Lawrence Alan, 332; Ronald Moore, 367; Shannon Lee, 367, 499; Tony, 335

B

Babock: Roger L., 353; Tracey Leigh, 353

Backensto: Eric Michael, 327; Michael McDonald, 327

Badillo: Ruth, 512

Baggett: Nadine, 175

Baich: Dan, 129; Yvonne, 129

Bailey: Kenneth (Hud) Marshall, 464; Martha, 121

Baily: Patricia, 455

Baker: Angie Renee, 531; Ashton Ladd, 527; Brian Albert, 527; Edna, 162; Eric Franklin, 532; Evan Marshall, 527; Francis Lea, 453; Jesslee, 478; Kedrick Farrell, 527; Michael, 478

Balch: Brian Keith, 479; Keith, 479; Rana, 386

Baldy: Justin William May, 470; Thomas Garvin, 470

Balentine: Brandon, 414; Brittany Denise, 345, 446, 489; Carolyn Joan, 148, 291; Cindy Lou, 148; Clifford, 245; Danny Eugene, 403; Deborah, 269, 443; Debra Annette, 148; Devin Andrew, 403; Dorothy (Dot) Gloria, 133, 269; Dorothy Ann, 530; Douglas, 269; Duane, 269, 443; Elmer Clyde, 240, 245, 417; Erma Ruth, 279; Ernest, 133; Evadean Joyce, 335, 396; Frances Pearl, 240, 400; Gertrude, 214; Glynis, 244; Goldie Yvonne, 519; Helen Sue, 441; Ida, 236; Jacqueline, 290; James Cecil Jr., 148; James Cecil Sr., 148; James Douglas, 133; James Eldon, 468; James Leon, 133, 269; Janice June, 133, 270; Jeffrey Wayne, 468; John Rich, 69, 126; John W., 290, 350; Joyce Marie, 465; Justin Aaron, 468; Katherine Jean, 148, 291; Lendon, 532; Letha Emmertian, 227; Lorena, 287; Lori Leigh, 532; Margie, 243, 335; Marilyn Jo, 148, 291; Martha Ann, 371; Martha Lee, 148, 291; Mary Lillian, 133; Matthew, 414; Nancy, 11; Nancy Carolyn, 350; Pamela Lois, 417; Pearl Belle, 126; Phillip S., 133; Robert, 133; Rocky Delane, 245, 414; Roger D., 345, 446; Sarah Pearl, 64; Sidney Houston, 64; Susie Ann, 92, 98, 130, 133; Thomas Lynn, 133; Tollie, 468; Tony Clyde, 403; Vera Inez, 286; Virginia (Virgie), 69; Whitney, 403; William Kenneth, 133

Ballard: Amy Nicole, 422, 524; April Michelle, 422, 524; Bernice, 206; Clara, 367; Mary, 375; Reginal, 73; Terry Glenn, 422; Thomas Crawford (T. C.), 240; Wilford Luvert, 422; Wilma Marcell, 240, 251, 399, 425, 439

Banks: Susan Diane, 306

Baptist: Dwight, 275; Jody, 275

Barackmra: Joy Deloris, 201

Barajas: Jose, 463

Barber: Calvin E., 440; Rebecca C., 403; Tracey, 440

Barbour: Patricia Ruth, 256

Bare: Anthony, 169

Barham: Jo Anne, 177

Barker: Bradford Glenn, 374; Brian Ray, 374, 504; Floyd, 217; Glenn Gary, 218, 374; Hairel Ray, 217, 374; Linda Gail, 218, 374; Lisa, 324; Malissa Dawn, 374; Margaret Elizabeth, 172; Michelle Leigh, 374, 504; Ralph, 194; Raymond Williard, 217

Barkley: Billy G., 466; Jerry L., 436; Mack, 136; Melissa Ann, 436; Victoria Starr, 466; William Brent, 466; William Chance, 466

Barksdale: Jaimy, 433; Mary Ruth, 531; Tracy Ellen, 433

Barlow: Luna Eugenia, 121

Barnell: Eunise, 392

Barnett: Abby Lane, 515; Arthur, 496; Billy Levon, 387; Brian Sidney, 514; Charles Reid, 494; Chase Levon, 514; Donawanna Nicholas, 515; Erick Dale, 441; Hollis Turner, 380; Holly Marie, 496; Jackie Wayne, 496; James Ovus, 387; Joshua (Josh) Aaron, 515; Mary Meagan, 496; Pamela Gail, 380; Sherri Sue, 494; Sherry, 380; Tamsey Virginia, 227; Tommy Leron, 387, 514; Tony Levon, 387, 514

Barns: Gary L., 333; Kenneth, 517; Patricia Rene, 333

Barrentine: Colon Ray Jr., 331; Savannah Rose, 331

Barrett: Bobby J., 469; Chuck Beauton Sr., 489; Jessica Lynn, 469; Joshua Ray, 523; Kristen, 489; Shannon Lynn, 469; Tim, 325

Barrett (adopting): A'Rheonna, 419

Barrier: Amy Nicole, 510; Benjamin Alan, 324; Bernice, 87, 176; Charles, 177; Danny Alan, 324; Donna Sue, 177, 321, 371; Haley Brooke, 477; Henry, 87; Henry Olen, 87, 176, 371; James (Bubba) Edward, 510; Jimmie, 177;

Joannie Lee, 324, 477; John Henry, 324; John Paul, 324, 477; Mary Ann, 177, 321; Matthew, 411

Barringer: Linda Gail, 531

Bart: Valery, 398

Barter: Hattie, 221

Bartlett: Jimmy Joe, 513; Jimmy Joel, 513

Barton: Nicholas James, 378; Sam, 378

Basdon: Dewey Scott, 444; Walker Joe, 444

Baskins: Carolyn, 519; David Doyle, 410; Jason Roy, 352; Jordan Lee, 352; Justin Dean, 352; Kimberly Renee, 248, 419; Margaret, 449; Marshall, 252; Oscar Edward, 352; Patricia (Patsy) Ann, 252; Robert Lee (B. J.) Jr., 410; Robert Lee (Bobby) Sr., 410; Roy Lee, 352; Tommy Lee, 248; Walter Amos, 248

Bass: Clara, 484; Flora Lee, 257; Patti Ann, 462

Baston: Dewey Edward, 444

Bates: Arthur Newton Jr., 232; Arthur Newton Sr., 232; Sandra Marie, 232, 394; Valerie Kay, 232; Wilburn N., 232

Bauchman: Fannie, 34

Baugus: Mamie, 121

Baxter: David, 531; Jasmyn Summer, 399; Jordan Christopher, 531; Larry Simpson Jr., 399; Larry Simpson Sr., 399; Luke Cody, 399; Savannah Danielle, 399

Beadle: Beverly Jean, 502; Timpest, 156

Beakey: Patricia Ann, 397

Bean: Martha Ann, 303

Beard: Audrey Dale, 255; Horace, 176; Kenny, 350; Polly, 176; Sharon, 176

Beasley: Joyce, 134; Mildred, 343; Shirley Louise, 287; Teresa Rae, 498

Beavers: Gladys, 68; Mattie, 133; Wanda Ealine, 279

Beck: Garey Leon, 524; Gwendolyn (Gwen) Joy, 524

Beckeet: Amanda, 502

Becker: Catherine Doris, 198, 350; Herman Guy, 198; Perry Lee, 198; Sybile Vilena, 198, 349; Sylvia Marie, 198, 349

Beckman: Mary, 35; Rosie, 75

Beddingfield: Dorothy J., 377

Bedford: Ellis Ray, 336; Jonathan David, 336; Tamara Leigh, 336

Bedingfield: Ida, 475; Ira Hobbs, 210; Mary, 475; Maude Helen, 210

Bedwell: Alexandria Michelle (Alli), 534; Cherokee, 499; Saloura, 533; Shane, 499, 533

Behel: Amanda Summer, 369; Carl Ricky, 432; Carla Dauphane, 432; Cortney Lane, 432, 525; Earl E., 369; Edward Mayfield Sr., 227; Hearil Ray, 432; Krista Nicole, 518; Lena Mae, 227; Thomas, 518; William Jimmy, 369

Belcher: Anna Clare, 415; Ben D., 245; Bennie Datson, 245, 415; Bennie LaDon, 245; Brodie Shannon, 415; Floyd, 442; Joseph Benjamin, 415; Mary Lewis, 442; Michael Ladon, 245, 414; Sherry Denise, 245, 414

Bell: Anthony Ray, 474; Aprel Marie, 438; Caarver Alexander, 528; Daughter, 528; Debra Kaye, 368, 501; Derrick, 361; Hugh, 368; James Anderson (Andy), 438; Jared Joseph, 438, 528; Lindsey Allison, 474; Mary Jane, 288; Raymond, 396; Sarah Ann, 312; Sonny, 438; Sonola L., 457; Sullivan Arwin, 528; Valerie Kay, 396

Bennett: Allison, 80; Barbara Patricia, 348; Barbara Sue, 80; Beatrice Lillie, 255; Charles, 282; Ella Finn, 282; Jean Marie, 80; Marcia, 340; Martin, 80; Mary, 80; Mary Mable, 35, 79; Oscar Lee Jr., 80; Oscar Lee Sr., 35, 80; Roy, 35, 79; Thomas Lee Jr., 363; Thomas Lee Sr., 363; William (Bill) Carl, 255; William W., 35

Benson: April Marie, 411; Beverly Jean, 522; Billy Carol, 411; Danny Wayne, 419; Elizabeth Anne, 402; Helen Christine, 487; Kimberly Marlene, 419; Lowell Ralph, 402; Patsy Jane, 345; Raymond, 268, 400; Ruth Ann, 340; Shirley, 348; Tina Rose, 400

Bentley: Billie Rae, 463; David Michael, 298, 462; John, 298; John Kevin, 298; Mitchell Eric, 462; Shawn Michael, 462; Tracie Marie, 298, 463

Berdett: Geraldine, 468

Berg: Neva Louise, 256

Bergbauger: Al, 144

Bergin: Elizabeth Gail, 452

Berkey: Albert, 141; Denise Lynne, 141, 281; Patricia Gail, 141, 281; Raymond C., 141; Ronald Chas, 141

Berner: Mitz, 296

Berry: Lila Jean, 335; Mary Louise, 278; Raymond (Ray), 152

Berryman: Arthur Calvin, 277; Christopher Louis, 256, 429; Douglas Greg, 429; Ether Leigh, 429; Grover Cleveland, 256; James Leonard Jr., 256, 429; James Leonard Sr., 256; Jeanice Michele, 256, 429; Lois M., 280; Marisa Shae, 429; Paula Louise, 277, 448; Samuel James, 429

Bertrand: Aghbert James (Ed), 340

Bevers: Donald Gene, 491; Marlyn, 291

Bevins: Clara Jean, 318

Bevis: Andrew Griffin, 236, 237, 238, 381; Arbie, 47, 99; Billy Daniel, 366; Billy Ray, 467; Brenda Sue, 237, 401, 412; Christie Lynn, 351; Edwin Dwayne, 236, 399, 425; Ethel, 318; George, 362; Hattie, 180, 364; James, 47, 265; James Celia, 47; Janet Lou, 236, 252, 399; Jarred Paul, 399; Jeffrey Louis, 451; Jerry Lynn, 351; Jessie Andrew II, 351; Justin Ross, 467; Kristopher Edwin, 399; Lennie, 218; Linda Gail, 265; Linnie Belle, 168; Lois Inez, 238, 251, 381, 416; Lonie Blake, 400; Lonnie Ray, 236, 399; Louie Andrew, 400; Louie Edwin, 236, 252, 425; Loyal Thomas, 451; Mary Alice, 68; Mary Delise, 362; Mary Lucille, 419; Matthew M., 92; Maudie Alice, 92; Melissa, 229; Melissa Kay, 451; Miceala Faith (KK), 399; Nan Young, 21; Nathaniel Wade, 400; Pride T., 467; Shirley Renee, 366; Stacey LeAnn, 351, 490; Steven Ray, 451; Terry Lynn, 237, 401; Vera Adelaide, 245; Virgie M., 137; Virginia, 119; Willie Dalton, 237, 412

Biggers: Carolyn Sue, 515

Biggs: Clara Kay, 92, 186; Delta Marie, 215, 364; Edward (Eddie), 92; Nellie Young, 43; Royal N. R., 92; Ruby, 92; William, 92

Billings: Mary, 447

Billingsley: Beverly, 199, 351; Brenda, 199, 351; Brian Eugene, 199, 352; Catherine Marie, 352; Deborah Alliene, 199, 352; Donna Faye, 199, 352; Elaine Renee, 199, 351; Grady Earl, 98, 199; James (Pete) Marshall, 98, 199; McArthur Andrew, 98; Michael Allen, 199; Millard Horace, 98, 199; Teresa Estell, 199, 351; Thomas Moore, 98, 199; Waymon, 227; William Eugene, 98, 199; William Marshall, 352

Bills: Elizabeth, 86; Evelyn, 86, 176; Fleeda, 86; Marlon, 86; Ollie E., 86; Virginia, 86

Bing: Carl, 240

Birch: Adam, 481; Ethan, 481; Nathan, 481

Bird: Robert E., 176

Birdsong: Ruth, 385

Birdwell: Connie, 390

Bishop: James O., 276; Lynne Carol, 276

Black: Kelvon Dwaine, 490; Kyle, 490; Peggy, 514; Vernice Louise, 138; William Larry, 490

Blackburn: Angela Carmon, 289, 457; Buford Clyde, 146; Charles Everett, 146, 289; John David (J. D.), 289; Nettie Bama, 199; Sampson Emmitt, 146

Blackhulen: Stella Marie, 469

Blackman: Greg Alan, 448

Blackstock: Ann, 460; Clifford H., 278; Patricia Diane, 278

Blackwell: Jack Martin, 363; Mildred Elaine, 363; Molly Darlene, 447; Robert Lane, 447

Blahuta: Bill, 338; Emma Grace, 483; John Corey, 338, 483

Blair: Mary Jane, 358

Blake: Martha, 281

Blakney: Lois Katherine, 219; W. C., 219

Blalock: Amelia Dawn, 394; Charles Christopher, 306, 394, 516; Charles Clifford, 306, 394; Charles Luke, 306; Noble, 394

Blanche: Lillian, 487

Bland: Leesa, 371

Blankenship: Delorease, 197; Ron, 191

Blansett: Cheryl Lynn, 424

Blanton: Ada, 60; Ida Lula, 32; R. Ben, 32, 60

Blasingame: Linda Louise, 450

Blenkisopp: Teresa, 428

Blevins: David, 165; Michael (Mickey), 470

Bloss: J. B., 81; Thelma Katherine, 81

Blount: Eustis, 174; Grace, 195; Marin, 56; Martha Ann, 134

Blowers: Windy, 512

Blythe: Charlotte L., 372

Boatright: Donald Douglas, 155, 297; James (Jim) W., 155; James Hoyt Jr., 297, 302, 461; James Hoyt Sr., 155, 297; James Madison, 155; John, 297; Jonathan Michael, 461; Richard, 297; Shane, 297; Shawn, 297, 462; Steven Mitchell Jr., 461; Steven Mitchell Sr., 297, 461; Tammy Alene, 302, 461, 530; Wernita Elizabeth, 155, 297

Bobbett: Ida L., 122

Bock: Barry, 517; Bradley, 517

Boesiger: Marion, 313

Boeswetter: Lona, 161; Otto, 161

Boggess: Donald Arthur Jr., 125, 256; Donald Arthur Sr., 125; Dorothy Ann, 125, 256

Boggs: Kelly, 262; Shawn, 262

Bogus: Bobby Ray, 441; Cody Steven, 441; Justin Ray, 441; Maud, 163; Timothy Ray, 441

Boldger: David John, 109

Boles: Gustavous Adolphus, 23; Matilda, 23

Bolger: Earl, 222; John, 222; Johnny, 222; Patricia Ann, 370; Ruth, 222

Bolick: Shirley Ann, 428

Bolton: Joseph Farrel, 393

Bompos: Fran, 203

Bone: Homer Oliver Sr., 452; Vera Amanda, 452

Bone'e, 424

Bonner: Betty Jane, 358; Rebecca Ann, 257; Willie Lake, 257

Boone: Kim, 261, 434; Thomas E., 261

Booten: George Russell, 280; Rose Marie, 280

Boothe: Darris Mae, 293; Myers Luther, 293

Borden: Alice, 482; Betty, 178; Christie Lynn, 427; Daniel Lawson, 178; Dannie, 178; Evelyn, 205; Gene, 485; Glenda, 405; Laura Ann, 502; Patricia Ann (Lucy), 316, 472; Roger Lee, 502; Steven, 526; Steven Chance, 526; Tamara (Tammy) Anne, 429

Bordon: Barbara Ann, 316; Linda Gail, 349

Bosler: Ed, 340; Mary Ann, 340

Bostick: Betty, 457; Flora, 398

Boston: Brian B., 351; Rachel E., 351; Shannon, 475; William Andrew, 351; William Terry, 351

Boswell: Virginia (Jenny) A., 186; Wilbur, 186

Bottomle: Remona, 394

Boulie: Josephine, 257

Bounds: Emily Louise, 60, 127; Izora Isabelle, 60; John, 60; Thomas Evertt, 60; William T., 60

Bourdon: Anita Joyce, 372

Bourgeois: David, 434

Bowen: Janice, 332

Bowes: Annie Margie, 149

Bowles: Maggie Myrtle, 136; Sarah Elizabeth, 52

Box: Baby, 29; Donald Andrew, 146, 289; Donna Jo, 289, 457; Erica Faith, 457, 530; George Daily, 29; Gladys, 67, 146; Gregory (Greg) Thomas, 289, 457; James (Jim) W., 29, 67; James Windell, 289, 457; Jared, 457; Jessica Lynn, 457; John Carroll (J. C.) Sr., 67, 146; John Craven, 29; Judy Darlene, 289, 457; Mutell Sue, 67; Rose Mary, 146, 289; Ruby Louise, 146, 289; Stella Mae, 67, 146; Teresa Ann, 289, 457; Thomas Carroll, 146, 289; Willie Carmen, 67, 146

Boyd: Charles, 90; Fannie Katherine, 90; Helen, 135; Rolland Norman, 324; Sharon Antoinette, 324

Boyette: Gayle, 506

Boyle: Katrina Marie, 474

Bracken: Charles Gordon, 99; Gordon, 99; James Edward, 99; Joanne, 99; Sharon Sue, 99, 202

Braden: Rhonda Denise, 471; Robert, 471

Bradfield: Alva A., 82

Bradford: Dawn Noell, 462; Earl, 462; Joe B., 377; Kimberly Sue, 415; Michael Eroy, 377

Bradley: Allen Clayton, 431; Casey Ann, 516; Edward, 194; Jackson, 431; James, 86, 164; Jonathan Craig, 431; Mary Maxine, 194; Sharon Rebecca, 431; Stephan Ray, 516; William Dustin, 431

Brandon: Clarence W., 229; Winnie Mae, 229

Brannon: Mary, 412

Brant: Lannie E., 405; Rebecca Aileen, 405; Robert Lannie, 405

Branyon: Laura Madden, 295, 460; Lawrence Madden, 295; Thomas Aaron, 295

Bratcher: Dustin, 503; Heather, 503; Kayla, 503; Ken, 373, 503; Kenneth L., 373; Kerri, 373, 503

Bratton: Imelda, 506

Brazier: Keith Ray, 476; Tatum Keauna, 476; Treyton Kade, 476

Breeden: Deanna Lee, 341; Lew Brian, 341

Brethrick: Dorothy Lucille, 280

Brewer: Alexia Chailey, 469; Amy Elaine, 413; Bess, 123; Collier B., 373; David Ricky, 373; Dewayne, 191; Elgena, 345; Elizabeth Francis, 164; Hazel, 183; Helen C., 346; Jarred Scott, 373; Jerrel, 191; Jimmie S., 502; Juston David, 373; Kelly Ashlane, 469; Kenneth, 191; Natalie, 507; Nate, 507; Pauline, 202; Thomas Dale, 413; Tony, 507; Willa Mae, 254; William Delane, 469; William T., 469

Brewington: Daniel Joseph, 406; Madison Clair, 520; Ray, 405; Tony Wayne, 405, 520

Briggs: Lola, 138

Bright: Ruthell, 468

Brink: Margaret Louise (Peggy), 491; William Lawrence, 491

Brinkley: Nancy, 214

Bristo: Robert, 291

Britnell: Charles (Chief) Wayne, 411; Crystal (Christy) Dawn, 411, 523; Marion Gilbert, 411

Broadfoot: Biddy Blessing, 439; Buck, 486; Dorothy Ellen, 182; Jordan Leigh, 305; Lee S., 305; Owen W., 182; Stephanie Laura, 486; Stephanie Paige, 305; Stephen Jay, 305; Violet Catherine, 70; William Howard II, 330; William Howard III, 330; Wilodean, 200

Broadway: D. B., 348

Brockwell: Aubrey Elaine, 388; E. W. Jr., 388; Wanda, 457

Brogan: Antonio, 449; Rolando, 449; Rolando Sean, 449

Bromley: Orenda Orlando, 70

Brooks: Andrew David, 328; Brain Matthew, 328; Charles, 208; Dennis Gray, 328; Donald Ray, 348; James, 208; Leann Elizabeth, 328; Robert Daniel, 348; Wayne, 208; William (Bill) D., 328

Brown: Aaron David, 466; Alice Elaine, 239; Allen Randall Jr., 360; Allen Randall Sr., 360; Allison Darnell, 360; Amanda, 519; Amanda Leann, 407, 521; Annie Marie, 242; Ashley Nicole, 349; Barbara Ann, 181; Bayle Levi, 521; Benjamin Franklin Jr., 96, 196; Benjamin Franklin Sr., 96, 339; Bernard Axle, 304; Bernita Sue, 344; Bessie, 244; Bessie Lou, 246, 414, 510; Bob Lee, 240, 521; Bobby Junior, 240, 407; Carrie, 210; Carrie Lee, 112, 201; Charles E., 275; Chastity Danielle, 511; Cheri Lynn, 346; Clarence E., 243, 246, 381; Clinton Jared, 407; Cody Lance, 458; Cody William, 304; Dewitt Anthony, 304; Dorothy (Dottie) Norene, 96, 197; Dorothy Mozelle, 243; Dustin Drew, 349; Dwight Gabriel, 324; Edwin O., 491; Elisha Faye, 349; Eloise Keech, 91; Emma Christine, 521; Emma Virginia, 74; Emmitt Louis, 291; Glenda Dale, 451; Glenn Thomas, 240, 407; Harleigh Alexzandrea Mae, 521; James Houston, 467; James Shannon, 467; Janet Ann, 360; Jeremy Christopher, 407; Jim, 383; Jimmie Nell, 96, 196; Jimmy Turner, 240, 407; John Henry, 291; Joyce, 332; Karon Denise, 324; Kenneth Wayne, 240, 407, 521; Kristin Leeann, 511, 534; Kyle Wayne, 407; Leonard Wilson Jr., 310; Leonard Wilson Sr., 310; Lewis, 112; Louis A., 346; Loyd Orvil, 239; Lucky David, 466; Margaret, 12, 13, 140; Marilyn, 451; Marvin, 240; Marvin Francis, 96, 310; Mary Agnes, 128; Oscar David, 466; Rachel Lane, 197; Ralph Lee, 197, 349; Ray, 381; Rebecca Leigh, 291; Richard Blake, 511; Ricky Lowell II, 349; Ricky Lowell Sr., 197, 349; Robbie Lorinan, 197; Robert Lance, 291, 458; Roger Lloyd, 197; Ronald Lynn, 197, 349; Ronnie Lowell, 96, 197, 339; Ronnie Matthew, 349; Sarah Jane, 304; Shannon Chase, 467; Shelia Ann, 275; Talina Shawn, 407, 521; Teresa Jo, 381, 511, 529; Terry, 430; Terry Richard, 382, 511; Theresa Gail, 349; Tiffany Darlene, 349; Travis Ray, 381, 511; Verla, 383; Yolanda Lynn, 407, 521

Bruce: Able, 108; Allen Wayne, 505; Amos, 108; Amos Jerry Jr., 219, 376; Amos Jerry Sr., 108, 219; Amy, 376; Ann Sharp, 51; Barbara Sue, 179, 324; Baylis Sr., 37; Becky, 221, 378; Becky Lou, 179, 325; Betty Jane, 220, 378; Bobby Joel, 220, 378; Brandon Dwight, 324; Brenda Ruth, 179, 324; Bryant Kyle, 506; Byrum, 108; Chad Adam, 377, 506; Charles William, 219, 377; Cleona, 108, 219; Collin Warner, 377, 507; Cyndra Kay, 218, 375; Cyrus, 108; Daniel Wayne, 324; David Joey, 378; David Paul, 179, 324; Donna Sue, 220, 378; Dora Smith, 51; Durwood Wiliam, 108; Edsel Glenn, 108; Edwin Dewayne, 218, 375; Elizabeth Irene, 505; Emily, 377, 507; Evelyn Katherine, 219, 377; Francis Laurene, 204, 358; Freddie Lee Jr., 376; Freddie Lee Sr., 219, 376; George "Dan" Robert, 51; George Owen, 51, 109; George Robert (Dan), 50; Gracie Jeanette, 218, 375; Granville Ray, 218, 375; Gregory Alan, 376, 505; Harding Abel, 108, 220; Harold Sherman, 219, 376; Hunter Cole, 324; Jackie Dewayne, 218, 375; James, 51; James Millard Jr., 376; James Millard Sr., 219, 375; James Pinkney Jr., 108, 218; James Pinkney Sr., 50, 108; Janice, 221, 378; Jessie D., 109, 224; Jewell, 108, 218; John C., 108, 221; John Daniel, 179, 324; John Gilbert Jr., 219, 376; John Gilbert Sr., 108, 218; John Paul, 218, 375; John Terry, 375, 504; Joseph (Joey) Paul, 376; July Jacqueline, 376; Kelly, 377, 507; Kern, 101; Kimberly, 506; Kimberly Jan, 376, 505; Lanny Warner, 220, 377; Laverne, 101, 204; Leacia Mae, 109, 224; Lewis, 101, 204; Lilly Eddie Levie, 51, 109; Margaret L., 108; Margie, 51; Margie Ann (Marjorie), 51, 110, 118, 120; Mary Leona, 108, 219; Mary Sue, 204, 358; Mattie Sue, 218, 374; Merita Kay, 220, 377; Michael Wayne, 179, 324; Mildred Diane, 375, 504; Mitzi Diane, 220, 378; Montez, 80; Nancy, 37, 105, 107, 110; Nancy Elizabeth, 114; Naomi Deborah, 108, 219; Natalie, 506; Nettie Bethel, 92, 108, 219; Pamela Jane, 376, 504; Pamela June, 218, 375; Patricia, 101, 204; Paul Byrum, 108, 179, 219; Paula Malin, 376, 504; Pearl, 51; Pearl I., 108, 218; Pinkton (Pinkerton), 50; Quennon Chancey, 376, 505; Rachel Annette, 219, 377; Reeda, 377, 507; Reeder, 108; Reeder Warner, 108, 220; Reggie Paul, 219, 376; Riggle, 108, 218; Robert Cyrus, 108, 220; Robert William, 50, 92, 108, 179; Samuel Lewis, 101; Sandra, 221; Scott Blakney, 377, 506; Shannon Kelly, 377, 506; Sheila, 221, 378; Sherri Lynn, 376, 505; Shirley Francis, 218, 375; Terry Lynn, 179, 324; Tracy, 221, 378; Tyler, 506; Viola T., 108, 221; Virginia Alice, 219, 376; Virginia Suzanene, 376, 505; William Carl Jr., 375, 504; William Carl Sr., 218, 374; Willie, 51; Willie Clyde, 108, 218; Zabrina Camilla, 376, 505

Brumley: Dorinda Elizabeth, 63

Bryan: Mary E., 284

Bryant: Betty Ruth, 376; Charles Kyle, 376; Cynthia, 253; Harry, 297; Lilly, 310; Marilyn, 297, 300; Rosie, 209

Buck: Geraldine, 395

Buckley: Charles Richard, 360; Hillary Ann, 360

Bullard: Clara Louise, 207

Bullock: Bob, 292

Bundy: Lynnessia Ann, 492

Burbalt: Roseann Kathryn, 234

Burbank: Allie, 413; Angie Marie, 416; Berl Reed, 372; Darnell Eunice, 121, 341; Dustin Craig, 417; Ethel, 417; Ethridge John, 121; Haley Savana, 413; Janice Marie, 247, 383, 416; John Ethridge, 244, 247; Karen Sue, 247, 416; Larry Bennett, 244; Lindsi, 413; Melissa (Lisa) Ann, 244, 413; Melissa Gaye, 372; Michael, 413; Michael (Mike) Larry, 244, 413; Patricia, 401; Patrick Ryan, 416; Roger Dale, 247, 416; Ronnie Dale, 247, 383

Burch: Betty, 468; Billie, 388; Eugene Paul, 260; Linda, 202; Ruth Ann, 420

Burcham: Judy, 252; Tracy Carol, 281; Walter J. Jr., 281

Burchell: Edna Pauline, 138

Burdette: Ann, 384

Burgess: Blant, 66; Martha June, 245; Mary Marguerite, 227; Theodore R., 227

Burgress: Irene, 392

Burk: Beth Nicole, 498; Bradley Kyle, 498; Charles Milton, 366, 498; Donald Oneal, 211, 366; Ezra Milton, 211; Jimmy Ray, 211, 366; Linda Sue, 366, 498; Lisa Lou, 366, 498; Lyonel, 211; Melissa, 366, 498; Milton Sharp, 211, 366

Burks: Gregory Gains, 320, 475; Marjorie, 353; William, 320

Burnett: Audrey Kay, 427; Claudie Howard, 253; Janet Darlene, 253; Stephen Ralph, 427

Burnette: Darryl Wendell Sr., 455; John Wendell Jr., 455; Johnny, 455; Kathryn May, 455

Burney: Bobby Shearil, 380; Farris Weldon, 460; Jim, 380; Melissa Faye, 380; Michelle, 380; Rebekah Cromwell, 460; Vincent Farris, 460

Burns: Allen Wayne, 171; Ben Turner, 278; Bertha L., 333; Bertha Lee, 391; Betty, 261; Bille J., 185, 325, 482; Cecil C., 163; Charles C., 459; Chester, 171; Daniel Gregory, 459; Edna Joe, 171; Francis Elizabeth, 278; George Luther, 241; Geraldine, 171, 317; Helen, 171; James Billy, 171; John Clark, 459; Joyce Sue, 171; June, 529; Lester, 171; Lillie Clara, 229; Louisa Dock (Loudocky), 52, 108; Marvin A., 185; Mary, 171; Mary Marie, 163; Melvin James, 353; Nannie, 142; Pamela Rachel, 459; Peggy Lou, 171; Rodney Perry, 171; Sarah Ann, 241, 442; Tommy Gelitha Jr., 171; Tommy Gelitha Sr., 171; Vester, 171

Burson: Christopher Evan, 300, 463; Francis Paul, 300, 463; Gloria Jean, 158, 300; Hubert Jeffrey Jr., 158, 300; Hubert Jeffrey Sr., 158; Jefferson Dean, 300, 463; Linda Kay, 158, 300; Roslyn Darleen, 158, 300

Burton: Archie Pride, 308; Charles Phillip, 482; James Smith, 308; Kimberly Elizabeth, 308; Kyle David, 482; Leonard, 400; Mary Janice, 400; Michael Alexander, 482; Oscar, 482

Busby: Delbert Lee, 422; Donald Ray, 422; Hubert Lee, 422; Lesa Michelle, 422; Raymond George, 422; Sara Louise, 422

Bush: Frances (Lucy Ann), 15

Butler: Annie Laura, 79; Bob, 79; Carol, 450; Cody, 442; Debbie Lee, 279; Elvin, 279; Emma Elizabeth, 212; Gerald Thomas (Tommy), 441, 534; Glenda Faye, 451; Helen Josphine, 181; Irene, 395; Jean Thompson, 356; Jesse, 181; Joye Darlene, 397; Nicole, 441, 529, 534; Robert Wesley, 356; Ruth, 257; Thomas M., 397; Wanda June, 420; William Gilbert, 356

Buttram: August Daniel, 327; Carter McDaniel, 327; Lindsey Katherine, 327, 478; Marvin McDaniel, 327

Buttrum: Cynthia (Cindy) Elizabeth, 374; Shelia, 449; Wilburn D., 374

Byard: Annie Mae, 73

Byars: Kenny, 386

Byrd: Annie Della, 218; Carl, 218; Jimmy Dale, 513; Marlene, 377; Mary M., 479; Michael Dale, 513; Tiffany Lashea, 513

Bysom: W. N., 98

C

Caddell: Marion C., 397; Toni Marie, 397

Cagle: Adrienne Linn, 456; Beatrice E., 66, 143; Brieanna Pollman, 456; David Leon, 144; Delora Jean, 144, 287; Denise Lynn, 144, 287; Evelyn Clara, 66, 143; Fayna (Faye), 66, 144; Francis Jeanette, 66, 144; Gwendolyn, 212, 368; Harold Ray, 144, 286; Harry, 212; Heather Ann, 286; Jewell Melinda, 211; Kierstyn Sarah, 456; Leisa Joann, 285, 456; Lindon Loyd, 143, 285; Lloyd Brooke, 66, 143; Martin Leonard, 212; Martin Luther, 211, 212; Mary Diane, 144, 286; Melissa Rene, 144, 287, 400; Robbie Linn, 285, 456; Teresa Yvonne, 144, 286; William Edward Jr., 66, 144, 400; William Edward Sr., 66

Cain: Chase Garrison, 320; Jim, 320; Mildred, 328

Caldwell: Doris Wanee, 204

Calhoun: Richey, 530; Tolby, 530

Call: Bessie Virgil, 60, 128; Bobby, 128; Clara Dean, 60; Connie Lynn, 129, 261; Daisy Ruth, 60, 129; Dana, 261; David Lee, 129, 261; Dennis Howard, 129, 261; Doris Ann, 128; Dorothy Louise, 60, 129; Ervin Howard, 60, 129; Floyd William, 60, 128; George William, 129; Greta, 129, 262; Heather Michelle, 262, 434; Ida Mae, 60, 128; Laura, 261, 434; Linda, 129, 261; Lisa, 261; Megan, 262; Robert T., 60; Robert Turner, 60, 128; Roy Lee, 60, 129; Solomon L., 60

Callahan: Joseph, 86; Mary Jane, 329; Robert, 329; W. L., 59

Calvert: Amy Camille, 426

Cambel: Gene, 187

Camfield: Kieron Wallace, 505; Moria Kathleen, 505

Campbell: Alice, 263; Cathy Marlene, 316, 472; Cheryl Renee, 316, 472; Eric Scott, 472; Francis Lynn, 375; J. Wesley, 142; Jason, 498; Mary Blanche, 142; Mary Jo, 354; Michael, 498; Patricia Ann, 483; Robert, 498; Robert Lee, 316; Ruth, 134; Sharon Lee, 316, 472; Stephanie, 498

Canerday: Dorothy, 484; Frances, 419

Canerdy: Arthur Lee, 293; Hilda Sue, 293

Cannon: Hewitt, 219; James B. Sr., 296; Robert Scott, 296; Sean Thomas, 296; William P., 219

Cantrell: Kenneth Ray, 287

Caperton: Fannie Florence, 128

Capley: Judy, 503

Capooth: Paul Albert, 316; Roger Dale, 316, 472

Carbine: Elizabeth Ann, 428; Eugene R., 428; James Ronald, 428; Kristan Renee, 428

Carden: Marion Monroe Jr., 207; Marion Monroe Sr., 207

Carder: Lillie Mae, 233

Carles: Ruth Ann, 160, 530

Carmack: Danny, 510; Lee, 510; Michael, 510; Wanda, 432

Carneg: Jo, 281

Carpenter: Andrew Elliot, 366, 497; Anna Noelle, 366; Cecil W., 253; Eva Dell, 161; George Elliot, 366; Juanita Ray (Nita), 253; Madge, 155; Oscar, 366

Carr: Andrew J., 57, 123; Douglas, 123; Doyle, 123; Edith, 123; Edward, 123; Glenn, 123; Griffin, 124; Griffith Putman, 57, 123; Hazel, 123; Iva Lee, 124; James, 123; Joseph Price Sr., 26, 30, 49, 57; Lee Shelton, 57, 123; Mamie Etta, 57, 124; Martha (Mattie) Jane, 26; Mary (Mollie) Elizabeth, 49; Meryl, 123; Minnie Ada, 57, 124; Noah Edgar, 57, 123; Odessia, 124; Ruby, 123; Ruby Whiton, 57; Sarah Lavinia (Vina), 30; Thelma, 124; William Turner, 57; Zelma, 124

Carrier: Hazel, 362

Carrigan: Ryan Paul, 504; Warren Thomas, 504; Warren Thomas Jr., 504; Warren Thomas Sr., 504

Carroll: Cornelius, 68; Dallas Freeman Jr., 301; Essie Mae, 384; James Thomas, 126; Jessie Augusta, 261; Kathy Lou, 258, 358; Mack, 174; Martha, 267; Mary Frances,

126; Melanie, 252; Moody, 67; Myra Catherine, 154; Orlen William, 252; Reeder Edward, 154; Stephanie Darcin, 439

Carson: Atheleen, 104; Columbus Ciscoe, 231; Danny Eugene, 231, 392; Danny Lee, 392; James David, 392; James Elmer, 231, 392; Owen, 104; Patsy Willodean, 231, 392; Randy Lee, 231

Carter: Alvin Grady, 248; Audean, 367; Dorothy Evelyn, 181; Edward Lacy, 181; Eric, 513; Floyd Kenneth (Kenny), 437; Gertrude, 179; Glenn, 308; James Henry Jr., 366; Jo Ann, 308; Jordan Marie, 437, 528; Joshua, 460; Kenneth Benjamin (Ben), 437; Marissa Marie, 528; Mary Elizabeth (Liz), 248; Mike, 460; Milton, 76; Norma Jean, 379, 508; Oliver Dewey, 379; Oscar W., 179; Rebecca LeAnn, 460; Robert Franklin, 81; Shirley Ann, 379, 507; Stephen (Chipper) L., 81; Sue, 379, 508; Virgil Ellis, 81; Vivian, 291

Carver: Roger Lynn, 472; Rusty Lynn, 472

Casey: Kelly, 493

Cash: Martha Jo, 259; Merrill Herschel, 259

Cassady: David, 359

Cassel: Angelia Leigh, 447; Buford Wayne, 447; Lonnie Eugene, 447; Ronda Kay, 447, 529

Casteel: Wanda Ann, 328

Castillo: Nubia, 528

Castleman: Vickie Kay, 424

Cathcart: Florence Alice, 208

Cayson: Bonnie Faye, 375

Cecil: Ollie, 142

Chambers: Annie Ruth, 388; Bessie, 280; Brenda Lee, 309, 466; Burton, 97; Burton Elias, 96; Cindy Gail, 309, 466; Donna Marie, 309, 466; Dorothy Marie, 349; Doyle Augustus, 309; Erica Michelle, 466; George, 309; Herbert Russell, 197; Hubert, 97; Mary, 96; Mary Geneva, 162; Melisa Kaye, 309, 466; Milford Faxon, 97, 197; Milford Harley, 197; Princess Inez, 97, 197; Rhonda Lynn, 309, 466; Richard Doyle, 309, 466; Samuel Elias, 97; Sheila Dianne, 309, 466; Thelma, 380; Woodrow, 97, 197

Chamers: Mary Denise, 273

Champaign: Eddie, 305; Macon, 305; Peri Leigh, 305

Champion: Candy, 170

Chandler: Carl Edward, 341; Deborah Jean, 253; Gregory Wayne, 495; James E., 253; Jeffery Craig, 495; Jerry Wayne, 364, 495; Joe James, 364; Jonathan David, 341; Teresa Kaye, 364, 495; Thomas Clifton, 364

Chaney: Mary Jane (Mollie), 28; Rosalie, 402

Chapman: Barbara Michelle, 357; Francis Jean, 357; Jason Carl, 357

Chappell: Howard, 434; Howard Stuart, 434

Charles: Dale Shipman, 347

Chastagner: Edward, 160

Cheatom: Kelly Lynn, 512

Cheek: Ida Dell, 370; Nettie Eliza, 211

Cherry: Carolyn Ann, 195; Haili, 195; James Edward, 195; James Steven, 195; Mary Katheryn, 342

Chesnutt: Johnny Bruce, 221, 378

Chickasaw: Charlotte Smith (Chealty), 19

Childers: Patsy Lynn, 507

Childress: Charlie Adron, 257; Christopher Douglas, 257, 430; Cynthia Dawn, 257, 430; Douglas Raymond, 257; Evelyn, 303; Laura Lee, 257, 430

Childs: Allison Brooke, 419; Rex Hayden Jr., 419; Rex Hayden Sr., 419

Choate: Beverly, 294; Tammy Melissa, 448

Chowning: Arthur E., 185; Bobbie Dean, 185, 331; John Coleman, 449; Kelvin Arthur, 449; Robert Monroe, 185; Willie Mae, 201

Christoff: Joan Louise, 256

Christopher: Tara Nico, 481

Cira: Brian Robert, 367, 499; Dana Michelle, 367, 499; Deborah Ann, 367; Robert James, 367; Timothy James, 367, 499

Clanton: Clyde, 101; Delora May, 101, 203; Eli, 101; Ida Malissie Eveline, 28; James R., 28; Martha Jane, 84; Murrell Wilson, 101, 203; William Carl, 101, 203

Clark: Ashley Michele, 359; Cecil Lamar, 337; Deborah Lynn, 341; Etta, 252; Kenneth, 359; Lynnie Mae, 223; Ruth, 117; Sybil Ann, 337

Claudo: Gabiel, 195

Clay: Dorothy, 466

Clayton: George, 499; Jennifer Morgan, 499; Jessica Leigh, 499; Kim, 499

Clement: Dan, 275

Clemmons: Ann, 135; Brenda, 525; Clyde, 135; E. J., 440; Gary E., 521; Georgia, 369; Georgie, 295; Goldie, 309; Jennifer, 521, 535; Larry, 321; Norma Marvell, 426; Olive Kathleen, 293; Tiffany Nichole, 519

Clemons: Ben C., 365; Benny, 484; Billy Gene, 440; Billy Kevin, 440; Bobby Gerald, 365; Boyce, 404; Carroll Eugene I, 241, 335, 404; Charles Thomas, 229, 247; Christy Dawn, 440, 529; Christy Lynn, 404, 519; Derrick Heath, 335; Dusty Wayne, 404; Eddie Wayne (Pete), 484; Francis Cordelia, 229; Gwin Ann, 465; Helen, 143; James Thomas, 143, 172; Jerod, 481; Kimberly Dawn, 404; Linda Mae, 413; Lonzie Clifford, 247; Marcella, 451; Margaret Sue, 501; Mickey Lewis, 404; Natasha Beth, 335; Patsy Joyce, 241; Robert P. III, 371; Ronnie, 335; Ruth, 391; Ryan Keith, 335, 481; Sandra Gail, 371; Sawyer, 481; Shannon Boyce, 404; Stella Ann, 390; Tammy Lynn, 404, 519; Virgie Elizabeth, 172

Clever: Jean, 390

Clifton: Kathleen, 360

Clonts: Linda Maureen, 184

Cloud: Allen, 208; Melba Glenda, 208

Clowdus: Diane Marie, 392; William L., 392

Clyne: Bill, 290

Coan: Joseph Adam, 472

Coates: Mary Ellen, 211

Coats: Barbara Joyce, 295; Betty, 466; Janet Lynn, 403; Willie O., 295

Cobb: Ada, 143; Aubrey Ray, 145; Donnie Ray, 145; Emmy Luetellace (Lou), 113, 231; Estelle Willis, 188; George Elmer, 113; Herman R., 207; Julia Loretta, 113, 231; Linda Kay, 261; Minnie Viola, 309; Richard Lewis, 207, 359; Richard S., 113; Robert Harold, 207; Stacie, 430; Terry, 447; Villace Lorene, 113, 231; Willis E., 145

Coburn: David Maury, 425; Patricia Ann, 499

Cochran: Brenda, 411; Charles Blake, 325; Clarence U., 337; Larry Charles, 325; Shirly Ann, 426; Tonya Shae, 337, 482

Cockrell: Mollie, 211

Cody: Sarah, 385

Coffman: Allison Marie, 527; Brian Scott, 527; Taylor Marie, 527

Cofield: Beth May, 169, 314; Billy Clay, 168; Crystal Alese, 169, 314; Lee Ann, 169, 314

Coggins: Rosella, 386
Coker: Paul F., 358
Colburn: Beatrice, 227
Cole: Aaron, 234; Billy Ray, 180, 428; Clifton L., 319; Connie
    Sue, 319; Danny Joe, 180, 326; Ethel, 252; Lori Beth,
    428; Matthew Kyle, 326; Onis M., 259; Owen, 180;
    Samuel Gage, 326; Willa Zoo, 259
Coleman: Aden J., 346; Annette, 230; Betty, 147; Brett
    Franklin, 436; Ethridge, 230; Gail, 147; Jennifer Dawn,
    436, 527; Jessie, 508; Jewel A., 287; Lawanna Lee, 346;
    Linda, 147; Lottie, 70; Michael, 147; Rachel Ann, 147;
    Rand Dwayne, 393; Ricky, 147; Thomas Alton, 147; Tyler
    Dwayne, 393; Wade, 147; William (Bill) Denny, 436;
    William (Billy), 147
Collie: Maxine Flora, 70; Walter J., 70
Collier: Kernest, 173
Collin: Andrea Lee, 257, 430; Betsy Lynn, 257; George A.
    Jr., 257
Collins: Amanda Michelle, 468; Amber Faith, 485; Ashley
    Nicole, 485; Bernie James, 302, 339; Calvin L., 468;
    David Maurice, 339, 485; Edwin, 237; Elton Dewitt, 237;
    Halley, 485; Jospeh Allen, 485; Keith Alan, 339, 485;
    Kiesha Marie, 485; Kristina Michelle, 237; Lois, 130;
    Margaret, 262; Martha, 389; Michael Leonard, 468;
    Michelle Anne, 302, 339, 485; Nathan Tyler, 485;
    Richard Lee, 339, 485; Shaylene Brooke, 519; Terry, 406;
    Timmy, 519
Collum; David Leon, 202; Cleburn, 202; Sherry Venetia,
    202; Cynthia (Cindy) Lynn, 202; Beatrice, 285; Sherry
    Venetia, 356; Cynthia (Cindy) Lynn, 356
Conaway: Harrell, 362; Joey, 362; Monica, 362, 493
Condrey: Charles Thomas Jr., 489; Charles Thomas Sr., 489;
    Clifford D., 420; Jerry Cliff, 420
Conn: Rose Mary, 440
Conner: Alan Martin, 484; Alisha Shay, 349; April Dawn,
    426; Billy, 484; Curtis Michael, 426; Steven Eldon, 349
Conway: Evelyn, 484; Ronald, 150
Cook: George Seaton, 428; Jimmy Linman, 428; Katherine,
    223; Lenora, 296; Ronald Lee, 267; Susan Lucille, 451;
    Willie L., 267
Cooksey: Joe, 317; Joseph Christopher, 317; Seth Michael,
    317; Shannon Renee, 317
Cooper: Claire Katherine, 445; Emma Elizabeth, 445; James
    Maxwell, 135; James Steven (Steve), 135, 272; Joe, 135;
    Joe Benny, 135, 271; Joshua Steven, 272, 445; Leatrice,
    457; Lois Ardene, 338; Lois Caroline, 448; Mackenlee
    Rian, 445; Michael Joe, 272, 445; Ola Mae, 374; Rusty
    Hudson, 445; Terri Kay, 271, 445; Zachary Ryan, 272,
    445
Copeland: Betty, 142; Brenda Kaye, 411; Francis, 246;
    Mary Ann, 416
Copos: Mary, 181
Corell: Elizabeth Jean, 272
Corlew: Jesse Anna Catherine, 302; John Jesse III, 302
Cornelius: Ross Jr., 352
Cortes: Victor Pena, 285
Corum: Betty Stevenson, 511
Cossey: Cassandra Lynn, 471; Cathy, 267; David Leon, 316;
    Deborah (Debbie) Faye, 316, 471; Dennis Ray, 316, 471;
    Donna Kay, 316, 471; George Lewis, 316; James Braden,
    471; James Daniel (Danny), 316, 471; James Edward,
    316; Lisa Danielle, 471; Patsy Marlene, 419
Costello: Millicent, 299
Costner: Alfred Eugene, 139

Cothurm: Phyllis, 469
Cottle: Willie Mae, 80
Cottrell: Da Ron, 302
Couch: Anthony Mark, 530; Betty Murl, 516; Lindsey
    Ryann, 530; William Mark, 530
Counts: Bessie, 102; Madge, 102
Covington: Cory Phillip, 534; Elgena, 345; Hadlee Rayanne,
    534; Phillip Oneal, 534
Cowan: Mary, 208
Cowaski: Cherise, 262; David, 262; Joseph, 262; Paul, 262
Cox: Andre Douglas, 261, 434; Andrew, 434; Angelia Lee,
    433, 525; Bethany Renea, 326; Bryant, 433; Charla
    Marie, 433, 525; Charles, 261; Diane, 261; Elbert Turner
    Jr., 260, 433; Elbert Turner Sr., 128, 260; Francis, 384;
    Francis Louise, 183; Frank Lee, 260, 433; Glenda
    Carolyn, 261, 434; Howard, 284; James (Jimmy), 261;
    Jimmie L., 485; Joe, 249; John, 261; Joyce Ann (Joe Ann),
    236; Julia Emma, 209; Key, 128; Lee Douglas, 128, 261;
    Lee Riley, 128; Lola Elizabeth, 75; Mageline, 237, 238,
    324; Martha Ann, 260; Mary Joe, 261; Maxine, 274; Otis
    Lee, 183; Price, 236; Ruth Ann, 433; Sandra Marie, 485;
    Thomas Wayne, 260, 434
Craft: Glenda Maxine, 308; Leo M., 308
Craig: Nicole Lynn, 401; Thomas Bartley, 401
Crandell: John Samuel, 505; Truman K., 505
Crapo: Robert Lee, 527; Tyler Austin, 527
Creasy: Annie Ruth, 270; Daniel A., 393; Donna Marie, 393;
    Jacob Alexander, 488; James Austin, 488; James Lynn,
    488; Jared Alexander, 488; Jennifer Faun, 528
Creekmore: Geneva Faye, 465
Creel: Donna Marie, 450
Creighton: Alex Logan, 481; Eric Allen, 481
Crespo: Ramon Vazquez, 424
Crews: Adam Ray, 506; Hannah Kelly, 506; Hunter Gray,
    506; Joe Marcus, 328; Joe Rex, 328; Ray, 506
Crider: Annie Viola, 54, 117; Austin Dakota, 410; Bertha
    Mae, 53, 116; Betty Ann, 116, 239; Catherine Lorene,
    115, 238; Donald Fay, 117, 241; Donald Wayne, 410,
    522; Dorothy, 117; Ed Louie, 144; Edgar Louis (Ed), 53,
    116; Edith Louise, 54, 117; Edward Joyce (E. J.), 117,
    241, 442; Etta Mae, 115, 238; Fannie Elizabeth (Sister),
    53, 116; George Washington, 53, 109; Ima Jean, 115,
    238; Infant Son, 117; James Albert, 54, 117; James
    Owen, 117; John Richard, 53, 116; Lois, 117, 241; Lula
    Pearl, 109; Margaret Alice (Maggie), 219; Marsha
    Leeann, 241, 410, 442; Marvin Turner, 53, 115; Mary
    Etta (Virgie), 53, 116; Megan Brooke, 410; Michael
    James, 241, 410; Patricia, 117; Paul Evertt, 115, 238;
    Peggy, 117, 241; Ricky Donald, 241, 410; Ruth C., 115,
    238; Samantha Faith, 410; Tony Lee, 241, 410; Tonya
    Renea, 241, 410; Vickie Lynn, 241, 410; William
    Jefferson (Jeff), 53; Zackery Taylor, 410
Crittenden: Betty J., 253; Clarence C., 386; Ida V., 38; John
    Wesley, 38; Karen Brooke, 386; Katie Beth, 386; Thomas
    Randall, 386; Thomas Wade, 386
Crockett: Laverne, 45; William Mullins, 44
Croley: Patsy Annette, 391
Cromwell: Charles Leon Jr., 460; Charles Leon Sr., 460;
    Cindy Renee, 390; Daniel Joseph, 460; Danny Allen, 505;
    Danny Wayne, 505; Elizabeth, 81; Jackson Paul, 505;
    Judy, 390; Lana Elizabeth, 505; Randall Lee, 507; Robert
    W., 355, 390; Terry Leroy, 507; Terry Randall, 507;
    Tracey Ann, 355
Cronk: Margaret Louise, 125

Crosslin: Billy Joe, 387; Cammie Jo, 387, 514; Carl L., 508; Donna Audrey, 508; Freda Karen, 387; Jack J., 392; James Leon, 246; Joan Rae, 246; Joe, 387; Waylon Jackson, 392

Crossno: Kimberly Kaylee, 353; Melanie Erin, 353; Rachel Amanda, 353; Thomas Dewey, 353

Crosswhite: Bobby Glen, 368; Debra Gail, 413; Francis, 129; James Fox, 368; Keith Glenn, 368, 500; Kelli Cheree, 368, 501; Ruby, 146

Crotts: Juanita, 493

Crowden: Gary William, 279; Mark Anthony, 279; Sara Margaret, 279; Tara Michelle, 279

Crowder: Dorothy Lee, 200; Howard Lemay, 200

Crowell: Betty Jo, 446; C. A., 100; Edward, 168; Jason Lee, 313; Jean C., 500; Jerry Trapp III, 313; Jerry Trapp Jr., 168, 313; Jerry Trapp Sr., 168; Marilyn Leigh, 168, 314; Mary Pauline, 183

Croy: Marvin Andrew Jr., 343; Marvin Andrew Sr., 343; William T., 343

Crum: William, 1

Crumley: Dona Jane, 150

Crunk: Amanda (Mandy) Lee, 353; Cecil Gerald Jr., 353; Cecil Gerald Sr., 353

Cruthis: David Lee, 423

Cuellar: Beth Ann, 474; Christopher Allan, 474

Culp: Ashley, 438; Carey, 438, 528; Denise, 438, 528; Frederick, 438; Whitney, 438; Zachary, 528

Culver: Brandon C., 480; Brandon Christopher, 480; Isabell (Belle), 19; Rebecca, 480; Robin, 480

Cummings: April Marie, 389; Bethany Grace, 389; Betty Carolyn, 229, 389; David, 112; Debra Mae, 229, 388; Elmer J., 112; Gary Dale, 229, 389; Gregory Lynn, 229, 389; Harold Lee, 229, 388; Joyce Dianne, 229, 388; Lucian (Jay) Jones II, 229; Lucian Jones (Jay) I, 112, 229; Margie, 306; Mary Frances, 112, 229; Patsy Correan, 229, 388; Paul Lee, 112, 229; Susan Cheri, 229, 388; Sybil, 337; Tammy Leigh, 388, 515; Thomas Arthur, 160

Curtis: Dimple Laverne, 155

Cypert: Jody Aaron, 201, 355; John Thomas, 201; Richard Wayne, 201

D

Dabbs: Andrea Gayle, 357; Codie Jared, 520; Damon Wayne, 357; Donavan Zane, 520; Dustin Zane, 520; Gaylen Wayne, 357; JulieAna Paige, 520

Dacus: Lela Mae, 358

Dail: Denise Danielle, 360, 492; Wilford Sylvester Jr., 360

Dailey: A. J. (Will) Sr., 94, 132; Ashley Renee, 443; Jeffery Lynn Jr., 443; Jeffery Lynn Sr., 269, 443; Jennifer Lynn, 443; Jerry Lynn, 133; Josephine Oneada, 132, 269; Kimberly Diane, 269, 443; Margaret Louise, 133, 269; Mary Ann, 133; William (Doc) Turner Sr., 94, 132, 191; William Turner Jr., 133, 269

Dale: Michael, 531

Dallas: Ruby, 288

Damaan: Ed A., 184

Daniel: Charles A., 355; Daphne Mirl, 232; Ester Marie, 143; Gregory Eugene, 501; Horace Olen, 501; James Christopher, 355; James William Jr., 485; John, 112; Kaden Gregory, 501; Kylan Glenn, 501; Modie Bentley, 143; Mykell Tatiana, 501

Daniels: Amy Joyce, 237; Bobby Louis, 237, 401; Clay Louis, 237; David, 324; Derek Robert, 324, 477; Felicia Dawn, 238, 403, 413; Ginger Leigh, 238, 402; Heather Nicole, 238, 403; Joey Clay, 237; Joseph McKinley, 238, 413; Julie Sue, 237, 402; Melvin Robert, 237, 238, 324; Minnie Pearl, 112, 236; Vickie Denise, 324, 477

Danley: Arthur Clyde, 328; Lisa Ann, 328; Mary Effie, 285; Thalia, 291; Zella, 259

Danner: Ella Sue, 137

Darby: Addie Lee, 152; Amanda Eloise, 385; B. L., 174; Beverly Jane, 258, 430; Charlene, 202; Elgenia, 148; Elizabeth (Betty), 241, 335, 404; George Allen, 258; Hobert, 269; Ira Joe, 269; Ivadale, 434; Jack, 269; James Bruce, 358, 491; James Thomas, 358; Joe White, 258, 358; Patsy Ann, 258, 430; Ross E., 385; Sharon, 258, 430; Steven, 530; Susan Rebecca, 358, 491; Teresa Gail, 258, 431; Thomas (Tommy) Eugene Jr., 326; Thomas Eugene Sr., 326; Thomas Riley (Ry), 326, 478; William Ethan, 491

Davenport: Bertha Rose, 443; Joyce, 346

Davey: Steven, 150

David: Carrie Elizabeth, 327; Kenneth, 327

Davidson: Charles Gary, 464

Davis: Alma Rachel, 192; Annie Lee, 126; Beverlia Mavline, 281; Bobby Gean, 516; Brian Keith, 516; Chad Dewayne, 515; Christopher Brent, 514; Cortez, 281; Daniel Murphy, 483; Dennis Eugene, 501; Devoron Kathleen, 288; Edsel C., 517; Eleanor, 329; Elizabeth Marie, 284; Erma Jane, 121, 244, 247; Ernest Harden, 501; Ernest Timothy, 514; Gerold Ray, 500; Hannah Adeline, 228, 264, 266; Hershel Price, 70; Ida, 236; Irene Francis, 213; James Tyndal (Ty) III, 295; James Tyndal Jr., 295; James Tyndal Sr., 295; John Henry, 70; Johnnie R., 332; Jonathan Loyce, 332; Joyce Elaine, 377; Judy Elaine, 467; Julia, 193; L. B., 193; Lavis Elizabeth, 55; Lloyd G., 377; Lloyd Thomas, 478; Louis L., 327; Martie, 515; Matthew, 524; Rania, 456; Richard Lee, 193; Rita Danielle, 478; Rita Faye, 327; Robert, 176, 483; Ronald Blane, 517; Roy, 142; Ruth Evelyn, 387; Samantha Gail, 500; Sara Elizabeth, 295; Sarah E., 89; Sarah Elizabeth, 483; Silvia Elizabeth, 260; Susan Marie, 193, 345; Sylvia, 337; Thomas Glenn, 478; Willie Frank, 213

Davison: Betty, 437

Dawson: Gloria Darlene, 384; Ida, 258; Shirley, 404; Willard, 384

Day: Cindy, 184; Louise Elizabeth, 452

De Lones: N. May, 261

Dean: Annie B., 289; Betty Jan, 205; Charles Mack, 173; Eliza Mae, 376; Francis, 286; Gertrude (Gertie) Odell, 263, 265; Jo Ann, 385; Thurza, 173, 182, 278; Zelda, 208

Dearen: Addie Louise, 44; Clara Edna, 43, 94; Clearmont, 45; Ed, 45; Edgar Lee, 94, 191; Era Marie, 44; Frances "Molly" Young, 44; Garland, 45; Hazel Inez, 93, 189; Hopkins Lee, 43; James Edgar, 43, 94; James Lindley (Jay), 44; Janet Leigh, 191; Jay, 45; Jeannette Rosiland, 342; Jessie Bell, 43, 93; Jim, 45; John Garland, 43; John Lemuel, 94, 190; John Lindley, 43, 45; John Michael, 190, 342; Lee, 45; Margie Etta, 43; Martha, 94, 191; Mary Gladis, 44; Mildred Pauline, 93, 189; Minnie Pearl, 43, 93; Nancy Leverne, 44; Nancy Ray, 94, 191; Pamela, 191; Robert Clearmont, 44; Ronald Gene, 191; Roy Edwin, 44; Shawn Leigh, 190, 342; Vera Mae, 93, 189; William Lee, 43, 93; William Merle, 94

Deatherage: Scott, 492

DeBoor: Breanne Justine, 356; Chelyse Danielle, 356; James, 356

Decerra: James Daniel, 438; Mary Jo, 438; Richard Jr., 438; Richard Sr., 438; Sherry Lynn, 438

Deck: Jeannie, 334

Decker: Blair, 477; Edana L., 322; James, 498; Jamie Christine, 498; Terri Ann, 438

Dees: Lodis Roosevelt, 452; Marsha Lynn, 452

Dehart: J. W., 30

Deitz: Sherrin, 459

Delano: Anita Gay, 493; Charles Austin, 493; Franklin Paul, 462; Paul Leonard, 462; Sonora Elizabeth, 462, 530

Delee: Carol, 273

Delong: Amanda, 518

DeLony: Preston, 276; Thelma Janice, 276

Delorse: Anthony, 429

Dena: Anthony, 457

DeNalla: Carnella, 329

Denardo: Emily Carroll, 257; John Dale Jr., 257; John Dale Sr., 257; Mary Rose, 257

Denman: Charles Emery (Chuck) Sr., 265

Dennis: Andrew Jackson, 94; Betty Sue, 192; Bonnie Sue, 192; Brandon, 489; Christine, 94, 192; Clarence L. V., 94, 191; Clarence W., 192; Curtis, 94, 192; Dalton L., 94, 192; Donald E., 192; Donnie L., 192; Dorothy W., 94, 193; Greg, 344; Herman, 192, 344; Hugh L., 192, 344; Jay, 209; Jerry, 192, 344; John, 94; John Albert, 94, 192; Johnnie Russel, 192, 344; Johnny A., 192; Judith Anne, 193, 345; Leigh Ann, 192, 345, 446; Mary, 192, 344; Michelle Renee, 490; Morrie Davis, 192; Ryan, 344; Sandra, 192; Sarah H., 209; Shawn, 344; Sherry, 344, 489; Shirley H., 192; Sue, 192, 344; Tina Marie, 193, 345; Troy Burlon, 94, 192; Troy Wayne, 192, 345; Wendall Dean, 192, 345

Denson: Sarah M., 32

Denton: Amanda Dawn, 448; Kevin, 480; Trevor, 480

Depoyster: Rusty, 532

Devaney: Dorothy, 416; Dorothy Betty, 402

Dewberry: Cheryl Evelyn, 212, 368; Claudeen, 212, 368; Edna Kaye, 212, 369; Homer Claude Jr., 212; Homer Claude Sr., 212; Jean Gay, 212, 368

Dewitt: Larry, 136; Vicki, 136

Diakus: Ella C., 34; Mattie, 78

Dial: Annie Fay, 232; Brenda Joyce, 344; Jana Lynn, 501; Kenneth Earl, 501; Monella Pauline, 294; Walter Yancy, 232

Dick: Denise, 321; Diana, 321; Donald, 321; Donna, 321

Dickerson: Margie Earnest, 397; Walter Alvin, 258; Walter Franklin, 258

Dickson: Lemuel Forrest, 74; Nettie Grace, 74

Diehl: Beth Rose, 495

Dill: Estelle, 261

Dillaka: David Allen, 357

Diller: Kathy, 525

Distafine: Debbie, 307

Dixon: Audrey Ruth, 142, 283; Clemeth Issac, 142; Fannie Pearl, 285; Mable, 143; Melissa Gail (Missy), 317; Myra, 292; Paula, 283, 454; Robert Dale, 142, 283; Travis Wayne, 317; Virgil Commadore, 142

Dizon: Alexander Le, 497; Andy T., 497

Dobbins: Sue, 494

Dobeck: Colleen Ann, 426

Dockey: Lewell, 368

Dodd: Allen Eugene, 412; Ann Jeanette, 161; Barbara, 508; Blanche, 373; Brandon Shane, 279; Christine (Christa) Lee, 279; Clifford, 139; Danny Rae, 139, 279; Gavin Payne, 450; Hershel H., 139; Jill Suzanne, 279; Jimmy Howard, 139, 278; Jody Lynn, 279, 450; Jonathan Craig, 412; Kacey Lashae, 412; Karen Elizabeth, 279; Kathy Lynn, 279, 450; Roger Anthony, 140, 279; Stacy Allen, 412; Stacy Michelle, 279, 450

Dollins: Sharon Kay, 357

Domonkos: Judy, 221

Donaldson: Blake, 462; Charles Ray, 519; Misty Yvonne, 519

Donaver: Annie Marie, 166

Doonley: Julia C., 319

Dorrah: Amberly Michelle, 502; James W., 502; Justin Scott, 502; Scott David, 502

Dorrough: Bonnie, 121

Doss: Ailee Belle, 526; Brian, 526; Celia Ilene, 115; Johnny Buford, 115

Dotson: Christine, 530; Patricia Ann, 188

Doty: Kathy Jo, 451

Doucette: Darin Martin, 426; Lionel Joseph, 426

Dover: Adron Pension, 56, 122; Blanche, 56; David Ray, 289; Estell, 56; Eurwin, 56; Florence, 56, 123; Gaylord, 56; Gertrude, 56, 122; Hattie, 56, 123; Jenetta, 56, 123; Josephine, 56, 122; William Edward, 56

Dow: Bobby, 506; Faith Ellisabeth, 506; Sophia Grace, 506; Stacy Ryan, 506

Dowdy: Addye Faye, 69, 151; Anna Claire, 518; Beulah Mae, 221; Blanche Lorene, 61; Charles Daniel, 318; Charlie Avery D., 29; Clarke Elise, 473; Clora Ovrille, 69, 150; Cynthia (Cindy) Lyn, 318, 473; Dorlea Francis, 151, 293; Esther L., 294; Franklin, 13; Gregory Allen, 318, 473; Hattie, 94; Homer Lee, 318; Horace Loyd, 69; Hosea (Hozie) Durille, 29, 69; Infant Daughter, 30; Infant Son, 30; James Ardis, 136; James Don, 136; James Floyd Jr., 151, 293; James Floyd Sr., 69, 151; Jamin Allen, 473; Jeffrey Wade, 318, 473; Jeremy Michael, 518; Jerry Michael (Mike), 518; Jesse A., 61; John Thomas, 29; Johnnie Charles, 30, 69; Juanita Ventelle, 69, 151; Kenneth Herschel, 151, 293; Laura Belle, 13, 30; Lee, 57; Mary, 13; Mary Alice, 28; Mary Angeline, 12; Nancy Ruth, 318, 473; Summer Brook, 473; Thomas, 12, 13; Thomas Jefferson, 13; William Alexander, 29; William Floyd, 29; Willie M., 136, 221

Downey: Bob, 370

Doyle: Madison Grace, 409; Robert, 409

Drake: Haley Lexis, 446; John Benjamin, 446; Tommy, 446

Draper: Lerlene, 372

Drew: Robert, 350

Drisdale: Emma Lile, 74; William E., 74

Droke: Lola M., 208

Drummond: Bonnie Mae, 492

Duffy: Penny Lee, 483

Dugan: Linda, 299

Dugger: Barbara Claire, 205; Gordon F., 205, 358; Jeanette Marion, 205; Margaret, 205, 358; Mary Sue, 358, 491; Thomas J., 205

Duke: Lisa, 324

Dumas: Jesse Aubrey, 208; Joyce, 208

Duncan: Amanda, 250; Amber Lynn Turner, 477; Donna, 250; Evie, 82; Joe Dayton, 477; Richard L., 457; Tyron Wayne, 457

Dunmire: W. L., 99

Dunn: Creda Ann, 181; David Emerson Jr., 372; David Emerson Sr., 372; Emerson, 372; Horace Clinton, 181

Dunnavant: Jeffrey Neil, 462; Ronald Glenn, 462

Dupree: Cynthia Jean, 252; Raleigh T., 252

Durham: Albert Morron, 361; Betty, 361; James, 361; Leonard E., 361, 492; Lillian, 123

Dye: Anthony, 480; Clarissa Joyce, 480; Jessica, 480; Robert, 480

Dyer: Jason, 506, 507; Lily, 506; Maggie, 507

E

Eads: Chester, 203

Eady: Callie Suzanne, 365, 497; George C., 365; James Ray II, 365, 497; James Ray Sr., 365; Margaret Elizabeth, 365, 497

Eagle: Carolyn Virginia, 79, 167; Don, 79; Miriam Ann, 79, 167

Easley: Martha Ruth, 479

Eaton: Linda Kay, 403

Eaves: Dorothy, 303; Lina C., 60; Shirley, 421

Ebray: Rosa, 103

Echols: George Walter Jr., 338; George Walter Sr., 338; Georgeanna Lee, 338, 483; Johnny Neal, 338, 483; Patrick Bryan, 483; William Bryan, 338, 483

Eck: Amy Christine, 325; Christy Lynn, 325; Holly Lynn, 325, 478, 514; John David, 511; Joseph H., 325; Patrick August, 325, 514; Susan Elizabeth, 511

Eckl: Carolyn, 511

Eddy: Christopher Blake, 466; David Lee, 466; Dubert, 147; Jordan Lee, 466; Missouri Elvina, 56; Royce L., 466

Edillion: Edwin (Dr.), 355; Eric Edwin, 355

Edward: Carol Sue, 285; Lawrence Jr., 285

Edwards: Charles Glenn, 169; David, 169; Greg F., 345; Janie, 189; Reate Lynn, 169

Egyed: John Eugene, 234; Mary Elizabeth, 234

Eisman: Debbie Lee, 389; Wallace J., 389

Elder: Comadell, 308

Ellidge: Annie, 138

Elliot: Dorothy Marvell, 137; Mable, 366

Elliott: Alecia Marlene, 256; Bradley Ralph, 256; David Brian, 256; David Ralph, 125, 256; Linda May, 125, 255; Patsy Ann, 125, 255; Sammie E., 125; Thomas (Tommy) Douglas, 125, 256; Thomas Ralph Sr., 125; Wanda Louise, 125; William Allen, 205

Ellis: Judy, 506; Michael, 405; Pat, 44

Ellison: Roy Lincoln, 74; Walter James, 74

Ellithorpe: Laurel Ann, 228

Elmore: Austin, 446; Dudley Guy I, 274; Dudley Guy II, 274; Dudley Guy III, 274, 446; Hilary Lanea, 446; Mattie Mae, 60; Tina Marie, 274, 446

Elrod: Deborah A., 362, 492; Lloyd Mack Jr., 362, 492; Lloyd Mack Sr., 362; Matthew, 492; Samuel, 362

Ely: Bryan David, 512; David William, 512; Matthew Coburn, 512; Preston William, 512

Emanus: Paula, 406

Emge: Richard, 336

Emmons: Gillus, 313; Phyllis Lee, 313

Emory: Margaret, 253

Endicott: Casey, 324, 477; Jack, 324; Timothy, 324, 477

England: Kathryn Reginia, 375; Ralph, 375; Waymon, 185

Engle: Clarence A., 494; Gary Michael, 494; Jana Michelle, 494; Lora Ashley, 494; Trey Michael, 494

English: Allen E., 392; Ricky Lynn I, 392; Ricky Lynn II, 392

Ensey: Hayley K., 432; Jeffrey Lee, 432; Jeffrey Tyler, 432; Kayla M., 432; Richard L., 432

Eppes: Mary Rebecca, 327

Epps: Helen, 214

Ergle: Crodelia, 315

Ester: Doris, 334

Eubanks: George Eaton, 258; George Pearson, 258; Jennifer Dawn, 258, 430; V. L., 183; Vernon Keith, 183

Evans: Chloe Reed, 506; Dwight Lamar, 377; Herbert E., 500; Ina Mae, 138; Kristopher Dwight, 377, 506; Lily Ryan, 506; Lori Ann, 377, 506; Rayne Evans, 506; Wanda Gail, 500; Willam (Bill) Buster, 377

Everhart: Virginia Lee, 505

Ezekiel: Ashley Marie, 406; Barbara Ruth, 239, 406; Billy Gene Jr., 471; Billy Gene Sr., 316, 471; Bobby Gene, 239, 406; Christine, 239, 405; Christopher Gene, 406; Christopher Lee, 471; Christopher Paul, 238, 402; Colin Earl, 239, 405; Dorothy Ann, 239, 406; Fannie Elizabeth, 118; James, 238; James Logan, 402; Janice Aileen, 239, 405; Jeffrey Earl, 405, 520; Jerry Anthony, 239, 405; Jesse James, 118, 239, 316; Jimmie Nell, 239, 405; Justin Paul, 406; Krista Louise, 402; Linda Faye, 239, 405; Michael Anthony, 405; Paul Howard, 238; Paula Kanisha, 238; Robert James (Bob), 239; Rodney Dale, 335, 481; Roger Dale, 335; Samantha Dawn, 471, 532; William Archie, 316

Ezell: Brett, 303, 464; Brooks Emerald, 464; Elizabeth Bailey, 464; Ella Jean, 431; Herbert E., 303; Hollis Lee, 390; Keith, 303; Mike, 303; Peggy Leah, 341; Sonia Meshell, 390; Theresa, 514

F

Fabian: Cynthia L., 130, 263; Donald N., 130, 263; Joseph Jr., 130; Joseph Sr., 130; Katie, 130; Kerri, 263; Michael, 130

Fair: Gayla Sue, 287; James A., 287

Faires: Amanda Joe, 102, 104; Laura Moody, 58; Volien, 443

Fairres: J. W., 185

Falls: Arch, 103

Fanning: Erica Lynn, 450; Judy, 278; Kendall Lynn, 450; Roye Lowe, 278

Farmer: Annabelle, 198; Cheri Lynn, 359, 492; Joseph Eugene, 359; Mary E., 64; Mary Francis, 359, 492; William Eugene Jr., 359; William Eugene Sr., 359

Farris: Dorothy Dell, 182; Enlow Franklin, 182; Grady Owen, 429; Norman Owen, 429; Rachel Marie, 429; Tyler Colby, 429

Faulkner: Cecile, 293; Dewey, 191; Earsly B., 192; Jimmy Daniel, 191, 275; Lena, 194; Lou, 190; Martina Ann, 191, 275, 343; Quinnie, 195; Tamara Faye, 191, 343, 481

Faust: Bruce, 183; Tonya, 415

Featherston: William (Bill), 316

Fell: Louise, 350; Michael Allen, 479; Morgan Alexis, 479; Patricia Lea, 401

Feltner: Lucy, 432

Felts: Frank Meredith, 487; Jerry, 487; Kimberly Janine, 487

Fergerson: Phillip Travis, 312; Price T., 312; Stanley Price, 312

Fernandez: Martha, 297

Ferrell: Dorothy, 178
Fertick: Kimberly Sue, 305
Fessler: Clifford Dean, 412; Clifford E., 412; Cory Todd, 412; Eric Wade, 412; Michael Dean, 412
Fielder: Alice Leona, 72; Callie, 72, 119, 215; Charlene, 410; Frances Charlene, 412; James Boyd, 72; Martha, 180
Fields: Charles Harrison, 185; David, 185; Glenda, 281; Heather Lynn, 262; Herbert Lee Jr., 262; Herbert Lee Sr., 262; Jacob Michael, 185; Wilma M., 376
Fink: Earl L., 454; Susan Dale, 454
Finn: Pope, 206
Fishburn: Betty Jo, 512
Fisher: Emma, 340; John Anderson, 156; Louise, 156
Fiske: Gordon, 447; Jennifer, 447
Flaherty: Claudia Ann, 273; William Henry, 273
Fleming: Billie Sue, 429; Connie Lorene, 323; Patricia Gale, 343
Fletcher: Amanda Louise, 492; Kathy, 314; Robert Wayne Jr., 492
Flint: Carolyn Sue, 447
Flippo: Charles D., 230; Martha Elizabeth, 483
Floore: Claudia Ray, 330; Elizabeth Ann, 330; Kevin James, 330; Scott Thomas, 330
Floyd: Joseph L., 482; Martha Jean, 482
Foiles: Beau Bradley, 456; Brad, 456; Kayla Nicole, 456; Mackenzie Jordan, 456; Ryelee Mae Morgan, 456
Fooshie: Patricia, 451
Forbes: Allen, 532; Bruce Jr., 470, 532; Bruce Sr., 470; Sammy, 470; Timothy, 470
Ford: Kay, 374; Margaret, 22, 24; Steve, 434
Formby: Rachel Margaret, 293
Forness: Lana, 446
Forrest: Mark, 352, 490
Forst: Ella, 179
Forsythe: Annie Ruth, 278
Fortner: Joyce Marie, 410
Fosier: Sara, 491
Foster: Alvin Eli, 296; Andrew Jackson, 210; Buck Byrum, 121; Eric Jame Jr., 296; Eric Jame Sr., 296; Gladys Fay, 210; Jessie Margaret, 159; Linda Brown, 498; Nola Eugene, 121; Tabatha Jenne', 296; Ted I., 418; Terry Lee, 418
Foust: Betty Joyce, 413; Etta, 54; James, 54; Ronnie, 415; Sarah A., 45
Fowler: Ann, 412; Carlton (C. J.) Elvin Jr., 253, 427; Carlton Elvin Sr., 253; Charles Edward, 390; Cora Belle, 140; Deborah, 515; Elvin C., 253; Maude Elizabeth (Libby), 89
Fox: Benjamin Paul, 372; Cecil Alexander, 461; Christopher Alan, 215, 372; Joan Marie, 461; John Lee, 215; Matthew Thomas, 372; Mitzi Kay, 215, 372; Paul Douglas, 215
Foy: Martha, 173
Francis: Vita Mae, 239
Franks: Archie Maruiel, 344; Bennie Earshell, 403; Bennie Reed, 403; Edwin Alex, 336; Ester Anna, 332, 336; Glenn Leek, 228; Gracie, 403; Jeanette, 161; Jerry Glenn, 228, 386; Larry Roland, 228, 386; Lon, 228; Mildred Aline, 400; Mollie, 363; Robert Matthew, 405; Sherron Diane, 228, 386; Timothy Allen, 405; Vernon, 405
Freeman: Effie May, 147; Nannie Mae, 90; Sarah, 20
French: Alice Jean, 359; Annie, 122; Nicholas (Nick), 326
Friend: Aaron Joseph, 480; Angelica Beth, 480; Crystal Leann, 401; David, 480; Evan, 480; John, 480; Nolan, 480; Ronald Nelson, 401

Frye: Anna, 486; Cora, 127
Fuller: Cary C., 76; Franklin, 449; Matthew Hiram, 449; Morgan Katherine, 449
Fulmer: Carolyn Courtney, 51; Chester, 282; Essie Amanda, 68; George Washington, 68; Jeanette Maurene, 443; John Leonard, 426; Nellie, 204; Robert, 426; Sidney J., 443
Fulton: Abigail, 74; Gertrude, 143; Martha Jane, 161
Fusrno: Patti, 280
Futrell: Janice Faye, 391; Lucille, 174; Thomas L., 391; William P., 174

G

Gaddy: Arlon N., 516; Carolyn Ann, 516
Galarza: David, 424; Juan-Samuel David, 424
Galbreath: Richard, 507; Tara Shae, 507
Gallagher: Peggy, 206
Gallien: Archie Hayes, 284; Sandra Gail, 284
Galp: Claire Thompson, 451
Gamble: Katherine Mallory, 332; Kerri Beth, 332, 479; Melanie Leigh, 332, 479; Robert A., 332; Robert Holland (Jody), 332
Gambrell: Edward, 502; Susan Dean, 502
Gamell: Raymond Lewis, 159
Gammel: Luther, 88
Gammill: Bernis Carl, 103, 207; Carl C., 103; Lida Mae, 106; Ora Elizabeth, 103, 207; Robert Arthur, 103, 207
Gann: Carlas Ann, 249, 422; Dona Lynn, 249, 422; Donna Carol, 229, 389; Eathon Tyler, 423; Eddie Junior, 249, 421; Floyd, 229; Francis Louise, 249, 422; Haley Breanna, 423; James Edward, 249; Janet Lynn, 249; Jeromey Emil, 370; Judy Ann, 249, 421; Kathrin Nicole, 421; Marvin Eugene, 370; Mary Decarla, 229, 389; Melvin C., 370; Preston Wayne, 249; Roy Dee (Pete), 229; Shannon (Shane) Eugene, 370; Timothy Bret Wayne, 423; Timothy Horace, 249, 423; Tina Renea, 249, 422; Verna Lee (Jenni), 249, 422; William Blake, 423; William Horace, 249; William Paul, 249, 423
Garett: Mary Ethel, 382
Gargas: Polly Marinda, 162
Gargis: Benny Wayne, 525; Claude, 430; Elizabeth Marlene, 244; Howard Kyle, 515; James Curtis, 273; Jennifer Lynn, 430; Katlin Leanne, 515; Megan, 525; Parke, 273; Rodney Brett, 525; Samuel Jackson, 430, 525; Shelby Jackson, 430
Garner: Bobbie Sue, 504; Christopher Lee, 431; Clyde E. Sr., 431; Diane, 216, 373; James Godwin, 216; James Jackson, 216; John Richard, 431; John Richard Jr., 431; Julia, 60; Lullie, 91; Mary C., 312; Sheila Diane, 411; Thomas, 411
Garrett: Calvin, 255; Jewell Virgie, 167, 310; Katherine (Katie) Evelyn, 61; Mable, 173; Rufus J., 167; Vera, 255; William R., 167
Garrison: Betty, 181; Bobbie Louise, 282; Mary Francis, 305
Gates: Theresa Renee, 353
Gatlin: H. Edwin, 188; Martha Elizabeth, 188; Michael Lynn, 426; Verlon O., 426
Gautney: Ladonna Larraine, 426
Gay: Laura Jean, 161; Samuel Albert, 161
Gean: Amy Leigh, 290; Andrea Marie, 443; Benjamin Gloyd, 443; Bradley Alan, 443; Carrol Marion, 189; Cheryl Darline, 148, 290; Cleo, 421; Clifford Dalton, 269;

Curtis, 105; Daisy L. Sharp, 105; Danielle Elizabeth, 529; Dannie Lee, 269, 442; Dona Suzanne, 442; Donnie Lynn, 269, 442; Doris Evelyn, 189; Dustin Aaron, 486; Eddo Neal, 367; Felix M., 105; Geneva L., 340; Geneva Yvonne, 189, 339; George Wiley, 189; Henry, 145; Henry Letherd, 148, 367; James Gloyd, 269; James Lee, 442; James Rickey, 269, 442; Kelsey Leanne, 486; Kenneth Aaron, 189, 339; Kenneth Edward, 148, 290; Kimberly Dawn, 339, 486; Kisha Leane, 339, 486; Koby Henderson, 486; Larry David, 148, 290; Lillie, 145; Lurlan Leathard, 148; Mackie Alan, 269, 443; Mary Kathleen, 189, 302, 339; Michael Aaron, 339, 485; Michael Dale, 443, 529; Michael Neal, 367, 499; Mildred Loriene, 189, 338; Nena Lee, 367, 499; Pamela Sue, 421; Rachel Elizabeth, 442, 529; Raymond Dale, 269, 443; Robert Andrew, 443; Russell Thomas, 290; Sharon Elaine, 189, 197, 339; Steven Miles, 442; Susan Lorene, 339, 486; Tabitha Lynn, 443; Thomas Steven, 269, 442; Timothy Daniel, 442; Tommy, 435; Tracy Maurene, 443, 529; Tyler Ryan, 442; Violet Beatrice, 372; Virgil Henderson Jr., 189, 339; Virgil Henderson Sr., 189, 197; Wanda Gail, 148, 290; Wylie Henderson, 105

Geans: Jesse P., 14; Ruby Mae, 243, 246, 381; Susan Tabatha, 14

Geist: Juanita Faye, 100

Gentile: George Jessie, 175; Jesse, 175

Gentry: Bobby, 251; Brett, 424; Bruce, 251, 424; Julie, 251; Karen, 251, 425; Mandy, 424; Susan, 251, 424; William Sanford, 251

George: Rachel Ann, 159

German: Linda, 191

Ghrigsby: Mary Evelyn, 333

Gibbons: Betty, 491

Gibbs: Dempsy Comer, 225; Forrest B., 140; Jeffrey Brown, 140, 279; Jeffrey Todd, 280; Lindsi Nicole, 280; Mabel Elois (Lady Maude), 225; Mary Annie, 125; Sandra Dee, 140, 279; William Alton, 140

Gibson: Carla Jo, 228, 387; Delilah Charlene, 495; Dennis Lee, 374; Glenn T., 374; Kyle, 374; Lisa Gaye, 228, 387; Mae Louise, 308; Ralph, 228; Thomas J., 495; Waymon, 181

Gifford: Jacob Warren, 448; Jessie Wheeler, 448; Rodney Warren, 448

Gilbert: Ann, 14; Emily F., 4; Frederick, 4; George, 4; John A., 14; John F., 14; Lovenia, 4; Minerva, 4; Nellie Joann, 390; Robert, 4, 14; Samuel, 4; Samuel L., 4, 14; William P., 14

Gilchrist: Christopher Columbus, 269; George (Trip) III, 522; Homer Allen, 269; Jackson Austin, 522; Kenneth Lee, 401, 519; Robert Stephen, 401; Steven Ray, 401; Vernon H., 254; Vivian Marsheila (Sheila), 254

Giles: Leon Dotson, 136; Lillian Maye, 136

Gillean: Lisa, 446

Gillis: Flora, 269; Gloria Dean, 328

Gilmore: Audrey Pauline (Pat), 162; Cordis Dee, 162; Nettie, 229, 247

Gist: Ida, 258; Laura May, 36; Mary L., 494; Pearl Gladys, 129

Givens: Billy Fred, 103, 208; Bobbie Carol, 208, 360; Francis Ann, 103, 208; Franklin, 103; Geri Lisa, 208, 361; Gina Gail, 208, 360; James Walter, 162; Joni Leslie, 208, 361; Lois Marie, 208, 360; Mark Bradley, 208, 361; Mary Francis, 208, 360; Mary Virginia, 103, 207, 275; Matthew Bryant, 208; Mildred Lorene, 162; Millicent Louise, 360; Orlan Wesley, 103; Robert (Bobby) Orlon Jr., 208, 360; Robert Orlan Sr., 103, 208; Robert Orlon III, 360; Scott Patton Jr., 360; Scott Patton Sr., 208, 360; Tabatha Ann, 360; Thomas Brent, 208, 361; Thomas Edsel, 103, 208; Zachery Craig, 361

Givers: Lorene, 314

Gladney: Avie Lona, 275; Willadean Dalphine, 496

Glasgow: Tina Jo, 401

Glason: Charles Mark, 533

Glass: Charlie F., 97

Glasscock: Alice Kay, 227, 384; Brenda, 227, 384; Bryan Mitchell, 384, 513; Cheri Ann, 227, 384; Cheryl Antoinette, 227, 384; Elizabeth Anne (Libby), 227; Ethel Lucille, 111, 226; Fred Jr., 227, 384; Fred Sr., 111, 226; Harold Owen, 111, 227; Irella, 111; Irene, 111, 226; James Arnold, 111, 227; James Fletcher, 111; John Elijah, 106, 111; John Owen, 227; Krista Kathryn, 384; Leigh Marie, 384, 513; Lonie Alberta, 106, 156; Quentin, 384; Sam Harold, 227, 384; Vicki Lynn, 227, 384; Vivian Veatrice, 111, 226; William Boyce, 111, 227

Glatz: Charlie, 61

Glaysher: Phyllis, 418

Glick: Andrew M., 350

Glisson: Mickie, 206

Glock: Charles A., 384; Larraine Elizabeth, 384

Glover: Birdie, 287; Brittney Rene'e, 465; Charles Elbert, 144; Claudie Clayton, 314; Dee, 465; Sean Dee, 465; Timothy Hilton, 465

Goad: Margaret, 443; Marion, 283

Gober: Hazel Lois, 418

Godsey: Dorothy J., 183

Goff: Charles, 361; Sharon, 361

Goings: Delphea, 166

Goins: Clara Ruth, 486; Hattie, 213; Lilly, 37

Golden: Florence, 73, 158; John, 73, 158; Martha Janice, 158, 299; Myron Dennis, 158; Willis, 73, 158

Goldstein: Donald Burt III, 296; Donald Burt Jr., 296; Donald Burt Sr., 296; Julie Trey, 296

Gomes: Johannes, 495; Johannes Hendrik, 495; Nicole Renee, 495, 533; Stephen William, 495, 533

Gonzales: Virginia, 506

Gonzalez: Julio Raul, 396

Gooch: Barbara Green, 334, 480; Benji Rena, 433; Betty, 126; Bobby Elizabeth, 500; Donnie Lee, 187, 334; Erica Lynn, 335, 481, 488; Grady Benjamin Franklin, 433; Homer Clyde, 187; Ida Dean, 139; Jacob Dannon, 334; Janet Faye, 187, 334; Jennifer Sherae, 335, 481; Jerry Dewayne, 187, 334; Johnson, 21; Joshua Harnell, 334; Kathy Ann, 187, 334; Larry Robert, 187; Linda Joyce, 187, 333; Lucile Gladys, 217; Marcia Lynn, 187, 335, 488; Marsha Kay, 187, 335; Martha C., 21; Minnie Salinia, 174; Perry Randal, 187; Ralph Roland, 187, 435; Roxie Mae, 278; Sharon Jean, 187, 334, 435, 489; Sonia Michelle, 334, 480; Timmy Lee, 187, 335

Goode: Charles Daniel, 337, 483; Charles Oshell, 188; Connie Faye, 365, 497; Helen, 283; Jess N., 188; Lauren Nicole, 497; Marshall Elbert, 188, 337; McKenzie William, 497; Megan Elizabeth, 497; Michael Ray, 365, 497; Orville, 365; Phillip Glenn, 365, 497; William Ray, 365

Goodman: Clifford Lee, 96; Deaner Beatrice, 96, 195; Drew, 431; Earline Inese, 96, 196; George, 514; John H., 78; Leigh, 431; Mary Mymer, 144; Rayborn Eugene, 96;

Terry Lee, 431; Tiffany, 431; William Claude Jr., 96; William Claude Sr., 96

Goodwin: Gordon, 472; Laura Beth (Shirley), 472; Louis H., 431; Mary Jane, 451; Willie Franklin, 215

Gordon: Catelynn Elaine, 460; Charles Elliote, 460; Charles Eugene, 460; Charles Samuel, 460; John C., 493

Gordy: Carolyn, 354

Goss: Eddie F., 270; Elaine, 270

Gothard: Callie Ann, 210

Gowan: Sherry, 514

Grace: Norma Sue, 427

Graham: Barry Lynn, 531; Joshua, 531; Ruby Pearl, 203; Shirley Jeanette, 357

Grant: Michelle, 289; Mike, 289

Grantham: Lucille H., 284

Graven: Elizabeth T., 29

Graves: Beverly Elaine, 416; Elizabeth Reece, 455; Granville O., 416; Joe David, 476; L. C., 391; Lisa Reae, 391; Mary Francis, 274; Pamphelia, 46; Rhett David, 476; Rodney, 455

Gray: Ashley Renea, 402; Bonnie, 142; Charles Edwin Jr., 387, 515; Charles Edwin Sr., 387; Charles Leon, 147, 290; Christopher Matthews, 290; Donna Jean, 289, 458; Eirt Benton, 370; Eliza Jane, 59; Fletcher Leon, 370; Gilbert, 127; Glenda Kay, 433; Granville Oneal, 402; Helen Joyce, 495; Henry, 147; Hines, 147; Jeffery Oneal, 402; John Hines, 147, 289; Kay Elizabeth, 289; Kayla Falawn, 402; LaDonna Kay, 387, 515; Leslie, 171; Lillie B., 388; Lizzie, 127; Manerva E., 28; Martha, 66; Miranda, 290; Otis, 387; Reba Juanita, 368; Rebecca P., 87; Sarah, 94; Thomas L., 368; Willehmia, 328; Zackary Oneal, 402

Greacher: Todd, 463

Green: Barry, 269, 443; Bill, 193; Carol, 409; Cecil (Red), 403; Cherie, 444; Donald, 269, 444; Earl, 355; Earline, 281; Edgar M. Jr., 269; Edgar M. Sr., 269; Francis Virginia, 158; Jewell, 404; John Robert, 298; Margaret, 169; Michael, 269, 444; Paul, 321; Rachel Marie, 403; Sandra Kay, 298; Shannon, 522; Tamela, 355; Tim, 269, 444

Greene: Adell Marie, 146; Anthony Mansfield, 423; Ashley Beth, 423; Bedford Ray, 250; Billy Joe Jr., 423; Billy Joe Sr., 249, 423; Bobby Ray Jr., 423; Bobby Ray Sr., 250, 423; Breanna Nicole, 423; Clell Marker Jr., 146, 289; Clell Marker Sr., 146; David Craig I, 146, 288; David Craig II, 288; Dustin Seth, 424; Haggard Franklin, 201; Johnny Walter, 249, 423; Mandi Eilee, 288, 457; Mansell, 249, 250; Pamela Kay, 250, 424; Roger Dale, 250, 424; Salena Jewel, 423; Sherry Mae, 249, 423; Taresa Ann, 249, 423; Walter Edward, 249

Greer: Ada Tennessee, 210, 475

Gregg: Nancy Jane, 15

Gregoire: Renee L., 143; Robert, 143

Gregory: Charles Lacey, 449; Jane, 452; John Andrew, 497; John Michael, 497; John Robert, 497; Sharon Denise, 449

Gresham: Sarah Adelene, 29; Willie L., 210

Gressham: Brenda Joyce, 419; Carol, 340

Griffin: Sonya Renee, 483

Griffith: Jennifer Lynn, 161

Grigsby: Amanda Michelle, 262; Andrew Taylor, 262; Ann Elizabeth, 262; Arthur Eugene, 129; Bertha, 199; Beverly, 333; Bryan David, 262; Cheryl Ann, 200, 352; Emily Ruth, 262; Erskin, 200; Ethel Mae, 303; Gary Ellis, 200, 352; James Howard Jr., 129, 262; James Howard

Sr., 129; Jarred Paul, 352; Joshua Nathaniel, 501; Kathy Lou, 275; Lindsey Beth, 352; Mark Anthony, 368, 501; Michael Owen, 129, 262; Paul Ellis, 200; Rachel, 440; Rachel Eleanor, 333; Sara Ileen, 432; Thomas Keith, 200, 352; Tony Paul, 200, 352; Virgil, 368; William Lloyd, 275

Grimes: Brenda Mae, 180; Fletcher, 180; Myra, 455; Tom, 123

Grisham: Marie, 248; Patricia Joann, 401

Grissom: Anna Kathryn, 359; Dexter, 359; Jack Leory, 359; Jacob, 359; Mary Leigh, 359

Gross: Dempsey, 347

Grove: Kevin, 477; Paul, 477; Preston, 477

Grubbs: Barry, 181; Gertrude, 230; Nell, 161; Rhonda, 181

Guderian: Myrtle, 61

Guerra: David Paul, 457

Guimberts: Brook Laura, 445; Scott, 445

Guinn: Blanche, 207

Gullett: Betty Jean, 91; Emily M., 427; Jimmy Lloyd, 427

Gully: Geraldine, 484

Guthrie: Billie Jane, 381; Grace, 337; Harry, 381; Loretta Suzanne, 395; Nellie Nell, 426

Guy: Jennifer Marie, 520; Jeremy Lynn, 520; Tommy David Jr., 520; Tommy David Sr., 520

Guyse: Bertha, 270; Columbus, 164

H

Haase: Jeffrey Taylor, 455; Jerry, 455; Julia Alexandria, 455

Haataja: Ann Pauline, 385; Austin Matthew, 349; Doris June, 385, 401; Elmer Matt, 197, 385; Evan Drake, 349; Larry Elmer, 197; Matthew Shannon, 197, 349; Scott Franklin, 197, 349

Haddock: Anthony Franklin (Bubba), 522; Clifford David, 410; Earl, 186; Edith Ann, 186; Gertha C., 346; Gilbert Lee, 519; Jewell, 377; Jon Stacy, 346; Linda Faye, 349; Lindsey Brianne, 522; Mary, 466; Stacie Darlene, 410; Tyler Lee, 519

Hadorn: August David, 222; Edward Fred, 222; Emma Jane, 222; Frank Raymond, 222; Fred Milton, 222; Gloria Ann, 222; Grave Levie, 222; James Edward, 222; Jessie Ray, 222; William Eugene, 222

Haeger: Eric Steven, 327; Karen Ann, 181, 327; Lewis, 181; Michael Fay, 181, 327; Michael Todd, 327; Paul Jerome, 181

Hager: Andrew Lewis, 372; Andrew Terry, 372; Christopher Andrew, 372

Haggard: Frances Lovella, 288; J. W., 288

Hahn: Estella, 340

Haigler: Alvin Hayne Jr., 499; Alvin Hayne Sr., 499; Brooke Lauren, 499

Haines: Harry A., 302

Hairell: Birdia, 99; Cynthia, 108; Dorothy Maurita, 108, 217; Emmett Comer, 108; Idna Cynthia, 108, 217; William (Billy), 108

Hairrell: Retha, 99

Haithcoat: Ruby, 418

Halasi: Marcia Ellen, 395

Halcombe: Adam David, 496; Adam Reid, 494; Alicia Carol, 363, 494; Allen Jones, 209; Anthony Lee, 362, 493; Arnold, 209, 363; Arthur Thomas, 190; Barbara Faye, 190; Beverly, 486; Brian Keith, 493; Bryan Lindsey, 364, 496; Carla Diane, 363, 494; Charles Herschel, 210, 364; Chase Lindsey, 496; Daniel Alvin, 418; Daniel Eric, 418,

524; Daniel Leon, 362, 493; Daniel Peter, 496; David Lawrence, 364, 496, 502; Derrick Allen, 493; Diona Lynn, 374; Doris Geraldine, 190, 339; Doris Jean, 362, 493; Drew Terrell, 496; Dwayne Charles, 364, 496; Edith Elizabeth, 210, 364; Edwin Ray, 209, 363; Elmer Patford, 104, 209; Erlene, 209; Ernest Powers, 104, 209; Garry Phillip, 363, 494; Gary Andrew, 494; Gary Boyce, 190; Geneva Bernice, 209, 363; Geneva Gwen, 362, 494; Grady Allen, 362, 493; Hazel Juanita, 210, 363; Helen Lee, 210, 365; Hubert Lee, 104, 210; James Lee, 209, 362; Jimmy Keith, 363, 494; Jimmy Leonard, 209, 363; Joshua Lee, 493; Jsaon Todd, 374; Kyle Austin, 494; Lanier, 190; Lanier Thomas, 374; Lawrence O'steen, 210, 364, 502; Mable Inez, 210, 364; Mark Allen, 363; Mary Beth, 496, 533; Milton Sarah, 104; Nina Ruth, 209; Pamela Rose, 372; Phillip Lee, 494; Reba Nell, 210, 364; Rhonda Sue, 364, 496; Ricky Lynn, 363, 494; Robbie Louellen, 190, 340; Ruben L., 418; Shane Dale, 493; Steven Lee, 362, 493; Terrence Kyle, 496; Terry Hubert, 364, 496; Thomas Edsel, 190, 340; Timothy Wayne, 362, 493; Tracy Lyn, 363, 494; Vera May, 100; Virginia, 296; Willard Lee, 209, 362; William Clyde (Willie), 372, 374; Willie Cletus, 209, 363

Hale: Andrea, 425, 524; Angela Louise, 277; Blair, 425; Gene, 456; Gina Ann, 456; Jospeh, 277; Joyelyn Holland, 162, 305; Lue Ella, 119; Mable Chester, 148; Mason, 425; Maudie, 311; Richard Howard Jr., 332; Tim, 425; Walter W. Jr., 75; Walter William Sr., 75; William Holland, 75, 162; Windolon, 435

Hall: Alma Thora, 181; Amanda Dawn, 309; Amy Denise, 275; Andrew David, 491; Barbara Kaye, 166, 310; Barry Alan, 309, 465; Bobbie, 246, 287; Bradford Alan, 491; Bradford Stanley, 491; Capothia Lynn, 309; Carlene, 165, 309; Charles Kevin, 303; Charles Parker, 303; Charles Ray (Dr.), 303; Chessie, 252, 392; Christopher Michael, 330; Clara Mae, 166, 309; Cristy Michele, 310; Dana Maria, 275; Dana Shay, 301; Daniel W., 330; David Nelson, 183, 330; Dewey W., 491; Diane Elizabeth, 182; Dianna Michele, 310; Donna J., 182, 329; Dovie Leigh, 165, 308; Flora, 141; Floyd Edward Jr., 166, 309; Floyd Edward Sr., 78, 166; Glenda Dale, 165; Grant, 300; Houston Alfred, 78; Howard Godsey, 183; Howard Thomas, 90, 183; Hubert F., 78, 166; James David, 234; James Doyle, 234; James Franklin Jr., 90, 183; James Franklin Sr., 90; James Ray, 182, 329; Jamie DeAnna, 310; Janet Marie, 182, 330; Jennifer H., 330; Jerry Dennis, 275; Jerry Michael, 166, 310; Joane Eileen, 182; Johnny Houston, 165, 309; Josesph Michael, 182, 330; L. E., 275; Leanne Marie, 329; Leslie Ann, 308, 464; Lester Lawrence Jr., 165, 308; Lester Lawrence Sr., 78, 165; Lindsey Thomas, 183; Lura Kathleen, 183, 330; Martha Bell, 165; Maureen Louise, 182, 329; Melissa Gail, 308, 464; Michael, 478; Michelle Lee, 234, 396; Miranda Kaye, 308, 465; Monica, 301, 463; Patricia Michelle, 330; Ray Arlen, 90, 182; Robin Michele, 165, 309; Ryan Heath, 466; Sara Jane, 166, 309; Sarah, 343; Shannon, 300, 463; Sharon Kay, 234, 396; Shirley Ann, 165, 308; Stephanie Amanda, 183, 330; Stephen M., 330; Steven Douglas, 361; Tonia Dee, 309, 465; Tricia Amanda, 329; Twila Gail, 309, 465; Wayne Joseph, 166, 310; Will, 90; William (Bill) Charles, 182, 330

Hallsen: David Michael Jr., 329; David Michael Sr., 329; Erica Leigh, 329; Magnus, 329

Ham: Ila M., 504

Hamilton: Adar Mae, 308; Ashley, 300; Blake, 300; Brenda Joyce, 244; Caine, 300; Helen Frances, 190; Richard Gaylon, 300

Hamm: Debra Kay, 369; Gene, 311; Glen, 472; Jeffery Lee, 524; John Bennett, 524; Josie, 316; Martha, 147; Whitney Dawn, 472

Hammond: BryLeigh Mae, 532; Emma Faith, 532; Joshua, 532; Lois Eliese, 259; Olivia Odell, 163; Wylie Edward, 259

Hamner: Velma Elizabeth, 200

Hanback: Alma Evelene, 143; Audrey Jean, 236, 287, 406; Barbara Jean, 348; Barry Lee, 151, 294; Charles Boyce, 125, 255; Charlotte June, 385, 513; Charlotte Kay, 255, 429; Colby Ray, 523; Danny Lynn, 242, 411; David Lynn, 455; Dawanda Ann, 255, 428; Deena Lynn, 385, 401, 513; Donald Ray, 242; Doris Ann, 227, 385; Dylan Lane, 411; Heather Leigh, 455; James Stanton, 125; Jess, 236; Jessie L., 143; Joel Dennis, 227, 385, 401; John Stewart, 151, 294; Koby Ray, 411; Lee Ellis, 125; Logan Dewayne, 523; Lowell, 227; Lucille, 157; Madison, 523; Obie R., 242; Pearl, 248; Phillip Wayne, 385; Ralph D., 151; Ray Winiford, 242; Roy Lee, 151; Tammula Denise, 255; Teddy Ray, 411, 523; Teresa Gaye, 349; Thomas Lee, 242, 411; Tommy Dewayne, 411, 522; Wylie Edward, 227

Hancock: Dylan Jacob, 512; Neal, 512

Hand: Hazel Ila Lou, 190

Handback: Mollie F., 106; Samuel E., 106

Handley: Irene, 102, 206; Marion Andrew, 102; Pauline, 102; Trula, 102, 206

Hankey: Louise, 203

Hanks: Mary Louise, 158

Hannah: Laura Francis, 393; Linda Sue, 283

Hanvey: Alfred, 348; Angelia Lenae, 348

Haraway: Martha Fern, 259

Harbin: Emerald C., 393; Janet Marie, 245, 414; John Edward Jr., 245; John Edward Sr., 245; Ryan Douglas, 393; Stephen Douglas, 393

Harbour: Elizabeth W., 3

Hardaway: Jean, 303

Hardeman: Mary, 373

Hardwick: Jack Carrol, 330; James Mason, 330; James Noel, 330; Matthew McCuin, 330

Hardy: Louise, 452

Hare: Richard Bryan, 429

Hargett: Patricia Ann, 252

Hargrave: Martha Jane, 375

Hargrove: Luther H., 128

Harlan: Connie Elizabeth, 274, 489; Thomas Leon, 274

Harman: Becky, 409

Harmon: Alan Jack, 322; Andrea Kay, 322; Anne, 322; Billy Jr., 322; Billy Thomas Sr., 178, 322; Gradie Marguerite, 178, 322; Grady Evan, 322; Grady Thomas, 178; Harold Mack, 178, 322; Jimmy Donald, 178; Mary Lou Faye, 178, 322; Michelle, 322; Norma Jean, 178, 323; Odie Jack, 178, 322; Patricia, 322; Phyllis, 322; Ronald, 323; Stephen Lyle, 322; Trina, 323

Harnsbery: Julie Carrol, 393

Harper: Donna Sue, 189, 338; Harold M., 189; John Wesley, 189

Harris: Beverly Jane, 318; Donnie Paul, 360; Evelyn, 209; Hazel, 325; Mae, 93; Martha Louise, 281; Miles Orlan, 360, 492; Nadine, 310; Paul Willis, 443; Tammie Renae, 443

Harrison: Alicia Dawn, 290; Ashleigh Elizabeth, 454; Bobby Joe Jr., 391; Bobby Joe Sr., 391; Carley Marie, 454; Carmelo Keith, 479; Carolyn Sue, 289; Donald M., 290; Donna H., 70; Earl Cherry, 182; Gregory Jones, 454; Herby Giles Sr., 309; Jacey Lee, 535; Jack Denton, 505; Joey Wayne, 391, 516; Johnny, 535; Jordan Thomas, 535; Justin Wayne, 516; Leonard, 391; Margaret Lou, 309; Mary Ethel, 182, 453; Matthew Bryant, 454; Misty, 483; Reece Mills, 454; Ross, 289; Scott, 87; Susan, 330; Thomas Edward, 479; Warren Bradley, 505

Harsh: May, 202

Hart: Adrian Lee, 343, 481, 488; Brenda Marie, 439; Charles (Chuck) Elton, 251, 409; Christina Ann, 343, 481, 489; Donald Eugene, 365, 496; Halle, 489; Hannah, 251, 425; Hazel, 215; Jack Eugene, 364; James Melvin, 343; Jennifer (Jenni) Leigh, 251, 409, 425; John Howard, 251; John Leland, 215, 364; Jordan Wade, 425; Michael Ray, 496; Robert Wayne, 496; Shanna Lynn, 481; Shirley Ann, 365, 496; Steven, 508; Steven Eugene, 508; Terry Melvin, 343, 481

Hartley: Buford, 313; James Douglas, 313

Harvell: J. D., 493; Sherry, 493

Harvey: Nettie Sue, 324

Haskins: Fannie Belle, 168

Hassel: Margaret Michelle, 456; Robert, 456

Hatcher; Jimmy, 304; Troy, 304

Hatchett: Charles Keith, 410; Kendra Nichole, 410

Hatfield: Shawna Kay, 272, 445

Haverkamp: Kelly Lynn, 451; William, 451

Haverwas: Marie, 168

Hawkins: Cheyenne, 522; Corey Ryan, 409, 522; Jack, 158; John, 158; Keith, 409; Matthew Richard, 491; Melissa Lauren, 491; Patsy, 158, 299; Richard Eugene, 490; Robert (Bob) Ellie, 158; Vernon Eugene II, 490; Whitney, 409

Hawks: Rossie, 454

Hayes: Ada, 129; Anne Davis, 370; Betty Adaline, 261; Beverly J., 497; Brenda, 393; Faye, 455; Fred Joel, 270; Freddie, 162; Gary Edward, 286; Greogry Lee, 466; Herbert Calvin III, 308, 464; Herbert Calvin Jr., 308; Herbert Calvin Sr., 308; James N., 412; Jamie Edward, 286; Jason Dwayne, 466; Jennifer Yvonne, 286, 456; Jesse Raymond, 162; Joyce, 162; Lindsey Ann, 298, 462; Linnie Ann, 98; Lloyd Thomas, 286; Mae, 164; Mary Lou, 337; Mildred, 162; Robert Lee, 466; Taylor Randolph, 261; Theresa Lynn, 270; Vicki Lynn, 412; Virginia, 211; William Edgar, 466; William Lester, 211; William Neal Jr., 298; William Neal Sr., 298

Haygood: Brittany Lee, 430; Eddie, 430; Estella Mary, 226; Justin Caleb, 430; Noah E., 226; Shirley, 253

Haynes: Bobby Gene, 177; Caleb Lee, 322; Carmel Inez, 87, 177; Carol Suzanne, 177; Christopher (Criss) Columbus, 40; Clarence, 40, 87; Columbus C., 40; Donna Suzan, 373; Doyle Odell, 87, 177; Edwin Lenard, 87, 177; Gary Doyle, 177, 321; Henry Harvey, 40; James Purnell, 88, 177; Jo Ann, 261; Josie Etta, 40, 87; Joyce Ann, 177, 321; Kathy Jane, 177; Leigh Ann, 177; Leonard A., 40, 88; Linda Sue, 177, 322; Lou Tishie, 40, 88; Myrtie, 297; Nyla Jane, 345; Phyllis Kay, 177, 322; Rebecca Lee, 177; Roxie W., 40, 88; Shirley, 453; Stewart Odell, 321; Tammy, 292; Thomas Edward, 373; Weldon Lewis, 87, 177

Haywood: H. D., 258; Miley Fulton, 258

Hayworth: Judy, 398

Head: William Joseph Jr., 431

Headley: Frances, 273

Heard: Bessie Florence, 162; Ruth Evelyn, 394

Hearin: Elijah David, 301; Joseph Norman II, 159; Joseph Norman III, 159, 301; Joseph Norman IV, 301; Thomas Taylor, 301

Hearn: Cecile H., 308

Heathcoat: Teresa Diane, 443; Thomas Leroy, 443

Heatherly: Peggy Sue, 471

Heck: Edgar Phillip, 187; Eugene Philip, 187; Kenneth Rowland, 187; Leisa Carol, 187, 335; Sandra Kay, 187; Vicki Ann, 187, 335

Heid: Harry Herbert, 289; Laurel Jane, 289

Heiger: James, 507

Heimdale: Robert Jess, 207

Heird: Murphy D., 366

Hellums: Delphia Alice, 274; Ginger Elizabeth, 496; Sandra (Sandy) Darlene, 494; Sidney L., 494, 496

Helm: Brittany, 425; Lisa, 425

Helton: Anne, 237; Leonard David, 279; Patricia Lynn, 279; Phyllis Elaine, 413

Henderson: Andrew, 221; Elfie Maude, 221; Joy Lee, 143; William, 143

Hendon: Chad Wesley, 281; Douglas Wesley Jr., 281; Douglas Wesley Sr., 281; Lisa Michelle, 281, 451; Lynn, 351

Hendrix: Charlie H., 494; Mable C., 467; Rhonda, 494

Henry: Annie Roberta, 363; Eulas P., 443; Grace Lee, 433; Shelia Marie, 443

Hensley: Brittany, 418; Emmaleigh, 443; Grace, 80; Jeffrey, 443; Ralph Garland, 418; Shelby R., 418; Victoria, 443

Henson: Anthony, 505; Carolyn, 443; Evelyn, 371; Lena, 149; Linda L., 288; Nancy Jane, 69, 126; Vermillion Mercedes, 505; Walter Lee, 288

Herbert: Herbert T., 281; Jacob Andrew, 281; Kelly Lynne, 281; Steve William, 281

Herd: Donald Lawson, 443; Ernest Doyle, 443

Herlong: Loretta, 499

Hermann: Michael Clark, 503; Michael Shane, 503

Hernadez: David Alexander, 394; Prisciliano, 394

Herring: Jennifer Dawn, 348

Herron: Dorothy, 297; Mary Elizabeth (Lizzie), 116, 117, 119

Herston: Barbara, 428; Clara, 106; Marilyn, 389; Ora, 143; R. P., 106; Shirley June, 465

Hess: Dennis, 348

Hester: Leigh Ann, 294; Loretta Marie, 427; Myra E., 303

Heupel: Betty Ruth, 394; Catherine, 327

Hibbett: Lester Lee, 313; Susan Elaine, 313

Hice: Chandler Jackson, 465; Jack Gwinn Jr., 465; Jack Gwinn Sr., 465

Hickman: Beverly Jane, 141; James Ervin Jr., 141, 281; James Ervin Sr., 141; Joel Scott, 141; Martha Francis, 281; Rufus T., 141

Hicks: Dewey Lee, 274; Inez, 188; Wanda Faye, 274

Higdon: Deloris Maxine, 309; James Andrew, 309

Higginbotham: Angel, 509

Higgins: Amanda Willine, 195; Fred Rayburn Jr., 476; Fred Rayburn Sr., 476; Irene, 129; Jeremy, 476; Joe Lewis, 216; Josiah, 19; Lou Jean, 461; Martha Jane, 19; William, 195

High: Wanda Faye, 467

Highland: David, 529; Jamie Dewayne, 529; Ruby Mae, 502

Hill: Ada (Adar) Elizabeth, 54, 224, 225; Barbara, 525; Bertha, 468; Beverly Diane, 145; Billie Faye, 326; Billy

Ray, 339; Bob, 339; Bradley Christopher, 288; Charles Henry Jr., 145, 288; Charles Henry Sr., 67, 145; Christine Vernon, 243; Denise, 488; Donald J., 66, 145; Donna S., 290; Edna, 133; Ellis Franklin, 70; Elsie Marie, 67, 146; Francis, 151; Francis Ruth, 24; Gilbert Roland Jr., 465; Grant Robert, 288; Ida E., 24; Inez, 314; James, 416; James Hamilton (Punkin), 280; Jennie Hester, 127; John Arthur, 145; John Quincey, 127; Jolly, 66; Jonna Leeann, 428; Julie Elaine, 516; Kyler Blake, 484; Laura, 24; Leanna, 24, 56; Leon, 428; Leslie Shawn, 465; Lester Eugene, 516; Martha, 24; Mary Francis, 273; Mary Opel, 66, 145; Matilda, 24; Max Eugene, 416; Melvin Douglas, 145, 287; Paula Elaine, 145, 288; Peggy, 396; Polly, 24, 56; Rachel Lindsey, 288; Randal Reed, 339, 484; Raymond A., 66, 145; Rita Faye, 67, 146; Roanna Renee, 339, 484; Ronnie Ray, 339, 484; Teresa Ann, 428; Vernel Andrew, 66; Walter, 70; William (Bill), 54; William (Bill) Jefferson, 24; William Henry, 67

Hillis: Frances Christinson, 76

Hillyard: Anna Michelle, 256; Michael Loyd, 256

Hines: Freda, 255; Joe P., 258

Hinkle: Holly Elizabeth, 432; Steven James, 432; William Charles, 432; William J., 432

Hinson: Alfreada, 394

Hinton: Amber Nicole, 299; Anita Louise, 158, 299; Barnie, 32; Billy Floyd, 286; Bonnie Ethel, 32, 73; Bradley Dewayne, 286; Bradley William, 301; Britt, 159, 301; Brooks, 301; Candy Jones, 158, 300; Carley Young, 301; Charlene Vada, 396; Christy Lee, 301, 464; Christy Louise, 286, 456; Curtis Melvin Jr., 158, 299; Curtis Melvin Sr., 73, 158; Cynthia Ann, 158, 300; Denice, 511; Ethel Ivadell, 364; Floyd V., 286, 369; Francis Marie, 195; Gene Arnold, 73; Glenda Gail, 369, 399; Gloria Mae, 73, 159; Hattie, 147; James Arnold, 158, 299; Jones Carlton, 73, 158; Jones Henry, 32, 73; Krista Marie, 299, 463; Larry Carlton, 158, 299; Lawson Benjamin, 32; Lloyd Thurston Jr., 159, 301; Lloyd Thurston Sr., 73, 159; Martha Ann, 73, 159; Marvin Lindsey, 364; Michael, 300; Michele Lee, 299; Nancy Michele, 300; Norma Susan, 159, 301; Ola Roselyn, 73, 159; Pallie, 32; Pearl, 32; Richard, 301; Richard George, 159, 301; Robert Lewis, 158, 299; Rosa, 32, 73; Sarah Elizabeth, 301; Scott Ryan, 299; Vernon Juanita, 73, 158; Vernon L. B., 32, 73; Wendy Estelle, 158, 300

Hipps: Andrea Marie, 326; Billy Sr., 343; Cathy Rouna, 364, 495; Clifford Allison, 328; Debra Lynn, 180, 326; Jackie Diane, 180, 326; James David, 180; Jennifer Rose, 495; Jesse James (Jamie), 180, 326; Jessica Danielle, 326, 478; Laurie Elizabeth, 495; Lizzie, 112; Lori Darlene, 326, 478; Mary Elizabeth, 328; Michael Allison, 328; Michael Bradley, 328; Nancy Carol, 180, 326; Shelia Diane, 364, 495; Susan Michelle, 364, 495; Teresa Ann, 343; Wilford Douglas, 364, 495; William Howard, 364; William Reeder, 180, 364

Hirth: Thomas Emil, 292

Hisey: Robert Erskin, 157

Hoagland: Jennifer Gayle, 424; Royce Edward, 424

Hodges: Ballie Rhea, 451; Bessie, 255; Casey Jay, 451; Cathy Sue, 287; Chester Hall, 287; Chester Roy, 140; Glenn, 280; Gregory Wade, 280, 450; Jason Larry, 281, 451; Jody Marion, 280, 451; Johnny Dale, 141, 281; Kayla Breanne, 451; Larry Joe, 140, 280; Lila Mae, 160; Rhonda Lynn, 280, 450; Roy Wade, 140, 280; Roy

Wilson, 140; Victor Wayne, 280, 451; Walter Warren, 280

Hoernig: Burno Cornelius, 260; Marie Anne, 260

Hogan: Margaret F., 182

Hogue: James William (Bill), 490

Holcomb: Teresa, 326

Holden: Arnold G., 286; Betty Muriel, 365; Brooke Leigh Ann, 413; Dorothy Lee, 414; Doug, 321; Gaylon, 413; Jackie R., 413; Jennifer, 321; Jeremy Ross, 286; Jessica Leann, 286; Larry Dean, 286; Luther, 365; Mary Lou, 333

Holderead: Brady, 299

Holderman: Stella, 462

Holland: David Eugene, 306; Eugene E., 306; John, 33; Jonathan William, 306; Louis E., 447; Nancy (Mattie) George, 33; Sallie Ann, 447; Sarah Kathleen, 332; Toni Beth, 447, 529; Tony Gary, 447

Hollander: Ashley, 509; Callie Michelle, 377; Danny Thomas, 377; Donald Thomas, 377; Drew Nathaniel, 377, 506; Marilyn D., 450; Samantha, 510; Stanley, 509

Hollin: Martha, 115

Hollingsworth: James Anthony (Tony), 372; James R., 372; Nicholas Keith, 372

Hollins: Carol Joyce, 411

Hollman: Curry, 66; Doyle, 117; June, 117; Les, 262; Mary Ellen, 66

Holloman: Mildred, 265

Holloway: Aquilla Faye, 509; Benjamin Dakota, 439; Bessie Marie, 28; Blaze, 438; Carissa LaShae, 439; Daniel Lynn, 439; David Lee Sr., 439; Derek, 438; Francis Elizabeth, 473; Heather, 438; James (Jim) Elbert, 265, 438; James Anderson, 265; John, 28; Julia May, 265, 438; Levi Daniel, 439; Lois, 334; Margaret, 438; Mary, 438; Mary Esther, 263; Pamela, 438; Robert Daniel, 473; Roger William, 265, 438; Samantha Mahshell, 438; Sandra Rickaya, 438; Steven, 515; Tammy Jean, 509; Troy, 438; William Anderson, 263, 265

Holt: Aaron Von Brown, 34; Annie Mae, 90; Barbara, 504; Bart Kenneth, 270, 444; Basil Donald, 270; Bobbie, 135, 271; Bradly Kane, 270, 444; Brian Keith, 270, 444; Britney, 441; Bryan Lee, 406; Burt, 226; Cecilia Ann, 81; Claude Ellis, 135; Edsel, 314; Effie, 354; Enoch Arden, 337; Essie L., 511; Evelyn, 468; Francis, 531; Gene Autry, 266; Grace E., 35, 80; Granville W., 468; Harold E., 469; Heather Marie, 306; Jean, 135; Jimmy Dale, 270; Jimmy E., 306; John E., 135; John Emerald, 503; Joshua Seth, 469; Joyce, 135, 271; Judy Carolyn, 337; Kathryn, 201; Kathy, 135; Kenny, 266, 441; Keoni, 441; Lea May, 503; Leslie Paul, 314; Mable, 285; Mary Ann, 135, 271; Mary Ella, 362; Mary K. (Polly), 53, 109; Nancy, 135, 271; Odie, 268; Pamela Gaye, 468; Penny, 135, 271; Regina, 266, 441; Ronald Edwin, 469; Ronnie, 266; Stanley Keith, 306; Stephanie Diane, 406, 520; Steven Mitchell, 406; Thomas Owen, 226; Thuney Etta, 143; Wayne, 266, 440; Wesley, 406; Wesley Dale, 314; Whitney Brooke, 306; William Cecil, 35, 81; William Charles, 81, 168; William Henry, 35

Holtsford: B. M., 81; Vivian Beatrice, 81

Holyfield: Jefferson Davis, 14

Honey: Leonard, 279; Susan, 279

Hood: James Robert, 421; Jeffery Paul, 421; Linda Sue, 423; Mary, 384; Ronald Barton, 421; Ronald Edward, 421; Tara Sue, 513; Teresa, 420; Thomas Harold Jr., 513

Hooden: Dora, 40

Hoover: Ruth, 462

Hopkins: Janice Kay, 417; Kelly Renee', 475; Robert, 417, 439; Susan Renee, 439

Hopper: Joe, 30

Hopson: Isabelle, 38

Horrison: Jim, 479

Horton: C. M., 42; Devon Wayne, 405; Elizabeth, 81; Era, 252; George, 81; Ida D., 131; James Harlan, 253; James Phillip (Phil), 253; James R., 332; Jean Ann, 253, 427; Jerry Wayne, 405; Joyce, 514; Kevin Austin, 405; Nancy Ann, 332; Terry Don, 377; Timothy (Tim) Wayne, 405; Virgie, 272; Viva, 191

Hosman: Cindy Lou, 422; Sharon Delores, 421

House: Ashley Michelle, 445; Bud, 392; Grady Alexander, 432; Hailey Ann, 445; J. Matt, 55; James David, 392; Janice Melissa, 432; Kylee Brooke, 445; Michael, 445; Tyler Michael, 445

Housman: Bob, 447; Patricia H., 447

Houston: Annalee Grace, 300; Jeffrey Allen, 300; Sara Rebekah, 300

Howard: Amanda Jean, 519; Bessie Laverne, 530; Edwin Staples III, 529; Elvin, 519; Hattie A., 188; Helen, 161; Jimmy Dale I, 354; Joyce Ann, 343; Mary, 354; Pat, 290; Thomas Eroy, 161

Howell: Ann Caroline (Callie), 25; Charles E., 80; Charles Edward, 81; J. C., 67; William Phillip, 25; Winifred Louise, 80

Howington: Janet, 432

Hoyt: Ralph Donald, 487

Hubbard: Alfred Willie, 233, 394; Billy Ray, 233; Brittney Dawn, 395; Charlie, 282; Clara Evelyn, 233, 306, 394; Della, 120; Dwight Corbin, 233, 395; Elizabeth Cathryn, 395, 517; Elmer John (E. J.), 233, 394; Janette Gaye, 394, 517; Jannice Maye, 394, 517; Jeanette Faye, 394, 517; Jennifer Kaye, 394, 517; Joan Louise, 203; John Hamilton, 203; John Washington, 120, 233; Joyce Ann, 427; Letha Mae, 243; Mae Leigh, 394, 516; Malissa Jean, 395; Mary Jane, 190; Mary Ruth, 233, 395; Neal Lee, 233, 394; Rebecca Anne, 395; Ressie Lenora, 282; Sandy Alphelia, 394, 517; Sheila Ann, 233, 395; Spencer Eugene, 233, 395; Willie Marshall, 233

Hubbert: Carrie Lynn, 333; Julie Elizabeth, 473; Katy Danell, 473; Paul L., 333; Roger Dale Jr., 473; Roger Dale Sr., 473; Wesley Dale, 473

Huckaba: Carolyn, 295; Sheron Kay, 279; William B., 279; William Boyd, 295

Hudson: Carl Tom, 257; Dolly, 445; Fronia C., 81; Jerry, 282; Marjorie, 227; Sam, 227; Samuel, 81

Huffman: Edna Mae, 264

Huggins: Donald, 323; Stacie, 323; Tracie, 323; Willie, 241

Hughen: Charlotte Ann, 277; James F., 277

Hughes: Billie Sue, 289; Carrie Lavenia, 137; Christina Ann, 355; Frances, 130; Glenn, 130; Kimberly, 472; Marcus Allen, 521; Mark, 521; Mrytle Eugene, 373; Ruth Virginia, 177

Humphrey: Annah, 459; Lillie Mae, 493

Humphreys: Amy, 518

Hunt: Austin, 457; David, 150; David Lee, 457; Dorothy Jean, 235; Evia E., 467; Jonah, 457; Joyce Ann, 517; Judy, 484; Myrtle, 128; Sam Clifford Jr., 74, 160; Sam Clifford Sr., 74; Travis Lynn, 457

Hunter: Aldon Leon, 313; Andrea Lynn, 313; Brad George, 313; Gregory Scott, 313

Hurley: Charles Edward, 302; Jason Michael, 302; Laura, 276; Lillian Emeline, 390

Hurn: Brenda, 479

Huskie: John, 85

Hutto: Alan, 425; Amy Earline, 450; Bruce, 150, 293; Buryl O., 150; Chelsie, 293; Felton, 303; James W., 450; Victor Barney, 150, 293

Hutton: Emily S., 12, 57

Hyde: Alexis Marie, 531; Dorothy, 30; Edith M., 434; Kristen Leann, 531; Margaret, 346; Raymond, 531; Ricky Lorey, 531; William, 30

I

Ibry: Francis Adele, 74, 160; William Donley, 74

Imhoff: Robert E., 359

Indelicato: Anthony Paul Jr., 388; Anthony Paul Sr., 388; Michael Lee, 388; Salvador Anthony, 388

Ingram: Allison, 314; Bama Inez, 119, 298, 382; Cecil, 314; Lige, 119; Sarah, 75; Timothy Alan, 184; Wayne, 314

Inman: Blake, 267; Bobby Vaill, 530; Perry Howard II, 425; Perry Howard III, 425; Ron, 267

Irions: Bessie, 193

Irons: Bobby, 440; Dorothy Marie, 294; Edith Evelyn, 493; Imogene, 458; Lois, 130; Melissa Beth, 331, 479, 526; Pamela Gail, 440; Pauline, 162, 270; Peggy, 435; R. C., 440; Robert Lee, 140; Roberta, 140; Roland Lynn, 331, 526; Roland O., 331; Timothy Wayne, 410

Irvin: Joseph Gibson, 387; Laura Jane, 387; Randy James, 387

Isbell: Doris, 276; Earl, 85; William C., 85

Isley: William (Will), 112

Isom: Jonel, 355

Ivey: Gary Wayne, 462; Kristy Leanne, 462

J

Jackson: Arelia Jeanetta, 179; Bertha Lucille, 232, 392; Bessie, 436; Carletta, 197; Chester, 223; Connie Joyce, 471; Dorothy, 222; Dorothy Jean, 420; Early Dean, 232; Elizabeth Virginia, 224, 225; Floyd, 309; George, 222; Jason Kyle, 309; John, 218; Kimberly Dawn, 309; Lawrence, 223; Mary Alice, 167; Mildred, 223; Ralph E., 309; Robert (Boots), 258; Robert Lee Jr., 223; Robert Lee Sr., 223; Robert Ray, 257; Thomas, 223; Turner, 218; Vadean, 391; Virginia Alice, 93; William, 222; William (Billy), 223; William Jack, 223; William Stephen, 482; Zelma, 218

Jacob: Georganne Roley, 473

Jacobs: Cynthia Leigh, 429; Kimberlie, 386, 514; Leonard Fred (Bucky), 386; Thomas E., 386

James: Bessie, 371; Charles, 460; Dannyle, 315; Ester Laverne, 231; Gwendale Gail, 483; Harold Lee, 141; Hillary Taylor, 282; Jennifer Leigh, 141, 282; Jerry Glynn, 141, 282; Joey Kynn, 141, 282; Joni Lisa, 141; Linnie, 194; Mae, 168; Melanie, 460; Robert Enoch, 141; Ruby Jean, 450; Shannon Douglas, 531

Jangaard: Arnt L., 305; Kevin Warren, 305; William (Will) Hale, 305

Jaronick: Ralph, 395

Jarvis: Ivy, 55

Jaynes: Amanda Dawn, 419; Francis Lucille, 311; Otis Theo, 139; Thomas O., 419; Thomas Willard, 311; Vernon, 139

Jean: Billie, 355; Mamie, 172; Shirley, 473

Debra Leigh, 182, 328; Dee, 21; Dewey Caleb, 36, 81; Dicey, 21; Dixie, 83, 171; Dolly Katherine, 90, 181; Donald, 84, 173; Donald Edward III, 168, 314; Donald Edward Jr., 81, 168; Donald Edward Sr., 36, 81; Donald Pace, 82, 169; Doris, 36, 82; Dorothy, 83, 171; Dudley, 37; Earl, 35; Edgar Bruce, 84, 173, 182, 278; Edgar Floyd (E. F.) Jr., 37; Edgar Floyd Sr., 15, 37; Edna Juanita, 167, 311; Edward (Ed) Price, 35, 79; Effie C. M., 37, 83; Elizabeth (Lizzie), 37, 84; Ellie, 21, 34, 48; Ellis, 83; Elsie, 36, 82; Elvin, 35; Emma, 34, 78; Emmit, 79; Emory, 79; Ernest, 34, 77; Estelle, 38, 86; Ethel M., 79, 167; Etta, 37, 85; Evie Jane, 37, 82; Floyd, 79; Gentry Aaron, 167, 311; George W., 34, 77; George William, 164, 308; Georgia Mae, 84, 172; Greenberry Lee Jr., 37, 84, 107; Greenberry Lee Sr., 17, 37, 105, 107, 110; Gregory Darrell, 174; Hannah Margaret, 37, 85; Harriet Lutisha, 21, 48; Heather Leshae, 470; Hector J., 37, 83; Helen Louise, 167, 312; Henry, 21, 78; Herschel Lee, 79, 166; Homer, 84; Howard, 84; Howard Carlos, 91, 183; Howard Shannon, 42, 91; Hubert, 35; Hunter, 19, 40; Iris Gail, 91, 183; J. Lewis, 34, 78; Jack Clayton, 90, 181; James Alex, 84, 173; James Bruce, 173, 319; James Harrell, 395; James Howard, 183; James Leonard, 91; James Tyler, 473; James Wayne (Jimmy), 470; Jamie Dianna, 314; Janie Margaret, 15; Janie Marie, 166; Jason, 474; Jason Craft, 308; Jason James, 319, 475; Jeanetta, 172; Jesse Mack, 38, 87; Jewell Lee, 166; John, 21; John David, 37, 84; John H., 17, 38; John Henry, 84, 173; John L., 5, 15, 35; John Phillip II, 15, 34; John S., 8, 21; Johnathan Jr, 20, 42; Joseph A., 15, 34; Joyce, 37; Judith (Judy) Lynn, 91, 185; Judy Jane, 166, 310; Julia Suzanne, 91; Julie (Julia), 17, 38; Justin, 314; Karey, 169; Katen Lewis, 78, 165; Kathyleen, 172, 318; Kelly Leann, 470, 531; Kerom William, 37, 83, 110; Lara, 22, 48; Larry Wayne, 311, 468; Laura, 41, 90; Laurel Lee, 168, 314; Leanna, 20; Leatha, 22; Lee Willie, 34, 78; Leora, 21; Lillie Mae, 34, 78; Lilly Mae, 82, 170; Linda Sue, 91, 183; Linnie I., 83; Lizzie O., 34, 77; Loraine, 78, 165; Lorane, 83; Lou Ann, 395; Louisa F., 21, 48; Louise, 35, 79, 173, 319; Lucelle (Lucy), 34, 77; Lucille, 83, 171; Lucretia (Lula), 19, 39; Lucy Claudette, 91, 184; Lula Mae, 15, 35, 36, 82; Luther, 78; Lynwood Clyde, 172, 318; Mable, 167, 311; Mae Virginia, 91, 183; Mamie G., 77, 164; Maraday (Merry Dee), 17, 37; Margaret Marie, 167, 311; Margie L., 38, 85; Mark Howard, 91; Martha (Bettie), 17; Marvin Elmer, 77, 164; Marvin Glenn, 42, 91; Mary, 20, 84, 173; Mary (Mittie), 34; Mary (Polly), 17, 19, 40; Mary Bernease, 84, 174; Mary Elizabeth, 164, 308; Mary Ellender, 42; Mary M. (Polly II), 8, 20; Mary Nell, 90, 183; Mary Odelle, 38, 87; Mary Polly, 8; Matilda, 17, 39; Mattie Sue (Susie), 83, 133, 172; Mazie Aileen, 36, 81; Melissa, 184, 331; Michael Shannon, 183; Mildred Etoyl, 79; Millard, 37, 82; Mollie Elizabeth, 15, 35; Nancy, 20, 42; Nancy (Fannie) Paralee, 15, 33; Nancy Elizabeth, 37; Neal, 319, 474; Nellie Mauvaline, 36, 82; Nelson McCaun, 42, 90; Nora, 83; Nora Louise, 78, 165; Ola, 34; Ola Mae, 82, 171; Ollie Lou, 37; Owen Wayne, 172, 318; Patricia Ann, 173, 278, 319; Patricia Elois, 91, 184; Patsy, 172; Paul J., 79; Pauline Myran, 41, 90, 319; Pearl, 78, 166; Pearlie, 83; Pete (J. R.), 83, 172; Phillip, 5; Rachel June, 165, 308; Ralph, 172; Ralph Nolan, 84, 174; Raymond Oneal, 173, 319; Reba, 78, 166; Rebecca, 312; Rebecca Ann, 81, 168; Rhonda Denise, 420; Rian Caleb, 315; Richard G., 91, 184; Robbi Nell, 86; Robbie Lee,

164, 308; Robert, 8, 19, 83, 85; Robert Andrew, 15, 36; Robert Russell, 168, 314; Ronald Gregg, 82, 169; Ronald Joseph, 169, 315; Sabrina Renee, 468; Samuel S., 37, 83, 105, 133; Sandra Gail, 311, 468; Sara Francis, 35; Sarah, 21, 48; Sarah Georganne Elizabeth, 473; Sarah Melissa, 167, 311; Sherrie Denise, 169; Shirley Jean, 311, 467; Son, 474; Susan Denise, 311, 468; Susan Maureen, 184; Susan Renee, 167, 312; Sylvester (Sill) B., 8, 17; Tellie Dora, 15, 36; Thomas, 8, 83; Thomas Alonzo, 82, 169; Thomas Arnett, 36, 82; Thomas G., 37, 83; Timothy Allen, 312; Tina Ann, 169; Todd, 319, 474; Turner, 38, 86; Velma, 83; Viola, 38, 86; Viola Beatrice, 82, 170; Wanda Gail, 166; Wheeler, 34; William, 20, 21; William A., 35; William Brian, 182, 329; William Dennis, 184; William Richard, 91, 184; William Travis, 329; Willie C. (Will), 34, 77; Willie May, 37; Winnie E., 41, 89; Zula Mason, 38, 86

Lingofelter: Kaelei-Lynne Nicole, 527; Mark Allen, 527; Ryan Allen, 527

Linham: Clarence, 124; Clifford, 124; Earl, 124; Mamie Etta, 124; Roy, 124

Linvile: Myrtle Alice, 169

Linville: Benjamin Lee, 326; Bob Edward, 431; Brittany Noelle, 431; Cawer, 431; Dorothy, 278; Jon Michael, 431; Krysta Lynn, 326, 478; Sam M., 326; Sammy Lee, 326; Tiffany Joy, 431; Velma, 152

Lipford: Carl Gene, 243; Tamara Lynn, 243

Litrel: Joshaway Mark, 454; Tabena, 454; Tomath (Tim), 454

Little: Albert Frank, 296; Barbara Ann, 296; Cynthia Dyanne, 444; George, 497; Ivan Paige, 497

Littrell: Carol Dawn, 515; Don Douglas, 211; John Allen, 211; Lawrence Terry, 515; Mary Ann, 211, 367; Maude Ellen, 211, 367

Llewellyn: Christine, 383

Lobeck: Annie, 260

Locke: Ann, 87, 176; Will, 87

Lockwood: Elaine Louise, 505

Logan: Linda Lou, 402; Maurice Robert, 278; Naomi Sue, 278

Long: Abbie Leona, 109, 222; Barbara Jane, 223; Betty Aileen, 223; Billy, 51; Carol Francis, 489; Carrie D., 109, 222; Dee, 51; Denise, 223; Dennis, 223; Doralene, 222; Ernest Steven Jr., 223; Ernest Steven Sr., 109, 223; George, 51; Hattie Marie, 222; Homer Dee, 222; Howard Cuelell, 222; Jack Rowland, 223; James Ireis, 109, 223; John, 109, 223; Johnny E., 223; Joyce Ann, 223; Joyce Audrey, 223; Katherine Ducky, 223; Larry, 223; Lillian, 109, 222; Lillian Aileen, 222; Lilly Bruce, 51; Lilly Lee, 223; Lynda Cheryl, 360; Magie Estelle, 109, 222; Margie Grace, 109, 223; Mildred Charlotte, 469; Patricia, 223; Raymond Andrew, 331; Ronald, 223; Turner, 51; Turner Cuelell, 109, 221; Virginia, 109, 223; William Dee, 109; William Joseph Jasper, 48

Longfellow: Tracy, 379

Look: Kathy, 518

Loosier: Verrin, 482

Lopp: Alberta, 391

Lott: Carrie Heather, 497; Diedre Suzanne, 396; James, 497; Ray T., 396

Lotte: Susan Nan, 442

Love: Dale, 476

Lovelace: Barbara Jean, 98, 202; Bennett Pope, 98; Billie Faye, 98, 201; Brittany Nicole, 468; David Harland, 468;

McMillan: Walden, 149

McMullens: Nellie, 87

McMurtrey: Arthur Spencer, 310; Ralph Edward, 310; Regina Lynn, 310, 467

McNair: Bobby, 384; Dana, 384, 513; David L. Sr., 384; David Lee Jr., 384; Dawn, 384, 512; Keely Leann, 384, 512

McPeters: Doris, 383; Nancy Elizabeth (Lizzie), 29; William A., 29

McRae: Donald K., 204, 358; Gail Jeane, 358, 490; Jacob Hamilton, 490; James Robert, 358, 490; James Thomas Jr., 204, 358; James Thomas Sr., 204; James William Chance, 491; Jason Neville, 490; Marsha Laurene, 358, 490; Wallace Bruce, 204; William Merrill, 358, 491

McRight: Emily Joy, 325; Joshua Conrad, 325; Martin Glenn, 325; Tulon Conrad Jr., 325; Tulon Conrad Sr., 325

McWilliams: Jeanie Corrina, 424; Jerry Fair, 424

Meador: Barbara Ann, 262; Christopher Bryan, 357; Daphna Michelle, 204, 357; Daryl Wayne, 204, 357; Karen Durelle, 204, 357; Melissa Shawn, 357; Michael Shane, 357; Michael Van, 204; Stephanie Kay, 357; Teresa Kay, 204, 357; Van Urbin, 204

Meadows: Ida Lee, 58, 126

Medford: James Allen, 464; Jonie Leigh, 464

Medley: Katherine Fay, 349; Laura Annie, 151; Margaret, 253; Samuel, 151; Susanna, 2

Medyette: Carol Jean, 360

Meisenheimer: Harold, 259

Melton: Annabelle Jeanette, 417; Beverly Jo, 221, 378; Boyd, 311; Buford Eldred Jr., 413; Buford Eldred Sr., 235, 382, 417; James S., 311; James Wylie (Jim), 220, 221; John T., 166; Joseph Wheeler (Joe), 221; Judy Ann, 235, 408, 501; Leonard S., 364; Lloyd Hardiman, 364; Mary Lucille, 220; Nancy Lynn, 382; Susie Jane, 166; Timothy (Tim) James, 221; Vanessa Rose, 413; Viola Bruce, 108

Menges: Dorothy, 150

Merel: Bertha, 339

Merrill: Damon Ashley, 300; Daniel Burson, 300; Eddie Paul, 300

Messer: Pearl, 451

Metz: Derek Mark, 354; Eric Douglas, 354; Jeremy Tyler, 354

Metzger: Mathias Wayne, 527

Michael: Betty Sue, 394; Bobbie Sue, 259; Clint, 467; Irene, 127; John, 259; Linda Gail, 260; Maranda Kaye, 467; Mary Catherine, 316; Odis Lee, 260; Taylor N., 394; Travis Chase, 467

Michaels: Christopher, 529; Christopher Allen, 529

Michaud: Bernard Ross, 359; Marc R., 359; Marc Ross, 359

Michen: Chad Stefan, 336; Raymon, 336

Mickey: Elizabeth, 130; Frank, 130

Midday: Margie, 438

Middleton: Gerald Scott, 478

Miles: Amanda Lynn, 445; Arda Mae, 141; Arvil L., 442; Beulah Lucille, 293; Billy Ray, 135, 272; Bonnie Fay, 135, 272; Brett Allen Jr., 445; Brett Allen Sr., 272, 445; Charles Dennis, 135, 272; Charles Dewey, 135; Charlie, 135; Denise Renae, 272, 445; Hannah Elizabeth, 272; James Hershel, 387; John Dalton, 267; Joshua Aaron, 272; Judy, 267; Lucas John, 272; Mary Francis, 135, 272; Sandra Kay, 135, 272; Susan Elizabeth, 442; Willard, 185

Milford: Alberta, 85; Allie Lee, 38; Anaziah Douglas (A. D.), 38, 46; Bertha M., 120; Etta Lee, 46, 97; Etta Maggie (Etter), 216; George Eddie, 38; George W., 38; Hettie,

46, 96; James William, 84; Lannie L., 84; Mamie Lee, 113; Mason Addie, 115; Mollie L., 38, 85; Olivia Pinkney, 38; Pearlie Ann, 38, 85; Ruby P., 38, 85; Samuel Douglas, 46; Sarah (Sallie) Frances Elizabeth, 110, 116, 170; Thomas Douglas, 113, 115; Verna Pearl, 224

Miller: Dorothy Christine, 380; Henry Edward, 379; Jack, 203; Lori Elizabeth, 505; Lydia, 510; Madison, 510; Rena Mae, 422; Sam, 487; Tommy, 510; William E. Jr., 505; William E. Sr., 505

Millett: Mary Grace, 330

Milligan: Tara Elease, 420

Mills: Crystal Ann, 497; Jennifer Lindsey, 469; Jessica Courtney, 469; Joan, 144; Joe H., 144; Mildred Gaither, 182; Randiff Jerell, 316; Woodrow W. Jr., 497

Milstead: Jane, 304

Milton: Madgie D., 66

Minor: Ruby, 351

Minton: Cynthia, 25; George J., 25; Harriet, 25; John, 25; Julia, 25; Laura, 25; Laura Ann, 113, 115; Nora, 322; Rosilee, 25

Mitchell: Aaron Lee, 500; Benton Thomas, 507; Bessie A., 297; Braden Kyle, 441; Brylee Celaine, 441; Bryndall Celeste, 441; Charles Kimball, 498; Christopher Chase, 507; David Nolan, 393; David Raymond, 393; Deanna Lynn, 368, 500; Della, 256; Eddie Kyle, 367, 441, 500; Edna Eloise, 410; Edward Earl, 379; Edward Lee, 212; Everette, 377; Harris Toney III, 303; Harris Toney Jr., 303; Harris Toney Sr., 303; James David, 349; James Mason, 212; James Ralph (Buddy), 212, 367, 441; Jeffrey Terrell (Terry), 367, 500; Jessie, 180, 298; Jim, 180; Johnny, 233; Judy Belle, 304; Judy Elaine, 212, 368; Kandi, 445; Kevin Bruce, 379, 507; Kimberly (Kim), 367, 499; Larry Steven, 368, 500; Lauren Constance, 498; Lillian, 63; Linda Faye, 417, 439; Margaret Ellen, 198; Martha Lee, 212, 367; Perry, 233; Phyllis, 233; Rebecca Susan, 281; Robert D., 297; Russell Edward, 368, 500; Russell Taylor, 212, 368; Selina Gail, 349; Sherrie Alane, 368, 500; Shirley F., 233; Steven Earl, 379, 507; Thomas Larry (Tommy), 212, 368; Trista Paige, 500, 534; Valleria, 175; W. E., 233; Wilma Lee, 386; Zachary Nolan, 393

Mitchum: Barbara B., 80, 168; Bobby, 80; Bufford Lee, 35, 80; Floyd, 35, 80; Glenda, 80; Marguerite, 80; Nellie, 35, 80; Tellie Ruth, 35, 80; Tom, 35; Tommy, 80

Mock: Shelby, 419

Moffett: Glen Allen, 471; Patrick Allen, 471

Moles: Betty, 469

Momow: Mary L., 454

Monroe: Thomas Franklin, 349

Montague: Michelle, 440

Montalvo: Alejanerino, 409; Alex Daniel, 409; Stephanie Elizabeth, 409

Montel: Susan, 462

Montgomery: Aaron Conner, 440; Alice Faye, 279; Alicia Joy, 326; Alvin E., 326; Alvin Mikel, 326; Ashley Danyelle, 465; Audrey Cordelia, 152; Betty Mae, 201; Brittany Rene, 326; Buren Allen, 201; Carlton Lee, 440; Connie Darlene, 419; Daniel Alan, 465; Ella Penola, 247; Freddie C., 419; Grayford E., 465; Henry Harrison Sr., 152; Herschel Vernon, 279; Inez Isabell, 145; James Hershel, 281; Jimmy Ray, 441; John Eric, 441; Judith Diane, 281; Kathleen M., 326; Lila Virginia, 141; Linnie Mae, 162; Mary Lucille, 232; Miley Greenberry, 141; Tony Ajill, 440

Moody: Arline Lee, 186; Elizabeth Ann, 257; Ernest Jeremiah, 186; Robbie, 253

Moomaw: Carolyn, 500; Ruth, 253

Moone: Michelle, 415

Moore: Ada S., 318; Barbara Fay, 195, 343; Berlin, 195; Betty, 222; Betty Jean, 496; Bobby Ray, 279; Clura Mae, 92; Doris, 455; Elizabeth Ann, 53, 103; Ernestine, 223; George Will, 92; Helen, 223; Herbert F., 469; Jacky Wayne, 309; Jacqueline Michele, 309, 465; James C., 314; Jasper Norman, 360; Lois Juanita, 140; Maggie Marie, 403; Mary Ann, 314; Mary Belle, 363; Maxie B., 140; Patricia Ann, 434; Ralph O., 469; Rebecca Lynn, 466; Robert D., 309; Robert E., 149, 434; Tara Jacinda, 309; Teresa Ann, 279; Tommy, 222; William, 466; William Franklin, 469

Morgan: Arnold C., 286; Betty Jo, 171, 317; Charles Edward, 171, 318; Charlie Daniel, 318; Dorothy Lorraine, 171, 317; Evaline, 171, 317; Ivey, 513; James Aubry Jr., 171; James Aubry Sr., 171; James Edward, 171; Jerry Wayne, 171; Kelly Lee Ann, 318; Lillie Belle, 373; Margie, 45; Melinda Ann, 286; Peggy, 171, 317; Sam Jones, 43; Sue, 171, 317

Morris: Abby Grace, 487; Addison Jo, 534; Anna Lindsey, 331; Charles, 178; Charles F. Sr., 182; Chelsea, 529; Derrick Randy, 511; Easter, 309; Emma Cate, 487; Francis Willadean, 371; Glenda, 453; Homer, 168; James C. Sr., 69; James Walter, 371; Jean Marie, 182; Larry, 453; Lois, 396; Marshal Earl, 511; Mavis Arlene, 460; Melissa Diane, 232, 393; Nisha Desiree, 529; Norman Glenn, 487; Perry Lee (Ed), 232; Preston Dane, 529; Preston Lee, 511, 529, 534; Randy Lee, 511, 529; Robert, 178; Ronald Gene, 453; Rose Marie, 168; Roy Dean, 331; Ruth, 384; Teresa, 373; Tiffany Dawn, 511, 534

Morrison: Braden Jacob, 461; Carol Jean, 358; Cynthia Emanola, 32; Holly Lee Waldrep, 461; Joseph Jr., 461; Lucille, 79; Michael Alexander (Alex), 461; Michael Anthony, 461; Nellie Mae, 151; Rhett Gannon, 461; Virginia, 297; Zebulon Pike, 32

Morrow: Bess, 123; Carrie, 75; James Madison, 75; Vera, 377

Morse: Mollie Lugenia, 106, 111

Moryan: Leslie Ellen, 433

Moseley: Jack, 388; John David, 388; John Michael, 388; Salonia I., 226

Mosley: Sarah Frances, 261

Moss: Anthony Gwynn, 408; Dona Pearl, 186; Elsie, 373; Girl, 522; Joseph Brandon, 408, 522; Laura Caitlin, 408

Mothler: Mary, 497

Moyers: Clara, 157

Muckey: Dale D., 262; Raynea Donanne, 262

Mullen: Norma Jane, 415

Mullins: Amanda Rachael, 241; Bobby, 455; Francis, 145; Phyllis, 291; Sherry Lynn, 455; William C., 128; William Curtis (Bill), 241

Muns: Luther W., 388; Mary Jeanette, 388

Muraloski: Alexander Jospeh, 505; David Wayne, 505

Murks: Helen, 508; Ina C., 394; Katherine Gail, 465; Pearline, 309

Murphy: Alice, 25, 57; Amanda Louisa, 24, 57; Angelia Leigh, 154, 296; Aundrea Leeann, 482; Barbara Hubbard, 243; Benjamin Kyle, 337; Bill, 252; Bobbie Joan, 188, 336; Carroll, 93; Charley B., 210; Clarence, 386; Danny William, 346; Darlene, 533; Daryl Wayne, 154; David, 25, 57; Dewey Arnold, 188, 332, 336; Dorothy (Dolly) Elizabeth, 25, 27, 57; Doyal Lee, 93, 188; Elbert, 269; Eldridge (Ajax), 134; Elizabeth Ann, 188,

337; Era, 397; Esther Loretta, 210; Eugene Whitfield Jr., 384; Gary Carl, 188, 337; Gary Lee, 336, 482; Herschel Alexander, 243; Ida, 25, 57; James R. Jr., 25; James Robert Sr., 24, 27; Jennifer Robin, 337, 483; Jenny Ione, 93, 188; Jessia Ann, 337, 483; Jessie, 45; Joan Denise, 336, 482; John, 17, 24; John Carroll, 24, 57; John Franklin, 154; Johnny Wayne, 154; Jones Elbert, 93; Joshua Dale, 482; Judy Irene, 332, 336, 482; Julia Ann, 467; Juston Lee, 337; Karl Jones, 93, 188; Kelley Lee, 189, 337; Kenneth Lee, 188, 337; Kristy Lynn, 154; Laura E., 25, 57; Lee, 129; Leona J., 131; Lloyd E., 346; Lois Marie, 129; Lola, 343; Luelus Peyton, 482; Margaret Ellen, 269; Margaret Sue, 188, 336; Marion E., 24; Martha Ann, 188, 337; Mary Etta, 93; Melissa Jill, 337, 483; Melody Anne, 384; Mirandey Jean, 482; Nancy Jane, 17; Odella L., 247, 367; Ora Kyleene, 93, 189; Paula Lane, 188; Rebecca Ann, 134, 252; Rebecca Ashley, 337; Robert Arnold, 93, 188; Roger Dale, 336, 482; Ruby L., 192; Samuel Tolbert, 384; Skip, 345; Tom Buford (Tinker), 192; Vernice, 83

Murtishaw: Jane, 183

Muse: Andrea Nicole, 327; Lauren Brittney, 327; Michael Allen, 327; William Thomas, 327

Myers: Jimmy, 259; John Barry, 389

Myhan: Cecil Coburn, 511; Danny Glen, 511; Ivadean Joyce, 492; Larry Dwight, 342; Linda Renee, 342; Ludie B., 273

Myrick: David, 463; Diane, 322; Dorothy Annett, 229; John Edward, 369; John Steven, 36; Juanita Elizabeth, 327; June, 414; Misty Dawn, 369; Reba Ruth, 36; Susie Ann, 144

N

Nands: Therese Ann, 319

Naples: Albert, 150; Helen, 150

Nappier: Gaynell, 386

Nard: Emma, 65

Narimore: David, 382

Narmore: Leona, 138; William (Bill) M., 138

Nash: Craig Richard, 446; Geraldine, 319; Melanie Renee, 395, 517; Michael (Mike) Edward Sr., 395; Michael Edward Jr., 395, 517; Millard Filmore, 419; Norme E., 395; Plum Smiley, 319; Russell Von, 419

Nations: Callie, 277

Neal: Jennifer Nicole, 445; Jill, 423; Preston Brian, 422; Vernon Dennis, 291

Neamtu: Stefan, 456

Nebel: Jeanett, 460

Neen: Mark, 342

Neher: Joseph William, 343; Stacy Lee, 343

Neill: Gwenda Gale, 324

Nelson: Bob, 171; LaDonna Mae, 286; Lucky Jean, 348; Millard O., 77; Richard, 172; Richard Lee, 286; Turner, 286

Nesbitt: Earl George II, 337; Emily Lane, 337; Erin Elizabeth, 337; George Dale Jr., 337

Newbern: Susie, 188

Newberry: David Glenn Jr., 460; David Glenn Sr., 460; Glenn Dale, 460; Virgil, 175

Newland: Amanda Lynn, 487; Donna Christine, 340, 486; Russell Glen, 340, 487; Shelly Jean, 340, 487; Willard Russell, 340

Newman: Armstead W., 4; Lavenia, 4; Nancy, 4; Parthenia, 4; Samuel, 4

Newport: Mildred, 363

Newson: Grace, 203

Newton: Baxter Paul, 231; Dana, 444; Glenda Mae, 231; Kelly, 377, 506; Reeda, 377, 507; Virginia, 252; William D., 377; William Kimberly (Kim), 377

Nichols: Anna Suzanne, 184; Arthur Lindsey, 184; Betty Jane, 162; Brittany Denise, 449; Carrie Donyalla (Dana), 245, 415; Carrie Mae, 277; Christy Leann, 448; Coy Oscar, 184; Fallon Michelle, 516; Gilbert C., 162; Haley Elizabeth, 353; James (Jimmy), 163; James Phillip, 277; Jerome Clay, 277, 449; John, 163; John Austin, 353; John Warren, 353; Marvin Laverne, 277; Mary Virginia, 163; Monica Leigh, 458; Paul Jr., 76, 163; Paul Sr., 76; Paula, 163; Robert, 356; Ronald Elroy, 458; Stella, 140; Thomas Edgar III, 516; Thomas Edgar Jr., 516; Thomas Edgar Sr., 516; Tony Philip, 277, 448; Vicki, 163

Nicholson: Dawn Alicia, 277; James Allen, 448; Nancy Ann, 448

Nielsen: James E., 526

Niezgodski: Irene, 186

Nipper: Mary, 79

Nivens: Carolyn R., 517

Nixon: Wanda, 255

Noble: Reba Dell, 402

Nobles: Ernest Jr., 243; Joyce Elizabeth, 243, 401, 415; Rosie, 309

Noe: Barbara, 436

Nolan: Phyliss, 460

Norad: Alice Elizabeth, 95

Norman: Deborah Kay, 369

Norris: James T. Sr., 303; Kendall Allen, 303; Nellie Sue, 374, 400

North: Ira, 126; Nathan M., 126

Northedge: Jason, 263; Ronald, 263

Norton: Brenda, 454

Norwood: Otha O., 259

Nowlin: Mary Ruth, 182

Nuszbomb: Ruth Lucille, 129

Nyeres: Linda, 347

O

O'Briant: Alex, 429

O'Bryan: Mary S., 192

O'Kelley: Christopher Michael, 286; Clara E., 66; De Nita, 286; James Edward, 319; James R., 319; James Wesley, 349; Jeffery, 319; Josh, 319; Mary Katryn, 287; W. M., 286; Wanda Darlene, 349; William Michael, 286

Oakley: Ada, 142; Austen Terry, 329; Bill, 329, 435; Billy Dewayne, 435; Chadrick Dewayne, 435; Colby Lee, 435; Eric Denton, 329; Jonathan William, 329; Sandra, 350; Tara Lashelle, 435; Terry Clyde, 329

O'Bryant: Pauline, 282

Odell: Helen Lorene, 339

Odom: Benjamin Jennings III, 410; Benjamin Jennings IV, 410; Bryan Mackenzie, 410; Geneva Mae, 181; James Macquire, 410; Jeremy Randal, 529; Meyson Jennings, 410; Morgan Shanelle, 410

Odum: Cheryl Annette, 321, 477; Deborah Diane, 321, 476; Grady Floyd, 177; Harry Wilbern Jr., 321, 476; Harry Wilbern Sr., 177, 321; Stell, 476

Offield: Virginia, 69

Ogletree: Annie, 488; Jimmy Daniel, 241; Shawna, 241, 411; Stephen, 241; Tony, 241

Okey: Ryan, 263

Olive: Brett Seaf, 354; Cef W., 200; Dolly, 149; Dona Sue, 200, 354; Douglas Gene Jr., 200, 354; Douglas Gene Sr., 200; James, 267; Margaret, 516; Mary Lee, 283; Mary Lou (Bonnie), 354, 490; William, 164

Oliver: Buford, 260; Leatha Pearl, 260; Shelia Ann, 516

Olsen: Dennis, 356; Kelsey Leigh, 356; Lacey Kristil, 356; Lindsey Ann, 356

Oneal: Boy, 30; Danny, 406; Danny Michael, 406; James Andrew, 30; Kathy, 167

Opsteph: Michael Ryan, 355; Paul Matthew, 355; Peter (Pete) John, 355

Organ: Jerry, 421

Orosch: John Joseph, 302; Karleen Joan, 302

Osterloo: Blake William, 527; Cole William Lee, 527; Gary William, 527

Overby: Louisa Francis, 80

Overholser: Madison Grant, 419; Meagan Allison, 419; Phillip Lamar, 419; Shawn Paul, 419

Overhulser: Abagail, 462; Paul, 462; Paul Gene, 462; Zachary, 462

Overton: May, 90

Owen: Joan, 253; Kristi, 449

Owens: Alma May, 365; Billy Henry, 389; Douglas Henry, 389; Joe Dare, 358; John Douglas, 389; Julia, 358, 491; Michael Scott, 389; Mona Sue, 513; Oscar B., 394; Sandra Kay, 394; Susan, 358, 491

P

Pace: Annie Myrtle, 58; Hattie M., 82; James Asgood Andrew, 58

Pack: J. L., 93; Lena, 93

Padron: Dennis, 300; Lawrence Jefferson, 300, 463; Michael Lawrence, 300; Susanna Marie, 300, 463; Valeria Lynn, 300, 463

Paff: Leonard, 462; Tina Louise, 462

Pagniozzi: Connie, 497

Painter: David Clifton, 486; Don, 486

Palmer: Andrea Hope, 402; Brella, 164; Chad Nolan, 402; Edna, 291; Henry W., 52; Iva Mae, 431; James Robert, 402; Jamie Sederall, 402; Lizzie (Pearl) R., 52; Robert F., 27; William O., 164

Pamella: Mary Grace, 150

Pankey: Elois, 362

Parham: Lawrence, 387

Paris: Jean Ann, 401

Parker: Alma, 128; Beverly, 188; Charles Edward, 365; Daniel Glenn, 500; David Oscar, 500; Edward B., 154; Edward O., 365; Elizabeth, 1; Heather Dawn, 427; Isabella, 215, 226; Jeanetta Irene, 154; Kathy, 494; Lora Leigh, 365; Mary, 42; Mary Lee, 242; Minnie, 226; Nelson Edward, 365, 497; Patricia, 442; Vicki Charlene, 365

Parks: Nora Ann, 346

Parnell: Aladee, 47, 99; Alonzo, 47, 99; Christeen, 99; Doyle, 99, 202; Edward Rufus, 47; Elbert, 47, 99; Ethel, 47; Howard, 99; J. C., 99; Jack, 99; James Hilton, 312; Joseph Heath, 312; Joseph Hilton Sr., 312; Lee, 47, 99;

Lenny, 99; Oma Mae, 47; Stephen Barrett, 312; Turner W., 47; Vertia Thora, 47, 99

Parrish: April Dawn, 333, 479; Arnelle, 355; Azalee Estell, 224; Bobby Lance Jr., 333; Bobby Lance Sr., 333; Carla, 424; Charles Ray, 523; Charles (Chuck) Lawrence, 523; Cindy Marie, 333; Clara Delores (Delo), 234; Darrel Lee, 486; David Franklin, 396; David Morgan, 396, 518; Della, 72; Fannie, 110; Freddie, 514; Grady L., 416; Hyson Pearline, 435; James Roy, 333; Jim Watson (Totch), 234; Jimmy L., 486; John David, 396; Jordan Chase, 523; Laura Elma, 240; Lillie, 395; Logan Daniel, 523; Lois Marie, 416; Margaret, 392; Mary Omie, 267; Michael Lee, 287; Pamela Gaye, 514; Rachel Renee, 248; Roland Lee Jr., 287; Roland Lee Sr., 287; Ruby Magdeline, 251; Samantha Jewel, 486; Sarah Ruth, 416; Thomas Watson, 248; Tyler, 518; Varnie William, 224; William Roy, 157

Parsons: Brenda, 162

Passarella: Christon, 530; Huston, 530; Mitch, 530

Pate: Cheyenne Kay, 488; Roger Walker Jr., 488; Roger Walker Sr., 488; Savannah Grace, 488

Paton: John Stuart Sr., 76

Patraw: Marvin, 338

Patrick: Grady Edward Jr., 196; Grady Edward Sr., 196; John William, 428; Joseph Buford (Jb) Jr., 134; Joseph Buford Sr., 134, 244; Kim Renee, 196, 348; Lorimer, 206; Patricia Carolyn, 134, 244, 271; Roy, 428; Tina Denise, 196, 348

Patterson: Catherine Agnes, 325; Emily Lee, 363; James A., 431; James Mack, 431; Mae, 430; Mattie, 227; Melanie, 431, 525; Meredith, 431; Michelle, 431; Peggy, 473; Tosha, 498

Patton: Gladys, 45; Mack Clifton, 217

Patty: Sandra, 371

Paulk: Donna Gail, 448; Guy J., 66; Inez, 66; Iris, 282

Pavisen: Michael, 338; Steve, 338

Payne: Beverly, 294; Lorin Chad, 503; Lovin Lucky, 503

Payton: Ashley Ann, 427; Jerry Jr., 427; Jerry Sr., 427

Pearl: Tim, 509

Pearson: David Martin, 331; Kenny M., 331; Laura Ann, 331

Peaveyhouse: Mary Beth, 522

Peck: Barbara, 306; Elipah Bradford, 469; Granville Allison, 144; Mary Elizabeth, 144; Nancy Jane, 389

Peden: Albert Grady, 295; Arthur (Arter), 116; Cynthia Ann, 295, 460; Edward J., 252; Ella Reenea, 295, 460; George, 295; Grace V., 418; Infant, 116; Jennie, 74; Kathie Jane, 252; Lorene, 412; Sandra Olean, 295, 460

Pendergrass: Anna L., 466; Bonnie, 250

Pendergrast: James Hugh, 307

Pendley: Stanley, 359

Pennick: Brandon Paul, 342; Brittney Ann, 342; Jessica Ashley, 342; Kenneth Jr., 342

Pennington: Amy Nicole, 371; Bridget Lashawn, 511; Charles A., 412; David Lee, 412; Douglas, 214; Douglas Reed, 372; Heather Michelle, 371; Henry, 214; James Otis, 511; Michael Dewayne, 214, 371; Terry Keith, 214, 372

Penrose: Allen, 290; Leo, 290; Susan, 290

Penya: Eric Ranier, 285, 456; Gonzalo, 285; Gregory Ernest Pena, 285, 456; Victor Scott Pena, 456

Pepper: Michael T., 168, 313; Patrick D., 168, 313

Peppers: Brittney Nicole, 305; Earnest G., 305; Makensie, 305; Steven Craig, 305

Peralita: Robert, 483

Perkins: Annie Lue, 97, 198; Chole Lane, 476; Connie Lee, 176, 320; Dianna Lynn, 176, 320; Edna Pearl, 87; Elsie, 97, 198; Florence Mabel, 189; Foster Edwin, 188; Freddie, 97, 198; George Stanley Jr., 226, 383; George Stanley Sr., 226; Henry Clayton, 304; Homer, 176; Homer Clyde III, 176, 320; Homer Clyde Jr., 176; Irish Virginia, 226, 383; James, 94; James Douglas, 97, 198; James Frederick (Fred), 97; James Wesley, 87; Jimmie Lee, 94; Joseph Lee, 97; Karen Anne, 176, 320; Leah Renee, 384; Mary Earline, 188; Mary Elaine, 226, 383; Michael Blake, 320, 476; Myra Evelyn, 226, 383; Myrtle Irene, 188; Nancy Delia (Dee), 97, 198; Noah Josiah, 226; Ozella (Ella), 116, 225; Pamela Sue, 176, 321; Phillip Dewayne, 320; Rachel Marie, 304; Randle Wayne, 304; Ryan Matthew, 304; Samuel Burton, 97, 198; Wanda, 345; Will, 188; Woodrow Wilson, 97, 198

Perry: Ardra Gwen, 322; Clara, 248; Danny, 436; Helen Gladys, 177; Marta Annette, 322; Melissa Ann (Missy), 436, 527; Rana Lynn, 322; Raymond Lee, 322

Perryman: Fronia, 81

Persall: Harry Vance, 284; Vance, 284

Peters: Arthur H., 96; Charles W., 414; David Michael, 305; Hernon D., 305; Hernon Randolph, 305; John Joe, 163, 516; Julie Deann, 163, 306, 516; Phillip David, 163; Phillip J., 163; Tonissi (Tony) Michele, 414

Peterson: Jessie, 464

Pettigrew: Vera, 283

Pettus: Felix Jeffrey, 518; Mary, 314; Rhonda Michelle, 518; Robert, 197

Phelps: Bobbie Lee, 393; Bruce Whiting, 149; Dorothy Ann, 149; Jack Davis, 512; Robert Alan, 512

Philippi: Justin Edward (Tiger), 352; Victor Edward, 352; Victor Grady, 352

Phillip: Ralph, 196

Phillips: Allen W., 418; Ashley Brook, 472; Barbara Lynn, 317; Billy Gerald, 224, 380; Briley Melinda, 512; Byron, 495; Clara Lavon, 224, 380; Clista Faye, 224, 379; Dana Colleen, 383, 512; Diannah Lynn, 493; Edith, 388; Edith Olean, 376; Elizabeth Lee, 224, 236, 237, 264, 268; Emmet Lee, 224; Emmet Walter, 224, 225; Ether Pauline, 209; Eva A., 209; G. W. (Dub), 316; Gary Wayne, 316, 472; Gaylon Ronald, 380, 509; George, 209; Gladys Whitney, 260; Gracie Mozella, 224, 379; Gregory Allen, 418; Gwendolyn Carmel, 383, 512; Henry Coburn, 383; Henry Shannon Jr., 383; Henry Shannon Sr., 383; Imogene, 458; Jacob Wayne, 472; Jason William, 495; Jerry Lynn, 287; Kathy, 292; Kevin, 433; Kevin Patrick, 383, 512; Kristy Elizabeth, 317; Laura Jane, 380, 509; Lisa, 510; Lucy, 103; Mable Rita, 224, 323, 379; Marcella Vernette, 224, 379; Marie Willard, 449; Michael (Mike) Dennis, 414; Milton Dale III, 510; Milton Dale Jr., 380, 510; Milton Dale Sr., 224, 380; Myron D., 414; Myrtle, 238; Pamela Denise, 383, 512; Patricia Diane, 380, 509; Rachel Marie, 414; Randy Lee, 380; Rhonda Kaye, 380; Roger Gene, 380; Ronald Eugene, 224, 379; Ruby Kaye, 414; Sarah E., 175; Sarah Juanita, 495; Serena Ann, 29; Sherry Ann, 380, 509; Sidney, 287; Tamesa, 380, 510; Tammy, 380, 510; Tara, 380, 510; Tina, 380, 509; Velma, 297; Virginia Ophelia, 225; Willie Eugene, 493

Pichard: Elizabeth, 301

Pickens: Adam Ray, 409; Bobby, 240; Casey Watson, 102, 205; Cecil Edgar, 102, 205; Era Viola, 102, 205; George Edgar, 102; Jeannie Diane, 240, 409; Jesse Aaron, 409; Joe Wilson, 102, 205; Kathy Ann, 240, 409; Linda Mae,

Q

R

Rahn: Deana M., 502; Norman, 502
Raines: Mamie, 131
Rainey: Danny Lynn, 269; Mary M., 131
Ramirez: Brooke, 525; William, 525
Ramsey: Amy Myrtle, 230; Thelma, 368
Randall: Nellie L., 252
Randolph: Abigail (Abbie), 48, 62, 63; Cora Mae, 99; Tabitha Jane, 108
Rasch: Paul E., 449; Paula Renee, 449
Ratcliff: John Christian, 446; John Michael, 446
Ray: Amy, 17; Brittany Belinda, 484, 532; David, 303; David Jonathan, 250; Evelyn, 207; Helen, 330; James Rufus, 250; Jarrod Nathaniel, 251; Jeremy Michael, 484, 532; Leighana Michelle, 532; Martha, 400, 485; Maude, 194; Norman Lester, 250; Thomas Duncan, 534; Thomas Wilson, 373; Tommy A. D., 534; Vina Mae, 373; William C., 484; William Gary, 484
Rayburn: Nolan, 147
Reatheford: Mary Sue, 279
Reaves: Adron, 24; Carol Dawn, 285; Cleatus Ray Jr., 285; Cleatus Ray Sr., 285; Jefferson Thomas, 24; Martha, 24; Ora Faye, 344; Williard E., 285
Redd: Carroll Josephine, 256, 429; Catherine Louise, 256, 429; Joseph (Joe) S., 125; Robert Carroll, 125, 256
Redding: Charlotte, 36; Duncan, 35; Lillie, 90; Melissa, 35
Redman: Imogene, 337; Jane, 305
Reed: Arther, 166; Christina Nicole, 394; Cleo William, 192, 344; Dennis Ray, 192, 344; Earnest, 192; Ethan Dean, 487; Ethel Marie, 166; James Fay, 192, 344; Leo Jasper, 192, 345; Lisha Anne, 496; Margaret Joyce, 256; Parker Roger, 496; Robert Earnest, 192, 344; Roger Dale, 192, 345; Tray Lynn, 192; William David, 394; Willie, 493
Reeder: Dora E., 96, 97
Reeves: Ethel Imogene, 121, 250; Jackie, 477; Jerry Ray, 420; Louise Phillips, 225, 382; Maggie Danielle, 477; Teresa Ann, 420; Tyler Wayne, 477
Reid: Ann Clementine, 161; Della, 115; Julius C., 161
Reilly: Thomas, 300
Rester: Anna Rea, 518
Retherford: Christa Leona, 140; Coy B., 140
Reyes: Lucy, 244
Reynolds: Albert, 176; Judy Ann, 447; Lucina, 1
Rhoden: Mary Elizabeth, 395
Rhodes: Abigail Grace, 519; Alexander Blair, 287; April Nicole, 246; Arlon Lee, 246, 287; Augusta, 261; Autry Paul, 519; Betty Faye, 193; Canadian Rosanna, 402; Cora, 216; Delbert Coy Sr., 458; Donald Ray Jr., 246; Donald Ray Sr., 246; Donna, 510; Greg Nelson, 287; James, 510; James Cleveland, 402; James Norman, 193; James Robert, 402; Kathelyn Elizabeth, 246; Lona, 331; Mary Dixie, 126; Mary Evangeline, 193; Mattie, 143, 144; Nancy, 50; Neal B., 458; Paul, 519; Roger Dale, 287; Rosa Mae, 186; Wesley Adam, 458; Will Evan, 458; William Mack, 261
Riccil: Mary, 374
Rice: Alice Marie, 292; Dan, 371; Jeanette, 190; Jennifer, 261; John Robert, 129; Johnny Winston, 129, 261; Myrtle, 314; Robert F., 371; Robert Neal, 320; William Winston, 129
Rich: Annie R., 440; Barry Joe, 514; Bobby, 512; Candace Delynn, 494, 533; Carol Lynn, 512; Casey Dwayne, 494; Earl Dwayne, 494; Eliane, 458; Gary, 465; Genevie, 332; Hazel, 337; Ida Jane, 276; James T., 514

Richards: Billy Ray, 337; Carlene M., 335, 482; Chris, 335, 482; Gregory Keith, 337; Heather Dawn, 186, 332; K. C., 337; Kenneth Moore, 186; Pad J., 186; Patrick William, 335; Shanie Leigh, 186, 332
Richardson: Bommer Gertrude, 364; Bradley, 288; Braily, 420; Brenda Sue, 461; Brent, 420; Catherine, 42; Cletis, 194, 347; David L., 457; Donna Nell, 462; Douglas Edward, 282; E. R., 203; Edna, 468; Emmitt, 194; Eric, 485; Eric Lee, 479; Frankie Alan, 483; Gladys, 375; Grandville, 479; Herbert Truman, 288; J. R., 194; Jacquelyn, 282; Jerry Ivon, 483; Jerry Mason, 420; Joe M., 287; John David, 451; Judith Elizabeth, 127; Julie Renee, 282; Kelly Faye, 451; Lee Alexander, 479; Linda Faye, 287; Mae, 173; Martha Faye, 320; Mary, 180; Michael Erick, 288, 456; Nancy, 431; Robbie Louise, 239; Robert, 173; Seth Bradford, 457; Terry David, 457; Theresa Marie, 528; Timothy Mason, 420; Tony Russell, 194; Trena, 507; Virgie L., 250; W. P., 282
Richey: Anthony Scott, 415; Cassidy Jean, 415; Francis, 254; Walter Anthony, 415
Richter: Frank J., 330; Margaret Kathryn, 330
Rickard: Bobby Lee Jr., 306; Bobby Lee Sr., 306; Chandler Scott, 483; Claude, 293; Deborah Louise, 466; Donald Scott II, 483; Hunter Lee, 483; James Edgar, 466; Janice Kathleen, 293, 461; Ruth, 330; Whitney Leigh, 306; William Hubert, 483
Riddle: Dollie, 145; Frances, 211
Rideout: Cathy Lynn, 471; Grady Lee, 387; Myra Sue, 387; Roy, 248; Shirley Jean, 248
Riggs: Derrick Cody, 495; Gregory Steven, 495; Noal Wesley Sr., 495; Shawn Nicholas, 495
Rikard: Gabriel, 293; Henry Wilber, 293; Kiley Ellen, 293; Megan Elizabeth, 293; Wilber Glenn, 293
Riley: Beulah, 77, 165; Charlotte, 516; Claude Edward, 77, 165; Gregory Lee, 287, 456; Homer Lee, 287; James N., 286; Johnny, 516; Johnny William, 287; Kerry Alicia, 287; Leonard, 77; Lillie, 77; Lillie Mae, 69; Mittie Rebecca, 77, 164; Nellie Catherine, 77, 165; Ora Gladys, 77, 165; Susie Holt, 504; Velmer, 77; Wanda Faye, 286; William Floyd, 77
Rinehart: Brian Earl, 204, 357; Brian Keith, 357; Cara Estelle, 203, 356; Christopher Lynn, 204; Earl Edward, 101; Essie Belle, 101; Infant Daughter, 101; Ocie Columbus, 101; Pamela Michelle, 203, 357; Tayler Denea, 357; Wallace Harold, 101, 203; William Porter, 101, 203; William Scott, 203
Risner: Alice, 334; Bobby Gene, 503; Bobby Myron, 503; Charles Thomas, 376; Doyle Fay, 334; Gregory Paul, 390; James Paul, 390; Kagen, 503; Lane Katherine, 390; Lorene, 309; Philip, 441; Ruby Lee, 368; Stephanie Roxanne, 388; Susan Gail, 376; Tina Louise, 376, 505; Tyler, 441; Walton Randall (Randy), 388; Wesley, 441; William T., 388; William Thomas, 376; Zachary Lane, 376
Ritchey: Annette, 338
Robbins: Bobby, 280; James Roland, 183; Melissa Ann, 183, 331; Vera Maelin, 183, 331
Roberson: Alba Faye, 398; Arthur H., 250; Bobby Joe, 227; Carolyn Faye, 228, 386; Cynthia (Cindy), 514; David Hilton, 385; David Lynn, 227, 385; Edith Faye, 460; Hunter Drake, 450; James Kevin, 450; James Terry, 450; Jerry Thomas, 228; John Sherman, 385; Jonathan Michael, 467; Judy Gail, 250; Larry Bruce, 227, 385; Larry Ryan, 386; Lenny Rhet, 386; Lori, 361; Magen Jane, 467; Martha Sue, 228, 386; Mary Nix, 385; Nathan

Carroll, 227; Nathan Harold, 227, 385; Nathan Tucker, 227; Paul Nathan, 385, 513; Timothy Dale, 227; Tommy Michael, 467; Virginia Ann, 227, 385, 478

Roberts: Eddie, 473; Elizabeth Julia, 284; Ernest Ray, 140; Frank, 83; Jeanette, 408; Lillie Virginia, 207; Martha Ernestine, 140; Mary Helen, 197; Mary Louise, 207

Robertson: Berry Lee (Buck), 215, 372; Charlotte Rose, 215, 372; Connie, 325; Daniel Scott, 372, 503; Dewey M., 196; Floyd, 325; Gary Lynn (Peanut), 215, 373; Joann, 215, 372; John Wesley, 211; Laura B., 124, 134; Mable, 352; Marie Powers, 211; Mills Berry, 215; Mitchell Joshua, 372; Nellie, 365; Roy, 215; Roy Lynn, 373; Suzanne Ray, 354; Thomas Berry, 373; Verta E., 172; Willie Jewel, 213

Robinett: Kate, 78

Robinette: Gertie Marie, 441

Robinson: Alonzo D., 297; Benjamin Wade, 504; Bobby William, 453; Brenda Sue, 297, 462; Carrie, 411; Charles B., 504; Daniel Keith, 504; Danny Ray, 411; Donald Keith, 504; Gayle, 257; Jackie Dale, 297, 462; James Otis, 257; Katherine Ann, 504; Kathleen Ophelia, 183; Leona Ruth, 143; Leroy, 143; Nelson, 183; Nikkie Dale, 462, 530; Peggy, 494; Phillip Nolan, 297; Roger Dale, 411; Sara Diane, 504; Sidney P., 514; Tracie Lynn, 453

Robison: Corey Wade, 473; Kenneth Ray, 473; Lindsey Michele, 473; William A., 473

Rochelle: Barbara Ann, 103, 207; Louis Jasper, 103; Thomas Edward, 103

Roden: Claude, 400; Donnie Jean, 400; Mary Caroline, 163; Thomas Alvine, 163

Roder: Rose Marie, 467

Rogers: Albert, 104; Albert Beverly Thomas, 53, 103; Albert G., 216; Amy Melissa, 373; Annie Maude, 104; Audrey Regina, 361; Ben Franklin, 104; Benjamin Franklin, 103; Bessie Etta Mary Ann, 62, 147; Bob R., 209, 362; Brian Kenneth, 373; Carolyn, 429; Christopher Steven, 362; Christopher Thomas, 373; Claudie Thomas, 104, 209; Clyde Norris Jr., 361; Clyde Norris Sr., 209, 361; Clydie B., 104, 209; Cora Blanch, 372, 374; Cornelia B., 63; De Anna, 505; Dorothy M., 209, 361; Edmon (Eddie) Falmer, 104, 208; Eliza Ann Moore, 104; Elizabeth, 209, 362; Emmet P., 104, 208; Ethel, 48, 145; Jim, 505; Jodie Woodrow, 216; Jody Boyd, 373; John T., 108; Julia (Junnie) C., 53; Kenneth Dale, 216, 373; Lillie Ann Sharp, 104; Mamie, 92, 108, 179; Mary Helen, 209, 362; Minnie Faye, 209, 361; Myrtle, 290, 350; Phillip David Jr., 362, 492; Phillip David Sr., 209, 362; Rebecca Ann, 362, 492; Robert Chris (Bob), 48, 62, 63; Robert W., 104, 209; Robert Wymon, 362; Roland E. Jr., 468; Roland E. Sr., 468; Ruthie Pearline, 369; Sarah Lynn, 362; Stephanie, 520; Stephanie Michelle, 373; Stephen Phillip, 216, 373; Velma, 103, 208; William Robert (Bob), 104; Woodson Chris, 104

Rohde: Charles Frederick Jr., 159

Roland: Ashley Lauren, 312; Chessie Diane, 312; Isabella Janice, 529; Junior, 529; Sarah Bethany, 312; Shayne, 312; Terrell Ray, 529

Rolin: Lorine, 304

Roll: Norma, 384

Rollan: Thomas, 422; Travis Dean, 422; Trinity Lee, 422

Rolston: Jacqueline Ann, 503

Romine: Charlotte Earl, 148, 291; Donna Diane, 168, 313; Howard James, 80, 168; James Earl, 148; James Howard, 168; James Thomas, 148; John Soloman, 148; Kathy

Raynell, 168; Linda Faye, 168, 313; Oatly Franklin, 80; Paul Franklin, 168; Peter Francis, 80; Rachel Kimberly, 313, 469; Richard Emmons, 313; Richard Leland, 80, 168; Richard Morris, 168, 313; Susan Marie, 168, 313; William Dean, 168, 313

Rook: Lucille, 44; Toy Katherine, 44

Rosado: Maria Vega, 424

Rosdick: Donna, 333

Rosenquest: Dorothy, 534

Ross: Charles Crawford, 226; Charles Travis, 226; Frankie Mae, 275

Rourke: Jeremy, 523; Joyce Leigh, 484

Roush: Albert Wesley, 478; Sandra Faye, 478

Roy: Guy, 169; James Martin, 169; James Matthew, 169; Samuel Martin, 169

Rozell: Debra, 433

Rucker: Brian Dearen, 338; Cynthia (Cindy) Lynn, 189, 338; Lauren Annette, 338; Thomas Monroe, 189; William (Bill) Dearen, 189, 338; William (Bob) R., 189

Ruffato: James, 299

Ruhlander: Pauline, 388

Rumble: Cody, 455; David Dwayne, 455; Deanna, 455; Magan, 455; Victor N., 455

Ruple: Myrtle Lou, 167; Tom, 167

Russell: Albert, 143; Alisa Ray, 267; Buddy, 519; Don, 143; Drexel Paul (Toad), 245, 251; Eddie Jerry, 251, 399; Fred, 168; Gordon Wade, 267; James Albert Jr., 286; James Albert Sr., 144, 286; Jeffery Aaron Blake, 519; Judith Paulette, 245, 439; Kathy, 143, 286; Kenneth, 267; Kimberly Ann, 267, 441; Kimberly Michelle, 286; Lawton Jeffery Leon, 519; Lindsey Allison, 267; M. C., 267; Margie, 205; Mark, 417; Mary, 319; Nathan Carroll, 286; Opal Asaline, 168; Patsy Jane, 524; Rebecca, 143, 285; Samuel Wayne, 267; Shirley Ann, 143, 285; Stewart Edward, 286; Vonda Lynn, 251, 399, 425

Rutherford: Beverly Jean, 295; Mattie Ruth, 390

Rutland: Francis, 278

Rzepka: Michael, 323

S

Saccoccio: David Jr., 526

Saddler: Ada Frances, 158; Charles Pugh, 114; Donald, 71; Ella Elizabeth, 63, 71; Infant Son, 71; James Lewis, 156, 297; James Louie, 71, 156; John Wesley Jr., 71; John Wesley Sr., 41, 71, 105; Lady Goldie, 71, 155; Laura Ethel, 41; Lillie Evelyn, 105; Mary Opal, 114; Vera Alean, 71, 155

Salasa: Judith Ann, 429

Salter: Betty Jean, 171; Bob, 171; James Earl, 171; Wilbert Lee, 229

Sample: Mollie, 33

Sampson: Candace April, 356; Randall Earl, 356; Raymond Douglas Jr., 356

Sandefur: William, 4

Sanders: Ashley Nicole, 409, 522; Charles Benjamin Jr., 198; Charles Benjamin Sr., 197; James (Jim), 265; Janell, 265, 439; Joanna Faith, 197, 349; Judith (Judy), 265, 439; Norman, 409

Sanderson: Charles C. (Chick), 258; Christina Marie, 489; Dennis Wayne, 258; Ester, 252; Gearldine, 313; J. C., 258; Joyce, 459; Paul Richard, 489

Sandlin: Janice Wyonell, 455

503; Arthur Lee (Dick), 120, 399, 408, 510; Aubrie Nicole, 524; Audrey Ellen, 137; Audrey Louise, 245, 251; Audrey Martin, 304; Avery Elise, 528; Barbara, 243; Beddie May, 131; Bethany, 417; Betty, 176, 321; Betty Ann, 496; Betty Jean, 370; Beulah Estelle, 131, 265, 381, 408, 415; Beverly Ann, 251, 425, 437; Billy, 385; Billy Rayburn, 247, 417; Billy Wayne, 249, 421; Boy, 436; Bradley Alan, 421; Brandi Gail, 440; Brandon Corey, 509; Brenda Darlene, 486; Brenda Faye, 503; Brett Matthew, 415; Brian Billy, 417, 523; Briar Mckenzie, 528; Butler Oscar, 264; Calvin Horton, 76; Cameron Don, 247, 417; Carlos Ray, 375; Carolyn Diane, 249, 421; Carolyn Estelle, 265, 437; Carrie Mildred, 157, 220; Carrie Virgie, 250; Casi, 307; Catassa Tennille (Tassa), 251; Catherine Ann (Cathy), 266, 440; Cellon Bill, 248; Charles Leon, 120, 251, 437; Charles Ray, 249, 421; Chase Cameron, 440; Chastidy Recale, 334, 481; Chester Owen, 224; Christine, 89, 180; Christine Elaine, 265, 438; Cindy Jo, 266, 440; Clarence, 370; Clyde E., 266; Codie Wayne, 415; Collin Christopher, 397; Colt Seaver, 400; Coy E., 142; Crystal Grace, 426; D. C., 266; Dallas Rose, 415; Dalton Harmon, 245; Dalton Wayne, 245; Daniel Maurice, 247; Dannie Lloyd, 238, 403; Dannie Ray, 266; Danny Russell, 247, 417; Darin Dwaine, 265, 440; David, 417; David Dink, 330; DeAnn, 265; Debora Louise, 142, 283; Deborah Fowler, 390; Delaina Brooke, 426; Della Vel, 159; Delmer, 419; Dewey J., 457; Dianna, 355, 390; Dill, 100; Dollie, 176, 321; Donna Machele, 247, 417; Donnie Ray, 264, 437; Dora Chlora Lee, 108; Dorothy Jean, 249, 421; Douglas Eugene, 253; Dustin Avery (Dusty), 251; Dusty Lyne, 425; Edna Pearl, 76; Edwin, 131, 265; Either Katherine, 131; Elbert Grady, 131, 381; Ella Bell, 179; Ellie Jeri, 242; Elsie, 225; Emily Suzanne, 283, 454; Emmett Oneal, 247, 367; Era, 421; Erma Lillian, 95, 270; Eugene Rufus, 253; Eulalia (Curly), 131, 266; Evan, 504; Evelyn Irene, 120, 251; Fern Lee, 205; Garnetta, 497; Gary Oneal, 334; Gayle Hoyt (Snuffy), 304; Gaylon E., 264; Girl, 436; Gladys Marie, 131, 264; Grace, 427; Grady Elbert, 131, 265; Gregory Wayne, 470, 531; Hagan, 146; Harold Dean, 470; Harold Lee, 459; Harriet, 204; Harvey Hamilton, 89; Hassell Lee, 264; Henry Littleton, 52, 108; Hollis Carter, 452; Isaac Don, 417, 524; Jack Wheeler, 266, 440; Jacob Bruce, 504; James Allen, 266, 440; James E., 330; James Floyd (Jimmy) Jr., 530; James Floyd Sr., 530; James Robert, 431; Jamie, 517; Jamie Craig, 517; Jean Harsh, 202; Jennifer, 398; Jennifer Gay, 264, 435; Jenny, 440; Jerald Wayne, 374; Jeremy Ray, 421; Jerry Wayne, 249, 422; Jesse Lynn, 264, 435; Jessica Ann, 422; Jessica Lynn, 295; Jessie Lynn, 265, 437; Jimmie Lee, 375; Jimmy, 431; Jimmy Lester (JL), 131, 265; Jimmy Ottis (Ott), 120, 248, 249; Joan Alice, 253; John, 22; John E., 531; John Leldon, 295; John S., 219; John Wesley, 374, 400; Johnny Dale, 264; Jonell, 249, 422; Joseph Spencer, 95; Joseph Wheeler, 131, 266; Julie, 440; Junior Ray, 264; Justin Duane, 341; Katherine Jewell, 246; Katherine Lindsey, 330; Kathy Jo, 265, 438; Kaye, 414; Kenneth David, 266; Kevin Lee, 400; Kierston Marie, 528; Lacey Danielle, 400; Laura Belle, 368; Laura Gail, 304; Laura Kay, 264, 435; Lavada (Slick), 131, 266; Layla, 480; Leah Nicole, 390, 515; Lena Pearl, 429; Lenly Loran, 341; Leo, 173; Leslie Amber, 421; Leslie Brooke, 503; Lila, 325; Lillie, 110; Lillie Rebecca, 312; Lisa Diane, 470, 531; Lloyd, 238, 348; Lloyd Robert, 348; Lola, 100; Lona, 174; Lonnie Nolan, 264, 334, 435; Lonnie Wayne (Boo), 264, 425, 437; Mallory Jean, 524; Mardie Wayne, 245, 415; Margie Louise, 249, 421; Margie Ruth, 120, 251, 399; Marguerite, 155; Marilyn Louise, 531; Marion, 142; Marion Luther, 137; Marissa Michele, 426; Mark Anthony, 417, 524; Marsha Lynn, 238, 403; Marvin, 89; Marvin John Jr., 131; Marvin John Sr., 131; Mary, 295, 375; Mary Ann, 367, 441; Mary Frances, 264, 425; Mary Katherine, 249, 420; Maryjane America, 22; Matthew, 440, 524, 528; Matthew Craig, 374; Mavis Lavern, 256; Melanie Joy, 417, 524; Mellisa Fay, 266; Menzo Lester, 131; Micah, 307; Michael, 425, 490; Michael Dewayne, 437, 528; Michael Ray, 253, 426; Mickey, 295; Mildred, 397; Minnie Melinda, 211, 212; Myra, 128; Myra Jeanette, 485; Myron, 202; Myrtle, 229, 370; Natalie Suzanne, 383; Nathan, 437; Noah (Sonny) L. V., 264, 334; Norma, 306; Olivia Anne, 459; Ollie B., 266; Opel Earline, 241; Otie Eugene, 253; Paige, 307; Patrick Allen, 528; Paulette, 437; Peanut, 251; Randle Arnold, 131, 264, 425; Ray J., 249; Regina Lynn, 417, 523; Ricky Dale, 120, 251, 399; Robin Grace, 330; Rodney Lee, 264; Roger, 307; Rollen, 249; Ronald, 398; Ronald E., 504; Ronnie (Red) Arnold, 264, 437; Roxie Bell, 143, 172; Rusty Evan, 437; Ruth, 185; Ruth Lucille, 131, 265; Sammy O., 253; Samuel (Sammie) Coy, 142, 283; Samuel Lee, 459; Sandra, 397; Sandra (Sandy) Renea, 518; Scott Alan, 348; Shaloe Amber, 417; Shannon Nole, 334, 480; Sherry, 437, 528; Shirley Ann, 248, 420; Skyler Waylon, 509; Stanley Morton, 235; Stephanie Nicole, 334, 480; Stephen Blair, 504; Susan Kay, 238; Terry Dwayne, 419; Theodore Roosevelt, 219; Thula Mae, 116; Timothy R., 397; Tommy Joe, 249, 421; Tracy Kyle, 264, 436; Tracy Michelle, 265; Travis Lynn, 120, 251, 510; Tyler Dewayne, 419; Vera, 224; Vicki Kay, 120, 251, 408; Victoria (Tori) Faith, 440; Walter, 85; Wanda Sue, 120, 251, 409; Wendell Gene, 264, 436; Wesley Daivd, 330; Wheeler Turner, 131; Whitney Blake, 419; Whitney Leigh, 440; Wilkes, 176; William (Bill), 110; William (Billy) Aaron Jr., 383; William Aaron Sr., 383

Smitherom: Patricia A., 374

Sneed: Randy, 485

Snell: Raymond Floyd Jr., 223; Raymond Floyd Sr., 223; Renaldi Marlene, 223; Robert Fay, 223

Snoddy: Charles Earl, 259; Emily Patricia (Pattie), 259, 432; Eric Earl, 259, 432; James Thomas, 259

Snow: Verda M., 100; William, 100

Solis: Andrew Ignatius, 297; Danielle (Dani) Wesley, 297; Jack Andrew, 297; Manvel Maurice, 297

Solomon: Jack L., 346; Sharon Jean (Jeanie), 346

Somers: Hazel, 442

Sommer: Emily Zane, 454; Jerry Lynn, 454

Sotherland: Janet Lee, 416

South: Hayen Lee, 488

South: Alfred Lynn, 333; Alonzo Allen, 284; Amanda Kay, 342, 488; Baylee Nicole, 488; Bobby Lance, 235, 397; Brandy Annette, 342, 488; Carrie LeeAnn, 343; Chad, 440; Charles, 440; Chester L., 440; Chester Linbergh, 333; Christopher Allen, 342, 488; Clara, 45, 96, 310; Dora, 57; Eva Leigh, 94, 191, 275; Hunter Ray, 488; Ida Edith, 185; Infant, 94; James, 94; James Cecil, 191, 342; James Claude, 94; Jeremy Clay, 342, 488; Jimmy Karl, 235; John T., 94; Kasi Nichole, 343; Mable Jewel, 185; Matthew Lynn, 343; Michael Allen, 343; Phillip Dale, 191, 343; Randal Keith, 191, 342, 348; Randi Marie, 343;

Rebecca Louise, 284; Ricky Lynn, 191, 343; Roger Allen, 191, 342; Rufus Allen, 94, 191, 348; Shelby Jean, 342; Steven Dewayne, 191, 343; Thomas Crayton, 235; Tisha Latonya, 343, 488; Vicki Lynn, 235; Wesley Tyler, 343; William Floyd, 235; William Tommy, 235, 397

South: Randi Marie, 488

Southerland: Luther, 374; Wanda Helene, 374

Southern: Helen Sue, 137; William R., 137

Sowders: Charles, 155, 297; Darrell C., 155; James, 155; Lamar S., 155

Spain: Jenell, 167; Noah Thomas, 167; Sue, 468

Sparks: Lillie Ollene, 392

Spencer: Frank Allen, 485; Kristy Marie, 485

Spiceland: Pat, 473

Spiegel: Marcus Avery, 198

Spiller: Houston Lane, 521; Hunter Blake, 521; John, 521; Jonathan Owens, 521; Stephen Lee, 521

Spillman: Marion, 239

Spires: Bertha Marie, 501; Christine, 448; Kathleen, 197, 385

Spivey: Ellie Juanita, 159

Springer: Bedford Forrest, 89; Emma Odell, 376; Francis, 271; Hardie Raymond, 89; James Dale, 368; James Lenon, 368; Lorene, 253; Mary E., 86; Raymond Glenn, 90, 181; Raymond Winston, 181; Sherrie Shelane, 368, 501; Suzanne, 368, 501

Springman: Larry, 438

Spulock: Howard Dewayne, 459; Howard Earl, 459; Mallory Danille, 459

Spurgeon: Susan Grace, 207

Stack: Dora, 151

Staggs: Brenda Gail, 388; Clifford Dalton, 162; Eddie, 235; Elizabeth (Beth) Arcella, 328; Elizabeth (Betty) Dean, 181; Jeremy Neal, 485; Lester Daniel Sr., 181; Lidie Jean, 162; Mary Elizabeth, 235; Roy Bennett, 388; Writher Odell, 328

Staley: Dale D., 533

Stanfield: Angela Michelle, 271, 445; Chris, 487; Harold, 271; Ida, 167; Jacob Daniel, 444; Kaylee Grace, 445; Margaret Evelyn, 428; Michael Harold Jr., 444; Michael Harold Sr., 271, 444; Riley Gail, 445; Robert, 414; Stacy Shawn, 271, 445; Theresa Lynn, 414

Stanford: Maggie, 269

Stanton: Aaron Moree, 482; Daniel, 482; Erin Nicole, 297; Jospeh Brian, 297; Kaitlin Lindsey, 296; Patrick Roy, 482; Paul Brian, 296; Walter G., 296

Stantz: Betty L., 279

Stanwich: Emily, 490

Stapleton: Brandon Duane, 509; Duane, 509

Starcher: Joe, 263

Staricks: Robert, 317

Starkey: James Cox, 402; Shelly Annette, 402

Starr: Thomas Charles Jr., 464

Startz: Betty Lou, 295

Stater: Virginia, 396

Statom: Betty Ruth, 65, 141; Dolly Francis, 65, 141; Frances Kay, 140, 280; Hilda Mae, 65, 141; James A., 64, 65; John Price Jr., 65, 141; John Price Sr., 65; John Tracey, 141; Jonathan Mark, 280; Lois Katherine, 65, 140; Martha Ann, 140, 280; Mattie Jo, 65, 141; Megan Lynn, 281; Morgan Leigh, 281; Nolan Sharp, 65, 140; Ollie Mitchell I, 64; Ollie Mitchell II, 65, 140; Ollie Mitchell III, 140; Robert Michael, 140, 280; Ryan Michael, 280; Sterling Josh, 141, 281

Stauber: Della, 361

Steele: Lanora Lynn, 452; Marshall Leroy, 452; Marshall Leroy Sr., 452; Melinda Anne, 452

Steely: Effie Lee, 371; Glydia, 269

Stenzet: Christa, 389

Stephens: Albert, 193; Betty, 193; James Mark Jr., 341; James Mark Sr., 341; Kimberly, 499; Robert Jeremy, 429; Tammy Annette, 477

Stephenson: Beverly Gail, 255, 429; Glenn Warner, 255; Kelvin Martin, 255, 429; M. H., 255; William Thomas, 429

Stepwith: Anthony W., 61; Eleanor, 61, 130; Sonny, 61

Stevens: L. Juanita, 378

Stevenson: Marilyn, 359; Michael Dale, 477; Minnie Mae, 74; Ryan Michael, 477; Tyler Dale, 477

Stewart: Charles Gomer, 75; Doris M., 315; Jack, 473; Jessie, 281; Jill Denise, 473; Kathy Sue, 468; Loncie Dunkin, 468; Loretta, 408; Mallie Denson, 75, 162; Mary, 128; Michael, 184; Mildred S., 375; Oscar, 375; Thelma Marion, 151; Tydus Austin, 326; Wildena, 432

Stidham: Cynthia Gail, 521; Eugene, 375; Ollie, 514

Stockard: Jessie, 311

Stocksberry: Annie, 413

Stone: James, 283; Jason Wayne, 422; Leslie Ann, 423; Lindsey Nicole, 423; Maranda Ann, 423; Mattie Sue, 240, 245, 417; Scotty Wayne, 422; Sylvia Ann, 331; Tanya Renea, 422; William H., 423; William Sanford, 331

Story: Kesha Annette, 320, 476; Robert Thomas (Tommy), 320; Tiffani LeNea (Tippi), 320, 476

Stotts: Wilma, 332

Stout: Amos Jerome, 398; David H., 398; Rebecca Dianna, 398

Stover: Jacob Brodie, 478; Mallorie Hope, 478; Michael, 478

Stowe: Charlotte Marie, 510; Herbert, 523; Tonya Renae, 523

Strait: Michael, 485

Strange: Corene Francis, 213; Mary Ann, 235; Sarah Frances, 157

Strawn: Mary Bertha, 234

Street: Eric Andrew, 298, 462; Erica Kaitlyn, 462; Kameron Andrew, 462; Mark Phillip, 298; Orton W., 298; Phillip Orton, 298

Streetman: Lois, 238

Strianese: Ryan Wayne, 357; Wayne Joseph, 356

Strickland: Gloyd, 236; Jessie, 301; Sandy Michelle, 301, 464; Tracy, 301

Stricklin: Anna Faye, 363; Bobby James, 340; Earl, 487; Ellis Monk, 340; Henry Ellis, 372; Jermiah Stephen, 487; Samantha Dawn, 487; Shelby Lynn, 487; Stephen Gene, 487; Tammy Lou, 340, 487; Thomas (Tommy) James, 340, 487; Tina, 444; Wanda Elizabeth, 372; William, 394; William T., 363

Stripling: Robert, 271

Strong: Charlotte, 214

Stroup: Marti, 520; Patricia Ann, 235

Struzick: Edward H., 303; Laura Evelina, 303

Stults: Andrea, 355; Bobby Joe Sr., 280; Bobby Joey Jr., 280, 450; Carter Blessin, 70, 139; Catlin Bryant, 460; Clint Jarrod, 295; Debra Lynn, 152, 295; Horace Calvin Jr., 295; Horace Calvin Sr., 151, 295; Hubert, 201; Janice Faye, 152, 295; Joel Thomas, 70; John Bobby, 70, 152; Judith Ann (Judy), 151, 295; Julia Christine, 70, 139, 151; Maddine Rose, 460; Mark Christopher, 292; Mary

Louise, 70, 151; Pauline, 288; Ponda Lynn, 295, 460; Raymond, 280; Sammy Carter Jr., 295, 460; Sammy Carter Sr., 151, 295; Sandra Jeanette, 201; Teresa Jean, 152, 295; Thomas Joel, 70, 151; Tommie Jo, 151, 295; William Carter, 460

Stump: Lisa Renee, 393

Stumpe: Mary Ellen, 310; Raymon Henry, 310

Stutts: Daniel Oneal Jr., 136, 273; Daniel Oneal Sr., 63, 136; Dolly Jane, 137, 273; Fannie Ethel, 63; John, 63; Kansas, 523; Mary, 386; William (Will) Jacob, 63; William Joel, 63

Sudden: Mary V., 310

Sudhoff: Christal Nova, 497; Frederick Albert, 497; Frederick W., 497; Michelle Lee, 497

Suggs: Charles W. Jr., 167; Kathleen Ann, 167, 312; Mary Louise, 167, 313; Michael T., 167; Patrick D., 168; Sandra Lee, 167, 312

Summerall: Kermit E., 189

Summers: Anita, 222; Anna Patricia, 469; C. Thomas, 222; David Leland, 222; Ira, 222; James Wayne, 395; Leland Elijah, 222; Lily Marquerite, 222; Mary Ann, 222; Phillip, 351; Robert Bruce, 222; Rose Marie, 222, 379; Shelly, 351, 490; Virgil Lee, 222

Sunderhaus: Edward Benjamin, 128; Rosemary, 128

Sutton: Bertha Lorine, 91

Suver: Larry, 344; Terri, 344, 489; Tina, 344, 489

Swaner: Lucille, 215

Sweeney: Scott Matthew, 495; William Raymond II, 495; William Raymond III, 495

Sweeny: Crystal, 422

Swinea: Willodean, 287

Swinford: Katherine (Katty), 22

Swink: Sue, 405

Swint: Cyril Agnes, 254; Emmitt Monroe, 254

Sylverius Meziere: Lillie Mae, 486

Szymczak: Barbara, 266; Donna, 266; Ed, 266; Edwin, 266

T

Tacker: Donald, 88; Dora Inez, 88, 177; Harold D., 88, 178; Harold D. Jr., 178; James Boyd, 178; Lillie, 88; Lou Tishie Haynes, 40; Loyd T., 178; Mary Bastine, 88, 178; Rebecca, 178; Retta Sue, 178; Tennie Louise, 88, 178; Virgie Hazel, 88, 178

Talbot: Larry, 438

Talley: Deloris, 469; Margie, 279; Mary Velma, 328

Tant: Sabrina, 66

Taravez: Wilhemina Guadalupe, 145

Tarpley: Roberta, 176

Tate: Aulton H., 283; Carol A., 426; Cornelia, 86, 175; Edna Mae, 86, 174; Eric Gerard, 393; Jamie Lynn, 283; Lisa Marie, 232, 393; Lyda Kathleen, 163, 306; Marie Lynn, 163, 306; Nichelous Ryan, 393; Robert William III, 393; Robert William Jr., 232, 393; Robert William Sr., 232; Simpson, 86; Stacy Leigh, 163, 307; William G., 163

Tatum: Karen Lynn, 407, 521; Tillman, 407; Wanda Lee, 407, 521

Tayes: Eddie Wayne, 314; Edison A., 314

Taylor: Alexis Brooke, 526; Amanda, 89, 180; Andy, 89; Andy Timothy, 356; Brandon Douglas, 526; Cary Allen, 253; Cathy, 89, 180; Christopher (Chris) Lee, 356; Christopher Thomas, 420; Deloris Marilyn, 274; Donnie, 420; Donnie Allen, 420; Doris Ann, 511; Edward (Edwin/Ed), 40; Elizabeth, 155; Elmer C., 253; Elza Raider, 40, 88; George W., 122; George Willis, 40, 89; Gussie, 257; Jennifer Sue, 420; Jimmy, 511; Joey Allen, 253, 427; Karen, 301; Lana Lynn, 246, 412; Linda Sue, 298; Lisa, 89, 180; Lyle Edward, 382; Marilyn L., 296; Marion Albert, 274; Martha (Mattie) Inez, 40, 88, 120, 220; Mary (Mollie), 88, 111; Michael Clay, 396; Montana Brooke, 467; Nancy, 122; Nancy Fay, 382; Norma Lynnett, 477; Oma, 326; Philip Neil, 361; Ralph Douglas, 526; Robert Dwayne, 467; Robert Oneal, 467; Roy Levell, 246; Sadie Bell, 336; Steve, 89; William Lynn, 356

Tays: Dustin Troy, 414; John Kenneth, 414; John Troy, 414

Teer: Bonnie Iness, 158, 299; Floyd, 158

Terrell: Cheryl Denise, 370, 496, 502; Donna Faye, 308; Edgar E., 308; Homer, 370; John, 459; Mary Alice, 432; William Howard, 370, 496

Terry: Annie, 269; Anthony Wayne, 466; Bobby Ray, 215; Bradley Wade, 466; Charlotte, 508; John Stanley, 427; Kim Dawn, 215; Meagan LeAnne, 427; Morgan Lane, 427; Patrick Brian, 427; Peggy Ann, 466; Susie, 120, 248, 249

Thacker: Ash'lee Darretanan, 505; Brett, 505

Thigpen: Bell, 229; Buford C. L., 502; Gayther Dellen, 511; James A., 335; John D., 433; John Gregory, 433; Judy Carol, 335; Marcus, 122; Martha Gail, 403; Nathan, 433; Pamela Kaye, 511; Susie Ann, 502; William Maple, 403; Zachery, 433

Thomas: Anthony Taylor, 422; Austin Allen, 422; Benjamin Walker, 490; Brooklyn Laurel Hope, 527; Camden Michael, 527; Carei Ann, 432; Cathy Allison, 435; Garon (Skipper) Coy, 390; Garon (Tommy) F., 390; Harry Hughes (Jitterbug), 351; Harry Joel, 351; Isaac Michael, 527; James Christopher, 422; James Taylor, 422; Joe Jr., 470; Joe Sr., 470; John Malcolm, 351; Kristie Dawn, 390, 515; Lewis E., 435; Lizzie Bell, 145; Logan Michael, 527; Madeline V., 160, 485; Mary Kathryn, 490; Michael Carl, 527; Mitchem Hugh, 490; Paul Douglas, 514; Paul F., 514; Percy Hugh, 351, 490; Robert Jason, 351; Robert M. Sr., 351; Russell A. Jr., 432; Tanner Michael, 527; Tonya Michelle, 391

Thomason: Carole Almeda, 252; James E., 252; Lester Hawkins, 82; Rena, 37; Robert Lee, 82

Thomison: Dorothy, 525

Thompson: Angie Kaye, 294, 459; Beth, 464; Bettie, 37; Bobby Lenard, 315, 470; Brian, 349; Brian Lee, 277, 448; Christopher, 471; Clarita May, 157; Dorothy, 346; Flora Belle, 274; Freddie Darryl, 483; Jackie M., 401; Jala Leigh, 483; James Rodger, 157; Jeff, 354; Jerry Dee, 276; Jon Michael, 263; Jon W., 263; Kathy Lynn, 276, 448; Kimberly, 480; Kimberly Ann, 277; Maria Gay, 401; Mark, 435; Mary Lucille, 366; Mary Paula, 294, 459; Robert, 315; Robert Earl, 294; Robert Earl Sr., 294; Shanna, 468; Sheilds, 276; Stacey, 435; Stella Kathryn, 296; Tera, 338; Terry, 471; William, 263; William Kelsie, 294; Winifred Lee, 356; Wriley, 480

Thorne: Janie Alberta, 167; Thomas Jr., 167; Thomas Sr., 167

Thornton: Blair, 270; Christine, 275; David Anthony, 439; Deborah Janice, 312, 469; Johnny B., 312; Kimberly Celeste, 312, 469; Lana Jane, 376; Mollie Jane, 439; W. G., 376

Thorp: Charles Minton, 427; Hunter Wade, 427; Wallace Wade, 427

Thorton: Jeanette, 159

Varnell: Gerlda Rena, 433

Vassaders: Robert, 356

Vasser: Frances Bell, 493; Linnie Yvonne, 402

Vaughn: Anthony (Tony) Reed, 383, 512; Connie Faye, 383, 511; Dorothy Sue, 262; Eric Jerome, 383, 512; Jason, 510; Joey Jay, 383; Kristy Dawn, 512, 534; Lura Dean, 460; Martha, 267; Mitchell Cline, 383; Pauline (Polly), 278; Rory Kyle, 512; Ryan Cole, 512; Sara Edna, 212; Thomas Roger Jr., 383; Thomas Roger Sr., 383

Vazquez: Christina Renee, 424

Vega: Raymon Vazquez, 424

Vermeulen: Lucienne Henriette, 302

Vernon: Gloria, 305

Verspett: Jennifer Lynn, 299; Joseph Ryan, 299; Phillip Michael, 299; Randy Leon, 299

Vickers: Benjamin F., 461; Betty Ruth, 302, 461

Vickery: Belle, 135; Linda Sue, 532; Margaret Lorene, 295; Vera, 286; William Jerry, 323

Vines: Francis Louise, 516

Vinson: Andrea Jean, 155, 296; Ida Florence, 148, 367; James Donald (Donnie), 155, 296; James Lindsey (Bo), 155; Louis Andrew, 155; Melanie Lynne, 155, 297; Rachel Ann, 296

Vliek: Anne Mae, 233

Volentine: Malcolm B., 312

Von Bargel: Beverly Joan, 526

Von Linsowe: Martin John, 376; Pamela Jo, 376

Voss: Caleb Cole, 431; Donald Wayne, 431; Rayford Delane, 431; Tessa Jean, 431

Voyles: Elizabeth Matilda, 55; Jacob, 55

W

Wachter: George Thomas, 392; Lori Renee, 392

Waddell: Calvin Lee, 311; Charles Edward, 311; Gentry James, 311; James, 311; John Pearl, 311; Kenneth Lynn, 312; Linda Jeanette, 311; Tammy Lou, 311; Trey, 507

Waddington: Stella Alice Marie, 491

Waddle: Nancy Anna, 262; Ralph David Jr., 262

Wadkins: Anne Marie, 529

Waggener: Frank Cameron, 103; Frank Wilson Jr., 207; Frank Wilson Sr., 103, 207; Gwendolyn, 103, 207

Wakelandis: Mary B., 100

Walden: Corey Eugene, 454; Eugene, 454; Jennifer Leigh, 454; Mary Lynn, 458

Waldrep: Holly Lee, 296, 461; Ladonice, 285, 455; Larry Angus, 296, 458; Leonard O., 285; Lyndell Shawn, 285, 455; Nikky Marie, 296, 458, 461; Roy Angus, 296

Walker: Anne Bell, 393; Billy Ray, 232; Billy Wayne, 232, 394; Bobby Sherrill, 129; Brittany Morgan, 393; Curtis D., 277; Eckard, 306; Elisa Lynn, 129, 262; Ellene Irene, 277; Elmore O'Neal, 518; Ester, 303; Gena Marie, 232, 393; Hazel, 232; John Hampton, 232; Kenneth David, 277, 449; Kristin Brady, 306; Lee Elton, 129; Linda Faye, 466; Luther, 238; Mark David, 277, 449; Marlow Ray, 232, 393; Rebecca Elaine, 262; Ronald Gene, 262; Son, 518; Terry Dewayne, 518; Wanda Kay, 232, 393; William, 495; William David, 277

Wall: Tammy Sue, 447

Wallace: Alma Ruth, 465; Andrew Gates, 353; Ashley Erin, 397; Betty Jean, 152; Bradley Shane, 397; Brenda Brooke, 200, 354; Brenda Jeannette, 328; Bruner Edward, 370; C. W., 186; Carrie, 191; Clinton Glenn, 354;

David Eugene, 234, 397; Dorman Glenn, 200; Dorman Richey, 200, 353; Edward Guy, 200; Elizabeth Marie, 353; Flora Marie, 186; Gladys Dean, 383; Gladys Marie, 139, 319; Glenda Jean, 200, 353; Grafford Eugene, 234; Harry Brooks, 200; Harry Mark, 200; Henry T., 467; Jacob Robert, 354; James David, 467, 531; James Henry, 467; James Thomas, 152; James W. Jr., 358, 491; James W. Sr., 358; James William, 139; Karen Anne, 200, 354; Lizzie Smith, 187; Lola Jean, 370; Louise, 201; Mable, 226; Madalyn, 490; Martha Gean, 234, 397; Martha Jean, 468, 531; Martha Nora, 165; Martin W., 358; Mary Elizabeth, 502; Mary L., 133; Mattie B., 141; Nancy Sue, 234, 397; Owen Wilburn, 234; Patricia, 278; Roger Lance, 200, 354; Thomas (Tommy) Wayne, 467, 531; Tony Keith, 234, 397; Victoria Leigh, 353; William, 328; William Shelby, 278

Waller: Patsy Ruth, 515

Walling: Heath Dewayne, 423; Jimmy D., 423; Jonathan Daniel, 423; Whitney Paige, 423

Walmer: Lilliam Gail (Pebbles), 475

Walter: Chris, 469

Walters: Mary Louise, 294

Walthall: Frances, 1

Walton: Era Irene, 240

Wambles: Sue, 258

Wanner: Bobby A., 320; Rhonda Charline, 320

Ward: Belvie H. Jr., 396; Kelly Daneen, 396; Mary Ann, 442; Ross, 442; Vickie Lynn, 490; William (Bill), 56

Warner: Jack A., 150

Warren: Donna Kaye, 349; Jack Gwynn, 349; Lucille, 280

Warrenfells: Elizabeth, 367

Wasserburger: Christy Ann, 471; Jesse Duane, 471, 532; Jesse Duane II, 532; Richard Duane, 471; Sean Thomas, 532

Watkin: Mary Alice, 140

Watkins: Archie Hopson, 151; Ashley Danean, 294; Bennie L., 443; Bobbie Sue, 151, 294; Buford Delmer, 395; Celsie Leiden, 314; Charles Lee, 151, 294; Earline, 151, 294; James Wilber, 314; Jana Lynn, 294, 460; Joshua Tracy, 314; Linda Sue, 443; Lucinda, 151; Mark Glenn, 314; Melissa Kay, 395; Nicklos Clay, 314; Omi Jean, 151, 294; Robert William, 490; Tom, 151; William Lewis, 98

Watson: Andrew Tyler, 481; Brianna Nicole, 481; Carolyn Lucille, 500; Clarence Blake, 76; Cody Lynn, 502; Jackson Call, 502; James Roy, 513; Jason, 433; Jennifer Rene, 513; Kathleen Margaret, 76, 163; Martha Faye, 466; Matthew, 481; Pearl, 297; Samuel Tyrus, 502; Taylor Ann, 433; William Gregory, 502

Wayland: Joyce Marie, 344

Wear: Edwin Dwayne, 508; Selena Nicole, 508; Shalane McKay, 508

Weatherby: Maggie, 200

Weatherington: James Edward, 341; M. O., 341, 346; Randy Wayne, 346

Weathers: Bayless Edward, 86; Minnie Lee, 86; Sarah Minnie Lee, 82

Weaver: Clara Oneita, 95, 194; Donna Douglas, 367, 498; Elaine Rena, 195; Harry Malcom, 195, 347; James, 195, 347; James Anderson (Andy) Jr., 367; James Anderson (Jim) III, 367, 498; James Anderson Sr., 367; James Paul, 95, 195; Jasper Clarence, 95; John Sidney, 95; Kasey Reigh, 498; Mary Boyd, 366; Mary June, 95, 195; Roxanne, 195, 348; Roxie Lucille, 95, 194; Verna, 134; Virtie Viola, 95, 194; William Clarence, 95, 195

Wiley: Mary Frances (Fannie), 51, 57, 83; Wm Jasper Newton, 51

Wilhite: Clyde, 116

Wilkes: Annie Mae, 138, 276; Anthony Charles, 277, 448; Aubrey Neal, 138, 277; Bethany Leigh, 448; Bonnie Faye, 139, 277; Callie Ann, 277; Charles Ashley Jr., 277; Charles Ashley Sr., 139, 277; Claire, 449; David Grant, 278; Debra Lynne, 277, 449; Donna Elizabeth, 278, 449; Earl Berry, 64, 139; Edward Earl, 139; Edwin Fay, 138; Elting, 64, 138; James Chambers, 64, 138; James Riley, 138, 276; Jason McKinley, 278, 449; Jeffrey Bruce, 276, 448; Jennah Kathryn, 448; Jimmy Carroll, 138, 276; Jimmy Kevin, 276, 448; Joe Wheeler, 138, 277; John Francis M., 64; John Jackson Jr., 278; John Jackson Sr., 139, 277; Laura Kaye, 276, 447; Levi (Lee) Grant I, 64, 152; Levi (Lee) Grant II, 64, 138; Levi Grant III, 138, 277; Lovie Lucille, 64, 139; Lya Janeen, 278, 449; Mandy DeAnne, 277; Mary Lee, 138, 277; Nathan Elting, 277; Nicole Elizabeth, 277, 448; Patsy Lee, 138, 276; Paula Christine, 278, 449; Ross Phillip, 277; Ruby Crystine, 64, 139; Rufus Grant, 139, 278; Rufus Jackson, 64, 139, 152; Sarah Kennedy, 448; Shirley Jean, 138, 276; Stefane Dawn, 277

Wilkins: Chester, 209

Wilkinson: Frances, 240; Kevin, 455; Linda Elaine, 352; Marty K., 455; Mary Ann, 207, 359; Robert H. Jr., 207, 359; Robert H. Sr., 207; Robert L., 352; William Frank, 207

Willard: Franklin Wayne, 391; Ned R., 391; Sabrena Rebecca, 391, 516; Sophia Diana, 391

Williams: Addie Lou, 359; Agnes Irene, 138; Andrea Florence, 282; Andrew, 146; Ankie, 77; Ann, 447; Annie, 226; Arleen Joyce, 345; Arthur J. Jr., 125, 256; Arthur James Sr., 125; Bette Carmen, 260; Carl Bedford, 190; Carla Lynn, 340, 487; Chloe Wheeler, 138; David Charles, 282; Debra Lynn, 190, 340; Delphie, 465; Donald Sandy, 476; Doyal, 487; Ebba Lou, 534; Elizabeth, 365; Eri Evelyn, 324; Genieve, 140; Ila M., 286; Imogene, 230; James Eugene, 298, 462; Jane Anne, 125, 256; Jerry Wayne, 190, 340; John, 190; John Frank, 230; Kaleb Hunter, 476; Katelyn Hannah, 476; Kathryn Elaine, 313; Katy Sue, 392; Kenneth Ray, 333; Larry David, 190, 340; Lillie, 325; Lorene, 353; Luther Burton, 317; Martha Evelyn, 81; Mary (Becky), 77; Mary Ethel, 146, 196; Mary Lois, 91; Mary Paige, 355; Nellie M., 494; Nora, 132; Norva, 161; Opel Bernice, 420; Patty Ann, 435; Ralph, 76; Ray, 333; Rebecca Ann, 312; Robert Oscar, 146; Ronald C., 392; Sarah Beatrice, 190, 340; Sharlene, 487; Shirley McBride, 492; Tammie Kaye, 298, 462; Thomas, 165; Thomas James, 462; Thomas Sanford, 312; Tom Raymond, 298; Tonya Ann, 340; Velma, 81; W. T., 91; Willis M., 435

Williamson: Courtney Lindsey, 183; Imogene, 366; Roger Dale, 183

Willingham: Marie, 447; Shawn Elizabeth, 449

Willis: Annie Belle, 65; Bobbie Sherry, 294; Christopher, 427; Dara Mae, 273; Doris Ann, 484; Ella F., 65; Haley Nicole, 427; James, 484; Robert Emmit, 294; Wesley, 65

Wilson: A. H., 165; Berlon Wayne, 322; Bertha, 195; Carrie Lynn, 322; Cecil Howard, 169; Eliza Henry, 127; Emily Elizabeth, 127, 260; James Earnest, 182; James Thomas, 227; John Phillip Bruton, 256; June Rose, 197; Kellie Rebecca, 322; Lawson Spence, 127; LEslie Allison, 322; Lillian Evelyn, 288; Lindsey Shay, 315; Margo Delores,

182; Nancy Spence, 127, 260; Nikkie Melissa, 322; Patsy, 320; Sarah Anna, 25; William (Pete) Harvey, 169; William (Will) Richard, 315; William Ricky (Ric), 169, 315

Wimpee: Janice Lanetta, 279; Martio Russell Sr., 279

Winborn: Bubba, 323; Donnie Joe, 179; Dossey W. Sr., 218; Douglas Ray, 179, 323, 369, 508; Edward Homer, 178; Ellen C., 334; Elsie Jeanette, 402; Glenda Gayle, 178, 323; Gregory, 323; Ida Mary, 218; James Leo, 178, 369, 508; Jimmy Glenn, 179; Kala, 323; Kasey, 323; Martha Faye, 179, 323; Michael Wayne, 323; Michelle Dawn, 323, 477; Pearl, 148; Ressie Jean, 401; Ricky Leo, 323; Sherry Denise, 457; Theresha, 323; Wanda Sue, 179, 323; Willard Leon (Pete), 179, 323; William C., 457; Wilson Leo, 179

Winchester: Erin, 291; John Charles, 291; Joseph Fred, 291; Laura Ellen, 291

Winders: Audrey Lynn, 405, 520; Bobby, 405; Jim Bob, 405; Lisa Renee, 405, 520

Winfree: Brandon Kyle Romer, 430; Dan, 430

Wingo: Jacob Joe, 384; Joe H. Jr., 384; Rich Allen, 384; William Luke, 384

Winsett: John T., 195; Wilma Earline, 195

Winsted: Chris, 531; Zachery Austin, 531

Winter: Bengamin Eastman, 291; James, 149; James Larry, 149, 291; James William, 149; Patrick William, 291

Winters: Glenda, 253

Wirington: Donald Mitchel, 292

Witt: Amie Alice, 201, 354; Andrea Jill, 201, 354; Andrew Michael, 353; Betty Lou, 98, 200; Carolyn Sue, 98, 200; Cathy Ann, 263, 434; Chadwick Todd, 201, 355; Charles D., 92; Chloe, 302; Craig Ryan, 201; Danny Price, 98, 201; Danny Ray, 263, 434, 479; David Lee, 353; David Lynn, 200, 353; Dewey Marlin, 92; Dorothy Jo, 98, 201; Elsie Irene, 92, 187; Eva, 130, 264, 381; Hannah Victoria, 435; Homer Lee, 130, 381; Ila Jean, 98, 200; James Arnold, 98, 200; James Michael, 200, 353; Jennifer Joy, 200, 353; Jennifer Lynn, 434; Johnelle, 133; Johnny Hulet, 133; Johnny R., 92, 98, 130, 133; Johnny Ray, 130, 263; Joshua Daniel, 434, 479, 526; Kara Loraine Mary, 434; Kimberly Jean, 434, 525; Letha Helen, 130, 263, 334; Linda Sue, 251, 437; Mary Etta, 98, 201, 231; Megan Celeste, 435; Minnie Ida, 136, 221; Olen L., 133, 243; Polly Ann, 133, 243, 270; Rachel Lee, 130, 264; Rachel Lynn, 353; Randy Lee Jr., 435; Randy Lee Sr., 263, 435; Raymond, 251; Ricky Dale, 263; Ruth Vernet, 98, 199; Sandra Dee, 200, 352; Sharon Lee, 200, 353; Shirley Diane, 98, 201; Thomas Clyde (T. C.) Jr., 98, 201; Thomas Clyde (T. C.) Sr., 98, 231; Virgil David, 98, 200; Virginia Francine, 98, 201

Wolf: Billy, 178; Donnie Lou, 178; Lameul, 178; Martha Ann, 178

Womble: Judy Diane, 217, 374; Kenneth Gene, 149, 291; Leslie Brooks, 217; Lester, 149; Lester Eugene, 149; Robert Clark, 217; Vera, 154; William Russell, 149

Wood: Abigail, 476; Ada Evelyn, 48, 101; Albert Weaver, 114; Alex Gregory, 415; Alexander Matthew, 518; Allisa Brielle, 534; Almon, 335, 396; Amanda Jean, 252; Amy Marie, 486; Andy, 522; Angela Gay, 252, 426; Anna Katelyn, 439; Annie Ruth, 88, 179, 220; Anthony Mark, 408, 522; Audrey Chambers, 486; Barbara, 89; Barbara Gail (Cookie), 170, 317; Barry Jason, 325; Barry Keith, 179, 325; Beadie May (Beckie), 114; Beatrice (Be-At), 225, 248, 265; Beatrice Marie, 170, 316; Benjamin McKinley, 116; Bennett A., 22, 24; Bennett Arvil (Ben),

118; Bennett Hampton (Hamp), 24; Bernice, 509; Bertha Mae, 48, 101; Beth, 442; Beth Elaine, 265, 440; Beth Rene, 486; Betty Sue, 116, 240; Bobby, 101; Bradley Kent, 325; Brandon, 253; Brandon Dale, 435; Brandy Nichole, 254, 427; Brian Keith, 180; Brian Kyle, 252; Britney, 413; Callie Pearl, 220, 221; Calvin Duane, 252, 425; Camron, 413; Carl Thomas, 116, 240; Carlos, 88; Carol Sue, 251, 381, 510; Cassidy Travis, 400; Charles Edward, 486; Charles Wayne, 116, 117, 119, 240, 408; Charles William, 116, 240, 400; Charlie Hampton, 116; Cheryl Elizabeth, 239, 404; Christina Ann, 434; Christopher Dale, 253; Christopher Lee, 493, 533; Clara Jean (Jeannie), 121, 253; Clara Nell, 119, 250; Clara Sue (Susie), 118, 242, 244; Claude Ellis Jr., 224, 264, 380; Claude Ellis Sr., 110, 224, 236, 237, 264, 268; Claudette, 170; Cletus, 228, 386; Connie Sue, 481; Cullin Dawson, 522; Curtis (Slick), 111, 228; Curtis Dwayne, 240, 409, 425; Cynthia Denise, 239; Daisy Marie, 434; Darren Lawrence, 244; Daryl Elmer, 101, 204; David Carl, 204, 357; David Paul, 240, 408; David Shane, 435; David Wayne, 264, 435; Dennis Almon, 396; Dennis Ray, 121, 253, 268, 442; Derrick Lee, 228; Destinee Starr, 416; Dewey Leora, 118, 239, 316; Doyle Lee, 434; Dustin Ray, 508; Dwight, 244, 413; Dylan Dwayne, 409; Edith Inez, 116, 240, 521; Eldred McKinley, 116, 239; Elizabeth Ann, 120, 252; Elizabeth Audrey Nicole, 521; Elizabeth Autumn, 518; Elmer Cecil, 48, 101; Elsie Elizabeth, 178; Elza Darlene, 88, 179; Emily Selena, 400, 518; Emily Suzanne, 476; Eric Wayne, 396, 518; Erlene, 111, 228; Estelle Eugene, 193, 266, 382; Eva Jean, 224, 236, 381, 513; Evelyn May, 101, 204; Finis Leonard (Phiney/Slim), 110, 118, 120, 170; Flora, 117, 237, 244; Floyde Leonard, 88, 120, 220; Floyde Virgil, 88, 179; Frank, 88; Franklin Delano, 170; Fred Amos, 88, 120, 178; Fred Calvin, 120, 252; Freda Marlene, 240, 407; Freddie Wayne, 508; Garland, 317; Garlin, 111; Gary Quinton, 413, 523; Gary Wade, 413; Gerald Glenn, 120, 252; Geraldine (Judy), 225, 381; Glen, 88, 179, 332; Glenna Joy, 179, 325; Gracie Elizabeth, 326; Grady, 88; Gregory Allen, 528; Gregory Dale, 265, 415, 439; Gregory Lynn, 252, 406, 426, 520; Grover, 509; Gwendolyn Michelle (Shelly), 406, 520; Harold Taylor, 89, 180; Harold Wade, 180, 326; Hazel Irene, 116, 239; Heath Nathan Ellis, 435; Heather Danielle, 408; Helen Faye, 396; Huell, 118; Hurbert (Herb) Lee, 116, 225; Infant Daughter, 118; Infant Son, 111; J. C. Sr., 493; Jack, 413; Jack Leon, 170, 316; James Edward, 89, 180; James Gregory, 180, 326; James Hampton (Jim) Jr., 111, 121; James Hampton (Jim) Sr., 88, 111; Jamie Michael, 254, 427; Jarrod Glen, 325; Jason Derek, 251, 425; Jason McKinley, 404, 519; Jason Ray, 382, 511; Jeffrey Curtis, 409, 522; Jeffrey Samuel (Sam) Sr., 239, 403; Jeffrey Samuel Jr., 404; Jennifer Lynn, 408; Jeremy Lynn, 382; Jerry Wayne, 120, 252; Jimmie Nell, 228, 386; Jimmy Carl, 493; Jo Carolyn, 225, 248, 382; Joanie, 244; Joey Lee, 265, 408, 439; John (Johnnie) Glenn, 335; John Eric (Elwood), 335, 488; John Franklin, 100, 203; John Hampton (Charlie), 48, 100; John Pugh, 110, 116, 170; John Robert, 119; Johnny Ray, 225, 382; Jonathan Elbert, 265, 439; Joseph, 111, 228; Joseph Thomas (Tommy), 381, 510; Josephine, 88, 180; Joshua (Josh) Lee, 408; Joshua Kyle, 435, 526; Judy Mae, 120; Karen Denise, 179, 325, 514; Katherine Viola (Susie), 316; Kathrine Marie, 528; Kathryn Lorraine (Lori), 240, 399, 408; Katy Jamys, 511; Keith Deran, 265,

439; Kelsey Brooke, 415; Kendall Allan, 440; Kendall Marie, 403; Kenneth Carroll, 120, 252; Kenneth Dale (K. D.), 239, 403; Kenny Daniel, 406, 520; Kent Maurice, 179, 325, 332; Kevin Duane, 408; Keyle, 244; Kris, 244; Kristin Blair, 520; Kylie Brooklyn, 526; Lady Carrie, 110, 224; Larry Ray (Soap), 224, 268, 381; Lauren Elizabeth, 440; Laurie Lee, 239, 404; Leigh Ann, 252, 426; Lemuel Carl, 48, 101; Leonard Earl, 110, 225, 248, 265; Lisa Rene, 179, 325; Louis Cola, 116, 240, 251, 399, 425, 439; Lowell Dale, 120, 253; Lula Ann, 111; Margaret (Peggy), 10; Marissa (Rissa) Kay, 251, 425; Mark Alan, 225, 382; Martha Jane, 121, 254; Mary Edith (Tootsie), 111, 228; Mary Elizabeth, 426; Mary Lou, 88; Mason Reed, 439; Matthew Dennis, 396; Matthew Ray, 253; Melissa Ann, 22; Melissa Evelyn (Aunt Eb), 41, 71, 105; Michael Balentine, 244; Michael Duane, 240, 408; Mittie Ethel, 48; Mittie Lou, 118; Mollie Joanna, 511; Monica Irene, 228; Monica Whitney, 416; Nadine, 119, 249; Nancy Ann, 239, 404; Nancy Carolyn, 119, 250; Nancy Mae, 264, 435; Nettie Louise, 119, 249; Nikki Laraine, 252, 426; Onita Katherine (Neat), 110, 120, 225, 254; Opal, 100, 203; Otha Oneal, 48, 101; Pamela Elaine, 239, 404; Patricia (Pat), 179, 324; Patsy Ann, 118, 245, 268, 416; Patsy Faye, 170, 316; Paul Douglas Jr., 239, 403; Paul Douglas Sr., 116, 239; Paula Marie, 239, 404; Paulette, 170; Pauline Inez, 110, 118, 225, 242, 268, 271; Pearlie Mae, 110, 118, 196, 224, 270; Peggy Ann, 225, 382; Peggy Sue, 240, 408; Phillis Ann, 225; Rachel Ann, 224, 237, 381; Rachel Anna, 116, 240; Rachel Diane, 325; Rachel Kathrine, 119, 249; Ralph, 88; Randall Thomas, 381, 416, 510; Rassie, 111, 228; Ray, 111, 121, 228; Regie Leon (Buck) Sr., 476, 534; Regie Leon Jr., 476, 534; Regina Faye, 509; Rejoyce Maree (Joyce), 116; Rhonda Sherae, 265, 439; Ricky Dale, 434; Ricky Louis, 240, 251, 408; Robbie Etoil, 119, 249; Robby Lee, 404; Robert Daniel, 250; Robert David, 120, 250; Robert Earl, 120; Ronnie Earl, 120, 253; Roxanna Gail (Roxie), 403; Roy Lynn, 88; Ruby Mae, 88, 178, 201, 369, 508; Rufus Ezra, 116, 239; Rutha (Ruthey) Barton Sharp, 24; Ruthie L., 224; Ryan Lee, 180; Sandra (Sandy) Jean, 179, 323; Sandra (Sandy) Kay, 252, 426; Sarah Elizabeth (Lib), 170, 315; Savana Elizabeth, 526; Selena Kay, 403; Shannon Lynn, 228; Sharon Louise, 240, 408, 439; Shawn Leigh, 523; Shelly Allison, 413; Sherman Daniel, 240, 406; Shirley Ann, 121, 253; Shirley Jean, 170, 316; Steven McKinley, 239, 404; Stevie Lawrence, 118, 244, 271; Tabitha Leann, 405; Tamra, 426; Tania Jo, 204; Tara Kayde, 413; Teresa Anna, 386, 514; Tesa Brayde, 413; Thelma Jean, 119, 249; Theresa Ann, 228; Thomas David, 408; Thomas Jake, 511; Thomas Moore, 225, 251, 381, 416; Timothy (Tim) Michael, 121, 254; Todd Allen, 404; Tonya Lynn, 403, 519; Tonya Michelle, 253, 426; Tracy Allen, 239; Tracy David, 225; Travis Lloyd, 240, 400, 406; Vella Mae, 435; Vincent Carl, 228; Virginia Elizabeth, 119, 248; Virginia Nell, 170, 315; Wallace Earl, 225, 265, 381, 408, 415; Wallace Ray, 110, 225; William Claude "Billy", Jr., 3, 6; William Clyde, 508; William Darin Ray, 521; William Derek, 508; William Hunter, 48, 100; William R., 48; Winfred Lynn, 335; Winston Churchill, 170; Zackery Lynn, 426

Woodall: Margaret Ellen, 245

Woodfin: Charles Micheal, 515; Christopher (Chris), 304; Helen Alean, 116; James (Jamie), 304; James Thomas,

304; Steve Keath, 304; Thomas (Tommy) Andrew, 515; Zebbie D., 116

Woods: Dale G., 459; Edith Rose, 198; Eunice Viola, 248; Ladusta Rae, 411; Margarette Darolyne, 321; Sherrie Lynn, 459

Woodson: Sarah, 1

Woodward: Audry, 199; Elvia, 199; Robert E., 106

Woody: Richard, 350

Woolfolk: Curtis Warren, 300; Virginia Leigh, 300; Willard Warren, 300

Woolwright: Joe E., 69

Wooten: Andy, 359; April Louise, 500; Drew, 359; Hazel, 267; James Orville, 500; Natalie Jo, 359

Worsham: Dakota Leon, 317; David Leon Wood, 171, 317; Ervin Ralph (Red), 170; Mary Katherine, 145; V. E., 145

Worted: Dorothy Irene, 366

Wright: Albert Lee Sr., 407; Alvin Washington, 247, 295; Anna Monique, 415; Bama, 217; Bertha, 231; Betty Ann, 295; Candace (Candi) Lynn, 293, 458; Carrie Emma, 25; Chase Wade, 354; Christopher Shannon, 293, 458; Clyde, 150; Cynthia (Cindy) Lea, 293, 458; Dalton Alex, 458; Danny Wade, 293; Debra (Debbie) Gail, 440; Dustin Andrew, 293; Edith Louise, 58, 125; Elinda Gaye, 199, 351; Elizabeth (Lizzie) Frances, 58; Emma Gertrude, 313; Ethan Elliot, 293, 458, 461; Etta Buna, 58, 124; Evelyn Virginia, 464; Flora Izadora, 167; George Moses (Mode), 25, 57, 110; Henry Washington, 247; Herschel Clyde, 150; Horace Lanny, 151, 293; Ida Mae, 25; Irene J., 387; J. T., 334; Jackie Juanita, 199, 351; James Lewis I, 407; James Lewis II, 407; James Phillip, 25, 58; Jerry Wade, 150, 293; Jess, 167; Kathy Renea, 247, 417; Katie, 117; Kim Debra, 444; Lauren Casey, 354; Louis Almon, 58; Mamie Odell, 199; Margaret Alliene, 199; Marjorie Ann, 493; Martha (Mattie) Jane, 25, 58; Mary Eula, 245; Mason Louise, 58, 124; Matthew Wayne, 293, 458; Mattie May, 58, 125; Mildred L., 416; Moses, 25; Nancy Minnie Irvin, 25; Norma Jean, 490; Olin E., 354; Opal Lorraine, 518; Paul Winford, 58; Percey Phillips (Pet) Jr., 199; Percy Phillip Sr., 199; Richard Washington, 25, 110; Ronnie Dale Sr., 523; Sandra Kay, 334; Scott Anthony, 293; Scottie Lee, 523; Shane Thomas, 458; Sidney H., 440; Terry Wade, 354; Timothy Elliot, 151, 293, 461; Walter William, 316; William Chad, 407

Wylie: Adam Barrett, 312; Alma June, 131; Beth, 270; Carrie Emalene, 181; Freddie Lee, 308; James Newton, 217; John Terry, 312; Marvin Edison, 339; Mary Evelyn, 217; Michael Andrew, 312; Odias Avon, 308; Richard, 270; Robert Jerry, 339; Robyn, 270; Scott Fredrick, 308, 464; Sharon Arlene, 308, 464; William P., 312

Wyman: Arthur, 157

Wynn: Dawanda Lou, 353

Y

Yarbrough: Janella Marie, 451

Yerby: Dennis A., 332; Edward (Dunk) L., 332; Ryan Chadwick (Chad), 332; Shana Nicole, 332, 479

Young: Ada, 46, 97; Ada V., 27, 63; Addie, 45; Agnes Gwindolin, 115, 237; Alana, 160; Alice Beulah, 115, 237, 243; Alysa Michelle, 402; Amanda Layne, 285, 455; Amanda Lee, 27, 30; Amy Dee, 195, 348; Andrew Cleveland, 31, 72; Angelia Diane, 236, 400, 406; Angie, 185; Annie Mae, 72, 157; Anthony Todd, 285, 455;

Arnold Andrew, 72, 157; Arnold Edward (Ed), 62, 133, 195; Arthur D., 342; Ashley Nicole, 455; Barbara Lynn, 132, 267; Barbara Sue, 114, 237; Bert Edward, 61; Bertha, 62, 133, 243; Betty Jane, 266; Betty Jean, 236, 401; Betty Ruth, 229, 387; Billy, 134; Billy Eugene, 285; Billy Gean, 236, 400; Bobbie Marlene, 256; Bobby Glenn Sr., 44; Bobby Turner, 62, 134; Bonnie Mae, 114, 236, 412; Boss C., 62, 133, 172; Boyce Edward, 133, 195, 270; Bradley Edward, 195, 348; Brenda Gaye, 186, 333; Bret Allen Jr., 336; Bret Allen Sr., 188, 336; Brianna Nicole, 401; Carl Robert, 119, 246, 414, 510; Carlene Vernial, 93, 187; Caroline, 54; Carrie Ann, 62, 132, 191; Catherine (Katie), 63, 136; Cathy, 132, 267; Catlin Gregory, 302; Cecil Arthur, 62, 135; Cecil Lloyd, 92, 186; Charles, 11; Charles (Sonny) Ruben II, 201; Charles Ruben I, 201; Charles Thomas, 201, 355; Charles Westbrook Jr., 74, 160; Charles Westbrook Sr., 32, 74; Chasity Dawn, 271, 444; Christine, 63, 131, 135, 266; Christopher, 273; Christopher David, 388; Clara Belle, 63, 135; Clara D., 62; Clara Estelle, 318; Clarence Roy, 73, 157, 247; Clarence W., 31, 72, 95; Clarence William (C. W.), 93, 187; Cleave Homer, 27, 63, 73; Cletus Dempsey (Skeet), 114, 236, 381, 513; Cleveland, 43; Colonel Carl, 318; Colton Will, 355; Condy, 46; Connie, 135; Cora, 31, 71; Daisy Evelyn, 268, 411; Danny, 157; Darrell Lee, 134; Dave D., 46, 97; David, 185; Dawn Marie, 188, 336; Deborah, 134, 271; Deborah (Debbie) Aletha, 236, 400; Deborah Sue, 115, 238, 413; Delia (Dee), 21, 46; Delia "Dee", 44; Della, 46, 98; Dennis, 185; Devenport (Deb), 42; Dewey, 46; Donald Alan, 187; Donald Kenneth, 115, 237; Donald L., 426; Donald Ray, 186, 332; Donnie, 160; Donnie D., 100, 202; Donnie Ray, 236, 400; Donnie Ray Jr., 387, 515; Donnie Ray Sr., 229, 387; Donny Joe, 135, 272; Dora K., 92; Dora Lee, 21, 47; Doris (Susie) Opel, 73, 158; Dorothy, 63, 136; Dorothy Mae, 115, 238; Douglas, 160; Douglas C. Jr., 136; Douglas C. Sr., 63, 136; Douglas E., 92; Doyal Lee Jr., 186; Doyal Lee Sr., 92, 186; Doyle Lee, 72, 119, 156; Dustin, 272; Dusty Joe, 271; Earnest Edward, 42, 92; Eddie, 20, 42, 43, 219; Edith Mae, 63; Edna G. (Birdie), 31, 63, 73; Edward, 382; Edward (Eddie) Earl, 186, 333; Elijah, 20, 27; Elizabeth (Lizzie), 380, 402, 406; Elizabeth "Lizzie", 21; Elizabeth Diane, 246, 416, 510; Ella Mae, 71, 155; Ellie Bert, 62, 115, 131, 243, 381; Elsie Sue, 132, 267; Elvin Bay, 62; Eric Dwayne, 236, 400; Ernest, 43; Etoile, 72; Eula, 31; Eula Beatrice, 62, 132, 237, 245, 381; Fay, 72; Felicia Lynn, 302; Florence Beulah, 31, 61, 72, 115; Frances Sybil, 193; Francis M., 42; Fred, 63; Fred Demphis, 114, 236; Garland, 47; Gary, 185; Gladys Lee, 62, 135; Gladys Myrtle, 32, 74; Glenda Sue, 157, 298; Goldie Sunshine, 351; Grace, 268; Grady L., 62, 134; Grayson Tobias, 355; Grover Cleveland, 42, 91; Harold Moore, 92, 186; Harvey Ross, 382; Hayley Anna, 332; Hazel Inez, 62, 132; Hazel Joyce, 92, 187; Heather Ruth, 447, 519; Homer David, 285; Hosea Leba, 48, 100; Hubert, 21; Hubert F., 72, 157; Hulet Edward, 27, 62, 72, 172, 191; Hurbert Franklin, 21; Infant, 20, 31, 62; Infant Daughter, 61, 114; Infant Son, 401; Irene Beulah, 62, 132; Isaac Benton, 44; J. Patton (Pat), 71, 155; James, 11; James (Jim) Calvin Jr., 46; James Calvin Sr., 46; James Charles (J. C.), 115, 237, 381; James Damon, 201, 355; James Lee, 100, 202; James Nicklaus, 61, 131; James Robert, 92, 185, 325, 482; James Roland, 236, 287, 400; James Wiley, 52; James Wylie (Jim), 27, 61, 72, 115;

Z

For additional information regarding the material covered in this publication, please contact Millie Mason (256-766-5623) or Sharon Wood (256-767-4440)

Bluewater Publications is a multi-faceted publishing company capable of meeting all of your reading and publishing needs. Our two-fold aim is to:

1) Provide the market with educationally enlightening and inspiring research and reading materials.

2) Make the opportunity of being published available to any author and or researcher who desires to be published.

We are passionate about preserving history; whether through the re-publishing of an out-of-print classic, or by publishing the research of historians and genealogists. Bluewater Publications is the *Peoples' Choice Publisher*.

For company information or information about how you can be published through Bluewater Publications, please visit:

www.BluewaterPublications.com

Also check Amazon.com to purchase any of the books that we publish.

Confidently Preserving Our Past,
Bluewater Publications.com
Formerly known as Heart of Dixie Publishing

amcontent.com/pod-product-compliance
Source LLC
burg PA
0840270326
CB00018B/4095

7 8 1 9 3 4 6 1 0 5 0 3 *